Foreign Policy
bulletin

The Documentary Record of United States Foreign Policy / Volume 1 / Number 1

July/August 1990

SUMMIT IN WASHINGTON

Also in this issue:

German Unification

China/MFN Status

Citizens Democracy Corps

The PLO/Talks Suspended

BULLETIN SPECIALS:
NELSON MANDELA, HELMUT KOHL,
GORBACHEV AT STANFORD

Foreign Policy
bulletin

Volume 1/Number 1
July/August 1990

The **FOREIGN POLICY BULLETIN** is published bimonthly (plus annual index) as a private publication, using the same format as the discontinued "Department of State Bulletin" and maintaining continuity with that publication while offering additional materials as well. Its purpose is to provide a timely and systematic record of United States foreign policy and of complementary documents from international sources. The **BULLETIN**'s coverage of official U.S. documents includes major addresses, diplomatic statements, and press conferences of the President and the Secretary of State; statements and congressional testimony by the Secretary and other administration officials; treaties and other agreements to which the United States is or may become a party; special reports; and selected press releases issued by the White House, the Department of State, and other agencies. Special features include speeches and other statements by foreign officials concerning U.S. policy; reports and other materials from international organizations relating to major issues confronting U.S. policy-makers; and background information about countries of particular interest to U.S. foreign relations.

PAUL E. AUERSWALD
Editor and Publisher

PHILIP AUERSWALD
Assistant Editor/Business Manager

HUGUETTE NIZARD
Subscriptions Manager

HOPE FUNG
Layout and Typesetting

J. LEONARD MAZUR
Marketing Consultant

Printed by
PRINTING SERVICE INTERNATIONAL

SUBSCRIPTIONS: Annual subscriptions to the **BULLETIN** are $35.00; outide the U.S. and Canada $53.00. Subscription orders should be sent to: Subscriptions, Foreign Policy Bulletin, 4812 Butterworth Place N.W., Washington, D.C. 20016.

SINGLE COPIES: Single copies, if still in print, can be obtained for $10.00 a copy plus postage by writing to the address below.

CORRESPONDENCE should be addressed to: Foreign Policy Bulletin, 4812 Butterworth Place N.W., Washington, D.C. 20016.

INDEXING: Arrangements are being made for online and printed indexing of the **FOREIGN POLICY BULLETIN**, including this issue. Complete information will be provided in the September/October issue.

CONTENTS

1 FEATURE: THE WASHINGTON SUMMIT, MAY 30–JUNE 3

FROM THE EDITOR:

Just as the "Department of State Bulletin" began publication on the eve of World War II and the years of Cold War that followed, so the FOREIGN POLICY BULLETIN begins at the dawn of what is certainly a new era in world affairs.

Our plan for this new periodical is to maintain continuity with its State Department predecessor, with all the advantages that accrue from a familiar and effective format, while at the same time gradually adding new material that will provide further perspective on this new era.

Modest departures in this issue are Nelson Mandela's speech to a joint session of Congress, Chancellor Helmut Kohl's commencement address at Harvard reflecting on the heritage of the Marshall Plan and the nature of European-American relations today, and President Mikhail Gorbachev's speech at Stanford University after the Washington Summit. There will be more of this, along with new "back of the book" lists and summaries, from other domestic and international sources important to the professional and the student.

During my years at the State Department, one of the things I enjoyed most about my job was communicating with the users of our numerous publications, users spanning the country and circling the globe. I am particularly pleased to be able to continue this communication, and indeed to have the opportunity to enlarge its scope to include many new readers. I look forward to the chance to provide the BULLETIN's audience with a documentary chronicle of the remarkable international events in which we are participating today. The contents of this first issue are ample illustration that these events will have a profound effect on all of our lives in the decade and the century ahead.

Paul E. Auerswald
Editor

Visit of President Mikhail Gorbachev of the Union of Soviet Socialist Republics

President Gorbachev made an official working visit to Washington, D.C., May 31 - June 3, 1990 to meet with President Bush and other government officials

Arrival Remarks, May 31, 1990 [1]

President Bush

Friends and distinguished guests, welcome to all of you, especially our guests from the Soviet Union. It is my great honor to welcome to the White House the President of the Soviet Union, Mikhail Gorbachev.

Mr. President, just over a year ago I said that the United States wanted to move beyond containment in its relations with the Soviet Union toward a new era, an era of enduring cooperation. When we last met in Malta, we agreed to accelerate our efforts on a full range of issues. Today differences remain, of course, but in the short six months since the Malta summit, we've made encouraging progress. I want this summit to take us farther still, and I know that that is your view as well, Mr. President.

We've seen a world of change this past year. Now, on the horizon, we see what, just one short year ago, seemed a distant dream: a continent cruelly divided, East from West, has begun to heal with the dawn of self-determination and democracy. In Germany, where the Wall once stood, a nation moves toward unity, in peace and freedom. And in the other nations of the most heavily militarized continent on Earth, at last we see the long era of confrontation giving way to the prospect of enduring cooperation in a Europe whole and free. Mr. President, you deserve great credit for your part in these transforming events. I salute you, as well, for the process of change you've brought to your own country.

As we begin this summit, let me stress that I believe we can work together at this historic moment to further the process of building a new Europe, one in which every nation's security is strengthened and no nation is threatened. Around the world, we need to strengthen our cooperation in solving regional conflicts and building peace and stability. In Nicaragua, for example, we've shown that we can work together to promote peaceful change. In Angola, our support for an early resolution of that country's tragic conflict – a resolution acceptable to the Angolan people – is now paying off. So, let us expand this new spirit of cooperation not merely to resolve disputes between us but to build a solid foundation for peace, prosperity, and stability around the world.

In that same spirit, Mr. President, let me quote the words of one of your nation's great minds, one of the world's great men in this or any age, Andrei Sakharov. Fourteen years ago, he wrote: "I am convinced that guaranteed political and civil rights for people the world over are also guarantees of international security, economic and social progress." Sakharov knew that lasting peace and progress are inseparable from freedom, that nations will only be fully safe when all people are fully free.

We in the U.S. applaud the new course the Soviet Union has chosen. We see the spirited debate in the Congress of People's Deputies, in the Soviet press, among the Soviet people. We know about the difficult economic reforms that are necessary to breathe new vigor into the Soviet economy. And as I've said many times before, we want to see *perestroika* succeed. Mr. President, I firmly believe, as you have said, that there is no turning back from the path you have chosen.

Since our meeting in Malta, we've reached agreements in important areas, each one proof that when mutual respect prevails progress is possible. But the agreements we've reached cannot cause us to lose sight of some of the differences that remain. Lithuania is one such issue. We believe that good faith dialogue between the Soviet leaders and representatives of the Baltic peoples is the proper approach, and we hope to see that process go forward.

Over the next four days, we're not going to solve all of the world's problems. We won't resolve all of the outstanding issues that divide us. But we can and will take significant steps toward a new relationship.

This summit will be a working summit in the strictest sense of the term, one where we mark the real progress we've made by signing new agreements and where we address the differences that divide us in a spirit of candor, in an open and honest search for common ground. In a larger sense, though, the success of this summit depends not on the agreements we will sign but on our efforts to lay the groundwork for overcoming decades of division and discord, to build a world of peace in freedom.

Mr. President, together, your great country and ours bear an enormous and unique responsibility for world peace and regional stability. We must work together to reduce tensions, to make the world a little better for our children and grandchildren. And to this end, I pledge you my all-out effort.

Mr. President, you've brought us a beautiful day, and you've brought back Mrs. Gorbachev—that brings joy to all of our hearts. A hearty welcome to her as well. So, it is my privilege to welcome you to the White House. And may God bless our peoples in their efforts for a better world. Welcome, sir.

President Gorbachev [2]

Mr. President, Mrs. Bush, ladies and gentlemen, comrades, thank you for this welcome. May I also greet all Americans on behalf of the peoples of the Soviet Union.

My present visit to the United States is a confirmation that Soviet-U.S. relations are acquiring greater stability, clarity, and predictability. I am convinced that both the Soviet people and the Americans approve such changes. I think that they are also properly appreciated throughout the world. Therefore, it is the great responsibility of the President and myself to make sure that the capital of trust and cooperation accumulated in recent years is protected and constantly increased.

I remember well my first visit to the United States, and not only because I saw America for the first time then. During those days in December 1987, President Reagan and I signed the treaty on the elimination of INF [intermediate-range nuclear force] missiles. That was truly a watershed not only in our relations but in the history of modern times. It was the first step taken together by two powerful countries on the road leading to a safe and sensible world.

Since then, our two great nations have traveled a long way toward each other. Thousands of American and Soviet citizens; dozens of agencies, private companies, and public organizations are involved in political and business contacts, humanitarian exchanges, scientific and technological cooperation.

In the same years, the world around us has also changed beyond recognition. Mr. President, this generation of people on Earth may witness the advent of an irreversible period of peace in the history of civilization. The walls which for years separated the peoples are collapsing. The trenches of the Cold War are disappearing. The fog of prejudice, mistrust, and animosity is vanishing.

I have come to the United States with the impressions still fresh in my mind of how our people celebrated the 45th anniversary of the victory over nazism and of my meetings with war veterans. I recently had many meetings with my countrymen. They all understand the importance of Soviet-U.S. relations. They look upon their improvement with the hope that the tragedies of the 20th century—those horrible wars—will forever remain a thing of the past. I think that this is what the Americans want, too.

Mr. President, living up to these hopes of our two nations is your mission and mine. This meeting is part of it. My colleagues and I have come to do serious work in order to make a decisive step toward an agreement reducing the most dangerous arms, which are increasingly losing their political significance, and to provide further impetus to interaction between our two countries—interaction and, of course, cooperation in solving international problems in trade, scientific, technological, and humanitarian fields; in cultural exchanges; in expanding information about each other; and in people-to-people contacts.

We want progress in relations between the Soviet Union and the United States of America. I am looking forward to meetings with the Americans and, to the extent possible, getting to know better your unique and great country.

On behalf of Mrs. Gorbachev and myself and of all those who have come with me to your Nation's Capital, I thank once again President George Bush and Mrs. Bush and all those present here for this warm welcome.

Excerpts of White House Fact Sheets on Scientific and Commercial Agreements, May 31, 1990 [3]

OCEAN STUDIES AGREEMENT

- Provides for a broad range of oceanographic research cooperation, use of port facilities in each other's countries, and far-reaching scientific exchanges.

- Intellectual property rights (IPR) provisions are included.
- Results of joint studies will be published openly.
- Shared use of research vessels will result in substantial savings for both sides.

EXPANDED CIVIL AVIATION AGREEMENT

- Total passenger and cargo flights per side would increase from 7.6 Boeing-727 equivalents/week to 15.1 immediately; to 42 on April 1, 1991; to 58 on April 1, 1992.
- U.S. airlines could increase services to Moscow and Leningrad. They would gain new rights over the North Atlantic to four additional cities and over the Pacific to two additional cities.
- Soviet airlines could increase services to New York and Washington. They would gain new rights over the Atlantic to two additional cities (with onward service to South America) and over the Pacific to two additional cities.
- Each side could designate up to seven airlines to serve the other, with no more than two passenger airlines per side serving a city pair.
- A charter article would be added guaranteeing each side annual approval of 100 charter flights over the Atlantic, within certain national constraints, and positive consideration of charter flight requests over the Pacific.
- Soviet airlines would retain unrestricted rights to sell tickets in the United States. Until Soviet currency becomes convertible for purchase of air transportation, U.S. airlines could only sell tickets in the U.S.S.R. for hard currency. To ensure U.S. sales access to Soviet citizens in absence of ruble convertibility, Soviet airlines would sell ruble tickets on U.S. airlines equal to 8.75 percent of our airlines' round-trip capacity, and remit the profits to U.S. airlines in hard currency.

MARITIME TRANSPORTATION AGREEMENT

- The agreement commits both parties to eliminate discriminatory treatment, although it permits Soviet shippers to pay Soviet carriers in rubles as an interim measure.
- The agreement contains no provisions for cargo-sharing, but does require Soviets to charter U.S.-flag carriers for Soviet Government controlled bulk cargoes whenever U.S. carriers are available on terms and conditions equal to or better than those offered by non-U.S. carriers. U.S. carriers wishing to participate in bilateral bulk trade are encouraged to inform Soviets of their interest, time availability, and price.
- The agreement establishes a forecast mechanism to trigger consultations on U.S. liner trade. The agreement goes into effect following the conclusion of first joint forecast, expected to take place within a few months of signature.
- It grants 2-day reciprocal notification access to 42 U.S. and 42 Soviet ports.
- Soviet-flag vessels are permitted to reenter U.S. cross-trades, subject to Soviet assurances with regard to past Soviet predatory rate practices.

Dinner Toasts, May 31, 1990 [3]

President Bush

Friends and distinguished guests, and especially President and Mrs. Gorbachev, Barbara and I are delighted to welcome you to the White House to share bread and salt with us on this special evening.

We're now nearing the end of a momentous day, the first of four in this Washington summit. And tomorrow, Mr. President, comes the moment that so many have been waiting for, a day when expectations will be at a fever pitch. That's right, tomorrow Barbara and Raisa go to Wellesley College. [Laughter]

And back here at the White House, sir, we will meet again, this time to sign our names to a series of agreements that signify the progress that our two nations have made in forging a new relationship, agreements on everything from nuclear testing and chemical weapons to expanded contacts between the people of America and the people of the Soviet Union. These agreements are a continuation of all that began in Malta just six months ago, a foundation we can build on, proof that differences can be resolved even while others remain. And let me assure President Gorbachev: Whatever deep differences divided us in the past, the United States and the American people approach every issue with a sincere belief that our two nations can find common ground. Indeed, because of our unique positions in the world, we must find common ground.

We meet at a time of great and historic change in the Soviet Union, in Europe, and around the world. Such profound change is unsettling, but also exhilarating. And we don't shrink from the challenges before us, but we welcome them, determined to build the foundations of enduring peace and security.

Mr. President, you deserve great credit for the course that you have chosen, for the political and economic reforms that you have introduced, and for creating within the Soviet Union this commitment to change. As I said this morning when I welcomed you to the White House, we want to see *perestroika* succeed. We want to see this transition now underway in the Soviet Union maintain its momentum.

Mr. President, it's said that your country is the land of possibilities. You have demonstrated the truth of that statement. And we've seen this past year that ours is a world of possibilities, that our time is a time of historic change, a time when men and nations can transform history, can turn possibility into progress, into peace. So, let us raise our glasses to our guests, President and Mrs. Gorbachev, to the growing friendship between American and Soviet people and to the possibilities now open to us, to the prospect of progress and lasting peace.

President Gorbachev [2]

Mr. President, Mrs. Bush, ladies and gentlemen, allow me on behalf of Mrs. Gorbachev and myself and all the members of our delegation to thank you for your warmth and for the kind words of President Bush.

We share the assessment of President Bush that we have done fruitful work today, and I'm sure that as a result of this meeting our countries will go to a new level of cooperation. Even now our relations, to which history assigned such an important role in the events and lessons of the 20th century, differ dramatically from what they were before the

1985 Geneva summit. To achieve this, we have worked together.

The enemy image is becoming a thing of the past. Ideological stereotypes are fading away. We have begun to understand each other's motives. As we are changing and becoming closer to each other, we have not ceased to be different. But it turns out that that is not so bad. Quite the opposite: it is useful, for diversity is a vital force of development.

The world, too, has changed beyond recognition. It has made significant progress toward a new period of genuine peace in its long history. I think we can say with confidence that the most important and decisive step in this direction was made by our countries. Our two countries had the will, common sense, and understanding of the situation and of the imperatives of the future to embark on a long and difficult road which led from Geneva via Reykjavik, Washington, Moscow, and New York to Malta, and now once again to Washington.

Today I would like to repeat here what I said to the President six months ago at Malta. The Soviet Union does not regard the United States as its enemy. We have firmly adopted the policy of moving from mutual understanding through cooperation to joint action. Today, when I was meeting some American intellectuals at the Soviet Embassy, I said to them this: "Yes, indeed, we used to be enemies, or almost enemies. Now we are, maybe, rivals, at least to some extent. And we want to become partners. We want to go all the way to become friends."

Improved Soviet-American relations have reduced the threat of war. This is the main achievement of these years. We have concluded close to 20 bilateral agreements in various fields. There has been an unprecedented expansion of exchanges among our people — and that is especially valuable — from schoolchildren to prominent personalities in the fields of science and the economy. I think that the work we have been doing together with President Bush during these days can be considered as another step toward a more humane and just world.

I cannot say yet how we are going to conclude this meeting, what the results would be. That would be premature. But I think that my talk today with the President and also the meeting of the delegations makes it possible to ex-

pect major results from this meeting, and maybe even major results, the biggest results, compared to all the other meetings in previous Soviet-American summits. Maybe I'm too optimistic, but let's wait and see. We have two days. I believe that maybe we will have those major results.

I feel that we're now witnessing the emergence of a general idea which is conquering people's minds on the eve of the 21st century: it is the idea of unity. To make this idea a reality is a truly monumental challenge. The world's diversity and its complex problems are such that we can only do it by synthesizing, or at least interlinking, the aspirations, values, achievements, and hopes of different nations.

In the world confronted with the nuclear, environmental, and other threats, global unity means a chance for the survival of our civilization. But mankind cannot be merely a community of survival. It should be a community of progress, progress for all, the East, the West, the North, the South, the highly developed, and the less fortunate. But today we have to rethink the whole idea of progress. Mankind's ascent toward the realization of the idea of its history should not result in irreparable damage to the environment, in the exploitation of man or entire nations, or in irreversible moral and ethical losses.

It is a difficult and novel task to build a new civilization. Coming from a country in which more than 100 nationalities live together, we know that, perhaps better than anyone else, our own house is in need of an overhaul and a fundamental restructuring along the lines of reason and justice. We are aware of the magnitude of this undertaking, unprecedented in the history of mankind.

Judging by the response of the rest of the world to our *perestroika*, we can conclude that it is a necessary and desirable element of mankind's political and philosophical potential. That is why, while rethinking that potential and restructuring ourselves, we believe that we are making a contribution to the cause of universal development and universal unity.

We have not yet completed the task of creating a durable democratic system in our country, but I am convinced that the reserves of our society's energy already committed to this great undertaking are enough to bring it to its completion. I can say this firmly: We

shall act on the basis of our values; we shall move resolutely but prudently.

The goal of our policy is to bring our society to a qualitatively new level. This will enable us to be predictable participants in the international process, partners to all who want a secure, just, and free world. In building this world, we count on long-term cooperation of the United States of America.

The most important developments in relations between our two countries and in world politics are probably yet to come. It is important not to lose sight of our goal, to resist the temptation of trying to secure unilateral advantages. Let us move ahead while overcoming both current and future problems and roadblocks. Let us cooperate and work together.

To the health of Mrs. Barbara Bush and to your health, Mr. President, to the success and well-being of all those present here, to a life worthy of today, and to our common and better future. Thank you.

Remarks on Signing Bilateral Agreements, June 1, 1990 [3]

President Bush

President Gorbachev, again, welcome to the White House. Mr. President, you and I set a course six months ago off the island nation of Malta. And at that time we agreed on an agenda, much of which was completed for this week's summit. Of course, our Malta agenda remains unfinished, but we've made great progress in the last six months and in the last two days.

We're about to sign agreements concerning many areas of vital interest to our countries and to the world, and to record specific understandings in joint statements that are being published today.

First, we'll sign a bilateral agreement that will, for the first time, eliminate the great majority of the chemical weapons that our countries have stockpiled over the years. And let this landmark agreement quickly lead to a global ban on chemical weapons.

Secondly, we will be signing protocols on limiting nuclear testing. After long, sometimes arduous negotiations, we both agreed on unprecedented improvements for on-site verification of the Threshold Test Ban Treaty and the Peaceful Nuclear Explosions Treaty.

Third, we will sign a major new agreement that updates and expands our 1973 agreement on the peaceful uses of atomic energy. This new agreement provides for substantial U.S.-Soviet cooperation in atomic energy research and civilian nuclear safety.

In addition, President Gorbachev and I are issuing a joint statement recording major agreed provisions of a strategic arms reduction [START] treaty as well as a joint statement in which we agree to future negotiations on nuclear and space arms designed to enhance stability and reduce the risk of war. We're also issuing a statement on the conventional armed forces in Europe [CFE], committing us to intensify the pace of the Vienna negotiations and to reach rapid agreement on all outstanding issues. You see, we agree that a CFE treaty is an indispensable foundation for the future of European security.

There are many other agreements the United States and the Soviet Union are signing or announcing during this summit, agreements that represent hard work and a lasting achievement not just by our governments but also for the peoples. For example, an agreement to establish a U.S.-Soviet park across the Bering Strait. This park will preserve the unique natural, environmental, and cultural heritage of the Bering Sea region of Alaska and Siberia. Just as a bridge of land once joined our two continents, so let a bridge of hope now reach across the water to join our two peoples in this spirit of peaceful cooperation.

In this same spirit, President Gorbachev and I will sign an agreement that realizes our Malta objective of expanding undergraduate exchanges by 1,000 students on both sides, allowing more of our young people to experience firsthand each other's culture and politics, to live as friends. And out of simple acts of friendship, a profound revelation eventually arises: the people of the world have more in common than they have in conflict.

In just a few moments, Secretary of State Baker and Foreign Minister Shevardnadze will also sign four important new agreements concerning maritime boundaries, ocean studies, civil aviation, and a long-term grains agreement. Minister Shevardnadze and Transportation Secretary Skinner will sign a fifth agreement on maritime

transportation. President Gorbachev and I are also signing a commercial agreement and are looking forward to the passage of a Soviet emigration law.

President Gorbachev, I am very gratified by what we've accomplished over the last few days and determined to build on this solid foundation. The agreements we record today and those yet to come will advance the cause of peace—agreements in the best interests of both our nations and all nations.

Not long ago, some believed that the weight of history condemned our two great countries, our two great peoples to permanent confrontation. Well, you and I must challenge history, make new strides, build a relationship of enduring cooperation. We may not agree on everything, and indeed we don't agree on everything, but we believe in one great truth: the world has waited long enough; the Cold War must end. And so, today with gratitude in my heart for all those on the Soviet side and the United States side that worked so hard at all levels to bring these agreements to fruition, I say let's renew our pledge and build a more peaceful world.

President Gorbachev [2]

Mr. President, ladies and gentlemen, comrades, first of all, I would like to thank President George Bush for presenting so well the results of our work that we've been doing over these days in Washington. So, I have a problem: What shall I talk about? [Laughter] So, I think that I will do some thinking aloud in this context.

I would say that maybe this room has seen many important events and many agreements signed, but I think that what is happening now and what you have listed as the results of our work together represents an event of momentous importance not only for our two countries but for the world.

President Franklin D. Roosevelt half a century ago spoke of a world in which four essential freedoms will triumph: freedom of speech, freedom of worship, freedom from want, and freedom from fear. And this ideal has not yet been attained in the world and it could not be attained in the world of animosity and confrontation. And therefore, while liberating the world from fear, we are making steps towards a new world; and this is the important work of our two nations, of our two peoples.

What is very important, I think, is that we do not just declare our commitment to moving toward a healthier international environment, toward better international relations, toward a non-violent world; we are taking practical steps in that direction. And what you have just listed and what we'll be signing during this visit, I think, is a confirmation that both our declarations are right in that they seek to justify the hopes of our peoples and that we're also taking those practical steps. The important steps that we are taking today illustrate the degree of agreement between our two countries, despite the fact that— and here I quite agree with you—that there are things on which we disagree and there are differing views that we have on certain questions. But that area of disagreement is being narrowed in the course of our work together. What we will be signing, I think, is the best demonstration that we are ready to participate at the level of our responsibility in building a new civilization.

There are still many difficult challenges awaiting us. It is evident that to dismantle that monumental artifact of the Cold War, the accumulated arsenals of mutual destruction, is not at all a simple or even an entirely safe thing to do. The slightest imbalance and due haste or lack of equilibrium in this process may dangerously destabilize the overall international situation. But I'm sure that if we take a balanced and responsible approach, if we take into account the concerns and positions of each other even when we disagree, if we do all that, I'm sure that we will be able to move ahead more resolutely and more vigorously.

Mr. President, you have just mentioned Malta. Mr. President, I'm pleased to note that the turbulent developments of recent months after Malta have not led us astray from the goal we set together. So, I believe that we have passed the first test.

Mr. President, let me reaffirm here something that I've been saying to you during our one-on-one talks. We have had many such talks during this summit, and I welcome this style of negotiating. But let me reaffirm to both of our peoples that the Soviet Union is committed to the objective set at Malta: completing before the end of this year the preparation of the START treaty. I believe that this goal is attainable even though it is difficult.

I also can confirm what you have said: that we have agreed during our talks that this year we will seek to sign a treaty at the Vienna talks. And of course, we believe that in that case that will be the CSCE [Conference on Security and Cooperation in Europe] European security summit meeting. I think we already have good results and a good potential to work.

I believe that this is all possible as a result of the efforts of both sides over the past few years, including the efforts in which you, sir, have participated vigorously and actively and with great foresight in order to expand our relationship and to build on the capital of trust in our relations.

It would seem that I've said even more than I intended to say. I think it means that I'm human in the sense that I'm emotional. I would like to say that we've done a great deal in order to assure the success, and I would like to congratulate our two nations. And I would like also to shake your hand, Mr. President, so that we congratulate each other.

Joint Statement on the Treaty on Strategic Offensive Arms, June 1, 1990 [3]

The President of the United States George Bush and the President of the Union of Soviet Socialist Republics Mikhail S. Gorbachev discussed the status of the Treaty on the Reduction and Limitation of Strategic Offensive Arms [START]. The two Presidents expressed their satisfaction with the great progress which has been made in the negotiations on this Treaty. In particular, they welcomed the mutually acceptable solutions which have been found in major issues in the talks and reaffirmed their determination to have the Treaty completed and ready for signature by the end of this year. They instructed their negotiating teams in Geneva to accelerate their work to complete the Joint Draft Text recording the details of these solutions in order to fulfill this goal.

The START Treaty will be a major landmark in both arms control and in the relationship between the United States of America and the Union of Soviet Socialist Republics. It results from the recognition by both sides of the special obligation they bear to reduce the risk of outbreak of nuclear war, enhance strategic stability, and strengthen peace and international security. As such, the START Treaty will signal a turning point in U.S.-Soviet arms control efforts toward a more rational, open, cooperative, predictable and stable relationship. The Treaty will complement to a remarkable degree the important political changes which have recently begun to remove the hostility and suspicion and will facilitate the reduction of the sizeable stockpiles of strategic offensive arms which now exist.

The benefits of this Treaty are many. For the first time ever, both sides will carry out significant reductions in strategic offensive arms—up to 50 percent in certain categories. More importantly, these reductions will be designed to make a first strike less plausible. The result will be greater stability and a lower risk of war.

Major agreed provisions of the Treaty are as follows:

The total number of deployed ICBMs [intercontinental ballistic missiles] and their associated launchers, deployed SLBMs [submarine-launched ballistic missiles] and their associated launchers and heavy bombers will be reduced to no more than 1600; within this total deployed heavy ICBMs and their associated launchers will be reduced to no more than 154;

The total number of warheads attributed to deployed ICBMs, deployed SLBMs and heavy bombers will be reduced to no more than 6000. Of these, no more than 4900 will be warheads on deployed ICBMs and deployed SLBMs, no more than 1540 will be warheads on heavy ICBMs, and no more than 1100 will be warheads on mobile ICBMs;

The aggregate throw-weight of the deployed ICBMs and SLBMs of each side will be limited to an agreed level which will be approximately 50 percent below the existing level of the aggregate throw-weight of deployed ICBMs and SLBMs of the Union of Soviet Socialist Republics as of a date to be determined. This limit will not be exceeded for the duration of the Treaty;

Heavy bombers equipped for long-range nuclear air-launched cruise missiles (ALCMs) will be distinguishable from other heavy bombers. Heavy bombers equipped for nuclear armaments other than long-range nuclear ALCMs will be counted as one delivery vehicle against the 1600 limit and will be attributed with one warhead against the 6000 limit;

Heavy bombers equipped for long-range nuclear ALCMs will be counted as one delivery vehicle against the 1600 limit and shall be attributed with an agreed number of warheads against the 6000 limit. Existing and future U.S. heavy bombers equipped for long-range nuclear ALCMs will be attributed with 10 warheads each. Existing and future Soviet heavy bombers equipped for long-range nuclear ALCMs will be attributed with 8 warheads each;

Within the 1600 limit on delivery vehicles the United States of America may have no more than 150 heavy bombers equipped for long-range nuclear ALCMs that are attributed with 10 warheads each. The Union of Soviet Socialist Republics may exceed that number of heavy bombers by 40 percent. If the United States of America exceeds the 150 number, each additional heavy bomber equipped for long-range nuclear ALCMs will be attributed with the number of long-range nuclear ALCMs for which it is actually equipped. If the Union of Soviet Socialist Republics exceeds 210 heavy bombers equipped for long-range nuclear ALCMs, each such heavy bomber will be attributed with the number of long-range nuclear ALCMs for which it is actually equipped;

Existing and future U.S. heavy bombers may be equipped for no more than 20 long-range nuclear ALCMs; existing and future Soviet heavy bombers may be equipped for no more than 12 long-range nuclear ALCMs;

Long-range ALCMs will be considered those with a range in excess of 600 kilometers. Future long-range non-nuclear ALCMs will not be considered nuclear if they are distinguishable from long-range nuclear ALCMs. There will be no restrictions on deploying such ALCMs on aircraft not limited by the Treaty.

Reductions will be carried out in three phases over a period of seven years. Specific, equal interim levels for agreed categories of strategic offensive arms will be achieved by the end of each phase of reductions;

The numerical limitations provided for by the Treaty will be achieved and complied with through conversion or elimination in accordance with agreed procedures.

Sea-launched cruise missiles (SLCMs) will not be constrained in the

START Treaty. Each side will provide the other with a unilateral declaration of its policy concerning nuclear SLCMs and, annually for the duration of the Treaty, with unilateral declarations regarding its planned deployments of nuclear long-range SLCMs, i.e., those with a range in excess of 600 kilometers. Those declarations will be politically binding. In the annual declarations the maximum number of deployed nuclear SLCMs for each of the following five Treaty years will be specified, provided that the number declared will not exceed 880. In the declarations of policy it will be specified that the United States of America and the Union of Soviet Socialist Republics will not produce or deploy nuclear sea-launched cruise missiles with multiple independently targetable warheads. The sides reaffirmed their 1987 Washington Summit Joint Statement to continue to seek "mutually acceptable and effective methods of verification."

Except as specifically prohibited, modernization and replacement of strategic offensive arms may be carried out.

The START Treaty will include specific prohibitions on certain categories of strategic offensive arms, basing modes and activities. The following are among the bans under the START Treaty:

— new types of heavy ICBMs;
— heavy SLBMs and launchers of heavy SLBMs;
— mobile launchers of heavy ICBMs;
— new types of ICBMs and SLBMs with more than 10 reentry vehicles;
— flight testing and deployment of existing types of ICBMs or SLBMs with a number of reentry vehicles greater than the number specified in the Washington Summit Joint Statement of December 1987;
— rapid reload of ICBM launchers;
— long-range nuclear ALCMs equipped with multiple independently targetable warheads.

The far-reaching reductions and other constraints contained in the Treaty will be accompanied by the most thorough and innovative verification provisions ever negotiated.

Taken together, the START Treaty's comprehensive verification regime will create a degree of transparency in the military sphere which would have been unthinkable only a short time ago. It will not only provide for effective verification of the obligations of the Treaty, but will also greatly increase the mutual confidence which is essential for a sound strategic relationship. In addition, this verification system can provide a model which may be incorporated into future agreements. The verification regime under development includes:

- On-site inspections: For the purpose of ensuring verification of compliance with the Treaty, each side will, on the basis of reciprocity, conduct twelve kinds of on-site inspections, as well as continuous monitoring of mobile ICBM production facilities, in accordance with agreed procedures. *Inter alia*, each side will conduct short-notice inspections at facilities related to strategic offensive arms, including inspections to verify the numbers of reentry vehicles on deployed ballistic missiles, inspections to verify elimination of strategic offensive arms and facilities related to them, suspect site inspections, and various exhibitions.
- National technical means of verification: For the purpose of ensuring verification, each side will use national technical means of verification at its disposal in a manner consistent with generally recognized principles of international law. The Treaty will include a series of cooperative measures to enhance the effectiveness of national technical means of verification. There will be a ban on interference with such means;
- Ban on denial of telemetric information: The sides agreed to make onboard technical measurements on ICBMs and SLBMs and to broadcast all telemetric information obtained from such measurements. Except for strictly limited exceptions, there will be a ban on any practice, including the use of encryption, encapsulation or jamming, that denies full access to telemetric information;
- Information exchange: Before signature of the Treaty the sides will exchange data on the numbers, locations and technical characteristics of their strategic offensive arms. These data will be updated on a regular basis throughout the lifetime of the Treaty;
- A comprehensive agreement on the manner of deployment of mobile ICBM launchers and their as-

sociated missiles and appropriate limitations on their movements so as to ensure effective verification of adherence to the numerical limitations provided for in the Treaty. In addition, the number of non-deployed ICBMs for mobile launchers will be limited and mobile ICBMs will be subject to identification through the application of unique identifiers, or tags.

To promote the objectives of the Treaty, the sides will establish the Joint Compliance and Inspection Commission.

The sides have agreed that the Treaty will have a duration of 15 years, unless superseded earlier by a subsequent agreement. If the sides so agree, the Treaty can be extended for successive five year periods, unless superseded.

The progress outlined above fulfills the aim, set forth by the Presidents of the United States of America and the Union of Soviet Socialist Republics during their Malta meeting, of agreeing upon the basic provisions of the strategic offensive arms Treaty by the time of their Washington meeting. The two Presidents express confidence that the Foreign Ministers and the delegations of the two countries at the Geneva talks will be able to reach agreement in the remaining months on the outstanding issues that are still being negotiated.

Joint Statement on Future Negotiations on Nuclear and Space Arms and Further Enhancing Strategic Stability, June 1, 1990 [3]

The United States of America and the Union of Soviet Socialist Republics, building on the results of the current negotiations, agree to pursue new talks on strategic offensive arms, and on the relationship between strategic offensive and defensive arms. The objectives of these negotiations will be to reduce further the risk of outbreak of war, particularly nuclear war, and to ensure strategic stability, transparency and predictability through further stabilizing reductions in the strategic arsenals of both countries. This will be achieved by seeking agreements that improve survivability, remove incentives for a nuclear first strike and implement an appropriate relationship between strategic offenses and defenses.

In order to attain these objectives, the sides have agreed as follows:

First. This year the sides will complete work on the Treaty Between the United States of America and the Union of Soviet Socialist Republics on the Reduction and Limitation of Strategic Offensive Arms [START]. Following the signing of the Treaty, the sides will hold consultations without delay regarding future talks and these important talks will begin at the earliest practical date. Both sides in these future talks will be free to raise any issues related to any strategic offensive arms.

Within the existing negotiating framework on Nuclear and Space Arms in Geneva, the two sides will continue negotiations on ABM (Antiballistic Missiles) and space without delay. Thus, in the future talks the two sides will discuss strategic stability issues of interest to them, including the relationship between strategic offensive and defensive arms, taking into account stabilizing reductions in strategic offensive arms and development of new technologies. The sides will work toward the important goal of reaching an early outcome in these negotiations.

Second. The United States of America and the Union of Soviet Socialist Republics, as is the case in the emerging START Treaty, will, in the new negotiations, seek to reduce their strategic offensive arms in a way consistent with enhancing strategic stability. In the new negotiations, the two sides agree to place emphasis on removing incentives for a nuclear first strike, on reducing the concentration of warheads on strategic delivery vehicles, and on giving priority to highly survivable systems.

In particular, the two sides will seek measures that reduce the concentration of warheads on strategic delivery vehicles as a whole, including measures related to the question of heavy missiles and MIRVed [multiple independently-targetable reentry vehicle] ICBMs. Effective verification will be provided by national technical means, cooperative measures, and on-site inspection.

Third. Having agreed on the need to ensure a predictable strategic relationship between the United States of America and the Union of Soviet Socialist Republics, the sides will, for the entire duration of the START

Treaty, exchange, at the beginning of each calendar year, information on planned changes in the numbers of strategic offensive arms as of the end of the current year.

Fourth. The sides will pursue additional measures to build confidence and ensure predictability of the military activities of the United States of America and the Union of Soviet Socialist Republics that would reduce the possibility of an outbreak of nuclear war as a result of accident, miscalculation, terrorism, or unexpected technological breakthrough, and would prevent possible incidents between them.

Fifth. The sides believe that reducing the risk of outbreak of nuclear war is the responsibility not only of the United States of America and the Union of Soviet Socialist Republics, and that other States should also make their contribution toward the attainment of this objective, in particular in the field of nonproliferation of nuclear weapons. They call upon all States to consider the new opportunities for engagement in mankind's common effort to remove the risk of outbreak of nuclear war worldwide.

Accordingly, the United States of America and the Union of Soviet Socialist Republics will give these future negotiations the highest priority so that the benefits of strengthened stability can be realized as soon as possible.

Joint Statement on Conventional Armed Forces in Europe, June 1, 1990 [3]

President Bush and President Gorbachev agreed that early conclusion of an agreement on conventional armed forces in Europe (CFE) is essential to the future stability and security of the continent. A CFE agreement will constitute the indispensable foundation for new European relationships and for a future security architecture in Europe. The Presidents reaffirmed the commitment they made at their meeting in Malta in December 1989 to conclude a CFE agreement by the end of 1990. They agreed further that the forthcoming summit of the CSCE nations should be held after the CFE agreement is ready for signature.

In the course of their talks, the Presidents committed themselves to in-

tensifying the pace of the negotiation in Vienna and to reaching rapid agreement on all outstanding issues.

Joint Statement on the Establishment of a Soviet-United States International Park in the Region of the Bering Strait, June 1, 1990 [3]

The Presidents of the United States of America and of the Union of Soviet Socialist Republics, expressing support for the expansion of bilateral cooperation in the field of environmental protection and in the preservation of cultural heritage, endorse the intention of the two countries to create, in the region of the Bering Strait, a U.S.-Soviet International Park embracing protected terrestrial and aquatic areas.

Both leaders recognize that elements of natural and cultural heritage of the Bering region represent a common heritage of the American and Soviet peoples. Thousands of years ago, across a land bridge uniting the Asian and American continents, the first arrivals came to North America. Later, the sea divided the continents but failed to destroy the ecological, cultural and spiritual community of the inhabitants of Beringia. This community has remained essentially undisturbed by the influences of historical change.

Both leaders recognize that the creation of an international park would facilitate permanent recognition of the unity of this heritage and secure a framework for joint efforts in its preservation.

During 1990-1991, both countries will undertake the following practical steps:

— preparation and signature of a protocol on the creation of a complex of specially designated protected terrestrial and aquatic areas; and

— determine all organizational details connected with the functioning of the park.

Continuing close cooperation regarding the international park, between the representatives of both countries, may take the form of regular meetings of senior park management officials, the exchange of park personnel for professional training and orientation, joint research and consultations on planning and exchange visits to both sides of the park for touristic and cultural purposes, in particular by native populations.

The two sides express their confidence that establishment of the international park will serve the development of U.S.-Soviet cooperation in the protection of nature, and the activities of local populations in preserving the unique natural and cultural heritage of the Bering region. [4]

Excerpts of White House Fact Sheets on Bilateral Agreements, June 1, 1990 [3]

TRADE AGREEMENT

At Malta, President Bush proposed targeting the June summit for completion of a MFN (most-favored-nation trade status) commercial agreement, provided that the Soviets approve and implement new emigration legislation. New emigration legislation passed the first reading in the Supreme Soviet in November. The Second Supreme Soviet reading, which would codify the law, was set for May 31. No serious opposition has appeared, but the press of other business could delay final passage. We have emphasized to the Soviets at all levels the importance of expeditious passage.

This agreement breaks much new ground in commercial agreements with the Soviets. Specifically, it:
- provides improved market access, for example, by prohibiting adoption of standards which are discriminatory or designed to protect domestic production;
- facilitates business by establishing expedited accreditation procedure for commercial offices, allowing offices to hire directly local and third-country employees on mutually agreed terms, permitting access to all advertising media, and allowing companies to engage and serve as agents and to conduct market studies; and
- offers strong intellectual property rights protections by reaffirming commitments to the Paris Convention and the Universal Copyright Convention, obligating adherence to the Bern Convention for the Protection of Literary and Artistic Works, providing copyright protec-

tion for computer programs and data bases and protection for sound recordings; providing product and process patent protection for virtually all areas of technology; and providing comprehensive coverage of trade secrets.

The Soviets have reaffirmed their commitment, once they receive MFN and USG [U.S. Government] lending restrictions (Stevenson and Byrd amendments) are lifted, to resume lend-lease repayments.

LONG-TERM GRAINS AGREEMENT

- The new agreement is to take effect January 1, 1991.
- The Soviets are required to buy a minimum of 10 million metric tons of grain from the United States annually (up from 9 million metric tons), including at least 4 million metric tons of wheat; 4 million metric tons of feed grains (corn, barley, or sorghum); and 2 million additional metric tons of either wheat, feed grains, or soybeans/soymeal, with soy measures counted double for purposes of quantity.
- The Soviets may buy up to 14 million metric tons annually (up from 12 million metric tons) without prior consultation with the Department of Agriculture.

CHEMICAL WEAPONS DESTRUCTION AGREEMENT

The U.S.-U.S.S.R. Bilateral Agreement

The key provisions of the destruction agreement are:
- Destruction of the vast bulk of declared stocks to begin by the end of 1992.
- Destruction of at least 50 percent of declared stocks by the end of 1999.
- Declared stocks are to be reduced to 5,000 agent tons by 2002.
- Both countries will stop producing chemical weapons upon entry into force of this agreement, without waiting for the global chemical weapons ban.
- On-site inspections during and after the destruction process to confirm that destruction has taken place.
- Annual exchanges of data on the stockpile levels to facilitate monitoring of the declared stockpiles.

- Details of the inspection procedures will be worked out by December 31, 1990.
- Both countries will cooperate in developing and using safe and environmentally sound methods of destruction.
- The United States and U.S.S.R. will take steps to encourage all chemical weapons-capable states to become parties to the multilateral convention.

Both countries took an initial step in this direction by exchanging data on declared chemical weapons stockpiles in December 1989 and by initiating verification experiments to build confidence and gain experience for a chemical weapons ban treaty.

This agreement will be submitted to Congress for its review and approval.

A Global Chemical Weapons Ban

The bilateral U.S.-Soviet agreement was designed to provide new impetus to the conclusion of a comprehensive, verifiable global chemical weapons ban at the earliest possible date. Toward that end:
- Both countries have agreed to accelerate their destruction of chemical weapons under a global chemical weapons convention so that by the eighth year after it enters into force, the United States and U.S.S.R. will have reduced their declared stocks to no more than 500 agent tons.
- The United States and U.S.S.R. will propose that a special conference be convened at the end of the eighth year of a multilateral convention to determine whether participation in the convention is sufficient to complete the elimination of chemical weapons stocks over the following 2 years.

THE NUCLEAR TESTING PROTOCOLS

Verification Method

- Two verification protocols being signed at the Washington summit will provide for effective verification of compliance with the treaties.
- Verification methods for Threshold Test Ban Treaty (TTBT) and Peaceful Nuclear Explosions Treaty (PNET) include hydrodynamic yield measurement, on-site inspection, and some seismic monitoring

on the territory of the testing party. The U.S. hydrodynamic method is CORRTEX [Continuous Reflectrometry for Radius versus Time Experiments] is the most accurate nonintrusive technique the United States has found. CORRTEX determines the yield by measuring, at the detonating site, the rate at which the supersonic shock wave in the ground crushes coaxial cable buried near the explosive device. On-site inspections permit each side to take core samples and rock fragments from the area of the explosion to confirm geological/geophysical data near the explosion. Seismic monitors measure distant shock waves produced by the explosion (as in measuring earthquakes) in order to arrive at an estimate of the explosive yield.

- National technical means also will be used to monitor all explosions.

How the Protocols Work

- PNET verification: Both sides have the right to hydrodynamic measurement (CORRTEX for the United States) for explosions with planned yields above 50 kilotons; the right to on-site inspections for explosions with planned yields above 35 kilotons; the right to a local seismic network for a group explosion above 150 kilotons.
- TTBT verification: the right to hydrodynamic measurements of nuclear weapons tests with planned yields above 50 kilotons; on-site inspection for tests with planned yields above 35 kilotons; in-country seismic monitoring for tests with planned yields above 50 kilotons, using three designated seismic stations off the test site but within the testing party's territory; special provisions for monitoring unusual cases: tests with nonstandard geometries, tests with multiple nuclear explosions in each of the first 5 years of the treaty, if a side does not have at least 2 tests with planned yields above 50 kilotons, the other side may use hydrodynamic measurement that year on up to 2 tests with planned yields below 50 kilotons.
- Required notifications under TTBT (PNET notifications are similar): Each June, the parties will inform each other of the number of ex-

plosions with planned yields above 35 kilotons and 50 kilotons for the following calendar year. No later than 200 days prior to the planned date of any explosion, the other side would have the right, under protocol provisions, to monitor; the testing party must provide notification of the planned date, location, and whether the planned yield exceeds 35 or 50 kilotons. Within 20 days of receipt of such notification, the verifying party must inform the testing party whether it plans to carry out verification activities, and, if so, which type.

- Under both treaties, joint commissions will be used to discuss implementation and verification issues.
- Once the protocols are signed, the administration will seek Senate advice and consent as to ratification of the TTBT and the PNET and their protocols.

CUSTOMS COOPERATION AGREEMENT

- The agreement provides for mutual assistance between the customs services of the United States and the U.S.S.R.
- The agreement provides the basis for cooperative activity in deterring and detecting narcotic trafficking.
- The agreement is designed to strengthen cooperative measures which the two services typically undertake.
- The agreement provides a formal basis for cooperation in areas of customs law enforcement assistance, export control, and commercial fraud.

MARITIME BOUNDARY AGREEMENT

- The parties agree that the line described as the "western limit" in the 1867 U.S.-Russia convention ceding Alaska is the maritime boundary along its entire length.
- Further, the agreement contains innovative provisions to ensure that all areas within 200 miles of either coast fall under the resource jurisdiction of one or the other party. The U.S.S.R. transfers to the United States jurisdiction in three "special areas" within 200 miles of the Soviet coast, beyond 200 miles of the U.S. coast, and on the U.S. side of the maritime boundary. The

United States transfers to U.S.S.R. jurisdiction in one "special area" within 200 miles of the U.S. coast, beyond 200 miles of the Soviet coast, and on the Soviet side of the maritime boundary.

CULTURAL CENTER AGREEMENT

- The Centers—constituted as nondiplomatic, nonprofit institutions—will be opened in Washington and Moscow.
- The Center Directors and one Deputy Director for each side are to have diplomatic titles and be accredited by their governments to their respective Embassies, with this exception: Center personnel, properties, and papers will not have diplomatic status.
- The Centers will carry out a variety of functions, e.g. operating libraries; sponsoring seminars, films, and performances; and providing student counseling and language instruction.
- The public is guaranteed free, unrestricted access to the Centers.
- The U.S. Center in Moscow has the right to use rubles to cover domestic operating expenses.
- Occupancy and opening dates will be determined by mutual agreement on basis of reciprocity.
- The agreement is to take effect after an exchange of notes confirming each side has completed the domestic measures required for implementation.

AGREEMENT ON EXPANSION OF UNDERGRADUATE UNIVERSITY EXCHANGES

- Increase existing exchanges (750 U.S. and 250 Soviet) by 250 students both ways in academic year 1991-1992.
- Increase targeted numbers to 1,500 each way by 1995-1996, subject to availability of funds.
- Mix of private and U.S. Government funding (arrangements to be determined) to cover the costs of the Soviet participants in the United States; the U.S.S.R. is to cover all in-country costs for Americans.
- Participants on both sides are to be chosen on basis of academic excellence and language proficiency.
- Participants would pursue full-time academic work in a variety of dis-

ciplines, including agriculture. The preferred length of the students' participation would be one year, though shorter periods would be considered.

MEMORANDUM OF UNDERSTANDING TO INCREASE CIRCULATION OF AMERICA AND SOVIET LIFE MAGAZINES

- The memorandum of understanding (MOU) amends the 1989-1991 Program of Cooperation under General Exchanges Agreement.
- The MOU provides for increased circulation of America and Soviet Life magazines up to 250,000 copies in 1991.
- The distribution of both magazines after 1991 is to be governed solely by demand.
- Each side may print commercial advertising and distribute unsold copies of its magazine at official premises, cultural centers, and exhibitions under its sponsorship.

Dinner Toasts, June 1, 1990 [5]

President Gorbachev

Mr. President, Mrs. Bush, ladies and gentlemen, comrades, we have completed the second full day of talks, but I would like to sum things up. This meeting is only a stage, though a major one, in the gigantic and forward-looking project of *perestroika* and Soviet-American relations.

We are going to have at least two more meetings with President Bush this year alone: one at the Conference on Security on Cooperation in Europe, where I hope a treaty reducing conventional arms in Europe will be signed, and the other to sign a treaty reducing strategic offensive arms.

I believe that the agenda for 1990 that we approved at Malta can be implemented. We may reach greater heights in building a new Soviet-American relationship only by setting our sights higher and higher while abandoning all that was nurtured by the ideology and geopolitics of the Cold War.

In assessing the outcome of our talks, I believe I can say that they have demonstrated a growing mutual understanding between the U.S.S.R. and the

United States, which means progress in sustaining the profound and positive changes underway in the world. In this regard, our in-depth discussion of the problems and prospects of the European process was no doubt a useful one. It has served to clarify views and positions, and brought in new arguments for consideration and exploration of acceptable solutions.

It is quite natural that we focused on the external aspects of German unification. As we see it, two processes should be completed: that of the final postwar settlement, and that related to the internal issues of interforming the two parts of Germany into a single state. We believe that those two processes form the substance of the period of transition which when completed will result in the cancellation of the rights of the four victorious powers; the rights which, incidentally, stem from the outcome of the war and not from the division of Germany. The transition will end in the emergence of a new sovereign state.

At the same time we believe that the discussion is not over, that it continues. And there may be more than one approach. We have to consider all of them together, including also our allies. What is acceptable in the final analysis is only a jointly developed approach which would not prejudice anybody's interest or erode the overall process of positive changes in Europe and in the world. Those changes are the principle achievement of recent years and the main product of growing trust between us and of the growing awareness that our civilization is one.

A very important result of this summit is the agreements we have signed today and the official statements we have made. They demonstrate that our joint policy of moving from constructive understanding to constructive interaction is bearing fruit. There is no doubt that this has been made possible — and I would say that what happened today is a confirmation of what I'm going to say — this has been made possible only in the environment produced by our meeting with President George Bush at Malta.

The Soviet Union and the United States had to conduct a major and, I would say, courageous reassessment of how they viewed each other and the world. They had to realize that our mutual isolation was an anomaly and that human civilization is indivisible. Therefore, it is quite logical that the agreements we have signed reflect our

common readiness to obtain greater interdependence from people-to-people communication and cooperation in vitally important areas and through reinforcing the legal framework of Soviet-American relations. The package of our new agreements also reflects the special role the Soviet Union and the United States play in building bridges of understanding and trust between the East and the West.

In particular, I would like to call your attention to the agreement on trade. This agreement takes on special relevance since it has been concluded at a time of a dramatic change of direction in the Soviet economy which is crucial for the future of *perestroika*. I am convinced that the Soviet people will appreciate the fact that the United States, the President of the United States, is signing this agreement to normalize Soviet-American commercial relations at this moment of special importance for our country.

Now that we have recorded the progress we have made and laid down guidelines for the future, I would like to express the hope that the ship of Soviet-American relations will continue to sail on this course. It is clear that there are still some disagreements between us as to the optimal structure of our relationship. But this area of disagreement is being narrowed while the area of trust, agreement, and cooperation is expanding. An indication of the sincerity and seriousness of our countries' intentions is that we have started a difficult process of revising what appeared to be eternal concepts of the role of military power in safeguarding national security. In taking a radically different approach to security, we should not forget people who were ahead of their time. Andrei Sakharov is one of them.

One of the fathers of nuclear super weapons, Sakharov had the courage of his convictions to uphold to the end that force could no longer play a role in relations among states. Sakharov taught us another lesson, too: One should not fear dogma, nor be afraid of appearing naive. Political decisions that truly meet peoples' best interests should be based on the realities of life, not on contrived schemes.

Today our society is going through a complex, and sometimes dramatic, but promising process of *perestroika* on a democratic and humane basis with full respect for human rights and freedoms. *Perestroika* is also a contribution to building a new world, for we are searching for answers to the questions that confront in one way or another with greater or lesser intensity all nations and, indeed, all mankind.

We believe that once we are clear of the thorns on this path we have chosen, we shall not only reach new frontiers in our country's history but also help to build a new civilization of peace. We are ready to do that, together with the United States of America.

I would like to propose a toast to a future of peace for the Soviet and the American people, and for all nations on Earth. To idealism and the idealists. To the health of the President of the United States of America, Mr. George Bush, and Barbara Bush. To the health and well-being of all present here. To the happiness of our children and grandchildren.

President Bush

Mr. President and Mrs. Gorbachev, Barbara and I would like to thank you for this splendid dinner and for your wonderful hospitality and for your most interesting and gracious remarks. Yesterday we welcomed the Gorbachevs back to Washington still filled with memories of the things we shared in Malta: friendship, cooperation, seasick pills. [Laughter]

For us here in this country, Mr. President, this week began with our observance of our Memorial Day, a day for not only remembrance of those who gave their last full measure of devotion but also for recommitment to the ideal that they shall not have died in vain.

And the week has now ended with a new memorial, a living memorial marked by historic agreements on both nuclear and chemical arms. And they've been shaped by a remembrance of shared interests and a recommitment to forging a just and lasting peace. And they stand as a memorial not to the past but to the future, a memorial to wars that need never be fought, to the hardship and suffering that need never be endured.

This afternoon we signed a landmark agreement to destroy the great majority of our chemical weapons. And we issued a joint statement recording major agreed provisions of a strategic arms reduction treaty. And the President and I also signed a commercial agreement, and we're looking for-

ward to the passage of a Soviet emigration law. And we also agreed on this long-term grain agreement.

But true peace takes more than just laying down of arms. It also requires the reaching out of hands. And you know, Americans and Soviets have often tended to think of our two countries as being on opposite sides of almost everything, including the opposite sides of the world. But we share an important northern border, and we are, in fact, next door neighbors across the Bering Sea.

Today, we've also signed an agreement fixing our maritime boundary in the Bering Sea area and announced our agreement to establish a U.S.-Soviet park across the Bering Strait, a new gateway to the Arctic and a new gateway to the future.

Mr. President, I learned that the name of your home town out in the northern Caucasus, Privolnoye, can mean spacious or free.

President Gorbachev

Thank you for mentioning it.

President Bush

I know my pronunciation was bad, but I'm sure I'm right when I say it means spacious or free. [Laughter]

President Gorbachev

Great pronunciation—can mean both.

President Bush

Well, anyway, it reminded me of the new breeze, the new spirit of freedom that we've seen sweep across Europe and around the globe. I sensed it last summer, speaking in front of the shipyard gates to the people of Gdansk. And I told them because Americans are so free to dream, we feel a special kinship with those who dream of being free. Today that kinship is quickly becoming a shared spirit, a spirit that inspires millions here in our nation, in your own, and around the world.

So, ladies and gentlemen, I invite all of you to join me in a toast to our gracious hosts, the President and Mrs. Gorbachev. To lasting peace, and to this wonderful spirit of freedom.

Exchange With Reporters Following Meetings at Camp David, Maryland, June 2, 1990 [5]

Q. President Bush, how was the meeting?

President Bush. Just a minute, wait until I get out of this thing. [Laughter] [6]

President Gorbachev. In today's discussions with the President I rate them no less than the conversations we had yesterday and the day before yesterday, over the past two days. We worked very constructively and fruitfully, and I think that had we not had this day like today my visit would have been different. But the discussions we have had today make it possible for me to state with full responsibility and in a balanced manner the full and two things: there is really ample opportunity for our cooperation, even though there are some real problems to which neither the President nor myself turn a blind eye to. And I set high store by the personal relationship that the President and myself have established, the personal rapport between us.

We showed a great responsibility, both to our people as well as to the peoples of other nations. But this kind of personal rapport that we have established enables us to approach all problems in a better way by presenting argumentation and reaching a certain balance.

Q. But will you reassess your position on Germany as a result of these informal talks?

President Gorbachev. We discussed that, and the President and myself are going to mention the subject tomorrow. We exchanged views on this question, too. But there's one point that has to be borne in mind: for all the importance of our positions and responsibilities, we must remember that we are all part of this process. There is also the six—the Two-Plus-Four formula. There are also interests of other European nations involved. And I think the President and myself took that into account. It's been a big day, indeed.

Q. On what issues did you make progress today?

President Bush. I would simply say that my assessment of the meetings and President Gorbachev's are in close parallel. He pointed out there's some differences, and I'll point out there's some differences. But as I said yesterday, I see this glass not half empty but half full, and more. And I think the point is, we've been able to discuss these differences and the common ground in a very civil way. I will repeat what I have said before: that President Gorbachev has presided over and, indeed, led in ways that have brought about significant change. That change benefits mankind and it benefits U.S.-Soviet relations.

So, some will argue that we haven't solved all the problems. To me, that's not the point. The point is, we have an awful lot of common ground. We sat there today and talked about regional problems, not in the sense of dividing up the world — maybe that would have happened years ago — but in terms of ironing out problems, achieving common ground as we looked at a lot of regional problems. We did the same thing yesterday and the day before on bilateral problems.

So, at the end of the day here in Camp David, no neckties, very relaxed. The only thing that went wrong is, I pride myself as a horseshoe player, and President Gorbachev picked up a horseshoe, never having played the game to my knowledge, and literally, literally — all you horseshoe players out there — threw a ringer the first time. [Laughter] Really. And I like to think — there's not much more to say.

President Gorbachev. Well, I couldn't give in, after all. [Laughter]

President Bush. But there's a more significant point. And that is that he pointed out in a very warm and friendly atmosphere at dinner that a horseshoe in the Soviet Union, when posted in one's house, symbolizes warmth and friendship. That made an impression on me.

Q. Mr. President, "close enough" is only good enough usually in horseshoes.

President Bush. Yes.

Q. But you went ahead and signed the trade agreement despite the differences on Lithuania.

President Bush. Exactly. And the maritime agreement and the grain agreement and a lot of other agreements, including arms control agreements.

Q. Despite the difference on Lithuania.

President Bush. And this, in my view, is the interest of the United States. The agreement we signed on arms, the agreement we signed on trade,

maritime, Bering Straits. Why do you single out one agreement? I look at the overall relationship. If somebody wants to argue with me, fine, we'll take him on. I'm doing what I think is in the best interest of the United States of America.

President Gorbachev. Goodbye.

President Bush. You got it. Thank you all.

President Gorbachev. Thank you.

President Bush. We'll see you guys.

Joint Statement on Ethiopia, June 2, 1990 [3]

The U.S. and U.S.S.R. discussed relief requirements and the prospects for a political solution to Ethiopia's internal conflict. They welcome the Ethiopian government's agreement to permit relief food to enter northern Ethiopia through the Port of Massawa under a U.N. sponsored relief effort, and they believe that such operations would not compromise the unity and territorial integrity of Ethiopia. They also welcomed the agreement expressed by the Ethiopian government to have U.N. representatives present in the course of the negotiations between the Ethiopian government and the Eritreans.

In addition, to deal with the growing problems of starvation, the U.S. and the U.S.S.R. are prepared to work together and combine their assets. U.S. food will be transported on Soviet aircraft to demonstrate our joint commitment to responding to this tragic humanitarian problem.

Recognizing the continuing political and military conflicts that exacerbate the problems of starvation and recognizing also the lack of momentum on peace talks, the U.S. and U.S.S.R. will support an international conference of governments under the auspices of the U.N. on settlement of conflict situations in the Horn of Africa.

Joint Statement on the Environment, June 2, 1990 [3]

During the state visit of Mikhail S. Gorbachev, President of the U.S.S.R., at the invitation of George Bush, President of the United States, the two sides affirmed their serious concern about the health of the global environment, and

their commitment to expand U.S.-Soviet cooperation in the field of environmental protection and the study of global change. Mindful of their obligations under international environmental conventions, and committed to continued international discussion aimed at other understandings on matters of common concern, the sides emphasized the need for practical and effective joint measures on environmental protection.

The United States and the U.S.S.R. attached great importance to full and open exchange of environmental data, and to careful coordination of existing global atmospheric, terrestrial and ocean monitoring systems. Accordingly, they endorsed intensified bilateral cooperation in areas of environmental, ecological and pollution monitoring, and in related research.

The United States and the Soviet Union noted with satisfaction their agreement to establish, by the end of 1991, a Beringian International Park in the region of the Bering Strait. On other bilateral matters, they also pledged to facilitate contacts and cooperation between their respective nongovernmental environmental organizations.

Joint News Conference, June 3, 1990 [5]

President Bush. Good morning, everybody. Please be seated. Well, when President Gorbachev and I were at Malta, we agreed that we would try to build a fundamentally different U.S.-Soviet relationship, one that would move beyond containment to an era of enduring cooperation. At the time, no one knew the momentous events that would unfold around the world. And our task is, if anything, more urgent, and the case for a new U.S.-Soviet relationship more compelling, because the opportunities before us are so great.

We've not shied away from discussing issues about which we disagree. There were some tough ones before us, particularly the aspiration of the Baltic peoples, a cause which the United States fully supports. I think it's a mark of how far the U.S.-Soviet relationship has come that in all our exchanges, whether about issues on which we agreed or disagreed, the spirit of candor and openness, a desire not just to understand but to build bridges, shone through.

President Gorbachev and I had intensive discussions on the transforming events in Europe, events that have put before us our best chance in four decades to see Europe whole and free. I stressed that the long-held aspirations of the German people should be met without delay. On the matter of Germany's external alliances, I believe, as do Chancellor [Helmut] Kohl [of the Federal Republic of Germany] and members of the alliance, that the united Germany should be a full member of NATO. President Gorbachev, frankly, does not hold that view. But we are in full agreement that the matter of alliance membership is, in accordance with the Helsinki Final Act, a matter for the Germans to decide.

Over the last six months and in Washington this week, we made great progress in our mutual effort toward building a more peaceful and stable world. We signed a very important chemical weapons accord, nuclear testing protocols and gave a political push to others, including negotiations to reduce U.S.-Soviet strategic nuclear forces and conventional military forces in Europe. I'm also hopeful that the good discussion between President Gorbachev and — the one we had about the importance of "open skies" — we'll revive those negotiations. We discussed regional issues and human rights in considerable detail, made progress in the economic sphere, concluding a commercial agreement, a long-term grains agreement.

In closing, let me say how productive I really feel the last few days have been. President Gorbachev and I have agreed to meet on a regular basis, perhaps annually. Both of us would like to think that we can get together more often with less formality because, you see, we're now at a stage in the U.S.-Soviet relationship, and indeed in world history, where we should miss no opportunity to complete the extraordinary tasks before us.

Mr. President, it's been a pleasure having you here, sir.

President Gorbachev. Ladies and gentlemen, comrades, what has happened over these days enables me to characterize this summit meeting as an event of enormous importance, both for our bilateral relations and in the context of world politics. President Bush has listed the results of the work that we have done together here, which enables you to see the scope, the scale, of this

work and, I think, confirms the conclusion that I have drawn.

I agree with President Bush fully, who many times emphasized that we took Malta as a point of departure. And it is Malta that added momentum to the process which, of course, given all the difficulties and disagreements which we have and which we do not deny, still leads us to a qualitatively new relationship with the U.S.S.R. and the U.S.A. The atmosphere and the results of this meeting make it possible for us to speak, really, of a new phase of cooperation, which the President has just mentioned.

I believe that this transition is both the result and a factor for further changes that affect all countries. The constructive spirit of these days, the spirit of responsibility in which we discussed all questions, have made our success possible; and that's very important because that has a stabilizing effect on the entire international situation at a time when we are addressing fundamental issues of civilization.

I would not want to now give a listing of all that we discussed, to mention all the agreements, all the important questions and statements that we have made and that have a lot of potential for the future. But let me still mention what is most important: We signed the main provision for a treaty on the reduction of strategic arms. And I would like to emphasize that this is the first time that we're not just limiting but we will be reducing the most devastating means of warfare. And I hope that we will sign the treaty itself this year. We also signed a statement about the future treaty negotiations on nuclear and space arms. We have agreed to make sure that we will complete the Vienna talks this year and sign an agreement on conventional arms at a European summit by the end of this year. Not everything depends on us, but this is our position; we want to achieve that.

We also discussed problems relating to the European process; specifically, external aspects of German unification. I cannot say that we have reached agreement, but that does not mean that our efforts were futile. Many new arguments emerged as a result of these discussions, and new, possible perspectives. We have clarified our positions, and it is our position that we will continue discussion in order to find a mutually acceptable solution. We could not resolve this issue in Washington

with the two of us. There is also the Two-Plus-Four formula and other European countries which are concerned and which want to see a mutually acceptable solution, a solution acceptable to all of us. The position of the Soviet Union is that we have to find solutions that would fit into the overall positive trend of changes in Europe and in the world that would strengthen and not erode security.

I would like, in particular, to emphasize the importance of our dialogue at Camp David, where we talked during the day yesterday; and this is a new phase in strengthening mutual understanding and trust between us. We really discussed all world problems. We compared our political perspectives, and we did that in an atmosphere of frankness, a constructive atmosphere, an atmosphere of growing trust. We discussed, specifically, such urgent international issues as the situation in the Middle East, Afghanistan, southern Africa, Cambodia, Central America. That is just some of what we have discussed. I would not want to go into detail right now. I think that you will probably seek to get clarification on this. But anyway I think that the Camp David dialogue was very important.

We have agreed to make a special statement on Ethiopia, to support efforts to reestablish peace there and also, with the help of the United Nations, to give humanitarian relief to the Ethiopian people.

Speaking of bilateral relations, we have some important political achievements here. Specifically, there is movement on such important areas as trade agreement, grain trade, agreement on civil aviation cooperation, maritime agreement, peaceful uses of the atomic energy science and technology, and education.

While we and the President were working — and our Ministers were also discussing things — there were important contacts and discussions with the various American companies. And some important decisions were made, such as Chevron, that will be participating in the exploration of the Tengiz oil fields. That will mean an investment of about 10 billion rubles. A group of our academicians were here with me, and they had a good discussion which resulted in the signing of a memorandum of intent with IBM, which will participate in the program of using computers for education in the Soviet

Union. I think that this economic area and other areas create a good foundation for our political dialogue and creates a kind of solid pillar of support for our cooperation.

I would like to express my profound gratification at this work that we have done together with President George Bush. I appreciate very much him as a political leader who is able, in a very human way and in a politically responsible way, to engage in dialogue and cooperation. We spent many hours together and were able to come to know each other very well. I don't know whether anyone will be ever able to say that we know each other totally well or completely. I think that would take many, many years. But now we have a good human relationship and, I think, a good human atmosphere between us.

The President has said, and I would like to confirm this, that we have decided to have regular meetings on a working basis in a businesslike manner, and this is really what is necessary. I would like to tell you that I've invited President George Bush, the President of the United States, to visit the Soviet Union, to come for a state visit to our country, in concluding — and that is something that is not within the framework of the official negotiations but was part of our visit.

I would like to say both to the Americans and to the Soviet people that here we — the Soviet delegation — we have felt very good feelings of the American people, feelings of solidarity, and a lot of interest from the Americans toward what we are doing in the Soviet Union for *perestroika*. I have felt that on many occasions in my short exchanges with the Americans and also in various talks. I would like to thank all Americans for that, and they certainly can expect reciprocity from the Soviet Union for that.

And finally, we, the two of us, were discussing things of concern to us, various regions, various problems affecting the lives of other countries; but that does not mean that we were trying to decide anything for others any way. We remembered always that what we were doing must be useful not only for our countries but for the world — and of course, specifically, for the Third World.

And let me, at this, wrap up my initial remarks at this press conference.

German Unification and NATO

Q. I'd like to ask both Presidents about Germany. President Bush, you've mentioned that you still have a disagreement about a united Germany being in NATO. In any concrete sense, did you narrow your differences on this subject, and are any alternatives being seriously considered?

President Bush. I'm not sure we narrowed them. I feel I understand President Gorbachev's position. But I know this for fact certain: I had every opportunity to explain in considerable detail why I felt a united Germany in NATO would be stabilizing, would be important for the stability of a post-German unification Europe.

So, I can't say whether we narrowed them; but the benefit of a meeting like this is, once again, you can talk in great frankness about it. I have no suspicion about his position, and I hope he has no suspicion about mine. And we've got collective decisions to take with NATO allies on matters of this nature, but in the final analysis, it's the question for Germany to decide that.

And maybe we're closer on that, but I would defer to President Gorbachev.

President Gorbachev. Since I have already made quite a few remarks on many occasions during these days on this subject, I will confine myself to comments which I think important in order to emphasize the thinking on this score and in order for us to understand better what we are after. We're not insisting that it should be an option of the Soviet Union. We are not saying that this should be a version by the United States of America or anybody else's option.

What we are talking about is an option — or a solution of external problems related to Germany unification which would organically incorporate the European process and improvement of international politics as a whole — so that a solution of these issues would help enrich this process and make it more stable and reliable. We're opposed to any options whatever it may come from. We ourselves are not going to offer one that would weaken these processes or create difficulties for the unfolding processes in the European continent. We've not going to put spokes in the wheels, as it were. So, I believe the fact that the President, myself, and our colleagues have devoted a great deal of time to this issue — we

have thrashed out this idea very, very thoroughly — I think has been very helpful and beneficial because we will continue our debates on this.

Rapport Between Two Presidents

Q. I have this question to address to you. You have just mentioned President Bush as having qualities of a statesman. Could you tell us what role they played in helping you make so many accomplishments at this summit meeting and advance in the solution of many problems that seem to be intractable?

President Gorbachev. I can reiterate what I have said, and I can add the following: Mr. Bush and I met each other a bit earlier before finding ourselves in this position together. And during my contacts with him, I felt — and it was during my first visit here in 1987 — that this is the kind of person to do business with, to build our relations with. Then we had contacts at Governors Island, which persuaded me even more of that.

We have maintained correspondence between us, and perhaps Malta was exactly the point where President Bush and I could get to know each other even better and to engage in some thinking on one-on-one meetings. I must say that everything began with discovering the fact that President Bush and myself have a desire to do business informally, which is very, very important. If we added to this the fact that each of us, while being himself and while representing their own people, should react in a responsible fashion to everything and in context of the real role played by the Soviet Union and the United States of America, we could very well imagine the human compatibility which exist between people and which enables them to create a kind of atmosphere that makes it possible to clarify the root causes of some particular processes.

I can say that this dialogue is well underway. And as to yesterday's meetings at Camp David, they were a great accomplishment in and by themselves. This is my assessment, and I think the fact that we have established a rapport will be very important.

Israeli Settlement of Occupied Territories

Q. This is a two-pronged question for both Presidents. Beyond words, what guarantees can you give the Palestinians that the decisions you made on emigration will not result in the further usurpation of their lands? And why is it that President Gorbachev has shown so much human sympathy for the Palestinians, while the U.S. vetoes even a U.N. look at their plight under military siege?

President Bush. Did you have a particular order you wanted us to answer that question in? [Laughter]

Q. If you can.

President Bush. The United States policy on settlement in the occupied territories is unchanged and is clear. And that is: We oppose new settlements in territories beyond the 1967 lines—the stated, reaffirmed policy over and over again. Now, we do not oppose the Secretary-General sending an emissary to the Middle East to look at this important question. The question is compounded, however, when you see, on the eve of the discussion of that, an outrageous guerrilla attack on Israel launched from another country. That is unacceptable to the United States. Having said that, the position of our country is we do not think that it needs U.N. troops or U.N. Security Council missions, but we do favor Mr. Goulding, a representative of the Secretary General, going there.

So, when the question came—and we differed with the Soviet Union; indeed, we differed with many of our other allies on this question—it is our view that the most productive way to handle that question was to have an emissary from the Secretary General, not, as the other countries in the Security Council favored, a Security Council delegation go there.

Q. But, Mr. President, you agree that there have been settlements, even though this has been our policy for many years?

President Bush. Yes, I agree there are settlements that go contrary to the United States policy; and I will continue to represent the policy, reiterate the policy, and try to persuade the Government of Israel that it is counterproductive to go forward with additional settlements in these territories. Our objective is to get the parties to the peace table. And our Secretary of State has worked diligently with the Israelis, and I've tried to do my best to get them talking. And that's what we think is the most immediate step that is needed. And I will continue to reiterate

American policy and continue to push for peace talks.

President Gorbachev. Just a moment. I'd like to respond, too. You formulated your question in precise terms, namely: What kind of guarantees can we issue so that those who want to leave—those who have chosen Israel as their place of residence—those who leave from the Soviet Union should not be resettled on occupied territories?

This is not a simple question, and this is what I have to say in this connection. The Soviet Union is now being bombarded by a lot of criticism from Arab countries lately. I have had meetings with President [Hafiz el-] Assad of Syria and President [Hosni] Mubarak of Egypt.

Those were very important talks with them. Nevertheless, this was the question that was also raised by them in acute terms—the question of guarantees now. We are facing the following situation.

Either, after these meetings and exchanges with the President of the United States of America on this particular issue, our concern would be heeded in Israel and they will make certain conclusions or else we must give further thought to it in terms of what we can do with issuing permits for exit. And some people are raising the matter in these terms in the Soviet Union, namely: As long as there are no assurances from the Israelis that this is not going to be done by them for the—to postpone issuing permits for exit, to put it off. But I hope they will heed what the two Presidents strongly advise them, that they should act in a wise fashion. Perhaps this is what I would like to express by way of reacting.

President Boris N. Yeltsin of the Russian Republic

Q. My question is addressed to Comrade Gorbachev. Your relationship with President Bush, *perestroika* activities well-assured inside, but there is a cooling of interest. Everybody's concerned with internal matters at home. Taking advantage of this opportunity, I'd like to ask you what do you think of your relationship with Yeltsin? Are you going to offer an olive branch of peace to each other?

President Gorbachev. I don't think you have chosen the best place for

clarifying our internal problems. [Laughter] But *c'est la vie*, as they say [laughter]—there is real life. There are certain processes underway back home. And I thought I tried to respond to this question when I was in Canada. As soon as I stepped out of the plane, they asked me this particular question. And I said that what I was worrying about most was a kind of an impasse which emerged at the Congress itself, because there is no strong preponderance. It took really three rounds for Comrade Yeltsin to gain a majority of votes, by just a few votes, to be elected. So, the situation remains.

And I said that in recent days something has happened which calls for thinking on our part. Comrade Yeltsin, with respect to some very serious, important, political, fundamental issues, has changed his position. At least he has introduced clarity. And I said if this is not a political gain for him to hold high office it is one thing. A certain approach can be adopted on the basis of that, and we could certainly forecast a certain kind of developments in the Supreme Soviet and in Russia.

But if this is nothing but a maneuver and he will return to what he has been doing in recent years—not only critical terms if Americans believe this is to be constructive but also in destructive activities, destructive efforts. He went as far as to fertilize in the framework of *perestroika* our efforts with ideas regarding forms of life where we are making a turnaround in all spheres. So, if he is going to come back to this, then, of course, his chairmanship will certainly complicate these processes. I should say that, after that he gave an interview and people began to see that he is changing again, the very next day he was interrogated at a session. He tried to explain his position.

In short, I always say life will place everything in proper perspective. Now that we have reached a phase of radical, fundamental change where everybody is supposed to show great responsibility for their country, where we're changing everything, now that we're about to make a radical change in our economy, it is all very serious. Everything will become clear pretty soon what Comrade Yeltsin is after.

Trade Agreement and MFN Status

Q. Mr. President, President Bush, I'd like to ask you about the trade

agreement that you signed yesterday, already a matter of some political controversy and criticism in this country. Secretary Baker has indicated it will not go to Congress for its action until the Soviet codification of its new emigration policies. Does that mean, sir, that when that law is passed in the Soviet Union that you are prepared to go ahead as well with most-favored-nation [MFN] trading status for the Soviet Union, or will that further step require some action, some loosening, some shift on the Baltics?

President Bush. We had a chance to discuss the Baltics, and I made clear that the Baltics—I think I said it at a U.S. press conference several weeks ago—caused some tensions. But the linkage is between the trade agreement and the emigration legislation. I'm not going to send that legislation up—and I've tried to be very frank—until the Soviet Union has completed action on the legislation guaranteeing the right of emigration.

Q. Well, what about, sir, the further step of actually granting most-favored-nation status?

President Bush. I've given our position in the linkages between the emigration, and that's it.

Q. May we take it, then, sir, that most-favored-nation status would then be forthcoming if this emigration law is codified?

President Bush. We'll cross that bridge when we get to it. But the trade agreement linkage is between the— MFN is hooked into the emigration law being passed. That's it.

We have other agreements—the grain agreement, and we have a maritime agreement. And the difference of position we have on the Baltics, you might say is one of the thorns in the side of an overall relationship. We've always had a difference on this. We have not recognized the incorporation of the Baltic States into the Soviet Union; that's been the historic position of the United States. But that concern, you might say, affects a wide array of issues that we have with the Soviet Union.

Frankly, I've been very pleased. First place, I've tried to be very frank with President Gorbachev not just here but before he came here, saying the difficulties that I face. And [Secretary of State] Jim Baker was very frank with [Soviet Foreign Minister] Eduard Shevardnadze, saying the problems we face. I think it is important in this emerg-

ing relationship that we share as directly as we can with the Soviet side the political problems we face. We've got a Congress that has its rights. They have every right to look at what I've signed and every obligation to do that and make their judgment as to whether it's in the best interests.

I signed the trade agreement because I am convinced that it is in the best interests of the United States. I believe the same thing about the grain agreement. I believe the same thing about the maritime agreement. But I don't want to mislead the American people and say that I have lessened my concern over the Baltic States. I've tried to be frank with the Soviet side on this. But the linkage (back to your question) the linkage with trade is on MFN— emigration law being passed. And then we go forward.

Negotiating Strengths and Weaknesses

Q. In connection with this meeting, there was a lot of speculation about weak and strong points—somebody speaks from a position of strength, someone from a position of weakness. How would you define what a strong position is, a position of strength? What is the place where a factor of force or strength holds? What are the components of force? What makes politics strong? This is a question that is addressed to both Presidents.

President Gorbachev. Let me begin first in order to let President Bush have a little rest. [Laughter] I think this is a certain speculation on this score. Both during the preceding period and in the course of our talks, we have been representing our peoples and countries, well aware of what the dialogue is all about. And I think to assume that someone— myself or President Bush—can dictate to each other or to the Soviet Union is absurd. This would be the greatest misconception, on the basis of which no progress could ever be made.

I think that this idea is suggested because at this point in time the Soviet Union is deep into profound change. And since fundamental change is involved, we are walking away from one particular way of life toward different forms of life: we're changing our political system; we're introducing a new model in economy. All these are fundamental things, indeed. Debates are underway. Doubts are being expressed. Views are being compared. And this is

very important because what is at stake is our destiny.

Of course, when you look from outside—well, we ourselves can feel the strain of our society; it is very much politicized. But a look from outside, without knowing all the subtleties, without knowing all the depth of sentiments—one could certainly arrive at some erroneous conclusions. Hence, the question of how long will Gorbachev stay in his office and how this whole *perestroika* will end and so on and so forth.

Even this, I think, fits into this process of profound change, and perhaps this is something we cannot do without. But the most important thing is that everything that is happening confirms not only the fact that we're cleaning up our courtyard, we are really revamping our entire society. We are trying to adapt it to human needs on the basis of freedom and democracy. We want to make it more open toward the outside world. That is the essence, and therein, Soviet people do not differ. And I hope there are no differences on that among the journalistic corps.

Perhaps some part of society thinks otherwise, but the question is how to do all this to avoid losing everything that we should keep and jettison everything that we don't need, that stands in the way. I don't think we have ever tackled tasks like this in the history of our country. I don't know whether anybody else has been able to resolve so many tasks within such a short period of time. So, it is for this particular reason that we appreciate so highly the fact that the whole world understands this correctly.

So, from this particular perspective, I wish to state—and this goes to show the farsightedness of President Bush and his colleagues, to say nothing of the American public, which overall understands what is happening in the Soviet Union today, understands that this is something that we need. Above all, of course, it's up to us to solve all of these problems; but of course, everybody understands full well that this is something that the whole world, all the nations, need. For without such changes, without a stronger, balanced, harmonized world, we will not accomplish our objectives.

So, today the pivotal point of world politics is *perestroika* in the Soviet Union, not because we are there but because this is an objective reality.

President Bush. May I simply add that the United States is not trying to deal from strength or weakness. I tried to say this at the welcoming ceremony for President Gorbachev. We have a unique responsibility to deal with world peace. No other countries have the same degree of responsibility that the Soviet Union and the United States have. So, we're not looking for winners or losers. We salute reforms that make our systems more compatible on the economic side, on the human rights side, the openness side. But we're not looking for trying to achieve advantage. We sat down here, one-on-one, and tried to hammer out agreements and get closer together on vital matters affecting other countries.

And it is because of the standing of the Soviet Union and the standing of the United States in the world that we have responsibilities. So, I can tell you — all the journalists from the Soviet side, the European journalists — the United States is dealing with mutual respect here. We salute the changes, of course. But we have a unique responsibility in the world. And I plan to — one of the things I'm pleased about in our agreement is that we will be meeting more often now, and we can't miss an opportunity to enhance stability and peace in the world. So, that's where I'm coming from on your question.

Press Secretary Marlin Fitzwater. Let's turn to the international press.

Soviet-U.S. Relations

Q. Following on President Bush's comment, on a scale that had adversaries at one end and allies at the other, would you now say that each other's country was more of an ally than an adversary?

President Bush. I don't want to get into semantics. "Alliances" have a connotation to some that they might not have for another. "Adversaries" sometimes convey the concept of hostility or enmity. In my view, we've moved a long, long way from the depths of the Cold War. We've moved towards a — I don't quite know how to quantify it for you, but we could never have had the discussions at Camp David yesterday or as we sat in the Oval Office a couple of days before with President Gorbachev 20 years ago. We all know that. So, there's been dramatic move. And the more this reform and openness takes place, the more compatible the relationship be-

comes. Neither of us tried to cover over the differences.

So, I know that's too general for you, but that's where I'd leave it.

NATO's Future and German Unification

Q. Question to President Bush, if I may, to follow up my colleague's one. Are there circumstances under which you would be prepared to recommend the total dissolution of NATO? What's the threat that still keeps it in business?

And a question to President Gorbachev, too. How long do you think the transition period should last before the responsibilities of the Four Powers run out — the four victorious powers in World War II?

President Bush. You want me to start with that one?

As I look at the world, the threat is unpredictability and stability — or instability is the threat. We feel that a continued U.S. presence in Europe should not be seen as hostile to the Soviet interests, but indeed, we hope a continued U.S. presence there will be seen as something that's stabilizing. And NATO is the existing machinery that we feel, with an expanded mission, can best provide that stability. And herein, we have a difference with the Soviet Union.

But it is that rather than some kind of Cold War mentality, that drives our decision to, one, remain in Europe and two, to try to have a broader role for NATO. Under article II of the NATO treaty, there is language put in there, I'm told, by Lester Pearson [former Prime Minister of Canada] years ago that provides a broader than just military assignment for NATO. So, we see this as not exclusive to an expanded role for CSCE [Conference on Security and Cooperation in Europe], not contradictory to the aspirations of many Europeans for an expanded EC [European Community], but as a way in which we can continue without hostility to anyone to provide a stabilizing presence.

President Gorbachev. I'd like to respond to this extremely important question if I may.

First, as an overall statement of the fact, it seems to me that if some kind of option is suggested, one that would replace or would be accompanied by replacing an isolation on the European continent, either of the United States of America or of the Soviet Union, then I

would say in no uncertain terms — and I could even make a forecast — that that particular option would be doomed. It would be doomed in the sense that it would be difficult to put into effect, but what matters most, it would lead to exacerbation rather than improvement in the situation. For that reason, we believe that we will not be able to make any further progress in restructuring international relations, including in the main European area, without an active participation of the United States of America and the Soviet Union. These are realities, and there's also a great sense of responsibility behind those realities. This is the first point.

The second point now. Yes, indeed, we believe that the option which we think will be found eventually and which will provide powerful momentum and which would contribute to the strengthening of the European process must necessarily include some kind of a transition period during which we could join our efforts to conclude a final document, exhausting thereby the rights we are endowed with as the victorious Four Powers under the results of the Second World War. These are the issues that were raised by history itself; and so, therefore, in the framework of international law it must be brought to conclusion.

A concurrent unification of Germany and its presence would mean the coincidence of these two events. This would mean that this would be an independent and sovereign state. I really don't know, and I wouldn't like to engage in speculation about the timeliness. But I think that we must be very, very active now so as to ensure some kind of synchronization between the internal processes which lead to the unification of Germany and the settlement of external aspects so that they would be combined.

I can see, and I offered, many options in our position. Those options are there, and it seems to me there are some points the American side has noticed. I am expressing my supposition. I am not saying that I heard this from the President. But I think they have something to think about, and I think we will give serious thinking to the U.S. position, too.

Q. President Gorbachev, on the subject of NATO membership for a united Germany, you have complained in the past about Western sensitivity to your security concerns. Some of your

aides say privately that a united Germany could belong to NATO and your security concerns could be satisfied by both a limited American presence in Germany and, primarily, by strict limits on German troops and armaments. The real problem, they say, is psychological: a matter of national pride. They say that if you accept Germany in NATO it will be a humiliating admission to the Soviet people that you've lost the Cold War.

In your talks with President Bush, were you frank about this? Is this a problem for you? And, President Bush, have you considered this problem yourself in your own thoughts?

President Gorbachev. First, I do not think that whatever I am saying on this extremely important question of world politics appears to be a complaint from me or from the Soviet Union—"this would be humiliating for the Soviet Union" to pass, you said, around, to come here to Washington or to Bonn or elsewhere—this is out of the question. And please bear that in mind. This is the first point.

The second point is: You know there is a process underway, a beneficial process, and look how far we have progressed in this process. We're entitled to raise the question in these terms. Each subsequent step must strengthen it rather than weaken it. We have a right to that. Take, for example, our negotiations on 50 percent reductions in strategic offensive arms. If this whole negotiating process were to be depicted to you in its entirety, you would certainly see the kind of battles we are having on each and every point. Why? Because nobody really wants his security to be diminished.

Incidentally, our own position is that we find it unacceptable that we should have greater security than the United States of America. In a situation like this, we won't be able to move forward. I would recommend to all our partners to give some thought to this position. If decisions are made of the kind that will cause concern to the Soviet Union, this would not be beneficial to the Soviet Union; this would not be beneficial to others as well.

So, the question arises: a united Germany, its advent on the horizon—all this is very important and serious. While applauding the Germans' desire to be united, we must at the same time think about ways of preserving the balance that has been emerging and taking shape for decades.

Here is the central point. If we were to adopt only one point of view, then I would think that it would not be complete, for it gives rise to concerns. And if that is the case, then if there were no other way out — but I believe that such a way out will be found to mutual satisfaction—but if this were to be the only option and some would like to impose it on us and say that we reject this, then we should go back and see where we are. What's happening to our security? What should we be doing with our armed forces, which we are both reforming and reducing? What should we do about Vienna? How should we behave there? All these are matters of strategic importance for everything happening in Europe; it is really the highest level of strategy.

This is one way, one pathway, which gives rise to some doubts or suspicions, one that can certainly slow down things. But there is another pathway that we are offering—let it be American or German or British. We are not claiming to have it as our own. We are claiming one thing only: We want to see an option that would strengthen everything in Europe rather than weaken things.

As to the second part: It's a question of pride? Well, I'd say that the problem is not pride, really, if today I have to remind you once again that we lost 27 million people in the fronts, in partisan detachments—27 million people during World War II. And 18 million people were wounded and maimed. Then I think it's not a matter of pride, but of justice—supreme justice. For these sacrifices of our people enable us to raise these matters with all nations, and we have a moral right to do so, so that everything that was obtained at such tremendous costs— that so many sacrifices would not spell new perils. So, this is what I wanted to say, and I think that this is what should be said.

President Bush. Mr. President, may I simply add, in answer to your question, the answer is "no" because our policy is not predicated on pride or on humiliation or on arrogance. It is predicated on what do we see, from the U.S. standpoint, is the best for the future, best for stability and peace in Europe and elsewhere. So, the considerations that you asked about have nothing to do with the formulation of U.S. policy on these important questions. I'm just going to do what I think is best for the United States and the rest of the free world and the Soviets. So, we're not dwelling on what you asked about.

Soviet Relations With Pacific Nations

Q. Mr. Gorbachev, you say that you have established new relations with the United States. Could you tell us how you are going to develop the process in the area of the Pacific Ocean and whether you're going to convene some kind of representative conference or meeting to discuss those matters with representatives of different zones?

President Gorbachev. It seems to me that I have already expressed myself in rather a great detail on this score. And it also seems to me that what I said back in Vladivostok, in Krasnoyarsk, remains today. And I reiterate that approach. And it seems to me that this is not a thing of the past, for the processes are beginning to develop in that region, too, which is inhabited by billions of people. One way or another things will be more complex with due regard for the real specifics over there. We must act with due regard for those specifics without copying blindly the European process, but borrowing something from it.

At this time, I can say that what happened with armaments, with INF [intermediate-range nuclear force] missiles along the border with China, and the kind of dialogue which is underway now between countries and, finally, the fact that we have traveled a certain distance toward a settlement of the situation of Afghanistan—all these are signs showing that there is a positive process emerging over there.

Of course, I think this road will be longer and more thorny. But still, it is especially necessary over there because those peoples need an opportunity to reallocate their resources to overcome a lot of social problems that have been accumulated. This is number one.

And number two, I'd like to say that, following the intensive contacts we have had and the dialogue that we are developing with India and now with China and other countries, such as Indonesia, I am planning to go on a visit to Japan so as to open that area for discussions. So, we're going to intensify our efforts in that direction.

I wish to say right away that here, too, we must cooperate with the United

States of America. I said this before in my statements; and now, too, I wish to reiterate it once again in the presence of the President of the United States of America.

Lithuanian Independence

Q. This question is directed to President Bush, but, President Gorbachev, feel free to join in, of course. Mr. President, about six weeks ago you suggested your patience was nearing an end in regards to the Lithuanian situation. I was wondering if that's still the case. If not, what has changed? And specifically, have you received any assurances that the embargo will be lifted?

President Bush. No, there have been no such assurances. I'm not sure anything has changed. I don't recall placing it that my patience is nearing an end. I've tried to make clear to everybody that we have not recognized the incorporation of these Baltic States into the Soviet Union and, therefore, we have a difference with the Soviet Union. They consider this an internal matter; and we say that, having not recognized the inclusion, why, we have a different problem.

But we had some good discussions of this. I've been encouraged to see discussions going on over there between various leaders. And let's hope the matter can be resolved, because I haven't lessened my view as to people's aspirations for self-determination, and I feel strongly about that. That's a hallmark of American belief and policy, and I haven't changed one bit on that. But I would turn it over to President Gorbachev, who has a different view on it.

President Gorbachev. I really don't even know what I can tell you now, because two days ago, in a meeting with representatives of the congressional leadership, I explained our position in great detail. It seems to me that our position is constructive and convincing.

Our Constitution has recorded the right for each people to make a choice for self-determination up to and including secession. We did not have a mechanism that would regulate the implementation of that right. Now we have it recorded in the law. So, we are reforming our federations. We are expanding the Republics' sovereign rights. And we hope that a full federation is something that we are in vital need of to resolve all the problems that have been

accumulated. This is our conviction; this is the way we're acting. And shortly, in the next few days, there is to be a Federation Council meeting convened to consider specific steps, dates, and ways of resolving this particular problem in specific, concrete terms.

Perhaps this particular process will develop in a way that would imply the presence of different levels of federative ties, just like various ties or links between the Republics. This will be a new process, new forms of links of the kind that would be in consonant with the purposes of our *perestroika*, with the goals of reforming our federation. This is one direction.

If, nevertheless, in the framework of this process, some Republic or other is going to raise this question—and I'm sure they will— they must be addressed and dealt with in the framework of the constitutional process. We want to see this happen precisely on the basis of the Constitution. Any other different approach leads only to an impasse. And the experience that we have by now not only with respect to Lithuania but also with respect to other Republics in terms of dealing with ethnic problems, where some people are trying to resolve the problem by different methods, without due regard for the Constitution, leads to exacerbation, aggravation, and confrontation. And this is not beneficial either for people, for their families, or for the economy, or for the overall atmosphere in our country.

The President of the Soviet Union, just like the President of the United States of America—and I happen to know the American Constitution—have as one of their main responsibilities to defend and protect the constitutional system. I swore an oath of allegiance to the Constitution; and for that reason, we are prepared and willing to address any issue, including those that have been raised by the Supreme Soviet of the Lithuanian SSR, in the framework of the constitutional process. This implies a referendum, incidentally. As to the referendum, those who have engineered this kind of solution, if I may say so, regarding the statehood of Lithuania, will also address our own option and let the people decide.

After they make a choice, I'm sure no fewer than 5 or 7 years would be required for us to sort things out. There will be this divorce proceeding underway, for there are 800,000 non-Lithuanians who live there. Defense,

missiles, navy—they're all there. Today Lithuania's territory includes five areas that used to belong to Byelorussia. Stalin ceded Klaipeda, which the Soviet Union, as the basis of the results of World War II, received just as it did Kaliningrad in Eastern Prussia. It received Lithuanian territories. So, they raise this question: to return to Russia these lands.

Recently, I held a press conference with President Mitterrand of France, just as I am doing now with President Bush here. And I said, Listen, in order to make a decision how to act with respect to overseas territories such as Caledonia, France has projected a period of 10 years. How is it possible for us to resolve issues such as this overnight, when people met pending the opening of the Third Congress of People's Deputies and put the question to the vote? Is that a responsible policy really, I ask myself. I really think that we are acting in accordance with the mandate from the Third Congress of People's Deputies. And we have a vast reserve of good will and constructive spirit; and we do our best in order to resolve, on the basis of constitutional approaches, this particular issue. But any other way would be unacceptable.

I keep referring to—well, I'm not asking the President to come over to us and bring order to our house. But I keep saying that President Bush would have resolved an issue like this within 24 hours, and he would have restored the validity of his Constitution within 24 hours in any State. [Laughter]

But we are going to resolve it. We are going to do it ourselves. With full responsibility, I wish to declare here now for all of you to know that we are anxious to see this issue resolved in such a way as everybody's interest would be taken into account and within the Constitution's framework.

Joint Statement on Nonproliferation, June 4, 1990 [3]

The United States of America and the Union of Soviet Socialist Republics oppose the proliferation of nuclear weapons, chemical weapons, missiles capable of carrying such weapons, and certain other missiles and missile technologies. The more nations that possess such weapons, the more difficult it will be to realize the desire of people everywhere to achieve effective arms control and disarmament measures and to reduce the threat of war. Weapons proliferation can provoke or intensify insecurity and hostility among nations, and threatens mankind with warfare of unprecedented destructiveness.

Our discussions over the past months point the way to a new era in relations between our two countries. We have taken major steps toward concluding agreements to reduce our own strategic nuclear arsenals, to bring limits on nuclear testing into force, and to reach a global ban on chemical weapons. Together with the nations of Europe, we are taking unprecedented steps to reduce existing conventional weaponry as part of a process of building a lasting structure of European security. The progress we are making and the commitments we have made in these bilateral and multilateral arms control efforts clearly demonstrate that arms reductions can contribute to increased security, even when there have been long-standing and deep-seated differences between countries.

The historic steps we have taken to improve U.S.-Soviet relations and to cooperate in the interests of international stability create the possibility of even closer and more concrete cooperation in the areas of nuclear, chemical, and missile non-proliferation.

With these considerations in mind, The United States and the Soviet Union:
- Declare their commitment to preventing the proliferation of nuclear weapons, chemical weapons, and missiles capable of carrying such weapons and certain other missiles and missile technologies, in particular those subject to the provisions of the Missile Technology Control Regime (MTCR);
- Agree to work closely together and with other members of the international community to develop and to put into action concrete measures against the proliferation of these types of weapons; and
- Call on other nations to join in a renewed commitment to effective nonproliferation measures as a means of securing international peace and stability and as a step toward the effective limitation worldwide of nuclear weapons, chemical weapons, missiles, and missile technology.

The two sides have taken specific actions to advance these commitments.

Nuclear Weapons Nonproliferation

In order to prevent the proliferation of nuclear weapons, the United States and the Soviet Union:
- Reaffirm their steadfast and long-lasting commitment to prevent the proliferation of nuclear weapons and to strengthen the international nuclear weapons nonproliferation regime;
- Reaffirm their strong support for the Treaty on the Nonproliferation of Nuclear Weapons (NPT) and agree that it continues to make an invaluable contribution to global and regional security and stability
- Urge all countries which have not yet done so to adhere to the NPT;
- Urge all NPT parties to implement scrupulously their International Atomic Energy Agency (IAEA) safeguards obligations under the Treaty;
- Affirm their intention to cooperate together and with other Treaty parties to ensure a successful 1990 Review Conference on the Treaty on the Nonproliferation of Nuclear Weapons which would reaffirm support for the objectives of the Treaty and its importance to international security and stability;
- Support the Treaty for the Prohibition of Nuclear Weapons in Latin America (the Treaty of Tlatelolco) and urge all countries in the region to bring it into force at an early date;
- Reiterate their continuing commitment to strengthening the IAEA, whose unique system of safeguards has contributed to the widespread peaceful use of nuclear energy for social and economic development
- Support increased international cooperation in the peaceful uses of nuclear energy under IAEA safeguards;
- Call on all non-nuclear-weapons states with unsafeguarded nuclear activities to place these activities under international safeguards;
- Agree on the need for stringent controls over exports of nuclear-related material, equipment and technology, to ensure that they will not be misused for nuclear explosive purposes, and urge all other nations capable of exporting

nuclear-related technology to apply similarly strict controls;
- Continue to support efforts to improve and strengthen the international nuclear export control regime;
- Support discussions among states in regions of nuclear proliferation concern for the purpose of achieving concrete steps to reduce the risk of nuclear proliferation, and, in particular, join in calling on the nations of the Middle East, southern Africa, and South Asia to engage in and pursue such discussions;
- Agree to continue their regular, constructive bilateral consultations on nuclear weapons nonproliferation.

Missile and Missile Technology Nonproliferation

In order to stem the proliferation of missiles and missile technology, the United States and the Soviet Union:
- Have signed the Treaty between the United States of America and the Union of Soviet Socialist Republics on the Elimination of Their Intermediate Range and Shorter-Range Missiles, demonstrating that controls on — indeed the elimination of — such missiles can enhance national security;
- Reaffirm their intention that the START Treaty be signed by the end of the year;
- Affirm their support for the objectives of the Missile Technology Control Regime, covering missiles, and certain equipment and technology relating to missiles capable of delivering at least 500 kilograms of payload to a range of at least 300 kilometers and they call on all nations that have not done so to observe the spirit and the guidelines of this regime;
- Are taking measures to restrict missile proliferation on a worldwide basis, including export controls and other internal procedures;
- Have instituted bilateral consultations to exchange information concerning such controls and procedures and identify specific measures to prevent missile proliferation;
- Agree to work to stop missile proliferation, particularly in regions of tension, such as the Middle East;
- To this end, affirm their intent to explore regional initiatives to reduce

the threat of missile proliferation, including the possibility of offering their good offices to promote such initiatives;

- Recall that they favor international economic cooperation including cooperation aimed at peaceful space exploration, as long as such cooperation could not contribute to missile proliferation;
- Appeal to all countries—to exporters of missiles and missile technology as well as purchasers—to exercise restraint, and express their willingness to continue their respective dialogues with other countries on the nonproliferation of missiles and missile technology.
- Are resolved, on their part, to continue to work to strengthen such international restraint with respect to missile and missile technology proliferation.

Chemical Weapons Nonproliferation

In order to stem the use and proliferation of chemical weapons, the United States and the Soviet Union:

- Declare that a multilateral, effectively verifiable chemical weapons convention banning the development, production and use of chemical weapons and eliminating all stocks on a global basis is the best long-term solution to the threat to international security posed by the use and spread of chemical weapons, and that nonproliferation measures are considered a step toward achieving such a convention;
- Will intensify their cooperation to expedite the negotiations in Geneva with the view to resolving outstanding issues as soon as possible and to finalizing the draft convention at the earliest date;
- Have instituted bilateral confidence building measures, including chemical weapons data exchange and reciprocal site visits;
- Have just signed a trailblazing agreement on destruction and nonproduction of chemical weapons and on measures to facilitate the multilateral convention on chemical weapons;
- Commit themselves in that agreement to take practical measures to encourage all chemical weapons-capable states to become parties to the multilateral convention;
- Having declared their possession of chemical weapons, urge other

states possessing chemical weapons to declare their possession, to commit to their destruction, and to begin immediately to address, through research and cooperation, the need for chemical weapons destruction capability;

- State that they themselves will not proliferate chemical weapons;
- Have instituted export controls to stem the proliferation of chemical weapons. These measures are not intended to hinder or discriminate against legitimate peaceful chemical activities;
- Have agreed to conduct bilateral discussions to improve the effectiveness of their respective export controls to stem the proliferation of chemical weapons;
- Conduct regular bilateral consultations to broaden bilateral cooperation, including the reciprocal exchange of information on the problems of chemical weapons proliferation;
- Confirm their intent to pursue political and diplomatic actions, where specific cases give rise to concerns about the production, use or spread of chemical weapons;
- Join with other nations in multilateral efforts to coordinate export controls, exchange information, and broaden international cooperation to stem the proliferation of chemical weapons;
- Reaffirm their support for the 1925 Geneva Protocol banning the use of chemical weapons in violation of international law;
- Are taking steps to strengthen the 1925 Geneva Protocol by:
  —Encouraging states that are not parties to accede;
  —Confirming their intention to provide active support to the United Nations Secretary General in conducting investigations of reported violations of the Protocol;
  —Affirming their intention to consider the imposition of sanctions against violators of the Protocol, including those under Chapter VII of the United Nations Charter;
  —Agreeing to consult promptly in the event of a violation of the Protocol to discuss possible bilateral and multilateral actions against the offender, as well as appropriate assistance to the victims of such violation;
- Agree that the presence and further proliferation of chemical weapons in areas of tension, such as

the Middle East, is particularly dangerous. The two countries therefore affirm their intent to explore regional initiatives in the Middle East and other areas, including the possibility of offering their good offices to promote such initiatives as:
—Efforts to broaden awareness of the dangers of chemical weapons proliferation and its negative impact on implementation of the multilateral convention on chemical weapons;
—Bilateral or multilateral efforts to stem chemical weapons proliferation, including the renunciation of the production of chemical weapons;
—Efforts to destroy chemical weapons in advance of the multilateral convention on chemical weapons, as the United States and the Soviet Union are doing

The United States and the Soviet Union call on all nations of the world that have not already done so to join them in taking comparable, effective measures to stem chemical weapons proliferation

Joint Statement on Bering Sea Fisheries Conservation, June 4, 1990 [3]

In the course of the state visit by the President of the Union of Soviet Socialist Republics to the United States of America, the sides reviewed problems posed by the development of an unregulated multinational fishery for pollock in the central Bering Sea. In light of the magnitude of that fishery, which accounts for more than one-third of the total annual catch of pollock in the Bering Sea, the situation is of serious environmental concern. In particular, there is a danger to the stocks from overfishing. This may result in significant harm to the ecological balance in the Bering Sea and to those U.S. and U.S.S.R. coastal communities whose livelihoods depend on the living marine resources of the Bering Sea.

The sides agreed that urgent conservation measures should be taken with regard to this unregulated fishery. The sides noted that, in accordance with international law as reflected in the relevant provisions of the 1982 United Nations Convention on the Law of the Sea, all concerned states, including coastal states and fishing states, should cooperate to ensure the conservation of these living resources. To this end, both sides noted that they would welcome cooperative efforts towards the development of an international regime for the conservation and management of the living marine resources in the central Bering Sea.

Joint Statement on Cooperation in Peaceful Uses of Atomic Energy, June 4, 1990 [3]

During the state visit of Mikhail S. Gorbachev, President of the U.S.S.R., at the invitation of George Bush, President of the United States, the sides concluded a new U.S.-U.S.S.R. Agreement on Scientific and Technical Cooperation in the Field of Peaceful Uses of Atomic Energy. This Agreement strengthens the longstanding framework for important research in a number of fields of mutual interest, including controlled thermonuclear fusion, fundamental properties of matter, and civilian nuclear reactor safety.

Recognizing the need to manage responsibly the development and utilization of nuclear power, the two sides have agreed on cooperation in the study of the health and environmental effects of past, present and future nuclear power generation, and in strengthening operational safety practices in civilian nuclear reactors. The sides intend to develop and implement promptly a mutually beneficial joint program of work in these fields under this Agreement. They also agreed to explore the possibilities for cooperation in the management of hazardous and radioactive waste.

Joint Statement on the International Thermonuclear Experimental Reactor, June 4, 1990 [3]

At their meeting in Geneva in 1985, the leaders of the United States and the Soviet Union emphasized the importance of the work aimed at utilizing controlled thermonuclear fusion for peaceful purposes, and advocated the widest practical development of international cooperation in obtaining this es-

sentially inexhaustible source of energy for the benefit of all mankind.

The International Thermonuclear Experimental Reactor (ITER) project, involving joint efforts by the U.S.S.R., the United States, Japan and the European Community, under the aegis of the International Atomic Energy Agency, is making significant progress towards this end. A conceptual design will soon be completed.

Noting with satisfaction the results being attained under this project, the United States and the Soviet Union look forward to continued international efforts aimed at promoting further progress in developing controlled thermonuclear fusion for peaceful purposes.

Joint Statement on Technical Economic Cooperation, June 4, 1990 [3]

The two sides reiterated their commitment to the program of technical economic cooperation outlined by Presidents Bush and Gorbachev at Malta in December and expressed a desire to expand the scope and number of joint projects. This program is a concrete expression of U.S. and Soviet commitment to work together in support of economic *perestroika*. Its goal is to advance the process of market-oriented economic reform by sharing experience and expertise regarding the problems and opportunities involved in building market structures and institutions.

Projects and contacts currently underway at the expert level include statistical cooperation, development of small businesses, establishment of financial markets, banking reform, and tax administration. The two sides also had useful discussions on economic policy issues during visits by the Soviet Minister of Finance and State Bank Chairman to Washington, and the Chairman of the President's Council of Economic Advisors and the Chairman of the Federal Reserve Board to Moscow.

The two sides will work to expand the scope of current cooperation projects and in particular to develop new projects in areas of special interest, including antitrust issues, enterprise management, and economic education. The two sides also noted that private exchanges and projects can be consistent with and complement technical coopera-

tion. Both sides believe that technical economic cooperation is in their mutual benefit in promoting the successful development of market-oriented reforms.

---

[1]Made on the South Lawn of the White House where President Gorbachev was accorded a formal welcome with full military honors (text from Weekly Compilation of Presidential Documents of June 4, 1990).

[2]President Gorbachev spoke in Russian, and his remarks were translated by an interpreter.

[3]Text from Weekly Compilation of Presidential Documents of June 4, 1990.

[4]The U.S.-U.S.S.R. joint report "International Park Program, Beringen Heritage Cooperation" was endorsed as the framework for establishing an international park by the end of 1991. The Bering Land Bridge National Reserve will be the initial companion site to be linked with a Soviet protected area on the Chukotskiy Peninsula.

[5]Text from Weekly Compilation of Presidential Documents of June 4, 1990. President Gorbachev spoke in Russian, and his remarks were translated by an interpreter.

[6]President Bush referred to the golf cart that he was riding in.

"The Transition to a New Age . . ."

Speech by Mikhail Gorbachev

Delivered at Stanford University, Stanford, California, June 4, 1990 [1]

Ladies and gentlemen, I feel enormous joy and satisfaction that, within the framework of my visit to the United States of America. I find myself here, among you, within the walls of a university that is celebrated and renowned throughout the entire world. Thank you for your warm welcome.

I think that those who work or study at your university are doubly lucky: it is in California, and this is a special place, even by international standards. And I say this, not to compliment the governor of this state, who is here with his wife, but I think that I am certifying a truth.

It is said that only five countries in the world produce a greater gross output than this state. In California, the ideas of tomorrow's technology are born. California is tightly tied economically with Europe, and with Asia, and with Latin America. Therefore, this is a fitting place—a place fit for living, and for me, in my position, a place fit for giving thought to the mutual situation of the Soviet Union and the United States, which are [positioned] on the dividing line between two decades, two centuries, two epochs, and on the coastline of the Pacific Ocean, which Alexander Herzen l9th century intellectual and social critic], our great countryman, prophetically called the Mediterranean Sea of the future.

Ending the Cold War

It is appropriate here to give thought now to the destiny of the world, especially since exactly 45 years ago, in San Francisco, the United Nations was founded. I think it is very symbolic that precisely this sunny city was chosen as the place from which to proclaim the creation of this organization, the effectiveness of which concerns us all very much. Let us look at what kinds of conclusions were drawn from the horrible war that had just ended. You see, the United Nations was created, and I quote: ". . . to maintain [international] peace and security and to eliminate the

political, economic, and social causes of war . . . to regulate disputes in conformity with the principles of justice and international law . . . and to develop [friendly] relations among nations based on [respect for] the principle of equal rights and self-determination of peoples, and . . . respect for human rights and for fundamental freedoms for all, without distinction as to race, sex, language, or religion...."

Beautiful words, a beautiful appeal. Alas, only in recent years have we been able to come closer to addressing these tasks in the sphere of practical politics. Only now is world politics really beginning to adapt itself to those stated ideas and principles. And already we have all felt how necessary the United Nations is for us, if we want to move on to a new world, to new relationships that are in the interests of all peoples and all nations.

For a long time, the Pacific Ocean, too, was a force-field with respect to confrontations and the arms race. Finding ourselves on its two opposing shores, our countries were on different sides of the barricades of Asian revolutions. But new winds are now blowing in Asia. Asia is developing rapidly according to its own logic and provides impressive examples of economic efficiency and international cooperation. The Japanese, the Chinese, the Koreans, and other Asian peoples are teaching the whole world lessons, and that includes you and us. And so that we might not fall by the wayside in the Pacific, not to mention in Europe, we must consider how most quickly to abandon our military political rivalry.

The Cold War has been left behind, and it is not worth squabbling over who won the victory.

Let us ponder the future. There are more than adequate grounds for our two countries to be its building partners, to be partners in the formation of new security structures, in

Europe, in the Asian regions, and the Pacific Rim, partners in the making of a truly global economy—and, most of all, partners in the creation of a new civilization. I do not sow illusions about the possibility of an accelerated rapprochement, or the convergence of our two societies. They are sufficiently different, and for a long time they developed along divergent lines. I suppose that, more likely than not, they will never become identical. And this, incidentally, is not at all necessary. It is important to see a major thrust toward a world without wars, towards a world of equal rights and freedom. As the departure point for a future-oriented interaction between countries and peoples, I would choose the fact that the Cold War has been left behind. And it is not worth squabbling over who won the victory.

In a cold war, as in a nuclear war, there can be no winners. This has already become an accepted point of view. You and we know this. All the remaining [discussion] comprises arguments about for whom the Cold War was profitable. This is political fraud and irresponsibility. Our countries, having experienced the burden of the arms race during these years, know this especially well. And this has fed our political thoughts, reasonings, political analysis, and, finally, our political choice, which led us to this new summit meeting, and to new and unprecedented decisions, which open a wide road to the collaboration of our two great peoples and our two great nations. Each of our countries bears its share of the responsibility for the fact that the postwar period in the history of mankind took on the character of an exhausting and dangerous confrontation. But, now, it is just as logical to declare that an enormous responsibility likewise lies on you and on us to dismantle the mechanisms of East-West military opposition.

There was a time when military procurement orders were considered, and in some places are still considered, the best stimulus for economic and technological progress. Californians, too, I will note, paid tribute to such an approach in its time. But, as I have been told, they, earlier than others, began to understand that a military economy is, in the final analysis, a dead end, even from the standpoint of practical benefit. And it is symbolic that already in the seventies, Santa Clara County, which ranked first in per capita military contracts, began to seek a path toward the demilitarization of its local economy. I want to believe, that in keeping with the improvement of Soviet-American relations, military procurement orders and participation in the arms race will become a thing of the past, not only for your beautiful state, but for both of our great powers.

Role of Science and Scholarship

The role of science and scholarship in the arms race is enormous, but science and scholarship were the first to make authoritative pronouncements against this insane occupation and to begin to seek a way out of this situation. Here we must not forget to credit the joint efforts of Soviet and American scientists and scholars, to which Stanford contributed substantially. I have in mind the elaboration of the scientific and scholarly bases of such conceptions as international security and strategic stability. Without a serious, objective approach to the nature of strategic stability and mutual security, without scholarly analysis, which takes into account all the factors — economic, political, scientific and scholarly, military-technical, and military-political — it is impossible to make correct decisions on the cardinal issues of nuclear and conventional arms reductions.

The scientists and scholars of our lands have made their joint estimates. They have discussed them more than once, approaching this work as a scientific and scholarly project, disassociating themselves from the political and military ambitions which, for a long time, hindered our finding the way out. Using this approach, they have helped to realize and implement major political decisions, including those that were adopted in Washington a day or two ago. Today I can mention with pleasure the names of Stanford University scientists and scholars who, over the course of many years patiently and persistently carried on this most important work. They all have very high academic reputations, and they all are united by a belief in the necessity for peace on earth, and the triumph of reason and justice. Among them I would like to distinguish Wolfgang Panofsky, Sidney Drell, William Perry, David Holloway, and others from CISAC [Center for International Security and Arms Control] and from the committee sponsored by the U.S. National Academy of Sciences.

Together with their colleagues from the Committee of Soviet Scientists and Scholars [for Peace] Against the Nuclear Threat — [Yevgenii Pavlovich] Velikov, Yurii Andreevich Osipian, [Roald Zinnurovich] Sagdeev, and others — they have done a great deal to build bridges of trust between our countries. I would like to take this opportunity to express deep gratitude to them all, and I hope that you will join me in this.

Stanford's scholars and scientists have greatly facilitated initial contacts between the defense-industry representatives of both countries with respect to the problems of conversion. This promising area of our relations can afford us all substantial dividends. New steps in the sphere of disarmament require serious restrictions on the creation of advanced weapons systems. Here also the Soviet and American scholars and scientists may work jointly to determine what are the limits of permissible modernization, and when is there a qualitative arms race. This must be kept in mind so that those arms, which on the face of it seem to be conventional arms [but are not], do not come to replace nuclear arms, for this would again leave us with weapons of mass destruction.

Warnings in this regard, it seems to me, are now necessary, timely, and pressing. One would like to see scholars, scientists, and engineers demonstrating not less, but more, ingenuity in the working out of these kinds of questions than they do on the creation of modern weapons. That is, that they expend more ingenuity on these questions and other problems of disarmament, which are connected, in part, with the prohibition of chemical warfare, with the Vienna negotiations, with the problems of tactical nuclear weapons. President Bush and I can attest that it is not so easy to part, once and for all, with this weaponry, even when the decision has already been made. A technology to destroy these dangerous arms is needed. And I think we should collaborate here as well, so as not to harm the ecological system and the health of people. Here again there are difficulties, but, I think, we will cope with these difficulties by uniting our efforts.

The scholars and scientists of Stanford, as I have heard, want to study ecological problems intensively together with their Soviet colleagues. This is also

a vital matter in the forefront of world development. I cannot help but note Stanford's contribution to Soviet-American collaboration on the problem of high-temperature superconductivity. Here, both of our countries lead the way. I would like to mention here the names of two Stanford professors [of applied physics], Ted Geballe and Malcolm Beasley, the organizers of the worldwide conference on superconductivity, in which more than 30 Soviet scholars and scientists participated here last summer.

The U.S.S.R. and the United States of America are leaders in such scientific fields as the study of the fundamental properties of matter, solid state physics, mathematics, physical chemistry, astronomy and space research, and the complex of biological sciences. Collaboration in the humanities would also be very interesting. I know of Stanford's unique library in Hoover Tower — the richest collection of materials on the Russian Revolution. For our part, we could invite Stanford scholars and scientists for joint work on the historical and literary archives in the Soviet Union. In a word, we are for the wide-ranging collaboration of free and strong minds, which are conscious of their responsibility for the future of all who are open to joint work and the unimpeded exchange of its achievements.

"Humanity is One"

Ladies and gentlemen, in our country, we have opted to make radical and fundamental changes. Our *perestroika* was born of profound processes taking place in our society. In five years, our country has become different. But it seems to me that the whole of mankind is making the transition into a new time of life, a new age, and that, in all of the world, some kind of different system of natural laws and rules has begun to operate, a system to which we are not yet accustomed. Fifty years ago, the great Russian scholar Vernadskii wrote: "Humanity is one. The life of mankind in all its multiplicity has become indivisible, one. The events, which happen at any point on any continent or ocean, affect and have repercussions, great and small, in a series of other places everywhere on the face of the earth."

I continue quoting: "The telegraph, telephone, radio, airplanes, and balloons have embraced the entire globe. Communications have become simpler and faster. Every year the level of their organization increases, and they grow rapidly. This process of man's totally settling the biosphere is conditioned by the historical course of human thought, and is inseparably linked with the rate of communication, with advances in transportation technology, with the possibility of instantaneous thought transmission, and with the simultaneous discussion of a thought everywhere on the planet."

I am delighted—after all, this was said 50 years ago—that this prediction has proved itself true. We are seeing the essential issues of international relations evolve toward ever-augmented, mass-scale, and open communications. In this connection, the role of today's creative, constructive policies is sharply increased. But the price of mistakes also grows, the mistakes which, to no small degree, stem from adherence to old dogmas, accustomed rules of action, old ways of thinking. All people must change so that a new type of progress might become the reality throughout the world. The alpha and omega of the new world order is tolerance. Without tolerance and a respectful attitude toward one's partner, no understanding of the other's cares and anxieties can be expected. This supposes the cultivation of an approach to security structures that is new and in keeping with the times. It requires cooperation and even alliance-building.

A New Concept of Alliances

I am convinced that we are on the threshold of revising our concept of alliance building. Until now, alliances were built on a selective, in essence, discriminatory basis, on the opposition of one party against another. They separated countries and peoples to a significantly larger degree than they united them. This system reached its peak during the years of the Cold War, having embodied itself in two twin antipodes: the North Atlantic Treaty Organization and the Warsaw Pact. But the time is approaching when the very principle of alliance-building should change. And its point is unity, a unity that enables us to achieve living conditions worthy of humankind as well as the preservation of the environment, unity in the war against hunger, disease, narcotics addiction, and ignorance. It is in the common interest of our two countries and peoples not to resist this trend toward a new cooperation, but to promote it. And I think that both the United States and the Soviet Union, if they understand this and will work together, can decisively contribute to ushering our entire civilization out onto the road of prolonged, peaceful development.

I see many young people here; true, there are many more outside the confines of this hall, and I am glad that I greeted as many of them as possible. Therefore, in conclusion, I would like to address them, the youth. Your generation, friends, must not only create a new world order, but live in it. Probably it will differ in many ways from that which we now imagine, and from the one that I now am talking about, as I share my ideas with you here today. But the main thing is that people in this new world should live better and freer. In large measure, this depends on you and on the people of scholarship and science. I wish you success in this great and unprecedented undertaking. Thank you.

---

[1]Text provided by News and Publication Service, Stanford University. Translated from the original Russian by Darlene Reddaway, Ph.D. candidate in the Department of Slavic Languages and Literatures.

President Bush Announces Citizens Democracy Corps for Eastern Europe

Commencement Address at the University of South Carolina, Columbia, May 12, 1990 (opening and closing remarks deleted). [1]

In the past year, one nation after another has pulled itself out from under communism, onto the threshold of democracy. Each has endured great suffering, tremendous economic damage. We've all seen the images of long lines and empty shelves. But what we can't see so easily, what's beneath the surface but no less real, is the moral damage, the deep scars on the spirit left by four decades of communist rule.

Because in these regimes, the human spirit was subject to systematic assault. Religion, morality, right and wrong—any challenge to the rule of the state became the enemy of the state. Believers were persecuted, churches and cemeteries razed. Citizens were turned one against the other, enlisted into the ranks of the regime's informers. Nothing stood outside the reach of the regime, not even the past. History—it was rewritten to suit the needs of the present, yesterday's heroes airbrushed from the pages of history. Milan Kundera, the Czech author, called it "organized forgetting."

Of course, these nations had laws. They had courts. They had constitutions. All in service to the state. They had, in name at least, rights and freedoms; in reality, the empty shell of liberty—not the rule of law but the perversion of law: rules made not to serve the will of the people but the whim of the party. That's how in Romania the law made it illegal for three or more people to have a conversation in the street. That's how in another country a man whose so-called crime was teaching others about religion was jailed for six months. The trumped up charge: walking on flower beds. We will never know how many dissidents were punished as common criminals and how many millions of others were frozen by fear into silence and submission.

That's the legacy, the landscape of moral destruction. The tragic consequence of four decades of Communist rule: a breakdown of trust. From ancient times, the great minds have recognized the link between the law and trust.

As Aristotle wrote: "Law is a pledge that the citizens of a state will do justice to one another"—the bond that makes the collection of individuals into a community, into a nation.

Reconstructing Trust

Fortunately, the moral destruction in Eastern Europe, as you all know, was not complete. Individuals somehow managed to maintain an inner strength, their moral compass, to sustain the will to break through the regime's wall of lies. They did so, as Vaclav Havel [President of Czechoslovakia] put it, by the simple act of "living in truth." They created "flying universities," where lecturers taught in private homes. They formed underground publishing houses and groups to monitor human rights, an authentic civil society beyond the reach of the ruling establishment. And today the builders of those civil societies no longer live underground. They are the new leaders of Eastern Europe. And they've begun to build, on the ruins of communist rule, democratic systems based on trust.

Today I want to focus on how America can help these nations secure their freedoms, become a part of a Europe whole and free. Early this year, in the State of the Union, I talked about America's role as a shining example, about the importance of America not as a nation but as an idea alive in the minds of men and women everywhere. And that idea was, without doubt, a guiding force in the Revolution of 1989.

Let me share a story with you about a recent American visitor to Romania who asked the people she met what they needed now, what was most important to them. This simple question produced some unexpected answers. In Timisoara, one woman pulled from her purse a worn copy of TV Guide, an issue from July 1987, containing a bicentennial copy of the United States Constitution. And she held it out to the American visitor. And she said, "What we need is more of these."

And there on the streets of Timisoara—in a country where food is in short supply, where homes are without heat and streets dark at night—there a woman pins her hopes on our

Constitution. What that Romanian woman wanted, what all the nations of Eastern Europe aspire to, is democratic life based on justice and the rule of law.

Poland, Czechoslovakia, and Hungary stand now, in the spring of 1990, as America stood in the summer of 1787. Who will be their Franklins, their Washingtons, their Hamiltons, their Madisons, their men and women of towering genius, the nation builders who will set in place the firm foundations of self-government? Some of them we know by name, the heroes of the Revolution of '89. But for Eastern Europe's constitution builders, the work has only now begun because the fate of freedom depends not just on the character of the people who govern but whether they themselves are governed by the rule of law.

And just as the framers of our own Constitution looked to the lessons of history, Eastern Europe's new democracies will look to their own parliamentary past, to Europe's example and, of course, to our own American Constitution. And that's why we must export our experience, our two centuries of accumulated wisdom on the workings of free government.

Already we're actively engaged with Eastern Europe and the Soviet Union with an ongoing series of exchanges bringing jurists and parliamentarians, political leaders here to the United States to meet their American counterparts. And today I'm pleased to announce four new initiatives, four steps that the United States will take to support democratic development in Eastern Europe.

Supporting Democratic Development

First, America will continue to act to advance economic freedom. In the past year, we've committed more than $1 billion in direct economic assistance to Eastern Europe. We've extended loans and credits, opened our markets through most-favored-nation (MFN) status, and promoted American investment. And today I'm pleased to announce yet another economic initiative: The Export-Import Bank will provide Poland a new line of medium-term export credits and loan guarantees for purchasing machinery, technology, and services from American suppliers.

Second, the United States will work to help ensure free and fair elections in Eastern Europe. Next week, we'll send a Presidential delegation to observe the elections in Romania and another team to next month's elections in Bulgaria.

Third, America will work to broaden the mandate of the CSCE, the Conference on Security and Cooperation in Europe. Less than a month from now, as one of the 35 nations of the CSCE, the United States will take part in a conference on human rights, including free elections, political pluralism, and the rule of law. And I've instructed Ambassador Max Kampelman, head of our delegation, to seek a new consensus on these cornerstones of freedoms, rights, and democracy. As I said last week at Oklahoma State University, we must work within the CSCE to bring Eastern Europe's new democracies into this commonwealth of free nations.

Fourth and finally, we will work to strengthen the foundations of free society in Eastern Europe. And I am pleased to announce today the creation of a Citizens Democracy Corps. Its first mission: to establish a center and a clearinghouse for American private sector assistance and volunteer activities in Eastern Europe. We know the real strength of our democracy is its citizens, the collective strength of individual Americans. We're going to focus that energy where it can do the most good.

America has much to contribute, much it can do to help these nations move forward on the path to democracy. We can help them build political systems based on respect for individual freedoms; for the right to speak our mind, to live as we wish, and to worship as our conscience tells us we must; systems based on respect for property and the sanctity of contract; laws that are necessary not to amass fortunes, not to build towers of gold and greed, but to provide for ourselves, for our families; systems that allow free associations — trade unions, professional groups, political parties — the building blocks of a free society. We've got to help the emerging democracies build legal systems that secure the procedural rights that preserve freedom and, above all, a system that supports a strict equality of rights, one that guarantees that all men and women, whatever their race or ancestry, stand equal before the law.

In this century, we've learned a painful truth about the monumental evil that can be done in the name of humanity. We've learned how a vision of Utopia can become a hell on earth for millions of men and women. We've learned, through hard experience, that the only alternative to tyranny of man is the rule of law. That's the essence of our vision for Europe: a Europe where not only are the dictators dethroned but where the rule of law, reflecting the will of the people, ensures the freedoms millions have fought so hard to gain.

There is still work to be done. In the Baltic States, where people struggle for the right to determine their own future, we Americans, so free to chart our own course, identify with their hopes and aspirations. For, you see, we're committed to self-determination for Lithuania and Latvia and Estonia. And ultimately, the Soviet Union itself, now committed to openness and reform, will benefit from a Europe that's whole and free. Democracy and freedom threaten absolutely no one.

We sometimes hear today that with freedom's great triumph — and, oh, what exciting times we're living in — that America's work is done. Nothing could be further from the truth. I want to close today with a story about the enduring power of the American idea and the unfinished business that awaits the generation that you proudly represent.

It's about a town called Plzen in Czechoslovakia; a town that just last week celebrated the day, 45 years ago, when it was liberated by American troops. Of course, within a few short years, Plzen's dream of freedom vanished behind the Iron Curtain, and with it, the truth about that day back in 1945. A generation grew up being taught that Plzen had been freed not by your fathers and granddads in the United States Army but by Soviet sol-

White House Fact Sheet on the Citizens Democracy Corps, May 12, 1990[1]

The President announced today the creation of a Citizens Democracy Corps. The objective of this major new program is to support democratic change and market-oriented economic reform in Eastern Europe by mobilizing and coordinating American private sector initiatives.

Since the President's historic visits to Poland and Hungary and the revolutions of 1989, private Americans and voluntary organizations have stepped forward with extraordinary generosity with offers to assist the process of democratic change in Eastern Europe. To make best use of the enormous energy and creativity of the American private sector, the President supports the creation of a new center to promote these volunteer initiatives and match them with requests for assistance from Eastern Europe.

The Citizens Democracy Corps will serve as an information clearinghouse for U.S. private volunteer assistance programs for Central and Eastern Europe. It will establish an information base of technical services and equipment available from the United States on a private, volunteer basis. The Democracy Corps will also be a recipient of requests from Central and Eastern Europe for assistance in such areas as constitutional law and parliamentary procedures; English-language training; journalism, broadcasting, and publishing; public health and medical support; market economics, banking, and financial services; business law, commercial practices and agriculture; and environmental protection.

The Citizens Democracy Corps will be the point of contact for U.S. businesses, voluntary organizations, and educational institutions that want to find out what is now being done and where further efforts are needed. The Democracy Corps could also launch new volunteer initiatives to meet the changing requirements of the region.

The President will ask prominent citizens representing a cross section of the American private sector to form a commission to direct the program and stimulate volunteer groups. The commission and the volunteers mobilized to provide assistance will be called the Citizens Democracy Corps. While the U.S. Government will help provide initial funding, the Democracy Corps will create its own financial base so that it can become, in the full sense of the term, "citizens democracy."

diers dressed in American uniforms. But the people of Plzen knew better. They never forgot. And today, finally free to speak the truth, the town invited their true liberators back. After 45 long years, those old American soldiers returned to the streets of Plzen, to the sounds of "The Star Spangled Banner," to a hero's welcome.

Those GI's, my generation, were your age in 1945. And now it falls upon you, the graduating class of this great university, to uphold our American ideals not in times of war, thank God, but in a time of tremendous excitement, helping these nations secure the freedom that your fathers and grandfathers fought for, the freedom millions only dreamed of until today.

---

1 Text from Weekly Compilation of Presidential Documents of May 21, 1990.

NATO and the U.S. Commitment to Europe

Address by President Bush at the Oklahoma State University commencement, Stillwater, May 4, 1990 (introductory remarks deleted).[1]

Postwar America was ready for peace and prosperity. But while the free world was recovering, the nations of Eastern Europe were being "consolidated" behind an Iron Curtain. So began four decades of division in Europe—and 40 long years of suspicion between superpowers.

Today, you graduate at the end of an era of conflict—but a contest of a different kind, a cold and abstract war of words and walls. Now Europe and the world have entered a new era, the "age of freedom."

I hope you'll forgive me if I use this great forum at your great university to handle a subject of a very serious nature... I'll be reflecting on the power and potential of democratic change in each of the commencement addresses I make this year. I begin today...with a few words on the changes and America's place in the new Europe.

A few of you may be wondering what a continent 4,000 miles away has to do with you. Throughout our history, great upheavals in Europe have forced the American people to respond, to make deep judgments about the part we

should play in European affairs. This has been true from the time of the French Revolution and the wars which followed it; to World War I and the flawed peace which ended it; to the Second World War and the creation of the postwar order. I believe that, now, we are poised at another such moment—a critical time in our strategic relationship with our neighbors across the Atlantic.

Many of the graduates of America's class of 1916 may have wondered why the faraway war making headlines in their newspapers would have anything to do with them. They might have agreed with President Wilson, who that year said, "We are not interested" in the causes of war, in "the obscure foundations from which its stupendous flood has burst forth." But a year later, those classmates—and their country—were swept up in the torrent, carrying them to the horror of the trenches in France.

Yet after the war, we again turned away from active involvement in European affairs. Instead, we sponsored a treaty to outlaw war and then, as the outlaws gained strength, the United States passed new neutrality laws. Another generation of Americans sat in the bright sun of commencement ceremonies at colleges across the country, thinking war in Europe would pass them by. But when war came, they paid an awful price for America's isolation.

When that war ended, those students no longer questioned our role in the future of Europe. They no longer asked what Europe had to do with them, because they knew the answer: everything.

About a year ago in Germany, I defined the kind of Europe our country is committed to: a peaceful, stable Europe, a Europe whole and free. Today that goal is within our reach.

A New Age of Freedom

We are entering a new "age of freedom" in a time of uncertainty but great hope. Emerging democracies in Eastern Europe are going through social, political, and economic transformations; shaking loose stagnant, centralized bureaucracies that have smothered initiative for generations.

In this time of transition, moving away from the postwar era and beyond containment, we cannot know what

choices the people of Eastern Europe will make for their future. The process of change in the Soviet Union is also still unfinished. It will be crucial to see, for example, whether Moscow chooses coercion or peaceful dialogue in responding to the aspirations of the Lithuanian people, and [other] nationalities within the Soviet Union. The only noble answer lies in a dialogue that results in unencumbered self-determination for Lithuania.

President Gorbachev has made profound progress in his country; reforms so fundamental that the clock cannot be turned back. Yet, neither can we turn the clock ahead, to know for sure what kind of country the Soviet Union will be in years to come. For the sake of the future we share with Europe, our policies and presence must be appropriate for this period of transition—with a constancy and reliability that will reassure our friends, both old and new.

My European colleagues want the United States to be a part of Europe's future. I believe they are right. The United States should remain a European power in the broadest sense—politically, militarily, and economically. And, as part of our global responsibilities, the foundation for America's peaceful engagement in Europe has been—and will continue to be—NATO.

Recognizing in peace what we had learned from war, we joined with the free nations of Europe to form an Atlantic community, an enduring political compact. Our engagement in Europe has meant that the Europeans accept America as part of their continent's future, taking our interests into account across the board. Our commitment is not just in defense; it must be a well-balanced mix of involvement in all dimensions of European affairs.

Because of our political commitment to peace in Europe, there has not been a war on that continent in 45 years. This "long peace" should be viewed through the long lens of history. Europe has now experienced the longest uninterrupted period of international peace in the recorded history of that continent. The alliance is now ready to build on that historic achievement and define its objectives for the next century. So the alliance must join together to craft a new Western strategy for new and changing times.

Call to a Summit

Having consulted intensively with Prime Minister Thatcher in Bermuda, President Mitterrand in Florida, Chancellor Kohl at Camp David, and by telephone or cable with NATO Secretary General Woerner and all of my other allied colleagues, I am calling for an early summit meeting of all NATO leaders. Margaret Thatcher, one of freedom's greatest champions of the last decade, told me that while NATO has been fantastically successful, we should be ready now to face new challenges. The time is right for the alliance to act.

The fundamental purpose of this summit should be to launch a wide-ranging NATO strategy review for the transformed Europe of the 1990s. To my NATO colleagues, I suggest that our summit direct this review by addressing four critical points:

One, the political role NATO can play in the new Europe.

Two, the conventional forces the alliance will need in the time ahead, and NATO's goals for conventional arms control.

Three, the role of nuclear weapons based in Europe—and Western objectives in new nuclear arms control negotiations between the U.S. and the Soviet Union.

Four, strengthening the Conference on Security and Cooperation in Europe—the CSCE—to reinforce NATO and help protect democratic values, in a Europe whole and free.

Future Political Mission of NATO

The first task the NATO Summit should consider is the future political mission of the alliance. As military threats fade, the political dimension of NATO's work—always there, but seldom noticed—becomes more prominent. So at the NATO Summit, we should look for ways to help our German friends sustain freedom and achieve unity—something which we and our allies have supported for over 40 years. And, we should reaffirm the importance of keeping a united Germany a full member of NATO.

The alliance needs to find ways to work more closely with a vigorous European Community that is rightly asserting its own distinct views. And in Eastern Europe, governments once our adversaries are now our partners in building a new continent. So we must also talk about how to encourage further peaceful democratic change in Eastern Europe and in the Soviet Union.

But even as NATO gives more emphasis to its political mission, its guarantee of European security must remain firm. Our enemy today is uncertainty and instability, so the alliance will need to maintain a sound, collective military structure with forces in the field, backed by larger forces that can be called upon in a crisis.

Review of Conventional Forces

Which brings me to the second task for the NATO Summit—a review of how the alliance should plan its conventional defenses. While we need to recognize that it will take some time before the Soviet military presence is gone from Eastern Europe and before the major reductions contemplated by both sides can be implemented, we need to develop our strategy for that world, now.

Obviously, Soviet actions will be critical. Yet even after all the planned reductions in its forces are complete—even if our current arms control proposals are agreed to and implemented—the Soviet military will still field forces, dwarfing those of any other single European state, armed with thousands of nuclear weapons. Militarily significant U.S. forces must remain on the other side of the Atlantic for as long as our allies want—and need—them. These forces demonstrate, as no words can, the enduring political compact that binds America's fate with Europe's democracies.

If the Soviet withdrawal continues and our arms control efforts are successful, we must plan for a different kind of military presence focused less on the danger of an immediate outbreak of war. We must promote long-term stability and prevent crises from escalating by relying on reduced forces that show our capability—and readiness—to respond to whatever may arise.

The conventional armed forces in Europe [CFE] treaty we have proposed, would be the most ambitious conventional arms control agreement ever concluded. We must finish the work on this treaty soon, and plan to sign it at a CSCE Summit this fall. But at the NATO Summit we need to look further ahead, preparing for the follow-on negotiations after the conclusion of a CFE treaty. The NATO Summit should develop the alliance's objectives for these talks.

Role of Nuclear Forces in Europe

Third, the NATO Summit should also assess the future of U.S. nuclear forces in Europe. As democracy blooms in Eastern Europe, as Soviet troops return home and tanks are dismantled, there is less need for nuclear systems of the shortest range. The NATO Summit should accelerate ongoing work within the alliance to determine the minimum number and types of weapons that will be needed to deter war—credibly and effectively.

In light of these new political conditions, and the limited range and flexibility of short-range nuclear missile forces based in Europe, I have reviewed our plan to produce and deploy newer, more modern, short-range nuclear missiles to replace the Lance system now in Europe. We have almost finished the research and development work for these new missiles. But I have decided, after consulting with our allies, to terminate the follow-on to [the] Lance program. I have also decided to cancel any further modernization of U.S. nuclear artillery shells deployed in Europe.

There are still short-range U.S.—and many more Soviet—nuclear missile systems deployed in Europe. We are prepared to negotiate the reduction of these forces as well, in a new set of arms control talks. At the NATO Summit, I will urge my colleagues to agree on the broad objectives for these future U.S.-Soviet negotiations and begin preparations within the alliance for these talks. I would also like to suggest that these new U.S.-Soviet arms control talks begin shortly after a CFE treaty on conventional forces has been signed.

In taking these steps, the United States is not going to allow Europe to become "safe for conventional war." There are few lessons so clear in history as this. Only the combination of conventional forces and nuclear forces have ensured peace in Europe.

But every aspect of America's engagement in Europe—military, political, and economic—must be complementary. And one place where they all come together is in the Conference on Security and Cooperation in Europe—an organization of 35 states of Europe and North America. The CSCE is already a beacon for human rights and individual freedoms. Now, it must take on a broader role.

Strengthening CSCE

So the fourth task for a NATO Summit is to reach common allied objectives for the future of CSCE. It can help the victorious forces of democracy in Eastern Europe secure their revolutions, and— as they join the commonwealth of free nations— be assured a voice in the new Europe

The CSCE should offer new guidelines for building free societies— including setting standards for truly free elections, adopting measures to strengthen the rule of law, and pointing the way in the needed, but painful, transition from centralized, command economies to free markets.

The CSCE can also provide a forum for political dialogue in a more united Europe. I agree with those who have called for regular consultations among senior representatives of the CSCE countries. We should consider whether new CSCE mechanisms can help mediate and settle disputes in Europe. I believe my allied colleagues and I should agree to take up these new ideas at a CSCE Summit later this year, in conjunction with the signing of a CFE treaty.

Stability and Peace

In Eastern Europe, in this hemisphere, the triumph of democracy has cast its warm light on the face of the world like a miraculous dawn. But the outcome of this struggle for freedom is not ordained, and it will not be the work of miracles.

All of you who graduate here today are part of a historic decision for America's engagement in the future of Europe. I am convinced that our work to protect freedom— to build free societies— will safeguard our own peace and prosperity.

The security of Europe and the world has become very complex in this century. But America's commitment to stability and peace is profoundly clear. Its motivation derives from the strength of our forefathers— from the blood of those who have died for freedom— and for the sake of all who would live in peace.

Every voice, every heart's commitment to freedom, is important. There is a story about a man trying to convince his son that in the struggle for freedom, every voice counts. They stood in a valley, watching the snow fall on a distant mountain. "Tell me the weight of a snowflake," the man said.

"Almost nothing," answered the boy.

As the snow swirled around them, up on the mountain they saw an avalanche whose thunder shook the earth. "Do you know which snowflake caused that?" the old man asked.

"I don't," answered the boy.

"Maybe," said the man, "like the last snowflake that moves a mountain, in the struggle for freedom, a single voice makes a world of difference."

America's mission in Europe, like millions of individual decisions made for freedom, can make a world of difference. The cry for freedom— in Eastern Europe, in South Africa, in this hemisphere— was heard around the world in the "revolution of 1989." Today, in this new "age of freedom," add your voice to the thundering chorus.

---

[1]Text from Current Policy 1276, Department of State, May 1990.

The Common European Interest: America and the New Politics Among Nations

Secretary Baker's address upon receiving the seventh annual Hans J. Morgenthau Memorial Award to the National Committee on American Foreign Policy on May 14, 1990. [1]

I am very pleased to receive the Hans J. Morgenthau Memorial Award and to join the prestigious company of the six preceding recipients. Of course, I have spent most of my life in the law, many of my last twenty years in public service, and much of that time concerned with domestic issues. So it is a real honor to be recognized here tonight for service to the foreign relations of the United States of America.

Above all, it is an honor to receive an award that remembers a man such as Hans Morgenthau.

Driven from Europe by Hitler, Hans Morgenthau spent the rest of his life educating America about the world beyond its shores. It was a world that seemed to be in headlong flight from civilization. As an international lawyer, Hans Morgenthau saw the League of Nations collapse. As a political philosopher, he witnessed the tragedies of fascism and Stalinism. As a diplomatic historian, he lived through two hot wars and then the ebb and flow of a cold one. A personal victim of politics gone bad, he was driven to shake America out of its traditional isolationist slumber. And he would do so using the lessons of history, the often-times bitter realities of international politics and, above all, the reason of national interest.

Nowhere was Hans Morgenthau more effective or more eloquent than in his 1946 classic, *Scientific Man versus Power Politics*. There he wrote, "The age is forever searching for the philosopher's stone, the magic formula, which, mechanically applied, will ... substitute for the uncertainties and risks of political action the certitude of rational calculation." And he continued: "Since, however, what the seekers after the magic formula want is simple, rational, mechanical, and what they have to deal with is complicated, irrational, incalculable, they are compelled to simplify the reality of international politics and to develop what one might call the 'method of the single cause'."

Hans Morgenthau believed there could be no single cause of war nor any single solution to the problems of power and peace. Most of his career was spent debunking those who followed the "method of the single cause."

Tonight, I would like to join company with Hans Morgenthau. I would like to argue against the "method of the single cause" as it applies to the most dramatic event of our time: Europe's recent dawn of freedom and unity.

The visible reduction in the Soviet threat has led some to assume that our only reason for being in Europe over the last 40 years was to contain that threat. Beyond containment, in their view, lies the end of the American role. And so as the alleged "single cause" of America's involvement — fear of Soviet aggression — recedes, America's position in Europe should recede with it.

This would be the most profound and strategic mistake of the generation. We must leave not only the Cold War behind but also the conflicts that preceded the Cold War. The reduction of the Soviet threat need not cause Europe to revert to an unsteady balance of power or a fresh outbreak of national rivalries and ethnic tensions.

Perestroika in the Soviet Union, the democratic revolutions of Central and Eastern Europe, and the unification of Germany create a new opportunity for Europe and for America: to cast our vision beyond the prevention of war to the actual building of peace.

To prevent war, we must continue to deter aggression and contain the residual threat.

To build the peace, however, America's role must go beyond balancing itself against remaining Soviet military power.

American engagement must be recast to suit the new circumstances. Removed by an ocean but bound historically, politically, economically, and strategically to Europe, we can be a guiding hand toward the common interest. Fostering the European common interest can be one of our key national interests. As Professor Morgenthau wrote years ago, "Diplomacy has here the new task of creating and maintaining new institutions and procedures through which new common interests of nations can be pursued."

So tonight, ladies and gentlemen, I want to outline for you America's new diplomatic tasks and to review with you those common interests: political legitimacy, economic prosperity, and military security. And I want to discuss America's role in helping to achieve those interests, both for ourselves and for Europe.

The First Common Interest: Political Legitimacy

The first task we face is fostering political legitimacy — or, to put it plainly, governments elected *by* the people and responsible *to* them. After sweeping away the dictators of the past, the peoples of Central and Eastern European are working to build legitimate political orders that can endure. America must continue to stand with them, reassuring them of our commitment to their new democracies.

The surest building block will be free and fair elections. Last May in Mainz, the President put forward a free elections proposal for the 35 nations of the Conference on Security and Cooperation in Europe (CSCE). He augmented it just two days ago, calling in his speech at the University of South Carolina [2] for CSCE to build a new consensus around free elections, political pluralism, and the rule of law. Next month in Copenhagen, we hope to see CSCE move forward on these ideas.

In order to ensure that the elections in Central and Eastern Europe this spring are free and fair, I proposed in February in Prague that the CSCE member states send observer delegations to these elections. The United States has sent observers to the elections that have already been held, and we will send Presidential delegations to the upcoming elections in Bulgaria and Romania. And I am pleased to report that many states have joined us in this effort.

But in some cases, observers may not be enough. We are concerned that a pattern of intimidation and violence may be undermining the election campaign in Romania.

As we consider institutions capable of fostering political legitimacy throughout Europe, CSCE can play an important part. It remains the one European organization that includes as members almost all European states as well as the United States and Canada. It is well placed to enhance the European consensus on the political and economic values that should be our guiding lights. It can become, if you will, the "conscience of the continent." To strengthen CSCE, we need to regularize its meetings, develop new guidelines for free societies, and promote it as a forum for political dialogue in the new Europe. In this way, the new democracies of the East can be assured a voice in the new Europe. While CSCE's Ten Principles embody Western values, NATO should remain the place where Western democracies join in guaranteeing the new peace of Europe. Alongside its role as a military alliance, NATO has for forty years been a primary political forum where democratic minds have met and resolved to go forward. The Alliance will remain a central forum for political consultations about Europe's future. Therefore, as the President has made clear, we believe NATO should use this summer's summit to accelerate its adaptation to new political realities in Europe.

This process has already begun. The Alliance has worked vigorously on implementing our proposal for a NATO arms control verification staff since we proposed the idea in Berlin in December. And since that time, the Alliance's political consultations have been enhanced, including a special Ministerial eleven days ago to discuss developments in the Soviet Union, the unification of Germany, and ways to strengthen CSCE.

In this regard, I would like to raise an idea that may be worth further consideration. Already, the North Atlantic Assembly has invited Eastern European parliamentarians to some meetings. The Western European Union (WEU) and NATO need to consider how they might reach out and reassure the peoples and governments of the East. These institutions should consider developing, for example, a solid political and military dialogue with the Central and Eastern Europeans and with the Soviets. In this way, we may be able to heighten understanding of the West's continuing commitment to legitimacy and stability.

Over the longer term, as democracy grows in Central and Eastern Europe, the United States will expand bilateral ties with the new democracies and add diplomatic resources and facilities in the region. We will open new cultural centers across Eastern Europe and do much more to satisfy the large demand for the teaching of English. Already, we have proposed a Fund for Independent Broadcasting and a Free Press.

Democracy can only flourish with extensive citizen participation. That's why the President has proposed a Citizens Democracy Corps[2]. By involving American citizens with private citizens and groups in Eastern Europe, and perhaps eventually the Soviet Union as well, the give-and-take of democracy can flourish across the Atlantic.

The Second Common Interest: Economic Liberty and Prosperity

Economic liberty and prosperity is the second common interest behind which all Europeans can unite. Europe, politically and economically, needs to be made an inclusive and integrated whole, open to the world.

Our bilateral economic efforts involve three areas. First, we are standing with those new democracies in crisis situations, providing desperately needed emergency aid. Second, we are actively supporting efforts aimed to facilitate the transition from Stalinist command economies to private sector-driven free markets. Third, we're working to integrate the new market democracies into the international economic system.

The United States has led the way on several key assistance issues, including the creation of the Polish stabilization fund to support Poland's courageous reforms. We have launched innovative Enterprise Funds for Poland and Hungary to assist the growth of the private sector in those countries. The United States will continue to broaden its trade and assistance programs with the emerging democracies – and the more market-oriented these economies become, the wider the avenue will be for our economic relations.

Institutionally, a European Community (EC) closely tied to the United States and open to association to the East can serve the interests of all. For the Western Europeans, it can provide expanded and freer markets. For Americans, it can provide an open door to all of Europe. And for the Eastern Europeans, it can open their emerging private sectors to both Western Europe and the United States, assuring them of a market for the products of their transformed economies.

We have taken many steps to increase our consultations with the EC on economics and politics. For example, our work together in the area of standards could help eliminate unintended trade barriers. We now have regularly scheduled Ministerials as well as President-to-President meetings. In the context of the European Political Cooperation (EPC) process, we are striving to intensify our dialogue on political issues, including Eastern Europe and regional conflicts.

Working together, an involved America, the G-24 [3], the EC, the OECD [Organization for Economic Cooperation and Development] Center for European Economies in Transition, and the new European Bank for Reconstruction and Development can create an inclusive, not exclusive, economic climate.

The Third Common Interest: Military Security

Political legitimacy and economic prosperity will need to be buttressed by military security. With conditions changing, the President has said we now need to develop our strategy for dealing with a new European strategic environment. As Soviet troops leave Central and Eastern Europe and Moscow proceeds with further reductions in its forces, we will be able to change NATO's strategy and forces significantly from those we've relied upon in the past. In thinking about the American conventional military presence in Europe, Soviet actions will remain critical. As the "new thinking" is translated into a new Soviet force structure, we will be able to alter our posture. Indeed, the opportunity to draw down our forces is due in no small part to President Gorbachev's withdrawing of Soviet troops and redefining more realistically Soviet security interests in Europe. Yet even if all Soviet armed forces return to the U.S.S.R. and conventional arms control moves forward, the Soviet military will retain forces many times larger than those possessed by any other single state.

American troops will, therefore, need to remain in Europe for as long as they are wanted. But the nature and composition of the American military presence in Europe should change with the threat. If we codify the political changes in democratic governments and the military changes in CFE [negotiations on conventional armed forces in Europe], we will need to plan differently. Thus, in the near future, we may be able to plan less for the danger of an immediate outbreak of war and more on how to promote long term military stability in Europe.

The President has also stressed the need for the NATO Summit to assess the future of U.S. nuclear forces in Europe. Here, too, military strategy must reflect political reality. Circumstances and conditions are changing. We need to pay close attention to the numbers, kinds, and deterrent missions of our nuclear weapons in Europe. As part of this reassessment, the President has called upon the Alliance to agree on broad objectives for future U.S.-Soviet negotiations on short-range nuclear missiles deployed in Europe.

Conventional and nuclear arms control must be a central element in our planning. As I stressed in San Francisco last October, arms control can lock in positive changes, require the Soviets to destroy weapons in an effectively verifiable manner, and make the changes difficult and costly to reverse. Not only should we sign a treaty on Conventional Forces in Europe (CFE) this year, but we must accelerate its follow-on negotiations to cope with those residual security concerns states may have even after CFE.

We must also strengthen our efforts at promoting strategic predictability in the confidence and security building measures talks (CSBMs) in Vienna. The Chairman of the Joint Chiefs of Staff is broadening military-to-military exchanges, both with the Soviets and with the East Europeans. On the civilian side, we should undertake a similar dialogue with our counterparts, focusing not on day-to-day events but rather the doctrinal concepts we use in thinking about war and peace.

As we adapt to changed conditions, let me stress one point: We cannot afford to allow Europe to become safe for any type of war. Deterrence must be maintained by an appropriate and reliable mix of conventional and nuclear forces.

As for the longer term, we are interested in exploring the possibilities of a CSCE mechanism for peaceful resolution of disputes. We encourage such efforts, provided they complement but do not supplant existing institutions like NATO and the WEU. Together, the old and the new can complement one another, creating multiple institutions to cope with evolving problems.

New Institutions and the Common Interest: Two-Plus-Four

From my discussion of our three common interests, I hope one point is clear: As there is no single cause for America's involvement in Europe, so too there can be no single tie which binds us together. Nor can any single institution embody our diverse involvement across the Atlantic. This is why we are interested in developing America's relations with the primary institutions of Europe - NATO, the EC, and CSCE.

But, as I noted last winter in Berlin and in Prague, new institutions and mechanisms may need to be created. For example, in Prague I stressed the role regional or voluntary associations might play in promoting common interests of Central and Eastern Europeans.

As Europe is reconciled and integrated, all of the common political, economic, and security interests overlap in a single project: the unification of Germany in peace and freedom. A unified Germany and the process which brings it about will put an indelible stamp on our hopes for the future.

The Two-Plus-Four process for German unification is a prime example of how mechanisms, even temporary ones, may need to be invented to assist in articulating the common interest while complementing the ongoing work of existing institutions.

Far from being an attempt to dictate the future of Germany or Europe, the Two-Plus-Four exists for a different purpose: to ratify the already clear will of the German people to unite in freedom and self-determination while providing a forum to discuss unification's external ramifications.

A primary task of the Two-Plus-Four will be to arrive at a formula by which all remaining Four Power rights and responsibilities, including over Berlin, will be terminated and transferred to a fully sovereign Germany—a Germany united within the territory of the FRG [Federal Republic of Germany], the GDR [German Democratic Republic], and Berlin.

In general, the Two-Plus-Four should act as a "steering group," directing to appropriate European fora those external issues related to German unification that can best be decided elsewhere—such as in the CFE and CSBM talks, the upcoming SNF (short-range nuclear missile forces) talks, or CSCE. This approach can involve the relevant European states and assure action on important external issues, without singling out Germany and thereby planting seeds of future instability. In this way, decisions can be reached in fora already created to support common interests.

The New Politics Among Nations

There is no single cause of the freedom that swept across Europe in the last year. And there can be no single solution to insure that Europe becomes and remains whole and free.

Effective solutions will demand the multiple talents that the American people have to offer their neighbors across the Atlantic. As Soviet troops return home, our military requirements for Europe's defense can be refashioned and many, though not all, of our troops can be brought home to the United States. With effectively verifiable arms control agreements in place, our overall military burden can be significantly reduced.

There is much talk of a "peace dividend." If the peace we are now building in Europe can be made solid and durable, there will be real dividends. They will be more than financial, more than a controlled and gradual reduction in the defense budget. Just as importantly, they will come in the form of new exchange opportunities for our students and cooperative ventures for our scientists, increased economic opportunities for our businessmen, and improved political understanding for our people.

But these returns require investments of a new type.

Precisely for that reason—to insure the peace and realize its benefits—as some of our troops depart Europe, our students, businessmen, and diplomats should arrive. And they should cross the Atlantic in numbers larger than ever before. But when they cross the Atlantic, they must do so with a firm understanding of America's purpose in the new Europe.

Articulating the common interest in a Europe whole and free and establishing institutions and procedures built on those interests are the key tasks of the nineties. The alternative is for Europe to drift back towards the familiar politics among nations described by Hans Morgenthau and so much feared by him.

I do not believe that anyone in Europe today—or any nation for that matter—wants to go back to "business as usual."

The history of our century, unfortunately, is full of well-meaning but failed experiments in collective security. They failed because nations either lost sight of common interests or lacked the wisdom and the courage to uphold them. As the world's preeminent democracy, we have sacrificed for two generations so that Europe's dream of unity and freedom might be realized. Now, the final impediments to that dream are being removed. As the President put it, a new commonwealth of nations is at hand.

The great Americans, hardened by World War II, who joined our nation's destiny to that of Europe's forty years ago must find their counterpart today in this generation. For we, too, have been hardened by a war — a war whose casualties can be seen in the ruined societies now being reborn on the other side of the breached Berlin Wall. It was a struggle that overshadowed our lives and the lives of our families and darkened the spirit.

Now that struggle draws to a close.

Surely the lesson that Hans Morgenthau taught, of America's necessary enrollment in the ranks of those striving for democracy and peace, is a lesson that transcends the Cold War. We must therefore pledge ourselves anew to secure those vital common interests in Europe and elsewhere which can redeem the sacrifices of the 20th century with peace and freedom.

In short, we must build the peace.

Then, indeed, shall we see a new politics among nations.

---

1 Department of State Press Release 68, May 14, 1990.

2 President Bush's commencement address at the University of South Carolina, May 12, 1990 (see previous section).

3 President Bush and the other leaders at the Paris economic summit meeting in July 1989 agreed on the need to coordinate Western assistance in support of political and economic changes in Poland and Hungary. The European Community Commission, which was chosen to coordinate the process, has convened a series of meetings of 24 interested countries known as the G-24.

Secretary Baker's Trips to Europe Prior to Washington Summit

INTERVENTION AT THE NORTH ATLANTIC COUNCIL MINISTERIAL MEETING, BRUSSELS MAY 3, 1990 (Excerpts) [1]

We begin today an Alliance consultation process on a wide range of truly historic issues. How we work together to resolve the issues before us will have much to do with the success of the newly emerging European political and security environment.

These consultations will continue within the Alliance at our June North Atlantic Council (NAC) meeting and hopefully at a North Atlantic Treaty Organization Heads of Government meeting this summer. NATO must and will adapt to the new conditions. We must grasp today's opportunities, confident that the Alliance will play — indeed, is playing — a vital role in managing the new political and military challenges that confront the West. That is what political consultations are all about.

NATO is, in fact, all about politics — the politics of international peace and security. The Alliance is founded on our shared commitment to common political ideals. This political commitment has kept the Alliance together for 40 years, even when we have had differences on military strategy. In this regard, NATO was not, is not, and cannot afford to become a narrow, technically-based, defense-only organization. Political and military interests work together and cannot be neatly separated.

This is particularly true today. As I pointed out in a speech I gave in Berlin in December and later stressed here at the Council, the Alliance needs to enhance its political role. In my view, our discussion here today of three essentially political questions — the Lithuanian crisis, German unification, and Conference on Security and Cooperation in Europe (CSCE) — is testimony already to our ability to change with the times.

In this spirit, before turning to discuss U.S.-Soviet relations in detail, I would first like to share with you the key elements from a speech President Bush will give tomorrow on European security issues. Today, the speech is

being previewed with the leaders of the Alliance, and the President has asked that I review it with you, also.

[Section omitted. See speech by President Bush, p. 29]

Let me now turn to an assessment of Soviet politics.

U.S.-Soviet Relations

In our view, *perestroika* has entered a critical, even paradoxical stage. On the one hand, [President Mikhail] Gorbachev's formal power has never been greater as he heads for the Party Congress this summer. On no single issue has he been successfully challenged. Ascending to the Presidency, he is positioned to push through the radical reforms he has so often extolled in the last six months.

The irony is that while Gorbachev may finally be able to push through radical reform, right now he may be reluctant to act, increasingly fearful that real reform could lead to a genuine implosion from below.

In light of these Soviet domestic realities, I suspect we are in for an uncertain two months until the Soviet Party Congress can clarify *perestroika's* political prospects more definitively.

Despite Gorbachev's internal problems, the President and I believe that the U.S.-Soviet summit which begins later this month could be quite successful. Most importantly, we hope to mark real progress in arms control. In strategic arms reduction talks (START), tomorrow I hope with Foreign Minister Shevardnadze to at least narrow the remaining differences over ALCMs (air-launched cruise missiles) and SLCMs (sea-launched cruise missiles). And while many differences remain, I do believe that with the necessary political will, all the major substantive issues can be resolved by the summit. However, we will just have to see if the political realities in the Soviet Union will permit this. Besides START, the verification protocols for the nuclear testing treaties are on track for signature. We are also working hard to complete a bilateral chemical weapons destruction agreement, and we expect to release a joint statement covering chemical weapons, missiles, and nuclear nonproliferation.

On other matters, the President will again have an extensive discussion on European issues. We will also raise various regional issues with President Gorbachev, looking in particular at how elections might be an acceptable mechanism for resolving the conflicts in Afghanistan and Angola. On human rights and democratization, we are getting closer to resolution of all divided family and refusenik cases. Finally, we look forward to progress on the rest of our agenda of transnational, bilateral, and economic issues.

Let me conclude with a few words on Lithuania—the one real threat to progress at the summit and continued improvements in U.S.-Soviet relations.

For all of us, Lithuania, Latvia, and Estonia present a dilemma, and we appreciate the consultations our Ambassadors have held here at NATO on the Lithuanian crisis. This is exactly the kind of political issue on which we need to consult. We should do it more often. It's exactly what we mean by enhancing NATO's political role.

Lithuania has, of course, presented Gorbachev with a dilemma, too. Gorbachev and [Soviet Foreign Minister Eduard] Shevardnadze have both indicated that they are under domestic pressure to take action against Vilnius, and this may account in part for Moscow's inconsistent signaling and waffling on this issue.

In the face of uncertainties in Soviet policy, we have sought to maintain a consistent approach. Our policy reflects three basic considerations.

First, we are determined to maintain our support for the right of the Lithuanian people to exercise self-determination. And we will continue not to recognize Moscow's forcible incorporation of the Baltics into the U.S.S.R.

Second, we do not wish to take any actions that could escalate the situation or make it more difficult for Moscow to maneuver itself out of the current impasse. Once Moscow imposed economic sanctions against Lithuania, we weighed our reaction carefully. We continue to keep under review the options we outlined to you in our consultations. I should note that in Congress there is growing opposition to a trade agreement with the Soviet Union under present circumstances.

Third, we have sought in our contacts with Moscow and Vilnius to promote dialogue between the two sides. We have suggested each side defuse the situation, step back from confrontation, and start a dialogue. We have worked quietly to try to promote such a dialogue—the only pathway to a solution.

Further Soviet action in Lithuania or elsewhere in the Baltics will certainly stimulate moral and political pressures on all of us to act. I will underscore this point with Foreign Minister Shevardnadze when I meet with him tomorrow. While we understand the pressures affecting the Soviet leadership, they too must understand that we have our own principles and are subject to our own political pressures.

Moreover, the reform process in the Soviet Union will be called into question if self-determination in Lithuania is denied. Democracy is not divisible. It won't be sustainable in some republics if it is denied in others.

We have sought to consult with you bilaterally, as well as here at NATO. We value these consultations highly. I would welcome your continuing assessments of events in Moscow and how we might jointly react to the Lithuanian problem.

Two-Plus-Four and German Unification

With the first Two-Plus-Four Ministerial about to be held, we are at an important moment in the process of unification. It is important that we enter this process on the basis of an unequivocal Alliance consensus in favor of German unity on terms that preserve and strengthen not only Western security but security in Europe as a whole.

The internal obstacles to German unity have now been largely overcome, reflected in the overwhelming East German support for those political parties that clearly favor unification.

While the Soviet Union has been willing to permit changes to take place in Central and Eastern Europe, clearly the process of German unification is, from the Soviet standpoint, the most sensitive of these changes. We want, therefore, to sustain Soviet willingness to cooperate in these changes.

We must avoid creating the image of winners and losers in the unification process. Indeed, there can and should be only winners. Creating a stable, united Germany within secure borders, as part of a free democratic alliance, hurts no one. The adaptation of NATO, the EC [European Community], and CSCE to new European realities is a gain for everyone.

We are prepared to listen to Soviet concerns, and we will make it clear that while Two-Plus-Four can discuss many issues, it will take decisions primarily on issues clearly related to Four Power rights and responsibilities. A united Germany must have full control over all of its territory without any new discriminatory constraints on German sovereignty.

Two-Plus-Four has an important role to play in steering the discussion of external aspects of unification into the proper fora. In this regard, many of the broader political-military issues raised by unification can only be resolved in other settings.

Thus, the question of a unified Germany's position in Western defense structures is a matter to be discussed and decided upon here at NATO. Similarly, a united Germany's relations with the European Community must be decided upon in the EC. Conventional arms control questions, including questions relating to German armed forces, should be addressed and decided in the follow-on to the CFE negotiations. Nuclear weapons should be addressed in the upcoming SNF (short range nuclear missile forces) negotiations. And broader arrangements for East-West cooperation can be pursued in fora in which all participants are represented, particularly in the 35-nation CSCE.

Overcoming the division of Germany is the essential component in overcoming the division of Europe, and has positive implications for broader East-West cooperation, including strengthening the CSCE process. That is a central subject for NATO to consider, to which we will return shortly.

It is important to emphasize that there is no substitute for the security and stability provided by NATO. Broader structures like CSCE can complement, but not substitute for, the mutual security structure provided by NATO. All of us have welcomed the FRG's [Federal Republic of Germany] unequivocal statement that a unified Germany will remain in NATO. A unified Germany, fully participating in NATO and in its mutual defense structure and in other forms of Western defense cooperation, is essential to long term European stability.

In bilateral meetings with the Soviets, as in discussions with Central and Eastern Europeans, we have made clear the importance we attach to continued full German participation in NATO and its integrated military structures. Ultimately, I hope and believe, the Soviet Union will recognize not only that a neutral Germany is in no one's interests, but also that a Germany that is fully a part of NATO is in Soviet long term interests.

As regards the Two-Plus-Four, Saturday's exchange will be the first among ministers. I expect it will involve an initial exchange on the agenda items that have been put forward and agreement to continue the process. I believe there is general agreement on the part of all Western participants that, if possible, we would like to complete the Two-Plus-Four's work by fall, before the CSCE Summit.

This is an ambitious agenda, however, and one which will require hard work. We will keep you fully informed as the process unfolds.

Let me note that I have followed closely the Council's discussions in recent weeks on the implications of German unification for NATO. These discussions have emphasized again the need for close consultations in this forum in advance of any decision being taken that might have broader implications for the Alliance. I share the view that these discussions should continue and that capitals should give them full attention. These discussions will ensure that the Alliance's efforts to adapt are reinforced in the Two-Plus-Four process.

CSCE Summit

Like many of you, I have given a great deal of thought recently to CSCE, and to how we might use that process to promote the goals we share for Europe's future. That is why I wrote each of you some ten days ago, outlining the importance we attach to the Helsinki process and our approach to the CSCE Summit. If you believe my letter represents a major effort on our part to enhance CSCE's role in the future of Europe, you're right.

This Council has a strong, guiding role to play in identifying common positions for us to put forward in order to shape future directions of the CSCE process. As we prepare for a summit, it is important that we have in mind a clear outline of what it can and cannot accomplish.

The President and I believe that a summit at which a CFE agreement is signed can register important gains for our common security. Signing a CFE agreement at the summit remains, in our view, critical to institutionalizing a legitimate security order for the new Europe.

A summit also offers the newly reforming countries of Eastern Europe an inclusive sense of greater community and can assist them as they seek to develop more open, democratic, and market-based structures—much along the lines of what we have in the West. It can pave the way to a new, democratic Europe that is inclusive and not exclusive.

As the President's speech tomorrow makes clear, the United States sees an expanded conception of human rights as a fundamental aspect of a CSCE summit. In this regard, we ask for your support for the following proposals:

—Endorsement by the 35 of the principle and content of free and fair elections, which we view as the key building block for making Europe free and whole. We and our cosponsors, the United Kingdom, will press hard for adoption of our elaborated free elections proposal at Copenhagen and seek your vigorous support, so that the summit can build on a strong base.

—Endorsement of efforts to explore possible mechanisms to assist in dispute management.

—And, similarly, agreement on a mechanism whereby CSCE states can request clarification of unusual military activities, thereby meeting the evolving needs of a new and changing Europe.

Parallel to these ideas, the President and I believe it is important that the CSCE process be built up. For that reason we have proposed that political consultations among the 35 be regularized at any of several levels. We also have proposed that review meetings be held more frequently to assess accomplishments that have been achieved and to chart future directions. For planning purposes, we believe these meetings should be of fixed duration. And we have suggested that the summit consider how existing organizations can be used to follow up on CSCE accomplishments, without creating costly or duplicative bureaucratic structures.

In putting forward these suggestions, we are seeking to use the CSCE process to its fullest potential.

Certainly CSCE has a role in security matters, as demonstrated by the solid record of success in the Stockholm Conference and follow-on Confidence and Security Building Measures (CSBMs) negotiations, as well as the related conventional force talks. And, CSCE can do more to enhance our mutual security, as underscored through some of the proposals the U.S. has put forward. CSCE can complement NATO. But it cannot replace the security guarantees that NATO provides.

This is something on which I think all of us can agree, and which we should make clear to our colleagues in the Soviet Union and the newly reforming states of Eastern Europe. And we should intensify our efforts to achieve a conventional forces agreement, which remains at the center of our thinking as regards the CSCE Summit.

These are some of the thoughts I wanted to convey to you as we consider the question of preparations for the CSCE Summit.

Thus far, the United States has devoted its attention to developing a common approach to the CSCE Summit among the countries represented here. We believe that much work remains to be done here in elaborating a common concept and would urge that the working group redouble its efforts to achieve that goal.

At the same time, we recognize the importance of moving ahead with preparations among the 35 for the summit. For that reason, I have proposed that a preparatory conference of the 35 begin in early July.

I have also offered to host a short meeting of foreign ministers this fall on the margins of the opening of the United Nations General Assembly, to review the status of CSCE Summit preparatory work.

I would welcome your views on these suggestions and hope we can move quickly to agreement on the way forward at our meeting today.

---

[1] Department of State Press Release 65, May 10, 1990.

OPENING INTERVENTION AT THE TWO-PLUS-FOUR MEETING, BONN, MAY 5 [1]

We are fortunate, each of us, to live in this age of great events. And today the six of us, working together, have a task to perform that pertains to one of the greatest events of this exceptional era.

As public servants, we bear a special trust, not just from our governments, but from the people of Europe and America—from generations past, present, and future. We face the challenge of rising above the past.

For we meet in recognition that an historical process is underway: the unification of Germany in peace and freedom. Today, we engage in an act of reconciliation—of a people too long separated, of a continent too long divided.

In helping Germany achieve freedom and unity, I believe all the states and peoples of Europe can be the winners. That should be our aim. That is a vision that looks to the future, not to the past.

For the United States, we see this as the realization of a goal we have shared with the German people for over forty years. So we believe that the primary purpose of this Two-Plus-Four process is to facilitate the unity of the two Germanys as the German people decide their future on the basis of free and democratic self-determination. We seek a unified, sovereign Germany, solidly built on universal democratic values, and acting with due consideration for the interests of others in the European and global community of nations. We are bound—legally and morally—to this end.

We believe that a united Germany will be a full and constructive partner—for all of us—in the building of a Europe whole and free. The history of the Federal Republic of Germany's involvement in world affairs over the past four decades provides the firmest indicator of the German people's commitment to peace and international cooperation. And the declaration of the German Democratic Republic's first democratically elected government makes clear that these aspirations are fully shared by the East German people.

The process of unification has already advanced significantly as the result of decisions democratically arrived at within the Federal Republic of Germany and the German Democratic Republic. The timing and form in which unification will occur has yet to be determined. In our view, and indeed according to the statement the six agreed to in Ottawa, these are internal issues to be decided by the Germans themselves through their democratically elected representatives.

Once a united and democratic Germany exists in mutually recognized borders, the Four Powers will have fully met their responsibilities. The basis for any remaining special rights will no longer exist. A primary task of this group, therefore, will be to arrive at a formula by which we will terminate and transfer all remaining Four Power rights and responsibilities to a fully sovereign Germany—a Germany united within the territory of the Federal Republic of Germany, the German Democratic Republic, and Berlin. We must focus our efforts on the substance of a final settlement, not on the symbols of the past.

We see this as the realization of a goal we have shared with the German people for over 40 years.

In doing so, we all should seek to promote full, equal, and cooperative relations between a united Germany and other members of the international community. There should be no effort to single out Germany. The imposition of limitations of a discriminatory nature on any sovereign state can only lead to resentment, instability, and conflict. Likewise, attempts to impede self-determination would harm the development of a legitimate and harmonious global order.

Unification will have important implications for each of us in our relations with Germany, as well as for Germany's place in the new, evolving European order. The United States recognizes that others among the Four have legitimate interests that may need to be addressed as part of this Two-Plus-Four process. We believe that this forum may be an appropriate place for discussions of such issues, but it is our view that this forum should take decisions only on those issues relevant to Four Power rights and responsibilities.

We come to this meeting, of course, with broader European interests in mind. But we—the Six—have received no mandate from other nations to represent their interests. Thus, many issues of significant interest to us here will require consultation and decision in other, more inclusive fora.

In our view, the Two-Plus-Four should in general act as a "steering group," directing to appropriate European fora those external issues related to German unification that can best be decided elsewhere—such as in the CFE and CSBM talks, the upcoming SNF talks, or CSCE. This approach can involve the relevant European states and assure action on important external issues, without singling out Germany and thereby planting seeds of future instability.

The unification of Germany should act as an incentive to strengthen and institutionalize more inclusive and cooperative structures for East-West interaction. As President Bush's speech yesterday made clear once again, we are ready to engage in that process. Our success here will represent a major step forward and give important impulse to our common efforts in other fora.

We have agreed on four agenda items. Let me briefly mention each.

On borders, the two Germanys and Poland have already begun to work together to remove any residual doubt as to their mutual commitment to the present frontier. Our position is clear. We respect the provisions of the Helsinki Final Act—that the current borders between signatories to the act are inviolable, subject only to peaceful change. We also believe that we all can agree that a united Germany should consist of the current territory of the FRG, the GDR, and Berlin—no more, no less.

On political-military issues, we believe that while the six can discuss many subjects, we should act primarily as a "steering group." Most of these issues have implications for states other than the six. They should as a consequence be decided in more inclusive fora, especially the CFE and CSBM talks. In this way, both German sovereignty and all-European interests can be respected and assured.

On Berlin, we look to end all Four Power authority in an orderly way.

Finally, we must prepare a Final Settlement under international law and terminate the Four Power rights and responsibilities. This effort must look to the future, not become absorbed with the legacy of the past. We should resolve these rights and responsibilities in an expeditious, straightforward, and legally binding way.

Let me close by making a point that builds on a fine phrase recalled by my friend, Foreign Minister [Hans-Dietrich] Genscher [of the Federal Republic of Germany]: We want a

European Germany. As the Berlin Wall crumbled last November ninth, we saw Germany being made whole again. But we also saw Europe being made whole. For it is impossible to have a Europe whole and free or to build a Common European Home, if Germany is not whole and free. In breaking down the Wall, the people of Berlin helped to unify Germany, and equally, they helped to unify Europe.

The inevitability and desirability of German unification is a fact. So, too, is the inevitability and desirability of European reconciliation and integration. Together here today, like the ordinary citizens of Berlin last November ninth, we take steps for Europe and for Germany.

This is our charge. It is an honorable duty, one that I am pleased we will have an opportunity to perform together.

——————————

1Department of State Press Release 62, May 5, 1990.

PRESS BRIEFING ENROUTE FROM WARSAW, POLAND MAY 6, 1990

(Excerpt)[1]

Q: Did the Polish officials you met seem to feel satisfied with whatever assurances you were bringing them, or did they have additional complaints or worries to bring to your attention?

A: I think they were very pleased to receive the letter inviting them to participate in the third meeting of the Two-Plus-Four, to be held in Paris in July, and to participate at the expert level in the preparatory meeting for that meeting.

I think they were somewhat reassured by our account of the discussion that took place in Bonn. And they, as you know, have begun having their own discussions with the two Germanys with respect particularly to the issue of borders.

I think that while the issue remains to be addressed and resolved, I think there is a much better atmosphere than there was several weeks ago, particularly before they engaged directly with the two Germanys.

Q: Did he ask you to talk to [Chancellor Hulmut]Kohl [of the Federal Republic of Germany] about signing a treaty with them? Did they ask you to use your influence with Chancellor Kohl to see if perhaps their desire to have an initial treaty on the borders might be useful?

A: They laid out their concerns and their position and their view of the status of their talks with the two Germanys. It's the position of the other countries in the Two-Plus-Four discussions, as you undoubtly know, that the preferable approach is for the Polish government, in discussion with the two German governments, to work out the mechanics and the details. I think that they are encouraged by the suggestions that there be a border treaty agreed to and that that border treaty be elaborated in resolutions of the two German parliaments. And I think that they understand that a border treaty with a unified Germany cannot be entered into until there is, in fact, a unified Germany in place to sign such a treaty.

And I'm not suggesting that there are not still some differences in approach, but I think that things are moving in a very positive direction.

——————————

1Made available to news correspondents by Department of State spokesman Margaret Tutwiler.

PRESS CONFERENCE FOLLOWING U.S.-U.S.S.R. MINISTERIAL, MOSCOW, MAY 19, 1990

(Opening Remarks) [1]

Ladies and gentlemen, we have just finished four days of long and detailed talks with President Gorbachev, Foreign Minister Shevardnadze, and their colleagues. These have been some of the most intensive discussions we have had with our Soviet counterparts during this administration. In the end game of negotiations, I think it is reasonable to expect both the intensity and the difficulty of the work to increase. In short, we have been engaged in some heavy lifting to lock in agreements by the time of the summit between President Bush and President Gorbachev.

I think that our discussions have resulted in some real accomplishments, and the progress that we have made here makes me optimistic that we can have a productive summit in Washington, beginning less than two weeks from now.

In the five hours of meetings with President Gorbachev, we covered a number of issues, including arms control; Baltic, particularly Lithuanian, desires for independence; German unification; and the Soviet economy. We had a full exchange of views on these issues.

I might just say that in the discussions that I had here on Lithuania, the parties expressed a desire to find a way to a peaceful dialogue. I can't say at this point that the Soviets and the Lithuanians have yet arrived at a common basis on which to proceed, but I do think that they are now more actively seeking to develop that basis, even though they are not there yet.

Let me briefly cover the results of our talks and where our relationship stands as we get ready for the summit.

On START, of course as you know, our goal has been to reach agreement on the major substantive issues by the time of the summit. We are in a position now, I think, to do so. While some issues remain, we have now reached agreement at this Ministerial on what have been two of the most vexing problems that we have faced in START: air-launched cruise missiles (ALCMs) and sea-launched cruise missiles (SLCMs). On ALCMs, we have agreed to a complicated formula which equitably meets the needs of both sides.

On SLCMs, we have agreed to a politically binding declaration which will stand outside of the START treaty itself. The declaration will enhance both strategic stability and predictability without creating verification problems for either side.

We resolved a number of other START issues and we also agreed to begin work on the objectives for follow-on negotiations on START.

On chemical weapons, we have reached agreement on what I think is a precedent-setting accord. I believe that this agreement is very significant, particularly as it provides a real pathway toward a global ban on horrific weapons that we already know from bitter experience actually get used.

Very simply put, this United States-Soviet accord is a trailblazing agreement that implements the President's initiative on chemical weapons.

On nuclear testing, we have completed work on the protocols to the nuclear testing treaties. These are now ready for signing at the summit.

We also have agreed to a summit joint statement on nuclear, chemical, and missile nonproliferation.

The one area where we made less progress in arms control than we had hoped for is CFE. We had come with ideas designed to push this process forward, but our counterparts, apparently, were not able to respond meaningfully at this time.

On regional issues, we had a full discussion on Afghanistan. I believe that we are closer to developing a common basis on which to move to free and fair elections—the surest path to reconciliation, peace, and legitimacy in that war-torn country.

On Central America, our discussions reaffirmed the importance of continued adherence to Esquipulas and the need to end the insurgency in El Salvador and to promote a political dialogue.

On human rights and democratization, we stressed our continuing concern over the remaining refusenik cases in the Soviet Union and the need to resolve all of these as soon as possible. I also raised our concerns about anti-Semitism and the vital need for the Soviet leadership to speak out strongly against it.

We had exchanges on economics, transnational and bilateral issues. We have finalized for signing at the summit several United States-Soviet agreements in the commercial area, including the Long-Term Grains Agreement and the Maritime Transportation Agreement.

In terms of transnational and bilateral issues, we are ready to sign a maritime boundary agreement, an agreement on oceans study, an accord to open cultural and information centers in Moscow and Washington, and perhaps other agreements. We also will be able to sign the Thousand-Thousand Agreement—an exchange of a thousand undergraduate students between our two countries.

In closing, let me simply say that we have worked to prepare the ground so that our Presidents can lock in and institutionalize mutual points of advantage in this relationship.

---

[1]Department of State Press Release 71, May 22, 1990.

CSCE: The Conscience of the Continent

Secretary Baker's address before the Conference on Security and Cooperation in Europe (CSCE) Conference on the Human Dimension, Copenhagen, June 6, 1990. [1]

We are present at the creation of a new age of Europe. It is a time of discussion of new architectures, councils, committees, confederations, and common houses. These are, no doubt, very weighty matters.

But all the deliberations of statesmen and diplomats, scholars and lawgivers, will amount to nothing if they overlook or forget a very basic premise. This premise, of course, is that "all Men are created equal, that they are endowed by their Creator with certain unalienable Rights, that among these, are Life, Liberty, and the Pursuit of Happiness." And it is "to secure these Rights"—secure them—that "Governments are instituted among Men, deriving their just Powers from the Consent of the Governed." And that, my friends, is why we are here.

Human rights is a modern phrase. But it recalls the words—and the spirit—of committed men and women throughout Europe's history. The codes of King Canute. The Magna Carta. The Bill of Rights. The Declaration on the Rights of Man. The Universal Declaration of Human Rights. And, yes, the Helsinki Final Act.

At times over the years, these words could not be heard because of yelling crowds, prison gates, and secret police. At times, these words have been burned and at times they have been banned. But they kept returning on the lips of successor generations. They could not be destroyed, because they are in the soul of man.

The very ideas that so stirred Jefferson and Montesquieu resonate today in the words of Havel and Geremek. They echo in our collective historical memory, and they illuminate our path to the future.

Time and again, we have seen how government's contempt for human dignity led to suffering on an unprecedented scale. Each generation, including ours, has learned what our forefathers discovered—that it is to our collective peril that we close our eyes to the suffering which is inflicted by in-tolerance and by oppression. Thomas Jefferson put it this way 200 years ago: We must swear "upon the altar of God, eternal hostility against every form of tyranny over the mind of man."

And so, today, we, representatives of the people of 35 nations, must rededicate ourselves to the cause of human rights; we must reaffirm the democratic values that are our legacy from the past.

Realizing the Helsinki Vision

We are now closer than ever, I think, to realizing CSCE's long-cherished vision of a Europe that is whole and a Europe that is free. But as we approach our work, as we consider grand designs and institutional concepts, it is useful to find our bearings by recalling another gathering 15 years ago. Then the peoples of Central and Eastern Europe still lived in an artificially divided Europe, isolated behind a wall—a dark curtain through which the light of world concern reached but very, very dimly.

It was at that dark time that a band of intrepid men and women in a small flat in Moscow risked their freedom to form the first Helsinki monitoring group. They rejected the darkness of tyranny, and they pledged to bring the denial of human rights to light. Their leader, Yuri Orlov, who is with us now, launched the Helsinki movement with a toast that was as sardonic as it was defiant: "To the success," he said, "of our hopeless cause!"

Dr. Orlov and his colleagues paid dearly for that pledge. They all suffered. One by one, they were persecuted, arrested, exiled. Some of them died. Yet, inspired by their selfless example, one by one, others throughout the Soviet Union and Central and Eastern Europe took up the spirit of Helsinki. And one by one, these courageous men and women breathed life into the Helsinki process. They infused the words with meaning.

Before long, these words inspired acts of bravery that dictators and one-party states could never comprehend. In Katowice, in Poland, democratic activists considered the Final Act to be so important that they braved the blows of security forces to distribute copies of it to their neighbors. And it was to the Madrid meeting of Helsinki signatory states that exiled Solidarity leaders appealed in the aftermath of martial law, proclaiming that there can be no social peace without social justice.

Time and again, Czechoslovakia's Charter '77 cited the Helsinki Final Act in defense of their unjustly persecuted countrymen. They were persecuted for "living in truth," for accepting the praiseworthy folly, as Vaclav Havel put it, of believing their words and ideals could really make a difference. Now the charter's original members—President Havel and Foreign Minister Dienstbier to name only two—are leading the new Czech and Slovak Federal Republic to democracy.

When Bucharest's beautiful old buildings were bulldozed and entire villages were threatened by the whim of a dictator, people turned to the CSCE human rights mechanism to spare further destruction of Romania's priceless cultural heritage.

Just before the Berlin Wall fell, scores of East German refugees sought to transit through Hungary to freedom. The reforming Hungarian government, confronted with demands from East German authorities to place old rules in the way of new freedoms, turned to a different set of rules. The Hungarians cited their CSCE obligations to justify the crucial act of safe passage.

And it was the holding in Sofia of a CSCE environmental meeting that coalesced the democratic opposition, precipitating the movement that has now brought unprecedented change in Bulgaria.

As we leave the Cold War behind us, we confront again many age-old national, religious, and ethnic conflicts that have so sorrowed our common civilization. CSCE, NATO, the EC [European Community], and other democratic institutions of Europe must now play a greater part in deepening and broadening European unity. We must ensure that these organizations continue to complement one another and to reinforce one another.

The North Atlantic Treaty Alliance will continue to serve as the indispensable guarantor of peace—and, therefore, the ultimate guardian of democracy and prosperity. The Alliance will work to lock in stabilizing arms control agreements, to reshape its defensive strategy to meet fundamentally changed conditions, and to build bridges of political cooperation to the newly emerging democracies of the East. As President Bush stressed with President Gor-

bachev at last week's Washington Summit, we believe NATO will remain a cornerstone to both military security and political legitimacy in the new Europe.

Working in concert, the G-24, the OECD [Organization for Economic Cooperation and Development], the European Community, the European Bank for Reconstruction and Development, the Council of Europe, the United States, and Canada can foster an inclusive European order, involving Central and East European nations and the Soviet Union in the new Europe by assisting market-based reform and the building of democratic institutions.

Building a New Europe

The prospects for the fulfillment and protection of human rights have never been greater. It is a time for CSCE to take on additional responsibilities—but never at the price of forgetting its fundamental purposes. If CSCE is to help build a new Europe, a Europe different from all those empires and regimes that rose and fell, it must build from the liberty of man.

Three challenges lie before us:

First, we must ensure that the freedoms so recently won are rooted in societies governed by the rule of law and by the consent of the governed.

Second, we must ensure that all peoples of Europe may know the prosperity that comes from economic liberty and competitive markets.

Third, we must ensure that we are not drawn into either inadvertent conflict or a replay of the disputes that preceded the Cold War.

CSCE is the one forum where our nations can meet on common ground to channel our political will toward meeting these challenges for the entire continent. CSCE's three baskets are uniquely suited to today's political, economic, and security challenges. Although it lacks military or economic power, CSCE can resonate with a powerful and irresistible voice. It can speak to Europe's collective concerns and interests. It can become, if you will, my friends, "the conscience of the continent."

Ensuring Freedom

Today, I would like to share with you our views on how a strengthened CSCE can meet the first challenge that we face: that of forging a deepened consen-

sus on human rights, political legitimacy through free elections, and the rule of law.

We are all familiar with the Danish author Hans Christian Andersen's tale, *The Emperor's New Clothes*. Although written over a century ago, it is an ageless parable. In it, imperious authority cloaks itself in attractive falsehoods, deluding itself in the process. But, in the end, the naked truth is revealed by a small, insistent voice that refuses to be hushed. It grows into a popular cry.

1989 was not kind to the Stalinist dictators who cloaked themselves with false authority and ignored the insistent voice and will of the people. Now in Central and Eastern Europe, the emerging democracies are working to construct legitimate and enduring political orders. CSCE can help by deepening our consensus on the key building blocks of freedom—the building blocks of genuine elections, political pluralism, and the rule of law.

The new social compacts between government and governed now being written in Eastern and Central Europe must be constantly renewed through free elections. As we all know well, democracy—like CSCE —is a process. Democracy evolves through give and take, consensus-building, and compromise. It thrives on tolerance, where the political will of the majority does not nullify the fundamental rights of the minority.

The free elections proposal that the United Kingdom and the United States tabled last year in Paris has gathered strength from the dramatic events of last fall and from the new elections of this spring. In my recent travels to Eastern and Central Europe, democratic activists enthusiastically supported this proposal. They also emphasized the importance they attach to the presence of international observers as their countries undergo the new experience of elections. In February, in Prague, I called upon the CSCE member states to send observer delegations to the elections in Eastern and Central Europe. And I am pleased to note that many states have now joined the United States in doing so.

Our revised proposal reflects our experience observing the elections—not only on voting day but also during the electoral campaign. We welcome the strong support that our text is receiving and we will work to see it adopted here in Copenhagen. And when the 35 consider proposals to institutionalize

CSCE, I urge all to start with mechanisms to ensure that governments are freely chosen by their people.

But first, of course, all countries here should embrace the concept for free elections by conducting elections without intimidation and without pressure, I am thinking specifically of the elections to be held in Bulgaria in just a few days.

But free and fair elections alone do not ensure that the new democracies are going to succeed. The irreducible condition of successful democracy, beyond legitimate elections, is clear: Fundamental individual freedoms must be guaranteed by restraints on state power. Where these guarantees are absent, there is really no true democracy. Indeed, where they are absent, the risk of dictatorship always looms.

For this reason, the watchword of reformers everywhere is the rule of law. As the late Andrei Sakharov said, democratic change must be accomplished through democratic methods—peacefully and through legal processes.

But what do we really mean by the rule of law? The law, after all, has been used as a tool of repression in societies where rulers make the rules to serve themselves as opposed to serving the people. As President Bush stressed last month in a speech at the University of South Carolina, the rule of law means the supremacy of laws written through democratic processes, applied in an equal fashion, and upheld by independent judiciaries.

Therefore, we strongly support efforts at this meeting to set forth for CSCE the elements of a democratic society operating under the rule of law. In this regard, President Bush told President Gorbachev how highly we value Soviet efforts to institutionalize the rule of law, *glasnost*, and democratization in the Soviet Union. To this same end, we are engaging in cooperative technical efforts to strengthen democratic political cultures and institutions in Central and Eastern Europe.

A closing thought on our human rights agenda: As we turn to the ambitious task of consolidating democracy in entire societies, we must not lose sight of individual liberty, for democracy begins and democracy ends with the citizen and his or her individual rights. Despite the dramatic gains in human rights that we witness today, men and women in some participating states are still made to suffer because they want to be free, they are still targets of intolerance, still cannot emigrate, still may not exercise their full Helsinki rights. So we must continue to press until CSCE's high standards of human rights prevail throughout all of Europe, until they extend to every individual.

Before turning to ways that we might strengthen CSCE, I would like to say a word about the Baltic States. At the Washington Summit, President Bush conveyed our very deep misgivings about Soviet policy toward Baltic independence. He stressed again our view that a systematic dialogue must be initiated so that the aspirations of the Baltic peoples can be achieved.

Strengthening CSCE

The scope for meaningful cooperation in CSCE, my friends, is widening, and our consensus is deepening in CSCE's human dimension. But in order to have CSCE fulfill its potential in this important area and in CSCE's other baskets, the Helsinki process itself is going to have to be enhanced.

I recently shared with colleagues six ideas on how we can work together to improve CSCE as a process by reinforcing CSCE's organization.

First, the United States favors regular consultations among the signatory states. Ministers may wish to meet at least once a year, and their senior officials should convene at least twice a year. Such exchanges will invigorate the CSCE as a forum for high-level political dialogue.

Second, we support the holding of CSCE review conferences on a more frequent basis, perhaps every two years, and with a fixed duration of about three months.

Third, to ensure that the political commitments we make in CSCE strengthen political legitimacy, we seek adoption in Copenhagen and confirmation at the summit of the principle of free and fair elections, political pluralism, and the rule of law.

Fourth, we seek confirmation at the summit of the Bonn Principles of Economic Cooperation. These principles make clear our mutual commitment to the supportive relationship between political liberty and economic liberty. Specifically, 35 nations will endeavor to achieve or maintain the free flow of trade and capital, market economies with prices based on supply and demand, and protection for all property, including private property and intellectual property.

Fifth, CSCE can play a major role in dispute management. We, therefore, hope that the CSCE summit will reinforce the mandate of the January 1991 Valletta Conference on Peaceful Settlement of Disputes so that that conference can achieve concrete results. We also believe CSCE can foster military openness and transparency through innovative proposals in the Vienna CSBM [confidence and security building measures] talks—for example, the proposal for a mechanism to request clarification of unusual military activities.

In particular, we believe that CSCE should consider a mechanism to improve communications among member states. Our approach might be similar in essence, if not in structure, to the mechanism that we have established in the human dimension area as well as to the one which we plan to establish for the conventional forces discussions [CFE]. We should find a way of constructively addressing compliance questions with regard to CSCE security obligations. This might include observations and inspection reports in accordance with the Stockholm agreement. We should provide for meetings to exchange information and to discuss the implications of military activities or other unusual occurrences having security implications.

And, *sixth,* I proposed that we begin preparatory work for a possible CSCE summit through a meeting of officials this summer—so I am, of course, pleased that the 35 nations have now agreed that our officials can meet next month in Vienna.

Also, I am very happy that the 35 have agreed to the offer of the United States to host a CSCE ministerial meeting this fall in connection with the United Nations General Assembly.

Then, at the CSCE summit, we would expect to sign a CFE agreement, and President Gorbachev last week indicated that he shared this view. At the 35-nation summit, we would also expect to review, record, and consolidate progress in all three Helsinki baskets; to strengthen CSCE as a process; and to plan ahead for the 1992 review conference.

Our work, both before the summit and during it, of course, also must address the subject of institutionalizing CSCE.

Until now, CSCE has shown a remarkable ability to both reflect and change with the times. I am confident that it will continue to do so, provided we preserve the flexibility that has made it effective. As we consider proposals for CSCE's development — either for adoption at the summit or for referral by the summit leaders to other upcoming meetings of the CSCE — the United States position will be guided by three principles.

One, proposals should reinforce fundamental democratic and market values.

Two, suggestions for new institutions should complement rather than duplicate roles assigned to existing institutions and fora.

Three, proposals should result in a stronger transatlantic process of dialogue and consultation regarding Europe's future.

The American delegation to this Copenhagen meeting, which is headed by Ambassador Max Kampelman, which, of course, has the complete confidence of President Bush and myself, will be guided by these criteria.

My friends, I began my remarks with a tribute to the Helsinki monitors who risked their lives and liberty to advance the cause of freedom for others. Many have lived to see the dawn of a much more hopeful day. Some of the monitors are with us in this chamber, and many of them serve as elected representatives of the newly emerging democracies of Central and Eastern Europe. One of the founding monitors of Charter '77 now honors us by leading the distinguished delegation from the Czech and Slovak Federal Republic.

Ambassador Hajek, you — and your courageous colleagues — are the very embodiment of CSCE's human dimension. You have given this process a heart, a mind, and a searching conscience. When many viewed CSCE with cynicism, you answered them with dynamism. You taught us to raise our sights and raise our voices.

The Danish author Isak Dinesen was another believer in the power of the human will. One of her favorite mottos was *Je responderay!* I will respond. She lived by that principle, and she was proud to recount how occupied Denmark lived by it during the dark days of the Second World War. The Danish people took it upon themselves to save the entire Jewish community of Denmark — thousands of men, women and children. By honoring human dignity

and the ties that bind all of us, by their efforts and to the grace of God, they succeeded beyond all expectation.

Their example is proof positive that commitment of will matters, that responsibility to others matters, and that individual freedoms to act and to think and to feel can shape not only the moment but the very future of one's country.

These same strengths must shape Europe's future. Channeled through

CSCE, they can truly become the conscience of the continent.

Thank you.

---

[1]Department of State Press Release 81, June 11, 1990.

Secretary Baker at the Spring NATO Ministerial Following the Washington Summit

EXCERPT FROM PREPARED INTERVENTION, TURNBERRY, SCOTLAND, JUNE 7, 1990 [1]

We laid out nine assurances [during the Washington summit] that we and others have offered and which we believe respond to many Soviet concerns.

First, we are committed to follow-on CFE (conventional armed forces in Europe) negotiations for all of Europe, which would also cover forces in the central region of Europe.

Second, we have agreed to advance SNF (strategic nuclear forces) negotiations to begin once the CFE treaty is signed.

Third, Germany will reaffirm its commitments neither to produce nor to possess nuclear, biological, and chemical weapons.

Fourth, NATO is conducting a comprehensive strategic review of both conventional and nuclear force requirements and strategy to fit the changed circumstances.

Fifth, NATO forces will not be extended to the former territory of the GDR [German Democratic Republic] for a transition period.

Sixth, the Germans have agreed to a transition period for Soviet forces leaving the GDR.

Seventh, Germany will make firm commitments on its borders, making clear that the territory of a unified Germany will comprise only the FRG [Federal Republic of Germany], GDR, and Berlin.

Eighth, the CSCE process will be strengthened.

Ninth, Germany has made it clear that it will seek to resolve economic issues in a way that can support *perestroika*.

While Gorbachev was reassured by these points, German membership in NATO — and the Soviet position in Europe after unification — remained his major concern. President Bush stressed that a unified, democratic Germany would pose no threat to Soviet security, and that Germany's membership in NATO was a factor for stability and security in Europe. He reiterated his support for Germany's full membership in NATO, including participation in its integrated military structures. He said that Germany must enjoy the right, as stipulated in the Helsinki Final Act, to chose freely its own alliance and security arrangements. Gorbachev seemed to accept this point.

We can and should be prepared to meet reasonable Soviet concerns. But we cannot acquiesce in an effort to block a full return to German sovereignty or to use ostensible security concerns over Germany as a surrogate for weakening the alliance...

---

[1] Text from Current Policy 1284, Department of State, June 1990.

PRESS BRIEFING AFTER THE MEETING, JUNE 8, 1990 (Excerpts) [1]

I would like to begin by thanking Prime Minister [Margaret] Thatcher, Foreign Minister [Douglas] Hurd, and our Scottish hosts for inviting us to this spectacular Atlantic setting. On behalf of the entire American delegation, I extend our special thanks for the warm hospitality you've offered us.

I was pleased to have this opportunity to brief my colleagues on President Bush's meetings with President Gorbachev. All seemed heartened by our progress in putting U.S.-Soviet relations on a sounder, more constructive footing.

All agreed with the line of reasoning President Bush outlined for President Gorbachev with regard to German unification—especially the nine point approach for engaging the Soviets. And all, of course, agreed that NATO membership, a decision freely made by the German people, is the best guarantee of long-term stability in Europe.

In addition, I shared with my colleagues here my impressions of what I think was a positive follow-up session with [Soviet] Foreign Minister [Eduard] Shevardnadze this past Tuesday in Copenhagen.

Here at Turnberry we spent much of our time laying the foundation for the NATO Summit a month from now in London. That summit will guide the ongoing strategic review of Alliance policy.

We discussed our conventional and our nuclear arms policy. On conventional arms control, we are working to complete the CFE agreement and we are developing an approach to follow-on negotiations to CFE. On nuclear arms control, we look forward to SNF talks that will begin once the CFE Treaty is signed. We reaffirmed our commitment to maintaining an appropriate mix of conventional and nuclear forces.

I am pleased that NATO agreed to establish the arms control verification staff that the United States proposed late last year. This is a useful example of how our Alliance has started, within a matter of months, to take concrete steps to adapt NATO to future requirements.

On Europe's political future, we are agreed that the Helsinki process should be strengthened to support further growth in democratic values across the continent. We all start from the premise, however, that CSCE has got to be a complement to NATO.

I believe we also all recognize NATO's significant potential for bringing the new democracies of Central and Eastern Europe, as well as the Soviet Union, within the orbit of a new European system based on the values that NATO and other democratic institutions have always promoted and defended.

I am particularly pleased that my ministerial colleagues decided to issue a special statement to underscore the importance of extending to the Soviet Union and all other European nations the hand of friendship and cooperation. This statement welcomes yesterday's declaration by the member states of the Warsaw Treaty Organization and looks forward to building confidence and closer relations between the member states of the two alliances, as well as with all other European countries.

All of us know that only NATO can continue to guarantee European security and stability. It will, however, be a new alliance, renewed and reinvigorated to develop and insure a Europe which is whole and free. Even while we fulfill the oftentimes painful but necessary task of preventing war, now we must meet the more positive task of building peace—a peace defined, I think, not by the absence of war from the Baltic to the Adriatic, but by a community of democratic values that extends from the Atlantic to the Urals.

Q. Mr. Secretary of State, reportedly you detect now a positive attitude by the Soviets on the German question. Is that in your opinion just another twist of the mood or the final, the good one?

A. I hope it's not just another twist of the mood. Let me simply say that as I mentioned in my opening statement, I did get a sense at least of movement from my meeting with Foreign Minister Shevardnadze in Copenhagen. As you know, it has been our position to try and encourage the Soviet Union to take a constructive approach to the question of German reunification, to take an approach that would not, in effect, isolate the Soviet Union, that would not create antagonisms and create resentment.

The next questioner will ask me, well give us some more specifics about that, so I'll give you what I can give you in answer to your question. I came away from that meeting more encouraged on the potential for completing a CFE agreement this year. I have reported that encouragement to my colleagues here. I came away from that meeting with the view that the Soviets recognize the importance to them of future good relations with the united Germany. And I came away from it with a generally more positive feeling regarding the question of solving the external aspects—solving the questions of the external aspects of German reunification.

* * *

Q. Mr. Secretary, I'm a little confused about the fifth U.S. point that was presented to Mr. Gorbachev. You stated in your intervention that NATO forces would not be extended to the former East Germany for a transition period. Do you mean that after some transition period NATO forces would, in fact, go into what is now East Germany?

A. No. I think what we're saying is that we're talking here about ultimately a sovereign, a completely and totally sovereign, unified Germany. And it is as simple as that. We have indicated a willingness to—we have advanced assurances to the Soviet Union specifically that there would be no extension of NATO forces to the territory that now constitutes the GDR. We haven't agreed with respect to the period of time, that's all. Does that answer your question?

Q. No. It sounds to me as if—if you haven't agreed to the period of time, then that leaves open the possibility that after some agreed period of time, indeed NATO forces would be extended to that territory.

A. That hasn't been determined. That hasn't been decided. That hasn't been the subject of discussion. What we're saying is, right up front, we would agree—at least the position of the United States is—that for a period of time to be determined there would be no such extension of forces. Just as one of the other points in the nine points is that there would be for some indeterminate period of time—a period of time to be determined, at least according to the Germans—be a willingness on their part to permit a continued presence for Soviet forces in the territory of the GDR.

Q. If I could just follow up though, that does still leave open the question of whether the United States would accept the concept of a permanent area within Germany in which NATO forces would not enter, or would not operate, and as you know, many Defense Department officials feel that that would make the idea of German membership in NATO less than—or in the integrated military command—less than meaningful if, in fact, all of German territory be included. So I know what you're saying that you haven't really addressed this yet. But what would be the U.S. view of having a permanent sphere of Germany that was not essentially part of NATO's operating area?

A. I really don't want to take it here this morning beyond where we've taken it, and I think we've been pretty clear with respect to it. The only question that has not been determined is whether we're talking about a discrete period of time, or whether we're talking about perpetuity, and I'm not willing to speculate with you on hypotheses here this morning in answer to that question.

Q. Mr. Secretary, if I may just divert your attention for a moment to another subject. There's a story making the rounds out of the White House press corps that Secretary of State Baker has made up his mind on the question of the continuing PLO [Palestine Liberation Organization] dialogue with the U.S. What is your view now of the PLO's response to the attack on Israel? And what is your view now of the PLO dialogue with the U.S.?

A. Well, we've said all along that this is a very, very serious matter. We have condemned what happened as far as the raid—or proposed raid—was concerned in the strongest possible terms. Terrorism is something that has to be taken very, very seriously. It is also important that we pursue peace in the Middle East in a serious manner. And peace in the Middle Bast is also a serious matter. So there is some perspective and responsibility required in dealing with this issue. Let me simply say to you that when we are satisfied that we know all we need to know about this issue we will act in a way, I think, that reflects our dual commitment to promoting peace but to being resolute in countering terrorism.

Q. Have there been any—since the first contact you had with the PLO in Tunis after the attack, have there been any further contacts?

A. I'm not going to get into who shot John with you on that and questions of confidential diplomatic exchanges. I'm simply not going to do that.

Q. Is the dialogue still on?

A. It has not been terminated.

Q. Mr. Secretary, when the dialogue began in November of 1988,

the U.S. Government, through [U.S.] Ambassador [to Tunisia] Pelletreau, communicated, we were told, certain understandings to the PLO about what the U.S. position would be if the PLO or any faction thereof engaged in terrorist actions. Do those conditions still pertain?

A. There has been no change in the original understandings that were entered into at the time that the dialogue was originally established.

* * *

Q. We understand that the British Foreign Secretary yesterday urged the United States to remain in the peace process, in the business of trying to promote it. Is that possible if the United States breaks off its dialogue with the PLO?

A. Well, let me just say that the position of the United States is that we would like to see peace in the Middle East. That's the position, I suppose, of everyone. And we want to do whatever we can do to advance the peace process in the Middle East, and we have worked very, very hard since we have been in office to try and do that. And we will continue to try and do that.

We will continue to be willing to remain engaged as long as the parties themselves want us to and will remain engaged themselves. So we are hopeful, as we have been before, that a new government will emerge in Israel that will be committed to moving forward with the peace process. We are willing to play our part in that to the extent that the parties want us to.

Q. Mr. Secretary, on that point, when you were discussing the reaction to the PLO raid you seemed to be setting up a dichotomy between pursuing the peace process and showing opposition to terrorism. Do you see the dialogue with the PLO as part of the peace process? And would the peace process be damaged in any way if that dialogue was terminated?

A. I don't intend to set up a dichotomy. I do not intend to be seen to be suggesting that we would in any way countenance terrorism in order even to advance the noble cause of peace, because terrorism, as I said earlier, is a very, very serious matter with us. Too many Americans have been victimized by this. It is something that we condemn in the strongest terms, and there is no such suggestion, if I may say so, in that original answer.

It is important that we try and move toward peace in the Middle East, so that we do not see escalation of violence, so that we do not see increased outbreaks of terrorism.

Q. Mr. Secretary, the other part of the question was, do you see the dialogue with the PLO as part of the peace process?

A. I do not mean to suggest that the dialogue with the PLO is a part of the peace process in terms of the process that we were working on prior to the collapse of the Israeli Government, because as you know we were working very hard to bring Israelis and Palestinians together. We were working very hard with Egypt to accomplish this.

[1]Department of State Press Release 83, June 8, 1990.

U.S.-Soviet Relations After the Washington Summit

Secretary Baker's statement before the Senate Foreign Relations Committee, June 12, 1990 [1]

It is a privilege to appear before your Committee this morning. My purpose is to review recent developments, especially those concerning U.S.-Soviet relations, and also to look ahead. We have just completed a U.S.-Soviet Summit, and now we are in the midst of preparations for a special NATO Summit. Your advice and counsel are important as we deal with these matters. As the President and I have often stressed, the United States can best meet the momentous challenges we face from the perspective of a truly bipartisan foreign policy.

Recent international developments, especially the trend toward democracy and economic reform, confirm our long held values and are clearly in our long-term interests. But, just as clearly, the aftermath of the political earthquakes of 1989 will be a complex period of rebuilding damaged structures, modifying others and, in some cases, constructing new ones. There will be aftershocks. There will also be great opportunities to create a more democratic, more prosperous, and more secure world.

Such opportunities depend in large measure on whether the United States and the Soviet Union can establish an enduring improvement in our relations. We are now fully engaged in trying to do that through the search for points of mutual advantage. This search is guided by our determination, as the President says, to go beyond containment, to build a new world that leaves behind both the Cold War and the conflicts which preceded it. It is also guided by the potential of *perestroika*, the Soviet Union's attempt to reform its economy and indeed its entire social system. *Perestroika* merits our support precisely because it offers the chance for more constructive Soviet foreign and defense policies and, eventually, a more democratic Soviet Union. We know that finding points of mutual advantage will not always be easy or swift. As [former Secretary of State] Dean Rusk wrote me last year, "We have much to remember and much to forget" before we conclude that the new era is here to stay. But

there has been progress, and there is promise of more progress.

I would now like to review for you what we have been able to do over the last several months in the major areas of U.S.-Soviet engagement.

A Whole and Free Europe

First, we have made headway toward the achievement of a whole and free Europe and within that Europe, a whole and free Germany. Last month I travelled to Bonn for the initial Ministerial of the Two-Plus-Four Talks. We have made clear that the purpose of this process is to ratify the clear will of the German people to unite in peace and freedom while providing a forum to discuss unification's external ramifications.

Discussions between the two German governments on all internal aspects of unification are proceeding rapidly. Meanwhile, we are trying to come to grips with the external ramifications of unification, including borders, Berlin, residual Four Power rights under international law, and political-military issues. Here the United States has emphasized that it would be counterproductive to perpetuate a special status for Germany or to prolong any limitations on German sovereignty.

I must believe that in the end the Soviet Union does not want to be isolated on this [NATO] issue.

Discriminatory limitations could only sow the seeds for future instability. For this reason we are opposed to using these discussions to put limits on strictly German military capabilities. Such limits and other confidence building measures belong properly to the CFE negotiations, the CSBM talks, and the upcoming SNF talks.

A united Germany begins a new chapter in post-war European politics. But this new chapter should contain the lessons we have learned from the old. The European Community and NATO represent the will of free peoples

cooperating on both sides of the Atlantic to assure democracy, peace, and prosperity. That is why we and so many Europeans, including the Germans, believe that the new Germany should be a full member of a vigorous NATO.

NATO, like all European institutions, will evolve to deal with the new situation. But of this we can be sure: It will remain a defensive alliance with an appropriate mix of nuclear and conventional forces designed to preserve peace and security, not to start war. And it will also continue to serve, as I told the CSCE Conference in Copenhagen last week, as the indispensable guarantor of peace.

The Soviet Union opposes full membership in NATO for a unified Germany. At the May Ministerial in Moscow and later at the summit, we explained to the Soviet leaders that NATO is a voluntary alliance of free peoples. Its purpose is not — and never has been — to threaten or to attack the Soviet Union, or anyone else, but rather to prevent aggression and to provide an anchor against the winds of uncertainty and instability.

The United States, in consultation with our NATO allies, has proposed a nine-point package of future security measures that substantiate our views. It includes the following elements: (1) follow-on CFE negotiations for all of Europe, which would also cover forces in the central region of Europe; (2) SNF negotiations to begin once a CFE Treaty is signed; (3) a reaffirmed German commitment neither to produce nor to possess nuclear, biological, or chemical weapons; (4) a NATO strategy review, of both conventional and nuclear force requirements and strategy to fit the changed circumstances; (5) non-extension of NATO forces into the former territory of the GDR for a transition period; (6) support of Germany's interest in a transition period for Soviet forces leaving the GDR; (7) final resolution of Germany's borders to comprise only the FRG, GDR, and Berlin; (5) willingness to strengthen CSCE; and (9) a resolution of Soviet-German economic issues in a way that can support *perestroika*.

To sum it up, we are trying to meet Moscow's security concerns, but it is also incumbent on the Soviets to understand why NATO is indispensable to us and, for that matter, to most European nations. I must believe that in the end the Soviet Union does not want to be isolated on this issue.

Before turning to the next area of our search for points of mutual advantage, I want to say a word on the recent elections in Central and Eastern Europe.

Two more countries have just faced the test of their first multi-party elections since the revolution of 1989. In Czechoslovakia, by all accounts both the spirit and the practice of free elections were upheld. Civic Forum and its Slovak counterpart, Public Against Violence, received the large plurality of votes, but the big winner was democracy.

On Sunday, Bulgarians went to the polls for the first round of voting for a new parliament. Official results indicate that the ruling Bulgarian Socialist Party—the former Communists —took almost half the vote, prior to parliamentary run-offs and the Presidential election. We cannot predict the composition of the parliament or what kind of coalition may be formed until we know the outcome of these races.

Questions about possible election day abuses are being explored by government and party representatives. We want to reserve judgment on these matters until we have reviewed the reports of Bulgarian and foreign election observers, including the U.S. observer delegation. We have made clear our dissatisfaction on several issues relating to the fairness of the campaign itself, including intimidation of opposition activists and supporters, serious inequalities in campaign resources and media access, and irregularities in voter lists.

We will continue to work with all Bulgarians for the development of political pluralism and democratic institutions.

Arms Control

The second area of our search for points of mutual advantage with the Soviet Union concerns arms control. Our broad objective is to enhance strategic stability and predictability and to preserve deterrence at lower levels of arms and with less risk of either misunderstanding or miscalculation. Both strategic and conventional arms control must be integrated in our policy because these two aspects of the strategic balance are closely related. Finally, we want to broaden the traditional arms control agenda to deal with new global dangers, such as missile

proliferation, and an old problem— chemical warfare—that unfortunately has been revived.

Progress can be reported in some, though not all, of these areas. At the summit, the President and Mr. Gorbachev signed a joint statement on START and on future Nuclear and Space Arms negotiations. The START statement records agreement on almost all the major issues. Before a treaty can be signed, however, a few very difficult problems must be resolved, and much complex, involved work must be completed. I believe, however, that we can overcome these final hurdles in time to meet both Presidents' objectives of actually signing a treaty later this year.

The United States and the Soviet Union are both committed to future negotiations on strategic arms. Our search to lower the danger of nuclear war will not stop with START. These future negotiations will seek to enhance strategic stability and predictability, especially through the reduction of incentives for a nuclear first strike. We are both committed to reduce the concentration of warheads on strategic arms, notably heavy missiles and MIRVed ICBMs.

On nuclear testing, we completed a long negotiating effort by signing the protocols to the Threshold Test Ban Treaty and the Peaceful Nuclear Explosions Treaty.

At the summit, the U.S. and the U.S.S.R. also signed a historic bilateral accord to destroy most of our chemical arms stockpiles. Both sides are to stop production; reduce to equal, low levels; and develop appropriate inspection procedures. We are also pledged to work together in persuading all nations to join us in the eventual elimination of all chemical weapons.

On conventional weapons in Europe, the CFE Treaty, which requires significant reductions in Soviet forces and equipment, is an essential building block of a Europe whole and free. The President and I have therefore been heartened by recent Soviet statements renewing their commitment to seek rapid agreement on CFE. I might add that at the summit, President Gorbachev agreed with our contention that no CSCE Summit take place until a CFE treaty is signed.

We and our NATO allies have agreed that talks on reducing short-range nuclear forces should commence once a CFE agreement is signed. Furthermore, as noted earlier, our nine

points on German unification include a follow-on CFE negotiation that would cover forces in the central region of Europe. It is essential that CFE keep up with the rapid political changes now occurring. The stakes for both sides are too high for foot-dragging.

Regional Conflicts

The third point of our search for mutual advantage concerns regional conflicts. In testimony to the Congress and throughout our public statements, we have stressed the importance of U.S.-Soviet cooperation in bringing to an end these terrible and unnecessary local wars. Over the past year, such cooperation has yielded good results in Southern Africa where an independent Namibia is the first but hopefully not the last achievement. In Central America, the victory of democracy through the Nicaraguan election has transformed prospects for peace. We are still concerned, however about Soviet support for Cuba and Cuban support for the rebels in El Salvador. Continued Soviet military assistance for Cuba is a striking exception to the Soviet Union's "new thinking" on regional issues.

We have stressed the importance of U.S.-Soviet cooperation in bringing to an end these terrible and unnecessary local wars.

President Bush and President Gorbachev had far-ranging discussions at the summit on all of the regional problems. As one result, both the United States and the Soviet Union issued a joint statement on June 2 concerning Ethiopia. In a remarkable example of our willingness to work together, we have agreed that U.S. food will be transported on Soviet aircraft to deal with the tragedy of starvation in that country. We and the Soviets also support an international conference of governments under the auspices of the U.N. to settle at last the disastrous conflicts in the Horn of Africa.

Economic Relations

The fourth and final point I want to discuss today is U.S.-Soviet trade. At the summit, the President signed a bilateral Commercial Agreement. Also, the Soviet Union agreed to a new Long Term Grains Agreement.

There is no direct relationship between the Grains Agreement and the Commercial Agreement. American grain has been sold under continuing arrangements to the Soviet Union since the early 1970s, and they are our biggest single foreign customers for this produce. The Grains Agreement replaces and expands an existing agreement that governed sales through the end of 1990.

Under the Jackson-Vanik legislation, the extension of most-favored-nation trading status requires both a waiver of Jackson-Vanik and the completion of a commercial agreement. But the waiver is conditional on Soviet emigration practices. The President has therefore indicated that he will neither waive the Jackson-Vanik Amendment nor send the Commercial Agreement to Congress until the Supreme Soviet passes its emigration law. I have been assured by Foreign Minister [Eduard] Shevardnadze that free emigration of Soviet Jews will continue and that President Gorbachev's recent comments on this issue were not intended to mean otherwise.

The President told Mr. Gorbachev what the Senate had already made clear and the House of Representatives reaffirmed. We do not believe that the Congress will approve the Commercial Agreement until the deadlock over Lithuania is broken. That is a fact of political life.

I wish I could report that the U.S. and Soviet positions were closer on Lithuania, but they are not. However, President Gorbachev reiterated his commitment to settling the Lithuanian crisis peacefully. We also believe we heard a commitment to compromise and are encouraged that Baltic leaders are in Moscow now. We hope this will lead not just to meetings with Soviet leaders, but to a systematic dialogue toward a peaceful resolution. But a practical narrowing of the Soviet and Lithuanian differences is yet to be seen.

Conclusion

Mr. Chairman, as you can see, we are fully engaged in several vital areas of U.S.-Soviet contact. Our purpose throughout is to find those points of mutual advantage that will provide a solid underpinning for a lasting improvement of U.S.-Soviet relations. The immense changes now sweeping away old dogmas and dictatorships offer both of our countries an historic opportunity. As I said in the opening of my statement, after earthquakes there are always aftershocks. The work of reconstruction and building anew has just begun. But I think that we have made a good beginning.

Part of that good beginning is the rapport we saw at the summit between President Bush and President Gorbachev. Differences notwithstanding, the tone and clarity and comfort of the discussions were unprecedented. I think that indicates an underlying desire to work problems out, an attitude that builds confidence for the future.

Another very important confidence builder is the progress we have just made at the North Atlantic Council meeting in Scotland. As you know, the President has called for a special NATO Summit next month to spell out NATO's political role and to adjust NATO's military strategy and structure in guaranteeing the peace of the new Europe. We have had very good discussions at Turnberry. I could summarize them by saying that NATO is preparing to do more than just prevent war, NATO is also willing and able to build the peace. We want to build a peace defined not just by the absence of war from the Baltic to the Adriatic. but by a community of democratic values that extends from the Atlantic to the Urals.

I would conclude now by reiterating what I said to the CSCE Conference on the Human Dimension in Copenhagen. At the urging of the United States and others, the CSCE is now going to quicken its pace and increase its activities in its role as the conscience of Europe. But we and all the other nations who participate in the upbuilding of the new Europe must never forget a fundamental purpose. We must build on the basis of an inalienable right: human liberty.

---

[1] Department of State Press Release 84, June 12, 1990. The complete transcript of the hearings will be published by the committee and will be available from the Superintendent of Documents, U.S. Government Printing Office, Washington, D.C. 20402.

The Closing of "Checkpoint Charlie"

Secretary Baker's remarks at the closing of "Checkpoint Charlie," Berlin, June 22, 1990 [1]

My fellow Foreign Ministers, Commandants, Mayors, Citizens of Berlin:

For 29 years, this street stood as a stark symbol—of a city divided by a concrete wall, of a nation and a continent split by an Iron Curtain. For 29 years, "Checkpoint Charlie" embodied the Cold War. Now, 29 years after this barrier was built, we meet here today to dismantle it and to bury the conflict that created it. And in its place, together we pledge to build a bridge between East and West, a bridge not of cement and steel but of peace and freedom.

At this checkpoint, the United States stood with its allies and the German people, resolved to resist aggression and determined to overcome the division of the Cold War. Now that time has come. Now we are gathered here for a new journey. We have come to extend hope and to reaffirm the dream. Men and women will be free. Berlin will be undivided. Germany will be united in peace and freedom. Europe will be whole, and it will be free.

The American people join all of you—the people of Berlin, of Germany, of Europe—on this new journey. "Checkpoint Charlie" now leads from the conflicts of the past to the reconciliation of the future. As we raise the gate of history, the spirit of liberty moves along this road to join this city, to unite this nation, to heal this continent.

---

[1] Made available to news correspondents by Department of State spokesman Margaret Tutwiler.

Joint Press Conference Following Second Two-Plus-Four Ministerial in Berlin

Following is the Transcript of Secretary Baker's Joint Press Conference with Foreign Ministers Markus Meckel of the German Democratic Republic, Roland Dumas of France, Eduard Shevardnadze of the Soviet Union, Douglas Hurd of the United Kingdom, and Hans-Dietrich Genscher of the Federal Republic of Germany in East Berlin, June 22, 1990.[1]

[After Opening Remarks by Foreign Minister Meckel:]

Foreign Minister Dumas. Ladies and gentlemen, as the first speaker, I ought perhaps to begin by thanking the authorities of the German Democratic Republic for the hospitality extended to us here. And I also want to say to the press here tonight, that the French delegation has every reason to feel satisfied with today's meeting. The meeting began with a highly symbolic ceremony this morning—the removal of "Checkpoint Charlie"—which provided an extremely felicitious augury for today's meeting.

And we have committed ourselves to making headway in our discussions, and indeed, I think we did make headway today in a constructive and warm climate as the German Democratic Republic's Foreign Minister has just stated. The French delegation made its contribution to the discussions, expressing its views, not least with respect to border questions, and we were happy to record the progress that has been made with respect to the five principles as defined by our experts. By the same token, important progress has been made, and was made, during discussion with respect to the next meeting which will also be attended by the Polish authorities. With that in mind, we and the other delegations' experts, to our satisfaction at the votes which took place only yesterday in the Bundestag and the Volkskammer on the Oder-Neisse frontier, France expressed its wish that between now and the end of the year, we should do everything we can to begin the drafting of a treaty which would enshrine the principles embedded in those resolutions. And that

also goes for what we have come to call the elements of a final settlement under international law. We, in France, gave our entire blessing to those elements which have already met with the agreement of our experts. We thought it was important to simultaneously ensure parallelism and contemporaneity in ensuring that full sovereignty of Germany is attained, concurrently with the establishment of German unity. We would not wish to see Germany in any way singularized under the terms of a final settlement, whilst of course reflecting the security interests of all the countries concerned. At the end of the day, what we wish to see is the relinquishment or disappearance of quadrapartite rights bequeathed by the wall. The most important thing seemed to be, and was certainly, as Mr. Meckel had said, the definition of a broad approach. An approach which we have handed down to our experts. And it's a difficult but important, indeed crucial, task for our experts between now and the next meeting in Paris on July 17th. They will have to compile a list of questions which individual delegations have raised on security matters.

Next Two-Plus-Four Meeting

Finally, ladies and gentlemen, we agreed on the arrangements for the next meeting, as I said, which has been scheduled for Paris on the 17th, with a view to completing our work—and it is our hope that we will be able to complete our work round about the end of the year, in order to reflect the concerns expressed by the German delegations. I, myself, said that I would do what I could to find a date which would bring forward the date of this CSCE [Conference on Security and Cooperation in Europe] Summit—therefore a summit which would no longer take place in December, but in November of this year. So we have worked out a timetable, a broad approach and underlined the overall principles which are designed to lead to the conclusion of our work.

Foreign Minister Meckel. Thank you very much. Now I'd like to call on Mr. Shevardnadze to continue.

Foreign Minister Shevardnadze. Thank you. Ladies and gentlemen, this second ministerial meeting of six countries has taken place on a day which is of special importance for our peoples and, in this context, I would like to emphasize the significance of that ceremony that took place this morning. The ceremony that impressed all of us and I'm sure has impressed all Berliners, and I would like to thank Secretary Baker for this initiative.

In characterizing the meeting that we have had today, I would like, first of all, to emphasize the business-like and constructive nature, and the increasing degree of agreement among the participants as regards the prerogatives of the future settlement under international law, the external aspects of German unity.

Soviet Proposal

The Soviet delegation welcomes the decision of the parliaments of the two German states as regards the border with Poland. It is very important that we have agreed that at the Paris meeting of the Six which will be attended by Minister Skubiszewski [of Poland], we will be able to achieve a definitive decision, a definitive settlement, of this issue. The Soviet delegation put forward for discussion today, the draft basic elements, basic principles, of the final settlement under international law with Germany. Of course, this is a draft but we believe that it is important in that it makes it possible to begin a more specific effort, more specific work to develop the content and the form of the future final document of our six. We were pleased to note that in the statements by our colleagues, they gave general support to the idea of beginning what is more formal work on the language of the document, or documents, which we will be adopting. There is also a general understanding that the group of experts, as has already been mentioned by my colleagues, will work more intensively, will have to work more intensively, perhaps in the mode that traditional negotiations go into at the phase of legal development of specific language. The provisions in our draft are not regarded by us as the final truth. We are ready to seek compromise approaches, mutually acceptable approaches, and judging by the meeting that we have had today, we can say confidently that we will be able to find such mutually acceptable approaches.

I would like to emphasize something which I believe is very important: we intend to have final agreement that will resolve all aspects of German unity before the end of this year. German settlement—what is more, the calendar of other talks and meetings including the summit meeting of the 35 CSCE countries—is also being built around the achievement of German unity, and you can see from this that our intentions indeed are very serious and very business-like. I understand of course that the reporters are interested to find out about the specifics—where we agree, where we differ, where we have greater clarity, and where there is some vagueness, and there is, of course, some vagueness, too. Of course, all of that exists, as in any negotiation. There are differences, there are opposing views, and there are different understandings. But, indeed it would be surprising if things were different right now, because we are discussing matters of extraordinary historic importance, I would say, and they cannot be agreed easily.

I would like to emphasize that we do have a rather high and broad degree of mutual understanding and willingness to understand each other, and to take into account the interests of all participants. I think that in this situation it would be counter-productive to dwell on the specific elements and to go into the essence of our differences. I think it is very encouraging that the problem with German unity is being examined, considered by all of us in its interrelationship with the institutionalization of the European process—the transformation of European alliances and the development of new relationships between the members of those alliances.

Importance of NATO Summit

A lot will depend on how the North Atlantic Alliance will respond to the changes that have taken place in Europe. The NATO session in London will show, and I would like to say in all responsibility and to emphasize that its

results can provide a powerful incentive to the process of overcoming the division of Germany and the division of our continent. We are leaving Berlin in a good mood and with great hopes that our work will be successful in the future.

As our host, our chairman today, Mr. Meckel, has said the next meeting will be in Paris. After Paris, we'll be meeting in Moscow. After Moscow, in New York, and, therefore, we do have a lot of difficult work to do, but this will be creative work, a common creative effort which we are sure will be successful. Thank you.

Secretary Baker. Ladies and gentlemen, my colleagues have mentioned the ceremony that was held earlier today. And at that ceremony, I said that as we raise the gate of history, the spirit of liberty will move through Berlin, joining this city, uniting this nation, and healing this continent. Our hosts, the democratically elected government of the German Democratic Republic, do indeed I think represent that spirit of liberty. It is really only because the people of the GDR chose the road of freedom that we are able to meet in Berlin, the symbol of a divided Germany and a divided Europe. Soon I think it will symbolize something new: Berlin undivided, Germany united peacefully and freely, and Europe whole and free.

So I begin by offering our appreciation for all those individual citizens of the German Democratic Republic, ordinary men and women, whose tremendous courage has given us this opportunity. To the church leaders and the many others whose search for national reconciliation and justice has been long and lonely, we offer our congratulations. And I offer my personal appreciation to Prime Minister de Maiziere and Foreign Minister Meckel, for their arrangements during the course of this meeting.

At the opening of these talks in May, I described the opportunity that I thought faced us in some plain language: to facilitate German unification in freedom and in peace. Four decades, four decades of division have left us with some very difficult and some very complex problems. But let there be no mistake about the outcome: a free, sovereign, united German state in mutually recognized borders.

It is the view of the United States that the process for attaining this outcome, and that's really what we've been spending a lot of our time on today, the

process for attaining this outcome really must be based upon two core principles. First, our actions should not singularize or discriminate against a united Germany. We think that would plant the seeds of future instability in Europe. And secondly, we should terminate Four Power rights at the time of unification so that there are no remaining restrictions on the sovereignty of Germany. I should acknowledge, I think up front, that while other participants agree with this view, a draft which was submitted by the Soviet Union I do not think does agree with this view. This draft would restrict German sovereignty, and I think it would do so for some years.

But let me briefly review our discussions here today.

Arrangements for Polish Participation

First of all, on borders, we made preparations for Polish participation at the next Ministerial in Paris in July, as my colleague Roland Dumas has mentioned. We believe Poland's legitimate concerns about the border must be met, and we have stressed here today that no decision on this matter should be taken without full consultations with the Poles.

I believe rapid progress on Germany's borders is both essential and realizable. Our position is very clear. A united Germany should consist of the current territory of the Federal Republic of Germany, the German Democratic Republic, and Berlin—no more, no less. There's no disagreement among the six of us on this point.

Second, we worked toward an agreement on the elements of the final German settlement document. The United States believes that this document should contain five elements. One, it should begin with a general political declaration noting the international context for unification. Secondly, it should also welcome the achievement of German unity through the unification of the Federal Republic of Germany, the German Democratic Republic, and Berlin. Third, it should end our remaining rights and responsibilities pertaining to borders. Fourth, it should include provisions lifting the Four Power status of Berlin. Fifth, the settlement should also codify the achievement of a united Germany's full and complete sovereignty and the end of the quadripartite rights and responsibilities.

Today we agreed tentatively to an interim outline for elements of a final settlement, referring to a preamble, to borders, and to Berlin. We further agreed to have our experts prepare a list of other issues of concern, and to determine, if they could, the appropriate fora for resolution of these issues.

To sum it up, let me simply say that we believe that a stable balance of interests can be attained. We are trying, for our part, to meet Moscow's appropriate security concerns, but I have to say that we think it is incumbent upon the Soviets to understand the concerns of the German states, others in Europe, and the United States as well.

When these talks began, I stressed our special public trust, a trust that transcended borders and even generations. Today, I think that point bears repeating. For too long, a Europe whole and free has really only been a dream while reality offered us the stark face of checkpoints, of walls and of confrontation.

That has been the past and until very recently that looked like it might even be the future. But here and now, in this city, and in this nation, I think we have the opportunity to banish the old reality and to establish in its place the Europe that I know all of us want to see. Thank you.

Foreign Minister Meckel. Thank you, Secretary Baker. I'd now like to call Mr. Hurd and ask him to address the press conference.

Foreign Minister Hurd. Thank you, Mr. Chairman. I'd like to thank you, and through you the government of the GDR, for the admirable arrangements which have been made for our meeting, and for your hospitality. I don't think anybody came here to this meeting, either among the participants, or among the commentators, expecting that there would be today some great breakthrough on substance. And nor has there been. The time is not, in practice, ripe for that. But nevertheless, I confirm what has already been said about the constructive, the workmanlike atmosphere in which the discussions took place, both in the sessions and in the lunch which the Ministers had together.

And we made some progress on borders, but obviously the main discussion of that must await the meeting in Paris, at which the Polish Foreign Minister will join us. We tackled what has been a very stubborn procedural point, and often points of procedure are the stubborn ones but when they are dealt with they unlock the way for real progress on substance. And we set our experts to examine rigorously what the problems are and, important in this matter, in which forum, in which discussion, those problems can best be solved. I believe that that focussing of our principal problems will enable us – I certainly hope will enable us – to make more rapid progress in the future.

Of course, we received the paper, the Soviet paper of which Mr. Shevardnadze has just informed us. And you listened to him just now, as we listened to him, saying that it was a basis for discussion, and compromise was not excluded. I would simply make two points: We are sure that it would be a mistake to try to pick out Germany and create a peculiar, special, limited status for one country in Europe. It's a mistake which was made before, regretted before, and we think it would be an element of instability rather than stability. Where there are thoughts and proposals which affect Germany, then of course they should be considered. But they should be considered alongside thoughts and proposals effecting other countries in Europe, and there are obviously ways and means of doing that.

Deadline for Completion

The second point is that we believe it is right and wise to plan on the basis that the political unification of Germany, brought about by the wishes of freely elected parliaments and governments in both Germanies, should coincide with the ending of the Four Power responsibilities inherited, surviving from the last war. If that synchronization is not achieved, then I think while again we may be piling up problems for the future. Now that is, it seems to me, a perfectly possible aim, even with the accelerated timetable for German unification which is now in prospect. And that is why this is good news that we decided that we would aim to complete the Two-Plus-Four work before the CSCE Summit in November, so that that summit could take account of what had been concluded.

Finally, ladies and gentlemen, I noticed again just now something which

Mr. Shevardnadze said which he said also more than once during the day about the central importance of the NATO Summit in London. We understand that as the host country, and I'm sure all the Allies understand that as we prepare for that summit. We entirely understand that that summit is going to be of central importance, for the Allies certainly, but also for the security of Europe as a whole. Thank you.

Foreign Minister Meckel. Thank you very much indeed, Mr. Hurd. I'd now like to call on Mr. Genscher.

Foreign Minister Genscher. Thank you very much indeed, Mr. Chairman. I spoke first in Bonn, and so, in accordance with what has become time-honored tradition I speak last at tonight's news conference.

The Federal Government was particularly satisfied with the statements made by the Foreign Ministers of the United States, United Kingdom, France and the Soviet Union – their statements welcoming the resolutions passed by both German states on the western frontier of Poland. They were decisions which we took independently, in full sovereignty, and in full exercise of our responsibility for the peace of Europe. Our meeting today got off to a hopeful start - with an act of great symbolism at "Checkpoint Charlie," and I say great symbolism because it represents tremendous evidence of the distance we've already covered as a result of the determination to obtain freedom of ordinary people. And it is a reflection too, of the responsibility shown and assumed by all the governments represented here.

Today, too, is a day of memories, of painful memories of 1941. And that is why it is particularly understandable that we as Germans, as we seek to settle the external aspects of German unity, we need to reflect and respect the security interests of the Soviet Union. Those interests we respect, as I say, and interests which we take into account. And we reached agreement that by the CSCE Summit conference the Two-Plus-Four talks will have been completed, so that we can communicate to the CSCE Summit conference the results of our work. And I'd like to express my gratitude to the French Foreign Minister for having expressed his intention to host the conference in Paris in November. I did inform my colleagues that it was our wish, the German people's wish, to hold all German elections in Germany in December—one single German election to reflect the wishes of the people in both German states, to make the wishes and their thinking. And my colleagues said at our meeting today that what had happened yesterday also reflected the wishes of the peoples in both Germanies. It's particularly important for us to ensure that the united Germany does not face problems which remain in abeyance, which remain in the air. Full sovereignty must be attained, contemporaneously and simultaneously with the completion of German unity. And it's equally important for a unified Germany not to be singularized, and not to suffer from discrimination. And that is the broad framework within which we are seeking solutions to the external aspects of German unification.

We know that those external aspects are imbedded in overall European trends. And that is why we are looking ahead to the CSCE Summit which will establish new structures, new institutions—institutions which will afford more stability and more confidence in Europe. But that is why, furthermore, we look ahead to the NATO Summit in London at which the views of the Western Alliance will be expressed—the views as to how the future can be fashioned. A summit at which too, we should also express our views on the relationship to be entertained by the states of the two alliances with each other. And here too, we look ahead to the result of the disarmament negotiations in Vienna. The first part of those negotiations we would wish to see concluded prior to the CSCE Summit. There is no clearer reflection than that, I think, of how the external aspects of the German unification process are embedded in a European process of agreement and understanding. It is for the experts now to produce an inventory of our problems, of the issues before us, and then we shall decide how and where solutions can be sought. All the states party to the Two-Plus-Four process will make their proposals—those proposals such as the suggestions that have already been tabled in four more documents, others which were tabled or will be tabled early in the future.

Like the previous speakers, like my colleagues, I myself, in the light of the spirit which prevailed in today's meet-ing, I'm absolutely convinced that we're all working towards a constructive solution within the time frame to which I have referred. And that is why I'm confident that that result will have been achieved by the CSCE Summit conference.

Mr. Chairman, I'd like to thank you and the government of the German Democratic Republic for the way in which you have hosted this meeting and we look forward with considerable expectations to our next meeting in Paris, which we intend to prepare extremely thoroughly indeed.

Foreign Minister Meckel. Thank you very much indeed. Perhaps having spoken initially as Chairman of the meeting, I might now make a couple of comments on behalf of the GDR.

We in the GDR embarked upon a peaceful revolution in the cause of liberty and democracy, and very quickly we found ourselves in a position where responsibility for this country had to be assumed. But a responsibility not only for Germany, but also for Europe, and that is why it is our contention that it is not only of importance for Germany but also for Europe, that no matters remain unresolved at the point of German unity. And in order to ensure that happens, we must seek to generate a consensus among each of us—the security interests of all of us must be reflected, in particular those of our eastern neighbours. As their one-time partner, seeking together to overcome the burdens of Stalinism, we must now reflect their security interests. Nobody must lose out in this process. Mr. Genscher has already drawn your attention to the historic importance of today's date, a date which was mentioned several times during today's meeting, June 22nd, 1941, when German troops invaded the Soviet Union. That too, is eloquent testimony to the responsibility we all shoulder today. Today questions of sovereignty were of paramount importance. The question of when Germany will attain, could attain, full sovereignty. It's our view that sovereignty is important for Germany, if Germany is to be a true partner of Europe. And it seems to us that one of the most important signs and symbols of sovereignty is a sense of a self-denying ordinance, if you will. Which is why we, as two German states, decided and are pledged to forswear the possession, the production, the proliferation and the deployment of nuclear, biological and chemical weapons.

Limiting German Armed Forces

And we have also said that we would be prepared to put our name to a declaration limiting armed forces to, say, three hundred thousand men—a fully sovereign decision that, in the hope that, it would be properly reflected as CFE [conventional armed forces in Europe] negotiations in Vienna. Without singularizing Germany, whilst at the same time, giving a genuine boost to the momentum leading to the CFE Vienna agreement which will, in itself, be of major importance to Central Europe, as it will lay down ceilings for force levels in that area. And in the future it will be particularly important to establish a proper organization for this security of Germany towards the East. Now no final settlement has yet been found for that, although a proposal was made that the member states of the Warsaw Treaty Organization and NATO should meet together just before the next CSCE Paris summit, in order to pass a joint declaration. And that joint declaration would state that they don't regard each other as enemies, but that, in accordance with their own military strategies, they will seek to forego violence and the use of force in their mutual dealings as their alliances change. Perhaps I could leave it there, and I'm sure we would be happy to take any questions you might have.

Q. A question for Secretary of State Baker: The Soviet draft suggests a timetable for limiting and going down to only token forces of other countries on German soil. Could you please react to that? Is that a worthwhile suggestion?

Secretary Baker. Our view of that is that the truest sign of German sovereignty is to permit the unified Germany to make its own decision with respect to matters such as the stationing of troops on its soil.

Q. If I understand the proposal, it would be the occupying powers that decide to remove their troops. I did indeed wonder if you saw it as a limitation on Germany? I thought it invites the other countries to get out of Germany. Is there anything wrong with that? A. Maybe we better let Minister Shevardnadze explain his proposal to you, since we just saw it for the first time today. But my understanding is, it would create a different situation for Berlin than it does for the rest of the GDR. It would require, for instance, that there be the removal of troops with respect to the city of Berlin and you would have a Berlin then, surrounded by some three hundred and eighty thousand Soviet troops. You ask me if I think that is a good idea, and I think you knew what the answer was when you asked the question. But, let me simply say: our position is this is really a matter for a sovereign unified Germany to determine.

Q. I thought there was another aspect of the proposal that foreign troops would be removed from the rest of Germany over a period of years.

A. I think there is another aspect of it. My answer to that would be, why not let the sovereign unified Germany make that determination, rather than imposing it upon it as a condition for its obtaining a final settlement?

Q. Mr. Shevardnadze, would you like to say something?

Foreign Minister Shevardnadze. Yes, I shall add a few words. We submitted such a proposal, and I must say that this is not the first time that we've mentioned it. We consider that that is a very fair way of putting the question. All who are present here know well the position and the principles the Soviet Union adheres to regarding the presence of any military forces on foreign territory. I'm more than convinced that, after a certain time shall elapse, the German nation and the German people will see toward regarding the presence of foreign troops. I do not know of any people which would approve of a military presence of other powers. We are looking at tomorrow. We want to build a new Europe. We want to overcome finally military confrontation and we would like to assure Germans and the German people of our will and therefore we think, and we are determined to put an end to foreign military presence on German soil.

Q. Minister Shevardnadze, if I may focus your attention also on what I think is a key issue in this obvious debate that you all had today over your proposal. Many of the items in your draft proposal seem to rely on the continuation of some kind of regulation of Germany after its unification. You talk even about small details such as preservation of war memorials and so on, and you say that all of these issues will

have — [Recording tape at end: rest of question not transcribed]

A. I think that the basic arguments regarding the external aspects of German unity must be developed within the framework of the Two-Plus-Four mechanism but it's important, and I ask you to pay special attention to this — it's very important, we agreed today, and it's a matter of principle, that the document on the settlement of the German question on the basis of international law will be submitted to a summit conference of the thirty-five states. We underline by this that every state has its interests, every state has its voice and its weight and its interest, in the optimal settlement of the question regarding the building of German unification.

Q. A question for Foreign Minister Shevardnadze: You said that the NATO Summit which is coming up is going to be pivotal and so did most of the other ministers. What is it that the Soviet Union regards as necessary to come out of that NATO Summit to ameliorate or to deal with some of your concerns? What do you need NATO to do at the summit?

A. I could mention very many elements, very many aspects as regards the wishes of the Soviet Union. But if we speak of what is most important, of the main tendencies to be supported, that tendency amounts to overcoming military confrontation on the European continent. That is the main, basic task of the present moment, of the present stage in the European process and the state of affairs in Europe. And I think that in this respect, the countries of the Warsaw Pact have said their voice, you know about the statement adopted in Moscow in this respect. We would imagine that the conference in London will define its attitude in principle to this declaration and will say its weighty word in the interests of overcoming military confrontation in Europe and the building of new relations between the two military alliances and the member states of these alliances.

Q. So you are looking for a specific set of declarations from NATO that would lead to the kind of inter-alliance assurances that you have been talking about. Can you tell us what specific things you need in the way of those assurances? A nonaggression statement? A non-enmity statement? Is that what you're looking for?

A. You are quite right. You point out two elements, but one could have

other elements in mind as well. Why shouldn't we set up some sort of mechanism for negotiations, a consultative council between the two treaties so as to carry on serious negotiations aimed at all the coming military confrontations, speak about the problems of safeguarding stability in Europe. There are many such elements, but the most important task is that we must deal with the most important question, namely that our two alliances do not consider each other to be military enemies.

Q. Can you please tell us, Mr. Genscher, what you think of the suggestion to withdraw all foreign troops within six months? Are you just as skeptical as the U.S. Secretary of State?

Foreign Minister Genscher. I already said in my introductory statement that it is our aim to achieve full sovereignty by unification. And if we achieve sovereignty, it also means the reply to the question on rights and responsibilities which do not concern just the whole of Germany but also Berlin. You should be most impressed by the fact that we are in complete agreement, that the CSCE conference in November will share the results of the Two-Plus-Four discussions. Thank you.

Q. Minister Genscher, at the last Two-Plus-Four meeting in Bonn, the Soviet Union made a proposal for a package approach so that the external questions of German reunification need not be settled at the same time as the internal questions. Now since then we've, the two Germanies, moved to clear away some of the underbrush that would stand in the way of German reunification but the Soviet proposal today sounds like a slight variation on that. Do you see some convergence of the Soviet position with the German position since then or has it actually stood in place?

A. I think that what is important is what Mr. Shevardnadze just said, namely that we try to bring the Two-Plus-Four talks to an end by the CSCE Summit because it will bring forward the inner unification of the two states and that became particularly clear yesterday when both German parliaments adopted a state treaty concerning economic, financial and other questions. All colleagues recognized that this development accords with the will of the Germans and we cannot put any obstacles in the way to German unification. This is why we want to negotiate intensively, consult intensively, not just on the level of experts but also on the level of foreign ministers so as to achieve our aim by this set date. Everybody is clear that we do not want European to lag behind German development. We want to synchronize it all and that means for me also complete sovereignty of a united Germany at the same time.

Q. This is mainly for Mr. Shevardnadze. You have repeatedly stressed today the Soviet Union's readiness for compromise in order to meet the timetable you have set out. But the proposals you have tabled leave you far away from the positions put forward by the other members in your group. How do you think this is going to be bridged in the relatively short time you have left?

Foreign Minister Shevardnadze. I am convinced that we shall overcome these disagreements. I would like to say the following: My colleagues were quite right when they said that the process of German reunification is developing very dynamically. I believe that we should do everything possible to create maximum, optimal conditions for the building of the external aspects of German reunification. That's one aspect. Secondly, we must try, and that is quite possible, we must try to ensure the same high degree of dynamism regarding the formation of all European structures of security. In other words, we must prepare seriously for the summit meeting of the thirty-five European states. We must achieve a high degree of dynamism at the Vienna talks. We must achieve real reductions in armed forces so as to help eliminate military confrontation on the European continent. And another aspect, and I mentioned it the other day, we must build new relations between the two political-military unions. This whole complex provides the basis and the conditions to find compromise decisions and I am optimistic.

Q. Mr. Genscher, Mr. Baker said that today was the first time he had seen Mr. Shevardnadze's proposals. You have had meetings recently with Mr. Shevardnadze. Are we to understand that these proposals were also not brought up in your meetings with Mr. Shevardnadze and this was the first time today that you had seen these proposals?

Foreign Minister Genscher. This proposal was submitted to all of us for the first time today. But in the past we did speak about what was to happen with Europe and I think that we should

not consider our conversations in isolation. If this is done, one might not notice that very important developments are to take place in 1990. I would like to repeat: first result, the conventional arms talks in Vienna before CSCE; the NATO Summit meeting decision on the relationship between the members of the two alliances; the CSCE Summit itself. We hope that Europe will gain new confidence and in this context there will be changes, changes during the next few months, changes towards improvement. We shall find a reply to many questions, replies which were impossible to find in the past. We think that in these new and altered conditions, we shall find an answer to them. In other words, it shows that the approaches of the two German governments during the unification and the road to German unification will not create new problems. It will solve problems and will make a serious contribution to peace and security in Europe. We consider that the German process of reunification will have a positive influence upon the development of the whole of Europe and we can see that in the whole content of our consultations. And this is how you can see why we are so confident, a confidence which we voiced today in spite of the fact that there are differences of opinion among us, we shall still try to work with greater intensity and we shall try to move forward within the whole European framework. We want to bring about a serious change for the better before the summit meeting of the CSCE. We think that by the CSCE Summit we shall be able to solve the German question, but in such a way that Germany would not be singularized.

Q. Foreign Minister Genscher, I'd like to ask you two specific questions about how to meet Soviet concerns about the size of the future German Bundeswehr. Do you see a basis for compromise here? Would you be willing to accept in a final settlement some kind of overall statement about an outer limit on any country's forces - say in the central zone - which would be negotiated in Vienna without naming Germany by name? Secondly, what do you think of Mr. Meckel's suggestion about some kind of a unilateral declaration by Germany about its intentions in this regard?

A. I think that we had a consensus during our talks today that within the framework of the negotiations of the

twenty-three in Vienna, we should try to achieve some result on the strength on the troops on German soil without any singularity of Germany. The talks in Vienna will be on such a level that they will satisfy all and therefore we think that Vienna is the correct forum. You will remember that we have agreed on the procedure, namely we shall define problems, we shall make a list of them, we shall decide where to settle them and which to settle. The questions which belong to Vienna will be settled in Vienna because they will not result in the singularization of Germany.

Foreign Minister Shevardnadze. I would like to state that my proposal is not any discrimination, it is a sovereign action of the Germans which will be put on a broader basis in Vienna by stressing Central Europe. So it will have the effect you mentioned. But I hope that it will proceed quicker and possibly even on a lower level if the Germans can pass such an act.

Q. Mr. Shevardnadze, the Western ministers starting with the French and then Mr. Baker and then Mr. Hurd all stated the principles in similar terms on which they see a settlement. Namely, the singularization of Germany and a synchronization of the lifting of allied rights at the same time as unification. Now your proposal seemed to go counter to both those two principles. So could you state for us whether you reject those two principles? Or how are we to understand your proposal?

A. No, we do not reject these four principles. We add something to them. We developed our arguments and we submitted them to the talks today. Those who are interested in our paper can study it and they can also read my statement where I tried to explain in detail the position of the Soviet Union on these questions. Apart from these principles which you mentioned and which you have in mind, there are others which also require a reply. These include the political-military status of a united Germany and other questions. So we are examining it all in one whole complex and I do not want to dramatize the situation. The negotiations are taking place. They will be continued. The experts have received certain instructions, guidance, I would say. And in about a month's time we shall meet in Paris and see the first results of the work and we shall try to find a compromise decision.

Q. For Foreign Minister Shevardnadze. Are you not concerned about the effect in Germany of singularizing or discriminating against Germany as each of the other foreign ministers has pointed out? Each of them has expressed some concern about this. But you have not. Why not?

A. Will you please repeat your question, sir?

Q. My question was: Each of the other foreign ministers has expressed his concern, to some degree or another, about the effect in Germany of singularizing or discriminating against Germany in the process of the Two-Plus-Four talks. But you have not. Why not?

A. We do not want any singularization of Germany or the German question. We emphasize the importance of finding complex decisions and contributing towards the building of German unity on the one hand, and on the other hand, we want to contribute to the development of a European process and European structures.

Q. [Warsaw Pact member states indicated] their readiness to reduce and transform the character of their union. So the question is, will NATO at its summit in London answer these steps of the East with a new conception of its military policy?

Secretary Baker. We have said for some time that there will be an enhancement of the political component of the NATO alliance. I have suggestions myself going all the way back to Decem-

ber of last year with respect to political undertakings that the alliance might consider concentrating on. I won't repeat all of these here. There is a changed situation in Europe. Will the NATO alliance remain a defense and security alliance? Yes, it will because it has always been first and foremost a defensive alliance. Those of us who are in it believe that it has been largely responsible for the fact that we have seen an absence of war for over forty years. But it will adapt, it will become more political. And I would simply refer you to the results of the NATO Summit meeting which is upcoming now in just two weeks in London. And I think after that summit takes place you will be able to measure exactly the degree to which there is more of a political adaptation to this alliance, the degree to which there will be a recognition on the part of this alliance with respect to the changed circumstances in Europe. And with respect to the declaration that came forth from the member states of the Warsaw Pact here not long ago. Thank you.

---

[1]Department of State Press Release 93, June 22, 1990.

Nelson Mandela Meets with President Bush and Addresses Congress

On June 25, 1990, Mr. Mandela, deputy president of the African National Congress (ANC), met with President Bush at the White House. [1]

President Bush

Welcome to all of you. It is a great pleasure, a sincere pleasure, for Barbara and me to welcome to the White House Mr. and Mrs. Mandela—Mr. Mandela, a man who embodies the hopes of millions. In our meetings this morning, he and I will talk about the future of South Africa, and it is my sincere hope that these talks will be productive discussions that will contribute to positive change toward true democracy and the dismantling once and for all of apartheid.

We meet at a time of transition for South Africa. We applaud the recent steps President [F.W.] de Klerk and the Government of South Africa have taken to expand the rights and freedoms of all South Africans. These are positive developments, steps toward a fully free and democratic future that we all wish to see for all of the people of South Africa. In order for progress to continue, we must see on all sides a clear commitment to change.

All parties must seize the opportunity to move ahead in a spirit of compromise and tolerance, flexibility and patience. And from all parties, we look for a clear and unequivocal commitment to negotiations leading to peaceful change. I call on all elements in South African society to renounce the use of violence in armed struggle, break free from the cycle of repression and violent reaction that breeds nothing but more fear and suffering. In the words of the great Martin Luther King, Jr., "Let us not seek to satisfy our thirst for freedom by drinking from the cup of bitterness and hatred."

Mr. Mandela, in the eyes of millions around the world, you stand against apartheid, against a system that bases the rights and freedoms of citizenship on the color of one's skin. That system is repugnant to the conscience of men and women everywhere, repugnant to the ideals that we in America hold so dear. No system that denies the rights that belong to each and every individual can endure forever. Apartheid must end.

The United States, committed to the concept of free market and a productive private sector, is ready to do its part to encourage rapid and peaceful change toward political and economic freedom. We will continue to urge American firms that are still doing business in South Africa to play a progressive role in training and empowering blacks and building a foundation for future prosperity.

But while the reform process has moved forward—and it has—apartheid remains a reality, and genuine democracy a dream. Our sanctions have been designed to support change. And when the conditions laid down in our law have been met, then, and only then, will we consider, in consultation with the Congress, whether a change in course will promote further progress through peaceful negotiations.

Mr. Mandela, we in this country support the struggle against apartheid. For two centuries, we had our own battles. America fought its own battles to promote the standard of equal rights. It was here at the White House—in a room now obscured by these coverings because we're repainting the White House—but it's right there, in the midst of the Civil War, that Abraham Lincoln signed the Emancipation Proclamation, that great beacon of light and hope. In the room where this historic document was signed, even now we feel the power of the undeniable truth that guided Lincoln's hand: that all men must be free.

In this past year, freedom has made great gains. A terrible chapter of oppression has ended for millions of men and women in Eastern Europe, in Asia, and in this hemisphere. People have defeated, through peaceful means, dictatorships that promised freedom and progress but delivered only poverty and repression. The triumph is far from universal. There are still those who rule through force and terror. But the events of this past year have been clear: The future belongs not to the dwindling ranks of the world's dictators but to democracy, the millions of friends of freedom the world over.

Mr. Mandela, you said many years ago, before the first of your 10,000 days in prison, that there is no easy walk to freedom. Your years of suffering, your nation's suffering—they've borne that out. But just as, this past year, so many millions of people in Eastern Europe and elsewhere tasted freedom, so, too, South Africa's time will come.

As Martin Luther King said on the steps of the Lincoln Memorial, we cannot walk alone. Sir, we here in America walk in solidarity with all the South Africans who seek through nonviolent means democracy, human rights, and freedom.

Once again, it is a sincere privilege to welcome you to the White House, and may God bless you and all the people of South Africa. Welcome, sir.

Mr. Mandela

Mr. President, it is an honor and a pleasure for my wife, my delegation, and I to be welcomed by you. This is a continuation of the rousing welcome which we have received from the people of New York and Boston, of black and white. That welcome has far exceeded our wildest expectations. We look forward to visiting Atlanta and other cities because we are confident that the warm welcome we have received is not confined to New York, Boston and Washington. That mood expresses the commitment of all the people of the United States of America to the struggle for the removal of apartheid.

One thing that is very clear, and it has been made even more clear in the remarks by the President, is that on the question of the removal of apartheid and the introduction of a nonracial democracy in our country we are absolutely unanimous. That is something that we have always known because the people of America and the President, in particular, have spoken in this regard in very clear and firm terms. And this has been a source of great encouragement to our people. To receive the support of any government is, in our situation, something of enormous importance; but to receive the support of the Government of the United States of America, the leader of the West, is something beyond words. If today we are confident that the dreams which have inspired us all these years is about to be realized, it is, in very large measure, because of the support we have got from the masses of the people of the United States of

America and, in particular, from the Government and from the President.

There are very important political developments that have taken place in our country today, and it is my intention to brief the President as fully as possible on these developments. We are doing so because it is necessary for him to understand not only in broad outline what is happening in our country, he must be furnished with the details which may not be so available to the public so that the enormous assistance that he has given us should be related to the actual developments in the country.

I will also ask the President to maintain sanctions because it is because of sanctions that such enormous progress has been made in the attempt to address the problems of our country.

I will also inform him about developments as far as the arms [armed? - ED.] struggle is concerned. The remarks that he has made here are due to the fact that he has not as yet got a proper briefing from us. I might just state in passing that the methods of political action which are used by the black people of South Africa were determined by the South African Government. As long as a government is prepared to talk, to maintain channels of communication between itself and the governed, there can be no question of violence whatsoever. But when a government decides to ban political organizations of the oppressed, intensifies oppression, and does not allow any free political activity, no matter how peaceful and nonviolent, then the people have no alternative but to resort to violence.

There is not a single political organization in our country, inside and outside Parliament, which can ever compare with the African National Congress in its total commitment to peace. If we are forced to resort to violence, it is because we had no other alternative whatsoever. But even in this regard, there have been significant developments which I hope to brief the President on. I am also going to brief the President on the key role which the ANC now occupies in the country as a result of his efforts to mobilize the entire country around the question of peace.

We have and are addressing the question of black unity. We are also addressing ourselves to means and methods of helping Mr. de Klerk to maintain his position with confidence and to go on with the negotiations

without looking over his shadow. We have already started important initiatives in trying to mobilize the white community, not only those who support him but even the right wing, because we are the only organization in the world that can help Mr. de Klerk to maintain his position.

And I am going to urge on the President not to do anything without a full consultation with the ANC in regard to any initiative which he might propose to take in order to help the peace process in the country. As people who are operating inside, and as the architects of the peace process, it is absolutely necessary for everybody who wants to be of assistance in the struggle of the black people inside the country and who want to help promote the

peace process to have a full consultation with the ANC before any step is taken.

Finally Mr. President, I would like to congratulate you and President Gorbachev for the magnificent efforts that you are making in order to reduce international tensions and to promote peace. It is my hope that governments throughout the world will follow your example and attempt to settle problems between governments, and between governments and dissidents inside its country, by peaceful methods. You and comrade Gorbachev have opened a chapter in world history which might well be regarded as the turning point in many respects. And here we congratulate you and wish you every success.

ADDRESS BY NELSON MANDELA, DEPUTY PRESIDENT OF THE AFRICAN NATIONAL CONGRESS, TO A JOINT SESSION OF CONGRESS, JUNE 26, 1990. [2]

Mr. Speaker; Mr. President; esteemed Members of the U.S. Congress; your excellencies, ambassadors and members of the Diplomatic Corps; distinguished guests, ladies and gentlemen:

It is a fact of the human condition that each shall, like a meteor, a mere brief passing moment in time and space, nit across the human stage and pass out of existence. Even the golden lads and lasses, as much as the chimney sweepers, come, and tomorrow are no more. After them all, they leave the people, enduring, multiplying, permanent, except to the extent that the same humanity might abuse its own genius to immolate life itself.

And so we have come to Washington in the District of Columbia, and into these hallowed Chambers of the U.S. Congress, not as pretenders to greatness, but as a particle of a people whom we know to be noble and heroic — enduring, multiplying, permanent, rejoicing in the expectation and knowledge that their humanity will be reaffirmed and enlarged by open and unfettered communion with the nations of the world.

We have come here to tell you, and through you, your own people, who are equally noble and heroic, of the troubles and trials, the fond hopes and

aspirations, of the people from whom we originate. We believe that we know it as a fact, that your kind and moving invitation to us to speak here derived from your own desire to convey a message to our people, and according to your humane purposes, to give them an opportunity to say what they want of you, and what they want to make of their relationship with you.

The Struggle for Democracy

Our people demand democracy. Our country, which continues to bleed and suffer pain, needs democracy. It cries out for the situation where the law will decree that the freedom to speak of freedom constitutes the very essence of legality and the very thing that makes for the legitimacy of the constitutional order.

It thirsts for the situation where those who are entitled by law to carry arms, as the forces of national security and law and order, will not turn their weapons against the citizens simply because the citizens assert that equality, liberty and the pursuit of happiness are fundamental human rights which are not only inalienable but must, if necessary, be defended with the weapons of war.

We fight for and visualize a future in which all shall, without regard to race, color, creed or sex, have the right to vote and to be voted into all elective organs of state. We are engaged in struggle to ensure that the rights of every individual are guaranteed and protected, through a democratic constitution, the rule of law, an entrenched bill of rights, which should be enforced by an independent judiciary, as well as a multiparty political system.

Mr. Speaker, we are acutely conscious of the fact that we are addressing an historic institution for whose creation and integrity many men and women lost their lives in the war of independence, the civil war and the war against nazism and fascism. That very history demands that we address you with respect and candor and without any attempt to dissemble.

What we have said concerning the political arrangements we seek for our country is seriously meant. It is an outcome for which many of us went to prison, for which many have died in police cells, on the gallows, in our towns and villages and in the countries of Southern Africa. Indeed, we have even had our political representatives killed in countries as far away from South Africa as France.

Unhappily, our people continue to die to this day, victims of armed agents of the state who are still determined to turn their guns against the very idea of a nonracial democracy. But this is the perspective which we trust Congress will feel happy to support and encourage, using the enormous weight of its prestige and authority as an eminent representative of democratic practice.

To deny any person their human rights is to challenge their very humanity. To impose on them a wretched life of hunger and deprivation is to dehumanise them. But such has been the terrible fate of all black persons in our country under the system of apartheid. The extent of the deprivation of millions of people has to be seen to be believed. The injury is made that more intolerable by the opulence of our white compatriots and the deliberate distortion of the economy to feed that opulence.

Transforming the South African Economy

The process of the reconstruction of South African society must and will also entail the transformation of its economy. We need a strong and growing economy. We require an economy that is able to address the needs of all the people of our country, that can provide food, houses, education, health services, social security and everything that makes human life human, that makes life joyful and not a protracted encounter with hopelessness and despair.

We believe that the fact of the apartheid structure of the South African economy and the enormous and pressing needs of the people, make it inevitable that the democratic government will intervene in this economy, acting through the elected parliament. We have put the matter to the business community of our country that the need for a public sector is one of the elements in a many-sided strategy of economic development and restructuring that has to be considered by us all, including the private sector.

The ANC holds no ideological positions which dictate that it must adopt a policy of nationalization. But the ANC also holds the view that there is no self-regulating mechanism within the South African economy which will, on its own, ensure growth with equity.

At the same time, we take it as given that the private sector is an engine of growth and development which is critical to the success of the mixed economy we hope to see in the future South Africa. We are accordingly committed to the creation of the situation in which business people, both South African and foreign, have confidence in the security of their investments, are assured of a fair rate of return on their capital and do business in conditions of stability and peace.

We must also make the point very firmly that the political settlement, and democracy itself, cannot survive, unless the material needs of the people, the bread and butter issues, are addressed as part of the process of change and as a matter of urgency. It should never be that the anger of the poor should be the finger of accusation pointed at all of us because we failed to respond to the cries of the people for food, for shelter, for the dignity of the individual.

We shall need your support to achieve the postapartheid economic objectives which are an intrinsic part of the process of the restoration of the human rights of the people of South Africa. We would like to approach the issue of our economic cooperation not as a relationship between donor and recipient, between a dependent and a benefactor.

We would like to believe that there is a way in which we could structure this relationship so that we do indeed benefit from your enormous resources in terms of your capital, technology, all-round expertise, your enterprising spirit and your markets. This relationship should however be one from which your people should also derive benefit, so that we who are fighting to liberate the very spirit of an entire people from the bondage of the arrogance of the ideology and practice of white supremacy, do not build a relationship of subservient dependency and fawning gratitude.

One of the benefits that should accrue to both our peoples and to the rest of the world, should surely be that this complex South African society, which has known nothing but racism for three centuries, should be transformed into an oasis of good race relations, where the black shall to the white be sister and brother, a fellow South African, an equal human being, both citizens of the world. To destroy racism in the world, we, together, must expunge apartheid racism in South Africa. Justice and liberty must be our tool, prosperity and happiness our weapon.

Mr. Speaker, distinguished representatives of the American people, you know this more than we do that peace is its own reward. Our own fate, born by a succession of generations that reach backward into centuries, has been nothing but tension, conflict, and death. In a sense we do not know the meaning of peace except in the imagination. But because we have not known true peace in its real meaning; because, for centuries, generations have had to bury the victims of state violence, we have fought for the right to experience peace.

On the initiative of the ANC, the process toward the conclusion of a peaceful settlement has started. According to a logic dictated by our situation, we are engaged in an effort which includes the removal of obstacles to negotiations. This will be followed by a negotiated determination of the mechanism which will draw up the new constitution.

This should lead to the formation of this constitution-making institution and therefore the elaboration and adoption of a democratic constitution. Elections would then be held on the basis of this constitution and, for the first time, South Africa would have a body of lawmakers which would, like yourselves, be mandated by the whole people.

Despite the admitted commitment of President De Klerk to walk this road with us, and despite our acceptance of his integrity and the honesty of his purposes, we would be fools to believe that the road ahead of us i s without major hurdles. Too many among our white compatriots are steeped in the ideology of racism to admit easily that change must come.

Tragedy may yet sully the future we pray and work for if these slaves of the past take up arms in a desperate effort to resist the process which must lead to the democratic transformation of our country. For those who care to worry about violence in our country, as we do, it is at these forces that they should focus their attention, a process in which we are engaged.

We must contend still with the reality that South Africa is a country in the grip of the apartheid crime against humanity. The consequences of this continue to be felt not only within our borders but throughout southern Africa which continues to harvest the bitter fruits of conflict and war, especially in Mozambique and Angola. Peace will not come to our country and region until the apartheid system is ended.

Continuing Sanctions

Therefore we say we still have a struggle on our hands. Our common and noble efforts to abolish the system of white minority domination must continue. We are encouraged and strengthened by the fact of the agreement between ourselves, this Congress as well as President Bush and his administration that sanctions should remain in place. Sanctions should remain in place because the purpose for which they were imposed has not yet been achieved.

We have yet to arrive at the point when we can say that South Africa is set on an irreversible course leading to its transportation into a united, democratic, and nonracial country. We plead that you cede the prerogative to the people of South Africa to determine the moment when it will be said that profound changes have occurred and an irreversible process achieved, enabling you and the rest of the international community to lift sanctions

We would like to take this opportunity to thank you all for the principled struggle you waged which resulted in

the adoption of the historic comprehensive Anti-Apartheid Act which made such a decisive contribution to the process of moving our country forward toward negotiations. We request that you go further and assist us with the material resources which will enable us to promote the peace process and meet other needs which arise from the changing situation you have helped to bring about.

The stand you took established the understanding among the millions of our people that here we have friends, here we have fighters against racism who feel hurt because we are hurt, who seek our success because they too seek the victory of democracy over tyranny. And here I speak not only about you, Members of the U.S. Congress, but also of the millions of people throughout this great land who stood up and engaged the apartheid system in struggle, the masses who have given us such strength and joy by the manner in which they have received us since we arrived in this country.

Mr. Speaker, Mr. President, Senators and Representatives; we went to jail because it was impossible to sit still while the obscenity of the apartheid system was being imposed on our people. It would have been immoral to keep quiet while a racist tyranny sought to reduce an entire people into status worse than that of the beasts of the forest. It would have been an act of treason against the people and against our conscience to allow fear and the drive toward self-preservation to dominate our behavior, obliging us to absent ourselves from the struggle for democracy and human rights, not only in our country but throughout he world.

We could not have made an acquaintance through literature with human giants such as George Washington, Abraham Lincoln and Thomas Jefferson and not been moved to act as they were moved to act. We could not have heard of and admired John Brown, Sojourner Truth, Frederick Douglass, W.E.B. DuBois, Marcus Garvey, Martin Luther King, Jr., and others—we could not have heard of these and not be moved to act as they were moved to act. We could not have known of your Declaration of Independence and not elected to join in the struggle to guarantee the people life, liberty and the pursuit of happiness.

We are grateful to you all that you persisted in your resolve to have us and other political prisoners released from jail. You have given us the gift and privilege to rejoin our people, yourselves, and the rest of the international community in the common effort to transform South Africa into a united, democratic and nonracial country. You have given us the power to join hands with all people of conscience to fight for the victory of democracy and human rights throughout the world.

We are glad that you merged with our own people to make it possible for us to emerge from the darkness of the prison cell and join the contemporary process of the renewal of the world. We thank you most sincerely for all you have done and count on you to persist in your noble endeavors to free the rest of our political prisoners and to emancipate our people from the larger prison that is apartheid South Africa.

The day may not be far when we will borrow the words of Thomas Jefferson and speak of the will of the South African Nation. In the exercise of that will by this united nation of black and white people, it must surely be that there will be born a country on the southern tip of Africa which you will be proud to call a friend and an ally, because of its contribution to the universal striving toward liberty, human rights, prosperity and peace among the peoples.

Let that day come now. Let us keep our arms locked together so that we form a solid phalanx against racism to ensure that that day comes now. By our common actions let us ensure that justice triumphs without delay. When that has come to pass, then shall we all be entitled to acknowledge the salute when others say of us, blessed are the peacemakers.

Thank you for your kind invitation to speak here today and thank you for your welcome and the attention you have accorded our simple message.

---

[1]Text from Weekly Compilation of Presidential Documents of July 2, 1990.
[2]Text from the Congressional Record, June 26, 1990

President Extends Most-Favored-Nation Trade Status for China

Excerpts from President Bush's press conference, May 24, 1990. [1]

Today, after long and thorough deliberation, I have determined that MFN [most-favored-nation] trade status for China should be extended for a year. MFN is not a special favor; it is not a concession; it's the basis of everyday trade. And taking MFN away is one thing I said I would not do; that is, in doing that, take steps that would hurt the Chinese people themselves. I do not want to do that.

To express America's outrage at the tragedy of Tiananmen, the Congress and my administration promptly enacted sanctions against China. These sanctions remain basically unchanged today. And while implementing those sanctions, I have repeatedly made clear that I did not want to hurt the Chinese people. And this was a difficult decision, weighing our impulse to lash out in outrage that we all feel—weighing that against a sober assessment of our nation's long-term interests.

I concluded that it is in our best interest and the interest of the Chinese people to continue China's trade status. Not to do so would hurt the United States. Trade would drop dramatically, hurting exporters, consumers, and investors. China buys about $6 billion a year of American aircraft and wheat and chemicals, lumber and other products. Lose this market, and we lose American jobs: aircraft workers in the West, farmers in the Great Plains, high-tech employees in the Northeast.

Our economic competition will not join us in denying MFN. Without MFN, an average of 40 percent higher costs for Chinese imports will turn into higher prices for American consumers. Hong Kong weighed on my mind. Hong Kong would be an innocent victim of our dispute with Beijing. Twenty thousand jobs and $10 billion could be lost in a colony that is a model of free enterprise spirit. The United Kingdom and China's neighbors have urged me to continue MFN. Korea, Japan, Thailand, Singapore, even Taiwan made clear that MFN should be retained.

In recent weeks, China has taken modest steps that appear intended to

show responsiveness to our concerns. Beijing lifted martial law in Tibet, restored consular access there, giving us a chance to judge the situation for ourselves. Two hundred eleven detainees were recently released and then their names provided for the first time. While we welcome these and earlier steps, they are, let's face it, far from adequate. And I am not basing my decision on the steps that the Chinese have taken so far.

Most important of all, as we mark the anniversary of Tiananmen, we must realize that by maintaining our involvement with China we will continue to promote the reforms for which the victims of Tiananmen gave their lives. The people in China who trade with us are the engine of reform, an opening to the outside world. During the past 10 years, we've seen our engagement in China contribute to the forces for justice and reason that were peacefully protested in Beijing. And our responsibility to them is best met not by isolating those forces from contact with us or by strengthening the hand of reaction but by keeping open the channels of commerce and communication.

Our Ambassador [James R. Lilley] came to see me here in the Oval Office the other day and told me that not only the people that he's in contact with but the students there, the intellectuals there, all favor— there in China—favor the continuation of MFN. So, this is why I've made the decision I have made.

* * *

Q. Mr. President, it's been a year now since the world has watched China mow its own people down in Tiananmen Square. How can we expect the prodemocracy movement fighters around the world to have faith in the United States when they see a reward to Beijing such as the MFN?

A. I made clear, Tom [Thomas Raum, Associated Press], I don't think this is a reward to Beijing. I think it is very important we keep these commercial contacts. I think it is in the interest of the United States that we keep these contacts. MFN is based on emigration, and emigration has continued from

China at respectable levels. And so, that is why I'm making this decision.

And what irks me is when some of the people up on the Hill accuse me of being less interested than they are in human rights. I think we're on the right track here. I've cited the number of countries that agree with us. I've cited the fact that the students and the intellectuals in China itself agree with what I've just done. And so, it is not a favor we're doing. I have cited the need to balance out the interest of others, including Hong Kong, which is under enormous pressure from the refugee situation there. And so, this decision is the proper decision. And it has nothing to do with saying we're condoning human rights excesses. I took the lead a year ago at the G-7 [economic summit of industrialized nations] meeting in Paris and got our allies to join in sanctions that still exist. So, I'm glad you asked it because then I vented a spleen here.

Q. But, sir, if it's not a favor, how do you square this with our policy on denying the same status to the Soviet Union, based on the fact that they haven't codified their emigration policy?

A. Because the MFN is related to emigration. And the Soviets have not passed the necessary emigration legislation.

Q. Mr. President, is it time now for—-

A. And China does have the proper policy.

* * *

Q. Mr. President, critics of this decision on China believe it is based too heavily on a blind faith that you have of those leaders based on your experience as envoy over there. What message does this send to the younger generation of Chinese leaders who are going to come along and replace those in power now?

A. It says that economic contacts are the best way to keep the economic reforms going forward. It says that the more economic contacts we have with China, the more they're going to see the fruits of free-market economies. I've told you that the students in China, according to our Ambassador, want to see this MFN continue. And so, it should send no message other than that isolation is bad and economic involvement is good.

And the whole fact that we've had economic involvement, I think, has moved China more towards reform than if we hadn't had it. And so, I want to see it continue. And that is the message to the people because it has — some will interpret the way you've said, and I will say it has nothing to do with that. It has nothing to do with that at all. We have certain sanctions in place; they remain in place. China has got an emigration policy going that qualifies, and you have the interests of — Taiwan says keep it going, Hong Kong says keep it going. Three editorials in this country — well, maybe many, many more, I think — who were upset with the fact that I opted for executive action instead of legislation all support continuation of MFN. And those people who were on my case, if you will, about the decision I took, which I still think was the correct decision, are now saying continue MFN.

Q. You're satisfied that these students, who now say that they favor the policy, aren't doing that under some duress since the crackdown by the regime in Beijing?

A. No, because I think you wouldn't see all these other interests out there if it was simply that. Maybe there's some pressure on them; I don't know. But that's not what our Ambassador is telling me.

---

[1]Text from Weekly Compilation of Presidential Documents of May 28, 1990.

U.S.-Philippine Exploratory Talks on U. S. Military Facilities

JOINT PRESS STATEMENT ISSUED BY THE U.S.-PHILIPPINES PANELS TO THE EXPLORATORY TALKS, MAY 18, 1990[1]

Representatives of the Government of the Republic of the Philippines and the Government of the United States of America, led by Secretary of Foreign Affairs Raul S. Manglapus and Special Negotiator Richard Armitage, respectively, have engaged in a productive week of exploratory talks. The talks were characterized by complete candor and amicability, as befits friends and allies.

On the subject of the termination date of the 1947 Military Bases Agreement, as amended, the Philippine panel presented the U.S. Special Negotiator with a diplomatic note stating that the agreement will be terminated as of September 16, 1991, and cannot be extended. The Foreign Secretary explained that this action was consistent with the 1987 constitution of the Philippines and the 1966 Ramos-Rusk exchange of notes. The U.S. Special Negotiator responded that the United States holds to its interpretation of the language of the 1947 agreement, as amended, according to which one year notice of termination could not be served until after September 16, 1991, but stated that this difference of view need not stand in the way of efforts to explore the future of Phillipine-U.S. relations.

Regarding the performance of obligations undertaken by both countries under the provisions of the 1988 Memorandum of Agreement (MOA) and the Reagan-Acquino letter of 17 October 1988, the Philippine panel expressed its concerns related to what it considers as shortfalls in American compensation to date relative to the "best efforts" pledges made by the U.S. in 1988. The U.S. panel explained its position that it was fulfilling its commitments including its continuing best efforts. Both sides engaged in extensive technical discussions which clarified each delegation's understanding of the other's positions and

resolved some points. The U.S. Special Negotiator also advised the Foreign Secretary of a series of ongoing efforts to provide excess U.S. military equipment, the possibilities of provisional medical equipment to the military, and additional food aid for the Philippines and three other countries. Additionally, the U.S. panel received a list of medical equipment desired for civilian government hospitals in the Philippines, and has undertaken to explore the possibilities of providing such equipment.

The Philippine side acknowledged these ongoing U.S. efforts to provide additional assistance, which the Philippine government will apply to the FY 1990 base compensation package of the 1988 MOA. The Phillipine government views these allocations in the following manner:

A. The excess military equipment to cover the amount of $59.9 million for the military assistance component and $14.7 million for the unused FMS [Foreign Military Sales] credits component, both the FY 1990;

B. The additional food aid (possibly rice and in grant) and medical equipment, instruments and supplies for the Philippine civilian government hospitals for the gap in the food aid and development assistance component which is presently in the amount of $28.8 million;

C. The medical equipment, instruments and supplies, for the Philippine civilian government hospitals to cover the Berry Amendment component for FY 1990 in the amount of $30 million; and

D. For ESF [Economic Support Fund], the U.S. administration shall continue to make its best efforts to provide the full level of ESF assistance set forth in the Reagan-Acquino letter of October 1988, including giving high priority to the allocation of fund[s] to the Phillipines should the assistance come from unearmarked funds,

The U.S. panel notes that it does not agree with the views of the Phillipine panel regarding the perceived shortfalls.

The Philippine and U.S. panels have established a joint technical committee to monitor ongoing efforts to implement the 1988 Memorandum of Agreement and the other assistance efforts which were discussed. The Foreign Secretary and the U.S. Special Negotiator will exchange letters regarding the creation of the joint technical committee and the respective terms of reference for each side.

The panels agreed that both countries were attempting to fulfill their responsibilities and deal with each other in a spirit of good faith and mutual trust. In view thereof, and the satisfactory resolution, to date, of the concerns which have arisen in relation to the implementation of the 1988 MOA, the two panels have decided to move on to discussions of the nature of U.S.-Philippine relations in the future. These discussions could include consideration of a new agreement concerning friendship, cooperation and security on the basis of a new relationship between the Phillipines and the U.S. and in the light of the changing global environment.

FINAL STATEMENT BY U.S. SPECIAL NEGOTIATOR RICHARD ARMITAGE, MANILA, MAY 18, 1990[1]

Mr. Foreign Secretary, Secretary Bengzon, distinquished members of the Philippine delegation, colleagues and friends:

When I first addressed you during our opening ceremonies last Monday, I stated that although we on the American panel have very definite opinions about how a future American presence on the Philippine military bases might best be managed, we are nevertheless keenly aware of whose bases they are and whose country this is.

The distinquished Foreign Secretary proved my point by presenting me and my Government with a termination notice right at the opening bell. Although we have a legal difference of opinion concerning termination of the 1947 Military Bases Agreement, there can be no question that in this country the Constitution of the Philippine Republic reigns supreme.

There were several points of a similar nature that I made in my opening statement, all of which can be boiled down to one central proposition: with respect to U.S. facilities on Philippine military bases, the Government of the Philippines will make the final decision. President Bush has made it very clear

that the United States will exercise good faith in the discussions of our future security relationship, but that we will leave if we are not wanted.

To all those Filipinos who contacted us during the week, whether at the hotel, the Embassy or elsewhere, with acknowledgement of the different tone of my opening statement, thank you for your sentiments and thank you for your interest. Although a negotiator must prepare for the worst and assume opposition at every turn, I am mindful of the fact that there are those who do support a continued U.S. presence on Philippine military bases. Notwithstanding this support, for which we are grateful, I must tell the Filipino friends of the United States that in the words of folksinger Bob Dylan, "The times they are a'changin'." I cannot predict the shape or even the likelihood of a future bases agreement between our two countries. I am certain, however, that whatever emerges will full reflect the strength, vitality and relevance of

---

President Bush has made it very clear . . . that we will leave if we are not wanted.

---

democracy in the Philippines.

Whenever discussions of this nature take place, very high priority is assigned, in the end, to selecting the best words to describe the atmospherics. We all know, for instance, that words such as "frank," "direct," and even "comradely" usually mask difficult discussion. Although our respective press spokesmen are expected and indeed required to produce descriptive adjectives about atmospherics, I propose instead to be a bit more specific.

The Philippine panel expressed to the U.S. side its deep disappointment with certain funding decisions made by the U.S. Government in the wake of the 1988 Memorandum of Agreement. It did so with dignity and in great detail. Although the Filipino criticism of our perceived performance was direct and pointed, it was not emotional or ad hominem. It represented, in short, the way friends commnunicate a sense of disappointment.

For our part, we received the criticism of our Filipino friends in the spirit it was given and reacted, I believe, appropriately. We pointed out that we are doing exactly as President Reagan committed the executive branch of the U.S. Government to do in his October 17, 1988 letter to President [Corazon] Acquino: We are exerting our best efforts to bring to fruition certain assistance levels for the Philippines. The U.S. side reaffirms that it will, between now and September 30, 1991, continue to exert its best efforts in the context of the Reagan-Acquino letter.

I must admit, however, to a sense of disappointment that the issues of compensation so dominated our time during these talks.

It is, in fact, the very idea of a direct relationship between U.S. facilities on Philippine bases and U.S. aid levels that has produced this unfortunate "shortfall" controversy. The plain fact is that U.S. assistance to the Philippines not linked to military facilities has increased dramatically since the EDSA revolution. The magnitude of this increase far outstrips any of the numbers used to describe the so-called "shortfall."

Yet my sense of disappointment with the pervasiveness and persistence of this compensation controversy has only marginally to do with the specific issues discussed this week in Manila. The U.S. taxpayer, the U.S. Congress and the administrations of Presidents Reagan and Bush have, in my view, nothing to be ashamed of when it comes to financial sacrifices for the sake of democracy and economic development in the Philippines. I deny the assertion that the United States has somehow fallen short in this respect. My sense of disappointment and frustration stems instead from the inappropriateness of constructing a renewed strategic relationship between our two peoples if it is simply on the basis of money.

I do not wish to be misunderstood on this point in particular. I am not suggesting that U.S. assistance to the Philippines be deemphasized. What happened in this country in 1986, just as what happened in Eastern Europe and Nicaragua in 1989, is most worthy of American support as a matter of fundamental national interest. In World War I, President Wilson told the American people they were fighting to "make the world safe for democracy."

In 1990 we Americans have come to understand that the spread of democracy makes the world a safer place for us and for all. When people in countries as far apart as the Philippines and Poland liberate themselves from autocracy and oppression, Americans have an obligation to help, an obligation rooted in enlightened self-interest. Our relationship with the Philippines transcends the issue of base rights and goes to the central tenet of our policy: unqualified supporrt for the leadership of President Corazon Acquino and the permanence of democracy in the Philippines.

My mission today, however, has little to do with the spread of democracy. My charter from President Bush is limited very specifically to the matter of the future status of U.S. military facilities on Philippines bases. I will tell you now that the future of these facilities hinges on how Filipinos choose to answer the following question: Of what value are these facilities to the Philippines? If the answer is expressed only in monetary terms, the American military presence cannot be sustained. It will be gone not because of a shortfall in U.S. support for democracy and economic development in the Philippines. Rather, it will be gone because, in a strategic sense, money alone cannot cement friendships or confirm alliances. When it comes to Filipino honor and sovereignty, my bedrock belief is that, in the final analysis, money is not the measure. Whatever cynical reactions this assertion may produce in certain quarters, this is the position I take.

I would like to conclude my remarks by conveying some sense of where I think we are in this process. Although I am filled with uncertainties, I start with the proposition that there exist certain basic, immutable facts. There is God, who, by giving us the ability to think and act freely, has created us in his image. There is the Philippines and there is the United States. There is an Asian-Pacific world in which these two countries are fated to coexist. There is a deeply rooted friendship that exists between the peoples of these two countries. Of all the forgoing, I am absolutely certain.

I am less certain however about that which awaits us in the coming years. What is to become of Philippine-U.S. friendship as we approach the 21st century? I do not have the answer. I do not think that any of us present, today, in this place, has the answer either. Together, let us find and, if need be, create an answer fully in harmony with our respective and common needs. I suggest we begin today.

Thank you, Mr. Secretary, and your distinguished colleagues, for all of the courtesies that you have extended to me and my colleagues. Thank you, sir, for your friendship that you have all conveyed. We find ourselves satisfied with the outcome and look forward to our future endeavors.

---

[1]Provided to news correspondents by Department of State spokesman Margaret Tutwiler.

Europe and America: Past and Future

by Helmut Kohl, Chancellor of the
Federal Republic of Germany

*Speech at Harvard University, June
7, 1990.*[1]

I deem it an honor to be able to address
you here today. This site is of special
symbolic significance for a German: 43
years ago George Marshall delivered
here his famous speech initiating the
reconstruction program for Europe. It
was the American response to a momentous challenge — generous and far-
sighted. Thirty-five years ago Konrad
Adenauer, the first Chancellor of the
Federal Republic of Germany, gave a
speech here. A few weeks earlier the
three Western powers had revoked the
Occupation Statute. The Federal
Republic of Germany had acquired its
sovereignty and become an equal
partner in the community of free nations. Against this background, today's
ceremony affords me a special opportunity to thank the American nation for
everything that it has done for the
benefit of Germany and Europe in the
past years and decades.

This is a time of joy, pride and
gratitude. The vision of Germany's and
Europe's freedom and unity is becoming reality. The dream of a free, peaceful and just world will materialize,
provided that we do not relax our common efforts. This dream is linked particularly closely to the ideals of the
American nation. The people in
Central, Eastern and Southeastern
Europe rebelled against dictatorship
with the words. "We are the people!"
Who was not reminded of the splendid
introductory words to the American
Constitution: "We the People"!

In many countries, the people have
smashed the chains of dictatorship, including my fellow countrymen in the
GDR [German Democratic Republic].
The unification of Germany is now
under way. It is a victory of the right to
self-determination. This is a cause for
joy just as much for our American
friends as for ourselves. The Americans
in particular have always struggled
against people being kept in tutelage by
foreign powers. In fact, the ideal of self-
determination is the true source of the
American nation.

The Legacy of George Marshall

For more than 40 years, the division of
Europe was a major cause of the tensions in East-West relations. Overcoming this division thus serves the goal of
peace. The unification of Germany will
in addition impart a strong impetus to
the process of European integration,
which will result not least in an
economic upswing from which many
will benefit. All in all, German unity will
be a gain in human, political and
economic terms not only for us Germans, but also for our neighbors and
friends.

When George Marshall delivered
his famous speech here at Harvard,
Europe lay in ruins. It was on the verge
of bleeding to death from the consequences of the war unleashed by the
Nazi tyranny. Left to its own devices,
Europe was too weak to defend itself
against Stalin's expansionary aspirations. Here in Harvard, George
Marshall's speech initiated one of the
great success stories

---

*By the end of this century, the
cornerstone will have been laid
for a United States of Europe.*

Today we face another historic challenge. We must overcome the economic
and ecological devastation and the
moral crisis in Eastern Europe. We
must firmly anchor democracy in a part
of the world where dictatorship
prevailed for decades — for over 57
years in the case of my fellow
countrymen in the GDR. Forty-three
years ago the primary objective was to
send a signal for overcoming despair
and hopelessness. Today we are about
to give effect to the grand vision which
George Marshall, too, had in his time:
At long last the people and nations in
Eastern Europe are to be able to live as
we in Western Europe have been able
to do for decades, above all thanks to
American assistance.

By virtue of America's assistance,
the Europeans are today in a position to
perform a major part of the necessary
reconstruction work through their own
efforts. But for this, too, we need continued partnership with our American
friends. If Europe and America combine their intellectual and material
resources for this task, they will invest in
their common future. It is an investment
whose yield will benefit all of us. This investment is therefore dictated not only
by solidarity, but also by common sense.
It is in our joint interest that flourishing
regions should again emerge in Central,
Eastern and Southeastern Europe and
that freedom, democracy and human
rights be established there, too, forever.
I cordially ask our American friends to
participate actively in this peace
enterprise.

In the past few weeks and months,
the United States has responded to the
changes in Europe and Germany with
exemplary foresight. In the context of
German-American partnership, close
cooperation and friendship with President Bush mean a great deal to me.
Above all I rate highly the keen awareness of historic opportunities that has
guided the U.S. government's actions.
Friendship proves its worth particularly
in difficult times. My message today is
this: German-American friendship is a
decisive prerequisite for Europe and
America managing to cope in unison
with the tasks of the future. And I am
certain that if we cultivate and expand
this friendship, we shall also be jointly
successful.

A United States of Europe

Europe will remain America's closest
partner, but the old continent will
change its appearance. By the end of
this century, the cornerstone will have
been laid for a United States of Europe.
I am firmly determined that this federation should not be an exclusive club confined to the present members of the
European Community. We are thus
acting in the spirit of those great men
and women who, after 1945, set about
bringing together the people and nations of the free part of Europe.
Vicariously for many I would like to
mention Winston Churchill and Konrad

Adenauer, Robert Schuman and Jean Monnet, Alcide de Gasperi and Paul-Henri Spaak — and not least eminent Americans like Harry S. Truman and James Byrnes.

The overwhelming success and appeal of European unification have made a decisive contribution to the change of outlook in Central, Eastern and Southeastern Europe. The hopes of the people and nations there are based on what has been achieved in Western Europe. The United States of Europe must therefore be open to countries like Austria, Sweden, Norway and Finland. It must not exclude the Poles, Czechs and Slovaks or Hungarians or any other Europeans who want to joint this federation. The United States of Europe will thus form the core of a peaceful order in which the nations of the old continent finally overcome former rivalry, chauvinist thinking and mutual prejudice. The present-day relations between Germany and France set an example in this respect.

Europe of the future will be a continent of diversity that affords the regions and nations new opportunities for self-development. This naturally includes above all the protection of ethnic, cultural and religious minorities. Europe of the future will be a continent of open borders. We Germans do not want to couple the unity of our fatherland with the displacement of existing borders. The border between Germany and Poland remains inviolable, but in future it should no longer separate Germans and Poles from one another. It must become open like the border between Germany and France. Without German-Polish friendship it will not be possible to complete the development of a free Europe.

Open borders also imply that the Europe of the future must not seal itself off by protectionist measures. Only free world trade generates prosperity. This is in the enlightened self-interest of everyone. And it would be a disservice to the partnership between Europe and America if, in the economic sphere, our relations were marked by unfair competition and short-sighted egoism on whichever side.

The Transatlantic Partnership

Despite different views on individual matters, Europe's and America's vital interests continue to be identical. We must therefore remain capable of jointly protecting our freedom. Although we are emerging from the shadow of the East-West conflict and are making progress in the field of disarmament, who can rule out risks in the future? Therefore vigilance is the price of our common freedom, as NATO's motto points out. Precisely because it does not derive its raison d'etre from any hostile stereotyping, the Atlantic alliance will remain in existence, though in a changed form and with an enlarged agenda.

The political dimension of European-American partnership is now becoming even more prominent. In the period ahead we must therefore intensify political coordination between Europe and America - if necessary, via new institutions. We have gained favorable experience in this respect within European political cooperation. We should use this experience to a greater extent for the transatlantic dialogue. It is more essential than ever for the Americans and Europeans to achieve the greatest convergence possible on important issues of foreign policy. This applies both to aspects of East-West relations and to subjects that move up the agenda for the future.

The Atlantic separates us only in a geographical sense. Even more than in the past we now have the opportunity to devote our combined energies to new goals. Transatlantic relations are today denser than ever. America will continue to have a firm position in Europe. It has a triple anchorage there: via Atlantic alliance, via increasing cooperation between the United States and the European Community and via America's active role in the CSCE process.

Agenda for the Future

On the threshold to the 21st century, the agenda for the future contains many topics that we can only tackle by a full-scale effort by all free nations. Europeans and Americans must together elucidate their vision of a better world in which coming generations can thrive. Let me name but one example that is particularly close to my heart: the protection of man's natural environment. Together we must strive for a world in which life in all its forms is respected. Creation was entrusted to mankind, and we bear responsibility for it. The destruction of tropical rain forests and the hole in the ozone layer over the Antarctic affect people in both America and Europe, and on all other continents. The threat of global climatic changes impinges on the vital nerve of all nations. The growth of the world's population compels us to use nonrenewable resources economically and to develop environmentally compatible sources of energy. We therefore need a worldwide partnership for the sake of the environment.

The splendid and dramatic developments in Europe and Germany must not divert our attention from the problems of the Third World. We must therefore continue to frame a development policy which energetically supports the poorest and weakest and above all helps them to help themselves. This is also an investment in our common future. With this in mind I proposed at world economic summits, for the first time at Toronto in 1988, that environment protection be linked to debt problems. For instance, debt relief for Third World countries should more often be made contingent on the funds released being used for tangible environmental measures wherever possible.

The tremendous damage to the environment in Eastern Europe proves that economic and ecological considerations can be reconciled only in a free and open society. This is another reason why we must not relax our struggle for human rights and self-determination. In furthering the cause of freedom, encouraging success has been achieved in Europe or South and Central America, but in many parts of the world, people are still arbitrarily arrested, humiliated, tortured or even murdered. They deserve our solidarity, and we shall continue to do everything possible to assist them.

Finally, allow me to address a few words to the young people on both sides of the Atlantic: It is my generation's duty to leave behind a world in which you feel at ease, a world in which more freedom prevails, peace is more secure and natural resources are conserved and protected more effectively. Soon you will yourselves bear responsibility. But you will need partners. It is therefore essential that young Europeans and

Americans get to know each other better right now.

Across generations a recognition must be maintained: freedom imposes duties. And let me add that education also imposes duties. This applies particularly to the graduates of such an outstanding university as Harvard. Studying here is a privilege. But such a privilege also implies special responsibility: that of placing your talents and knowledge at the service of your fellow human beings. At the end of this century, which has seen so much suffering and misery, today's young generation has a chance like hardly any preceding one: the chance of a full life in peace and freedom. And the young generation has every reason to be optimistic in its pursuit of happiness.

————————

[1]Text from Statements and Speeches, Volume XIII, No. 16, German Information Center, New York.

Department of State Statements on Elections and Violence in Romania

MAY 10, 1990[1]

The Secretary [of State] has asked the U.S. Ambassador to Romania, Alan Green, Jr., to return to Washington this week for consulations regarding the May 20 elections in that country, the first multiparty elections there in over 40 years. The decision has been taken in light of reports of irregularities in the Romanian electoral process which raise questions about whether those elections will be free and fair. Ambassador Green will return to his post before the May 20 balloting.

Among the electoral problems which concern us is the incidence of organized acts of intimidation and harassment directed against some opposition parties and candidates. We have urged the interim Romanian Government to take more vigorous steps to maintain order and to protect the rights of all candidates in these elections. We are also concerned about complaints that several major parties still encounter obstacles in obtaining their fair share of broadcast time on the publicly-controlled radio and television and in distributing their campaign literature through the mails, as well as problems with distributing independent newspapers.

The U.S. has repeatedly stated that free and fair elections on May 20, conducted through a truly secret ballot, are crucial to the further progress of democratization in Romania and to the future of the bilateral relations between our two countries. We call upon all Romanians to conduct themselves as befit the citizens of an emerging democracy and, especially, to vote on May 20. They now have the power and the responsibility to choose who will lead them in the years to come.

MAY 25,1990 [1]

The United States has concluded that serious distortions and irregularities marked the Romanian electoral process which unfairly favored the National Salvation Front to the disadvantage of its competitors.

These included organized acts of intimidation and violence directed primarily against opposition candidates and their sympathizers, the Front's virtually unrestricted use of government resources for campaign purposes, and impediments to equitable access by the major opposition parties to public television and to assured deliveries nationwide of opposition campaign literature and independent newspapers. There has also been concern that secret police activity marred the electoral process.

The government, led by the National Salvation Front, bore direct responsibility for the conduct of the electoral process and in our view failed to take sufficiently vigorous steps to remedy the irregularities or to discourage acts of intimidation and violence that took place during the campaign.

Irregularities occurring on election day included instances of inadequate physical control over ballot boxes, inappropriate "assistance" to some voters inside the voting booths, and questions over the status of certain printed ballots and voter identity cards. Although these conditions also concerned us, we observed that the overwhelming number of Romanians were able, freely and without visible coercion, to cast their ballots. We lack substantiating evidence that these voting day irregularities were of sufficient weight to have altered the outcome of the elections.

The Romanian people have given their new leaders a mandate for more democracy. As one U.S.-based observer team said, the burdens and responsibilities for democratization now fall fully on the shoulders of the National Salvation Front. The Front will have to establish its democratic credentials, to the satisfaction of the Romanian people and the international community, by building a pluralistic, democratic political environment in which all opinions and parties can compete freely and equally. They must write a democratic constitution, establish a meaningful political dialogue with the opposition parties, ensure continued respect for human rights and the rule of law, encourage the growth of independent print and broadcast media free from government control, and bring the large security apparatus finally under democratic control.

The democratic process means more than just a single vote count. The United States is committed to working with Romania to see the process of democratization through to its successful attainment.

The Department wishes to express its special appreciation to the Presidential Election Observer Mission, the international delegations organized by the National Democratic Institute for International Affairs and the National Republican Institute of International Affairs, and the other American and international observers for their support for democracy.

JUNE 14, 1990 [1]

The United States condemns in the strongest possible terms the Romanian government's brutal suppression, including the use of deadly force, of legitimate forms of dissent and political protest. We deplore as well government-inspired vigilante violence by workers and others against Romanian citizens. These actions, as well as the attacks by protesters on government buildings and the Romanian television station depart from the commonly accepted norms of democracy and the rule of law. These violent events follow elections held less than one month ago which were intended to bring democracy to post-Ceausescu Romania, and take place at a time when Romania is seeking to reintegrate itself into the Helsinki process through its participation in the CSCE Conference on the Human Dimension in Copenhagen.

We call upon [Romanian] President Iliescu to use his electoral mandate to resolve the present crisis peacefully, establish the rule of law and implement his stated commitment to genuine democratization. Restraint, tolerance and good-faith democratic measures are now urgently required if Romania expects to promote the goals of the December Revolution.

Threats to the democratic process in Romania are not only of concern to the United States. They jeopardize the goal of a Europe whole and free. We call upon the democratic nations of Europe to make their concerns known to the Romanian leadership and encourage all Romanians to avoid violence. The success of Romania's democratic experiment will require encouragement and support from abroad.

June 15, 1990 [2]

Actions authorized by President Iliescu and his government in the past few days strike at the very heart of Romanian democracy.

Organized attacks against the offices of opposition political parties and independent newspapers and beatings of political figures who pursued democratic goals through peaceful means, by workers summoned to Bucharest by President Iliescu himself, threaten to return Romania to authoritarianism.

We call upon President Iliescu and his government to halt immediately any further action against Romania's fledgling democratic process.

Specifically, he should clear all worker vigilantes from the streets and

publicly pledge that they will not be encouraged or allowed to return, provide public guarantees of safety for leaders and members of all political parties and those who exercise their legitimate right of expression and dissent, and reopen all independent newspapers and magazines attacked on Thursday.

Further, we urge President Iliescu and his government to engage opposition parties and other groups in a dialogue to repair the damage to Romanian democracy caused by the events of recent days.

Until the democratic process is restored, the United States has decided to withhold all nonhumanitarian economic support assistance that Romania might be eligible for.

Ambassador Alan Green, who was in Washington this week on consultations, has been instructed to return to Bucharest to convey to the Romanian leadership the seriousness of our cconcerns about recent events.

---

[1]Provided to news correspondents by Department of State spokesman Margaret Tutwiler.
[2]Provided to news correspondents by Department of State deputy spokesman Richard Boucher.

Alexander Dubcek on the "Prague Spring"

Excerpt from address by Mr. Dubcek, Chairman of the Czechoslovak Federal Assembly, at The American University, May 13, 1990. [1]

...Despite our contribution to European history, to European culture, our country began to fear a loss of identity after August 21, 1968. An act of violence and malevolence relegated us to the role of a pawn in a great game of politics. Once again, we were reminded that our country lies at the front line, at the frontier of the Cold War.

"Prague Spring" was to be our contribution to the history of politics. We would contribute a pinch of tolerance and freedom, a bit of cooperation between nations, striving to build a socially just society—what we called "socialism with a human face." Today, the phrase "democracy with a human face" is the buzz word.

Our people's resistance without violence to a far greater force of tanks and armed forces, their great moral strength, has left an impression on Europe, who was terrified at the thought of military conflict, and of Soviet soldiers, whose armaments stood against the great moral strength of the Czech and Slovak people.

As I stood in front of the television cameras, debating with General Jer-

shov, one of the leaders of the August 1968 attack, I again felt our people's moral victory. 1968 was a crucial year, and all of Eastern Europe and even the Soviet Union were deeply affected by its tremendous consequences.

In a letter he wrote to me shortly before his death, Andrei Sakharov wrote: "The year 1968 influenced my fate. Spring brought hope...But it is impossible to think without bitterness of the years that followed on the heels of the storm of 1968, years during which time stood still. But fire burned beneath the ashes. I am convinced that the breath of truth that the Czechs and Slovaks inhaled...is the prologue to today's bloodless revolutions in the countries of Eastern Europe."

If that is indeed true, then "Prague Spring" is part of the history of Europe. And in this sense, "Prague Spring" is the source of ideas that have resulted in the revolutionary changes presently taking place in our country, which are taking place in the Soviet Union, in Eastern Europe...

---

[1]Text provided by the Office of Media Relations, The American University, Washington, D.C.

Suspension of Talks with the PLO

Excerpts from President Bush's Press Conference, Huntsville, Alabama, June 20, 1990. [1]

Based on the recommendation of the Secretary of State, I have decided to suspend the dialogue between the United States and the PLO [Palestine Liberation Organization], pending a satisfactory response from the PLO of steps it is taking to resolve problems associated with the recent acts of terrorism, in particular, that May 30th terrorist attack on Israel by the Palestinian Liberation Front, a constituent group of the PLO.

By way of background, on December 14, 1988, Yasser Arafat, speaking on behalf of the PLO Executive Committee, recognized Israel's right to exist. He accepted the United Nations Security Council Resolutions 242 and 338, and he renounced terrorism. Now, subsequently, the United States announced that because the PLO had met our longstanding conditions for dialogue we would begin a substantive dialogue with the PLO. And at the time, we applauded Chairman Arafat for taking these essential steps. And we have conducted such a dialogue with the PLO through our Embassy in Tunis.

Over the past 18 months, representatives of the United States and the PLO regularly exchanged views about the political and security situation in the region. On balance, we believe that these exchanges contributed to progress in the peace process.

On May 30th, 1990, the Palestinian Liberation Front attempted a seaborne terrorist infiltration into Israel. Palestinian Liberation Front Leader Abu Abbas represents the PLO on the Executive Committee of the PLO. The size of the force and the geographical target area strongly indicate that civilians would have been the target.

That day we issued a statement deploring this attempted terrorist attack. On May 31st, we raised this incident with the PLO in Tunis. We told them that it could not avoid responsibility for an attempted terrorist action by one of its constituent groups and needed to take steps to deal with the matter by condemning the operation, disassociating itself from it, and by also beginning to take steps to discipline Abu Abbas, the perpetrator.

We've given the PLO ample time to deal with this issue. To date, the PLO has not provided a credible accounting of this instance or undertaken the actions outlined above. The U.S. does take note of the fact that the PLO has disassociated itself from this attack and issued a statement condemning attacks against civilians in principle, but as we previously indicated this is not sufficient — this alone is not sufficient.

The U.S.-PLO dialogue has demonstrated that it can advance the Arab-Israeli peace process. And at the same time, the dialogue is based on the assumption that the PLO is willing to abide by the conditions it accepted in December, 1988, including renunciation of terror.

At any time that the PLO is prepared to take the necessary steps, we are prepared to promptly resume the dialogue. In the meantime, we would hope and expect that the peace process would proceed as intended and without delay. We remain committed to the pursuit of a comprehensive settlement of the Arab-Israeli conflict and to a just and lasting peace. And as is often stated, it is our view that such a peace must be based on those two resolutions, U.N. Resolution 242 and 338, and the principle implicit therein of territory for peace, and provide for Israel's security and Palestinian political rights.

We believe that Palestinian participation is vital to any successful process and that there are real opportunities for Palestinians in this process. We strongly hope that Israelis, Palestinians, and the Arab States will recognize these opportunities and take the necessary steps to create an environment in which a viable peace process can thrive.

We denounce violence in the area and call upon all parties to eschew violence and terror and opt instead for dialogue and negotiation. We're prepared to continue working with the parties toward this end.

I'll be glad to take a few questions.

Q. Mr. President, doesn't your announcement of today, coupled with Secretary Baker's words that the Israelis should call the White House when they're serious, mean that the U.S. position in the peace process, though, in the Middle East is dormant right now?

A. John [John Mashek, Boston Globe], it's not moving forward right now. And the offer still stands. I have sent a letter to Prime Minister Shamir [of Israel]. I have very specifically asked questions that relate to seriousness about the peace process. But I would like to see the peace process move forward. Nothing herein should indicate anything different. Because here we are simply taking a narrow shot at terrorism.

*　　　*　　　*

Q. Is it true that none of our allies, with the exception, of course, of the Israelis, wanted you to suspend these talks with the PLO? And you said you have given the PLO enough time. I mean, why now? Is there some reason it's happening today?

A. No, I don't think of any reason today, and I didn't set in my mind x numbers of days. But, John [John Cochran, NBC News], I think there will be a lack of agreement with what I've done here on the part of some of our strongest allies. And I know this is true on the part of some of the most reasonable and moderate Arab States. But I would simply remind them of the conditions upon which the dialogues started in the first place, and I would also remind them that if they look at this statement and remedial action is taken the dialogue from the U.S. side can promptly be restored.

Q. Mr. President, at the same time you're having this trouble with the PLO, you've also got a new Israeli government that has an avowed policy of settling in the West Bank more rapidly than it's been settled in the past. How are you going to deal with that government? What's your policy going to be on aid toward that government, specifically on housing guarantees for Soviet emigrants?

A. Jerry [Gerald Seib, Wall Street Journal], my position on settlement in the territories is probably as well known as anything. And our policy is not to have new settlements, and our policy is certainly not to finance new settlements. Is that responsive, or is there another part to your question?

Q. This is a specific question now, though, of whether we'll provide housing guarantees for Soviet emigrants — $400 million.

A. But not to settle in the post-'67 territory — in the territories beyond the '67 lines.

Q. Are you going to seek specific new guarantees from this new government that that won't happen with that money?

A. Well, I will, and I hope I'm successful. But I think there is no question that the Shamir government knows my position on this, knows the standing position of the United States.

* * *

Q. Back on the PLO. One of the theories passed around in your own administration was that the intent of this terrorist attack was to derail the peace process. Are you at all concerned that by suspending the dialogue you're playing into the hands of the hardliners like Abu Abbas? And is there also a danger—

A. Yes. Let me stop you there just to respond so I don't forget the question. Yes, I am concerned about that. Go ahead.

Q. Well, if you're so concerned about it, then why did you take the stand?

A. Well, because we had to weigh the whole question; and the question was complicated by the fact that there were three specific undertakings, one of which, a very important one in my view, has clearly been violated. It's not an easy call because I know some feel that the PLO dialogue is totally unproductive, and as I indicated in this statement, I don't. The question up here was, Well, do our allies — will they agree with the steps that I've taken here in Huntsville today? And the answer is no; some of them will not agree because they do feel that the dialogue has kind of helped calm things in some parts of the Middle East.

So, what the answer to it is, is for the PLO to take the action that I've called for and to satisfy us that those who were responsible will be disciplined

and condemn this specific act. It's not enough to simply reiterate one's concern on terror.

Q. If I may follow up?
A. Please.

Q. Is there a danger, too, that those Palestinians who had put some hope in the dialogue between the PLO and the U.S. might now throw up their hands in desperation and resort to violence?

A. Well, I hope that's not the case, and yet I would refer you to my last paragraph or two of the statements when I did call for no violence. And I think it's fair to say that anytime you're dealing with something as complicated as the Middle East you worry about that. But I hope that's not the case. And I hope they'll see in my statement a rather temperate view here: that we're specific in calling for the condemnation of this particular terrorist act; that once that is done, in keeping with Arafat's undertaking, that we can resume talks.

There has been a frustration, Jim [Jim Miklaszewski, NBC News], in the Arab world that this dialogue has not resulted in more progress. And I understand the frustration. I don't happen to agree with it. I think things are better because we've had the dialogue. But Israel has strongly objected to it; and some Palestinians have been, as we can clearly see, concerned about it. But I believe we ought to try to find a way to get it back at some point.

Q. But the flip side of that coin, if I might: As you grappled with this, did you worry, and are you worried now, that Israel will just take this and say, See, we've been right about the PLO all along, and we won't talk to them?

A. I'm not so troubled on that because I think they will see here that I am not accepting the premise that there is no good to come from talking to the PLO. So, I don't worry too much about that point.

Q. Do you see Mr. Shamir as too hardline, as the kind of leader who is going to say, Well, we were right, and therefore, we'll stay away from the table even longer?

A. Well, I'm hoping that's not the case. And one of the reasons I sent him this long and lengthy letter was to make clear to him that it is our view the peace process ought to go forward. And it's going to be difficult for him, but it must go forward. And it must go forward along the lines of what originally was the Shamir plan, and then it became —

Mubarak [President Hosni Mubarak of Egypt] got interested and he played a useful role in it. Then Jim Baker got involved and has done a heroic job in trying to get the talks going.

So, I hope that the U.S. will have a useful role to play, regardless of the step I've taken here on the PLO, because as we all know, we were not proposing that the PLO be at the table. This was a charge made against us by some in Israel, and that doesn't happen to be the case. And I think the government knows that.

* * *

Q. Mr. President, you specified that the PLO dialogue has been positive and productive, but you haven't really told us in what way. Could you be a little more specific bout that? What productivity do you see in it?

A. I think the very fact we are talking can — and that's one of the reasons I would hope that it can be restored — can eliminate differences. And I would like to feel that the PLO, because of our dialogue, doesn't see us as quite the hostile country that once they did. There's all kinds of small points that are taken up by our Ambassador Pelletreau in Tunis that I think have reduced the levels of misunderstanding.

I don't want to leave you the wrong impression: that I think the dialogue has resulted in a more dynamic peace process. But I do think that it's good, and I think that it encourages moderation within the PLO ranks. I think we lose sight of the fact that Arafat did something that was predicted no Palestinian leader could do when he recognized Israel's right to exist as a state. And some might say, Well, it's about time. And I'm one of them. But that was quite a step forward. It was quite a step forward when he recognized Resolution 242, and I think that was positive. And then I think we've had a chance to solidify those gains, modest though they might have been, through dialogue. But I can't point to the fact that that has really solved the question of Middle East peace. I just feel that talking offers more potential than stiff-arming each other. And yet we can't digest it as long as this terroristic act is sticking in our throat. And properly so, as a country that decries international terrorism.

* * *

Q. Was there not a need here, sir, to not appear to be indulging to the PLO at a time when the administration has been tougher than perhaps any recent administration has been with Israel?

A. That's not what made my decision. And I don't know that we've been tougher. I'm the President of the United States. The United States has a policy. And I'm supposed to, I think, go forward with our policy. And one of the big problems we've had is the question—between ourselves and the Israeli Government—is this question of settlements. But I wouldn't read my decision here to go as follows: He made this decision because he's concerned about a complicated relationship with Israel at this point. That's not why I made the decision, but some may read it as that. But we're staying with our concept on the peace process, and we are staying with our policy on settlements. And this action that I've taken today is consistent with our policy on antiterror.

Q. Mr. President, do you feel that Israel has committed acts of terrorism when it bombs Palestinians?

A. We spoke out on the recent violence in the Gaza. And please note my last comment calling for peaceful resolution to these questions as opposed to violence and international terror. And that's the way I would respond on that.

---

[1]Text from Weekly Compilation of Presidential Documents of June 25, 1990.

Iran-U.S. Settlement of Small Claims

The following is a Department of State Fact Sheet (Rev.) issued May 14, 1990. [1]

On May 13, 1990, the United States and Iran signed an agreement that will settle claims of less than $250,000 ("small claims") of U.S. nationals against Iran. This agreement will shortly be submitted to to the Iran-United States Claims Tribunal in The Hague. (The Tribunal was established under the 1981 Algiers Accords, which resolved the hostage crisis.) In addition, the agreement will also settle a claim of the United States Government against Iran arising out of certain assistance loans. A single lump sum of $105 million will be paid to the United States from an escrow account held in the Dutch Central Bank once the Tribunal approves the settlement.

Originally 2,795 U.S. small claims were filed with the Tribunal. The Tribunal has decided only 36 of these. Another 72 cases have been settled by the parties, with these settlements approved by the Tribunal. The settlement agreement covers 2,361 small claims still pending at the Tribunal; 10 dismissed by the Tribunal for lack of jurisdiction; 326 filed with the Tribunal but subsequently voluntarily withdrawn, and 415 submitted to the State Department but not filed with the Tribunal because the time limit for filing had expired.

The small claims will be transferred to the Foreign Claims Settlement Commission, an agency within the U.S. Department of Justice. Legislation enacted in 1985 authorized this Commission to receive and determine the validity and amounts of these claims. In due course, the Commission will inform claimants and the public of the procedures and deadlines that will be applicable to its adjudication of claims. The Commission's processing of the claims will be much quicker than the Tribunal's.

There is no connection between the recent hostage release and the small claims negotiations. The settlement negotiations have been ongoing several months. The objective throughout has been to obtain the best possible results for the claimants. The claims talks are exclusively legal and financial in nature.

The Tribunal's caseload of U.S. small claims has now been settled. In addition, to date the Tribunal has previously disposed of 1,310 cases of the 3,856 cases filed: 13 disputes concerning interpretation of the Algiers Accords, 65 claims of Iran or the United States against each other, 797 claims of U.S. nationals against Iran for $250,000 or more ("large claims"), and 435 small claims. The Tribunal has awarded U.S. claimants $1.3 billion. After the small claims settlement, there will remain at the Tribunal 12 interpretive disputes, 11 disputes between the governments, 160 U.S. large claims, 2 Iranian large claims and 108 Iranian small claims. Included, for example, among the remaining claims are claims by U.S. oil companies against Iran and Iran's claim against the U.S. Government arising out of the Iranian Foreign Military Sales Program.

---

[1]Provided to news correspondents by Department of State spokesman Margaret Tutwiler.

The Andean Strategy to Control Cocaine

by Melvin Levitsky

Statement before the Subcommittee on Western Hemisphere Affairs of the House Foreign Affairs Committee, June 20, 1990. Mr. Levitsky is Assistant Secretary of State for International Narcotics Matters. [1]

I welcome the opportunity today to discuss the President's Andean strategy and outline our policy goals and objectives in this area. Cocaine control is our number one priority and our main focus has been, and will continue to be, the Andes.

The President's historic meeting in Cartagena in February signalled a new era in narcotics cooperation with our Andean partners. No longer is the drug issue simply a law enforcement problem. We are working with Colombia, Bolivia and Peru to explore ways to strengthen law enforcement, military, intelligence, and economic cooperation, including opportunities for expanded trade and investment in order to attack the drug trade in a comprehensive way. The President's Andean strategy seeks to bolster these countries' capabilities on all fronts. The programs we have are cooperative programs. We cannot do the job without a strong effort from the Andean countries, the countries that surround the Andean region and the transit countries through which cocaine passes.

The Andean Strategy is a multi-faceted approach to the complex problem of cocaine production and trafficking. Of course, the main front in this war is here at home. But as we work to diminish our own demand for and consumption of drugs, we must also work hard to reduce the international supply; otherwise, it will be more difficult to sustain effective domestic programs in law enforcement, education, prevention and treatment.

In 1989, the administration completed a comprehensive plan to work with the three Andean governments to disrupt and destroy the growing, processing and transportation of coca and coca products within the source countries, in order to reduce the supply of cocaine entering the United States. In September 1989, the President's National Drug Control Strategy directed that a five-year, $2.2 billion counter-narcotics effort begin in FY 1990 to augment law enforcement, military, and economic resources in Colombia, Bolivia and Peru. After careful negotiations between the United States and each of the individual cooperating governments, implementation plans have been prepared to ensure effective use of the assistance.

The administration's $2.2 billion plan provides a cooperative approach for working with the three major Andean governments to disrupt and destroy the growing, processing, and transportation of coca and coca products within the source countries in order to reduce the supply of cocaine from these countries to the United States. Congress has authorized and appropriated funds for the first year of this plan. For FY 90, approximately $230 million in economic, military and law enforcement assistance is being offered to the three Andean countries for counter-narcotics related initiatives. In 1991, we are asking for $423 million, including narcotics-related economic assistance.

Objectives

The Andean strategy has three major objectives.

First, through concerted action and bilateral assistance, it is our goal to strengthen the political will and institutional capability of the three Andean governments to enable them to confront the Andean cocaine trade. With new governments in Colombia and Peru, it will be essential for the U.S. Government to help them address the full range of their drug-related problems .

Second, we will work with the Andean Governments to increase the effectiveness of the intelligence, military and law enforcement activities against the cocaine trade in the three source countries, particularly by providing air mobility for both military and police forces and making sure they are well equipped and trained and that they cooperate in an integrated strategy. It has become clear that the Andean countries cannot conduct effective anti-narcotics operations without the involvement of their armed forces; this is especially true where the traffickers and insurgents have joined forces, as in Peru. Specific objectives include efforts to isolate key coca growing areas, block the shipment of precursor chemicals, identify and destroy existing labs and processing centers, control key air corridors, and reduce net production of coca through aerial application of herbicides when it is effective to do so.

Our **third** goal is to inflict significant damage on the trafficking organizations which operate within the three source countries by working with host governments to dismantle operations and elements of greatest value to the trafficking organizations. By strengthening ties between police and military units and creating major violator task forces to identify key organizations, the bilateral assistance will enable host government forces to target the leaders of the major cocaine trafficking organizations, impede the transfer of drug-generated funds, and seize their assets within the United States and in those foreign nations in which they operate.

Intelligence is a critical component of this strategy. We have worked closely with the intelligence community and law enforcement agencies to focus intelligence collection on these targets. In short, we have developed a strategy that is coherent, focused, and determined.

A major tenet of this strategy is the incorporation of expanded economic assistance beginning in FY 1991 directed toward offsetting the negative economic dislocations we know will occur. This assistance will, in turn, strengthen the political commitment of the three Andean nations to carry out an effective counter-narcotics program. U.S. economic assistance is, in general terms, linked to counter-narcotics performance and to follow-through with economic policy reform. In harmony with the views of the three Andean governments, our direct economic assistance and other initiatives support economic alternatives for those directly involved in the cultivation of and trade in coca. Examples of such assistance include crop substitution and other economic alternative activities, drug awareness, administration of justice, balance of payments and export promotion. The assistance reflects our conclusion, incorporated in the Declaration of Cartagena, that a comprehensive, intensified counter-narcotics strategy must include understandings regarding economic cooperation, alternative development, and encouragement of trade and investment. As vigorous host government programs against the drug trade and economic policy reform initiatives become more effective, our economic assistance will increase in the outyears of the Andean strategy. We are not seeking to impose law enforcement, security or economic assistance on these countries. These are programs that require cooperation and mutual agreement. Our intensive dialogue with the Andeans is refining a common understanding of what is needed and what is possible on both sides.

Role of the Military

Let me deal directly with concerns which have been raised regarding the role of the Andean militaries in the drug war and potential human rights abuses. There is no reason to expect that U.S. military aid will undermine democracy or civilian rule in the Andes. On the contrary, I believe it will help to strengthen both democracy and the international struggle against illegal narcotics for the following reasons:

- U.S. security assistance will be negotiated with and delivered through the civilian governments;
- An impoverished, poorly trained, and equipped military, unable to feed its troops, is far more susceptible to corruption and human rights abuses; and
- The military is far more likely to take a constructive approach if actively engaged in the drug war, as opposed to being left to criticize civilian efforts from the sidelines. The involvement of the military, as in our own country, can bring a significant resource in the war against drugs if properly coordinated and directed by civilian authorities.

I would also like to set out a number of points that address misconceptions that have grown up in recent months about the so-called militarization of the U.S. counter-narcotics effort. Like many slogans, the use of emotionally-charged and sometimes politically motivated words like "militarization" is a gross oversimplification that does not do justice to the effort either to understand or deal with the complex problems of international narcotics.

In the first place, the level of our security assistance is only a part of our total effort. Of some $129 million in counter-narcotics funds requested for Peru in FY91, for example, only about $40 million is for military assistance, and much of that is for maintenance support and infrastructure improvement. Nor do we contemplate large levels of U.S. military presence in the Andes. We have never maintained such a presence and our strategy includes as one of our tenets the determination not to Americanize the effort to work with local governments.

We cannot gloss over [human rights] abuses in some countries... But neither should we succumb to the romantic notion of downtrodden peasant masses protesting in arms against social injustice...

Secondly, our decision to encourage greater participation of the local militaries in the counter-narcotics efforts parallels the evolution of our own policy that projects a greater role for the Department of Defense in the war on drugs in the U.S. Indeed, the militaries in the Andean states are an important component of the governments and their involvement is a sign of greater overall national commitment in dealing with the problem.

Thirdly, while we believe the militaries of the Andean states need to play a more constructive role, we never have nor will force military assistance on these countries. Nor is the assistance we are providing of a nature to create large, new forces in the region. We are developing the specialized skills and units required to conduct or support meaningful counter-narcotics operations, not creating major combat units. We should remember the immense size of the countries we are dealing with and that the narcotics processing facilities and growing areas are spread over large areas often in remote locations. Narcotics law enforcement units are neither equipped nor trained to address the increasingly paramilitary nature of the problem. Further, as the case of Bolivian military support for counter-narcotics operations demonstrates, military support in some cases can be an effective way to avoid duplicating a parallel military capability within police narcotics enforcement agencies.

The financial resources of the narcotics traffickers, such as those in Colombia, enable them to hire private armies and terrorists on a national and international scale. Their ability to buy manpower and equipment surpasses the police capability and, in some cases, calls into question even the military's ability to respond effectively. These capabilities permit the narco-traffickers to challenge or defy the sovereignty of local governments in a way unprecedented in our experience.

U.S. counter-narcotics policy, therefore, should not be characterized as a "militarized" effort, but rather one that seeks to provide legitimate governments with the tools and assistance to help defend their political sovereignty.

But the problem does not end there. There is now a further complicating factor and that is the degree to which so-called guerrilla organizations are becoming involved in narcotics trafficking, either in providing protection in return for profit or in engaging in the production and sale of coca.

The effort of the U.S. to help these countries deal with "narco-insurgents" has raised the specter of counter-insurgency—specifically, whether the U.S. should engage in supporting Andean militaries, some with past records of human rights abuses, in waging a struggle against insurgent groups which are clearly involved in many aspects of narcotics trafficking. We cannot gloss over past abuses in some countries. We do not support these and never will. But neither should we succumb to the romantic notion of downtrodden peasant masses protesting in arms against social injustice, nor depict organizations like the _Sendero Luminoso_ (Shining Path) of Peru or the FARC (_Fuerzas Amadas Revolucioarias de Colombia_ — Armed Revolutionary Forces of Columbia) in Colombia as champions of human rights. Moreover, these groups are now becoming narcotics traffickers themselves, profiting from the environment of drugs and using drug monies to finance further violence.

In such groups, we are dealing with professional organizations of tight-knit cadres whose record of human rights abuses, indiscriminate bombings of civilian targets, the use of torture, terrorism on a national scale, and of barbaric brutality are plainly part of the public record in Colombia and Peru. While the U.S. attitude toward these problems is well known, the United States has not provided significant financial assistance to any of the Andean nations to deal with these specific problems. We are focusing our effort on counter-narcotics not on counter-insurgency, but we cannot lose sight of the fact that it is the insurgents who have become involved in narcotics and, along with the traffickers, created a militarized situation.

Let me also point out the following. At this point we have not concluded a security assistance agreement with the Government of Peru. We have done some advance planning and held discussions with officials of the Government, but no programs of assistance can go forward without such an agreement. While it is our belief that the narcotics situation in the Upper Huallaga Valley cannot be dealt with effectively without the involvement of the Peruvian military, this is a Peruvian government decision. And, of course, it will be a decision as to whether the counter-narcotics performance of the Peruvian institutions involved in the struggle will justify the provision of economic assistance. Our request for economic assistance for Peru in 1991 is based on the assumption of effective counter-narcotics performance.

Our counter-narcotics work in Bolivia does not create a significant military capability; it, too, focuses on improving the military's ability to support counter-narcotics efforts. This includes improvements in riverine programs by the Andean navies to interdict the flow of precursor chemicals and drugs on Bolivia's waterways.

The involvement of the Colombian military in supporting counter-narcotics law enforcement operations over the past two years proves the effectiveness of this approach. Recently, the Colombian military, using equipment supplied by the United States, with the police seized over 18 tons of cocaine in one transportation complex deep in the Colombian jungle.

It is basic to our policy that human rights remain under continuous review to determine whether government policies justify, reinforce, or call into doubt our continued assistance relationship. State Department human rights reports on Colombia and Peru have been candid in their criticisms, and, in fact, received praise from human rights groups. We will work with the Andean militaries to eliminate human rights abuses as they increase their involvement in anti-narcotics operations. Our training, in fact, will emphasize human rights and civic action.

Involvement of U.S. military personnel and organizations is clearly defined, limited and subject to continuing review. The U.S. military role is to provide support and development of host country capabilities. It will provide training and operational support, materiel, advice, and technological and maintenance support to cooperating nations' counter-narcotics organizations. Defense personnel will not participate in actual field operations.

Contrary to some media reports, the levels of counter-narcotics based economic assistance planned for in the President's Andean strategy outweigh the levels of military assistance being offered. Over the five years that the strategy covers, from FY 1990 to 1994, economic assistance will total over $1.1 billion, versus approximately $676 million in security assistance. Moreover, this does not include other economic assistance such as food aid and trade preferences for the Andean region.

Further Initiatives

We are, of course, living up to the economic commitments made at the Cartagena summit. We are implementing the initiatives contained in the President's November 1 Andean trade package, including working with the countries in the region to develop further initiatives:

— In February, Administration officials met with representatives from the Economic Community, Canada and Japan to discuss ways we can help the Andean countries improve their trade performance.

— In March, the Office of U.S. Trade Representative (USTR) announced that 129 products were accepted for review under the U.S. generalized system of preferences

(GSP) special Andean review. Final results of the review will be announced in July.

— We have also conducted successful technical seminars on the GSP program in Colombia, Bolivia, Peru, Ecuador, and Venezuela to help the Andean countries take full advantage of the GSP. A U.S. team is in the Andes the week of June 18 to conduct seminars on the U.S. textile program.

— We have scheduled a workshop in Washington for the Andean countries the week of July 9 on ways to expand U.S.-Andean trade and investment opportunities.

— We are exploring areas of potential cooperation with the multilateral development banks and have emphasized U.S. support for World Bank efforts in the area of trade policy reform.

— On May 8, the U.S. and Bolivia signed an agreement to establish the U.S.-Bolivia Trade and Investment Council, whose objectives are to monitor trade and investment relations, identify opportunities for expanding trade and investment, and negotiate agreements where appropriate.

— We also renewed our commitment to seek a new International Coffee Agreement (ICA).

— We have offered to accelerate negotiations on tariff and non-tariff measures in the international trade negotiations now ongoing in Geneva. Andean participants have not yet responded to our offer.

In addition to the bilateral aspects of the Andean strategy, we are also working with the international community to gain support for Andean initiatives. The strategy suggests that a consultative mechanism with other developed countries be established to encourage closer coordination of international counter-narcotics efforts. I will be travelling to Europe at the end of this month to further this goal.

We are pleased with the work of the G-7 Financial Action Task Force on money laundering; the U.S. hopes to expand the number of countries that embrace the action recommendations of the task force to ensure that all countries have comprehensive domestic programs against money laundering and cooperate to the maximum extent possible in international money laundering investigations and prosecutions. Narcotics is also on the agenda of the Houston economic summit next month, and there we hope to gain greater G-7 support for precursor chemical control. As our own controls become more effective, the drug traffickers look to Europe and the surrounding countries for supply of these chemicals, and so we must bolster international efforts to limit their use to legitimate industry. Without essential chemicals, cocaine cannot be produced. We have just completed a State-Drug Enforcement Administration (DEA) mission to Europe to promote the control of essential and precursor chemicals. We will be conducting similar missions to Latin American countries.

In closing, I would like to take this opportunity to say that I believe that during the coming year, we and the Andean governments will have many opportunities for progress as we work together to attack all aspects of the cocaine trade. We are optimistic. The price of coca leaf is down in Peru and Bolivia. As a result, in Bolivia voluntary eradication of coca is up—this year has already surpassed last year's total—and increasing numbers of growers are moving out of the illegal industry. DEA laboratory analysis indicates that purity levels of cocaine at both the wholesale and retail levels are down and prices have increased at the wholesale level in many areas throughout the nation. Cartagena ended the argument over who is to blame for the drug crisis; we now have a consensus on the nature of the problems we face and a solidifying common front against the drug trade.

Success will not happen overnight, but we are beginning to see that our efforts are having an impact in the Andes, and on the streets of the United States. Provided we are prepared to sustain our activities and not allow our thinking to be clouded by false analogies and over simplifications, I believe we will continue to make progress toward a goal the American people have made clear that they support.

---

[1]The complete transcript of the hearings will be published by the committee and will be available from the Superintendent of Documents, U.S. Government Printing Office, Washington, D.C. 20402.

Secretary Baker Meets with Central American Presidents

Following is the text of Secretary of State Baker's press conference following meetings with the six Central American Presidents, Antigua, Guatemala, June 18, 1990. [1]

Ladies and Gentlemen, I have a statement and then I'll be delighted to respond to your questions.

As I said to the six Presidents this morning, they have completed I think, an historic summit meeting, and it is a symbol of the changes that are transforming this region. For the first time in history, all of the Presidents attending their summit have been democratically elected. Also, for the first time, the principle subject for discussion is regional economic development, not the resolution of conflicts. And, of course, Panama is attending for the first time.

Here in Antigua, the Presidents have adopted a far-reaching agenda for regional economic integration and development and we congratulate them on this achievement. When President Bush took office this was a region in crisis and many argued that the United States faced only two choices — accommodation to dictatorship or disengagement.

President Bush instead has pursued a new regional policy with four elements. First, support for the regional peace process begun in Esquipulas. Secondly, enlisting the cooperation of the Soviet Union to end the conflicts in this region. Third, engaging our European allies and Japan in support of regional democratization and development. And fourth, building a bipartisan base in the United States for our policy toward Central America.

We believe that this region has an historic opportunity today to realize three goals: democracy, disarmament and development. We also recognize that there are fears in Central America that the United States and the industrial democracies will be diverted by the changes in Eastern Europe and ignore this region at this moment of historic opportunity.

I'm here today at the request of President Bush to make it very clear that the United States will continue to be fully engaged and fully supportive of this regional peace process. That's why we are exploring with Japan, with the European Community, Canada and other industrial democracies, possible ways to achieve more support for democracy and development in Central America. I have discussed these proposals with the six Presidents and they tell me that they welcome this effort. We will continue to consult closely about the best way to proceed.

The bottom line, I think, is this — Central America is poised as never before to consolidate democracy, achieve lasting peace and disarmament, and create the conditions for growth and opportunity in which all of the peoples of this region, particularly the poor, can share.

The United States wants to do everything that it can to help this region's leaders seize this historic opportunity.

Any questions?

Q. An American official today said that he felt that the arms levels in Central America were excessive and pointed to Costa Rica as an example to be emulated in the future. I would like to ask you, Mr. Secretary, if you agree with that and if you think that the help to be offered by the G-24 will have to be preceded by cuts in both levels in armaments and troops in the region?

A. I would not anticipate that the G-24 would expressly condition their willingness to support democracy, disarmament and development, by requiring total disarmament in advance. So I would not see that as an absolute precondition. Costa Rica, of course, has a rich tradition of pursuing democracy and freedom and disarmament and it is a tradition that the United States has supported for many, many years in the past and continues to support.

Remember, there are three goals: democracy, disarmament and development. And in trying to encourage additional support from the G-24, we would be trying to encourage support for all three goals.

Q. I understand that the G-24 is not going to operate on the basis of preconditioning, but there will be some kind of ordering of assistance on the basis of predefined projects. Isn't that right?

A. Yes, and there will be as it appropriately should be, conditionality with respect to G-24 efforts, just as there is conditionality with respect to the efforts the G-24 has made to support democracy and freedom in Eastern Europe. For example, there were certain events in Romania here during the course of the last several days which did not move in the direction of respect for human rights, freedom and democracy. And the G-24, at least for the time being, put on hold or temporarily suspended its efforts with respect to Romania.

Q. In the past, when the United States participated in efforts of this kind, it imposed a number of conditions, one of which was the establishment of democratic regimes. I would like to ask in this case, what requirements the United States intends to impose in order for countries to get assistance and get it on a timely basis, because the pressure of poverty and misery in the countries at this time does not allow them to continue under the present circumstances.

A. First of all, if it was a cooperative effort through the G-24, whatever conditions were imposed would be imposed through the cooperative efforts of the G-24 countries and not just the United States. But, secondly, the United States conditions its assistance now on respect for human rights, freedom, democratic traditions and we make no bones about that. We're quite proud of that, because these are principles that we believe very strongly in. Furthermore, we believe these principles more and more are being adopted by countries around the world, not just in Eastern Europe, not just in Central America, but indeed in Africa and Asia as well.

Q. In order to cooperate in this disarmament effort is the United States willing to reduce its military aid to El Salvador, for instance, and the presence of its military advisors?

A. Well, the United States only has 55 advisors there and that's the same number we had, if I'm not mistaken, when I first came to Washington with President Reagan in 1981. But further to the point of your question—the United States is for the first time willing to condition its military assistance to El Salvador and we are in the process of having discussions with our Congress to that effect now. We should be careful not to interpret that in the wrong way.

There is a major insurgency going on in El Salvador in which some are seeking to reverse the results of the ballot box with bullets and bayonets. That's not our idea of democracy and that's not our idea of an approach to freedom.

Q. Mr. Secretary, you mentioned the Soviet Union and I would like to ask you what might be the political and economic contribution of the Soviet Union to the development of Central America to which the United States and the other countries in the G-24 are going to be contributing?

A. Well, hopefully, the Soviet Union will stop supporting regimes in this hemisphere that support attempts to reverse decisions at the ballot box with bullets and bayonets, as I said a moment ago.

The Soviet Union has indicated to us that they are prepared to do this, and so we hope that's one contribution. We think it was a contribution with respect to what happened in Nicaragua. We've had discussions with the Soviet Union about the prospects of their continuing the assistance to Nicaragua that they furnished during the period of time of the Sandinista government. We make the point that it would be nice to see them support a freely, democratically elected government in this hemisphere since they themselves now profess to support the idea of democratization. We'll see whether or not they're able to do that although they've indicated to us some prospect that they will be able to continue some assistance to this freely elected democratic government in Nicaragua.

---

[1]Department of State Press Release 88, June 18, 1990.

Chile: Agreement Signed in Letelier Case

The following statement was released by the Department of State on June 12, 1990. [1]

Representatives of the Governments of the United States of America and Chile signed yesterday an Agreement setting forth procedures for settlement of the civil claims arising from the deaths of Orlando Letelier and Ronni Moffitt in Washington, D.C. on September 21, 1976. These claims derive from a judgment entered on November 5, 1980 by the United States District Court for the District of Columbia awarding compensation to the families of the victims. The government of the United States has espoused these claims.

Without admitting nor pronouncing itself on the liability of the Chilean State in the matter, the Government of Chile has agreed to make an ex gratia payment to the Government of the United States, to be received on behalf of the families. The ex gratia payment which the government of Chile will make is a frequently used procedure in contemporary international law that will be carried out in accordance with the constitution of Chile.

An international commission, established in accordance with provisions of the 1914 Treaty for the Settlement of Disputes that May Occur Between the United States and Chile, will determine the amount of such compensation. The agreement referring the determination of the amount of compensation to the commission will be submitted to the Chilean Congress for approval.

While this agreement is designed to resolve one of the aspects of the existing dispute between the United States and Chile, that is just compensation for the families of the victims, both Governments recognize that bringing to trial those responsible for the murders of Orlando Letelier and Ronni Moffitt is of the utmost importance.

The Government of Chile reiterates its commitment to cooperate by all the means within its power in clarifying these crimes within the framework and in complete compliance with its legal system.

For its part, the Government of the United States is pleased by the Government of Chile's commitment to seeing justice done in this case, which President Aylwin has described as a "moral obligation" of his government. In addition, the Government of the United States considers this agreement an important step forward which will contribute to a relationship with Chile free of extraordinary legal restrictions or limitations and permit a full range of normal relations.

---

[1]Provided to news correspondents by Department of State spokesman Margaret Tutwiler.

An Agenda to Promote Inter-American Cooperation

by Lawrence S. Eagleburger

Address before the General Assembly of the Organization of American States (OAS), Asuncion, Paraguay, June 5, 1990. Ambassador Eagleburger is Deputy Secretary of State.

Let me begin by expressing my sincere appreciation and praise to you [the assembly president, Paraguayan Foreign Minister Luis Argano] and your government. Appreciation for your generous hospitality and for the highest standards that have characterized the organization of this assembly. Praise for your country's struggle to realize democracy's full promise. Please convey to President [Andres] Rodriguez our deep respect and support.

This, the 100th anniversary of the Inter-American system, is a historic occasion that comes at a time of revolutionary change throughout the world. We find ourselves in the midst of one of those revolutionary outbursts that, as in 1830 and 1848, occasionally have punctuated the course of human events. But there is a difference: the revolution underway today, for the first time in history, is occurring on a truly global scale.

This global revolution has one universal and defining feature: the democratic form of government has come to be recognized as the embodiment of political legitimacy. It is not a revolution that has been imposed from without; rather, the democratic idea has become irresistible precisely because it is now an indigenous force the world over, from Poland to Paraguay, and from China to Chile. It has not triumphed everywhere, to be sure; not all men and women today live under freedom and democracy. But we have reached the point where all are demanding to live under freedom and democracy as their God-given right. Democracy's ideological foes, on the left and the right, have been discredited. The political and economic systems they fashioned stand today in ruins. The Western Hemisphere can justly take pride in having launched the epochal worldwide transition from dictatorship to democracy, first in Argentina, Brazil, Bolivia, and Ecuador, and lately in Chile, Panama, and Nicaragua. Think of the open wounds that still festered in our midst when this assembly last met only seven months ago, and you will realize how far we have traveled toward achieving an unprecedented degree of mutual respect and common purpose among the nations of this hemisphere.

The attention of the world has been drawn in the last year to a similar transformation in Eastern Europe. I know that many in Latin America wonder whether we have become unduly preoccupied with the revolutionary saga now unfolding in the old world. Yet it should be remembered that the United States has been deeply involved in European affairs for the last 50 years. We have been so engaged because it was there that two systems and two military alliances stood poised on the brink of conflict and where the fate of humanity hung in the balance. I know that our friends in this hemisphere will understand and support our continued engagement in Europe to assure that the Cold War is brought to a peaceful and successful conclusion. Surely this is a responsibility we must bear, not only on our own behalf, but in the broader and common interest of all mankind.

The Twin Revolutions

The United States has another, equally compelling responsibility— and that is a responsibility to what [Bolivian] President [Jaime] Paz Zamora so movingly described yesterday as our common home, *"El Hogar de las Americas."* We are, first and foremost, citizens of the Americas, and we fully recognize the significance of the fact that, as President Paz noted, two revolutions have taken place in Latin America, one political and one economic. The conversion of almost the entire hemisphere to representative government and to the principles of rational economic management opens up the possibility of closer ties than we have ever enjoyed between ourselves and our Latin neighbors. It is no accident that President Bush, whose keen interest in Latin America is a secret to no one, asked Ambassador [Carla] Hills to represent him at this historic gathering. The world into which we are moving is one in which national security will be defined less in terms of military strength than in terms of economic well-being. Increasingly, the weapons of war will give way to the building blocks of economic integration and interdependence—trade and investment.

The facts speak for themselves. Any concern about where U.S. interests and attention lie must be weighed against the fact that our two-way annual trade with Latin America today exceeds $100 billion, and that U.S. investment in the region is in excess of $50 billion. In a hemisphere in which we have been engaged, through this organization, for 100 years, it is simply inconceivable that we would turn our backs on our fellow American states. It is equally inconceivable that five nations in the heart of Europe could substitute, in our minds, in our commercial, political, and security relationships and, indeed, in our sympathies, for our many friends in this hemisphere.

There is, however, another factor at work today that, although imperceptible to most observers, already has begun to transform the nature of the relationship between my country and the nations and peoples of the Americas. For what the United States is seeking to accomplish in Europe today and what, I am confident, we will accomplish, is really the closing of an old chapter. It needs to be recognized that if we are successful in this endeavor to end the Cold War once and for all, we will have opened a new chapter in [the] foreign policy of the United States, one in which our attention and our energies inevitably will be drawn toward building, in partnership, a Western Hemisphere of freedom, peace, progress, and prosperity.

Ladies and gentlemen, the ties that bind my country to the nations of this hemisphere—ties of history, geography, and natural affinity—are great indeed. For more than 200 years, we have been the champions— imperfect champions—of democracy. Now that our democratic ideals are triumphing, we face—all of us in this hemisphere face— the monumental challenge of making those ideals work in practice. For the first time, working in partnership with one another and through the Organization of American States [OAS], we, the nations of the Americas, have a unique opportunity to fashion a diplomacy among democracies in pursuit of the consolidation of democracy. The revolutionary changes through which we are passing will require more, not less, of this organization.

The framers of the OAS Charter were forward-looking and visionary. Our charter is not a timid document committed to the status quo. If we are true to its purposes and to our vast potential as a regional community, we will endeavor together:

- to forge our rightful and progressive policy in a world liberated from the authoritarian state and the command economy, taking advantage of increasing global interdependence and competition for markets;
- to address the underlying causes of outstanding conflicts and defeat new threats to peace, such as those created by the traffic in illicit drugs; and
- to cooperate to preserve the natural resources of this hemisphere.

An Agenda for the Future

One hundred and two years ago, U.S. Secretary of State [James] Blaine issued a call for an inter-American Congress and declared the willingness of the United States to "enter into the deliberations of the Congress with the loyal determination to approach any proposed solution . . . as a single member among many coordinate and co-equal states." At that first Inter-American Conference, the United States made eight proposals. To mark that historic occasion, I would like today to propose a new agenda of eight points with the hope that together we may open a new century of inter-American progress.

First, we should recommit ourselves to the OAS as the natural forum for hemispheric dialogue.

The hemisphere is stirring with new life. The OAS must harness its energy, broaden its scope, and deepen its impact. Already, the OAS is showing new strength and demonstrating its great potential. Secretary General [Joao] Baena Soares is leading a critical OAS contribution to the delicate equilibrium of peace, national reconciliation, and demobilization in Nicaragua. The CICAD (OAS Drug Abuse Control Commission) is in the vanguard of international efforts to combat the traffic in

illicit drugs. The Inter-American Commission on Human Rights is forging a new regional consciousness.

For a decade, however, the OAS has been hamstrung by lack of resources. Many members, including the United States, have fallen behind in their payments. Last year the Secretariat was forced to release almost one-third of all personnel. The OAS has become dependent on special voluntary contributions even to support peace in Central America.

This General Assembly has the duty of developing a consensus on a new quota system that will distribute the organization's costs equitably. For my part, I can inform you that the United States shortly will pay more than $20 million to the OAS. With other U.S. payments this year, this means that the Secretariat will have the money it needs to work more effectively for us all. For Fiscal Year 1991, President Bush has requested the money to begin paying U.S. arrearages as well as the full U.S. assessment. Congressional attitudes toward this request will be significantly affected by our success in developing a new quota system.

Second, the consolidation of democracy must be at the top of our agenda.

The great democratic revolution that is sweeping across the Americas has created, fortuitously, the conditions under which we can begin to act as a community that is both sovereign and democratic and, thereby, transcend over time an issue that long has driven this hemisphere and this organization. Building on the OAS Charter's call for a "land of liberty," we can create a "system of liberty." We can, in short, now develop systematic means of ensuring democracy's future in the fullest conformity with the hallowed principles of this organization.

We are on the right track. The OAS observation mission in Nicaragua made an invaluable contribution to a peaceful, democratic transition. It demonstrated the organization's effectiveness, the dedication of its personnel, and the competence and vision of its leadership.

Today, we in the OAS cannot be indifferent or settle for halfway measures when our Haitian brothers and sisters are asking for our help. We must do everything we can to heed Haiti's call for electoral assistance. To aid responses in such cases, the United States sup-

ports the Canadian initiative urging the Secretary General to create a permanent institutional mechanism to coordinate OAS support for democracy.

Third, human rights must remain at the core of our cooperative efforts. At its 30th anniversary last year, Secretary Baker saluted the Inter-American Human Rights Commission as a pioneering organization. It is a well-established, experienced, and unique body, rightfully called the "conscience of the Americas." The United States encourages the commission to expand its activities to include technical assistance and training

Fourth, we must unleash the hemisphere's economic potential.

The triumph of democracy has handed us a unique and historical opportunity to reduce longstanding political and security challenges in this hemisphere to manageable challenges of an economic nature. We must not squander this opportunity, and risk seeing the reemergence of old security challenges by allowing the economic problems that brought down Marxists and dictators to undermine the stability of their democratic successors. Our new democratic order will be blessed with peace and stability only if the fruits of democracy—growth deriving from a free market economy—are available to all.

In just six months, the Uruguay Round of the GATT [General Agreement on Tariffs and Trade] will conclude. We must continue to move toward more open and liberal trading practices. The cost of economic autarky is isolation, stagnation, and decline. Wide-ranging participation in the global economy does not exclude greater regional integration. Our objective must be to increase trade among ourselves even as we work together to open up trade opportunities throughout the world.

We in the United States applaud the courageous efforts underway throughout the region to increase Latin America's global competitiveness. We believe the hemisphere cannot afford to lag behind the free-market revolution if it is to survive and to flourish economically in a world where competition for capital is growing more intense. For our part, we pledge to redouble our efforts to confront and defeat protectionist pressures in our country. We will not counsel freer trade in the Americas while permitting new barriers to trade to arise in the United States.

Fifth, we must commit ourselves firmly to the rule of law. I am referring here not only to this organization's traditional stance against the governmental abuse of freedom but, more particularly, to the emergence of transnational threats to our democratic form of government and to our national sovereignty. Clearly, the most immediate threat to the rule of law today comes from the drug cartels. When we contemplate the great toll in human lives and the frontal assault on the rule of law carried out daily by the drug cartels, we should rise as one in indignation. And we should rise in homage to the people of Colombia who last week again defied the cartels to elect a new president in free, multiparty elections.

In February, the summit attended by the presidents of Bolivia, Colombia, Peru, and the United States gave birth to a powerful new anti-drug consensus. In April, the CICAD brought together attorneys general and ministers from throughout the hemisphere to press for ratification of the 1988 U.N. Anti-Narcotics Treaty and approve model legislation to control chemicals and machines used in the manufacture of cocaine. Last week, CICAD developed the first international program of action for education to prevent drug abuse.

The United States supports CICAD's vital work, including its new experts group to develop model legislation to stop money laundering and to seize illegal assets.

Sixth, we must ensure that we bequeath to future generations a hemisphere that can sustain human life — our children's lives.

Exploiting nature is necessary to mankind's progress; preserving nature is necessary to mankind's survival. We have a common stake in the prudent use of our environmental assets — air, water, plant, and animal life. As with the war on drugs, no one nation can defend the earth in isolation.

The United States believes this General Assembly should use the Secretariat's proposal on an "Inter-American System for Nature Conservation" to develop an action program by the next General Assembly. The OAS clearly has a vital role to play in the environmental arena. We recognize that this issue is particularly sensitive. Therefore, we ought to be examining ways in

which we can address those sensitivities and do whatever is in our power to preserve the patrimony of generations yet to come.

Seventh, we must make the substantial investments in education needed to support democracy and human development.

Education is clearly a matter that is closely linked to the hemisphere's economic future and the viability of its democratic institutions. Last year, here in Asuncion, ministers of education discussed informatics [information science] as an educational tool. We believe that the Secretariat for Education, Science, and Culture should take advantage of its regional outlook and multilateral experience to propose a strategy for enhanced cooperation.

Eighth, we must find in ourselves the impartiality and constancy that are essential to the peaceful resolution of conflicts.

From the earliest inter-American plan for arbitration to today's OAS efforts in support of national reconciliation in Nicaragua, the need for active, collective involvement in the making of peace has been an essential and widely accepted purpose of our cooperation.

Recently, OAS support of the Central American peace process has deserved our full support. OAS work in Nicaragua, first on elections and now on national reconciliation, is making clear the links between peace, democracy, and development. We call upon other members of this body to join us in making voluntary contributions to support the OAS in Nicaragua, and we urge OAS members to contribute to the Donors' Conference on Nicaragua that starts in Rome tomorrow [June 6, 1990].

We express our gratitude to the Secretary General for his leadership and urge him to intensify his efforts in El Salvador to promote peace on the basis of constitutional democracy, impartial justice, and full respect for human rights.

It is important to note as well that ONUCA [United Nations Peacekeeping Force in Central America] is providing a stabilizing external presence today without which the joint efforts of the OAS and the U.N. in Nicaragua would be jeopardized. We are pleased that Venezuela, a member of the OAS, is contributing a reinforced battalion to ONUCA. At the same time, we note the absence of contributions by member

countries through the OAS as such. My government does not have a specific proposal but would welcome a review of how we might most effectively utilize existing OAS institutions, such as the Inter-American Defense Board and the Inter-American Defense College, in ways supportive of peace and democracy in the hemisphere.

A Call to Action

The late president of Colombia and secretary general of the OAS, Alberto Lleras Camargo, said of the OAS in 1954 that, "It is what the member governments want it to be and nothing else . . . the weaknesses of the organization, if it has them, are weaknesses of the governments; weakness in their capacity to act in coordination and jointly with each other. The strength of the organization, when it is evident, lies precisely in the action of the governments." United by the practical commitment to democracy, our governments are developing a working partnership. Partners approach each other freely and as equals, with mutual respect. Partners look to fix problems, not to affix blame. Partners accept the notion of co-responsibility. And when they disagree, they air their dialogue openly.

A heavy responsibility weighs upon this generation in the Americas. The dreams and aspirations of our forefathers for a hemisphere united in a universal commitment to democracy are finally on the verge of being realized. But history is no friend of the status quo; our democratic triumph will be short-lived if we do not meet the challenge now of making democracy work. We in the United States believe that our national well-being is linked to the successful consolidation of democracy and the emergence of genuine prosperity throughout Latin America. We believe that through our collective efforts we can defeat the threats to democracy — drugs, debt and underdevelopment. We can do so, above all, by tapping fully the great potential of our unique hemispheric asset, our privileged forum for dialogue, cooperation, and collective action — the Organization of American States.

---

[1] Department of State Current Policy 1283, June 1990.

Current Actions

*Note: This is the first listing of current treaty actions since the discontinuation of the **Department of State Bulletin**. It was released by the Department of State in June 1990 as "Current Treaty Actions, January-March 1990." Subsequent lists will be published here as soon as they are available, until the gap between the two publications is closed and the regular schedule can be resumed.*

MULTILATERAL

Agriculture-Diseases
International agreement for the creation at Paris of an International Office for Epizootics, with annex. Done at Paris Jan. 25, 1924. Entered into force Jan. 17, 1925; for the US July 29, 1975. TIAS 8141.
Accession deposited: Burma, Aug. 24, 1989.

Atomic Energy
Amendment of Article VI.A.1 of the Statute of the International Atomic Energy Agency of Oct. 26, 1956, as amended (TIAS 3873, 5284, 7668). Done at Vienna Sept. 27, 1984. [Senate] Treaty Doc. 99-7.
Acceptances deposited: Cote d'Ivoire, Oct. 27, 1989; Jamaica, Dec. 28, 1989; Luxembourg, Jan. 11, 1990.
Entered into force: Dec. 28, 1989.

Aviation
Convention on offenses and certain other acts committed on board aircraft. Done at Tokyo Sept. 14, 1963. Entered into force Dec. 4, 1969. TIAS 6768.
Accession deposited: German Democratic Republic, Jan. 10, 1989;[1] Marshall Islands, May 15, 1989; Zimbabwe, Mar. 8, 1989.

Convention for the suppression of unlawful acts against the safety of civil aviation. Done at Montreal Sept. 23, 1971. Entered into force Jan. 26, 1973. TIAS 7570.
Accession deposited: Vanuatu, Nov. 6, 1989.

Protocol for the suppression of unlawful acts of violence at airports serving international civil aviation. Done at Montreal Feb. 24, 1988. Entered into force Aug. 6, 1989.[2] [Senate] Treaty Doc. 100-19.
Senate advice and consent to ratification: Nov. 22, 1989.

Protocol relating to an amendment (Article 56) to the convention on international civil aviation (TIAS 1591). Done at Montreal Oct. 6, 1989. Enters into force on the date on which the 108th instrument of ratification is deposited.

Protocol for the suppression of unlawful acts of violence at airports serving international civil aviation, supplementary to the convention of Sept. 23, 1971 (TIAS 7570). Done at Montreal Feb. 24, 1988. Entered into force Aug. 6, 1989.[2]
Ratifications deposited: Austria, Dec. 28, 1989; Chile, Aug. 15, 1989; Denmark, Nov. 23, 1989, France, Sept. 6, 1989.[1]

Coffee
Extension of the international coffee agreement, 1983.[4] Done at London July 3, 1989. Entered into force Oct. 1, 1989.
Acceptances deposited prior to Oct. 1, 1989: Angola, Benin, Bolivia, Burundi, Cameroon, Canada, Colombia, Costa Rica, Cote d'Ivoire, Dominican Republic, El Salvador, Equatorial Guinea, Fiji, Finland, France, Gabon, Fed. Rep. of Germany, Ghana, Guatemala, Guinea, Haiti, Honduras, India, Indonesia, Kenya, Liberia, Madagascar, Malawi, Mexico, Nicaragua, Norway, Panama, Papua New Guinea, Paraguay, Philippines, Portugal, Rwanda, Sri Lanka, Sweden, Switzerland, Tanzania, Thailand, Togo, Uganda, US, Zaire, Zambia, Zimbabwe.
Notifications of provisional application deposited prior to Oct. 1, 1989: Belgium, Brazil, Central African Rep., Cuba, Denmark, Ecuador, Ethiopia, European Economic Community, Greece, Ireland, Italy, Japan, Luxembourg, Netherlands, Nigeria, Peru, Spain, UK, Venezuela
Accessions deposited: Trinidad and Tobago, Nov. 13, 1989; Singapore, Nov. 28, 1989; Sierra Leone, Nov. 29, 1989.

Conservation
Convention on international trade in endangered species of wild fauna and flora, with appendices. Done at Washington Mar. 3, 1973. Entered into force July 1, 1975. TIAS 8249.
Ratification deposited: Poland, Dec 12, 1989.
Accession deposited: Burkina Faso, Oct. 13, 1989.

Consular Relations
Optional protocol to the Vienna convention on consular relations, concerning the compulsory settlement of disputes. Done at Vienna Apr. 24, 1963. Entered into force Mar. 19, 1967; for the US Dec. 24, 1969. TIAS 6820.
Accessions deposited: Hungary, Dec. 8, 1989; Nicaragua, Jan. 9, 1990.

Containers
International convention for safe containers, with annexes, as amended. Done at Geneva Dec. 2, 1972. Entered into force Sept. 6, 1977; for the US Jan. 3, 1979. TIAS 9037, 10220, 10914.
Accession deposited: Dem. People's Rep. of Korea, Oct. 18, 1989; Indonesia, Sept. 25, 1989.

Copyright
Berne convention for the protection of literary and artistic works of Sept. 9, 1886, as revised at Paris July 24, 1971, and amended on Oct. 2, 1979. Entered into force for the US Mar. 1, 1989. [Senate] Treaty Doc. 99-27.
Accession deposited: Honduras, Oct. 24, 1989.
Ratification deposited: UK, Sept. 29, 1989.

Diplomatic Relations
Optional protocol to the Vienna convention on diplomatic relations concerning the compulsory settlement of disputes. Done at Vienna Apr. 18, 1961. Entered into force Apr. 24, 1964; for the US Dec. 13, 1972. TIAS 7502.
Accession deposited: Hungary, Dec. 8, 1989; Nicaragua, Jan. 9, 1990.

Human Rights
International covenant on civil and political rights. Done at New York Dec. 16, 1966. Entered into force Mar. 23, 1976.[2]
Ratification deposited: Ireland, Dec. 8, 1989.[5]

International covenant on economic, social, and cultural rights. Done at New York Dec. 16, 1966. Entered into force Jan. 3, 1976.[2]

Ratification deposited: Ireland, Dec. 8, 1989.

Maritime Matters
Convention for the suppression of unlawful acts against the safety of maritime navigation and protocol for the suppression of unlawful acts against the safety of fixed platforms located on the Continental Shelf. Done at Rome Mar. 10, 1988.[6] [Senate] Treaty Doc. 101-1.
Senate advice and consent to ratification: Nov. 22, 1989.

International convention on maritime search and rescue, 1979, with annex. Done at Hamburg Apr. 27, 1979. Entered into force June 22, 1985.
Ratification deposited: Greece, Sept. 4, 1989.[1]

International convention on standards of training, certification, and watchkeeping for seafarers, 1978. Entered into force Apr. 28, 1984.[2]
Accession deposited: Cape Verde, Sept. 18, 1989.

International convention on load lines, 1966. Done at London Apr. 5, 1966. Entered into force July 21, 1968. TIAS 6331, 6629, 6720.
Accession deposited: Dem. People's Rep. of Korea, Oct. 18, 1989.

International convention on tonnage measurement of ships, 1969, with annexes. Done at London June 23, 1969. Entered into force July 18, 1982; for the US Feb. 10, 1983. TIAS 10490.
Accession deposited: Dem. People's Rep. of Korea, Oct. 18, 1989.

Convention on the International Maritime Organization. Done at Geneva Mar. 6, 1948. Entered into force Mar. 17, 1958. TIAS 4044.
Acceptance deposited: Monaco, Dec. 22, 1989.

Convention on facilitation of international maritime traffic, with annex. Done at London Apr. 9, 1965. Entered into force Mar. 5, 1967; for the US May 16, 1967. TIAS 6251.
Accession deposited: Seychelles, Dec. 13, 1989.

Migration
Amendments to the constitution of the intergovernmental committee for migra-

tion of Oct. 19, 1953 (TIAS 3197). Adopted at Geneva May 20, 1987.
Entered into force: Nov. 14, 1989.

Narcotic Drugs
United Nations convention against illicit traffic in narcotic drugs and psychotropic substances, with annex and final act. Done at Vienna Dec. 20, 1988.[6] [Senate] Treaty Doc. 101-4.
Senate advice and consent to ratification: Nov. 22, 1989.
Instrument of Ratification signed by the President: Feb. 13, 1990.
Signatures: Brunei, Oct. 26, 1989; Gabon, Dec. 20, 1989; Pakistan Dec. 20, 1989; Switzerland, Nov. 16, 1989.
Ratifications deposited: China, Oct. 25, 1989; Nigeria, Nov. 1, 1989; Senegal, Nov. 27, 1989.

Nuclear Accidents
Convention on assistance in the case of a nuclear accident or radiological emergency. Done at Vienna Sept. 26, 1986. Entered into force Feb. 26, 1987; for the US Oct. 20, 1988. [Senate] Treaty Doc. 100-4.
Accession deposited: Saudi Arabia, Nov. 3, 1989.[1]
Ratification deposited: Austria, Nov. 21, 1989.[1]

Convention on the early notification of a nuclear accident. Done at Vienna Sept. 26, 1986. Entered into force Oct. 27, 1986; for the US Oct. 20, 1988. [Senate] Treaty Doc. 100-4.
Accession deposited: Saudi Arabia, Nov. 3, 1989.[1]

Nuclear Weapons — Nonproliferation
Treaty on the nonproliferation of nuclear weapons. Done at Washington, London, and Moscow July 1, 1968. Entered into force Mar. 5, 1970. TIAS 6839.
Ratification deposited: Kuwait, Nov. 17, 1989.

Patents
Patent cooperation treaty, with regulations. Done at Washington June 19, 1970. Entered into force Jan. 24, 1978. TIAS 8733.
Ratification deposited: Canada, Oct. 2, 1989.

Pollution
Convention for the protection of the ozone layer, with annexes. Done at Vienna Mar. 22, 1985. Entered into

force Sept. 22, 1988. [Senate] Treaty Doc. 99-9.
Ratification deposited: Argentina, Jan. 18, 1990.
Accessions deposited: China, Sept. 11, 1989; Tunisia, Sept. 25, 1989; Syrian Arab Rep., Dec 12, 1989; United Arab Emirates, Dec. 22, 1989; Fiji, Oct. 23, 1989; South Africa, Jan. 15, 1990; Sri Lanka, Dec. 15, 1989; Syrian Arab Republic, Dec. 12, 1989; Zambia, Jan. 24, 1990.

Montreal protocol on substances that deplete the ozone layer, with annex. Done at Montreal Sept. 16, 1987. Entered into force Jan. 1, 1989. [Senate] Treaty Doc. 100-10.
Accession deposited: Tunisia, Sept. 25, 1989; Syrian Arab Rep., Dec 12, 1989; United Arab Emirates, Dec. 22, 1989; Fiji, Oct. 23, 1989; Guatemala, Nov. 7, 1989; South Africa, Jan. 15, 1990; Sri Lanka, Dec. 15, 1989; Zambia, Jan. 24, 1990.

Convention on the prevention of marine pollution by dumping of wastes and other matter, with annexes. Done at London, Mexico City, Moscow, and Washington Dec. 29, 1972. Entered into force Aug. 30, 1975. TIAS 8165.
Accession deposited: Malta, Jan. 19, 1990.

Prisoner Transfer
Convention on the transfer of sentenced persons. Done at Strasbourg Mar. 21, 1983. Entered into force: July 1, 1985. TIAS 10824.
Signature: Iceland, Sept. 19, 1989.

Property — Industrial
Nice agreement, as revised, concerning the international classification of goods and services for the purpose of the registration of marks. Done at Geneva May 13, 1977. Entered into force Feb. 6, 1979; for the US Feb. 29, 1984.
Notification of accession deposited: Japan, Nov. 20, 1989.

Property — Intellectual
Convention establishing the World Intellectual Property Organization. Done at Stockholm July 14, 1967. Entered into force Apr. 26, 1970; for the US Aug. 25 1970. TIAS 6932.
Accessions deposited: Thailand, Sept. 25, 1989; People's Dem. Rep. of Yemen, Sept. 27, 1989.
Ratification deposited: Madagascar, Sept. 22, 1989.

TREATIES

Red Cross
Protocol additional to the Geneva conventions of Aug. 12, 1949 (TIAS 3362, 3363, 3364, 3365), and relating to the protection of victims of international armed conflicts (Protocol I), with annexes. Adopted at Geneva June 8, 1977. Entered into force Dec. 7, 1978.[2]

Protocol additional to the Geneva conventions of Aug.12, 1949 (TIAS 3362, 3363, 3364, 3365), and relating to the protection of victims of non-international armed conflicts (Protocol II). Adopted at Geneva June 8, 1977. Entered into force Dec. 7, 1978.[2]
Accession deposited: Algeria, Aug. 16, 1989.[7]
Ratifications deposited: Bulgaria, Sept. 26, 1989; Byelorussian SSR, Oct. 23, 1989;[7] Cote d'Ivoire, Sept. 20, 1989; Liechtenstein, Aug. 10, 1989;[7,8] Luxembourg, Aug. 29, 1989; Peru, July 14, 1989; USSR, Sept. 29, 1989.[9]

Rubber
International natural rubber agreement, 1987, with annexes. Done at Geneva Mar. 20, 1987. Entered into force provisionally Dec. 29, 1988; definitively Apr. 3, 1989. [Senate] Treaty Doc. 100-9.
Accession deposited: Nigeria, Nov. 28, 1989.

Safety at Sea
Amendments to the international convention for the safety of life at sea, 1974 (TIAS 9700), concerning passenger ro-ro ferries. Adopted at London Apr. 21, 1988.
Entered into force: Oct. 22, 1989.

Satellite Communications Systems
Agreement relating to the International Telecommunications Satellite Organization (INTELSAT), with annexes. Done at Washington Aug. 20, 1971. Entered into force Feb. 12, 1973. TIAS 7532.
Accession deposited: Mozambique, Nov. 15, 1989.

Operating agreement relating to the International Telecommunications Satellite Organization (INTELSAT), with annex. Done at Washington Aug. 20, 1971. Entered into force Feb. 12, 1973. TIAS 7532.
Signature: Empressa Nacional de Telecomunicacoes de Mocambique, Nov. 15, 1989.

Convention on the International Maritime Satellite Organization (IN-MARSAT), with annex. Done at London Sept. 3, 1976. Entered into force July 16, 1979. TIAS 9605.
Accession deposited: Cuba, July 25, 1989.
Ratification deposited: Turkey, Nov. 16, 1989.

Sugar
International sugar agreement, 1987, with annexes. Done at London Sept. 11, 1987. Entered into force provisionally Mar. 24, 1988.
Accession deposited: Jamaica, Jan. 25, 1990.

Taxation — Assistance
Convention on mutual administrative assistance in tax matters. Done at Strasbourg Jan. 25, 1988.
Signature: Finland, Dec. 11, 1989.[6]

Torture
Convention against torture and other cruel, inhuman, or degrading treatment or punishment. Done at New York Dec. 10, 1984. Entered into force June 26, 1987.[2]
Signature: Paraguay, Oct. 23, 1989.

Trade
United Nations convention on contracts for the international sale of goods. Done at Vienna Apr. 11, 1980. Entered into force Jan. 1, 1988. [52 Fed. Reg. 6262]
Accession deposited: Ukrainian SSR, Jan. 3, 1990.
Ratifications deposited: Chile, Feb. 7, 1990; Fed. Rep. of Germany, Dec. 21, 1989.

Whaling
International whaling convention and schedule of whaling regulations. Done at Washington Dec. 2, 1946. Entered into force Nov. 10, 1948. TIAS 1849.
Notification of withdrawal: Solomon Islands, Nov. 23, 1989; effective June 30, 1990.
Amendments to the schedule of the international convention for the regulation of whaling, 1946 (TIAS 1849). Done at San Diego, June 12-16, 1989.
Entered into force: Sept. 25, 1989.

Wheat
Wheat trade convention, 1986. Done at London Mar. 14, 1986. Entered into force July 1, 1986; definitively for the US Jan. 27, 1988. [Senate] Treaty Doc. 100-1.

Food aid convention, 1986. Done at London Mar. 13, 1986. Entered into force July 1, 1986; definitively for the US Jan. 27, 1988. [Senate] Treaty Doc. 100-1.
Acceptance deposited: Netherlands, Dec. 29, 1989.
Ratification deposited: Argentina, Feb. 1, 1990.

BILATERAL

Argentina
Agreement regarding the consolidation and rescheduling or refinancing of certain debts owed to, guaranteed by, or insured by the US Government and its agencies, with annexes. Signed at Buenos Aires Dec. 14, 1989. Entered into force Jan. 22, 1990.

Australia
Agreement concerning defense communications services, with annexes. Signed at Canberra Nov. 6, 1989. Entered into force Nov. 6, 1989.

The Bahamas
Treaty on mutual assistance in criminal matters. Signed at Nassau June 12 and Aug. 18, 1987.[8] [Senate] Treaty Doc. 100-17.
Senate advice and consent to ratification: Oct. 24, 1989.

Bangladesh
Agreement amending and extending the agreement of Feb. 19 and 24, 1986, as amended, relating to trade in certain apparel categories. Effected by exchange of notes at Washington June 23 and Aug. 23, 1989. Entered into force Aug. 23, 1989; effective Feb. 1, 1989.

Barbados
Memorandum of understanding concerning the operation of the INTELPOST service, with details of implementation. Signed at Bridgetown and Washington Oct. 18 and 26, 1989. Entered into force Feb. 15, 1990.

Belgium
Treaty on mutual legal assistance in criminal matters, with attachment. Signed at Washington Jan. 28, 1988. [Senate] Treaty Doc 100-16.
Senate advice and consent to ratification: Oct. 24, 1989.[10]

Belize
Memorandum of understanding concerning a cooperative medical research program. Signed at Belmopan Dec. 12, 1989. Entered into force Dec. 12, 1989.

Benin
Agreement regarding the consolidation and rescheduling of certain debts owed to, guaranteed by, or insured by the US Government and its agency, with annexes. Signed at Cotonou Nov. 20, 1989. Entered into force Dec. 28, 1989.

Bolivia
Agreement extending the swap agreement of Sept. 15, 1989, between the US Treasury and the Central Bank of Bolivia/Government of Bolivia. Signed at La Paz and Washington Dec. 15, 1989. Entered into force Dec. 15, 1989.

Swap agreement among the US Treasury and the Central Bank of Bolivia/Government of Bolivia, with related letter. Signed at Washington and La Paz Dec. 27, 1989. Entered into force Dec 27, 1989.

Burundi
International express mail agreement, with detailed regulations. Signed at Bujumbura and Washington Nov. 10 and Dec. 13, 1989. Entered into force Jan. 15, 1990.

Canada
Treaty on mutual legal assistance in criminal matters, with annex. Signed at Quebec Mar. 18, 1985. [Senate] Treaty Doc. 100-14.
Senate advice and consent to ratification: Oct. 24, 1989.[10]

Treaty on mutual legal assistance in criminal matters, with annex. Signed at Quebec City Mar. 18, 1985. [Senate] Treaty Doc. 100-14.
Instrument of ratification signed by the President: January 2, 1990.[10]
Instruments of ratification exchanged: Jan. 24, 1990.
Entered into force: Jan. 24, 1990.

Agreement extending the memorandum of understanding of June 4, 1979 (TIAS 9585), for cooperation in the research and development of tar sands (oil sands) and heavy oil. Signed at Washington, Edmonton, and Ottawa Oct. 27, Nov. 9, and Dec 1, 1989. Entered into force Dec. 1, 1989.

Chile
Memorandum of understanding regarding cooperation in establishing and implementing emergency procedures to ensure the safety of fresh fruit exported to the US from Chile. Signed at Washington Oct. 27, 1989. Entered into force Oct. 27, 1989.

Air transport agreement, with annexes. Signed at New York Sept. 27, 1989. Enters into force on a date to be determined in an exchange of notes indicating that all internal procedures have been completed by both parties.

Colombia
Agreement amending the agreement of Jan. 6 and Mar. 1, 1988, relating to trade in cotton sateen fabrics. Effected by exchange of notes at Bogota Jan. 6 and Sept. 20, 1989.
Entered into force: Sept. 20, 1989; effective Jan. 1, 1989.

Congo
Treaty concerning the reciprocal encouragement and protection of investment, with annex. Signed at Washington Feb. 12, 1990. Enters into force 30 days after the date of exchange of instruments of ratification.

Cuba
Agreement extending provisional application of the maritime boundary agreement of Dec. 16, 1977. Effected by exchange of notes at Washington Dec. 26, 1989. Entered into force Dec 26, 1989.

Czechoslovakia
Agreement amending and extending the agreement of June 25 and July 3 and 22, 1986, as amended, relating to trade in certain textile products. Effected by exchange of notes at Prague June 12 and Aug. 10, 1989. Entered into force Aug. 10, 1989; effective June 1, 1989.

Denmark
Agreement amending and extending the agreement of June 11, 1984, concerning Faroese fishing in fisheries off the coasts of the US. Effected by exchange of notes at Washington Mar. 28, 1989.
Entered into force: Nov. 15, 1989; effective July 1, 1989.

Dominican Republic
Agreement for the exchange of information with respect to taxes. Signed at Santo Domingo Aug. 7, 1989.
Entered into force: Oct. 13, 1989.

Egypt
Third amendment to the grant agreement of Sept. 26, 1984, for Cairo Sewerage 11. Signed at Cairo June 14, 1989. Entered into force June 14, 1989.

Project grant agreement for power sector support. Signed at Cairo Sept. 27, 1989. Entered into force Sept. 27, 1989.

El Salvador
International express mail agreement, with detailed regulations. Signed at San Salvador and Washington Aug. 29 and Oct. 6, 1989. Entered into force Oct. 30, 1989.

Agreement amending and extending the agreement of Mar. 2 and Apr. 30, 1987, as amended, relating to trade in cotton textiles. Effected by exchange of notes at San Salvador Dec. 18 and 27, 1989. Entered into force Dec. 27, 1989; effective Jan. 1, 1990.

France
Agreement concerning the wreck of the CSS Alabama. Signed at Paris Oct. 3, 1989. Entered into force Oct. 3, 1989.

Guatemala
International express mail agreement, with detailed regulations. Signed at Guatemala and Washington Nov. 7 and Dec. 19, 1989. Entered into force Feb. 15, 1990.

Guinea
Agreement regarding the consolidation and rescheduling of certain debts owed to, guaranteed by, or insured by the US Government and its agencies, with annexes. Signed at Conakry Nov. 22, 1989. Entered into force Jan. 22, 1990.

Honduras
Agreement on mutual cooperation to combat the production of and illicit trafficking in drugs. Signed at Tegucigalpa Nov. 14, 1988.
Entered into force May 15, 1989.

Hong Kong
Agreement amending the agreement of Aug. 4, 1986, as amended, relating to trade in certain textiles and textile products. Effected by exchange of letters at Washington Dec. 20 and 21, 1989, and Jan. 5, 1990. Entered into force Jan. 5, 1990.

Hungary

Agreement regarding new chancery facilities in Budapest, with associated agreement on purchase of lots. Signed at Budapest Sept. 29, 1989. Entered into force Sept. 29, 1989.

Investment guaranty agreement. Signed at Budapest Oct. 9,1989. Entered into force Dec. 27, 1989.

Air transport agreement, with annex and memorandum of understanding. Signed at Budapest July 12, 1989. Entered into force definitively: Feb. 8, 1990.

India

Agreement amending the agreement of Feb. 6, 1987, as amended, relating to trade in textiles and textile products. Effected by exchange of letters at New Delhi Dec. 6 and 21, 1989. Entered into force Dec. 21, 1989.

Indonesia

Agreement extending the agreement of Dec. 11, 1978, as amended and extended (TIAS 9609), for cooperation in scientific research and technological development. Effected by exchange of notes at Jakarta Sept. 16 and 28, 1989. Entered into force Sept. 28, 1989.

Ireland

Agreement amending the agreement of Feb. 3, 1945, as amended relating to air transport services (EAS 460, TIAS 1620, 4007, 7660). Effected by exchange of notes at Dublin Jan. 25, 1988, and Sept. 29, 1989. Entered into force Sept. 29, 1989.

Israel

Memorandum of understanding regarding transfers of materials, supplies, and equipment for cooperative research and development programs. Signed at Washington Sept. 8, 1989. Entered into force Sept. 8, 1989.

Agreement amending and extending the agreement of May 6, 1985, in the field of health. Signed at Jerusalem Jan. 7, 1990. Entered into force Jan. 7, 1990.

Jamaica

Agreement relating to the agreement of Jan. 15, 1987, as amended, for sales of agricultural commodities. Signed at Kingston Nov. 24, 1989. Entered into force Nov. 24, 1989.

Japan

Agreement extending the agreement of May 2, 1979, as extended (TIAS 9463), on cooperation in research and development in energy and related fields. Effected by exchange of notes at Washington Oct. 31, 1989. Entered into force Oct. 31, 1989.

Agreement concerning cooperation regarding the Geotail Scientific Satellite Program. Effected by exchange of notes at Tokyo Sept. 25, 1989. Entered into force Sept. 25, 1989.

Agreement extending the agreement of Sept. 10, 1982, as amended and extended, concerning fisheries off the coasts of the US (TIAS 10480). Effected by exchange of notes at Washington Oct. 6, 1989. Entered into force: Dec. 31, 1989.

Agreement amending and extending the agreement of May 2, 1979, as extended (TIAS 9463), on cooperation in research and development in energy and related fields. Effected by exchange of notes at Washington Feb. 1, 1990. Entered into force Feb. 1, 1990.

Jordan

Agreement regarding the consolidation and rescheduling or refinancing of certain debts owed to, guaranteed by, or insured by the US Government and its agencies, with annexes. Signed at Amman Oct. 31, 1989. Entered into force Dec 6, 1989.

Agreement concerning the reciprocal exemption from income tax of income derived from the international operation of ships and aircraft. Effected by exchange of notes at Amman Apr. 7, 1988. Entered into force: Apr. 7, 1988.

Kenya

International express mail agreement. Signed at Washington Dec. 11, 1989. Entered into force Jan. 30, 1990.

Korea

Agreement regarding the high seas squid driftnet fisheries in the North Pacific Ocean, with record of discussions and exchange of letters. Effected by exchange of notes at Washington Sept. 13 and 26, 1989. Entered into force Sept. 26, 1989.

Kuwait

Agreement on investment guaranties. Signed at Kuwait April 24, 1989. Entered into force Oct. 24, 1989.

Laos

Memorandum of understanding concerning cooperation on narcotics issues. Signed at Vientiane Jan. 9, 1990. Entered into force Jan. 9, 1990.

Marshall Islands

Agreement amending the governmental representation provisions of the Compact of Free Association of June 25, 1983. Signed at Washington Mar. 18, 1988. Entered into force Sept. 6, 1989.

Agreement regarding augmentation of educational assistance. Signed at Washington Sept. 7, 1988. Entered into force Sept. 7, 1988.

Agreement concerning the reciprocal exemption from income tax of income derived from the international operation of ships and aircraft. Effected by exchange of notes at Majuro Dec. 5, 1989. Entered into force Dec. 5, 1989; effective with respect to taxable years beginning on or after Jan. 1, 1987.

Mexico

Treaty on cooperation for mutual legal assistance. Signed at Mexico City Dec. 9, 1987.[6] [Senate] Treaty Doc. 100-13. Senate advice and consent to ratification: Oct. 24, 1989.[10]

Agreement on the development and facilitation of tourism. Signed at Washington Oct. 3, 1989. Enters into force upon receipt of the later notification of the completion of necessary legal requirements in each country.

Agreement for the exchange of information with respect to taxes. Signed at Washington Nov. 9, 1989. Enters into force upon an exchange of notes confirming their mutual agreement that both sides have met all constitutional requirements necessary to effectuate agreement.

Agreement amending the agreement of Feb. 13, 1988, as amended, concerning trade in cotton, wool, and manmade fiber textiles and textile products. Effected by exchange of notes at Mexico and Washington Oct. 2 and Nov. 1, 1989. Entered into force Nov. 1, 1989.

Exchange stabilization agreement among the US Treasury and the Banco de Mexico/Government of Mexico. Signed at Washington and Mexico Jan. 12, 1990. Entered into force Jan. 12, 1990.

Micronesia
Agreement amending the governmental representation provisions of the Compact of Free Association of Oct. 1, 1982. Signed at Washington Mar. 9, 1988. Entered into force Aug. 24, 1989.

Agreement relating to radio communications between amateur stations on behalf of third parties. Effected by exchange of notes at Kolonia Apr. 4 and Sept. 12, 1989. Entered into force Oct. 12, 1989.

Agreement concerning certain technical assistance to be provided by the Department of the Army. Signed at Honolulu Sept. 21, 1989. Entered into force Sept. 21, 1989.

Nepal
Agreement amending and extending the agreement of May 30 and June 1, 1986, as amended, relating to trade in cotton textiles. Effected by exchange of notes at Kathmandu Dec. 21, 1989, and Jan. 10, 1990.

Netherlands
Memorandum of understanding regarding the joint training of Royal Netherlands Air Force and United States Air Force aircrews on the F-16 weapons system in the US. Signed at The Hague Oct. 30, 1989. Entered into force Oct. 30, 1989.

Protocol to the agreement on social security and administrative arrangement of Dec. 8, 1987. Signed at The Hague Dec. 7, 1989. Enters into force upon entry into force of the agreement of Dec. 8, 1987.

Agreement on mutual administrative assistance in the exchange of information in securities matters. Signed at The Hague Dec 11, 1989. Enters into force on the first day of the second month following the date on which the parties have informed each other in writing that their constitutional procedures have been complied with.

Norway
Memorandum of understanding concerning scientific and technical cooperation in the earth sciences, with annexes. Signed at Reston and Trondheim Sept. 14 and Oct. 12, 1989. Entered into force Oct. 12, 1989.

Panama
Mutual cooperation for reducing demand, preventing illicit use, and combating illicit production and traffic of drugs. Signed at Panama Jan. 10, 1990. Entered into force Jan. 10, 1990.

Peru
Agreement for the exchange of tax information. Signed at Cartagena Feb. 15, 1990. Enters into force upon an exchange of notes confirming that both sides have met all constitutional and statutory requirements necessary to effectuate agreement.

Agreement relating to trade in cotton, wool, and manmade fiber textiles and textile products, with annexes. Signed at Lima July 26, 1989. Entered into force July 26, 1989; effective May 1, 1984.

Philippines
Agreement amending the agreement of May 16, 1988, regarding the consolidation and rescheduling of certain debts owed to, guaranteed by, or insured by the US Government and its agencies. Effected by exchange of notes at Manila Apr. 25, 1989. Entered into force Apr. 25, 1989.

Agreement regarding the consolidation and rescheduling or refinancing of certain debts owed to, guaranteed by, or insured by the US Government and its agencies, with annexes. Signed at Manila Nov. 3, 1989. Entered into force Dec. 13, 1989.

Poland
Agreement on the development and facilitation of tourism. Signed at Warsaw Sept. 20, 1989. Enters into force on the date on which each party has informed the other that it has completed all necessary legal requirements.

Agreement for sales of agricultural commodities. Signed at Warsaw Nov. 30, 1989. Entered into force Nov. 30, 1989.

International express mail agreement, with detailed regulations. Signed at Washington Dec. 11, 1989. Entered into force Feb. 1, 1990.

Romania
International express mail agreement, with detailed regulations. Signed at Washington Dec. 14, 1989. Entered into force Feb. 15, 1990.

Spain
Arrangement for the exchange of technical information and cooperation in nuclear safety matters, with patent addendum. Signed at Vienna Sept. 27, 1989. Entered into force Sept. 27, 1989.

Swaziland
Agreement for economic, technical, and related assistance. Signed at Mbabane Dec. 5, 1989. Entered into force Dec 5, 1989.

Sweden
Arrangement for the exchange of technical information and cooperation in nuclear safety matters, with patent addendum. Signed at Stockholm Oct. 4, 1989. Entered into force Oct. 4, 1989.

Thailand
Treaty on mutual legal assistance in criminal matters, with attachments. Signed at Bangkok Mar. 19, 1986.[6] [Senate] Treaty Doc. 100-18. Senate advice and consent to ratification: Oct. 24, 1989.

Air transport agreement, with annexes. Signed at Bangkok Dec. 7, 1979. Entered into force Dec. 7, 1979. TIAS 9704.

Memorandum of understanding relating to annex 1 of the 1979 air transport agreement. Signed at Washington June 15, 1984. Entered into force Oct. 10, 1984. Notice of termination: Presented by Thailand, Oct. 31, 1989, effective Nov. 2, 1990.

Trinidad and Tobago
Agreement for the exchange of information with respect to taxes. Signed at Port of Spain Jan. 11, 1989. Entered into force: Feb.9, 1990.

Tunisia
Supplementary protocol to the convention for the avoidance of double taxation and the prevention of fiscal evasion with respect to taxes on income of June

17, 1985. Signed at Tunis Oct. 4, 1989. Enters into force upon the exchange of instruments of ratification of the convention and the supplementary protocol.

Agreement relating to the agreement of Mar. 16, 1988, for sales of agricultural commodities. Signed at Tunis Sept. 28, 1989. Entered into force Sept. 28, 1989.

Uganda
Agreement regarding the consolidation and rescheduling of certain debts owed to, guaranteed by, or insured by the US Government and its agencies, with annexes. Signed at Kampala Dec. 19, 1989. Entered into force Jan. 26, 1990.

U.S.S.R.
Memorandum of understanding on cooperation in geoscience, with annexes. Signed at Washington and Moscow May 6, 1989. Entered into force May 6, 1989.

Memorandum of understanding concerning cooperation in the pursuit of Nazi war criminals. Signed at Moscow Oct. 19, 1989. Entered into force Oct 19, 1989.

Agreement on the prevention of dangerous military activities, with annexes and agreed statements. Signed at Moscow June 12, 1989. Entered into force Jan. 1, 1990.

Memorandum of understanding regarding a bilateral verification experiment and data exchange related to prohibition of chemical weapons. Signed at Jackson Hole, Wyoming, Sept. 23, 1989. Entered into force Sept. 23, 1989.

Agreement on reciprocal advance notification of major strategic exercises. Signed at Jackson Hole, Wyoming, Sept. 23, 1989. Entered into force Jan. 1, 1990.

Agreement concerning mutual visits by inhabitants of the Bering Straits region. Signed at Jackson Hole, Wyoming, Sept. 23, 1989. Enters into force on the date the parties exchange notes notifying each other that necessary internal procedures have been completed.

Agreement extending the agreement of June 19, 1973, on cooperation in studies of the world's oceans (TIAS 7651, 9349). Effected by exchange of notes at

Moscow Dec. 11 and 15, 1989. Entered into force Dec. 15, 1989.

Agreement extending the agreement of June 21, 1973, as amended and extended (TIAS 7655, 10757), on scientific and technical cooperation in the field of peaceful uses of atomic energy. Effected by exchange of notes at Moscow Nov. 21 and Dec 12, 1989. Entered into force Dec 12, 1989.

Agreement relating to trade in certain cotton textile fabric products, with annexes. Effected by exchange of letters at Washington Dec. 28, 1989. Entered into force Dec. 28, 1989; effective Jan. 1, 1990.

United Kingdom
Memorandum of understanding concerning the exchange of reserve officers. Signed at Washington Sept. 11, 1989. Entered into force Sept. 11, 1989.

Treaty concerning the Cayman Islands relating to mutual legal assistance in criminal matters, with attachments, protocol, and exchange of notes. Signed at Grand Cayman July 3, 1986.[6] [Senate] Treaty Doc. 100-8. Senate advice and consent to ratification: Oct. 24, 1989.[1]

Agreement extending the agreement of Apr. 14, 1987, as extended, concerning the British Virgin Islands and narcotics activities. Effected by exchange of notes at Washington Nov. 9, 1989. Entered into force Nov. 9, 1989; effective Nov. 12, 1989.

Agreement extending the agreement of July 26, 1984, as extended, concerning the Cayman Islands and narcotics activities. Effected by exchange of notes at Washington Nov. 28, 1989. Entered into force Nov. 28, 1989.

Agreement extending the agreement of Mar. 11, 1987, as extended, concerning Anguilla and narcotics activities. Effected by exchange of notes at Washington Dec. 21, 1989. Entered into force Dec. 21, 1989; effective Dec. 27, 1989.

Vanuatu
Memorandum of understanding on the establishment of a Peace Corps program in Vanuatu. Signed at Port Vila

Oct. 2, 1989. Entered into force Oct. 2, 1989.

Venezuela
Agreement on the development and facilitation of tourism. Signed at New York Sept. 27, 1989. Entered into force Sept. 27, 1989.

Yugoslavia
Memorandum of understanding relating to the air transport agreement of Dec. 15, 1977, as amended (TIAS 9364), and the nonscheduled air services agreement of Sept. 27, 1973, as amended (TIAS 7819, 9460). Signed at Belgrade June 28, 1989. Entered into force provisionally June 28, 1989; enters into force definitively on the date of an exchange of notes indicating approval by both parties in accordance with their constitutional requirements.

Agreement amending the agreement of Dec. 5 and 26, 1986, as amended, relating to trade in certain cotton, wool, and manmade fiber textiles and textile products. Effected by exchange of notes at Belgrade Dec. 19, 1989, and Jan. 3, 1990. Entered into force Jan. 3, 1990; effective Jan. 1, 1990.

Zaire
Agreement regarding the consolidation and rescheduling of certain debts owed to, guaranteed by, or insured by the US Government and its agencies, with annexes. Signed at Kinshasa Dec. 23, 1989. Entered into force Feb. 5, 1990.

---

[1] With reservation(s).
[2] Not in force for the US.
[3] Not applicable to the Faroe Islands.
[4] Certain provisions of the agreement were suspended.
[5] With declaration(s).
[6] Not in force.
[7] With declaration(s) concerning Protocol I.
[8] With reservation(s) concerning Protocols I and II..
[9] With declaration(s) concerning Protocols I and II..
[10] With understanding(s).

Department of State

Press releases may be obtained from the Office of Press
Relations, Department of State, Washington, D.C. 20520-6810.

No.	Date	Subject
60	5/4	Baker: press conference following NATO meting, Brussels, May 3.
*61	5/4	Baker: press conference with Ireland Foreign Minister Gerard Collins and EC President Jacques Delors following EC foreign ministers meeting, Brussels, May 3.
62	5/5	Baker: opening intervention at Two-Plus-Four ministerial meeting, Bonn, May 5.
*63	5/7	Program for the official working visit of Jaime Paz Zamora, President of the Republic of Bolivia.
*64	5/8	Baker: remarks at the unveiling of the portrait of the Honorable George P. Shultz, May 8.
65	5/10	Baker: excerpts from intervention at the NATO ministerial meeting, Brussells, May 3.
*66	5/10	Baker: press conference with other foreign ministers following Two-Plus-Four meeting, Bonn, May 5.
*67	5/11	Program for the state visit of Zine el Abidine Ben Ali, President of the Republic of Tunisia, May 14-17.
68	5/14	Baker: Speech to National Committee on American Foreign Policy, New York, May 14.
69	5/18	*Foreign Relations of the United States,* 1955-57, volume XVI, Suez Crisis, July 26-December 31, 1956, released.
*70	5/22	Baker: interview by Dan Rather, CBS-TV, Moscow, May 16.
71	5/22	Baker: press conference following U.S.-U.S.S.R. ministerial, Moscow, May 19.
*72	5/23	Baker: pre-summit press conference, May 23.
*73	6/7	Charles E. Redman, Ambassador to Sweden (biographic data).
*74	6/14	Program for the official working visit of General Chatichai Choonhavan, Prime Minister of Thailand, June 13-15.
*75	5/29	Baker: interview by Lesley Stahl, "Face the Nation," CBS-TV, May 27.
*76	5/31	Baker, interview by Bernard Shaw, "World Today," CNN, May 29, 1990.
*77	5/31	Baker: interview by Charles Gibson, "Good Morning America," ABC-TV, May 31.
*78	6/10	Baker: press briefing during Washington Summit, June 1.
*79	6/4	Baker: interview on "Meet the Press," NBC-TV, June 3.
*80	6/6	Baker: interview by Ralph Begleiter, CNN, and John McWethy, ABC, June 3.
81	6/11	Baker: speech to CSCE Conference on the Human Dimension, Copenhagen, June 6.
82	6/11	Baker: excerpts from prepared intervention at North Atlantic Council ministerial, Turnberry, Scotland, June 7.
83	6/8	Baker: press briefing at the NATO ministerial meeting, Turnberry, Scotland, June 8.
84	6/12	Baker: statement before the Senate Foreign Relations Committee, June 12.
*85	6/13	Baker: statement before the House Foreign Affairs Committee, June 13.
*86	6/18	Baker: remarks following meeting with Taro Nakayama, Foreign Minister of Japan, San Francisco, June 15.
87	6/19	*American Foreign Policy:* Foreign Affairs Press Briefings and Treaties, 1988. Supplement, released (microfiche publication).
88	6/18	Baker: press conference following meetings with Central American Presidents, Antigua, Guatemala, June 18.
*89	6/20	Baker: remarks at luncheon commemorating 30th anniversary of U.S.-Japanese security treaty, June 20.
*90	6/25	Reginald Bartholemew. Under Secretary of State for International Security Affairs (biographic data).
*91	6/21	Baker: remarks with Hans-Dietrich Genscher, Foreign Minister, Federal Republic of Germany, East Berlin, June 21.
*92	6/22	Baker: remarks with Foreign Minister Eduard Shevardnadze, U.S.S.R., Berlin, June 22.
93	6/22	Baker: press conference with other foreign ministers following Two-Plus-Four meeting, East Berlin, June 22.

* Not printed in the Bulletin.

Foreign Relations Volume on Suez Crisis [1]

The Department of State, on May 18, 1990, released *Foreign Relations of the United States, 1955-1957*, volume XVI, Suez Crisis, July 26-December 31, 1956.

The unexpected nationalization of the Suez Canal Company by Egyptian President Nasser on July 26, 1956, caused deep consternation among British and French leaders. Britain and France promptly imposed economic sanctions against Egypt, began joint military planning and mobilization of forces for a possible seizure of the Canal, and requested U.S. support for their activities.

U.S. officials believed that the use of force would be disastrous for Western interests in the Third World and emphasized to Britain and France that military force should be used only as a last resort if all diplomatic effort failed. At U.S. initiative, an international conference was held in London between August 16 and 23, during which a proposal for international operation of the Canal was adopted. Nasser rejected the proposal. The United States then proposed a Suez Canal Users Association; this became operative on October 1 after a second international conference. The U.N. Security Council discussed the matter at Anglo-French initiative between October 5 and 13. Meanwhile, the United States reaffirmed on several occasions to Britain and France its opposition to the use of force. Britain and France temporarily suspended their military preparations to allow time for diplomacy.

In keeping with its pledge under the 1950 Tripartite Declaration to oppose aggression in the Middle East, the United States protested Israel's mobilization and its subsequent invasion of the Sinai Peninsula on October 29. When the United States sought Anglo-French support for action in the U.N. Security Council, the two nations rebuffed the United States and instead issued an ultimatum that Israel and Egypt must withdraw 10 miles on either side of the Canal and that Egypt must allow the stationing of Anglo-French forces along the Canal. When Egypt refused, Britain and France bombarded the Canal Zone and later invaded the environs of Port Said with paratroopers. The United States

remained firmly opposed to the use of force and supported action in a special session of the U.N. General Assembly that led to the creation of the United Nations Emergency Force. The United States stood firmly by its Allies, however, when the Soviet Union threatened to intervene militarily in the area after crushing the Hungarian revolt on November 4.

Having obtained a cease-fire by November 7, the United States mobilized its efforts to obtain an Israeli, French, and British withdrawal from territories seized during the fighting. The last British and French troops left Egyptian territory on December 22. Israel withdrew from approximately one-half of the Sinai Peninsula, but insisted on further assurances before completing its withdrawal from Sharm al-Sheikh and the Gaza Strip.

This volume presents the comprehensive official historical documen-

tary record of U.S. diplomacy in the events discussed above. Its 1,344 pages were gathered from the White House, the Department of State, the Dwight D. Eisenhower Presidential Library, and other government agencies. Nearly all the documents selected were declassified for this publication.

Copies of volume XVI (Department of State Publication No. 9740, GPO Stock No. 044-000-02251-6) may be purchased for $41.00 (domestic postpaid) or $51.25 (foreign postpaid) from the Superintendent of Documents, U.S. Government Printing Office, Washington, D.C. 20402. Checks or money orders should be made out to the Superintendent of Documents.

American Foreign Policy: Foreign Affairs Press Briefings and Treaties, 1988, Supplement Released [2]

The Department of State, on June 19, 1990, published on microfiche the complete transcripts of the formal daily press briefings conducted by the Department's spokesman and the special press briefings by senior Department and White House officials on foreign policy issues during 1988. Also included in this publication are the treaties, protocols, and conventions signed by the United States in 1988, specifically those international agreements requiring formal Senate consent in the ratification process. This microfiche publication supplements the official record of principal messages, addresses, statements, and briefings in the printed volume, *American Foreign Policy: Current Documents, 1988.*

A major theme documented in the briefings is the continued improvement in U.S.-Soviet relations. The briefings discuss the expectations and results of ministerial and summit conferences as well as the more issue-specific U.S.-

Soviet meetings on arms control, human rights, and Afghanistan. Other briefings highlight regional European concerns, including NATO and individual countries' positions on arms control and weapons deployment and the European Community's plans for creating a single European market in 1992.

The briefings also cover Middle Eastern issues such as the cease-fire between Iran and Iraq, the U.S. Navy's downing of an Iranian commercial jetliner over the Persian Gulf, and the U.S. opening of contacts with the Palestine Liberation Organization. A major portion of the briefings concerning Africa discuss the progress of the Angolan-Namibian talks and relief efforts in Ethiopia. Important issues in Central America include U.S. sanctions against the Noriega regime and the continuing U.S. effort to insulate the region against the Sandinista regime in Nicaragua. U.S. concerns in Asia center around the expansion of U.S.-Chinese relations and the achievement of an equitable trading relationship with Japan. U.S. positions and attitudes are also revealed in the frequent State Department and White House briefings covering visits to the United States of foreign dignitaries.

The documents are presented in two parts. Part I contains Department of State daily press briefings, and the Department of State and White House Special Briefings and Press Conferences held in 1988. Following many of the daily briefings are "posted statements," which are the typewritten responses to reporters' specific inquiries the Spokesman did not fully answer during the daily press briefings. Part II contains treaties, protocols, and conventions signed by the United States in 1988. An

accompanying 71-page printed guide contains lists of all briefings and treaties included in the microfiche, the names and positions of all on-the-record briefers, and a comprehensive index for both parts.

In addition to the 1988 printed volume, annual printed editions for 1981 through 1987 have also been published, as have annual microfiche supplements for 1981 through 1986. Supplements for 1987 and 1989 are in preparation.

This microfiche publication was prepared in the Office of the Historian, Bureau of Public Affairs, Department of State. It comprises about 470 press briefings and 17 treaties, totaling about 5,800 pages on 60 microfiche cards.

Copies of this microfiche publication (Department of State Publication No. 9728, GPO Stock No. 044-000-02278-8) may be purchased for $20.00 from the Superintendent of Documents, U.S. Government Printing Office, Washington, D.C. 20402. Checks or money orders should be made out to the Superintendent of Documents.

---

[1] Department of State Press Release 69.
[2] Department of State Press Release 87.

INDEX

INDEX

FOREIGN POLICY BULLETIN
4812 Butterworth Place, N.W.
Washington, D.C. 20016

Foreign Policy

bulletin

The Documentary Record of United States Foreign Policy / Volume 1 / Number 2

September/October 1990

MILITARY AIRLIFT COMMAND

THE PERSIAN GULF CRISIS

Also in this issue:

Breakthrough to German Unification

Economic Summit in Houston

Cambodia/Policy Shift

Secretary Baker's Asian Trip

BULLETIN SPECIALS:
WORLD BANK REPORT ON POVERTY
UN, ARAB LEAGUE RESOLUTIONS

An independent publication with editorial autonomy • No government affiliation

Foreign Policy

bulletin

Volume 1/Number 2
September/October 1990

The **FOREIGN POLICY BULLETIN** is published bimonthly (plus annual index) as a private publication, using the same format as the discontinued "Department of State Bulletin" and maintaining continuity with that publication while offering additional materials as well. Its purpose is to provide a timely and systematic record of United States foreign policy and of complementary documents from international sources. The **BULLETIN's** coverage of official U.S. documents includes major addresses, diplomatic statements, and press conferences of the President and the Secretary of State; statements and congressional testimony by the Secretary and other administration officials; treaties and other agreements to which the United States is or may become a party; special reports; and selected press releases issued by the White House, the Department of State, and other agencies. Special features include speeches and other statements by foreign officials concerning U.S. policy; reports and other materials from international organizations relating to major issues confronting U.S. policy-makers; and background information about countries of particular interest to U.S. foreign relations.

PAUL E. AUERSWALD
Editor and Publisher

PHILIP AUERSWALD
Assistant Editor/Business Manager

HUGUETTE NIZARD
Subscriptions Manager

HOPE FUNG
Layout and Typesetting

J. LEONARD MAZUR
Marketing Consultant

Printed by
PRINTING SERVICE INTERNATIONAL

ISSN 1052-7036

SUBSCRIPTIONS: Annual subscriptions to the **BULLETIN** are $35.00; outside the U.S. and Canada $53.00. Subscription orders should be sent to: Subscriptions, Foreign Policy Bulletin, 4812 Butterworth Place N.W., Washington, D.C. 20016. To subscribe by phone, call (202) 966-1553.

SINGLE COPIES: Single copies, if still in print, can be obtained for $10.00 a copy plus postage by writing to the address below.

CORRESPONDENCE should be addressed to: Foreign Policy Bulletin, 4812 Butterworth Place N.W., Washington, D.C. 20016. Telephone: (202) 966-1553

INDEXING: Included in the PAIS (Public Affairs Information Service) indexes: the PAIS Bulletin, PAIS on CD-ROM, and online through Dialog, BRS, and Data-Star. Information about other indexing services will be provided in subsequent issues.

CONTENTS

The Persian Gulf Crisis: Phase 1

White House Statement, August 1, 1990 [1]

The United States strongly condemns the Iraqi military invasion of Kuwait and calls for the immediate and unconditional withdrawal of all Iraqi forces. We have conveyed this message to the Iraqi Ambassador in Washington and to the Iraqi Government through our Embassy in Baghdad. We deplore this blatant use of military aggression and violation of the U.N. Charter. Together with Kuwait, we are calling for an emergency session of the U.N. Security Council.

White House Statement, August 2, 1990 [1]

National Security Adviser Brent Scowcroft has been chairing an interagency task force in the Situation Room monitoring the Iraqi invasion of Kuwait. The President was informed of the initial signs of the Iraqi action at approximately 9 p.m. yesterday by National Security Adviser Scowcroft and has been receiving periodic updates since.

The United States is deeply concerned about this blatant act of aggression and demands the immediate and unconditional withdrawal of all Iraqi forces. We do not have exact details at this time concerning the extent of the Iraqi action, although it is clearly extensive. We have no reports of any harm to American citizens. The State Department is in constant contact with our Embassy in Kuwait concerning the status of U.S. citizens.

At the urging of Kuwait and the United States, the United Nations Security Council will be meeting early this morning to consider this matter. In addition, we have been informed that the Arab League and the Organization of the Islamic Conference will be convening to review the situation. We are urging the entire international community to condemn this outrageous act of aggression.

The United States is reviewing all options in its response to the Iraqi aggression.

United Nations Security Council Resolution 660, August 2, 1990 [2]

The Security Council,
Alarmed by the invasion of Kuwait on 2 August 1990 by the military forces of Iraq,

Determining that there exists a breach of international peace and security as regards the Iraqi invasion of Kuwait,

Acting under Articles 39 and 40 of the Charter of the United Nations,

1. Condemns the Iraqi invasion of Kuwait;

2. Demands that Iraq withdraw immediately and unconditionally all its forces to the positions in which they were located on 1 August 1990;

3. Calls upon Iraq and Kuwait to begin immediately intensive negotiations for the resolution of their differences and supports all efforts in this regard, and especially those of the League of Arab States;

4. Decides to meet again as necessary to consider further steps to ensure compliance with the present resolution.

President's Remarks and Exchange With Reporters, August 2, 1990 [1]

Let me make a brief statement here about recent events. The United States strongly condemns the Iraqi military invasion of Kuwait. We call for the immediate and unconditional withdrawal of all the Iraqi forces. There is no place for this sort of naked aggression in today's world, and I've taken a number of steps to indicate the deep concern that I feel over the events that have taken place.

Last night I instructed our Ambassador at the United Nations, Tom Pickering, to work with Kuwait in convening an emergency meeting of the Security Council. It was convened, and I am grateful for that quick, overwhelming vote condemning the Iraqi action and calling for immediate and unconditional withdrawal. Tom Pickering will be here in a bit, and we are contemplating with him further United Nations action.

Second, consistent with my authority under the International Emergency Economic Powers Act, I've signed an executive order early this morning freezing Iraqi assets in this country and prohibiting transactions with Iraq. I've also signed an executive order freezing Kuwaiti assets. That's to ensure that those assets are not interfered with by the illegitimate authority that is now occupying Kuwait. We call upon other governments to take similar action.

Third, the Department of State has been in touch with governments around the world urging that they, too, condemn the Iraqi aggression and consult to determine what measures should be taken to bring an end to this totally unjustified act. It is important that the international community act together to ensure that Iraqi forces depart Kuwait immediately.

Needless to say, we view the situation with the utmost gravity. We remain committed to take whatever steps are necessary to defend our longstanding, vital interests in the Gulf, and I'm meeting this morning with my senior advisers here to consider all possible options available to us. I've talked to Secretary [of State] Baker just now; General Scowcroft [Assistant to the President for National Security Affairs] and I were on the phone with him. And after this meeting, I will proceed to deliver a longstanding speech. I will have consultations — short ones — there in Aspen with Prime Minister Thatcher [of the United Kingdom], and I will be returning home this evening, and I'll be here in Washington tomorrow.

I might say on a much more pleasant note, I just hung up from talking to Mr. and Mrs. Swanson, the parents of Tim Swanson, the Peace Corps volunteer who has been held against his will — held hostage or kidnaped — there in the Philippines. And I want to thank everybody in the U.S. Government that was so instrumental in working for his release. And, Bob [Robert M. Gates, Assistant to the President and Deputy for National Security Affairs], I hope you'll convey that to the Ambassador and others in our Philippines country team.

Q. Mr. President?

"Iraq's unprovoked aggression is a political test of how the post-Cold War world will work ... a first opportunity to limit such dangers, to reinforce the standards for civilized behavior found in the United Nations Charter ..."

— *Secretary of State Baker,*
September 4, 1990

A. Yes, Helen [Helen Thomas, United Press International]?

Q. **Do you contemplate intervention as one of your options?**

A. We're not discussing intervention. I would not discuss any military options even if we'd agreed upon them. But one of the things I want to do at this meeting is hear from our Secretary of Defense [Richard B. Cheney], our Chairman [Gen. Colin L. Powell, Chairman of the Joint Chiefs of Staff], and others. But I'm not contemplating such action.

Q. **You're not contemplating any intervention or sending troops?**

A. I'm not contemplating such action, and I again would not discuss it if I were.

Q. **What is the likely impact on U.S. oil supplies and prices?**

A. This is a matter that concerns us, and I don't know yet. Again, I'm going to hear from our experts now. Our Secretary of Energy [James D. Watkins] is here, if you'll note, and others who understand this situation very well indeed—our Secretary of Defense. And we'll be discussing that. But this is a matter of considerable concern, and not just to the United States, I might add.

Q. **Are you planning to break relations?**

A. You've heard me say over and over again, however, that we are dependent for close to 50 percent of our energy requirements on the Middle East. And this is one of the reasons I felt that we have to not let our guard down around the world.

Q. **Are you contemplating breaking diplomatic relations?**

A. I'm discussing this matter with our top advisers here in just a minute.

Q. **Is this action in your view limited to Kuwaiti'**

A. There's no evidence to the contrary. But what I want to do is have it limited back to Iraq and have this invasion be reversed and have them get out of Kuwait.

Q. **Do you think Saudi Arabia is threatened or any of the other Emirates?**

A. I think Saudi Arabia is very concerned; and I want to hear from our top officials here, our Director of Intelligence [William H. Webster] and others, as to the worldwide implications of this illegal action that has been condemned by the United Nations.

Q. **And you were taken by surprise?**

A. Not totally by surprise because we have good intelligence, and our intelligence has had me concerned for some time here about what action might be taken.

Thank you all very much. And I expect I will say something further because I'm having a joint press meeting with Margaret Thatcher and, at that time, I might be able to take a few more questions on this subject. But the main thing I want to do now is hear from our advisers, and then we will go forth from this meeting all on the same wavelength. I'm sure there will be a lot of frenzied diplomatic activity. I plan to participate in some of that myself, because at this time, it is important to stay in touch with our many friends around the world, and it's important that we work in concert with our friends around the world.

Q. Gorbachev?

A. Thank you very much. Obviously—Helen, you might be interested—this matter has been discussed at very high level between Secretary Baker and the Foreign Minister of the Soviet Union [Eduard A. Shevardnadze]. And so far I've been pleased with the Soviet reaction.

Q. Well, do you expect to make decisions?

A. That's all I've got to say right now. We've got to go on with this meeting.

Executive Order 12722 Blocking Iraqi Government Property and Prohibiting Transactions With Iraq, August 2, 1990 [1]

By the authority vested in me as President by the Constitution and laws of the United States of America, including the International Emergency Economic Powers Act (50 U.S.C. 1701 et seq.), the National Emergencies Act (50 U.S.C. 1601 et seq.), and section 301 of title 3 of the United States Code.

I, George Bush, President of the United States of America, find that the policies and actions of the Government of Iraq constitute an unusual and extraordinary threat to the national security and foreign policy of the United States and hereby declare a national emergency to deal with that threat.

I hereby order:

Section 1. All property and interests in property of the Government of Iraq, its agencies, instrumentalities and controlled entities and the Central Bank

of Iraq that are in the United States, that hereafter come within the United States or that are or hereafter come within the possession or control of United States persons, including their overseas branches, are hereby blocked.

Section 2. The following are prohibited, except to the extent provided in regulations which may hereafter be issued pursuant to this Order:

(a) The import into the United States of any goods or services of Iraqi origin, other than publications and other informational materials;

(b) The export to Iraq of any goods, technology (including technical data or other information controlled for export pursuant to Section 5 of the Export Administration Act (50 U.S.C. App. 2404)) or services from the United States, except publications and other informational materials, and donations of articles intended to relieve human suffering, such as food, clothing, medicine and medical supplies intended strictly for medical purposes;

(c) Any transaction by a United States person relating to transportation to or from Iraq; the provision of transportation to or from the United States by any Iraqi person or any vessel or aircraft of Iraqi registration; or the sale in the United States by any person holding authority under the Federal Aviation Act of 1958, as amended (49 U.S.C. 1514), of any transportation by air which includes any stop in Iraq;

(d) The purchase by any United States person of goods for export from Iraq to any country;

(e) The performance by any United States person of any contract in support of an industrial or other commercial or governmental project in Iraq;

(f) The grant or extension of credits or loans by any United States person to the Government of Iraq, its instrumentalities and controlled entities;

(g) Any transaction by a United States person relating to travel by any United States citizen or permanent resident alien to Iraq, or to activities by any such person within Iraq, after the date of this Order, other than transactions necessary to effect such person's departure from Iraq, or travel for journalistic activity by persons regularly employed in such capacity by a newsgathering organization; and

(h) Any transaction by any United States person which evades or avoids, or has the purpose of evading or avoiding,

any of the prohibitions set forth in this Order.

For purposes of this Order, the term "United States person" means any United States citizen, permanent resident alien, juridical person organized under the laws of the United States, or any person in the United States.

Section 3. This Order is effective immediately.

Section 4. The Secretary of the Treasury, in consultation with the Secretary of State, is hereby authorized to take such actions, including the promulgation of rules and regulations, as may be necessary to carry out the purposes of this Order. Such actions may include prohibiting or regulating payments or transfers of any property or any transactions involving the transfer of anything of economic value by any United States person to the Government of Iraq, its instrumentalities and controlled entities, or to any Iraqi national or entity owned or controlled, directly or indirectly, by Iraq or Iraqi nationals. The Secretary may redelegate any of these functions to other officers and agencies of the Federal government. All agencies of the United States government are directed to take all appropriate measures within their authority to carry out the provisions of this Order, including the suspension or termination of licenses or other authorizations in effect as of the date of this Order.

This Order shall be transmitted to the Congress and published in the Federal Register.

[Filed with the Office of the Federal Register, 9:44 a. m., August 2, 1990]

Executive Order 12723 Blocking Kuwaiti Government Property, August 2, 1990 [1]

By the authority vested in me as President by the Constitution and laws of the United States of America, including the International Emergency Economic Powers Act (50 U.S.C. 1701 et seq.), the National Emergencies Act (50 U.S.C. 1601 et seq.), and 3 U.S.C. 301.

I, George Bush, President of the United States, find that the situation caused by the invasion of Kuwait by Iraq constitutes an unusual and extraordinary threat to the national security, foreign policy and economy of the

United States and have declared a national emergency to deal with that threat.

I hereby order blocked all property and interests in property of the Government of Kuwait or any entity purporting to be the Government of Kuwait, its agencies, instrumentalities and controlled entities and the Central Bank of Kuwait that are in the United States, that hereafter come within the United States or that are or hereafter come within the possession or control of United States persons, including their overseas branches.

For purposes of this Order, the term "United States person" means any United States citizen, permanent resident alien, juridical person organized under the laws of the United States or any person in the United States.

The Secretary of the Treasury is authorized to employ all powers granted to me by the International Emergency Economic Powers Act to carry out the provisions of this Order.

This Order is effective immediately and shall be transmitted to the Congress and published in the Federal Register.

[Filed with the Office of the Federal Register, 9:45 a.m., August 2, 1990]

President's Remarks and Session With Reporters Following a Meeting With Prime Minister Thatcher, Aspen, Colorado, August 2, 1990 [1]

Let me first welcome Prime Minister [Margaret] Thatcher [of the United Kingdom] back to the United States. It's a very timely visit, and as you can well imagine, we have been exchanging views on the Iraq-Kuwait situation. Not surprisingly, I find myself very much in accord with the views of the Prime Minister. I reported to her on contacts that I've had since I left Washington: personal contacts with King Hussein [of Jordan]; Mr. Mubarak of Egypt, President Mubarak; President Salih of Yemen—a long conversation just now. I can tell you that [Secretary of State] Jim Baker has been in close touch with the Soviet leadership, and indeed, the last plan was for him to stop in Moscow on his way back here.

We are concerned about the situation, but I find that Prime Minister Thatcher and I are looking at it on exactly the same wavelength: concerned about this naked aggression, condemning it and hoping that a peaceful solution will be found that will result in the restoration of the Kuwaiti leaders to their rightful place and, prior to that, a withdrawal of Iraqi forces.

Prime Minister, welcome to Colorado and to the United States. And if you care to say a word on that, then we can take the questions.

The Prime Minister. Thank you, Mr. President, and thank you for the welcome.

We have, of course, been discussing the main question as the President indicated. Iraq has violated and taken over the territory of a country which is a full member of the United Nations. That is totally unacceptable, and if it were allowed to endure, then there would be many other small countries that could never feel safe.

The Security Council acted swiftly last night under the United States leadership, well supported by the votes of 14 members of the Security Council, and rightly demanded the withdrawal of Iraqi troops. If that withdrawal is not swiftly forthcoming, we have to consider the next step. The next step would be further consideration by the Security Council of possible measures under Chapter VII.

The fundamental question is this: whether the nations of the world have the collective will effectively to see the Security Council resolution is upheld; whether they have the collective will effectively to do anything, which the Security Council further agrees, to see that Iraq withdraws and that the government of Kuwait is restored to Kuwait. None of us can do it separately. We need a collective and effective will of the nations belonging to the United Nations—first the Security Council and then the support of all the others to make it effective.

Q. Mr. President, when Kuwaiti shipping was in danger in the Gulf war, you put those ships under American flags. Now Kuwait itself has been invaded. The Kuwaiti Ambassador says that they're desperate for help and that American intervention is of paramount importance. Will you answer that call, and how will you?

The President. I answer that we're considering what the next steps by the United States should be, just as we

strongly support what Prime Minister Thatcher said about collective action in the United Nations.

Q. Are you still not contemplating military intervention?

A. No. I mentioned at the time we were going to discuss different options, which I did after that first press conference this morning. And we're not ruling any options in, but we're not ruling any options out. And so, that is about where we are right now. We had thorough briefings— you know who was at the meeting today— by General Powell [Chairman of the Joint Chiefs of Staff], General Schwarzkopf [Commander-in-Chief of the U.S. Central Command, USA] and others. But I think it would be inappropriate to discuss options.

Q. What are the chances of U.S.-Soviet cooperation in restoring peace to the Gulf?

A. I would say they're very good. I reported to Prime Minister Thatcher on a conversation that I had with Jim Baker on the plane flying out here. And I think you could say that he would not be stopping in Moscow unless there would be a good degree of cooperation between the Soviet Union and the United States. But again, the Soviet Union is a member of the United Nations. They voted with the United Kingdom and with the United States. And so, I think there is a good level of cooperation with the Soviets and, hopefully, with other permanent members and, hopefully, with the rest of the members of the Security Council.

Q. We understand that the Soviets have announced that they are cutting off arm shipments to the Iraqis. Are the French, which is the other big arms supplier to Baghdad, also planning to cut off arms shipments?

A. I've not talked today—I believe you had contact, Prime Minister, at some level with the French Government, but I can't answer that question.

The Prime Minister. We had contact. Douglas Hurd [British Foreign Secretary], I believe, had contact with Mr. Dumas [French Foreign Minister]. This was about the Security Council resolution which France, of course, fully supported.

Q. Mr. President, isn't Saddam Hussein [President of Iraq] at the root of this problem? Hasn't he replaced Qadhafi [leader of Libya] as sort of the bad boy of the region? Would you like to see him removed? And what can you do about him?

A. I would like to see him withdraw his troops and the restoration of the legal government in Kuwait to the rightful place, and that is the step that should be taken. I might say that I am somewhat heartened by the conversations I had with Mubarak and with King Hussein, Mr. Salih—all of whom I consider friends of the United States—and all of them who are trying to engage in what they call an Arab answer to the question, working diligently behind the scenes to come to an agreement that would satisfy the United Nations and the rest of the world. So, there are collective efforts beginning to be undertaken by these worthy countries, and let's hope that they result in a satisfactory resolution of this international crisis.

Q. But, Mr. President, Saddam Hussein has been the source of the most recent mischief in the region—nuclear triggers, missiles, the big gun—as Prime Minister Thatcher knows about. Is he going to be a constant source of problems there in that region?

A. If he behaves this way, he's going to be a constant source. We find his behavior intolerable in this instance, and so do the rest of the United Nations countries that met last night. And reaction from around the world is unanimous in being condemnatory. So, that speaks for itself.

The Prime Minister. Did I hear someone say Prime Minister?

The President. You hope you did. [Laughter] Please.

The Prime Minister. I'm sorry. I told you I'd finished. [Laughter] But so, I thought that that guy shouldn't have it all. [Laughter]

Q. Prime Minister, is there any action short of military intervention that Britain or the other United Nations countries could take—

The Prime Minister. Yes, of course.

Q. —that would be effective against Iraq?

A. Yes, of course. Yes, of course there is—you know, the whole Chapter VII measures. And that, of course—obviously we're in consultation now as to which measures we could all agree on so the Security Council would vote them. And then they'd become mandatory. The question then is whether you can make them effective over the rest of the nations. And obviously, the 14 couldn't do it on their own. And so, there will be a good deal of negotiation as to what to put in the next Security

Council resolution if Iraq does not withdraw.

Q. But are you confident that you'd be able to mobilize that kind of international support?

A. I believe that further Chapter VII measures would have a good chance of getting through. We certainly would support them.

The President. May I add to that, that the United States has demonstrated its interest in that by the action that I took this morning by executive order: cutting off imports from Iraq to this country.

Q. Mr. President, can I ask both of you to answer this: How does the fact that they apparently have chemical weapons now affect your decision making and narrow your options?

The Prime Minister. I don't figure it affects it at all. What has happened is a total violation of international law. You cannot have a situation where one country marches in and takes over another country which is a member of the United Nations. I don't think the particular weapons they have affects that fundamental position.

Q. But doesn't it affect what actions we can take? And doesn't it make military action—

The Prime Minister. No, I do not think it necessarily affects what actions we can take.

The President. I would agree with that assessment.

Q. What did the Arab leaders that you talked to ask the United States to do? Did they ask you to either restrain yourself or to become militarily involved? And have you contacted Israel?

The President. We've had contact with Israel, yes. I have not personally, but we have. And they asked for restraint. They asked for a short period of time in which to have this Arab solution evolve and be placed into effect. And they are concerned, obviously, with this naked aggression. But it was more along that line: Let us try now, as neighbors and Arabs, to resolve this. And I made clear to them that it had gone beyond simply a regional dispute because of the naked aggression that violates the United Nations Charter.

Q. What did Israel say it would do at this point?

The President. I would have to think back to the details of it; but offering cooperation, I think, was about where I would leave it there.

Q. Mr. President, we're hearing reports now that some of the

Americans, particularly in the oil fields, may have been rounded up by Iraqi troops. Do you have anything to that? How does that affect your reaction?

A. Well, I don't have anything on that right now. And secondly, it would affect the United States in a very dramatic way, because I view a fundamental responsibility of my Presidency as protecting American citizens, and if they're threatened or harmed or put into harm's way, I have certain responsibilities. But I hadn't heard that, Charles [Charles Bierbauer, Cable News Network], and I hope that that is not correct.

Q. May I also ask about British citizens? Any word? Are they safe?

The Prime Minister. We have some British citizens in Kuwait. You probably know that there was a British Airways flight there on its way to Africa, and the passengers there are now in a hotel in Kuwait. So, we have some there, and of course, we have a number of other British citizens in Kuwait. And we, too, are concerned for their safety.

Q. Mr. President, some of the smaller nations in the Persian Gulf—Bahrain, the Emirates, and the others—obviously have reason to worry about what has happened here. What can the United States and Great Britain say to those countries and those people who are feeling very concerned today?

The President. Well, the United States can say that we are very much concerned for your safety. And this naked aggression would understandably shake them to the core. And so, what we are trying to do is have collective action that will reverse this action out and to make very clear that we are totally in accord with their desire to see the Iraqis withdraw—cease-fire, withdraw, and restitution of the Kuwaiti Government. And that would be the most reassuring thing of all for these countries who, whether it's true or not, feel threatened by this action.

Q. At the risk of being hypothetical, if Iraq does not move out quickly and has gained a foothold among the smaller Gulf nations, what can the United States and other nations do militarily?

The President. We have many options, and it is too hypothetical, indeed, for me to comment on them. And I'd refer that also to the Prime Minister.

The Prime Minister. That's precisely why you're looking at the next stage in the Security Council; second, what other measures can be put into action mandatorily; and why the very nations to whom you refer — we should also need their cooperation in putting other actions into effect.

Q. Mr. President, have you dispatched the U.S.S. Independence to the region, and have you heard from Saudi Arabia?

The President. Well, I would not discuss movement of any U.S. forces. And what was the second part of your question?

Q. Have you heard from Saudi Arabia?

The President. No, but I have a call to King Fahd, and I was supposed to have taken that call before now, but it's been delayed by a few minutes. And so, I hope before I leave here I will talk to him. I think it is very important I do talk to him. And I'd leave it there.

Q. What do you expect him to say?

The President. Well, that's too hypothetical, too. I know he'll be expressing the same kind of concern that we feel.

Q. Prime Minister, if I could, the President's executive order this morning established a U.S. embargo on trade with Iraq. When you mentioned chapter VII measures, would you support in the Security Council a call for an international embargo on Iraqi oil?

The Prime Minister. We are prepared to support in the Security Council those measures which collectively we can agree to and which collectively we can make effective. Those are the two tests. We have already frozen all Kuwaiti assets. Kuwaitis have very considerable assets, and it's important that those do not fall into Iraqi hands. Iraq, we believe, has only very, very small assets and rather a lot of debts, so the position is rather different with her.

White House Statement on the President's Telephone Conversation With King Fahd of Saudi Arabia, August 2, 1990 [1]

President Bush and King Fahd of Saudi Arabia discussed the Iraq attack on Kuwait in a telephone call at approximately 4:45 p.m. MDT. The two leaders spoke for nearly one-half hour. They agreed that the attack on Kuwait was absolutely unacceptable, and they discussed possible options for dealing with the situation. President Bush

described the conversations he had earlier in the day with other Arab leaders and with Prime Minister Thatcher. The President emphasized the United States demand for the immediate and unconditional withdrawal of Iraqi forces.

Joint Statement, Secretary of State Baker and Foreign Minister Eduard Shevardnadze of the Soviet Union, Moscow, August 3, 1990 [3]

The Soviet Union and the United States, as members of the United Nations Security Council, consider it important that the Council promptly and decisively condemn the brutal and illegal invasion of Kuwait by Iraqi military forces. The United States and the Soviet Union believe that now it is essential that the Security Council Resolution be fully and immediately implemented. By its action, Iraq has shown its contempt for the most fundamental principles of the United Nations Charter and international law.

In response to this blatant transgression of the basic norms of civilized conduct, the United States and the Soviet Union have each taken a number of actions, including the Soviet suspension of arms deliveries and the American freezing of assets. The Soviet Union and the United States reiterate our call for the unconditional Iraqi withdrawal from Kuwait. The sovereignty, national independence, legitimate authorities, and territorial integrity of the State of Kuwait must be completely restored and safeguarded. The United States and the Soviet Union believe the international community must not only condemn this action, but also take practical steps in response to it.

Today we take the unusual step of jointly calling upon the rest of the international community to join with us in an international cutoff of all arms supplies to Iraq. In addition, the Soviet Union and the United States call on regional organizations, especially the League of Arab States, all Arab governments, as well as the Nonaligned Movement and the Islamic Conference to take all possible steps to ensure that the United Nations Security Council Resolution is carried out. Governments that engage in blatant aggression must know that the international community cannot and

will not acquiesce in nor facilitate aggression.

Secretary of State Baker and Foreign Minister Shevardnadze, Joint Press Conference, Moscow, August 3, 1990 [3]

Foreign Minister Shevardnadze. Good evening ladies and gentlemen. This has been a rather unusual meeting and talk with the Secretary of State. This meeting has taken place because of the events that are very disturbing to the entire world, and of course, I am referring to the Iraqi invasion into Kuwait. The Secretary of State and I discussed this situation in Irkutsk [U.S.S.R., where they met August 1 and 2]. And I'll say this to you, the Secretary of State at that time said that he was concerned about the concentration of Iraqi forces near the Kuwait border. And frankly, at that time, I was almost sure that there would be no further deterioration. I really did not think at that time that the Iraqis would so openly engage in aggression against such a defenseless country. A country that is no threat to anyone.

Anyway, at that time we agreed that if the situation does deteriorate, we'll meet and consult. And as you know, now that this has happened and what has happened is very unfortunate and I will say tragic, and so we felt that it was necessary for us to meet here in Moscow. We have now discussed the situation, the situation that has evolved — is evolving in the Persian Gulf as a result of this invasion in Kuwait and we have decided to make a joint Soviet-American statement about these events. You know that yesterday we published some documents that reflect the position of the Soviet Government. Let me tell you that it was a rather difficult decision for us to make the kind of statements that we made yesterday and also to be making this joint statement because of the long standing relations that we have had with Iraq and that have been evolving for decades. But despite all this, despite the traditional good relations that we've had with that country, we are being forced to take these steps, and to make these statements because what is being done in Kuwait and this aggression is inconsistent with the principles of new political thinking and in fact, with the principles of civilized relations between nations.

Secretary Baker and I have decided to read for you the text of this joint statement. [Reads statement in Russian.] So this is the agreed text of the joint statement and we are now communicating this statement to you.

Secretary Baker. Let me simply join with the Minister in condemning what is indeed, as he characterized, a very tragic action by Iraq against Kuwait. I said at a press conference earlier in Mongolia that this was an outlaw action. It does indeed run counter to the principles of civilized behavior. I think it is natural, today, that the United States and the Soviet Union would find themselves in agreement with respect to their view of what's happened. This would not necessarily have been the case at an earlier time and we might be viewing this very tragic action—we might have been in earlier days viewing this very tragic action through an East-West prism. But we don't today and the Minister has indicated that there was some difficulty on the part of the Soviet Union in coming to this agreement. We understand that and I think it makes the fact of our joint statement and joint agreement even more meaningful.

Now I'd like to read the joint statement in English. [Reads statement.]

Q. The question from the Kuwait News Agency: Please tell us what specific steps you intend to take to make sure that this conflict between Iraq and Kuwait is settled as soon as possible and whether the Soviet Union is in direct contact with Iraq on this question.

Foreign Minister Shevardnadze. Well, what we read out to you—the agreed text of the joint statement—contains our political assessment of what has been happening. Of course, we have not stopped and we do not intend to suspend our direct contacts with the leaders of Iraq. Yesterday the Soviet leadership sent a special letter to the President of Iraq, President Saddam Hussein. We are also in touch through our Ambassadors in Moscow and in Baghdad.

The second point is about the possible other political measures or steps on the part of the Soviet Union or the United States. I think one of the main avenues is for us to work jointly to cooperate within the Security Council of the United Nations. You know that one Security Council resolution has already been adopted on this conflict. And if that resolution is not implemented, naturally we will have to think about the adoption of another resolution, in order to give us an appropriate basis for taking practical steps in order to put an end to this conflict. And we have a good degree of mutual understanding about working together within the Security Council with other partners.

The Secretary of State and I both believe that the Arab countries themselves can do a great deal. And also the nonaligned movement, the League of Arab countries and other regional organizations. And we will work hard to get those countries and those organizations to act.

Secretary Baker. Let me simply add to what the Minister has said in answer to your question that we are taking similar political steps, diplomatic steps, in terms of our consultations with other governments around the world. We look forward to working cooperatively with other governments in the United Nations with respect to this matter. In addition, the United States is instituting certain economic sanctions and taking certain economic actions against Iraq as a consequence of this action.

I think that it would be perhaps important to take note of one of the provisions in here calling for other nations to join the United States and the Soviet Union in an international arms embargo against Iraq. These steps that we have outlined are a lot more than simply rhetoric. They are specific and concrete actions.

Q. Mr. Secretary, if the actions taken so far and the diplomatic efforts fail to achieve the desired result, are the U.S. and the Soviet Union considering further cooperation against Iraq, perhaps in the area of economics or even military?

Secretary Baker. The Minister and I have agreed that we will—the two governments—will stay in close touch, in close contact with respect to this issue and further developments regarding this issue. I've already told you what the United States has done and is doing from an economic sanctions standpoint. As I mentioned in my press conference this morning, I don't think it is useful to speculate with respect to questions involving military actions.

Foreign Minister Shevardnadze. Just a couple of points here. We still continue to hope that the Iraqi leadership will have enough courage, enough resolution and political wisdom to make sure that this very bad situation—this action, very bad for the world community and for its own people—that this is ended. If that does not happen we will work together both bilaterally and also on a collective international basis.

Q. This is a question from TASS to Foreign Minister Shevardnadze. What is happening to the Soviet citizens there, specifically the military specialists who are there in those countries, and the second question is whether the cut-off of Soviet military supplies to Iraq is on a temporary or permanent basis, and also a question to the Secretary of State. Do you rule out the possibility that Iraq might also attack other Gulf states and if that happens, would you contemplate military action?

Foreign Minister Shevardnadze. I've said already that with Iraq we have a long standing relationship of cooperation and it is no secret that that cooperation includes cooperation in the military field. Yesterday we decided to cut off arms supplies and arms deliveries to that region—to that country. And as for the other areas we shall act taking into account the evolution of the situation.

Secretary Baker. Let me answer the question that you directed to me by saying that in light of the action that the Government of Iraq has taken here with respect to Kuwait, I don't think that you should prudently, rule out anything.

With respect to military responses, I've already answered that by saying I don't think it's useful to speculate with respect to military actions.

Q. The question to Foreign Minister Shevardnadze: You've said that you've been in touch with the Iraqis and can you say what the answer has been to your demands or to your contacts and secondly, would you rule out Soviet military intervention in this situation?

Foreign Minister Shevardnadze. We have not yet had any official reply from the Iraqi leadership. In Baghdad, we have had contacts at various levels and we have been assured that very soon the Iraqs will pull out their troops. As for military intervention, the Soviet Union does not have any such plans for any such operations and I understand the United States has no such plan at this time.

Q. A question from Soviet television to Foreign Minister Shevardnadze, whether the question of possible military action, military intervention by the United States or the Soviet Union was discussed at this meeting.

Foreign Minister Shevardnadze. As I said there are no such plans and if there are no such plans then there is no need to discuss this.

Q. Have the two governments asked China to join in the arms embargo against Iraq and what has the response been?

Foreign Minister Shevardnadze. We have not yet talked to the Chinese leadership about this, but we certainly will be in touch with them.

Q. Mr. Shevardnadze, can you tell us how many Soviet citizens there are at the present time in Iraq and in Kuwait, whether you have any concern about their safety, whether you have any plans to evacuate them and, Mr. Secretary, can you answer the same question please?

Foreign Minister Shevardnadze. In Kuwait, the total number of Soviet citizens there is about 900 persons. As for Iraq, there is a large group of Soviet specialists there, a large Soviet colony. The total number is from 7-8,000 persons, and that is a very old number. We expect that the security and safety of Soviet citizens there will be safeguarded. Otherwise there might be very, very severe consequences. I hope, I think that it will not come to that.

Secretary Baker. With respect to the (inaudible) of Americans, let me simply say in exactly the same terms that the Minister has used, we expect the safety and welfare of Americans to be safeguarded and there could be very serious consequences if that were not to be the case. I cannot give you the exact number of Americans in Iraq, but there are roughly 3,800 Americans in Kuwait.

United Nations Security Council Resolution 661, August 6, 1990 [2]

The Security Council,
Reaffirming its Resolution 660 (1990) of August 2, 1990,

Deeply concerned that that resolution has not been implemented and that the invasion by Iraq of Kuwait continues with further loss of life and material destruction,

Determined to bring the invasion and occupation of Kuwait by Iraq to an end and to restore the sovereignty, independence and territorial integrity of Kuwait,

Noting that the legitimate Government of Kuwait has expressed its readiness to comply with Resolution 660 (1990),

Mindful of its responsibilities under the Charter of the United Nations for the maintenance of international peace and security,

Affirming the inherent right of individual or collective self-defense, in response to the armed attack by Iraq against Kuwait, in accordance with Article 51 of the Charter,

Acting under Chapter VII of the Charter of the United Nations,

1. Determines that Iraq so far has failed to comply with paragraph 2 of Resolution 660 (1990) and has usurped the authority of the legitimate Government of Kuwait;

2. Decides, as a consequence, to take the following measures to secure compliance of Iraq with paragraph 2 of Resolution 660 (1990) and to restore the authority of the legitimate Government of Kuwait;

3. Decides that all States shall prevent:

(a) The import into their territories of all commodities and products originating in Iraq or Kuwait exported therefrom after the date of the present resolution;

(b) Any activities by their nationals or in their territories which would promote or are calculated to promote the export or transshipment of any commodities or products from Iraq or Kuwait; and any dealings by their nationals or their flag vessels or in their territories in any commodities or products originating in Iraq or Kuwait and exported therefrom after the date of the present resolution, including in particular any transfer of funds to Iraq or Kuwait for the purposes of such activities or dealings;

(c) The sale or supply by their nationals or from their territories or using their flag vessels of any commodities or products, including weapons or any other military equipment, whether or not originating in their territories but not including supplies intended strictly for medical purposes, and, in humanitarian circumstances, foodstuffs, to any person or body in Iraq or Kuwait or to any person or body for the purposes of any business carried on in or operated from Iraq and Kuwait, and any activities by their nationals or in their territories which promote or are calculated to promote such sale or supply of such commodities or products;

4. Decides that all States shall not make available to the Government of Iraq or to any commercial, industrial or public utility undertaking in Iraq and Kuwait, any funds or financial or economic resources and shall prevent their nationals and any persons within their territories from removing from their territories or otherwise making available to that Government or to any such undertaking any such funds or resources and from remitting any other funds to persons or bodies within Iraq or Kuwait, except payments exclusively for strictly medical or humanitarian purposes and, in special humanitarian circumstances, foodstuffs;

5. Calls upon all States, including States nonmembers of the United Nations, to act strictly in accordance with the provisions of the present resolution notwithstanding any contract entered into or license granted before the date of this resolution;

6. Decides to establish, in accordance with rule 28 of the provisional rules of procedure of the Security Council, a Committee of the Security Council consisting of all the members of the Council, to undertake the following tasks and to report on its work to the Council with its observations and recommendations:

(a) To examine the reports on the progress of the implementation of this resolution which will be submitted by the Secretary General;

(b) To seek from all States further information regarding the action taken by them concerning the effective implementation of the provisions laid down in this resolution;

7. Calls upon all States to cooperate fully with the Committee in the fulfillment of its task, including supplying such information as may be sought by the Committee in pursuance of this resolution;

8. Requests the Secretary General to provide all necessary assistance to the Committee and to make the necessary arrangements in the Secretariat for the purpose;

9. Decides that, notwithstanding paragraphs 4 through 8, nothing in the present resolution shall prohibit assistance to the legitimate Government of Kuwait, and calls upon all States:

(a) To take appropriate measures to protect assets of the legitimate Government of Kuwait and its agencies; and

(b) Not to recognize any regime set up by the occupying Power;

10. Requests the Secretary General to report to the Council on the progress of the implementation of the present

resolution, the first report to be submitted within thirty days;

11. Decides to keep this item on its agenda and to continue its efforts to put an early end to the invasion by Iraq.

Secretary of Defense Richard B. Cheney, Excerpt from Department of Defense Press Briefing, August 8, 1990 [4]

I thought I would open with a brief statement about my trip this past weekend. The decision was made on Saturday for me to travel to Saudi Arabia, the planning began on Saturday. The actual decision to go wasn't finalized until Sunday. I left Sunday afternoon accompanied by Bob Gates, General Scowcroft's deputy; by General Schwarzkopf who is our CINC [Commander-in-Chief] in charge of that part of the world; Paul Wolfowitz, the Under Secretary [of Defense] for Policy; and our Ambassador to Saudi Arabia, Mr. [Charles] Freeman, who was in the country at the time.

We arrived in Saudi Arabia on Monday, met with King Fahd on Monday evening, as well as the Crown Prince and other officials.

At that time, we discussed in general the intelligence that was available to us on the situation in the Gulf, reviewed with them the diplomatic developments and all of the work that had been underway by the President with respect to efforts to impose economic and political sanctions on Iraq in regard to its invasion of Kuwait. We then discussed with them in some detail the military situation on the ground in the Persian Gulf region, and we also presented to the King a rundown on our military capabilities.

Subsequent to those discussions the King made the request for the deployment of U.S. forces to the Kingdom of Saudi Arabia. I conveyed that request, by telephone, to the President. The President authorized me to deploy those forces, and I subsequently then gave instructions for those deployments to the Chairman [of the Joint Chiefs of Staff Colin L. Powell] by telephone back here in Washington, and of course to General Schwarzkopf who was with me in Jeddah, Saudi Arabia.

Subsequent to that, I had a meeting the next morning with Prince Sultan who is the Saudi Defense Minister. We discussed in greater detail the deployments that are now underway. When I left Saudi Arabia, at the direction of the President, I stopped and visited, as I think has been announced, President Mubarak in Alexandria, Egypt, and then last evening King Hassan in Rabat, Morocco.

Presidential Address to the Nation Announcing the Deployment of Forces to Saudi Arabia, August 8, 1990 [5]

In the life of a nation, we're called upon to define who we are and what we believe. Sometimes these choices are not easy. But today as President, I ask for your support in a decision I've made to stand up for what's right and condemn what's wrong, all in the cause of peace.

At my direction, elements of the 82d Airborne Division as well as key units of the United States Air Force are arriving today to take up defensive positions in Saudi Arabia. I took this action to assist the Saudi Arabian Government in the defense of its homeland. No one commits America's armed forces to a dangerous mission lightly, but after perhaps unparalleled international consultation and exhausting every alternative, it became necessary to take this action. Let me tell you why.

Why U.S. Forces Were Deployed

Less than a week ago, in the early morning hours of August 2d, Iraqi armed forces, without provocation or warning, invaded a peaceful Kuwait. Facing negligible resistance from its much smaller neighbor, Iraq's tanks stormed in blitzkrieg fashion through Kuwait in a few short hours. With more than 100,000 troops, along with tanks, artillery, and surface-to-surface missiles, Iraq now occupies Kuwait. This aggression came just hours after Saddam Hussein [President of Iraq] specifically assured numerous countries in the area that there would be no invasion. There is no justification whatsoever for this outrageous and brutal act of aggression.

A puppet regime imposed from the outside is unacceptable. The acquisition of territory by force is unacceptable. No one, friend or foe, should doubt our desire for peace; and no one should underestimate our determination to confront aggression.

Four simple principles guide our policy. First, we seek the immediate, unconditional, and complete withdrawal of all Iraqi forces from Kuwait. Second, Kuwait's legitimate government must be restored to replace the puppet regime. And third, my administration, as has been the case with every President from President Roosevelt to President Reagan, is committed to the security and stability of the Persian Gulf. And fourth, I am determined to protect the lives of American citizens abroad.

Immediately after the Iraqi invasion, I ordered an embargo of all trade with Iraq and, together with many other nations, announced sanctions that both freeze all Iraqi assets in this country and protected Kuwait's assets. The stakes are high. Iraq is already a rich and powerful country that possesses the world's second largest reserves of oil and over a million men under arms. It's the fourth largest military in the world. Our country now imports nearly half the oil it consumes and could face a major threat to its economic independence. Much of the world is even more dependent upon imported oil and is even more vulnerable to Iraqi threats.

We succeeded in the struggle for freedom in Europe because we and our allies remain stalwart. Keeping the peace in the Middle East will require no less. We're beginning a new era. This new era can be full of promise, an age of freedom, a time of peace for all peoples. But if history teaches us anything, it is that we must resist aggression or it will destroy our freedoms. Appeasement does not work. As was the case in the 1930's, we see in Saddam Hussein an aggressive dictator threatening his neighbors. Only 14 days ago, Saddam Hussein promised his friends he would not invade Kuwait. And four days ago, he promised the world he would withdraw. And twice we have seen what his promises mean: His promises mean nothing.

In the last few days, I've spoken with political leaders from the Middle East, Europe, Asia, and the Americas; and I've met with Prime Minister Thatcher [of the United Kingdom], Prime Minister Mulroney [of Canada], and NATO Secretary General Woerner. And all agree that Iraq cannot be allowed to benefit from its invasion of Kuwait.

We agree that this is not an American problem or a European problem or a Middle East problem: it is the world's problem. And that's why, soon after the Iraqi invasion, the United Nations Security Council, without dissent, condemned Iraq, calling for the immediate and unconditional withdrawal of its troops from Kuwait. The Arab world, through both the Arab League and the Gulf Cooperation Council, courageously announced its opposition to Iraqi aggression. Japan, the United Kingdom, and France, and other governments around the world have imposed severe sanctions. The Soviet Union and China ended all arms sales to Iraq.

And this past Monday, the United Nations Security Council approved for the first time in 23 years mandatory sanctions under Chapter VII of the United Nations Charter. These sanctions, now enshrined in international law, have the potential to deny Iraq the fruits of aggression while sharply limiting its ability to either import or export anything of value, especially oil.

I pledge here today that the United States will do its part to see that these sanctions are effective and to induce Iraq to withdraw without delay from Kuwait.

But we must recognize that Iraq may not stop using force to advance its ambitions. Iraq has massed an enormous war machine on the Saudi border capable of initiating hostilities with little or no additional preparation. Given the Iraqi government's history of aggression against its own citizens as well as its neighbors, to assume Iraq will not attack again would be unwise and unrealistic.

And therefore, after consulting with King Fahd [of Saudi Arabia], I sent Secretary of Defense Dick Cheney to discuss cooperative measures we could take. Following those meetings, the Saudi Government requested our help, and I responded to that request by ordering U.S. air and ground forces to deploy to the Kingdom of Saudi Arabia.

Let me be clear: The sovereign independence of Saudi Arabia is of vital interest to the United States. This decision, which I shared with the congressional leadership, grows out of the longstanding friendship and security relationship between the United States and Saudi Arabia. U.S. forces will work together with those of Saudi Arabia and other nations to preserve the integrity of Saudi Arabia and to deter further Iraqi aggression. Through their presence, as well as through training and exercises, these multinational forces will enhance

the overall capability of Saudi armed forces to defend the Kingdom.

Defensive Nature of Deployment

I want to be clear about what we are doing and why. America does not seek conflict, nor do we seek to chart the destiny of other nations. But America will stand by her friends. The mission of our troops is wholly defensive. Hopefully, they will not be needed long. They will not initiate hostilities, but they will defend themselves, the Kingdom of Saudi Arabia, and other friends in the Persian Gulf.

We are working around the clock to deter Iraqi aggression and to enforce U.N. sanctions. I'm continuing my conversations with world leaders. Secretary of Defense Cheney has just returned from valuable consultations with President Mubarak of Egypt and King Hassan of Morocco. Secretary of State Baker has consulted with his counterparts in many nations, including the Soviet Union, and today he heads for Europe to consult with President Ozal of Turkey, a staunch friend of the United States. And he'll then consult with the NATO Foreign Ministers.

I will ask oil producing nations to do what they can to increase production in order to minimize any impact that oil flow reductions will have on the world economy. And I will explore whether we and our allies should draw down our strategic petroleum reserves. Conservation measures can also help; Americans everywhere must do their part. And one more thing: I'm asking the oil companies to do their fair share. They should show restraint and not abuse today's uncertainties to raise prices.

Standing up for our principles will not come easy. It may take time and possibly cost a great deal. But we are asking no more of anyone than of the brave young men and women of our armed forces and their families. And I ask that in the churches around the country prayers be said for those who are committed to protect and defend America's interests.

Standing up for our principles is an American tradition. As it has so many times before, it may take time and tremendous effort, but most of all, it will take unity of purpose. As I've witnessed throughout my life in both war and peace, America has never wavered when her purpose is driven by principle. And on this August day, at home and abroad, I know she will do no less.

Thank you, and God bless the United States of America.

President's Letters to the Speaker of the House and the President Pro Tempore of the Senate, August 9, 1990 [5]

Dear Mr. Speaker: (Dear Mr. President:)

On August 2, 1990, Iraq invaded and occupied the sovereign state of Kuwait in flagrant violation of the Charter of the United Nations. In the period since August 2, Iraq has massed an enormous and sophisticated war machine on the Kuwaiti-Saudi Arabian border and in southern Iraq, capable of initiating further hostilities with little or no additional preparation. Iraq's actions pose a direct threat to neighboring countries and to vital U.S. interests in the Persian Gulf region.

In response to this threat and after receiving the request of the Government of Saudi Arabia, I ordered the forward deployment of substantial elements of the United States Armed Forces into the region. I am providing this report on the deployment and mission of our Armed Forces in accordance with my desire that Congress be fully informed and consistent with the War Powers Resolution.

Two squadrons of F-15 aircraft, one brigade of the 82nd Airborne Division, and other elements of the Armed Forces began arriving in Saudi Arabia at approximately 9:00 a.m. (EDT) on August 8, 1990. Additional U.S. air, naval, and ground forces also will be deployed. The forces are equipped for combat, and their mission is defensive. They are prepared to take action in concert with Saudi forces, friendly regional forces, and others to deter Iraqi aggression and to preserve the integrity of Saudi Arabia.

I do not believe involvement in hostilities is imminent; to the contrary, it is my belief that this deployment will facilitate a peaceful resolution of the crisis. If necessary, however, the forces are fully prepared to defend themselves. Although it is not possible to predict the precise scope and duration of this deployment, our Armed Forces will remain so long as their presence is required to contribute to the security of the region and desired by the Saudi Government to enhance the capability of Saudi armed forces to defend the Kingdom.

I have taken these actions pursuant to my constitutional authority to conduct our foreign relations and as Commander in Chief. These actions are in exercise of our inherent right of individual and collective self-defense. I look forward to cooperation with the Congress in helping to restore peace and stability to the Persian Gulf region.

Dear Mr. Speaker: (Dear Mr. President:)

On August 2, 1990, I reported to the Congress that, pursuant to section 204(b) of the International Emergency Economic Powers Act, 50 U.S.C. section 1703(b), and section 201 of the National Emergencies Act, 50 U.S.C. section 1621, I exercised my statutory authority to declare a national emergency and to issue two Executive orders that imposed a comprehensive economic embargo against Iraq and blocked both Iraqi and Kuwaiti government property within the jurisdiction of the United States or under the control of U.S. persons.

In the days after the imposition of U.S. economic sanctions, the Iraqi government has tightened its unlawful grip over the territory of Kuwait and has installed a puppet regime that in no way represents the people or legitimate Government of Kuwait. On August 6, the United Nations Security Council, to bring the invasion and occupation of Kuwait to an end and to restore the sovereignty, independence, and territorial integrity of Kuwait, decided that all nations shall impose sweeping economic sanctions against both Iraq and Kuwait.

Today, I have taken additional steps to respond to these developments and to ensure that the economic measures we are taking with respect to Iraq and Kuwait conform to United Nations Security Council Resolution 661 of August 6, 1990. Specifically, pursuant to section 204(b) of the International Emergency Economic Powers Act, 50 U.S.C. section 1703(b), section 201 of the National Emergencies Act, 50 U.S.C. section 1621, and the United Nations Participation Act, 22 U.S.C. section 287(c), I have issued two new Executive orders.

The order I have issued with respect to Iraq:

— prohibits exports and imports of goods and services between the United States and Iraq, and any activity that promotes or is intended to promote such exportation and importation;

— prohibits any dealing by a U.S. person in connection with property of Iraqi origin exported from Iraq after August 6, 1990, or intended for exportation to or from Iraq to any country, and related activities;

— prohibits transactions related to travel to or from Iraq or to activities by any such person within Iraq, except for transactions necessary for prompt departure from Iraq, the conduct of official business of the United States Government or of the United Nations, or journalistic travel;

— prohibits transactions related to transportation to or from Iraq, or the use of vessels or aircraft registered in Iraq by U.S. persons;

— prohibits the performance by any U.S. person of any contract in support of certain categories of projects in Iraq;

— prohibits the commitment or transfer of funds or other financial or economic resources by any U.S. person to the Government of Iraq, or any other person in Iraq;

— blocks all property of the Government of Iraq now or hereafter located in the United States or in the possession or control of U.S. persons, including their foreign branches; and

— clarifies that the definition of U.S. persons includes vessels of U.S. registry.

In a separate order, I have extended to Kuwait all economic sanctions currently in effect against Iraq. Specifically, that order:

— prohibits exports and imports of goods and services between the United States and Kuwait, and any activity that promotes or is intended to promote such exportation or importation;

— prohibits any dealing by a U.S. person in connection with property of Kuwaiti origin exported from Kuwait after August 6, 1990, or intended for exportation to or from Kuwait to any country, and related activities;

— prohibits transactions related to travel to or from Kuwait or to activities by any such person within Kuwait, except for transactions necessary for prompt departure from Kuwait, the conduct of official business of the United States Government or of the United Nations, or journalistic travel;

— prohibits transactions related to transportation to or from Kuwait, or the use of vessels or aircraft registered in Kuwait by U.S. persons;

— prohibits the performance by any U.S. person of any contract in support of certain categories of projects in Kuwait;

— prohibits the commitment or transfer of funds or other financial or economic resources by any U.S. person to the Government of Kuwait, or any other person in Kuwait;

— blocks all property of the Government of Kuwait now or hereafter located in the United States or in the possession or control of U.S. persons, including their foreign branches; and

— clarifies that definition of U.S. persons includes vessels of U.S. registry.

Today's orders provide that the Secretary of the Treasury, in consultation with the Secretary of State, is authorized to take such actions, including the promulgation of rules and regulations, as may be necessary to carry out the purposes of those orders.

The orders were effective at 8:55 p.m. EDT, August 9, 1990.

The declarations of national emergency made by Executive Orders 12722 and 12723, and any other provision of those orders not inconsistent with today's orders, remain in force and are unaffected by today's orders.

I am enclosing a copy of each of today's orders.

[The texts of Executive Orders 12724 and 12725 were filed with the Office of the Federal Register on August 10, 1990.]

King Fahd of Saudi Arabia Addresses His Nation, August 9, 1990 [6]

An official Saudi source made a statement to the Saudi Press Agency in which he said, "The government of the Kingdom of Saudi Arabia wishes to express its sincere gratitude to all the brotherly Arab countries, and to the friendly nations that have promptly responded to the Kingdom's desire of dispatching troops from their countries to assist the Saudi armed forces in defending its integrity and its economic potentials, in the current circumstances, as explained by King Fahd bin Abdul-Aziz, the Custodian of the Two Holy Mosques and the Supreme Commander of the Saudi armed forces, in his speech to the citizens today, Thursday, the 18th of Muharram 1411.H."

The source added, "The response of our Arab brothers and our friends in the West shows the extent of those countries' understanding of the dangers faced by the Arab Nation in these critical moments of its history. That response also signifies the interest of these countries in the stability and security of the Arab Gulf region and consequently the return to normalcy to the State of Kuwait, the restoration of the legitimate government and the removal of all consequences resulting from ther Iraqi invasion of Kuwait."

The source concluded by saying, "The Kingdom of Saudi Arabia, while expressing its gratitude to the nations whose forces have already arrived in the Kingdom and those nations whose forces will arrive today and tomorrow, emphasizes that the objective of the presence of such forces is strictly defensive and temporary. Their mission will end as soon as the reasons for their participation in the maintenance of peace and security of all the nations of the Gulf end."

Saddam Hussein Asserts Kuwait "Merger" with Iraq, August 9, 1990 [7]

President Saddam Hussein has said that Iraq's decision to accept the Kuwaiti new free interim government's appeal for a full merger with Iraq is final and irreversible, warning that those who are trying to hamper this decision will reap nothing but defeat and humiliation. The President's warning was made during a session of the National Assembly on Wednesday and a meeting with the top officials of the Arab Bath Socialist Party on Tuesday.

The President described the merger decision as a historical turning point which would leave its imprint on coming resolutions. Today's turning point means new will, determination and firmness when things have to be rectified, the President said.

He said the return of Kuwait to Iraq is the return of the branch to its origin. It is the return of Kuwait to its people, in all parts of Iraq. It is the return of the part which has been torn away from Iraq, the party where all nationalist and human values have been assassinated, the President said.

The President went on to say that it is time for justice to appear and new Iraq to be able to face up to the enemies, no matter how huge their numbers are. We are not aggressors, we don't intend to launch aggression, but he who ventures to launch an aggression

(against Iraq) will regret it and Iraq's will would remain intact from the land of Zakho (in northernmost Iraq) to the sea in Al-Ahmadi and Kuwait, the President said.

The President told the party members that Iraq had decided to put things back to normal underlying the fact that Iraq and Kuwait are one people, one country, and one future. The decision implies a challenge to those who try to obstruct the movement of history as desired by the Bath (Party). We tell those who are frustrated and conspirators that we will not bow to anybody but to God and that the will that took the decision shall not compromise, the President stressed.

The President warned that those who have not had an experience with Iraq and the Bathist can try their fortune to finally find themselves defeated in all fields. I ask you and the people to accept the enemies' challenge, to prove in the name of the people that you are capable of inflicting a heavy defeat on them, regardless of their names or how big their fleets and geographical areas are. They will be defeated along with division, and unity shall triumph, the President said.

U.N. Security Council Resolution 662, August 9, 1990 [2]

The Security Council,
Recalling its resolutions 660 (1990) and 661 (1990),
Gravely alarmed by the declaration by Iraq of a "comprehensive and eternal merger" with Kuwait,
Demanding, once again, that Iraq withdraw immediately and unconditionally all its forces to the positions in which they were located on 1 August 1990,
Determined to bring the occupation of Kuwait by Iraq to an end and to restore the sovereignty, independence and territorial integrity of Kuwait,
Determined also to restore the authority of the legitimate Government of Kuwait,
1. Decides that annexation of Kuwait by Iraq under any form and whatever pretext has no legal validity, and is considered null and void;
2. Calls upon all States, international organizations and specialized agencies not to recognize that annexation, and to refrain from any action or deal-

ing that might be interpreted as an indirect recognition of the annexation;
3. Further demands that Iraq rescind its actions purporting to annex Kuwait;
4. Decides to keep this item on its agenda and to continue its efforts to put an early end to the occupation.

Statement to the Security Council by Ambassador Thomas R. Pickering, U.S. Permanent Representative to the United Nations, August 9, 1990 [8]

Mr. President, we are pleased and gratified by the unanimous approval of the Council of Resolution 662. The United States does not recognize Iraq's outrageous and unlawful declaration that Kuwait is part of Iraq.

My government, therefore, is eager to support the legitimate government of Kuwait through the consensus resolution which we have adopted which declares that any such charade is null and void, and without legal effect. Iraq repeatedly over the last several days has shown its scorn for the international community and for the resolutions of this body. Iraq's declaration is further proof of its continuing threat to the world community and its disdain for international law. For our part, at the request of governments in the region, the United States has increased its presence in the area. Mr. President, we are in the course of informing this Council officially by appropriate letter of our action taken under Article 51 of the Charter. As President Bush said yesterday, this is entirely defensive in purpose, to help protect Saudi Arabia, and is taken under Article 51 of the United Nations Charter and indeed in consistency with Article 41 and Resolution 661.

As Resolution 661 affirms, Article 51 applies in this case. The Iraqi invasion of Kuwait and the large military presence on the Saudi frontier creates grave risks of further aggression in the area. This being the case my government and others are, at the request of Saudi Arabia, sending forces with which to deter further Iraqi aggression.

Why is this resolution necessary? It is necessary because Iraq is attempting to extinguish the sovereignty of a member state of the United Nations.

There is something repugnant, chilling and vaguely familiar about the statement issued yesterday by the Iraqi Revolutionary Command Council. We have heard that rhetoric before. It was used about the Rhineland, the Sudetenland, about the Polish corridor, about Mussolini's invasion of Ethiopia and about the Marco Polo Bridge incident in China. It was used to divide and to swallow up sovereign states contrary to international law. The world community did not react. The result was global conflagration.

We believe the international community has learned this lesson well. We here will not and cannot let this happen again. We have finally learned the grim lesson of the 1930's which was succinctly articulated by a Soviet Foreign Minister of the era, Maxim Litvinov. He said "Peace is indivisible." We agree.

My government is heartened by the response from the world community to Resolution 661 and we are confident that the procedures to implement it are well underway by the member states and in the United Nations. Resolutions 660 and 661 should be used not only to contain this cancerous act of aggression but also to require Iraq to withdraw its forces immediately, unconditionally, and totally.

The Council also again today calls for the restoration of the legitimate authority, sovereignty, and territorial integrity of Kuwait.

By this resolution the international community again reaffirms that this crisis is not a "regional" matter alone; that it threatens us all and that we have learned the lessons of history. We cannot allow sovereign state members of the United Nations to be swallowed up. The United States stands ready to return to the Council as circumstances warrant to seek further Council action to implement Resolution 660. We are gratified that the Council continues to work expeditiously and effectively in its efforts to deal with this crisis.

League of Arab States Resolution Condemning Iraqi Aggression, August 10, 1990 [9]

The Arab Summit which convened in Cairo August 10, 1990 has decided:
— To confirm a resolution passed by the Arab League Council August 3

and a resolution issued by the Islamic Conference Organization August 4.
— To confirm Security Council Resolutions 660 dated August 2, 661 dated August 6, and 662 dated August 9 as an expression of legitimacy.
— To condemn Iraqi aggression against the brotherly state of Kuwait and not to recognize Iraq's decision to annex Kuwait or any other results arising from the invasion of Iraqi troops of Kuwaiti territory. It demands Iraq withdraws its troops from Kuwait immediately and returns it to the state it was before August 1.
— To confirm Kuwait's sovereignty, its independendence and regional security being a member state in the Arab League and the United Nations. It also insists on the return of its legitimate government which was present before the Iraqi invasion. It supports all measures taken to free its land and fulfill its sovereignty.
— To denounce Iraqi threats to gulf Arab states and to denounce Iraq's buildup of armed forces on the borders of Saudi Arabia. It confirms total Arab solidarity with the Kingdom and the other gulf Arab states.

It supports measures taken by Saudi Arabia and other gulf Arab states to defend their legitimate rights according to Article Two of the joint Defense and Economic Cooperation Pact between Arab League states and Article 51 in the United Nations Charter and Security Council Resolution 661, dated August 6. These measures should be stopped immediately after the total withdrawal of Iraqi troops from Kuwait and the return of Kuwait's legitimate authority.
— To respond to Saudi Arabia and other gulf Arab states' request to transfer Arab forces to support their armed forces to defend their land and regional security against any outside aggression.

The emergency Arab summit has commissioned the Arab League Secretary General to follow up the execution of this decision and to issue a report on it within 15 days to the league's council to take appropriate measures.

Intervention by Secretary Baker at Special Session of the North Atlantic Council, Brussels, August 10, 1990 [10]

We have assembled here today to deal with an act of aggression that threatens both our moral principles and our material interests.

Only one week ago, the Government of Iraq attacked and occupied its neighbor, the sovereign state of Kuwait. This premeditated, unprovoked assault has already cost many innocent lives. Oil and financial markets have been thrown into turmoil. Above all, hopes have been jeopardized that as the Cold War winds down, a new era of freedom and peace will begin for all nations.

The issue we face, therefore, goes beyond the fate of a single state or, for that matter, the price and supply of oil. It is not only Kuwait that has been attacked. It is not only economic progress that is threatened. If might is to make right, then the world will be plunged into a new dark age.

This is a sudden and tragic turn of events. Over the past year, we have gathered around this table to celebrate extraordinary historical events. Our alliance, faithful to its principles, has kept the peace of Europe for over 40 years. We have worked hard for the day when Europe would be whole and free. Now, as that day approaches, NATO is adapting to a new situation on the continent — one full of promise.

Far sooner than anyone could have predicted, however, the members of NATO must adapt to a different situation outside of Europe, this one full of peril. Iraq has just emerged from a decade of carnage in a war with neighbors and many nations represented in this room were helpful to the cause of Baghdad in that terrible struggle. Many believed, and there was reason to believe, that Iraq would close the book of war and write a new book, beginning with a chapter on peaceful relations with its neighbors. Surely that was in Iraq's interest. Just as surely, that remains the true interest of the people of Iraq today.

Instead, we have seen a continuous and unrelenting buildup of arms. The Iraqi dictator, Saddam Hussein, has spared no expense to sustain a vast force, far out of proportion to any conceivable threat. Hundreds of thousands of soldiers remain under arms. Iraq deploys some 5,700 modern tanks, the fourth largest tank army in the world. And Iraq's 10,000 other armored vehicles rank it third after the Soviet Union and the United States.

Despite all international appeals, Saddam has continued to develop the chemical weapons that he used against Iran and, yes, even against his own people. He has amassed hundreds of rockets, with which he once attacked Iranian cities. He continues a vigorous nuclear research program, with ominous implications.

Why was the leader of a nation, needing so badly to heal it own wounds, wasting its resources on yet more arms? Now we have the answer. Those arms were for aggression — to intimidate and to attack, to bend to Saddam's will the sovereignty of his neighbors.

We need not waste any time on the argument that this large, very powerful and battle-hardened Iraq was mortally threatened by the allegedly aggressive acts of the Amir of Kuwait. Nor should we concern ourselves with the lies about a popular revolution that overthrew the Amir and invited Iraqi help to restore order. All of us here have heard such falsehoods before. They echo down through the corridors of this century's tragic history, the very history we have sworn never to repeat.

The stakes involved in the current crisis in the Gulf are very high for all of us around this table. Since 1949, every American president has said that the Gulf is a vital U.S. and Western interest and that we could not allow any hostile power to gain a stranglehold over its energy resources. Now Saddam Hussein poses just such a threat. Given the central importance of Gulf oil to the global economy, all of us share an interest in thwarting this dictator's ambitions. We all have a very critical stake in this.

And all of us also have a broader stake in stability in the Middle East — an already violent neighborhood made worse by Saddam's bellicosity. Indeed, one of the strategic anchors of our alliance, Turkey, lies critically exposed along its southern borders to dangers aggravated by Iraq's aggression.

And finally, all of us share a deep interest born of bitter experience in demonstrating that aggression does not pay. We know the history of the 1930s and how appeasement whets the appetite of aggressors. I can think of few examples in recent history of aggression more callous or more brutal than

Saddam's invasion of Kuwait. If all our hopes for a new and more peaceful international order are ever to become a reality, we must act now to blunt Saddam Hussein's menacing ambitions.

In the face of this grave challenge, President Bush has laid out four basic objectives to guide American policy. *First,* we seek the immediate, unconditional and complete withdrawal of all Iraqi forces from Kuwait. *Second,* Kuwait's legitimate government must be restored to replace the puppet regime. *Third,* we remain committed to the security and stability of the Gulf. And *fourth,* we are determined to protect the lives of our citizens abroad.

From our extensive consultations in recent days, I think it is fair to say that all of us share those fundamental goals. The question now is how best can we coordinate our actions to achieve them. The comprehensive response of the international community, to which all of us have contributed in different ways, has been extraordinary and remarkable.

The United Nations Security Council has acted swiftly to condemn Iraq, call for its withdrawal from Kuwait and approve for the first time in 23 years mandatory sanctions under Chapter VII of the U.N. Charter. These measures will take time to make an impact on Saddam, but they can be very powerful if we are patient and resolute. And if we are diligent and vigorous in preventing exemptions and cheating.

A sure sign of new times is that the Soviet Union has joined the community of nations in condemning Iraq. The unprecedented joint statement and its call to action that the United States and the Soviet Union issued in Moscow laid the groundwork, I believe, for the almost unanimous vote on sanctions in the Security Council. It has helped to cement the strong international consensus, and helped ensure Iraq's isolation in the Middle East. I have stayed in close contact with [Soviet Foreign Minister] Eduard Shevardnadze, on an almost daily basis, believing strongly that we have to keep the Soviets engaged. And, as part of this ongoing effort, I will meet with the Soviet Ambassador here in Brussels who has been designated to be the Soviet liaison to NATO — another example of our changing times and our evolving alliance.

Comprehensive international sanctions are one crucial step toward blunting Saddam's aggression. Our work here today at NATO is another part of the answer. A new danger has arisen,

coming from a distant place but with the capacity to strike all of us. Even as traditional threats have dramatically diminished (and shaped our hopes for the future), we now see a threat that poses a new challenge and new dangers. We are reminded that our security and well-being can be challenged from new directions and new sources. And some of our member states, like Turkey, may acquire even greater strategic importance as we cope with a changed security environment.

Our consultations on this crisis, on this challenge, are a reminder of our changing circumstances and our adapting alliance.

This alliance, spanning the Atlantic, is a symbol of Western unity, and it is here that we should demonstrate our solidarity in the present crisis. We need to block further aggression; we need to buy time for U.N. sanctions to undo the aggression that has already occurred; and we need to cooperate to ensure these sanctions are effective. We are not alone. Yet the world will look to us — to the nations represented here today — for leadership. We should provide it.

There are four messages I hope can emerge from today's meeting. *First,* that the members of this alliance will contribute — each in their own way — to stopping further Iraqi military aggression. We have taken steps of our own. I should note that the military deployments we are making are coming at the Saudis' request, following Iraqi broken promises and an ominous and continuing buildup.

We know from our discussions with them that the Saudis and other nations of the Gulf hope that multinational force assistance will be as broad as possible, both from the Arab world and from the West. Some among you have already made decisions to join us in dispatching military assets to the Gulf area. These contributions are vital, politically and militarily. We endorse the goal of a multinational effort, and we urge each of you to examine how you might help.

A *second* message I hope we can send is that we are ready to stand by our collective defense obligations. I have just come from Ankara, where I had the opportunity to talk with President Ozal, Prime Minister Akbulut, and Foreign Minister Bozer. President Bush asked me to strengthen our contacts with a key ally and a bulwark for the alliance on its southern flank. In our discussions, President Ozal and his colleagues reemphasized their strong commitment to NATO and the West, and it is fortunate for us that they have such a commitment.

We should therefore emphasize, publicly and privately, the cohesion of our alliance and the indivisibility of our mutual security. This means the unequivocal reaffirmation of our clear and unconditional obligations under Article Five of the North Atlantic Treaty, which provides that an armed attack against any member of the alliance shall be considered an attack against all the members of this alliance. This council should be prepared to meet at any time, pursuant to Article Four of the Treaty, should the territorial integrity or security of any NATO member state be threatened. Such a meeting would discuss possible collective action that would supplement the immediate right of self-defense recognized by the U.N. Charter and the automatic duty of each NATO member to assist another member that has been the victim of an armed attack. I hope we will never need to have such a meeting. But our clear readiness to do so is the best way to prevent it. There should be no miscalculations about our resolve.

In addition to deterring further Iraqi aggression, we should cooperate to undo the aggression which has already taken place.

Our *third* message should thus be that this alliance endorses actions which member states may take in order to enforce the mandatory sanctions put in place by U.N. Security Council Resolution 661. If these U.N. sanctions fail, despite enjoying such a rare unanimity of support, then it is hard to imagine how any U.N. sanctions could ever succeed. The United Nations, as an institution, will have suffered a mortal blow—just as the League of Nations did before it, under analogous circumstances. We do not want this to happen. There is no need today to dwell on what may need to be done. An international blockade is certainly a possibility. But first we should give the sanctions some time to work, and give ourselves time to see what else is needed to make them effective. We should show, however, that we will do whatever must be done in order to enforce the will of the United Nations.

Finally, we should send a signal that NATO is a place where we can consult and work together to meet a common crisis. As our heads of state and government announced, in May 1989, "Worldwide developments which affect

our security interests are legitimate matters for consultation and, where appropriate, coordination among us. Our security is to be seen in a context broader than the protection from war alone." This challenge from Iraq has an additional feature. Turkey, one of our members, is in the frontline of potential conflict. I know this is a sensitive point for some of you. My suggestion is simple. Members of the Alliance should exchange information in NATO about their political and military activities, to facilitate practical cooperation in whatever channels—bilateral or multilateral—are most useful.

I want to conclude with this thought. What we do here today, I am convinced, carries significance far beyond the situation in the Persian Gulf. This is the first crisis of the postpostwar era. Our challenge, as I have often said, is to leave behind not only the Cold War but also the conflicts which preceded it. Now acting together we have the opportunity to do so.

Secretary Bakers's Press Conference Following the North Atlantic Council Special Session, Brussels, August 10, 1990 [11]

First of all, let me say that over the past year we've met often here in Brussels to discuss and to review and to celebrate some very historic and extraordinary events. This Alliance, faithful to its principles, has kept the peace of Europe for over 40 years. We have worked hard to the day when Europe would be whole and Europe would be free. Now, as that day approaches, NATO is adapting to a new situation on the continent—one that I think is full of promise.

Far sooner than anyone could have predicted, however, the members of NATO are adapting to a different situation outside of Europe, this one full of peril. Saddam Hussein's wanton aggression has raised the stakes for all of us. Since 1949, every American president has reaffirmed that the Gulf is a vital Western interest, and that we could not allow any hostile power to gain a stranglehold over its energy resources.

Never historically has that a threat been as real or as immediate as it is today. Given the central importance of Gulf oil to the global economy, we all share an interest in thwarting Iraq's menacing and unlimited ambitions.

NATO members also have a broader stake in the stability of the Middle East—an already violent neighborhood made worse by Iraqi bellicosity. Indeed, a strategic anchor of our alliance, Turkey, lies critically exposed along its southern borders to dangers aggravated by Iraq.

And finally, all of us share a deep interest born of bitter experience in demonstrating that aggression does not pay.

The reaction to Iraq's threat from the international community—to which all of NATO's members have contributed in different ways—has already been remarkable. The U.N. Security Council has approved for the first time in 23 years mandatory sanctions under Chapter VII of the U.N. Charter.

Comprehensive international sanctions are one crucial step towards stopping Iraqi aggression. Our work here today at NATO is another part of the answer.

I think that today's meeting was extremely useful. It demonstrated unmistakable resolve and solidarity on the present crisis.

I proposed four points and there was very strong support for all of them. *First,* that the members of the Alliance support President Bush's decision to deploy forces to Saudi Arabia and will contribute each in their own way to blocking further Iraqi aggression.

Second, we stand by our collective defense obligations to Turkey.

Third, the alliance support actions which member states may take to help enforce U.N. sanction. We agree that we must do what must be done in order to enforce the will of the United Nations.

And *fourth,* we sent another signal that NATO is a place where we can consult and where we can work together to meet a common crisis. The pressure of recent events has demonstrated NATO's vitality as a forum for political consultations on the most urgent challenges we face—a role that we have discussed for the Alliance over the course of the past year. We all recognize the practical value of NATO as a forum for exchanging information and consulting about ongoing military activities.

Let me conclude with this thought. What the members of NATO do in response to the Iraqi threat carries significance far beyond the situation in the Gulf. This is the first crisis of the postpostwar era. Our challenge is to demonstrate that armed aggression still doesn't pay.

Acting with other nations, the members of NATO are demonstrating our unity in confronting a common danger. We are demonstrating, I think, that in a new era we can work together in dealing with threats from new sources and from new directions.

I'd be glad to take your questions.

Q. In your statement here and in your intervention you declaim, deplore what Saddam Hussein has done. You call him a dictator, etc. You talk about a war-weary country. Is he so out of sync with his people that the United States would like to see the Iraqi people remove, overthrow, do away with Saddam Hussein as being out of step?

A. I'm not going to suggest that that is something that the United States is interested in or pursuing. That's a matter for the people of Iraq to determine — that is who will constitute their leadership. But I am suggesting that the entire world community has risen up in almost complete unity to condemn the aggression that has taken place by Iraq under the leadership of Saddam Hussein and has called for the immediate withdrawal of Iraqi forces from Kuwait and for the imposition of mandatory sanctions for the first time in 23 years.

Q. Are the Westerners being held against their will in Iraq hostages now, and what is the U.S. position? What is the U.S. prepared to do about it?

A. Well, the United States is very disturbed about the restrictions on the freedom of travel of all foreign nationals in Iraq and in Kuwait, including, of course, American government officials and American citizens. And you know the high priority that President Bush has placed upon the safety and welfare of our citizens. Most, if not all, foreign nationals are being prevented from leaving Iraq and Kuwait against their will. As far as we know, nothing has been asked or demanded for their freedom. Their restraint is, though, against all international norms. We are not calling them hostages because discussions are ongoing even as we speak here this afternoon about obtaining permission for them to leave. As best we can tell — so far, at least — they have not been mistreated.

Q. As a result of your consultations today, could you tell us whether the Allies on an individual basis will be sending any help to stand beside American troops in Saudi Arabia or elsewhere if they are needed?

A. A number of members of the NATO Alliance have indicated that they do intend to send military support to the efforts that are currently under way in Saudi Arabia and in the Persian Gulf. The United Kingdom and France and the United States, of course, have been quite specific about the types and the nature of the support that they intend to furnish. Germany, Belgium, and Canada have expressed indications, or gave indications that they will be having announcements to make in due course respecting some sort of support. Of course those announcements are for them to make and not for me to make. I do think it's not inappropriate for me on behalf of the United States to express our gratitude to the countries I've just mentioned and to the countries of Italy, Spain, and Portugal, who have been very forthcoming insofar as our use of bases on their territory is concerned in the current crisis.

Q. Secretary General Woerner explained why NATO as an organization could not engage in any kind of military support, but it does seem to some of us sitting here that certainly NATO, rather than just saying it supported what other states have done in the military sphere, could have said that, for instance, it urged all its members to lend support. Were you disappointed at all in the degree of support that you got for the President's military action?

A. Well, I was not disappointed in the slightest, and we got what I think is very, very strong and forthcoming support from everyone for the actions that the President has taken. Not only that, there were absolutely no reservations expressed whatsoever. Let me suggest to you that when we talked earlier this year about a NATO Alliance adapting to the changed circumstances in Europe and to new challenges, we talked about a NATO Alliance that would serve as a forum for extensive political consultations among its members with respect to matters that might affect a number of the members of the Alliance. I think we've seen a very good example of that today and I would say — and I saw some of the Secretary General's press conference, not all of it — but I would suggest to you that not only have we had extensive consultations here today, but that we have had extensive coordination today.

Certainly on the political side we are coordinating our political response. We are coordinating our response in terms of our approach to the sanctions that the United Nations has announced, everyone having agreed that we must do everything we can to enforce those sanctions. The only area where there is not a coordination is in the military area. And of course the Alliance by treaty can coordinate military action by forces under a NATO command only where the territory of a member state has been attacked. So I think that we should recognize the distinction between military coordination on the one hand, and significant political consultation and coordination on the other.

Q. In the last 18 months or so — certainly since you've come into office — there was a lot of talk bout Germany and Japan really supplanting the United States at the vanguard of the Western alliance. Do you feel now in some way vindicated that this crisis has demonstrated that, given the fact that it is only the United States that can project power, that a lot of this talk about the United States being supplanted was nothing more than hot air?

A. Germany and Japan are close allies of the United States. The United States is a close ally of Germany and Japan, so your question is phrased in a way that would have me responding adversely and I don't want to do that. Let me speak personally for myself. I have never really felt that that argument was valid. I think that these three nations, as three of the major economies of the world, together with other member states of this Alliance can continue as we have in the past to act jointly to support freedom and democracy around the world. And that's what I think you're seeing happening here today.

I think I mentioned to a number of you that are travelling with me that you shouldn't expect, you shouldn't look for, coordinated military action coming out of this meeting. But there has been significant political coordination and action and there has been a clear recognition here, I'm very happy to say, on the part of all of the NATO member states, of the collective defense obligations that we all owe our ally Turkey in the event she is attacked — being located strategically as she is in the region.

Q. Has the Soviet Union cut off arms sales or supplies to Libya as well as Iraq?

A. I don't have the answer to that for you. I have not had any recent discussions with representatives of the Soviet Union respecting arms sales to Libya.

Q. Qadhafi says that they have.

A. He says they have?

Q. Yes.

Q. In the case of either the multinational force, a blockade which you said is a possibility, or any other action, have you had discussions with the other ministers or elsewhere about the command structure? Will the United States—will these forces be under U.S. command, under Saudi command, or under multinational command?

A. We've had discussions to the effect generally that it is the view of some of us that we have the legal authority necessary to—to institute such an embargo or blockade. Provided that the request comes from the legitimate Government of Kuwait, the authority exists under Article 51 of the U.N. Charter. I don't know how many of the NATO Alliance countries adopt that view. Let me simply say the United States does, and I know some other major countries do. The only other discussions we have had with regard to that subject, quite frankly, are that there will have to be agreed upon some sort of coordinating mechanism. That has not yet—not as yet been done. It will have to be done, as the Secretary General, I think, mentioned to you, by the governments that are involved in the effort jointly and, of course, by—with the full concurrence and participation of the Government of Saudi Arabia with respect to operations that might take place on the ground.

Q. Two questions please. First, what will be the U.S. reaction to an eventual forced removal of embassies and diplomatic representation from Kuwait? And second, meeting the Soviet Ambassador, I believe, will be in a few hours, or a half an hour—are you expecting any kind of message back from the Kremlin, or will it just be for information purposes?

A. I'm meeting with the Soviet Ambassador to Belgium because he is the designated Soviet liaison to NATO, in keeping with the call in the London Declaration for a diplomatic liaison relationship from the member states of the Warsaw Pact. So I will be meeting with him at the conclusion of this press conference in his capacity as the Soviet liaison here to NATO.

We are considering the other question that you asked. There are meetings ongoing now in Washington. I do not think a decision has as yet been taken. But let me simply say that, of course we do not recognize and we condemn and view as null and void the so-called "an-

nexation" of Kuwait by Iraq, and we think that the legitimate Government of Kuwait is the government of Kuwait that existed eight or nine or ten days ago. And we have concern and regard for the safety of the some 3,500 to 3,800 private American citizens that are resident in Kuwait, or that are now in Kuwait.

Q. We hear you got strong support here from your colleagues. Many of those same colleagues met this morning as Ministers of Foreign Affairs of EC [Economic Community] countries. And so 11 of the 12 of them afterwards came here. Now, the EC communique speaks about the necessity of working under the U.N. coordination, of good links with the Arabs and has not one word on the United States. Do you think that's a bit schizophrenic that 11 ministers have not a word for the United States?

A. No, I don't think its schizophrenic in the least. They knew they were coming over here to fully embrace and endorse and enthusiastically support what the United States had done. That's how I explain that.

Q. There are reports out of Cairo this morning that Egyptian officials are floating the idea of the opponents of Iraq saying that if Iraq will withdraw from Kuwait, all forces will be withdrawn from Saudi Arabia and elsewhere that have been put in place. Is the United States prepared to withdraw from Saudi Arabia if Iraq withdraws from Kuwait?

A. Well, the United States has long said that we want to see an immediate Iraqi withdrawal, but we also want to see a restoration to power of the legitimate Government of Kuwait. We also want to be assured of the safety and welfare of American citizens and for that matter, we think the safety and welfare of all foreign nationals should be assured. And we would want to make certain that there was no threat to freedom of navigation in the Gulf and to the security and stability of the Gulf. But the withdrawal of Iraqi forces from Kuwait and the restoration of the Kuwaiti leadership are something that we have been calling for for a long time—before any decision was made, I might say, to respond to the request of the Government of Saudi Arabia for defensive assistance.

Q. Two Soviet officials yesterday voiced uneasiness about military action in the Gulf that did not get the explicit sanction of the United Nations. Are

strains appearing in your cooperation with the Soviets, and can you tell if the United States would seek a U.N. endorsement of the military action that is currently underway?

A. Well, first of all, let me say that I don't think any strains are appearing in the relationship, and I would repeat what I said that evening in Moscow when we had our joint U.S.-Soviet statement on this incident of Iraq aggression. Think what we [would] think about the difference in the situation if we were viewing this in an East-West prism, the way we would have been perhaps viewing this kind of a crisis as recently as a year or 18 months ago. I talked again with the Foreign Minister of the Soviet Union last night, and it is not my sense that there is any problem developing in our relationship, that is, the U.S.-Soviet relationship. Now with respect to the question of U.N. participation—whether it is economic or political or military—the broader the participation can be in opposition to this Iraqi aggression, the better off we are. And there was no reason why we would not welcome a U.N. condemnation of this action, a further condemnation of this action by Iraq. So that's the best way I know to answer your question.

Q. Given that the world is changing, do you think it might be necessary for NATO to consider revising its constitution so it might be able to deal in military fashion with out-of-area incidents?

A. Well, that is a very broad question and it's premature for me to even try and address it here. I think the London Declaration goes a long way toward reflecting the awareness on the part of the member states of the need to adapt to the changed circumstances. But that would, of course, be taking adaptation the full length, and I think it's a little premature perhaps to start that debate.

Q. I would like to ask you if there is a possibility to make use of Incirlic Airbase against Iraqi forces within the context of the Security and Economic Cooperation Agreement signed between Turkey and the United States.

A. That's really a question I would prefer that you direct to the authorities of the Turkish Government.

Q. Is there any new indication of an Iraqi troop buildup on the Turkish border? There's been conflicting reports and also conflicting confirmations from Washington.

A. There is some evidence of increased activity up there, up north.

There is furthermore—there is further evidence of continued movement south through Iraq toward Kuwait of additional Iraqi forces.

Q. What do you think of the attitude of French, which has refused to join the multinational force and has moved in the Gulf on its own?

A. We welcome the announcement that was made by the Government of France, I think it was last night or early this morning, that they are going to send some significant assets to the Gulf, both naval and air. And so, we welcome that very much. Again, let me say that the question or questions of coordinating any multilateral force in the Gulf or on the ground is a matter that is going to have to be, and will be, addressed by the countries that have forces in the Gulf or on the ground and the sovereign governments that might be affected.

Q. Would you clear up a point, please? You said the other day that France and the Soviet Union had agreed to consider sending naval assets to the Persian Gulf. The Soviets now apparently are saying that they would only send any sort of military help in this crisis in the context of a U.N. solution. What is it?

A. I think that is the Soviet position. What I said was, the Soviets had sent a ship to the Gulf. They have. They would want to do any coordinated action, I think, only under a U.N. command. I'm not sure that's the case with France. I think that France would be, perhaps—I shouldn't speak for France, and I won't, so go ask them. But they're sending significant assets to the Gulf, just as many other countries are. And if, for instance, you're going to talk in terms of a blockade, there will have to be a traffic cop as there was before. And someone or some collection of countries or individuals will have to coordinate this. That is something that is being considered and being discussed.

U.N. Security Council Resolution 664, August 18, 1990 [2]

The Security Council,
Recalling the Iraqi invasion and purported annexation of Kuwait and resolutions 660, 661 and 662,
Deeply concerned for the safety and well being of third state nationals in Iraq and Kuwait,

Recalling the obligations of Iraq in this regard under international law,
Welcoming the efforts of the Secretary General to pursue urgent consultations with the Government of Iraq following the concern and anxiety expressed by the members of the Council on 17 August 1990,
Acting under Chapter VII of the United Nations Charter:
1. Demands that Iraq permit and facilitate the immediate departure from Kuwait and Iraq of the nationals of third countries and grant immediate and continuing access of consular officials to such nationals;
2. Further demands that Iraq take no action to jeopardize the safety, security or health of such nationals;
3. Reaffirms its decision in resolution 662 (1990) that annexation of Kuwait by Iraq is null and void, and therefore demands that the government of Iraq rescind its orders for the closure of diplomatic and consular missions in Kuwait and the withdrawal of the immunity of their personnel, and refrain from any such actions in the future;
4. Requests the Secretary General to report to the Council on compliance with this resolution at the earliest possible time.

Statement by Ambassador Pickering to the U.N. Security Council, August 18, 1990 [12]

At the outset, let me express the gratification of my government at the unanimous adoption of this very important resolution.

Yesterday this Council expressed its concern and anxiety over the situation regarding foreign nationals in Iraq and Kuwait. In the succeeding 24 hours the Iraqi regime answered the deep and unanimous concern of the Security Council with new actions and threats against those innocent people, which we find dismaying and revolting.

In the meantime, the Secretary General has moved swiftly. We warmly welcome his announcement that he will immediately send a special mission to the area.

Following our meeting yesterday, Baghdad continued to deny consular access to American and other nationals in Kuwait and in Iraq. Just a few hours later, Iraq crossed the Rubicon when the speaker of the Iraqi Parliament an-

nounced that foreign nationals were being detained and sent to camps and other housing, either inside or close to military and other strategic installations in Iraq.

As if that were not enough, we heard this morning that Iraq was also going to take special action against the weakest and most innocent of this group of foreign visitors and residents in Iraq and Kuwait. The regime of Saddam Hussein singled out infants for special food restrictions. It also pointed to the aged and their special needs and indicated that they would be denied food. The announcement did not distinguish between foreigners. It made it clear that all foreigners in those categories would be treated alike.

Finally, the announcement completely ignored the major concern of the Security Council that those foreign nationals who wish to leave Iraq and Kuwait should be permitted to do so. Obviously, instead of talk about the mutual sharing of food shortages under sanctions, such persons should be permitted to leave Iraq and Kuwait immediately, as is their right under international law and in accordance with all common standards of human decency. Instead, we were told that they are being placed in the most sensitive areas, militarily speaking, of Iraq and Kuwait. The lesson is obvious: blatant rejection of the concern and appeal of the council is clear. That is why we are back, meeting here again today.

This adds one more serious insult and injury to the many which the Iraqi regime has already heaped upon the family of nations:
— It attacked without provocation a state member of the United Nations.
— It then, contrary to its own protestations, baldly annexed the territory of that state.
— It has attempted in all possible ways to flout the Security Council resolution calling for immediate and unconditional withdrawal of is forces.
— It has attempted to find all possible means to escape the sanctions imposed upon it under Security Council Resolution 661 (1990).
— It has continued in other ways flagrantly to violate international law and its obligations with respect to its treatment of the third State citizen community in Iraq and Kuwait, including an order to shut down embassies and consulates in Kuwait and withdraw the diplomatic immunities of their personnel.

— It has rejected the international community's condemnation of its invasion and aggression.

— And now it has begun to round up and concentrate in Kuwait the innocent citizens of the United States and other countries friendly to the United States. It has begun also to relocate the civilian citizens of third countries, obviously separating them from the protection of their governments, and is planning to use them as human shields around military and strategic installations in Iraq and Kuwait.

Each of the above actions is unacceptable to the international community. The cumulative effect of all these actions is intolerable. No nation can allow such steps to be taken against its own citizens without the fullest possible response. This is an action on the part of Iraq which requires the full and concerted solidarity of all states. This council is the place where that action can and must be taken.

In that regard, the Security Council's resolution will send an unequivocal and clear message to Saddam Hussein. He and his regime must bear the responsibility for the health, security and safety of third country citizens now locked up in his country. He must bear full responsibility before the family of nations and international public opinion for his treatment of those human beings. It is contrary to international law and to all the norms of Arab hospitality to use guests as military shields. Both the civil rights and the human rights of these individuals are clearly being violated, and we believe that the international community should speak out clearly, with one voice — and now — about the problem.

Throughout this crisis the international community, as represented here in this Council, has remained united in its resolve. Now it is time to continue to show that resolve. It is imperative, in the view of my government, that the Security Council should record clearly and forcefully that Iraq has solemn obligations under the Charter of the United Nations which it must respect. We must call a spade a spade. When Iraq tears up international law, seeks to use innocent civilians as a military shield and indicates that it no longer respects its solemn obligations under the Charter and international law, we must speak clearly, firmly and forcefully, as we have.

In particular, we can do no less today because the lives of hundreds or thousands of foreign nationals from countries all over the world are being put at risk. We must move now to put on the record our clear efforts to secure their release. The resolution the council has just adopted is a solid document. It calls on Iraq immediately to permit such persons to depart from Iraq and Kuwait, and it rejects fully and completely the efforts of Iraq to close the diplomatic and consular missions in Kuwait which help to protect those people.

Each of us has a duty and an obligation to protect our own citizens. Today we make it clear that it is not only our individual but our collective determination to do all we can to protect the lives, the safety, the security and the health of innocent citizens now caught up in this malign conspiracy of aggression and prevarication. My delegation worked hard to help prepare the resolution just adopted by the Security Council; we supported its adoption and will support is full implementation. Thank you, Mr. President.

White House Statement on the Treatment of Foreign Nationals in Iraq and Kuwait, August 18, 1990 [13]

On several occasions since the Iraqi invasion and subsequent occupation of Kuwait, the President has stated publicly his interest in the well-being of American citizens and all foreign nationals in both Iraq and Kuwait. The President thus views yesterday's statement by the Speaker of Iraq's National Assembly [Sadi Mahdi], that Iraq will "play host to the citizens of these aggressive nations as long as Iraq remains threatened with an aggressive war," to be totally unacceptable. He is deeply troubled by the indication that Iraqi authorities intend to relocate these individuals within Iraq against their will. The President is also deeply concerned about today's announcement by the Government of Iraq that foreign nationals may not have access to adequate quantities of food.

The use of innocent civilians as pawns to promote what Iraq sees to be its self-interest is contrary to international law and, indeed, to all accepted norms of international conduct. We urge that Iraq immediately reconsider its refusal to allow any foreign national desiring to leave to do so without delay or condition. We would also hope that Iraq would take note of yesterday's statement by the U.N. Security Council President expressing the Council's concern and anxiety over the situation of foreign nationals in Iraq and Kuwait and calling upon the Secretary General to take all appropriate steps. The United States intends to consult with other governments with citizens being held in Iraq and Kuwait to determine what additional measures ought to be taken.

President's Remarks to Conference of the Veterans of Foreign Wars [Excerpt], Baltimore, August 20, 1990 [13]

Throughout history, we have learned that we must stand up to evil. It's a truth which the past 18 days have reaffirmed, and its lessons speak to America and to the world.

The first lesson is as vivid as the memories of Normandy, Khe Sanh, Pork Chop Hill. We have been reminded again that aggression must and will be checked. So, at the request of our friends, we have sent U.S. forces to the Middle East — reluctantly, but decisively — knowing, as Teddy Roosevelt said, that America "means many things, among them, equality of rights and, therefore, equality of duty and obligation."

Yet we are not acting alone but in concert, helping to protect our own national security interests as well as those of the broader community of nations, which brings me to the second lesson reaffirmed by the past 18 days. By itself, America can do much. Together with its friends and allies, America can do much more — for peace and for justice.

Think back with me to World War II, when together allies confronted a horror which embodied hell on earth, or Korea, where United Nations forces opposed totalitarianism. Today, once again, many nations — many of them Moslem — have joined to counter aggression and, thus, to restore the peace.

Our Saudi friends, under the wise leadership of King Fahd, asked for our help in deterring further aggression by Iraq. I salute the many countries who have courageously responded to Saudi Arabia's request. I also salute those governments who were responding to the Amir of Kuwait's call for the full enforcement of United Nations sanctions.

We must not delude ourselves: Iraq's invasion was more than a military attack on tiny Kuwait; it was a ruthless assault on the very essence of international order and civilized ideals. And now, in a further offense against all norms of international behavior, Iraq has imposed restrictions on innocent civilians from many countries. This is unacceptable. And that's why the United Nations Security Council voted unanimously Saturday night to condemn Iraq's action, just as it earlier voted to condemn the invasion itself. They know, as we do, that leaders who use citizens as pawns deserve and will receive the scorn and condemnation of the entire world.

And so, to the leaders of Iraq, I will now make two points clear: In moving foreign citizens against their will, you are violating the norms of your own religion. You are going against the age-old Arab tradition of showing kindness and hospitality to visitors. And so, my message is: Release all foreigners now! Give them the right to come and go as they wish. Adhere to international law and U.N. Security Council Resolution 664.

We've been reluctant to use the term "hostage." But when Saddam Hussein [President of Iraq] specifically offers to trade the freedom of those citizens of many nations he holds against their will in return for concessions, there can be little doubt that whatever these innocent people are called, they are, in fact, hostages. And I want there to be no misunderstanding. I will hold the Government of Iraq responsible for the safety and well-being of American citizens held against their will.

Let me also take a moment to thank President Gorbachev for his recent words condemning the Iraqi invasion. He has shown—if anyone doubted it—that nations which joined to fight aggression in World War II can work together to stop the aggressors of today.

Excerpt, President's Press Conference Announcing Mobilization of U.S. Reserves, August 22, 1990 [13]

Let me make a brief opening statement, and then I'll be glad to take any questions.

First, Secretary [of Defense] Cheney and General Powell [Chairman of the Joint Chiefs of Staff] have just given me a very full and, I would say, encouraging briefing on the status of our deployment to the Persian Gulf. This has been a very complicated mission calling for precision, calling for maximum coordination with Saudi Arabia and the other nations providing forces. The process has gone smoothly, and we've now moved what amounts to a medium sized American city completely capable of sustaining itself all the way over to the Middle East.

And the Secretary reports that the men and women in the armed forces have performed with extraordinary ability, their morale is high, and they've accepted the challenge of their mission with extraordinary dedication to duty. And I'm very proud of each and every single one of them, and I want them to know that the American people are behind them 100 percent, supporting them strongly.

And it's also crucial that everyone understand that we are not in this alone. We stand shoulder to shoulder right there in the Middle East with the armed forces of 22 other nations from the Middle East, from Europe, and around the world.

Secretary Dick Cheney reports an impressive alliance of multinational forces that stands behind the United Nations resolve that Iraq completely and unconditionally withdraw from Kuwait with the restoration of the legitimate government in that country. The United Nations has provided enormous leadership to the whole world community in pursuing this objective and voting the sanctions necessary to carrying it out. And let's be clear: As the deployment of the forces of the many nations shows and as the votes in the United Nations show, this is not a matter between Iraq and the United States of America; it is between Iraq and the entire world community, Arab and non-Arab alike. All the nations of the world lined up to oppose aggression.

And as our forces continue to arrive, they can look forward to the support of the finest Reserve components in the world. We are activating those special categories of reservists that are essential to completing our mission. The United States considers its Reserve forces to be an integral part of the total military command. These essential personnel will soon be joining the cohesive organization required to support the

military operations in and around the Arabian Peninsula, and I have the highest confidence in their ability to augment the Active forces in this operation.

We continue to pursue our objectives with absolute determination. I might add that I talked to the four leaders of Congress today, and I am very pleased that they are giving us the strong support they have been—the Speaker, Senator Mitchell [majority leader], Senator Dole [minority leader], Congressman Michel [Republican leader]. And the world simply cannot waiver in its opposition to the threat that Iraq has placed on the doorstep of all nations who cherish freedom and the rule of law.

U.N. Security Council Resolution 665, August 25, 1990 [2]

The Security Council,
Recalling its resolution 660 (1990), 661 (1990), 662 (1990) and 664 (1990) and demanding their full and immediate implementation,

Having decided in resolution 661 (1990) to impose economic sanctions under Chapter VII of the Charter of the United Nations,

Determined to bring an end to the occupation of Kuwait by Iraq which imperils the existence of a Member State and to restore the legitimate authority, and the sovereignty, independence and territorial integrity of Kuwait which requires the speedy implementation of the above resolutions,

Deploring the loss of innocent life stemming from the Iraqi invasion of Kuwait and determined to prevent further such losses,

Gravely alarmed that Iraq continues to refuse to comply with resolutions 660 (1990), 661 (1990), 662 (1990) and 664 (1990) and in particular at the conduct of the Government of Iraq in using Iraqi flag vessels to export oil,

1. Calls upon those Member States cooperating with the Government of Kuwait which are deploying maritime forces to the area to use such measures commensurate to the specific circumstances as may be necessary under the authority of the Security Council to halt all inward and outward maritime shipping in order to inspect and verify their cargoes and destinations and to ensure strict implementation of the

provisions related to such shipping laid down in resolution 661 (1990);

2. Invites Member States according-ly to cooperate as may be necessary to ensure compliance with the provisions of resolution 661 (1990) with maximum use of political and diplomatic measures, in accordance with para-graph 1 above;

3. Requests all States to provide in accordance with the Charter such assis-tance as may be required by the States referred to in paragraph 1 of this resolu-tion;

4. Further requests the States con-cerned to coordinate their actions in pursuit of the above paragraphs of this resolution using as appropriate mechanisms of the Military Staff Com-mittee and after consultation with the Secretary General to submit reports to the Security Council and its Committee established under resolution 661 (1990) to facilitate the monitoring of the im-plementation of this resolution;

5. Decides to remain actively seized of the matter.

The Persian Gulf Crisis in a Global Perspective

Secretary Baker's statement before the House Foreign Affairs Committee, September 4, 1990[14]

I have come here today to speak to you—and through you to the American people—about the conflict in the Per-sian Gulf and what it means for the United States.

I would like to use my statement today to place this crisis in a larger con-text. The entire world has mobilized to redress aggression against a small country in a distant place. Already, we're paying higher prices when we pull up to the local gas pump. And thousands of our finest young men and women now stand guard in the heat of the Persian Gulf.

The President has made it plain we have a straightforward responsibility to the American people: Openly and clearly, we have a duty to state what is at stake as a result of Saddam Hussein's invasion of Kuwait. We have a duty to tell our people what our immediate goals are in this conflict. And we have a duty to explain how we plan to achieve those goals in order to further our long run interests in the gulf and beyond.

The Stakes

Let me start by discussing what's at stake.

First, Iraq's unprovoked aggression is a political test of how the post-Cold War world will work. Amidst the revolu-tions sweeping the globe and the trans-formation of East-West relations, we stand at a critical juncture in history. The Iraqi invasion of Kuwait is one of the defining moments of a new era—an era full of promise but also one replete with new challenges. While the rules of the road developed during the Cold War did, in the end, preserve East-West peace in Europe, the task now is to build an enduring peace that is global in scope, not limited just to Europe and not rooted in confrontation and tension.

If we are to build a stable and more comprehensive peace, we must respond to the defining moments of this new era, recognizing the emerging dangers lurk-ing before us. We are entering an era in which ethnic and sectarian identities could easily breed new violence and conflict. It is an era in which new hos-tilities and threats could erupt as mis-guided leaders are tempted to assert regional dominance before the ground rules of a new order can be accepted.

Accordingly, we face a simple choice: Do we want to live in a world where aggression is made less likely be-cause it is met with a powerful response from the international community, a world where civilized rules of conduct apply? Or are we willing to live in a world where aggression can go unchek-ed, where aggression succeeds because we cannot muster the collective will to challenge it?

Sadly, Saddam Hussein's attack on Kuwait will not be the last act of aggres-sion that international society will face. So long as ruthless aggressors remain, the reality of international life is that such predatory designs will emerge from time to time. But the current crisis is a first opportunity to limit such dangers, to reinforce the standards for civilized behavior found in the United Nations Charter, and to help shape a more peaceful international order built on the promise of recent trends in Europe and elsewhere. We must seize this opportunity to solidify the ground rules of the new order.

Second, from a *strategic* standpoint, we must show that intimidation and force are not successful ways of doing business in the volatile Middle East—or

anywhere else. The combination of un-resolved regional conflicts, turbulent so-cial and political changes, weapons of mass destruction, and much of the world's energy supplies makes the Mid-dle East particularly combustible. No one is immune from conflicts in the Mid-dle East. And no one can feel safe when the danger of war escalating in the Mid-dle East is so high.

If we want to encourage peaceful change and preserve the security of all our friends in the area, we must remain a reliable partner for peace. We must help demonstrate that Saddam Hussein's violent way is an anachronism, not the wave of the future.

Third, and perhaps most obviously, what is at stake *economically* is the de-pendence of the world on access to the energy resources of the Persian Gulf. The effects on our economy and our people are already being felt. But this is not about increases in the price of a gal-lon of gas at your local service station. It is not just a narrow question of the flow of oil from Kuwait and Iraq. It is about a dictator who acting alone and unchal-lenged could strangle the global economic order, determining by fiat whether we all enter a recession, or even the darkness of a depression.

A sustained oil price spiral—similar to what happened in 1973 and again in 1979—could easily cause higher inflation and interest rates worldwide, sending us all into a sustained recession-ary slide. The burden could become par-ticularly great for the new democracies of Eastern Europe, threatening to undo the revolutions of 1989. It would also be painfully felt in the poorer countries of Central America, South Asia, and Africa—threatening those who are now embracing market-oriented reforms and striving to improve living standards for their impoverished millions.

Simply put, these are the stakes raised by Iraq's invasion against Kuwait. How have we and the international com-munity responded to them?

Our Objectives

For the United States, the President has identified four immediate goals:

One, the immediate, complete, and unconditional withdrawal of all Iraqi forces from Kuwait as mandated in United Nations Security Council Resolution 660;

Two, the restoration of Kuwait's legitimate government;

Three, the protection of the lives of American citizens held hostage by Iraq, both in Iraq and in Kuwait; and

Four, a commitment to the security and stability of the Persian Gulf.

Our strategy is to lead a global political alliance to isolate Iraq — politically, economically, and militarily. In this way, we aim to make Iraq pay such a high price for its aggression that it will be forced to withdraw from Kuwait and release Americans and others held hostage. This in turn will allow the restoration of Kuwait's legitimate government. It will also improve the opportunities for long term security and stability in the Persian Gulf in a way that builds on the unprecedented international consensus that has already been formed.

Implementing the Strategy

Our strategy has moved on two mutually supporting tracks toward these aims. Let me summarize our efforts.

Diplomatically, we have worked from the beginning to foster a coordinated international response to Iraq's aggression. The results have been extraordinary and unprecedented. Five unanimous United Nations Security Council resolutions have been passed. And Iraq is now isolated.

We are gratified by the responsible and productive work we have been able to undertake with the other Permanent Members — Britain, France, the Soviet Union, and the People's Republic of China — as well as the support the Arab League and the Nonaligned Movement have provided.

In particular, the Soviet Union has proven a responsible partner, suggesting new possibilities for active superpower cooperation in resolving regional conflicts. The President will work to further strengthen our ties of partnership when he meets President Gorbachev in Helsinki this Sunday. In taking the long view, we should remember what this conflict would have looked like if old style zero-sum thinking was still driving Soviet policy in the Gulf.

NATO, the EC [European Community], and the West European Union have pitched in magnificently. Our NATO ally, Turkey, should also be singled out for its fast, effective, and courageous cooperation. Finally, a broad regional coalition — including Egypt, Saudi Arabia, Kuwait, the Gulf states, and Syria — have done much to foster an international cohesion.

In this regard, let me make a larger point: From the early days of this administration, we have made a concerted effort — with our friends in Asia and Europe, with the Soviets, and with organizations like NATO and the EC — to focus on the explosive dangers inherent in regional conflicts. In response to Iraq's invasion, we have drawn upon the new international ties being shaped by this strategy.

The Kuwaitis themselves deserve our compassion and respect. They have suffered a brutal invasion, their country pillaged, their lives traumatized. There has been a tragic loss of life, and thousands of Kuwaitis have fled to neighboring states, escaping in many cases with only the clothes on their back.

The Kuwaitis, however, are fighting back heroically. They are not collaborating with the Iraqi occupiers. All elements of Kuwaiti society — from religious conservatives to secular liberals — have voiced support for the restoration of the government. An indigenous Kuwaiti resistance has emerged. It carries on the struggle against Iraqi aggression from inside Kuwait. Moreover, the government of Kuwait in exile is providing financial aid to support our military effort and to help alleviate economic disruptions that have occurred in such states as Egypt.

In short, Kuwait has been occupied, not conquered.

The political coalition, bound by the principle that Saddam Hussein must be denied the fruits of aggression, has created an economic embargo under U.N. auspices that is solidly in place. Iraq's import-dependent economy is beginning to feel the strain, and international pressures will continue to grow over time as shortages mount. Sanction busters may be tempted by the lure of financial profits, but Security Council Resolution 665 which permits enforcement by appropriate means should ensure that Iraq's opportunities to export its oil and import key materials will be severely constrained over time.

Saddam Hussein's aggression has exacted a broad range of economic costs for countries across both the region and globe. The destruction of the Kuwaiti economy by Iraqi invaders has caused major economic dislocations for our friends in the region, notably Egypt and Turkey. Other countries with fragile economies, especially in Eastern Europe, are bearing heavy costs. The need to offset the burden of our own military efforts must also be addressed.

As the President announced last Thursday, we have initiated an action plan to meet these needs. Our friends around the world are responding. Saudi Arabia is meeting a large share of the fuel costs for this effort. And other Gulf states are providing fuel and financial resources to the affected states.

The President has also asked [Treasury] Secretary Brady and myself to go to key nations in the gulf, Europe, and Asia to help mobilize and coordinate the international effort. We will attempt to ensure that the costs and responsibilities are shared equitably and that our various efforts complement one another. The aim is to address the vital needs of affected parties and to maintain the solidarity of the international coalition.

Time can be on the side of the international community. Diplomacy can be made to work.

On the military track, over twenty five countries are now supplying men and material in support of the Security Council resolutions. U.S. military objectives are to deter an Iraqi attack on Saudi Arabia and to insure the effective implementation of the United Nations sanctions. Our military forces are also there to protect American lives and to provide an effective and decisive military response should Iraq escalate its aggression to active combat with the multinational force.

Once the present danger passes, however, we must not let its lessons go unheeded. We have a responsibility to assure the American people that a decade from now, their sons and daughters will not be put in jeopardy because we failed to work toward long run solutions to the problems of the Gulf.

The historic international consensus we have built can become a solid foundation for successfully meeting our immediate objectives and building a safer future. It can foster a future Gulf environment that will protect our interests and help us avoid having to make this kind of massive diplomatic and military effort again.

In the long run, we seek a stable Gulf in which the nations of that region and their peoples can live in peace, free of the fear of coercion. We seek a region in which change can occur and legitimate security concerns can be preserved peacefully. And we seek a region in which energy supplies flow freely.

We will need to work together with governments in the Gulf and outside of it to build a more durable order. We will want to ensure that our friends in the area have the means to deter aggression and defend themselves, making it less necessary to send American men and women to help them. And we will work with the rest of the regional and international community to prevent further Iraqi expansionism as well as Iraqi efforts to acquire and produce weapons of mass destruction.

Resolution of today's threat should also become a springboard for a sustained international effort to curb the proliferation of chemical, biological, and nuclear weapons and ballistic missiles in the region and elsewhere. It can become a springboard for revived efforts to resolve the conflicts which lie at the root of such proliferation, including the festering conflict between Israel and its Palestinian and Arab neighbors.

It is not enough to demonstrate that aggression and intimidation don't pay; we must show that a pathway to reconciliation and peace does exist, and that it can be found with good will and good faith on all sides.

The Implications for America's Role in the World

Mr. Chairman, let me conclude by placing Saddam Hussein's invasion of Kuwait in historical perspective.

For over four decades, the central fact of international relations was the conflict between East and West. The Cold War reverberated across the globe, affecting everyone everywhere. Much of America's foreign policy was either driven by, or derivative of, our efforts to contain Stalinist aggression.

Now, the central dispute of the postwar period—the East-West conflict over the future of Europe—has been transformed. Last year's people power revolutions in Central and Eastern Europe swept away the dictatorships of the past. In their place, the people are finding freedom. Europe is becoming whole and free, and Germany will be united in peace and freedom.

An enlightened Soviet leadership has encouraged peaceful, democratic change as the only legitimate road to progress. This administration has actively engaged the new thinkers and reformers in the Soviet Union. Together, we are finding common interests that will unite East and West. Partnership is replacing conflict.

As I have said many times before, America's role in this sea change in world politics is straightforward: We must leave behind not only the Cold War but also the conflicts that preceded it.

And this is why—as the President has said from the outset—Iraq's aggression cannot stand.

The line in the sands of Arabia is also a line in time. By crossing into Kuwait, Saddam Hussein took a dangerous step back in history. Maybe he thought the world would consider Kuwait expendable, that we would think of it as just a small, faraway country of which we knew and cared little. Possibly he remembered the 1930s when the League of Nations failed to respond effectively to Mussolini's aggression against Abyssinia, what is today Ethiopia. Clearly, Saddam Hussein thought his crime would pay.

But the world has decided otherwise. He must not be allowed to hold on to what he stole.

The President has made our position clear: The world must stand united to defend the principles enshrined in the United Nations Charter.

In this effort, America must lead and our people must understand that. We remain the one nation that has the necessary political, military, and economic instruments at our disposal to catalyze a successful collective response by the international community.

Geographically, we stand apart from much of the world, separated by the Atlantic and the Pacific. But politically, economically, and strategically, there are no oceans, and in a world without oceans, a policy of isolationism is no option at all. Only American engagement can shape the peaceful world our people so deeply desire.

We believe this coordinated and comprehensive international isolation of Iraq is the only peaceful path to meeting the objectives set by the President. Our efforts will, however, take time and that is what we ask most of the American people: Stand firm. Be patient. And remain united so that together we can show that aggression does not pay.

---

[1] Text from Weekly Compilation of Presidential Documents of August 6, 1990.
[2] Text provided by United Nations Information Center, Washington.
[3] Department of State Press Release 115, August 6, 1990.
[4] Excerpt from Transcript of Department of Defense News Briefing, August 8, 1990, as released by the Office of the Assistant Secretary of Defense (Public Affairs).
[5] Text from Weekly Compilation of Presidential Documents of August 13, 1990.
[6] Text as provided by the Royal Embassy of Saudi Arabia Information Office, Washington.
[7] Text printed as released by Iraqi [official] News Agency, provided by the Iraqi Press Office, Embassy of Iraq, Washington.
[8] U.S. Mission to the United Nations Press Release 62 (90), August 9, 1990.
[9] Partial text provided by the Arab League Information Center, League of Arab States, Washington.
[10] Department of State Press Release 118, August 10, 1990.
[11] Department of State Press Release 119, August 10, 1990.
[12] U.S. Mission to the United Nations Press Release 64 (90), August 18, 1990.
[13] Text from Weekly Compilation of Presidential Documents of August 27, 1990.
[14] Department of State Press Release 125, September 12, 1990.

Publication Summary

World Development Report 1990: Poverty

© 1990 THE WORLD BANK

The following summary was released by THE WORLD BANK to accompany the publication of its annual World Development Report for 1990. The English language version of the report was published by Oxford University Press, New York. [1]

The Extent and Nature of Poverty

More than one billion people — about one-third of the total population in developing countries — live in poverty; that is, their annual per capita consumption is less than $370. Being poor means being unable to attain a minimal standard of living and having insufficient money to purchase adequate food, clothing, and housing. It also means low life expectancies, high death rates among infants and children, and few opportunities to obtain even basic education.

Poverty remains high despite good economic performance in much of the developing world over the past several decades. In many countries the gains stemming from economic growth have been offset by rapid population increase. And one entire region — Sub-Saharan Africa — has not participated in economic advance at all. Per capita consumption is no higher in Sub-Saharan Africa today than it was 25 years ago. In South Asia gains have been made in consumption, but nearly half of the developing world's poor still live in that region.

Poverty presents many different faces in different countries. But certain tendencies prevail:

- Poverty is at its worst in rural areas. In India, 77 percent of the poor are rural, as are 80 percent of the poor in Kenya.
- Nevertheless, urban poverty is increasingly significant, especially in Latin America. In Venezuela, 85 percent of the poor live in urban areas, as do 69 percent in Mexico. Most of the urban poor — as many as 75 percent in Brazil — have jobs in the informal sector, generally the ones that pay the least.
- Agriculture is still the main source of income for the world's poor. But the rural poor usually have little land or are completely landless. In Bangladesh the mean per capita monthly income among those owning more than 7.5 acres of land is four times greater than among those with less than one acre.
- Poor households tend to be large — in Pakistan in 1984 the poorest 10 percent of households had, on average, almost eight members.

Countries that have been successful in reducing poverty have adopted a strategy that has two equally important elements. The first element is the promotion of the productive use of the poor's most abundant asset — labor ... The second is the provision of basic social services to the poor.

- Women face all manner of cultural, social, legal, and economic obstacles that men, even poor men, do not. In South Asia the literacy rate for women is only about half that for men. In rural areas of Pakistan only about 20 percent of girls are enrolled in primary school.
- The poor spend nearly all their incomes on consumption. At least half of their consumption — as much as 70 percent in Cote d'Ivoire and Peru — is in the form of food.
- The poor suffer disproportionately from environmental degradation. They must frequently eke out an existence on marginal rural lands or live in shantytowns on the urban periphery. They are thus both victims and perpetrators of a deteriorating environment.

The staggering numbers of the developing world's poor should not obscure the progress that has been made. Between 1965 and 1985 consumption per capita in developing countries increased from $590 to $985 (in 1985 dollars), and in some countries poverty decreased dramatically. In Indonesia the proportion of the population living in poverty fell from 58 to 17 percent between 1970 and 1987; in Thailand it declined from 67 to 26 percent between 1962 and 1986. Brazil, Colombia, Costa Rica, India, Malaysia, Morocco, Pakistan, Singapore, and Sri Lanka are other countries in which poverty, as measured by consumption, declined noticeably.

In addition, health, education, and other social indicators improved in most countries even when average incomes did not increase. Life expectancy in the developing world increased from 50 to 61 years between 1965 and 1985, and enrollment in primary school rose from 73 to 84 percent of the primary school age group.

Poverty, nevertheless, increased in many countries during the 1980s, and economic performance differed markedly among regions. But the 1980s was not a lost decade for all, or even most, of the world's poor. Many Asian countries, especially those in East Asia, continued to grow, and poverty declined rapidly. Growth in Latin America and Sub-Saharan Africa, however, was negative over the decade, and that in Eastern Europe was stagnant. Countries in all three regions experienced sharp increases in poverty during the 1980s.

Countries that have been successful in reducing poverty have adopted a strategy that has two equally important elements. The first element is the promotion of the productive use of the poor's most abundant asset — labor — through policies that harness market incentives, social and political institutions, infrastructure, and technology. The second is the provision of basic social services to the poor. Primary health care, family planning, nutrition, and primary education are especially important.

Economic growth is the key factor in reducing poverty — it is the basis for a rise in incomes. Investment in human capital is also essential because it enables the poor to take advantage of the income-earning opportunities that arise as a consequence of growth. Some countries — Sri Lanka is an example — have improved social indicators even under conditions of slow growth. Others — such as Brazil and Pakistan — have lagged in converting growth into social progress.

Public policy must include a sustained commitment to improving the conditions of the poor, and political factors are crucially important in the effort to reduce poverty. The main tradeoff is not between growth and reducing poverty; it is between the interests of the poor and of the nonpoor. Poverty reduction has generally proved more politically feasible where it has been possible to build coalitions that unite the poor with nonpoor groups that have an interest in reform.

Policies for Reducing Poverty

Growth that improves income-earning opportunities for the poor requires two broad sets of policies — policies designed to stimulate rural development and to foster job creation in urban areas.

Many policies that were meant to benefit the rural poor failed to have the desired results. For example:

- Taxation of agriculture has often been excessive and has contributed to poor agricultural performance (as in Ghana, Nigeria, Senegal, and Tanzania).
- Land reform has generally led to only modest gains for the poor (except when they stemmed from postwar or revolutionary situations, as in the Republic of Korea and Japan).
- Subsidized credit programs have often benefitted the rich instead of the poor and have run into serious problems with repayment of loans.

More promising avenues include strong public support for the development of appropriate rural infrastructure, increased access of small farmers to technical innovations through improved agricultural extension programs, efforts to strengthen linkages between farm and nonfarm economies, and the development of rural financial institutions (including group lending).

On the urban side the message is similar. Government efforts to intervene on behalf of the urban poor — through minimum wage legislation, job security regulations, and the like — have, on balance, led to diminished employment in the formal sector. Regulations have tended to hinder investment and job creation in urban areas. Governments can be more successful in creating jobs by avoiding distortions in product and factor markets and by providing suitable urban infrastructure.

Both in rural and in urban areas more needs to be done to improve the participation of the poor in growth by involving the intended beneficiaries in the design and implementation of programs, paying more attention to institutional development, and making room for a greater role for non-governmental organizations and local groups of the poor.

Social progress for the poor has generally depended on government policies and efforts. Countries that have achieved progress are distinguished by political commitment, by budgetary provisioning (Costa Rica spends 23 percent of its governmental budget on health), and by attention to the institutional and organizational aspects of providing social services, including decentralization and the construction of physical infrastructure, especially in rural areas.

Despite the progress that has been made in many countries, an immense task remains. About 15 million children under age 5 die every year from causes that are not usually fatal in developed countries. About 110 million children worldwide receive no primary education at all. Governments are responsible for the bulk of successes in providing social services to the poor, but they are also to blame for most of the failures. In most countries government spending on social services is skewed away from the people who need it most — the poor. In health, an estimated 70 to 85 percent of the developing world's total spending goes for treatment of illness, which in practice mainly benefits the nonpoor, rather than for preventive care, which could make an immense difference for poor people. In education, too, governments have generally favored higher-level training over services that would benefit the poor. Yet policies that would improve the health and education of the poor would be to the advantage of the entire economy because of the strong links between education and economic growth, education and agricultural productivity, and workers' health and productivity.

Family planning services are vital for poverty reduction. In many countries, notably in Sub-Saharan Africa, the population is growing at 3 to 4 percent a year. Few countries can invest enough to absorb such increases. Low wages and growing poverty are the likely results. Where strong family planning programs have been implemented — as in Costa Rica, Indonesia, Korea, and Singapore — birthrates and the incidence of poverty have declined sharply.

Many poor people may fail to benefit, at least in the short term, from improved income-earning opportunities or from the provision of social services. People who may at some time need extra help include the old, the disabled, widows and orphans, and those vulnerable to natural catastrophes and macroeconomic shocks. They can be helped by a system of income transfers or by safety nets: that is, some form of income insurance to help people through short term stress and calamities. Governments have an important part to play in providing these safeguards — the more so since the evidence is that in many developing countries family and ethnic ties are dissolving and community support systems are becoming weaker. Some mechanisms are more practicable or useful than others in given circumstances.

- General food price subsidies — those in Egypt are a good example — tend to be expensive and are difficult to confine to the poor. "Targeting" the subsidies — for example, by limiting them to commodities that are consumed mainly by the poor — works better.
- "Rationed" food subsidies, which provide a quota of subsidized food to poor households with unlimited sales permitted on the open market, are an improvement over unrestricted subsidies. An example is the general rice ration in Sri Lanka (1942-78), which greatly benefitted the poor. Food stamp programs, such as Jamaica's, also generally yield a more progressive pattern of transfers.
- Public employment schemes can be effective in providing the poor with jobs, building infrastructure with labor-intensive methods, and — in their food-for-work variant — feeding the poor during droughts and famines. In two large rural public

works schemes in South Asia—the Employment Guarantee Scheme in Maharashtra State, India, and the Food for Work Programme in Bangladesh—the proportion of participants below the poverty line was at least 90 percent in the early 1980s.

- By contrast, efforts to transplant formal social security schemes to developing countries have met with little success, although Chile and Costa Rica are prominent exceptions. The nonpoor tend to benefit more from such formal schemes, and many needy elderly and other poor individuals have not been reached.

The shocks of the early 1980s confronted most developing countries with the need to adjust their economies. Over the medium and long term, restructuring—including adjustment of fiscal policies, realignment of exchange rates, liberalization of trade regimes, deregulation of industries, and privatization of state enterprises—is broadly consistent with a shift toward a pattern of growth and human capital formation that effectively reduces poverty. In the short run, however, some of the poor may be losers. This is especially true of the urban poor if the demand for their labor is reduced. Short-run stabilization may also threaten social services, transfers, and safety nets that help the poor.

The experience with adjustment in the 1980s underlines the crucial importance of appropriate national policies. Some countries such as Indonesia and Malaysia acted decisively to stabilize their economies and establish a framework for economic restructuring that was fully consistent with the continued reduction of poverty. Poverty actually declined—slightly in Malaysia, significantly in Indonesia—during their adjustment episodes. The situation was quite different in Brazil, where the public sector deficit remained high and the currency became overvalued, contributing to high inflation and other distortions in the economy. Brazil's policies made the poor worse off, and poverty increased sharply between 1981 and 1987. Ghana undertook many of the policy requisites for adjustment, but many other Sub-Saharan African countries avoided difficult policy choices altogether, with adverse consequences for the poor.

Experience also shows that it is possible to restructure public expenditures during adjustment—Chile, Indonesia, and other countries protected services to the poor while adjusting. Moreover, a number of countries put programs in place to protect the poor during the inevitable short-run difficulties. Public employment schemes, such as those undertaken in Chile and Peru, appeared most effective. Both countries' programs successfully targeted the poor and provided social security to the unemployed during recessions.

In short, generalizations about the uniformly adverse effects of adjustment on the poor are difficult to sustain. Whether the poor suffered from adjustment depended in large measure on policy performance.

International Factors

Although domestic policies are the essential ingredients of a strategy for reducing poverty, international factors play an important part. Three are of particular importance: world trade, international debt, and foreign aid.

A solid case for a greater volume of aid can be made, but only if more countries seriously pursue the reduction of poverty and aid donors learn better the lessons of experience.

Many trade barriers put up by industrial countries harm the poor in developing countries. The immediate effects of trade liberalization by the industrial countries, however, would vary greatly among developing countries. Most middle-income countries would gain, but many poor countries—especially exporters of primary commodities—would not gain (and might even lose) in the short term because of supply rigidities, the loss of existing preferences, and possible net losses from increased prices of food imports. Over the longer term trade liberalization would benefit even low-income countries. But this would depend on whether they adopted policies to encourage diversification away from excessive reliance on a few commodities. Since this reorientation will take time, external assistance will continue to be important for many low-income countries over at least the next decade.

Debt burdens currently place an enormous strain on the economies of severely indebted low-income countries with large numbers of poor people. Although the international community has taken steps to deal with the problems, these initiatives have not made a large dent in debt burdens. (For example, converting concessional loans to grants has canceled only about 3 percent of the outstanding debt of low-income African countries.) Additional debt relief would facilitate an increase in investment and in the consumption of the poor. But further relief should be conditional on appropriate policy reform in the countries concerned.

Developing countries received $51 billion in aid in 1988, and some impressive successes have been achieved. Korea and Indonesia are among the countries that have put large volumes of aid to good use and have taken important steps on behalf of the poor. The extension of aid for agricultural research, the construction of rural infrastructure, the provision of primary education, basic health care, and nutrition programs, and relief from natural and man-made disasters has benefitted many poor people.

Aid has often been an effective instrument for reducing poverty. But its contributions have not always come up to full potential. There are various reasons for this.

- Donors, especially bilateral donors, have many different motives for supplying aid—political, strategic, commercial, and humanitarian. Reducing poverty is only one, and it is usually far from the most important.
- Some recipients—including Haiti, Sudan, Tanzania, and Zaire—have fallen into "aid dependency."
- Many poverty-oriented projects funded by aid have failed to reach the poor.

Aid can be made a more effective instrument for reducing poverty by linking it more directly to the antipoverty impact of countries' overall policies. Thus, countries that receive substantial volumes of aid should generally be those which are attempting to pursue policies that generate income-earning opportunities and efficiently provide social services for the poor. Where countries have large numbers of poor people but public policies are not conducive to poverty reduction, the appropriate response is to direct limited quantities of aid in a highly targeted fashion toward the poorest groups. Thus, aid could support health clinics serving poor women and children, immunization programs for children, or well-targeted feeding programs. Many countries represent intermediate cases in which informed judgments will have to be made about the initiatives that aid can usefully support to reduce poverty.

A solid case for a greater volume of aid can be made, but only if more countries seriously pursue the reduction of poverty and aid donors learn better the lessons of experience. Aid would increase to only $64 billion in the year 2000 if it grows at 2 percent a year in real terms from now to then (the projection of the OECD's Development Assistance Committee), but it could increase to $73 billion if it grew in line with the projected increase of 3 percent a year in donors' GNP. It could increase to $108 billion or $144 billion if respective aid/GNP ratios of 0.5 and 0.7 percent were attained by those donors currently below these ratios while those above them maintained their current proportions.

Expanded provision of social services for the poor and a greater emphasis on growth that makes productive use of labor could sharply reduce poverty in the developing world over the next decade. The incidence of poverty would fall from its 1985 level of 33 percent to 18 percent by 2000, and the number of poor people would decline from 1.1 billion to 825 million. Regional experience would vary markedly, however. Only in Sub-Saharan Africa would the number of poor increase, from 180 million to 265 million.

Such estimates, although considered reasonable approximations, are nevertheless contingent on a number of variables. The downside risks are high. A less buoyant external environment, including contractions in world trade or diminished flows of financial resources to developing countries, would leave many more people in poverty in 2000 than the estimates suggest. Likewise, a failure to undertake requisite policy reforms or to safeguard social services and real incomes where progress has already been made would sharply reduce the potential gains.

The challenge is particularly great in Sub-Saharan Africa. Even with a supportive policy environment including greater provision of social services, a

growth rate of 5.5 percent a year—nearly 2 percent higher than the projected rate—would be needed to raise per capita consumption by enough to prevent the number of poor from increasing. Challenges abound elsewhere as well. At the projected growth rates, strong measures will be needed to prevent poverty from increasing significantly in Bangladesh over the next decade. A squeeze on investment could slow growth and threaten projected gains in reducing poverty in India. Given its resources, Latin America should be able virtually to eliminate poverty, but its exceptionally high degree of income inequality is an obstacle. Raising all the poor in the continent to just above the poverty line would cost only 0.7 percent of regional GDP—the approximate equivalent of a 2 percent income tax on the wealthiest one-fifth of the population.

The challenges vary in different regions, but they are not insurmountable. Preventing the number of poor from rising in Sub-Saharan Africa while reducing the number elsewhere in the developing world by nearly 400 million is an ambitious—but achievable—target for the end of the century.

General Ordering Information

WORLD DEVELOPMENT REPORT 1990

World Development Report 1990 is published in paperback editions in Arabic, Chinese, English, French, German, Japanese, Portuguese, and Spanish; a hardcover edition is also available in English. The Report may be purchased from World Bank distributors in a number of countries. Publication dates and prices vary by country. To facilitate wider dissemination in developing countries, special prices have been arranged with many of the distributors. For more information, write to World Bank Publications, Box 7247-8619, Philadelphia, PA 19170-8619, U.S.A.

WORLD DEVELOPMENT INDICATORS 1990: Data on Diskettes

These diskettes contain all the data in the WDI annex to *World Development Report 1990.* The World Bank's new STARS software allows users to create tables by selecting data from a

wealth of indicators, from selected time series including the most recent period available, and from 120 countries and regional and economic groups. Basic data are also provided for 65 more countries that have less than 1 million population or are not members of the World Bank. Two formats are included in each set—5 1/4 inch and 3 1/2 inch double-density diskettes—for use on PCs with a hard disk and MS-DOS version 2.0 or higher. A user's guide and a complimentary copy of *World Development Report 1990* accompany each set. Stock #11532/$95.

Representative State Department Statements on the Civil War in Liberia

Following are selected excerpts from recent Department of State statements and press guidances concerning the civil war in Liberia through August 1990 [1]

JUNE 7, 1990

Due to the potential threat to lives, all Americans are strongly advised to depart Liberia immediately. In order to assist Americans, we have arranged special commercial flights to transport American citizens and their immediate families from Liberia to the neighboring country of Cote d'Ivoire. From Cote d'Ivoire, transportation is being arranged back to the United States.

The U.S. Embassy in Monrovia has announced these special flights to the Americans in Liberia. All Americans still in Liberia have been urged to contact immediately the Consular Section of the U.S. Embassy located at 111 United Nations Drive, Monrovia, to obtain the details of these flights. All Americans should also inform the embassy of their whereabouts and current intentions. Three special commercial flights will be departing from Spriggs-Payne Airfield in Monrovia for Abidjan this Sunday. The embassy will broadcast this announcement over a radio net to American citizens three times daily until further notice.

Through travel advisories and press statements, the U.S. Government has been advising Americans for almost two months to depart Liberia. As the security situation has deteriorated, our embassy has been urging Americans to leave through daily broadcasts over shortwave radio networks and missionary radio stations, news releases and regular briefings for the American community. We have reduced our embassy staff and families from over 600 to a minimal staff of 70 essential personnel. Several thousand private American citizens have left Liberia already. Those Americans remaining are strongly advised to depart Liberia immediately until the security situation stabilizes.

JULY 6, 1990

The current situation in Monrovia greatly hampers organizing a relief effort. However, throughout the crisis, we have contributed food and nonfood aid. Through the Bureau of Refugee Programs, we have donated $1.2 million to the UNHCR [United Nations High Commissioner for Refugees]. We also contributed $200,000 to the ICRC for work with displaced persons. 19,200 metric tons of rice have been allocated for use in assisting refugees and displaced persons.

Today, the Office of Disaster Assistance (OFDA) made a $50,000 grant to Medecins Sans Frontieres to assist civilians who have taken refuge on church compounds in Monrovia.

JULY 29, 1990

President [Samuel K.] Doe met with members of the diplomatic corps Tuesday and then privately with [American] Ambassador [Peter] de Vos. President Doe has not requested our assistance in departing Liberia. Our offer to assist him in leaving the country still stands, if the situation on the ground permits.

Liberians have sought refuge on a number of U.S. facilities. While it is difficult to determine exact numbers, there are over 7,000 on the Greystone compound, a residential complex, and approximately 12,000 on the VOA [Voice of America] compound. There are some 18,000 refugees at the telecommunications facility near Brewerville. All U.S. facilities continue to function.

JULY 30, 1990

Last night, some 200 Liberians who sought refuge at the Lutheran church in Monrovia were massacred by Armed Forces of Liberia soldiers. Dozens of others were wounded. We condemn this senseless act of terror and call again on all sides to refrain from inflicting violence on helpless and innocent men, women, and children. All parties to the conflict should respect their obligations under the Geneva Convention on the Protection of Victims of Armed Conflict to prevent murder and the carrying out of executions without due process. We renew the appeal, which we have made both publicly and privately throughout this tragic conflict, for both sides to forgo a military solution and follow the path of negotiation.

AUGUST 1, 1990

We are extremely concerned over the fighting and bloodshed in Liberia. Since the fighting in Liberia intensified in April, the United States has been engaged in a sustained diplomatic effort to bring about a peaceful resolution of the conflict and to create the conditions for the emergence of democracy in Liberia. We have focussed our efforts on a number of fronts.

We have been in regular contact with both the Government and the National Patriotic Front to urge both sides to settle their differences at the negotiating table. We have met with representatives of the contending sides both in Washington and in the region. We provided our embassy in Freetown as the site for the first round of peace talks in mid-June. In the interest of bringing an end to the conflict, we have offered to assist President Doe to leave Liberia should he decide to do so. [2]

In Monrovia, we have been in touch with Liberians of all political persuasions and supported their efforts to bring about a peaceful settlement, most prominently those of the Liberian Council of Churches.

We have interceded with foreign governments to desist in their material support for both sides.

Since April, we have also consulted on a regular basis with Liberia's neighbors. We actively and publicly supported the mediation effort of the regional ECOWAS [Economic Community of West African States] group, which led to the second round of talks in Freetown in mid-July.

We facilitated the diplomatic initiative of the Organization of African Unity, including supporting Assistant Secretary General Haggag's trip to the region to talk with the neighboring countries and the contending parties.

We are now engaged in consulations at the United Nations to see what constructive role the Secretary General might play in addressing the crisis in Liberia. In the meantime, we are continuing our consultations with African states and other interested parties in our ongoing efforts to stop the killing in Liberia.

AUGUST 5, 1990

Because of an increased threat to our embassy and its facilities, at approximately 9 a.m. Monrovia time (0500 Washington time) August 5, a reinforced rifle company of American Marines was helicoptered from the Marine Amphibious Readiness Group (MARG) to the compound of the American Embassy in Liberia. At the same time, a number of embassy employees and private citizens were removed by helicopter from the embassy compound and two communications sites near Monrovia.

The purpose of this operation was to draw down the number of Americans at the embassy and to provide additional security for those who remain. Our embassy in Monrovia will continue to have as its principal tasks assistance to American citizens and exercise of American diplomatic influence to bring an end to the fighting in Liberia.

The Marine presence does not indicate or constitute any intention on the part of the U.S. Government to intervene militarily in the Liberian conflict. We call on all parties to that conflict to ensure the safety of American citizens.

American citizens who remain in Monrovia should contact the embassy.

AUGUST 15, 1990

The U.S. Government has expressed its support for the objectives contained in the ECOWAS Communique: a ceasefire in Liberia, the calling of a national conference and formation of an interim government, and the holding of free and democratic elections.

The ECOWAS mediation group is preparing to place a monitoring group (ECOMOG) into Liberia to achieve those objectives.

It is important that the parties to the Liberian conflict agree to the introduction of the monitoring group so that it can take place peacefully. A diplomatic effort to bring that about is under way.

In that regard, the U.S. Government has sent a liaison team to Freetown to interact with the ECOMOG's Commander, General Arnold Quainoo, and other appropriate officials. The team will help us determine how the prospect for a peaceful deployment of ECOMOG can be achieved, and what the United States can do to be helpful in that context.

The team, which will be headed by the U.S. Ambassador to Sierra Leone, will consist of him and four State and Defense Department officers from Monrovia.

AUGUST 28, 1990

Marines continue to provide security to the U.S. Embassy. Five people were evacuated yesterday—2 U.S. citizens and 3 foreign nationals. This brings the total evacuations to 1,705, including 141 U.S. citizens and 1,566 foreign nationals.

The Marines and Sailors previously assigned to Mediterranean Amphibious Ready Group 2-90 have been relieved to allow a turnover of units. Three ships—the USS Saipan (LHA-Assault Helicopter Carrier), USS Sumter (LST-Tank Landing Ship), and USS Ponce (LPD-Amphibious Transport Dock Ship) are steaming home and an official announce[ment] of their arrival will be made five days prior. The fourth ship, the USS Peterson (DD-Destroyer), is currently deployed in the Mediterranean. During their 80 consecutive days off the coast of Liberia MARG 2-90 evacuated 1700 people (139 Americans and 1,561 foreign nationals).

The USS Whidbey Island (Amphibious Transport Dock Ship) and the USS Barnstable County (Tank Landing Ship) form a joint task force under the U.S. European Command. The remainder of MARG 3-90, which includes four amphibious ships, are operating in the Mediterranean.

We will maintain a presence off the coast as long as necessary to complete the mission.

---

[1] Selected from texts provided by the Bureau of African Affairs, Department of State; August 28 text prepared by the Department of Defense.

[2] On September 9, 1990, President Doe was captured by forces loyal to rebel leader Prince Johnson and subsequently killed.

Congress Debates Cambodian Policy

**STATEMENT BY SENATOR
GEORGE J. MITCHELL REGARD-
ING AMERICAN POLICY TOWARD
CAMBODIA,
JUNE 11, 1990** [1]

Following the close of the U.S.-Soviet summit, we are reminded how many significant changes have occurred in the world in the past few years. We are also reminded that not all of America's policies have adapted to these changes in the international environment.

Regional conflicts, a recurrent theme of discussion in U.S.-Soviet relations, continue across the globe. Some, as in Nicaragua and Namibia, have been peacefully resolved. New conflicts threaten to break out, as between India and Pakistan. Others, such as Afghanistan and Angola, simply continue on.

To some extent, these continuing conflicts reflect the legacy of the past, a cold war, zero-sum battle of proxy forces and puppet governments. For external powers fueling such conflicts, there appears to be a lack of courage and commitment to reexamining the basis of their policies and creatively addressing the need for a peaceful solution. Nowhere is this more obvious and tragic than in the case of American policy toward Cambodia.

Bush Administration's Policy Criticized

The Bush administration's Cambodia policy, to the extent that a thorough and conscious policy can be said to exist, has been shaped by several factors: the legacy of bitterness and misunderstanding from earlier American involvement in Southeast Asia; the Bush administration's unwillingness to confront China or cooperate with the Soviet Union in the search for peace in Cambodia; and the administration's unwillingness to act unless immediate, positive results are guaranteed.

For over a decade, United States policy toward Cambodia has been seen through the prism of the superpower conflict. Because the Soviets backed the Vietnamese who invaded Cambodia, the U.S. automatically joined with the Association of Southeast Asian Nations (ASEAN) and with China to counter Soviet expansionism—even if it meant de facto support for the genocidal communist rebels known as the Khmer Rouge. The U.S. reflexively supported a policy that could produce an outcome far worse than the problem it purported to address.

The Bush administration has thoughtlessly continued this policy, despite changes both in Southeast Asia and in superpower relations. Those changes have destroyed the only rationale used to justify that policy. The President has failed to reexamine U.S. interests in this conflict, failed to disentangle our policy from that of China for fear of "upsetting" the Chinese Government. The Bush administration continues its policy in Cambodia despite overwhelming evidence of the dangerous result it makes more likely.

In the literal sense of the word, the administration's Cambodia policy is incredible. It is insupportable. It must be changed.

The Khmer Rouge Threat

China's clients, the Khmer Rouge, are communists who have fought to control Cambodia for over twenty years. When they succeeded and did control Cambodia, from 1975-1979, they wrought unspeakable horror. It is virtually impossible to describe their methodical terror, what is now called "autogenocide"—the systematic destruction of one's own people.

The Vietnamese invaded Cambodia in 1979, not for humanitarian reasons, but in response to Khmer Rouge attacks. They drove the weakened Khmer Rouge into the western fringes of the country and into Thailand.

The U.S. subsequently "winked" in encouragement as the Chinese and Thai resurrected Pol Pot's Khmer Rouge troops with arms and supplies. The United States joined China, North Korea and members of ASEAN to help support two alternative non-communist guerrilla groups. The Reagan administration then encouraged the non-communists to a make a formal alliance with the Khmer Rouge. This failure to distinguish between murderers and non-communists—at the U.N., on the ground, in negotiations—is a grave mistake that haunts current U.S. policy.

The Khmer Rouge have many times—we don't know exactly [how many times]—the number of troops of each other faction. In Prince Sihanouk's own words, the Khmer Rouge are "the most effective, disciplined and well trained military force." Unquestionably the strongest resistance force is that of Khmer Rouge headed by Pol Pot.

The faction led by Son Sann reportedly is the second most active group, although it is the smallest of the three.

The least powerful of all is the group led by deposed Prince Sihanouk, who joined the Khmer Rouge to oppose the Cambodians who ousted him in 1970. Sihanouk now says that the Khmer Rouge aren't criminals anymore, but patriots.

These factions, while they do not trust or like each other, rely on the same primary benefactor, China. China wants them to cooperate. Prince Sihanouk, once revered as Cambodia's "God-King," provides the only imaginable shred of legitimacy for the Khmer Rouge. But Prince Sihanouk is nothing on the ground. His main military

---

Four Cambodian Factions

- The Sihanouk National Army (ANS), under former monarch and head of state Norodom Sihanouk.

- The Khmer People's National Liberation Front (KPNLF), headed by former Prime Minister Son Sann. The ANS and KPNLF together form the non-communist resistance.

- The Khmer Rouge, a Marxist-Leninist group headed by Pol Pot that took power in 1975 and established one of the most murderous regimes in modern world history.

- The People's Republic of Kampuchea (PRK), led by Hun Sen and Heng Samrin. This regime, which includes former Khmer Rouge officials and was installed and sustained by the Vietnamese in the wake of their invasion, now calls itself the State of Cambodia.

leverage is derived from the battlefield success of the Khmer Rouge.

When the Vietnamese had nearly 200,000 troops in Cambodia and held the Khmer Rouge at bay, the world isolated and ignored Cambodia. No one bothered to seriously consider that Chinese policies were strengthening the murderous Khmer Rouge.

By the end of 1989, when the Vietnamese withdrew the bulk of their troops and left the country in the hands of the government they had installed, the world awoke. The possibility of a Khmer Rouge return to power became real.

Surely this is not what we seek, nor is it in our interest.

U.S. Interests in Cambodia

What are U.S. interests in Cambodia? A stable regional peace, a Cambodia that no country—Vietnam, the Soviet Union, or China—can use to project its own power. A Cambodia that will prosper economically and become a trading partner. A Cambodia that will not destroy itself once again, as it nearly did under the Khmer Rouge.

The Vietnamese have withdrawn either all or most of their troops from Cambodia. They have turned inward, trying to confront their massive economic failure at home. While one day Vietnam might again turn outward, this is most likely if hostile Cambodian forces again attack, as the Khmer Rouge did. The Soviets are seeking disengagement from the region. They want to reduce the financial burden of support; they want a peaceful solution. Whatever residual threat of Vietnamese or Soviet expansion in the region exists, it is not, in my view, outweighed by the threat of the return of the Khmer Rouge.

The Hun Sen regime is tainted by its foreign installation and by its leaders' former association with the Khmer Rouge. Like the Laotian government with which we have relations, the Cambodian communists have undertaken social reforms, opened the government to former opponents, and allowed some economic freedoms.

The current regime is not ideal. But it is not the Khmer Rouge.

The administration does not believe it faces a choice between the two. It believes that all factions can be brought into a comprehensive peace that would lead to Prince Sihanouk's election as head of a peaceful and democratic Cam-

bodia. It desperately wants to believe that this is possible, so that it can avoid a choice between the evil and unattractive. I wish it were that simple.

It is not.

Indirect Support of Khmer Rouge

The crux of the problem is that the Bush administration assumes that China and its client the Khmer Rouge, if brought into a settlement, will abide by its terms. Whether this is an inclusive coalition government or an internationally administered election, such an accommodating approach requires cooperation. But our policy should not be based upon any assumption that China would be satisfied with anything less than ultimate Khmer Rouge domination, or upon the expectation that the Khmer Rouge will mend their ways.

The Bush administration has been slow to realize the inherent danger of its current policy—that it in effect sanctions the return of the murderous Khmer Rouge.

It does so first by providing non-lethal assistance to the two non-communist groups without adequate control over the use of that assistance.

These groups receive much of their support from China. Joined in a coalition, they do not fight against the Khmer Rouge. They fight with the Khmer Rouge. Increasingly there are reports of tactical and strategic military cooperation between Sihanouk's forces and the Khmer Rouge. Prince Sihanouk has stated that the noncommunists take ammunition and heavy weapons from the Khmer Rouge. It is alleged that all factions share intelligence information during battlefield operations.

There are also reports of the existence of a Cambodian working group in which the resistance factions coordinate planning and strategy as well as coordinate outside assistance.

Congress in 1985 barred the use of funds "for the purpose or with the effect of promoting, sustaining, or augmenting, directly or indirectly, the capacity of the Khmer Rouge or any of its members to conduct military or paramilitary operations."

That was the American Congress' response to the terror perpetrated by the Khmer Rogue.

It appears that there is reason to question whether this law is being obeyed. Accordingly, at my request the Senate Intelligence Committee will con-

duct new oversight hearings on the administration's policy in Cambodia, and the administration's compliance with the law.

The second way the U.S. indirectly promotes the return of the Khmer Rouge is through its diplomatic policy. The U.S. and most other nations preferred to leave the Cambodia seat at the United Nations occupied by the Khmer Rouge rather than see the Vietnamese-installed government represented in the U.N. In 1982, the Reagan administration encouraged Sihanouk and Son Sann to join a coalition with the Khmer Rouge and jointly occupy the seat—although the Khmer Rouge in effect control the seat. This U.S.-engineered coalition gives the Khmer Rouge international legitimacy it does not deserve.

It is time to abandon this charade and withdraw support for any coalition, regardless of its title or its flag, that includes the Khmer Rouge. Rather an empty seat than one stained by the crimes of the Khmer Rouge.

The third aspect of the Bush administration's policy that facilitates Khmer Rouge dominance is its conscious penalizing of the Cambodian people. The U.S. has been the single most important factor in ensuring Cambodia's isolation.

The Administration refuses to allow licenses for rehabilitation or development projects in Cambodia. It makes it very time-consuming and difficult for private voluntary organizations to provide even strictly defined humanitarian aid. Administration policies have in effect denied Cambodia international assistance to restore the damage done by the Khmer Rouge, let alone make progress toward the country's 1969 standard of living.

Administration policymakers apparently fear that humanitarian relief, economic development and international interactions with Cambodia will strengthen the Hun Sen regime—and that this is more important than the well-being of the Cambodian people. They seem to forget that keeping Cambodians weak and powerless helps the Khmer Rouge most.

The Administration refuses even to talk to representatives of the Hun Sen regime. We have diplomatic relations with Laos, even though Vietnamese troops remain in that country. Secretary Baker has met with Angolan President dos Santos, even though the U.S. funds a guerrilla force in his country. But the administration will have nothing to do with Hun Sen.

How can the U.S., without any contact with Cambodia, fully understand what is happening inside the country?

There are so many basic facts we don't know for certain—from the strength and popular support for the Khmer Rouge to the effects of the economic reforms of the Hun Sen government. We are not aware of facts that should be crucial factors in our policy toward that country.

But this administration apparently believes that this lack of knowledge is worth a political point.

In its efforts to promote a peaceful resolution of the conflict, the administration intends that the Khmer Rouge be given an entree, a chance to participate in elections, to be included in a settlement. But unless the United States changes its current priorities, this approach could facilitate domination by the Khmer Rouge.

Khmer Rouge domination is not what the administration intends. I believe that. But it is made more likely, rather than less likely, by the administration's policy.

I believe U.S. policy toward Cambodia cannot be based on a solution that emphasizes satisfying China and the Khmer Rouge. Their interests are not ours. U.S. policy in Cambodia should be first and foremost aimed at isolating the Khmer Rouge.

Policy Changes Proposed

What changes in policy would this require?

We must first remove the fig leaf of legitimacy that we bestow upon the Khmer Rouge in the international community. The first symbolic step should be the withdrawal of U.S. support for the occupation of Cambodia's seat at the United Nations by a coalition government that includes the Khmer Rouge.

Second, the administration should work to convince the ASEAN countries that fund the non-communist resistance that it is time to divorce Sihanouk and Son Sann from the Khmer Rouge.

Together, the United States and ASEAN should work to convince the noncommunist forces that such a split is a necessary step toward restoring their political autonomy and legitimacy. They are stained by association with the Khmer Rouge; they must begin to demonstrate independence from the

forces that nearly destroyed the Cambodian people.

Third, the President should clearly state that the U.S. will not support a negotiated solution that would give the Khmer Rouge a role in Cambodia's future or increase the likelihood of a Khmer Rouge military victory.

If the recent Tokyo talks presage a bipartite solution that would exclude the Khmer Rouge, those talks were positive. But it is troubling that the process established by the Tokyo Communique would not necessarily preclude Khmer Rouge participation, as is it troubling that Prince Sihanouk hopes the Khmer Rouge will yet join him.

That the Khmer Rouge continue to insist on an equal diplomatic role will, I believe, prompt the administration unequivocally to reject a quadripartite solution.

The United States should strongly support elections in Cambodia, but those elections must be conducted in a manner that will minimize the possibility of a return of the Khmer Rouge.

Fourth, the administration must ensure that the law barring any direct or indirect U.S. support for the Khmer Rouge is being obeyed. The American people deserve a guarantee that their money is not in any way helping the forces of murder and genocide. If the U.S. government cannot provide this guarantee, then funding for the noncommunists should be reexamined.

America does not promote democracy abroad by directly or indirectly enhancing the strength of the communist, murderous Khmer Rouge.

Fifth, the United States should talk to the Hun Sen regime. As I stated earlier, to deny all contact in order to make a political point does not serve American interests. We must be better informed about the situation within Cambodia and capable of some form of dialogue with the ruling regime.

Finally, the administration should ease restrictions on humanitarian and development aid to Cambodia. The Senate recently took a positive step by adopting the Cranston/Kerrey amendment to provide $5 million of emergency aid to Cambodian children through international relief agencies. I urge the administration to use this money to help the children of Cambodia.

We should begin interacting with Cambodia, exchanging people and ideas. We should not enforce Cambodia's isolation and poverty, be-

cause isolation and poverty is not a stable basis on which to build a peaceful and democratic future.

In order to take these steps, the administration must confront three major factors affecting its current policy.

First, the administration will be forced to face the fact and admit that China is the problem, not the solution, in Cambodia. The U.S. must decouple its Cambodia policy from that of the Chinese. China cannot be our partner in the search for peace as long as it supports the Khmer Rouge.

American officials have repeatedly made personal requests that China reduce that support. Yet according to the press, even administration officials admit that China has since sent large new weapons shipments to the Khmer Rouge. Is this what the President is getting in return for continuing business as usual after the massacre in Tienanmen Square? If so, he's getting nothing.

The administration must recognize that China's interests are not ours. It is time to admit that China does not share our goals in Cambodia. It is time for American policy to reflect American goals.

Second, the Bush administration will be forced to abandon the cold war prism through which it views Cambodia. The administration remains wedded to an outmoded analysis of the conflict which has blinded officials to the dangerous result their policies may bring about.

Until the administration can objectively evaluate the situation, it will be unable to consider the Hun Sen government as part of the solution.

But just as we dealt with South Africa in Namibia and the Sandinistas in Nicaragua, so, too, will we have to deal with the Hun Sen regime if we are to bring peace and democracy to Cambodia and prevent a return of the Khmer Rouge.

Finally, the administration will be forced to take risks, to devote energy and time to an uncertain outcome. This is difficult for an administration that engages itself only when the costs are negligible and the victory is certain. The Bush administration is so risk-averse that it appears unwilling to take the steps necessary to restore morality and sanity to our Cambodia policy. But it must do so, now.

I am certain that no American wishes to help return the nightmare of the murderous Khmer Rouge to the

Cambodian people. It is time to change America's Cambodia policy accordingly.

---

[1] Text Provided by the Office of the Majority Leader, United States Senate, released June 11, 1990.

REMARKS BY REPRESENTATIVE STEPHEN J. SOLARZ, JUNE 27, 1990 [1]

Mr. Chairman, my amendment, which is offered together with the gentleman from Michigan [Mr. Broomfield] is designed to permit the program of non-lethal assistance to the non-communist resistance forces whom we have supported for many years in Cambodia to continue, while simultaneously prohibiting any assistance directly or indirectly to the Khmer Rouge.

The amendment would strike a provision in the bill before Members which would prohibit any and all assistance, even nonlethal assistance, to the non-communist resistance forces in Cambodia. Mr. Chairman, I think we have three main objectives which we need to consider in Cambodia. The first is to prevent Pol Pot and the Khmer Rouge from returning to power. The second is to bring the fighting in that country to an end. The third is to make it possible for the people of Cambodia, at long last, to have the opportunity for self-determination.

Mr. Chairman, I will submit that the provision in the bill which completely prohibits any assistance whatsoever to the non-commnunist resistance forces would strike a deadly blow against our efforts to prevent the Khmer Rouge from returning to power, to make a free and fair election possible, and to bring the fight in Cambodia to an end. Indeed, I would suggest that if our amendment is defeated and the language in the bill is preserved, it would play right into the hands of the Khmer Rouge. It would play into the hands of the Khmer Rouge by greatly diminishing the prospects for a political settlement of the Cambodian conflict which would bring the fighting to an end, which would facilitate the introduction of a large United Nations peacekeeping force, and which would make possible an internationally supervised free and fair election.

In a free and fair election, Pol Pot and the Khmeer Rouge would have no chance whatsoever. The anti-Khmer Rouge elements in Cambodia will not need Roger Ailes to make negative spots in order to defeat the Khmer Rouge in an election. However, if there is no political settlement and the fighting continues, then Pol Pot and the Khmer Rouge, who have 40,000 men still under arms and constitute the most formidable and fanatical of the various Cambodian factions in the field, could very easily battle their way back to power in Phnom Penh over the next few years.

The reason that the defeat of this amendment and the adoption of the language in the bill would diminish the prospects for a political settlement, thereby playing into the hands of Pol Pot, is that it would greatly diminish the incentive which Vietnam has to agree to a political settlement. We are now closer to achieving a political settlement of the Cambodian conflict than at any time in the last 15 years. The five permanent members of the [United Nations] Security Council are essentially in agreement on how to do it, by bringing in the United Nations, and by having an internationally supervised free and fair election. China is behind it, the Soviet Union is behind it, the United States is behind it, but Vietnam and the puppet government in Cambodia are not. If we now abandon the non-communists, we will be sending a signal to the Vietnamese that time is on their side, and their incentive to make the concessions necessary to get a settlement will be greatly diminished.

Now, it will be said by the opponents of my amendment that the aid we have given to the non-communists in the past had ended up in the hands of the Khmer Rouge. That is simply not true. I have looked into it. I have had closed briefings on it, and there is not a shred of credible evidence that any of our aid to the non-communists in the past has ended up in the hands of the Khmer Rouge. If it were true, I would be leading the fight to cut off this aid to the non-communists, but it is not true. It will also be said by opponents of my amendment that Prince Sihanouk, who we are trying to help, is a front man for the Khmer Rouge. This is hogwash. The best evidence that it is hogwash is the fact that one month ago the Japanese convened a conference in Tokyo to move the peace process on Cambodia forward. All the Cambodian factions were present, and at the end of the conference they had a communique calling for a cease-fire and a political settlement. Hun Sen signed it. Sihanouk signed it. Son Sann signed it, but the Khmer Rouge did not sign it. If Sihanouk is a front man to the Khmer Rouge, why would he be signing agreements opposed by the Khmer Rouge and which exclude the Khmer Rouge from power?

I urge Members, as does the administration, as do all the ASEAN [Association of Southeast Asian Nations] ambassadors, to support my amendment and prevent the Khmer Rouge from returning to power.

---

[1] Text from the Congressional Record, June 27, 1990

Secretary Baker Announces U.S. Policy Shift on Cambodia

Replies by Secretary of State Baker to press questions after his meeting with Soviet Foreign Minister Eduard Shevardnadze, Paris, July 18, 1990 (brief opening remarks omitted). [1]

Q. Both countries have an interest in Cambodia and Vietnam. There's a story now in the Los Angeles Times that the administration has finally concluded that the Khmer Rouge really is the strongest of the insurgents, and that there are bigger dangers than the Cambodian government, which some people insist is not a puppet of the Vietnam government. In any event, has the administration changed horses, so to speak?

A. One of the major objectives of our administration, of course, was to see the withdrawal of Vietnamese forces from Cambodia. We have now seen that accomplished and it is very important, we think, to do what we can to prevent a return to power by the Khmer Rouge. This has also been an objective of administration policy. In keeping with that objective, we have determined that we will open a dialogue with Vietnam about Cambodia, we will be prepared to enhance our humanitarian assistance to Cambodia, and we will be prepared to and will in fact change what has been our policy regarding the seat at the United Nations which has been held by a coalition that includes the Khmer Rouge. I discussed this matter with the Minister and I advised him of this change in policy by the United States.

Q. Does that mean, Mr. Secretary, that the United States no longer backs the coalition which includes the Khmer Rouge?

A. It means that with respect to the seat in the United Nations that is certainly the case. The United States continues to support the non-communist resistance, it continues to support those forces that are loyal to Son Sann and Prince Sihanouk.

Foreign Minister Shevardnadze. [Inaudible] our approaches on the Cambodian problem in principle have become much closer.

*   *   *

Q. Does this Cambodian policy mean the resumption of U.S. relations with Vietnam?

Secretary Baker. The change in policy does not constitute a decision to normalize relations with Vietnam. It is a decision simply to begin a dialogue with Vietnam about Cambodia. The progress or lack of progress of that dialogue, as well as continuing efforts by Vietnam with respect to our POWs and MIAs, will have a lot to [do] with whether or not we can move toward normalization.

Q. Did you get any indication that the Soviets are also changing their position to withdraw or reduce support for the Vietnamese-backed government?

A. No, I did not get that impression. I did not ask him that question, though.

Q. Doesn't this undercut Sihanouk now? You're really purposely trying to undermine his effort as a result of withdrawing recognition?

A. No, not at all. In fact, it works in the other direction in our view because in the absence of the bipartisan policy approach, I think it will be ever more difficult to continue to generate the funds that we need from the Congress to continue this support to the non-communist resistance. And as you know, we've recently had an adverse vote in that connection.

Q. Does that mean that this change in policy was something that you worked out with people on Capitol Hill and that they've agreed with this?

A. I think you'll find that there's quite a bit of agreement in the Congress with respect to this. It's not something that we worked out in that sense. This was not a negotiated agreement between us and the Congress.

Q. Did they agree to the idea of opening a dialogue in Vietnam or did they agree with the idea of reducing support that ends up in the hands of the Khmer Rouge?

A. Some will agree with some aspects of this and others will disagree. So it's pretty hard — you can't answer that question yes or no.

Q. What was the key factor in the reshaping of your own thinking on this issue? Obviously, you've had this policy now for the first 15-18 months of the administration. What was it that forced you to draw a different conclusion?

A. Well, we had a goal of seeking Vietnamese withdrawal from Cambodia. We have realized that. That was one of our policy goals. Another policy

goal was to prevent the return of the Khmer Rouge to power. We've not been able to achieve that goal and in fact, it would appear that the risks are greater as we move forward that that might, in fact, occur. So we want to do everything we can to prevent a return of the Khmer Rouge to power. That has been one of our policy goals all along that we've not been able to achieve.

The third policy goal is that we would like to see free elections in Cambodia. And we hope that this will enable us to move that third policy goal forward as well. So, we've achieved one of our policy goals, we still have two to go.

Q. Did you inform the Chinese before that you were going to take this move?

A. We've done some consultations, I can't tell you exactly the scope and extent of how much — who's been contacted. I know we've contacted our ASEAN [Association of Southeast Asian Nations] partners.

Q. Have you changed your opinion about the government in Cambodia? The Reagan policy has been that it was a puppet government of Vietnam. A lot of people question that and think compared to the Khmer Rouge it's not a bad choice. Do you still think they're puppets?

A. Our goal is to prevent a return to power of the Khmer Rouge. That doesn't require, I don't think, that we make those kind of judgments vis-a-vis the government in Cambodia. It certainly was a puppet government while Vietnam troops were in the country supporting it. Those Vietnam troops have now gone and that's one of our policy goals that we've been able to achieve.

Q. [What does] dialogue with Vietnam mean? Can you define what you hope to get out of this dialogue?

A. What it means is we want to talk to Vietnam, because we think they have influence with the Cambodian government, about using that influence to help us construct or create the conditions that would permit the election of a free government in Cambodia. That's, again, one of our policy goals that we have not as yet been able to achieve. We have a dialogue going with Vietnam on POWs and MIAs through General Jack Vessey and, of course, that will be continuing. But we do have now Vietnam troops out of Cambodia, so that's one thing that we will not have to be discussing with Vietnam — except to the extent that evidence might suggest there may be some remaining in Cambodia and we'll want to talk about that.

Q. Does this not possibly complicate matters with China which has shown no sign of giving up its support for the Khmer Rouge?

A. I'll let China speak for itself with respect to this. It's not up to me to give you the Chinese reaction. I would simply say it's our view, and it's a view that's shared by many around the world, that the last experience with Khmer Rouge rule in Cambodia was extraordinarily tragic for many, many Cambodians. And a major policy goal of ours continues to be to prevent the return to power of the Khmer Rouge. We hope and believe that this will help move us in that direction.

Q. How close are they to regaining power? It sounds like you're really afraid that that could happen.

A. I don't know, I can't quantify that for you except to say that they are still out there — for over a year now we've been trying to have a political dialogue through the Cambodian conference that was convened here a year ago in Paris. The Khmer Rouge has succeeded in turning that political dialogue into a dialogue of the battlefield. And the fighting continues and Cambodians continue to suffer and Cambodians continue to die. It is important, we think, to focus our attention in the way that I've just suggested.

---

[1] Department of State Press Release 104, July 18, 1990.

Implementing a Political Settlement in Cambodia

by Richard H. Solomon and John R. Bolton

Statements before the Subcommittee on East Asian and Pacific Affairs, Senate Foreign Relations Committee, July 20, 1990. Mr.Solomon is Assistant Secretary of State for East Asian and Pacific Affairs and Mr. Bolton is Assistant Secretary of State for International Organization Affairs. [1]

Assistant Secretary Solomon. Today's hearing is particularly timely, in view of Secretary Baker's announcement on July 18 of several revisions in our policy on Cambodia, as well as my having just returned from the fifth meeting of the representatives of the U.N. Security Council permanent five [2] in Paris.

I welcome this opportunity to discuss the administration's efforts to maintain bipartisan support for our policy of a political settlement to the conflict in Cambodia and to review the considerable progress that I believe was attained by the permanent five in Paris earlier this week.

U.S. Objectives

I would begin by stating my belief that we share the same objectives regarding a Cambodian settlement. We seek to do all that we can to ensure that the Cambodian people have the right of self-determination through free and fair elections; are at last freed from the burden of foreign invasion and civil warfare; and, especially, that they never again fall subject to rule by the murderous Khmer Rouge. As Secretary Baker noted on July 18, the fighting continues, Cambodians continue to suffer and die. Our efforts are designed to turn the battlefield conflict into a competition at the ballot box.

U.S. national interests in Cambodia focus on our moral concerns. Beyond our commitment to the security of our allies and friends in the Association of Southeast Asian Nations (ASEAN), we seek only an opportunity for the Cambodian people to choose their own government through free and fair elections and to have a future of security and national independence. For the most part, our effort to influence events

there is limited to the diplomatic sphere. But I believe that the objectives we seek justify, indeed compel, our continuing involvement in the search for peace and national reconciliation.

Our efforts over the past year have been shaped by the judgment that the best way to achieve our objectives is through a negotiated, comprehensive settlement which would bring to bear the concern and commitment of the international community through the United Nations. To that end, we have been working to achieve:

- The verified withdrawal of all foreign forces;
- The creation of a neutral political process culminating in free and fair elections centered around a role for the United Nations;
- The preservation of a viable non-communist alternative for the Cambodian people which can be present at the negotiating table and at the polls; and
- Above all, a settlement that has reliable guarantees that the Khmer Rouge will not again impose its violent rule on the Cambodian people.

I believe we have made significant progress toward each of these goals, and in a moment I would like to say something about each. Before doing so, however, I want to make one more general point.

The United States can only be successful in helping shape developments in Cambodia if we have strong support—bipartisan support in the Congress and from the American people. We know that this is a complex problem with many ambiguities and moral dilemmas. Cambodia is a small and distant country torn asunder by two decades of warfare, and it is not at the top of our national priorities. Moreover, our approach to the problem is burdened by the complex feelings held by the American people for developments in Indochina. Thus, building a national consensus is no easy task.

It is no secret that, of late, there has been much more intense debate over the direction of our policy. In my estimation, this debate has not been over its basic thrust—and particularly over the objective of preventing a Khmer Rouge return to power. Rather, differences seem to focus on the tactics employed to attain a solution, including our stress on a U.N. role in the settlement process. Since we cannot be effective in our diplomatic efforts without your support, there has been considerable consultation with the Congress since the beginning of this administration. As a result of those consultations, and as a reflection of the progress we believe we are making in our overall strategy, we are now in a position to make certain revisions in our policy. These are designed to encourage flexibility on the part of the key participants in this conflict and to maintain strong support at home for our efforts. Later in my testimony, I will elaborate on the details of these adjustments, but first let me give you an update on the Paris meeting from which I just returned.

Results of the Paris Meeting

I am pleased to report that during our two days of meetings, the permanent five representatives were able to make what our joint summary statement called "significant progress" on two of the most difficult elements of a political settlement process: transitional arrangements regarding the administration of Cambodia during the preelection period and military arrangements after an agreement, and a cease-fire, go into effect. All five representatives were able to agree on the need for establishment of a U.N. Transitional Authority in Cambodia (UNTAC) with a military, as well as civilian, component. We agreed upon a role for UNTAC in verifying the withdrawal of all foreign forces from Cambodia, the regrouping of all Cambodian forces with weapons stored under U.N. supervision, and a phased program of arms reduction. UNTAC will also have as its mission ensuring the cessation of all outside military assistance to Cambodia.

I should emphasize that all five permanent members of the Security Council—and here I would like to make special mention of the Soviet and Chinese delegates—displayed a willingness to compromise in order to move to an agreement. The negotiation also achieved significant progress on the political structure that would exist in the period leading up to free elections. A Supreme National Council should be established and composed of individuals representing "all shades of opinion

among the people of Cambodia." The permanent five approach envisages an important role for the UNTAC on the civil side and will provide for U.N. supervision or control of existing administrative structures in order to ensure a neutral political environment conducive to free and fair general elections.

If these measures are implemented, these steps will permit the holding of free and fair elections, a necessary step to both peace and a legitimate government.

I am encouraged that the permanent five process—which Secretary Baker first proposed to his permanent five and ASEAN colleagues during last fall's General Assembly session—has reached consensus on some of the most important elements of a comprehensive framework agreement. The five are determined to sustain the momentum developed in Paris, and they will meet again in New York toward the end of August. At that time, they will also deal with the election process, with measures to protect human rights, and international guarantees of Cambodia's independence.

Despite this recent progress, I should say frankly that any prognosis for success must be guarded. The issues are difficult and complex; and, in view of the violence that has plagued Cambodia over the past two decades, it is not surprising that there is great distrust among the Cambodian parties to the conflict. But the growing consensus among the permanent five is a good sign that the major powers, whose interests have long been caught up in this conflict, can work together in an effort to construct a political process culminating in elections.

U.S. Role in the Settlement Process

Let me stress our conviction that the United States has an important and continuing role to play in this diplomatic effort. And our ability to do so—to be a credible player and to provide the Cambodian people the alternative of an election with other than communist options—is critically dependent on our continuing to provide nonlethal assistance to the non-communist groups. These people have, against great odds, struggled to maintain a non-communist alternative for the Cambodian people. We would totally undercut their position, and our own credibility, were we to cut off aid abruptly to the only groups in

Cambodia with which we share important basic values. It would be especially self-defeating now that the diplomatic progress is gaining momentum.

Questions on U.S. Assistance

Let me speak directly to the question that has been on the minds of many regarding our assistance. It has been suggested that some of our aid may be finding its way to the Khmer Rouge, or that it is indirectly assisting that group. I want to stress that nothing would be more abhorrent to me, to the Secretary, or to the President. We will do, and we are doing, all that is possible to ensure that this does not occur.

We continuously review this situation and find no evidence that a diversion of our material assistance has occurred or that there is systematic battlefield cooperation such that our assistance enhances the combat capacity of the Khmer Rouge.

The issue of such cooperation has been raised repeatedly with the non-communist resistance leaders themselves, including recently by a distinguished member of Congress, Representative Stephen Solarz. We have a written response from one leader confirming that no aid provided by the United States has gone to the Khmer Rouge and outlining new and clear directives to his field commanders designed to doubly ensure against such an occurrence, or of military cooperation, in the future. We will continue to monitor this situation closely. I want to assure you that the administration will immediately cease its material support for any non-communist resistance organization if reliable intelligence demonstrates that the law has been broken.

My presentation would not be balanced if I did not air the other side of our dilemma; that is, that cutting off our assistance would leave the non-communists largely dependant on support from China, and perhaps even the Khmer Rouge. If we were to end assistance in the absence of truly solid evidence, we might well bring about the very outcome we seek to avoid by leaving the Khmer Rouge the only resistance force in the field. This could only prolong the war and the suffering of the Cambodian people.

Results of Policy Review

Let me now turn to the revisions in our approach which Secretary Baker announced in Paris. As you may recall, over the past two months, both President Bush and Secretary Baker have publicly commented on periodic reviews of our policy. These continuing assessments have reaffirmed that our overall strategy of seeking a political solution through free and fair elections conducted with significant U.N. support is the course that is most likely to attain our objectives.

Yet circumstances are changing. We have attained our strategic objective in the withdrawal from Cambodia of the bulk of Vietnamese military forces. Political momentum toward a solution is now building. The Chinese have shown flexibility; the Soviets have shown flexibility. We now need to convince Hanoi and Phnom Penh that participation in a comprehensive political settlement holds the key to the future. We want to encourage both Vietnam and China to use their considerable influence with their clients to accept the procedures that are being developed by the permanent five.

We thus decided upon a number of new steps, including an enhancement of our dialogue with Hanoi about Cambodia. This will complement efforts underway with the Vietnamese on POW/MIA and other humanitarian issues. We are also considering contacts with the Phnom Penh regime, although we would do so only if it would advance our goal of free and fair elections. We will also be looking carefully at additional humanitarian programs for Vietnam and Cambodia that would both help these suffering people as well as express our openness to a new relationship once the Cambodian conflict is resolved. And we will implement a new program designed to aid Cambodian children — both those within the country as well as in camps along the Thai-Cambodian border.

We will no longer support the CGDK [Coalition Government of Democratic Kampuchea] as the holder of Cambodia's U.N. seat. We want the seat to be occupied by a freely elected government — and, pending that development, by Cambodians firmly committed to the holding of free and fair elections. This latter adjustment is designed to make it crystal clear that we will do nothing, even indirectly, which

seems to give legitimacy to the Khmer Rouge as an organization.

In conclusion, I believe the options before us are as clear as they are stark. The prospects for Cambodia are either for a negotiated settlement or for continuing warfare. While the diplomatic approach is difficult and may present us with some controversial choices, the alternative of ongoing warfare is unacceptable. It would be the course on which the Khmer Rouge would have its best chance for a return to power. As I noted earlier, our ability to influence events in Cambodia is limited, but if there is to be a chance for a peaceful resolution of this tragic conflict, we — the Congress and the executive branch — must work closely together. I have come here today in that spirit.

Assistant Secretary Bolton. I appreciate this opportunity to appear before you once again to discuss the role of the United Nations in facilitating and implementing a comprehensive political settlement to the Cambodian conflict. When I last spoke to you in February, I indicated that we believed the United Nations could play an important and salutary role in moving the peace process in Cambodia forward and in ensuring that the Cambodian people do not have to experience another decade of war and tragedy. Today, we are still convinced that the United Nations has a central role to play in bringing peace to Cambodia — a peace that will be lasting, a peace that will ensure that the human rights of the Cambodian people are protected and that they will never again have to suffer through the depredations of the Khmer Rouge period.

The Bush administration has emphasized constantly, and I wish to repeat it here, that the United States is unalterably opposed to a return to power of the murderous Khmer Rouge. In all international fora of which the United States is a member, we have made explicit our abhorance of the Khmer Rouge. My colleagues in New York and Geneva, and at all international meetings, have no contact with Khmer Rouge representatives. At the recent meeting of the World Health Assembly, for example, I proclaimed "our abhorance of the appalling human rights record of the Khmer Rouge" and "our firm reservations about the representation of such a regime in this forum."

We have never been reticent about stating that one of the central motivations underpinning our efforts at fashioning a comprehensive Cambodian settlement is to create a structure of peace that contains effective measures to prevent the Khmer Rouge from returning to power. Under no circumstances will we countenance roles for the leaders responsible for the past Khmer Rouge atrocities in Cambodia's future.

We have continually reviewed our policy on Cambodia in the light of changing circumstances to ensure that it could best meet our objectives, including denying the Khmer Rouge the chance to regain power. As Secretary Baker stated in Paris on July 18, we have realized our goal of seeing the Vietnamese withdraw from Cambodia. Unfortunately, we are far from satisfied that conditions exist to ensure that the Khmer Rouge will not once again prevail in Cambodia; indeed, it would appear that the risks are greater as we move forward that that might, in fact, occur. To underline our seriousness in preventing a Khmer Rouge return, we have decided that at this fall's U.N. General Assembly, we will vote against a renewal of the credentials of the former Coalition Government of Democratic Kampuchea — now known as the National Government of Cambodia — as long as that coalition includes the Khmer Rouge. We also will actively oppose any attempt by the Phnom Penh regime to gain the Cambodian U.N. seat.

Cambodian Representation in the United Nations

A credentials fight in the United Nations this autumn will serve no constructive purpose and will do nothing to hasten a comprehensive settlement to this conflict. We hope that the Cambodian parties clearly understand this and, in an act of statesmanship as well as self-interest, will obviate the need to put this contentious issue to a vote by refraining from carrying their battle in Cambodia to the floor of the General Assembly. If the non-communist resistance, those organizations headed by Prince Sihanouk and Mr. Son Sann, were to divorce themselves from the coalition with the Khmer Rouge, the United States would happily support their application to represent Cambodia in the United Nations.

The administration firmly believes that this decision, as well as the others addressed by Dr. Solomon, will have a significant impact on moving the peace process further along and bringing relief to the Cambodian people, who have suffered so tragically for more than a decade.

U.N. Framework for Peace

Since February, the five permanent members of the Security Council have continued their search for a framework for a settlement which could be recommended to the Cambodian parties. We met in Paris in March, in New York in May, and, as you know, again in Paris this week. At each of these meetings, we have made encouraging progress in developing a workable and acceptable framework for a comprehensive settlement.

The core goal around which the U.N. operation will be structured continues to be the conduct of free and fair elections to permit the Cambodian people to determine their own destiny. We continue to believe that no institution other than the United Nations has the ability, resources, and experience to ensure that the playing field is sufficiently level—that no party has any unfair advantage—to enable the Cambodian people to exercise their franchise freely. The U.N.'s successes in Namibia and Nicaragua demonstrate that this is a realistic mandate for the United Nations.

The exact extent of the U.N. role is still being worked out. However, as the permanent five consultations continue, and the zone of agreement on the nature of the U.N.'s role is expanded, we can begin to sketch out the components of what we are calling an enhanced U.N. role in Cambodia This week's Paris talks made significant progress in defining the peacekeeping tasks of a U.N. operation. These tasks would include:

- Monitoring the cease-fire;
- Verifying the withdrawal of foreign forces from Cambodia;
- Liaising with neighboring governments to ensure developments in their territory do not endanger the settlement;
- Monitoring the cessation of outside assistance to all the Cambodian parties;
- Locating and confiscating caches of weapons; and

- Organizing mine-clearing training programs.

Once the ceasefire is formalized, the Cambodian forces would move to cantonments under U.N. supervision and their arms would be stored under U.N. supervision. The United Nations would then initiate a phased process of arms control and reduction to stabilize the security situation and build confidence among the parties.

The meeting also discussed the concept of a Supreme National Council which would be the embodiment of Cambodian sovereignty but would delegate all necessary powers to ensure the implementation of the comprehensive settlement to the United Nations.

The permanent five agreed at the Paris meeting to continue their consultations and to accelerate their efforts to flesh out further the U.N.'s role in the conduct of free and fair guarantees which will be part of the settlement.

U.N. Survey Missions

Since the beginning of the year, in anticipation of the role it may be requested to play in implementing a comprehensive settlement, the United Nations and its specialized agencies have sent four survey missions to Cambodia to begin building the data base which will be needed to plan for a U.N. operation. The U.N. Development Program (UNDP) dispatched a mission to look at the country's reconstruction needs; the Secretariat sent a group to examine the governmental and political structures; U.N. High Commissioner for Refugees (UNHCR) personnel visited Cambodia to assess how the repatriation of refugees should be handled; and a combined Secretariat/specialized agency mission went to follow up on the information developed by earlier groups. Before discussing their findings, I wish to note that the U.S. Government has neither approved their main conclusions nor has it undertaken any commitments regarding costs or sources of funding. These will have to be addressed at a later stage.

In all candor, the picture these missions have brought back of conditions in Cambodia is sobering; the United Nations will be faced with a daunting task logistically as well as politically. The UNDP mission estimated that the cost of upgrading the road, rail, port, civil aviation, and telecommunications systems to an acceptable "minimal level for

the effective deployment of a United Nations operation" would be approximately $30 million. This preoperational phase would require six months, UNDP estimates. To highlight some of the problems which would have to be rectified:

- The rail and road systems would have to be substantially rehabilitated.
- It will be necessary to provide basic radio communications, navigational aids, and air traffic control facilities to upgrade the civil aviation system to international standards.
- The country's communications system, both domestic and international, will need urgent improvement.
- The ports and inland waterways will require extensive rehabilitation.

Similar conclusions were drawn by the UNHCR mission. UNHCR estimates that $37 million and four months would be required to prepare the country for the return of its refugees. The lack of any national transportation infrastructure obviously will make a repatriation difficult for the 300,000 Cambodians now estimated to live on the Thai-Cambodian border. Of even greater magnitude is the problem of how the returning refugees will be employed once they are inside Cambodia again.

In addition to the obvious logistical difficulties of moving these refugees back into the country, a significant problem which will need to be rectified first is the virtual absence of medical and public health facilities. Tropical diseases are endemic in the areas in which refugees will be ultimately settled, and it is estimated that 95% of Cambodia's water supply is contaminated.

Needless to say, a serious additional problem which impacts on the resettlement operation is the necessity to deal with the significant number of mines which have been laid throughout the country.

Whatever the exact configuration of the total U.N. operation and the job it must accomplish in Cambodia, this operation will be unprecedented in its complexity, degree of difficulty, size and scope, and, obviously, cost. The United Nations and its specialized agencies have previously undertaken many of the tasks we envisage for them to do in Cambodia. The United Nations has also carried out integrated operations, in Namibia and Central America for example, which combined peacekeeping, election monitoring, and repatriation. However, the operation being contemplated for Cambodia will be unique. It will require the United Nations to plan and implement a multifaceted operation which will include peacekeeping; ensuring a free and fair election and guarding against manipulation by the incumbent regime; the repatriation of 300,000 refugees; and a coordinating role in the reconstruction of this devastated country.

This is not an enterprise about which we should have any illusions. It will not be easy. The peacekeeping aspect of the U.N. operation will require the United Nations, for the first time, to monitor a ceasefire in a guerrilla war in which there are multiple parties and no clear lines of demarcation among the conflicting forces.

As we work with the United Nations to realize our goal of free elections in Cambodia, we will be especially mindful of the need to keep the U.N. operation as efficient and cost-effective as possible, consistent with its ability to fulfill its mandate.

---

[1] Department of State Current Policy 1291, August 1990. The complete transcript of the hearings will be published by the committee and will be available from the Superintendent of Documents, U.S. Government Printing Office, Washington, D.C. 20420.
[2] The five permanent members of the U.N. Security Council: China, France, the United Kingdom, the U.S.S.R., and the United States.

Sixty-six Senators Urge Further Change in Cambodian Policy

Letter to President Bush signed by 66 Members of the United States Senate, July 24, 1990 [1]

Dear Mr. President:

As Senators deeply concerned about the continuing war in Cambodia, we are writing to ask that you reexamine American policy toward that country. We are pleased by the policy revisions recently announced by Secretary Baker. With the withdrawal of the majority of Vietnamese troops from Cambodia, there are several additional steps which we believe the administration should now take, even as the Perm Five process continues.

We believe that it is counterproductive for the United States to decline all contact with the Hun Sen regime

---

We believe that the Khmer Rouge represents an unacceptable threat to the people of Cambodia and that the American policy should be based, first and foremost, upon preventing the return of the Khmer Rouge. We appreciate that you share our concern about the Khmer Rouge, as Secretary Baker clearly expressed on Wednesday at his meeting with Soviet Foreign Minister Shevardnadze. However, we believe that American policy can and should more clearly and effectively help prevent future Khmer Rouge domination of Cambodia.

Specifically, we urge you to clearly state that the U.S. will not support a negotiated solution that would give the Khmer Rouge a role in Cambodia's future or increase the likelihood of a Khmer Rouge military victory.

We commend you for the decision to end U.S. support for any Cambodian representation in the United Nations that includes the Khmer Rouge. We look forward to active efforts by the United States to deny the resistance coalition's credentials in the United Nations as long as the Khmer Rouge is a member of that coalition.

We are concerned about reports that the non-communist resistance is cooperating militarily with the Khmer Rouge. While we are aware administration officials maintain that there is no consistent pattern of cooperation, we urge you to thoroughly investigate these reports to ensure that there is no tactical or strategic cooperation.

As you know, U.S. law prohibits the provision of funds which would have "the effect of promoting, sustaining, or augmenting, directly or indirectly, the capacity of the Khmer Rouge or any of its members to conduct military operations in Cambodia or elsewhere in Indochina."

We also urge you to make it a high priority of U.S. policy to press the Chinese government to end all support of and aid to the Khmer Rouge.

The continued isolation of Cambodia not only harshly and unfairly penalizes the Cambodian people, it undermines American efforts to promote a diplomatic solution and support self-determination for Cambodians. We welcome the decision to ease licensing restrictions on humanitarian projects in Cambodia and hope you also will allow development aid to be provided to Cambodia. We are pleased that the administration will implement the program appropriated by Congress to provide aid to children inside Cambodia.

We believe it is counterproductive for the United States to decline all contact with the Hun Sen regime. The United States should gain a better understanding of the political and military situation on the ground as well as a firsthand knowledge of the regime's goals and motivations. Since Hun Sen has committted the regime to hold "general, free, fair and democratic elections organized and supervised by the U.N.," we hope that you will see value in opening up direct contacts with representatives of the regime in Phnom Penh.

We fully share your belief in the importance of free and fair, internationally supervised elections in Cambodia. Rather than emphasizing an interim power-sharing arrangement, the U.S. diplomatic effort should focus on achieving an agreement to hold such elections at the earliest possible time, which should include the return and full participation of the non-communist elements currently in camps along the Thai-Cambodian border.

We believe that after 20 years of turmoil and tragedy, the people of Cambodia deserve an opportunity to determine their own future free of fear of the Khmer Rouge. We hope that you will see the aforementioned actions as important steps toward ensuring this goal and helping to build a new future for Cambodia. Thank you for considering our recommendations. We look forward to hearing from you.

---

[1] The letter was signed by Senators Mitchell, Danforth, Boren, Cohen, Byrd, Hatfield, Pell, Kassebaum, J. Robert Kerrey, John F. Kerrey, Cranston, Robb, Wallop, Warner, Kennedy, Chafee, Leahy, D'Amato, Levin, Jeffords, Sanford, Lugar, Burdick, Boschwitz, Bryan, Dixon, Mikulski, Ford, Lieberman, Kohl, Nunn, Reid, Akaka, Shelby, Daschle, Biden, Simon, Bentsen, Dodd, DeConcini, Harkin, Rockefeller, Gore, Wirth, Sarbanes, Heflin, Moynihan, Bingaman, Riegle, Bumpers, Inouye, Pryor, Glenn, Exon, Graham, Breaux, Metzenbaum, Baucus, Sasser, Adams, Hollings, Conrad, Bradley, Heinz, Lautenberg, and Specter. Text provided by the Office of the Majority Leader, United States Senate, July 26 release.

Secretary of State's Trip to Asia

STATEMENT BEFORE THE ASEAN POST-MINISTERIAL CONFERENCE, JAKARTA, INDONESIA, JULY 27, 1990 [1]

When we last met one year ago in Brunei, none of us could have predicted the political upheaval that is now shaking the European continent and reshaping East-West relations. Militarily, politically, and economically, Europe is being transformed. Yet so, too, is Asia.

While Eastern Europe has surged forward dramatically and abruptly, East Asia and the Pacific (as I noted in our meeting a year ago) had a start on today's twin revolutions of democracy and economic liberty. In recent years, individual freedom and private initiative have been expanding here. But continued progress will require intensified work and a strengthened partnership in the region.

Here, as in other regions, we face three fundamental challenges to greater progress: first, ensuring regional security and stability; second, consolidating democracy's advance and guaranteeing human rights; and third, perpetuating economic prosperity.

Our task in Jakarta, at this ASEAN Post-Ministerial Conference, is to enhance our transpacific partnership in meeting the challenges of security, democracy, and prosperity.

The third challenge, economic prosperity, is being actively pursued by all of us individually, bilaterally, and in other fora, for example the Uruguay Round and APEC. So, today, I would like to focus on how we can best ensure security, promote democracy, and meet a major humanitarian need. Clearly, the two most intractable problems in the region today — the Cambodian conflict and Indochinese refugees — are urgent examples of these challenges and, just as importantly, of the need for continuing cooperation.

The United States has been and will remain a Pacific power. In spite of our activities and responsibilities in Europe we have been actively engaged in shaping the postwar order in Asia. Indeed, this is my fourth trip to the Pacific in the 18 months our administration has been in office. Our historical and cultural ties to this region are longstanding and deeply held. And our shared interests are growing as transoceanic economic and political interdependence increases. We know our security is a mutual challenge, and we remain committed to a forward-based strategic presence to ensure stability and security across the Pacific and East Asia.

Our forward-based strategy will continue to rely upon cooperative security arrangements. We are pleased to be expanding cooperative military ties with Singapore that will complement our basing arrangements with the Philippines. And we hope that our current discussions with the Philippine Government on the future of our relationship will result in mutually beneficial agreements, taking into account our longstanding friendship as well as new realities.

Developments in Cambodia

Our most immediate security problem lies in Indochina — that seemingly endless center of conflict. The war in Cambodia continues to drain the lifeblood of a people that have suffered too long and too deeply.

Our common approach to Cambodia has, for a decade, focused on three goals: (1) a verified withdrawal of Vietnamese troops; (2) the prevention of the return of power of the Khmer Rouge; and (3) genuine self-determination for the Cambodian people through free elections. These are our common goals today just as they were when we met one year ago. Our current challenge, and our new opportunity, is to move them towards resolution by the time we meet next year.

This past year has seen unprecedented diplomatic activity in the search for a political solution: in Paris, in Jakarta, in Tokyo, and at the United Nations. Working together, we have helped achieve the withdrawal of Vietnam's regular combat units from Cambodia. That is a worthy success. But it should be neither our ultimate achievement, nor the high water mark of our cooperative effort.

Now, we must look beyond. We must set our sights on the achievement of a just, durable and comprehensive peace in Cambodia. Yet, we do ourselves, and the Cambodians, a great disservice if we blur this vision through a failure to recognize the steady, threatening movement of brutal men through the jungles.

So, our efforts to achieve our third objective, self-determination through elections, must not be pursued irrespective of our second: preventing the Khmer Rouge from shooting their way back into power. Can there be any doubt that a Khmer Rouge return to power through violence will make a mockery of all our efforts in Cambodia?

We face new circumstances—not just because of the increased danger from the Khmer Rouge, but also because of new opportunities to shape different diplomatic solutions. Given the progress we have made in the Permanent Five discussions recently, with signs of flexibility by both the Soviet Union and the PRC [People's Republic of China], the United States believes we need to widen the possibilities for political engagement.

In an effort to broaden and intensify the search for peace, we have chosen to pursue an active dialogue with Hanoi about Cambodia—a step that most (if not all) of you have already taken. The Vietnamese withdrawal gives us cause to see whether Hanoi is now prepared to support a process of political reconciliation in Cambodia culminating in free and fair elections. We are also considering contacts with the Phnom Penh regime, though we will do so only if we determine that it will also advance our elections goal. These moves will complement both our work with the Soviet Union to transform East-West tensions into joint constructive action, and our ongoing support for the non-communists.

This diplomatic opening must be combined with a greater effort to control the Khmer Rouge military threat—to move the conflict from the battlefield to the ballot box. To this end, we will no longer support the Coalition Government of Democratic Kampuchea (CGDK) as the holder of Cambodia's seat in the U.N. if that coalition includes the Khmer Rouge. Continued support for the coalition at the U.N. is only providing the Khmer Rouge diplomatic cover for its military maneuvers.

Both the CGDK and the PRK [People's Republic of Kampuchea] are vestiges of the past—polar creations of invasion and occupation. Rather than engage in sterile debates over these relics, we should look to the future we want to create. That means Cambodia's

U.N. seat should belong to a freely elected government—or, as a transitional arrangement, to Cambodians committed to fair and free elections in the context of a comprehensive settlement that includes a cease-fire and a halt of violence against civilians.

If we are serious about the objective of Cambodian self-determination, we need to give additional impetus to the Perm Five effort: to urge the formation of a Supreme National Council (SNC) and to hold U.N.-organized elections. That impetus can come from offering new diplomatic incentives, and from showing no tolerance for the KR's dialogue of death.

Recently, some have proposed a different approach—the path of critical finger-pointing—and they seem willing to risk the collective, comprehensive effort that has accomplished so much.

Now, we know full well that the chances for achieving Cambodian self-determination while preventing a military resurgence of the Khmer Rouge are much better if we work together. That is why I am encouraged that the approach I have outlined is very close to that set forth in ASEAN's joint settlement of July 23. Let me say again: our common goals remain the same, and our approach toward achieving them differs only very slightly.

Delaying Tactics of Burmese Military Regime

Before discussing the problem of Vietnamese boat people, I would like to say a word about Burma. We welcome the May 27 elections there. However, in recent weeks there have been disturbing indications that the military regime intends to impose conditions which would significantly delay, if not indefinitely put off, the transfer of power to an elected civilian government. It appears that Burma's rulers appear not only out of step with the worldwide movement toward democracy, but also heedless of the desires of the Burmese people.

We are concerned that growing public impatience with the regime's delaying tactics and apparent disregard of the election results could lead to

renewed popular discontent and further military repression. The United States believes we should all work toward the release of all political prisoners and assist the Burmese people in their effort to achieve a representative civilian government based on the results of the May elections.

Indochinese Refugees

The tide of refugees over the past years has presented all of us a staggering humanitarian challenge. Together, we have cooperated to accommodate temporarily and resettle almost two million Vietnamese and Cambodians who have fled warfare and oppression in their homelands. When the history of this century is written, the sacrifices made by the ASEAN nations to try to maintain first asylum will warrant significant recognition.

As free nations committed to fundamental human rights, we must now continue to hold high the practice of first asylum. Here, too, we face a challenge of recommitment to achieving common objectives. In doing so, we recognize and respect your sacrifices on behalf of our fellow men and women.

Because we have recognized our mutual responsibilities, our nations developed a Comprehensive Plan of Action (CPA). It shared benefits and obligations for all parties to achieve a common goal. My nation believes that commitment is worth preserving.

Recently, some have proposed a different approach—the path of critical finger-pointing—and they seem willing to risk the collective, comprehensive effort that has accomplished so much. We believe this would be a mistake. It would leave the nations of this region to reap a whirlwind of humanity without international support.

But if we start down this path, each of us should be willing to point first at ourselves. What has each of us done? What will each of us do? The facts make it clear the United States has met its commitments.

First, we have met our financial obligations by pledging $21 million to the UNHCR [U.N. High Commissioner for Refugees] this year out of a total of $53 million received. *Second,* we are ahead of schedule in resettling the pre-cutoff date refugee population. We pledged to take 18,500 of a total of 46,000 within three years, and we've already resettled 12,000 of that number. *Third,* we pledged to take half of all newly screened-in refugees. In fact, we've taken two thirds of the small numbers processed so far. And we'll keep that pledge as the first asylum nations get their screening operations up and running, and begin identifying more refugees. *Fourth,* the United States is not a newcomer to these responsibilities. Since 1975, we've resettled 900,000 of 1.7 million Southeast Asian refugees, and taken 120,000 more through the Orderly Departure Program with Vietnam.

Frankly, we believe the CPA is working. Over the past 12 months, more than 3,000 people have returned voluntarily from Hong Kong to Vietnam — and new arrivals to Hong Kong are way down. As other nations implement their voluntary return programs, and as the UNHCR expands its information program within Vietnam, we believe the flight of Vietnamese to the ASEAN nations will also recede. Indeed, today there exists a backlog of voluntary returners.

Nevertheless, we understand that a comprehensive multilateral effort must meet the concerns of all of its contributors. That's why we're willing to accept suggestions made by U.N. High Commissioner for Refugees Stoltenberg for some adjustment in procedures. In particular, while we continue to oppose involuntary repatriation, we are willing to support UNHCR's suggestion for a new category of returnees — "those who do not object." And we are willing to join with others in a new "best efforts commitment" to resettle or return all asylum seekers by the end of 1992. These are significant moves — especially because Vietnam has stated, and restated, that it will not accept involuntary repatriation. The CPA approach, with these changes in the repatriation system, remains the one workable approach.

To be direct, the U.S. has demonstrated its willingness to compromise so as to support the UNHCR's efforts to maintain the CPA. We recognize that much more can be accomplished if we work together. We know the alternative is inhuman chaos and loss of life. It is our hope, indeed it's our request, that we can all avoid the path of finger-pointing and instead work with the UNHCR to strengthen the CPA — or at a minimum not to prematurely terminate or disregard it.

Finally, we all must recognize that the CPA is only dealing with the symptoms of the refugee problem. Its

source lies in Vietnam, in failed economic, political, and social policies. Over the long run, we must see that Vietnam fulfills its humanitarian commitments as well as its obligations to contribute to a stable political solution to the Cambodia conflict. Ultimately resolution of these twin challenges of Cambodia and the asylum seekers requires that Vietnam end its isolation and seek to reconcile itself with the dominant trends of our times.

In conclusion, I am pleased to have this opportunity to be with you again. There is no doubt we have significant work to do. Our shared challenges offer hard evidence that while we are separated by a vast ocean, we are drawn together by converging interests — in matters of security, economics, democracy and human rights. And that is what this dialogue is all about.

---

[1] Department of State Press Release 108, July 27, 1990.

JOINT PRESS BRIEFING AFTER THE CONFERENCE, JULY 29, 1990 [1]

Transcript of Secretary Baker's Joint Press Conference with Foreign Ministers Ali Alatas of Indonesia, Taro Nakayama of Japan, Abu Hassan Bin Haji Omar of Malaysia, Joe Clark of Canada, Wong Kan Seng of Singapore, Raul Manglapus of the Philippines, and European Community Commissioner Abel Matutes, July 29, 1990. [1]

Foreign Minister Alatas. May I call the meeting to order. Good morning ladies and gentlemen of the press. As being the tradition at the end of every post-ministerial conference [PMC], my distinguished colleagues and I are pleased to be able to sit here today with you and to tell you about some of the things that we discussed and did during the past two and a half days of the PMC. I shall not be engaging in a long introduction, and furthermore, I notice that from day to day you have had briefings either from me or from my other colleagues, so you are quite up to date with the developments.

Let me simply say that we have had a very productive dialogue and it proceeded in the traditional atmosphere of friendship and frankness among friends. We discussed, in the

plenary session, most of questions of common interest and concern to all of us. Of course, some questions have caught your attention more particularly than others, but I can tell you that we did not only talk about the Cambodian issue or refugees, but we had wide-ranging and, I think, very enlightening discussions about other issues.

We look[ed] forward to what kind of a political, economic and security environment that East Asia and the Pacific would present us in the time ahead. And I think I can express the feelings of all my colleagues when I say that this PMC session has again shown the value of this kind of discussion and dialogue among friends, and that this dialogue session shows that it is the kind of event that is continually expanding, not only in its scope of subjects discussed, but also in the way in which we can communicate with one another — the quality of communication with one another.

Q. A question to the U.S. Secretary of State: **Mr. Baker, in the light of the letter sent by 66 Senators to President Bush** [2] **asking you to go beyond — asking the administration to go beyond the July 18th statement, what kind of follow-up steps are you contemplating now in order to comply with some of the questions in that letter?**

Secretary Baker. Let me say that the letter that you mention has just been received by us. I think that, while the letter from 66 of our United States Senators suggests that we go further, it also recognizes the steps that we have taken to date in terms of adjustments in our policy approach, and it supports — these Senators, I might say — support those steps. Some of them, as the letter indicates, would like to see us go further.

I have said during the course of the discussions here that we are giving some thought to discussions with Phnom Penh. But whether we have discussions with Phnom Penh will depend upon whether or not we are satisfied that they could be productive in terms of achieving the overall goals that, I think it's fair to say, everyone up at this dais and every country represented here shares.

I'd like to take this occasion to make clear something else I said during the course of these meetings. That is that the fundamental goals of ASEAN and its dialogue partners with respect to the problem of Cambodia remain exactly the same today as they were one year ago when we met, and as they have for some years. There are slight differences among us—very slight differences—with respect to questions of tactics and strategy.

Q. I have a question for the Foreign Minister of Japan, Mr. Nakayama. Why did you see the need to deplore the past war during your Six-Plus-One meeting? And what is your next step after the Tokyo meeting in seeking a solution to the Cambodian question?

Foreign Minister Nakayama.[3] The threat of the Soviet Union is decreasing and the Japanese may appear as an increased threat. And in this new environment, ASEAN must be (inaudible) so I should like to relate the Japanese view. It is true that U.S. public opinion, after the reduced threat of the Soviet Union, (inaudible) the Chinese threat, Japan with its large economic clout may be seen as a new threat. That is on the process of the U.S. public opinion.

So I can explain that I should like to make it abundantly clear that the Government of Japan has under our constitution renounced any belligerence and it is the consensus of the Japanese people that we approach peace through and through. Also, the Japanese policy of defense is that Japan's Self Defense Forces are strictly for defensive purposes. But since they would not be adequate to defend Japan, we have the bilateral security pact with the United States.

The international community should understand that Japan will not become a military power and needs this security pact with the United States. Japan is a maritime nation and the United States is protecting the safety of the seas. That U.S. presence, I believe, is the basis for the development of security in this region.

I also mentioned that this policy of having defense forces is for strictly defensive purposes and they will never become a threat to the region. I also mentioned that the presence of U.S. naval forces in the Pacific would be extremely important for maintaining security in the region. Also, in response to the views of ASEAN, we expect that Japan, having caused damages and sufferings to the peoples of ASEAN and the United States, that we have modestly, and with humility, learned a lesson from that past experience.

Next year being the 50th year since the outbreak of the Pacific War, we should like to state that after the war, having renounced militarism, Japan has developed its economy on its own ef-

forts, by importing resources from overseas and by adopting democracy. We can certainly well understand the suffering has been caused for various people. We have no intention whatsoever of becoming a military power, although we have become an economic power, and together with the ASEAN countries and the Asian countries, Japan intends to serve as a partner in the interest of the prosperity to this region and we shall consider seriously what we can do in the best interests of that end.

Foreign Minister Alatas. Our closed sessions appear not to be so very closed after all.

Q. I would like to address the Japanese Foreign Minister as well. I just realized that you are seated at the far end. I thought that you should have been seated at the center of the panel. I don't know whether you want to comment on that. But my question was: Before you came here, there were two different reports in the local media. One said Japan is siding with the ASEAN position in the Cambodian conflict, and the other said Japan is not. Which one do you think is closer to the truth?

Foreign Minister Nakayama.[3] At the Tokyo meeting on Kampuchea held earlier in Tokyo, we believed it will be extremely important to establish the Supreme National Council [SNC] in order to attain peace in Kampuchea. That point has been reaffirmed. And so we hope that in the interests of peace in Kampuchea the Supreme National Council will be established as early as possible so that free elections will be held under the supervision of the United Nations. That is the basic position of Japan. And we believe that all countries concerned should cooperate as much as possible for the earliest attainment of that goal.

Q. I'd like to ask Mr. Baker the difference between the Khmer Rouge in the Supreme National Council and the Khmer Rouge in the CGDK [Coalition Government of Democratic Kampuchea].

Secretary Baker. If the Khmer Rouge were to participate in the Supreme National Council, there would of necessity be a significant difference. First of all, I think it is certainly the view of the United States and perhaps the view of others as well, that there should be no role in a Supreme National Council for anyone who wants to pursue power through the battlefield rather than through the ballot box. That's what

the Supreme National Council is all about. The Permanent Five have agreed that the Supreme National Council should be composed of individual Cambodians acceptable to one another. The requirement that they be acceptable to one another is a condition, in our view, that establishes some constraint. Given the purpose of the Supreme National Council, as opposed to the CGDK's retention, or not, of a seat at the United Nations—given the purpose of the Supreme National Council, the Cambodians who compose that council will of necessity be committed to free and fair elections. They will be committed to a ceasefire, and they will be committed to ending the violence against civilians. That, I think, is a significant difference.

Q. I wanted, if I may, to address the question to both the Chairman and Secretary Baker. Given that one of the significant differences of opinion over the Cambodian issue is what to do about the seat in the forthcoming General Assembly of the United Nations, I wondered if both of you could confirm or deny the suggestion that the United States has promised not to lobby for the vacancy of that seat or otherwise the demanding of that seat by the CGDK at the forthcoming General Assembly?

Secretary Baker. Let me give you the United States' answer. The United States has promised nothing other than to support its policy position, which is we can no longer support the CGDK for that seat. I think we made that very, very clear, and that's one of the things that we think when we say it's important that we do what we can to prevent a return to power of the Khmer Rouge. One of the things we're talking about is to oppose actions that would give the Khmer Rouge legitimacy, such as actions which might tend to support their participation in a coalition that holds that seat.

Foreign Minister Alatas. I think that Secretary Baker has correctly described the position that now emerges on this question. As he said it, on the fundamentals we remain united. It's only on some tactics and some tactical aspects that we differ. It is here that we differ, that we continue to differ, but of course we now understand better the United States position—why it believes that it can no longer support the CGDK. That was the gist of our discussions. We understand it, and we take note of it.

We have a different view, but what is more important is that now not only the United States and ASEAN, but all the participants of this dialogue meeting are agreed that, therefore, in pursuance of the common objective that we share—that we fully share—we should now try to contribute to efforts to have an SNC formed between now and the General Assembly session. And I would rather stress this point than any other point. And as I indicated in my briefings yesterday and day before yesterday, there was also a convergence—a general convergence—of views among all the participants of the PMC that perhaps the two cochairmen of the Paris conference, France and Indonesia, should now exert more active efforts again to contribute to this goal of trying to get the four Cambodian parties to agree on an SNC. Because, of course, you will concede that they will have to decide. We cannot decide for them on an SNC. This is one aspect on which they will have to agree. And, as I've indicated, I have been communicating and I will continue to communicate with my colleague, [French] Foreign Minister Roland Dumas, and hopefully we can inform you later on—not now—what we are going to do.

Q. There is discussion on the Asia-Pacific Security Dialogue Forum, or something to that effect. I would like to get an explanation from Secretary Baker as to what the U.S. view is and also what the ASEANs say about this, if Mr. Alatas could go on record.

Secretary Baker. Let me start by subscribing to what our chairman said in his opening comments with respect to the fact that we, I think, have had some very solid and productive and very, very substantive talks during the course of this post-ministerial conference. They've been perhaps even more substantive than before because things are changing around the world. During the course of these discussions we reaffirmed ASEAN's importance to meeting the security and political, as well as economic, challenges facing the region. We talked quite a bit.

A number of countries had suggestions to make with respect to how institutions might be adapted to meet some of these new challenges. I think it's fair to say that all of us agreed that the first step is to begin adapting those institutions and organizations that work—ASEAN, for instance; the U.S.-Japanese security relationship, for another example.

We need to build on some of the cooperative efforts we've already begun in the economic sphere, and I have particular reference when I say that to APEC [Asia-Pacific Economic Cooperation], which I think holds great promise. But whatever evolution occurs here in the Pacific, consequent to the changes that are taking place in other parts of the globe, let me say that you can be assured of one simple reality and that is that the United States, we think, has been—and we certainly intend to remain—engaged, fully engaged, as a partner in the Pacific working with our friends and allies to expand our common interests here.

Foreign Minister Alatas. Let me add to what you have just correctly described as the gist of our discussions in the closed sessions. As I said earlier, we look forward and we try to extend views and perceptions on what possible changes would occur in the political, economic and security environment of the Asia-Pacific. As Secretary Baker already said, it was a good exchange of views. There were new ideas put forward by certain participants. We discussed them. But in the course of those discussions I simply inserted what I thought was a necessary element of these discussions, namely, that we in ASEAN, too, have been for some time now working on a kind of a blueprint for greater peace and stability, not only in our own subregion of Southeast Asia but hopefully of benefit also for the larger Asia of East Asia and the Pacific.

So I explained a little bit the underlying ideas under ZOPFAN [Zone of Peace, Freedom, and Neutrality], so the threat perceptions — of the way the ASEAN perceived possible threats to its security and to peace in the area, the hopes that ASEAN countries have for a new kind of a situation where there is mutual restraint, both on the part of the subregional and regional countries as well as on the part of the external countries.

I think Indonesian journalists are quite aware of these ideas that have been worked out by ASEAN now for several years. And that was the essence of our exchange of views. I believe that it was useful to our dialogue partners to know a little bit more about our thinking on ZOPFAN as our input into the discussions of what the future may bring to us. Certainly ASEAN will continue now. We have agreed in the AMM to continue among ourselves a dialogue on security, very much anchored on our

ZOPFAN ideas, but looking forward also to see whether, in the light of these very rapid and very fundamental changes taking place in the world, there need to be further adjustments.

Q. In your view, is ASEAN satisfied that the United States has shown sufficient flexibility, and has Secretary Baker been persuasive enough, to forestall the individual members from taking any unilateral action on the forced repatriation of refugees or any other unilateral actions that might jeopardize first asylum?

A. Well, on the refugee question we know that there is a divergence of views, but during the PMC we had active discussions among ourselves. We in ASEAN recognize that the United States has moved in its position. You are aware that it now is prepared to consider a category called "those who do not object."

Secretary Baker explained the United States views on a paper worked out by the UNHCR. Secretary Baker also said that the United States was willing, on a best-effort commitment, to work toward the final resolution of this problem either by way of repatriation, or by resettlement by the end of 1992. We appreciate this move, but in fairness and in all candor, we in ASEAN think that they do not yet go far enough. But ours is not a negative attitude; both sides are continuing to talk about this. Both sides are continuing discussions.

I think now, taking it a little bit wider, on this whole question of refugees I think all the participants are agreed that the CPA [Comprehensive Plan of Action] is a worthwhile format, is a worthwhile document or agreement to work on, and none of us in ASEAN wants it to be scuttled. But I think we should continue to talk and try to narrow the differences further.

Q. Mr. Baker, can you tell us whether you discussed with the ministers, and can you share with us, at what point the United States, and under what circumstances the United States would be prepared to resume normal diplomatic relations with Vietnam?

Secretary Baker. We didn't discuss that during the course of our meetings. Our policy with respect to resumption of relations with Vietnam, I think, is well known in the United States. The new ingredient, of course, is that we have concluded that it would be, in our view at least, helpful—perhaps helpful—in resolving the problems of Cambodia if we had a dialogue with Vietnam on Cambodia. We talk to Vietnam now, as you undoubtedly know, about the Orderly Departure Program and we have had for some time a dialogue going with Vietnam with respect to our POWs and MIAs.

The question of normalization is not before us right now. We want to first see if we can have a productive discussion with Vietnam with respect to Cambodia. There are a number of things that would have to happen before we would be prepared to fully normalize relations with Vietnam — having to do with continued cooperation with respect to POWs and MIAs, having to do with steps that Vietnam is capable of taking and should take to assist in the goals that everyone up here shares for resolving the Cambodian problem, and having to do, of course, with fundamental considerations of human rights and that sort of thing affecting Vietnam.

Q. I have a question for the Foreign Minister of Malaysia on refugees. Will Malaysia continue to support the Comprehensive Plan of Action or the proposal being developed by the U.N. High Commissioner for Refugees if they do not explicitly give the first asylum countries the option of involuntarily repatriating refugees?

Foreign Minister Abu Hassan. Well, as you know, I was chairman of the International Conference on Refugees in Geneva and the CPA was adopted at that international conference. So we are fully committed to the implementation of the CPA, provided that the other parties as well would together implement, not only just the first asylum countries, but also the resettlement countries as well as Vietnam. All the three parties should contribute positively towards the implementation of the CPA. And there is also the time frame, that is, by June 1992 we would see the end of this problem.

Q. Mr. Clark, I'd like to know if Canada sees itself as having a role to play bringing the United States and ASEAN closer together, finding a solution to the Cambodian conflict. If so, what is that role?

Foreign Minister Clark. I think that this meeting, as both Mr. Alatas and Mr. Baker have remarked, has demonstrated the remarkable closeness of purpose not only between the United States and members of ASEAN but among all of the dialogue partners and members of ASEAN. On the question

of the Supreme National Council, the seat, indeed on the question of refugees, I think this meeting has marked a determination to find some common purpose and to move forward on that. Canada, of course, wants to play a continuing role, as other countries do, in resolving that problem, but I don't think it would be apt or correct to suggest any polarizing of views here. We have put forward, as has Gareth Evans of Australia and others, some proposals about next steps that might be considered in the development of security arrangements in institutions and structures in Asia and the Pacific. We think those are worth looking at.

We frankly think that those modest proposals we put forward will grow on people. With that in mind, Canada intends to convene a couple of informal meetings in the next two or three months. On one level, security specialists from the security sessions will be invited from nations at this table. For the second meeting, officials from nations at this table will be invited just to see if there is any point in looking at further elaboration of structures or institutions that might build on the excellent example of dialogue that ASEAN has established.

Q. I would like to ask Secretary of State Baker, please. You've made the U.S. position on the Khmer Rouge very clear in the past few days. What about the Khmer Rouge as a physical force on the ground? Even if China stops supplying arms to the Khmer Rouge, they can still go on fighting for some considerable length of time. Then who's to say they won't get arms from somewhere else? Do you have any plans and have you had any discussions at this meeting about what to do about the Rhmer Rouge as a physical threat in Cambodia? For example, have you had talks with the Thai Foreign Minister about perhaps eradicating Khmer Rouge camps from Thai soil to eliminate their chance of taking refuge in Thailand?

Secretary Baker. There's been no discussion with respect to the last specific point that you articulated. We have had, I think, a fair amount of discussion about our common objective of preventing a return to power of the Khmer Rouge. After all, this has been one of the objectives that we have jointly articulated for over ten years.

As we have seen the withdrawal of combat troops by Vietnam, it seems to the United States that it is more important than ever that we concentrate on

what was stated as our second policy goal, even though it was not stated as being subordinate to getting the Vietnamese out. And frankly, the advances that the Khmer Rouge has made on the battlefield, and to which you allude, was one of the motivating forces for the position which the United States has articulated. Having said that, let me say once again, we have not changed our goals and objectives, and ASEAN and all of its dialogue partners still have the same goals and objectives, one of which is preventing the return to power of the Khmer Rouge.

One thing is for sure, though, our past policy approach — let me rephrase that. To suggest that somehow our policy adjustment will give aid and comfort to the Khmer Rouge, I think, misses the point. Because our past policy — and I'm not suggesting you did that in your question — but our past policy approach has certainly not kept the Khmer Rouge from moving toward power, because they have moved significantly on the battlefield. We have had discussions here about how we might counter that. One way that we could counter it diplomatically, of course, is for those who have influence with either the Khmer Rouge or their sponsor, or sponsors, to use that influence and to prevail upon them to seek a solution within the SNC format. So we've had a discussion of it to that extent.

One other thing I think we might do is to continue to try and help establish the non-communist resistance as a significant force and, as you know, the United States hopes to continue to be able to provide assistance to the non-communist resistance. In that respect we totally share the objectives of ASEAN and its dialogue partners.

Q. I would like to address this question to Secretary Baker. When Vice President Dan Quayle visited Jakarta last year, he was talking a little bit about the possibility that the U.S. would extend lethal aid to the Cambodian resistance forces, and the vice president said that it could be extended either overtly or covertly. If it is extended overtly, there would be a public announcement about that. So far I haven't heard anything about that public announcement, so my question is what is that lethal aid consisting of and has the United States extended it covertly?

A. You're talking about aid to the non-communist resistance?

Q. The so-called lethal aid.

A. We extend aid of a nonlethal character to the non-communist resistance overtly . What we might or might not do other than overtly, of course, I will not comment on.

Q. Could I take up a point Secretary of State Baker made about the sponsors of the Khmer Rouge and ask him whether and to what extent — underlying a certain confidence that a certain one can be reached — is a shift of position in China's attitude towards Cambodia reflected in the P[ermanent] Five and whether we could perhaps elaborate a bit on that shift. And if I could ask the chairman: How important is Cambodia going to be as a subject, a side subject admittedly, when Li Peng comes to Jakarta shortly?

A. Obviously China's position with respect to the Khmer Rouge is fundamental. I think that it is the view of the United States that China has exhibited a positive approach during the course of our Perm Five discussions to this problem. I think that it is our view that China would like to see a resolution of this problem just as other Perm Five members would.

Foreign Minister Alatas. The prospective visit of Prime Minister Li Peng to Indonesia is, as of course you also know, dedicated to another purpose. That is the resumption of normal diplomatic relations between the two countries. So whether during that visit there will be an exchange of views on the Cambodian question, I cannot ascertain. It perhaps will happen, if not at the head of government level, more probably at the foreign ministers level, because with my colleague, Minister Qian Qichen, we have at all times had a running dialogue about it, the last time when I was in Beijing. So that could happen again when he comes here in Jakarta.

Q. I would like to follow up on the boat people and ask a question of Mr. Matutes. Commissioner, what was your response to the EC [European Community] proposal and why is there any time frame in the — in your proposal?

Commissioner Matutes. We have presented our initiative for assistance to boat people returning to Vietnam, and we have consulted the ASEAN countries and other dialogue partners. I am pleased to say that despite the short notice, our initiative has been extremely well received by all those concerned, in particular the timing of our proposal is seen as very helpful.

On the second part of the timing for further development, it could be as follows. In August we will work with United Nations High Commissioner for Refugees and others on technical details of the program. In mid-September, we will discuss it with the EC foreign ministers in the framework of our Council of Ministers. In the course of these developments, we will be in touch with ASEAN, with dialogue partners, and of course, with Vietnam and others interested with us. Then by the end of September we hope to be able to come up with a comprehensive program acceptable by all those concerned.

Foreign Minister Alatas. Let me add, I'm glad this question was asked because I had wanted to also say about this that we in ASEAN do appreciate the intention of the European Community to set up a comprehensive regional program for the boat people, just the same as we are appreciative of other efforts that have been indicated, for example, by countries like Australia and the United States in helping the UNHCR meet this question financially and with funds.

We in ASEAN have said in our statement that the burden of boat people on the first asylum countries is getting to the point that it's almost unbearable politically, economically. We of course acknowledge that some of our friends around the dialogue table have been forthcoming in various ways in trying to lighten the burden and we would not want to appear unthankful for that. We believe that an integral solution is necessary, but we acknowledge these positive efforts, the most recent one being the one offered by the EC in the course of this dialogue.

Q. Foreign Minister Alatas, you mentioned ZOPFAN. Could you tell us whether the U.S. proposal for access to military facilities in Singapore is or is not compatible with your concept of ZOPFAN?

A. From what we understand it to be, and I stand to be corrected if I have not understood it well, it is a question of the United States making use — making more expanded use of Singapore facilities.

So, in our understanding, that comes nowhere near the definition of a military base. If that is the situation, then we don't think that it goes against what we envisage in ZOPFAN. What do we envisage in ZOPFAN and what do we in Indonesia think about military

bases? That you know already, namely, we think eventually these bases will disappear because they are temporary in nature. You are very conversant with this phrase in the basic document of ASEAN, but we would leave it to the countries concerned to determine for themselves in the light of their own national interest how temporary is going to be executed. So that is in short term my answer to your question on the Singapore facility.

The Foreign Minister of Singapore has an addition?

Foreign Minister Wong Kan Seng. I have no addition. I just want to confirm your understanding that the proposed use of the facilities in Singapore by the United States is correct.

Foreign Minister Alatas. Now, we are nearing the end. Can I entertain a last question?

Q. Can you describe the talks on economic issues between ASEAN and the dialogue partners and what to expect from this meeting yesterday?

A. Well, there were of course two levels of discussions. One concerned the actual dialogue — relations in the economic, trade, investment and industrial cooperation field. The other level was an exchange of views on international as well as regional economic issues.

Now on the international issues, we spent a lot of time and, I think, very productively, on such questions as the Uruguay Round which concerns us all and on questions such as commodities and the result of the G-7 [Economic] Summit and APEC, what APEC was going to move toward, and so on. On the actual relations, dialogue or cooperative relations between ASEAN and its dialogue partners, I can say, they are moving very well.

Every time we meet it strikes me that new and sometimes innovative programs are being added while existing programs are being implemented.

Of course, there remain obstacles, but we are all trying to remove them from our paths. Obstacles in trade, in access to markets, obstacles perhaps or slowness in developing industrial cooperation with certain dialogue partners and other things. I think, on the whole we are quite satisfied with the economic relations between the dialogue countries and ASEAN.

Foreign Minister Manglapus. I just want to comment on a question from this side regarding ZOPFAN and the presence of military bases in Southeast

Asia. The dialogue that was proposed by the Philippines, and which was incorporated in the joint communique of the AMM, is intended precisely to seek consensus in the region about the achievement of ZOPFAN. Against the background of the temporary character of these military bases, there have been a variety of opinions aired about how to achieve this. The Philippines feels that, in view of the developments in Europe and other parts of the world, that it is time that Southeast Asia talk openly about its own security.

Q. I would like to ask the Foreign Ministers of the Philippines and Malaysia if they could describe to us how they would like the United States to further modify its policy on the Vietnamese boat people.

Foreign Minister Abu Hassan. Well I already said so earlier, but insofar as the question of the boat people, everybody should be committed to the full implementation of the Comprehensive Plan of Action which was adopted in Geneva last year. This means that all the parties concerned, not just the first asylum countries but also the resettlement countries, Vietnam, UNHCR, should work together towards the full implementation.

There is the question of time frame there—three years from the time we had the international conference. Secondly, we have to address the question of those who are determined not to be refugees. Now the screening process is taking place in all the first asylum countries while there is full commitment by those third countries that those who are screened in will be taken to be resettled. But there is a question of how to address the issue of those screened out. This is where there is a difference of opinion between us and the United States. Therefore, we have to discuss this further — how best we can arrive at some consensus within the next few months and how best we can achieve the target of full implementation by 1992.

Foreign Minister Manglapus. Yes, in the matter of the screened-outs, there is an issue and that is the opposition of some countries to the idea of what is called involuntary repatriation to Vietnam. The Philippines, of course, as you perhaps know, has gone beyond all agreements in accommodating refugees in the Philippines in our territory. However, in the matter of the screened-outs, we would like to see something worked out, as the Malaysian Foreign Minister

has indicated, so that the countries of first asylum are not left with these screened-outs not knowing what to do with them. We believe that the countries that oppose involuntary repatriation should take some initiatives in providing us with alternatives to absorb the screened-outs.

---

1 Department of State Press Release 109, July 29, 1990.
2 See page 40.
3 Unofficial interpretation.

ADDRESS AT THE ASIA-PACIFIC ECONOMIC COOPERATION (APEC) OPENING SESSION, SINGAPORE, JULY 30, 1990 [1]

I am delighted to be here in Singapore for the second Asia-Pacific Economic Cooperation [APEC] meeting. Working together, we've made considerable progress since Canberra in setting out an ambitious program for this new group.

In the past year, truly historic changes have ushered in a new era in world politics and economics. We are seeing the rise of economic liberty and market oriented principles. Hand in hand with economic freedom, democracy is taking root around the world.

I know many of you are concerned about the amount of attention that Central and Eastern Europe and the Soviet Union have received in the last year. It's true that our diplomatic focus has been heavily concentrated on that region, but the pace and scope of events have demanded that.

But our global efforts are helping the Asia-Pacific region, too. Everyone in this room will benefit from our achievements in Europe. For example, the easing of military and political tensions will allow greater resources to flow into more productive areas. In the United States, we will be better positioned to reduce our budget deficits. At the Houston Summit, we worked hard to get commitments to move forward on agricultural issues in the Uruguay Round. In fact, the highest international economic policy priority of the United States is a successful outcome to the Uruguay Round. This will benefit the entire world economy as well as the Asia-Pacific region.

The accomplishments of this region have stood as an important example and

a stimulus to change in other parts of the world. The economies of Asia and the Pacific are to a relatively large extent open to market forces and have long achieved impressive results.

Importance of Asia-Pacific Region

I would like to emphasize that we remain firmly committed to the Asia-Pacific region. As I said in Jakarta last Friday, the United States has been and will remain a Pacific partner for security, democracy, and prosperity. Cooperation will grow in the region as we strengthen our bilateral ties and multilateral institutions.

We regard ASEAN as a core political and economic institution in Southeast Asia. Having just completed a highly successful ASEAN Post-Ministerial Conference, we look forward to continuing our work together with ASEAN in APEC meetings today and tomorrow. We believe APEC is an important new multilateral forum for all of us to work together in ways that promote economic growth and political stability in the region.

APEC provides our highly interdependent economies the opportunity to compare experiences and to share information; to arrive at improved mutual understanding; and to engage in cooperative activities. We are a relatively successful group of countries and we are all clearly doing many things right. So there are great benefits to sharing our experiences with each other. We can develop ways multilaterally to overcome macroeconomic barriers to more efficient flows of capital, trade and technology. If we are successful, we can enhance mutual economic growth and increase living standards.

APEC's Work Program

Only nine months ago, we met in Canberra to launch the APEC process. Congratulations are due to APEC senior officials who have produced, in a very short time period, a seven point work program which is now underway. In our view, the work program should move toward identifying those activities which have the greatest impact on the economic growth and development of the region. We are particularly pleased to see areas such as human resources, energy, and telecommunications included.

We think work program activities should accomplish the following objectives: increase information; identify impediments to closer cooperation and improved performance; and facilitate private sector action, by far the largest source of capital and technology.

We have three aims for this ministerial. *First,* we hope to give further impetus to the work program, including the subject of transportation which we have proposed should be added to the program.

Second, we want APEC to give a strong endorsement to a timely, successful conclusion to the Uruguay Round.

Third, we look to have a wide-ranging discussion of the economic outlook for the region in the current global context, a subject to which I would now like to turn.

Economic Outlook

We see the global economic outlook as generally favorable for the Asia-Pacific region economies. Growth in the industrial countries as a group will be lower than in 1988 and 1989. But it still should be close to 3 percent for 1990 and 1991, despite relatively slow U.S. growth this year. Thus, in our view, the industrial countries will continue to provide a solid base for developing country expansion, with world trade growth still strong. While the Central and Eastern European countries are engaged in a difficult transition to democratic, market-oriented systems, their reconstruction should be beneficial over the medium term for the global economy as well as for themselves. Over the long term, Soviet economic reform should also positively affect the global economy. But it is unclear what impact Soviet reform will have in the short run.

We've probably seen the worst of industrial country inflation, though we remain committed to a vigilant and firm approach. Inflation rates have started to fall in the United States, Japan, Canada, and elsewhere. Part of this improvement is the result of firm anti-inflation policies, part simply the passing of some special factors which tended to exaggerate underlying inflationary pressures.

I recognize that some of the developing countries in Asia have particular concerns about higher inflation, and I am glad to see appropriate steps being taken to arrest it. Substantial correction of external imbalances has occurred, with the U.S. and Japanese imbalances now down to about 2 per-

cent of GNP. But further reductions are needed. This will require action by both surplus and deficit countries.

Our basic conclusion is that while some global macroeconomic problems remain, they are manageable. Prospects for the global economy remain bright. So do the prospects of this region. And it is my hope and expectation that the work of APEC in reducing barriers to growth will prove a catalyst to further expansion and prosperity — first for the region, and through this region's increasing influence, for the world economy. We are very pleased to note the Government of Thailand has offered to host our 1992 Ministerial and the United States would like to offer to host the 1993 Ministerial.

---

[1] Department of State Press Release 110, July 30, 1990.

APEC PARTNERSHIP FOR EDUCATION

Statement at the APEC Meeting, Singapore, July 31, 1990 [1]

Today, I would like to announce an American initiative that will expand our ties and bonds across the Pacific. The initiative is in the area of human resources development—specifically, education. As President Bush has made clear, education is a critical building block for a more tolerant, democratic society—domestically and globally. We believe that investing in education is investing in the future. Education is vital to the continued growth and prosperity of the APEC region.

As many of you know, the United States has in fact a comparative advantage in higher education. We have been an education magnet. Far more foreign students are enrolled in universities in America than in any other country. Some 350,000 foreign students were enrolled in U.S. universities in 1986 and over half of these were from East Asia and the Pacific.

We have learned throughout our history that effective education requires a partnership of both the public and private sectors. The private sector is especially important because it offers resources and provides a "real life" classroom for training the business leaders of tomorrow.

To enhance educational links across the Pacific, I am pleased to announce today the "APEC Partnership

for Education." This Partnership will include the U.S. and other interested APEC governments, education institutions throughout the region, and private enterprises.

This program will have three components: first, support for educational partnerships between American and other APEC institutions in science, engineering, business and management; second, widening of private sector internships and other outreach programs for APEC students studying in the U.S.; and third, expansion of U.S. Government-sponsored private sector training programs in the U.S. and in APEC member countries.

Our overall objective is to help train the transpacific leaders of the next century through expanded educational opportunities. Over the next five years, we aim through the Partnership to:

- Establish 10-15 partnerships between leading U.S. educational institutions and their APEC counterparts;
- Involve a minimum of 20,000 Asia-Pacific students studying in the United States directly in on-campus activities sponsored by the Partnership, such as specialized courses and seminars focused on the particular needs of the region;
- Enroll 5,000 of these students in private sector internships and cooperative education programs;
- Train 2,500 Asian private sector employees in their countries and, from this number, select 500 for additional short term courses in America; and
- Reach more than half of the almost 200,000 Asia-Pacific students in the United States through newsletters and other outreach channels that will keep them current on Partnership-sponsored activities and events.

The APEC Partnership for Education will emphasize the various programs of the Agency for International Development and the United States Information Agency. Both are very active across the region in solidifying society-to-society ties. These agencies fund a variety of scholarship activities, including the Fulbright Program, and support university linkages, international visitor and youth exchanges, and other programs.

Combined private and public sector resources should reach $30 million over the next five years. We have already had preliminary contacts with U.S. academic institutions which have reacted with great interest. Other APEC members may want to join us with parallel programs.

We look forward to discussing with you our ideas for an APEC Partnership for Education at the next session of the Human Resources Working Group.

---

[1] Department of State Press Release 111, July 31, 1990.

VISIT TO MONGOLIA

Toast by Secretary Baker at welcoming dinner hosted by the Mongolian Government, Ulaan Baatar, August 2, 1990. [1]

It is a great pleasure to be here in Mongolia and to bring you greetings from President Bush. On this occasion, we celebrate a major step forward in cooperation between our two countries. Mongolia, like my native Texas, is a land of wide open spaces. And I know that we share together great satisfaction at Mongolia's recent wider opening to both political and economic change. We all welcome Mongolia's movement toward the openness of choice implied by democracy, the openness of free markets and international trade, and the openness of expanded contacts with the rest of the world community, regardless of differences.

We welcome and encourage Mongolia's greater involvement in world affairs because we believe that both the world and Mongolia will benefit from it. The sharing of democratic values will certainly foster friendship among free peoples. Free and fair trade will enrich Mongolians and their partners alike. For too long Americans and Mongolians have been strangers. Now, we have the opportunity to become friends.

I am especially happy to be here at this crucial time in Mongolia's long history. Your government and your people are moving forward together toward a common goal of greater democracy, greater protection of human rights, and economic reform. These developments have been most encouraging to the United States. I know that the United States and Mongolia are separated by a great distance from one another. But cooperation and understanding can bridge any distance and respect can overcome any differences. We have begun to build that bridge and to use that respect as the basis for all of our growing exchanges. The cultural agreement we signed last year was one very important step in this process.

Let me take a few moments now to review the new steps that we have taken this very day.

Allow me now to propose a toast: To the Mongolian people as they move toward freedom and democracy, and to the future of friendship and cooperation between the United States and Mongolia.

First, the Peace Corps. We have signed a Peace Corps agreement with Mongolia, which will allow us to send our volunteers to work directly with the Mongolian people in English language instruction and in other areas that will benefit both peoples.

Second, a consular convention. The conclusion of our consular convention provides our nations with the necessary framework of mutual. protection as travel between our countries — in tourism, business, and academic exchange — increases.

Third, a trade agreement. The initialling of a bilateral trade agreement reflects our awareness of the important reforms Mongolia has committed to undertake. It is an important step in the future growth of our economic relations.

Fourth, a television satellite link. As part of this growing interchange in people, information, and ideas, we are also very pleased to offer Mongolia a satellite link antenna that will give Mongolian television access to American programming.

Fifth, an assistance package. America is committed to working with Mongolia as it faces the challenge of transforming its institutions at home and reorienting toward the outside world. We are, therefore, pleased to offer scholarships, exchange opportunities, and expert assistance in business management, banking, and law; biotechnology and agriculture; computers and information management; and democratic institution building.

These achievements indicate that our countries have made important progress in constructing a new relationship. We look forward to building on this solid foundation of bilateral cooperation as Mongolia continues to build its own new foundation of democracy.

This is a memorable moment for Mongolia. You have joined many other countries around the world on the road to reform. It is not an easy road to travel, but the destination of democracy, human rights, and a market economy promise a better life for all. I am sure that your continued progress will further improve U.S.-Mongolia relations while increasing our mutual respect.

I want to close with this thought. Before 1920, I am told, there was a local landmark called "American Hill" here in Ulaan Baatar. It symbolized America's presence. Now that new joint business ventures between our two nations have been established, I look forward to the day when a new "American Hill" can serve as a living symbol of U.S.-Mongolian friendship and cooperation.

---

[1] Department of State Press Release 113, August 7, 1990.

"Permanent Five" Agree on Framework for a Cambodia Settlement

Statement adopted at meeting of the Five Permanent Members of the U.N. Security Council (China, France, the U.S.S.R., the United Kingdom, and the United States), August 28, 1990. [1]

The Five Permanent Members of the U.N. Security Council have held in Paris and New York six meetings in 1990 at the Vice Ministerial level in order to define the key elements of a comprehensive political settlement of the Cambodia conflict based on an enhanced U.N. role.

At the end of their sixth meeting, held in New York on August 27-28, 1990, the Five reached final agreement on a framework for a settlement. The framework document is composed of five sections comprising the indispensable requirements for such a settlement:

I. Transitional arrangements regarding the administration of Cambodia during the preelection period;

II. Military arrangements during the transitional period;

III. Elections under United Nations auspices;

IV. Human rights protection;

V. International guarantees.

This document will be made public after it has been communicated to the interested parties.

The Five also recalled the two documents elaborated by the 1989 Paris Conference on Cambodia on repatriation of refugees and displaced persons and on reconstruction.

Taken together, these documents outline a settlement process based on national reconciliation and involving an enhanced United Nations role which would ensure a just and lasting political solution to the conflict.

The basic principle behind the Five's approach is to enable the Cambodian people to determine their own political future through free and fair elections organized and conducted by the United Nations in a neutral political environment with full respect for the national sovereignty of Cambodia.

Implementation of this approach requires the full support of all parties to the Cambodia conflict. The Five therefore urge the acceptance of this framework document in its entirety as the basis for settling the Cambodia conflict.

The Five thus now call on the Cambodian parties to the conflict to commit themselves to this process and to form the Supreme National Council [SNC] as soon as possible on the basis outlined in the framework document.

To this end. the Five support Indonesia's efforts to convene in Jakarta a meeting with the Cambodian parties. They urge the two cochairmen of the Paris Conference to commend the framework to the Cambodian parties and to pursuade them to form the Supreme National Council accordingly.

To sustain the momentum of this process, the Five will continue to work with all those concerned with the Cambodia conflict and the U.N. Secretary General. To this end, they have agreed to convene another meeting in Paris at an appropriate time before mid-October.

---

[1] Text provided by the United Nations Information Center, Washington.

U.S. Diplomatic Follow-up to Framework Agreement

by Robert Kimmitt

Excerpt from statement before the Asian and Pacific Affairs Subcommittee, House Foreign Affairs Committee, September 12, 1990. Mr. Kimmitt is Under Secretary of State for Political Affairs. [1]

The past two months have seen a dramatic upswing in the prospects for a peaceful settlement to the Cambodian conflict. As a result of a combination of diplomatic efforts by a number of countries— including, I'm pleased to say, some well-timed initiatives by the United States— a major step has been taken toward a comprehensive political settlement. Reflecting the new spirit of the post-Cold War era, the Perm Five have produced a settlement framework

that has been welcomed around the world and that was accepted by the four Cambodian parties on September 10 at a pivotal meeting in Jakarta. Contributing to this result were the policy revisions announced by Secretary Baker on July 18 in Paris which led to our opening of talks with the Vietnamese [in New York twice in August], and well as our decision to begin a dialogue with the Hun Sen regime. [2] The flexibility and constructive approach of the Soviets and the Chinese have also contributed to this successful first step.

We join the Congress in unalterable opposition to the Khmer Rouge shooting its way back into power. As Secretary Baker has repeatedly stressed, we want to move the conflict

off the battlefield, where the Khmer Rouge thrive, to the negotiating table. We seek a neutral political process under U.N. auspices culminating in the free and fair election of a legitimate government, which we hope will end the death and suffering in Cambodia.

---

[1] The complete transcript of the hearings will be published by the committe and will be available from the Superintendent of Documents, U.S. Government Printing Office, Washington, D.C. 20402.

[2] Direct discussions were initiated with Phnom Penh representatives in Vientiane, Laos, the only capital in Southeast Asia where both the U.S. and the Phnom Penh regime have embassies.

Assistance and Reform: Eastern Europe and Central America

by Secretary of State James A. Baker, III

Remarks at the G-24 Ministerial Meeting, Brussels, July 4, 1990 [1]

Almost one year has passed since leaders at the Paris Economic Summit asked the European Commission to coordinate Western assistance in support of fundamental reform in Poland and Hungary. Since then, the Commission and the member states of the G-24 have committed more than $14 billion in economic assistance and investment credits to support the transition of these two countries to democratic governments and market-oriented economies. I would like to congratulate President [of the European Community Jacques] Delors and his colleagues, especially Vice President Andriessen, as well as the Commission as a whole for their highly capable efforts.

This is a transition never before undertaken by so many so quickly. The G-24's broad support for reform in Poland and Hungary is based on the recognition of a simple fact: the people of these two countries are determined as never before to shake off the mistakes of the past. In April 1989, President Bush indicated that our support for Poland was predicated on tough decisions that only the Polish people could make. Under the leadership of Prime Minister Mazowiecki, the Polish Government supported by a majority of the people has not hesitated to make such tough decisions.

We have also begun to work constructively with Prime Minister Antall and the other members of the new, freely elected Hungarian Government. We are pleased that on September 6, this new Government will open the Budapest Environmental Center, an idea first proposed by President Bush last year. With a Hungarian executive director, an American program manager, and broad European support, the Center will become a prime example of transnational cooperation for progress in Central and Eastern Europe.

We look forward to hearing assessments from our Polish and Hungarian colleagues on the progress they have made and on how our efforts can be channeled to meet the challenges ahead.

But, today, we have another important task before us—to welcome Czechoslovakia, Yugoslavia, Bulgaria, and the German Democratic Republic into this process. In December, we opened the way for G-24 coordinated assistance for these countries as soon as they met the political and economic criteria for such assistance. Now, they have done so.

Newly Eligible Nations

In the June 8-9 elections, the Czech and Slovak people firmly endorsed the velvet revolution and the leadership of Vaclav Havel, Civic Forum, and the Public Against Violence.

Yugoslavia has embarked on an ambitious program of economic and political reform. Just last week, the Markovic government announced a broad expansion of its economic reform program. We believe this program charts a solid course for Yugoslavian prosperity. The Republics of Slovenia and Croatia have recently held free elections, and other republics are expected to hold such elections in the near future.

This is a transition never undertaken by so many so quickly.

Set against this progress, however, are rising internal tensions, particularly in the province of Kosovo. This concerns us greatly. We of the G-24 should collectively call upon the people, and the leaders, of Yugoslavia and its republics to resolve their difficulties peacefully and with full respect for human rights. Political and economic reform, even when fully supported and nurtured by friends and neighbors, cannot succeed if it is undermined by intolerance from within.

In Bulgaria, we have expressed our deep concern about the fairness of the recent elections. Nevertheless, pending formation of the new Bulgarian Government and assuming continued democratization, we believe that progress toward reform has been sufficient for Bulgaria to be eligible now for G-24 assistance. The United States will continue to monitor closely the process of democratization and free-market reform in Bulgaria. We are prepared to provide tangible support for this

process. At the same time, we need to keep in mind that G-24 conditionality is not a one time threshold, but a continuing requirement.

The German Democratic Republic [GDR] is, of course, a special case and needs to be treated as such. I believe the events of this week are the first steps toward a bright economic and political future for all the people of Germany. Pending German political unification, however, it is appropriate for the G-24 to recognize the tremendous progress that has been made in the GDR toward political and economic reform.

Unfortunately, Romania has not yet met the conditions required for G-24 support. The Iliescu regime's complicity with the miners' violent repression of demonstrators, and the arrest of the political opposition, raises serious questions about its commitment to democratic reform and basic human rights. We look forward to the day when we can include Romania in the G-24 process. However, we will require demonstrable progress on both political and economic reform and respect for human rights before that day can come.

Criteria for Assistance

The United States believes it is essential that we maintain the integrity of the G-24 process. As I noted at the outset, this process was established to support Poland and Hungary as they moved to embrace the principles of political and economic freedom. Following those principles, the G-24 has helped both countries to follow through on their own decisions to join the community of democratic nations. Our decision to expand the process to the other countries of Central and Eastern Europe recognizes their progress in political and economic reform. The Commission, working with the G-24 member states, has developed the following five criteria that should determine eligibility for G-24 coordinated assistance:

First, adherence to the rule of law; *second,* respect for human rights; *third,* the introduction of multi-party systems; *fourth,* the holding of fair and free elections; and, *fifth,* the development of market-oriented economies.

These criteria—the criteria that our CSCE [Conference on Security and Cooperation in Europe] meetings in

Bonn and Copenhagen have set for all of Europe — send a clear message to reformers and old thinkers alike. Western assistance is designed to support fundamental political and economic reform. Its purpose is not to maintain the status quo or to revert to the problems of the past.

We also appreciate the contributions of the IMF [International Monetary Fund], World Bank, OECD [Organization for Economic Cooperation and Development], and the Paris Club. These institutions are playing major roles in assisting the political and economic transition of Central and Eastern Europe. And our policies of assistance should complement the programs of these international institutions.

We believe that other international institutions that play significant roles should also be invited to participate in G-24 ministerials and senior experts meetings. For example, the ILO [International Labor Organization] plays an important part in the working group on training, and the effective handling of labor issues is essential to successful economic reform in Central and Eastern Europe.

We also need to be creative about adapting current institutions to meet new needs. Therefore, I propose that the OECD create a new affiliate status to meet a new need. This new status would be available for those states that have developed democratic political systems, committed themselves to creating market economies, participated in the OECD Center for European Economies in Transition, and shown an interest in eventual OECD membership. Affiliate involvement in OECD activities would be tailored to their unique needs and interests. Affilitate status would, in short, be one more way to foster a greater sense of inclusion for the newly democratizing countries.

Assistance to Central America

Before closing, I would like to say a few words about our proposal for a G-24 effort in Central America. Recognizing the great success of the G-24 mechanism in Europe, the United States has proposed to the 12 EC [Economic Community] Foreign Ministers, President Delors, Japan, and Canada that we develop a G-24-like mechanism to broaden support for democracy and development in Central America. President Bush has discussed this with President Delors. I have discussed it with a number of you and with the Central American Presidents.

At their June 18 economic summit, the Presidents welcomed the idea as a way of maintaining international attention on the region's economic and political progress, despite competing events in Eastern Europe and the Soviet Union. They believe, as we do, that we cannot let the great events of Europe lead us to overlook other opportunities and needs elsewhere.

We have not yet worked out specifics of the structure and functioning of the mechanism, because we wanted to solicit views from the Central Americans and other interested governments. Although inspired by the East European G-24, the mechanism for Central America would be a separate and distinct process, reflecting the different realities of the two regions.

At this point, we see the mechanism serving two main functions: (1) bringing together developed countries and the Central American states to discuss needs and resources, and (2) acting as a clearing house for information. It might also prove useful for: (3) preparing coordinated needs assessments, and (4) pursuing a small number of joint projects too large for any single donor nation.

Let me close with this observation. Last year when the European Commission and the member states of the G-24 undertook the task of coordinating Western assistance to Poland and Hungary, it was truly a leap into the unknown. Now we are fully engaged in a task with a great redeeming purpose: helping to bring the long-denied benefits of democracy and economic liberty to the nations of Central and Eastern Europe. Working through the Commission and the G-24, our collective efforts must continue to quicken the courage of the peoples we have promised to help in their quest for freedom and prosperity.

---

[1] Department of State Press Release 97, July 4, 1990. The Group of 24 [G-24] comprises the 24 countries of the Organization for Economic Cooperation and Development. At the July 1989 Paris economic summit meeting, the leaders agreed on the need to coordinate Western assistance to support political and economic reform in Poland and Hungary. The European Community Commission, which was asked to coordinate the process, has convened a series of meetings of the 24 countries.

The 1990 Houston Economic Summit, July 9-11

The 16th Economic Summit of Industrialized Nations was hosted by the United States. In addition to President Bush, the summit was attended by Prime Minister Brian Mulroney of Canada, President Jacques Delors of the European Community (EC), Chancellor Helmut Kohl of the Federal Republic of Germany, President Francois Mitterand of France, Prime Minister Giulio Andreotti of Italy, Prime Minister Toshiki Kaifu of Japan, and Prime Minister Margaret Thatcher of the United Kingdom. The leaders were accompanied by their foreign and finance ministers.

1990
ECONOMIC SUMMIT
OF
INDUSTRIALIZED
NATIONS
HOUSTON, TEXAS

Political Declaration: Securing Democracy, July 10, 1990 [1]

1. We, the Leaders of our seven countries and the Representatives of the European Community, salute the men and women around the world whose courage and wisdom have inspired and brought about the historic advances of democracy we have witnessed over the past year. As we enter the final decade of this century, which we intend should be a Decade of Democracy, we reiterate our commitment to support the strengthening of democracy, human rights, and economic reconstruction and development through market-oriented economies. We emphasize the important opportunity provided in this forum for representatives from Europe, Japan, and North America to discuss critical challenges of the coming years.

2. Europe is at the dawn of a new era. We welcome enthusiastically the profound and historic changes sweeping the continent. The London Declaration on a Transformed North Atlantic Alliance [*see* Europe] provides a new basis for cooperation among former adversaries in building a stable, secure, and peaceful Europe. We are determined to seize all opportunities to achieve a Europe whole and free and recognize the European Community's contribution to that effort. We applaud the unification of Germany, which is a tangible expression of mankind's inalienable right to self-determination

and a major contribution to stability in Europe. We welcome the replacement of repressive regimes in Central and Eastern Europe by governments freely chosen by their peoples. We applaud the introduction of the rule of law and the freedoms that are the bedrock of a democratic state. We urge Romania, following recent events, to adhere to the positive trend taking place in other countries of Central and Eastern Europe.

3. We welcome the intention of the Soviet Union to move toward a democratic political system, as well as Soviet attempts to reform their economy along market principles. We commit ourselves to working with the Soviet Union to assist its efforts to create an open society, a pluralistic democracy, and a market-oriented economy. Such changes will enable the Soviet Union to fulfill its responsibilities in the community of nations founded on these principles. We are heartened by indications that a constructive dialogue is underway between the Soviet Government and the Baltic States, and we urge all sides to continue this dialogue in a democratic spirit.

4. The advance of democracy accompanied by market-oriented economic reforms is not just a European phenomenon. Since we last

met, we have witnessed the spread of democratic values in many parts of the world. In Asia, there are encouraging signs of new political openness in Mongolia and Nepal. In the Philippines, the government continues to engage in courageous efforts to consolidate democracy. We acknowledge some of the recent developments in China, but believe that the prospects for closer cooperation will be enhanced by renewed political and economic reform, particularly in the field of human rights. We agree to maintain the measures put into place at last year's summit, as modified over the course of this year. We will keep them under review for future adjustments to respond to further positive developments in China. For example, in addition to existing lending to meet basic human needs, we will explore whether there are other World Bank loans that would contribute to reform of the Chinese economy, especially loans that would address environmental concerns.

5. In Africa, we hope that Namibia's attainment of independence and democracy will be a positive example for freedom, pluralism, and market-oriented economic reform throughout the continent. We also welcome the positive developments that have taken place in South Africa, espe-

cially the launching of talks between the government and representatives of the black majority. We hope this will lead to a peaceful transition to a nonracial democracy and the complete dismantlement of the apartheid system. We will continue to support this process and we call on all parties to refrain from violence or its advocacy.

6. In Latin America, we welcome the reestablishment of freedom and democracy in Chile. We applaud the recent fair and free elections in Nicaragua, as well as progress on the path to peace through dialogue in El Salvador and Guatemala. We encourage the efforts of the Panamanian government to reestablish democracy and the rule of law. We note with satisfaction the positive evolution in Haiti. We hope that Cuba will take steps to join the democratic trend in the rest of Latin America.

7. While we applaud the reduction of ideological conflicts that have divided much of the world since the end of the Second World War, we note with deep concern the reemergence of intolerance affecting ethnic and religious groups. We agree that such intolerance can lead to conflicts, which can threaten fundamental human rights, as well as political and economic development.

8. We reaffirm our commitment to the fundamental principles we seek to realize in our own societies, and we underscore that political and economic freedoms are closely linked and mutually reinforcing. Each of us stands ready to help in practical ways those countries that choose freedom through the provision of constitutional, legal, and economic know-how and through economic assistance, as appropriate.

In drawing from our different constitutional and historical experiences, we stand ready, individually and jointly in relevant fora, to:

- assist in the drafting of laws, including bills of rights and civil, criminal, and economic framework laws;
- advise in the fostering of independent media;
- establish training programs in government, management, and technical fields;
- develop and expand people-to-people contacts and exchange programs to help diffuse understanding and knowledge.

In the same spirit, the recent [July 4] G-24 Ministerial agreed to extend its

assistance in Central and Eastern Europe in parallel with progress in political and economic reform.

We agree the challenge facing the industrialized democracies is to continue the effort already underway in Europe while expanding efforts to support political reform and economic development in other parts of the world. We call on our people and the people of other democracies to join in this great endeavor.

Statement on Transnational Issues, July 10, 1990 [1]

Terrorism

We, the Heads of State or Government, reaffirm our condemnation of terrorism in all its forms, our commitment to make no concessions to terrorists or their sponsors and our resolve to continue to cooperate in efforts to combat terrorism. We demand that those governments which provide support to terrorists end such support immediately. We are determined not to allow terrorists to remain unpunished, but to see them brought to justice in accordance with international law and national legislation.

We welcome the recent release of several hostages, but remain deeply concerned that hostages are still being held, some for more than five years. Their ordeal and that of their families must end. We call for the immediate, unconditional and safe release of all hostages and for an accounting of all persons taken hostage who may have died while being held. We call on those with influence over hostage takers to use their influence to this end.

We note with deep concern the continuing threat presented to civil aviation by terrorist groups, as demonstrated by such outrages as the sabotage of civil aircraft over Lockerbie, Scotland on December 21, 1988, above Niger on September 19, 1989, and over Colombia on November 27, 1989. We reiterate our determination to fight terrorist assaults against civil aviation.

Accordingly, we will continue our cooperation to negotiate a convention requiring the introduction of additives into plastic explosives to aid in their detection. We pledge to work to strengthen international civil aviation security standards. Consistent with this

objective, we note the importance of making available training and technical assistance to other nations. We support initiatives undertaken through the International Civil Aviation Organization (ICAO) regarding this issue. We will work together with ICAO to expand such assistance.

Nonproliferation

We discussed the threat to international security posed by the proliferation of nuclear, chemical and biological weapons, and of ballistic missile weapons delivery systems.

With regard to nuclear proliferation, we take special note of the recent declaration issued by the European Council in Dublin on that subject. That document underscored the great importance attached to the maintenance of an effective international nuclear nonproliferation regime and the need to make every effort to contribute to strengthening nonproliferation and encouraging the participation of further countries in the regime. The Treaty on Nonproliferation of Nuclear Weapons (NPT) is an important element of that regime. We further endorse the EC's call for all states to apply IAEA [International Atomic Energy Agency] safeguards on as universal a basis as possible.

We also urge all nuclear suppliers to adopt nuclear export control measures equivalent to the Nuclear Suppliers Group Guidelines.

Whether NPT parties or not, we commit ourselves to working actively to secure a satisfactory outcome to nuclear nonproliferation discussions in the forthcoming months, including those at the Fourth Review Conference of the NPT.

We hope that these discussions will contribute to the achievement of as broad a consensus as possible in favor of an equitable and stable nonproliferation regime. Such a regime should be based on an indispensable balance between the nonproliferation of arms and the development of peaceful and safe uses of nuclear energy.

The global community has focussed for decades on nuclear proliferation, especially when combined with advanced missile delivery systems. Today we also face new and growing problems from the proliferation of chemical and biological weapons.

With regard to chemical and biological proliferation, we commit ourselves to pursue efforts to prevent the diversion of chemical precursors at a national level, as well as in the relevant Western fora. We similarly commit ourselves to be vigilant about the danger of potential diversions in the field of biological technologies.

We endorse a complete ban on chemical weapons, through an effective and verifiable treaty, as the only long term guarantee against the proliferation of chemical weapons. We believe an important step toward achieving such a treaty was made in the recent U.S.-Soviet agreement on destruction and nonproduction of chemical weapons and the recent declaration of intent by NATO states to become original signatories to the Chemical Weapons Convention. We reiterate our determination, first expressed at the 1989 Paris Conference on Chemical Weapons, to redouble the effort at the Conference on Disarmament in Geneva to resolve the remaining issues and to conclude the convention at the earliest date. We also urge all states to become parties as soon as it is concluded. Similarly, as the 1991 Review Conference on the Biological Weapons Convention approaches, we call on all nations that have not become party to the convention to do so and to participate in confidence building measures designed to strengthen its effectiveness.

We wish to highlight the importance of dealing with the related threat of ballistic missiles capable of delivering nuclear, chemical and biological weapons. We note especially the contribution of the Missile Technology Control Regime (MTCR) to our joint efforts to control missile proliferation. We applaud the recent decisions of additional nations to adhere to the MTCR, and we call upon all nations to observe the MTCR Guidelines.

Press Briefing by Secretary Baker, Opening Statement, July 10, 1990 [2]

Ladies and gentlemen, you have before you, I think, copies of the Political Declaration and statements on terrorism and nonproliferation. I'd like to, by way of opening this up, summarize those for you, and then I'll be glad to respond to your questions.

The Political Declaration that we're releasing today celebrates the historic advance of democracy since the Seven last met in Paris. In the Declaration, we reiterate our support for the peaceful democratic movement that's bringing freedom to Central and Eastern Europe and that is uniting Germany.

But the great events in Europe should not lead us to overlook other opportunities and other needs. During the course of our discussions, we cited Namibia as a positive model for democratic evolution elsewhere—on the African continent, for instance. Most of the leaders here have met recently with Nelson Mandela [Deputy President of the African National Congress]. Some of them have met with [South African] President [F.W.] de Klerk.

We think that the focus of our efforts should be on encouraging negotiations to bring about a nonracial democracy in South Africa.

In Central and South America, we welcome the return of democracy to Chile and Panama, and we welcome free and fair elections in Nicaragua.

The winds of freedom have not bypassed Asia either. We are witnessing very important changes now taking place in Nepal as well as Mongolia. We acknowledge some recent actions taken by the Chinese government in this Political Declaration. But for now, the measures that were put in place at last year's Economic Summit remain.

We will explore, however, whether there are World Bank loans that would contribute to reform of the Chinese economy, especially to meet environmental concerns.

We also devoted considerable discussion to the evolution of events in the Soviet Union and how a reforming Soviet Union can play an important role in addressing both old and new challenges facing the international community. President Bush will review that discussion for you in more detail tomorrow.

The Declaration closes by suggesting actions that Western nations can take to help secure and promote democracy's advance in all regions of the world. The Declaration notes that political freedom and economic liberty are mutually reenforcing, and they cannot flourish in an environment of intolerance.

A separate statement was issued on the transnational problems of terrorism and the proliferation of nuclear, chemical, and biological weapons as well as ballistic missiles. These dangers, like the elicit trade in narcotics that will be addressed in tomorrow's communique, of course, know no boundaries.

In the case of nuclear proliferation, the deliberations here, I think, take on added significance in this 20th anniversary year of the Nuclear Nonproliferation Treaty.

In addition to the topics covered in the documents released today, regional conflicts were discussed. We recognize each conflict's unique nature and the responsibility of the parties on the ground to take the lead in seeking negotiated solutions. We think, however, that free and fair elections have a key role to play in bringing peace to these regions.

In Afghanistan, in Cambodia, and in Angola, we want to see negotiated settlements providing for cease fires, arms cutoffs, and transition periods supported by the United Nations and regional organizations, all leading to free elections.

We discussed the current situation in the Middle East. And although different approaches were raised, we all agreed on the need for movement in the peace process. We expressed the hope that the cycle of violence and repression would give way to early dialogue between Israel and Palestinians that will lead to free democratic elections and to negotiations.

Regarding the human tragedy in the Horn of Africa, we discussed, among other actions being taken, the recent agreement between the United States and the Soviet Union to launch a joint effort to deal with starvation and conflict in Ethiopia.

We also noted with particular concern developments related to Kashmir. These events threaten regional stability and they could imperil the growth of political and economic freedoms in two democracies, India and Pakistan. We are encouraged by recent moves toward dialogue between the two countries, and we agreed to use all means at our disposal to encourage and support this process.

We expressed our concern that the Asia and Pacific region has yet to see the same process of conciliation, military disengagement, and reduction of tensions that has characterized East-West relations in Europe.

In this regard, we support the early resolution of the Northern Territories issue as an essential step leading to the normalization of Japanese-Soviet relations.

The Korean Peninsula remains an area of sharp concern, especially because the North has yet to sign and implement a nuclear safeguards agreement. We welcome the recent talks between North and South Korea, and we hope that they mark a turning point in inter-Korean relations.

In sum, the summit partners share the imperative of our time: to help promote and to help secure democracy around the world. We are committed to turn the hope of today into the solid achievements of tomorrow.

Economic Declaration, July 11, 1990 [1]

1. We, the Heads of State and Government of the seven major industrial democracies and the President of the Commission of the European Communities, meeting in Houston for our annual Economic Summit, celebrate the renaissance of democracy throughout much of the world. We welcome unreservedly the spread of multiparty democracy, the practice of free elections, the freedom of expression and assembly, the increased respect for human rights, the rule of law, and the increasing recognition of the principles of the open and competitive economy. These events proclaim loudly man's inalienable rights: When people are free to choose, they choose freedom.

2. The profound changes taking place in Europe, and progress toward democracy elsewhere, give us great hope for a world in which individuals have increasing opportunities to achieve their economic and political aspirations, free of tyranny and oppression.

3. We are mindful that freedom and economic prosperity are closely linked and mutually reinforcing. Sustainable economic prosperity depends upon the stimulus of competition and the encouragement of enterprise—on incentives for individual initiative and innovation, on a skilled and motivated labor force whose fundamental rights are protected, on sound monetary systems, on an open system of international trade and payments, and on an environment safeguarded for future generations.

4. Around the world, we are determined to assist other peoples to achieve and sustain economic prosperity and political freedom. We will support their efforts with our experience, resources, and goodwill.

The International Economic Situation

5. In recent years, substantial progress has been achieved in promoting a stronger world economy through sound macroeconomic policies and greater economic efficiency. The economic expansion in our countries, now in its eighth year, has supported notable income growth and job creation in the context of rapid growth of international trade. However, unemployment remains high in a number of countries. Inflation, although considerably lower than in the early 1980s, is a matter of serious concern in some countries and requires continued vigilance. External imbalances have been reduced in the United States and Japan, whereas in other cases they have increased. Continuing adjustment remains a priority in order to counter protectionist pressures, alleviate uncertainties in financial and exchange markets, and contribute to avoiding pressures on interest rates. Sound domestic macroeconomic policies, which may differ according to conditions in each country, will make a major contribution to further external adjustment.

6. In the developing world, the experience of the late 1980s varied widely. Some economies, particularly in East Asia, continued to experience impressive domestic growth rates. The economies of a number of other developing countries have been stagnant or declined. Nonetheless, serious efforts—in some cases by new leadership—to implement economic adjustment and market-oriented policies have begun to yield positive results and should be continued.

International Monetary Developments and Policy Coordination

7. At a time of growing economic interdependence, the summit countries have developed a cooperative process based on a common appreciation of the need for market-oriented policies and the importance of sound domestic budgetary and monetary policies. This process has contributed importantly to the strengthened performance of the world economy and to improved stability of exchange rates by concentrating attention on multilateral surveillance and close coordination of economic policies, including cooperation on exchange markets. It is important to continue and, where appropriate, to strengthen this cooperative and flexible approach to improve the functioning of the international monetary system and contribute to its stability.

8. To sustain the present economic expansion to the benefit of all countries, each nation must pursue sound policies. Balanced expansion of demand with increasing productive capacity is key, while external imbalances and structural rigidities require correction. Price pressures warrant continued vigilance.

9. Countries with sizable current account deficits should contribute to the adjustment process by the reduction of fiscal deficits, and undertake structural reforms to encourage private saving and increase competitiveness.

10. Countries with large external surpluses should contribute to the adjustment process by sustained noninflationary growth of domestic demand with structural reform in order to improve the underlying conditions for growth and adjustment and to promote increased investment relative to saving.

11. The investment needs of the world as a whole are expected to grow in the coming years, particularly in Central and Eastern Europe and in developing countries undertaking market reforms, as well as in some industrial countries. To meet these needs industrial and developing countries alike should foster saving and discourage dissaving.

12. The market-oriented restructuring of Central and Eastern European economies should stimulate their growth and increase their integration into the global economy. We support these changes and seek to assure that this difficult transformation will contribute to global growth and stability.

13. Within the European Community, the European Monetary System is leading to a high degree of economic convergence and stability. We note the European Community's decision to launch the Intergovernmental Conference on Economic and Monetary Union and the beginning of the first stage of that union. During this first stage, closer surveillance and coordination of economic and monetary policies will contribute toward noninflationary growth and a more robust international economic system.

14. We welcome the prospect of a unified, democratic Germany which enjoys full sovereignty without discriminatory constraints. German economic, monetary, and social union will contribute to improved noninflationary global growth and to a reduction of

external imbalances. This process will promote positive economic developments in Central and Eastern Europe.

15. We call on the member countries of the International Monetary Fund (IMF) to implement the agreement by the IMF to increase quotas by 50 percent under the Ninth General Review of Quotas and to strengthen the IMF arrears strategy.

Measures Aimed at Economic Efficiency

16. Considerable progress has been made over the past few years in supplementing macroeconomic policies with reforms to increase economic efficiency. We welcome the progress in the realization of the internal market in the European Community and the continuing efforts to reduce structural rigidities in North America and Japan. Nonetheless, we emphasize the widespread need for further steps to promote regulatory reform and liberalize areas such as retail trade, telecommunications, transport, labor markets, and financial markets, as well as to reduce industrial and agricultural subsidies, improve tax systems, and improve labor force skills through education and training.

17. We welcome the major contributions of the Organization for Economic Cooperation and Development (OECD) in identifying structural policy challenges and options. We encourage the OECD to strengthen its surveillance and review procedures, and to find ways of making its work operationally more effective.

The International Trading System

18. The open world trading system is vital to economic prosperity. A strengthened General Agreement on Tariffs and Trade (GATT) is essential to provide a stable framework for the expansion of trade and the fuller integration of Central and Eastern Europe and developing countries into the global economy. We reject protectionism in all its forms.

19. The successful outcome of the Uruguay Round has the highest priority on the international economic agenda. Consequently, we stress our determination to take the difficult political decisions necessary to achieve far-reaching, substantial results in all areas of the Uruguay Round by the end of this year. We instruct our negotiators to make progress and in particular to agree on

the complete profile of the final package by the July meeting of the Trade Negotiations Committee.

20. We confirm our strong support for the essential broad objectives of the negotiations: reform of agricultural policies; a substantial and balanced package of measures to improve market access, strengthened multilateral rules and disciplines; the incorporation of new issues of services, trade-related investment measures, and intellectual property protection within the GATT framework; and integration of developing countries into the international trading system.

21. As regards agriculture, achieving the long term objective of the reform of agricultural policies is critical to permit the greater liberalization of trade in agricultural products. Experience has shown the high cost of agricultural policies which tend to create surpluses. The outcome of the GATT negotiations on agriculture should lead to a better balance between supply and demand and ensure that agricultural policies do not impede the effective functioning of international markets. We therefore reaffirm our commitment to the long term objective of the reform, i.e., to allow market signals to influence agriculture production and to establish a fair and market-oriented agricultural trading system.

22. The achievement of this objective requires each of us to make substantial, progressive reductions in support and protection of agriculture — covering internal regimes, market access, and export subsidies — and develop rules governing sanitary and phytosanitary measures. Variations among countries in the mechanisms of agricultural support reflect differences in the social and economic conditions of farming. The negotiations on agriculture should therefore be conducted in a framework that includes a common instrument of measurement, provides for commitments to be made in an equitable way among all countries, and takes into account concerns about food security. The framework should contain specific assurances that, by appropriate use of the common measure as well as other ways, participants would reduce not only internal support but also export subsidies and import protection in a related way.

23. Agreement on such a framework by the time of the July meeting of the Trade Negotiations Committee is critical to the successful completion of the Uruguay Round as a

whole. Accordingly, we commend to our negotiators the text submitted by the Chairman of the Agricultural Negotiating Group as a means to intensify the negotiations. We intend to maintain a high level of personal involvement and to exercise the political leadership necessary to ensure the successful outcome of these negotiations.

24. Negotiations on market access should achieve agreement on a substantial and balanced package of measures. As regards textiles, the objective is to liberalize the textile and clothing sector through progressive dismantling of trade barriers and its integration, under a precise timetable, into GATT on the basis of strengthened GATT rules and disciplines.

25. Negotiations on multilateral rules and disciplines should strengthen GATT rules in areas such as safeguards, balance of payments, rules of origin, and updated disciplines for dumping and antidumping measures. Concerning subsidies, rules are needed which will effectively discipline domestic subsidies so as to avoid trade distortions, competitive subsidization, and trade conflicts. Improved disciplines must also cover countervailing measures so that they do not become barriers to trade.

26. As regards the new areas, the aim is to develop new rules and procedures within the GATT framework, including a framework of contractually enforceable rules to liberalize services trade, with no sector excluded a priori; an agreement to reduce trade distorting effects of trade-related investment measures; and an agreement to provide for standards and effective enforcement of all intellectual property rights.

27. A successful Uruguay Round is essential for industrialized and developing countries alike. We seek the widest possible participation of developing countries in the Round and their further integration into the multilateral trading system. To achieve this objective, developed countries are prepared to accept greater multilateral disciplines in all areas and to offer improved market access in areas of interest to developing countries such as textiles and clothing, tropical products, and agriculture.

28. For their part, developing countries should substantially reduce their tariffs and increase the percentage of tariffs that are bound; subscribe to balanced and effective restraints on all forms of exceptions, including measures imposed for balance of payments dif-

ficulties; and participate meaningfully in agreements covering the new areas. The end result should be a single set of multilateral rules applicable to all GATT contracting parties, although some developing countries, especially the least developed, may need longer transition periods or other transitional arrangements on a case by case basis.

29. The wide range of substantive results which we seek in all these areas will call for a commitment to strengthen further the institutional framework of the multilateral trading system. In that context, the concept of an international trade organization should be addressed at the conclusion of the Uruguay Round. We also need to improve the dispute settlement process in order to implement the results of the negotiations effectively. This should lead to a commitment to operate only under the multilateral rules.

Direct Investment

30. Free flows of investment increase global prosperity by complementing the open international trade system. In particular, foreign direct investment can help restructure the economies of developing and Central and Eastern European countries, create new jobs, and raise living standards.

31. All countries should therefore seek to reduce their barriers to investment and resist protectionist pressures to discourage or discriminate against such investment. The OECD and the GATT should continue to promote investment liberalization. The multilateral development banks and the IMF should require investment liberalization in their programs in Central and Eastern Europe and developing countries.

Export Credits

32. We welcome the important negotiations that are underway in the OECD on a balanced package of measures to strengthen multilateral disciplines on trade- and aid-distorting export credit subsidies. This package, to be completed by spring of 1991, should reduce substantially, through improved discipline and transparency, distortions resulting from the use of officially supported commercial and aid credits. It is also important to avoid introducing trade distortions in financial flows to the nations of Central and Eastern Europe.

Reform in Central and Eastern Europe

33. We welcome the political and economic reforms taking place in Central and Eastern Europe. At the recent Conference on Security and Cooperation in Europe (CSCE) in Bonn and by the agreement to establish the European Bank for Reconstruction and Development (EBRD), the participating countries of the region accepted the key principles underpinning market economies. However, the degree of implementation of economic and political reform varies widely by country. Several countries have taken courageous and difficult measures to stabilize their economies and shorten the transition to a market economy.

34. We and other countries should assist Central and Eastern European nations that are firmly committed to economic and political reform. Those providing help should favor countries that implement such reforms.

35. Foreign private investment will be vital in the development of Central and Eastern Europe. Capital will flow to countries with open markets and hospitable investment climates. Improved access for their exports will also be important for those Central and Eastern European countries that are opening up their economies. Western Governments can support this process by various means, including trade and investment agreements. The recent decision by the Coordinating Committee for Multilateral Export Controls (COCOM) to liberalize export controls is a positive step.

36. We commend the work done by the Commission of the European Communities on the coordination by the Group of 24 (G-24) of assistance to Poland and Hungary inaugurated at the [1989 Economic] Summit of the Arch which has made a significant contribution to helping these countries lay the foundation for self-sustaining growth based on market principles. We welcome the decision of the G-24 to enlarge the coordination of assistance to other emerging democracies in Central and Eastern Europe, including Yugoslavia.

37. We recognize that these countries face major problems in cleaning their environment. It will be important to assist the countries of Central and Eastern Europe to develop the necessary policies and infrastructure to confront those environmental problems.

38. We also welcome the recent initiatives in regional cooperation, e.g., in transport and the environment, that will make a positive contribution to economic progress and stability in the region.

39. We expect the new EBRD to play a key role in fostering investment in those countries and to contribute to orderly transitions toward market economies and a sound basis for democracy. We urge the rapid entry into force of the Bank.

40. The Center for Cooperation with European Economies in Transition at the OECD will encourage reforms and strengthen relations between these countries and the OECD, as will the OECD's follow up work from the CSCE Economic Conference in Bonn.

41. We invite the OECD to consider a closer relationship with those Central and East European countries that are committed to political and economic reform.

The Soviet Union

42. We discussed the situation in the Soviet Union, and exchanged views regarding the message that Soviet President Gorbachev sent us several days ago on his economic plans. We welcome the efforts underway in the Soviet Union to liberalize and to create a more open, democratic, and pluralistic Soviet society, and to move toward a market-oriented economy. These measures deserve our support. The success of *perestroika* depends upon the determined pursuit and development of these reform efforts. In particular, we welcome President Gorbachev's suggestion for a sustained economic dialogue.

43. We have all begun, individually and collectively, to assist these reform efforts. We all believe that technical assistance should be provided now to help the Soviet Union move to a market-oriented economy and to mobilize its own resources. Some countries are already in a position to extend large scale financial credits.

44. We also agreed that further Soviet decisions to introduce more radical steps toward a market-oriented economy, to shift resources substantially away from the military sector and to cut support to nations promoting regional conflict will all improve the prospect for meaningful and sustained economic assistance.

45. We have taken note of the decision of the European Council in

Dublin on June 26. We have agreed to ask the IMF, the World Bank, the OECD and the designated president of the EBRD to undertake, in close consultation with the Commission of the European Communities, a detailed study of the Soviet economy, to make recommendations for its reform and to establish the criteria under which Western economic assistance could effectively support these reforms. This work should be completed by year's end and be convened by the IMF.

46. We took note of the importance to the Government of Japan of the peaceful resolution of its dispute with the Soviet Union over the Northern Territories.

47. The host Government will convey to the Soviet Union the results of the Houston Summit.

The Developing Nations

48. We reiterate that our commitment to the developing world will not be weakened by the support for reforming countries in Central and Eastern Europe. The poorest of the developing nations must remain the focus of special attention. The International Development Association replenishment of SDR 11.6 billion, agreed to last December, will provide needed resources for these countries, and marks the incorporation of environmental concerns into development lending. It is our intention to take a constructive part in the Paris Conference on the least developed countries in September.

49. The advanced industrial economies can make a number of major contributions to the long run development of the developing countries. By sustaining economic growth and price stability, we can offer stable, growing markets and sources of capital for the developing world. By providing financial and technical support to developing countries undertaking genuine political and economic reform, we can reinforce their ongoing liberalization. The industrialized nations should continue to make efforts to enhance their development aid and other forms of assistance to the developing countries, including reinforcing the effectiveness of the aid.

50. In the developing world, there is a growing acceptance of the view that growth can be encouraged by a stable macroeconomic framework, sectoral reform to provide more competition, and an opening of markets. Open,

democratic, and accountable political systems are important ingredients in the effective and equitable operation of market-oriented economies.

51. Important contributions to a hospitable investment climate can be made by the protection of intellectual property, and by liberalization of investment regimes, including transparent and equitable investment rules, and equality of treatment for foreign and domestic investors.

52. The recent Enterprise for the Americas initiative announced by the U.S. President will support and encourage more market-oriented policies in Latin America and the Caribbean. We believe that such U.S. efforts hold great promise for the region and will help improve prospects for sustained growth in the Americas through the encouragement of trade, open investment regimes, the reduction of U.S. bilateral concessional debt, and the use of debt for equity and nature swaps.

53. In a number of countries, sustainable development requires that population growth remains in some reasonable balance with expanding resources. Supporting the efforts of developing countries to maintain this balance is a priority. Improved educational opportunities for women and their greater integration into the economy can make important contributions to population stabilization programs.

54. In the Mediterranean basin, the initiatives of economic integration, which are underway, deserve encouragement and support.

Third World Debt

55. Significant progress has been made during the past year under the strengthened debt strategy, which has renewed the resolve in a number of debtor countries to continue economic reforms essential to future growth. In particular, the recent commercial bank agreements with Chile, Costa Rica, Mexico, Morocco, the Philippines, and Venezuela involve significant debt and debt service reduction. Important financial support for debt and debt service reduction is being provided by the IMF and the World Bank, as well as by Japan. The Paris Club has agreed, in order to support medium term IMF-supported reform and financing programs, to provide adequate restructuring agreements, notably through mul-

tiyear reschedulings and through lengthening of the repayment period. The combination of debtor reform efforts and commercial bank debt reduction has had a notable impact on confidence in debtor economies, as clearly demonstrated through flows of both new investment and the return of flight capital to Mexico, in particular.

56. These measures represent major innovations in the case by case debt strategy and are potentially available to all debtor nations with serious debt-servicing problems which are implementing economic adjustment policies.

57. The adoption by debtor nations of strong economic reform programs with the IMF and World Bank remains at the heart of the debt strategy, and a prerequisite for debt and debt service reduction within commercial bank financing packages. It is vital that debtor countries adopt measures to mobilize savings and to encourage new investment flows and the repatriation of flight capital to help sustain their recovery. In this connection, the recent U.S. Enterprise for the Americas initiative to support investment reform and the environment in Latin America needs to be given careful consideration by Finance Ministers.

58. For countries implementing courageous reforms, commercial banks should take realistic and constructive approaches in their negotiations to conclude promptly agreements on financial packages including debt reduction, debt-service reduction and new money.

59. Creditor nations will continue to play an important role in this process through ongoing contributions to the international financial institutions, rescheduling of official debt in the Paris Club, and new finance. We encourage the Paris Club to continue reviewing additional options to address debt burdens. In the case of the lower middle income countries implementing strong reform programs, we encourage the Paris Club to lengthen the repayment period, taking account of the special situations of these countries. We welcome the decisions taken by France with respect to Sub-Saharan Africa and by Canada with respect to the Caribbean to alleviate the debt burden of the lower middle income countries.

60. Creditor governments have also provided special support for the poorest countries through the implementation of Toronto terms in Paris

Club reschedulings. All of us have canceled official development assistance (ODA) debt for the poorest countries. We encourage the Paris Club to review the implementation of the existing options that apply to the poorest countries.

61. We note and will study with interest the Craxi Report on debt commissioned by the U.N. Secretary General.

The Environment

62. One of our most important responsibilities is to pass on to future generations an environment whose health, beauty, and economic potential are not threatened. Environmental challenges such as climate change, ozone depletion, deforestation, marine pollution, and loss of biological diversity require closer and more effective international cooperation and concrete action. We as industrialized countries have an obligation to be leaders in meeting these challenges. We agree that, in the face of threats of irreversible environmental damage, lack of full scientific certainty is no excuse to postpone actions which are justified in their own right. We recognize that strong, growing, market-oriented economies provide the best means for successful environmental protection.

63. Climate change is of key importance. We are committed to undertake common efforts to limit emissions of greenhouse gases, such as carbon dioxide. We strongly support the work of the Intergovernmental Panel on Climate Change (IPCC) and look forward to the release of its full report in August. The Second World Climate Conference provides the opportunity for all countries to consider the adoption of strategies and measures for limiting or stabilizing greenhouse gas emissions, and to discuss an effective international response. We reiterate our support for the negotiation of a framework convention on climate change, under the auspices of the United Nations Environment Program (UNEP) and the World Meteorological Organization (WMO). The convention should be completed by 1992. Work on appropriate implementing protocols should be undertaken as expeditiously as possible and should consider all sources and sinks.

64. We welcome the amendment of the Montreal Protocol to phase out the use of chlorofluorocarbons (CFCs) by the year 2000 and to extend coverage of the Protocol to other ozone depleting substances. The establishment of a financial mechanism to assist developing countries to tackle ozone depletion marks a new and positive step in cooperation between the developed and developing worlds. We applaud the announcement in London by some major developing countries, including India and China, that they intend to review their position on adherence to the Montreal Protocol and its amendments. We would welcome their adherence as a crucial reinforcement of the effectiveness of the Protocol, which would ultimately lead to a worldwide phaseout of ozone depleting substances. We urge all parties to ratify the amended Protocol as quickly as possible.

65. We acknowledge that enhanced levels of cooperation will be necessary with regard to the science and impacts of climate change and economic implications of possible response strategies. We recognize the importance of working together to develop new technologies and methods over the coming decades to complement energy conservation and other measures to reduce carbon dioxide and other greenhouse emissions. We support accelerated scientific and economic research and analysis on the dynamics and potential impact of climate change, and on potential responses of developed and developing countries.

66. We are determined to take action to increase forests, while protecting existing ones and recognizing the sovereign rights of all countries to make use of their natural resources. The destruction of tropical forests has reached alarming proportions. We welcome the commitment of the new Government of Brazil to help arrest this destruction and to provide sustainable forest management. We actively support this process, and we are ready for a new dialogue with developing countries on ways and means to support their efforts. We are ready to cooperate with the Government of Brazil on a comprehensive pilot program to counteract the threat to tropical rain forests in that country. We ask the World Bank to prepare such a proposal, in close cooperation with the Commission of the European Communities, which should be presented at the latest at the next Economic Summit. We appeal to the other concerned countries to join us in this effort. Experience gained in this pilot program should immediately be shared with other countries faced with tropical forest destruction. The Tropical Forestry Action Plan must be reformed and strengthened, placing more emphasis on forest conservation and protection of biological diversity. The International Tropical Timber Organization action plan must be enhanced to emphasize sustainable forest management and improve market operations.

67. We are ready to begin negotiations, in the appropriate fora, as expeditiously as possible on a global forest convention or agreement, which is needed to curb deforestation, protect biodiversity, stimulate positive forestry actions, and address threats to the world's forests. The convention or agreement should be completed as soon as possible, but no later than 1992. The work of the IPCC and others should be taken into account.

68. The destruction of ecologically sensitive areas around the world continues at an alarming pace. Loss of temperate and tropical forests; developmental pressures on estuaries, wetlands and coral reefs; and destruction of biological diversity are symptomatic. To reverse this trend, we will expand cooperation to combat desertification; expand projects to conserve biological diversity; protect the Antarctic; and assist developing countries in their environmental efforts. We will work within UNEP and other fora to achieve these objectives, and will participate actively in UNEP's work to protect biodiversity.

69. Efforts to protect the environment do not stop at the water's edge. Serious problems are caused by marine pollution, both in the oceans and in coastal areas. A comprehensive strategy should be developed to address land-based sources of pollution; we are committed to helping in this regard. We will continue our efforts to avoid oil spills, urge the early entry into force of the existing International Maritime Organization (IMO) Convention, and welcome the work of that organization in developing an international oil spills convention. We are concerned about the impact of environmental degradation and unregulated fishing practices on living marine resources. We support cooperation in the conservation of living marine resources and recognize the importance of regional fisheries organizations in this respect. We call on all concerned countries to respect the conservation regimes.

70. To cope with energy-related environmental damage, priority must be given to improvements in energy efficiency and to the development of alternative energy sources. For the countries that make such a choice, nuclear energy will continue to be an important contributor to our energy supply and can play a significant role in reducing the growth of greenhouse gas emissions. Countries should continue efforts to ensure highest worldwide performance standards for nuclear and other energy in order to protect health and the environment, and ensure the highest safety.

71. Cooperation between developed and developing countries is essential to the resolution of global environmental problems. In this regard, the 1992 U.N. Conference on Environment and Development will be an important opportunity to develop widespread agreement on common action and coordinated plans. We note with interest the conclusions of the Siena Forum on International Law of the Environment and suggest that these should be considered by the 1992 U.N. Conference on Environment and Development.

72. We recognize that developing countries will benefit from increased financial and technological assistance to help them resolve environmental problems, which are aggravated by poverty and underdevelopment. Multilateral development bank programs should be strengthened to provide greater protection for the environment, including environmental impact assessments and action plans, and to promote energy efficiency. We recognize that debt-for-nature swaps can play a useful role in protecting the environment. We will examine how the World Bank can provide a coordinating role for measures to promote environmental protection.

73. In order to integrate successfully environmental and economic goals, decisionmakers in government and industry require the necessary tools. Expanded cooperative scientific and economic research and analysis on the environment is needed. We recognize the importance of coordinating and the sharing the collection of satellite data on earth and its atmosphere. We welcome and encourage the ongoing discussions for the establishment of an International Network. It is also important to involve the private sector, which has a key role in developing solutions to environmental problems. We encourage the OECD to accelerate its very useful work on environment and the economy. Of particular importance are the early development of environmental indicators and the design of market-oriented approaches that can be used to achieve environmental objectives. We also welcome Canada's offer to host in 1991 an international conference on environmental information in the 21st Century. We support voluntary environmental labelling as a useful market mechanism which satisfies consumer demand and producer requirements and promotes market innovation.

74. We note with satisfaction the successful launching of the Human Frontier Science Program and express our hope that it will make positive contributions to the advancement of basic research in life science for the benefit of all mankind.

Narcotics

75. We urge all nations to accede to and complete ratification of the U.N. Convention Against Illicit Traffic in Narcotic Drugs and Psychotropic Substances (the Vienna Convention), and to apply provisionally terms of the Convention.

76. We welcome the conclusion of the U.N. Special Session on Drugs and urge the implementation of the measures contained in the Program of Action it has adopted.

77. We support the declaration adopted at the ministerial meeting on drugs convened by the United Kingdom that drug demand reduction should be accorded the same importance in policy and action as the reduction of illicit supply. Developed countries should adopt stronger prevention efforts and assist demand reduction initiatives in other countries.

78. We endorse the report of the Financial Action Task Force (FATF) and commit our countries to a full implementation of all its recommendations without delay. As agreed at the May meeting of Task Force Finance Ministers, the FATF should be reconvened for a second year, chaired by France, to assess and facilitate the implementation of these recommendations, and to complement them where appropriate. All OECD and financial center countries that subscribe to the recommendations of the Task Force should be invited to participate in this exercise. The report of the new FATF would be completed before we next meet. We also invite all other countries to participate in the fight against money laundering and to implement the recommendations of the FATF.

79. Effective procedures should be adopted to ensure that precursor and essential chemicals are not diverted to manufacture illicit drugs. A task force similar to the FATF should be created for this purpose, composed of Summit participants and other countries that trade in these chemicals, with the involvement of representatives of the chemical industry. The task force should address the problems which concern cocaine, heroin and synthetic drugs and report within a year.

80. We support a strategy for attacking the cocaine trade as outlined in particular in the Cartagena Declaration. We recognize the importance of supporting all countries strongly engaged in the fight against drug trafficking, especially Colombia, Peru, and Bolivia, with economic, law enforcement, and other assistance and advice, recognizing the need to make contributions within the framework of actions against drug trafficking carried out by the producer countries.

81. The heroin problem is still the most serious threat in many countries, both developed and developing. All countries should take vigorous measures to combat the scourge of heroin.

82. We should support an informal narcotics consultative arrangement with developed countries active in international narcotics control. Such a group could strengthen efforts to reduce supply and demand, and improve international cooperation.

83. We welcome the current review of U.N. drug abuse control agencies and urge that it result in a more efficient structure.

Next Economic Summit

84. We have accepted the invitation of Prime Minister Thatcher to meet next July in London.

President's Press Conference Following Summit, July 11, 1990 [1]

Thank you all very much. And I have a brief opening statement, and then I'll be glad to respond to your questions.

My colleagues from France and the United Kingdom, Germany, Canada, Italy, Japan, and the European Communities and I have just completed this 16th meeting of the leaders of the largest industrialized democracies. This, the first economic summit of the [post-] postwar period, celebrates the resurgence of democracy and free markets around the world. Over the past three days, we've had full discussions on the key issues of our times: advancing political and economic freedom; promoting sustained economic growth, both in developed and in developing countries; assisting the transition to market economies in Central and Eastern Europe and, indeed, in the Soviet Union; and protecting the environment. We are united in a common goal to extend to those who seek political and economic freedom a helping hand with our resources, talents, and experience. As our declaration states, when people are free to choose, they choose freedom.

We identified the successful completion of the Uruguay Round of global trade talks as one of the highest economic priorities. We recognize that agreement on fundamental reform of agriculture is critical to achieving this goal. We commended the report by the chairman of the GATT agricultural group, the De Zeeuw report, to our negotiators as a vehicle to move these talks forward, and we also committed to maintain our personal involvement and to exercise political leadership at every step along the way as we move toward the final ministerial meeting in December.

On the Soviet Union, we discussed our common efforts to assist the Soviet reform effort, the success of which is in our common interest. In addition to offering the Soviets technical assistance, we've asked the IMF [International Monetary Fund] to coordinate a major study of the Soviet economy and make recommendations for its reform. In keeping with the agreements reached here, I will be conveying to President Gorbachev the results of our deliberations.

We achieved major progress on the environment, particularly on climate change and forests. We committed to finish the negotiations on a framework climate change convention by 1992. In a first, we agreed that implementing protocols should consider all sources and sinks of greenhouse gases, consistent with the comprehensive approach that we recommend. We agreed to launch a special effort to address the deforestation in the rain forests, a concern that was very forcefully raised by Chancellor Kohl [of the Federal Republic of Germany]. I found a very receptive audience for my proposal that a freestanding global forest convention be negotiated without delay, and we agreed to move ahead on this rapidly.

In short, this was a summit that addressed itself to a rapidly changing world. We agreed to welcome, respond to, and manage the changes on behalf of free markets, free political systems, and a better life for people everywhere. It is no small achievement that we came to a positive and unanimous conclusion on so many important and difficult issues, and I would stress those two words: positive and unanimous.

And I want to congratulate my colleagues on the results of the collective effort. I think they left feeling good. We had a very generous letter to our Secretary of State just now from Prime Minister Mulroney [of Canada], and he's a veteran of these summits. And I must say to the Canadians here: I once again benefited from not only his commitment — learned from his commitment on certain issues like the environment but benefited from his advice.

I also want to thank the two Secretaries that were at my side, Secretary [of State] Baker and Secretary [of the Treasury] Brady, Ambassador Carla Hills [U.S. Trade Representative], Secretary [of Agriculture] Yeutter, Secretary [of Commerce] Mosbacher, who worked with their colleagues and others at this summit. I want to thank the sherpas. I understand they all stayed up until 4 o'clock this morning in ironing out this Final Communique.

So, it was a team effort, and I think most of our — well, I think all of our summit participants left feeling good about this particular summit.

And now I think Terry Hunt [Associated Press] has the first question.

Q. Mr. President, I'd like to ask you about Soviet aid. Is this six-month study of Soviet needs a way of delaying the political decision on aid, or at the end of that, will the United States make a commitment to send some cash to Moscow?

A. It's not an effort to delay anything. It is, as we said in the report, a step towards assisting the reforms. And I'll make clear to President Gorbachev that he ought to view this outcome of this summit very positively. You may remember that in London only a few days ago I gave my views on the U.S. lending money at this time. So, it's not an effort to forestall anything; it's an effort to move forward, encourage forward motion, and be helpful to the Soviet Union in terms of reform. They need much, much more reform, and they're the ones that say this. And in Gorbachev's letter, he asked for assistance in many areas — personnel management and how they change their systems. And we've already started bilaterally, as have other countries, in trying to assist. So, it's really a coordinated effort to help the Soviet Union.

Q. Well, in six months, then, can Mr. Gorbachev expect that the United States would be sending some financial assistance to meet these needs?

A. Not particularly. Not necessarily. But what he can expect is that we will have been helpful to him in the reforms that he knows that he has to undertake, and maybe this could lead to support. But there are things that have to happen, and I've been very up front with him personally and then in public statements as to what has to happen for the United States to send money. And incidentally, I don't — I'm trying to think on the Gorbachev letter — I don't think there was a request for sending money. And then I also told our Soviet partners that we had some problems — legal problems — the settlement of this Kerensky debt for example, before we would be free to give more, like financial support.

So, I wouldn't set a time frame on when and if the United States decides to go forward. But I must say that I hope the Soviets will view this as positive. And, indeed, I've contacted Mr. Gorbachev already by cable telling him I want to talk to him about the summit and telling him why I felt that it is positive and also congratulating him on his landslide win. Certain readings I was doing before then — I wasn't sure that it was going to work out quite that way.

But he's in the political arena, and he did pretty darn well, and I congratulated him.

Q. Mr. President, for 40 years we've spent untold billions to fight the Soviet Union. Is it conceivable, as you and Secretary Baker have portrayed, that the American taxpayer would not be willing to spend a dime to help them now?

A. We are trying to help them now; and I think we're going to send the kind of help that, in the long run, will be most beneficial to them. And they need reform, and they know it. And we're going to try in every way to facilitate that reform because we are in a very different age. But we have some problems. I'm not particularly enthusiastic about the intercontinental ballistic missiles aimed at U.S. cities. I find it a little contradictory to think that they will continue to spend $5 billion a year for Cuba, a totalitarian system whose leader is swimming against this tide of democracy and freedom that is lifting up most hopes in the Soviet Union. So, certain things have to happen before I, as President, will make recommendations for direct financial aid. So, what we're trying to do is carry our part of the load in helping the reforms.

Q. In your discussions, why did Germany and other countries think it's necessary now?

A. Well, Germany has some very special interest that we understand. As I said over in London, Helen [Helen Thomas, United Press International], we're not urging everybody to march in lockstep, just as in our programs for Central America—I want to see more help from the G-7 and the G-24 and anybody else who will listen to help the democracies in Central and South America.

And they've got certain priorities, and I hope they will be able to help in this way. But if we go forward as we have in assisting Nicaragua and Panama, I don't feel that everybody has to move in lockstep on that support for democracy.

Q. Mr. President, the Final Communique here reflecting your views in no small part on agriculture subsidies calls upon each nation to "make substantial progressive reductions in support and protection of agriculture." Does this mean, sir, that you're prepared to ask Congress to abolish some of the more notorious forms of support and subsidy that are part of our farm program?

A. Absolutely! And we have to do it, and it's a two way street. And I expect there would be some political opposition because, like many of these countries, we protect. But I am convinced, and I believe Congress would support the concept, that if we all do this and we all reduce barriers and we all make a freer trading system, that the United States can compete. But I'm sure I would have some obstacles from the supporters of certain programs that have been in existence for a long time.

But that's a little down the road now, and I think as far as the EC [European Community] goes, it's a little down the road. So what we're trying to do is move the whole thing forward without saying that we have to have tomorrow totally unprotected trade. I'd like to shoot for that some day. I've said that before.

Q. Well, how soon, sir, will you be going to Congress with a legislative package to begin to undo—

A. As soon as we see what progress is made in the GATT. That's where the next action is, is in these talks that are coming up—I think it's just on the 23d of this month or sometime. That's why I think this language that we worked out and that all of you have, I think, now is encouraging, because we all know that agriculture has been a major stumbling block.

And my special trade representative, Carla Hills, impressed on me the need to move that particular category forward, and we did get agreement. But the next step before we talk about needing a legislative package is to get agreement out of the GATT.

Economic Assistance for the Soviet Union

Q. Mr. President, if the study delays a decision on aid to the Soviet Union beyond German reunification, would it not be expected that there would be a lessening of interest in the summit countries in helping the Soviets if the German unification question is resolved by that time?

A. No. I think events are changing so fast that different countries are going to look at this with slightly different senses of priority. But in the meantime, this study will go forward. We have sent, in a bilateral sense, many missions to the Soviet Union. Alan Greenspan [Chairman of the Federal Reserve Board] was over there on his own. We've had [Attorney General] Dick

Thornburgh over there talking about helping reorder the justice system. We have people from the stock markets over there. We've had a wide array of individuals and groups of business people go. And so, that process of trying to assist in change and in reform is underway bilaterally.

But this look that the IMF will coordinate and be done by these other agencies will kind of give an official—at least for the G-7, we will look at it in rather an official way and then see if we can decide on more collective action at the next summit or whether we proceed individually on a case by case basis.

Environmental Policies

Q. Mr. President, on the question of the environment, you, in the past, and your Chief of Staff [John H. Sununu], to say at least two, have always said that there has not been enough information—you needed to study more. Now you're prepared to move, particularly on the global warming question. Who twisted your arm? What changed your mind, sir?

A. I think we're moving forward because we recognize there is a problem. I thought we called for more data in here. Clearly, we need more. When you take the NASA study—and then some people point to that as challenging the concepts of global climate change—why, I think everybody—well, put it this way, everybody at this summit agreed that we needed more scientific information.

But the steps that we've recommended here in this communique we can enthusiastically endorse. So, I think we came out with a reasoned position, not a radical position that's going to throw a lot of American men and women out of jobs. And yet we've done an awful lot (and I think others at the summit recognized it) in terms of cleaning up the air. We've got a proposal, and I told them proudly of it, to redo our Clean Air Act, and they were very much impressed with that. You might have heard Prime Minister Mulroney's supportive comments about that. So, there's a lot of things working bilaterally in terms of emissions, and I think we have a very reasonable position at this point.

Q. If I could follow, there seems to be a little wiggle room on CO_2. Are you making a clear commitment to do something about it?

A. I wouldn't read anything into these texts beyond what is actually printed there.

Arms Control

Q. I understand that it would take some time for the Soviet economy to reform. But are you suggesting, when you link Soviet aid to arms control, that you could never imagine any direct aid so long as there are any Soviet weapons aimed at the West?

A. No, I didn't say that. But I would really prefer to stand on what I've simply said. The world is changing very fast. But they know that we've got some big difficulties on the regional questions and on the fact that a lot of missiles are aimed at the United States. A good way to start in doing something about that is to have a successful conclusion on the START [strategic arms reduction] treaty. So, I don't want to go beyond where we are right now. If you'd have asked me last year at this time if I could have predicted the rapidity of change, the changes that have taken place, I couldn't have predicted them. So, I don't know exactly where we will be, but I do know that this proposal we've made is sound.

Q. Do you think if the IMF does say that some direct aid is necessary that perhaps that would spur greater arms control movement?

A. Excuse me, the IMF says what?

Q. If the IMF study suggests that direct aid is appropriate, do you think that in turn could stimulate or speed up the arms control on behalf of the Soviets?

A. I would hope so. I think Gorbachev is committed to a fast track on strategic arms.

Q. On aid to the Soviets, you keep saying that the American people simply aren't ready to give cash to Gorbachev. Now, if the IMF comes back with a report, Gorbachev accepts some of those recommendations, they cut way back on aid to Cuba — largely which consists of oil shipments, after all, not money — he does these things you want, are you ready before the 1992 Presidential campaign to go out there and tell the American people you would send American cash or supply credits to Gorbachev?

A. Your question is too hypothetical. I can't go into a hypothesis like that. And we will wait and see. We've taken a path. It's based on the facts right now. And I would just say that I think Mr.

Gorbachev understands that at this juncture sending money from the United States is not in the cards. And he knows what needs to be done to change the formula, and I'd like to think he's going to try. And maybe he'll come out of this Congress where many predicted his demise and feel encouraged to go forward. But I'm not going to answer a hypothetical question of that nature.

Q. Let me ask you this. You got some sort of a delay on aid to the Soviets because of this study, which will not be completed until December. A lot of people are painting this summit as they did the NATO Summit: as a victory for George Bush across the board, whether it's cutting agricultural subsidies for Europeans or whether it's the environment. What didn't you get at this summit that you wanted? What did you lose here?

A. In the first place, I don't — I'm glad to hear that — but really, honestly, we don't look at it as a victory for one side and a defeat for another. That's the good thing about this G-7 group. And so, there weren't any winners or losers in it, but there was compromise along the way. But again, I'm not going to reopen the hard work that went into this agreement by saying what we would like to have had that was different. But it did work out in a way that I can strongly support. But again, excuse me for not projecting winners or losers or helping you with what we got and what we didn't get.

Q. Mr. President, at the NATO Summit and then again here, it seems as though you have developed a special working relationship with Chancellor Kohl. I wondered — one of the German delegation also said that after you had supported him on Soviet aid he couldn't come back and not support you on the environment. Can you describe that relationship, and would you say that's a fair assessment?

A. It's not a fair assessment because he's a bulldog when it comes to the environment. He's a fighter for what he believes in. And I think he felt satisfied with what he got. And maybe he would like to have had more. But when we focused in on this forestry agreement and on the question of the rain forests, I think Chancellor Kohl felt that he had achieved something that he came here to achieve.

But the relationship is — it's hard to explain. I do think that the Germans appreciate the fact that we have stood at their side on this question of German

reunification. I think that's an element. But there isn't any quid pro quo. There was no "I owe you one" or "I want to pay you" for taking what we feel is a principled position in terms of German reunification. And he fought hard. And there were some compromises in terms of wording. But I think the declaration in terms of reforestation and the forestry agreement and the Amazon all speak to his keen interests. And so, I hope that he will be able to tell his constituencies and all the German people that there is a new awareness and a heightened awareness because of the eloquence that he brought to bear on the question.

Q. Would you say, however, that you find more common ground or common interest with Chancellor Kohl than you would perhaps with [Prime Minister of the United Kingdom] Margaret Thatcher?

A. No, I wouldn't say that at all. But I find plenty of common ground with both. Nice try. [Laughter] You're going to get me in trouble; they haven't even left town here.

Q. I have two questions about the summit's kind of do-your-own-thing on Soviet aid. One, is it really good for the alliance? And number two, doesn't it bode poorly for America's leadership in the alliance?

A. No, I think, without reopening the hypothesis of the earlier question about how the Americans fared, I think we're doing all right in the alliance. And it doesn't work, Craig [Craig Hines, Houston Chronicle], that you have to march in lockstep on all these questions. I don't feel that I have to defer on a lot of questions that we initiate on loans to the G-7. And I don't think they should have — these individual countries who have very special agendas and special relationships — I don't think that they should defer to us on these questions.

Now, when you get into some arms control initiatives or matters of that nature, why, obviously, you want to stay together as much as you can. And as the world — I don't worry about that; I don't worry about it all.

Q. Isn't it drawing it a little fine, though, to say arms control, yes, but aid to the Soviets — which, really, there were no conditions placed on, that could be used for anything, German aid that could be used for anything. Isn't that —

A. Well you may be a little ahead of me on what the Soviets plan to use the

German aid for, aid that has not yet been forthcoming. I understand that Chancellor Kohl is going to Moscow, I think—is that correct?—within the next couple of weeks. But we don't know that as to what conditions will be on the funding and how it will be used in the Soviet Union. But I gave him our position. He gave me his. But that's not enough to break up a strong alliance and a very comfortable and strong bilateral relationship between the Federal Republic and the United States.

Reforestation and Agricultural Subsidies

Q. Mr. President, on the forestry issue, there are a number of sentences in the declaration talking about the importance of preserving forests globally. What impact would that have on the American domestic field? Would it, for example, change the balance that your administration has been trying to strike on the issue of the Pacific Northwest forests and the spotted owl there?

A. No, we are committed to prudent forest management, but we're also committed to planting a billion trees a year and putting real emphasis on reforestation. So, I don't think there's any contradiction. Some would argue—some of the purists in the environmental movement—that you've got to stop where we are, not harvest any lumber at all. And some of it would be done in the protection of the owl, and some because they're opposed to harvesting the old growth forests. I don't share that view. And I do think we can find a balance where the net is an increase in the numbers of trees.

Q. If I could follow up: What response do you have to the people in Third World countries who argue that you're asking them to make sacrifices on their economic development, that you're not willing to ask American workers to make parallel sacrifices?

A. I think we have to find ways to assist those who would take that view. And I think many of our countries will move forward (and did not have great respect for the environment and now are doing a good job on it, and I would put the United States in that category—with pride, I might say) [and] should find ways to assist these countries.

Q. Back on agriculture, Mr. President. You said that you were encouraged about the language on agricultural subsidies. Could you say

why, specifically, when the U.S. gave in on the key question of allowing one common measure to be used for all subsidies? And also, on a separate matter, could you tell us whether you got any commitment for help from your allies on the Latin American aid initiative?

A. Not being a technical expert on these highly technical GATT negotiations, I relied heavily on advice from experts like Carla Hills, who is one—such an expert. And Clayton Yeutter, Bob Mosbacher, involved also. And these people who have been wrestling with the technicalities of the trade question were very pleased at the formulation we came up with. They felt without such formulation the whole successful conclusion of the GATT round was at stake. But they think that the wording we have that refers peripherally to this De Zeuuw report is enough now to move the agricultural discussion forward when they meet soon again.

What was the second part? I don't know on the others. I know that some of them have expressed an interest in helping, but I didn't ask for a collective decision out of the G-7 on that question.

Economic Assistance for the Soviet Union and China

Q. Mr. President, the Soviets have already reacted negatively to advance word of the part of the communique that says that reform would help them get further aid. What would you tell Mr. Gorbachev when you speak to him—why he should not view this as the allied countries saying: The Cold War is over; you lost. Here's what you have to do; here are our conditions for integrating you back into Western society?

A. I think you phrase it well, because we've got to be careful that we don't send the signal that we don't want to send. But I don't worry about this one because I sat up there at Camp David with Mr. Gorbachev in a very frank discussion and told him the problems that I have with going forward with financial aid. I've been quite open about it in the press conference following a highly successful NATO Summit.

And incidentally, I think the reaction from the Soviet Union on the NATO Summit has been extraordinarily positive, extraordinarily so; and some of that, I think, has been masked by the understandable attention given to the G-7 meeting here. But it's been extraordinarily positive.

And so far, I think—put it this way: It just totally diminishes the risk of the kind of misunderstanding that your question implies. Now, you saw the lively debate in the Peoples Congress [Soviet Union's Communist Party Congress]. It looks like our own Congress up there—yelling at each other and debating and calling people names and doing all these frantic things. So, I'm not saying that somebody's not going to jump up, having finished trying to filet Gorbachev, and jump on me for the way we've reacted in this summit. I am saying that I am not going to have misunderstanding creep in because of failure to communicate. And, indeed, I've already sent off a communication to Mr. Gorbachev, and I will be in touch with him personally very soon to discuss this. But I don't think there's too much of a danger of that.

Q. If I could follow up: In his letter to you in your role as host of this summit, did he ask for direct cash aid?

A. I need help on that, but I think not. My reaction is that he did not ask for that. I know he didn't have a price tag on it, but he listed several categories of places where we could give support, including credits.

Bob [Robert D. Blackwill, Special Assistant to the President and Senior Director for European and Soviet Affairs at the National Security Council], was that a proper answer? I don't want to—okay. So, I was right.

Q. Some of your colleagues accused you of a double standard, Mr. President, in supporting language yesterday that opened the door to lending to China, particularly if it moves toward economic reforms, and yet taking the much less flexible position regarding the Soviet Union. How do you respond to that?

A. I respond by saying we already have sanctions on China because China has not moved forward far enough on human rights. Those sanctions remain. We have offered the hope that if they take further steps in the human rights field more can be done. We've said that all of us together would consider World Bank loans— which right now are discouraged by the G-7—consider World Bank loans that would contribute to the reform of the Chinese economy. And then I think we added a little thing about especially those that would help on this world environmental problem.

So, my answer to those is that they're wrong and that the pressure is still on. And let's hope it will not be counterproductive. Again, my position is — and I think every summit leader there agrees with me, everyone, I believe — that we should not further isolate China. There have been some things that we can take some encouragement from. But the sanctions are on China. We took the lead on this question a year ago at the G-7 summit, and some who criticize me fail to realize that. But I want to see them move forward, and I want to see restored good relations with China. But we're not there yet.

Q. Do you believe that financial aid could play a role in stimulating reforms in the Soviet Union?

A. Well, some think that. I don't particularly agree with that. I think when you see the Japanese move forward, as they plan to do, to keep a commitment — they feel a solemn commitment — to China for this third yen loan, that they feel that way. I have great respect for Prime Minister Kaifu, and I had a long talk with him about that. As you know, they plan to move forward. Just as I can't get all exercised over what Chancellor Kohl does, I feel the same way about what Prime Minister Kaifu is doing. But he feels that the step he is about to take would encourage reformers. I'm not sure that he's right in this regard, and I think that the people in power there can build on the steps that they've taken in a way to satisfy the rest of the people in the G-7 that we should go back to more normal relations.

Q. Mr. President, a followup on Craig's question. In the past, the United States did call the tune on allied relations with the Soviet Union. Now that we're seeing key allies going their own way on aid to the Soviet Union, aren't we seeing at least a subtle change in the way the United States has to lead the alliance? Aren't you having to give a little more leeway to the allies now that the Cold War is over?

A. We're dealing in entirely different times. Earlier on, in terms of the alliance, we had a much more formidable military opposition. Now we see the Warsaw Pact in almost a state of disarray: we see troops coming out; we see democracies replacing totalitarian systems. So, you have an entirely different era. For the United States side, I think we have very good understanding inside the G-7 about the Soviet Union. But if your question is, Is it bad or does it alter the U.S. role if Chancellor Kohl,

for very special reasons, goes forward, I would argue that it does not.

President Gorbachev's Political Power

Q. Mr. President, there's a lot of concern over President Gorbachev's ability to hold on to power. Does his victory yesterday suggest he will be around for a good while despite his serious economic problems?

A. I don't know yet, but certainly he's surprised a lot of us in this room, hasn't he — including me. Who would have thought he'd have a three to one victory or whatever it was? I had the figures at the tip of my tongue a while back, because it was an impressive landslide inside a body where, if I had gone by just some impressions, I wouldn't have thought he had gotten quite that big a landslide. So, I don't know. And I think there's some discontent inside the Soviet Union. I think he's got enormous problems. I hope that what we're doing to help here will help with those problems. But certainly, I'd have to leave it there because I couldn't go beyond that. And I think if you go to experts you'll find divisions on that question.

Q. You don't think the election proves that he has a grip on power now?

A. Well, I think it does at this juncture, certainly in terms of the party. And certainly I think, the way he's handling his foreign affairs is probably getting great credit at home. I do understand there's consumer concern and that everybody, including Mr. Gorbachev and Mr. Shevardnadze, recognize that they have enormous economic problems inside the Soviet Union.

---

[1] Text from Weekly Compilation of Presidential Documents of July 16, 1990.
[2] Department of State Press Release 102, July 10, 1990.

Breakthrough to German Unification

LONDON DECLARATION ON A
TRANSFORMED NORTH ATLANTIC
ALLIANCE,
JULY 6, 1990 [1]

Issued by the Heads of State and Government participating in the meeting of the North Altantic Council in London [the NATO Summit], July 5-6, 1990

1. Europe has entered a new, promising era. Central and Eastern Europe is liberating itself. The Soviet Union has embarked on the long journey toward a free society. The walls that once confined people and ideas are collapsing. Europeans are determining their own destiny. They are choosing freedom. They are choosing economic liberty. They are choosing peace. They are choosing a Europe whole and free. As a consequence, this Alliance must and will adapt.

2. The North Atlantic Alliance has been the most successful defensive alliance in history. As our Alliance enters its fifth decade and looks ahead to a new century, it must continue to provide for the common defense. This Alliance has done much to bring about the new Europe. No one, however, can be certain of the future. We need to keep standing together, to extend the long peace we have enjoyed these past four decades. Yet our Alliance must be even more an agent of change. It can help build the structures of a more united continent, supporting security and stability with the strength of our shared faith in democracy, the rights of the individual, and the peaceful resolution of disputes. We reaffirm that security and stability do not lie solely in the military dimension, and we intend to enhance the political component of our Alliance as provided for by Article 2 of our Treaty.

3. The unification of Germany means that the division of Europe is also being overcome. A united Germany in the Atlantic Alliance of free democracies and part of the growing political and economic integration of the European Community will be an indispensable factor of stability, which is needed in the heart of Europe. The move within the European Community towards political union, including the development of a European identity in the domain of security, will also contribute to Atlantic solidarity and to the establishment of a just and lasting order of peace throughout the whole of Europe.

4. We recognise that, in the new Europe, the security of every state is inseparably linked to the security of its neighbors. NATO must become an institution where Europeans, Canadians and Americans work together not only for the common defense, but to build new partnerships with all the nations of Europe. The Atlantic Community must reach out to the countries of the East which were our adversaries in the Cold War, and extend to them the hand of friendship.

5. We will remain a defensive alliance and will continue to defend all the territory of all of our members. We have no aggressive intentions and we commit ourselves to the peaceful resolution of all disputes. We will never in any circumstance be the first to use force.

6. The member states of the North Atlantic Alliance propose to the member states of the Warsaw Treaty Organization a joint declaration in which we solemnly state that we are no longer adversaries and reaffirm our intention to refrain from the threat or use of force against the territorial integrity or political independence of any state, or from acting in any other manner inconsistent with the purposes and principles of the United Nations Charter and with the CSCE [Conference on Security and Cooperation in Europe] Final Act. We invite all other CSCE member states to join us in this commitment to nonaggression.

7. In that spirit, and to reflect the changing political role of the Alliance, we today invite President Gorbachev on behalf of the Soviet Union, and representatives of the other Central and Eastern European countries to come to Brussels and address the North Atlantic Council. We today also invite the governments of the Union of Soviet Socialist Republics, the Czech and Slovak Federal Republic, the Hungarian Republic, the Republic of Poland, the People's Republic of Bulgaria and Romania to come to NATO, not just to visit, but to establish regular diplomatic liaison with NATO. This will make it possible for us to share with them our thinking and deliberations in this historic period of change.

8. Our Alliance will do its share to overcome the legacy of decades of suspicion. We are ready to intensify military contacts, including those of NATO Military Commanders, with Moscow and other Central and Eastern European capitals.

9. We welcome the invitation to NATO Secretary General Manfred Worner to visit Moscow and meet with Soviet leaders.

10. Military leaders from throughout Europe gathered earlier this year in Vienna to talk about their forces and doctrine. NATO proposes another such meeting this autumn to promote common understanding. We intend to establish an entirely different quality of openness in Europe, including an agreement on "Open Skies".

11. The significant presence of North American conventional and U.S. nuclear forces in Europe demonstrates the underlying political compact that binds North America's fate to Europe's democracies. But, as Europe changes, we must profoundly alter the way we think about defense.

12. To reduce our military requirements, sound arms control agreements are essential. That is why we put the highest priority on completing this year the first treaty to reduce and limit conventional armed forces in Europe (CFE) along with the completion of a meaningful CSBM (confidence and security building measures) package. These talks should remain in continuous session until the work is done. Yet we hope to go further. We propose that, once a CFE Treaty is signed, follow-on talks should begin with the same membership and mandate, with the goal of building on the current agreement with additional measures, including measures to limit manpower in Europe. With this goal in mind, a commitment will be given at the time of signature of the CFE Treaty concerning the manpower levels of a unified Germany.

13. Our objective will be to conclude the negotiations on the follow-on to CFE and CSBMs as soon as possible and looking to the follow-up meeting of the CSCE to be held in Helsinki in 1992. We will seek through new conventional arms control negotiations, within

the CSCE framework, further far-reaching measures in the 1990s to limit the offensive capability of conventional armed forces in Europe, so as to prevent any nation from maintaining disproportionate military power on the continent. NATO's High Level Task Force will formulate a detailed position for these follow-on conventional arms control talks. We will make provisions as needed for different regions to redress disparities and to ensure that no one's security is harmed at any stage. Furthermore, we will continue to explore broader arms control and confidence building opportunities. This is an ambitious agenda, but it matches our goal: enduring peace in Europe.

14. As Soviet troops leave Eastern Europe and a treaty limiting conventional armed forces is implemented, the Alliance's integrated force structure and its strategy will change fundamentally to include the following elements:

— NATO will field smaller and restructured active forces. These forces will be highly mobile and versatile so that Allied leaders will have maximum flexibility in deciding how to respond to a crisis. It will rely increasingly on multinational corps made up of national units.
— NATO will scale back the readiness of its active units, reducing training requirements and the number of exercises.
— NATO will rely more heavily on the ability to build up larger forces if and when they might be needed.

15. To keep the peace, the Alliance must maintain for the foreseeable future an appropriate mix of nuclear and conventional forces, based in Europe, and kept up to date where necessary. But, as a defensive Alliance, NATO has always stressed that none of its weapons will ever be used except in self-defense and that we seek the lowest and most stable level of nuclear forces needed to secure the prevention of war.

16. The political and military changes in Europe, and the prospects of further changes, now allow the Allies concerned to go further. They will thus modify the size and adapt the tasks of their nuclear deterrent forces. They have concluded that, as a result of the new political and military conditions in Europe, there will be a significantly reduced role for substrategic nuclear systems of the shortest range. They have decided specifically that, once negotiations begin on short range nuclear

forces, the Alliance will propose, in return for reciprocal action by the Soviet Union, the elimination of all its nuclear artillery shells from Europe.

17. New negotiations between the United States and the Soviet Union on the reduction of short range nuclear forces should begin shortly after a CFE agreement is signed. The Allies concerned will develop an arms control framework for these negotiations which takes into account our requirements for far fewer nuclear weapons, and the diminished need for substrategic nuclear systems of the shortest range.

18. Finally, with the total withdrawal of Soviet stationed forces and the implementation of a CFE agreement, the Allies concerned can reduce their reliance on nuclear weapons. These will continue to fulfil an essential role in the overall strategy of the Alliance to prevent war by ensuring that there are no circumstances in which nuclear retaliation in response to military action might be discounted. However, in the transformed Europe, they will be able to adopt a new NATO strategy making nuclear forces truly weapons of last resort.

19. We approve the mandate given in Turnberry to the North Atlantic Council in Permanent Session to oversee the ongoing work on the adaptation of the Alliance to the new circumstances. It should report its conclusions as soon as possible.

20. In the context of these revised plans for defense and arms control, and with the advice of NATO Military Authorities and all member states concerned, NATO will prepare a new Allied military strategy moving away from "forward defense", where appropriate, towards a reduced forward presence and modifying "flexible response" to reflect a reduced reliance on nuclear weapons. In that connection, NATO will elaborate new force plans consistent with the revolutionary changes in Europe. NATO will also provide a forum for Allied consultation on the upcoming negotiations on short range nuclear forces.

21. The Conference on Security and Cooperation in Europe (CSCE) should become more prominent in Europe's future, bringing together the countries of Europe and North America. We support a CSCE Summit later this year in Paris which would include the signature of a CFE agreement and would set new standards for the establishment, and

preservation, of free societies. It should endorse, inter alia:
— CSCE principles on the right to free and fair elections;
— CSCE commitments to respect and uphold the rule of law;
— CSCE guidelines for enhancing economic cooperation, based on the development of free and competitive market economies; and
— CSCE cooperation on environmental protection.

22. We further propose that the CSCE Summit in Paris decide how the CSCE can be institutionalised to provide a forum for wider political dialogue in a more united Europe. We recommend that CSCE governments establish:
— a program for regular consultations among member governments at the heads of state and government or ministerial level, at least once each year, with other periodic meetings of officials to prepare for and follow up on these consultations;
— a schedule of CSCE review conferences once every two years to assess progress toward a Europe whole and free;
— a small CSCE secretariat to coordinate these meetings and conferences;
— a CSCE mechanism to monitor elections in all the CSCE countries, on the basis of the Copenhagen Document;
— a CSCE Centre for the Prevention of Conflict that might serve as a forum for exchanges of military information, discussion of unusual military activities, and the conciliation of disputes involving CSCE member states; and
— a CSCE parliamentary body, the Assembly of Europe, to be based on the existing parliamentary assembly of the Council of Europe, in Strasbourg, and include representatives of all CSCE member states.

The sites of these new institutions should reflect the fact that the newly democratic countries of Central and Eastern Europe form part of the political structures of the new Europe.

23. Today, our Alliance begins a major transformation. Working with all the countries of Europe, we are determined to create enduring peace on this continent.

PRESIDENT'S PRESS CONFERENCE FOLLOWING THE NATO SUMMIT, LONDON, JULY 6, 1990 [EXCERPTS] [1]

I'd like to begin by thanking Prime Minister Margaret Thatcher for hosting this splendid meeting, and I want to express my appreciation also to [NATO Secretary General] Manfred Woerner not only for his kind remarks just now but for his outstanding leadership in NATO and in this alliance which is at a turning point in its history.

I'm pleased to announce that my colleagues and I have begun a major transformation of the North Atlantic alliance, and we view it as a historic turning point. NATO has set a new path for peace. It's kept the peace for 40 years and today charted a new course for stability and cooperation in Europe.

We, as you know, are issuing a document, the London Declaration; and it makes specific proposals and establishes directions for the future in four key areas.

First, the London Declaration transforms our relationship with old adversaries. To those governments who confronted us in the Cold War, our alliance extends the hand of friendship. We reaffirm that we shall never be the first to use force against other states in Europe. And we propose a joint declaration between members of the alliance and member states of the Warsaw Pact which other CSCE states could join in, making a solemn commitment to nonaggression. We say to President Gorbachev: Come to NATO. We say to all the member states of the Warsaw Pact: Come to NATO and establish regular diplomatic liaison with the alliance.

And second, the London Declaration transforms the character of NATO's conventional defenses. We can start, and must start, by finishing the current CFE [conventional forces in Europe] talks this year. Once CFE is signed, we would begin follow-on negotiations to adopt additional measures, including measures to limit manpower in Europe. With this goal in mind, a commitment will be given when the CFE treaty is signed concerning the manpower levels of the armed forces of a united Germany. We will also seek in the nineties to achieve further far-reaching measures to limit the offensive capability of conventional armed forces. We'll change our strategy for a conventional defense. We agreed to move away from NATO's current strategy of forward defense to a reduced forward presence. We agreed, in addition, to make the principle of collective defense even more evident by organizing NATO troops into multinational corps.

And third, the London Declaration transforms NATO's nuclear strategy. For 23 years we've had a nuclear strategy called flexible response, developed to meet a danger of sudden overwhelming conventional attack. As that danger recedes, we've agreed to modify flexible response.

Nuclear deterrence has given us an unprecedented period of peace, and it will remain fundamental to our strategy. But by reducing its reliance on nuclear weapons, NATO in the new Europe will adopt a new strategy making its nuclear forces truly weapons of last resort.

This new strategy will require different forces. We've decided that once negotiations begin on short range nuclear forces we are prepared to eliminate all NATO nuclear artillery shells from Europe in return for reciprocal action by the Soviet Union. We agreed that this review should report its conclusions as soon as possible.

And fourth, the London Declaration transforms the alliance's vision for the CSCE and the structure for building a Europe whole and free. We know the CSCE process — bringing together North America and all of Europe — can provide a structure for Europe's continued political development; and that means new standards for free elections, the rule of law, economic liberty, and environmental cooperation. And we agreed today on six initiatives to give life to CSCE's principles and realize its potential.

As you can see, the London Declaration will bring fundamental change to every aspect of the alliance's work. This is indeed a day of renewal for the Atlantic community. For more than 40 years, we've looked for this day — a day when we have already moved beyond containment, with unity on this continent overcoming division. And now that day is here, and all peoples from the Atlantic to the Urals, from the Baltic to the Adriatic, can share in its promise.

I'd be glad to take some questions. Helen [Helen Thomas, United Press International]?

Q. Mr. President, with the end of the Cold War, the drawdown in forces, and eventual denuclearization of Europe, are you now ready to give some economic help — as other allies want — to include the Soviet Union and Eastern Europe so that they can get back on their feet, as we did after World War II with Germany and Japan?

A. Well, we have given substantial help to certain countries in Eastern Europe. I have had a discussion — not here at NATO but with Mr. Gorbachev and others at different times — about support for the Soviet Union. We are most interested in helping them go forward with their reforms.

But there was no decision taken, certainly, to send money to the Soviet Union. I have some big problems with that one. I think the American people do. But there are ways that we can assist in this transformation, in this reform that is taking place in the Soviet Union.

Q. Well, you're not opposed to other countries giving it?

A. If the Germans decide they want to do that, that's their business. But I have made very clear to those who have spoken to me about this that at this juncture we have some serious problems, and I've not been under any false colors about that at all.

Q. President Gorbachev has imposed a two year deadline on himself and the communist leaders for reversing their country's economic tailspin. Does your reluctance to give the Soviets any financial aid complicate his chances for success in meeting that deadline?

A. I hope not, because as you know, not only have I spoken very fondly of and enthusiastically about what he's trying to do in terms of reform but I've spoken about him personally and about our interest in seeing him succeed. And he's got some extraordinarily difficult problems, but I don't think our position on financial aid at this time should — hopefully, it will not complicate his standing. He deserves support for this reform.

Q. Do you view Western aid for the Soviet Union now as a subsidy for its military machine?

A. I'll tell you, we've got some problems that I've been very frank with concerning the Soviets. And one of them is a great percentage of their GNP going into the military. Another is some regional problems that perhaps are unique to the United States, but things that concern me — spending $5 billion a year in Cuba, for example, to sustain a totalitarian regime that is highly critical of the Soviet Union from time to time. So, we have some regional problems. We have some reform problems that should take place before financial support can be given. But perhaps there are ways that we can assist them as we go forward with credit or other matters before we go to direct government loans.

U.S. Armed Forces in Europe

Q. Mr. President, with the threat receding, in the way your communique describes, do you think it's inevitable that at some point in the next few years the Europeans will decide it's better that American troops just go home? And what do you say to American taxpayers to convince them that it's worth continuing to pay the bill to have them in Europe?

A. I don't think the American troops will stay against the will of the host country. I don't want to see American forces deployed where American forces are not wanted. I don't want to see Soviet forces deployed where Soviet forces are not wanted. And I expect the same would be true of other nationalities' forces as well. But I don't foresee that day because I think the alliance has spoken rather eloquently about the need for a common defense. And all the members of the alliance are united in their view that a U.S. force presence in Europe is stabilizing and very, very important. So, I don't see that day looming up on the horizon.

Q. But do you fear that American taxpayers' support for that continuation might be eroding?

A. I see some attacks on this, and I think this NATO declaration should help in that regard. But I view it as my responsibility to make clear to the American taxpayer why it is in our interest to help keep the peace. And that's exactly what these forces are engaged in.

Economic Assistance for the Soviet Union

Q. Mr. President, in light of the stress that's been placed here on the continued cohesion within this alliance, sir, would it not be a major breach of that cohesion if a country like West Germany were to provide direct aid to the Soviet Union in light of the deep concerns which you have expressed about such aid from the West?

A. No, I don't feel that that's a breach of alliance cohesion. The Germans have their own bilateral relationship with the Soviet Union, and it doesn't concern me one bit. I've not made one single effort to try to have the Germans look differently at that question.

Q. Mr. President, would it not then be possible that aid from our ally West Germany would, at least arguably or indirectly, flow to a country like Cuba?

A. Well, if you want to say that anything that goes to the Soviet Union facilitates aid to Cuba, I suppose we could say the same about our trade. But I don't think that would be a fair charge to make against the Germans.

* * *

Eastern European Membership in NATO

Q. Mr. President, back to the declaration. You're inviting the Warsaw Pact countries to come to NATO as observers. What if they want to become members of NATO — Hungary, for instance, or even Poland? Are you saying by inviting them to just be observers that you do not look favorably on them becoming full members?

A. I'm saying NATO views this as an open invitation, and who knows what will happen in terms of membership down the line? That's not in the cards right this minute. We're just coming out of an adversarial environment of varying — I think there's varying degrees of enthusiasm for what you're talking about amongst the members of the Warsaw Pact at this juncture, so I'd say it's premature.

Q. Would you oppose any country — for instance, Hungary — becoming a member of NATO?

A. Not forever. But at this juncture, I support the NATO doctrine.

Modernization of Strategic Nuclear Weapons

Q. Mr. President, in your communique you talk about nuclear weapons becoming truly weapons of last resort. You say the fundamental strategy of the alliance is being transformed here. As part of this review, are you considering going back home and taking another look at some of the strategic nuclear modernization programs that you have supported — looking at some of the very expensive weapons programs that some say should be a bonus, a part of the "peace dividend"?

A. Not as a result of anything that's transpired here in NATO, no. We are interested in strategic arms agreements with the Soviets. The Soviets, as we all know, have indeed modernized their forces. We're on the horns of a dilemma in that question, you might say, because we have not [modernized] to the degree they have. But that was not a consideration here at NATO, nor has anything transpired here that will make me go home with a different approach to strategic arms.

Q. If I may follow up: So, you'll proceed across the board with strategic modernization? Your commitment to that —

A. Yes. I will proceed in negotiating with the Soviets to achieve a strategic arms agreement.

NATO Policy

Q. Mr. President, how much did threats to *perestroika* and reforms in the Soviet Union play in changes you've announced today at NATO?

A. You mean, what's going on at the Congress [28th Communist Party Congress of the Soviet Union]? None, in my view. I mean, I think what's contributed to the changes in our approach — NATO — are the changes that have taken place, particularly since our last meeting, in terms of Eastern Europe and in terms of the Soviets' willingness to withdraw forces, hopefully, through a CFE agreement. So, I don't think anything was short — that there was short term thinking as a result of the debates that are going on in Moscow this very day.

Q. Well, if I can follow up then: What kind of messages do the changes announced today send to Gorbachev?

A. They send to him that here's an alliance that you should view, Mr. Gorbachev, as defensive and not threatening. And, please, convince your military and others in the Soviet Union of this fact.

You see, from my discussions with Mr. Gorbachev and others, I've had the feeling that they have viewed NATO as much more threatening to them than the way in which I've looked at NATO. But now, as a result of the actions that we've taken here, I think it should be clear to the Soviet military, to Mr. Gorbachev, to his adversaries and to his friends inside the Soviet Union that NATO is changing. And to the degree they had seen it as a threat to their shores or to their borders, they should look at it as not a threat to their borders or to their people.

Anytime you sit down with people from the Soviet Union, they tell you of the fact that they lost from 20 million to 27 million lives. It's ingrained in them.

They do it not as a defensive mechanism but they do it because they feel very strongly about that. I hope that they will look at the changes that NATO has taken and say: Well, if NATO had been a threat to us, it no longer is a threat to us. And then I hope we can go forward to further document that spirit by mutual agreements on arms control.

Q. How are you going to communicate what's in this document to Mr. Gorbachev and the people there? Are you going to talk with him personally? Did the NATO leaders decide on some other method of communication with him to let him know what it means, what the communique means?

A. The NATO leaders have decided that the Secretary General will be going there, and that will be a very good face-to-face chance to discuss these matters. I believe our Secretary of State is meeting soon with Mr. Shevardnadze [Soviet Foreign Minister], and you can be sure the matters will be discussed then. And then, in all likelihood, I will discuss it personally by telephone with Mr. Gorbachev.

I think it's very important that the leader of the United States and the leader of the Soviet Union stay in touch. In fact, when he was here in Washington, we talked about more such contacts. So, perhaps within the next couple of weeks, I will be talking to him about what transpired, because I want to make some of these points here again, particularly that they ought not to view NATO as a threat and certainly ought not to view it as a roadblock to progress in arms control or withdrawal of conventional forces or whatever it might be.

Soviet Response to NATO Policies

Q. Mr. President, what kind of tangible response would you like to see from President Gorbachev now to this? And I'm thinking particularly of the issue of Germany and NATO.

A. In terms of the question of Germany and NATO, I would like to see the tangible response be an acceptance of the concept that a unified Germany in NATO is not only good but that it certainly is no threat to them. And we've had long talks with Mr. Gorbachev about that. And perhaps this declaration will be a document that he can use to convince others that a unified Germany in NATO is in the interest of stability and world peace. So, I think that is probably the most important message. And then I'd like to think that out

of this he would feel more confident in going forward with arms control, bringing the Two Plus Four talks to a conclusion, and there's a wide array of other things as well.

*   *   *

NATO Invitation to President Gorbachev

Q. Mr. President, Mikhail Gorbachev is already under fire from conservatives for essentially giving away Eastern Europe. Are you at all concerned, sir, that by inviting him to speak to NATO you're further undermining him? And I have a followup.

A. No, not only do I think we're not undermining him but I would think that would send a signal that NATO has no hostile intentions to the Soviet Union. So, I would hope nobody at home would consider this an effort to undermine Mr. Gorbachev, nor would it have the effect of undermining a man who has clearly tried to move forward, who has presided over the Soviet Union at a time when this fantastic change towards democracy and freedom has taken place in Eastern Europe. And you're seeing that same kind of quest for change – democratic change and economic change – inside the Soviet Union. So, I don't think it would have the effect that the question suggests.

Q. If he accepts your invitation, sir, will you attend that meeting, or would it be an occasion for some sort of a superpower summit?

A. The level of the Gorbachev meeting at NATO has not been determined. And I would be guided by what the other NATO members think is appropriate. The level at which Mr. Gorbachev would speak to NATO has not been set. If it was a head of state level, why, of course, I would attend. Others have addressed NATO at varying levels.

East-West Relations and Political and Economic Change

Q. Having attended quite a number of these things, these NATO conferences, I'd like to ask a question, Mr. President, that I asked – [inaudible] – is this to some extent a celebration of the victory of NATO in the Cold War – the Cold War is over and NATO has won? Or don't you believe it's the idea that NATO has won the Cold War?

A. Excuse me, back up, now. I've tried to avoid code words, and the Cold

War being over is something that I'd rather not comment on. I don't think we're dealing in terms of victory and defeat. We're dealing in terms of how do we stabilize and guarantee the peace and security of Europe. So, to the degree a chief of state or head of government dwells on the kinds of rhetoric that you understandably ask about, I think it is counterproductive. Does that answer it?

Q. Would you say that NATO has to a great extent caused Gorbachev to be – that the whole changes in Eastern Europe have to some extent been caused by what's been going on in Western Europe for the last 40 years?

A. I would say to some degree that the changes in Eastern Europe and in the Soviet Union have been because they have seen the success of market economies. They've seen a craving for freedom and democracy on the parts of people. And to the degree NATO countries contributed to that proper perception, so be it. I'd like to think that – I'm convinced that NATO's solidarity during the last 40 years has guaranteed the peace for Europe. And when you look back at history, it is a long peace, given some of the conflagrations on this continent. So, I think NATO deserves a lot of credit.

But I think the yearning for freedom and democracy is pretty fundamental. NATO has nothing to do with the changes in our own Western Hemisphere, and yet you're seeing now the emergence of democracies, and you've seen the emergence of free people there. So, it's fundamental: People want democracy and freedom. But I think NATO's major contribution has been to keeping the peace, and yet it has set an example that I think many in Eastern Europe now want to follow.

Changes in the Soviet Union

Q. Mr. President, how do you square your concern over stability in Europe, which is the new purpose of NATO, with increasing signs of instability in the Soviet Union, particularly on the political and economic front? And what can you do to put those two pieces of the puzzle together?

A. A very good and very difficult question because, frankly, one thing we do is stay out of the internal affairs of the Soviet Union. I realize that some think that I'm not staying out of the internal affairs of the Soviet Union when I speak pleasantly about Mr. Gorbachev.

But I think they have to sort it out now. They have to decide what they want, how much of their gross national product ought to go into arms, whether the threat is much less than they have historically perceived. And once they take that decision, then we in the West will stand ready to work very cooperatively with them. But I think the next move, what I'm saying, is up to them. I think they have to make these determinations. And in the meantime, NATO, having seen the changes that have taken place in Eastern Europe and the predicted changes in terms of force levels, can go forward with what I think people will view as a historic document.

Excuse me, I did tell you I'd get over here.

Nuclear Artillery Shells

Q. Thank you very much. How conditional is the proposal to remove nuclear artillery from Europe? Are you actually saying that you will not do this unless the Soviet Union does likewise? Are you saying it should be part of negotiations, or are you actually merely inviting the Soviet Union to withdraw their nuclear artillery?

A. Well, I'd certainly invite them to do it, and the document is fairly clear on that point. I think that the withdrawal of nuclear artillery on the part of the West is conditioned on the withdrawal of Soviet nuclear artillery.

German Membership in NATO

Q. On paragraph 12—"manpower levels of united Germany"—what happened to nonsingularization of Germany?

A. Well, I don't see that as singularization. That was a question that had to be addressed anyway. And I think that you're going to see the United States addressing its force levels through CFE talks. So, I would think that this is not what I have always thought of as singularization, trying to single Germany out, for example— a united Germany—from being a part of NATO. I think what it simply says is this question, at an appropriate time, will be addressed. And we are going forward, addressing ourselves now to U.S. force levels under our conventional force talks. So, I don't see any contradiction in that.

East-West Relations

Q. Would you say that you are hoping that Gorbachev can convince other people that through this document that they do not have to fear NATO? Are you saying that some of the people in the Soviet Union are imposing this fear to NATO—to Mr. Gorbachev, and who are these people? I have a followup question, please.

A. If I got the first part of it correctly, I think there's been a historic fear on the part of some about the West because of the Soviets' own history. I happen to believe that that fear has been misplaced all along. But to the degree people still have that fear, and they look at this document, it would seem to be de minimus. I can't single out which people they are, but I think there has been a historic concern on the part of the Soviets because of their own history in—certainly as recently as World War II, with an enormous loss of life. I think over the years, as we have improved our relations with the Soviet Union and, indeed, as they have changed, those fears have diminished. I think—given the new openness, the *glasnost*—I think they're going to diminish even more.

What was the followup?

Q. How do you expect that Mr. Gorbachev can be helped in his present problems in the Soviet Union with this London Declaration?

A. I think he will say: Look, NATO has indeed changed in response to the changes that have taken place in Eastern Europe. If I were him, I'd say: I've been right. They're changing. And now I want to go forward with the United States and negotiate some more deals. I want to see us reform. I want to see us stop some of what we've been doing in various regions around the world that others view as detrimental to the interests of freedom and democracy. And so, if I were him, I would take a hard look at this document. I'd listen carefully to what he hears from Manfred Woerner when he goes there. And I would think he could say, We've been right to reach out as we have tried to do to the United States and, indeed, to improve relations with countries in Western Europe. They're changing. They have now changed their doctrine because of steps that I, Mr. Gorbachev, have taken. And I get on the offense. Then let the rest of us help him with some of his hardliners. And there's plenty of work to do.

But I would think that he would view this as a very positive step forward

and one that vindicates some of the moves that he's made over the past year or two.

EIGHT POINT SOVIET-GERMAN [FRG] AGREEMENT ON GERMAN UNIFICATION, JULY 16, 1990 [2]

1. German Unification will include the Federal Republic [of Germany], the GDR [German Democratic Republic] and Berlin.

2. When unification is completed, Four Power rights and responsibilities will be abrogated, granting the unified German state full sovereignty, beginning at the moment of unification.

3. Exercising its full sovereignty, a unified Germany will be able to choose freely and independently whether it wants to belong to a military alliance, and, if so, which one, in keeping with the CSCE Final Act. I [Chancellor Kohl] have made clear the view of the Federal Republic Government that unified Germany should be a member of the Atlantic Alliance and I am certain this is also the view of the Government of the GDR.

4. Unified Germany will conclude a bilateral treaty with the Soviet Union regulating troop withdrawals from the GDR, to be completed in three to four years. In addition, a transitional agreement on the effects of introducing the Deutschmark in the GDR will be concluded with the Soviet Union for this three to four year period.

5. As long as Soviet troops continue to be stationed on the territory of the former GDR, NATO structures will not be expanded to include this part of Germany. This will not stand in the way of the immediate application of Articles 5 and 6 of the NATO Treaty right from the outset. The Federal Republic's non-integrated units, i.e. its territorial defense units, can be stationed in Berlin and on the territory of the present day GDR immediately after German unification.

6. We feel that troops of the three Western Powers should remain in West Berlin after unification for the duration of the Soviet military presence on the territory of the present day GDR. The Federal Government will request this of the Western Powers and will settle details concerning the stationing of troops with the individual governments.

7. The Federal Government is prepared to make a pledge at the ongoing Vienna talks [on conventional

forces] to reduce the strength of unified German forces to 370,000. Reductions will commence when the first Vienna treaty goes into effect.

8. A unified Germany will refrain from the manufacture, possession, and use of ABC weapons and will remain a party to the [Nuclear] Nonproliferation Treaty.

PRESIDENT'S STATEMENT ON UNIFIED GERMANY'S MEMBERSHIP IN NATO, JULY 16, 1990 [3]

I welcome President Gorbachev's statement, at his press conference with Chancellor Kohl, accepting a united Germany's right to choose to remain a member of NATO. This comment demonstrates statesmanship and strengthens efforts to build enduring relationships based on cooperation. It can be seen as a response, perhaps in part, to the outcome of the NATO Summit in London, where the alliance displayed its readiness to adapt to the new realities in Europe and reach out to former adversaries in the East.

Five months ago, in February, Chancellor Kohl and I agreed that a united Germany should remain a full member of the North Atlantic alliance, including its military structures. East German Prime Minister de Maiziere joins us in supporting continued German membership in NATO. The Helsinki Final Act guarantees Germany's right to make this choice. And we think this solution is in the best interests of all the countries of Europe, including the Soviet Union.

---

[1] Text from Weekly Compilation of Presidential Documents, July 9, 1990.

[2] Excerpt from FRG Chancellor Helmut Kohl's statement at a joint press conference with Soviet President Mikhail Gorbachev, Zheleznododsk, U.S.S.R. Text provided by the Press Department, Embassy of the Federal Republic of Germany, Washington.

[3] Text from Weekly Compilation of Presidential Documents, July 23, 1990.

Joint Press Conference Following Third Two-Plus-Four Ministerial in Paris

Following is the Transcript of Secretary Baker's Joint Press Conference with Foreign Ministers Roland Dumas of France, Hans Dietrich Genscher of the Federal Republic of Germany, Markus Meckel of the German Democratic Republic, Krzysztof Skubiszewski of Poland, Douglas Hurd of the United Kingdom, and Eduard Shevardnadze of the Soviet Union in Paris, July 17, 1990 [1]

Foreign Minister Dumas. Ladies and gentlemen, we are going to report on the work we have done today. There were three rounds, so to speak. In the morning we met, the Two-Plus-Four. The six: the Ministers of the Federal Republic of Germany and the Democratic Republic of Germany, the United States, the United Kingdom, France and the USSR. The second period was taken up by a working luncheon which included the Minister of Foreign Affairs of Poland. And the third period or round this afternoon with the participation of the Polish Minister. And during the third part of this meeting we dealt especially with Polish affairs and questions.

Now ladies and gentlemen, the process of the German reunification puts an end to the sorry period of the Cold War, the division of the German people, and the division of our European continent. Of course, the reunification of Germany is something that the German people themselves have to do, and we are happy to note that everything goes all right. But since the partition of Germany was very hard to deal with, as well as the legal situation after the Second World War it gave rise to, we had to take into account the external circumstances—the effects of such a reunification that was referred to in Strasbourg at the European Council meeting in December last year, on the initiative of the President of the French Republic. It has been said then that the problem of borders should be solved. That was the reason for which the group of the six has been set up. The six, the Two-Plus-Four, have already met in Bonn and Berlin. These two meetings clarified the issues. And it has been agreed in Berlin, for instance, that our goal should be to reach a consensus and cogency between the reunification of

Germany and its regaining its sovereignty. And it has also been agreed that the group of six should end its work for the summit of the CSCE to be held on the 19th of November in Paris.

Events Since Last Meeting

I think we should be happy for the decisions taken since then in several institutions, that is, since our last meeting in Berlin. In particular, I refer to the summit meeting of the countries of the Atlantic Alliance, 5 and 6 July, which put a definitive end to the Cold War and established a new type of relationship and security in Europe. That was started in London. And the recent meetings between Mr. Gorbachev and Mr. Genscher in Moscow led to very substantial progress in relations between the Soviet Union and Germany, and a very important step was therefore taken in Moscow.

The ministers of Foreign Affairs, who met today in Paris, took note with great satisfaction of the statement of Chancellor Kohl and Mr. Gorbachev. After these brief remarks on behalf of my country, I could say that there's no obstacle for a united Germany to be reestablished with sovereignty before the end of the year. And it's in full conformity with what France asked for and negotiated for quite a long time. It's a very important step in the setting up of a solid and free Europe, entirely freed from past conflicts.

Achievements Today

Now, today's meeting. A few words about that. This meeting is to be considered within this general framework and it enabled us to do away with several obstacles and therefore to make another and probably decisive step towards what we call a definitive settlement. We are agreed that Germany herself would decide on the role in the military and political systems that is to be found in the Final Act of Helsinki. The question of Soviet troops in the present territory of the GDR, that will be settled by a bilateral agreement between the U.S.S.R. and the united Germany. It has been asked from our political directors to start drafting the final settlement I alluded to. But you understood it, I am sure. The main part of our meeting had to do with the problem of borders and especially Oder-Neisse border. The Polish Foreign Minister participated in that part of our work, and even at the lunch, as provided for when the Ottawa group decided upon it. I think I speak for all my colleagues that we rejoiced in this participation of the Polish Minister. And it has been a very fruitful meeting and very positive.

I could say that our meeting enabled us to register a general agreement on the way in which one could settle the problem of the border between Germany and Poland as regards principles and ways and means and the calendar of that settlement.

On the invitation of the Soviet Foreign Minister, our next meeting — ministerial meeting — will be held on the 12th of September in Moscow. Therefore, this meeting today ends with the satisfaction of all concerned. I am very happy especially that Poland participated in this today and in the general satisfaction we all feel. I am especially happy that this meeting could have taken place in Paris. Now I will give the floor to the Polish Foreign Minister.

Foreign Minister Skubiszfewski. Thank you, Mr. Chairman. I would like to express the thankfulness and the joy of the Polish government because my country was represented during this conference and participated in the debate. Especially I am happy that this meeting has taken place in Paris, in France, and of the results obtained. And I believe that as regards the problem of the border between Germany and Poland, on both sides, that the two German states and Poland are equally satisfied. Raising that was my main purpose — the question of the confirmation of that border — and decisions have been taken and language has been decided which are entirely satisfactory.

Polish-German Agreement

As you know, Poland proposed some time ago that a treaty be concluded between a united Germany and Poland on the basis of a draft we submitted as to where the provisions regarding the border were. The main features and the treaty now will concentrate only on the topic of the border in order to facilitate things, and it is within the realm of legal texts and constitutions, inter-

national law and national law of Germany and Poland. But I also think that — and there we concur with our German friends — that one should, as soon as possible, conclude another treaty in order to settle all questions of good neighbors between Poland and united Germany. That is something which will take place later.

The border, as I said, has been confirmed. And you know that starting with the Potsdam Agreement in 1945, one always stressed, on both sides, the Polish stand: that we needed a peace settlement in order to determine and delineate that border. After today's decision, it is no longer necessary because we achieved final results.

In my contribution to the meeting, I referred to other problems also of concern to Poland, in particular the economic question. And I'm in a position to tell you that in this field also we felt that Germany was fully understanding. We had a very favorable proposal from Minister Genscher about a meeting between Germany and Poland this summer in order to discuss the very difficult economic problems rising for Poland as a result of the past situation. And I am prepared to reply to questions you would care to put to me.

Foreign Minister Dumas. Mr. Baker has the floor.

Secretary Baker. Ladies and gentlemen, about six months ago in Ottawa we started this Two-Plus-Four process. It was a new process designed to fit new times. I think it would be fair to say that our aim was ambitious, but none too ambitious for this new age of European hope and freedom.

Our aim, of course, was to facilitate the peaceful and democratic unification of Germany, as well as the reconciliation of Europe, and today I think we draw much nearer to that target. We are keeping to the pace that's necessary to complete our work and to meet the target, to terminate the residual Four Power rights and responsibilities and to accord Germany its full sovereignty at the time of unification in 1990.

Only six weeks ago at the Washington summit, President Bush presented President Gorbachev nine points designed to assure the Soviet Union of our firm intention to address the legitimate political, security and economic interests of the Soviet Union.

Only two weeks ago in London, the NATO nations issued a declaration that translated this intention into instruc-

tions, specific commitments to extend a hand to the East, to modify NATO's defensive doctrine and strategies, to expand our commitment to arms control, and to gradually construct new CSCE institutions for the whole of a Europe enjoying freedom and peace.

Only yesterday, the Federal Republic of Germany and the Soviet Union in Stavropol agreed on eight points that will enable us to terminate Four Power rights at the time of unification, restoring Germany's full sovereignty and full prerogatives under the Helsinki Final Act, and thereby creating a sound basis for European security and European stability.

Today, of course, we meet with our Polish colleague, Minister Skubiszewski, in recognition of the special interest that all of us have taken in assuring the definitive character of the Polish-German border. We all agree that a unified Germany will consist of the Federal Republic of Germany, the German Democratic Republic, and Berlin. No more, no less. We also agreed, after discussion with and adjustment by our Polish colleague, on a set of principles to guide the final settlement of the border issue. And, of course, we were pleased by the German statement committing to act on the border treaty in the shortest possible time after unification, in line with the commitments already given by the German parliaments. Next, our officials will begin to use the list of external issues they assembled to prepare a draft final settlement document.

German Unification Imminent

In conclusion, the United States is very pleased that we are moving toward a sovereign and united Germany, and we are moving toward a stable security environment for Europe. We are replacing the historical national interests that divided us with a common European and Atlantic interest that unites us. The outcome that has so long eluded us is now within our reach.

By the anniversary of our Ottawa meeting, I expect the United States and the other four powers will welcome the advent of a united, sovereign and democratic Germany, a valuable contributor to the promotion and preservation of a Europe which is whole and a Europe which is free.

Foreign Minister Dumas. Thank you. And I shall now give the floor to

Mr. Genscher, Foreign Minister of the Federal Republic of Germany.

Foreign Minister Genscher. Ladies and gentlemen, I should like to begin by thanking our host, Mr. Dumas, for the excellent way in which he chaired our meeting today. And I should like to express, too, my particular pleasure at the presence of our Polish colleague, Foreign Minister Skubiszewski, who for many years has worked to strengthen understanding between Poland and Germany. Today, during the sessions in which he participated, we considered the principles which will underline the resolution of the border issue. Of course, we are well aware of the darkest periods of the historical relationship between Germany and Poland.

Today, we have had agreement on these basic principles, not just among those participating in the Two-Plus-Four negotiations, but also with our Polish colleague. And I should like to take this opportunity to express the determination of the government of the Federal Republic of Germany to ensure that, within the shortest possible time after unification and the return of sovereignty, there will be a border treaty with Poland, which will then be submitted to the Parliament of the united Germany for ratification.

In our discussions today, we also took up the issue of the results of our discussions with the Soviet leadership in recent days in the Soviet Union. These discussions and the results of those discussions have been welcomed by all participants today. We consider that they represent a success for Europe as a whole, for the new Europe, and that these results have confirmed our expectations that it should be possible to conclude the Two-Plus-Four discussions before the CSCE summit meeting, which will take place in Paris in November. We should be able to complete that before the CSCE summit meeting. In this way we should be able to sign the final document this year so that German unification, and return of full sovereignty to Germany, should be possible within this year.

Given this development, which has been accompanied by the successful preparatory work for the CSCE summit meeting and the results of the NATO conference in London, which represented a new relationship between the member countries of the different alliances — of the two alliances — that this dynamic process of German unification is clearly exhibiting a positive influence on Europe as a whole. German unification as a contribution to ensuring the unity, the stability, of Europe and to maintaining peace in Europe.

We Germans, of course, are fully aware of the responsibility which this development places upon us, and we welcome the fact that following today's discussions, it is now clear that German unification will be complete by the end of this year. And I should like to thank all of my colleagues who participated in this negotiation; I should like to thank them for their very constructive approach. Thank you.

Foreign Minister Dumas. Thank you, Mr. Genscher, and I shall now give the floor to the foreign affairs Minister of the Soviet Union.

Foreign Minister Shevardnadze. Ladies and gentlemen, I share the general assessments of the meeting that has just taken place, the ministerial meeting that has just taken place, the assessments as outlined by Mr. Dumas and by my other colleagues that preceded me. By the time of the Paris meeting, very important events have taken place that give us reason for confidence that an agreement about the final settlement of the external aspects of German unity will be reached and will be linked up with the process of German unification.

I would like to note the important work that has been done during the first two rounds of the meeting of the six, and also during the ministerial contacts at a bilateral level. It was during those contacts that we reached an understanding about the conditions and the kind of political evolution that would make possible the resolution of issues related to the German settlement.

Importance of Recent Summit Meetings

In particular, let me emphasize the fact that over the past few months there have been contacts among the top leaders of the countries that participated in the Two-Plus-Four mechanism. The meeting between the President of the U.S.S.R., Mikhail Gorbachev, and Federal Chancellor Mr. Kohl completed this series of intensive negotiations at the summit level.

So, now, we have before the six the mutual understandings that evolved, that emerged both during the broad political dialogue of the four powers and the two German states, and those that have been made possible as a result of the far-reaching changes taking place within the Warsaw Treaty, NATO, and within the overall European context.

The central problem that we faced at our talks in Ottawa was the determination of the responsibilities and rights of the four powers, and the granting of a full sovereignty to the future united Germany, and the problem of the political, military status of Germany.

For us, from the very outset there was no question — we did not question the fact that the process of the establishment of German unity is taking place on a democratic basis, that we can trust the German people in both parts of Germany, who over the postwar period have proven their commitment to peace and shown their determination to create a kind of society and state that would not threaten anyone and that would be a sound partner for all countries in the West and in the East.

Broader European Agreements

But we, just like others, had to recognize that until very recently, there were certain realities that stood in the way of resolving the issues related to Germany.

So, from the very outset, during the work of our mechanism of the six, we established a link between German unification and three other processes: that of reducing military confrontation in Europe and sharing a transition of European countries to defensive doctrines that implement the principle of defense efficiency; that of creating European structures of security and political cooperation; and that of transforming military blocs into political alliances and establishing relationships of partnership between the states that participate in the two alliances.

After the meeting of the political consultative committee of the Warsaw treaty in Moscow and the meetings of our partners in Dublin and London, we have seen a dramatic change, a dramatic headway in all these three areas. We can say without exaggeration that we have a qualitatively new political-military situation evolving in Europe today. And that makes it possible to consider the possibility of synchronizing the external and the internal aspects of German unity and of terminating the responsibilities of the Four Powers at the time of unification of the two German states and the granting of the future Germany of full sovereignty. And that means that, as a sovereign state, Germany will decide itself which alliance it is going to belong to. A choice in favor of NATO created difficulties for us, serious problems for us, in a situation when NATO was holding on to its positions of the past. But the forthcoming transformation of this alliance is making it possible for us to take a new look at the role and place of the changing NATO in Europe.

I think that the interests of all European countries are well served by the political statements of the leaders of the FRG and the GDR, that the future Germany will have no weapons of mass destruction, that the size of the Bundeswehr will be limited—will be substantially limited—and also that the military structures of NATO will not extend to the territory of the GDR. Together with the agreement about the stationing of Soviet troops on the territory of Germany for a few years, these constraints will serve as material guarantees of stability in Europe.

Soviet Treaty with United Germany

We also have a firm understanding that the Soviet Union and a united Germany will conclude a treaty in which the two sides will not consider themselves as adversaries, will not use force against each other, and will closely cooperate in the political, economic and other areas. We expect that shortly new European structures of security will emerge, and first of all, a center to prevent and resolve crises. I would like to recall that during the first meeting of the six in Bonn, the Soviet side said that a change in the political-military situation in Europe will make it possible for the U.S.S.R. to take a different look, to take a new look, at the issues of German unity that looked difficult at the time. Currently, we have reason to do so and we can say that we have really taken a constructive and a goodwill approach to the resolution of these issues.

At the current meeting of the ministers, we have decided, as my colleagues have announced here, to arrange our work in practical terms so as to make sure that, by the time of the Moscow meeting on the 12th of September, we have a draft agreement between the six that the ministers could adopt as a basis and then complete work on it and submit it to the European summit meeting here in Paris.

Today will also go down in history, I'm sure, as a day when the question of the German-Polish border has been definitively settled, settled to the com-

plete satisfaction of our Polish friends. We value the contribution of Minister Skubiszewski to the resolution of this issue, and I would like sincerely to congratulate him and Mr. Genscher, and Mr. Meckel, and the delegation of those three countries on this important occasion.

And finally, I would like to thank my friend, Mr. Roland Dumas, for his effective chairmanship and also for providing a beautiful and elegant setting for our meetings here in Paris.

Foreign Minister Dumas. Thank you. I should like to thank you, my dear friend, and I shall now give the floor to the foreign affairs Minister of the United Kingdom, Sir Douglas Hurd.

Foreign Minister Hurd. Well, Mr. Chairman, you have been a very skillful chairman for us and it will turn out that today we have cracked two nuts: the question of the Polish borders and the shape of the final settlement. But as someone said quite recently—I can't quite remember who—we do have strong teeth. But this couldn't be taken for granted, even a few weeks ago, because several times in this series of talks, doubts have been expressed about the strength of purpose and the prospects for success in completing our task before the end of the year. Those doubts are now retreating. Mr. Shevardnadze talked this morning to us about patient, serene negotiation. Well, that's been practiced here today, it's been practiced at many meetings in the last few months, and because of that, it's coming out right.

Importance of NATO Summit

When we have met before in the Two-Plus-Four machinery, Mr. Shevardnadze has emphasized that a united Germany would not fit easily into the landscape of a new Europe if everything else remained the same. And he drew particular attention in advance to the importance of the NATO Summit in London. And we took serious note of what he then said, and as you have heard today, the London Declaration has not disappointed him. And as a result of the particular hard work of the governments of the Soviet Union and the Federal Republic of Germany, we are now within sight of reconciling the freedom of a united Germany to choose its own alliance, its own place in Europe, reconciling with the legitimate concerns of the Soviet Union.

Over lunch and this afternoon, we reached agreement on the border question—Polish-German border question. Now, we British have very strong sympathies for historical reasons, for reasons of today also, with the Poles. I have held several long and fruitful conversations on this problem with Mr. Skubiszewski. It's a great relief, a great satisfaction to us, that agreement has been reached on this. Here are two countries with a very checkered history together—two countries which are now going to be divided, but divided by an agreed international frontier, but united in their commitment to a Europe which is democratic, free, and which sorts out its differences peacefully. That is how it ought to be.

Foreign Minister Dumas. Thank you very much. I call on the Foreign Minister of the German Democratic Republic, Mr. Meckel.

Foreign Minister Meckel. I should like to begin, once again, by thanking the foreign affairs minister of France for the way in which he chaired the meeting today. And I think that during our discussion, and indeed over the last days and weeks since June 22nd, our meeting in Berlin, we have achieved quite a lot of progress, and I think we have taken a major step forward. We have come much closer to resolving the issues which have brought us together. I would mention in particular the summit meeting in London recently, the meeting in Moscow in recent days. In this respect, in the area of security, much progress has been made, and I think this has taken account of the way in which the situation in Europe has developed. That's a point I wanted to bring up.

The new relationship between the member countries of NATO and the Warsaw Pact, and the progress which has been made towards an institutionalization of the CSCE process, and just how important this is in security terms is something that was said very clearly: that the concept of security must not be seen in purely military terms, that security is a broader concept. It's not a question of arming against adversaries, but rather working together to attain security and it also has political and economic dimensions.

We consider that what has been said with regard to conventional armed forces is a very positive starting point. We are very glad indeed that the Federal Republic has taken up our suggestion, namely, that both German states take the initiative to set a ceiling on German forces, go along with this proposal to Vienna, and in the area of conventional forces we are going to propose a Central European solution.

In recent days, the Soviet Union has agreed to German unification and a return of full sovereignty to Germany. The fact that these events have taken place at the same time, we consider a very major step forward. We think, too, that the international treaties which concern these allied rights and responsibilities, we need to study such treaties to see whether they contain restrictions, limitations on sovereignty which correspond to the rights and responsibilities of the allies.

Withdrawal of Soviet Forces

We are particularly pleased that the Soviet Union has stated that it is willing to withdraw Soviet troops from the territory of the German Democratic Republic in the next few years, and we think that this is a very positive development. This is the starting point of the treaty proposed between Germany and the Soviet Union, which concerns not just security issues, but all issues concerning our relations. We consider that this should be based on the renunciation of force on both sides. This is linked to the withdrawal of Soviet nuclear weapons from German territory and the agreement that on the present territory of the GDR no nuclear weapons should be based there in the future. We think this is a very important undertaking. It is a first important step forward on the road to a situation whereby, on German territory as a whole, no nuclear weapons should be stationed. And we consider that there is, quite simply, in the new Europe, no need for such nuclear weapons on German territory. We consider that security can be maintained without nuclear weapons on German territory.

And I am very pleased that in today's meeting, Mr. Skubiszewski has taken part in the discussion about this issue of the German-Polish border. We have made progress. This, in fact, is an issue which we can now consider as having been resolved. We consider that this is in keeping with the responsibility of Germans, who when they consider the past, the checkered history of our relations between our countries, this is something we must be very much aware of.

It's particularly significant that shortly after Federal Chancellor Kohl's visit to Moscow—that so shortly after this agreement—we have been able today to attain agreement. Now, yesterday the agreement concerned German-Soviet relations; today German-Polish relations. This represents a very good prospect for the future. We never again want to see a situation whereby the relationship between Germany and the Soviet Union could represent a danger to Poland.

We are particularly satisfied that Poland has obtained assurances regarding its security today—security, that is, of its border. This is something which has been based on the principle: firstly, of signing a border treaty with Germany as soon as possible subsequent to the unification of Germany; and, then, there will be, subsequent to that, negotiations on a general treaty covering relations between both states. We consider that this is a major step forward. We consider that German unification is closely linked to this key question of the definitive nature of the border between Germany and Poland. Today, we have clearly stated that we are prepared, before unification, to engage in trilateral discussions with Poland, covering those issues which are of mutual interest.

Foreign Minister Dumas. Thank you very much. Now, you can put your questions to all the ministers. Will you kindly start by telling to whom you're addressing your question, and tell us what paper you represent. You have the floor.

Q. I have a question for Minister Skubiszewski. Would you say that what happened today actually foretells the possibility for Poland to become part of united Europe?

Foreign Minister Skubiszewski. An important step in the direction you have indicated. There is no question of a united Europe without a united Germany and vice versa. The final regulation of the — or the confirmation of the frontier issue is an important contribution to the stability on the European continent.

As to Poland's return to Europe, I think this can be taken only in the relative terms because Poland was always present in Europe even in the worst times of its postwar history. We have always been part of cultural Europe and part of European civilization. At the present time, we are taking steps to become a member of the Council of Europe in Strasbourg and we also are making preparations for negotiations on the conclusion of an agreement of association with the European Community, to mention just two important steps which are elements of the Polish European policies.

Q. You make reference to economic talks this summer with West Germany. Please give us some details. And everybody's made reference to the border being finally settled, and terms of that settlement. But I haven't heard any of the terms except that the border is where the border is. Can you give us some idea of what the other terms are?

A. As to the economic talks, I can't give you any details regarding our future talks with Federal Germany and possibly also with the German Democratic Republic because this is only the beginning of our thinking about it. In any case, we are involved in talks with the German Democratic Republic on the fate of our various treaties and arrangements of an economic nature which will change—at least, some of them will change—as a result of German unification. And this is an important problem for Poland because the German Democratic Republic has been an important economic partner for Poland.

As to your second question, I cannot speak in detail about the provisions of the instrument that had been discussed today because this is a confidential matter, but I can tell you one thing. Poland was always puzzled by constant references to peace settlement or peace treaty as the final moment of the recognition or confirmation of the frontier. That condition, or requirement, of peace treaty or peace settlement has now disappeared. That's as a result of this conference—a stabilizing result.

Q. A question for Mr. Genscher. Herr Genscher, there seem to be many questions here and other places from the Soviets, from Poland about Germany's future, good behavior. What reassurances have you been able to give your dialogue partners here?

Foreign Minister Genscher. I would say that Germany's behavior was not a matter we discussed today. The matter we discussed is that which was pointed out by our German—and I would like to just emphasize here, to underline what the Foreign Minister of the Soviet Union said when he spoke about the confidence, the trust which his country has in both German states and the peoples of both German states, and this is a trust which is shared by all participants in this conference.

Q. I have two questions, if I may, to Mr. Genscher. In connection with what Mr. Meckel just said, I would like to know what you think about the positioning of nuclear arms throughout the territory of the GDR. I would like to hear from you how you foresee the future.

My next question is to Mr. Dumas. Are there any elements which perhaps did not go into the general outline of the settlement which are of concern to you in connection with the unification of Germany, be they of economic, political or military nature?

A. During our discussions yesterday with the Soviet leadership, we did attain agreement, and this agreement is one which is shared by the participants of today's conference, according to which it is up to the united Germany to decide as to which, and if it wants to belong to an alliance. And in our discussions with the Soviet leadership, and as our Federal Chancellor said in the press conference in the Soviet Union, he clearly stated that Germany wants to remain a member of the Western alliance for the—into the future. Over a period of three to four years, Soviet troops will continue to be based on the territory of the GDR. This will be based on a treaty which a united and sovereign Germany will sign with the Soviet Union, and at the same time, in the territory of the present GDR forces of the united Germany will be based which will not be under NATO command, which will be responsible for territorial defense.

Following the withdrawal of Soviet troops, German forces—and that includes German forces under NATO command—will be based in the territory of the GDR. These forces will not, however, have nuclear arms at their disposal. This is a clear description of the situation as it will apply to Germany, in agreement, too, with the Soviet Union, that the Articles 5 and 6 of the NATO treaty will apply as soon as unification takes place. That these provisions, provisions of Articles 5 and 6 of the NATO treaty, will apply also to the territory of the GDR.

Foreign Minister Dumas. To answer your last question, as you know, the Ottawa group was set up to deal with the external aspects of German unification. It being understood that internal issues are dealt with preference of the two countries. Among them, there was the question of frontiers between Poland and Germany and to identify the problems which occurred. The

working group submitted to us five essential points which we considered also today. The Minister of Foreign Affairs of Poland raised a number of additional problems which will not enter into the final document of the Two-Plus-Four Conference but to which he was able to receive replies in the course of the meeting. These replies, some of them, find their way into the final settlement. In other cases, they will be in the shape of declarations that we work into this conference, so you need not worry because there will not be any questions which were not dealt with.

Q. For Ministers Genscher, Meckel and Skubiszewski, and the question is, did you refer today to the question of German Constitution in the context of the borders? Thank you.

Foreign Minister Genscher. The Federal Republic of Germany at an early stage in the framework of the Two-Plus-Four negotiations clearly expressed that those provisions of the Constitution of the Federal Republic which concern German unification will be either deleted or modified because the unification of the Federal Republic of Germany and the German Democratic Republic, and Berlin. Once this unification has taken place, German unification will have been completed, and in this way the goal of the Constitution—the objective of the Constitution will have been attained.

Foreign Minister Skubiszewski. It is true that we talked today about the constitutional problems. A constitution is the highest law of the land, and when you provide that the Constitution will take account of certain international changes such as the unification of Germany and the confirmation of the border, you thereby imply that you'll have various legal changes which to some extent are subject to international regulations. Others belong to the sovereign decision of the respective countries. I think that part of our debate was very useful.

Foreign Minister Meckel. The constitution, of course, is the supreme law of any state. It's a matter for the sovereignty of that country. As has been said, following German unification, it will be necessary to modify the Constitution in certain respects. The preamble, in this respect has been mentioned. This specifies that Article 23, that this is something which will not in the future be present in the German Constitution. Today, we did not actually discuss this matter but there was agree-

ment that the constitutional issues of this kind should not be part of a treaty with another state. There was discussion as to what extent other legal provisions should be mentioned.

We agreed that it is purely self-evident that domestic law must be in line with international law and international obligations, and it is not necessary to specify this in a treaty. And I say this because, and I underline this because I myself have lived in a state for many years which signed many international treaties. However, the domestic law of the GDR quite simply was not adapted to that—was not in line with our international undertakings, and we are particularly sensitive and particularly aware of this issue and to ensure that this is not the case in the future in Germany.

Nuclear Weapons

Q. This is both for Mr. Shevardnadze and Mr. Genscher. Mr. Meckel referred just now to his hopes for the denuclearization of Germany. To Mr. Shevardnadze, is it still the Soviet Union's goal that the whole of Germany should be denuclearized? And Mr. Genscher, what is your view on this issue?

Foreign Minister Shevardnadze. That would be an ideal solution. Yesterday, in Stavropol and also in Moscow we discussed the question of the military-political status of the territory of what is now GDR. And an understanding has been reached that, on that territory, during the presence of the Soviet troops and also after Soviet troops withdraw, there will be no stationing of nuclear weapons. As for the other aspects of that problem, we have a good degree of mutual understanding that after the completion of the Vienna talks—of the first phase of the Vienna talks, we will begin a dialogue about reducing and maybe eventually eliminating tactical nuclear weapons from Europe.

Foreign Minister Genscher. Mr. Shevardnadze, I think, has clearly stated that in the territory of the present-day GDR, following the withdrawal of the Soviet troops—up to that withdrawal—German troops will be stationed, and indeed following that, they will not dispose of nuclear weapons. The remaining issues will be discussed within the alliance and will be discussed at an international level.

Q. Secretary Baker, does the fact that the arrangements between the

Soviet Union and the Germans were concluded by them and not by this conference directly, the fact that the United States is no longer in a position to wield the kind of economic clout it once did, and the fact that you haven't been asked a question up to this point at this news conference combine to indicate that American influence in Europe is not what it once was, nor will it be?

Secretary Baker. I'm glad you're asking your question. You know, I was really beginning to wonder—respond to you by saying that we are extremely happy to see the announcement that came out of the Soviet Union yesterday, because we have worked very long and very hard for exactly this result.

The terms of agreement that were reached between Chancellor Kohl and President Gorbachev are terms that the United States has supported since as early as last December when we called for a unified Germany as a member of the NATO alliance. So, the terms please us very much. And we would draw your attention, if we could, to the nine points that I mentioned in my opening statement and which we have discussed with all of our colleagues here from time to time, particularly with Minister Shevardnadze and President Gorbachev of the Soviet Union. So we're very pleased to see this result. It is a result that we've supported for a long time, and a result that we have worked very hard to achieve.

Foreign Minister Genscher. My answer to this, to add to what Mr. Baker has just said, is that Germany has welcomed from the very outset that the United States has supported Germany's march towards unification, and our view of Germany's continued membership of NATO, which will be the result of the free decision on our part, but also the principle of not extending the structure of NATO to the territories of the GDR. This is the result of the joint appraisal of this matter, and we have greatly appreciated the United States' support in this respect. And I still remember what President Gorbachev said yesterday in the final conference with the Federal Chancellor, in which he referred to the importance of the results attained in the London NATO Summit, which represented the starting point of a fundamental change in Europe which enabled the Soviet Union to reach agreement with the Federal Republic yesterday. And in this respect, I should just like to emphasize how important a role the President of the United States and the

Foreign Minister—Secretary of State of the United States have played in attaining the result at the London NATO Summit.

Q. This is to Herr Genscher. In terms of economic aid, what kind of price do you expect to have to pay for the Soviet Union's agreement to German unification? And could you oblige by answering in English please for British television.

A. Yes, but unfortunately, I would prefer to speak in German. I do not think that it is in keeping with the status of our relations with the Soviet Union and the peoples of the Soviet Union, that it is not in keeping to talk about a price paid to buy Soviet agreement. I do not think that's appropriate—a view of that kind is not appropriate. One cannot buy approval; one cannot buy agreement. That is not something we want to do and something that we could not do.

The Federal Republic of Germany and the Soviet Union, however, do agree that a united Germany will be able to contribute to strengthening relations between our two countries and to do so much more effectively than a continuation of the division of Germany. And for this reason, we have agreed that in a treaty which should be signed within twelve months, these prospects for future relations between Germany and the Soviet Union, we will develop these and we will sign an agreement to this effect. We are convinced that our contribution to insuring the success of the economic reform policy in the Soviet Union, this is, we are convinced, not just beneficial to the Soviet Union, but indeed to the development of Europe as a whole. We have a new approach to this matter, and we are convinced that this is something which is clearly going to be to the benefit of all countries of Europe and we believe that all countries are aware of this. Now, when I talk about "we", I'm not just referring to the Soviet Union and the Federal Republic of Germany, I am also referring to all the states present at this table and, indeed, I believe all those states participating in the CSCE process.

Foreign Minister Shevardnadze. Please bear with me. I would like to react—to respond to your question, too. In such terms as the establishment of a state, sovereignty of a nation, national unity, and the self-determination of nations, there is no trade and we're not

going to trade. And I fully agree with Mr. Genscher on this.

Q. A question for Minister Baker or Minister Skubiszewski. Mr. Baker, you referred to adjustments by the Polish Minister on the principles of the border treaty. I wonder if either of you can please elaborate on what the adjustments were?

And secondly, for Minister Shevardnadze, you referred to "partners", "our partners in Dublin and London." Do you now regard the NATO countries as partners? And to bring up the question that came up in Bonn, are you preparing to somehow formalize that partnership, if not by an application to NATO, then what comes next?

Secretary Baker. Our perhaps joint answer, Minister, by saying that we have adopted five general principles that guide us in addressing the question of borders as it relates to the external aspects of German unification. And the Minister made several suggestions for changes in those principles. I think I'm probably at liberty to certainly mention one of those in which he requested that we have a statement to the effect that the confirmation of the definitive nature of Germany's borders represents an important contribution to the order of peace in Europe, or words generally to that effect. And we picked up on that suggestion and added that to our five principles. There were other suggestions that were made which were followed as well.

Foreign Minister Dumas. As chairman of this meeting I'd like to confirm that this amendment was adopted and will figure in the final. Minister Skubiszewski?

Foreign Minister Skubiszewski. Mr. President, you spoke up about adaptations. In fact, there were no particular adaptations, but we enlarged on certain issues. We adopted certain clarifications in various ways, as the Secretary of State said, some of them were incorporated into the five principles, others were subject of statements by the interested states. All of this boils down to confirmation of the frontier.

Foreign Minister Shevardnadze. When we speak about partnership, I think there should be nothing surprising in that in fact the relations of partnership are something that we are already building with the United States, France, the FRG, Britain, and other countries. And as for the future, well, yes, I am fully confident that we will be real partners because what we are doing is building new relations between countries that belong to the different military-political alliances today.

Many things are changing in the world today. We are entering a period of peace in the development of world civilization. And in that context, we have to build new relations and there is nothing surprising about the fact that we, the adversaries of yesterday, countries that belong to confronting political-military alliances, will become real partners and will cooperate on the basis of the principles of equality and mutual trust.

Q. Could you please be a bit more specific about the changes that you wanted? Did you ask for a change in the preamble to the West German Constitution, for example? Did you ask for Article 23 to be taken out of the Constitution? Did you ask for a timetable to be put into the Two-Plus-Four agreement to bind the German states to recognize the frontier as quickly as possible?

Foreign Minister Skubiszewski. I didn't ask for the changes in the preamble of the Constitution nor in Article 23, because I was told some time ago by our German partners that these changes would be brought about. So that was not a subject of discussion today. And so the change of the Constitution is a matter to be decided by the country which is responsible for that Constitution.

We have received satisfactory assurances at — not only we — it was a matter which was first of all discussed in the Two-Plus-Four talks. As to the timetable, there was indeed a problem of various consultations prior to this meeting, and it was also mentioned during this meeting. Our interest is in the speedy conclusion of the bilateral treaty, the treaty between Poland and united Germany, and we have received the assurance that that treaty would be concluded as soon as possible after the unification of Germany. That corresponds to the Polish position from the outset.

We always envisaged that the signing and ratification of the treaty will take place after unification. But we insisted on the usefulness of talks preparatory to the treaty now, prior to unification, because that might be helpful for what would happen after unification. That I would say is a pragmatic approach.

Foreign Minister Dumas. Thank you very much. I would like to thank my six colleagues. Thank you, ladies and gentlemen for participating in this exchange.

---

[1] Department of State Press Release 105, July 20, 1990.

President's Proposal for a Global Forest Convention

White House Fact Sheet, July 11, 1990 [1]

President Bush today proposed to the leaders of the [economic] summit of industrialized nations that negotiations begin on an international convention on forests.

Background

The U.S. Forest Service estimates that the world is losing about 27 million acres of tropical forest each year. A recent study estimated even higher losses, in the range of 40-50 million acres per year. Severe and widespread forest declines have occurred in eastern and western Europe, and a body of evidence is accumulating that forests in North America and elsewhere are being damaged by stresses caused by air pollution.

The world's forests are the lungs of the Earth, absorbing carbon dioxide from mankind's activities and releasing oxygen critical to human existence. Forests serve as air conditioners and filters to protect us against heat, dust, and pollutants. They are essential in the protection of water supplies on which agriculture, industry, and cities depend. Not only are they a vital source of wood for fuel and shelter but we are increasingly learning of other resources which can be extracted in a way that provides economic benefits. And forests provide vital habitat for all manner of animal species. The Amazon Basin alone contains over 50,000 species of higher plants and a fifth of all the species of birds on Earth.

The U.S. Proposal

President Bush today proposed at the summit of industrialized nations to begin negotiations as expeditiously as possible on a global convention on forests. This would be a freestanding convention, similar to the highly successful Vienna convention on chlorofluorocarbons. The President proposed that negotiations be completed and the convention be ready for signing by 1992. The President expressed the hope that the convention would, to the maximum extent possible, emphasize market-based mechanisms and flexibility for achieving its goals.

The President outlined several areas in which international cooperation could help to address threats to the world's forests and could lead to positive action:

Research and Monitoring. The convention could accelerate cooperative research in programs to protect natural forests and to improve forest management practices, the development of more cost effective reforestation techniques, and the development of sustainable yield strategies consistent with each country's economic, environmental, and forest management objectives. The President suggested, as a first step, that the Tropical Forestry Institute in Puerto Rico be expanded into a full-fledged International Tropical Forests Institute.

The President proposed the launching of a worldwide network to monitor the world's forests to improve understanding of their health and vigor, the effects of pollution, and the rate at which they are being converted to other uses. The President called for cooperation in developing an inventory of the resources of the world's forests, as a tool for analyzing their potential for new products and uses.

Education, Training, and Technical Assistance. The convention could help establish vehicles for formal and technical training in forest conservation and forest practices, reforestation, and related subjects; for the provision of technical assistance, extension services, and project expertise.

Reforestation and Rehabilitation. The convention could be used to develop national and international strategies for reforestation, timber stand improvement, and restoration of the health of the world's forests. The President highlighted the commitment of the United States to reforestation through his proposal to plant a billion trees a year in America. That proposal is now awaiting funding by the U.S. Congress.

Noting the importance of economics and trade, the President reaffirmed U.S. support for the International Tropical Timber Organization.

Tropical Forestry Action Plan Reform. The President also reiterated U.S. support for the goals of the Tropical Forestry Action Plan and called for

strengthening and reform of the programs contained therein, with an emphasis on wise stewardship and sustainable management.

Reduction of Air Pollution. International action is needed to curb acid rain and tropospheric ozone, which are believed to cause damage to forests. This is essential to relieving stress on forests in Europe and to ensure that the restoration and replanting of forests in eastern Europe will be successful. The President has proposed in his Clean Air Act legislation dramatic reductions in emissions which contribute to acid rain (sulfur dioxide and nitrogen oxides) and ozone formation (volatile organic compounds). The Clean Air Act proposal has passed both Houses of Congress and is awaiting final action by a House-Senate conference committee. The convention could lay the groundwork for bilateral and multilateral agreements with respect to air pollution.

Bilateral and Multilateral Assistance Program. The convention might also address the need for a review of bilateral and multilateral assistance programs to put greater emphasis on conservation of forest areas and sustainable use of forest resources. In addition, it could explore possible ways to promote sound forestry practices and reforestation and to ensure that such programs are not designed in ways which adversely affect forests.

Debt-for-Nature Swaps. The convention could promote sound use and protection for forests through debt-for-nature swaps, particularly with the support of the multilateral development banks. In addition, it could encourage local currency environmental trust fund programs and similar devices to help finance environmental programs. The United States recently proposed to pursue such arrangements in Latin America as part of its Enterprise for the Americas Initiative [see Western Hemisphere].

Removal of Harmful Subsidies. The convention could address itself to identifying and, where appropriate, changing subsidies and other market distortions which inadvertently encourage deforestation or discourage afforestation of lands which could be best used as forest. One possibility is the reduction of subsidies that encourage the conversion of marginal lands that are economically more productive as forest lands into crop or grazing lands.

---

1 Text from Weekly Compilation of Presidential Documents of July 16, 1990.

The Legal Aspects of German Unification

by Michael K. Young

Statement before the Senate Foreign Relations Committee, July 12, 1990. Mr. Young is Deputy Legal Adviser, Department of State.[1]

On behalf of the Department of State, I would like to thank the committee for giving me this opportunity to outline the legal aspects of our work on a final settlement on Germany.

From its postwar beginnings to the present day, our German policy has been one of remarkable consistency. In 1946, in Stuttgart, Germany, then Secretary of State Byrnes said:

"While we shall insist that Germany observe the principles of peace, good-neighborliness, and humanity, we do not want Germany to become the satellite of any power or powers or to live under a dictatorship, foreign or domestic. The American people hope to see peaceful, democratic Germans become and remain free and independent. [2]

Throughout the intervening 45 years, we have consistently voiced this conviction, constantly reaffirming our support for a unified, democratic, peaceful Germany, fully sovereign and fully integrated into the community of democratic, peaceful European states. Now, we stand on the threshold of the realization of this goal.

The clarity and simplicity of our position in no way diminishes the long and difficult path to its accomplishment. Nor should it detract from the considerable sacrifices made by both the American and German people, as well as others in the Western alliance, in our joint quest for a prosperous, democratic, united Germany. The division of Germany during more than four decades was the symbol, as well as the most dramatic expression, of the division of Europe into opposing camps. Germany's division was itself — as we experienced during crises from the 1948 Berlin blockade to the building of the Berlin Wall in 1961 — a source of dangerous tension as well. Management and control of the instability and conflict occasioned by this division have required great effort and energy.

We are now engaged in a process — along with the United Kingdom, France, the Soviet Union and the two Germanys — to resolve the legal vestiges from the war prolonged by this conflict. In our view, the ultimate goal of this process, the so-called Two-Plus-Four process, is a united Germany that is fully sovereign and free to determine its own future. When such a goal is realized, we consider it important — as Chancellor Kohl and other German political leaders have made abundantly clear — that a unified Germany will choose to remain firmly anchored in Western institutions.

A central element in a successful conclusion of these negotiations must be, in our view, a termination of the remaining rights and responsibilities of the four powers allied against Germany during World War II. We must avoid the perpetuation of any discriminatory limits on Germany. Limitations must only be entered into by Germany of its own sovereign will. But in the Two-Plus-Four process, the imposition of unilateral restrictions on Germany would fundamentally undermine perhaps our most important principle, that of self-determination. Such an imposition would also be inconsistent with our desire to insure the full sovereignty of the German nation. Moreover, as we learned from the catastrophic consequences of the 1918 Versailles Conference, the imposition of punitive and one-sided limitations can be fundamentally destructive of democracy.

The Current Legal Situation

I would now like to sketch out the extent of our current legal rights and responsibilities with regard to Berlin and Germany as a whole. These rights are at the heart of the current Two-Plus-Four negotiations between the two Germanys and the Four Powers on the external aspects of German unification. Thereafter I will say a few words on what we view as the legal and political context within which we are negotiating an end to these rights and the creation of a fully sovereign, democratic and united Germany.

In agreements concluded during and immediately after the Second World War, the U.S., U.K. and U.S.S.R (and later France) agreed that Germany, as part of its unconditional surrender, would be occupied by the four powers. The wartime allies divided Germany into three and, with the addition of France, four zones. The Soviets occupied what is now the GDR [German Democratic Republic], the former British, French and American zones now comprise the FRG [Federal Republic of Germany].

The four powers were careful to make clear from the very beginning of the occupation that:

- they were not annexing Germany;
- "Germany" as a state would continue to exist under international law;
- they reserved a voice in Germany's ultimate borders and government.

Despite repeated efforts on the part of the Western allies and the emerging West German government to merge all four occupation zones and establish a democratic and united German government, agreement could not be reached with the Soviet Union concerning all-German elections and the terms for a peace treaty with Germany. The Four Powers have long since individually ended the state of war between themselves and Germany.

The FRG was founded with the approval of the three Western allies on September 21, 1949. As of May 5, 1955, the Western allies ended the occupation regime in the FRG, reserving their rights with respect to Germany as a whole, a peace settlement, the setting of Germany's ultimate boundaries and Berlin. This was accomplished in the "Convention on Relations between the Three Powers and the Federal Republic of Germany." Article 7 of the Convention states that it is the common aim of the three Western powers and the FRG to achieve by peaceful means "a unified Germany enjoying a liberal-democratic constitution, like that of the Federal Republic, and integrated within the European Community." A parallel process took place in the Soviet zone. On October 7, 1949 the Soviets authorized the establishment of the GDR. The Soviet Union formally granted sovereignty to the GDR on March 25, 1954.

As a result of the September 12, 1944 London Protocol, Berlin was divided into three and, with the addition of the French, later four sectors to be jointly governed by the Allied Kommandatura ("AK"), made up of the military commandants of the four powers. Even though the Soviets left the AK on July 1, 1948, the AK remains the supreme authority with respect to all of greater Berlin. But since 1948 the Western allies have been able to exercise their authority through the AK in practice only in the three Western sectors of Berlin.

In 1949 and 1950 the Western allies precluded the FRG and Berlin authorities, who were drafting their respective constitutions, from making Berlin a state of the FRG. This was necessary in order to preserve Berlin's occupation status, and thereby allied and West German access to the city. In the "Declaration on Berlin" of May 5, 1955 the three Western allies granted the West Berlin city government substantial authority to govern the internal affairs of the Western sectors of Berlin. The Declaration provides that the three powers would normally confine the exercise of their authority to allied security and immunities, disarmament and demilitarization, foreign relations, satisfaction of occupation costs and police matters.

Although Berlin was not formally incorporated into the FRG, the Western sectors of Berlin have been increasingly merged into the legal, economic and social structure of the FRG. In 1971 the Four Powers concluded the Quadripartite Agreement on Berlin, which left the Soviet and Western divergent legal views on Berlin and Germany as a whole untouched, but which largely removed Berlin as a friction point between the superpowers and brought about considerable practical improvements in civilian access, communications, trade, and other areas between West Berlin and the FRG.

West Berlin remains legally occupied by U.S., British and French troops and greater Berlin remains legally subject to the occupation rights of the four powers. Although the exercise of allied rights does not significantly affect the day-to-day life of Berlin, these rights have been crucial to the survival of the city. It is these rights that have provided the legal basis for the allied presence in, and protection of, Berlin and enabled not only allies, but also Berliners and West Germans, unhindered transit, and particularly air transit, through Soviet-occupied GDR.

In sum, the FRG has been sovereign since 1955 and become one of our closest and most reliable allies, and Berlin has been formally self-governed since 1955 and been increasingly incorporated into the FRG. Nevertheless, the Western allies have preserved basic rights regarding Berlin and Germany as a whole, including those rights regarding the affirmation of Germany's final borders and the conclusion of a final settlement. They have done so with consistent Western support in order to underline the fact that the German question remains open, the division of Germany unacceptable, and the goal of a Germany united in democracy and peace our common objective.

These rights and responsibilities form the framework within which the Four Powers and two Germanys are meeting to work out the external aspects of German unification. As Secretary Baker noted at the first Two-Plus-Four ministerial meeting, our sole task is to fulfill those responsibilities and to terminate our rights.

The Two-Plus-Four Negotiations

One of the issues confronting us in the Two-Plus-Four negotiations is the German borders. Both German parliaments passed last month resolutions confirming the current Oder-Neisse Line as the Polish-German border and forswearing any future German claims to territory. In transmitting the texts of the resolution, [FRG] Foreign Minister Genscher informed the Polish Government that the Government of the Federal Republic of Germany had adopted the resolution as FRG government policy as well. The Polish and German Governments have also agreed to negotiate a treaty, binding under international law, that will reconfirm treaties the two Germanys already have with Poland establishing their common border. Thus, we are confident that we will be able to negotiate in the Two-Plus-Four talks a suitable affirmation of Germany's borders.

We are also negotiating the complete termination of all reserved Four Power rights, leaving a united Germany fully sovereign. We believe that political-military aspects of German unification, such as Germany's membership in NATO and its troop force levels, are issues more properly discussed by a sovereign Germany and in the fora that have been specifically established for such issues, such as the conventional arms talks in Vienna or NATO. We have nevertheless agreed to hear Soviet concerns on these issues in the Two-Plus-Four negotiations. Finally, we are working out in the Two-Plus-Four negotiations the terms of a final settlement that will resolve all outstanding Four Power issues regarding Germany in a manner consistent with the goal of a Germany free from any vestiges of the occupation era.

The United States has considerable flexibility regarding the form and contents of the settlement document. Our approach reflects the fact that the central element in resolving the German question—the ending of Germany's tragic and artificial division—is coming about as a result of the sea change in Eastern European politics and through the actions and decisions of the Germans themselves. The settlement document is not the instrument that will end Germany's division. Instead, it is a coda, albeit an important one, to the central work being carried on peacefully and democratically by the Germans themselves. The settlement document is needed, in our view, solely to provide an uncontested basis for full German sovereignty.

Thus, we believe that the settlement document should be brief. It must make a few important but technical adjustments to make the legal situation in Germany correspond to the new political realities there. No more is needed. Moreover, the Final Settlement on Germany is not the appropriate document in which to address the many detailed technical policy issues between the various parties. These can and will be settled elsewhere, bilaterally and multilaterally, as sovereign acts of a united Germany.

Not all of the participants in the negotiations agree with our preferred approach. Some—particularly the Soviets—want to use the settlement to create important new obligations and commitments involving Germany. However, if our preferred approach prevails, the German settlement will direct itself to the fulfillment of Four Power responsibilities and the termination of Four Power rights. To the extent the new situation gives rise to new obligations, these will be undertaken in other documents—for instance, in multilateral agreements on conventional arms limitations in Europe.

The Form of the Agreement

Against this background, Mr. Chairman, let me briefly address some of the general issues regarding the Senate's role on German treaty matters and survey the criteria that we will look at — together with the views of this committee and others in the Congress — in making the final judgment as to the appropriate domestic form for the settlement.

The Senate has already played a significant role in the adoption of the individual pieces of the conclusion of peace with Germany, with the result that the few remaining matters are generally technical in nature:

First, Congress and the President ended the state of war with Germany on October 24, 1951 when the President issued a proclamation pursuant to a joint resolution of Congress.

Second, the Senate gave its advice and consent on July 13, 1953 to the Agreement on German External Debts, which resolved reparations and other key issues that would normally have been addressed in a peace treaty.

Third, on July 1, 1952 and April 1, 1955 the Senate gave its advice and consent to the Convention on Relations between the Three Powers and the Federal Republic of Germany and its related Protocol on the Termination of the Occupation Regime in the FRG, which resolved other key issues necessary to normalizing our relationship with West Germany.

Unlike the case of Italy, Japan and the other Axis powers, the business of regulating the peace with Germany was never addressed in a single document. But through a series of documents in the early 1950s, the Senate has already given its advice and consent to the elements of such a peace treaty with Germany.

The allied rights and other subjects which remain for negotiation, as part of the final settlement, are set forth and reconfirmed in executive agreements, not treaties. I am referring to such documents as the August 1, 1945 Potsdam Protocol, the June 5, 1945 Declaration Regarding the Defeat of Germany and the Assumption of Supreme Authority and the September 3, 1971 Quadripartite Agreement on Berlin.

I should also note that the desire to avoid a "peace treaty" is felt very keenly in Bonn. We have been at peace with Germany for 45 years, a peace officially declared by Congress in 1951. During 35 of those years the West Germans have been our trusted ally and they have won our confidence and admiration. They have long since ceased to be a vanquished foe and we do not wish to do anything that makes it appear as if we have approached the final settlement on Germany from opposing sides, rather than as the close allies that we are.

Criteria for Submission to the Senate

The Department of State's regulations on international agreements, contained in the Foreign Affairs Manual (11 FAM 720), set forth the general criteria we review in resolving the question of submission to the Senate. The *first* criterion — and the most important — is the extent to which the settlement will involve commitments or risks affecting the nation as a whole. As I have noted, we do not intend to enter into new obligations in the settlement document, but merely to solemnize our fulfillment of an old one — our obligation to promote the emergence of a democratic, sovereign, unified Germany within a community of democratic states. The settlement will not create new rights.

The Department's *second* criterion is whether the settlement is intended to affect state laws. The settlement as we now see it would not.

Third is whether the agreement can be given effect without the enactment of subsequent legislation. No legislation would be required to implement the settlement we foresee.

Fourth is past U.S. practice regarding similar agreements. As I have noted, the settlement in all likelihood will address those issues that we have traditionally included in executive agreements not submitted to the Senate.

Fifth, the criteria highlight the preference of the Congress as to the particular type of agreement.

Sixth is the degree of formality of the settlement. It is simply too early to assess this criterion. I would note, however, that it has been Bonn's strong desire, and also our preference, not to present this settlement as a peace treaty dividing victors and vanquished. This may effect the degree of formality desired.

Seventh, the criteria refer to the proposed duration of the agreement, the need for its prompt conclusion, and the desirability of concluding a routine or short term agreement. The proposed settlement is intended to resolve permanently the comparatively narrow issues it will probably cover. Once the parties reach agreement, the sheer pace of events in Germany will make it desirable to bring the settlement into force expeditiously.

Finally, the criteria refer to the general international practice as to similar agreements. Some of the other parties may submit it to their parliaments. Others may not. However, this is a criterion we must treat with caution because the other states concerned have very different legal systems — as well as legal traditions that commend a different range of documents, with quite different legal form and criteria, to legislative consideration, while simultaneously sharply limiting the role of parliamentary review of these agreements.

Mr. Chairman, these are the criteria we will weigh in addressing the proper form for U.S. adherence to the eventual settlement document. I cannot say what final conclusion they will support but I am confident that as the matters become clearer the Department will remain in close touch with you and your colleagues.

A United, Democratic Germany

Returning to the Two-Plus-Four agenda, I would also like to say a few words about why this goal of a united and democratic Germany free from Four Power reserved rights is in the U.S. interest. These allied rights must be seen and understood within their historical context. The United States made a firm decision not to impose a punitive peace upon a defeated Germany. We sought guarantees that Germany would not again threaten peace on the European continent and felt that the greatest guarantee would be in the establishment of a free and democratic Germany. The only reason these rights have continued to be of significance 45 years after the war is that the goal of a unified and democratic Germany could not be achieved in the postwar years. These reserved rights must be seen within the context of our ongoing responsibility to all the German people to facilitate the establishment of a unified and democratic Germany.

Thus, it would be a mistake to view these allied rights as rights vis-a-vis the Federal Republic or even the German Democratic Republic. They are rather rights which the Western allies, in close consultation with our West German ally, have preserved and maintained precisely to preserve the freedom of Germans living in the Western sectors of Berlin and to keep open the question of, and demonstrate our commitment to, a unified and democratic Germany. With the events leading up to and following the November 9, 1989 fall of the Berlin Wall, we have seen a courageous popular revolt in East Germany and the startling and, if I may say, exhilarating, process of reintegration of the two Germanys. The internal aspects of unification have already progressed to an advanced stage, with the two countries now sharing a common currency and economic regime and rapidly progressing to full social and economic unity.

Political unity has also progressed rapidly and its formal establishment is only a matter of time. The expansion of a liberal democracy, with a market economy and close ties to the Western alliance, to all of Germany is clearly in the interests of the Western alliance. It is, in fact, a triumph of democracy made possible by that alliance. We are not engaged in the Two-Plus-Four negotiations regarding the external aspects of unification in order to come to terms with the FRG regarding Germany unity. We, as well as the British and French, are already in full accord with the FRG regarding the end point of this process—the establishment of a democratic and united Germany enjoying full sovereignty and free to choose its own alliances.

We are now making the effort in the Two-Plus-Four negotiations, in coordination with our Western allies, to persuade the Soviet Union that it is also in its interest to support the establishment of a unified, democratic Germany, without future impediments on its sovereignty. We firmly believe it is not in the interests of anyone, including the Soviet Union, to singularize Germany and thereby create the potential for future resentment and instability.

In the decades since the establishment of the Federal Republic and its acquisition of full sovereignty, we have studiously preserved these rights as a means, perhaps the only means, of achieving a goal we share with West Germany—a German people living in peace and freedom and, as we have sought for over forty years, in unity.

These phrases of peace, freedom and unity often have a trite ring to them. I think it is a token of the times in which we are privileged to work that there are no others to describe the process that is now taking place on the European continent. Nothing, in our view, furthers U.S. interests more than contributing to that process.

---

[1] The complete transcript of the hearings will be published by the committee and will be available from the Superintendent of Documents, U.S. Government Printing Office, Washington, D.C., 20402.

[2] "Restatement of U.S. Policy on Germany," address by Secretary of State James F. Byrnes, Stuttgart, Germany, September 6, 1946. Department of State Bulletin, September 15, 1946, pp. 496-501.

President Announces Enterprise for the Americas Initiative

Remarks by President Bush before members of the business community at the White House, June 27, 1990. [1]

In the past 12 months, every one of us, from the man in the White House to the man on the street, has been fascinated by the tremendous changes, the positive changes, taking place around the world. Freedom has made great gains not just in Eastern Europe but right here in the Americas; and we've seen a resurgence of democratic rule, a rising tide of democracy, never before witnessed in the history of this beloved hemisphere. And with one exception, Cuba, the transition to democracy is moving towards completion, and we can all sense the excitement that the day is not far off when Cuba joins the ranks of world democracies and makes the Americas fully free.

With one exception, that's the case. But the political transformation sweeping the rest of Latin America and the Caribbean has its parallel in the economic sphere. Throughout the region, nations are turning away from the statist economic policies that stifle growth and are now looking to the power of the free market to help this hemisphere realize its untapped potential for progress. A new leadership has emerged, backed by the strength of the people's mandate, leadership that understands that the future of Latin America lies with free government and free markets. In the words of Colombia's courageous leader, Virgilio Barco — President Barco: "The long-running match between Karl Marx and Adam Smith is finally coming to an end" with the "recognition that open economies with access to markets can lead to social progress."

For the United States, these are welcome developments, developments that we're eager to support. But we recognize that each nation in the region must make its own choices. There is no blueprint, no one size fits all approach, to reform. The primary responsibility for achieving economic growth lies with each individual country. Our challenge in this country is to respond in ways that support the positive changes now taking place in the hemisphere. We must forge a genuine partnership for free market reform.

Back in February, I met in Cartagena [Colombia] with heads of the three Andean nations, and I came away from that meeting convinced that the United States must review its approach not only to that region but to Latin America and the Caribbean as a whole. And I asked Treasury Secretary Brady to lead a review of U.S. economic policy towards this vital region, to make a fresh assessment, if you will, of the problems and opportunities we'll encounter in the decade ahead. That review is now complete, and the results are in. The need for new economic initiatives is clear and compelling.

All signs point to the fact that we must shift the focus of our economic interaction towards a new economic partnership because prosperity in our hemisphere depends on trade, not aid. And I've asked you here today to share with you some of the ideas, some of the ways we can build a broad-based partnership for the 1990s — to announce the new Enterprise for the Americas Initiative that creates incentives to reinforce Latin America's growing recognition that free market reform is the key to sustained growth and political stability.

The three pillars of our new initiative are trade, investment, and debt. To expand trade, I propose that we begin the process of creating a hemisphere-wide free trade zone; to increase investment, that we adopt measures to create a new flow of capital into the region; and to further ease the burden of debt, a new approach to debt in the region with important benefits for our environment.

Trade

In the 1980's, trade within our hemisphere trailed the overall pace of growth in world trade. One principal reason for that: over-restrictive trade barriers that wall off the economies of our region from each other and from the United States, at great cost to us all. These barriers are the legacy of the misguided notion that a nation's economy needs protection in order to thrive. The great economic lesson of this century is that protectionism still stifles progress and free markets breed prosperity. To this end, we've formulated a three-point trade plan to encourage the emerging trends toward free market reform that are now gathering forces in the Americas.

First, as we enter the final months of the current Uruguay Round of the world trade talks, I pledge close cooperation with the nations of this hemisphere. The successful completion of the Uruguay Round remains the most effective way of promoting long term trade growth in Latin America and the increased integration of Latin nations into the overall global trading system. Our aim in the Uruguay Round is free and fair trade.

Through these talks we are seeking to strengthen existing trade rules and to expand them to areas that do not now have agreed rules of fair play. And to show our commitment to our neighbors in Latin America and the Caribbean, we will seek deeper tariff reductions in this round on products of special interest to them.

Second, we must build on the trend we see toward free markets and make our ultimate aim a free trade system that links all of the Americas — North, Central, and South. We look forward to the day when not only are the Americas the first fully free, democratic hemisphere but when all are equal partners in a free trade zone stretching from the port of Anchorage to the Tierra del Fuego.

I'm announcing today that the United States stands ready to enter into free trade agreements with other markets in Latin America and the Caribbean, particularly with groups of countries that have associated for purposes of trade liberalization. And the first step in this process is the now-announced free trade agreement with Mexico.[2] We must all recognize that we won't bring down barriers to free trade overnight; changes so far-reaching may take years of preparation and tough negotiations. But the payoff in terms of prosperity is worth every effort, and now is the time to make a comprehensive free trade zone for the Americas our long term goal.

And **third,** I understand that some countries aren't yet ready to take that dramatic step to a full free trade agreement. And that's why we're prepared to negotiate with any interested nation in the region bilateral framework agreements to open markets and develop closer trade ties. Such agreements already exist with Mexico and Bolivia. Framework agreements will enable us to move forward on a step-by-step basis to eliminate counterproductive barriers to trade and towards our ultimate goal of free trade. And that's a prescription for greater growth and a higher standard of living in Latin America and, right here at home, new markets for American products and more jobs for American workers.

Promoting free trade is just one of three key elements in our new Enterprise for the Americas Initiative. And our second pillar is increased investment.

Investment Reform

The competition for capital today is fierce. And the key to increased investment is to be competitive, to turn around the conditions that have discouraged both foreign and domestic investment, reduce the regulatory burden, clear away the thicket of bureaucratic barriers that choke off Latin America's aspiring entrepreneurs.

In one large Latin city, for instance, it takes almost 300 days to cut through the red tape to open a small garment shop. In another country, the average overseas caller has to make five phone calls to get through, and the wait for a new telephone line can be as long as five years. And that's got to change.

Investment reform is essential to make it easier to start new business ventures and make it possible for international investors to participate and profit in Latin American markets. In order to create incentives for investment reform, the United States is prepared to take the following steps:

First, the United States will work with the Inter-American Development Bank to create a new lending program for nations that take significant steps to remove impediments to international investment. The World Bank could also contribute to this effort.

Second, we propose the creation of a new investment fund for the Americas. This fund, administered by the IDB, could provide up to $300 million a year in grants in response to market-oriented investment reforms in progress in privatization.

The United States intends to contribute $100 million to the fund, and we will seek matching contributions from Europe and Japan.

But in order to create an attractive climate for new investment, we must build on our successful efforts to ease the debt burden. That's the third pillar of this new Enterprise for the Americas Initiative.

Easing the Debt Burden

Many nations have already undertaken painful economic reforms for the sake of future growth. But the investment climate remains clouded, weighted down by the heavy debt burden. Under the Brady plan, we are making significant progress. The agreements reached with Mexico and Costa Rica and Venezuela are already having a positive impact on investment in those countries.

Mexico, to take just one example, has already seen a reversal of the destructive capital flight that drained so many Latin American nations of precious investment resources. That's critical. If we restore confidence, capital will follow.

As one means of expanding our debt strategy, we propose that the IDB add its efforts and resources to those of the International Monetary Fund (IMF) and the World Bank to support commercial bank debt reduction in Latin America and the Caribbean, and, as in the case of World Bank and IMF, IDB funds should be directly linked to economic reform.

While the Brady plan has helped nations reduce commercial bank debt, for nations with high levels of official debt — debt owed to governments rather than private financial institutions — the burden remains heavy. And today, across Latin America, official debt owed to the U.S. Government amounts to nearly $12 billion, with $7 billion of that amount in concessional loans. In many cases, the heaviest official debt burdens fall on some of the region's smallest nations, countries like Honduras and El Salvador and Jamaica.

That's a problem we must address today. As the key component in addressing the region's debt problem, I am proposing a major new initiative to reduce Latin America and the Caribbean's official debt to the United States for countries that adopt strong economic and investment reform programs with the support of international institutions.

Our debt reduction program will deal separately with concessional and commercial types of loans. On the con-

cessional debt, loans made from AID or Food for Peace accounts, we will propose substantial debt reductions for the most heavily burdened countries. And we will also sell a portion of outstanding commercial loans to facilitate these debt-for-equity and debt-for nature swaps in countries that have set up such programs. These actions will be taken on a case by case basis.

Strengthening Environmental Policies

One measure of prosperity and the most important long term investment any nation can make is environmental well-being. As part of our Enterprise for the Americas Initiative, we will take action to strengthen environmental policies in this hemisphere.

Debt-for-nature swaps are one example, patterned after the innovative agreements reached by some Latin American nations and their commercial creditors. We will also call for the creation of environmental trusts, where interest payments owed on restructured U.S. debt will be paid in local currency and set aside to fund environmental projects in the debtor countries.

These innovative agreements offer a powerful new tool for preserving the natural wonders of this hemisphere that we share. From the vistas of the unspoiled Arctic to the beauties of the barrier reef off Belize to the rich rain forests of the Amazon, we must protect this living legacy that we hold in trust. For an increasing number of our neighbors, the need for free market reform is clear. These nations need economic breathing room to enact bold reforms, and this official debt initiative is one answer, a way out from under the crushing burden of debt that slows the process of reform.

A Closer Partnership for the Americas

I know there is some concern that the revolutionary changes we've witnessed this past year in Eastern Europe will shift our attention away from Latin America. But I want to assure all of you here today, as I've assured many democratic leaders in Central and South America and the Caribbean and Mexico, the United States will not lose sight of the tremendous challenges and opportunities right here in our own hemisphere. And indeed, as we talk with the leaders of the G-24 about the emerging democracies in Europe — I've been talking to them also about their supporting democracy and economic freedom in Central America. Our aim is a closer partnership between the Americas and our friends in Europe and in Asia.

Two years from now, our hemisphere will celebrate the 500th anniversary of an epic event: Columbus' discovery of America, our New World. And we trace our origins, our shared history, to the time of Columbus' voyage and the courageous quest for the advanc ement of man. Today the bonds of our common heritage are strengthened by the love of freedom and a common commitment to democracy. Our challenge, the challenge in this new era of the Americas, is to secure this shared dream and all its fruits for all the people of the Americas — North, Central, and South.

The comprehensive plan that I've just outlined is proof positive the United States is serious about forging a new partnership with our Latin American and Caribbean neighbors. We're ready to play a constructive role at this critical time to make ours the first fully free hemisphere in all of history.

---

[1] Department of State Current Policy 1288, June 1990.

[2] On June 11, 1990, Presidents Bush and Salinas endorsed the goal of a comprehensive free trade agreement between the United States and Mexico. The Presidents have directed their trade ministers to undertake the consultations and preparatory work needed to initiate such negotiations and to report back to them before the two Presidents meet again in December 1990.

must do more to confront and reduce demand in our own society, and we pledge our best efforts and resolve. In Mexico, the challenge is to confront production or transit of drugs through Mexican territory. The inevitable problems that emerge in meeting these challenges get the headlines. But the truth is the United States and Mexico have never done more in their history to cooperate together to combat narco-trafficking than we have in this past year. I applaud the strong commitment of the Salinas government to making progress in this crucial war on drugs.

Third, the Problem of Immigration. Together, we live on opposite sides of a 2,000 mile long border which is crossed 250 million times every year. We must find solutions that protect both the dignity of the migrant and the concept of national sovereignty and controlled borders, and I am convinced that we will.

Fourth. Protecting the Environment. The United States and Mexico both agree that a way must be found to reconcile economic growth while also safeguarding our environmental heritage. We should not pass on to our children and our grandchildren a legacy of poisoned air, polluted water, and dying landscapes. Here the United States and Mexico have much to offer each other and much to gain through greater cooperation.

U.S.-Mexico Binational Commission Meeting

Remarks by Secretary of State Baker at the Commission plenary session, Excerpt, Washington, August 8, 1990 [1]

The United States and Mexico are both heirs to old traditions. Yet together we are engaged in a great new experiment. We are trying to turn the focus of our relationship from the past to the future, from managing irritants to creating opportunities. We confront each new problem with the words, "We shall work together." That is what this Binational Commission is really all about.

These meetings are becoming almost routine, a fact that reflects how far we have come together as partners for change. Yet this meeting is unique in today's world. Not many other nations routinely come together with the highest officials of their respective governments for sustained, serious dialogue on the fundamental issues of our time. There is no more important relationship to us than U.S.-Mexican relations. And the best way to improve that relationship is to set for ourselves great projects and then bring to those projects our respective strengths.

This commitment was begun by our Presidents during their meeting in Houston and continued during President Salinas' two visits to Washington last October and this June. The two Presidents developed a vision of cooperation, mutual benefit, and the

requirement for each of us to reach our full potential in a very competitive, fast-changing world. They also charged us with developing more effective mechanisms, such as this BNC, to manage our relations. Today, therefore, is a day dedicated to both vision and the practical steps we should take to create new realities.

We have come a long way in the last two years, as our Presidents had hoped and believed. Each of our ten working groups has an impressive array of issues to explore and work to resolve in our mutual interest. These represent our opportunities for the future and the means with which our societies will confront new international challenges.

Today, I would call your attention to four such challenges that will shape our future.

First, a Free Trade Agreement. Two months ago, President Salinas and President Bush endorsed a Free Trade Agreement as a major goal. By opening our markets and further reducing the barriers between us, we can create a new, more powerful engine of economic progress. And that engine will be driven by the immense creative energy of our peoples, as we move together toward the historical achievement of one market uniting both our nations and a better life for all our citizens.

Second. the War Against Drugs. The drug war is a challenge for both of our countries. We in the United States

Our working groups, of course, are going to consider the full range of cooperative areas beyond these four, including tourism, commerce, border, and global issues. For the first time at a Binational Commission Meeting, we welcome today the participation of our Ministries of Agriculture and of Education. As we work our way through these issues, we should do so with a renewed sense of confidence in the future. We are creating after all, a new model of international cooperation: two diverse nations amicably and intelligently drawing on their full potential.

What the United States and Mexico do together, as President Bush made clear in his "Enterprise for the Americas" proposal, will resonate throughout this hemisphere and, indeed, throughout the world. Our ability to advance in free trade, structured dialogue, and better lives for our citizens clearly marks a path for other nations to follow.

---

[1] Department of State Press Release 116, August 8, 1990.

Current Actions:

April-May 1990 and June-July 1990

These listings were released by the Department of State as "Current Treaty Actions, April-May 1990" and "Current Treaty Actions, June-July 1990."

I. April-May 1990

MULTILATERAL

Aviation
International air services transit agreement. Done at Chicago Dec. 7, 1944. Entered into force Jan. 20, 1945; for the US Feb. 8, 1945. EAS 487.
Acceptance deposited: German Dem. Rep., Apr. 2, 1990.

Convention on international civil aviation. Done at Chicago Dec. 7, 1944. Entered into force Apr. 4, 1947. TIAS 1591.
Adherence deposited: German Dem. Rep., Apr. 2, 1990.

Customs
Customs convention on containers, 1972, with annexes and protocol. Done at Geneva Dec. 2, 1972. Entered into force Dec. 6, 1975; for the US May 12, 1985.
Accession deposited: Trinidad and Tobago, Mar. 23, 1990.

Genocide
Convention on the prevention and punishment of the crime of genocide. Done at Paris Dec. 9, 1948. Entered into force Jan. 12, 1951; for the US Feb. 23, 1989.
Accession deposited: Bahrain, Mar. 27, 1990.

Human Rights
International covenant on economic, social, and cultural rights. Done at New York Dec. 16, 1966. Entered into force Jan. 3, 1976. [1]
Accessions deposited: Burundi, May 9, 1990;, Korea, Rep. of, Apr. 10, 1990; Somalia, Jan. 24, 1990.

International covenant on civil and political rights. Done at New York Dec. 16, 1966. Entered into force Mar. 23, 1976. [1]

Accessions deposited: Burundi, May 9, 1990; Korea, Rep. of, Apr. 10, 1990, [3] Somalia, Jan. 24, 1990.

Judicial Procedure
Additional protocol to the Inter-American convention on letters rogatory, with annex. Done at Montevideo May 8, 1979. Entered into force June 14, 1980; for the US Aug 27, 1988. [Senate] Treaty Doc 98-27.
Accession deposited: Chile, Jan. 11, 1990. [3]

Maritime Matters
Convention for the suppression of unlawful acts against the safety of maritime navigation. Done at Rome Mar. 10, 1988. [4] [Senate] Treaty Doc. 101-1.
Ratification deposited: Italy, Jan. 26, 1990.

Pollution
Protocol of 1978 relating to the international convention for the prevention of pollution from ships, 1973. Done at London Feb. 17, 1978. Entered into force Oct. 2, 1983.
Accessions deposited: Togo, Feb. 9, 1990; Djibouti, Mar. 1, 1990. [2]

International convention relating to intervention on the high seas in cases of oil pollution casualties, with annex. Done at Brussels Nov. 29, 1969. Entered into force May 6, 1975. TIAS 8068.
Accessions deposited: China, Feb. 23, 1990; Djibouti Mar. 1, 1990.

Protocol relating to intervention on the high seas in cases of pollution by substances other than oil. Done at London Nov. 2, 1973. Entered into force Mar. 30, 1983. TIAS 10561.
Accession deposited: China, Feb. 23, 1990.

Racial Discrimination
International convention on the elimination of all forms of racial discrimination. Done at New York Dec. 21, 1965. Entered into force Jan. 4, 1969. [1]
Notification of succession deposited: St. Lucia, Feb. 14, 1990; effective Feb. 22, 1979.

Accession deposited: Bahrain, Mar. 27, 1990.

Safety at Sea
International convention for the safety of life at sea, 1974, with annex. Done at London Nov. 1, 1974. Entered into force May 25, 1980. TIAS 9700.
Accession deposited: New Zealand, Feb. 23, 1990. [3]

Protocol of 1978 relating to the international convention for the safety of life at sea, 1974 (TIAS 9700). Done at London Feb. 17, 1978. Entered into force May 1, 1981. TIAS 10009.
Accessions deposited: New Zealand, Feb. 23, 1990; [3] Saudi Arabia, Mar. 2, 1990.

Slavery
Convention to suppress the slave trade and slavery. Done at Geneva Sept. 25, 1926. Entered into force Mar. 9, 1927; for the US Mar. 21, 1929. TS 778.

Protocol amending the slavery convention signed at Geneva on Sept. 25, 1926 (TS 778), and annex. Done at New York Dec. 7, 1953. Entered into force Dec 7, 1953, for the protocol; July 7, 1955, for the annex to the protocol; for the US Mar. 7, 1956. TIAS 3532.

Supplementary convention on the abolition of slavery, the slave trade, and institutions and practices similar to slavery. Done at Geneva Sept. 7, 1956. Entered into force Apr. 30, 1957; for the US Dec. 6, 1967. TIAS 6418.
Notification of succession deposited: St. Lucia, Feb. 14, 1990; effective Feb. 22, 1979.
Accession deposited: Bahrain, Mar. 27, 1990.

Terrorism
International convention against the taking of hostages. Adopted at New York Dec. 17, 1979. Entered into force June 3, 1983; for the US Jan. 6, 1985.
Accessions deposited: Australia, May 21, 1990; Mali, Feb. 8, 1990; Nepal, Mar. 9, 1990; Sudan, June 19, 1990; Romania, May 17, 1990.

Convention on the prevention and punishment of crimes against internationally protected persons, including diplomatic agents. Done at New York Dec. 14, 1973. Entered into force Feb. 20, 1977. TIAS 8532.
Accession deposited: Nepal, Mar. 9, 1990.

Timber
International tropical timber agreement, 1983, with annexes. Done at Geneva Nov. 18, 1983. Entered into force provisionally Apr. 1, 1985; for the US Apr. 26, 1985.
Accession deposited: Colombia, Mar. 27, 1990.

Torture
Convention against torture and other crueL inhuman, or degrading treatment or punishment. Done at New York Dec. 10, 1984. Entered into force June 26, 1987. [1] [Senate] Treaty Doc 100-20.
Signature: Paraguay, Oct. 23, 1989.
Ratification deposited: Paraguay, Mar. 12, 1990.
Accessions deposited: Guatemala, Jan. 5, 1990, [5] Somalia, Jan. 24, 1990.

Trade
United Nations convention on contracts for the international sale of goods. Done at Vienna Apr. 11, 1980. Entered into force Jan. 1, 1988. [52 Fed. Reg. 6262]
Accession deposited: Switzerland, Feb. 21, 1990.

Treaties
Vienna convention on the law of treaties, with annex. Done at Vienna May 23, 1969. Entered into force Jan. 27, 1980. [1]
Accessions deposited: Liechtenstein, Feb. 8, 1990; Switzerland, May 7, 1990.
Ratification deposited: Sudan, Apr. 18, 1990.

Vienna convention on the law of treaties between states and international organizations or between international organizations, with annex. Done at Vienna Mar. 21, 1986. [4]
Accessions deposited: Liechtenstein, Feb. 8, 1990; Switzerland, May 7, 1990.

UN Industrial Development Organization (UNIDO)
Constitution of the United Nations Industrial Development Organization, with annexes. Adopted at Vienna Apr. 8, 1979. Entered into force June 21, 1985. TIAS 1985.

Ratification deposited: Liberia, May 10, 1990.
Accession deposited: Burma, Apr. 12, 1990.

Women
Convention on the elimination of all forms of discrimination against women. Done at New York Dec. 18, 1979. Entered into force Sept. 3, 1981. [1]
Signature: Belize, Mar. 7, 1990.
Ratifications deposited: Belize, May 16, 1990; Bolivia, June 8, 1990; Trinidad and Tobago, Jan. 12, 1990.

Convention on the political rights of women. Done at New York Mar. 31, 1953. Entered into force July 7, 1954; for the US July 7, 1976. TIAS 8289.
Ratification deposited: Paraguay, Feb. 22, 1990.

BILATERAL

Australia
Arrangement concerning trade in certain steel products, with appendices. Effected by exchange of letters at Washington Mar. 9, 1990. Entered into force Mar. 9, 1990; effective Oct. 1, 1989.

Framework for an arrangement on steel trade liberalization, with appendices, and related letters. Effected by exchange of letters at Washington Mar. 9, 1990. Entered into force Mar. 9, 1990.

Austria
Arrangement concerning trade in certain steel products, with appendices. Effected by exchange of letters at Washington and Vienna Nov. 20 and Dec. 7, 1989. Entered into force Dec. 7, 1989; effective Oct. 1, 1989.

Bahamas
Agreement amending and extending the implementing arrangement of Apr. 5, 1984, to the agreement concerning US defense facilities in The Bahamas. Effected by exchanges of notes at Nassau Aug 20, 1987, and Jan. 25, Feb. 3 and 23, 1988. Entered into force Feb. 23, 1988; effective Jan. 26, 1988.

Bolivia
Agreement supplementing and amending the agreement of Feb. 24, 1987, as revised, concerning cooperation to combat narcotics trafficking, with annexes. Effected by exchange of notes at Washington May 9, 1990. Entered into force May 9, 1990.

Brazil
Arrangement concerning trade in certain steel products, with appendices. Effected by exchange of letters at Washington Feb. 26 and Mar. 5, 1990. Entered into force Mar. 5, 1990; effective Oct. 1, 1989.

Agreement regarding the consolidation and rescheduling of certain debts owed to, guaranteed by, or insured by the US Government and its agencies. Signed at Brasilia Mar. 14, 1990. Entered into force Apr. 19, 1990.

Agreement on steel trade liberalization, with appendices and related letter. Effected by exchange of letters at Washington Feb. 26 and Mar. 5, 1990. Entered into force Mar. 5, 1990.

Cameroon
Agreement regarding the phased discharge of certain debts owed to the Government of the United States, with annexes. Signed at Yaounde Jan. 3, 1990. Entered into force Jan. 3, 1990.

Agreement regarding the consolidation and rescheduling of certain debts owed to, guaranteed by, or insured by the US Government and its agencies, with annexes. Signed at Yaounde Jan. 3, 1990. Entered into force Feb. 12, 1990.

Canada
Agreement for the establishment of a binational educational exchange foundation. Signed at Ottawa Feb. 13, 1990. Entered into force Feb. 13, 1990.

Central African Republic
Agreement regarding the consolidation and rescheduling of certain debts owed to, guaranteed by, or insured by the US Government and its agencies, with annexes. Signed at Bangui Mar. 22, 1990. Entered into force May 3, 1990.

China
Arrangement concerning trade in certain steel products, with appendices. Signed at Washington Apr. 19, 1990. Entered into force Apr. 19, 1990; effective Oct. 1, 1989.

Agreement extending the agreement of Jan. 31, 1979 (TIAS 9179), relating to cooperation in science and technology. Effected by exchange of notes at Beijing Oct. 24 and 30, 1989. Entered into force Oct. 30, 1989.

Agreement extending the agreement of Jan. 31, 1979 (TIAS 9179), on cooperation in science and technology, as extended. Effected by exchange of notes at Beijing Apr. 30 and May 1, 1990. Entered into force May 1, 1990.

Costa Rica

Agreement regarding the consolidation and rescheduling of certain debts owed to, guaranteed by, or insured by the US Government and its agencies. Signed at San Jose Feb. 22, 1990. Entered into force Apr. 9, 1990.

Swap agreement among the US Treasury and the Central Bank of Costa Rica/Government of Costa Rica. Signed at Washington and San Jose May 18, 1990. Entered into force May 18, 1990.

Customs Cooperation Council

Tax reimbursement agreement, with annex. Signed at Brussels Jan. 26, 1990. Entered into force Jan. 26, 1990.

Czechoslovakia

Agreement on trade relations, with related exchanges of letters. Signed at Washington Apr. 12, 1990. Enters into force on the date of exchange of written notices of acceptance.

Ecuador

International express mail agreement with detailed regulations. Signed at Quito and Washington Mar. 20 and Apr. 11, 1990. Entered into force Mar. 30, 1990.

European Communities

Arrangement concerning trade in certain steel products, with appendices. Effected by exchange of letters at Washington and Brussels Nov. 20, 1989. Entered into force Nov. 20, 1989; effective Oct. 1, 1989.

Arrangement concerning trade in steel pipes and tubes, with appendices. Effected by exchange of letters at Washington and Brussels Nov. 20, 1989. Entered into force Nov. 20, 1989; effective Oct. 1, 1989.

Agreement on steel trade liberalization, with appendices. Effected by exchange of letters at Washington and Brussels Nov. 20, 1989. Entered into force Nov. 20, 1989.

European Space Agency (ESA)

Memorandum of understanding concerning the Solar Terrestrial Science Program, with related exchange of letters. Signed at Washington Nov. 30, 1989. Entered into force Nov. 30, 1989.

Finland

Arrangement concerning trade in certain steel products, with appendices. Effected by exchange of letters at Washington and Helsinki Feb. 16 and Mar. 7, 1990. Entered into force Mar. 7, 1990; effective Oct. 1, 1989.

Agreement on removal of trade distorting practices in steel, with appendix and related exchange of letters. Effected by exchange of letters at Washington and Helsinki Feb. 28 and Mar. 23, 1990. Entered into force Mar. 23, 1990.

France

Memorandum of agreement concerning a cooperative program of information exchange and development of cooperative research projects on free electron laser technology. Signed at Paris Jan. 31, 1990. Entered into force Jan. 31, 1990.

Gabon

Agreement regarding the consolidation and rescheduling or refinancing of certain debts owed to, guaranteed by, or insured by the US Government and its agencies, with annexes. Signed at Libreville Mar. 5, 1990. Entered into force Apr. 9, 1990.

German Democratic Republic

Arrangement concerning trade in certain steel products, with appendices. Effected by exchange of letters at Washington and Berlin Nov. 21 and Dec 8, 1989. Entered into force Dec 8, 1989; effective Oct. 1, 1989.

Germany, Federal Republic of

Memorandum of understanding concerning the joint research, development and demonstration of advanced armor protection systems (AAPS), with annexes. Signed at Washington and Bonn Jan. 4 and 11, 1990. Entered into force Jan. 11, 1990.

Memorandum of understanding on the mutual exchange of documents. Signed at Bonn and Washington Jan. 18, 1989, and Feb. 9, 1990. Entered into force Feb. 9, 1990.

Ghana

International express mail agreement, with detailed regulations. Signed at Accra and Washington Feb. 9 and Mar. 1, 1990. Entered into force Apr. 16, 1990.

Greece

Agreement amending the agreement of Sept. 8, 1983 (TIAS 10814), on defense and economic cooperation. Effected by exchange of notes at Athens Feb. 27, 1990. Entered into force Feb. 27, 1990.

Agreement extending the interim agreement on air services, with memorandum of understanding, of Apr. 9, 1985, as amended and extended. Effected by exchange of notes at Athens Apr. 18 and 25, 1990. Entered into force Apr. 25, 1990.

Guatemala

Agreement relating to the employment of dependents of official government employees, with agreement and addendum. Effected by exchange of notes at Washington Mar. 22 and 23, 1990. Entered into force Mar. 23, 1990.

Honduras

Project grant agreement for the economic stabilization and recovery program III. Signed at Tegucigalpa Mar. 29, 1990. Entered into force Mar. 29, 1990.

Hungary

Arrangement concerning trade in certain steel products, with appendices. Signed at Washington Sept. 27, 1989. Entered into force Sept. 27, 1989; effective Oct. 1, 1989.

India

Mutual cooperation agreement for reducing demand, preventing illicit use of and traffic in drugs, and for matters relating to licit trade in opiates. Signed at New Delhi Mar. 29, 1990. Entered into force Mar. 29, 1990.

International Telecommunication Union (ITU)

Tax reimbursement agreement, with annex. Signed at Geneva Jan. 19, 1990. Entered into force Jan. 19, 1990.

Israel

Agreement amending the agreement of Jan. 18, 1989, concerning the construction of diplomatic facilities. Effected by exchange of notes at Tel Aviv Jan. 22 and 30, 1990. Entered into force Jan. 30, 1990.

Memorandum of understanding on scientific and technical cooperation in the field of water resources development, with annexes. Signed at Washington and Haifa Jan. 26 and Feb. 8, 1990. Entered into force Feb. 8, 1990.

Jamaica
Agreement amending the agreement of July 6, 1989, regarding the consolidation of debts. Effected by exchange of notes at Kingston Nov. 27, 1989, and Jan. 18, 1990. Entered into force Jan. 18, 1990.

Japan
Arrangement concerning trade in certain steel products, with appendices. Effected by exchange of letters at Washington Feb. 14, 1990. Entered into force Feb. 14, 1990; effective Oct. 1, 1989.

Framework on steel trade liberalization, with appendix. Signed at Washington Feb. 14, 1990. Entered into force Feb. 14, 1990.

Agreement concerning the acquisition and production in Japan of the Sparrow Missile System (AIM-7M). Effected by exchange of notes at Tokyo Mar. 27, 1990. Entered into force Mar. 27, 1990.

Agreement amending the agreement of Mar. 31, 1989, concerning the acquisition and production in Japan of the SH-60J and UH-60J aircraft. Effected by exchange of notes at Tokyo Mar. 30, 1990. Entered into force Mar. 30, 1990.

Agreement regarding squid and large-mesh driftnet fisheries, with annexes and attachment. Effected by exchange of letters at Tokyo and Silver Spring Apr. 12, 1990. Entered into force Apr. 12, 1990

Korea
Arrangement concerning trade in certain steel products, with appendices. Effected by exchange of letters at Washington Apr. 20, 1990. Entered into force Apr. 20, 1990; effective Oct. 1, 1989.

Framework agreement for agreements on steel trade liberalization, with appendices and exchange of letters. Signed at Washington Apr. 20, 1990. Entered into force Apr. 20, 1990.

Malaysia
Agreement concerning reciprocal exemption with respect to taxes on income of shipping and air transport enterprises. Signed at Kuala Lumpur

Apr. 18, 1989. Entered into force: Mar. 12, 1990.

Malta
Agreement concerning the provision of training related to defense articles under the United States International Military Education and Training (IMET) Program. Effected by exchange of notes at Floriana Feb. 6 and 13, 1989. Entered into force Feb. 13, 1989.

Mauritania
Agreement regarding the consolidation and rescheduling of certain debts owed to, guaranteed by, or insured by the US Government and its agency, with annexes. Signed at Nouakchott Feb. 4, 1990. Entered into force Mar. 12, 1990.

Mexico
Arrangement concerning trade in certain steel products, with appendices. Signed at Washington Oct. 3, 1989. Entered into force Oct. 3, 1989; effective Oct. 1, 1989. Agreement on steel trade liberalization, with appendices. Signed at Washington Oct. 3, 1989. Entered into force: Oct. 3, 1989.

Agreement for the exchange of information with respect to taxes. Signed at Washington Nov. 9, 1989. Entered into force: Jan. 18, 1990.

Swap agreement among the US Treasury and the Banco de Mexico/Government of Mexico, with memorandum of understanding. Signed at Washington and Mexico Mar. 23, 1990. Entered into force Mar. 23, 1990.

Agreement regarding the consolidation and rescheduling or refinancing of certain debts owed to, guaranteed by, or insured by the US Government and its agencies. Signed at Mexico Mar. 14, 1990. Entered into force Apr. 23, 1990.

Agreement on maritime search and rescue. Signed at Mexico Aug. 7, 1989. Entered into force: June 25, 1990.

Mozambique
Agreement regarding the consolidation and rescheduling of certain debts owed to, guaranteed by, or insured by the US Government and its agencies. Signed at Maputo Mar. 6, 1990. Entered into force Apr. 23, 1990.

Nigeria
Agreement regarding the consolidation and rescheduling of certain debts owed

to, guaranteed by, or insured by the US Government and its agencies. Signed at Lagos Dec. 4, 1989. Entered into force Jan. 22, 1990.

NATO Maintenance and Supply Organization
Amendment one to the basic agreement of Feb. 2, 1982, on mutual support. Signed at Stuttgart and Capellen Apr. 30 and May 7, 1990. Entered into force May 7, 1990.

Norway
Agreement concerning the reciprocal exemption from income tax of income derived from the international operation of ships and aircraft. Effected by exchange of notes at Washington May 24, 1990. Entered into force May 24, 1990.

Pakistan
Memorandum of understanding on co-assembly and co-production of AN/UAS12A night sight equipment, with appendix. Signed at Rawalpindi Jan. 27, 1990. Entered into force Jan. 27, 1990.

Panama
Memorandum of agreement concerning assistance in developing and modernizing Panama's civil aviation infrastructure, with annexes. Signed at Panama and Washington Jan. 24 and Feb. 15, 1990. Entered into force Feb. 15, 1990.

Papua New Guinea
Memorandum of understanding concerning joint and combined military activities by Papua New Guinea defense forces and US military forces in independent Papua New Guinea, with appendices. Signed at Port Moresby Mar. 26, 1990. Entered into force Mar. 26, 1990.

Philippines
Agreement continuing the operations of the US Department of Veterans Affairs in the Philippines. Signed at Manila May 3, 1990. Entered into force May 3, 1990; effective Oct. 1, 1989.

Project grant agreement for the family planning assistance project. Signed at Manila May 10, 1990. Entered into force May 10, 1990.

Poland
Treaty concerning business and economic relations, with annex, protocol and related exchanges of letters. Signed at Washington Mar. 21,

TREATIES

1990. Enters into force on the 30th day following the date of exchange of ratifications.

Arrangement concerning trade in certain steel products, with appendices. Signed at Washington Sept. 12, 1989. Entered into force Sept. 12, 1989; effective Oct. 1, 1989.

Investment guaranty agreement. Signed at Warsaw Oct. 13, 1989. Entered into force Feb. 21, 1990.

Romania
Arrangement concerning trade in certain steel products, with appendices. Effected by exchange of letters at Washington and Bucharest Oct. 27 and Mar. 13, 1990. Entered into force Mar. 13, 1990; effective Oct. 1, 1989.

Spain
Convention for the avoidance of double taxation and the prevention of fiscal evasion with respect to taxes on income, with protocol. Signed at Madrid Feb. 22, 1990. Enters into force upon the exchange of instruments of ratification.

Sri Lanka
International express mail agreement, with detailed regulations. Signed at Colombo and Washington Feb. 1 and 14, 1990. Entered into force Mar. 30, 1990.

Thailand
Memorandum of agreement concerning mapping, charting, and geodesy. Signed at Bangkok and Fairfax Feb. 27 and Mar. 15, 1990. Entered into force Mar. 15, 1990.

Trinidad and Tobago
Arrangement concerning trade in certain steel products, with appendices. Effected by exchange of letters at Port-of-Spain and Washington Mar. 9 and 21, 1990. Entered into force Mar. 21, 1990; effective Oct. 1, 1989.

Air transport agreement, with annexes. Signed at Port-of-Spain May 23, 1990. Entered into force May 23, 1990. Supersedes agreements of Feb. 11, 1946 (TIAS 1507), Nov. 22, 1961 (TIAS 4955), and Sept. 27 and Oct. 8, 1962 (TIAS 5209).

Agreement on removal of trade distorting practices in steel trade, with appendices and exchange of letters. Effected by exchange of letters at Washington and Port-of-Spain Mar. 29 and Apr. 12, 1990. Entered into force Apr. 12, 1990.

Tunisia
Treaty concerning the reciprocal encouragement and protection of investment, with protocol. Signed at Washington May 15, 1990. Enters into force 30 days after exchange of ratifications.

Turkey
Memorandum of understanding concerning the operation of the BUREAUFAX service. Signed at Ankara and Washington Feb. 14 and Mar. 14, 1990. Entered into force Mar. 15, 1990.

Treaty concerning the reciprocal encouragement and protection of investments, with protocol. Signed at Washington Dec. 3, 1985. Entered into force: May 18, 1990.

USSR
Agreement on principles of implementing trial verification and stability measures that would be carried out pending the conclusion of the US-Soviet treaty on the reduction and limitation of strategic offensive arms. Signed at Jackson Hole, Wyoming, Sept. 23, 1989. Entered into force Sept. 23, 1989.

Agreement on a mutual understanding on cooperation in the struggle against the illicit traffic in narcotics. Signed at Washington Jan. 31, 1990. Entered into force Jan. 31, 1990.

Agreement concerning the conduct of reciprocal demonstrations of reentry vehicle inspection procedures, with appendix. Effected by exchange of letters at Geneva Jan. 22, 1990. Entered into force Mar. 23, 1990.

United Kingdom
Memorandum of understanding concerning cooperation in the development of a satellite communications modulator/demodulator and associated equipment resistant to electronic counter-measures and nuclear effects (Universal Modem), with annexes. Signed at Washington and London Oct. 25 and Dec. 8, 1989. Entered into force Dec 8, 1989.

Agreement extending the agreement of Apr. 14, 1987, as extended, concerning the British Virgin Islands and narcotics activities. Effected by exchange of notes at Washington Feb. 9, 1990. Entered into force Feb. 9, 1990; effective Feb. 12, 1990.

Agreement extending the agreement of Apr. 14, 1987, as extended, concerning the British Virgin Islands and narcotics activities. Effected by exchange of notes at Washington May 9, 1990. Entered into force May 9, 1990; effective May 12, 1990.

Memorandum of understanding concerning the establishment of a radar site in the Cayman Islands as part of the Caribbean Basin Radar Network (CBRN). Signed at Washington Feb. 26, 1990. Entered into force Feb. 26, 1990.

Memorandum of understanding concerning the provision, trial, and operation of a relocatable over the horizon radar (ROTHR) in the United Kingdom, with annex. Signed at Washington Apr. 20, 1990. Entered into force Apr. 20, 1990.

Agreement extending the agreement of Mar. 11, 1987, as extended, concerning Anguilla and narcotics activities. Effected by exchange of notes at Washington Mar. 26, 1990. Entered into force Mar. 26, 1990; effective Mar. 27, 1990.

Agreement extending the agreement of May 14, 1987, as extended, concerning Montserrat and narcotics activities. Effected by exchange of notes at Washington May 29, 1990. Entered into force May 29, 1990; effective June 1, 1990.

Venezuela
Arrangement concerning trade in certain steel products, with appendices. Signed at Washington Feb. 1, 1990. Entered into force Feb. 1, 1990; effective Oct. 1, 1989.

Swap agreement among the US Treasury and the Central Bank of Venezuela/Government of Venezuela, with memorandum of understanding. Signed at Washington and Caracas Mar. 16, 1990. Entered into force Mar. 16, 1990.

Yugoslavia
International express mail agreement, with detailed regulations. Signed at Belgrade and Washington Jan. 22 and Mar. 1, 1990. Entered into force Mar. 30, 1990.

Zambia
Agreement relating to the employment of dependents of official government employees. Effected by exchange of notes at Lusaka June 26, 1989, and Jan. 4, 1990. Entered into force Jan. 4, 1990.

---

[1] Not in force for the US.
[2] Does not accept optional annexes.
[3] With declaration.
[4] Not in force.
[5] With reservation(s).

II. June-July 1990

MULTILATERAL

Atomic Energy
Amendment of Article VI.A.1 of the Statute of the International Atomic Energy Agency of Oct. 26, 1956, as amended (TIAS 3873, 5284, 7668). Done at Vienna Sept. 27, 1984. Entered into force Dec 28, 1989. [Senate] Treaty Doc. 99-7.
Acceptances deposited: Mali, Mar. 13, 1990; South Africa, May 25, 1990.

Agreement regarding protection of information transferred into the United States in connection with the initial phase of a project for the establishment of a uranium enrichment installation in the United States based upon the gas centrifuge process developed within the three European countries [Fed. Rep. of Germany, Netherlands, UK]. Signed at Washington Apr. 11, 1990. Entered into force Apr. 11, 1990.
Parties: Germany, Fed. Rep., Netherlands, UK, US.

Coffee
International coffee agreement, 1983, with annexes, done at London Sept. 16, 1982, as extended July 3, 1989. [1]
Entered into force Oct. 1, 1989.
Acceptances deposited: Ethiopia, Mar. 26, 1990; Japan, July 17, 1990; Peru, Mar. 14, 1990; Venezuela, Mar. 2, 1990.
Accession deposited: Jamaica, Mar. 22, 1990.

Cultural Property
Statutes of the International Centre for the Study of the Preservation and Restoration of Cultural Property. Adopted at New Delhi Nov.-Dec. 1956, as amended at Rome Apr. 24, 1963, and Apr. 14-17, 1969. TIAS 7038.
Accession deposited: Mali, Oct. 9, 1989.

Convention on the means of prohibiting and preventing the illicit import, export, and transfer of ownership of cultural property. Done at Paris Nov. 14, 1970. Entered into force Apr. 24, 1972; for the US Dec. 2, 1983.
Acceptance deposited: Australia, Oct. 30, 1989. [2]
Ratifications deposited: Belize, Jan. 26, 1990; Madagascar, June 21, 1989.

Customs
Convention establishing a Customs Cooperation Council, with annex. Done at Brussels Dec. 15, 1950. Entered into force Nov. 4, 1952; for the US Nov. 5, 1970. TIAS 7063.
Accessions deposited: German Dem. Rep., Mar. 27, 1990; Iraq, June 6, 1990; Togo, Feb. 12, 1990.

Finance
Agreement establishing the European Bank for Reconstruction and Development, with annexes. Done at Paris May 29, 1990. Enters into force when instruments of ratification, acceptance, or approval have been deposited by signatories whose initial subscriptions represent not less than two-thirds of total subscriptions set forth in Annex A.
Signature: US, May 29, 1990.

Pollution
Convention on the prevention of marine pollution by dumping of wastes and other matter, with annexes. Done at London, Mexico City, Moscow, and Washington Dec. 29, 1972. Entered into force Aug. 30, 1975.
Accession deposited: Cyprus, June 7, 1990.

Pollution — Ships
Annex V to the international convention for the prevention of pollution from ships, 1973. Done at London Nov. 2, 1973. Entered into force Dec. 31, 1988. [Senate] Treaty Doc. 100-3.
Acceptances deposited: Ecuador, May 18, 1990; Switzerland, Apr. 30, 1990.

Protocol of 1978 relating to the international convention for the prevention of pollution from ships, 1973. Done at London Feb. 17, 1978. Entered into force Oct. 2, 1983.
Accession deposited: Ecuador, May 18, 1990.

Poplar Commission
Convention placing the International Poplar Commission within the

framework of the Food and Agriculture Organization.
Approved at Rome Nov. 19, 1959. Entered into force Sept. 26, 1961; for the US Aug 13, 1970. TIAS 6952.
Acceptance deposited: Chile, Jan. 29, 1990.

Rubber
International natural rubber agreement, 1987, with annexes. Done at Geneva Mar. 20, 1987. Entered into force provisionally Dec. 29, 1988; definitively Apr. 3, 1989. [Senate] Treaty Doc. 100-9.
Accession deposited: Sri Lanka, July 11, 1990.

Safety at Sea
International convention for the safety of life at sea, 1974, with annex. Done at London Nov. 1, 1974. Entered into force May 25, 1980. TIAS 9700.
Accession deposited: Sudan, May 15, 1990.

Satellite Communications Systems
Agreement relating to the International Telecommunications Satellite Organization (INTELSAT), with annexes. Done at Washington Aug. 20, 1971. Entered into force Feb. 12, 1973. TIAS 7532.
Accession deposited: Romania, May 7, 1990.

Operating agreement relating to the International Telecommunications Satellite Organization (INTELSAT), with annex. Done at Washington Aug. 20, 1971. Entered into force Feb. 12, 1973. TIAS 7532.
Signature: Ministry of Posts and Telecommunications of Romania, May 7, 1990.

Convention on the international maritime satellite organization (INMARSAT), with annex. Done at London Sept. 3, 1976. Entered into force July 16, 1979. TIAS 9605.
Accession deposited: Mozambique, Apr. 18, 1990.

Operating agreement on the international maritime satellite organization (INMARSAT), with annex. Done at London Sept. 3, 1976. Entered into force July 16, 1979. TIAS 9605.
Signature: Mozambique, Apr. 18, 1990.

Taxation — Assistance
Convention on mutual administrative assistance in tax matters. Done at Strasbourg Jan. 25, 1988. [Senate] Treaty Doc. 101-6.[3]
Ratification deposited: Sweden, July 4, 1990.[2]

Timber
International tropical timber agreement, 1983, with annexes. Done at Geneva Nov. 18, 1983. Entered into force provisionally Apr. 1, 1985; for the US Apr. 26, 1985.
Accession deposited: Togo, May 8, 1990.
Acceptance deposited: US, May 25, 1990.

Trade
UN convention on contracts for the international sale of goods. Done at Vienna Apr. 11, 1980. Entered into force Jan. 1, 1988. [52 Fed. Reg. 6262.]
Ratification deposited: Czechoslovakia, Mar. 5, 1990[2]
Accession deposited: Bulgaria, July 9, 1990; Iraq, Mar. 5, 1990.

United Nations
Charter of the United Nations and Statute of the International Court of Justice. Signed at San Francisco June 26, 1945. Entered into force Oct. 24, 1945. 59 Stat. 1031, TS 993.
Admitted to membership: Namibia, Apr. 23, 1990.

Weights and Measures
Convention establishing an International Organization of Legal Metrology. Done at Paris Oct. 12, 1955. Entered into force May 28, 1958; for the US Oct. 22, 1972, as amended Jan. 18, 1968. TIAS 7533.
Accession deposited: Saudi Arabia, Oct. 19, 1989.

BILATERAL

Australia
Agreement amending the agreement of May 29, 1980, as amended (TIAS 9781, 10198), providing for the continuation of a cooperative program facilitating space flight operations. Effected by exchange of notes at Canberra Jan. 17 and May 2, 1990. Entered into force May 2, 1990.

Botswana
Agreement extending the agreement of Mar. 28, 1980 (TIAS 9741), providing for a radio facility for the purpose of relaying Voice of America programs to areas in Africa. Effected by exchange of notes at Gaborone Mar. 13 and 20, 1990. Entered into force Mar. 20, 1990; effective Mar. 28, 1990.

Bulgaria
Memorandum of understanding concerning the operation of the INTELPOST service, with details of implementation. Signed at Sofia and Washington Apr. 20 and June 13, 1990. Entered into force June 25, 1990.

Cameroon
International express mail agreement, with detailed regulations. Signed at Yaounde and Washington Apr. 25 and June 22, 1990. Entered into force Aug. 1, 1990.

Indonesia
Agreement amending the agreement of Sept. 25 and Oct. 3, 1985, relating to trade in cotton, wool, and manmade fiber textiles and textile products. Effected by exchange of notes at Jakarta May 7 and 19, 1990. Entered into force May 19, 1990.

Kirabati
Investment incentive agreement. Effected by exchange of notes at Suva and Tarawa Jan. 22, 1990. Entered into force Jan. 22, 1990.

Nigeria
Postal money order agreement, with attachments. Signed at Lagos and Washington June 14 and 28, 1990. Entered into force Sept. 1, 1990.

Panama
Agreement relating to the establishment of a Peace Corps program in Panama. Effected by exchange of notes at Washington May 1, 1990. Enters into force upon Panamanian notification to US that constitutional requirements have been completed.

Papua New Guinea
Development cooperation agreement. Signed at Port Moresby May 7, 1990. Entered into force May 7, 1990.

Peru
Agreement extending the air transport services agreement of Dec 16, 1986. Effected by exchange of notes at Lima June 6 and 7, 1990. Entered into force June 7, 1990.

Poland
Agreement for collaboration to demonstrate an emerging retrofit of clean coal technology at a powerplant in Cracow, Poland, with annexes. Signed at Washington Mar. 15, 1990. Entered into force Mar. 15, 1990.

USSR
Agreement on the maritime boundary, with annex. Signed at Washington June 1, 1990. Enters into force on the date of exchange of instruments of ratification.

Agreement regarding certain maritime matters, with annexes. Signed at Washington June 1, 1990. Enters into force upon an exchange of notes certifying completion of the first forecasting requirements provided for in Annex III.

Agreement on cooperation on ocean studies, with annexes. Signed at Washington June 1, 1990. Entered into force June 1, 1990.
Supersedes the agreement of June 19, 1973, as amended and extended (TIAS 7651, 9349).

Civil air transport agreement, with annexes. Signed at Washington June 1, 1990. Entered into force June 1, 1990.
Supersedes the agreement of Nov. 4, 1966, as amended (TIAS 6135).

Agreement on expansion of undergraduate exchanges. Signed at Washington June 1, 1990. Entered into force June 1, 1990.

Memorandum of understanding to increase distribution of the magazines America and Soviet Life. Signed at Washington June 2, 1990. Entered into force June 2, 1990.

Agreement on scientific and technical cooperation in the field of peaceful uses of atomic energy, with annex. Signed at Washington June 1, 1990. Entered into force June 1, 1990.

Agreement regarding cooperation and mutual assistance between their customs services. Signed at Washington June 2, 1990. Enters into force on the 90th day following an exchange of notes in which the parties notify each other that they have accepted its terms and that all necessary legal requirements have been fulfilled.

Agreement on the supply of grain.
Signed at Washington June 1, 1990.
Entered into force June 1, 1990.

Protocol to the treaty of July 3, 1974, on
the limitation of underground nuclear
weapon tests. Signed at Washington
June 1, 1990. Enters into force on the
date of entry into force of the treaty.
[Senate] Treaty Doc. 101-19.

Protocol to the treaty of May 28, 1976,
on underground nuclear explosions for
peaceful purposes. Signed at
Washington June 1, 1990. Enters into
force on the date of entry into force of
the treaty. [Senate] Treaty Doc. 101-19.

Agreement on trade relations, with related exchanges of letters. Signed at
Washington June 1, 1990. Enters into
force upon an exchange of notes in
which the parties notify each other that
all necessary legal requirements have
been fulfilled.

Venezuela
Investment incentive agreement. Signed
at Washington June 22, 1990. Entered
into force June 22, 1990.

Zimbabwe
Investment incentive agreement. Signed
at Harare June 20, 1990. Entered into
force June 20, 1990.

---

[1] Certain provisions of the agreement
suspended.
[2] With reservation(s)/declaration(s).
[3] Not in force.

PRESS RELEASE

Department of State

Press releases may be obtained from the Office of Press Relations, Department of State, Washington, D.C. 20520-6810.

No.	Date	Subject
*94	6/28	Baker: pre-NATO Summit press conference, June 28.
95	6/29	Release of Foreign Relations of the United States, 1955-57, volume XVII, Arab-Israeli Dispute, 1957.
*96	7/2	Curtis Bohlen, Assistant Secretary of State for Oceans and International Environmental and Scientific Affairs (biographic data).
97	7/4	Baker: remarks at the G-24 ministerial meeting, Brussels, July 4.
*98	7/4	Baker: press conference following G-24 ministerial meeting, Brussels, July 4.
*99	7/6	Shirin Tahir-Kheli, Ambassador and U.S. Alternate Representative for Special Political Affairs to the United Nations (biographic data).
*100	7/7	Baker: interview by Robert Novak and Charles Bierbauer, CNN, Houston, July 7.
*101	7/8	Baker: interview on "This Week with David Brinkley," ABC-TV, Houston, July 8.
102	7/10	Baker: press briefing on the economic summit political communique, Houston, July 10.
*103	7/13	David Passage, Ambassador to Botswana (biographic data).
104	7/18	Baker: remarks with Foreign Minister Eduard Shevardnadze, U.S.S.R., Paris, July 18.
105	7/20	Baker: press conference with other foreign ministers following Two-Plus-Four meeting, Paris, July 17.
*106	7/20	Program for the official working visit of Rodrigo Borja Cevallos, President of the Republic of Ecuador, July 22-24.
*107	7/30	Program for the official working visit of Gnassigbe Eyadema, President of the Republic of Togo, July 30-August 1.
108	7/27	Baker: statement before the Six-Plus-Six open session of the ASEAN post-ministerial conference, Jakarta, July 27.
109	7/29	Baker: press conference with other foreign ministers after ASEAN post-ministerial conference, Jakarta, July 29.
110	7/30	Baker: address at opening session of second Asia-Pacific Economic Cooperation meeting, Singapore, July 30.
111	8/31	Baker: statement at the APEC meeting, Singapore, July 31.
*112	8/7	Baker: press conference with Foreign Minister Eduard Shevardnadze, U.S.S.R., Irkutsk, August 2.
113	8/7	Baker: toast at welcoming dinner hosted by Mongolian Government, Ulaan Baatar, August 2.
*114	8/3	Baker: press conference with Mongolian Foreign Minister Gombosuren, August 3.
115	8/6	Baker: joint statement and press conference with Foreign Minister Eduard Shevardnadze, Moscow, August 3.
116	8/8	Baker: opening remarks at plenary session of U.S.-Mexican Binational Commission, August 8.
*117	8/14	Baker: departure remarks after discussions with Government of Turkey, August 9.
118	8/10	Baker: intervention at special session of North Atlantic Council, Brussels, August 10.
119	8/10	Baker: press conference following special NAC session, Brussels, August 10.
*120	8/13	Charles E. Cobb, Jr., Ambassador to Iceland (biographic data).
*121	8/13	Richard Anthony Moore, Ambassador to Ireland (biographic data).
*122	8/13	Baker: interview on "This Week with David Brinkley," ABC-TV, August 12.
123	9/5	Release of Foreign Relations of the United States, 1955-57, volume XX, Regulation of Armaments and Atomic Energy .
*124	9/7	Baker: interview by Tom Brokaw, NBC-TV, September 4.
125	9/12	Baker: statement before the House Foreign Affairs Committee, September 4.
*126	9/14	Baker: statement before the Senate Foreign Relations Committee, September 5.

*Not printed in the Bulletin.

Foreign Relations Volumes on Arab-Israeli Dispute and on Arms Control Negotiations, 1955-57

The Department of State, on June 29, 1990, released Foreign Relations of the United States, 1955-1957, volume XVII, Arab-Israeli Dispute, 1957. [1]

U.S. efforts in the Middle East during 1957 first concentrated on resolving the diplomatic problems arising from the 1956 Suez Crisis. Primary among these was Israel's refusal to withdraw from the Gaza Strip and the eastern edge of the Sinai Peninsula down to Sharm al-Sheikh without certain guarantees. U.S. officials believed that Israel's continued occupation exacerbated anti-Western sentiment in the Arab world and impeded the prompt reopening of the Suez Canal and a speedy resolution of a Canal settlement.

Moreover, a strong movement within the Afro-Asian bloc in the U.N. General Assembly to adopt a resolution imposing far-reaching sanctions on Israel caused particular problems for U.S. officials. U.S. compliance with such a resolution would require the U.S. Government to outlaw the sale of Israeli bonds and the extension of private gifts to Israel. Congressional and other domestic opposition to a U.S. vote for sanctions grew substantially during this period.

During lengthy discussions with Israeli officials in February, the United States offered a series of assurances concerning Israeli passage through the Strait of Tiran off Sharm al-Sheikh that became a basis for Israel's withdrawal. Following intensive diplomacy in early March, an Israeli agreement to turn Gaza over to the U.N. Emergency Force was reached, and Israel subsequently withdrew its forces from Sinai and Gaza.

After Israel's withdrawal, the United States sought to obtain Egyptian agreement to a Canal settlement that would limit Egypt's control of the Canal. These efforts were unsuccessful, and the Suez Canal reopened for traffic on April 24 without the desired concessions.

U.S. interest in resolving the Arab-Israeli dispute also led to an indepth review of the Palestinian refugee question. The additional problem remained of how to deal with Nasser, whose influence in the Middle East remained extensive, and toward year's end U.S. officials were considering means of seeking a rapprochement.

This volume presents the comprehensive official historical documentary record of U.S. diplomacy in the events discussed above. Its 863 pages were gathered from the White House, the Department of State, the Dwight D. Eisenhower Presidential Library, and other government agencies.

Copies of volume XVII (Department of State Publication No. 9741 (GPO Stock No. 044-000-02253-2) may be purchased for $33.00 (domestic postpaid) and for $41.25 (foreign postpaid) from the Superintendent of Documents, U.S. Government Printing Office, Washington, D.C. 20402. Checks or money orders should be made out to the Superintendent of Documents.

The Department of State, on September 5, 1990, released Foreign Relations of the United States, 1955-57, volume XX, Regulation of Armaments and Atomic Energy. [2]

The volume presents the official documentary record of U.S. diplomacy in the fields of disarmament, nuclear testing, proliferation of nuclear weapons, reduction of conventional forces, and the participation of the United States in the Subcommittee of the U.N. Disarmament Commission. Documents were gathered from the Department of State, the Dwight D. Eisenhower Library, and other governmental agencies. Nearly all of the documents selected were declassified for this publication.

The volume also contains an expanded preface that provides information on the methodology followed in preparing the volume as well as guides to the files and other materials consulted in the volume's preparation. The preface explains the method of indicating material withheld in the declassification review process and other editorial methodology. The preface also outlines particular problems encountered in the course of compilation.

The first part of the volume reviews the discussion within the U.S. Government over the merits and parameters of disarmament. The Department of Defense argued that disarmament would impair U.S. security unless the outstanding political problems between the United States and the Soviet Union were first resolved. The Department of State took a more flexible position. This first period also features the discussions which led to the naming by President Eisenhower of Harold E. Stassen as the chief coordinator of U.S. disarmament policy in March 1955. Following his appointment, Stassen immediately set to work drafting a proposal which the U.S. delegation could use as a basis for discussion at the London meetings of the U.N. Disarmament Subcommittee. His plan was revised first to take account of Defense Department concerns about solving political problems and subsequently at the end of the summer to incorporate the "Open Skies" proposal for aerial inspection made by President Eisenhower at the Geneva Summit Conference, July 18-23, 1955.

The second part of the volume documents U.S. efforts to include aerial inspection in any disarmament plan. For the next two years the United States sought to convince first its allies and then the Soviet Union of the merits of the concept. The volume also examines the many revisions of Stassen's disarmament plans within the U.S. Government and his attempts to limit nuclear testing, which the Atomic Energy Commission consistently opposed; prevent the proliferation of nuclear weapons; and reduce conventional arms. All his efforts failed, and in late May 1957 Stassen revealed the latest Western disarmament proposal to the Soviet delegation at the London Subcommittee talks in an attempt to reach agreement. Many felt he acted prematurely. By the end of 1957 no substantive progress had been made on disarmament.

Copies of volume XX (Department of State Publication No. 9759; GPO Stock No. 044-000-02261-3) may be purchased for $30.00 (domestic postpaid) or $37.50 (foreign postpaid) from the Superintendent of Documents, U.S. Government Printing Office, Washington, D.C. 20402. Checks or money orders should be made out to the Superintendent of Documents.

---

[1] Department of State Press Release 95, June 29, 1990
[2] Department of State Press Release 123, September 5, 1990.

INDEX

INDEX

Name Index

FOREIGN POLICY BULLETIN ORDER FORM
(Photocopy to send)

TO: **FOREIGN POLICY BULLETIN**
       4812 Butterworth Place, N.W.
       Washington, D.C. 20016

Please enter _____ subscription(s) for _____ year(s) to the FOREIGN POLICY BULLETIN at $35.00 per year or $53.00 outside the U.S. and Canada.

_____   Payment is enclosed.

_____   Please send an invoice.

Please Type or Print
Organization or Personal Name   _____

Additional Address/Attention Line   _____

Street Address   _____

City, State, Zip Code   _____

Daytime Phone, Including Area Code   _____

FOREIGN POLICY BULLETIN
4812 Butterworth Place, N.W.
Washington, D.C. 20016

Foreign Policy
bulletin

The Documentary Record of United States Foreign Policy / Volume 1 / Number 3

November/December 1990

ONE GERMANY, A NEW EUROPE

Also in this issue:

Persian Gulf/War or Peace?

Violence in Jerusalem Condemned

Congress Cuts El Salvador Aid

BULLETIN SPECIALS: Yevgeny Primakov, Gorbachev's Persian Gulf Envoy, Yitzhak Shamir on Security Council Votes, Senator Kerry on Gulf Policy, Helmut Kohl on Principles Guiding Germany

An independent publication with editorial autonomy • No government affiliation

Foreign Policy

bulletin

Volume 1/Number 3
November/December 1990

The **FOREIGN POLICY BULLETIN**
is published bimonthly (plus annual
index) as a private publication, using
the same format as the discontinued
"Department of State Bulletin" and
maintaining continuity with that publication while offering additional materials
as well. Its purpose is to provide a timely and systematic record of United
States foreign policy and of complementary documents from international
sources. The **BULLETIN's** coverage of
official U.S. documents includes major
addresses, diplomatic statements, and
press conferences of the President and
the Secretary of State; statements and
congressional testimony by the
Secretary and other administration officials; treaties and other agreements to
which the United States is or may become a party; special reports; and
selected press releases issued by the
White House, the Department of State,
and other agencies. Special features include speeches and other statements by
foreign officials concerning U.S. policy;
reports and other materials from international organizations relating to major
issues confronting U.S. policy-makers;
and background information about
countries of particular interest to U.S.
foreign relations.

PAUL E. AUERSWALD
Editor and Publisher

PHILIP AUERSWALD
Assistant Editor/Business Manager

HUGUETTE NIZARD
Subscriptions Manager

HOPE FUNG
Layout and Typesetting

J. LEONARD MAZUR
Marketing Consultant

Printed by
**PRINTING SERVICE INTERNA-
TIONAL**

ISSN 1052-7036

SUBSCRIPTIONS: Annual subscriptions to the **BULLETIN** are $35.00;
outside the U.S. and Canada $53.00.
Subscription orders should be sent to:
Subscriptions, Foreign Policy Bulletin,
4812 Butterworth Place N.W.,
Washington, D.C. 20016.
To subscribe by phone, call
(202) 686-5230.

SINGLE COPIES: Single copies, if still
in print, can be obtained for $10.00 a
copy plus postage by writing to the address below.

CORRESPONDENCE should be addressed to: Foreign Policy Bulletin,
4812 Butterworth Place N.W.,
Washington, D.C. 20016.
Telephone: (202) 686-5230

INDEXING: Included in the PAIS
(Public Affairs Information Service) in-
dexes: the PAIS Bulletin, PAIS on CD-
ROM, and online through Dialog, BRS,
and Data-Star. Information about other
indexing services will be provided in
subsequent issues.

CONTENTS

2 FEATURE: ONE GERMANY, A NEW EUROPE

THE PERSIAN GULF CRISIS

One Germany, A New Europe

Treaty on the Final Settlement with Respect to Germany, September 12, 1990 [1]

The Federal Republic of Germany, the German Democratic Republic, the French Republic, the Union of Soviet Socialist Republics, the United Kingdom of Great Britain and Northern Ireland and the United States of America,

Conscious of the fact that their peoples have been living together in peace since 1945;

Mindful of the recent historic changes in Europe which make it possible to overcome the division of the continent;

Having regard to the rights and responsibilities of the Four Powers relating to Berlin and to Germany as a whole, and the corresponding wartime and postwar agreements and decisions of the Four Powers;

Resolved in accordance with their obligations under the Charter of the United Nations to develop friendly relations among nations based on respect for the principle of equal rights and self-determination of peoples, and to take other appropriate measures to strengthen universal peace;

Recalling the principles of the Final Act of the Conference on Security and Cooperation in Europe, signed in Helsinki;

Recognizing that those principles have laid firm foundations for the establishment of a just and lasting peaceful order in Europe;

Determined to take account of everyone's security interests;

Convinced of the need finally to overcome antagonism and to develop cooperation in Europe

Confirming their readiness to reinforce security, in particular by adopting effective arms control, disarmament and confidence building measures; their willingness not to regard each other as adversaries but to work for a relationship of trust and cooperation; and accordingly their readiness to consider positively setting up appropriate institutional arrangements within the framework of the Conference on Security and Cooperation in Europe;

Welcoming the fact that the German people, freely exercising their right of self-determination, have expressed their will to bring about the unity of Germany as a state so that they will be able to serve the peace of the world as an equal and sovereign partner in a united Europe;

Convinced that the unification of Germany as a state with definitive borders is a significant contribution to peace and stability in Europe;

Intending to conclude the final settlement with respect to Germany;

Recognizing that thereby, and with the unification of Germany as a democratic and peaceful state, the rights and responsibilities of the Four Powers relating to Berlin and to Germany as a whole lose their function;

Represented by their Ministers for Foreign Affairs who, in accordance with the Ottawa Declaration of February 13, 1990, met in Bonn on 5 May 1990, in Berlin on 22 June 1990, in Paris on 17 July 1990 with the participation of the Minister for Foreign Affairs of the Republic of Poland, and in Moscow on 12 September 1990;

Have agreed as follows:

Article 1

1. The united Germany shall comprise the territory of the Federal Republic of Germany, the German Democratic Republic and the whole of Berlin. Its external borders shall be the borders of the Federal Republic of Germany and the German Democratic Republic and shall be definitive from the date on which the present Treaty comes into force. The confirmation of the definitive nature of the borders of the united Germany is an essential element of the peaceful order in Europe.

2. The united Germany and the Republic of Poland shall confirm the existing border between them in a treaty that is binding under international law.

3. The united Germany has no territorial claims whatsoever against other states and shall not assert any in the future.

4. The Governments of the Federal Republic of Germany and the German Democratic Republic shall ensure that the constitution of the united Germany does not contain any provision incompatible with these principles. This applies accordingly to the provisions laid down in the preamble, the second sentence of Article 23, and Article 146 of the Basic Law for the Federal Republic of Germany.

5. The Governments of the French Republic, the Union of the Soviet Socialist Republics, the United Kingdom of Great Britain and Northern Ireland and the United States of America take formal note of the corresponding commitments and declarations by the Governments of the Federal Republic of Germany and the German Democratic Republic and declare that their implementation will confirm the definitive nature of the united Germany's borders.

Article 2

The Governments of the Federal Republic of Germany and the German Democratic Republic reaffirm their declarations that only peace will emanate from German soil. According to the constitution of the united Germany, acts tending to and undertaken with the intent to disturb the peaceful relations between nations, especially to prepare for aggressive war, are unconstitutional and a punishable offense. The Governments of the Federal Republic of Germany and the German Democratic Republic declare that the united Germany will never employ any of its weapons except in accordance with its constitution and the Charter of the United Nations.

Article 3

1. The Governments of the Federal Republic of Germany and the German Democratic Republic reaffirm their renunciation of the manufacture and possession of and control over nuclear, biological and chemical weapons. They declare that the united Germany, too, will abide by these commitments. In particular, rights and obligations arising from the Treaty on the Nonproliferation of Nuclear Weapons of 1 July 1968 will continue to apply to the united Germany.

2. The Government of the Federal Republic of Germany, acting in full

"President Mikhail Gorbachev made an inestimable contribution towards overcoming the division of our fatherland. He recognized the right of nations to follow their own path. Without the new thinking in Soviet foreign policy, we would not have experienced the day of German unity so soon."

— Chancellor Helmut Kohl
October 4, 1990

agreement with the Government of the German Democratic Republic, made the following statement on 30 August 1990 in Vienna at the Negotiations on Conventional Armed Forces in Europe [CFE]:

"The Government of the Federal Republic of Germany undertakes to reduce the personnel strength of the armed forces of the united Germany to 370,000 (ground, air and naval forces) within three to four years. This reduction will commence on the entry into force of the first CFE agreement. Within the scope of this overall ceiling no more than 345,000 will belong to the ground and air forces which, pursuant to the agreed mandate, alone are the subject of the Negotiations on Conventional Armed Forces in Europe. The Federal Government regards its com-

mitment to reduce ground and air forces as a significant German contribution to the reduction of conventional armed forces in Europe. It assumes that in follow-on negotiations the other participants in the negotiations, too, will render their contribution to enhancing security and stability in Europe, including measures to limit personnel strengths."

The Government of the German Democratic Republic has expressly associated itself with this statement.

3. The Governments of the French Republic, the Union of Soviet Socialist Republics, the United Kingdom of Great Britain and Northern Ireland and the United States of America take note of these statements by the Governments of the Federal Republic of Germany and the German Democratic Republic.

Article 4

1. The Governments of the Federal Republic of Germany, the German Democratic Republic and the Union of Soviet Socialist Republics state that the united Germany and the Union of Soviet Socialist Republics will settle by treaty the conditions for and the duration of the presence of Soviet armed forces on the territory of the present German Democratic Republic and of Berlin, as well as the conduct of the withdrawal of these armed forces which will be completed by the end of 1994, in connection with the implementation of the undertaking of the Federal Republic of Germany and the German Democratic Republic referred to in paragraph 2 of Article 3 of the present treaty.

2. The Governments of the French Republic, the United Kingdom of Great Britain and Northern Ireland and the United States of America take note of this statement.

Article 5

1. Until the completion of the withdrawal of the Soviet armed forces from the territory of the present German Democratic Republic and of Berlin in accordance with Article 4 of the present treaty, only German territorial defense units which are not integrated into the alliance structures to which German armed forces in the rest of German territory are assigned will be stationed in that territory as armed forces of the united Germany. During that period and subject to the provisions of paragraph 2 of this Article, armed forces of other states will not be stationed in that territory or carry out any other military activity there.

2. For the duration of the presence of Soviet armed forces in the territory of the present German Democratic Republic and of Berlin, armed forces of the French Republic, the United Kingdom of Great Britain and Northern Ireland and the United States of America will, upon German request, remain stationed in Berlin by agreement to this effect between the Government of the united Germany and the Governments of the states concerned. The number of troops and the amount of equipment of all non-German armed forces stationed in Berlin will not be greater than at the time of signature of the present Treaty. New categories of weapons will not be introduced there by non-German armed forces. The Government of the united Germany will conclude with the Governments of those states which have armed forces stationed in Berlin treaties with conditions which are fair taking account of the relations existing with the states concerned.

3. Following the completion of the withdrawal of the Soviet armed forces from the territory of the present German Democratic Republic and of Berlin, units of German armed forces assigned to military alliance structures in the same way as those in the rest of German territory may also be stationed in that part of Germany, but without nuclear weapon carriers. This does not apply to conventional weapon systems which may have other capabilities in addition to conventional ones but which in that part of Germany are equipped for

a conventional role and designated only for such. Foreign armed forces and nuclear weapons or their carriers will not be stationed in that part of Germany or deployed there.

Article 6

The right of the united Germany to belong to alliances, with all the rights and responsibilities arising therefrom, shall not be affected by the present Treaty.

Article 7

1. The French Republic, the Union of Soviet Socialist Republics, the United Kingdom of Great Britain and Northern Ireland and the United States of America hereby terminate their rights and responsibilities relating to Berlin and to Germany as a whole. As a result, the corresponding, related quadripartite agreements, decisions and practices are terminated and all related Four Power institutions are dissolved.

2. The united Germany shall have accordingly full sovereignty over its internal and external affairs.

Article 8

1. The present Treaty is subject to ratification or acceptance as soon as possible. On the German side it will be ratified by the united Germany. The Treaty will therefore apply to the united Germany.

2. The instruments of ratification or acceptance shall be deposited with the Government of the united Germany. That Government shall inform the Governments of the other Contracting Parties of the deposit of each instrument of ratification or acceptance.

Article 9

The present Treaty shall enter into force for the united Germany, the French Republic, the Union of Soviet Socialist Republics, the United Kingdom of Great Britain and Northern Ireland and the United States of America on the date of deposit of the last instrument of ratification or acceptance by these states.

Article 10

The original of the present Treaty, of which the English, French, German and Russian texts are equally authentic,

shall be deposited with the Government of the Federal Republic of Germany, which shall transmit certified true copies to the Governments of the other contracting parties.

AGREED MINUTE TO THE TREATY ON THE FINAL SETTLEMENT WITH RESPECT TO GERMANY OF SEPTEMBER 12, 1990

Any questions with respect to the application of the word "deployed" as used in the last sentence of paragraph 3 of Article 5 will be decided by the Government of the united Germany in a reasonable and responsible way taking into account the security interests of each Contracting Party as set forth in the preamble.
For the Federal Republic of Germany
Hans-Dietrich Genscher
For the German Democratic Republic
Lothar de Maiziere
For the French Republic
Roland Dumas
For the Union of Soviet Socialist Republics
Eduard Shevardnadze
For the United Kingdom of Great Britain and Northern Ireland
Douglas Hurd
For the United States of America
James W. Baker III

ACCOMPANYING LETTER, SEPTEMBER 12, 1990

Letter from Foreign Minister Hans-Dietrich Genscher (Federal Republic) and Prime Minister Lothar de Maiziere (German Democratic Republic) to the Foreign Ministers of the United States, France, United Kingdom, and the Soviet Union, concerning the Treaty on the Final Settlement with Respect to Germany. [2]

Mr. Foreign Minister,

In connection with the signing today of the Treaty on the Final Settlement with Respect to Germany, we would like to inform you that the Governments of the Federal Republic of Germany and the German Democratic Republic declared the following in the negotiations:

1. The Joint Declaration of June 15, 1990, by the Governments of the Federal Republic of Germany and the German Democratic Republic on the settlement of outstanding property mat-

ters contains, inter alia, the following observations:

"The expropriations effected on the basis of occupation law or sovereignty (between 1945 and 1949) are irreversible. The governments of the Soviet Union and the German Democratic Republic do not see any means of revising the measures taken then. The Government of the Federal Republic of Germany takes note of this in the light of the historical development. It is of the opinion that a final decision on any public compensation must be reserved for a future all-German parliament."

According to Article 41 (1) of the treaty of August 31, 1990, between the Federal Republic of Germany and the German Democratic Republic establishing German unity (Unification Treaty), the aforementioned Joint Declaration forms an integral part of the Treaty. Pursuant to Article 41 (3) of the Unification Treaty, the Federal Republic of Germany will not enact any legislation contradicting the part of the Joint Declaration quoted above.

2. The monuments dedicated to the victims of war and tyranny which have been erected on German soil will be respected and will enjoy the protection of German law. The same applies to the war graves, which will be maintained and looked after.

3. In the united Germany, too, the free democratic basic order will be protected by the Constitution. It provides the basis for ensuring that parties which, by reason of their aims or the behavior of their adherents, seek to impair or abolish the free democratic basic order as well as associations which are directed against the constitutional order or the concept of international understanding, can be prohibited. This also applies to parties and associations with National Socialist aims.

4. On the treaties of the German Democratic Republic, the following has been agreed in Article 12 (1) and (2) of the treaty of August 31, 1990, between the Federal Republic of Germany and the German Democratic Republic establishing German unity:

"The contracting parties agree that, as part of the process of establishing German unity, the international treaties concluded by the German Democratic Republic shall be discussed with the contracting parties in terms of the protection of bona fide rights, the interests of the states concerned and the treaty obligations of the Federal Republic of Germany as well as in the

light of the principles of a free democratic basic order founded on the rule of law and taking into account the responsibilities of the European Communities in order to regulate or ascertain the continuance, adjustment or termination of such treaties.

The united Germany shall lay down its position on the continuance of international treaties of the German Democratic Republic after consultations with the respective contracting parties and with the European Communities insofar as their responsibilities are affected."

Accept, Mr. Foreign Minister, the assurances of our high consideration.

Joint Press Conference Following Two-Plus-Four Signing of Treaty on Germany

Following is the transcript of the joint press conference of Secretary Baker and Foreign Ministers Eduard Shevardnadze of the Soviet Union, Hans-Dietrich Genscher of the Federal Republic of Germany [FRG], Lothar de Maiziere of the German Democratic Republic [GDR], Douglas Hurd of the United Kingdom, and Roland Dumas of France in Moscow, September 12, 1990. [3]

Foreign Minister Shevardnadze. My colleagues have asked me to outline the results of all the work here in Moscow within the Two-Plus-Four mechanism. Let me start by saying that, on September 12, this day will go down in history as a date important in many ways for both Europe and the world at large. We are going through an emotional and historic event. A few moments ago the Foreign Ministers of the six countries, in the presence of Mikhail Gorbachev, President of the U.S.S.R., signed a treaty on a final settlement with respect to Germany, which records decisions on a whole set of issues related to the external aspects of German reunification. We have drawn the line under World War II, and we have started counting the new time of the New Age.

Seven months ago in Ottawa we decided to establish the Two-Plus-Four negotiating mechanism. Those seven months were filled with important work, and I believe that at the beginning of that process none of the participants in

that process could even imagine that we would come to the closure in September. Too important were the disagreements. Too many hurdles appeared insurmountable. Sometimes there was lack of mutual understanding and trust; however, we did find enough strength to begin moving toward each other and consequently to move forward to an agreement.

The meetings between ministers of foreign affairs in Bonn, Paris and Berlin gave important impetus to our work. The meetings of the President of the U.S.S.R. took place with — he met with Chancellor Kohl in June, in Moscow and in Stravropol. They found a number of important solutions. I will not conceal the fact that difficult discussions around a number of political-military issues went on until the very last moment. However, eventually, we succeeded in clearing even those final hurdles. The result of all our giant work is the treaty that we have signed today.

We believe that that treaty certainly is a successful one. This is a document of importance and integrity, taking into account the balance of legitimate interests of all the participants in this process. This is a future-oriented document, a document that expresses our common vision of the constructive role and place that Germany will have in Europe, in accordance with the provisions of that treaty, at the end of this millenium and beginning of the third millenium.

The Content of the Treaty

Let me outline briefly the content of the treaty that has just been signed. The treaty contains a politically important preamble and ten articles. The treaty governs all the aspects of the questions related to borders in a very reliable manner. It determines the border of a reunited Germany, it records renunciation of any territorial claims. Let me particularly emphasize the fact that the article dealing with borders was specifically considered on the 16th of July in Paris.

Instructed by the ministers, the Soviet side will send a copy of the treaty to the Government of Poland. An important element of the treaty is the provision regarding political-military matters, which solemnly reaffirmed the commitment of the Governments of the FRG and the GDR that only peace will emanate from the soil of Germany, as well as their renunciation of the production or possession of weapons of mass destruction.

They will reduce over three to four years the troop strength of German armed forces to 370,000 men. The treaty says that the U.S.S.R. and the united Germany will settle on the treaty basis— the terms for, and the conditions for the stay of Soviet armed forces in the territory of what is now the GDR, as well as the terms for their withdrawal before the end of 1994. In other words, the terms, the deadlines, will have to be met within four years.

Let me draw your attention to the provision of the treaty dealing with the political-military status of what is now the territory of the GDR. Those provisions provide that prior to the withdrawal of Soviet troops from the GDR, only German units, territorial defense units not integrated in the NATO command, will be stationed there. Whereupon in the territory of what is now the GDR, other German units may be stationed; however, they must not have nuclear delivery vehicles. Foreign troops, equipment or delivery vehicles cannot be stationed in that part of Germany. The new treaty comes to replace the rights and obligations of the Four Powers. It stands to reason that that will take place as soon as the treaty enters into force.

Let me particularly dwell upon a very important subject. And that it is, that it is no secret that the German issue, for well known reasons, has always been a sensitive issue to the Soviet peoples and all the peoples of Europe. There are widespread concerns that the new country may do damage to the security of the Soviet Union and of Europe. We took that concern into account as we drew up the Treaty on the Final Settlement for Germany, as well as the bilateral aspects in our relations with united Germany. I believe that we have received all the necessary safeguards, commitments and guarantees consistent with the actual situation in Europe.

I must say that the same security guarantees are extended also to the united Germany, as well as all the other European nations. However this is only one element. We cannot continually live in the past. We have to think about the future, based upon the realities of today and the prospects for the development of the international situation.

Among those realities is the fact that we are now dealing with a new Germany, which has drawn its lessons from

history. We cannot overlook the fact that the age of the confrontation between the blocs and the age of the Cold War is receding into the past. The European landscape is changing tangibly.

There are good prospects for ensuring European security on a new basis within the CSCE [Conference on Security and Cooperation in Europe] structures. We have come close to practically beginning their construction. Let me also advise you that we received a letter from Mr. Genscher, with respect to the succession of rights, with respect to the treaties concluded earlier by the GDR with the U.S.S.R. and other countries. That letter will be incorporated by the sides in the ratification process.

We are going through an emotional and historic event.

The same letter also governs the important issues, such as the viability of monuments to the victims of antifascism in Germany. It also contains clear-cut statements to the effect that National Socialist partisan organizations cannot function in Germany.

Historic Importance

In conclusion, let me emphasize the historic importance of this document, which provides reliable conditions for a constructive participation of the democratic, united, peaceful Germany in the life of the world community and the nations of the world for the foreseeable future. As was agreed from the very beginning, the treaty on the final international settlement of external aspects of German unity will be submitted for consideration by the CSCE Summit, and that will be done by the French side. I think that on behalf of all my colleagues, participants in the Two-Plus-Four mechanism, I can express my satisfaction with the results of the work that has been done. The tasks that had been set have been fully accomplished.

It is very important also that the joint work within the framework of the six has provided us with a unique historic experience, which will be put to good use in the future.

Let me also express my hope that the results of the work of the six, as well as the Treaty on the Final Settlement with Respect to Germany itself, will be regarded favorably by the CSCE participants. Let me avail myself of this opportunity to wish the best of success, prosperity and well-being to the people of Germany within the framework of a new, reunited Germany. Let me also thank all those who made their concrete contribution to the elaboration of that treaty—to those countries which extended their fine hospitality to the members of the Two-Plus-Four mechanism—and to the reporters for their objective coverage of our important and complex work.

In conclusion, let me also say this. European and world history will be developing along new lines as of today, opened up by this treaty. I think that we have done the right thing. We have found the right solutions. Future generations will say that we acted in the spirit of wisdom and responsibility. I think this thinking is shared by all my colleagues and by all those who used their faith and their heart and their work in elaborating that treaty. Thank you.

Foreign Minister Genscher. Ladies and gentlemen: In this hour, we remember the victims of war and totalitarian domination; the agony, not only of those peoples represented here in Moscow— we're particularly thinking about the Jewish people. We would not want that agony to ever be repeated. Less than twelve months after the peaceful revolution in the GDR, we have sealed the reunification of Germany in freedom and justice, and it is going to find its place in Europe.

The final settlement with respect to Germany signed today announces the unity of Germany and supercedes the rights and responsibilities of the Four Powers with respect to Berlin and Germany as a whole. The reunited Germany, following the entry into force of that treaty, will acquire full sovereignty over its internal and external affairs. We believe that this sovereignty connotes some other responsibility with respect to Europe. This document demonstrates the goodwill of all the participants and seeks to insure a better future for Europe.

I want to thank my colleagues for having participated in this work. I want to thank President Gorbachev, President Bush, President Mitterrand, and Prime Minister Thatcher for their contribution.

Let me also emphasize that we are implementing what was set forth in the preamble to our Constitution, which reads that Great Britain, the United States and France recorded in that treaty with Germany in 1945 what we also recorded in the letter on German unity at the end of the Moscow treaty, as an expression of our search for German unity. Germans want their new unity to serve peace. This is what the preamble of our constitution says. The treaty, which we signed a few moments ago, means that only peace will emanate from the German soil. The policies of reunited Germany will be the policy of peace and the spirit of our basic law. We want to make our contribution to [the] establishment of peace and stability in Europe.

New security and unity for Europe connotes a lot of responsibility for us, but this does not translate into a desire for more power. President Gorbachev, following his meeting with Federal Chancellor Kohl on February 8, 1990, said that German unity must and can take place in a way that would contribute to a constructive European development. The meeting between President Gorbachev and Chancellor Kohl in July 1990 made it possible to achieve that goal. We know that the establishment of nationhood and unity of Germany does not create new problems for Europe, but rather promotes the solution of the existing problems.

Our current task now is to establish a new, peaceful European order. Relations with our neighbors in Eastern Europe, particularly with the Soviet Union acquire special importance to us. The accompanying document that we are initialling will attach special relevance to relations between Germany and the U.S.S.R. The key element of the new order is the question of borders. The treaty finally puts a final seal on the issue of borders of the reunited Germany.

On October 1st and 2nd, within the framework of the CSCE Foreign Ministers meeting in New York, and then at the Paris Summit, we all [will share our thinking about] the results of this meeting with all the CSCE members, and we are pleased that this reunification process takes place within the framework of the CSCE. Each CSCE participant will clearly see that the final settlement is fully consistent with the principles of the CSCE.

As of today, we are providing external conditions that will enable our

people to regain their nationhood and sovereignty and unity, and those hopes will be justified, just as we will justify the hopes of all the peoples of the world and all those present here now. The Germans have always had great hopes for this day, and have sought the achievement of this goal. I want to pay credit, tribute, to all those who suffered in all these years — all those who promoted the establishment of democracy in the Federal Republic of Germany and all those who made a contribution to the peaceful revolution in the GDR.

To us Germans, this is a day of joy and jubilation. This is a day which encourages us. At the same time it is a day of remembrance and a day of gratitude. In this day and age, the world is watching Germany to understand and realize that responsibility. Germans have nothing but a possibility and chance to live in freedom and as good neighbors with all the nations in the world and in Europe.

To us Germans, this is a day of joy and jubilation.

Foreign Minister de Maiziere. Ladies and gentlemen, German unity and freedom and peace in accordance with the desires of the American democracy and our neighbors fills the hearts of the Germans with joy. The treaty on final settlement for Germany is an historic document, which records what has been taking place in the postwar period and places a cornerstone for the building of a new Europe of peace and trust. I am convinced that this day will open a new chapter, a chapter of peace, which will come to replace the age of "peace-loving activities."

I believe that after we have overcome the division of Europe, we will insure a better future for the policy of good neighborliness for the benefit of all the peoples in Europe. This was a victory for wisdom, and I place great hopes on this treaty, in the sense that the new Germany will intensively, much more actively than in the past, turn toward its Eastern European neighbors. We have succeeded in achieving agreement with the peoples of Eastern Europe, and I think now that our

renewed energies will be directed toward Eastern Europe. And I am convinced that European states in the years to come, and beginning as of today, will become the richer for that. I think that our common history and cultural heritage will bear that out.

We have achieved a new dimension in our European activities. European states, together with North American democracies, can meet the challenge of the third millenium by eliminating the disagreements between the North and the South, by protecting their environment. I want to thank all the ministers, all the heads of governments, who participated in drawing up the treaty, particularly my thanks go to Mikhail Gorbachev, whose policies of *perestroika* and new thinking have, from the very beginning, filled with hope the hearts of all the Europeans. It has made this possible. I thank you.

Secretary Baker. Ladies and gentlemen, our meeting today is truly, I think, a rendezvous with history. We began the Two-Plus-Four process last February in the midst of a political revolution, as the German people sought unification in peace and freedom. Today, as we conclude the final settlement with respect to Germany, we of course complete the diplomatic portion of that political revolution. Six governments, from both sides of old lines dividing Europe, have facilitated successfully the unification of Germany. The restraints on German sovereignty dating from World War II are being removed.

We have settled the external aspects of German unity; but, perhaps even more important for the future, the Two-Plus-Four talks have created a new vocabulary. Words like openness, cooperation, partnership, have replaced a Cold War dialogue of secrecy, confrontation and antagonism. And I think it's fair to say as well that these words have been matched with deeds. As has already been said, a year ago I think few would have imagined this outcome.

Of course, hopes had risen before only to be bashed upon the hard rocks of reality. The division of Europe and Germany seemed permanent facts, etched in the concrete of the Berlin Wall; and, then, with a stunning swiftness that could not have been foreseen, the wall was breached. And through that breach poured the rekindled hopes of millions of people. Hopes for a world of freedom: freedom to speak, freedom to worship, freedom to work, freedom to choose, freedom above all from fear of the policeman's knock in the dead of the night.

And the plain ordinary people who breached the [wall], and who tore asunder the Iron Curtain shutting out the light, put into the hands of these governments, I think, a very special trust: trust that we could fashion agreements that would leave the Cold War behind; trust that we could consign to history forever one of the most corrosive conflicts of this century; trust that we could create a Europe whole and free, so that their children could enjoy the light of peace and freedom. Today I think that our countries have proved fully worthy of that trust.

Consider, please, these results: a Germany that is unified in peace and freedom, responding to the interests of the German people; a unified and sovereign Germany that is democratic, a member of NATO and the European Community and a willing partner in the building of Europe; a Germany that is reconciled with its neighbors to the East and West; a Germany with definitive borders, confirmed by mutually binding international legal agreements. And now we have a final treaty, fully supported by Germany's allies, Germany's neighbors and the international community.

For the United States of America, this represents the end of a 45-year journey. Since 1945, every American president and every American congress has endorsed the goal of a sovereign, democratic, united Germany. And now we hail the achievement of this goal, and we look forward to a bright future with our friend and ally.

Other new partnerships have been forged in the course of this diplomatic revolution. The Soviet Union's new thinking has offered a fresh vision of Soviet interests that is far more compatible with constructive international action. Eduard Shevardnadze's persistence and imagination have been instrumental in bringing us to this important day. Indeed, the same can be said of all my colleagues here today.

The secret of Two-Plus-Four has been dedication to a sincere search for a common interest that reflects the will of the people; and, if I might say so, this is a lesson that I think we can offer a world which is badly in need of it. Even as we meet, all nations are beset by a new challenge, an aggression in the Persian Gulf that threatens the peace, threatens the new world order, and

which, of course, must be resisted by collective action.

And now, even as history is made, we should look to the future. The old terminology of rights and responsibilities is already yesterday's language. The new Germany is here. New partnerships must be nurtured and expanded. Vital forces, such as NATO, the European Community, and CSCE must be adapted to new times. There is a new Europe, too, a new Europe based on free elections, the rule of law and the free market. And so, let our legacy be that 45 years after the end of World War II, we have finally got the political arithmetic right. Two-Plus-Four adds up to one Germany in a Europe that's whole and free.

For the United States of America, this represents the end of a 45-year journey.

Foreign Minister Hurd. Mr. Chairman, today marks the end of one long road, a road 45 years long, the period during which Germany has been divided; a period for almost all Germans alive today which has consumed the greater part of their lifetimes; a period of deep unhappiness for many, many thousands of Germans divided from their families, their friends, from the other half of their country. A period of danger for peace in Europe, precisely because of that division of one of the great countries of Europe.

Now the German people have long willed an end to that division. In the last seven months, the six governments have worked on the external side of that division. There have been differences. You have followed these differences at our meetings in this series. There have been differences, not just of rhetoric, but of substance based on history; and it has required a spirit, going beyond the ordinary coming and going of diplomacy, to make possible a reconciliation of those differences, and it is right, Mr. Chairman, that this series of meetings should conclude here in Moscow, because there is no doubt that the welcome new thinking of the Soviet Union has been one of the keys to this process. I do not think any of us should underestimate the effort which Presi-

dent Gorbachev and you yourself have made in that direction.

So it's the end of one long road, but it is also a milestone on the new road, the new road of a more secure, more harmonious world order, based on continuing collective effort for security and a greater respect and understanding for each other's rights and points of view.

Now, that new world order is facing a substantial test in the Gulf at the moment, as James Baker has just mentioned. It has other tests facing it in Europe. We have to conclude the CFE negotiations in Vienna. We have to make a success of the summit meeting after that in Paris, designed to create a new dimension, a new strength for the CSCE process. So we have many milestones yet, we have many tasks ahead of us in Europe and the rest of the world. Now, after October 3, a united Germany will be a part of this process, will add strength to the process. This owes much to the farsightedness and the determination of Chancellor Kohl, of Hans-Dietrich Genscher and of Prime Minister de Maiziere. The impetus, the firmness with which they have pursued this goal, the wisdom in which they have negotiated the various steps, have been formidable. So I think we can all say that the results are results of which we and history can be pleased and proud. It has been a notable day. As Winston Churchill said to the Council of Europe in 1949, "a united Europe cannot live without the health and the strength of Germany."

Foreign Minister Dumas. Ladies and gentlemen, today having signed here in Moscow, in the country which has suffered so much from the last world war, this treaty we give to Germany full and absolute sovereignty, I express the satisfaction of the French Government over the results which we have achieved as a result of the signing of this document. Here we have turned the page over on one of the most abnormal situations, which is a legacy of the Second World War.

We intend to remember the past. However, having started a new page of history, we have started a page of a new and democratic Europe, which is the result of the changes in the east of this continent and, first of all, here in Moscow. The European countries, under conditions of equality and liberty, can look in peace towards a single future.

As for France, this future is the future of the acceleration of building one structure, which will continue to be the

French-German friendship. However, the time today is such that we have to strengthen friendship between all the peoples of Europe so that all of them—all of the nations of Europe—can take the fullest possible part in the promotion of the movement of this continent towards the confederation of which the French President spoke, and I quote: "Today Europe has turned toward its history and its geography, and has come back to its own home."

Two aspects remain: disarmament, peace and cooperation. We shall be discussing these matters in Paris during the summit meeting of the CSCE. We are facing new prospects, and we entertain new hopes that this treaty will promote the establishment of a new world legal order, based on freedom and cooperation, rather than fear and confrontation.

France is to play its own role within the limits of this new world order. It is doing so through its presence in the Persian Gulf, in order to promote the solution of the crisis which has been mentioned here by Mr. Baker and Mr. Hurd. This crisis threatens the new world order before it is firmly established, but we are moving.

Q. I have a question for Mr. Shevardnadze. Some people were speaking about the sellout of Eastern Europe. Do you expect, during the debate in the Supreme Soviet on the ratification, there will be such problems? Secondly, what are the most complex problems for you for the withdrawal of Soviet troops from Germany? I thank you.

Foreign Minister Shevardnadze. When we assume and make serious, weighty political decisions, and determine our attitudes of principle toward nations, including neighboring nations, I think we should not be guided by all kinds of men in the street and vulgar approaches. You know the principles of the new political thinking. They are the foundation of the foreign policy of the Soviet Union, and we are guided by these principles in determining our stance on the reunification of Germany.

What problems shall we face in withdrawing our troops from Germany? There will be, of course, many problems because this is a complicated process. It is well known that we have quite a few troops serving there, but we have to welcome the fact that all the aspects, I mean legal aspects and financial aspects of the withdrawal of Soviet troops, are being resolved in a very fundamental manner to the satisfaction of both sides.

Calmly and fundamentally seriously we are discussing these questions and the talks are being completed.

Q. Bulgaria, Zemli I Ochestko Znamya newspaper. Distinguished Mr. de Maiziere and Mr. Genscher, we the Bulgarians greet you. We in our history also had a similar treaty of reunification. We would like to ask you whether you are satisfied and happy as Germans, but are you afraid of anything? Does fear still persist with you and, if yes, of what? Are you happy as German people?

Foreign Minister de Maiziere. Since I was asked the first, I will answer the first. I am not very well-versed in Bulgarian history, and I don't know the dates and the terms of that reunification treaty to which you refer, but people in my country in the last few weeks and days have gone through a major event.

For one thing it was July the 1st of 1990, when we made the first major step toward reuniting Germany by creating a currency, social and economic union, where we adopted a functioning market economy of the Federal Republic of Germany and reaffirmed that we in our part of Germany still have to overcome major difficulties; but we were fully confident of overcoming those difficulties.

Secondly, it was August the 31st, which was quite a recent date, when we signed the treaty on unification. That treaty was concluded in order to change the constitution, and thus we have equated the legal systems in both countries and resolved social, cultural and other problems as a result. From the very beginning it was clear that our people were eager to see their country reunited as soon as possible and, therefore, we were working hard to settle the external aspects of the reunification within the framework of the Two-Plus-Four process. I'm very happy, and I have already said today that I'm full of satisfaction that we have succeeded in concluding this treaty before October the 3rd, that is, before the date of the German reunification.

Looking into the future, we believe that we must have more grounds to be optimistic. As for fears, yes, of course, there are certain problems which, in the next few days and months, will be regarded as difficult problems for the people of my country, but we shall look into the future in order to meet the challenge that we have. Mr. Genscher?

Foreign Minister Genscher. We Germans are, of course, happy and thankful. We feel elated. We know that

the process of unification will create important personal problems for our citizens, because the problem of unification is not only something where governments are involved, but it involves every citizen. We are aware that, in completing the process of German unification, we are by no means creating yet a united Europe. And all our efforts will be aimed at contributing to such a Europe, so that such a Europe would be responsible not only for itself, but throughout the world it would be responsible for ensuring peace, economic development, social justice and the protection of [the] natural environment.

Several days ago, President Gorbachev and President Bush met in Helsinki. They faced a sort of challenge by the aggressor to the world community and order (inaudible). In having overcome those difficulties, we were able to be united in the face of the aggressor, and what has evolved in the world is not only the triumph for the people and states of North America and Europe, it is also a gain for all those who want to ensure peace throughout the world, and this is something we are engaged in. At the same time it is a contribution to a greater stability and greater social security throughout the world.

Q. Novosti Information Agency. What is the impact of today's treaty on the future of the new relations between the Warsaw Pact and the NATO Alliance? I would ask Minister Shevardnadze and Secretary Baker to express their views on that.

Foreign Minister Shevardnadze. You have perhaps noted that my colleagues and myself have emphasized that, in the initial stages of our work, we had confronted a number of serious challenges and difficulties, and yet, we have managed to achieve a number of important decisions, and the external aspects of German unity have been settled. The treaty is now signed. It is my view that everything that is taking place now in Europe, everything that has taken place thus far, but these processes have been particularly vigorous lately—of course, I'm speaking about the development of the CSCE Helsinki process; the development of new security structures; the development of new structures of relations among the members of the political-military alliances; as well as new European structures—have all converged to provide the necessary conditions for our negotiations to allow us to achieve important decisions in a very short time. That is number one.

Secondly, I believe that the unification of the two Germanys, the building of German unity, the spirit in which the two German states have been reunited, will certainly promote further development of the CSCE and the European process and a far greater dynamism to the formation of new European security structures.

That is what I have to say on that.

Secretary Baker. Let me simply add to that, of course, the united Germany will be a member of the NATO alliance, but it will be a member of the NATO alliance in the context of this treaty, which gives due regard to the security concerns of Germany's neighbors. The recent NATO Summit, the London Declaration at the recent NATO Summit, shows a clear intent and purpose on the part of the NATO alliance to adapt to the new realities in Europe.

It called for the establishment of liaison relationships by member states of the Warsaw Pact with NATO, and that process is ongoing. It called for the negotiation and execution of a nonaggression statement or agreement between NATO member states and Warsaw Pact member states; and this treaty, in my opinion, will go a long way towards ending the tensions and confrontation and, frankly, the risk of conflict that has existed under the prior structures. We have a situation, as some of us indicated in our formal remarks, where we see a united Germany ending the division of Europe, and that would be my response to your question as to how this will affect the NATO alliance and the Warsaw Pact.

Q. The Polish Newspaper Gazieta Vwiborcha, a daily newspaper. To Prime Minister de Maiziere and Minister Genscher: Are you disappointed that foreign troops will remain in Berlin? And do you consider that to constitute an obstacle to establish the capital of United Germany in Berlin? Thank you.

Foreign Minister de Maiziere. The troops of the United States, France, Great Britain and the Soviet Union will remain at the levels at which they are currently present in that city. Thus far, Soviet troops are stationed in what is known today as the GDR. We do believe that those forces will remain in that city for some time and that is a good thing. They will maintain contacts with the Bundeswehr.

Foreign Minister Genscher. I have nothing to add to that.

Q. Is the United States willing to exclude troop levels and aircraft levels from the conventional forces agreements, in order to get to an agreement which could be signed at a CSCE Summit in November? For Foreign Minister Shevardnadze, how would the Soviet Union react to that?

Secretary Baker. The position of the United States is that it is very important that we conclude a CFE agreement so that we can have a CSCE Summit. It has been and remains the position of the United States and, I think, of some other countries as well, that there should not be a CSCE Summit, in fact, unless we get a conventional forces agreement.

Much has already been agreed upon. What has been agreed upon could serve as the basis for a rather substantial conventional forces agreement. It has never been intended that manpower generally be a part of the initial conventional forces agreement. With respect to aircraft, that was originally intended to be a part of a conventional forces agreement, but there remain substantial differences between the parties. Our preference would be to find a way to bridge those differences, so that we could have aircraft included in a conventional forces agreement. But we would want a conventional forces agreement in any event. We would not unilaterally take a position that aircraft should be excluded without first talking to our allies.

Foreign Minister Shevardnadze. In principal, I agree with what Mr. Baker said. I believe that the main element in the coming European summit will, of course, be the signing of a conventional forces agreement. We have covered much ground, many problems have been resolved. Still, there is some work to be done, some complicated problems to be discussed. Yesterday, during our meeting with Secretary Baker, we discussed that. We have discussed that at length with other colleagues and we do believe that that dialogue should be continued. Several new proposals will be tabled within a few days by the Soviet delegation to the CFE conference, and I am convinced that before the Paris Summit, we will well be able to complete our work on the CFE agreement.

Q. My question is for the Foreign Ministers of the FRG and the Soviet Union. What is the status of the treaty on partnership and cooperation and

good-neighborliness between the Soviet Union and the united Germany, and what is your assessment of the importance of that future treaty?

Foreign Minister Shevardnadze. Well, I can respond if you wish. You mean the treaties, in the plural, between the Soviet Union and the future reunited Germany. There are several treaties: The so-called large treaty, the large agreement, namely, basic principles for the building of relations between the united Germany and the Soviet Union. That paper has been drawn up already by joint effort and tomorrow the Foreign Ministers will be able to initial that document. The next document, which is still being developed and is nearing its completion, is related to our economic, scientific, technological and other types of cooperation, plus some of the financial, fiscal and economic relations related to the withdrawal of our troops, plus the status of the Soviet forces in a united Germany, etc.

All those issues are being very rigorously debated, and I think that within a few days those negotiations will be completed. Therefore, I do believe that we can take satisfaction in the dynamics and the pace and the quality of the work that has already been done toward building new relations between the two countries.

Foreign Minister Genscher. Well, the signing, rather the initialing of the comprehensive treaty that will take place tomorrow emphasizes the intention of our two countries, following the reunification of Germany, to open up new and better prospects for our relations. Therefore, we take into account the importance of our relations with the U.S.S.R. in the future Europe. There are also three other treaties which will be concluded, and Minister Shevardnadze has already referred to them, which are designed and intended to govern our future relations. We believe that the set of treaties provides a sound foundation for our future relations.

Foreign Minister Shevardnadze. Let me merely add to that — there are a number of treaties which the German Democratic Republic concluded with the Soviet Union. And all those treaties, including the treaty on the reunification of Germany, contained a provision to the effect that all the international legal treaties remain in force, that both states must make sure that the obligations assumed by the two countries be amended or carried out by Germany.

Q. Two questions to Minister Genscher. The treaty signed today provides for definitive borders of Germany. In Bonn, several members of parliament have launched complaints regarding the definitive status of those borders. Do you think that could affect your negotiating partners? And question number two: by whom, when and how can maneuvers be carried out in the Eastern part of Germany?

Foreign Minister Genscher. On your first question, that initiative of the deputies will not hamper or impede German unity and will not reverse the course of history. On your second question, the treaty contains sufficient information regarding the possibility for the movement of Soviet troops in the territory of what is now the FRG as well as the movement of our allied forces in the territory of what is now known as the GDR and the FRG. That applies to the four-year period during which the Soviet forces will continue to be stationed in Germany. We have noted and stated together that all issues related to the application of word "deployment," as mentioned in paragraph three of article five, will be decided by the government of the united Germany responsibly and reasonably, taking into account the interests of the contracting parties, as set forth in the preamble. If you read the text of the treaty, you will understand even better the purpose and the meaning of that phrase.

In order to clarify what I said, I want to go to our first question, the question of borders. Let me say both Bundestag and the People's Chamber have adopted decisions regarding the border between Germany and Poland and sent copies of those papers to Poland. The treaty on reunification also will require amendments to the constitution that make it absolutely clear where the borderline should be traced. Our Western border is definitive, so there are no ambiguities regarding our border with Poland.

Q. From the Financial Times (London), to Mr. Shevardnadze and Mr. Baker. Mr. Shevardnadze, in your introduction you said that this treaty drew a line under the Second World War, but there are clearly some issues that still remain to be resolved. Could you say what your reaction is to the request addressed to you all from the Baltic Council last week, that the issue of the status and the sovereignty of the Baltic Republics should be resolved in an international negotiation, and not simply between the Baltic Republics and the Soviet government? Could I ask that of Mr. Shevardnadze and Mr. Baker?

Foreign Minister Shevardnadze. As for the Union Republics of the U.S.S.R. and their status, these questions are internal and questions of our state. That is our position with regard to the question you have asked.

Secretary Baker. The position of the United States of course is different, and that is no secret between us. The United States does not recognize the incorporation of the Baltic States into the Soviet Union, and, in fact, we still fly the Baltic flags in the auditorium of our State Department. With respect to the question insofar as it pertains to this treaty, this treaty of course deals only with Germany and doesn't pretend to deal with anything else.

Q. Buck English from The Wall Street Journal, to both Minister Shevardnadze and Secretary Baker. Now that the Ottawa understandings on U.S. and Soviet troop levels have been overtaken by events, and the Soviet Union has pledged to withdraw all of its troops from Germany over the next four years, I wonder if the Soviet Union is requesting from the United States any sort of pledge, even if it is not in the CFE treaty, on the number of troops the United States intends to maintain in Europe, and to Secretary Baker, does the United States intend to offer in some form such a pledge?

Foreign Minister Shevardnadze. The question which you are asking is being discussed between myself and the Secretary of State, and I would not rule out that tomorrow this question would not be a matter of discussion.

Secretary Baker. It has in fact been raised as recently as yesterday. I would agree with my colleague that it will probably be discussed tomorrow. Let me simply make it clear that the Ottawa understandings, we do agree, have been overtaken by events indeed, with all Soviet forces leaving the German Democratic Republic over the course of next four years or so. But it was never intended that the manpower be covered in the Conventional Forces Agreement and the Ottawa understandings were separate and apart from that Conventional Forces Agreement — just to clear up any confusion that might have been left, with respect to John Dancy's question. The United States will continue to discuss this matter, and not only with the Soviet Union, but with our allies and internally as well, and these questions have not been decided.

Foreign Minister Shevardnadze. And I would like to add one more thing. After Ottawa such changes have taken place in Europe, and we have to consider now the results of the agreement, which show that the Ministry of Foreign Affairs is not very strong on the forecasting side.

Q. The Tass agency — Mr. Ratkov. I have a question to all the participants in the talks, if I can. The Two-Plus-Four mechanism has a — is seen as a very effective instrument, and it would not be a good business practice to stop that machine from running. Do you envisage any sort of standing consultations, "One-Plus-Four," to resolve planetary issues?

Foreign Minister Shevardnadze. I am asking my colleagues why, why don't you think about it? Probably, it would be a good thing not to let this machinery stop, since we have built this structure already. And I do believe that we have other structures as well: Vienna talks, where we can use and adopt the positive experience that we have accumulated over these few months.

[All others declined to respond.]

Q. Reuters, asking Mr. Genscher. The treaty has been initialed, and on the 3rd of October there will be a reunited Germany, and you have spoken more than once on the subject of rights of different states. Have you discussed this matter here in Moscow or have you discussed that the rights and responsibilities of superpowers will be removed?

Foreign Minister Genscher. We were interested in having end on October the 3rd (inaudible) the rights and responsibility of the occupation powers. It could be referred only to a part of the country or to the entire country, but the process of reunification will take time, and it is only when the last reunification instrument is handed in that the treaty will enter into force.

We have decided today that we are all ready on October the 1st, 1990 in New York, before we start a meeting of CSCE Foreign Ministers, to sign a document which would suspend the rights and responsibilities of the Four Powers, as of October 3rd, would legally maintain their rights until the treaty finally enters into force, but not use those rights and responsibilities. Therefore, on October 3rd, a reunited Germany would no longer be pinched by those laws—that is, starting from October 3rd.

Q. The ministers of the Four Powers—as you have resolved collectively the German question—as you are dealing collectively with the Gulf crisis, are you prepared in the Security Council of the United Nations to resolve collectively the Palestinian question?

Secretary Baker. Let me answer for the United States by saying that we have never, nor do we now, rule out the possible utility of an international conference to deal with this question at an appropriate time. And, when that time might come, it would seem appropriate that the process would begin within the Permanent Five [Permanent Five Members of the U.N. Security Council] mechanism.

Foreign Minister Shevardnadze. I would like to add to what has been said by Mr. Baker that this question in some detail has been discussed recently in Helsinki during the summit, and an understanding was reached, that at a certain stage, we shall start active consultations in order to promote global settlement of the Middle East problem. That matter was discussed yesterday, and we conclude that, probably, we shall have bilateral and multilateral talks to step up our work and efforts, in order to remove those threats and those dangers which are widely discussed, and exist, in fact, in this region and in order to achieve an equitable solution.

Foreign Minister Hurd. Perhaps I could very briefly comment on the last two questions. This Two-Plus-Four machinery has worked well, has worked very well, because it is rooted in a particular piece of history and a particular set of legal rights, arising out of the end of the war with Germany. When we come to wider matters, other peoples have interests, other peoples have rights. The last question raised one of these wider matters. It has long been clear to us, I think to all the members of the European Community, as we have frequently said, that the Arab-Israel dispute is a poisonous dispute, which will need to be tackled. It cannot be tackled around the same table as the question of the aggression against Kuwait, but it will need to be tackled by the international community, and I have noticed with great interest what Jim Baker has just said about how that might start. Thank you.

[Minister Unidentified.] The composition of the Two-Plus-Four talks is

determined by the problems which were supposed to be resolved by this machinery. You can't just transfer this machinery to solve other matters, but the spirit by which all the participants in the Two-Plus-Four talks were governed could be used in order to resolve many other complex international issues. I recall that for many decades we have been discussing the question, which was closed today when this document was signed, and this issue was the most intractable one in world politics. If responsibility and the recognition of the interests of all the participants, as well as wisdom, were godfathers of those talks, then we believe that this spirit can govern us in all other talks, and we can have more optimism looking into the future. I think this can be a good example.

[Minister Unidentified.] A few words about the last question asked. Indeed the Two-Plus-Four mechanism is a good thing. It has been efficient, and today's meeting is a proof of that, but I believe Two-Plus-Four, that is the six, are the countries directly involved in the problem, which has been long ripe for solution, and to transfer these mechanism to the solution of other conflicts and problems in the would would, in my view, be a mistake, because the situation there is different.

But we meet often amongst ourselves—I mean the members of the six—in our bilateral talks and in multilateral fora. The crisis in the Persian Gulf should be discussed by the organs which have been created for that purpose. We believe, for instance, that the Middle East problem should be decided at an international conference, but there is still the U.N. Security Council, there are the Five Permanent Members of the Security Council, and their moves have demonstrated that these organs are useful and they can be tapped for the sake of promoting the solution, as well as for thinking over how to achieve solutions in general.

Presidents's Message to the Senate Transmitting the Treaty, September 25, 1990 [4]

To the Senate of the United States:

I submit herewith, for Senate advice and consent to ratification, the Treaty on the Final Settlement with Respect to Germany and a Related Agreed Minute,

signed by the United States, the Federal Republic of Germany, the German Democratic Republic, the French Republic, the Union of Soviet Socialist Republics, and the United Kingdom of Great Britain and Northern Ireland in Moscow on September 12, 1990. I transmit also, for the information of the Senate, a report of the Department of State with respect to this Treaty.

The Treaty that I am submitting today is the culmination of six months' negotiation among its six signatories in what has come to be called the "Two-Plus-Four" forum, established for this purpose at Ottawa in February 1990. This agreement will end the artificial division of Germany and Berlin; it provides for the full withdrawal of all Soviet forces over the next four years; and it terminates all remaining Four Power rights and responsibilities for Berlin and for Germany as a whole. It thus creates the basis for the emergence of a united, democratic, and sovereign Federal Republic of Germany, capable and ready to assume a full and active partnership in the North Atlantic Alliance, the European Community, and in the many other fora for international cooperation to which the Federal Republic of Germany has already contributed significantly.

The Treaty makes clear that the current borders of the Federal Republic of Germany and German Democratic Republic shall be the final and definitive borders of a united Germany. All the provisions relating to Germany's border with Poland were worked out with the participation and approval of the Government of Poland.

The Treaty specifies that the right of a united Germany to belong to alliances with all the rights and responsibilities arising therefrom shall not be affected by any of its provisions.

The Treaty provides for the withdrawal of all Soviet troops from the territory of a united Germany by the end of 1994. The Treaty also provides for the continued presence of British, French, and American troops in Berlin during the interim period at the request of the German government. During this period the German government shall have complete freedom regarding the stationing of territorial defense units of its own armed forces within the territory of the former German Democratic Republic, and these armed forces shall remain outside the integrated NATO military command structure. Following the departure of Soviet troops by 1994, there shall be no remaining limitations regarding the location of German armed forces throughout Germany and their integration with NATO structures. Non-German Allied forces and nuclear weapons systems shall not be stationed or deployed within the territory of the present German Democratic Republic. The Agreed Minute, for which I am also seeking your advice and consent, provides a special rule for application of the term "deployed."

The Treaty contains a number of assurances provided by the Federal Republic of Germany and the German Democratic Republic on behalf of a united Germany. Among these are a reaffirmation of their renunciation of nuclear, biological, and chemical weapons, and their stated undertaking to reduce the personnel strength of the German armed forces to 370,000 within three to four years.

Finally, the Treaty provides for the termination of all remaining Four Power rights and responsibilities for Berlin and Germany as a whole.

I would also like to draw to the attention of the Senate the texts of three letters that were exchanged on issues arising in the context of the unification of Germany (enclosed as attachments to the report of the Department of State). The first is a letter from Secretary of State Baker to Foreign Minister Genscher of the Federal Republic of Germany dated September 11, 1990; the second is a letter from Foreign Minister Genscher and Prime Minister and Foreign Minister de Maiziere of the German Democratic Republic to their counterparts in the Two-Plus-Four negotiations dated September 12, 1990; and the third is a letter dated September 18, 1990, from Foreign Minister Genscher to Secretary Baker.

In their letter of September 12 to their counterparts in the Two-Plus-Four negotiations, Foreign Minister Genscher of the Federal Republic of Germany and Prime Minister and Foreign Minister de Maiziere of the German Democratic Republic formally convey several additional assurances. Among these are their declaration that the constitution of a united Germany will protect the free democratic order and provide the continuing basis for prohibiting parties and associations with National Socialist aims. In his letter of September 18 to Secretary Baker, Foreign Minister Genscher also makes clear that the Government of a united Germany accepts responsibility for the

resolution of unresolved claims against the German Democratic Republic, both of American citizens, and of Jewish victims of the Nazi regime. In this letter he commits his government to seek, shortly after unification, to provide expeditious and satisfactory resolution of claims of Jewish victims of the Nazi regime against the German Democratic Republic. In this same letter he states that the Federal Republic of Germany will, shortly after unification, resolve through negotiations with the United States Government the claims of U.S. nationals that were previously under discussion with the German Democratic Republic. The commitments contained in these two letters are further evidence that the Government of the united Germany will sustain and build on the exemplary record of the Federal Republic of Germany in promoting democratic values.

This transformation is testimony to the power of the principles in the founding charter of the CSCE, the Helsinki Final Act.

The Treaty represents a major achievement for our German allies, who have not forgotten the past or the role Germany once played in the horrors of 1933-45, but who have demonstrated over four decades of steadfast support for democracy and the Western alliance what the world can expect from the united Germany.

The Treaty is also a tribute to the courage and the determination of the people of Germany to achieve unity in peace, freedom, and concord with their neighbors.

The emergence of a free, united, and democratic Germany, linked to the United States and to its European neighbors by indissoluble ties of friendship, common values, and mutual interests, and ready to act as a full partner within a broader community of democratic nations, has been an enduring goal of American foreign policy for over 40 years. Seldom has any President had the privilege of submitting for the Senate's advice and consent an agreement which so fully realizes our national purposes. This agreement is the result of decades of steadfast effort and resolve on the part of past Presidents

and Congresses, and our Allies. It is an achievement of which we can all be proud.

It is wholly fitting that Germany formally and irrevocably achieve its unified status at the earliest possible moment, unfettered by Four Power rights, shared by the Soviet Union, which are now outmoded and unnecessary. I therefore ask the Senate to act expeditiously in giving its advice and consent to ratification of the Treaty and the Related Agreed Minute.

President's Remarks to CSCE Ministerial, New York, October 1, 1990 [5]

On behalf of the American people, it is my great pleasure to welcome all of you to the United States. It's especially fitting that this meeting of the Conference on Security and Cooperation in Europe, the first ever on American soil, comes at this time of momentous change. For just as Europe enters a new and promising era, so, too, do America's relations with Europe.

We Americans are bound to Europe by a shared heritage and history and the common bonds of culture. Through the Atlantic alliance and the broader partnership that binds our two continents and peoples together, we have brought about the end of Europe's division and set our eyes on a new Europe, whole and free. Together we can forge a new transatlantic partnership at the CSCE, a commonwealth of free nations that spans the oceans between us.

In this past year, we would all agree, we've witnessed a world of change. Moments ago, right here in this building, the Foreign Ministers of France and Great Britain, the Soviet Union and the United States signed the document suspending all remaining Four Power rights and responsibilities in Germany, effective at the moment of German unification. I must say that just before I left from the hotel I saw that on television. And for me, and I think for many of the American people, it was a very moving moment, because with those final strokes of the pen really ends an era of discord and division. The way is now open for a united, sovereign, and democratic Germany. We rejoice with the German people that their nation is unified once more, and we will soon welcome a united Germany into the CSCE's community of states.

Germany's long-awaited day of celebration is the culmination of a year of change that, indeed, transformed a continent. This transformation is testimony to the power of the principles in the founding charter of the CSCE, the Helsinki Final Act. There, in the human rights and fundamental freedoms set down in Helsinki 15 years ago, we find the cause and catalyst of what I refer to as the Revolution of '89.

In the darkest days of dictatorship, those principles blazed forth a bright star, inspiring ordinary people to extraordinary acts. Think of Walesa, the father of Solidarity; of Sakharov and his unflinching humanity in the face of repression; of Havel, Mazowiecki, and Antall, not so very long ago political prisoners, now President and Prime Ministers of three of the world's newest democracies, 6 and Zhelev, another ex-political prisoner, now President of Bulgaria. Think of all the millions of ordinary men and women at long last free to speak their minds, free to live, work, and worship as they wish.

CSCE shares in this monumental triumph of the human spirit. Our challenge now is to keep pace with the tremendous political transformations that have changed the face of Europe, to create a CSCE that consolidates these great gains for freedom and bring East and West together—in Eastern and Central Europe, a CSCE capable of helping hard-won democratic principles take root and draw strength; a CSCE that can help secure a firm foundation for freedom in the new Europe now emerging.

In July, at the London Summit, the leaders of the Atlantic alliance put forward a series of proposals aimed at strengthening the CSCE and channeling its energies in new directions. We urge the member nations of the CSCE: to create a Center for Prevention of Conflict, to build on the CSCE's success in establishing confidence and security building measures that have done so much to reduce the risk of war by accident or miscalculation and to conciliate disputes; to establish a small permanent secretariat to serve the CSCE, one that could support an accelerated schedule of the CSCE consultations and review conferences; to create a CSCE elections office to foster free and fair elections, the fundamental democratic principle from which all others follow. And on behalf of the United States, let me say that

I hope that these new institutions can be situated wherever possible in the new democracies of Central and Eastern Europe.

And finally, at the London Summit, we issued an invitation to member nations to convene an Assembly of Europe, a parliament where the growing family of democracies, old and new, can chart a common course towards this new Europe, whole and free.

Today, as we prepare for a summit of the CSCE nations, I urge the ministers to make this meeting a milestone in the history of the CSCE. And to this end, let me mention one more area where rapid progress is critical: the ongoing negotiations of conventional forces in Europe.

An agreement to reduce conventional forces remains the cornerstone of a new security architecture for Europe. And for that reason, the United States believes a conventional arms accord is an essential prerequisite to a CSCE summit. And today I now call on the negotiators now working in Vienna to redouble their efforts in the weeks ahead. And I can pledge you the United States will cooperate in every way possible. We must resolve outstanding issues and reach agreement so that a summit can be held this year.

Fifteen years ago, in a Europe divided East from West, the CSCE offered a vision of a Europe united, whole and free. Today, with that new Europe within our reach, the CSCE remains central to all that Europe can become.

So, once again, welcome to the United States. And may the spirit that has carried Europe forward guide your discussions, and may you meet with every success. Thank you all very, very much.

CSCE Communique, New York, October 2, 1990 [1]

1. Foreign Ministers of the 35 states participating in the Conference on Security and Cooperation in Europe met in New York October 1-2, 1990 to review progress on preparations for a meeting of their heads of state and government in Paris. This was the first meeting of the CSCE ever held in the United States.

2. Ministers attached great importance to the comprehensive nature of the CSCE process, which brings

together the peoples and governments of Europe, the United States, and Canada. The CSCE process proved its vitality in the difficult years of East-West confrontation and mistrust, and has developed into an important foundation for the new Europe. In the new era of relations among CSCE states, the objectives set out in Helsinki in 1975 have been realized to a degree unforeseen even a few years ago. Ministers agreed that the role of the CSCE must be enhanced to respond to new opportunities for cooperation.

3. In that connection, Ministers discussed the work of the CSCE Paris Summit Preparatory Committee, which has been meeting in Vienna since July 10. Their discussion reflected a convergence of views regarding the scope and objectives of the Paris Summit Meeting, and the major new steps which are now possible for the CSCE process. They expressed the hope that through the elimination of tension and the growth of cooperation the CSCE countries will be able to make an even greater contribution to the lessening of tensions in other parts of the world.

4. Ministers approved the Agenda for the Paris Summit, which is annexed to this communique. They agreed that the Summit would take place as planned on November 19-21, 1990. However, they recognized that it was considered essential that a Treaty on Conventional Armed Forces in Europe be ready for signature at that time. They also expressed the hope that the Summit would endorse a set of substantial confidence and security building measures.

5. Ministers welcomed the Treaty on the Final Settlement with Respect to Germany, noting it as a historic step toward a Europe whole and free. Ministers were unanimous in acknowledging that German unification is an important contribution to stability, cooperation, and unity in Europe.

6. Ministers expressed their profound gratitude to the people and Government of the United States for the excellent organization of the New York Meeting and the warm hospitality extended to the participants in the Meeting.

Secretary Baker's Press Conference Following CSCE Ministerial, New York, October 2, 1990 (Opening Statement) [7]

As host of the first CSCE Ministerial ever held in the United States, I would like to start by expressing my appreciation to all involved for their unstinting efforts. Many people made this meeting a success, and on behalf of our American delegation and our guests, I want to thank all of them.

Here in America, I think we've done much to solidify the European architecture that we outlined previously in Berlin, in Prague, and in Copenhagen.

First of all, we've moved the consensus forward on institutionalizing and strengthening CSCE. We've done so, I think, in a way which reaffirms the transatlantic alliance of values that underpins the complementary institutions of the new Europe: NATO, CSCE, and the EC. We are especially gratified that the proposals first put forward in the NATO London Declaration have attracted very broad support here at this Ministerial.

In particular, we've advanced proposals to institute a high-level dialogue, to facilitate planning for systematic meetings, and to establish a small permanent administrative secretariat.

Second, since the peaceful revolutions of last fall in Central and Eastern Europe, the United States has fully supported efforts to consolidate these democratic revolutions in enduring representative democracies. At this CSCE Ministerial, we have moved forward proposals to create an elections monitoring mechanism.

Third, we have taken steps to establish a Conflict Prevention Center. This Center will aim to promote military predictability, transparency, and confidence and to facilitate the conciliation of disputes.

It is our position that the Conflict Prevention Center, the elections monitoring mechanism, and the secretariat should—if feasible—be located in the new democracies of Central and Eastern Europe. This would do much to ensure that CSCE remains an all-European institution—one that includes, not excludes, the peoples of the East.

Fourth, we have made some good progress, I think, toward completing a CFE Treaty, and I will be meeting with Foreign Minister Shevardnadze again tomorrow to further these efforts. As I stressed in my remarks closing this Ministerial, it is the view of the United States that completion of a CFE Treaty remains a prerequisite for convening a CSCE Summit.

Finally, in yesterday's German signing ceremony, we closed the old book on conflict and opened a new book on cooperation.

Here in New York, in ending the division of Germany and furthering the construction of the new Europe, we reaffirmed, I think, what has long been clear, and that is, that the ocean between us is a bridge, not a barrier, and that together Americans and Europeans can define common interests and shape a common future.

President's Address to the German People on German Unification, October 2, 1990 [5]

It is with great pleasure that I congratulate Chancellor Kohl and the German people at this historic moment. And it is my distinct honor to address the people of the united Germany.

In Berlin and Bonn, from Leipzig in the east to western towns along the Rhine, people are celebrating the day that all of Germany has been waiting for, for 45 long years. For the world, those 45 years were a time of tension and turmoil. For your nation, fate was particularly cruel. For 45 years, at the heart of a divided continent stood a divided Germany, on the fault line of the East-West conflict, one people split between two worlds.

No more. Today begins a new chapter in the history of your nation. Forty-five years of conflict and confrontation between East and West are now behind us. At long last the day has come: Germany is united; Germany is fully free.

The United States is proud to have built with you the foundations of freedom; proud to have been a steady partner in the quest for one Germany, whole and free. America is proud to count itself among the friends and allies of free Germany, now and in the future. Our peoples are united by the common bonds of culture, by a shared heritage in history. Never before have these common bonds been more evident than in this past year as we worked in common cause toward the goal of German unity. Today, together, we share the fruits of our friendship.

In this past year, we've witnessed a world of change for the United States, for the united Germany, for the Atlantic alliance of which we are a part. Even as Germany celebrates this new beginning, there is no doubt that the future holds new challenges, new responsibilities. I'm certain that our two nations will meet these challenges, as we have in the past, united by a common love of freedom. Together, building on the values we share, we will be partners in leadership.

This day, so full of meaning for Germany, is full of meaning for the world. Meters away from the walls of the Reichstadt, scene of the first session of the newly united German Parliament, stood the Berlin Wall, the stark and searing symbol of conflict and Cold War. For years, free men and women everywhere dreamed of the day the Berlin Wall would cease to exist, when a world without the Wall would mean a Germany made whole once more—when Germany, united and sovereign, would contribute in full measure as a force for peace and stability in world affairs.

Today the Wall lies in ruins, and our eyes open on a new world of hope. Now Germany is once more united. Now the Wall no longer divides a nation and a world in two. The last remnants of the Wall remain there at the heart of a free Berlin, a ragged monument in brick and barbed wire, proof that no wall is ever strong enough to strangle the human spirit, that no wall can ever crush a nation's soul.

Today the German nation enters a new era; an era, in the words of your national anthem, of "unity and justice and freedom." At this moment of celebration, as we look forward with you to a future of hope and promise, let me say, on behalf of all Americans, may God bless the people of Germany.

Next Steps in Soviet-American Relations

Secretary Baker's remarks upon receiving the George Kennan Award from the American Committee on U.S.-Soviet Relations, October 19, 1990. [8]

Ambassador Kennan, Chairman Kendall, Ladies and Gentlemen: I am honored to address this important audience and to share with my friend Eduard Shevardnadze the distinguished George Kennan Award. It is an honor because Ambassador Kennan has served his country long and ably, as both diplomat and historian.

Ambassador Kennan, you have been an eyewitness to and participant in the historic events of our time. The establishment of relations with the Bolsheviks. The construction of the Marshall Plan. And the ebb and flow of the Cold War.

I was particularly struck, however, by an account in your memoirs about that spring day in Moscow in 1945 when the happy crowd swarmed around you simply because you were an American and the war was over. Your Russian words captured the moment: "Congratulations on the day of victory. All honor to the Soviet allies."

But that moment, that springtime, was fleeting. It was soon chilled by the excesses of Stalinism. The grand alliance and its hopes for a postwar order turned into a long, Cold War.

Now, we live in new days of promise.

The epoch of the Cold War is over. Any lingering doubts have been dispelled by the events of the past month.

The Cold War in Europe ended quietly in New York on October 1: Foreign Minister Shevardnadze and I joined with our German, British, and French colleagues in signing away the rights of the World War II victors, recognizing a new united Germany and the trust among former adversaries that made it possible.

The Cold War that was played out across the rest of the globe ended more dramatically. It was closed by the partnership against Iraqi aggression that President Bush and President Gorbachev forged at the Helsinki Summit.

But the new epoch is just beginning. An important determinant of its future will be the change in the Soviet Union itself—a revolution that is transforming both Soviet foreign policy and Soviet society. While the people of the United States can take justifiable pride that their nation was a trustee of freedom throughout the Cold War, I am also pleased to recognize that President Gorbachev's revolution of new thinking and *perestroika* is, in large part, responsible for the end of the Cold War. And that is why President Gorbachev is so deserving of the Nobel Peace Prize.

From Containment to Points of Mutual Advantage

Five years ago, the internal contradictions of Stalinist power, successfully contained, started to lead to what Ambassador Kennan once termed a "mellowing," and what President Gorbachev calls *"Perestroika," "Glasnost,"* and "New Thinking."

Eighteen months ago, President Bush gave our government a new direction, too. He told us to move beyond containment.

And a year ago this week, I presented the details of the President's new course. Before the Foreign Policy Association in New York, I advocated that the United States pursue a creative search for points of mutual advantage with the Soviet Union. This, I believed, was the surest way to turn the promise of *perestroika* and new thinking into the reality of Soviet policy beneficial to the West. By standing pat, I contended, we would gain nothing and lose this chance to transform East-West relations.

So together, we began a revolution in U.S.-Soviet relations. We helped end the Cold War.

Now, we need to look forward to the time after the Cold War. We began with a search for points of mutual advantage. Next, we need to mark pathways of cooperation for addressing the post-Cold War challenges.

This could prove a unique historical opportunity.

I should start by examining how our pursuit of points of mutual advantage has achieved results on which we can build. Over the past year, we broadened and deepened our relationship with the Soviet Union by working on five topics: making Europe whole and free; resolving regional conflicts; stabilizing and reducing the arms competition; promoting human rights and democratic institutions; and assisting economic reform. In each, we've begun a fundamental change.

First, the changes in Europe over the past year may be the most hopeful ones of this century. Germany has unified, peacefully and freely. The peoples of Warsaw, Budapest, Prague, Sofia, and even Bucharest are struggling to establish democracies and ensure economic liberty.

This movement of, by, and for the people could not have succeeded peacefully without the courageous, farsighted cooperation of President Gorbachev, Foreign Minister Shevardnadze, and the other new thinkers in Moscow. They were the first Soviet leaders to understand that security ultimately rests on the legitimacy that can only be granted by the consent of the governed.

But this also came to pass because the United States and others in the West simultaneously reached out to Moscow.

We developed new mechanisms and adapted long-standing institutions to handle this sensitive transition. For example, we initiated the Two-Plus-Four mechanism to reconcile competing interests into a common European interest. President Bush called for and then led the first stage of NATO's adaptation that culminated in the London Summit Declaration. We supported the people power revolutions in Central and Eastern Europe in a way that assured Moscow that a free Europe would better serve true Soviet interests than a steel curtain or a concrete wall. And we worked to strengthen the Helsinki process, the conscience of the continent, so it can better support political freedom and economic liberty from North America to the Soviet Union.

Second, we have made great progress in resolving regional conflicts outside of Europe.

Most notable has been the solidarity we have shared with Moscow over Iraq's invasion of Kuwait, especially in the Helsinki Joint Statement. In it, President Bush and President Gorbachev set the international community's bottom line: "Nothing short of complete implementation of the United Nations Security Council Resolutions is acceptable."

Yet Iraq is only the most obvious example of a regional conflict resolution policy we've built, step by step, since the spring of 1989.

Our first real effort was in Central America, where we combined a U.S. diplomatic approach toward Nicaragua with limits on Soviet arms shipments to give the people of that wounded nation a chance to determine their own future. The Soviets joined us in a commitment to respect both the electoral process and its result. Peace and democracy were the outcome. Now we are trying to stop the killing in El Salvador, too, so as to give democracy a chance there as well.

In Africa, our joint efforts with Moscow led to full Namibian independence. Now, we are working together to achieve a ceasefire and multiparty elections in Angola. And we have tried to bring basic, humanitarian aid to the war-torn Horn of Africa.

In Asia, we began a Perm Five process to draw the Cambodian factions together behind another elections plan. In Southwest Asia, we have narrowed our differences over Afghanistan and are working to find a way to help move this conflict from the battlefield to the ballot box under United Nations auspices. I'm hopeful we'll get there soon.

Third, our points of mutual advantage may be most noticeable in conventional arms control. The Soviet conventional force imbalance, which for decades spawned fears of a continent-wide offensive, will disappear through a CFE [Conventional Forces in Europe] Treaty. Tens of thousands of pieces of military equipment will be destroyed. A military revolution this fall will match the political revolutions of last autumn.

We also continue to make progress on START [Strategic Arms Reduction Talks] — an agreement that will lock in substantial reductions, including a roughly 50% cut in the most destabilizing nuclear weapons. And nuclear testing treaties that were hung up for 15 years have now been ratified.

Perhaps even more important for the post-Cold War world, the Soviet Union and the United States are making a concerted effort to address the problems of spreading weapons of mass destruction. We are cooperating in implementing the chemical weapons initiative the President presented to the United Nations last year. Soviet and American bilateral destruction of the bulk of each of our chemical weapons stockpiles will move us along a realistic path toward our mutual goal: a global

ban on these weapons of horror. The two of us are also working multilaterally on the control of missile technology.

Fourth, we have supported Soviet political reform. We have made real progress on "zeroing" out human rights cases, although our work is not yet done. We have also instituted programs to help the Soviets build democratic institutions and the rule of law.

Finally, we have launched a wide range of economic contacts. Our technical economic cooperation already covers a breadth of activities — from market education to small business development. We are making efforts to introduce American businesspeople to the Soviet Union and to introduce the Soviets to the steps that will create a conducive climate for private investment. Some of these businesses are also helping to train Soviet managers. Over time, we hope to expand our efforts to help Republic and even some city leaders. In the international sphere, we have helped open up possibilities for the Soviets to participate in and learn from international market institutions.

From Points to Pathways of Mutual Advantage

Our search for points of mutual advantage has been productive. And the search must continue in new, more ambitious ways. We now need to pursue our hopes for the post-Cold War future. We need to build a new international order — what the President has called a "new partnership of nations." Any policy toward the Soviet Union, however, must begin with a sober appreciation of the twin revolutions in motion: the first, the Soviet government's relations with the outside world; the second, the changes within Soviet society.

I will begin with the external revolution — the transformation of Moscow's foreign and defense policies. New thinking and reasonable sufficiency have become essential elements of this leadership's policy. We have never enjoyed greater possibilities for cooperation between our governments.

U.S.-Soviet relations will always be unique. But our relations could become more like those we have with many other governments. Cooperation could become the norm, and disagreements could be limited to specific disputes. A "normal" relationship, possibly even a genuine partnership, may be in reach.

In our search for points of mutual advantage, we have tested whether new

thinking could guide Soviet policy, even when it confronted hard choices. This Soviet leadership has shown it can make the right hard choices.

Now we need to pose a different question: Can we build on our points of mutual advantage to create something more durable, something that strengthens and accelerates our ability to achieve results to our mutual advantage?

An answer to this question will depend to a great degree on continued new thinking in Moscow.

But for our part, we hope to build pathways of mutual advantage from the points we've begun.

The notion of pathways assumes that continuous, even lasting cooperation, not just intermittent or episodic agreements, may be possible. This idea assumes cooperation can operate in a regular, almost day-by-day fashion, to manage problems as they evolve. A pathway assumes that cooperation may prevent future problems as well as resolve past ones. And the pathways concept assumes that *mechanisms* and *processes,* built on democratic values and practices, will be the key to maintaining U.S.-Soviet cooperation as we search for answers to the complex problems of the future.

This concept, in short, proceeds from the premise that cooperation can become the norm, not the exception; that common problems can best be solved mutually, not unilaterally; and that many of our difficulties may stem not from U.S.-Soviet differences but from the complications inherent in leaving behind the Cold War and building a new international order.

We might look to build pathways and mechanisms of cooperation in three broad areas: eliminating the old vestiges of Cold War; addressing the new threats to the post-Cold War order; and dealing with the transnational dangers to peoples all over the globe.

One, we need to chart pathways to eliminate the remnants of the Cold War and prevent a resurgence of the conflicts that preceded it. Some of these concerns will be alleviated by CFE and its follow-on talks; by the adaptation of NATO and the EC to new needs; and by strengthening CSCE, politically and institutionally.

But working in concert with our Allies and the new European democracies, we can do more. We can deepen our dialogue with the Soviets to exchange regularly our ideas about

European challenges that concern all of us. We should focus our dialogue on ways democracy, economic liberty, reconciliation, and tolerance could be fostered across Europe within the CSCE context. We might also address our common interest in easing the economic transition of the new democracies in Central and Eastern Europe, which face problems of energy supply, disrupted markets, and debt, among others.

The Cold War could also be left further behind, as I stressed last fall in a speech in San Francisco, by broadening our dialogue to explore more fully the "software" side of the arms competition: *strategy* and *doctrine*. This would be a natural addition now to our attempts to constrain or reduce destabilizing military capabilities — the "hardware" side. In U.S.-Soviet arms control negotiations, we are working to constrain and reduce weapons. We should open up a complementary mechanism to learn more about the doctrine and strategy Soviet leaders follow for use of those weapons, in peace and war.

Therefore, I will propose to Foreign Minister Shevardnadze that we also set up a working group on deterrence, reassurance, and stability. This would complement discussions the Chairman of the Joint Chiefs and the Secretary of Defense are pursuing with their counterparts.

Our dialogue must also be broadened by talks on defense conversion. The Secretary of Defense is exploring this topic in his meetings in Moscow this week. A defense conversion dialogue with the Soviets can be a pathway to greater openness as well as to building down the possibilities of future war even further.

Two, the United States and the Soviet Union need pathways and mechanisms for managing new threats to the emerging international order. Iraq's brutal subjugation of Kuwait leaves no doubt that even though the danger of U.S.-Soviet confrontation has eased, the world remains a dangerous place. The world community's condemnation of Iraq also demonstrates that when the United States and Soviet Union lead, others are likely to follow.

U.S., Soviet, and multilateral cooperation needs to anticipate regional conflicts and to try to resolve them before they lead to war. Regional *conflict prevention* must become a goal of U.S.-Soviet cooperation.

Hand in hand with these discussions of regional conflicts, we plan to move more vigorously to cope with the new security agenda I detailed in San Francisco last October. The incipient nuclear programs of Iraq and North Korea are the best argument that our nonproliferation effort needs a new impetus to cope with a new danger. We cannot approach proliferation in a business-as-usual manner. I believe Foreign Minister Shevardnadze agrees.

We both see proliferation as perhaps the greatest security challenge of the 1990s. We concur that it is unconscionable that Iraq, with a leader who used chemical weapons against his own people, should be in a position where it could acquire nuclear weapons in the future. And we agree that stopping and countering proliferation must be a central part of our agenda.

Working together, we may be able to inspire a more comprehensive approach to nuclear, chemical, biological, and missile proliferation. Just as our bilateral agreement on destroying our chemical weapons stocks set a critical example — and makes a global ban more achievable — so now the two of us can help lead the way on the other weapons of mass destruction.

We must work with others, improving existing mechanisms and developing new ones to cut off the supply of necessary technology and reduce the demand for acquiring weapons of mass destruction. Our experience in Europe in developing confidence building measures (CBMs) may also be useful in different regions of the world, possibly providing mechanisms for gradually reversing proliferation where it has occurred.

And we will work with the Soviets to explore sanctions, both bilateral and multilateral, that might be imposed against those states that violate international nonproliferation norms or use weapons of mass destruction.

Developing together a pathway for countering the danger of nuclear, chemical, biological, and missile proliferation will be essential to any new, peaceful order. Here, again, I'll propose a ministerial working group to keep channels open and promote continual cooperation.

One instrument for fashioning a new international order is the United Nations. The Iraqi conflict has shown how much the Security Council can do when the Perm Five, especially the old adversaries the United States and the

Soviet Union, are united. We are particularly pleased with the U.S.-Soviet Joint Statement on the United Nations that we issued in New York during the General Assembly. We hope to build on it in the months ahead.

Three, we need to build pathways to cope with those transnational dangers that threaten all peoples and all nations. That's why I added the transnational issues of drug trafficking, terrorism, and environmental degradation to the formal U.S.-Soviet agenda early in 1989. But we need to achieve greater results.

We should explore the idea of an International Center for Ecological Research at Lake Baikal. The Center could become a pathway to more precise knowledge of our global environment for Soviet, American, and other scientists. Situated on Lake Baikal, the world's largest body of fresh water, it could stand for our commitment to end man's despoiling of nature's resources.

In addition, I propose that we advance energy efficiency as a topic for discussion. This could enhance prospects for economic growth, limit environmental degradation, and reduce our vulnerability to supply disruptions. We would invite the private sector and nongovernmental organizations and develop new U.S.-Soviet exchanges. Oil extraction would be another potential area for discussion.

We will also continue to build a pathway with Moscow to cooperate to counter international terrorism. On civil aviation, we have already begun discussions on procedures for handling crises such as hijackings. We are also exploring possibilities for cooperation in ending state-supported terrorism.

Pathways to a Democratic Dialogue

Let me turn now to the other Soviet revolution — the changes in Soviet society.

The internal revolution, in contrast to the new thinking in foreign and defense policy, presents an altogether different challenge to American policy. And it presents a novel opportunity for the American people.

Like most revolutions, *perestroika* has become a mix of paradoxical elements. On one side, we see remarkable, previously unthinkable progress. The Supreme Soviet is asserting its parliamentary powers. In key cities and regions, democrats — with a small "d" — run the government. The Communist

Party has formally surrendered its political monopoly, and alternative parties are beginning to form. The ideas of private property and market pricing are accepted now in mainstream Soviet economic debates. And Moscow is abandoning the Stalinist principle of empire, where the Center dictated everything, and seems to be moving toward a confederation through negotiation.

All of this is fundamentally to the good. It represents the "normalization" of Soviet society: the pluralization of political power, the decentralization of economic life, and the long overdue recognition of the need for a voluntary multinational union.

Unfortunately, this "normalization" is matched and oftentimes exceeded by a deterioration in Soviet life. Fragmentation equals or exceeds pluralization in many Soviet political debates. Standards of living are deteriorating, shortages are spreading, and the harvest is rotting. Freedom has unleashed age-old ethnic animosities that often shout down the voices of tolerance.

This other, darker side of the Soviet revolution concerns all of us. We all must be understanding of the hardship a great people is now enduring. In this, all must remember that democratic change must come through peaceful, democratic means—as Andrei Sakharov, another Nobel Laureate, so often reminded us.

The Cold War image of a single totalitarian monolith is gone, replaced by a confusing, jumbled mosaic that presents danger as well as hope.

The danger is that the breakdown of the old Stalinist system will outstrip the development of a new system—one built on universal democratic values and the rule of law. The hope is that devolution of political authority and decentralization of economic power will prevail over deterioration and decay.

As President Gorbachev has stated plainly, the Soviet future depends ultimately on the choices the Soviet peoples make. He is right. Their choices are their own. Building a new system will take all the courage and hard work and hope the men and women of the Soviet Union can muster.

But their choices will be less hard if we in the West stand by their side. Our influence may only be marginal. But help, however offered and however marginal, can still make a difference. The American people can make a difference.

Here is how they can help.

At the height of the Cold War, dialogue was practically impossible. The Iron Curtain had few openings. This made it necessary for most contacts with the Soviet Union to pass from our diplomats in Washington to Soviet leaders in Moscow. The path of formal government-to-government contact was often the only one.

But this was, as we always knew, abnormal. Indeed, the determination of Stalin and his successors to close off the Soviet people to normal exchanges and dialogue with the outside world stood as both hallmark and linchpin of Stalinist repression. And it is perhaps the main reason for the backwardness and poverty in which much of the Soviet economy is mired today.

Glasnost and democratization have created an opportunity our people have long sought: the chance to reach out to the Soviet people directly. The Cold War destroyed much, but it never destroyed the good will or hope between our peoples—peoples who fought and died together in World War II.

Almost from the very outset of this administration, I have stood on the side of hope—hope for a new Soviet Union built on democratic values. I intend to continue to stand there. That's why today I urge the American people, along with state and local governments, to join us in reaching out to the Soviet Union to help the Soviet peoples build better lives.

We can build *pathways between peoples*—pathways built on mutual respect for universal democratic values and a common interest in freedom, security, prosperity, and justice. Pathways to a true *democratic dialogue*.

These paths should cross at all levels: among persons, groups, firms, institutions, cities, and states. In joining at the local or city level, we can help create models or demonstrations of success. That can give hope.

To lend momentum to this effort, I want to announce today the President's decision to include the Soviet Union in the Citizens Democracy Corps.

We know a Europe whole and free must include the Soviet Union. We know Soviet reform can be accelerated by multiplied contacts with the American people. Through the Citizens Democracy Corps, we will try to help the leaders of the new Soviet Union by increasing their knowledge of democratic processes and market economics, by increasing their oppor-

tunities for interchange with our citizens and institutions, and above all, by giving them greater hope.

After the Cold War

Ambassador Kennan, I began by recounting a different time of hope 45 years ago.

Now, we are at the end of another war—the Cold War.

But today Stalin and his perverse ideology are truly gone.

Instead, new Soviet leaders welcome us. They welcome us to join with the peoples of the Soviet Union in a new revolution—a revolution of openness, of growing democratic change.

We should accept their invitation.

For if by our example and assistance, their world is made the better, both our peoples and our governments will be the better.

And if by our work, we rekindle some of the values of our experience—hard work, individual liberty, initiative, and tolerance—that will be all for the good, too.

---

1 Provided to news correspondents by the Office of Press Relations, Department of State.

2 Text from the German Information Center, New York.

3 Department of State Press Release 136, September 12, 1990.

4 Text from Weekly Compilation of Presidential Documents of October 1, 1990.

5 Text from Weekly Compilation of Presidential Documents of October 8, 1990.

6 President Vaclav Havel of Czechoslavakia, Prime Minister Tadeusz Mazowiecki of Poland, and Prime Minister Joszef Antall of Hungary.

7 Department of State Press Release 160, October 7, 1990.

8 Department of State Press Release 166, October 19, 1990.

The Principles Guiding the All-German Government

Statement by Helmut Kohl

Delivered at the plenary meeting of the German Bundestag, Berlin, October 4, 1990 (excerpts). [1]

I

Today's plenary meeting of the all-German Bundestag marks the beginning of parliamentary work in the united Germany. In both domestic and foreign affairs we are faced with great tasks, which will absorb all our energies in the period ahead.

In this policy statement I would like to ... set out the principles governing the activities of the first all-German Government. The policies of this Government will be marked by an awareness of German history in all its aspects. Only those who are familiar with their origin, and acknowledge it, have a compass guiding their path to the future.

We shall not forget those to whom we owe the unity of our fatherland. Many have contributed, first and foremost the people in the former GDR. Particularly here in Berlin I would like to mention the United States of America, above all President George Bush, and our friends in France and the United Kingdom. We are grateful to our partners in the European Community and the Atlantic alliance for their solidarity. Special thanks are also due to the reform movements in Central, Eastern and Southeastern Europe. Just over a year ago Hungary allowed the refugees to leave, thus knocking the first brick out of the Wall. The movements for freedom in Poland and Czechoslovakia encouraged the people in the GDR to stand up for their right to self-determination.

President Mikhail Gorbachev made an inestimable contribution towards overcoming the division of our fatherland. He recognized the right of nations to follow their own path. Without the new thinking in Soviet foreign policy, we would not have experienced the day of German unity so soon.

When has a nation ever had the opportunity to overcome decades of painful separation in such a peaceful manner? We have been able to restore German unity in freedom without war and violence, without bloodshed, in full agreement with our neighbors and partners. This is an important asset for our future. The united Germany follows the tradition of those movements for freedom in our history which neither war nor tyranny were able to suppress...

In acknowledging all aspects of German history, we Germans will not omit the dark chapters. We must never forget, suppress or play down the crimes committed in this century by Germans, the suffering inflicted on people and nations. By jointly shouldering this burden, we shall prove ourselves worthy of our common freedom. We owe it to the victims to keep alive the memory of the darkest chapter of our history. Above all we owe this to the victims of the Holocaust, the unparalleled genocide of European Jews.

In acknowledging all aspects of German history, we Germans will not omit the dark chapters.

At this juncture we are also guided by the firm will to build lasting bridges over the gulfs of the past, thus serving the common cause of understanding, peace and reconciliation founded on respect for human rights—both at home and abroad.

Continuity and a new beginning—the united Germany stands for both. We are able to build on the proven foundations established and developed in the Federal Republic of Germany, and we abide by our commitment to European unification and to the Atlantic alliance ...

It is now essential to ensure that Germany is also swiftly reunited in economic and social terms. This will call for great exertions, and we shall also have to make sacrifices. But I am certain we shall succeed if we Germans now hold to each other. At this decisive point in our history, we must more than ever practice solidarity. By doing so, we shall also overcome the deep intellectual, economic and ecological crisis left behind by socialism and communism. We must now openly take stock, and at the same time embark on a new beginning. The SED dictatorship's legacy is devastating.

II

... The economic situation in the former GDR is determined by the difficult transition from a socialist command economy to a social market economy. This task is unprecedented. Over decades two incompatible economic and social systems developed in opposing directions. Now we must jointly shape the future in freedom. We have every opportunity to jointly meet this challenge.

Industry and enterprises have to be radically adapted and reoriented ... We want to promote this process jointly by the swift modernization of enterprises and by intensified retraining and further training for employees. We are providing the necessary support through extensive skill enhancement schemes, investment allowances and regional economic aid. On the basis of the economic support currently envisaged, an investment volume of roughly DM 50 billion can soon be achieved ...

We have initiated a far-reaching infrastructure program for the former GDR. The main aim is to repair and modernize the road, railway and telephone systems. An efficient infrastructure is the prerequisite for lasting economic recovery...

Let me also stress this: The Unification Treaty enables the cities, towns and rural districts to make land and buildings available without delay for the purpose of job-creating investment. Immediate use should be made of this opportunity for the sake of promoting employment ...

In our view, economic recovery and ecological rehabilitation go hand in hand. Enterprises and plants posing a high threat to public health and the environment have already been shut down. And we are working at top speed on an ecological rehabilitation and development program, especially for highly polluted areas. ...

The former command economy has failed. But in many respects the contours of the new economic system are not yet clearly discernible. As a result, the people are understandably anxious about their own future, about their jobs, about their earnings or pensions, about their homes, about the new demands that a competitive economy will make on them. ... This also gives rise to expectations, which sometimes exceed the short-term capabilities of public and private aid and support. ...

The destruction caused in the course of four decades cannot be set right within a few weeks and months. And financial demands come up against the limits set by the need to keep the Mark stable and maintain a sound financial base for the country as a whole. After all, this is the foundation on which we all stand today and on which we want to build our common future.

It is thus all the more important that the public debate should not just focus on the cost entailed by this new beginning... Investments in our common future certainly involve costs – yet not only costs, but also returns. ...

It must be borne in mind that the united Germany lies at the heart of a no longer divided, but merging Europe. This bridging function will obviously yield tangible economic benefits for us and our partners ... Apart from the costs, we are also aware of the encouraging prospects emerging for the united Germany and for Europe as a whole.

Costs, returns and prospects are inextricably interlinked. This naturally includes intangible benefits that cannot be measured in Marks and Pfennigs – first and foremost, individual freedom. ...

All of this shows that we have every reason to tackle with confidence the task of reconstruction between the rivers Elbe and Oder. When have we ever been better prepared for this task than today? ... And it is already obvious that, after only three months of monetary, economic and social union, gratifying advances have been made:

- There has been a spate of company launches. This year alone almost 170,000 companies have been set up, 40 % of them since the introduction of the Mark and a social market economy. ...
- The privatization, rehabilitation and, where necessary, closure of former combines and enterprises under the auspices of the Trust Agency are making good headway. The urgently needed reorganization of the Agency's branch offices is also clearly progressing. ...
- The Treaty Establishing a Monetary, Economic and Social Union and the Unification Treaty have laid the foundation for an economic upswing and prosperity in the whole of Germany. ...

III

From the outset ... we have endeavoured to interlink the internal and external aspects of German unification as closely as possible. Our precept continues to be this: Germany is our fatherland, the united Europe our future.

We have always realized that the path to German unity would prompt many people in Europe and elsewhere to ask certain questions and even give rise to uneasiness and anxiety among quite a few of them. We understand and respect these feelings. But we are also able to point to the stable democracy based on the rule of law that has existed in the Federal Republic of Germany for over forty years. The years ahead will show that the united Germany is a gain for the whole of Europe. There is all the more cause for confidence in view of the mutual trust that marked the Two-Plus-Four talks on the external aspects of Germany unity. ...

At home and abroad we want to be good neighbors. There will be no separate German paths or isolated nationalistic efforts in the future either. Faithful to the preamble to our Constitution, we want to serve the peace of the world as an equal partner in a united Europe. This mandate embodies our conception of sovereignty. We are willing to share it with others in line with our Constitution, which authorizes us to transfer sovereign powers to intergovernmental institutions and – by consenting to a limitation of our sovereign rights – to enter systems of collective security.

We are immutably committed to our alliance, to solidarity and to the community of values with the free democracies of the West, especially with the United States of America. ...

Germany and Europe as a whole will need partnership and friendly cooperation with the U.S.A. and Canada in future, too. We want to reaffirm this in a transatlantic declaration that will provide an even broader basis on which to build. The North American democracies must be anchored in Europe in three ways: through the Atlantic alliance, through ever closer cooperation with the EC and through their participation in the CSCE process.

The agenda for the coming years includes the establishment of a European Union and the creation of a pan-European peaceful order. The accomplishment of German unity is proving to be an opportunity to accelerate the process of European unification.

In Munich a few days ago, President Mitterrand and I reaffirmed that France and Germany will continue to be the engines of European unification and that together we want to help structure the peaceful order in Europe. This cooperation is a further indication of the fundamental importance we attach to the partnership between France and the united Germany.

As a result of our joint initiative, and in close cooperation with the Italian Presidency, the intergovernmental conferences on economic and monetary union and on political union will be opened before the end of the year. These steps towards integration are imperative if the European Community is to live up to its growing political and economic role and responsibility.

The European Union we seek is to provide a solid foundation for the coalescence of the whole of Europe and to form its core. Together with France, we are resolved to work towards the creation of a European confederation in which all states on our continent work together as equal partners.

The united Germany is aware of the fact that the process of security and cooperation in Europe, the CSCE, has made an essential contribution to closing the gulfs dividing our continent.

We will do all in our power to support the further expansion of the CSCE. Our aim in doing so is to ensure greater protection for human and civil rights. We also want to advance towards permanent institutions. The focus of our interest at present is a Conflict Prevention Center. The summit meeting of the heads of state and government of the 34 CSCE countries, due to take place next month, should lay the tracks in all these directions.

Similarly we want the member states of NATO and the Warsaw Pact to extend to one another the hand of friendship and new partnership in a joint declaration in Paris. We hope that the remaining CSCE partners will thereafter join us in solemnly reaffirming their rejection of the use of force. We view all these aspects as elements for security and cooperation structures extending throughout Europe...

A first agreement on conventional disarmament in Europe will be completed very soon and signed at the CSCE Summit in November.

The Vienna negotiations will be continued immediately afterwards. Germany has acted as pacesetter in this context: in the Vienna negotiating forum we undertook on 30 August 1990 to cut the forces of the united Germany to 370,000 within three to four years.

We assume that in follow-on negotiations the other participants, too, will make their contribution to consolidating security and stability in Europe, not least through measures to restrict force strengths.

Together with its partners in the Alliance, the Federal Government is also energetically pursuing progress in other areas of disarmament and arms control. This applies particularly to a worldwide ban on chemical weapons, as well as the reduction of strategic nuclear weapons and of the short-range nuclear systems of the Soviet Union and the United States.

I have already expressed grateful recognition of the fact that the sweeping changes which took place in Central, Eastern and Southeastern Europe considerably eased our path to German unity. From the beginning we did our utmost to encourage and support these reform processes.

The extensive development of German-Soviet relations plays a key role in pan-European responsibility. During our talks in the Caucasus, President Gorbachev and I created the necessary conditions for lending a new quality to German-Soviet relations. ...

The Treaty on Good-Neighborliness, Partnership and Cooperation which has already been concluded serves this aim. It is gratifying that President Gorbachev will come to Germany to sign with me this groundbreaking treaty...

We envisage a comparable work for peace of pan-European significance with the Republic of Poland.

We are aware of the heavy burden imposed by the history of this century. But, equally, the history of both nations contains many good chapters on which we can build today. The time is now ripe for lasting reconciliation between the German and Polish people...

We will continue to follow the reforms in Hungary with friendly counsel and helpful assistance, as we will those in Czechoslovakia. The Federal Government is resolved to make these countries a focus of its cultural relations.

We have offered all reforming states in Central and Southeastern Europe the chance of being more close-ly linked with the European Community through an association tailored to their needs.

Developments in Europe and our obligations on this continent, however, never allow us to forget the conflicts, the anxieties and problems facing people in other parts of the world.

Many peoples in Africa, Asia and Latin America suffer poverty, hunger, need and overpopulation. Excessive debts undermine their political, economic and social stability. We will continue to demonstrate solidarity in helping people in need...

It is gratifying that President Gorbachev will come to Germany to sign with me this groundbreaking treaty.

We realize that greater responsibility is incumbent on the united Germany in the community of nations, not least for the preservation of world peace. We will shoulder this responsibility in the United Nations, the European Community and the Atlantic alliance as well as in our relations with individual countries. We intend to create clear constitutional conditions for this.

We most strongly condemn the Iraqi aggression against and subsequent annexation of Kuwait and the abduction of foreign, including German, citizens in violation of international law. This is an affront to the community of nations and the United Nations; at the same time, it is a test of their resolution... We have made our contribution to international solidarity and will continue to do so.

The Federal Government will also cooperate actively in the solution of the global problems of mankind:

- Humanity's natural resources of life must be preserved for future generations. We are especially concerned to protect the tropical rain forests.
- We want to help break the vicious circle of poverty, population growth and environmental destruction.
- We will step up the fight against drugs, epidemics and international terrorism.
- Endeavours towards greater worldwide protection of human rights — especially the rights of national, ethnic and religious minorities — are and will remain a central concern of our foreign policy. In view of the history of this century, we want to help prevent mass exoduses of refugees throughout the world and to guarantee people a life in their original homeland marked by dignity and secure rights. In whatever remains to be done in shaping our policy towards asylum seekers and foreigners we must remember that in a Europe of open borders, in a world which is growing ever closer together, the causes of these refugee flows have to be tackled at their source.

In the first Article of our Basic Law, the "German people acknowledge inviolable and inalienable human rights as the basis of every community, of peace and of justice in the world". This is the decisive moral force behind the policies of the united Germany.

Today we can say to the young generation in Germany and Europe, to our children, and grandchildren: you have every chance to live a life in peace and freedom. You have every chance to shape your life as you wish, and to find personal happiness in your career and family life.

Certainly, this will require some personal effort. But when did a young generation in Germany ever have more reason to view the future with confidence?

It is more rewarding than ever to play one's part in shaping the future. The all-German Government will make its contribution, too.

---

1 Excerpted text provided by the Embassy of the Federal Republic of Germany, Washington.

U.S.-Soviet Summit on Persian Gulf Crisis

JOINT STATEMENT, HELSINKI, FINLAND, SEPTEMBER 9, 1990 [1]

With regard to Iraq's invasion and continued military occupation of Kuwait, President Bush and President Gorbachev issue the following joint statement:

We are united in the belief that Iraq's aggression must not be tolerated. No peaceful international order is possible if larger states can devour their smaller neighbors. We reaffirm the joint statement of our Foreign Ministers of August 3, 1990 and our support for United Nations Security Council Resolutions 660, 661, 662, 664 and 665. Today, we once again call upon the Government of Iraq to withdraw unconditionally from Kuwait, to allow the restoration of Kuwait's legitimate government, and to free all hostages now held in Iraq and Kuwait.

Nothing short of the complete implementation of the United Nations Security Council resolutions is acceptable.

Nothing short of a return to the pre-August 2 status of Kuwait can end Iraq's isolation.

We call upon the entire world community to adhere to the sanctions mandated by the United Nations, and we pledge to work, individually and in concert, to ensure full compliance with the sanctions. At the same time, the United States and the Soviet Union recognize that U.N. Security Council Resolution 661 permits, in humanitarian circumstances, the importation into Iraq and Kuwait of food. The Sanctions Committee will make recommendations to the Security Council on what would constitute humanitarian circumstances. The United States and the Soviet Union further agree that any such imports must be strictly monitored by the appropriate international agencies to ensure that food reaches only those for whom it is intended, with special priority being given to meeting the needs of children.

Our preference is to resolve the crisis peacefully, and we will be united against Iraq's aggression as long as the crisis exists. However, we are determined to see this aggression end, and if the current steps fail to end it, we are prepared to consider additional ones consistent with the U.N. Charter. We must demonstrate beyond any doubt that aggression cannot and will not pay.

As soon as the objectives mandated by the U.N. Security Council resolutions mentioned above have been achieved, and we have demonstrated that aggression does not pay, the Presidents direct their Foreign Ministers to work with countries in the region and outside it to develop regional security structures and measures to promote peace and stability. It is essential to work actively to resolve all remaining conflicts in the Middle East and Persian Gulf. Both sides will continue to consult each other and initiate measures to pursue these broader objectives at the proper time.

JOINT NEWS CONFERENCE, PRESIDENT BUSH AND PRESIDENT MIKHAIL GORBACHEV, HELSINKI, SEPTEMBER 9, 1990 [1]

President Bush. I've been advised that I'm to take the first question. And if so, I would identify Helen Thomas, of the UP [United Press International].

Q. I'd like to ask both Presidents whether we are going to have a war in the Persian Gulf. And I'd like to follow up.

President Bush. Well, with your permission, Mr. President, I hope that we can achieve a peaceful solution, and the way to do that is to have Iraq comply with the United Nations resolutions. And I think the part of our joint statement, two short lines, said it most clearly: Nothing short of the complete implementation of the United Nations Security Council resolutions is acceptable. As soon as Saddam Hussein realizes that, then there certainly will be a peaceful resolution to this question.

Q. How about President Gorbachev — what do you think?

President Gorbachev. In replying to your question I should like to say that the whole of our seven hours of meeting today were devoted to the quest for a political resolution of that conflict. And I believe that we're on the right road.

Q. Mr. President, if I may follow up with you, President Bush. You are indicating that hostilities could break out if this is not resolved peacefully.

President Bush. The question is what?

Q. I said, you are indicating that there could be hostilities.

A. No, the United States is determined to see these resolutions enforced, and I'd like to feel that they will be enforced and that that will result in a peaceful resolution.

Q. Do you think, Mr. President, that the conflict of the Gulf gives the opportunity to solve the Palestinian problem through an international peace conference for the Middle East? And my second question is, was this problem discussed today with Mr. Gorbachev?

A. Well, let me say that I see the implementation of the United Nations resolutions separate and apart from the need to solve the other question. That question has been on the agenda of many countries for many years, and it is very important that that question be resolved. The Secretary of State said the other day, and I strongly support that, that under certain circumstances the consideration of a conference of that nature would be acceptable. Indeed, it's been a part of our policy from time to time. But the thing that I feel strongly about is that these issues are not linked. And any effort to link them is an effort to dilute the resolutions of the United Nations.

Q. This question to President Bush from Soviet radio and television. How long will the United States troops be present in the Persian Gulf area?

A. They will be present in the area until we are satisfied that the security needs of the area have been met and that these resolutions have been complied with. And the sooner they are out of there, as far as I'm concerned, the better. I made very clear to President Gorbachev, as I think he will confirm, that we have no intention keeping them a day longer than is required. So, I'd leave it right there.

President Gorbachev. I'd like to add something and to confirm what the President of the United States has just said to me in our conversation — that the United States of America does not intend to leave their forces in the zone. And in connection with the change or the normalization of the situation, the United States administration and, personally, the President will do everything possible to ensure that the forces are withdrawn from the region, from the zone. And that is a very important statement.

Q. I have a question for both Presidents. The unity that you're expressing doesn't ignore the fact that there is still some irritants between the two countries. President Bush, are you more sympathetic to suggestions of Western economic aid to the Soviet Union? And President Gorbachev, would you be willing to withdraw the Soviet military advisers from Iraq?

President Bush. For my part, I am very much interested in assisting to be sure that *perestroika* is successful. We, indeed, have a mission of high-level businessmen on their way to the Soviet Union—right now they happen to be in Helsinki. This is but one manifestation of the fact that we are trying to encourage economic cooperation in as many ways as possible. And we had a good, long discussion in our expanded meeting this afternoon about that. And I am—given the common stand that the Soviet Union and the United States have taken at the United Nations, it seems to me that we should be as forthcoming as we possibly can in terms of economics, and I plan to do that. There are certain constraints, as you say. There are certain nuances of difference; there are certain differences—real differences.

But on the other hand, I have said before—and I'll repeat it here in front of all these journalists from all around the world—we, of course, want *perestroika* to succeed. It is an internal matter of the Soviet Union. But I think this remarkable cooperation that has been demonstrated by the Soviet Union at the United Nations gets me inclined to recommend as close cooperation in the economic field as possible. And I will be saying this to the Congress when I get back. We still have problems. Look, we've got some big problems ourselves in our economy, and we are not in the position, operating at the enormous deficits, to write out large checks. Having said that, there are many ways that we can endeavor to be of assistance to the emerging economy in the Soviet Union.

President Gorbachev. There was a question also addressed to me. I would like, nevertheless, on the question which did appear also to be addressed to me—the Western assistance to the Soviet—I would like to continue. The conversation with President Bush is continuing on the Western assistance to the Soviet Union. I see that there is an attempt

being made to link, to establish a link between this and disagreements or the lack of disagreements. In response to that, I would say the following:

We began our conversation today together by reviewing the situation and realizing that the whole of world society and our two great states are undergoing a trial. This is a test of the durability of the new approach to resolving world problems. And as we enter upon a new peaceful period and as we emerge from the Cold War, we see that no less efforts are necessary in order to find ways and means in this period of peace to meet the new situation and to tackle all problems that may arise. I think if it hadn't been for Malta it would have been very difficult for us to act in the very difficult situation which arose in Eastern Europe—in Europe and in the situation connected with the unification of Germany.

I think that if, following that, there hadn't been Washington and Camp David and the other meetings on this level with other partners in international relations, we would now be in a difficult situation facing the crisis in the Persian Gulf. And the fact that today we have taken a common approach to such difficult problems—problems which may well have tragic consequences for the whole world, not just for the peoples of that region—demonstrates that we still are moving forward in the right direction and that we are capable of resolving the most difficult and the most acute problems and to find appropriate responses to the challenges of our time. And the greater part of our conversation together was devoted to this. I believe that this is the most important point to bear in mind. Differences, nuances in the differences of view, arguments, these can be—these are natural. It's natural those should arise. But what we have seen today is that we have confirmed the most important progress of recent time.

Now I should like to say something about the Iraqi question—but, in fact, I haven't quite finished on the first subject. I wouldn't want President Bush's reply to give rise to the opinion that the Soviet Union is going to align a certain sum with a certain behavior. We are acting in a difficult situation. We are finding a solution. We shall find a solution which will be satisfactory and, above all, which will remove the danger of an explosion. And this is becoming a normal element of the new kind of cooperation—in trade, in technology, in human

exchange. All of these elements characterize the new peaceful period upon which we are just now embarked, which we have to get used to.

It would be very oversimplified and very superficial to judge that the Soviet Union could be bought for dollars because, although we do look forward to cooperation in this very serious time of far-reaching changes in our economy—and that's normal—let's remember the reforms of recent years in a number of states. They always, in addition to the principal efforts made by the peoples concerned themselves, they always involved also the participation of the world community in one form or another. So if anybody wants to try to impose a different view, that's unacceptable to us. It's unacceptable to the United States, it's unacceptable to the Soviet Union, and it would be unacceptable to any other state.

Now, to move on to the second part of your question concerning our experts in Iraq. They are not so much advisers as specialists or experts who are working under contract. And their number is being reduced. Whereas at the beginning of the conflict I think there were still 196 of them, there are now some 150 of them. And the Iraqi leadership looks upon the matter thus: that if they haven't completed their work, their normal work under contract, even though it may be a matter of weapons, then they are nevertheless leaving Iraq and the process is going forward. So, I don't really think there's a problem.

Q. A question to both. Did you discuss any possible military options for curbing Iraqi aggression? And what would be the conditions, and what would be the point where you would consider that the political options were exhausted and it was time to go to the Security Council and talk about, through the Security Council, demanding an Iraqi withdrawal from Kuwait?

President Bush. The answer to your question is, no, we did not discuss military options. And your question is too hypothetical. And I would like to see this matter peacefully resolved.

President Gorbachev. I would like to support what was said by President Bush. And I stress once more that the whole of our time together was spent on talking about this conflict in a mutual search for a political solution. And I think we can look with optimism, in the final analysis, on the efforts being taken by the international community working together within the Security Council of the U.N.

Q. You were just saying that if Iraq doesn't withdraw its forces peacefully, then it will be necessary to take military steps. What kind of Soviet contribution will there be to those military steps? And what will happen then to the Soviet citizens who are in Iraq now? And what will the Arab factor be?

A. Firstly, I did not say that if Iraq does not withdraw peacefully we're going to have recourse to military methods. I did not state that. I do not state that. And moreover, in my view, that would draw us into consequences which we can't at this stage forecast. Therefore, our country and the United Nations as a whole has a whole range of possibilities of finding a political solution to this problem. Therefore, I would limit ourselves to that and, therefore, the second part of your question is irrelevant.

Q. If I could ask President Gorbachev specifically: Iraq had been your ally. What directly have you done in contact with Saddam Hussein to reverse the situation there? And, President Bush, what specifically have you asked Mr. Gorbachev to do directly? Have you asked him to make a direct contact with Saddam Hussein?

A. I should say that from the start of the crisis we've been actively exchanging views and carrying forth dialogue, not only within the Security Council, not only with the administration of the U.S.A. These types of contacts have great importance to us, but we are also holding active dialogue with the leadership of China, of India, of all the other European states, especially those which are members of the Security Council. And in my view, it's this dialogue which has helped us towards the Security Council resolution which was passed.

On top of that, we're also actively cooperating with the Arab States, the countries of the Arab world. And here our dialogue is no less intensive than with our partners in the countries I previously mentioned, including dialogue with President Hussein. And I can state that what we have announced publicly is also being said to President Hussein in our dialogue with him. Which all means that the President and the leadership of Iraq are expected to show a reasonable approach, to stop and to understand what is implied by the position taken by the Security Council on this issue. This is the dialogue which we have undertaken with him. And we are trying to

make sure that our arguments are convincing. We discussed various options for ending the situation with him. And we are also attempting, as I already said, to make it quite clear to Saddam Hussein that if Iraq were to provoke military action then the result would be a tragedy first and foremost for the Iraqi people themselves, for the whole of the region, and for the whole of the world.

You know, this is, of course, a dialogue in a very difficult situation, but we consider it's a very useful dialogue. And we don't exclude the possibility of establishing new contacts, of having new meetings at various levels. And the type of communication which we have had up until now with the Iraqis gives us hope that those links we have with them can be used positively for the sake of all of us, for the sake of finding a peaceful solution to this problem and especially of preventing the situation turning into aggression in the situation.

President Bush. My answer would simply be that there is no need to ask President Gorbachev to contact Saddam Hussein. Clearly, from his answer you can see that— President Gorbachev answered the question about the contact with Saddam Hussein. And clearly, if your question to me is: Have I asked him to contact Saddam Hussein? The answer is no.

But the Soviet Union is in contact. He himself, received the Foreign Minister, [Tariq] Aziz. But I would just simply sum it up by saying the best answer to Saddam Hussein— or the best contact is the contact that took place at the United Nations when there was worldwide condemnation of the aggression. And I happen to feel that this statement showing the Soviet Union and the United States in essential agreement here is another good statement for Saddam Hussein. And hopefully, he will see that he is not going to divide us and divide other countries and that he will do what he should have done some time ago, and that is comply with the United Nations sanctions. But I did not ask him to do that because they're way ahead of us on that. They are having contacts and trying to be helpful in that regard.

Q. I have a question to Mr. Bush. Mr. President, what is your position on the question of signing a treaty limiting strategic offensive weapons? And when do you think that such a treaty will, in fact, be signed?

A. We still remain committed to a strategic arms treaty. We vowed that we

would encourage our negotiators to move forward more rapidly on both the strategic arms treaty and the conventional force agreement. And I'm still hopeful that by the end of the year we will have such an agreement.

President Gorbachev. I'd like to confirm what President Bush has just said: that we really have agreed to make fresh efforts to give further instructions because we see that there is a possibility successfully to complete the negotiating process in those two fora and to come up with positive results in the course of this year.

Q. My question is for President Bush. And I would also like to hear President Gorbachev's comment on that. President Bush mentioned that you fail to see the link between the Palestinian question and the present situation. I would like to know how come it is so important to implement U.N. resolutions in this particular instance when other standing ones have been frozen and overlooked and disregarded for so long? So I'd like to know how come this situation is so different from other ones. And I would also like to add that I personally feel that the Palestinian dilemma and question needs the attention of the superpowers more than ever. Thank you very much.

President Bush. I agree that it needs it and we are very much interested in implementing Resolution 242 of the United Nations. We've been zealously trying to do that, as have many other powers for many years. But the fact that that resolution hasn't been fulfilled when it calls for withdrawal to secure and recognized boundaries— and it should be, and hopefully we can be catalytic in seeing that happen— does not mean that you sit idly by in the face of a naked aggression against Kuwait. And the United Nations has moved, and the United Nations resolutions should be implemented on their face without trying to tie it in to some other unresolved dispute. But I couldn't agree more that it is important. It is very important that that question eventually, and hopefully sooner than later, be resolved.

President Gorbachev. I think that everything that is taking place in the Middle East is a matter of concern to us— of equal concern. And even more than in the case of the Persian Gulf, we need to act more energetically in order to resolve the complex of problems in the Middle East and to come up with decisions and to devise a system to devise guarantees that would ensure the interests of all peoples and of the whole world community because it's a matter which is of vital concern to all of us.

And it seems to me that there is a link here because the failure to find a solution in the Middle East at large also has a bearing on the acuteness of the particular conflict we've been talking about here.

Q. A question for both Presidents, please. In your statement, you pledged to work individually and in concert to ensure full compliance with the U.N. sanctions against Iraq. May I inquire what, if any, specific and concrete steps you have agreed to take in furtherance of that?

President Bush. We didn't agree to specific and concrete steps. I think President Gorbachev in the contacts he's had with Saddam Hussein—I mean with the Iraqis—and if they continue, will be a step in that direction. Clearly, this message itself will be a step in the right direction. But we did not sit at this meeting and try to assign each other or ask each other to undertake specific measures in keeping with that particular paragraph.

President Gorbachev. I'd like to add to that that the emphasis here is on the significance of the political fact that we feel necessary to reflect in this statement and which testifies to our political will to act jointly or in parallel, independently really in search of these new steps toward a peaceful resolution of the problem.

I think that, therefore, the meeting and the document that we've just adopted is more important than our enumerating various steps that might have been taken here. That forms the basis for the further active quest for solutions.

Q. I also have a question to the Presidents of both countries—Mr. President, Mr. Gorbachev, first of all. Since the last meeting, it seems to be that you've had a good mutual understanding. Have you succeeded in deepening that mutual understanding in the course of today's meeting? And how, in general—what bearing, in general, is that factor having on the results of your negotiations?

President Bush. I think clearly there has been a developing mutual understanding over the years. I like to feel, and I think President Gorbachev agrees, that our meeting in Malta had

something to do with furthering that understanding. I'm convinced that our meeting in the United States, at Camp David particularly, furthered that understanding. I think the world sees clearly that if this had occurred 20 years ago, there wouldn't have been this cooperative feeling at the United Nations. And I think it's very important.

So, I don't know how one quantifies mutual understanding, but I feel we're moving on the right track. Neither of us, when we talk, try to hide our differences. Neither of us try to indicate that we look at exactly every problem exactly the same way. But the very fact we can talk with that degree of frankness without rancor, I think, enhances mutual understanding. And then, when we see us on a question of this nature, standing shoulder to shoulder with many other countries at the United Nations, I think it is [an] obvious manifestation of this developing mutual understanding.

It's a very broad philosophical question. But differences still remain. But the common ground, in my view at least, surges ahead of these differences. And we will continue to cooperate with President Gorbachev.

President Gorbachev. I don't know if I would be allowed to tell you a secret here. I haven't asked President Bush if he'll let me. But I must admit that I'm dying to take the risk and tell you. [Laughter] But it's too important to give you an answer to this particular question. But that last sentence does really give me the hope that we'll get by. In our talks, the President said, "You know, there was a long time when our view was that the Soviet Union had nothing to do in the Middle East—had no business being there." This was something that we had to talk through during this meeting here in Helsinki. And what was said here is that it's very important for us to cooperate in the Middle East, just as it is on other issues of world politics.

So, that is—in answer to your question, it is very important that at each meeting we move forward, we enrich our relationship, and I think I should say that we increase our trust. If trust is engendered between the leaders of two such nations during meetings of this kind—then I'm sure you'll agree with me that that is for the good of all of us, whether we want it or not. History dictates that a lot is going to depend on whether the two countries can work

together. That's not our ambition, it's just the way that history has gone. So far from excluding such a possibility, we intend to cooperate with all sorts of other countries as well, more and more. That's how we see our role in the world developing.

And my last comment is also very important. It seems to me that the way the world is, the way the world is changing, in today's world no single country, however powerful, will be able to provide the leadership which individual countries formerly tried to provide, including some countries which are represented here. We can only succeed if we work together and solve our problems together. That is what is emerging from these negotiations, and that we consider the most important aspect.

Q. I'm going to speak French, if I may. Could I ask Mr. Gorbachev whether the Soviet Union is still Iraq's friend, as Minister Tariq Aziz declared in Moscow last week? Are you still the friend of Saddam Hussein? And another question also directed to Mr. Gorbachev—President Saddam Hussein stated yesterday that the Soviet Union would demonstrate that it is a great power by resisting George Bush's pressure and by supporting the Baghdad regime. Could you indicate to me, if you would, what your reply would be to Saddam Hussein?

President Gorbachev. I want to reply to you and so to repeat it also to Saddam Hussein—the same reply that I've given to previous questions—my position is unchanged. We see our role and our responsibility, and within the framework of that responsibility we shall act in cooperation with the other members of the Security Council. And, in this instance, I can once again say since we are sitting here, two Presidents together, I should interact and cooperate with the President of the United States.

I'd very much like to express the hope that President Saddam Hussein will display—I really hope that he will display sobriety, will look carefully at the whole situation and will respond to the appeals and the demands of the world community, and that he will take steps that are suitable to the situation, that are carefully weighed in their worldwide implications and in their implications for the Arab world, too. No one has any intention of trying to exclude Iraq from the community of nations, but what the present Iraqi leadership is doing is driving it into a dead end. And I hope that President Saddam Hussein will heed this appeal to him.

Q. I'd like to ask Mr. Gorbachev if you have ruled out the possibility of a Soviet military participation in this effort in any sense, either as part of the naval blockade or as part of some future peacekeeping force in the region? And I would follow up with a question to Mr. Bush—to what degree that would be a disappointment to you if that's Mr. Gorbachev's position?

A. I don't see the point of doing that now. And we shall continue to act in cooperation within the Security Council and in strict compliance with all of its decisions.

President Bush. I'm not disappointed in that answer. [Laughter]

Q. I mean, you said you're determined to see this aggression end and current steps are being considered. What does this mean? What comes next?

President Bush. It's too hypothetical. We want to see the message get through to Saddam Hussein. We want to see him do what the United Nations calls on him to do. And that statement can be interpreted any way you want to interpret it, but it's out there. And I would simply not go into any hypothetical questions that would lead me beyond what that statement says.

President Gorbachev. Could I add a couple of words? Please, if you would excuse me, I'll add a couple of words just to what Mr. Bush has already said. You know in my view, I have the impression that both the press and public opinion in some countries is in some ways saying that there's a lack of decision on somebody's part, that we're withdrawing in the face of those who are trampling on international law. I cannot agree with that view. In fact, it's a view which causes a certain amount of embarrassment to the leadership of nations which are acting through the Security Council in this respect.

What has been done up until now in answer to Iraqi aggression is very important because action has been taken not only within the framework of the Security Council, but there has been unanimous world opinion, a kind of solidarity which has never been expressed before in the history of the world. And we have prevented the aggression going any further. We have preserved the functioning of the structures which are of economic importance which would affect so many other countries as well.

And finally, the resolution has been taken on an embargo, which is a very stiff measure, in reaction to the aggression. In my view, this is a strategic way of tackling the question which has been tackled successfully at the first stages. And we are convinced that the next stage of a political solution achieved politically, to put an end to this acute international crisis and make sure that a political settlement should be possible— that in this situation, decisiveness, will power, and responsibility, and political faith in the possibility of a political solution to this very difficult issue shows that the political leaders of the world are being responsible to their own nations and to the world. And we do not want to get caught up in arguments about prestige and so on.

Q. Concerning the humanitarian aid, does your joint statement mean in practice that you consider that food should be now allowed to Iraq?

President Gorbachev. The Presidents felt it necessary to reflect in our joint declaration that we see the need to uphold what was decided by the Security Council on this subject. And the Security Council was prepared to admit, for humanitarian purposes, the supply of medicines and of foodstuffs required first and foremost for children. We've actually stated this quite plainly in our statement. And so, we've taken a very clear-cut position on that. But we've also made it clear that this mistake [sic] is within the framework of certain international organizations and being monitored by them at all stages of the operations. So I think that this is being stated in the correct terms.

President Bush. I agree with President Gorbachev on that point and that the language is very good because it does express the concern that both countries feel in the event there actually are children and others who are suffering because of lack of food. I hope that nobody around the world interprets this as our view that now there should be wholesale food shipments to Iraq. Because I can speak only here for the United States when I would call attention to the fact that we need some kind of international agencies to see that there is this humanitarian concern, as expressed, this exception in the United Nations embargo for humanitarian purposes—and not only is it required for this humanitarian circumstance but that the food gets where it is supposed to go.

So, this should not be, from the U.S. standpoint, interpreted as a wholesale big hole in this embargo. It was not our intention, and I think the language is very clear on that point.

Q. A few things if you could clear up for us. First of all, you seem to disagree on the military option when you talk about further steps being taken to implement the U.S. sanctions. President Bush, you seem to be saying the military option is still out there. President Gorbachev seems to disagree. Do you disagree on that? Did you ask President Gorbachev to pull his experts out of Iraq? And did you ask him to send troops into the Gulf region?

President Bush. I did not ask him to send troops in. If the Soviets decided to do that at the invitation of the Saudis, that would be fine with us. But I did not ask him to do that. I believe with the 23 countries that are participating on the ground—23 countries that are participating on the ground and at sea that the security of Saudi Arabia is close to safeguarded.

What were the other two points?

Q. Did you ask him to pull the experts out of Iraq? And do you disagree on the use of military force? You seem to say it's still an option. He seems to say it's not an option ever.

President Bush. We may have a difference on that. As I think I've answered over and over again at home, I'm not going to discuss what I will or won't do. And President Gorbachev made an eloquent appeal, to which I agree, that a peaceful solution is the best. So I've left it open. He can comment on the other.

Again, John [John Cochran, NBC News], I'm sorry—the second point.

Q. The experts, pulling the experts out.

President Bush. Well, I think it would facilitate things. But on the other hand, he's given his answer here. And that is not a major irritant. You've said that—I think he said that he is reducing the numbers there. But I think I tried to make clear that this was a question that was widely being raised in the United States, and it would facilitate things if they were out of there in terms of total understanding. But I heard his answer, listened to it very, very carefully, and must say that I would let it stand at that. If I was just saying, would I like to see them all out of there, I think I'd say, absolutely. But I'd let him add to that.

President Gorbachev. In answer to all these questions which you gave us such a clear list of, I've already given answers. I really don't have anything to add to the answers I've already given.

Q. A question to the two Presidents, please. You mentioned something about the security arrangements. Is the Soviet Union going to participate in any kind of security arrangements, and what is the role of the region and the countries of that region of the Middle East?

President Gorbachev. To the first question, as we began, we intend to continue to cooperate closely and actively in the framework of the Security Council. And on the basis of the decisions that have been adopted we shall act accordingly. That's the first point.

Secondly, as concerns the role of the countries of the region, yes, I think that, generally speaking, I would stress the importance of the Arab factor not yet really having been brought to bear in efforts to help resolve this crisis situation. I don't want to offer you an analysis right now as to why that's the case, but nevertheless, I am convinced that there is an obvious activation of the quest on the part of Arab States to find the response to the urgent situation which faces us all here. We cooperate with all the Arab countries and I might say, not unusefully. The outlines of possible steps are beginning to emerge, but it is too soon to be specific. We are continuing our cooperation with Arab countries, and at a certain stage when the situation has changed and when the tension has been reduced, then perhaps we might carry this further. But we shall continue in the Security Council, the United Nations Security Council, to guarantee security.

I have no doubt that we shall succeed in resolving the problem by political means.

President Bush. May I comment on that one, please? I am very glad that the Arab States—the Arab League, and in other ways—have stated their condemnation of Saddam Hussein. He is trying to make this a contest between the Arab world and the United States. And it is no such thing—if you will look at how the United Nations has overwhelmingly condemned him. So the Arab States have a very key role in this. Many Arab States have responded in the defense of Saudi Arabia—Syria, Morocco Egypt, [to] say nothing of the GCC [Gulf Cooperation Council] countries. So, it is not Saddam Hussein and the Arab world against the United States; it is Saddam Hussein against the United Na-

tions and against a majority of the Arab League. And that is a very important point that I will continue to make, because the Arab League itself has stood up to him and urged his compliance with the sanctions and condemned his aggression.

So, in this case, I see the Arab States as having a very important role to play in the resolution of this question. And they have not been taken in by his attempt to make this the Arab world versus the United States of America when it is nothing of the kind.

White House Press Secretary Marlin Fitzwater. Thank you very much.

President Gorbachev. I want, the President and myself, to conclude this press conference by stressing our deep sympathies and feelings for the people of Finland, for the hospitalities extended to us on this soil, and to appreciate highly the contribution made by the President of this country and his wife to make these excellent arrangements for these meetings.

President Bush. May I simply add that President Koivisto and Mrs. Koivisto have been most hospitable. And I agree with this. We owe them a great debt of gratitude, and the people of Finland.

Secretary Baker's Press Conference Following Special Session of North Atlantic Council, Brussels, September 10, 1990 (Opening Statement) [2]

Before taking your questions, let me review quickly the key points of our discussions here today.

First, as I told our Congress last week and the North Atlantic Council today, we believe Iraq's unprovoked invasion and continued occupation of Kuwait is a political test of how the post-Cold War world will work.

The manner in which we and a coalition of democracies respond will be a measure of how well the institutions of Western security, that is NATO and the WEU, can adapt to today's dangers and tomorrow's threats.

Second, I reviewed the responsibility-sharing mission that our Secretary of the Treasury and I have been pursuing in the last week. We refer to this mission as "responsibility sharing" quite deliberately.

The costs of undoing Iraqi aggression undoubtedly will be a burden to all of us. But the overriding responsibility of building a more peaceful world justifies such a burden.

Trip to Gulf States and Egypt

My trip to the Gulf states and Egypt, I think, was particularly productive: politically, economically, and militarily. I found a regional coalition that is cemented in its stand against Iraqi aggression. In Egypt, President Mubarak made both political and military commitments to support a regional alliance against Saddam Hussein. And the Gulf states have made an extremely significant commitment. Having just spoken to our Ambassadors in Saudi Arabia and the UAE on my way to NATO today, I am pleased to announce that the commitments of Saudi Arabia, Kuwait, and the United Arab Emirates [UAE] for the remainder of this year now approximate 12 billion dollars. This commitment includes economic assistance to countries such as Egypt and Turkey on the front lines of the economic embargo with Iraq.

Roughly half of this 12 billion dollars will go to offset the costs of the American military effort in the Gulf. A substantial part of their contribution will be "in-kind" payments: fuel, water, food, and other essential material.

This points, I think, to a central fact of the responsibility-sharing effort, and that is that money alone is not enough. The billions of dollars that have been pledged are invaluable. But all the money in the world cannot create the airlift and sealift capabilities that are required today to move heavy forces into place and to return refugees home. The industrialized democracies of Europe and Asia who have extensive airlift and sealift capabilities can help by making ships and planes available for this critical need. And I heard from my colleagues around the table this morning that there is a willingness to respond positively in this area.

Helsinki Summit

Third, I reviewed President Bush's meeting with President Gorbachev yesterday.

From the outset of this conflict let me say that the Soviets have been very reliable partners in the worldwide coalition that has successfully isolated Saddam Hussein.

In his discussions with President Bush, President Gorbachev reaffirmed his commitment to seeing the Iraqi aggression reversed. There were really no major substantive differences between the two leaders as to how the conflict in the Gulf should be managed. In particular, I'd like to stress Soviet support for the bottom line reflected in yesterday's joint statement: "Nothing short of the complete implementation of the U.N. Security Council resolutions is acceptable." Around the table today here at NATO, our NATO colleagues also united behind this idea or principle of no partial solutions.

Looking to the Future

And *finally,* I told my colleagues of the need to look to the future. Once our short-term objectives are met and this particular case of Iraqi aggression is redressed, we are still going to need to stand together to prevent potential future Iraqi aggression.

Clearly, peace-loving governments in the Persian Gulf and the international community will need to consider creative, multilateral arrangements to insure against future aggression.

Governments in the region, along with the Permanent Members of the U.N. Security Council, need to consider intrusive, internationally sanctioned measures and procedures to diminish the threat of Iraqi weapons of mass destruction. Clearly, the Nonproliferation Treaty needs strengthening and perhaps other measures will be needed as well if an outlaw like Saddam Hussein can be only years away from having a nuclear capability. So the bottom line is simple: Saddam Hussein's aggression against Kuwait cannot stand, and the world has got to know that he will be incapable of future aggression, as well.

President's Address to Joint Session of Congress (Excerpt), September 11, 1990 [1]

Mr. President and Mr. Speaker and Members of the United States Congress, distinguished guests, fellow Americans, thank you very much for that warm welcome. We gather tonight, witness to events in the Persian Gulf as significant as they are tragic. In the early morning hours of August 2nd, following negotiations and promises by Iraq's dictator Saddam Hussein not to use force, a powerful Iraqi army invaded its trusting and much weaker neighbor, Kuwait. Within three days, 120,000 Iraqi troops with 850 tanks had poured into Kuwait and moved south to threaten Saudi Arabia. It was then that I decided to act to check that aggression.

At this moment, our brave servicemen and women stand watch in that distant desert and on distant seas, side by side with the forces of more than 20 other nations. They are some of the finest men and women of the United States of America. And they're doing one terrific job. These valiant Americans were ready at a moment's notice to leave their spouses and their children, to serve on the front line halfway around the world. They remind us who keeps America strong: they do. In the trying circumstances of the Gulf, the morale of our servicemen and women is excellent. In the face of danger, they're brave, they're well trained and dedicated.

A soldier, Private First Class Wade Merritt of Knoxville, Tennessee, now stationed in Saudi Arabia, wrote his parents of his worries, his love of family, and his hope for peace. But Wade also wrote, "I am proud of my country and its firm stance against inhumane aggression. I am proud of my army and its men. I am proud to serve my country." Well, let me just say, Wade, America is proud of you and is grateful to every soldier, sailor, marine, and airman serving the cause of peace in the Persian Gulf. I also want to thank the Chairman of the Joint Chiefs of Staff, General Powell; the Chiefs here tonight; our commander in the Persian Gulf, General Schwartzkopf; and the men and women of the Department of Defense. What a magnificent job you all are doing. And thank you very, very much from a grateful people. I wish I could say that their work is done. But we all know it's not.

So, if there ever was a time to put country before self and patriotism before party, the time is now. And let me thank all Americans, especially those here in this Chamber tonight, for your support for our armed forces and for their mission. That support will be even more important in the days to come. So, tonight I want to talk to you about what's at stake—what we must do together to defend civilized values around the world and maintain our economic strength at home.

U.S. Objectives in the Gulf

Our objectives in the Persian Gulf are clear, our goals defined and familiar: Iraq must withdraw from Kuwait completely, immediately, and without condition. Kuwait's legitimate government must be restored. The security and stability of the Persian Gulf must be assured. And American citizens abroad must be protected. These goals are not ours alone. They've been endorsed by the United Nations Security Council five times in as many weeks. Most countries share our concern for principle. And many have a stake in the stability of the Persian Gulf. This is not, as Saddam Hussein would have it, the United States against Iraq. It is Iraq against the world.

As you know, I've just returned from a very productive meeting with Soviet President Gorbachev. And I am pleased that we are working together to build a new relationship. In Helsinki, our joint statement affirmed to the world our shared resolve to counter Iraq's threat to peace. Let me quote: "We are united in the belief that Iraq's aggression must not be tolerated. No peaceful international order is possible if larger states can devour their smaller neighbors." Clearly, no longer can a dictator count on East-West confrontation to stymie concerted United Nations action against aggression. A new partnership of nations has begun.

We stand today at a unique and extraordinary moment. The crisis in the Persian Gulf, as grave as it is, also offers a rare opportunity to move toward an historic period of cooperation. Out of these troubled times, our fifth objective, a new world order, can emerge—a new era, freer from the threat of terror, stronger in the pursuit of justice, and more secure in the quest for peace. An era in which the nations of the world, East and West, North and South, can prosper and live in harmony. A hundred generations have searched for this elusive path to peace, while a thousand wars raged across the span of human endeavor. Today that new world is struggling to be born, a world quite different from the one we've known. A world where the rule of law supplants the rule of the jungle. A world in which nations recognize the shared responsibility for freedom and justice. A world where the strong respect the rights of the weak. This is the vision that I shared with President Gorbachev in Helsinki. He and other leaders from Europe, the

Gulf, and around the world understand that how we manage this crisis today could shape the future for generations to come.

The test we face is great, and so are the stakes. This is the first assault on the new world that we seek, the first test of our mettle. Had we not responded to this first provocation with clarity of purpose, if we do not continue to demonstrate our determination, it would be a signal to actual and potential despots around the world. America and the world must defend common vital interests. And we will. America and the world must support the rule of law. And we will. America and the world must stand up to aggression. And we will. And one thing more: In the pursuit of these goals America will not be intimidated.

What is at Stake

Vital issues of principle are at stake. Saddam Hussein is literally trying to wipe a country off the face of the Earth. We do not exaggerate. Nor do we exaggerate when we say Saddam Hussein will fail. Vital economic interests are at risk as well. Iraq itself controls some 10 percent of the world's proven oil reserves. Iraq plus Kuwait controls twice that. An Iraq permitted to swallow Kuwait would have the economic and military power, as well as the arrogance, to intimidate and coerce its neighbors — neighbors who control the lion's share of the world's remaining oil reserves. We cannot permit a resource so vital to be dominated by one so ruthless. And we won't.

Recent events have surely proven that there is no substitute for American leadership. In the face of tyranny, let no one doubt American credibility and reliability. Let no one doubt our staying power. We will stand by our friends. One way or another, the leader of Iraq must learn this fundamental truth. From the outset, acting hand in hand with others, we've sought to fashion the broadest possible international response to Iraq's aggression. The level of world cooperation and condemnation of Iraq is unprecedented. Armed forces from countries spanning four continents are there at the request of King Fahd of Saudi Arabia to deter and, if need be, to defend against attack. Moslems and non-Moslems, Arabs and non-Arabs, soldiers from many nations stand shoulder to shoulder, resolute against Saddam Hussein's ambitions.

We can now point to five United Nations Security Council resolutions that condemn Iraq's aggression. They call for Iraq's immediate and unconditional withdrawal, the restoration of Kuwait's legitimate government, and categorically reject Iraq's cynical and self-serving attempt to annex Kuwait. Finally, the United Nations has demanded the release of all foreign nationals held hostage against their will and in contravention of international law. It is a mockery of human decency to call these people "guests." They are hostages, and the whole world knows it.

Prime Minister Margaret Thatcher, a dependable ally, said it all: "We do not bargain over hostages. We will not stoop to the level of using human beings as bargaining chips ever." Of course, of course, our hearts go out to the hostages and to their families. But our policy cannot change, and it will not change. America and the world will not be blackmailed by this ruthless policy.

We're now in sight of a United Nations that performs as envisioned by its founders. We owe much to the outstanding leadership of Secretary-General Javier Perez de Cuellar. The United Nations is backing up its words with action. The Security Council has imposed mandatory economic sanctions on Iraq, designed to force Iraq to relinquish the spoils of its illegal conquest. The Security Council has also taken the decisive step of authorizing the use of all means necessary to ensure compliance with these sanctions. Together with our friends and allies, ships of the United States Navy are today patrolling Mideast waters. They've already intercepted more than 700 ships to enforce the sanctions. Three regional leaders I spoke with just yesterday told me that these sanctions are working. Iraq is feeling the heat. We continue to hope that Iraq's leaders will recalculate just what their aggression has cost them. They are cut off from world trade, unable to sell their oil. And only a tiny fraction of goods gets through.

The communique with President Gorbachev made mention of what happens when the embargo is so effective that children of Iraq literally need milk or the sick truly need medicine. Then, under strict international supervision that guarantees the proper destination, then food will be permitted.

Sharing the Burden

At home, the material cost of our leadership can be steep. That's why Secretary of State Baker and Treasury Secretary Brady have met with many world leaders to underscore that the burden of this collective effort must be shared. We are prepared to do our share and more to help carry that load; we insist that others do their share as well.

The response of most of our friends and allies has been good. To help defray costs, the leaders of Saudi Arabia, Kuwait and the UAE, the United Arab Emirates, have pledged to provide our deployed troops with all the food and fuel they need. Generous assistance will also be provided to stalwart front-line nations, such as Turkey and Egypt. I am also heartened to report that this international response extends to the neediest victims of this conflict — those refugees. For our part, we've contributed $28 million for relief efforts. This is but a portion of what is needed. I commend, in particular, Saudi Arabia, Japan, and several European nations who have joined us in this purely humanitarian effort.

There's an energy-related cost to be borne as well. Oil producing nations are already replacing lost Iraqi and Kuwaiti output. More than half of what was lost has been made up. And we're getting superb cooperation. If producers, including the United States, continue steps to expand oil and gas production, we can stabilize prices and guarantee against hardship. Additionally, we and several of our allies always have the option to extract oil from our strategic petroleum reserves if conditions warrant. As I've pointed out before, conservation efforts are essential to keep our energy needs as low as possible. And we must then take advantage of our energy sources across the board: coal, natural gas, hydro, and nuclear. Our failure to do these things has made us more dependent on foreign oil than ever before. Finally, let no one even contemplate profiteering from this crisis. We will not have it.

I cannot predict just how long it will take to convince Iraq to withdraw from Kuwait. Sanctions will take time to have their full intended effect. We will continue to review all options with our allies, but let it be clear: we will not let this aggression stand.

Our interest, our involvement in the Gulf is not transitory. It predated Saddam Hussein's aggression and will survive it. Long after all our troops come home — and we all hope its's soon, very soon — there will be a lasting role for the United States in assisting the nations of the Persian Gulf. Our role then: to deter future aggression. Our role is to help our friends in their own self-defense. And something else: to curb the proliferation of chemical, biological, ballistic missile and, above all, nuclear technologies.

Let me also make clear that the United States has no quarrel with the Iraqi people. Our quarrel is with Iraq's dictator and with his aggression. Iraq will not be permitted to annex Kuwait. That's not a threat, that's not a boast, that's just the way it's going to be...

United Nations Security Council Resolution 666, September 13, 1990 [3]

The Security Council,

Recalling its resolution 661(1990), paragraphs 3 (c) and 4 of which apply, except in humanitarian circumstances, to foodstuffs,

Recognizing that circumstances may arise in which it will be necessary for foodstuffs to be supplied to the civilian population in Iraq or Kuwait in order to relieve human suffering,

Noting that in this respect the Committee established under paragraph 6 of that resolution has received communications from several Member States,

Emphasizing that it is for the Security Council, alone or acting through the Committee, to determine whether humanitarian circumstances have arisen,

Deeply concerned that Iraq has failed to comply with its obligations under Security Council resolution 664 (1990) in respect of the safety and well-being of third State nationals, and reaffirming that Iraq retains full responsibility in this regard under international humanitarian law including, where applicable, the Fourth Geneva Convention,

Acting under Chapter VII of the Charter of the United Nations,

1. Decides that in order to make the necessary determination whether or not for the purposes of paragraph 3 (c) and paragraph 4 of resolution 661

(1990) humanitarian circumstances have arisen, the Committee shall keep the situation regarding foodstuffs in Iraq and Kuwait under constant review;

2. Expects Iraq to comply with its obligations under Security Council resolution 664 (1990) in respect of third State nationals and reaffirms that Iraq remains fully responsible for their safety and well-being in accordance with international humanitarian law including, where applicable, the Fourth Geneva Convention;

3. Requests, for the purposes of paragraphs 1 and 2 of this resolution, that the Secretary-General seek urgently, and on a continuing basis, information from relevant United Nations and other appropriate humanitarian agencies and all other sources on the availability of food in Iraq and Kuwait, such information to be communicated by the Secretary-General to the Committee regularly;

4. Requests further that in seeking and supplying such information particular attention will be paid to such categories of persons who might suffer specially, such as children under 15 years of age, expectant mothers, maternity cases, the sick and the elderly;

5. Decides that if the Committee, after receiving the reports from the Secretary-General, determines that circumstances have arisen in which there is an urgent humanitarian need to supply foodstuffs to Iraq or Kuwait in order to relieve human suffering, it will report promptly to the Council its decision as to how such need should be met;

6. Directs the Committee that in formulating its decisions it should bear in mind that foodstuffs should be provided through the United Nations in cooperation with the International Committee of the Red Cross or other appropriate humanitarian agencies and distributed by them or under their supervision in order to ensure that they reach the intended beneficiaries;

7. Requests the Secretary-General to use his good offices to facilitate the delivery and distribution of foodstuffs to Kuwait and Iraq in accordance with the provisions of this and other relevant resolutions;

8. Recalls that resolution 661 (1990) does not apply to supplies intended strictly for medical purposes, but in this connection recommends that medical supplies should be exported under the strict supervision of the Government of

the exporting State or by appropriate humanitarian agencies.

Secretary Baker's Joint Press Conference with Fahrouk Shara, Foreign Minister of Syria, September 14, 1990 [4]

Secretary Baker. Ladies and gentlemen, let me just make a very brief comment about the topics that were covered in my meeting with [Syrian] President Asad and Foreign Minister Shara. We talked at length as you would expect about the Gulf crisis and about ways in which we can cooperate in order to implement the United Nations resolutions. We talked about the United Nations sanctions and the importance of enforcement of those sanctions.

We talked as well about the subject of terrorism and the real problems that the United States has with Syria on this subject. In fact, we had a very extensive discussion of that topic. We talked about United States hostages in Lebanon. We talked about Lebanon and the Taif Accords.

We talked about the prospects for the peace process and particularly about the fact that we agreed that this issue should not be linked with the issue of the Gulf crisis. Do you want to say anything, Minister?

Q. Mr. Secretary, there are reports that the Kuwaiti embassies of the U.S., Britain, and France have been invaded by Iraqi soldiers. Do you have anything on that?

A. I've been in a meeting with President Asad for the last four and a half hours and I don't have anything specifically on it.

Q. Mr. Secretary, what level of forces is Syria going to send to Saudi Arabia and are the Soviets going to be transporting those troops?

A. Well, I would invite the Foreign Minister to speak to the level of forces that Syria will be sending to Saudi Arabia. I would only say that Syria has indicated that it intends to send or volunteer substantial forces for the common effort and there has been no indication, that I am aware of, that the Soviet Union has offered to transport those forces, but maybe the Minister would like to speak to that.

Q. Mr. Secretary, on the hostages, you said you discussed the hostages.

Did you get any indication from President Asad that some of the hostages might be released soon?

A. President Asad did not indicate any expectation that they would be released soon. We discussed the importance, of course, to the United States that our hostages in Lebanon be released and I thanked President Asad and Foreign Minister Shara for the efforts they have made in the past to secure the release of some of the hostages.

Q. Mr. Minister, did the Secretary of State give you any assurances that if and when the Gulf crisis is resolved the United States will put extra effort into resolving the Arab-Israeli dispute?

Foreign Minister Shara. Let me first express our satisfaction for the visit that Secretary Baker has made to Syria and the talks that he has had with President Asad. I think the talks generally speaking have been positive and constructive. We certainly discussed the bilateral relations between Syria and the United States. We hope that these relations will improve to preserve the interest of the two countries and peace and stability in the region.

Q. Did Mr. Baker give you any assurance (inaudible) —

A. Let me answer your question. We believe that an Iraqi unconditional withdrawal from Kuwait in implementation of U.N. Security Council resolutions would certainly pave the way after that for an Israeli withdrawal from the occupied Arab territories, because we believe that the recent dramatic developments in our region, and also if we take into consideration the post-Cold War, then it is important and imperative that this region should witness genuine peace and stability.

The immediate issue now is to get the Iraqi forces from Kuwait out and the restoration of the legitimate Government of Kuwait and then, certainly, if you want genuine stability in the region, then we should work for a comprehensive and just settlement of the Arab-Israeli conflict.

Q. Mr. Secretary, is that also the American position?

Secretary Baker. No, not exactly.

Q. Can you explain the American position?

A. Yes, I'd be delighted to. First of all, as I indicated, I think, in my opening remarks, we had a full and complete discussion of the importance of trying to move the peace process forward, but in

no way linking it with the Gulf crisis, because the two are not linked. I, therefore, don't think there ought to be any linkage. We talked about various ways in which the peace process might be moved forward simply exploring, for the first time, at least between the United States and Syria, this prospect. We had a quite extensive discussion of that subject, as I said.

Foreign Minister Shara. Let me first make it clear here that I don't mean there is the linkage between the two questions. We are not linking the Gulf crisis with the Arab-Israeli conflict at all. But, what I am saying from a theoretical point of view is that the unconditional withdrawal of the Iraqi troops from Kuwait would pave the way for a comprehensive and just solution for the Arab-Israeli conflict.

Q. Mr. Foreign Minister, can I please ask you to tell us why your country does not close down the offices of the PFLP-GC in light of evidence that it was involved in several terrorist incidents abroad?

A. Because we don't have evidence, so far. We made it very clear that if there was hard evidence to link any Palestinian group, then we would take the necessary action—to link any Palestinian group that is staying in Syria with any terrorist act, then in this case, those responsible will be brought to trial.

Secretary Baker. Let me follow up on that by saying that there is, and this is no secret, a disagreement between us with respect to the sufficiency of the evidence. We will work to resolve that disagreement. But, the point is, and I think it's obvious from what the Minister just said, we have had an extensive discussion of this subject.

This subject is very, very important as far as the United States is concerned. We have had, indeed, an extensive discussion of the question of Pan Am 103 and so we will continue to discuss this problem between us to see if we can arrive at some solution.

Now, the fact that those problems exist does not and should not prevent our trying to cooperate together to achieve what is a goal of the entire international community and that is a reversal of Iraq's unprovoked aggression against Kuwait.

Q. Mr. Secretary, is the United States about to propose aerial sanctions, additional sanctions through the air, and, if they are, what are aerial sanctions?

A. The United States has no plans at this time to propose anything, but there are a number of additional things that I think can be looked at, were it necessary to do so. I don't think anyone can tell you today, could give you today, a calendar which would lay out in objective detail exactly when and how much the sanctions that are now in place—when and to what degree they are going to be effective. There are varying estimates; however, most people think that they will be effective at some time.

Now it may be that the nations that have voted unanimously for the imposition of these sanctions will conclude that, in an effort to resolve this matter in a peaceful and diplomatic way, it is important that additional sanctions be looked at or sought from the United Nations. That decision has not as yet been taken, at least as far as the United States is concerned.

Q. (Inaudible) long term security structure with the Syrians and did they oppose a long term presence of United States forces in the Persian Gulf?

A. Let me say that we had a full discussion of the principle that we must find a way to promote stability in this very volatile region of the world. Consideration can and should be given to some sort of a regional security structure. But it is important to understand that a regional security structure should be led by the countries in the region and they should be at the forefront of any such regional security structure. And I made it clear to President Asad and to Foreign Minister Shara—reconfirmed, if you will—what President Bush has said on a number of occasions and that is that the United States does not seek and, in fact, does not wish to have a permanent presence on the ground in Saudi Arabia.

At the same time, I think we have to understand that we are, we the United States, are committed to the free flow of oil from the Gulf. We are committed to the preservation of security and stability in the Gulf region. We have had naval forces in the Persian Gulf since 1947, and we have no intention or desire to establish a permanent military ground presence in this region. And as soon as this crisis would permit our armed forces to be brought back to the United States, as President Bush has said, this is exactly what we want to do.

Q. Would Israel be part of that structure since it is one of the countries in the region?

A. I think when you talk about a regional security structure, you cannot exclude any of the countries in the region nor should you exclude, in my view at least, any country from outside the region. We have no preconceived ideas or notions on exactly the form that such structure would take except to say, as I have just said, the countries in the region would have a prominent or paramount role to play.

Q. Has the U.S.-Syrian relationship improved as a result of your coming here today after two years of having no U.S. Secretary of State come to Syria? If both gentlemen could answer the question.

Secretary Baker. Well, let me say that we have a common goal; we share a common purpose with respect to the problems today. But we make no secret about the fact that there are still problems revolving around this question of terrorism. And we must find a way to resolve those problems before the relationship can get what you might characterize as very close. We've got to find a way to resolve these problems. I have said before that our policy cannot and never will be amoral. We can have close relations only with countries that share our fundamental values. That is not to say that we cannot improve our relations where we have a common goal and a common interest as we have in this case. We can substantially improve our relations if we can overcome these problems we have with terrorism.

Foreign Minister Shara. Let me clarify our position vis-a-vis terrorism, because as you have already noted that Secretary Baker said that the question of terrorism stands in the way of improving the relations between Syria and the United States. We certainly want a better relation with the United States and at the same time we believe that the media in the West have made a major role in exaggerating the terrorism issue in our region.

Now, for instance, Syria has condemned terrorism in all its forms. Syria has condemned hostage taking, hijacking of airplanes. We consider any violent act outside the occupied territory is a terrorist act. But, at the same time, we cannot consider the legitimate struggle against the occupation forces as a terrorist act. Now we are talking about Kuwait, for instance. The Kuwaiti resistance to the Iraqi occupation is legitimate in every sense of the word.

We believe that so far, so far, Syria was put on the terrorist list without any justification. We believe that the Pan Am 103, the disaster of that flight, did not, until this moment, bring hard evidence to who is responsible and for who is behind that terrorist act. But in our estimation, the accusation addressed to Syria in this respect is meant for political objectives rather than analyzing an objective situation.

Nevertheless, we have agreed that we have to follow up the Lockerbie incident and whenever it is found that there is genuine evidence or hard evidence against Jabril or any other Palestinian faction that is residing in Syria, then the Syrian government will take necessary action and they will bring the persons involved to trial.

Q. Mr. Minister, are the Soviets going to help you send your troops to Saudi Arabia? What troops are you sending there?

A. President Asad made it very clear in his speech two days ago that Syria is committed to the Arab Summit resolution and in that resolution, which we strongly supported and are still supporting, Saudi Arabia can ask for Syrian troops and we said we would respond positively to any Saudi request. There was no ceiling on the number of troops. This is very much the desire of the Saudis and we will respond positively to any request.

Question: What other forms of cooperation did you and Mr. Baker agree on regarding how to roll back the Iraqi invasion? If you could both answer that.

Minister Shara. I think we have agreed, and I am sure that Secretary Baker would agree with what I am going to say, that the full implementation of U.N. Security Council resolutions is very important for everybody to pursue a political solution to the Gulf crisis.

Q. No military one?

A. Not a military one. For the time being, we believe that the adherence to the Security Council resolutions is very important to achieve a political solution and, of course, this political solution of the Gulf crisis should be based on unconditional withdrawal of Iraqi troops from Kuwait and restoration of the legitimate Government of Kuwait.

Secretary Baker. And we talked, as well, about the importance of this being an Arab solution. And one thing I think that is demonstrated, if I may say so, by the fact of my presence here today is

that this is indeed largely an Arab solution that we are trying to implement. You were with me when I went to Egypt and we had our discussions with President Mubarak. You were with us when we went to the Persian Gulf and talked to three of the nations there and six of those nations, as you know, are contributing forces. Syria is contributing forces. Egypt is contributing forces. Morocco is contributing forces. There are Moslem nations that are non-Arab that are contributing forces. So I think it is important for people, particularly in this part of the world, to realize that Arabs are in the forefront of the solution to this problem.

Press Briefing by Chancellor Helmut Kohl of the Federal Republic of Germany and Secretary Baker, Bonn, September 15, 1990 [5]

Chancellor Kohl. Ladies and gentlemen, I would like to say that first of all the part of our conversation which, I think, is most interesting to you has been concluded. First of all, with my statement here on what I perceive as the result of our meeting here and after that, Secretary Baker is going to give his statement.

First of all, allow me to underline once again how pleased I am to have Jim Baker with us here today. Over the last two weeks I've talked repeatedly with the President about this visit. And let me say that, and I said this here very clearly in these talks, we would like to make it very clear that we would like to give full support within the limits available to us to our American friends and partners who are at present active in the Middle East, in the Gulf area, because they are also active on our behalf in defending our interests in the region.

The invasion of Kuwait by Iraq in this act of aggression against a neighboring country represents a violation of the spirit of the international community and cannot in any way be tolerated by us. Let me say that the acts which we have witnessed over the past few days, and indeed hours, these attacks on individual persons, representatives of foreign countries, and now there is also an attack on the person of a representative of the French Republic, are acts of barbarism that cannot be tolerated.

Let me say how very pleased I am about the very clear decisions taken within the framework of the United Nations. Let me say at the same time how very much we regret that our Constitution, the Constitution of the Federal Republic of Germany, does not allow us at present to assume our full responsibility there in the area, something which I regret very much.

I hope that right after the elections, indeed at the beginning of the new year 1991, we will be able to come to an agreement in the legislative bodies, both the Bundestag and the Bundesrat, to initiate a change of our Constitution so that we may be in a position to fully assume our share of the responsibility. And, we underline once again, fully assume our share of the responsibility within the framework of the decisions taken by the United Nations. Let me say very frankly that I am dismayed that in this present situation, because of all these reasons which I have mentioned, we are not completely free to act in the interests of the community of nations the way we would like to act.

Let me say that also with regard to the moral stance, the moral position of Germany, and also and particularly the reunified Germany, I think it is totally unacceptable that in this particular situation we are not able to fully assume our share of the responsibility that we are tops in the field of exports on the other hand, but that we are not fully assuming our responsibility.

We talked about what we can do now; immediately as immediate help. And let me give you the figures as we have discussed them here. For us, all the assistance which we would give within this overall framework of help connected with the Persian Gulf, we are talking about a figure here of 3.3 billion Deutsche Mark. In this sum is included the German share in the overall assistance given by the EC [European Economic Community]. That is to say a share in the 1.5 billion ECU contribution which the EC had declared itself prepared to give, and of that the German share would be 420 million Deutsche Mark. Everywhere where the EC gives money, the Germans have a share of 27 percent.

We have to differentiate now between two different positions here. First, as to what we have agreed upon directly between ourselves and the United States, and between the help that we are going to give to those

countries who are suffering, particularly under the present situation in the region. That is to say help given towards Egypt, Jordan and Turkey.

We have agreed that the Federal Republic of Germany provide the United States of America with equipment in the following areas: wheeled vehicles, radio equipment, equipment used for engineering units, car trains, generators, water tanks, etc., material to counter ABC attacks and similar equipment. And all of this being modern material. This is worth one billion Deutsche Mark.

Under a different heading comes a particular form of assistance which was requested by our American friends and which is very important to them: 60 ABC detection tanks of the Fox type. That amounts to a value of 200 million Deutsche Mark. Then we will give a contribution of 400 million Deutsche Mark toward covering transportation costs — for shipping transport and similar transport. That brings us to a total of 1.6 billion Deutsche Mark of help given to our American friends.

The Federal Republic of Germany has agreed to give 200 million Deutsche Mark as a particular contribution towards commodity aid to Egypt. In the field of development aid, and we're talking here about immediate aid and project-related aid, we will give a contribution of 775 million Deutsche Mark to Egypt. So that Egypt will receive a total of 975 million Deutsche Mark.

A direct cash contribution towards commodity aid to Jordan of 200 million Deutsche Mark will also be given. And 110 million Deutsche Mark in commodity aid will be given to Turkey.

To Turkey, as it is a NATO member and as that puts us in a somewhat different position as regards our constitution, we will give aid in defense material to a very substantial order. I am not yet free to give you the exact sum of that because currently negotiations are underway with the Turkish government, particularly with Mr. Ozal. But it certainly is a sum which will have to be added to the sums which I have already mentioned.

Mr. Secretary, ladies and gentlemen, in this way the Federal Republic of Germany is trying to give a particular form of contribution as a support to all those who have assumed a particular share of responsibility in connection with the crisis in the Persian Gulf. And we know about our own

responsibility. I have already mentioned our particular situation and I think that what I have said bears testimony to the fact that we are aware of this responsibility, that we are willing and ready to assume our full share of responsibility within the scope of what is possible to us at the present time.

Secretary Baker. Chancellor, thank you very much. First let me say how appreciative we are, and I know President Bush is, for your receiving our delegation today, on a Saturday, and particularly receiving us here at your home. I must tell you also how pleased we are with the report that you've just given. It pleases us just as the progress that has been recently made in our joint efforts toward fulfilling what has been a goal of the United States for over 40 years — German unification.

We think that as Germany unifies and becomes larger and becomes greater, its international responsibilities, indeed, do increase, and we, of course, discussed this. It seems to me that being more, means doing more, and I think based on the report that you've just given, Chancellor, no one could draw any conclusion but that Germany is doing more.

We are very appreciative of these contributions, both the economic as well as the military. We see them as very positive and very forthcoming, and I don't suppose I'm giving any secrets away to suggest that they go beyond what we had privately discussed in our earlier communications and substantially so. I know that the President will be pleased and I am sure that the American people will be pleased as well.

I should make the point, I think, Chancellor, that we are talking about immediate contributions, both of material and equipment and economically. That is, we are not talking about something that might happen in another budget year or next year, we're talking about right now.

And for the benefit of our American friends here, I might just say that this translates into $2 billion, roughly equally divided into economic and material and equipment-type assistance. And, of course, that $2 billion is over and above the roughly $500 million that would be represented by Germany's share of the EC contribution. So, in total we are talking about a sum in the neighborhood of $2.5 billion for the balance of this year. And I think that speaks for itself.

Q. Chancellor Kohl, this effort has been going for about six weeks, and still there are thousands of hostages, the Iraqis have moved into embassies. Can you see your goal met in any means short of war?

Chancellor Kohl. I hope so. I'm not a prophet. Of course, this is a situation [in] which [it] is of the utmost importance that we stand firmly together and that each and everyone assumes his own share of responsibility and gives his own contribution towards averting or stopping that aggression, and averting a recession into a Cold War situation. And let me say that in spite of all of the difficulties, I do see a chance here because Iraq does have to acknowledge that in the present situation, really, the world community, or the largest share of the world community, is against it. I think that this is a fact that cannot be underlined enough.

But in this very critical situation, the United States of America and the Soviet Union are both working together in the same direction. And I think that this is very easy to see how important this is if one thinks back only twelve years ago where Brezhnev would have been President and Secretary General and Ustinov would have been Defense Minister in the Soviet Union—that indeed is a message which I would like to give to our American friends assembled here, not to Jim Baker and the representatives of the administration, obviously, but to our Americans friends here among the journalists. Now is the time that we can actually reap the benefits, and we see how very important it was that we did something in order to stabilize the countries of the Central and East and Southeast Europe.

You will remember the headlines of newspapers back in June when it was written about the decision which we had taken here and in which I tried very actively to promote in this country, that we would stand surely—that we will guarantee indeed this 5 billion Deutsche Mark loan to the Soviet Union. And, indeed, the stabilization programs which we have embarked upon with Hungary and Poland also have to be seen in this context.

Q. Mr. Chancellor, should Germany take any additional steps to absolutely shut down German trade with Iraq? And should there be any additional steps taken in the justice system in Germany to be sure that Iraq or Iraqis are not in any way rewarded at this time of difficult relations?

A. You know that we have not delivered weapons into Iraq. But let me say that I deeply regret the fact that there were Germany companies who over the past few years, indeed, participated in programs in this field. Let me remind all of us of Rabta. I do know at the same time, of course, that other countries, nearly all Western countries, participated in this kind of trade. But let me say just for the record this is, of course, no excuse at all for the participation of German companies.

You may know that we are radically altering, radically changing, our legislation on this point and we are introducing very harsh penalties for this. Because let me say that for me it is totally unacceptable that these business transactions are being made simply for profit.

I do have to concede, however, that the problem with a number of these deliveries which have been made into the region is that they can be used for both military and civilian purposes. And this is the problem which we face. You know that Ludwigshafen is indeed the stronghold of the German chemical industry, and we're one of the leading exporters of chemical goods in the world, which is why of course we're more affected than other countries. But let me say again for the record, that I am totally committed towards prohibiting in the future—doing everything in order to prohibit and to prevent such transactions from happening.

Quite apart from the legal changes necessary in order to ensure that, I would wish that in the Federal Republic of Germany, in the whole of Germany, we will come to a situation where we declare such behavior to be utterly despicable from a moral point of view.

United Nations Security Council Resolution 667, September 16, 1990 [3]

The Security Council,

Reaffirming its resolutions 660 (1990), 661 (1990), 662 (1990), 664 (1990), 665 (1990) and 666 (1990),

Recalling the Vienna Conventions of 18 April 1961 on diplomatic relations and of 24 April 1963 on consular relations, to both of which Iraq is a party,

Considering that the decision of Iraq to order the closure of diplomatic and consular missions in Kuwait and to withdraw the immunity and privileges of these missions and their personnel is contrary to the decisions of the Security Council, the international Conventions mentioned above and international law,

Deeply concerned that Iraq, notwithstanding the decisions of the Security Council and the provisions of the Conventions mentioned above, has committed acts of violence against diplomatic missions and their personnel in Kuwait,

Outraged at recent violations by Iraq of diplomatic premises in Kuwait and at the abduction of personnel enjoying diplomatic immunity and foreign nationals who were present in these premises,

Considering that the above actions by Iraq constitute aggressive acts and a flagrant violation of its international obligations which strike at the root of the conduct of international relations in accordance with the Charter of the United Nations,

Recalling that Iraq is fully responsible for any use of violence against foreign nationals or against any diplomatic or consular mission in Kuwait or its personnel,

Determined to ensure respect for its decisions and for Article 25 of the Charter of the United Nations,

Further considering that the grave nature of Iraq's actions, which constitute a new escalation of its violations of international law, obliges the Council not only to express its immediate reaction but also to consult urgently to take further concrete measures to ensure Iraq's compliance with the Council's resolutions,

Acting under Chapter VII of the Charter of the United Nations,

1. Strongly condemns aggressive acts perpetrated by Iraq against diplomatic premises and personnel in Kuwait, including the abduction of foreign nationals who were present in those premises;

2. Demands the immediate release of those foreign nationals as well as all nationals mentioned in resolution 664 (1990);

3. Further demands that Iraq immediately and fully comply with its international obligations under resolutions 660 (1990), 662 (1990) and 664 (1990) of the Security Council, the Vienna Conven-

tions on diplomatic and consular relations and international law;

4. Further demands that Iraq immediately protect the safety and well-being of diplomatic and consular personnel and premises in Kuwait and in Iraq and take no action to hinder the diplomatic and consular missions in the performance of their functions, including access to their nationals and the protection of their person and interests;

5. Reminds all States that they are obliged to observe strictly resolutions 661 (1990), 662 (1990), 664 (1990), 665(1990) and 666 (1990);

6. Decides to consult urgently to take further concrete measures as soon as possible, under Chapter VII of the Charter, in response to Iraq's continued violation of the Charter, of resolutions of the Council and of international law.

President's Address to the People of Iraq, September 16, 1990 [6]

I'm here today to explain to the people of Iraq why the United States and the world community has responded the way it has to Iraq's occupation of Kuwait. My purpose is not to trade accusations, not to escalate the war of words, but to speak with candor about what has caused this crisis that confronts us. Let there be no misunderstanding: We have no quarrel with the people of Iraq. I've said many times, and I will repeat right now, our only object is to oppose the invasion ordered by Saddam Hussein .

On August 2nd, your leadership made its decision to invade, an unprovoked attack on a small nation that posed no threat to your own. Kuwait was the victim; Iraq, the aggressor.

And the world met Iraq's invasion with a chorus of condemnation: unanimous resolutions in the United Nations. Twenty-seven States—rich and poor, Arab, Moslem, Asian and African— have answered the call of Saudi Arabia and free Kuwait and sent forces to the Gulf region to defend against Iraq. For the first time in history, 13 States of the Arab League, representing 80 percent of the Arab nation, have condemned a brother Arab State. Today, opposed by world opinion, Iraq stands isolated and alone.

I do not believe that you, the people of Iraq, want war. You've borne untold suffering and hardship during eight long years of war with Iran; a war that touched the life of every single Iraqi citizen; a war that took the lives of hundreds of thousands of young men, the bright promise of an entire generation. No one knows better than you the incalculable costs of war, the ultimate cost when a nation's vast potential and vital energies are consumed by conflict. No one knows what Iraq might be today, what prosperity and peace you might now enjoy, had your leaders not plunged you into war. Now, once again, Iraq finds itself on the brink of war. Once again, the same Iraqi leadership has miscalculated. Once again, the Iraqi people face tragedy.

The True Situation

Saddam Hussein has told you that Iraqi troops were invited into Kuwait. That's not true. In fact, in the face of far superior force, the people of Kuwait are bravely resisting this occupation. Your own returning soldiers will tell you the Kuwaitis are fighting valiantly in any way they can.

Saddam Hussein tells you that this crisis is a struggle between Iraq and America. In fact, it is Iraq against the world. When President Gorbachev and I met at Helsinki [September 9, 1990], we agreed that no peaceful international order is possible if larger states can devour their neighbors. Never before has world opinion been so solidly united against aggression.

Nor, until the invasion of Kuwait, has the United States been opposed to Iraq. In the past, the United States has helped Iraq import billions of dollars worth of food and other commodities. And the war with Iran would not have ended two years ago without U.S. support and sponsorship in the United Nations.

Saddam Hussein tells you the occupation of Kuwait will benefit the poorer nations of the world. In fact, the occupation of Kuwait is helping no one and is now hurting you, the Iraqi people, and countless others of the world's poor. Instead of acquiring new oil wealth by annexing Kuwait, this misguided act of aggression will cost Iraq over $20 billion a year in lost oil revenues. Because of Iraq's aggression, hundreds of thousands of innocent foreign workers are fleeing Kuwait and Iraq. They are stranded on Iraq's borders, without shelter, without food, without medicine, with no way home. These refugees are suffering, and this is shameful.

But even worse, others are being held hostage in Iraq and Kuwait. Hostage-taking punishes the innocent and separates families. It is barbaric. It will not work, and it will not affect my ability to make tough decisions.

I do not want to add to the suffering of the people of Iraq. The United Nations has put binding sanctions in place not to punish the Iraqi people but as a peaceful means to convince your leadership to withdraw from Kuwait. That decision is in the hands of Saddam Hussein.

The pain you now experience is a direct result of the path your leadership has chosen. When Iraq returns to the path of peace, when Iraqi troops withdraw from Kuwait, when that country's rightful government is restored, when all foreigners held against their will are released, then, and then alone, will the world end the sanctions.

What Iraq Must Do

Perhaps your leaders do not appreciate the strength of the forces united against them. Let me say clearly: There is no way Iraq can win. Ultimately, Iraq must withdraw from Kuwait.

No one—not the American people, not this President—wants war. But there are times when a country, when all countries who value the principles of sovereignty and independence, must stand against aggression. As Americans, we're slow to raise our hand in anger and eager to explore every peaceful means of settling our disputes; but when we have exhausted every alternative, when conflict is thrust upon us, there is no nation on Earth with greater resolve or stronger steadiness of purpose.

The actions of your leadership have put Iraq at odds with the world community. But while those actions have brought us to the brink of conflict, war is not inevitable. It is still possible to bring this crisis to a peaceful end.

When we stand with Kuwait against aggression, we stand for a principle well understood in the Arab world. Let me quote the words of one Arab leader, Saddam Hussein himself: "An Arab country does not have the right to occupy another Arab country. God forbid, if Iraq should deviate from the right path, we would want Arabs to send their armies to put things right. If Iraq should become intoxicated by its power and move to overwhelm another Arab State, the Arabs would be right to deploy their armies to check it."

Those are the words of your leader Saddam Hussein, spoken on November 28, 1988, in a speech to Arab lawyers. Today, two years later, Saddam has invaded and occupied a member of the United Nations and the Arab League. The world will not allow this aggression to stand. Iraq must get out of Kuwait for the sake of principle, for the sake of peace, and for the sake of the Iraqi people.

Elimination of Egypt's Foreign Military Sales Debt

Statement by Lawrence S. Eagleburger before the House Appropriations Subcommittee on Foreign Relations, September 19, 1990. Mr. Eagleburger is Deputy Secretary of State. (Excerpt) [7]

Egypt's Critical Role

At the moment of gravest danger, when lesser men might have succumbed to the intimidation or blandishments of the aggressor, Egyptian President Hosni Mubarak stepped alone to the fore and rallied an Arab consensus upon which all subsequent international efforts have been based. His actions have been timely, they have been bold, and they carry with them obvious political and military risks and economic costs.

President Mubarak quickly mobilized Arab opposition to Saddam, convening in Cairo an Arab League ministerial meeting that condemned the invasion and demanded an Iraqi withdrawal. He immediately sent 5,000 Egyptian troops to Saudi Arabia to join the international force gathering to defend that country from Iraqi aggression; he is now sending an additional 15,000 troops. Egyptian strategic cooperation also has been essential for our deployment under Operation Desert Shield. In short, President Mubarak is and must continue to be the solid foundation of Arab leadership in the Gulf crisis.

President Mubarak has done the right thing; we are all in his debt as a result. But his actions have had very

direct political and economic costs to him and to the people of Egypt. An Egyptian economy that was strained before August now faces serious difficulties that are the consequence of Iraq's invasion of Kuwait and of the Egyptian government's courageous response.

Costs to Egypt's Economy

It is estimated that, on an annual basis, remittances from Egyptian workers in Kuwait and Iraq will decline by $500 million to $1 billion. Suez Canal receipts will fall by $150 million to $200 million. Revenues from tourism will decline by $500 million to $1 billion. And another estimated $500 million a year will be lost because of exports, service contracts, etc.

And on top of all of these burdens, President Mubarak will have to come up with the means to absorb one-half million Egyptians — workers and their families — who are now returning to Egypt as a result of the crisis. Housing will have to be built; jobs will have to be created; and services will have to be provided. Failure to meet these needs could threaten political stability in Egypt, with potentially serious consequences for everything we and our Egyptian friends are now doing to resist Saddam's aggression. The exact costs of absorbing these Egyptians back into the fabric of Egypt's economy are difficult to predict with accuracy at this time, but they are conservatively estimated to run between $500 million to $1 billion.

The President's Proposal

In light of Egypt's critical role in the current Gulf crisis, the longstanding, close political relationships between the governments and people of the United States and Egypt, and the potentially overwhelming financial burdens for Egypt that have resulted from the crisis, the President decided to do two things.

First, he instructed Secretaries Baker and Brady to approach the gulf states and the industrialized countries around the world, countries that are vitally dependent on the free flow of oil, to encourage them to share in the burden of opposing Saddam. This burden-sharing, or responsibility sharing, is aimed at increasing direct contributions of military forces, where possible, to the Gulf region; helping defray incremental U.S. military costs associated with Operation Desert Shield; and helping

front-line states — such as Egypt, Turkey, and others — absorb some of the economic burdens brought on by the crisis.

Second, he proposed the elimination of Egypt's $6.7 billion of FMS [Foreign Military Sales] debt, the subject of today's hearing.

As you know, we have made important progress on the first part of our program. Significant, generous pledges have been made by several of our key friends and allies.

We are still engaged in the process of clarifying the pledges and developing a follow-up system to ensure that the funds are distributed appropriately — unconditionally at the outset (that is, through the rest of this calendar year) and integrated with appropriate conditionality through the medium term, which we have defined as calendar year 1991.

We believe that the second part of the President's program, the forgiveness of Egypt's FMS debt, is as important as the first.

President Mubarak's stand in the Gulf crisis can be compared with no risk of exaggeration to Egypt's decision to sign a peace treaty with Israel in 1979. Indeed, Egypt's current efforts to turn back Iraqi aggression should be viewed against the backdrop of more than a decade of constancy and cooperation with the United States on the Middle East peace process. Egypt paid a high price for its decision to choose peace, having been kicked out of the Arab League and ostracized by most Arab states. Nevertheless, it never altered its course and, today, is back as the leader of an Arab League which has rejected the extremism of a decade ago.

Another important result of the treaty with Israel was that Egypt abandoned its dependence on Soviet-made military equipment and turned instead to the United States as a military supplier. Today, U.S. equipment is being used by Egyptian soldiers who are standing shoulder to shoulder with American soldiers in Saudi Arabia.

Between 1979 and 1984, Egypt incurred $4.5 billion of FMS loans that carried interest rates comparable to Treasury's cost of borrowing. Interest rates on some of these loans are as high as 14 percent.

By 1984, the debt service burden on these loans — loans that by their military nature drained rather than stimulated economic activity — was beginning to strain Egypt's ability to pay. Between 1984 and 1990, the burden of servicing Egyptian FMS debt became the largest political irritant in U.S.-Egyptian relations. President Mubarak consistently stated his view that FMS debt was political debt and should be forgiven. We, in turn, consistently maintained that debt was debt and had to be paid.

Because of the Brooke/Alexander amendment and its requirement that military and economic assistance be cut off if a country were to go more than one year in arrears on its military debt service payments, the Egyptian government began to make its required payments just short of the one-year trigger. By the fall of 1989, Egypt's economic situation had reached the point where we expected that Egypt would have to reschedule its official debt in the Paris Club and that it would have to do so for at least the next five years. Our FY [fiscal year] 1991 budget estimates reflected this judgment. President Mubarak told us in increasingly strong messages that he would not be able to meet even these "brink of Brooke" payments, which in 1990 would exceed $700 million; our own analysis supported his conclusion.

Let me make it perfectly clear, however, that we were not prepared to seek cancellation of Egypt's FMS debt on the basis of these factors. Our decision to do so now is solely related to the unique circumstances and, in particular, to the urgent political and military challenges Egypt is facing as a consequence of the ongoing crisis in the Gulf. Our proposal should by no means be viewed as setting any kind of a precedent for any future action on the part of the United States.

Let me make another important point. We recognize that when the dust settles in the Middle East, Egypt has a formidable task in front of it in the area of economic reform. The United States will continue to work with Egypt and the international financial institutions to insure that the difficult choices are made, choices that will be necessary to get Egypt's economy on a sound footing. The forgiveness of FMS debt, in short, will not lessen in any way our commitment to engaging the Egyptians on the kinds of structural reforms which alone will enable them to profit economically from the climate of stability which we expect to prevail in the wake of this crisis.

These are not normal times. Egypt's bold and courageous leadership in generating and maintaining Arab sup-port for the efforts against Saddam Hussein, and the sacrifices Egypt is making incident to this exercise in leadership, make this the unique case it is and make the forgiveness of Egypt's FMS debt the right thing to do, and now the right time to do it. We do not support FMS debt forgiveness for any other country. No other country meets the unique combination of political, military, and economic factors that I have described here today.

U. N. Security Council Resolution 669, September 24, 1990 [3]

The Security Council,
Recalling its resolution 661(1990) of 6 August 1990,
Recalling also Article 50 of the Charter of the United Nations,
Conscious of the fact that an increasing number of requests for assistance have been received under the provisions of Article 50 of the Charter of the United Nations,
Entrusts the Committee established under resolution 661(1990) concerning the situation between Iraq and Kuwait with the task of examining requests for assistance under the provisions of Article 50 of the Charter of the United Nations and making recommendations to the President of the Security Council for appropriate action.

U.N. Security Council Resolution 670, September 25, 1990 [3]

The Security Council,
Reaffirming its resolutions 660 (1990), 661 (1990), 662 (1990), 664 (1990), 665 (1990), 666 (1990), and 667 (1990);
Condemning Iraq's continued occupation of Kuwait, its failure to rescind its actions and end its purported annexation and its holding of third State nationals against their will, in flagrant violation of resolutions 660 (1990), 662 (1990), 664 (1990) and 667 (1990) and of international humanitarian law;
Condemning further the treatment by Iraqi forces of Kuwaiti nationals, including measures to force them to leave their own country and mistreatment of persons and property in Kuwait in violation of international law;
Noting with grave concern the persistent attempts to evade the measures laid down in resolution 661 (1990);
Further noting that a number of States have limited the number of Iraqi diplomatic and consular officials in their countries and that others are planning to do so;
Determined to ensure by all necessary means the strict and complete application of the measures laid down in resolution 661(1990);
Determined to ensure respect for its decisions and the provisions of Articles 25 and 48 of the Charter of the United Nations;
Affirming that any acts of the Government of Iraq which are contrary to the above-mentioned resolutions or to Articles 25 or 48 of the Charter of the United Nations, such as Decree No. 377 of the Revolution Command Council of Iraq of 16 September 1990, are null and void;
Reaffirming its determination to ensure compliance with Security Council resolutions by maximum use of political and diplomatic means;
Welcoming the Secretary-General's use of his good offices to advance a peaceful solution based on the relevant Security Council resolutions and noting with appreciation his continuing efforts to this end;
Underlining to the Government of Iraq that its continued failure to comply with the terms of resolutions 660 (1990), 661 (1990), 662 (1990), 664 (1990), 666 (1990) and 667 (1990) could lead to further serious action by the Council under the Charter of the United Nations, including under Chapter VII;
Recalling the provisions of Article 103 of the Charter of the United Nations;
Acting under Chapter VII of the Charter of the United Nations:
1. Calls upon all States to carry out their obligations to ensure strict and complete compliance with resolution 661(1990) and in particular paragraphs 3, 4 and 5 thereof;
2. Confirms that resolution 661 (1990) applies to all means of transport, including aircraft;
3. Decides that all States, notwithstanding the existence of any rights or obligations conferred or imposed by any international agreement or any contract entered into or any licence or permit granted before the date of the present resolution, shall deny permis-

sion to any aircraft to take off from their territory if the aircraft would carry any cargo to or from Iraq or Kuwait other than food in humanitarian circumstances, subject to authorization by the Council or the Committee established by resolution 661(1990) and in accordance with resolution 666 (1990), or supplies intended strictly for medical purposes or solely for UNIIMOG;

4. Decides further that all States shall deny permission to any aircraft destined to land in Iraq or Kuwait, whatever its State of registration, to overfly its territory unless:

(a) The aircraft lands at an airfield designated by that State outside Iraq or Kuwait in order to permit its inspection to ensure that there is no cargo on board in violation of resolution 661(1990) or the present resolution, and for this purpose the aircraft may be detained for as long as necessary; or

(b) The particular flight has been approved by the Committee established by resolution 661(1990); or

(c) The flight is certified by the United Nations as solely for the purposes of UNIIMOG;

5. Decides that each State shall take all necessary measures to ensure that any aircraft registered in its territory or operated by an operator who has his principal place of business or permanent residence in its territory complies with the provisions of resolution 661(1990) and the present resolution;

6. Decides further that all States shall notify in a timely fashion the Committee established by resolution 661(1990) of any flight between its territory and Iraq or Kuwait to which the requirement to land in paragraph 4 above does not apply, and the purpose for such a flight;

7. Calls upon all States to cooperate in taking such measures as may be necessary, consistent with international law, including the Chicago Convention, to ensure the effective implementation of the provisions of resolution 661(1990) or the present resolution;

8. Calls upon all States to detain any ships of Iraqi registry which enter their ports and which are being or have been used in violation of resolution 661 (1990), or to deny such ships entrance to their ports except in circumstances recognized under international law as necessary to safeguard human life;

9. Reminds all States of their obligations under resolution 661(1990) with regard to the freezing of Iraqi assets,

and the protection of the assets of the legitimate Government of Kuwait and its agencies, located within their territory and to report to the Committee established under resolution 661(1990) regarding those assets;

10. Calls upon all States to provide to the Committee established by resolution 661(1990) information regarding the action taken by them to implement the provisions laid down in the present resolution;

11. Affirms that the United Nations Organization, the specialized agencies and other international organizations in the United Nations system are required to take such measures as may be necessary to give effect to the terms of resolution 661 (1990) and this resolution;

12. Decides to consider, in the event of evasion of the provisions of resolution 661(1990) or of the present resolution by a State or its nationals or through its territory, measures directed at the State in question to prevent such evasion;

13. Reaffirms that the Fourth Geneva Convention applies to Kuwait and that as a High Contracting Party to the Convention Iraq is bound to comply fully with all its terms and in particular is liable under the Convention in respect of the grave breaches committed by it, as are individuals who commit or order the commission of grave breaches.

Secretary Baker's Remarks Concerning Resolution 670, U.N. Security Council, September 25, 1990 [8]

Our meeting here today is extraordinary. This marks only the third time in the 45-year history of this organization that all of the Perm Five Foreign Ministers of the Security Council are meeting. Rarely has the United Nations been confronted by so blatant an act of aggression as the Iraqi invasion of Kuwait. Rarely has the international community been so united and determined that aggression should not succeed.

Acts have consequences. The stakes are clear. For international society to permit Iraq to overwhelm a small neighbor and to erase it from the map would send a disastrous message. The hopes of the world for a new, more peaceful post-Cold War era would be dimmed. The United Nations Charter

would be devalued—at the very moment when its promise is closer to fulfillment than at any time in its history.

Speaking for the United States, I want to tell the Council that our hopes for a better world are real. The United Nations Charter embodies the values of the American people and people everywhere who know that might alone cannot be allowed to make right.

Elementary justice and a prudent regard for our own interests have brought together an unprecedented solidarity on this issue. We are engaged in a great struggle and test of wills. We cannot allow our hopes and aspirations to be trampled by a dictator's ambitions or his threats.

Our purpose must be clear and clearly understood by all, including the Government and people of Iraq. Security Council Resolutions 660 and 662 establish the way to settle the crisis: complete, immediate, and unconditional Iraqi withdrawal from Kuwait, the restoration of Kuwait's legitimate government, and the release of all hostages. Until that time, the international community through Resolution 661 and its successor resolutions has set a high and rising penalty upon Iraq for each passing day that it fails to abandon its aggression.

These penalties are beginning to take effect, and bellicose language from Baghdad cannot compensate for the perils of isolation. Threats only prolong the needless suffering of the Iraqi people. Iraq has been quarantined because its brutal actions have separated it from the community of nations. There can be no business as usual. In fact, there can be no economic exchanges with Iraq at all.

Today, the United States, together with other members of this Council, supports a new resolution and additional measures:

First, the Council explicitly states that United Nations Security Council Resolution 661 includes commercial air traffic. This demonstrates again that the international community is prepared to plug any loophole in the isolation of Iraq.

Second, we agree to consider measures against any government that might attempt to evade the international quarantine. No temptation of minor gain should lead any government to complicity with Iraq's assault on international legality and decency. I would even say that the more effective the enforcement of sanctions, the more likely the peaceful evolution of this conflict.

Third, we remind the Government of Iraq that it is not free to disregard its international obligations, especially the humanitarian provisions of the Fourth Geneva Convention. Each day that Iraqi officials flout norms of elementary decency makes it that much more difficult for Iraq to resume its place in the international community and to repair the damage it has done. On this point, I would note the call of the Arab League for reparations.

Many thousands of innocent people have been dislocated as well. That is why the United States supports a coordinated and unitary approach to refugee assistance and relief efforts. The appointment of Saddrudin Aga Kahn is a major step in this direction.

Fourth, the Council puts the Government of Iraq on notice that its continued failure to comply could lead to further action, including action under Chapter Seven. The international community has made clear its desire to exhaust every peaceful possibility for resolving this matter in accordance with the principles of the United Nations Charter. But we are all well aware that the Charter envisages the possibility of further individual and collective measures to defend against aggression and flagrant violations of international humanitarian law.

[Soviet Foreign Minister] Eduard Shevardnadze spoke for all of us when he said earlier today: "This is a major affront to mankind. In the context of recent events, we should remind those who regard aggression as an acceptable form of behavior that the United Nations has the power to suppress acts of aggression. There is ample evidence that this right can be exercised. It will be, if the illegal occupation of Kuwait continues."

It is important to emphasize that the sanctions we have adopted are aimed at reversing the aggressive policies of the Iraqi government. They are not aimed at the people of Iraq, who are being forced to live with the consequences of a misguided policy.

The Council has acknowledged that its sanctions, as with any disruption, can be costly to many of our member states. We have a duty to make sure that no nation is crippled because it stood for the principles of international order. The United States has worked with other nations to coordinate an international ef-

fort to provide assistance to those desperately in need.

Mr. President, Members of the Council, the passing of the Cold War has meant many things — above all, a rebirth of hope. The horizons of democracy, of human rights, of national dignity, and of economic progress have all been extended. The result has been a rebirth of the United Nations as well. Suddenly, the vision of the Charter and the promise of international cooperation seem within reach. In Central America, in Namibia, and perhaps soon in Cambodia and Afghanistan, this organization makes signal contributions as a peacemaker. We are beginning to control at last the proliferation of conflicts, major and minor, that have exacted so high a price from humanity.

Now, together we all confront a supreme challenge to the United Nations and all that it represents. If the United Nations is to fulfill its mission, if peace is to prevail, then Iraq's leader must not be allowed to gain from his assault on decency and basic human values. We must do what justice, honor, and international peace demand that we do: reverse Saddam Hussein's brutal aggression.

President's Meeting with Amir Jabir al-Ahmad al-Jabir Al Sabah of Kuwait, September 28, 1990 [9]

The President. Well, it is my great pleasure to welcome His Highness Sheik Jabir Sabah to the United States. His Highness is visiting Washington for the first time. What normally would be a pleasurable occasion instead is a time for sobriety and sorrow. Our meeting has taken place with the backdrop of the tragedy that has been vested on Kuwait and its people by a ruthless and ambitious dictator.

Iraqi aggression has ransacked and pillaged a once peaceful and secure country, its population assaulted, incarcerated, intimidated, and even murdered. Iraq's leaders are trying to wipe an internationally recognized sovereign state, a member of the Arab League and the United Nations, off the face of the map.

To them and to the world, I will state what I told His Highness, the Amir. Iraq will fail. Kuwait — free Kuwait — will endure. And I have reaf-

firmed to the Amir that America's resolve to end this aggression against Kuwait remains firm and undiminished. Kuwait's sovereignty and territorial integrity will be restored, the stability and security of the Persian Gulf region is assured, and the safety of all innocent citizens is secured. And this is consistent with our longstanding interests endorsed by all my predecessors since Harry Truman. And this is consistent with the will of the world community, endorsed by the United Nations in eight Security Council resolutions. And just yesterday, the standing ovation that greeted the Amir's moving address to the U.N. General Assembly was one more powerful expression of international support for a free Kuwait.

His Highness and I reaffirmed our support for the U.N. Security Council resolutions as the means to bring about a peaceful end to the crisis. But ultimately, that is up to Saddam Hussein . I reiterated our strong belief that we just continue to stand on the principles by which the United States and the rest of the civilized world are governed. And that means that no nation should be allowed to conduct its relations with another on the basis of threats or the use of brute force. And finally, His Highness and I agreed that we must keep all our options open to ensure that Iraq's unlawful occupation of Kuwait is ended and Kuwait's legitimate government restored. We also discussed the key role that His Highness, his government, and the Kuwaiti people are playing and will continue to play in the international effort to achieve these efforts.

I want to thank the Amir for his generous support for those who are being asked to make sacrifices. And I also want to single out the valiant efforts of the Kuwaiti resistance who are continuing to fight vigorously for their country. Despite incalculable risks, many are willing to pay the highest price to rid their country of foreign occupation and to protect innocent citizens, including Americans, from harm. And many have already paid the ultimate price.

His Highness and I will continue to stay in close touch and to work together to find a solution to this tragedy. As I stated in my address to the nation earlier this month, we will stand by our friends.

And to my guests, let me, sir, say one more thing, sir. I look forward to the day that I can visit you and the Kuwaiti people in your rightful home, Kuwait.

Thank you for coming.

The Amir. Mr. President, I am pleased to have visited the capital of your great nation. And I wish I could have had the pleasure of receiving you in Kuwait City, the capital of my country, were it not for the Iraqi aggression which has denied us that opportunity temporarily, God willing. Nevertheless, the people of Kuwait, as well as myself, look forward to receiving you, Mr. President, in liberated, independent Kuwait.

I take pleasure in expressing to you once again, Mr. President, and to your great people the deep feelings of friendship and appreciation Kuwait feels for you. Our stand together in the face of treachery and aggression is proof that relations between our two countries are based on the solid foundation of common values and principles that, in turn, provides guidance for the fruitful cooperation that evolved and developed in various fields between the United States and Kuwait.

Your principled, courageous, and decisive position in face of the Iraqi aggression on Kuwait is a true expression of the unabated faith and commitment of the American people to the humanitarian morals on which and for which the United States of America was founded. The unity of the international community in support of our position against aggression and occupation, the two most flagrant violations of human rights, conclusively indicates the determination of all nations and peoples of the world to put a definitive end to armed aggression as any country's foreign policy tool. This unity takes on added relevance given the world's entrance to an era dominated by an atmosphere of peace, rapprochement, cooperation, and optimism.

We look with admiration to the role you Mr. President, and your nation have played in inaugurating and enhancing the foundation of this era. Mr. President, your just position by the side of Kuwait in this ordeal represents a categorical rejection of aggression in all its forms and manifestations whatever its source or pretext. The unity and support shown by the friendly American people towards the position and measures taken by you, Mr. President, against Iraq's aggression, whose first and foremost victims are the human

rights of the Kuwaiti people, are perfectly compatible with the unflinching faith in the standards of justice and fairness for which the American people stand. This is the faith that brings together the nations and peoples of the civilized world.

I am fully satisfied by the identical views we hold on issues covered in our talks this morning with you. Truly, this mutual agreement reflects the advanced stage in relations our two friendly countries and peoples have reached.

Thank you, Mr. President.

White House Statement on Emergency Military Assistance for Israel, October 1, 1990 [10]

On September 30, the President decided to provide two Patriot air defense fire units to Israel on an urgent basis under provisions of the law that allow for emergency military assistance from U.S. military stocks. The President's decision followed notification of Congress on September 29. The Patriot system will help Israel to upgrade its air defenses, including against an increased threat from ballistic missiles in the Iraqi inventory. In making this decision, the President reaffirmed his strong commitment to U.S.-Israel friendship and to the security of Israel.

CSCE Statement, New York, October 2, 1990 [11]

Consistent with the principles contained in the Helsinki Final Act, which guide our mutual relations, we, the Foreign Ministers of the Participating States of the Conference on Security and Cooperation in Europe (CSCE), meeting in New York, join the United Nations in condemning Iraq's invasion and occupation of Kuwait. These actions jeopardize the just and peaceful world order to which more cooperative European relations are making an important contribution.

We call upon the Government of Iraq to withdraw from Kuwait immediately and without conditions. Seeking a peaceful solution, we support fully all of the relevant resolutions adopted by the United Nations Security Council and

are determined to ensure their full and effective implementation.

We express our support for those countries that have particularly suffered because of the crisis created by Iraq and reaffirm our determination to work together to ensure that the burdens of standing against aggression are shouldered equitably by all.

We wish to contribute to the security and welfare in the area, in order to foster peace, tolerance, stability, and economic cooperation and development, and therefore we are determined to support efforts aimed at resolving the conflicts there and attaining a just, comprehensive, and lasting peace in compliance with the relevant resolutions of the United Nations Security Council.

Statement on Behalf of European Community, CSCE Ministerial, New York, October 2, 1990 [12]

Conclusions on Financial Assistance to the Countries Most Immediately Affected by the Gulf Crisis

The [EC] Council remains convinced that a complete implementation of the embargo decided by the Security Council with regard to Iraq is the essential condition for bringing about a peaceful solution to the crisis. The European Community and its Member States are fully implementing the embargo and call on all members of the international community to do likewise.

The Council is conscious of the grave burden which the present crisis imposes on the economy of many countries and in particular that stemming from a rigorous application of the embargo, and has therefore decided that the Community and its Member States will provide short-term financial assistance of 1.5 billion ECU to the countries most immediately affected : Egypt, Jordan and Turkey.

The contribution of the Community budget to such program of assistance will be 500 million ECU. The remaining amount will be made up of voluntary bilateral contributions from Member States, already announced or to be announced.

The Community's contribution will be entirely imputed to the 1991 budget.

The Council, for its part, will act speedily on any necessary revision of the financial perspectives.

This Community assistance through its budget will be mainly given in the form of grants, but provisions will also be made for the possibility of according loans or other forms of financial assistance.

Certain countries other than the three most immediately affected will also bear a very heavy economic cost. As agreed by the General Affairs Council on 17 September, the Community and its member States have committed themselves to examine the possibility of economic assistance in favour of these countries.

The Community will seek to join efforts with other donors and in particular with the Arab countries over this assistance. The Presidency and the Commission will undertake the contacts necessary to ensure the appropriate coordination.

The Council calls on the Commission to take the necessary action to ensure the urgent adoption of the formal legal decision.

Sale of Defense Equipment to Saudi Arabia

Excerpts from statement by Reginald Bartholemew before the Senate Foreign Relations Committee, October 4, 1990. Mr. Bartholemew is Under Secretary of State for International Security Affairs. [7]

We have come before you this morning to discuss the administration's plans to proceed expeditiously with an important sale of defense equipment to Saudi Arabia. As you know, two weeks ago we began consultations with Members of the Congress on Saudi Arabia's urgent requests for defense equipment. Following those consultations, the President directed us to proceed with the sale in two phases, the first of which we notified last week.

This morning, we will ask you to consider, as we have, how this sale bears on U.S. interests and objectives in the current Gulf crisis and beyond, not only vis-a-vis Saudi Arabia, but also for the region as a whole. In that context, the administration believes that this sale is but one step—an important step—in assisting the nations of the area in the current crisis, and in building lasting stability in the region.

*   *   *

The Iraqi aggression is a watershed. Even after Iraqi aggression is undone, it will be necessary to take steps to establish and maintain a stable balance—to deter and defend against aggression and to ensure the security and confidence of our friends in the Gulf, regardless of the fate of Saddam Hussein. We must work with our friends to achieve this objective.

This will require more planning and consultation. But we know already that lasting security in the Gulf should not depend on the long-term presence of U.S. forces. Nor should it depend solely on a willingness to repeat Desert Shield. Ultimately, lasting regional stability will require that our friends in the region do more to help themselves, in close cooperation with the United States.

Purpose of Sale

We seek through this sale to:
(1) help build an increased capability to deter and defend against potential aggressors;
(2) buy more time, in the event deterrence fails, for mobilization of support from friendly governments;
(3) develop the interoperability that will allow the U.S. and other friendly forces to reinforce the Saudis more effectively should that ever again be necessary; and
(4) help contribute to stronger and more stable post-crisis security arrangements.

Neither the states in the region, nor we, think that they can build, by themselves, the full range of force that in itself can deter and defeat potential aggressor states—states which have a far larger population base than our Desert Shield partners enjoy. Support by the United States and others for security relationships in the Gulf is now and will continue to be an element essential to the success of any such endeavor.

But Saudi Arabia and the other Gulf States themselves must collectively serve as the principal partners in any such security arrangement. They must have the defensive strength to raise the initial costs to an aggressor high enough to help deter aggression and, if deterrence should fail, they must be able to delay an aggressor until help arrives. This would be a marked improvement upon the situation that prevailed on August 2.

The Equipment to be Sold

The Saudis and the other GCC [Gulf Cooperation Council] States have made clear to us that they want to do more in their defense, both in the current crisis and in the long term. Their troops have been deployed in the front lines since the early days of the crisis. In the ensuing two months, we and the Saudis have discussed what was needed and available to enable them to assist in defending against the Iraqi threat. The first Saudi arms package, announced in August, partially met those needs by providing 24 F-15C/D air defense aircraft, stinger missiles, M60A3 tanks, and M833 depleted uranium ammunition. But, important as that sale was, it was only an initial response.

We are now proposing a larger response, in phases, to bolster Saudi Arabia and its GCC partners as they continue to face armor and air attack threats. The items in Phase I, which have been notified for your review, address specific Saudi requirements:

For air defense: We propose to bolster Saudi capabilities, against both aircraft and short-range ballistic missiles, by providing six Patriot missile combat fire units.

For anti-armor: We propose a significant enhancement of Saudi armor capabilities by making available 150 M1A2 Abrams tanks, 200 Bradley fighting vehicles, support vehicles, 150 TOW 2A launchers with 1750 missiles, and 12 Apache helicopters with 155 missiles. In addition, we are planning to furnish 27 M60A3 tanks to the Bahrainis who also have forces in Saudi Arabia.

For fire support: We plan to provide the Saudis nine Multiple-Launch Rocket System (MLRS) launchers with 2880 rockets.

For logistical support: We intend to provide 10,000 tactical wheeled vehicles, 7 KC-130 aerial tankers, 10 C-130H airlift aircraft, and 8 UH-60 Black-hawk medical evacuation helicopters.

For command, control and communications: We propose to provide an upgrade of Saudi naval communications.

Phase II, which we are planning to submit for your consideration in January, would continue the improvement of Saudi and Gulf State abilities to defend against Iraqi or other aggressor-state threats. While we expect its components to evolve with circumstances in the area, we anticipate it also would focus on meeting armor and air attack threats.

What we have proposed to sell to our friends in the Gulf, and what we will propose to sell them, constitute the elements of a force that can provide a basic, defensive capability and can be absorbed. This will not provide the Saudis or other Gulf States with a major offensive capability. Rather, by providing a substantially strengthened deterrent, that defensive capability will meet the need for a better balance of regional forces in the Persian Gulf—a need that has been underscored by Iraq's aggression.

Israel's Security

Mr. Chairman, let me reassure you on one particularly important point. As we always do, we have considered the potential impact of this sale on the security of Israel. Though the President and the members of his Cabinet have underscored this point in recent days, it bears repeating here today: This Administration's commitment to the security of Israel is unshakable. A crucial part of this is our commitment to help maintain Israel's qualitative superiority over its potential adversaries. We do not believe that enhancing the deterrent and defensive capabilities of our Saudi and Gulf partners will detract from this fundamental commitment. We believe that security and stability in the Gulf region will support Israel's security as well.

Secretary Basker's Statement Before the Senate Foreign Relations Committee, October 17, 1990, and House Foreign Affairs Committee, October 18, 1990 [13]

Six weeks ago, it was my privilege to speak to this committee and through you, to the American people, about Iraq's aggression against Kuwait. At that time, I outlined the President's goals:

First, the immediate, complete, and unconditional withdrawal of all Iraqi forces from Kuwait as mandated in United Nations Security Council Resolution 660;

Second, the restoration of Kuwait's legitimate government;

Third, the protection of the lives of American citizens held hostage by Iraq, both in Iraq and in Kuwait; and

Fourth, a commitment to the security and stability of the Persian Gulf.

I also described our strategy for achieving these goals.

The key element of that approach is American leadership of a global alliance that isolates Iraq—politically, economically, and militarily.

Today, I would like to discuss with you what we have done to carry out that strategy since early September, including how responsibilities are being shared and what results have been achieved.

Maintaining the Coalition

First, we have been working successfully through the United Nations Security Council to isolate Iraq politically and to impose penalties for its refusal to comply with the U.N. resolutions. That effort is continuing today as the Council considers its tenth resolution on the Gulf.

Second, we have secured notable cooperation from the Soviet Union. We have described this conflict as the first real crisis of the post-Cold War period. The positive approach of the Soviet Union has validated that label. In their Helsinki Joint Statement, President Bush and President Gorbachev declared, "We are united in the belief that Iraq's aggression must not be tolerated. No peaceful international order is possible if larger states can devour their smaller neighbors."

Since then, I have met with Foreign Minister Shevardnadze on several occasions, both in Moscow and in New York, and have talked to him on the phone frequently. The Soviets continue to support the objectives of the Security Council resolutions.

Third, from the beginning, we recognized that maintaining such an unprecedented international coalition would necessitate special efforts. The United States could lead—indeed, had to lead—but we should not carry the responsibility alone. The principle of shared responsibility had to be observed.

We must jointly face the military threat. But we must also act collectively to support the many nations observing the economic embargo or contributing forces for the defense of Saudi Arabia. Iraq's pillage of Kuwait continues to dis-

place hundreds of thousands of workers, straining the resources of neighboring states and the fragile economies of their homelands.

Immediately after testifying before this committee early last month, I left at the President's request to visit our major allies and partners in the Arabian Peninsula, the European Community, Italy, and Germany to put responsibility sharing into effect. The Secretary of the Treasury led a similar mission to London, Paris, Tokyo, and Seoul. This exercise in sharing responsibilities produced commitments of $20 billion in resources, equally divided between support for the front line states of Egypt, Turkey, and Jordan and assistance to the multinational military effort. This includes support for a substantial portion of our incremental defense costs, now running about $1 billion per month.

I would summarize the results of our ongoing efforts as follows:

- Fifty-four nations have contributed or offered to contribute militarily and/or economically to the Gulf effort.
- The three Gulf states of Saudi Arabia, Kuwait, and the United Arab Emirates have agreed to contribute more than $12 billion to this effort in 1990. All of the states in the Gulf Cooperation Council have contributed troops to the multinational force in Saudi Arabia and are providing access and services in support of U.S. forces. Host nation support for our deployed forces includes the free use of ports, logistical facilities, bases, and fuel.
- The U.K. is deploying over 6,000 combat troops, over 50 aircraft, and 12 warships.
- France has deployed over 4,000 combat troops, 30 aircraft, and 12 warships.
- Japan has pledged $4 billion: $2 billion in support of the military effort plus $2 billion in economic aid. And we hope to see that commitment fulfilled promptly and in a form immediately usable.
- Germany has pledged $2 billion: $1 billion in support of the military effort plus $1 billion in economic aid.
- The European Community has pledged $670 million in economic aid, along with member state commitments of an additional $1.3 billion.

- Italy has deployed 4 warships and 8 aircraft.
- Korea has pledged $220 million: $95 million in support of the military effort plus $125 million in economic aid.

To coordinate timely and effective economic assistance to the front line states, the President launched the Gulf Crisis Financial Coordinating Group on September 25. This group unites the major donors of Europe, Asia, and the Gulf under U.S. chairmanship, with technical support from the IMF and World Bank. We see it as an important vehicle for maintaining the international coalition.

The most important demonstration of America's commitment to bolstering the economic stability of our front-line allies is the President's proposal to cancel Egypt's FMS debt. No other signal would send the same powerful message to our friends in the region that we are determined to stand by them, even on the toughest issues. Last Thursday's assassination of the Speaker of Egypt's Parliament is a tragic reminder of how far Egypt's enemies are prepared to go to divert President Mubarak from his responsible and courageous course. Strong Congressional endorsement of Egyptian debt cancellation would provide Egypt critical economic relief and send a powerful and timely signal that the United States stands by its friends.

Mr. Chairman, the political and economic isolation of Iraq has been achieved. The costs and responsibilities for enforcing this isolation are being fairly distributed. Economic leakage is minimal. The Iraqi economy will suffer badly and the Iraqi war machine will be hurt, too.

The Military Track

A discussion of diplomacy and economic sanctions, however, should not blind us to the other essential track of our policy: the military buildup in the Gulf. I have just detailed for you the contributions made by our allies, including combat units, aircraft, and warships. In addition, Arab states such as Egypt and Syria are sending major units. There are now many thousands of Arab and Muslim soldiers deployed with the multinational forces in and around Saudi Arabia. And, of course, very large numbers of American marines, soldiers, sailors, and airmen are there already.

All told, over 25 countries are now supplying men or material in support of the Security Council resolutions.

Our military objectives are to deter an Iraqi attack on Saudi Arabia and to ensure the effective implementation of the U.N. sanctions. Economic sanctions against an aggressor like Saddam Hussein would never be effective unless the international community could help ensure the security of those nations, such as Saudi Arabia and Turkey, who must apply those sanctions. Our military forces are also there to protect American lives and to provide an effective and decisive response should Iraq escalate its aggression to active combat with the multinational force.

Saddam Hussein must know that he lacks not only the political and economic options of holding Kuwait but also the military option to succeed with his aggression. The political, economic, and military aspects of our strategy reinforce each other.

Some may urge action for action's sake. But the only truly effective action we can take now is to continue to heighten Iraq's political, economic, and military isolation.

The Need for Time

As the strategy takes effect, we face a difficult task. We must remain firm, not wavering from the goals we have set or our focus on the blatant aggression committed by Iraq. We must exercise patience as the grip of sanctions tightens with increasing severity.

Some may urge action for action's sake. But the only truly effective action we can take now is to continue to heighten Iraq's political, economic, and military isolation. Every day—in Washington, in New York, in the region—we continue our search for a peaceful solution.

Action that moves toward a partial solution would be self-defeating appeasement.

And should there be any doubt about the awful consequences of a partial solution, I would urge a close look at what Saddam Hussein is doing to the people of Kuwait. Because Saddam Hussein controls access to the true story

of Kuwait, this is a story that is not told frequently enough. So I commend the Congress' effort to secure eyewitness testimony of the brutalities now taking place.

It is the rape of Kuwait. Hospitals have been looted without regard for the sick. Parents have been tortured and executed in front of their children. Children have been tortured and executed in front of their parents. Even after his military conquest, Saddam has continued to make war on the people of Kuwait.

Let me be blunt: Saddam Hussein has invaded and tortured a peaceful Arab neighbor purely for self-aggrandizement. He is not raping Kuwait to advance the Palestinian cause.

We cannot allow this violent way to become the wave of the future in the Middle East. Saddam Hussein must fail if peace is to succeed. The prospects for a just and lasting peace between Israel and its Arab neighbors will be shattered if he prevails.

It is time to clear the air once and for all about the relationship between Saddam's aggression in Kuwait and other conflicts and problems in the region. I will put it to you simply: Does anyone seriously think that if this aggression succeeds, that prospects will be better for peace between Israel and the Palestinians? Can anyone seriously believe that if Iraq wins this contest with the international community, it will be easier to eliminate chemical weapons or biological weapons or nuclear weapons in the region?

Of course not.

Every hope for peace in this conflict-ridden region depends on stopping Iraq's aggression and ultimately reversing its capacity for future aggression.

Defeating Aggression

Let me sum it up.

Since we met last, a great coalition of nations has gathered to isolate Iraq and its dictator. Where before his aggression Saddam Hussein found allies of consequence, today he finds none. Where before the invasion, the Iraqi economy had important international links, today it has none. And where once there were prospects for successful Iraqi aggression against Saudi Arabia, today there are none.

Unity remains essential. I do not believe we could have come this far if most nations did not agree with President Bush that we all have a stake in a world where conflicts are settled peacefully. And that unity, expressed in political, economic and military terms, remains the best hope for a peaceful solution to this conflict as well.

Mr. Chairman, it is gratifying that the vast majority of Americans have rallied behind the President in support of both our goals and our strategy in the Persian Gulf. Indeed, most of the world has done so, as well. Saddam Hussein cannot be allowed to ruin the region. He cannot be allowed to spoil this time of hope in the world for a more secure and prosperous future. There is a morality among nations. That morality must prevail.

Excerpts from Q&A Following Secretary Baker's Statement, Senate Foreign Relations Committee, October 17, 1990 [14]

Senator Lugar. You expressed in your statement the need for unity of the people of the United States, and our Chairman [Senator Pell] in his introductory statement has gone through, I think correctly, the litany that all of us hope for a peaceful resolution of the Middle Eastern situation, that it is a dangerous situation and we have great commitments there now, and we have applauded the President for how well he has handled things, and likewise your own leadership.

But I come back to the Chairman's paragraph that we learned from the Vietnam experience that the support of the American people as expressed through 535 representatives in Congress is essential, and more fundamentally, shared responsibility for war is what the founding fathers of our country intended, and we should be faithful to that intent...

*　　　*　　　*

Senator Kassebaum. I would just like to comment on Senator Lugar's comments. The Administration is to be commended for a lot of consultations, that is true. But it goes beyond, I think, more than just leadership.

We have seen what has happened as far as just the summit on the budget and I think even more in this respect. The Congress represents, for better or worse, 535 of us, who represent constituents. And I feel very strong that what Senator Luger was saying is terrib-

ly important for the administration to remember. It is not just the consultation of the few, which I think is important, but it is the voice of all of us which is representative of the public even though they might disown us at this point.

Secretary Baker. I agree with that. But may I just also say, and in partial response to what Senator Sarbanes said, which I did not say at the time because we did not have time, but we do have a disagreement, of course. We should not have a constitutional argument, it does not seem to me, about whether or not the President, as Commander in Chief, has the constitutional authority to commit forces. It has been done going all the way back, I think, to World War II.

You can look at Grenada, Panama, Libya, even at the unhappy experiences, too, such as Vietnam and so forth. We are not going to resolve that constitutional argument here.

It is important and I have said it is important, we think, the President thinks, and I know that it is important that we have the support of the American people. One way you get that is to have the support of the elected representatives. Therefore, we will consult.

But if we were under an obligation to come back here and have hearings that might extend, hopefully not as long as the budget hearings, but that might drag out for a while while we debate, well, now wait a minute. If you are really talking about sending this force here and that one over there, is this the right thing to do and you really ought not to do that.

I just want to make sure we all understand the position that that would put the Commander in Chief in. So we do have a constitutional—different view, I suppose, on the constitutional question of the authority to commit forces. But we do not have any difference of view on the importance of being unified and the importance of trying to move together.

Senator Kassebaum. I am not a supporter of the War Powers Resolution, but it is a law of the land. Since it is, I think, that again we have got to make sure it works or else some of us would like to see it, of course, banned. But that is a legislative action where there is serious disagreement. But as long as it is there and as long as it is the law of the land, I think we have to adhere to it.

Remarks by Senator John F. Kerry, October 24, 1990 (Excerpt) [15]

Mr. President, I rise not just to predict what we will face when we return in January, but also because I am deeply concerned that our departure will complete another kind of convergence, a convergence of forces pulling us toward war in the Persian Gulf.

For this month we leave more than Washington. We also leave over 200,000 American troops and their commanders stationed in the gulf—hot, frustrated, impatient. We leave with the Army commander asking the President for authority to deploy an additional 100,000 GI's.

We leave a President who has been known to use force when Congress was out of session. We leave a Secretary of Defense who confided "it was an advantage that Congress was out of town" when he first deployed troops to the Gulf. We leave a Secretary of State who says it is impossible to rely on advance congressional authorization before using force in the Gulf. And we leave an administration, on the verge of midterm elections, the strength of its convictions newly challenged, grappling with a bungled budget, a looming recession, and declining popularity.

I do not believe this or any President would ever unleash a war for political purposes. But I am not convinced this administration will do everything in its power to avoid war with this constellation of influences tugging at it to take action.

Mr. President, if ever there was an avoidable war, it is this one. If ever there was a circumstance where the political leaders with the responsibility to make the final decisions are afraid of the political consequences of failing, it is this one.

The United States and the broad international coalition we have assembled have the upper hand in the Gulf. Our hand has been strengthened by an unprecedented, effective economic and military blockade; strengthened by eight U.N. resolutions; strengthened by the successful assembly of troops that stopped Iraqi aggression at the Saudi border; strengthened by the determined certainty that atrocities by the Iraqi military and Mukhabarat against innocent Kuwaiti and foreign nationals will be indelibly recorded in the outrage of civilized humanity and the docket of international courts of law.

What weakens our hand is the administration's constant worrying about the appearance of rewarding aggression. The Secretary of State recently fretted: "It would be a terrible mistake in terms of establishing a new world order if we began by working deals that would permit unprovoked aggression to pay."

Never mind that scarcely 100 days ago his State Department was doing just that: Working deals, through diplomatic signals, that would permit Saddam Hussein to grab Kuwait's northern oil fields. The question is: Where does the administration's principled unwillingness to pursue diplomatic solutions lead? It could lead to the kind of overreaction to terrorism that has crippled U.S. foreign policy more than once in recent history. It could lead to the martyrdom of Saddam Hussein. It could lead to an expenditure of American blood and treasure which has been authorized by neither the American public nor its Representatives in Congress.

Lessons of the Cold War and Vietnam

I have lived through two wars — one cold and one hot. I confess that the results of each of those wars changed my initial thoughts about their merits. I did not fight in World War II, although I may have been born because of it. My memories begin instead with fragments from the early days of the Cold War: duck and cover drill; Weekly Reader and Readers Digest stories about the dangers of Communist subversion. Although I grew up amid the violent energy of those who feared the red tide, my Cold War experiences did not make me a passionate anti-Communist.

My participation in the fight against the Communists of North Vietnam was a much more direct consequence of the draft and a sense of duty than it was a response to the call to "pay any price, bear any burden." The more advanced my military training the less thought I gave to the political objectives of my enemy.

But after returning to the United States and upon my release from the Philadelphia Hospital I was asked: For that cause, and this cost, would I do it again? My answer was " No, I would not"

I denied my own bitterness and confusion. Consumed by anger toward leaders and promised peace with honor, secret plans to end the war, and other noble sounding disguises for their own political retreat, I grew to distrust anyone whose call to arms appeared phony and insincere. That distrust has not disappeared. I remain deeply skeptical whenever I hear we have no choice but to send our troops into battle. And while I know there are times we must use force, I do not apologize for my cynicism. I believe it can be constructive. It is usually warranted.

That experience stands in sharp contrast to the verdict I have reached about the Cold War, some four decades after my earliest memories of it. Today I look at the new freedom and promise that fill people's lives in the former Eastern bloc. I hear the grateful words of Vaclav Havel and Lech Walesa. And I know that while they have secured their own liberty, our nation made an important contribution to Eastern Europe's freedom with our patient policy of quiet pressure and firm containment.

Mr. President, if ever there was an avoidable war, it is this one.

We were right, across those decades, to commit our resources; to draw the line; to expose the egalitarian rhetoric of Stalin and his heirs as a flimsy front for the hard realities of persecution, murder, and the gulag. Likewise, we were right to stand up for Nelson Mandela and others whose humanity has been denied by apartheid in South Africa.

We are right, in the same way, to stand up to Saddam Hussein. We are right if we exercise the same patient firmness in our embargo of Iraq that brought victory in the Cold War. But we are wrong if the pull of money obscures the goal of freedom.

We are also wrong, if we weaken our hand by firing the first shot. We are wrong if we reject diplomacy in the name of honor. Peace with honor has almost always meant peace with the honor of elected politicians intact.

If war occurs, the outcome is predictable: A lot of people will die; a lot of people will have their bodies torn

apart but will live; a lot of people will make a lot of money selling arms, building bases, repairing equipment; and a lot of people will look at the scene ten years from now and wonder why we did it.

The Course to Follow

There is a better course, and it must be stated clearly before we leave town. *First,* the administration needs to confirm what Americans already sense: That we have achieved a victory here. The first objective of the deployment of troops to the Gulf was to prevent an Iraqi invasion of Saudi Arabia.

The President should declare: We were the only nation with the capacity to deploy a force big enough and fast enough to deter further Iraqi aggression. We succeeded. American troops again deserve the world's gratitude. They accomplished their mission.

Second, the President should announce the start of phase two: a transition into a genuinely international force under U.N. auspices to continue enforcement of the embargo and protection of Saudi Arabia and other Gulf States. The President should refute dangerous suggestions that we must launch an American offensive now because international unity cannot be sustained over time. That is not true for our economic response. Surely it takes less effort to manage the discipline of a blockade than to manage the fury of a war. No one has suggested we will suffer 20,000 casualties dispatching our diplomats to plug up leaks in the blockade. Nor is it true that an international force is inferior if fighting does occur. Indeed, a truly international force — not one where nearly two-thirds of the ground troops are American — will draw strength from the greater presence of nations with a more immediate stake in the conflict. In short, a genuinely international force will keep Saddam Hussein isolated and threatened. The effectiveness of our response will not deteriorate because the makeup of the force has been altered.

Third, the President should signal a receptivity to the thoughtful proposals from the Senate Foreign Relations Committee and others on Capitol Hill to establish a consultative process, especially while Congress is adjourned. If they are not willing, then Congress should pass legislation establishing a consultative process.

Fourth, this administration should worry less about being perceived as weak if they find a peaceful solution. The American people will not perceive a negotiated settlement within the context of the U.N. resolutions as a failure of resolve. There are many diplomatic efforts yet to be tried. This is the challenge of the second phase of the Gulf conflict. If the administration rises to this challenge – rather than yielding to the lethal gravity that tugs it now toward war – it will have performed honorably and acted wisely on the lessons of the past 45 years.

Finally, the President must find the leadership to return our nation's attention from the martial distractions of the Gulf to the real battle for our way of life here at home. For we will not find our moment of opportunity out on the midnight sands of the Arabian Peninsula. That opportunity is here, in the spirit of our families; in the hands of our workers; in the minds of our students; in the hopeful eyes of our children. I pray President Bush will understand and remember that during the weeks to come.

Statement of House Speaker Thomas S. Foley and Senate Majority Leader George J. Mitchell, October 24, 1990 [16]

As the Congress approaches adjournment *sine die,* we will be taking several steps to facilitate the exercise of Congress's constitutional authorities with respect to war powers. We intend to ensure that the concurrent adjournment resolution provides that, in consultation with House Republican Leader [Robert H.] Michel and Senate Republican Leader [Robert] Dole, we will be able to recall the Congress to Washington as necessary.

We also have decided to ask members of the joint bipartisan leadership and the leaders of the House and Senate committees of jurisdiction to make themselves available as a group for regular consultation with the President. After Congress adjourns, this group would be available for consultation on developments in the Persian Gulf region. Presidential consultation with Congress is required by law under certain circumstances. We believe that regular consultation is necessary and

useful, particularly given recent developments in the Persian Gulf.

The members designated to be available for consultation are as follows:

Speaker Thomas S. Foley (D-WA), Senate Majority Leader George J. Mitchell (D-ME), House Majority Leader Richard A. Gephardt (D-MO), President Pro Tempore Robert C. Byrd (D-WV), House Republican Leader Robert H. Michel (R-IL), Senate Republican Leader Robert Dole (R-KS), Congressman Dante Fascell (D-FL), Senator Claiborne Pell (D-RI), Congressman William S. Broomfield (R-MI), Senator Jesse Helms (R-NC), Congressman Les Aspin (D-WI), Senator Sam Nunn (D-GA), Congressman William L. Dickinson (R-AL), Senator John Warner (R-VA), Congressman Anthony C. Beilenson (D-CA), Senator David L. Boren (D-OK), Congressman Henry J. Hyde (R-IL) and Senator William S. Cohen (R-ME).

U. N. Security Council Resolution 674, October 29, 1990 [3]

The Security Council,

Recalling its resolutions 660 (1990), 661 (1990), 662 (1990), 664 (1990), 665 (1990), 666 (1990), 667 (1990) and 670 (1990)

Stressing the urgent need for the immediate and unconditional withdrawal of all Iraqi forces from Kuwait, for the restoration of Kuwait's sovereignty, independence and territorial integrity, and of the authority of its legitimate government,

Condemning the actions by the Iraqi authorities and occupying forces to take third state nationals hostage and to mistreat and oppress Kuwaiti and third State nationals, and the other actions reported to the Council such as the destruction of Kuwaiti demographic records, forced departure of Kuwaitis, and relocation of population in Kuwait and the unlawful destruction and seizure of public and private property in Kuwait including hospital supplies and equipment, in violation of the decisions of this Council, the Charter of the United Nations, the Fourth Geneva Convention, the Vienna Conventions on Diplomatic and Consular Relations and international law,

Expressing grave alarm over the situation of nationals of third States in

Kuwait and Iraq, including the personnel of the diplomatic and consular missions of such States,

Reaffirming that the Fourth Geneva Convention applies to Kuwait and that as a High Contracting Party to the Convention Iraq is bound to comply fully with all its terms and in particular is liable under the Convention in respect of the grave breaches committed by it, as are individuals who commit or order the commission of grave breaches,

Recalling the efforts of the Secretary-General concerning the safety and well-being of third State nationals in Iraq and Kuwait,

Deeply concerned at the economic cost, and at the loss and suffering caused to individuals in Kuwait and Iraq as a result of the invasion and occupation of Kuwait by Iraq,

Acting under Chapter VII of the United Nations Charter,

Reaffirming the goal of the international community of maintaining international peace and security by seeking to resolve international disputes and conflicts through peaceful means,

Recalling also the important role that the United Nations and its Secretary-General have played in the peaceful solution of disputes and conflicts in conformity with the provisions of the United Nations Charter,

Alarmed by the dangers of the present crisis caused by the Iraqi invasion and occupation of Kuwait, directly threatening international peace and security, and seeking to avoid any further worsening of the situation,

Calling upon Iraq to comply with the relevant resolutions of the Security Council, in particular resolutions 660 (1990), 662 (1990) and 664 (1990),

Reaffirming its determination to ensure compliance by Iraq with the Security Council resolutions by maximum use of political and diplomatic means.

A

1. Demands that the Iraqi authorities and occupying forces immediately cease and desist from taking third State nationals hostage, and mistreating and oppressing Kuwaiti and third State nationals, and from any other actions such as those reported to the Council and described above, violating the decisions of this Council, the Charter of the United Nations, the

Fourth Geneva Convention, the Vienna Conventions on Diplomatic and Consular Relations and international law;

2. Invites States to collate substantiated information in their possession or submitted to them on the grave breaches by Iraq as per paragraph 1 above and to make this information available to the Council;

3. Reaffirms its demand that Iraq immediately fulfil its obligations to third State nationals in Kuwait and Iraq, including the personnel of diplomatic and consular missions, under the Charter, the Fourth Geneva Convention, the Vienna Conventions on Diplomatic and Consular Relations, general principles of international law and the relevant resolutions of the Council;

4. Reaffirms further its demand that Iraq permit and facilitate the immediate departure from Kuwait and Iraq of those third State nationals, including diplomatic and consular personnel, who wish to leave;

5. Demands that Iraq ensure the immediate access to food, water and basic services necessary to the protection and well-being of Kuwaiti nationals and of nationals of third States in Kuwait and Iraq, including the personnel of diplomatic and consular missions in Kuwait;

6. Reaffirms its demand that Iraq immediately protect the safety and well-being of diplomatic and consular personnel and premises in Kuwait and in Iraq, take no action to hinder these diplomatic and consular missions in the performance of their functions, including access to their nationals and the protection of their person and interests, and rescind its orders for the closure of diplomatic and consular missions in Kuwait and the withdrawal of the immunity of their personnel;

7. Requests the Secretary-General, in the context of the continued exercise of his good offices concerning the safety and well-being of third State nationals in Iraq and Kuwait, to seek to achieve the objectives of paragraphs 4, 5 and 6 and in particular the provision of food, water and basic services to Kuwaiti nationals and to the diplomatic and consular missions in Kuwait and the evacuation of third State nationals;

8. Reminds Iraq that under international law it is liable for any loss, damage or injury arising in regard to Kuwait and third States, and their nationals and corporations, as a result of

the invasion and illegal occupation of Kuwait by Iraq;

9. Invites States to collect relevant information regarding their claims, and those of their nationals and corporations, for restitution or financial compensation by Iraq with a view to such arrangements as may be established in accordance with international law;

10. Requires that Iraq comply with the provisions of the present resolution and its previous resolutions, failing which the Council will need to take further measures under the Charter;

11. Decides to remain actively and permanently seized of the matter until Kuwait has regained its independence and peace has been restored in conformity with the relevant resolutions of the Security Council.

B

12. Reposes its trust in the Secretary-General to make available his good offices and, as he considers appropriate, to pursue them and undertake diplomatic efforts in order to reach a peaceful solution to the crisis caused by the Iraqi invasion and occupation of Kuwait on the basis of Security Council resolutions 660 (1990), 662 (1990) and 664 (1990), and calls on all States, both those in the region and others, to pursue on this basis their efforts to this end, in conformity with the Charter, in order to improve the situation and restore peace, security and stability;

13. Requests the Secretary-General to report to the Security Council on the results of his good offices and diplomatic efforts.

Statement to the Security Council by Ambassador Thomas R. Pickering, U. S. Permanent Representative to the United Nations, October 29, 1990 [17]

Mr. President, the resolutions of the Council on Iraq are clear. Since August 2, the international community has acted together to condemn Iraq's unprovoked aggression against [Kuwait and] worked to take appropriate and measured steps to implement its resolution calling for immediate and unconditional withdrawal. Concerted action under Article 41 is already having an ef-

fect, signaling to Baghdad international resolve that aggression upon a sovereign member state of the United Nations must not be rewarded. Should Iraq continue to try to ignore and deny the international community, we believe that the Council will have to take further measures as prefigured in this resolution. The United States will actively support such efforts.

Iraq's continued unacceptable breach of international norms requires the international community to speak out yet again. It is speaking out today clearly against Iraq's efforts to destroy the sovereign state of Kuwait through organized looting, destruction, and even murder. By its systemic terrorizing of local and foreign innocent citizens, Baghdad has defied the world community, this Council and widely accepted standards of international conduct.

The Council further demands that Iraq honor its obligations under the Vienna convention towards diplomatic and consular personnel and missions and ensure immediate access to supplies of food, water and basic services to those missions, to allow these missions to exercise their functions for the protection of foreign nationals, to assure the immunities of their premises and personnel, and to allow the departure of all diplomatic and consular personnel who wish to leave. The fundamental principles of international conduct among states are being challenged by Baghdad's deplorable and illegal conduct, and we reject that conduct.

This resolution also makes clear that Iraq is liable for full restitution or compensation for the losses and damages it has caused by its illegal invasion and occupation of Kuwait. We anticipate the Council will address this question more fully in the days ahead. Baghdad must hear from us clearly: unprovoked aggression entails crippling costs, and Iraq must not be allowed to profit from its unacceptable disregard for the sovereignty and territorial integrity of another state.

It is the solemn duty of every state to protect its citizens. My government takes this responsibility most seriously. We join the other members of this body in demonstrating solidarity and resolve to condemn Iraqi violations of the rights of Kuwaitis and third State nationals present in Kuwait and Iraq. The continued denial of food, water and basic services, the refusal to permit the departure of any and all who seek to depart, the imposition of a virtual siege and terror—these are unacceptable. By today's action, the Council demands that Iraq cease its deliberate mistreatment of innocent citizens. I want to leave no doubt on this issue: We join the Council in this demand, and we urge the Government of Iraq to comply. But I want to underscore one point very clearly. Every nation has a duty to protect its citizens. This is a fundamental obligation. The United States will do that which is necessary to meet its obligation to its own citizens. Thank you, Mr. President.

Why America is in the Gulf

Address to the Los Angeles World Affairs Council by Secretary Baker, October 29, 1990 (opening remarks omitted). [18]

These are days of great upheaval. And today I'd like to speak to you about one of the most important of those upheavals: the situation in the Persian Gulf. As members of this World Affairs Council, you have long understood how distant international events can affect us at home. But I will say here today that rarely has such an event as Iraq's invasion of Kuwait been more challenging to our future and the future of many other nations.

At this moment, there are many thousands of Americans who are standing guard in the sands of Arabia. Maybe your son or daughter—a marine or soldier or sailor or airman, who was stationed at Fort Ord, or Camp Pendleton, or the Alameda Naval Air Station, or trained at 29 Palms is among them. Maybe you know a neighbor whose job has been affected by the economic dislocation of the conflict. And certainly we are all paying higher prices at the gas pump.

This conflict was not something we sought. But it won't go away by itself. It is a vital struggle in which we and the international community must prevail.

What's At Stake

So let me tell you just what's at stake.

First, Iraq's aggression challenges world peace. We live in one of those rare transforming moments in history. The Cold War is over, and an era full of

promise has begun. Just this month, we welcomed a new Germany united in peace and freedom. The peoples of Central and Eastern Europe have freed themselves through democratic, peaceful revolutions. After decades of conflict, the United States and the Soviet Union are writing new rules of cooperation. And after a long period of stagnation, the United Nations is becoming a more effective organization. The ideals of the United Nations Charter are becoming realities.

But it is also an era full of challenges and dangers. Ethnic and sectarian conflicts are intensifying. Nuclear, chemical, and biological weapons and advanced means for delivering them are proliferating. Terrorism and narcotics are scourges without boundaries or limits.

Saddam Hussein's aggression shatters the vision of a better world in the aftermath of the Cold War. As President Bush and President Gorbachev stated jointly in Helsinki: "No peaceful international order is possible if larger states can devour their smaller neighbors."

The rest of the world is trying to go forward with the 1990s.

But Saddam Hussein is trying to drag us all back into the 1930s.

And we know what that means: The tempting path of appeasing dictators in the hope that they won't commit further aggression. The self-defeating path of pretending not to see what was really happening as small nations were conquered and larger nations endangered. And then, finally, war at terrible cost.

In the 1930s, the aggressors were appeased. In 1990, the President has made our position plain: This aggression will not be appeased.

While the international community tries to build on the successful ending of the Cold War, Saddam Hussein seems hell-bent on a revival of hot war. He marries his old-style contempt for civilized rules with modern destructive methods: chemical and biological weapons, ballistic missiles, and—if he could—nuclear weapons.

What can be the long term meaning of Iraq's extensive chemical and biological weapons programs? Why is the Iraqi dictator spending billions of dollars to build weapons of mass destruction, including a nuclear bomb? And why has he turned Baghdad into a haven for international terrorists?

Surely not because he expects this aggression—first against Iran, now against Kuwait—to be his last.

So Iraq's invasion of Kuwait is a clear, indeed historic, challenge to the rest of the international community.

If we reverse his aggression, we'll help define the world that lies beyond the Cold War as a place where civilized rules of conduct apply.

If we do not, the bright promise of the post-Cold War era could be eclipsed by new dangers, new disorders, and a far less peaceful future.

Second, Iraq's aggression is a regional challenge. While might makes right is bad policy anywhere, it is especially dangerous in the Middle East. Just as when an event occurs can give it greater significance, where it happens gives it meaning, too. As we know, the Middle East is already disturbed by unresolved conflicts, sectarian and social strife, and vast economic disparities. When you add weapons of mass destruction and much of the world's energy supplies, it becomes an explosive mix. Today, the Middle East is truly at a crossroads. One road leads to peace, the other to war.

If there is one lesson we have learned, it is that no one is immune from the effects of conflict in the Middle East. There can be no hope of resolving other problems in the region unless peaceful change becomes the wave of the future in the Middle East and the Gulf. But Saddam Hussein's way is not the way of peace. His is a prescription for war. And I will say this bluntly: If his way of doing business prevails, there will be no hope for peace in the area.

Third, Iraq's aggression challenges the global economy. Obviously, we must do more to reduce our energy dependence. But for better or worse, the health of the global economy will depend for the foreseeable future on secure access to the energy resources of the Persian Gulf. Neither we nor the rest of the international community can afford to let one dictator control that access.

Just consider the consequences. If the entire world were to be thrust into a deep recession by an Iraqi stranglehold on Gulf energy resources, American industry, farmers, and small businesses would be hit especially hard. So would the democratic reformers of Eastern Europe. So would the other emerging democracies—in Latin America, Africa, and Asia. All would suffer profound setbacks in their ability to deliver the economic growth needed to sustain confidence in the democratic process.

All of us would lose from this economic tyranny. And all of us know how Saddam Hussein would seek to exploit his economic leverage in pursuit of his larger ambitions.

What the International Community is Doing

Led by the United States, the international community has recognized these vital stakes. President Bush has outlined four goals for our policy:

- *One,* the immediate, complete, and unconditional withdrawal of all Iraqi forces from Kuwait as mandated in United Nations Security Council Resolution 660;
- *Two,* restoration of Kuwait's legitimate government;
- *Three,* protection of the lives of American citizens held hostage by Iraq, in both Iraq and Kuwait; and
- *Four,* commitment to the security and stability of the Persian Gulf.

To achieve these goals, we and our international allies have sought to isolate Iraq: politically, economically, and militarily.

Let me try to put in perspective what we've accomplished to date.

On the *diplomatic* track, the United Nations Security Council has now passed ten resolutions. The last one was passed earlier today. Each has steadily increased the pressure on Iraq. Passage of today's Security Council Resolution refocuses international outrage on Iraq's pillage of Kuwait and strengthens the case for whatever further actions prove necessary to reverse Iraq's aggression.

Never in its existence has the potential of the U.N. as a force for peace and stability been clearer. That's due in no small part to unprecedented cooperation between the United States and the Soviet Union — cooperation unthinkable during the Cold War. It's also due to the support of the Arab League and the Nonaligned Movement, and indeed to the virtually unanimous sentiments of the international community.

Never in recent memory have so many nations acted to condemn aggression and cruelty.

The result has been Iraq's political and economic isolation. Economic sanctions are beginning to have an impact on Iraq. Iraq's oil income has been cut off. Shortages of spare parts will take their toll on Iraqi industry and, even more importantly, on the Iraqi war machine. Sanctions take time to bite, but as they do, they will impose a very high cost on Iraq's import-dependent economy.

Baghdad recognizes this; that's why it is working desperately to probe for weakness, splinter the international coalition, and overcome the sanctions. And that's why we must continue to stand firm — until Saddam Hussein stops trying to break the sanctions and starts rejoining civilized society by complying with the Security Council Resolutions.

On the *military* track, we and some 27 other countries have sent troops or material to the Gulf in support of the Security Council Resolutions. Many thousands of Arab and Moslem soldiers in Saudi Arabia now stand guard together with Americans and Europeans. And this multinational force on land has been joined by powerful multinational forces at sea and in the air.

In contrast, only fourteen other countries contributed military forces during the Korean War.

We must be clear about our military mission. Our military objectives are to deter an Iraqi attack on Saudi Arabia, protect American lives, and to ensure the effective implementation of the Security Council Resolutions. Without such forces, Iraq's neighbors would be subject to attack if they tried to enforce economic sanctions.

Our military forces are also there to provide an effective and decisive military response should the situation warrant it.

Saddam Hussein must realize there is a limit to the international community's patience. He must also realize that should he use chemical or biological weapons, there will be the most severe consequences.

The President has made our position clear: We strongly prefer a peaceful solution consistent with the mandate of the Security Council Resolutions. We are exhausting every diplomatic avenue to achieve such a solution without further bloodshed.

All options, however, are being considered.

And let no one doubt: We will not rule out a possible use of force if Iraq continues to occupy Kuwait.

Since the invasion, I've spent a lot of time travelling, visiting our allies and friends and bringing the message that we all share responsibilities for seeing this matter through. And they have responded. Our friends in the Gulf, Europe and Asia have committed an additional $20 billion in resources to support both "front line" states hardest hit economically by the crisis — namely Egypt, Turkey, and Jordan — and our own military buildup. We are confident that additional support will be forthcoming should the conflict carry over into 1991. All told, fifty-four nations are contributing militarily or economically to the effort against Iraq's aggression.

So we're on course. Every day, as the sun sets, Iraq is weaker. Every day, as the sun rises, the international community remains firmly committed to implementation of the the Security Council Resolutions. Sooner or later, and we all hope sooner, even the Iraqi dictator is going to notice that he's in deep trouble and the trouble is getting deeper.

Sooner or later, one way or another, Iraq will have to comply with the Security Council Resolutions. When it does, the prospects for peace in the Gulf and the Middle East will undoubtedly brighten. When it does, the prospects for a peaceful international order will brighten, too.

Meanwhile, the United States opposes any attempt to reward Iraq for its aggression — even if it plays the siren song of a "partial solution."

And should there be any doubt about the awful consequences of a partial solution, I would urge a close look at what Saddam Hussein is doing to the people of Kuwait. And because he controls access to the true story of Kuwait, this is a story that is not told frequently enough.

It is a story of barbarism in its most crude and evil form, the rape of Kuwait. Many of the reports seem unbelievable. There is the report of a couple, taking two sick children to hospital. On their way, they were stopped at an Iraqi checkpoint and when they asked for mercy, to be allowed to continue on their way, the Iraqi soldier summarily shot their children, "curing them" in his words.

And consider the Kuwait City zoo. Iraqi soldiers released the lions and tigers, and then tried to shoot them for target practice. Their efforts, however, were not completely successful. A lion escaped and mauled a young Kuwaiti girl.

He's also making political and economic war on our citizens still in Iraq and Kuwait. At strategic installations in Iraq, more than one hundred American citizens are being held hostage as human shields. These Americans are forced to sleep on vermin-ridden concrete floors. They are kept in the dark during the day and moved only at night. They have had their meals cut to two a day. And many are becoming sick as they endure a terrible ordeal. The very idea of Americans being used as human shields is simply unconscionable.

Life for those who have escaped Saddam's soldiers is no less odious. Their days are lived with terror. Obtaining food and water — the most basic of human necessities — carries with it the risk of death.

We all agonize for these people — innocent Americans and nationals of other countries, trapped by Saddam Hussein's deadly ambitions. In most cases, we cannot communicate our concern and sympathy directly to these Americans. But that does not lessen the pain we feel at their plight nor diminish our desire to banish all spectres of Iraq's aggression.

We understand the concerns of their families, here at home. The courage they have shown in the face of Saddam Hussein's manipulations is great. We salute their will and spirit, their unity in the face of adversity. We shall not forget them either.

This aggression extends beyond our citizens to the small band of American diplomats, men and women who still fly the American flag high over Kuwait. They are denied supplies of food, water, or electricity. But they are not without courage. Since August 2, I've spoken often to Ambassador Howell, most recently last week. He and our other diplomats in Kuwait continue to serve our nation in a superb fashion. They continue to fight back.

They are not giving in. And neither are we.

The Gulf and America's Role in the World

At the beginning of this conflict, the President and I and all of those con-cerned with the problem had to ask ourselves the same questions you must be asking: Why must America take the lead? Why must our kids be out there in the desert? Now that the Cold War is over, can't we pass this one up?

Ladies and gentlemen, this struggle is about the kind of world we want to live in, the kind of nation we are, and the kind of legacy we want to leave for our children.

The Cold War is over, all right. We fought and sacrificed and persisted for over forty years because we would not accept a world that was safe for the likes of Joseph Stalin.

The American people have not come this long hard way to make the world safe for the likes of Saddam Hussein.

Let no nation think that it can devour another nation and the United States will turn a blind eye. Let no dictator believe that we are deaf to the tolling of the bell, as our principles are attacked. And let no one believe that because the Cold War is over, the United States will abdicate its international leadership.

May I remind you that America's involvement in world politics came about from conviction based on hard and terrible experience. We're not in the game just to play one inning and then go home. We cannot be short of breath for the long haul. And whatever the noise of naysayers, our moral principles and our material interests make us a leader.

That's why we are in the Gulf.

That's why we must prevail.

Will we have the courage, the fortitude to stand up for what we know in our hearts is right? Is Saddam Hussein's kind of world the legacy we want to leave for our children? Are the nations of the world gathered in vain to defend the principles of the United Nations Charter?

I think you know the answer to these questions. There is a morality among nations. Aggression cannot be permitted to succeed.

America will do what is right.

1 Text from Weekly Compilation of Presidential Documents of September 17, 1990.

2 Department of State Press Release 135, September 12, 1990.

3 Text provided by United Nations Information Center, Washington.

4 Department of State Press Release 137, September 17, 1990.

5 Department of State Press Release 140, September 19, 1990.

6 Text from Weekly Compilation of Presidential Documents of September 24, 1990. The address was recorded on September 12.

7 The complete transcript of the hearings will be published by the committee and will be available from the Superintendent of Documents, U.S. Government Printing Office, Washington, D.C. 20420.

8 Department of State Press Release 146, September 25, 1990.

9 Text from Weekly Compilation of Presidential Documents of October 1, 1990.

10 Text from Weekly Compilation of Presidential Documents of October 8, 1990.

11 Provided to news correspondents by the Office of Press Relations, Department of State.

12 Released by the Italian Delegation to the CSCE Ministerial, New York, October 2, 1990.

13 Department of State Press Release 165, October 18, 1990.

14 Verbatim excerpt provided by Congressional Quarterly. The complete transcript of the hearings will be published by the committee and will be available from the Superintendent of Documents, U.S. Government Printing Office, Washington, D.C. 20420.

15 Text from the Congressional Record, October 24, 1990.

16 Released the Office of the Majority Leader, U.S. Senate, October 24, 1990.

17 U.S. Mission to the United Nations Press Release 99(90), October 29, 1990.

18 Department of State Press Release 169, October 29, 1990.

Interview of Yevgeny Primakov, President Gorbachev's Special Persian Gulf Representative

Interviewed by Igor Belyayev, political commentator of Literaturnaya Gazeta. Published by Literaturnaya Gazeta on November 7, 1990. Mr. Primakov is a member of the Presidential Council of the U.S.S.R. [1]

Q. Will there or will there not be a war? I mean a real live war in the Persian Gulf. This almost Shakespearian question arises as a result of the dreadful events that have taken place since Iraq's invasion of Kuwait. The new international order, still in the first stages of its development, is at stake.

You have just returned from a trip to the Middle East. And before that you had made tours of the Middle East, and of Western Europe and the United States. Might all this travelling come under the heading of "Primakov's Mission," and what is the essence of your mission?

A. First of all, I would like to say that all those trips are part of one plan, but it would be wrong to call it "Primakov's Mission." My meetings and discussions with the leaders of different countries—twice in Iraq, in Jordan, Italy, France, Great Britain, the United States, Egypt, Saudi Arabia, Syria, Kuwait and with the Palestinian Liberation Organization—were undertaken on the initiative of President Gorbachev. During these meetings, above all I was guided by the instructions of the Soviet President.

And now to the essence of recent events.

So, suddenly Iraq invaded and then annexed Kuwait. This action evoked the condemnation of the world community. The U.N. Security Council passed a number of resolutions, demanding that Iraqi troops be withdrawn from Kuwait. The resolutions also provided for economic sanctions against Iraq. Some of them are being enforced. The position of the Soviet Union on this score does not differ from that of the world community.

We would like Iraq to withdraw from Kuwait and we would like to see a return to the situation which existed before August 2. At the same time, we do not want Iraq to benefit from the annexation of another state and member of the United Nations.

Q. I think that our approach here should be interpreted broadly. It is not simply a question of the annexation of Kuwait by Iraq. A very serious precedent has been set, which runs counter to efforts in the interests of a world without war and aggression.

It seems to me that Saddam Hussein has an obvious case of what I would call a "Massada Complex."

A. Of course, the position taken by the Soviet Union is significant not only with regard to events in the Persian Gulf. Clearly, the world is coming out of a period of Cold War. We need new "rules of behaviour," a new world order to be based on the impossibility of force being used to promote the narrow, egoistical interests of one state or another. In our country, we remember the sad events of the 1930s. Today, we must do everything to avoid a repetition of this experience. The end of the Cold War and fierce confrontation between East and West must not be replaced by a new period of all-permissiveness among those (in this case, Third World countries) who, in comparison with their neighbors, possess relatively extensive military capabilities. Naturally, this holds not only for the Third World, but also for the world community as a whole.

Q. So, the mission initiated by the President of the U.S.S.R. was intended to liquidate the results of the Iraqi invasion of Kuwait and force Iraq to withdraw its troops?

A. Absolutely. But it would be wrong to limit the tasks set by the President to this alone.

As is known, at the request of Saudi Arabia itself, the United States and other countries have sent troops to Saudi Arabia and the territory of the United Arab Emirates. Naval forces have been sent to the Persian Gulf. This force, the bulk of which is made up of

American troops, is performing a military function. In other words, this is being done to show Iraq that if it refuses to withdraw its troops, it will be faced with a military challenge. According to the view of the Soviet leadership, all opportunities should be taken to secure the withdrawal of Iraqi troops by political means. But what shape are such political means likely to take?

President Saddam Hussein of Iraq, in a speech on August 12, linked the withdrawal of Iraqi troops to the settlement of the Arab-Israeli conflict and the situation in the Lebanon. In the same speech Hussein claimed that Kuwait is part of Iraq and that, under these circumstances, consent to withdraw Iraqi troops would be an act of goodwill. It is quite clear that such a package of measures is quite unacceptable. It must be viewed as an attempt on the part of Iraq to make capital out of what it has done.

Possibility of a Political Settlement

However, such a determinedly negative attitude ought not to be allowed to slam the door on the possibility of a political settlement. A plausible scenario might look like this: Iraq unconditionally withdraws its troops from Kuwait, but after that certain decisions would have to be taken to stabilise the situation in the region in accordance with the interests of many states. As a matter of fact, this line was taken by President Gorbachev at the summit meeting in Helsinki. Any settlement of the Gulf crisis must give impetus to the solution of other problems in the region, and, above all, of the Arab-Israeli conflict, at the heart of which is the Palestinian problem. This idea was expressed in the Joint Soviet-American Declaration which followed the summit meeting in Helsinki.

Q. A question arises. Given all these circumstances, do you think there is a possibility of Iraqi troops withdrawing from Kuwait?

A. I think this is the most important question. As I have mentioned, I have had the opportunity of meeting Saddam Hussein twice this month, on October 5 and 28. You will agree, of course, that in order to understand the situation fully, it is important to appreciate the nuances in dialogues, to see what is emphasised in this or that context and to recognise when there is an evident desire to avoid addressing one issue or another. On the basis of a careful comparative analysis of my two conversations with Saddam Hussein, it seems to me that the withdrawal of Iraqi troops from Kuwait on the basis of a political agreement is not out of the question. And this is a very serious conclusion. Certainly, a military solution could lead to a whole chain of processes with such negative consequences that it is difficult to evaluate them, even in general terms, today. I am not talking about victims or damage. Among politicians in the West such cynical expressions as "unacceptable losses" are commonly used. In fact, all losses are unacceptable, but if we are to use this Western expression, then in the case of war, losses on both sides would exceed acceptable levels. Further, we should not forget that in the theatre of operations and near it are the richest deposits of oil in the world. Many believe that in the event of war, they would be blown up, which would result not only in the cessation of oil extraction, but in an ecological disaster. We might make the following conclusion: a military outcome would lead to the destabilization of many regimes in the region, considerably aggravating the situation.

Q. But a no less important question is this: What role is to be played in a political settlement by those in the Arab world who would like to see an end to Iraqi aggression and its consequences?

A. From the many conversations I have had in Arab countries, my impression is that the overwhelming majority of Arabs realize the dangers involved in a military option. But that is not to say that they do not want Iraq to withdraw from Kuwait. So a political solution based on the principle of Iraq withdrawing from Kuwait does exist.

None of the Arab leaders reject the idea of talks between Iraq and Kuwait on controversial territorial and economic issues, but only after the withdrawal of troops.

One more thing has become clear as a result of these conversations. After the withdrawal of Iraqi forces the Arab States and, of course, the United States and other countries with troops in the area of the Persian Gulf, will also have

to decide the question of the cessation of the current military presence in Saudi Arabia. Why do I say, the "current" military presence? Because if Saudi Arabia asks for the military forces now in the region to be replaced by Arab ones—with or without the participation of other Moslem States—then, as has been pointed out by many of those with whom I have had discussions, such a request would most likely be granted. In actual fact, this would be in line with official statements made by the United States. At a press conference in Helsinki, President George Bush said in no uncertain terms that after the solution of the crisis United States forces would return home.

Iraq's Nuclear Potential

Q. But Iraq possesses weapons capable of causing mass destruction and, it would seem, is soon to have a nuclear capability. Under these circumstances, is it realistic to say that the withdrawal of Iraqi troops from Kuwait would stabilise the situation there?

A. No, I cannot say so. The issues raised in your question are very serious, and the world community is concerned that Iraq's not insubstantial military capability might be used against neighboring countries. Under these circumstances, without further measures, there can be no guarantee that other countries will be safe. That is why the Soviet Union (and this thought can be found in the Joint Soviet-American Declaration made at Helsinki) is doing everything it can to settle the Gulf crisis, and to promote strategic security in the region. Of course, the whole of the Middle East is concerned in this, including Israel.

The Helsinki Model

The Italian Prime Minister, Andreotti, and the Minister of Foreign Affairs, de Michelis, in their conversations with me, stressed that the Helsinki experience should be taken into account in the Middle East. I think this idea deserves some attention. But this experience cannot be applied without modification, because the main idea of the Helsinki security system has to do with the recognition of postwar borders in Europe and their inviolability. Until the Arab-Israeli conflict is settled in the Middle East, there can be no recognition of borders, never mind their inviolability. There are also territorial disputes between Turkey and

Iraq, and Turkey and Syria. At the moment these problems are just smoldering, but they could flare up at any moment. In any case, interest in these problems will increase when the question of the recognition of borders is raised. This is necessary, but there is no chance of its realization until the Arab-Israeli conflict is resolved.

Q. A system of strategic security is needed in the Middle East anyway.

A. In drawing up such a system, besides the question of borders, the following issues must be taken into account: arms exports to the region, all countries in the region joining the Nonproliferation Treaty and consenting to the consequent inspections of IAEA [International Atomic Energy Agency], and their becoming a part of the Chemical Weapons Treaty, which, hopefully, will soon be signed in Geneva. Provision may also be made for agreements of nonaggression and no first use of force.

But there is another side of the coin. Talking to Saddam Hussein I felt—and it seems to me not unreasonably—that he was "obsessed" with the idea that "since its military victory over Iran" Iraq has become in effect a "besieged fortress." It seems to me that Saddam Hussein has an obvious case of what I would call a "Masada Complex." Masada was the last fortress left standing in a war against the Jews and its defenders, realising the hopelessness of their position, declared that they were prepared to die but not to surrender. As far as I was able to gather, Saddam Hussein is considering the future and may think that Iraq will be attacked even if he withdraws his forces from Kuwait. Will the economic sanctions be lifted in the event of his forces being withdrawn? Such fears of Iraq are heightened by statements that suggest some of those who are in favor of a military solution have the goal not only of forcing Iraq out of Kuwait, but also of putting an end to the current regime in Iraq, if not breaking up Iraq altogether.

Q. In a joint press conference given by the Presidents of the U.S.S.R and France, when you were in the Middle East, Mr. Gorbachev said that in his opinion in the interests of political settlement it would be worthwhile to emphasise the Arab factor. This proposal, to judge from reactions in the press, was quite unexpected and was not, as far as I can judge, received in the same way throughout the world.

A. Such diversity of reaction was mainly the result of deliberate, interested commentaries on the part of some news agencies. In fact, where the resolution of the Gulf crisis is concerned, there is no question of passing the buck to the Arabs. Far from it. However, under current circumstances, the active participation of Arabs could lead in the direction of a political settlement, given, of course, the withdrawal of Iraqi troops from Kuwait. But Arab initiatives must not be isolated from the efforts of the world community, and above all of the Five Permanent Members of the U.N. Security Council.

Sometimes another argument is put forward: it is suggested that the Arab world is disunited and that it is unrealistic to expect consensus among the Arabs. Certainly, the attitude of Arab countries to Iraq's invasion of Kuwait has split the Arab world into two camps. The majority of Arab governments have denounced the Iraqi aggression. In my view, this attitude is not shared by the majority of the citizens in Arab countries. That Iraq has thrown down the gauntlet to the all-powerful West appeals to some of them, others like it that the Iraqi leadership has linked firmly the withdrawal of its troops from Kuwait to the settlement of the Palestinian problem. One way or another there is no uniformity in the Arab world. Under these circumstances, the convocation of an all-Arab summit (and in this respect I fully agree both with President Mubarak of Egypt and King Fahd of Saudi Arabia) would not be a panacea. It is possible that such a summit would produce little more than demonstrations of disagreements, mutual reproaches and excursions into the past to justify positions. But Arab efforts may take other forms. There is the Arab League, and there is also the possibility of uniting Arab efforts in other ways.

Soviet Citizens in Iraq

Q. Mr Primakov, we have spoken only of the political aspects of efforts undertaken by the Soviet Union. But there is another problem that worries us all. Your trips to the Middle East have had to do with the essential task of arranging a safe departure from Iraq for all Soviet citizens wanting to leave. On the basis of a brief announcement by TASS, we know only that an agreement with the Iraqi President provides for the return home of all Soviet citizens

who want to go. That is all. We have no particulars. Would you please give us some details?

A. During our first trip (I was then in Baghdad with the Vice Chairman of the Council of Ministers of the U.S.S.R., I.S. Byelousov) we raised the question of the return home of Soviet specialists. Of course, of those who wanted to go home. This question was not an unreasonable one ... Many attempts to settle this matter with Iraq's authorities were unsuccessful. Aeroflot flights to Baghdad became irregular, because there were no passengers for flights back to Moscow. During our first meeting with Saddam Hussein, Byelousov and I managed to make some progress with this issue. The Iraqi leader said that Soviet people in his country were not being delayed for political reasons. A schedule for the departure of 1,500 of our specialists was prepared within a month, that is to say by November 5.

It must be said that there was no deviation from this schedule. But there were 5,000 of our people in Iraq. And Iraq's authorities made special arrangements for Soviet military specialists. By the time I arrived in Baghdad for the second time 36 military specialists, who had served out their terms, observed all the formalities and had all the documents necessary for their departure, were almost taken off the plane. This caused considerable anxiety among Soviet citizens in Iraq, especially those in the south of the country.

During my second meeting with the President of Iraq, under strict instructions from the President of the U.S.S.R., I made it abundantly clear that all questions associated with Soviet people in Iraq must be resolved. In my presence Saddam Hussein called his secretary and ordered him to see that all Soviet citizens wishing to leave Iraq should be allowed to do so. A clear instruction was given with regard to Soviet military specialists. All who had served out their contracts were coming home. The 36 military specialists, whom I have mentioned, arrived in Moscow on an Aeroflot flight on the morning of November 2. An additional schedule has been prepared for the departure of another thousand Soviet citizens by the end of November. Incidentally, this number exceeds the number of applications made by Soviet specialists to Soviet organisations in Iraq to leave the country. Thus, between October 5 and the end of November 2,500 Soviet

people will return home. According to the agreement reached between the two countries, the number of flights will no longer be limited. It will only depend on the desire of specialists to leave Iraq.

Q. There are rumors that you brought from Baghdad one of our specialists, who had been kept for two and a half years by the Iraqi authorities in connection with a car accident which claimed lives. If this is so, can you give us some of the details of what happened? I am sure that our readers ought to know about this.

A. Yes, it is true. The driver was a resident of Kiev, in Iraq under contract. Twice an Iraqi court found him not guilty. Nevertheless, he was not allowed to leave the country, and his case was continually being reopened. After a while the man became discouraged. He was now living alone in Iraq, without his family. He was on the verge of desperation. Under instructions from Mr. Gorbachev, I discussed this case separately with the President of Iraq. This is because the fate of every Soviet citizen, and especially of one in such a serious position, is of great importance. The President of Iraq resolved this question to our satisfaction. Today the driver, who returned home with me from Baghdad, is with his loved ones in the Ukraine.

We are not only concerned with our own people, although, obviously, their fate is our first priority. In conversation with Saddam Hussein I raised the question of American, European and Japanese hostages. I still hope that the Iraqi leadership will reconsider this issue.

International Reactions to Trip

Q. Your trip received considerable attention throughout the world. It even caused a little drama when Yu. M. Vorontsov, a Soviet representative at the United Nations, made a request in your name that a resolution on Iraq by the Security Council be delayed for two days. Why?

A. It is not just a matter of drama. I asked that voting at the Security Council on this resolution be delayed from Saturday, October 27, to Monday, October 29. Making the request, of course I realized that one conversation with Saddam Hussein, due to take place on the Sunday, could not achieve a breakthrough, but it seemed to me that such a delay would create a favorable atmosphere for talks in Baghdad. And that is how it turned out. But since we did not receive any indication that Iraq was ready to withdraw its forces from Kuwait, the voting went ahead last Monday. And a Soviet representative at the U.N. was one of the authors of the resolution. And that, I think, accurately reflects the Soviet line. We are in favor of achieving a set goal: the withdrawal of Iraqi troops from Kuwait. But we want to make use of all the political means at our disposal.

As for reactions in the press, there was a diversity of views. The overwhelming majority in the world media understood the efforts of the Soviet Union and showed interest in their continuation. I am referring to both Western and Arab newspapers and television.

Of course, the anxiety in certain Western countries over my trip can be understood. I also understand the concern lest the forces in favor of the withdrawal of Iraqi forces from Kuwait be divided. And lest some take ad-

vantage of the situation to keep a military presence in the Persian Gulf. But the Soviet Union is firmly in favour of the obligatory withdrawal of all troops once the crisis ends. Naturally, there were other reactions to my trip. The authors of some of them predicted a failure of political efforts in order to suggest that a military solution was the only option. There were also those who ascribed to the Soviet representative goals which had nothing to do with reality. Unfortunately, this came to light in Izvestia, our quasi-official newspaper, which chose to base its comments on a trip by the Special Representative of the Soviet President entirely on Western sources.

Mr. Belyayev. In conclusion, I would like to point out that after your many meetings and exchanges of views with such a wide range of politicians, statesmen, heads of state and governments from all over the world, and your meetings with Saddam Hussein in Bagh-

dad, there is still a chance that war in the Persian Gulf will be averted. I think that such an outcome to the efforts of the Soviet leadership to prevent a war in the Persian Gulf, which is quite close to our southern borders, have been a great success. The withdrawal of Iraqi troops from Kuwait may, I think, be achieved without a war, though, to be frank, there is still some cause for concern.

---

1 Text provided by Novosti Information Agency, U.S.S.R.

South African President de Klerk Meets with President Bush

On September 24, 1990, President F.W. de Klerk of South Africa met with President Bush at the White House. [1]

President Bush. To our friends from South Africa, once again, welcome to the White House. We've just come from an extraordinarily useful meeting. President de Klerk and I have conversed on the phone several times in the past, but it was a great pleasure to hold this face-to-face meeting with the first South African leader to visit the United States in more than 40 years. President de Klerk described for me in detail what he is trying to accomplish in South Africa: the process of ending apartheid and negotiating a new political reality for all. We talked of this very promising, sometimes difficult situation, especially the recent violence. And I think all Americans recognize that President de Klerk is courageously trying to change things. After all, we have seen in other parts of the world the culture of political violence overwhelm the culture of dialogue, and this must not happen to South Africa. The Government has a special responsibility to maintain order, but all political parties and groups have a special responsibility to support the process of peaceful transition.

One thing is apparent in this process of change: The move away from apartheid toward a new political reality is indeed irreversible. And much has already happened. Leading political figures, including Nelson Mandela [African National Congress leader] have been released from prison. The Government and the ANC, the African National Congress, have reached an agreement on a plan for the release of the remaining political prisoners. Political organizations banned for years are now free to conduct peaceful political activities, and restraints on the media have largely been removed. A framework has been agreed to between the ANC and the Government to lead to negotiations over the political future of the country. Other groups are invited to join in. Except for the beleaguered Natal, the nationwide state of emergency has been lifted through the country.

Who among us only a year ago would have anticipated these remarkable developments? Clearly, the time has come to encourage and assist the emerging new South Africa. The United States clearly endorses the principle of constitutional democratic government in South Africa, and I'm here to tell you that I have enormous respect for what President de Klerk and Nelson Mandela are trying to achieve together in pursuit of this principle. And it is not simply this President. I believe, sir, it's the entire American people that feel that way.

South Africa needs a constitutional system based on regular and free elections with universal suffrage, a civil society where authority is responsible in every sense of the word. South Africa needs an unvarying respect for human rights and equal opportunity for all its citizens. And we also would like to see an economic system that's based on freedom and individual initiative and market forces. We believe that only a society that opens equal opportunity to all can remedy the social and economic deprivations inflicted on so many people for so many years by apartheid. And President de Klerk agrees with this principle of equal opportunity for all.

Clearly, the time has come to encourage and assist the emerging new South Africa.

And it is in such a context that the issue of sanctions often arises. Although our meetings today were not about sanctions, obviously, we discussed it; the topic did come up. And let me just say a quick word. As I stated, we believe the process of change in South Africa is irreversible, a fact that we'll bear squarely in mind as we consider specific issues in the future. Our goal must be to support the process of change and of course, I will consult fully with the Congress on these issues. And as you know all the conditions set in our legislation have not yet been made, in spite of the dramatic progress that we salute here today. But let me emphasize that these conditions are clear-cut and are not open to reinterpretation, and I do not believe in moving the goalposts.

Finally, we will be in touch with our traditional allies in Western Europe and elsewhere on what we can do to help build democracy in South Africa. It is only in this way that South Africa can again be fully accepted into the wider international community.

Apartheid has long hindered South Africa from within, depriving it of the talent and very dreams of millions of men and women. Little wonder then that the end of apartheid holds the promise of unleashing the creative energies of the restless millions, and that's why the end of apartheid can really mean the beginning of a greater South Africa.

Mr. President, if you're successful in this effort, South Africa around the world will become a beloved country not for one people but for all. And for that—your efforts, your courage—you leave with our gratitude, our appreciation, and a hearty Godspeed. Good luck to you, sir, in this wonderful endeavor. We're pleased you're here, very pleased, indeed.

President de Klerk. Mr. President, ladies and gentlemen, may I, at the outset, also say publicly how appreciative we are of the very kind reception which we have had here in the United States of America. For us it is, indeed, an historical occasion for me to be the first State President ever to visit the shores of America from South Africa.

From the moment we set foot here, we've been overwhelmed with friendliness. And in particular, Mr. President, I want to thank you for the very frank, very open, and very fruitful discussions which we were able to have today for over two hours.

I want to say, Mr. President, that from the people of South Africa I bring a message, a message of recognition for the awesome responsibility which rests upon your shoulders in the handling of the very difficult situation in the Gulf. We admire you for the strong leadership which you have shown, and South Africa has fully identified itself with that leadership. You can count on us, as we have publicly stated, to support the steps you have taken to assure that democracy, and that the political process of dialogue and the political process of keeping all channels open will also be maintained in that part of the world. We will support you, sir, in the very definite steps you have taken to assure that the unacceptable form of aggression which manifested itself there will be withstood; and South Africa will play its part in that regard. We wish you well in handling this awesome and tremendous responsibility.

Mr. President, I want to thank you for the acknowledgment of the new reality which exists in South Africa. There is, indeed, as you have stated, sir, a new reality; and the process in South Africa is indeed an irreversible one. There will be negotiations, and from those negotiations there will come about a new constitutional situation, a new constitution which will offer full political rights within the framework of internationally acceptable definitions of what democracy really is.

There will be a vote of equal value to all South Africans. There will be effective protection of the very values which you in the United States of America hold so dearly: values such as an independent judiciary; such as effective protection of the rights of the individual in the form of a bill of rights, of checks and balances to prevent the abuse of majority power to the detriment or suppression of minorities and smaller communities. There will be, in South Africa, the protection of fundamental values with regard to the assurance of an economic system which will create sufficient growth to meet the tremendous challenges which we face in the field of addressing the problems of poverty and illiteracy and housing and urbanization.

There will be in South Africa—the process is irreversible—through negotiation a new constitutional and economic dispensation which will offer equal opportunities and full democratic rights to all its people. In that sense of the word, the international community can rely on us. We will not turn back. The fact, sir, that you have today given recognition to this fact will serve as inspiration to us. We stand on the threshold of a tremendously exciting period in the history of our country. We are adamant to use the window of opportunity which history has given us to assure that we will bring about a new and just South Africa.

In that process, the Government of South Africa won't be acting unilaterally. Our goal is to bring about this fundamental change, to bring about this new and just South Africa on the basis of building and achieving a broad consensus between all the leaders with proven constituencies, whether they be large or small, in South Africa.

We are making headway with that. There are some stumbling blocks in the way. We have a problem of volatility to deal with which sometimes erupts into violent situations which are totally unacceptable. We've taken steps in an impartial manner, through the use of our security forces, curbed the violence. We are as anxious as you are, sir, that we should move as soon as possible to a situation where also in the province of Natal the state of emergency can be lifted and where the political process in South Africa can be fully normalized. We've already taken great steps in that direction.

I view, Mr. President, today as an important moment where real progress has been attained in normalizing our country's situation with regard to the international community. You, sir—as leader of the strongest country in the world, economically speaking and militarily speaking—your acknowledgment of the progress which we have made and your encouragement with regard to the progress which we are committed to make in the future is, for us, extremely important.

I thank you for the warm reception. And I look beyond the immediate problems and the historical problems, forward also to the day when South Africa, the new South Africa, with a new constitution and a new government, will, together with the United States of America and other important powers—being one of the strongest regional powers in the Southern Hemisphere, being the hope of the rebuilding of prosperity and opportunity for almost the whole continent of Africa—where South Africa will, by taking hands as we are now already doing with you and with others, will play a constructive role in ensuring stability on the globe, in ensuring that the vision which we share with you of peace between all countries, where we can make a contribution to ensure that that vision will also become reality.

We wish you, sir, and the American people everything of the best. We invite you to play the constructive role which you have spelled out here today. South Africa is going to overcome its problems. South Africa will become once again a proud member of the international community. And South Africa will be a trustworthy friend of the United States of America in maintaining the very values on which your system is built.

My country, ladies and gentlemen, today finds itself in step, in step with the basic value systems of this great country, the United States of America.

And we say to you, sir, thank you for a kind reception. Everything of the best in your endeavors to assure global peace. You will not find South Africa lacking in support when you need it.

---

1 Text from Weekly Compilation of Presidential Documents of October 1, 1990.

Department of State Warns of Massive Starvation in Sudan in 1991 [1]

The United States is the principal donor to a major international relief program in Sudan known as Operation Lifeline Sudan (OLS). Despite numerous obstacles, some imposed by the Government of Sudan, the OLS operation fed people displaced by Sudan's civil war and last year it succeeded in moving 100,000 tons of food. It is responsible for 70,000 tons of food going to hungry people so far this year.

However, we will have a much larger problem next year. The rains this year in Sudan have been poor and crops are likely to be well below average. The result will be a nationwide food shortage—perhaps as large as one million tons—in 1991. This will require a much larger relief program than heretofore. We estimate that as many as 8-9 million Sudanese may be at risk of starvation next year.

The full cooperation of the Government of Sudan will be absolutely necessary to organize such a relief program. We have urged the Government to do so but so far there has been little response. We have and will continue to make known our views at the highest levels of the Sudanese Government. We are making our own plans for dealing with the problem. The United States stands ready to provide up to 100,000 tons of relief food, plus additional food for commercial distribution, subject to budgetary restrictions. We are also urging other donors to make substantial contributions of their own. We believe that immediate action by the Sudanese government is needed in order to avoid another major human tragedy.

---

1 Provided to news correspondents by Department of State deputy spokesman Richard Boucher on October 26, 1990.

Philippine-American Cooperation Talks Begin

Excerpt from statement prepared for Kenneth M. Quinn, Deputy Assistant Secretary of State for East Asian and Pacific Affairs, and delivered by James P. Nach, Office of Philippine Affairs, before the Subcommittees on Asian and Pacific Affairs, House Foreign Affairs Committee, October 3, 1990. [1]

U.S. Policy Towards the Aquino Government

United States support for the Philippine Government remains firm and constant. It would be a great tragedy for the people of the Philippines and for U.S. interests in that country and in the region if democracy suffered another blow at the hands of coup plotters and self-seeking elements whose goal is to take power for themselves and turn back the clock. Military rule has no more chance than the discredited tenets of Communism to bring to the Philippines the success it needs in combatting poverty, corruption, and deficiencies in essential social services.

Democratic government is not the easy way, but it is the way the Filipino people have chosen for themselves, and they deserve our full and continued support in this effort to make democracy successful.

Our policy towards the Philippines is, therefore, clear and straightforward: We continue our unequivocal support for the democratically elected government of President Aquino, and we will continue to assist the Philippine Government and Filipino people. U.S. law is also clear. Assistance to any country whose democratically elected head of government is deposed by military coup or decree will be suspended. Those who are engaged in efforts to destabilize the constitutional government and who may be considering another coup attempt need to be aware that the U.S. Government is united in this view.

We have a unique relationship with the Philippines, one which has grown over the years into a mature relationship between two equal and sovereign nations with shared interests and aspirations. Our assistance takes many forms, befitting the complex relationship we have shared with the Philippines for nearly a century. Unfortunately, all too often some have sought to measure this relationship in terms of foreign assistance levels or military bases. Its true strength is based not on money, but on common values and common aspirations. Filipinos and Americans have worked together in many areas that are less well known but perhaps more indicative of these shared values. To mention only two, Filipino and American doctors pioneered together an oral rehydration formula which has saved the lives of millions of children all over the world; and it was Philippine and American initiatives that helped save so many of the boat people from Indochina over the last decade.

Mr. Chairman, the world is changing rapidly, and so too our relationship with the Philippines has been and must continue to change. We remain firmly linked as allies and partners, but the shape of the relationship needs to be adjusted from time to time. The Philippine-American Cooperation Talks — PACT, for short — that began in Manila last month are a reflection of this process. In these talks, we are discussing not only the security dimension but also the many other aspects of where we want our bilateral ties to lead.

This is a time for frankness among friends as well as vision about the future. It is an of opportunity to forge new relationships, new strengths, and new cooperation for the future. Success will be in terms of mutual benefits and cooperation in keeping with the shared history of our two nations.

The Philippines faces difficult challenges. While there is a role for the United States and other nations in encouraging and assisting reform and development, the greatest burden will be borne by the Filipino people. It is our firm conviction that democratic government remains the only acceptable course for the Philippines. Experience has shown that a democracy has the best chance of implementing lasting solutions to economic and social problems. As the Aquino Government continues its agenda, we hope to see continued change and acceleration of economic and military reforms designed to deal with the serious problems facing the country.

Philippine-American Cooperation Talks

Our goal in the Philippine-American Cooperation talks that began in Manila last month is to forge a new relationship with the Philippines consistent with our common interests. The existing 1947 Military Bases Agreement, amended many times, will be replaced. Although we do not share the Philippine Government's interpretation of termination timing, we agreed to enter into negotiations for a new agreement.

The first round of talks — our side is led by Special Negotiator Richard L. Armitage — ended September 22 with general agreement on the need for a long-term defense relationship and cooperation in non-defense areas. The GOP [Government of the Philippines] made clear its sovereignty concerns and expressed a desire to take full control of facilities at Clark Air Base by September 1991. The GOP gave no position on Subic Naval Base. We agreed to explore the possibility of cooperation in the areas of science and technology, health, education and cultural affairs, veterans affairs, and economic issues. Technical experts will exchange views prior to the next round of negotiations to be held soon in Manila. The first round of talks helped to examine the views and desires of both sides. There were no final decisions. With PACT discussions continuing, it is premature to comment on any specifics related to the talks, or to speculate on the outcome.

Since World War II, our use of military facilities in the Philippines has contributed to stability in one of the most economically and strategically important regions in the world. In a time of rapidly shifting world priorities and changing threats, the U.S. military presence has enhanced Philippine security and underscored our support for stability and economic growth throughout [the] East Asia and Pacific region. Training and maintenance of our Pacific air and naval forces are currently enhanced by the use of these facilities.

Our interest in the economic and democratic development of the Philippines is also served by the U.S. security presence. Our total contribution to the Philippine economy directly related to the bases is over a billion dollars annually, about evenly distributed between base-related military and economic assistance and spending by U.S. forces and personnel.

1 The complete transcript of the hearings will be published by the committee and will be available from the Superintendent of Documents, U.S. Government Printing Office, Washington, D.C. 20402.

Secretary Baker Meets with Vietnamese and Laotian Foreign Ministers

DEPARTMENT OF STATE STATEMENT, SEPTEMBER 27, 1990 [1]

Secretary Baker will meet with Vietnamese Deputy Prime Minister and Foreign Minister Nguyen co Thach during the Secretary's bilateral consultations in New York. The meeting is scheduled for September 29 at 9:30 a.m., and will last approximately thirty minutes.

The Secretary decided to take advantage of Deputy Prime Minister Thach's presence in New York to have this meeting for two reasons. First, he wanted to acknowledge the real progress made toward a settlement in Cambodia, including the acceptance of the framework agreement of the Five Permanent Members of the United Nations by the Cambodian factions and Vietnam. In that regard, he will want to discuss the successful formation of the Cambodian Supreme National Council and its early assumption of its seat in the U.N. Second, the Secretary wanted to press upon the Vietnamese our interest in accelerating activity on the POW/MIA issue.

This will be the fourth meeting between U.S. and Vietnamese officials since the Secretary's announcement on July 18 that we would begin a direct dialogue with Vietnam on Cambodia. It is also the highest level meeting to date. The last meeting took place on September 20 between Assistant Secretary Solomon and Vice Foreign Minister Le Mai. The normal channel for contacts between the U.S. and Vietnam will, however, continue to be between Deputy Assistant Secretary of State Kenneth Quinn and Vietnamese Permanent Representative to the United Nations Trinh Xuan Lang.

REMARKS BY SECRETARY BAKER AND FOREIGN MINISTER NGUYEN CO THACH OF VIETNAM AT BEGINNING OF MEETING, NEW YORK, SEPTEMBER 29, 1990 [2]

Q. Mr. Secretary, does this mean that the United States plans to open full diplomatic relations with Vietnam?

Secretary Baker. We're going to talk this morning about two issues,

primarily. The first issue is one — it's of extraordinary importance to me, to the President, I'm sure to the American people — and that's the issue: POWs and MIAs and Vietnam. And then we're going to spend the balance of our time on Cambodia.

Q. What else does Vietnam have to do about POWs and MIAs to satisfy the U.S.?

A. The pace — the Minister knows that the pace and the scope of our ability to move toward normalization of [relations with] Vietnam is going to depend upon further progress on the POW/MIA issue.

Q. But you're not ready to move toward normalization at this point?

A. We have to first talk, as I said, Ralph, we've got to first talk about the POW/MIA issue and we've got to talk in some depth and detail about Cambodia.

But let me say on Cambodia that I'm sure the Minister probably shares my pleasure at the recent developments respecting the possibility of a solution to the tragic circumstances of Cambodia. I think the Vietnamese Government has been taking some action to move that process forward just as the United States Government has.

Q. Mr. Minister, is Vietnam prepared to remove all of its military advisors from Cambodia now?

Foreign Minister Thach. We have promised to have international monitoring of our withdrawal.

Q. But are you prepared to withdraw all of your advisors?

A. We have withdrawn our forces, and we will withdraw all our advisors.

DEPARTMENT OF STATE STATEMENT, OCTOBER 2, 1990 [1]

Secretary Baker will meet on October 3 with Lao Foreign Minister Phoun Sipraseuth to discuss ways to continue the recent positive trend in bilateral relations. This will be the highest-level U.S.-Lao meeting since the current Lao Government came to power in 1975, though the two countries have maintained diplomatic relations. The Secretary looks forward to discussing recent Lao cooperation on the

POW/MIA and narcotics issues and to encouraging further progress in these important areas. He also expects the talks to cover Lao economic reforms as well as ongoing efforts to achieve a comprehensive political solution for Cambodia based on the recent agreement by the Five Permanent Members of the U.N. Security Council.

---

1 Provided to news correspondents by Department of State spokesman Margaret Tutwiler.

2 Department of State Press Release 156, October 29, 1990.

President's Speech to IMF and World Bank Annual Meeting

Remarks by President Bush at the Annual Meeting of the Boards of Governors of the International Monetary Fund [IMF] and World Bank Group, September 25, 1990. [1]

Thank you very much, and my special thanks to my good friend, our Secretary of the Treasury, Nick Brady, for those kind words and for the outstanding job that he's doing as our Secretary. To Chairman Saitoti and Mr. Camdessus and my old friend and former seatmate on the [House] Ways and Means Committee, Barber Conable, [2] it really is a pleasure to be back with you this year to welcome you all to Washington for this very important work. And it's a particular pleasure today to welcome the new members here from Bulgaria, the Czech and Slovak Republic, and Namibia and, of course, the special invitees from the Soviet Union. Your presence here reminds us all of how events of the past year are producing a new partnership of nations—a fundamental, indeed, inspiring change in the world's political and economic order.

The movement toward democratic rule, already strong throughout the 1980s, accelerated during what I call the Revolution of '89. The rights of the individual have been reaffirmed with greater adherence to the rule of law. The freedom to choose political leaders, and even political systems, has triumphed in countries that only a year ago were ruled by single party regimes. And hand in hand, new economic freedom has begun to emerge as well. Today leaders around the world are turning to market forces to meet the needs of their people, and of course—and I understand this—change has not come easily. But as I said last year at this same meeting: The jury is no longer out; history has decided.

And today the results of that global experiment are unmistakable. Today the consensus is this: Governments by themselves cannot deliver prosperity. Rather, the key to economic growth is setting individuals free—free to take risks, free to make choices, free to use their initiative and their abilities in the marketplace. We are seeing this, for example, in the restoration of private ownership in countries where the state once controlled every single aspect of economic life.

And for efficient production, private ownership is still the most powerful incentive known to man.

Matched by the rejuvenation of markets the ability to make individual economic choices is the fastest, more effective way to achieve and sustain broad-based economic growth. And that is why leaders everywhere are undertaking difficult economic reforms; building stronger, more versatile private sectors; improving efficiency; and making government decisionmaking much more rational.

That process takes time. Economic adjustment is often difficult. And in recent months, a new challenge has arisen which could hinder this process of change, and of course, I'm talking about Iraq's illegal and unprovoked aggression against the sovereign nation of Kuwait. Clearly, the greatest harm is to Kuwait and its people. When the Saudi border was opened, Kuwait's newest refugees brought fresh tales of cruelty and horror inflicted on the Kuwaiti people and foreign nationals as well by the occupying forces of Saddam Hussein.

Economic Effects of Gulf Crisis

And today other countries, already facing painful economic and political transformations, must now deal with additional hardships. Serious challenges have emerged for countries rocked by unpredictable tides in the flow of oil, trade, displaced workers and—God bless them—the refugees. This staggering burden, which is pressing upon these most seriously affected countries, calls for a generous response from the world community. Toward that end, we have already begun to mobilize financial resources for the front-line states to ensure responsible sharing among creditors.

The initial response to that effort has been impressive. Now, in order to transform commitments into concrete contributions, I am pleased to announce the formation of a Gulf crisis financial coordination group under the chairmanship of Secretary Nicholas Brady, our Secretary of the Treasury, with the aim of achieving effective, timely, and sustained financial support to these most seriously affected countries.

But let us not forget an even larger group of countries represented here will suffer from higher oil prices and other economic dislocations. While world attention has rightly focused on those countries closest to the situation and bearing the heaviest economic burden, I can tell you that the rest of the world is certainly not forgotten and never will be.

This gathering here of world financial leaders gives us an opportunity to discuss how we can work together to address the special financial burden of this crisis, and do so in a way that will sustain the dramatic worldwide transition to free markets. The IMF and World Bank, given their central role in the world economy, are key to helping all of us through this situation by providing a combination of policy advice and financial assistance. The political leadership of the U.N. must be matched by the economic leadership of the IMF and the World Bank.

Secretary Brady will be making some specific suggestions in his remarks for possible means of utilizing current IMF and World Bank programs more effectively. But let me say it again: We are determined not to allow the brutal behavior of one aggressor to undermine the historic process of democratic change or to derail the movement towards market-oriented economic systems.

Goals for the World Economy

Let me continue more broadly with a vision of the role of the United States and of a world economy we can all share.

First, we believe that the United States should contribute to economic stability and growth. And perhaps the greatest contribution that the United States can make to the health of the international economy is to get our own house in order. Our budget deficit must be brought under control and reduced.

And *second,* the United States is strongly committed to promoting development and growth in the newly emerging democracies of Latin America, Central and Eastern Europe, Africa, and Asia. We're working in all four regions to ease debt burdens under the Brady plan. In this hemisphere, where debt overhang holds back progress—impedes progress—we announced the Enterprise for the Americas Initiative to promote economic growth by expanding trade and investment, to reduce debt owed to the United States Government, and to provide funds for needed local environmental projects. In Eastern Europe, where massive restructuring is needed, we are working with other nations to provide billions of dollars in assistance to the newly emerging democracies. And in Africa, where undevelopment hangs on so stubbornly, many of the lowest income countries have already benefitted from reductions in debt owed to the United States.

Third, the United States is committed to the central role of the IMF and World Bank in helping bring about economic reforms. Reform efforts can only be successful if countries carry through on their responsibilities; and that means regulatory reform and privatization, sound macroeconomic and structural policies, and open borders for trade and investment.

This is why your work here in Washington this week is so important. For more than 40 years, the Fund and the Bank have quietly been enlisting the talents and the energies of the developed and developing world in a global struggle against poverty. And today, in a world where ideology no longer confronts and big power blocs no longer divide, the Bank and the Fund have become paradigms of international cooperation. Indeed, we especially appreciate your efforts in carrying out a study of the Soviet economy that is unprecedented in its scope. This study will produce recommendations for economic, financial, and structural reform.

As the coming week unfolds, part of your task will also be to plan for the future of your two great institutions. And I pledge the continued support of the United States for a World Bank and IMF, which so clearly advance our common struggle to improve the quality of life for all people everywhere. For this reason, we strongly support the IMF quota increase and the strengthening of the IMF arrears policy. And we would also like to challenge both institutions to intensify their focus on building dynamic private sectors in member countries, one of the most important stimulants for energizing these new market economies.

And we would also ask the World Bank to place a high priority in three other issues vital to sustain growth. First

is protecting the environment. As I said here last year, environmental destruction knows no borders. Second, eradicating poverty must continue to be a central mission of the Bank. And third, we strongly support greater efforts to integrate women into the development process.

The Uruguay Round

Finally, as we plan for the future, we must work together for success in another important international economic institution: the GATT [General Agreement on Tariffs and Trade]. As we meet today, less than 70 days remain in the four-year Uruguay Round of global trade talks. Lasting reform is essential for developed and developing countries alike, and it's the key to a successful round which establishes new rules and opportunities for all countries. These negotiations are one of the world's greatest economic opportunities of the decade, but much remains to be done.

The round is not just a trade issue: it is a growth issue. And it's not just an exercise for bureaucrats in Geneva. The trade talks are the last train leaving the station, and countries throughout the world must jump aboard. It can be the engine of economic growth that carries us into the 21st century.

The round promises to remove barriers in four crucial areas, areas untouched in previous rounds: services, investment, intellectual property, and agriculture. As a matter of fact, agriculture reform remains a major stumbling block. Indeed, it threatens to bring down the rest of the round. We must let farmers compete with farmers, instead of farmers competing with the deep pockets of government treasuries. We need a successful resolution of the agricultural issues if we are to have an agreement.

If countries around the globe don't muster the political courage to face these tough issues in the time remaining, we will forfeit new markets for our businesses, impose higher prices on our consumers, and forgo new jobs and higher incomes for workers in all countries. Worst of all, we will endanger a vital, proven framework of international cooperation. A collapse of the round will inevitably encourage increased protectionist pressure and political instability; and that, frankly, is something that we can ill afford as we forge a new

partnership of nations against aggression in the Persian Gulf.

I urge you to work actively within your governments to ensure success, and I urge my counterparts around the world—as we did at the Houston Economic Summit—to instruct your negotiators to bring all the components of the Uruguay Round to a successful conclusion by December.

In all these efforts, there is so much at stake. Almost 35 years ago, President Eisenhower first appeared at an IMF-World Bank meeting, and he spoke of the lessons that he learned while waging a war that brought together so many different soldiers from so many different lands. Ike noted, as I do now, that there were people in the audience who were our allies in that grand effort. And he said: "We early found one thing. Without the heart, without the enthusiasm for the cause in which we were working, no cooperation was possible. With that enthusiasm, subordinating all else to the advancement of the cause, cooperation was easy."

As the unity of the nations has demonstrated in the past two months, the worldwide enthusiasm for today's noble cause, the cause I've described as a new partnership of nations, is not only unprecedented but truly remarkable. And I urge you to seize that enthusiasm in your meetings this week, to forge the new levels of cooperation needed to succeed.

Thank you very much for coming to Washington, D.C. I hope you feel welcome, because you are. Good luck this week in the meetings ahead, and God speed you in your travels home. Thank you all very, very much.

1 Text from Weekly Compilation of Presidential Documents of October 1, 1990.
2. George Saitoti, Chairman of the International Monetary Fund and the World Bank Group; Michel Camdessus, Managing Director and Chairman of the Executive Board of the International Monetary Fund; and Barber B. Conable, President of the World Bank Group.

U.S. Deplores Violence in Jerusalem

SECRETARY BAKER'S REMARKS (PRESS CONFERENCE EXCERPT), OCTOBER 8, 1990 [1]

Q: Mr. Secretary—Mr. Baker—do you have any response to today's violence in the Occupied Territories?

A. We don't have all of the details yet about that violence. But this tragic loss of life is obviously a cause for great sadness. Each side is pointing to provocation by the other. We do not see any linkage to the Gulf situation. We will continue to work on the peace process, but we do not think that that has anything to do with the issue of reversing Iraq's aggression.

As I said, we really do not have, as we sit here now, all of the facts. But I do think it's fair to say that Israel needs to be better prepared and to exercise restraint in handling disturbances of this nature. And, of course, our condolences go out to all of the families of the victims.

REMARKS BY PRESIDENT BUSH (PRESS CONFERENCE EXCERPT), OCTOBER 9, 1990 [2]

Q. Mr. President, yesterday Israeli forces used the live ammunition to put down demonstrations in Israel, killing 19 Palestinians. Today Saddam Hussein is using that incident in an attempt to rally Arab support against Israel and, essentially, against the United States in the region. Do you think this incident could create a crack in the alliance against Iraq? And what's your reaction to the incident?

A. Well, I don't think it could do that. But, look, let me just express my strong feelings about this. First, my sorrow at this tragedy. It is particularly saddening, given the sanctity of the holy places and observances there, that violence shattered all of this. And I want to echo what [Secretary of State] Jim Baker said earlier: that Israeli security forces need to be better prepared for such situations, need to act with greater restraint, particularly when it comes to the use of deadly force. And at this point, what is needed most of all is calm on all sides.

I don't think I need to say this, but let me just state that we want to see the longstanding policy of maintaining open access to the holy places preserved, tempered only by mutual respect for people of other faiths. So, I am very, very saddened by this needless loss of life, and I would call on all for restraint. The action will shift to the United Nations now.

To the other part of your question, Jim [Jim Miklaszewski, NBC News], there's no relationship here. Saddam Hussein has tried to, from the very beginning, justify the illegal invasion of Kuwait by trying to tie it in to the Palestine question. And that is not working. The Arab world is almost united against him. If he tries now to use this unfortunate incident to link the two questions, I don't think that will be successful. And certainly, I will be doing what I can to see that it is not successful.

Having said that, I hope nobody questions our interest in seeing a solution to the Palestine question, to the implementation of the Security Council resolutions. And that's what Jim Baker has been working so hard on for such a long time. But let's separate out this violence and say: We deplore it and it must not happen, and regret it—the loss of life—for everybody.

U.N. SECURITY COUNCIL RESOLUTION 672, OCTOBER 12, 1990 [3]

The Security Council,

Recalling its resolutions 476 (1980) and 478 (1990),

Reaffirming that a just and lasting solution to the Arab-Israeli conflict must be based on its resolutions 242 (1967) and 338 (1973) through an active negotiating process which takes into account the right to security for all States in the region, including Israel, as well as the legitimate political rights of the Palestinian people,

Taking into consideration the statement of the Secretary-General relative to the purposes of the mission he is sending to the region and conveyed to the Council by the President on 12 October 1990,

1. Expresses alarm at the violence which took place on 8 October at the Al Haram Al Shareef and other Holy Places of Jerusalem resulting in over twenty Palestinian deaths and to the injury of more than one hundred and fifty people, including Palestinian civilians and innocent worshippers,

2. Condemns especially the acts of violence committed by the Israeli security forces resulting in injuries and loss of human life,

3. Calls upon Israel, the occupying Power, to abide scrupulously by its legal obligations and responsibilities under the Fourth Geneva Convention, which is applicable to all the territories occupied by Israel since 1967;

4. Requests, in connection with the decision of the Secretary-General to send a mission to the region, which the Council welcomes, that he submit a report to it before the end of October 1990 containing his findings and conclusions and that he use as appropriate all of the resources of the United Nations in the region in carrying out the mission.

STATEMENT TO THE SECURITY COUNCIL OF AMBASSADOR THOMAS R. PICKERING, U. S. PERMANENT REPRESENTATIVE TO THE UNITED NATIONS, OCTOBER 12, 1990 [4]

Mr. President, my Government supports this resolution on the tragic event which occurred in Jerusalem on October 8. My government extends its condolences to the families and friends of those many innocent persons and worshippers who were victims of violence on that sad day.

This is an incident which never should have happened. The Security Council tonight grieves for those lost and injured, condemns the acts of violence—both provocative and reactive—and reaffirms the obligations and responsibilities conferred upon the occupying power by the Fourth Geneva Convention. Moreover, we recall and reaffirm—properly and urgently I might add—that a just and lasting solution to the Arab-Israeli conflict must be based on Security Council Resolutions 242 and 338.

Mr. President, my Government is dedicated to doing whatever it can to bring the parties closer to a negotiated peace. We want to be clear for the record that this resolution, however, should not be misinterpreted: the Council's action tonight does not empower it to address any subject beyond the matters directly contained in this resolution. Most obviously and certainly this resolution makes clear it does not address in any way the status of the Middle East peace process nor does it change in any way the role of the United Nations in that regard. We expect the Secretary-General's mission to examine the circumstances of the October 8 incident and report back. We look forward to reviewing that report.

On behalf of the United States and in accordance with this resolution I would like to call on all sides to exercise restraint in words and actions so that calm can be restored and the holy places of all faiths respected. Thank you, Mr. President.

SECRETARY BAKER'S REMARKS (PRESS CONFERENCE EXCERPTS), OCTOBER 16, 1990 [5]

Q. Mr. Secretary, last June the U.S. ceased its discourse with the PLO, concluding that the PLO had not fulfilled its commitment renouncing terrorism. Is there any evidence the State Department has found of PLO involvement in the disorders on the West Bank and in Jerusalem, especially the melee last Monday in which Jewish worshipers were injured and 21 Palestinians were killed?

A. There is no evidence that I am aware of, Barry, that we now have, although as you know the investigation of this incident has just begun by the Israeli Government itself. The United Nations Security Council, as you are aware, has passed a resolution asking that a mission from the Secretary-General go to the region and report back. There is, again, as you know, to say the least, some question about whether that mission will take place.

Q. How do you feel, sir — may I follow up quickly — about Israel's reluctance to give more than just tourist attention to the U.N. investigators?

A. We are hopeful that the Israeli Government will make it possible for the Secretary-General's team to complete its mission. I think our reaction — the spokesman characterized it for you yesterday, our reaction to the initial response of the Israeli Cabinet.

Let me simply say that this resolution is one that the United States would have voted for had there been no Iraq-Kuwait issue or crisis because we were and remain deeply disturbed by the killings that took place. At the same time, we were also disturbed by the violence against innocent worshipers at the Western Wall. We don't think there's

any excuse for that either. The resolution does refer to the attacks on innocent worshipers.

* * *

Q. Israel again. How far is the U.S. willing to push Israel to follow the U.N. resolutions? There are some suggestions in the Arab world that unless you push as hard as you're pushing against Saddam Hussein, there's a double standard here.

A. Well, you know, we've made clear, I think, our view that it would be good if Israel would admit the Secretary-General's representative. We've said that it is only in that way, we think, that Israel will be able to make its case to the Secretary-General's mission, and not to admit the mission, we think, moves Israel and moves our effort in the Gulf in the wrong direction. We've made that very clear.

* * *

Q. Basically, how did we get to this point in the U.S.-Israeli relationship? First of all, obviously the tension we see today isn't the result of this single incident.

A. Well, Tom, you're the expert. You wrote the book on the region. I'm nowhere near —

Q. You're the Secretary. (Laughter)

A. — as well equipped to answer that question as you are.

But let me go back to the answer I gave you a minute ago on this question of the U.N. Security Council resolution. I said that the United States would have voted for this resolution if there had been no Gulf crisis. And the suggestion that somehow we are voting to condemn the killings that took place — the killing of 20 people and the injuring of some 150 through live fire, simply because we want to maintain a coalition on the Gulf is not — it's not accurate to suggest that.

Do we want to maintain the coalition on the Gulf? Yes.

Do we think it is appropriate that world attention be focused upon the rape of Kuwait? Yes.

Do we think it's inappropriate to link that with the Arab-Israeli problem? Yes.

Have we said for the full 20 months that we've been in office that we think it's extraordinarily important that there be a peace process? Yes.

Would we like to see a peace process develop? You bet.

Do we think that is in the interests of the United States and Israel? Yes, we do.

And we stand ready, willing and able to work on the development of a peace process.

Q. Mr. Secretary, yesterday you were quoted in the Israeli press as saying that if Israel does not comply with the latest U.N. resolution and allow this U.N. team in, it would be — that some would compare them to Saddam Hussein's not abiding by U.N. resolutions.

First of all, do you stand by those words? And, second of all, are you concerned that the Israelis, whom you had asked to remain silent when this crisis first began, might now feel that the deal is off and begin to be more public?

A. Well, let me say — I've said a number of times since the Gulf crisis started that we are very appreciative of the approach that was taken by the Israeli government — that is, the low profile approach that they took to this issue. And I would hope, and we would hope, that we would be able to get back to that.

And that was one of the points of my message to the Foreign Minister that I sent before the Israeli Cabinet had met, because I wanted to tell the Foreign Minister personally that I thought that it was important that the Secretary-General's mission be allowed to come to Israel, just as a similar mission was allowed to come in June of this year.

I do not stand by the quote as you have expressed it, because it is not accurate. What I said was, "I fear that some will try to make that comparison." I said, "quite unjustifiably," or something like that — words to that effect — that it would be unfair and unjustified. But that I would worry that that argument would be made in New York if the Secretary-General is not — his mission is not permitted to come to Israel.

EXCERPT FROM SPEECH BY PRIME MINISTER YITZHAK SHAMIR OF ISRAEL, OCTOBER 18, 1990 [6]

These are not easy days for Israel. We are still in the midst of the blessed mass immigration; and the ire of the Gulf Crisis, which has pushed the entire Middle East into an atmosphere filled with danger and tension, has been sprung upon us.

From the outset of the crisis, the State of Israel, of its own free will and without external pressure or demands, adopted a balanced and responsible policy, while strictly ensuring its future security, and in an effort not to be dragged into disputes which do not concern it. The Iraqi tyrant, who is trying for the second time to buy with rivers of blood the leadership of the Arab world, desires at any cost, to pull us into the whirlpool in order to grant the conflict between Iraq and nearly the entire civilized world, the character of an Israeli-Arab conflict. We have no interest in assisting him in carrying out his scheme and we welcome the establishment of a broad coalition against the tendencies of evil and extreme fanaticism. Fate has conspired these very days, before the crisis reached its peak, when the bloody and very painful incident on the Temple Mount fell upon us like a blow during the Succot holiday in Jerusalem. We have expressed our sorrow at the loss of life. We have no interest in bloodshed, not of Arabs, nor of Jews.

But hostile elements have succeeded, through wild hateful incitement and zealotry known to us all, in pushing the Arab-Israeli dispute into the flow of events in the region. And suddenly, an attempt was made to transform the anti-Iraqi coalition into an anti-Israeli coalition, whose objective was to forfeit the Jewish people of its sovereignty over the holy city of Jerusalem, the capital of Israel, and to harm the very heart of the Jewish-Israeli entity.

The primary element within the camp fighting against evil in the Middle East, made a grave error when it tried to purchase the unity of the camp by humiliating and endangering the State of Israel.

We desire no quarrel with the U.S. We do not welcome disputes. Nobody in Israel wants to cut the ties of alliance and friendship which bind the largest democracy in the world with the only democracy in the Middle East.

But in my opinion, there is no way Israel can sign, with its own hands, a verdict of humiliating surrender and forfeit its sovereignty over Jerusalem.

The wording of the latest Security Council resolution, which ignores the attack on hundreds of Jewish pilgrims who gathered to celebrate their festival at the Western Wall on the Temple Mount, the remnant of our holiest site, shocked all Jewish hearts and deeply hurt our feelings.

I would like to hope that the world has learnt something as a result of the lamentable and futile bloodshed, from which someone succeeded in gaining political fortune.

We call upon our friends to turn over this miserable page, to erase it, and to refocus on the central issue of destroying the terrible danger of bloody fanaticism which is raging in the region.

When the eruption of evil is contained, and the criminals are brought to justice, the region will be wiser, and many will realize that the only road to coexistence is through sincere peace negotiations. Only then will blessings come to this part of the world which is full of danger and opportunity. Until peace comes, and until a halt is put to tendencies of evil and violence, we, in Israel, will continue with perseverance and national unity to work toward realizing our main nationalist objectives: to absorb immigration, to develop the economy, to heal agriculture, to expand industry, and more than all, to consolidate our security — all this within an environment of love of Israel and a growing sense of Jewish solidarity.

And to ourselves we say: let us view the balance of forces in the war against us — the Arab world is fragmented and disunited. The PLO is paralyzed, deteriorated and embarrassed. After the halt in the famous U.S. dialogue its prestige is deteriorating. After three years, the intifada has brought nothing to the Arabs and those fighting against us. They have lost the support of the Communist world which constituted a large source of their strength. Israel is progressing in all spheres, and I do not need to elaborate.

Only irrational and unnecessary developments can assist our enemies and alter this positive balance: a harsh internal war within our country, for what? About marginal inconsequential matters which border on gossip and detective novels?

Or a U.S. and Western diversion from cooperation with democratic and peace-loving forces in the world and in the region — and the granting of aid to destructive elements, terrorists and warmongers.

We must hope that positive and logical considerations in the east and west as well as within the Arab world prevail, paving the way for true peace negotiations between Israel, which is gaining in strength, and those elements in the Arab environment which tend

toward peace. Peace will come as a result of negotiations.

U. N. SECURITY COUNCIL RESOLUTION 673, OCTOBER 24, 1990 [3]

The Security Council,

Reaffirming the obligations of Member States under the United Nations Charter,

Reaffirming also its resolution 672 (1990),

Having been briefed by the Secretary-General on 19 October 1990,

Expressing alarm at the rejection of Security Council resolution 672 (1990) by the Israeli Government, and its refusal to accept the mission of the Secretary-General,

Taking into consideration the statement of the Secretary-General relative to the purpose of the mission he is sending to the region and conveyed to the Council by the President on 12 October 1990,

Gravely concerned at the continued deterioration of the situation in the occupied territories,

1. Deplores the refusal of the Israeli Government to receive the mission of the Secretary-General to the region;

2. Urges the Israeli Government to reconsider its decision and insists that it comply fully with resolution 672 (1990) and to permit the mission of the Secretary-General to proceed in keeping with its purpose;

3. Requests the Secretary-General to submit to the Council the report requested in resolution 672 (1990);

4. Affirms its determination to give full and expeditious consideration to the report.

---

1 Department of State Press Release 167, October 10, 1990.

2 Text from Weekly Compilation of Presidential Documents of October 15, 1990.

3 Text provided by United Nations Information Center, Washingtion.

4 U.S. Mission to the United Nations Press Release 79(90), October 12, 1990.

5 Department of State Press Release 164, October 16, 1990.

6 Embassy of Israel (Washington) Background Paper, "Shamir's Address Before the Farmers Association," October 19, 1990.

President Establishes 1991 Refugee Admission Levels

Memorandum for the United States Coordinator for Refugee Affairs, October 12, 1990. [1]

In accordance with section 207 of the Immigration and Nationality Act ("the Act") (8 U.S.C. 1157), and after appropriate consultation with the Congress, I hereby make the following determinations and authorize the following actions:

a. The admission of up to 131,000 refugees to the United States during FY 1991 is justified by humanitarian concerns or is otherwise in the national interest, provided however, that this number shall be understood as including persons admitted to the United States during FY 1991 with Federal refugee resettlement assistance under the Amerasian admissions program, as provided in paragraph (b) below.

Ten thousand of these admissions numbers shall be set aside for private sector admissions initiatives, and may be used for any region. The admission of refugees using these numbers shall be contingent upon the availability of private sector funding sufficient to cover the reasonable costs of such admissions.

b. The 131,000 admissions shall be allocated among refugees of special humanitarian concern to the United States as described in the documentation presented to the Congress during the consultations that preceded this determination and in accordance with the following regional allocations; provided, however, that the number allocated to the East Asia region shall include the number of persons admitted to the United States during FY 1991 with Federal refugee resettlement assistance under section 584 of the Foreign Operations, Export Financing, and Related Programs Appropriations Act of 1988, as contained in section 101(e) of Public Law 100-202 (Amerasians and their family members):

Africa	4,900
East Asia	52,000
Soviet Union	50,000
Eastern Europe	5,000
Near East/South Asia	6,000
Latin America/Caribbean	3,100
Not Designated	10,000 [2]

Utilization of the 121,000 federally funded admissions numbers shall be limited by such public and private funds as shall be available to the Department of State and the Department of Health and Human Services for refugee and Amerasian admissions in FY 1991. You are hereby authorized and directed to so advise the judiciary committees of the Congress.

Unused admissions numbers allocated to a particular region within the 121,000 federally funded ceiling may be transferred to one or more other regions if there is an overriding need for greater numbers for the region or regions to which the numbers are being transferred. You are hereby authorized and directed to consult with the judiciary committees of the Congress prior to any such reallocation.

The 10,000 privately funded admissions not designated for any country or region may be used for refugees of special humanitarian concern to the United States in any region of the world at any time during the fiscal year. You are hereby authorized and directed to notify the judiciary committees of the Congress in advance of the intended use of these numbers.

An additional 5,000 refugee admissions numbers shall be made available during FY 1991 for the adjustment to permanent resident status under section 209(b) of the Act (8 U.S.C. 1159[b]) of aliens who have been granted asylum in the United States under section 208 of the Act (8 U.S.C. 1158), as this is justified by humanitarian concerns or is otherwise in the national interest.

In accordance with section 101(a)(42) of the Act (8 U.S.C. 1101(a)(42)), I also specify, after appropriate consultation with the Congress, that the following persons may, if otherwise qualified, be considered refugees for the purpose of admission to the United States while still within their countries of nationality or habitual residence:

a. Persons in Vietnam and Laos who have past or present ties to the United States or who have been or currently are in reeducation camps in Vietnam or seminar camps in Laos, and their accompanying family members.

b. Present and former political prisoners, persons in imminent danger of loss of life, and other persons of compelling concern to the United States in countries of Latin America and the Caribbean, and their accompanying family members.

c. Persons in Cuba who are (1) in immediate danger of loss of life and for whom there appears to be no alternative to resettlement in the United States, or (2) are of compelling concern to the United States, such as former or present political prisoners, dissidents, or human rights and religious activists, or (3) were employed by the United States Government for at least one year prior to the claim for refugee status; and their accompanying family members.

d. Persons in the Soviet Union and Romania.

You are hereby authorized and directed to report this determination to the Congress immediately and to arrange for its publication in the *Federal Register*.

George Bush
cc: The Secretary of State
The Attorney General
The Secretary of Health and Human Services

---

1 Presidential Determination No. 91-3. Text from Weekly Compilation of Presidential Documents of October 22, 1990.

2 Funded by the private sector.

President Bush: A New Partnership of Nations

President's address before the 45th Session of the U. N. General Assembly, New York, October 1, 1990. [1]

Mr. Secretary-General, distinguished delegates to the United Nations, it is really a great privilege to greet you today as we begin what marks a new and historic session of the General Assembly. My congratulations to the Honorable Guido de Marco on your election, sir, as President of the General Assembly. And on a personal note, I want to say that, having witnessed the unprecedented unity and cooperation of the past two months, that I have never been prouder to have once served within your ranks and never been prouder that the United States is the host country for the United Nations.

The Vision of San Francisco

Forty-five years ago, while the fires of an epic war still raged across two oceans and two continents, a small group of men and women began a search for hope amid the ruins. And they gathered in San Francisco, stepping back from the haze and horror, to try to shape a new structure that might support an ancient dream. Intensely idealistic and yet tempered by war, they sought to build a new kind of bridge: a bridge between nations, a bridge that might help carry humankind from its darkest hour to its brightest day.

The founding of the United Nations embodied our deepest hopes for a peaceful world, and during the past year, we've come closer than ever before to realizing those hopes. We've seen a century sundered by barbed threats and barbed wire give way to a new era of peace and competition and freedom.

The Revolution of '89 swept the world almost with a life of its own, carried by a new breeze of freedom. It transformed the political climate from Central Europe to Central America and touched almost every corner of the globe. That breeze has been sustained by a now almost universal recognition of a simple, fundamental truth: The human spirit cannot be locked up forever. The truth is, people everywhere are motivated in much the same ways. And people everywhere want much the same

things: the chance to live a life of purpose, the chance to choose a life in which they and their children can learn and grow healthy, worship freely, and prosper through the work of their hands and their hearts and their minds. We're not talking about the power of nations but the power of individuals, the power to choose, the power to risk, the power to succeed.

This is a new and different world. Not since 1945 have we seen the real possibility of using the United Nations as it was designed: as a center for international collective security.

The changes in the Soviet Union have been critical to the emergence of a stronger United Nations. The U.S.-Soviet relationship is finally beyond containment and confrontation, and now we seek to fulfill the promise of mutually shared understanding. The long twilight struggle that for 45 years has divided Europe, our two nations, and much of the world has come to an end.

Much has changed over the last two years. The Soviet Union has taken many dramatic and important steps to participate fully in the community of nations. And when the Soviet Union agreed with so many of us here in the United Nations to condemn the aggression of Iraq, there could be no doubt — no doubt then — that we had, indeed, put four decades of history behind us.

We are hopeful that the machinery of the United Nations will no longer be frozen by the divisions that plagued us during the Cold War, that at last — long last — we can build new bridges and tear down old walls, that at long last we will be able to build a new world based on an event for which we have all hoped: an end to the Cold War.

Two days from now, the world will be watching when the Cold War is formally buried in Berlin. And in this time of testing, a fundamental question must be asked, a question not for any one nation but for the United Nations. And the question is this: Can we work together in a new partnership of nations? Can the collective strength of the world community, expressed by the United Nations, unite to deter and defeat aggression? Because the Cold War's battle of ideas is not the last epic battle of this century.

The Guns of August 1990

Two months ago, in the waning weeks of one of history's most hopeful summers, the vast, still beauty of the peaceful Kuwaiti desert was fouled by the stench of diesel and the roar of steel tanks. Once again the sound of distant thunder echoed across a cloudless sky, and once again the world awoke to face the guns of August.

But this time, the world was ready. The United Nations Security Council's resolute response to Iraq's unprovoked aggression has been without precedent. Since the invasion on August 2nd, the Council has passed eight major resolutions setting the terms for a solution to the crisis.

The Iraqi regime has yet to face the facts, but as I said last month, the annexation of Kuwait will not be permitted to stand. And this is not simply the view of the United States; it is the view of every Kuwaiti, the Arab League, the United Nations. Iraq's leaders should listen: It is Iraq against the world.

Let me take this opportunity to make the policy of my government clear. The United States supports the use of sanctions to compel Iraq's leaders to withdraw immediately and without condition from Kuwait. We also support the provision of medicine and food for humanitarian purposes, so long as distribution can be properly monitored. Our quarrel is not with the people of Iraq. We do not wish for them to suffer. The world's quarrel is with the dictator who ordered that invasion.

Along with others, we have dispatched military forces to the region to enforce sanctions, to deter and, if need be, defend against further aggression. And we seek no advantage for ourselves, nor do we seek to maintain our military forces in Saudi Arabia for one day longer than is necessary. U.S. forces were sent at the request of the Saudi Government, and the American people and this President want every single American soldier brought home as soon as this mission is completed.

Let me also emphasize that all of us here at the U.N. hope that military force will never be used. We seek a peaceful outcome, a diplomatic outcome. And one more thing: In the aftermath of Iraq's unconditional departure from Kuwait, I truly believe there may be opportunities for Iraq and Kuwait to settle their differences permanently, for the states of the Gulf themselves to build new arrangements for stability, and for all the states and the peoples of the region to settle the conflicts that divide the Arabs from Israel.

But the world's key task — now, first and always — must be to demonstrate that aggression will not be tolerated or rewarded. Through the U.N. Security Council, Iraq has been fairly judged by a jury of its peers, the very nations of the Earth. Today the regime stands isolated and out of step with the times, separated from the civilized world not by space but by centuries.

Iraq's unprovoked aggression is a throwback to another era, a dark relic from a dark time. It has plundered Kuwait. It has terrorized innocent civilians. It has held even diplomats hostage. Iraq and its leaders must be held liable for these crimes of abuse and destruction. But this outrageous disregard for basic human rights does not come as a total surprise. Thousands of Iraqis have been executed on political and religious grounds, and even more through a genocidal poison gas war waged against Iraq's own Kurdish villagers.

Eliminating Chemical Weapons

As a world community, we must act not only to deter the use of inhumane weapons like mustard and nerve gas but to eliminate the weapons entirely. And that is why, one year ago, I came to the General Assembly with new proposals to banish these terrible weapons from the face of the Earth. I promised that the United States would destroy over 98 percent of its stockpile in the first eight years of a chemical weapons ban treaty, and 100 percent — all of them — in ten years, if all nations with chemical capabilities, chemical weapons, signed the treaty. We've stood by those promises. In June the United States and the Soviet Union signed a landmark agreement to halt production and to destroy the vast majority of our stockpiles. Today U.S. chemical weapons are being destroyed.

But time is running out. This isn't merely a bilateral concern. The Gulf crisis proves how important it is to act together, and to act now, to conclude an absolute, worldwide ban on these weapons. We must also redouble our efforts to stem the spread of nuclear

weapons, biological weapons, and the ballistic missiles that can rain destruction upon distant peoples.

A New World Order

The United Nations can help bring about a new day, a day when these kinds of terrible weapons and the terrible despots who would use them are both a thing of the past. It is in our hands to leave these dark machines behind, in the Dark Ages where they belong, and to press forward to cap a historic movement towards a new world order and a long era of peace.

We must join together in a new compact...to bring the United Nations into the 21st century, and I call today for a major long-term effort to do so.

We have a vision of a new partnership of nations that transcends the Cold War: a partnership based on consultation, cooperation, and collective action, especially through international and regional organizations; a partnership united by principle and the rule of law and supported by an equitable sharing of both cost and commitment; a partnership whose goals are to increase democracy, increase prosperity, increase the peace, and reduce arms.

And as we look to the future, the calendar offers up a convenient milestone, a signpost, by which to measure our progress as a community of nations. The year 2000 marks a turning point, beginning not only the turn of the decade, not only the turn of the century, but also the turn of the millennium. And ten years from now, as the 55th session of the General Assembly begins, you will again find many of us in this hall, hair a bit more gray perhaps, maybe a little less spring in our walk; but you will not find us with any less hope or idealism or any less confidence in the ultimate triumph of mankind.

I see a world of open borders, open trade and, most importantly, open minds; a world that celebrates the common heritage that belongs to all the world's people, taking pride not just in hometown or homeland but in humanity itself. I see a world touched by a spirit like that of the Olympics, based not on

competition that's driven by fear but sought out of joy and exhilaration and a true quest for excellence. And I see a world where democracy continues to win new friends and convert old foes and where the Americas — North, Central, and South — can provide a model for the future of all humankind: the world's first completely democratic hemisphere. And I see a world building on the emerging new model of European unity, not just Europe but the whole world whole and free.

This is precisely why the present aggression in the Gulf is a menace not only to one region's security but to the entire world's vision of our future. It threatens to turn the dream of a new international order into a grim nightmare of anarchy in which the law of the jungle supplants the law of nations. And that's why the United Nations reacted with such historic unity and resolve. And that's why this challenge is a test that we cannot afford to fail. I am confident we will prevail. Success, too, will have lasting consequences: reinforcing civilized standards of international conduct, setting a new precedent in international cooperation, brightening the prospects for our vision of the future.

A New and Vital Role for the U.N.

There are ten more years until this century is out, ten more years to put the struggles of the 20th century permanently behind us, ten more years to help launch a new partnership of nations. And throughout those ten years, and beginning now, the United Nations has a new and vital role in building towards that partnership. Last year's General Assembly showed how we can make greater progress toward a more pragmatic and successful United Nations. And for the first time, the U.N. Security Council is beginning to work as it was designed to work. And now is the time to set aside old and counterproductive debates and procedures and controversies and resolutions. It's time to replace polemic attacks with pragmatic action.

And we've shown that the U.N. can count on the collective strength of the international community. We've shown that the U.N. can rise to the challenge of aggression just as its founders hoped that it would. And now is the time of testing. And we must also show that the United Nations is the place to build international support and consensus for meeting the other challenges we face.

The world remains a dangerous place; and our security and well-being often depends, in part, on events occurring far away. We need serious international cooperative efforts to make headway on the threats to the environment, on terrorism, on managing the debt burden, on fighting the scourge of international drug trafficking, and on refugees, and peacekeeping efforts around the world.

But the world also remains a hopeful place. Calls for democracy and human rights are being reborn everywhere, and these calls are an expression of support for the values enshrined in the United Nations Charter. They encourage our hopes for a more stable, more peaceful, more prosperous world.

Free elections are the foundation of democratic government and can produce dramatic successes, as we have seen in Namibia and Nicaragua. And the time has come to structure the U.N. role in such efforts more formally. And so, today I propose that the U.N. establish a Special Coordinator for Electoral Assistance, to be assisted by a U.N. Electoral Commission comprised of distinguished experts from around the world.

As with free elections, we also believe that universal U.N. membership for all states is central to the future of this organization and to this new partnership we've discussed. In support of this principle and in conjunction with U.N. efforts to reduce regional tensions, the United States fully supports U.N. membership for the Republic of Korea. We do so without prejudice to the ultimate objective of reunification of the Korean Peninsula and without opposition to simultaneous membership for the Democratic People's Republic of Korea.

Building on these and other initiatives, we must join together in a new compact — all of us — to bring the United Nations into the 21st century, and I call today for a major long-term effort to do so. We should build on the success — the admirable success — of our distinguished Secretary-General, my longtime friend and yours, my longtime colleague I might also say, Javier Perez de Cuellar. We should strive for greater effectiveness and efficiency of the United Nations.

The United States is committed to playing its part, helping to maintain global security, promoting democracy and prosperity. And my administration

is fully committed to supporting the United Nations and to paying what we are obliged to pay by our commitment to the Charter. International peace and security, and international freedom and prosperity, require no less.

The world must know and understand: From this hour, from this day, from this hall, we step forth with a new sense of purpose, a new sense of possibilities. We stand together, prepared to swim upstream, to march uphill, to tackle the tough challenges as they come not only as the United Nations but as the nations of the world united.

And so, let it be said of the final decade of the 20th century: This was a

time when humankind came into its own, when we emerged from the grit and the smoke of the industrial age to bring about a revolution of the spirit and the mind and began a journey into a new day, a new age, and a new partnership of nations.

The U.N. is now fulfilling its promise as the world's parliament of peace. And I congratulate you. I support you. And I wish you Godspeed in the challenges ahead.

---

1 Text from Weekly Compilation of Presidential Documents of October 8, 1990.

Joint U.S.-Soviet Statement: Responsibility for Peace and Security in a Changing World

Released by the United States and the Soviet Union in New York, October 3, 1990. [1]

The 45th session of the United Nations General Assembly is taking place amidst the most profound changes in international affairs that have occurred since the Second World War. The confrontational nature of relations between East and West is giving way to a cooperative relationship and partnership. The U.N. is fast becoming a real center for agreed common actions and the Security Council is reestablishing its crucial role in the maintenance of international security, peaceful settlement of disputes, and prevention of conflicts. Yet there remain many challenges to meet and problems to solve on the way to a peaceful and prosperous future.

Reaffirming the resolution presented last year by the United States and Soviet Union and unanimously adopted by the U.N. General Assembly, our two countries will attach special importance in the United Nations and its specialized agencies and programs to promoting practical, multifaceted solutions to the issues of international peace and security, political, economic, social, cultural and humanitarian problems.

To accomplish this we will pursue cooperation with all member states in attainment of the following:

- Strengthen the U.N.'s efforts to promote international peace and security in all its aspects by working to improve U.N. peacekeeping, peacemaking and crisis prevention functions, by encouraging more active use of the Secretary-General's good offices and, at the request of individual countries, electoral assistance;
- Establish a new sense of responsibility at the U.N. by encouraging the trend away from rhetorical excess toward efforts to deal pragmatically with the major issues of the 1990s, including transnational issues like narcotics, the environment, development, terrorism, and human rights;
- Promote a new way of conducting diplomatic efforts within the U.N. system to eliminate duplicative programs and activities and ensure that the U.N. system is utilized in the most efficient manner possible — we call this a "unitary U.N.";
- Ensure the availability of sufficient resources to the U.N. for it to function effectively and efficiently by

timely payment of financial obligations to the U.N.

Promoting Peace and Security In All Its Aspects

Joint efforts have contributed significantly to the easing of tensions in Southern Africa and Central America, and are part of efforts to prepare a peaceful settlement in Cambodia. But serious problems still remain. Our search continues for workable solutions to conflict and instability in the Persian Gulf, the Middle East, Afghanistan, and El Salvador.

In the Persian Gulf, we face a most serious threat to the integrity of the emerging international system. The United States and the Soviet Union are working together with other members of the Security Council to fashion a concerted response, unprecedented in U.N. history, to this crisis. The swift reaction of the international community to Iraq's dangerous and unwarranted aggression serves as a sobering reminder to any future aggressor; the international community will not tolerate the kind of wanton aggression which Iraq has committed. We call upon all United Nations members to continue to support the sanctions invoked by Security Council Resolutions 661 and 670 until Iraq abides by the call of the Security Council to withdraw its forces from Kuwait immediately, totally and unconditionally. We call also for the restoration of the legitimate government of Kuwait.

The rapidly changing structure of international relations requires a United Nations that, while remaining faithful to its original purposes, can also respond flexibly and effectively to new challenges as they occur, like drugs, the environment, and the need to ensure the protection of human rights.

Tangible examples of the U.N. movement away from divisive rhetoric and political excess were last December's Special Session of the General Assembly on Apartheid and the resumed session last month, where the world community underscored its resolute opposition to apartheid while agreeing, by consensus, on a positive approach based on dialogue among all South African parties. We will work for equally positive results st the General Assembly this year.

The U.N. Special Session on International Economic Cooperation in April 1990 also reflected the growing convergence of views worldwide on the need for more effective approaches to national economic development, in the context of a supportive international economic environment. Our two countries will continue working together to promote further convergence in this direction. We will also support efforts to ensure careful and pragmatic preparation for the 1992 Conference on Environment and Development. We want to see the Conference fashion a realistic action plan to set the U.N.'s course in the coming decades.

Another area in which the U.N. is actively promoting peaceful change is in facilitation of free and fair elections. U.N. assistance in Namibia and Nicaragua was dramatically successful, and there are many other situations where the U.N.'s services are being requested. Our two countries will work with other U.N. members and the Secretary-General to structure a U.N. electoral assistance process to enable the organization, at the request of countries concerned, to carry out effectively this important new effort.

Promoting a Unitary U.N. and Assuring Needed Financial Resources

An important area of our bilateral and multilateral cooperation has been the administration and management of the United Nations, particularly its budget. As major contributors to the United Nations, we believe it is essential that all views on the budget are taken into account, and that the agreement of all major contributors is required in order to approve the budget.

For there to be consensus, the U.N. system must improve the setting of priorities and improve coordination among various U.N. programs. The aim should be to eliminate duplicative programs and activities and ensure that the various components of the United Nations are utilized in the most efficient manner possible. For priority setting and coordination to be effective, members will need clearer and more comprehensive data on what the U.N. and the specialized agencies are doing with assessed and voluntary contributions.

Our two countries provide an important element of U.N. resources. As such, we recognize our responsibility to pay assessments promptly so that the United Nations has the resources required to perform its tasks as expeditiously as possible, keeping in mind the necessity of strengthening the administrative and budgetary reforms that have taken place in recent years.

We intend to work for further enhancing the efficiency of the executive machinery of the Organization.

Establish a New Sense of Responsibility for Peace

The challenges before the international community and the U.N. are great. So, too, are the opportunities for more and better multilateral cooperation to confront and master the problems of our time.

In all spheres of U.N. activities the renunciation of sterile and rigid positions dictated by ideology rather than by practicality constitutes an essential prerequisite for creating an atmosphere of confidence within the United Nations among all United Nations members.

The United Nations can play a leading role on issues of global concern. We will actively support efforts, throughout the U.N. system, to implement and strengthen the principles and the system of international peace, security and international cooperation laid down in the Charter.

---

1 Department of State Dispatch, October 15, 1990.

United Nations World Summit for Children

Remarks by President Bush at the Opening Ceremony, September 30, 1990. [1]

I'm proud to address you here today as the President of this country, in which this special summit is being held. And at the outset, let me join all in expressing our appreciation to UNICEF [United Nations International Children's Emergency Fund] and then to the kids here with us today.

President Traore, our thanks to you, sir. And may I extend my special respects and special thanks to the Prime Minister of Canada.[2] It was largely his foresight and persistence that resulted in this impressive turnout.

In recent days, the world community has acted decisively in defense of a principle: that small states shall not become souvenirs of conquest. It was just three weeks ago that I spoke to the American people about a new world order, a new partnership of nations — freer from the threat of terror, stronger in the pursuit of justice, more secure in the quest for peace. Today we are holding this unprecedented world summit to work for the well-being of those who will live in and lead this new world. Their voices are still faint and unheard. So, we've come together, more than 70 strong — heads of state, chiefs of government — chiefs of state and heads of government — to speak for the children of the Earth.

Saving Sick and Starving Children

But first, we should acknowledge that for many children the only blessing they will ever know is their innocence. The facts are as stark as they are oppressive: There are almost 3 billion young people on Earth today, and more than 14 million of them will die this year. In the next hour alone, 1,000 babies will perish. But I think we're all gathered here to defy these statistics. We've seen children — swollen bellies. We've seen the pleading eyes of starvation. We've heard the cries of children dying of disease. So, let us affirm in this historic summit that these children can be saved. They can be saved when we live up to our responsibilities not just as an assembly of governments but as a world community of adults, of parents.

In my time as President, I've heard the heartrending cries of AIDS babies. I've stood helpless over infants born addicted to cocaine, their tiny bodies trembling with pain. But I've also been to many classrooms across America where the influence of love and well-being can be seen instantly in bright faces and wondering eyes. From all these experiences and many more, I've learned that our children are a mirror, an honest reflection, of their parents and their world. Sometimes, the reflection is flattering. At other times, we simply don't like what we see. So, we must never turn away.

So, let me tell you what the American people intend to do. This month, our Secretary of Health and Human Services, Dr. [Louis W.] Sullivan, announced ambitious new health objectives that we as a nation — citizens, families, business, and government — hope to reach by the year 2000. We seek to reduce infant mortality and low-weight births, to increase child immunization levels and improve the health of both mothers and children. And we want to see the day when every American child is a part of a strong and stable family.

We're working in partnership with other governments and international organizations to eliminate child-killing diseases. Of course, many diseases are but a manifestation of an even more basic disorder: malnutrition. And to combat world starvation, the United States will continue to help food production in many countries, and we will send almost 150 million metric tons of food abroad this year.

And sadly, there is another child-killer loose in the world that knows no cure: AIDS. And nowhere is this killer taking more lives than in Africa. So, I've asked Dr. Sullivan and Dr. Ronald Roskens, the Administrator of AID [Agency for International Development], to go to Africa to see what else America and the world can do to advance child survival across that continent and across the world.

Education for Every Child

So far, I've spoken here just briefly of the most urgent issues of survival, but simple survival is not enough for a child lacking in health or learning, or denied the love of family and time for play. One year and two days ago, I met with the Governors of our 50 States on a single topic of national importance. We agreed to set ambitious education goals for the year 2000. For America, this is a stiff challenge, self-imposed. I see among us today many leaders who should take pride in giving the world examples of educational excellence, examples the next generation of Americans will not leave unchallenged.

But of course, education is a mystery to the 100 million children not in school. It's an outrage that so many spend their childhood in mines, in factories, in the twilight world of the streets. The United States outlawed most forms of child labor decades ago. Let us strive together to make education the primary work of all children.

So, all children must be given the chance to lead happy, healthy, and productive lives. Let me be the first to say that the United States can learn from many of the nations represented here today, but what my countrymen have learned from hard experience is that progress begins when we empower people, not bureaucracies. Programs can best enhance the welfare of children by strengthening the mutual responsibilities of public institutions and individual families. We should also look to the private sector as an essential partner. Public efforts on behalf of children should encourage experimentation among neighborhoods and local governments, not stifle it. So, when it comes to improving the welfare of children, empowerment should begin first with their parents, as President Salinas [of Mexico] a minute ago so eloquently stated.

Saving one child is a miracle. As world leaders, we can realize such miracles, and then we can count them in millions. My friends and colleagues, thank you very much. And may God bless the children of this world.

---

1 Text from Weekly Compilation of Presidential Documents of October 8, 1990.

2 President Moussa Traore of Mali and Prime Minister Brian Mulroney of Canada, cochairmen of the Summit.

Congress Withholds Fifty Percent of El Salvador's Military Aid

REMARKS BY SENATOR PATRICK J. LEAHY (EXCERPT), OCTOBER 19, 1990 [1]

Mr. President, it has been almost a year since the Senate last considered the issue of military aid to El Salvador. In fact, I clearly recall the debate a year ago in the Senate when we considered military aid to El Salvador. That was just four days after the six Jesuit priests and their housekeepers were brutally murdered by Salvadoran soldiers. A few days after that massacre, a massacre that was greeted with revulsion throughout the world, the U.S. Senate voted 99 to nothing for a resolution demanding that those responsible for the murders be brought to justice and punished.

We stood up and spoke with unanimity we rarely ever see on a foreign policy issue in this body. Mr. President, some of us, however, have gone back and looked at what happened after we spoke so strongly. Let me tell you what happened.

Let me quote what the distinguished Member of the other body, Congressman [Joe] Moakley who chairs the House task force on El Salvador, said recently. Congressman Moakley said:

"The High Command of the Salvadoran armed forces is engaged in a conspiracy to obstruct justice in the Jesuits' case. Salvadoran military officers have withheld evidence, destroyed evidence, falsified evidence and repeatedly perjured themselves in testimony before the judge."

Mr. President, I remind every Senator, those 99 who voted last year, that if they really felt that that amendment meant something, if they felt they were doing something more than a symbolic gesture, if they meant that vote honestly, they should vote overwhelmingly for the amendment that is before us which is basically the Dodd-Leahy amendment.

Except for the changes I mentioned, it is identical to the language that the Appropriations Committee of the U.S. Senate voted out. It is known as the Dodd-Leahy provision: Senator Dodd and I put it together after being on opposite sides of this issue last year.

Senator Dodd had very strong feelings on the one side of the issue. But both of us were looking, I believe, for the same thing, that is, an end to the killings in El Salvador, and a bill to bring those who have been involved in the killings to justice. Although we had different points of view regarding a solution, we both knew what we wanted to find. As a result we put together this amendment, the Dodd-Leahy amendment, and we are joined by 26 cosponsors here in the U.S. Senate.

Also, the provision is very similar to the one passed in the House earlier this year, the so-called Moakley-Murtha provision.

What the FMLN Must Do

If anything is going to change in El Salvador, the United States has to apply pressure on both sides to negotiate in good faith at the United Nations. That kind of pressure from the United States is what is applied in the Dodd-Leahy provision. It caps military aid at last year's level, $85 million. But it withholds 50 percent of that aid unless the President, and I emphasize the President of the United States, determines that the FMLN is not abiding by any one of several conditions. The FMLN must:

Negotiate in good faith in the United Nations. In fact, if the President of the United States determines, after consulting with the Secretary-General of the United Nations, that the FMLN is stalling or it is not acting in good faith, then he has the unfettered discretion to simply release the aid.

The FMLN has to accept a plan put forward by the Secretary-General for a cease fire, if such a plan has been accepted by the Government of El Salvador.

The FMLN must not start an offensive which threatens the survival of the government.

And, they must not receive significant shipments of weapons. Again, we give the discretion to the President of the United States to determine this.

They must not attack civilian targets.

If the President reports that the FMLN violates any of these conditions,

then the military aid that has been withheld is released to the Government.

We have gone the extra hundred miles in this amendment.

Provisions Concerning the Government of El Salvador

The amendment also imposes some conditions on the Government. The Government has to support the U.N. peace process, it must accept a U.N. proposal for a cease-fire, and it must prosecute those responsible for murdering the Jesuits. Also, the Salvadoran Army must refrain from attacking civilians.

It is amazing, Mr. President, that the United States, which is asked to give virtually a blank check to a country, even has to include an amendment asking the military of that country not to attack civilians. I mean, that is a basic tenet of international law. We routinely, routinely send through this body senses of the Senate condemning those countries where the military attacks civilians. But yet here is one where we bankroll, we bankroll the whole shebang and unless we pass this amendment, we are willing to say to them, you cannot go out with our U.S. arms and our U.S. bankroll and kill civilians. That is not what a military is supposed to do.

If the President determines that the Government is not satisfying these conditions, then the military aid stops.

Mr. President, for more than ten years civil war has raged in El Salvador. I have been there many times, and I have seen the results of it. We know about the corruption. We know about the tremendous cost in human life and American aid. We also know we are going to send them another $328 million this year. That is almost more than what we spend in all of Eastern Europe, where democracy is breaking out, where the United States has enormous interests, where the potential is so great to bring about the democracy that we preach, where the economic and commercial opportunities are enormous. And yet, look at the priorities. We put our greatest priority on little tiny El Salvador where we have thrown away billions of dollars with no result whatsoever. We put as much priority there as we do all of Eastern Europe.

Mr. President, this goes beyond symbolism over substance. This is foreign policy gone haywire. This is wacko. This makes no sense whatsoever.

The Agenda for Negotiations

Earlier this year, the two sides in El Salvador finally agreed to negotiations under the auspices of the United Nations. Everyone—the administration, President Cristiani [of El Salvador], the top commanders in the Salvadoran military, the FMLN—has said the U.N. negotiations are the only real chance for real peace in El Salvador.

On April 4 in Geneva the two sides agreed on the terms and procedures for the negotiations, on April 4 in Geneva. An agenda for the negotiations, listing the issues to be resolved, was agreed to on May 21 in Caracas. These two documents were signed by both sides, and the Secretary-General's representative.

There have been four meetings since then. It is interesting, Mr. President, the Salvadorans have had fewer hours at the bargaining table trying to settle a ten-year war that has killed tens of thousands of their people than we spent so far this year debating the Federal budget.

The agenda for the negotiations is very clear.

It lists the key political elements of a peace settlement. Those issues include reform of the armed forces and the judicial system, protecting human rights, and verification by the United Nations.

Once there are agreements on those issues, the agenda calls for a cease-fire.

President Cristiani, in a letter dated September 14, 1990, reaffirmed this agenda, which includes a cease-fire within the framework of a political settlement. President Cristiani said:

"The basic framework of the talks calls for a two stage process: political agreements to be reached on issues agreed upon in Caracas, Venezuela, followed by a cease-fire and reintegration of the FMLN into the civilian and political life of the country."

Let me read that again:

"a two stage process: political agreements to be reached on issues agreed upon in Caracas, followed by a ceasefire. . ."

Mr. President, this amendment, and the language reported to the Senate by the Senate Appropriations Committee, is carefully written to strengthen the U.N. peace process. It does contain for the first time real incentives for both sides to negotiate in good faith. It highlights the importance of adhering to the terms and procedures for the negotiations they agreed to in Geneva and Caracas.

It requires both sides to accept a plan for a cease-fire put forward by the Secretary-General.

Mr. President, we are convinced that the only real hope for a peace that lasts in El Salvador is through the U.N. peace process. The goal of this amendment is to breathe new life into that process.

Mr. President, after a vote on the Dodd-Leahy provision I understand there will be another amendment offered. The proponents of that amendment will argue that it will bring a cease-fire. I disagree.

What their amendment would do is require both sides to cease fire before agreement on any of the key political issues to a settlement of the conflict. In fact, I do not think it would lead to a cease-fire. I think it would give the FMLN an excuse to drop out of all negotiations.

It is a clever amendment. Like so many clever amendments around here, it seems so reasonable. Nobody wants to vote against a cease-fire. I do not. I am sure the distinguished Presiding Officer does not. I am sure nobody does.

We are going to hear over and over again what we need is a cease-fire. I will concede that point. I suspect all 100 Senators want a cease-fire. But anyone who has spent time in El Salvador, knows El Salvador, studies the situation in El Salvador, understands also that the amendment that will be offered is not going to bring a cease-fire but will have just the opposite effect. I will have more to say at that time.

Time to Act

Let me tell you this: A year ago the Senate chose not to withhold military aid to El Salvador. We said, as we have said over and over and over again when the issue comes up, we will give them one more chance, one more chance. I have heard this almost since I came to the Senate. A majority of Senators wanted to give the Government a chance to prove they could rein in the military and punish those responsible for murdering the Jesuit priests.

By [any] standard that case has been a disaster. It has been proven beyond any doubt that President Cristiani—who, I believe, is a well-meaning person—is unable to get the military to stop lying about who ordered that massacre. And if we cannot, with all the pressure and international attention, get them to stop lying about that case, how in Heaven's name are we going to get them to stop lying about the thousands of other cases and thousands of other brutal murders in El Salvador?

Year after year, the administration has said it would cut military aid if human rights abuses do not improve and year after year the Congress has said it will cut military aid if the situation does not improve. And year after year, it does not improve; it gets worse. But out comes the checkbook.

At the same time that we are cutting virtually every program in the United States of America, we shuffle the money by the carload down to El Salvador and get absolute nothing back in return. That, Mr. President, is not a foreign policy. That is not a domestic policy. That is crazy, Mr. President, and I cannot believe any taxpayer in this country, if it were put to a referendum, would agree with that.

So today, $4 billion later, it is time to say, "Enough already. Cut it off." The Dodd-Leahy amendment is a modest attempt to put some sense into a policy that, by any objective analysis, has failed. For me, for many others, it does not go far enough, but we have offered it in a sense of compromise hoping that finally the Congress can speak in one voice. We want to end the bloodshed. This amendment is a first step.

No Murder Convictions

Mr. President, I recall so well my first trip to El Salvador years ago, seeing beside the road the second dead body I had seen in a space of a mile or so.

When I was a prosecutor, I went to many murder scenes or death scenes. I am well aware of what dead bodies look like and usually can tell pretty quickly if it is somebody recently killed. This particular one stuck in my mind because not only was the man recently killed, in a matter of hours at best, but the attitude of everybody around showed that it was such a commonplace matter. People on their way to work or to stores just walk by, barely glance. Two other people had shovels out and were starting to dig a grave right here beside the road, it was that commonplace a matter. Mr. President, I thought of that on subsequent trips.

Also, when I went down to talk with the investigators of the Jesuits' murder—I must say again, I want to emphasize over and over again, I mentioned the Jesuit murders because they were so abhorrent, because they got so much attention in this country and everywhere else that it is hard to believe that there is anybody not familiar with them. But they are no less abhorrent than the murders of thousands of other innocent civilians in El Salvador over the years. They bear in relationship to the thousands of other murders two things: One, the sheer animal brutality of these murders; and, second, the fact that nobody, nobody, has ever been convicted of any of these thousands of murders.

I talked with the investigators of that murder. I asked them who they talked with, what leads they had found, looked at the evidence they had gathered.

Mr. President, when I was a prosecutor, if any of the lowest assistants in my office had bungled a case as badly as they bungled that, he or she would have been fired.

Mr. President, that was the attitude I had as I left, but then I began thinking to myself: No, if I had assistant prosecutors in my office who bungled a case that badly, I would not fire them. I would probably try to indict them because it is obvious they were on the take; it was obvious they were trying to literally get away with murder.

Mr. President, as I said last year, it is going to be a cold day in Hell before we see anybody brought to trial and convicted of these murders. That was a year ago. Not only are we [no] closer to a conviction, we are further away. Some people say, well, maybe we should send a team of specialists or investigators down there.

To what? To a crime scene that a year ago was wiped clean, to look at evidence that no longer exists? Do you think they are going to be allowed to talk to the same people that the military has protected ever since then and has kept off limits to the investigators? Of course not.

At 2 a.m. this morning the U.S. Senate voted a budget package which, when returned from conference, will guarantee that virtually every single program of importance to the people of the United States will be cut. We voted at 4 o'clock in the morning on a committee conference on the farm bill which guarantees that every single farmer in this country will find his or her income lower because of cuts. We will guarantee in the final budget that will be

signed by the President, that there will not be one single program in this country of importance to the senior citizens, to children in school lunch programs, to those in health care, in education, in rebuilding the infrastructure of the country that will not be affected—I guarantee every one of them will see cuts. But not El Salvador. Just pour another $328 million down there—here it comes, boys; no strings attached; have a good day.

I would like to hear how anybody who might vote against the Dodd-Leahy amendment can go home and explain that the next time they are at a senior citizens feeding program; or the next time they are in a school; or anywhere else they might be—let them explain, sorry you did not get the money you want but stand proud because El Salvador got it.

TEXT OF AMENDMENT AS INCLUDED IN FOREIGN OPERATIONS BILL [2]

SEC. 531. (a) STATEMENT OF POLICY.—United States military assistance to the Government of El Salvador shall seek three principal foreign policy objectives, as follows: (1) to promote a permanent settlement and cease-fire to the conflict in El Salvador, with the Secretary-General of the United Nations serving as an active mediator between the opposing parties; (2) to foster greater respect for basic human rights, and the rule of law; and (3) to advance political accommodation and national reconciliation.

(b) MAXIMUM LEVEL OF MILITARY ASSISTANCE.—Of the funds available for United States military assistance for fiscal year 1991, not more than $85,000,000 shall be made available for El Salvador.

(c) PROHIBITION OF MILITARY ASSISTANCE.—(1) PROHIBITION.—Subject to paragraph (2), no United States military assistance may be furnished to the Government of El Salvador if the President determines and reports in writing to the Congress that—

(A) after he has consulted with the Secretary-General of the United Nations, the Government of El Salvador has declined to participate in good faith in negotiations for a permanent settlement and cease-fire to the armed conflict of El Salvador;

(B) the Government of El Salvador has rejected or otherwise failed to support an active role for the Secretary-General of the United Nations in mediating that settlement;

(C) the Government of El Salvador has rejected a plan for the settlement of the conflict which—

(i) has been put forward by the Secretary-General of the United Nations in accordance with the terms and procedures in the April 4, 1990 Geneva Communique and the May 21, 1990 Caracas Accord between the Government of El Salvador and the FMLN;

(ii) includes a proposal for an internationally-monitored cease-fire; and

(iii) has been accepted, within 15 days from its announcement, by the FMLN and is being complied with by the FMLN;

(D) the Government of El Salvador has failed to conduct a thorough and professional investigation into, and prosecution of those responsible for the eight murders at the University of Central America on November 16, 1989; or

(E) the military and security forces of El Salvador are assassinating or abducting civilian noncombatants, are engaging in other acts of violence directed at civilian targets, or are failing to control such activities by elements subject to the control of those forces; or

(F) the Government of El Salvador has failed to actively seek and encourage a law enforcement service from outside El Salvador, such as Scotland Yard or INTERPOL, to accompany and monitor investigators of the Government of El Salvador in their investigation into the eight murders at the University of Central America on November 16, 1989.

(2) REQUIREMENT FOR RESUMPTION OF ASSISTANCE.—Assistance prohibited under paragraph (1) may only be resumed pursuant to a law subsequently enacted by the Congress.

(d) WITHHOLDING OF MILITARY ASSISTANCE.—(1) IN GENERAL.— Fifty per centum of the total United States military assistance allocated for El Salvador for fiscal year 1991 shall be withheld from obligation or expenditure (as the case may be) except as provided in paragraphs (2) and (3).

(2) RELEASE OF ASSISTANCE.—The United States military assistance withheld pursuant to paragraph (1) may be obligated and ex-

pended only if the President determines and reports in writing to the Congress that—

(A) after he has consulted with the Secretary-General of the United Nations, the representatives of the FMLN—

(i) have declined to participate in good faith in negotiations for a permanent settlement and cease-fire to the armed conflict in El Salvador, or

(ii) have rejected or otherwise failed to support an active role for the Secretary-General of the United Nations in mediating that settlement;

(B) the FMLN has rejected a plan for the settlement of the conflict which—

(i) has been put forward by the Secretary-General of the United Nations in accordance with the terms and procedures in the April 4, 1990 Geneva Communique and the May 21, 1990 Caracas Accord between the Government of El Salvador and the FMLN;

(ii) includes a proposal for an internationally monitored cease-fire, and

(iii) has been accepted, within 15 days from its announcement, by the Government of El Salvador and is being complied with by the Government of El Salvador;

(C) the survival of the constitutional Government of El Salvador is being jeopardized by substantial and sustained offensive military actions or operations by the FMLN;

(D) proof exists that the FMLN is continuing to acquire or receive significant shipments of lethal military assistance from outside El Salvador, and this proof has been shared with the Congress; or

(E) the FMLN is assassinating or abducting civilian noncombatants, is engaging in other acts of violence directed at civilian targets, or is failing to control such activities by elements subject to FMLN control.

(3) EXCEPTION. — Notwithstanding any other provision of law, funds withheld pursuant to paragraph (1) of this subsection may be disbursed to pay the cost of any contract penalties which may be incurred as a result of such withholding of funds under this subsection.

(e) CONDITION FOR TERMINATION OF ALL UNITED STATES ASSISTANCE. — (1) PROHIBITION. — Subject to paragraph (2), no United States assistance may be furnished to El Salvador if the duly-elected head of Government of El Salvador is deposed by military coup or decree.

(2) REQUIREMENT FOR RESUMPTION OF ASSISTANCE. — Assistance prohibited under paragraph (1) may only be resumed pursuant to a law subsequently enacted by the Congress.

(f) ESTABLISHMENT OF A FUND FOR CEASE-FIRE MONITORING, DEMOBILIZATION, AND TRANSITION TO PEACE. — (1) ESTABLISHMENT OF FUND. — There is hereby established in the Treasury of the United States a fund to assist with the costs of monitoring a permanent settlement of the conflict, including a cease-fire, and the demobilization of combatants in the conflict in El Salvador, and their transition to peaceful pursuits, which shall be known as the "Demobilization and Transition Fund" (hereafter in this section referred to as the "Fund"). Amounts in this Fund shall be available for obligation and expenditure only upon notification by the President to the Congress that the Government of El Salvador and representatives of the FMLN have reached a permanent settlement of the conflict, including a final agreement on a cease-fire.

(2) TRANSFER OF CERTAIN MILITARY ASSISTANCE FUNDS. — Upon notification of the Congress of a permanent settlement of the conflict, including an agreement on a cease-fire, or on September 30, 1991, if no such notification has occurred prior to that date, the President shall transfer to the Fund any United States military assis-

tance funds withheld pursuant to subsection (d) of this section.

(3) USE OF THE FUND. — Notwithstanding any other provision of law, amounts in the Fund shall be available for El Salvador solely to support costs of demobilization, retraining, relocation, and reemployment in civilian pursuits of former combatants in the conflict in El Salvador, and of the monitoring of the permanent settlement and cease-fire.

(4) DURATION OF AVAILABILITY OF FUNDS. — Notwithstanding any other provision of law, amounts transferred to the Fund shall remain available until expended.

(g) STRENGTHENING CIVILIAN CONTROL OVER THE MILITARY. — In order to strengthen the control of the democratically-elected civilian Government of El Salvador over the armed forces of that country, United States military assistance for any fiscal year may be delivered to the armed forces of El Salvador only with the prior approval of the duly elected President of El Salvador.

(h) SUPPORT FOR DEMOCRACY — (1) ESTABLISHING A PROGRAM. — The Secretary of State, through agreement with the National Endowment for Democracy or other qualified organizations, shall establish and carry out a program of education, training, and dialogue for the purpose of strengthening democratic political and legal institutions in El Salvador.

(2) ELECTION MONITORING. — Of the amounts made available to carry

---

U.S.-SOVIET JOINT STATEMENT ON EL SALVADOR, OCTOBER 18, 1990 [1]

Secretary of State James A. Baker, III, and Soviet Foreign Minister Eduard Shevardnadze directed that officials of the United States and the Soviet Union responsible for Latin America — Assistant Secretary for Inter-American Affairs Bernard Aronson and his Soviet counterparts, Mr. Valery Nikolayenko and Mr. Yuriy Pavlov — meet in Washington last week. In these meetings, the two sides expressed their continued support for a peaceful solution in El Salvador, as the Government of El Salvador and the FMLN have committed themselves to in the Geneva and Caracas Agreements. The Soviet and American participants considered it desirable that the parties in conflict intensify their negotiations with a view toward reaching political agreements and a cease-fire as quickly as possible. They also consider that both sides in the dialogue should refrain from military actions that would damage the prospects for peace

---

1 Department of State Dispatch, October 22, 1990.

out this subsection, up to $2,000,000 may be used for support for monitoring the 1991 municipal and National Assembly elections in El Salvador, and for monitoring the registration and campaign processes leading up to those elections, by appropriate organizations such as the United Nations, the Organization of American States, the Carter Center, the National Democratic Institute for International Affairs, the National Republican Institute for International Affairs, and the Center for Electoral Assistance and Promotion (CAPEL) of San Jose, Costa Rica.

(3) ASSISTANCE. – Up to $10,000,000 of funds appropriated under the heading "Economic Support Fund" for fiscal year 1991 may be used to carry out this subsection.

(i) REPORTING REQUIRE-MENTS. Sixty days after the date of enactment of this Act and every 180 days thereafter, the President shall submit to the Congress a report describing –

(1) the willingness or unwillingness of the Government of El Salvador and the FMLN to negotiate seriously and in good faith for the purpose of achieving a permanent settlement to the conflict

in El Salvador, including a cease-fire, and providing appropriate information regarding criteria described in subsections (c) and (d)(2); and

(2) the status of investigations into the politically motivated murders listed in section 538 of this Act.

(j) DEFINITIONS. – For purposes of this section –

(1) the term "United States assistance" has the same meaning as is given to such term by section 481(i)(4) of the Foreign Assistance Act of 1961 (22 U.S.C. 2291(i)(4)) and includes United States military assistance as defined in paragraph (2); and

(2) the term "United States military assistance" means –

(A) assistance to carry out chapter 2 (relating to grant military assistance) or chapter 5 (relating to international military education and training) of part II of the Foreign Assistance Act of 1961; and

(B) assistance to carry out section 23 of the Arms Export Control Act.

_____

1 Text from the Congressional Record, October 19, 1990.

2 Text provided by Senator Patrick J. Leahy's office, Washington.

may be applied. If foreign components are used to produce an article, the final product must be substantially transformed into a "new and different article of commerce" in one or more of the beneficiary countries. Products not qualifying under these three requirements will be dutiable.

Products that are particularly sensitive to import competition will still be dutiable. These products include textiles and apparel; footwear; canned tuna; petroleum and petroleum products; and watches and watch parts. Handbags, luggage, flat goods, work gloves, and leather wearing apparel also will continue to be dutiable, but will be subject to the same duty reduction program as has been made available to products from the Caribbean Basin. Duty-free entry of sugars, syrups, and molasses is provided consistent with the tariff-rate quotas on these products.

The proposal includes provisions for general import relief and emergency relief to safeguard domestic industries. Specific relief provisions are also included to safeguard domestic industries producing perishable products (i.e., live plants and fresh cut flowers, certain fresh or chilled vegetables, certain fresh fruit, and concentrated citrus fruit juice).

To assess the effects of the legislation on the U.S. economy and on particular industries producing like or directly competitive articles, the U.S. International Trade Commission would be required to issue reports to the Congress. The first such study will assess the effectiveness of the Act during its first 2 years, with annual reports thereafter. The proposal also requires the Secretary of Labor to report to the Congress annually on the impact of the Act on U.S. labor.

Enactment of the Andean Trade Preference Act of 1990 will permit the United States to support the efforts of the Andean countries to eliminate the production, processing, and shipment of illicit drugs. In conjunction with other Andean trade measures announced on July 23 and the Enterprise for the Americas Initiative announced on June 27, it will also increase the prospects for economic growth and prosperity in the Andean countries and throughout the hemisphere. I look forward to working closely with the Congress to enact this vital initiative.

_____

1 Text from Weekly Compilation of Presidential Documents of October 8, 1990.

Andean Trade Preference Act Submitted

President's Message to Congress, October 5, 1990. [1]

I am pleased to transmit a legislative proposal entitled the "Andean Trade Preference Act of 1990" and a section by section analysis. The Andean nations are engaged in a serious struggle to combat illegal narcotics trafficking. It is incumbent upon the United States to aid them in their efforts to develop legitimate trading opportunities for their people. Their struggle is our struggle as well.

This proposal would implement my Andean Trade Preference Initiative of July 23, 1990. It would create a trade preference program patterned after the Caribbean Basin Initiative (CBI) for four Andean countries – Bolivia, Colombia, Ecuador, and Peru.

The Andean Trade Preference Initiative is intended to:

• fulfill, in part, my commitment at the Cartagena Summit to expand economic alternatives for these four Andean countries;

• complement the program of economic assistance, drug control, and the economic reforms agreed on with the Andean countries; and

• provide U.S. economic support to those Andean countries that are fighting to eliminate the production, processing and shipment of drugs.

Just as CBI did for the countries of the Caribbean Basin, the Andean Trade Preference Act of 1990 will provide the authority to establish duty-free treatment of imports from the four Andean countries. These trade preferences would be granted for a period of ten years.

The legislation outlines the rule-of-origin requirements for duty-free entry. Articles must be imported directly from a beneficiary country. These imports must consist of at least 35 percent value-added in one or more of the beneficiary countries, or one or more of the CBI countries, to which 15 percent of the total value from U.S.-made components

Current Actions:

August, September, October 1990

These listings were released by the Department of State as "Treaty Actions" on, respectively, September 10, October 15, and November 12, 1990.

I. August 1990

MULTILATERAL

Coffee
International coffee agreement, 1983, with annexes, done at London Sept. 16, 1982, as extended July 3, 1989. [1]
Entered into force Oct. 1, 1989.
Acceptance deposited: Cuba, Aug 3, 1990.
Accessions deposited: Congo, July 30, 1990; Vietnam, Aug. 3, 1990.

Containers
International convention for safe containers, with annexes, as amended. Done at Geneva Dec. 2, 1972. Entered into force Sept 6, 1977; for the US Jan. 3, 1979. TIAS 9037, 10220, 10914.
Accession deposited: Morocco, July 5, 1990

Health
Statute of the International Agency for Research on Cancer. Done at Geneva May 20, 1965. Entered into force Sept. 15, 1965. TIAS 5873.
Notification of withdrawal: Australia, June 29, 1990; effective Dec. 29, 1990.

Satellite Communications Systems
Convention relating to the distribution of programme-carrying signals transmitted by satellite. Done at Brussels May 21, 1974. Entered into force Aug. 25, 1979; for the US Mar. 7, 1985. [Senate] Treaty Doc 98-31.
Accession deposited: Australia, July 26, 1990.

Trade
Agreement on technical barriers to trade (standards code). Done at Geneva Apr. 12, 1979. Entered into force Jan. 1, 1980. TIAS 9616.
Acceptance deposited: Israel, Feb. 16, 1990.

Agreement on interpretation and application of articles VI, XVI, and XXIII of the General Agreement on Tariffs and Trade (subsidies and countervailing duties code).
Done at Geneva Apr. 12, 1979.
Entered into force Jan. 1, 1980. TIAS 9619.
Acceptance deposited: Colombia, May 7, 1990. [2]

United Nations convention on contracts for the international sale of goods.
Done at Vienna Apr. 11, 1980. Entered into force Jan. 1, 1988. [52 Fed. Reg. 6262]
Accession deposited: Spain, July 24, 1990.

BILATERAL
Australia
Agreement concerning cooperative development of the digital chart of the world. Signed at Washington June 22, 1990.
Entered into force June 22, 1990.

Austria
Agreement on social security, with administrative arrangement. Signed at Vienna July 13, 1990. Enters into force on the first day of the third month following written notification by the parties of compliance with all statutory and constitutional requirements.

Brazil
Postal money order agreement. Signed at Brasilia and Washington July 19 and Aug. 14, 1990.
Entered into force Oct. 15, 1990.

Chile
Agreement concerning compensation in the deaths of Orlando Letelier and Ronni Moffitt, with annex. Signed at Santiago June 11, 1990. Enters into force upon notification to the US by Chile that it has completed the proceedings necessary under Chilean law.

China
Agreement amending and extending the agreement of July 23, 1985, as amended, concerning fisheries off the coasts of the United States. Effected by exchange of notes at Washington Mar. 14 and 22, 1990.

Entered into force: Aug. 8, 1990; effective July 1, 1990.

Congo
Agreement concerning the establishment of a Peace Corps program in the Congo. Effected by exchange of notes at Brazzaville Apr. 21, 1990. Entered into force Apr. 21, 1990.

Ecuador
Postal money order agreement. Signed at Quito and Washington Aug. 1 and 8, 1990. Enters into force Oct. 15, 1990.

Egypt
Grant agreement to assist Egypt with its balance of payments. Signed at Cairo July 9, 1990.
Entered into force July 9, 1990.

Ethiopia
Memorandum of understanding concerning the operation of the INTEL-POST service, with details of implementation. Signed at Addis Ababa and Washington Mar. 26 and July 16, 1990.
Entered into force Aug. 15, 1990.

German Democratic Republic
Agreement extending the agreement of Apr. 13, 1983, as amended and extended (TIAS 10687), concerning fisheries off the coasts of the United States. Effected by exchange of notes at Washington Jan. 16 and Apr. 5, 1990. Enters into force: Aug. 3, 1990; effective July 1, 1990.

Guyana
Swap agreement among the US Treasury and the Bank of Guyana/Republic of Guyana, with memorandum of understanding. Signed at Georgetown and Washington June 19 and 20, 1990. Entered into force June 20, 1990.

Honduras
Swap agreement among the US Treasury and the Central Bank of Honduras/Government of Honduras, with memorandum of understanding. Signed at Tegucigalpa and Washington June 27 and 28, 1990. Entered into force June 28, 1990.

Hungary
Swap agreement among the US Treasury and the National Bank of Hungary/Government of Hungary, with memorandum of understanding. Signed at Washington and Budapest June 19, 1990. Entered into force June 19, 1990.

Agreement concerning the operations of the US Peace Corps in Hungary. Signed at Budapest Feb. 14, 1990. Entered into force July 12, 1990

Israel
Agreement extending the agreement of June 3, 1984, as extended, on cooperation in energy research and development. Effected by exchange of letters at Washington and Jerusalem May 18 and June 11, 1990. Entered into force June 11, 1990; effective June 3, 1990.

Lesotho
International express mail agreement, with detailed regulations. Signed at Maseru and Washington June 19 and July 20, 1990. Entered into force Aug 30, 1990.

Mexico
Agreement on cooperation in combating narcotics trafficking and drug dependency. Signed at Mexico Feb. 23, 1989. Entered into force July 30, 1990.

Memorandum of understanding for the exchange of technical information and for cooperation in the field of air quality research. Signed at Washington July 19, 1990. Entered into force July 19, 1990.

Agreement on cooperation for the protection and improvement of the environment in the metropolitan area of Mexico City. Signed at Washington Oct. 3, 1989. Entered into force Aug. 22, 1990.

Agreement of cooperation regarding international transport of urban air pollution, with appendix. Signed at Washington Oct 3, 1989. Entered into force Aug. 22, 1990.

Mongolia
Agreement on cooperation through the US Peace Corps in Mongolia. Signed at Ulaanbaatar Aug. 2, 1990. Entered into force Aug. 2, 1990.

Mozambique
International express mail agreement, with detailed regulations. Signed at Maputo and Washington July 9 and 23, 1990. Entered into force Aug. 30, 1990.

Multinational Force and Observers
Agreement concerning the settlement of claims by the United States against the Multinational Force and Observers (MFO). Effected by exchange of notes at Rome May 3, 1990. Entered into force May 3, 1990.

Peru
Agreement concerning scientific and technical cooperation in the earth and mapping sciences, with annexes. Signed at Lima July 19, 1990. Entered into force July 19, 1990

Poland
Agreement concerning the program of the US Peace Corps in Poland. Signed at Warsaw Feb. 23, 1990. Entered into force Feb 23, 1990.

Seychelles
Agreement amending the agreement of June 29, 1976, as amended (TIAS 8385,10173), relating to the establishment, operation, and maintenance of a tracking and telemetry facility on the island of Mahe. Effected by exchange of notes at Victoria May 29 and June 15, 1990. Entered into force June 29, 1990.

Spain
Agreement regarding mutual assistance between customs services. Signed at Madrid July 3, 1990. Enters into force on the 90th day following notification by the parties that they have accepted the agreement's terms and that all necessary national legal requirements have been fulfilled.

USSR
Visa arrangement concerning textiles and textile products, with attachment. Signed at Washington July 2, 1990. Entered into force Sept. 1, 1990.

United Kingdom
Agreement extending the agreement of Mar. 11, 1987, as extended, concerning Anguilla and narcotics activities. Effected by exchange of notes at Washington June 26, 1990. Entered into force June 26, 1990; effective June 27, 1990.

Memorandum of understanding on collaboration in energy research and development. Signed at Washington June 11, 1990. Entered into force June 11, 1990.

Western Samoa
Status of forces agreement. Signed at Apia June 25, 1990. Entered into force June 25, 1990.

Yugoslavia
Agreement regarding mutual assistance between customs administrations. Signed at Belgrade Apr. 11, 1990. Enters into force on the 90th day following notification by the parties that all necessary national legal requirements have been fulfilled .

Zaire
International express mail agreement, with detailed regulations. Signed at Kinshasa and Washington June 29 and July 20, 1990. Entered into force Aug. 30, 1990.

---

1 Certain provisions of the agreement suspended.
2 With declaration(s).

II. September 1990

MULTILATERAL

Arbitration
Inter-American convention on international Commercial arbitration. Done at Panama City Jan. 30, 1975. Entered into force June 16, 1976.
Ratification deposited: US, Sept. 27, 1990. 1
Entered into force: Oct. 27, 1990.

Conservation
Convention on international trade in endangered species of wild fauna and flora, with appendices. Done at Washington Mar. 3, 1973. Entered into force July 1, 1975. TIAS 8249.
Accessions deposited: Brunei, May 4, 1990; Guinea-Bissau, May 16, 1990; Cuba, Apr. 20, 1990; United Arab Emirates, Feb. 8, 1990.

Customs
Customs convention on containers, 1972, with annexes and protocol. Done at Geneva Dec. 2, 1972. Entered into force Dec. 6, 1975; for the US May 12, 1985.
Accession deposited: Morocco, Aug. 14, 1990.

TREATIES

Finance
Articles of agreement of the International Monetary Fund, formulated at Bretton Woods Conference July 1-22, 1944. Entered into force Dec. 27, 1945. TIAS 1502.

Articles of agreement of the International Bank for Reconstruction and Development, formulated at Bretton Woods Conference July 1-22, 1944. Entered into force Dec. 27, 1945. TIAS 1501.
Signatures and Acceptances: Czechoslovakia. Sept. 20, 1990; Bulgaria and Namibia, Sept. 25, 1990.

Germany
Treaty on the final settlement with respect to Germany, with agreed minute and related letters. Done at Moscow Sept. 12, 1990. Enters into force on the date of deposit of the last instrument of ratification or acceptance.
Signatures: France, German Dem. Rep., Germany, Fed. Rep. of, UK, US, USSR, Sept. 12, 1990.

Maritime Matters
Convention on facilitation of international maritime traffic, with annex. Done at London Apr. 9, 1965. Entered into force Mar. 5, 1967; for the US May 16, 1967. TIAS 6251.
Accession deposited: Mauritius, June 18, 1990.

Nuclear Weapons – Nonproliferation
Treaty on the nonproliferation of nuclear weapons. Done at Washington, London, and Moscow July 1, 1968. Entered into force Mar. 5, 1970. TIAS 6839.
Accession deposited: Mozambique, Sept. 12, 1990.

Oceanographic Research
Agreement concerning the continuation of marine geoscientific research and mineral resource studies in the South Pacific region, with annex. Signed at Washington September 10, 1990. Entered into force September 10, 1990.

Pollution
Convention for the protection of the ozone layer, with annexes. Done at Vienna Mar. 22, 1985. Entered into force Sept. 22, 1988. [Senate] Treaty Doc. 99-9.
Accessions deposited: Bangladesh, Aug. 2, 1990; Brunei, July 26, 1990; The Gambia, July 25, 1990; Poland, July 13, 1990.

Montreal protocol on substances that deplete the ozone layer, with annex. Done at Montreal Sept. 16, 1987. Entered into force Jan. 1, 1989. [Senate] Treaty Doc. 100-10.
Accessions deposited: Bangladesh, Aug. 2, 1990; The Gambia, July 25, 1990; Poland, July 13, 1990.

Safety at Sea
International convention for the safety of life at sea, 1974, with annex. Done at London Nov. 1, 1974. Entered into force May 25, 1980. TIAS 9700.
Accession deposited: Morocco, Jun. 28, 1990.

Terrorism
Convention on the prevention and punishment of crimes against internationally protected persons, including diplomatic agents. Done at New York Dec. 14, 1973. Entered into force Feb. 20, 1977. TIAS 8532.
Accession deposited: Maldives, Aug. 21, 1990.

Tonnage
International convention on tonnage measurement of ships, with annexes. Done at London June 23, 1969 . Entered into force July 18, 1982; for the US Feb. 10, 1983.
Accession deposited: Morocco, June 28, 1990

Trade
United Nations convention on contracts for the international sale of goods. Done at Vienna Apr. 11, 1980. Entered into force Jan. 1, 1988. [52 Fed. Reg. 6262].
Accession deposited: USSR, Aug. 16, 1990.

Treaties
Vienna convention on the law of treaties between states and international organizations or between international organizations, with annex. Done at Vienna Mar. 21, 1986. [2]
Ratification deposited: Argentina, Aug 17, 1990.
Accession deposited: Spain, July 24, 1990.

Trusts
Convention on the law applicable to trusts and on their recognition. Done at The Hague July 1, 1985. [2]
Ratifications deposited: Italy, Feb. 21, 1990; UK, Nov. 17, 1989. [1,3,4]

BILATERAL

Argentina
Agreement extending the annexes of the air transport agreement of Oct. 22, 1985, as amended and extended. Effected by exchange of notes at Buenos Aires June 22 and July 27, 1990. Entered into force July 27, 1990.

Australia
Protocol amending the treaty on extradition of May 14, 1974 (TIAS 8234). Signed at Seoul Sept. 4, 1990. Enters into force on date on which the parties have exchanged written notification that they have complied with their respective requirements.

Belize
Agreement concerning grants of defense articles and services to Belize from US military stocks. Effected by exchange of notes at Belize and Belmopan Aug. 6 and 23, 1990. Entered into force Aug. 23, 1990.

Czechoslovakia
Agreement concerning trade in certain steel products, with arrangement. Effected by exchange of letters at Washington and Prague Oct. 27, 1989, and Aug. 10, 1990. Entered into force Aug. 10, 1990; effective Oct. 1, 1989.

Ecuador
Agreement regarding the consolidation and rescheduling or refinancing of certain debts owed to, guaranteed by, or insured by the US government and its agencies, with annexes. Signed at Washington July 30, 1990. Entered into force Sept. 12, 1990.

Egypt
First amendment to the grant agreement of Sept. 27, 1989, for power sector support. Signed at Cairo Aug. 21, 1990. Entered into force Aug. 21, 1990.

Fourth amendment to the grant agreement of Sept. 26, 1984, for Cairo Sewerage II. Signed at Cairo Aug. 21, 1990. Entered into force Aug. 21, 1990.

Sixth amendment to the grant agreement of Sept. 22, 1981 (TIAS 10277), for irrigation management systems. Signed at Cairo Aug. 21, 1990. Entered into force Aug. 21, 1990.

Grant Agreement for cash transfer. Signed at Cairo Aug. 31, 1990. Entered into force Aug. 31, 1990.

German Democratic Republic
International express mail agreement, with detailed regulations. Signed at Berlin and Washington Aug. 6 and Sept. 7, 1990. Entered into force Oct. 15, 1990.

Indonesia
Agreement amending the air transport agreement of Jan. 15, 1968 (TIAS 6441), as amended. Effected by exchange of notes at Jakarta April 12 and June 19, 1990. Entered into force June 19, 1990

Mexico
Minute 283 of the International Boundary and Water Commission: Conceptual plan for the international solution to the border sanitation problem in San Diego, California/Tijuana, Baja California. Signed at El Paso July 2, 1990. Entered into force August 8, 1990.

Agreement amending the agreement of Feb. 13, 1988, as amended, concerning trade in cotton, wool, and man-made fiber textiles and textile products. Effected by exchange of notes at Mexico July 19 and Aug. 3, 1990. Entered into force Aug. 3, 1990.

Mongolia
Agreement concerning the reciprocal issuance of visas to government officials. Effected by exchange of notes at Ulaanbaatar Aug. 2, 1990. Entered into force Aug. 2, 1990.

North Atlantic Treaty Organization
Tax reimbursement agreement, with annex. Signed at Brussels July 18, 1990. Entered into force: July 18, 1990; applicable with regard to tax reimbursements for institutional income earned after Feb. 29, 1984.

Pakistan
Project grant agreement for Balochistan road project. Signed at Islamabad Aug. 9, 1990. Entered into force Aug. 9, 1990.

Senegal
Agreement regarding the consolidation and rescheduling of certain debts owed to, guaranteed by, or insured by the US government and its agencies, with annexes. Signed at Dakar July 13, 1990. Entered into force Sept. 5, 1990.

Singapore
Agreement amending the air transport agreement of March 31, 1978, as amended (TIAS 9002, 9654). Effected by exchange of notes at Singapore May 18 and June 15, 1990. Entered into force June 15, 1990.

Thailand
Agreement on research collaboration related to HIV infection and AIDS [acquired immune deficiency syndrome] in Thailand, with annex. Signed at Bangkok and Atlanta July 24 and Aug. 3 and 8, 1990. Entered into force Aug. 8, 1990.

USSR
Implementing agreement concerning cooperation in the space flight of a Soviet Meteor-3 satellite employing a US Total Ozone Mapping Spectrometer (TOMS). Signed at Moscow July 25, 1990. Entered into force Aug. 24, 1990.

United Kingdom
Agreement extending the agreement of Apr. 14, 1987, as extended, concerning the British Virgin Islands and narcotics activities. Effected by exchange of notes at Washington Aug. 9, 1990. Entered into force Aug. 9, 1990; effective Aug. 12, 1990.

Venezuela
Agreement extending the agreement of Dec. 26, 1984, as extended (TIAS 10652), establishing a Venezuela-United States Agriculture Commission. Effected by exchange of notes at Washington Feb. 15 and July 31, 1990. Entered into force July 31, 1990; effective Dec. 27, 1989.

---

1 With reservation(s).
2 Not in force.
3 With declaration.
4 Territorial Application: Isle of Man, Bermuda, British Antarctic Territory, British Virgin Is., Falkland Is., Gibraltar, St. Helena, St. Helena Dependencies, South Georgia and the South Sandwich Is., UK Sovereign Base Areas of Akrotiri and Dhekelia in the Is. of Cyprus (Nov. 17, 1989) and Hong Kong (Mar. 30, 1990).

III. October 1990

MULTILATERAL

Agriculture
International plant protection convention. Done at Rome Dec. 6, 1951. Entered into force Apr. 3, 1952; for the US Aug. 18, 1972. TIAS 7465.
Adherence deposited: St. Kitts & Nevis, Apr. 17, 1990.

Maritime Matters
Convention on facilitation of international maritime traffic, with annex. Done at London Apr. 9, 1965. Entered into force Mar. 5, 1967; for the US May 16, 1967. TIAS 6251.
Accession deposited: Portugal, Aug. 6, 1990.

Nuclear Weapons – Nonproliferation
Treaty on the nonproliferation of nuclear weapons. Done at Washington, London, and Moscow July 1, 1968. Entered into force Mar. 5, 1970. TIAS 6839.
Accession deposited: Albania, Sept. 12, 1990.

Pollution
Annex V to the international convention for the prevention of pollution from ships, 1973. Done at London Nov. 2, 1973. Entered into force Dec. 31, 1988.
Acceptance deposited: Australia, Aug. 14, 1990.

Convention for the protection of the ozone layer, with annexes. Done at Vienna Mar. 22, 1985. Entered into force Sept. 22, 1988. (Senate) Treaty Doc. 99-9.

Montreal protocol on substances that deplete the ozone layer, with annex. Done at Montreal Sept. 16, 1987. Entered into force Jan. 1, 1989. (Senate) Treaty Doc. 100-10.
Accessions deposited: Brazil, Mar. 19, 1990; Iran, Oct. 3, 1990.

Protocol to the 1979 convention on long-range trans-boundary air pollution concerning the control of emissions of nitrogen oxides or their transboundary flows, with annex. Done at Sofia Oct. 31, 1988. [1]
Ratifications deposited: Luxembourg, Oct. 4, 1990; UK, Oct. 15, 1990.

Torture
Convention against torture and other cruel, inhuman, or degrading treatment or punishment. Done at New York Dec. 10, 1984. Entered into force June 26, 1987. [2] (Senate) Treaty Doc. 100-20.
Senate advice and consent to ratification: Oct. 27, 1990. [3]

BILATERAL

Canada
Agreement on fisheries enforcement. Signed at Ottawa Sept. 26, 1990. Enters into force upon notification by the par-

ties that they have completed their internal procedures.

Egypt
Grant agreement for commodity imports. Signed at Cairo Sept. 30, 1990. Entered into force Sept. 30, 1990.

Indonesia
Agreement extending the agreement of Dec. 11, 1978 (TIAS 9609), for scientific and technical cooperation. Signed at Jakarta Oct. 4 and 5, 1990. Entered into force Oct. 5, 1990.

Ireland
Agreement amending the agreement of Feb. 3, 1945 (EAS 460), as amended, relating to air transport services, with annex. Effected by exchange of notes at Dublin July 25 and Sept. 6, 1990. Supersedes agreement of June 11, 1973 (TIAS 7660).

Italy
Memorandum of understanding relating to the air transport services agreement of June 22, 1970 (TIAS 6957), as amended, with related exchange of letters. Signed at Rome Sept. 27, 1990. Entered into force Sept. 27, 1990, except for amendment to Article 10, which shall enter into force on the 15th day following the date of exchange of notes covering the Italian instrument of ratification.

Namibia
General agreement for special development assistance. Signed at New York Sept. 28, 1990. Entered into force Sept. 28, 1990.

Netherlands
Agreement on social security, with administrative arrangement. Signed at The Hague Dec. 8, 1987.

Protocol to the agreement on social security and administrative arrangement of Dec. 8, 1987. Signed at The Hague Dec. 7, 1989.
Entered into force: Nov. 1, 1990.

Nicaragua
Grant agreement to provide balance-of-payments support and to assist Nicaragua in its efforts to stabilize the economy. Signed at Washington Sept. 26, 1990. Entered into force Sept. 26, 1990.

Philippines
Grant agreement for natural resources management program. Signed at Manila Sept. 28, 1990. Entered into force Sept. 28, 1990.

Poland
Agreement regarding the consolidation and rescheduling of certain debts owed to, guaranteed by, or insured by the US government and its agencies, with annexes. Signed at Warsaw Aug. 24, 1990. Entered into force: Oct. 22, 1990.

Senegal
Treaty concerning the reciprocal encouragement and protection of investment, with annex and protocol. Signed at Washington Dec. 6, 1983. (Senate) Treaty Doc. 99-15. Entered into force: Oct. 25, 1990.

USSR
Agreement regarding certain maritime matters, with annexes. Signed at Washington June 1, 1990. Entered into force: Oct. 1, 1990.

Venezuela
Agreement amending the annex to the air transport services agreement of Aug. 14, 1953, as amended (TIAS 2813, 7549, 8433). Effected by exchange of notes at Washington July 19 and Oct. 10, 1990. Entered into force Oct. 10. 1990.

---

1 Not in force.
2 Not in force for the US.
3 With reservations, declarations, understandings, and a proviso.

PRESS RELEASES

Department of State

Press releases may be obtained from the Office of Press Relations, Department of State, Washington, D.C. 20520-6810.

No.	Date	Subject
*127	9/7	Baker: remarks to U.S. Air Force men and women, Saudi Arabia, September 7.
*128	9/8	Baker: press conference with President Hosni Mubarak of Egypt, Alexandria, September 8.
*129	9/9	Baker: interview by Tom Brokaw, NBC-TV, Helsinki, September 9.
*130	9/12	Baker: press briefing after Helsinki Summit, September 9.
*131	9/12	Baker: interview on "Newsmaker Sunday," CNN, Helsinki, September 9.
*132	9/14	Baker: interview on "Face the Nation," CBS-TV, Helsinki September 9.
*133	9/14	Baker: interview by Dan Rather, CBS-TV, Helsinki, September 9.
*134	9/10	Baker: opening statement at press conference following North Atlantic Council (NAC) ministerial, Brussels, September 10
135	9/12	Baker: press conference following NAC ministerial including opening statement, Brussels, September 10.
136	9/12	Baker: press conference with other Two-Plus-Four ministers following signing of treaty on Germany, Moscow, September 12.
137	9/17	Baker: press conference with Foreign Minister Fahrouk Shara of Syria, Damascus, September 14.
*138	9/17	Baker: press briefing with Foreign Minister Gianni de Michelis of Italy, Rome, September 14.
*139	9/18	Baker: press briefing with Foreign Minister Hans-Dietrich Genscher, Federal Republic of Germany, Bonn, September 15.
140	9/19	Baker: press briefing with Chancellor Helmut Kohl, Federal Republic of Germany, Bonn, September 15.
*141	9/19	Baker: press briefing following meetings with Chancellor Kohl and Foreign Minister Genscher, Bonn, September 15.
*142	9/21	Program for the official working visit of Frederick Willem de Klerk, President of the Republic of South Africa, September 23-25.
*143	9/24	Baker: interview on "Meet the Press," NBC-TV, September 23.
*144	9/27	Program for the official working visit of Shaikh Al-Ahmad, Al-Sabah, Amir of the State of Kuwait, September 28.
*145	10/4	Edwin D. Williamson, Department of State Legal Adviser (biographic data).
146	9/25	Baker: remarks at meeting of United Nations Security Council, New York, September 25.
*147	9/25	Baker: remarks following Security Council meeting, September 25.
*148	9/26	Baker: remarks with Foreign Minister Eduard Shevardnadze, U.S.S.R., at beginning of bilateral meeting, New York, September 26.
*149	9/26	Baker: remarks with Foreign Minister Shevardnadze after bilateral meeting, September 26.
*150	9/26	Baker: remarks before bilateral meeting with Foreign Minister Sabah Al-Sabah of Kuwait, New York, September 26.
*151	9/26	Baker: remarks before bilateral meeting with Foreign Minister David Levy of Israel, New York, September 26.
*152	9/27	Baker: remarks before bilateral meeting with Foreign Minister Saud Al-Faisal of Saudi Arabia, New York, September 27.
*153	9/27	Baker: remarks with Foreign Minister Eduard Shevardnadze, U.S.S.R., before bilateral meeting, New York, September 27.
*154	9/27	Baker: remarks with Foreign Minister Shevardnadze after bilateral meeting, September 27.
*155	9/28	Baker: remarks before bilateral meeting with Foreign Minister Habib Boulares of Tunisia, New York, September 28.
156	9/29	Baker: remarks with Foreign Minister Nguyen Co Thach of Vietnam, New York, September 29.
*157	10/1	Baker: remarks at beginning of CSCE ministerial meeting, New York, October 1.
*158	10/2	Baker: closing remarks at CSCE ministerial meeting, October 2.
*159	10/2	Baker: remarks before bilateral meeting with Foreign Minister Sten Sture Andersson of Sweden, New York, October 2
160	10/2	Baker: press conference after CSCE ministerial meeting, October 2.
*161	10/3	Baker: remarks with Foreign Minister Eduard Shevardnadze, U.S.S.R., before bilateral meeting, New York, October 3.
*162	10/3	Baker: remarks while with Baltic Foreign Ministers Meri of Estonia, Jurkans of Latvia, and Saudargas of Lithuanaia, New York, October 2.
*163	10/3	Baker: remarks with Foreign Minister Eduard Shevardnadze, U.S.S.R., after bilateral meeting, New York, October 3.
164	10/16	Baker: press conference on terrorism information rewards program, October 16.
165	10/18	Baker: statement before Senate Foreign Relations Committee, October 17, and House Foreign Affairs Committee, October 18.
166	10/19	Baker: remarks to the American Committee on U.S.-Soviet Relations, October 19.
*167	10/10	Baker: press conference with Secretary of Defense Richard Cheney and Foreign Minister Gareth Evans and Defense Minister Robert Ray of Australia following ministerial meeting at Blair House, October 8.
*168	10/4	Baker: press conference at the White House on agreement in principle of CFE Treaty, October 4.
169	10/29	Baker: speech to Los Angeles World Affairs Council, October 29.
170	10/30	Release of *Foreign Relations of the United States,* 1955-57, volume XIX, National Security Policy.
171	11/1	Release of *Foreign Relations of the United States,* 1955-57, volume XXV, Eastern Europe.
*172	10/31	Baker: remarks at luncheon in honor of Citizens Democracy Corps, October 31.
*173	10/31	Baker: interview by Tom Brokaw, NBC-TV, October 31.

*Not printed in the Bulletin.

Foreign Relations Volumes on National Security Policy and Eastern Europe, 1955-57

The Department of State, on October 30, 1990, released Foreign Relations of the United States, 1955-1957, volume XIX, National Security Policy. [1]

This volume covers the internal evolution of U.S. policy on basic national security, estimated threats to the nation, the emphasis on nuclear weapons over conventional forces, missile and and other weapons programs, and civil defense.

The preface provides information on the methodology followed in preparation of the volume and includes guides to the files and lists of materials consulted in its preparation. It also provides information on the method of indicating the absence of material withheld in the declassification review process and on particular problems encountered in the course of compilation.

This volume documents the extensive discussions of the February 1955 report prepared by a committee headed by James R. Killian, Jr., President of M.I.T. The Killian Committee report made sweeping recommendations to reduce U.S. vulnerability to possible surprise attack and emphasized the urgency and importance of U.S. missile programs. As part of its emphasis on nuclear weapons, President Dwight D. Eisenhower's administration began to develop tactical nuclear armament. Strategic doctrine evolved gradually so that by 1957 the administration was considering less than "massive retaliation" responses to foreign conflicts. While continuing to integrate nuclear weapons in U.S. military forces, the administration also began to place more emphasis on mobile and easily deployable forces to respond to aggression "in a manner and on a scale best calculated to avoid hostilities from broadening into general war."

President Eisenhower and Secretary of State John Foster Dulles recognized the importance of educating the public on the distinction between tactical nuclear weapons that might be used by conventional armed forces against strictly military targets and large nuclear bombs with high levels of radioactive fall-out. But the warnings of Secretary Dulles and other administration officials that attempts to inform the American public on the destructive effects of nuclear weapons in a "dramatic, nationwide" educational campaign might create hysteria instead of informed judgment persuaded Eisenhower to adopt a more gradual strategy of working with elite opinion groups to disseminate the administration's perspective.

President Eisenhower also resisted the costly recommendations of the report of a special panel headed by H. Rowan Gaither, Jr., Chairman of the Boards of the Ford Foundation and the Rand Corporation, in November 1957. The report proposed not only a modest shelter program but accelerated missile programs, improved readiness for the Strategic Air Command, and increased emphasis on scientific research and conventional armed forces. He received strong support from Secretary Dulles who argued that the Gaither report focused too narrowly on the military struggle with international communism at the expense of political and economic aspects. Dulles also objected to any elaborate shelter program.

Nearly all of the documents were declassified for this publication.

Copies of volume XIX (Department of State Publication No. 9758; GPO Stock No. 044-000-02275-3) may be purchased for $28.00 (domestic postpaid) and for $35.00 (foreign postpaid) from the Superintendent of Documents, U.S. Government Printing Office, Washington, D.C. 20402.

The Department of State, on November 1, 1990, released Foreign Relations of the United States, 1955-1957, Volume XXV, Eastern Europe. [2]

Documentation in this 706-page volume was selected from previously classified records of the White House, Department of State, and other government agencies. The preface describes the methodology followed in preparing the volume and the principles followed in selecting documents. It also explains the method of indicating material withheld in the declassification review process as well as particular problems encountered in the course of compilation and declassification.

The documents published in this volume demonstrate that in early 1955 the Eisenhower administration was not optimistic concerning its aim to detach major East European Soviet satellites. There seemed little hope of fostering "National Communism" and loosening Moscow's grip behind the "Iron Curtain." Intelligence estimates concluded that at least through 1960, Soviet control of East Germany, Poland, Czechoslovakia, Hungary, Romania, Bulgaria, and Albania would remain intact.

The situation in the Soviet bloc changed rapidly after Soviet First Secretary Nikita Khrushchev denounced the late Joseph Stalin at a secret session of the Soviet Communist Party Congress in early 1956. Khrushchev's speech encouraged East Europeans to criticize their Stalinist leaders and consider changing their Stalinist regimes. By June 1956, Polish workers rioted, and a reform-minded, more nationalist Communist leadership came to power in Poland. Closer U.S.-Polish relations evolved thereafter.

The wave of Eastern European awakening and unrest culminated with the Hungarian uprising of October 1956 when for a brief moment it appeared that a nationalist, anti-Soviet popular revolt might overthrow Soviet control. Eisenhower and his advisers had discussed such a possibility, but when the rebellion occurred the Eisenhower administration could offer the Hungarians no more than moral support. In early November 1956, the Soviet Union crushed the rebellion and many Hungarians felt betrayed by the United States, believing that it had encouraged their revolt and then stood by and watched the Soviet Union suppress it. The volume published here shows how the U.S. Government struggled to understand the rebellion and its aftermath.

Copies of volume XXV (Department of State Publication No. 9760; GPO Stock No. 044-000-02263-0) may be purchased for $28.00 (domestic postpaid) or $35.00 (foreign postpaid) from the Superintendent of Documents, U.S. Government Printing Office, Washington, D.C. 20402.

---

1 Department of State Press Release 170, October 30, 1990, with minor deletions.
2 Department of State Press Release 171, November 1, 1990, with minor deletions.

INDEX

INDEX

Name Index

Subscribe to
THE FOREIGN POLICY BULLETIN

for only $35 a year

Use the order form below
and/or submit your own purchase order
— or you may enter your subscription
through a subscription agency

For further information, call: (202) 686-5230

FOREIGN POLICY BULLETIN ORDER FORM
(Photocopy to send)

TO: **FOREIGN POLICY BULLETIN**
4812 Butterworth Place, N.W.
Washington, D.C. 20016

Please enter _____ subscription(s) for _____ year(s) to the FOREIGN POLICY BULLETIN at $35.00 per year or $53.00 outside the U.S. and Canada.

_____ Payment is enclosed.

_____ Please send an invoice.

Please Type or Print
Organization or Personal Name _____

Additional Address/Attention Line _____

Street Address _____

City, State, Zip Code _____

Daytime Phone, Including Area Code _____

FOREIGN POLICY BULLETIN
4812 Butterworth Place, N.W.
Washington, D.C. 20016

BULK RATE
U.S. POSTAGE
PAID
WASHINGTON, D.C.
PERMIT NO. 4393

Foreign Policy
bulletin

The Documentary Record of United States Foreign Policy / Volume 1 / Number 4 & 5

January/February 1991
March/April 1991

SPECIAL DOUBLE ISSUE

War and Peace
in the Persian Gulf

From November 8th announcement
doubling U.S. Forces
to February 27th suspension
of offensive operations

Also in this Issue:

Shevardnadze's Resignation

Paris Summit for a New Europe

U.S.-Japan Economic Relations

President Visits South America

BULLETIN SPECIALS:

Congressional Hearings and Debate on Persian Gulf,
Interview with New Soviet Foreign Minister Bessmertnykh,
Shamir on Scud Missiles, Mitterand on Paris Summit,
Gorbachev on New Europe, Baltic States and Gulf War

An independent publication with editorial autonomy • No government affiliation

Foreign Policy *bulletin*

Volume 1/Number 4 & 5
January/February 1991
March/April 1991

PHOTO AND GRAPHIC CREDITS:

1)Cover photo of American troops in Saudi Arabia, Department of Defense.

2)Page 5 photo of Secretary of Defense Richard B. Cheney and Joint Chiefs of Staff Chairman Colin L.Powell testifying before Senate Armed Services Committee, Department of Defense.

3)Page 94 map of European Community membership, Department of State.

The **FOREIGN POLICY BULLETIN** is published bimonthly (plus annual index) as a private publication of Mediacom, Inc. It uses the same format as the discontinued "Department of State Bulletin" and maintains continuity with that publication while offering additional materials as well. Its purpose is to provide a timely and systematic record of United States foreign policy and of complementary documents from international sources. The **BULLETIN's** coverage of official U.S. documents includes major addresses, diplomatic statements, and press conferences of the President and the Secretary of State; statements and congressional testimony by the Secretary and other administration officials; treaties and other agreements to which the United States is or may become a party; special reports; and selected press releases issued by the White House, the Department of State, and other agencies. Special features include speeches and other statements by foreign officials concerning U.S. policy; reports and other materials from international organizations relating to major issues confronting U.S. policymakers; and background information about countries of particular interest to U.S. foreign relations.

PAUL E. AUERSWALD
Editor and Publisher

PHILIP AUERSWALD
Assistant Editor/Business Manager

HUGUETTE NIZARD
Subscriptions Manager

HOPE FUNG
Layout and Typesetting

J. LEONARD MAZUR
Marketing Consultant

Printed by
PRINTING SERVICE INTERNATIONAL

ISSN 1052-7036

SUBSCRIPTIONS: Annual subscriptions to the **BULLETIN** are $35.00; outside the U.S. and Canada $53.00. Subscription orders should be sent to: Subscriptions, Foreign Policy Bulletin, 4812 Butterworth Place N.W., Washington, D.C. 20016. To subscribe by phone, call (202) 686-5230.

SINGLE COPIES: Single copies, if still in print, can be obtained for $10.00 a copy plus postage by writing to the address below.

CORRESPONDENCE should be addressed to: Foreign Policy Bulletin, 4812 Butterworth Place N.W., Washington, D.C. 20016. Telephone: (202) 686-5230

INDEXING: Included in the PAIS (Public Affairs Information Service) indexes: the PAIS Bulletin, PAIS on CD-ROM, and online through Dialog, BRS, and Data-Star. Information about other indexing services will be provided in subsequent issues.

SPECIAL DOUBLE ISSUE

In order to release full documentation of the Persian Gulf War and the events preceding it as soon as possible, we have published a "double issue"--including both the January/February and March/April issues. Although this meant some delay in releasing the first of the two issues, it speeds up considerably publication of documentation of the war period and provides the entire chronology in one place. In all, it covers the four months from November 1990 through February 1991. We are excited about this "double issue" and the range and volume of the materials it offers. We hope those interested in the study of U.S. foreign relations will share our enthusiasm.

Paul E. Auerswald
Editor

CONTENTS

FEATURE: WAR AND PEACE IN THE GULF

Part I: November 8, 1990 - January 11, 1991

Part II: January 12, 1991 - February 27, 1991

CONTENTS

PARIS SUMMIT: "A GRAND TURN IN THE COURSE OF HISTORY"

War and Peace in the Gulf
Part I: November 8, 1990 - January 11, 1991

President's Press Conference Announcing Major Troop Increase, November 8, 1990 [1]

On August 6th, in response to the unprovoked Iraqi invasion of Kuwait, I ordered the deployment of U.S. military forces to Saudi Arabia and the Persian Gulf to deter further Iraqi aggression and to protect our interests in the region. What we've done is right, and I'm happy to say that most Members of Congress and the majority of Americans agree.

Before the invasion in August, we had succeeded in the struggle for freedom in Eastern Europe, and we'd hopefully begun a new era that offered the promise of peace. Following the invasion, I stated that if history had taught us any lesson it was that we must resist aggression or it would destroy our freedom. Just ask the people of Kuwait and the foreign nationals in hiding there and the staffs of the remaining embassies who have experienced the horrors of Iraq's illegal occupation, its systematic dismantling of Kuwait, and its abuse of Kuwaitis and other citizens.

The world community also must prevent an individual clearly bent on regional domination from establishing a chokehold on the world's economic lifeline. We're seeing global economic stability and growth already at risk as, each day, countries around the world pay dearly for Saddam Hussein's aggression.

From the very beginning, we and our coalition partners have shared common political goals: the immediate, complete, and unconditional withdrawal of Iraqi forces from Kuwait; restoration of Kuwait's legitimate government; protection of the lives of citizens held hostage by Iraq both in Kuwait and Iraq; and restoration of security and stability in the Persian Gulf region.

To achieve these goals, we and our allies have forged a strong diplomatic, economic, and military strategy to force Iraq to comply with these objectives. The framework of this strategy is laid out in ten United Nations resolutions, overwhelmingly supported by the United Nations Security Council. In three months, the U.S. troop contribution to the multinational force in Saudi Arabia has gone from 10,000 to 230,000 as part of Operation Desert Shield. General Schwarzkopf [commander of the U.S. forces in the Persian Gulf] reports that our forces, in conjunction with other coalition forces, now have the capability to defend successfully against any further Iraqi aggression.

I have today directed the Secretary of Defense to increase the size of U.S. forces committed to Desert Shield...

After consultation with King Fahd [of Saudi Arabia] and our other allies, I have today directed the Secretary of Defense to increase the size of U.S. forces committed to Desert Shield to ensure that the coalition has an adequate offensive military option should that be necessary to achieve our common goals. Toward this end, we will continue to discuss the possibility of both additional allied force contributions and appropriate United Nations actions.

Iraq's brutality, aggression, and violations of international law cannot be allowed to succeed. Secretary Baker has been consulting with our key partners in the coalition. He's met with the Amirs of Bahrain ['Isa bin Salman Al Khalifa] and Kuwait [Jabir al-Ahmad al-Jabir al-Sabah], King Fahd, President Mubarak [of Egypt], as well as the Chinese Foreign Minister [Qian Qichen], President Özal [of Turkey], [Soviet] Foreign Minister Shevardnadze, President Gorbachev. He also will be meeting with Prime Minister Thatcher [of the United Kingdom] and President Mitterrand [of France]. I've been heartened by Jim's appraisal of the strong international solidarity and determination to ensure that Iraq's aggression does not stand and is not rewarded.

But right now, Kuwait is struggling for survival. And along with many other nations, we've been called upon to help. The consequences of our not doing so would be incalculable because Iraq's aggression is not just a challenge to the security of Kuwait and other Gulf nations, but to the better world that we all have hoped to build in the wake of the Cold War. And therefore, we and our allies cannot and will not shirk our responsibilities. The state of Kuwait must be restored, or no nation will be safe and the promising future we anticipate will indeed be jeopardized.

Let me conclude with a word to the young American GI's deployed in the Gulf. We are proud of each and every one of you. I know you miss your loved ones and want to know when you'll be coming home. We won't leave you there any longer than necessary. I want every single soldier out of there as soon as possible. And we're all grateful for your continued sacrifice and your commitment.

Q. Mr. President, it sounds like you're going to war. You have moved from a defensive position to an offensive position, and you have not said how many more troops you are sending or, really, why.

A. Well, I've said why right now. And I hope it's been very clear to the American people.

Q. Are there new reasons that have moved this posture?

A. No, it's just continuing to do what we feel is necessary to complete our objectives, to fulfill our objectives, that have been clearly stated.

Q. Well, are you going to war?

A. I would love to see a peaceful resolution to this question, and that's what I wanted.

The heart of our effort, if there is a theme underlying U.S. policy over the last four months, has been the fact that we have not "gone it alone" . . . we have, indeed, functioned as part of a world-wide international coalition.

Secretary of Defense Cheney,
December 3, 1990

Q. What made the change from the defense to offense?

A. I would like to see a peaceful solution to this question. I think Saddam Hussein should fully, without condition, comply to the U.N. resolutions. And if this movement of force is what convinces him, so much the better.

Q. You said last week that the sanctions haven't had the impact that you wanted. Some members of the coalition are urging a go-slow approach. The President of Egypt says you've got to wait two or three months before you judge whether the sanctions have worked. Are you willing to wait that long?

A. Wait for what?

Q. To see if the sanctions have worked?

A. I think from talking to Jim Baker and recently to President Mubarak that we are in total sync with him. But I hope that the sanctions will work within a two month period. But I don't think we've got a difference with Egypt on this at all, Terry [Terence Hunt, Associated Press].

Q. The question is how long are you willing to give the sanctions?

A. Well, I can't tell you how long. If I knew, I certainly wouldn't want to signal that to Saddam Hussein.

Q. Prime Minister Thatcher said yesterday that if, indeed, Saddam doesn't withdraw from Kuwait that you and the allies will use force. I haven't heard you say that before. You've talked about wanting to retain the option of war, but would you use force?

A. Well, I don't want to say what I will or will not do. But certainly, I noted what Prime Minister Thatcher said, one of the strongest members of this coalition. And she's an eloquent spokesman for her views and speaks in a way that shows that we're all together. So, I have not ruled out the use of force at all, and I think that's evident by what we're doing here today.

Q. Sir, can I just follow that up by going back to the speech you gave at the Pentagon back in August, when you talked about oil, protecting Middle East oil reserves, and you talked about American jobs, in fact the American way of life being endangered. Yet when you went out on the campaign trail, you seemed to shy away from oil. You said demonstrators don't seem to

understand that we're not going to go to war for oil. But that was one of the things you talked about. And in fact, isn't oil part of the American national interest? Isn't that a main reason we're there?

A. It is a part of it, but it is not the main reason—or I'd say, a main reason. The main reason we're there is to set back aggression, to see that aggression is unrewarded. My argument with some of the protestors is that they seem to suggest that oil is the sole reason that we are involved in this enormous commitment. And that is simply not correct. There's a lot of other interests, and the restoration of the security and stability in the Persian Gulf region clearly relates to the world's economic interest. I'm not denying that, and I'm not backing away from the fact that all the Western world has real interest in that. But my argument with those people is that they are missing the point. The point is: It is the aggression against Kuwait that has caused this coalition to come together as it has.

Q. Do you feel that you are free to take offensive action without any kind of U.N. resolution authorizing it?

A. Yes, we have authority. But we've been great believers in going to the United Nations. I think one of the major successes has been the ability to have world opinion totally on our side because of U.N. action. The peacekeeping function of the United Nations has indeed been rejuvenated by the actions of the Security Council.

Q. Mr. President, do you yet have the support you need in order to secure an additional resolution from the U.N. Security Council to explicitly authorize the use of force? Do you now have sufficient support on the Security Council to get that?

A. I would say that the Baker mission is—what it is about is consultation. That subject will be discussed in some ways, I'm sure, but that's not why he's there. We're talking about a wide array of issues and so I'd say we have not tried to specifically poll the other 14 members of the Security Council along those lines. So, I can't answer whether we would or not.

Q. If I may follow: Has any country told you they would block such a resolution?

A. Some may have said such a thing, but it's not been brought to my attention at all. And again, I think I'd know if that were the case. But I don't think so.

Q. Mr. President, it would seem that the situation at the U.S. Embassy in Kuwait is crucial to the future of the overall situation in the Gulf. What is the latest there? What is the situation with their food and water supplies? And do you have any plan in the works to resupply them?

A. I think it's unconscionable to try to starve people out and to isolate them from food and supplies of all kinds, and that's exactly what's going on. In terms of how long they can survive, I'm not sure I could give you a specific answer, but I believe the answer would be a few weeks, something of that nature.

Q. Are there plans to resupply them when they run out or—

A. Well, if there were, given the hostile environment in which these people are living, it would be unproductive to discuss it.

Q. Mr. President, what has happened in the last two weeks that has led you to put now an offensive force into Saudi Arabia?

A. Well, we have not only offensive but defensive forces there already. And what leads me to do this is just because I believe, upon the advice of our able Secretary of Defense and others, that this is in the best security interests of our people that are there and of the coalition. I think it is just a guarantee of the safety of all, and I think it sends a very strong signal—another strong signal—to Saddam Hussein that we are very, very serious about seeing the United Nations resolutions complied to in their entirety, without any kind of watering down.

Q. Would you say that we're in a critical phase now between a peaceful solution and a possible armed conflict?

A. I wouldn't phrase it that way.

Q. Mr. President, the longer that you wait and the longer that no action is taken in Kuwait, the less and less there seems to be of Kuwait. What's the point of waiting if there's not going to be anything left of that country when you finally decide to go in?

A. Well, I've told you that I would like to feel that Saddam Hussein would come to his senses and comply under economic pressure with the sanctions that have been taken in the United Nations and with the objectives. I would like to think the economic sanctions would compel him to do that which he has been unwilling to do. Regrettably, he keeps reiterating his view that this is not Kuwait but Province 19, and that is

unacceptable to the United States and to our partners. So, I think we're giving these sanctions time to work. We're giving world opinion time to mobilize and impress on him that we're all serious. But now we're moving up our forces for the reasons I've given you.

Q. But there might not be much left of Kuwait.

A. Well, that worries me. It worries me very much, as do the lives of those who have been forced into hiding by his brutality and his violation of international law. Of course, it concerns me deeply. And I've spoken about that, the dismantling of Kuwait and the systematic brutality that is exercised against the citizens of Kuwait. And as each day goes by it's worse. So, I take your point that it's—I guess it's your point—that it's a very bad situation. But I just keep reiterating my determination to see our objectives fulfilled here.

Q. Sir, on your consultation that your Secretary of State's doing now in Moscow, could you just spell out for us what your understanding is as of today with Mikhail Gorbachev on the use of force?

A. Well, I talked to Jim Baker—it's a very timely question because I talked to him, just before coming in here, from Moscow; and he had a long series of consultations and discussions there with the Foreign Minister and with Mr. Gorbachev. I am convinced, from what the Secretary has told me, that we are on the same wavelength in terms of the objectives that I spelled out here. But I can't go in with you into what the Soviet position will be on the use of force. I don't think they've been asked to send forces. Is that—maybe I missed the question.

Q. Mr. Shevardnadze on the record today said that they, too, would not rule out the use of force, while they still wanted a peaceful solution. Does that at least help you send the kind of signal to Saddam Hussein that you're also trying to send here?

A. I think it is very helpful. But I think the signal of solidarity between the United States and the Soviet Union and the rest of the Security Council has already gone out. But, no, I think that it is very helpful to have a position like that stated and restated, because that's the way the whole world feels. And it is good to have this solid front between ourselves and the Soviet Union. And I think Jim felt that he had a constructive visit with the Chinese Foreign

Minister. And he's looking forward to his meetings with President Mitterrand and Prime Minister Thatcher in the next couple of days. But his trip has been extraordinarily helpful in sending that signal of solidarity and determination on the part of those that are involved here, strong determination.

Q. I understand that we're going to be getting [a briefing from Secretary of Defense Cheney] and General Powell [Chairman of the Joint Chiefs of Staff] will speak later, but can you please give us some sense of the numbers and types of reinforcements that you're sending to the Gulf? And do you believe that this will be the final deployment? We keep seeing the numbers ratcheting up and hearing that this should be sufficient to do the job.

A. Let me simply say we're talking about substantial numbers. I will defer, with your permission, of course, to the Secretary of Defense and the Chairman of the Joint Chiefs, who will be able to help more than I will on the details of this move. But I can't say whether—after this is completed—whether there will be anything else done or not. I mean, I am still hopeful that Saddam Hussein will get the message that he is not going to prevail and that he has to get out of Kuwait without condition, and that the rulers have to come back and that the stability of the Gulf must be guaranteed. So, I would simply leave it there and, if you would, let the defense experts take the rest of it.

Q. As you have consulted—if I may follow up—on this deployment and, in fact, on the military situation overall with the other countries involved in the multinational forces, there have been complaints, observations out of Israel that, were there to be offensive action, there needs to be coordination or some sort of chain of command involving the Israelis, too, where they may end up being involved. To what extent are you communicating with the Israelis, and to what extent do you envision any role or possible role for the Israelis should this come to war?

A. I think the whole world knows that the United States has a very special relationship with Israel—a strong relationship. I think we are in close touch with the key players there in terms of our objectives, and I think they have conducted themselves regarding all of this very well, indeed. But I am not going to discuss any more details than that. But I feel that we're

on a good wavelength there. We had some differences, obviously.

Q. Mr. President, to follow up on Wyatt's [Wyatt Andrews, CBS News] question: After Foreign Minister Shevardnadze made his comments today, President Gorbachev seemed to say that it was too early to talk about the use of force. Are the Soviets sending us mixed signals—

A. No—

Q.—or is this just an indication that, like President Mubarak made earlier in the week, that some of our allies want more time to try to find a diplomatic solution before use of force?

A. I don't get the feeling we're getting any mixed signals at all from the Soviets, particularly after I've talked to Jim Baker. I know there was some feeling there were mixed signals because of Mr. Primakov's [Soviet Presidential Council member] mission, but upon the completion of that, I think people recognize that we are still very much in agreement with the Soviets on matters as it relates to the Gulf. It's good, Ann [Ann Devroy, Washington Post], and it's strong. And I just can't worry about that point at all, after talking to Jim Baker.

Q. Does Jim Baker have an explanation for the difference between Mr. Shevardnadze's remarks and Mr. Gorbachev's remarks today?

A. No. He made the point that we were together with them, and that was not discussed—any differences.

*   *   *

Q. Some members of your administration are convinced that Saddam Hussein will not move until the eleventh hour, or 11:59 p.m., when he is totally convinced that you are about to use military force. Why is he not convinced now, do you think? How do you expect that you will be able to get to that 11:59 minute?

A. Well, I'm not sure I accept the 11:59 analogy. But if there has ever been any doubt in his mind about the seriousness of the West and of the other Arab countries and of the coalition—put it that way—I think that those doubts are rapidly being dispelled. You see, I do believe that when he moved into Kuwait I think he felt he was going to have just an easy time of it and that the world would not rise up in arms against the aggression. I think he miscalculated there. I believe he thought he could just take over Kuwait and then there would be a lot of talk

and discussion and he would be able to turn Kuwait, a sovereign nation, a member of the Arab League, a member of the United Nations, into Province 19.

And the United States, along with other countries, said, No, we're not going to permit this aggression to stand, because an unchecked aggression today could lead to some horrible world conflagration tomorrow. And so, I think there's where the miscalculation originally was. I find it hard to believe that today, November 8th, he does not understand that he's up against a determined, unprecedented alliance.

And so, I hope that he is rethinking his position of unyielding opposition to the will of the rest of the world. And I would think that when he surveys the force that's there, the force that's going, what other countries are doing in this regard, he will recognize that he is up against just a foe that he can't possibly manage militarily. Margaret Thatcher touched on that yesterday, and I thought she did it very well, indeed. And so, if nothing else happens, I'm convinced that this move will show him how serious we are as a significant partner in this coalition. I think it's a good thing, and it will have strong support from others around the world. Let's hope he comes to his senses and does tomorrow that which he should have done weeks ago, because this aggression simply will not stand.

Statement of Senate Majority Leader George J. Mitchell, Senate Foreign Relations Committee Chairman Claiborne Pell, and Senate Armed Services Committee Chairman Sam Nunn, November 13, 1991 [2]

Last week, the President announced that he would deploy another 200,000 American troops to the Persian Gulf.

On August 7, when the first of the 200,000 troops now in the Gulf were deployed, the President told the nation that the action had four basic goals:

- "... the immediate, unconditional and complete withdrawal of all Iraqi forces from Kuwait.
- "... Kuwait's legitimate government must be restored to replace the puppet regime.

- to ensure "... the security and stability of the Persian Gulf ..."
- "... to protect the lives of American citizens abroad."

The President made clear this was "not an American problem or a European problem or a Middle East problem" but a world problem. He successfully engaged the United Nations to condemn the invasion and call for an economic embargo against Iraq.

The President could not have made more clear the purpose of American armed forces in the region. He said:

"The mission of our troops is wholly defensive. Hopefully, they will not be needed long. They will not initiate hostilities, but they will defend themselves, the Kingdom of Saudi Arabia and other friends in the Persian Gulf...

"Standing up for our principles will not come easy. It may take time and possibly cost a great deal. ... most of all, it will take unity of purpose."

The President emphasized that our troops' purpose was defensive and that our broader goal was to enforce the sanctions and induce Saddam Hussein to leave Kuwait through economic sanctions.

Now the President has said that we will almost double the armed forces in the Gulf. Secretary Baker says the purpose of that movement is to shift from a defensive to a potentially offensive posture.

Yet there is no statement from the President as to what has required a change in our posture. He has not said that the economic sanctions have failed. He has not made the judgment that the sanctions must be abandoned, or if he has made that judgment he has not made it public.

The Congress and the nation stand behind our troops in the Gulf.

But if it is the President's intention to ask the American people to stand behind a military mission that goes beyond deterring Iraq from an attack on Saudi Arabia, the President owes the American people the fullest possible explanation of what our military mission is in that region and how he hopes to achieve that goal.

The doubling of troop strength provides the President with additional flexibility in seeking to demonstrate to Saddam Hussein that aggression carries a price.

But in the face of the troop buildup, the President owes the people of the nation a clear description of our goals in the region, the potential costs of achieving those goals, and the purposes we intend to achieve there.

The Armed Services and Foreign Relations Committees of the Senate will hold hearings to explore these issues.

The American people deserve a fuller national debate about our goals in the Gulf and the potential costs of achieving those goals.

Statement by Senator Richard J. Lugar, November 13, 1990 [3]

The United Nations Security Council has resolved that Iraq must withdraw its military units from Kuwait and must pay reparations to Kuwait and other nations injured by its aggression. President Bush has stated clearly that aggression must not have any rewards and that Iraqi withdrawal from Kuwait is a basic precondition to further negotiations on Middle East security.

In return, President Saddam Hussein of Iraq has stated that Kuwait is a permanent province of Iraq and that Iraq's military forces will never move. Apparently, he has found United Nations and United States resolutions incredible and believes that he can wait out various statements and shows of strength.

The announcement by President Bush that additional American troops will go to Saudi Arabia in the next two months should give further credibility to the United Nations and United States messages to Iraq. But President Bush's decision has also stimulated comment by Arab nations, members of the U.N. Security Council, and members of Congress. Some of these comments question the offensive use of military force against Iraq, suggest that any force be applied only in Kuwait as opposed to Iraqi territory, suggest that use of force be calibrated in order that injury to Iraq's military power should be limited, and suggest that the specific objectives of the U.N. forces be more sharply defined and focused quickly.

Saddam Hussein may find the U.N. resolutions and President Bush's statements to be incredible, but I believe that President Bush has set the United States on a collision course in which Iraq will either withdraw from Kuwait or be forced to do so by military means.

United States commitment to that course of action has already been very substantial and expensive.

I am also convinced that so long as Saddam Hussein and the rest of the world has any doubt about the unified resolve of the United States in this matter, the chances for miscalculation and tragic mistakes loom much too large.

The most certain path to peace in this situation is the credibility of the United States. That credibility can be insured if the President states as clearly as possible specific missions for United States military forces and his reasons for employing those forces.

Then, the President and congressional leadership should call the Congress to Washington to debate and to vote on authorizing the President to commit United States military forces and United States financial resources to complete fulfillment of United States missions in the Middle East.

Our aims must be clear. The unity and the staying power of the American people represented by the votes of their Congressional members must be equally clear. The clarity and certainty of our American voice is the primary reason that Iraq may leave Kuwait without military confrontation and that American leadership in this crisis will be taken much more seriously by potentially wavering allies.

In the worst case of actual full scale war, the resolution of the American people to win will be of the essence. That will can be expressed only under our Constitution by the Congress as representative of all of the American people.

There is no other issue of greater importance on the American agenda. A date for the Congress to meet should be set immediately.

President's Letter to the Speaker of the House and the President Pro Tempore of the Senate, November 16, 1990 [4]

Dear Mr. Speaker: (Dear Mr. President:)

There have been a number of important developments in the Persian Gulf region since my letter of August 9, 1990, informing you of the deployment of U.S. armed forces in response to Iraq's invasion of Kuwait. In the spirit of consultation and cooperation between our two branches of government and in the firm belief that working together as we have we can best protect and advance the nation's interests, I wanted to update you on these developments.

As you are aware, the United States and Allied and other friendly governments have introduced elements of their armed forces into the region in response to Iraq's unprovoked and unlawful aggression and at the request of regional governments. In view of Iraq's continued occupation of Kuwait, defiance of ten U.N. Security Council resolutions demanding unconditional withdrawal, and sustained threat to other friendly countries in the region, I determined that the U.S. deployments begun in August should continue. Accordingly, on November 8, after consultations with our Allies and coalition partners, I announced the continued deployment of U.S. armed forces to the Persian Gulf region. These forces include a heavy U.S. Army corps and a Marine expeditionary force with an additional brigade. In addition, three aircraft carriers, a battleship, appropriate escort ships, a naval amphibious landing group, and a squadron of maritime prepositioning ships will join other naval units in the area.

I want to emphasize that this deployment is in line with the steady buildup of U.S. armed forces in the region over the last three months and is a continuation of the deployment described in my letter of August 9. I also want to emphasize that the mission of our armed forces has not changed. Our forces are in the Gulf region in the exercise of our inherent right of individual and collective self-defense against Iraq's aggression and consistent with U.N. Security Council resolutions related to Iraq's ongoing occupation of Kuwait. The United States and other nations continue to seek a peaceful resolution of the crisis. We and our coalition partners share the common goals of achieving the immediate, complete, and unconditional withdrawal of Iraqi forces from Kuwait, the restoration of Kuwait's legitimate government, the protection of the lives of citizens held hostage by Iraq both in Kuwait and Iraq, and the restoration of security and stability in the region. The deployment will ensure that the coalition has an adequate offensive military

option should that be necessary to achieve our common goals.

In my August 9 letter, I indicated that I did not believe that involvement in hostilities was imminent. Indeed, it was my belief that the deployment would facilitate a peaceful resolution of the crisis. I also stated that our armed forces would remain in the Persian Gulf region so long as required to contribute to the security of the region and desired by host governments. My view on these matters has not changed.

I appreciate the views you and other members of the congressional leadership have expressed throughout the past three months during our consultations. I look forward to continued consultation and cooperation with the Congress in pursuit of peace, stability, and security in the Gulf region.

President's Remarks to Allied Armed Forces Near Dhahran, Saudi Arabia, November 22, 1990 (Excerpt) [5]

With us today, we have four very special guests out here. The leaders, if you will, the top leadership of the United States Congress: the Speaker of the House, Tom Foley; the leader of the Senate, George Mitchell, next to him, Senator Mitchell; Congressman Bob Michel, the Republican leader, minority leader in the House; and Senator Bob Dole [Senate minority leader].

*　　*　　*

No President is quick to order American troops abroad. But there are times when any nation that values its own freedom must confront aggression. Czechoslovakia—they know firsthand about the folly of appeasement. They know about the tyranny of dictatorial conquest. And in the world war that followed, the world paid dearly for appeasing an aggressor who should and could have been stopped. We're not going to make that mistake again. We will not appease this aggressor.

As in World War II, the threat to American lives from a seemingly distant enemy must be measured against the nature of the aggression itself: a dictator who has gassed his own people—innocent women and children —unleashing chemical weapons of mass destruction, weapons that were con-

sidered unthinkable in the civilized world for over 70 years.

And let me say this: Those who would measure the timetable for Saddam's atomic program in years may be seriously underestimating the reality of that situation and the gravity of the threat. Every day that passes brings Saddam one step closer to realizing his goal of a nuclear weapons arsenal. And that's why more and more, your mission is marked by a real sense of urgency. You know, no one knows precisely when this dictator may acquire atomic weapons, or exactly who they may be aimed at down the road. But we do know this for sure: He has never possessed a weapon that he didn't use. What we're confronting is a classic bully who thinks he can get away with kicking sand in the face of the world.

So far, I've tried to act with restraint and patience. I think that's the American way. But Saddam is making the mistake of his life if he confuses an abundance of restraint—confuses that with a lack of resolve.

Over the past four months, you have launched what history will judge as one of the most important deployments of allied military power since 1945. And I have come here today to personally thank you. The world is watching. Our objectives in the Gulf have never varied. We want to free and restore Kuwait's government, protect American citizens abroad, safeguard the security and stability of the region. The united world has spelled out these objectives in ten United Nations Security Council resolutions. To force Iraq to comply, we and our allies have forged a strong diplomatic, economic, and military strategy. But the Iraqi dictator still hasn't gotten the message.

Maybe he's confused by his own propaganda, this ridiculous radio broadcast that I understand the Marines have labeled "Baghdad Betty." [Laughter] Well, she plays all the oldies, so one guy suggested we send Iraq a tape of M.C. Hammer and a note that says: This is how we entertain ourselves. Just imagine how we fight.

We have been patient. We've gone to the United Nations time and time again. I'm prepared to go another time. We still hope for a peaceful settlement, but the world is a dangerous place. And we must make all of these options credible. Those in uniform, it seems to me, will always bear the heaviest burden. We understand something of what you endure—the waiting, the uncertainty, the demands of family and military life. And we want every single troop home. We want every Brit to be able to go home as soon as possible. We want every single American home. And this I promise: No American will be kept in the Gulf a single day longer than necessary. But we won't pull punches; we are not here on some exercise. This is a real-world situation. And we're not walking away until our mission is done, until the invader is out of Kuwait. And that may well be where you come in.

As we meet, it is dawn in America. It is Thanksgiving Day. The church bells ring an hour of prayer, a day of rest, a nation at peace. And especially today, Americans understand the contribution that you all are making to world peace and to our country. Year after year on this special day, no doubt each of you has given thanks for your country. This year, your country gives thanks for you. Thanksgiving is a day of prayer, a day when we thank God for our many, many blessings. And I have done that today. This has been an unforgettable visit, an unforgettable visit.

And I leave—as I know our Congressmen do, and I know Barbara does—with pride in our heart, a prayer on our lips. God bless you all. God bless our faithful allies, the United Kingdom. God bless the Marines, and may God bless the greatest, freest country on the face of the Earth, the United States of America. Thank you and bless you all. Good luck to all of you guys.

Secretary Baker Calls for Meeting of U.N. Security Council, November 24, 1990 [6]

Having concluded our consultations with nearly all United Nations Security Council Member States, we are, in our capacity as Council President, inviting these countries to a ministerial-level Council session in New York on November 29. At that time, we will consider what additional steps the Council might take to achieve implementation of the ten resolutions already adopted in response to Iraq's unprovoked invasion and continuing occupation of Kuwait.

As members of the Security Council, we have a special responsibility to the rest of the world. When the Council takes actions under the U.N. Charter to restore international peace and security, those actions must be implemented. Our determination to ensure their implementation should demonstrate to Saddam Hussein the need to resolve this crisis peacefully and promptly.

U.N. Security Council Resolution 677, November 28, 1990 [7]

The Security Council,
Recalling its resolutions 660 (1990) of 2 August 1990, 662 (1990) of 9 August 1990, and 674 (1990) of 29 October 1990;
Reiterating its concern for the suffering caused to individuals in Kuwait as a result of the invasion and occupation of Kuwait by Iraq,
Gravely concerned at the ongoing attempt by Iraq to alter the demographic composition of the population of Kuwait and to destroy the civil records maintained by the legitimate Government of Kuwait,
Acting under Chapter VII of the Charter of the United Nations,
1. Condemns the attempts by Iraq to alter the demographic composition of the population of Kuwait and to destroy the civil records maintained by the legitimate Government of Kuwait;
2. Mandates the Secretary-General to take custody of a copy of the population register of Kuwait, the authenticity of which has been certified by the legitimate Government of Kuwait and which covers the registration of population up to 1 August 1990;
3. Requests the Secretary-General to establish, in cooperation with the legitimate Government of Kuwait, an Order of Rules and Regulations governing access to and use of the said copy of the population register.

Secretary Baker's Remarks as Security Council President Introducing the Debate on Resolution 678, November 29, 1990 [8]

I would like to begin by thanking my fellow Foreign Ministers for joining us here today. Your very presence here (only the fourth time in the Security Council's history that the Foreign Ministers have assembled) symbolizes the seriousness of the situation.

I would like to begin today's discussion with a quotation that I think aptly sets the context for our discussions today:

"there is ... no precedent for a people being the victim of such injustice and of being at present threatened by abandonment to an aggressor.

"Also there has never before been an example of any government proceeding with the systematic extermination of a nation by barbarous means in violation of the most solemn promises, made to all the nations of the earth, that there should be no resort to a war of conquest and that there should not be used against innocent human beings terrible poison and harmful gases."

Those words could well have come from the Amir of Kuwait but they do not. They were spoken instead in 1936, not 1990. They come from Haile Selassie, the leader of Ethiopia, a man who saw his country conquered and occupied, much like Kuwait has been brutalized since August 2. Sadly, his appeal to the League of Nations fell ultimately upon deaf ears.

The League's efforts to redress aggression failed, and international disorder and war ensued.

History now has given us another chance. With the Cold War behind us, we now have the chance to build the world envisioned by the founders of the United Nations. We have the chance to make this Security Council and this United Nations true instruments for peace and justice across the globe.

We must not let the United Nations go the way of the League of Nations. We must fulfill our common vision of a peaceful and just post-Cold War world. But if we are to do so, we must meet the threat to international peace created by Saddam Hussein's aggression.

That's why the debate we are about to begin will rank as one of the most important in the history of the United Nations. It will surely do much to determine the future of this body.

Our aim today must be to convince Saddam Hussein that the just, humane demands of this Council and the international community cannot be ignored. If Iraq does not reverse its course peacefully, then other necessary measures—including the use of force—should be authorized. We must put the choice to Saddam Hussein in unmistakable terms.

U.N. Security Council Resolution 678, November 29, 1990 [7]

The Security Council,

Recalling and reaffirming its resolutions 660 (1990) of 2 August 1990, 661(1990) of 6 August 1990, 662 (1990) of 9 August 1990, 664 (1990) of 18 August 1990, 665 (1990) of 25 August 1990, 666 (1990) of 13 September 1990, 667 (1990) of 16 September 1990, 669 (1990) of 24 September 1990, 670 (1990) of 25 September 1990, 674 (1990) of 29 October 1990 and 677 (1990) of 28 November 1990.

Noting that, despite all efforts by the United Nations, Iraq refuses to comply with its obligation to implement resolution 660 (1990) and the above-mentioned subsequent relevant resolutions, in flagrant contempt of the Council,

Mindful of its duties and responsibilities under the Charter of the United Nations for the maintenance and preservation of international peace and security,

Determined to secure full compliance with its decisions,

Acting under Chapter VII of the Charter of the United Nations,

1. Demands that Iraq comply fully with resolution 660 (1990) and all subsequent relevant resolutions and decides, while maintaining all its decisions, to allow Iraq one final opportunity, as a pause of goodwill, to do so;

2. Authorizes Member States cooperating with the Government of Kuwait, unless Iraq on or before 15 January 1991 fully implements, as set forth in paragraph 1 above, the foregoing resolutions, to use all necessary means to uphold and implement Security Council resolution 660 (1990) and all subsequent relevant resolutions and to restore international peace and security in the area;

3. Requests all States to provide appropriate support for the actions undertaken in pursuance of paragraph 2 of this resolution;

4. Requests the States concerned to keep the Council regularly informed on the progress of actions undertaken pursuant to paragraphs 2 and 3 of this resolution;

5. Decides to remain seized of the matter.

Secretary Baker's Remarks Following Vote on Resolution 678, November 29, 1990 [9]

Today's vote marks a watershed in the history of the United Nations. Earlier this week, members of this Council heard testimony of crimes committed against the citizens of Kuwait. There can be no doubt that these are crimes incompatible with any civilized order. They are part of the same pattern that includes the taking of innocent hostages from many nations.

Today's resolution is clear. The words authorize the use of force. But the purpose, I truly believe, is to bring about a peaceful resolution.

The entire international community has been affronted by a series of brutal acts:

- Iraqi forces have invaded and seized a small Arab neighbor.
- A once prosperous country has been pillaged and looted.
- A once peaceful country has been turned into an armed camp.
- A once secure country has been terrorized.

The nations of the world have not stood idly by. We have taken political, economic, and military measures to quarantine Iraq and to contain its aggression. We have worked out a coordinated international effort involving over 50 states to provide assistance to those nations most in need as a consequence of the economic embargo of Iraq. And, military forces from over 27 nations have been deployed to defend Iraq's neighbors from further aggression and to implement U.N. resolutions. The 12 resolutions passed by the Security Council have established clear-

ly that there is a peaceful way out of this conflict: the complete, immediate, unconditional Iraqi withdrawal from Kuwait, the restoration of Kuwait's legitimate government, and the release of all hostages.

I do not think all of this could have taken place unless most nations shared our vision of what is at stake. A dangerous man has committed a blatant act of aggression in a vital region at a critical moment in history. Saddam Hussein's actions, the vast arms he possesses, the weapons of mass destruction he seeks, indicate clearly that Kuwait was not only not the first but probably not the last target on his list. If he should win this struggle, then there will be no peace in the Middle East, only the prospect of more conflict and a far wider war.

If Saddam should come to dominate the resources of the Gulf, his ambitions will threaten all of us here and the economic well-being of all nations. Finally, if Iraq should emerge from this conflict with territory or treasure or political advantage, then the lesson will be clear: Aggression pays. As I said earlier today, we must remember the lesson of the 1930s: Aggression must not be rewarded.

Since August 2, many nations have worked together to prove just that. Many unprecedented actions have been taken. The result is a new fact: a newly effective U.N. Security Council, free of the constraints of the Cold War.

Yet the sad truth is that the new fact has not yet erased the old fact of Iraqi aggression and that, and that alone, is the ultimate test of success. We must ask ourselves why Saddam Hussein has not recoiled from his aggression. We must wonder why he does not understand how great are the forces against him and how profound is the revulsion against his behavior.

The answer must be that he does not believe we really mean what we say. He does not believe that we will stand united until he withdraws. He thinks that his fact of aggression will outlast our fact: an international community opposed to aggression.

We are meeting here today therefore, first and foremost, to dispel Saddam Hussein's illusions. He must know from us that a refusal to comply peacefully with the Security Council resolutions risks disaster for him.

Members of the Council, we are at a crossroads. Today we show Saddam that the sign marked "peace" is the direction he should take.

Today's resolution is clear. The words authorize the use of force. But the purpose, I truly believe, is to bring about a peaceful resolution. No one here has sought this conflict. Many nations here have had good relations with the people of Iraq. But the Security Council of the United Nations cannot tolerate this aggression and still be faithful to the principles of the U.N. Charter.

With passage of today's resolution, we concur with other Council Members that this should lead to a pause in this Council's efforts, assuming no adverse change in circumstances. We do so while retaining our rights to protect our foreign nationals in Iraq and mindful of the terms of the Fourth Geneva Convention and the Geneva Protocol of 1925, should Saddam Hussein use chemical or biological weapons.

"A Pause for Peace"

By passing today's resolution—a pause for peace—we say to Saddam Hussein: "We continue to seek a diplomatic solution. Peace is your only sensible option. You can choose peace by respecting the will of the international community. But if you fail to do so, you will risk all. The choice is yours."

If we fail to redress this aggression, more will be lost than just peace in the Persian Gulf. Only recently, in Europe, the nations party to the Cold War assembled to bury that conflict. All the peoples of Europe and North America, who had nothing to look forward to except an unending, twilight struggle, now have a fresh start, a new opportunity. Conflict and war are no longer the watchwords of European politics.

Members of the Council, we meet at the hinge of history. We can use the end of the Cold War to get beyond the whole pattern of settling conflicts by force, or we can slip back into ever more savage regional conflicts in which might alone makes right. We can take the high road toward peace and the rule of law, or Saddam Hussein's path of brutal aggression and the law of the jungle.

Simply put, it is a choice between right and wrong.

I believe we have the courage and the fortitude to choose what's right.

President's Press Conference Announcing Offer for Talks with Iraq, November 30, 1990 (Excerpts) [5]

...Yesterday's United Nations Security Council resolution was historic. Once again the Security Council has enhanced the legitimate peacekeeping function of the United Nations. Until yesterday, Saddam may not have understood what he's up against in terms of world opinion, and I'm hopeful that now he will realize that he must leave Kuwait immediately.

I'm asking Secretary Jim Baker to go to Baghdad to see Saddam Hussein.

I'm continually asked how effective are the U.N. sanctions that was put into effect on August 6th. I don't know the answer to that question. Clearly, the sanctions are having some effect, but I can't tell you that the sanctions alone will get the job done. And thus, I welcome yesterday's United Nations action.

The fledgling democracies in Eastern Europe are being severely damaged by the economic effects of Saddam's actions. The developing countries of Africa and in our hemisphere are being victimized by this dictator's rape of his neighbor Kuwait. Those who feel that there is no down side to waiting months and months must consider the devastating damage being done every day to the fragile economies of those countries that can afford it the least.

As Chairman Alan Greenspan [of the Board of Governors, Federal Reserve System] testified just the other day, the increase in oil prices resulting directly from Saddam's invasion is hurting our country, too. Our economy, as I said the other day, is at best in a serious slowdown, and if uncertainty remains in the energy markets, the slowdown will get worse.

"The Things That Concern Me Most"

I've spelled out once again our reasons for sending troops to the Gulf. Let me

tell you the things that concern me most. First, I put the immorality of the invasion of Kuwait itself. No nation should rape, pillage, and brutalize its neighbor. No nation should be able to wipe a member state of the United Nations and the Arab League off the face of the Earth.

I'm deeply concerned about all the hostages—innocent people held against their will in direct contravention of international law. Then there's this cynical and brutal policy of forcing people to beg for their release, parceling out human lives to families and traveling emissaries like so much chattel.

I'm deeply concerned about our own embassy in Kuwait. The flag is still flying there. A handful of beleaguered Americans remain inside the embassy unable to come and go. This treatment of our embassy violates every civilized principle of diplomacy. It demeans our people; it demeans our country. And I am determined that this embassy, as called for under Security Council Resolution 674, be fully replenished and our people free to come home. What kind of precedent will these actions set for the future if Saddam's violation of international law goes unchallenged?

I'm also deeply concerned about the future of Kuwait itself. The tales of rape and assassination, of cold-blooded murder and rampant looting are almost beyond belief. The whole civilized world must unite and say: This kind of treatment of people must end. And those who violate the Kuwait people must be brought to justice.

I'm deeply concerned about Saddam's efforts to acquire nuclear weapons. Imagine his ability to blackmail his neighbors should he possess a nuclear device. We've seen him use chemical weapons on his own people. We've seen him take his own country, one that should be wealthy and prosperous, and turn it into a poor country all because of insatiable appetite for military equipment and conquest.

Not Another Vietnam

I've been asked why I ordered more troops to the Gulf. I remain hopeful that we can achieve a peaceful solution to this crisis. But if force is required, we and the other 26 countries who have troops in the area will have enough power to get the job done.

In our country, I know that there are fears about another Vietnam. Let me assure you, should military action be required, this will not be another Vietnam. This will not be a protracted, drawn-out war. The forces arrayed are different. The opposition is different. The resupply of Saddam's military would be very different. The countries united against him in the United Nations are different. The topography of Kuwait is different. And the motivation of our all-volunteer force is superb.

I want peace. I want peace, not war. But if there must be war, we will not permit our troops to have their hands tied behind their backs. And I pledge to you: There will not be any murky ending. If one American soldier has to go into battle, that soldier will have enough force behind him to win. And then get out as soon as possible, as soon as the U.N. objectives have been achieved. I will never—ever—agree to a halfway effort.

Let me repeat: We have no argument with the people of Iraq; indeed, we have only friendship for the people there. Further, I repeat that we have no desire to keep one single American soldier in the Gulf a single day longer than is necessary to achieve the objectives set out above.

No one wants to see a peaceful solution to this crisis more than I do. And at the same time, no one is more determined than I am to see Saddam's aggression reversed.

Lastly, people now caution patience. The United States and the entire world have been patient. I will continue to be patient. But yesterday's U.N. resolution, the 13th by the Security Council, properly says to Saddam Hussein: Time is running out. You must leave Kuwait. And we've given you time to do just exactly that.

Offer to Talk with Iraq

Many people have talked directly to Saddam Hussein and to his Foreign Minister Tariq Aziz. All have been frustrated by Iraq's ironclad insistence that it will not leave Kuwait. However, to go the extra mile for peace, I will issue an invitation to Foreign Minister Tariq Aziz to come to Washington at a mutually convenient time during the latter part of the week of December 10th to meet with me. I'll invite Ambassadors of several of our coalition partners in the Gulf to join me at that

meeting. In addition, I'm asking Secretary Jim Baker to go to Baghdad to see Saddam Hussein. And I will suggest to Iraq's President that he receive the Secretary of State at a mutually convenient time between December 15th and January 15th of next year.

Within the mandate of the United Nations resolutions, I will be prepared, and so will Secretary Baker, to discuss all aspects of the Gulf crisis. However, to be very clear about these efforts to exhaust all means for achieving a political and diplomatic solution, I am not suggesting discussions that will result in anything less than Iraq's complete withdrawal from Kuwait, restoration of Kuwait's legitimate government, and freedom for all hostages.

Q. Mr. President, now that you have a clear-cut U.N. resolution on use of force, doesn't that force you into a position if these talks between the Secretary of State break down—doesn't this force you into the position of having to use force on January 15th if Saddam Hussein hasn't left? And if not, won't we be perceived as the one who blinked first?

A. No, the date was not a date at which point force had to be used.

Q. If I could just follow up with another question. Are you going to ask Congress for approval of this resolution—would you like to see Congress pass the same kind of resolution that the U.N. passed?

A. I'd love to see Congress pass a resolution enthusiastically endorsing what the United Nations has done, yes. But we're in consultation on that, and I have no plans to call a special session. I'm not opposed to it, but we're involved in consultations right now. I have talked to several Members of Congress. I've talked to leaders in the House. I've talked to several on the Republican side and Democratic side in the Senate. And I want to be sure that these consultations are complete.

Some feel a lame duck session is not good, that the new Members should have a right to have a say. Others feel that we ought to move right now. The Congress, as you know, in their adjournment resolution, had a provision in there that they could come back and take this up. They are a coequal branch of government; they can do that if they want to. But we will continue our consultations. They'll follow, incidentally, today, this with a meeting

with the leadership. So, I'll get a little better feel for that as we go along.

Q. Mr. President, you say you're confident that American troops will prevail against Saddam if they're called upon?

A. Oh, absolutely.

Q. But at what price? How many Americans?

A. Oh, I can't give you any figures, of course. But I can say that the movement of this additional force safeguards the lives of every American and every one of our allies in the Gulf.

Q. Mr. President, in recent days, senior members of the administration have emphatically rejected the idea of any special emissaries or diplomatic envoys to or from Iraq to discuss this on your part. What changed your mind, sir?

A. The United Nations resolution, I think, has a good chance of making Saddam Hussein understand what it is he's up against. I have not felt that he got the message. I hope this will do it. But I am convinced that these two direct meetings that I've discussed here will guarantee to all the people of the world, certainly to the American people, that Saddam Hussein not misunderstand, not misinterpret. I keep hearing, Well, people won't give him the news. Unlike the President of the United States, who gets good news and bad news very faithfully, I am told that Saddam Hussein's troops don't bring him the bad news; and I'm told that he is somewhat isolated. And I think this U.N. resolution will help de-isolate him, and I think the two proposals that I have made here will help. So, it's just going the extra step, Brit, that's what it is. And it's a decision that I personally made.

Q. You indicate that this date is not actually a deadline for the use of force, merely a date after which force would be permissible. How do you avoid the impression, should that date come and go without military action, that the U.S.-led coalition has, in fact, blinked?

A. Well, we've got to look at events at the time, but I don't think there will ever be a perception that the United States is going to blink in this situation. That's why I had some of the words in this statement that I had.

Q. Mr. President, you've just spoken about the weapons of mass destruction—nuclear weapons—and also that one of your goals is to try to

reach stability in the region. Can you reach stability in the region with Saddam Hussein in power?

A. I think most countries, members of the United Nations, feel that there have to be some safeguards put into effect in terms of guaranteeing the security and stability of the Gulf. And so, I would think that the status quo ante will not be enough. And I think there are sanctions in place now, and I think it would be very proper to discuss what those safeguards should be after there has been a total compliance with the United Nations resolutions.

*   *   *

Q. Mr. President, Arab experts suggest that Saddam Hussein has hinted in his remarks that he would like to have some sort of deal, but he wouldn't necessarily hold to his demands. Now you're saying you're willing to meet with him. Are you willing to offer him anything in these meetings in return for a pullout, such as a conference on the Middle East?

A. No. Those two items are totally separate. We've made that very, very clear. And what I have said is that these discussions will be done within the U.N. mandate. I'm not all that hopeful that we'll get big results out of all of this. It's going the extra mile. It's taking the extra step. But I can't tell you that I think we're going to have great success on all of this because our partnership in the world is together on the fact that we cannot stop short of total fulfillment, without condition, of the United Nations resolutions.

Q. What then is the point of the meeting? Are you just delivering ultimatums?

A. No, this isn't an ultimatum at all. And I hope what it does is demonstrate that we are prepared to go face to face and tell him how committed we are to the United Nations resolutions. I've told you I don't think he has felt this commitment. As I said earlier, he may feel it a little more strongly now that we did what many skeptics thought couldn't happen—that the United Nations Security Council did, and that is come together and pass this very important resolution.

So, one thing is he has got to understand what the alternatives are to complying with the United Nations resolutions. And the best way to get that across is one on one—Baker look-

ing him right in the eye. I've been told that he doesn't necessarily believe that I am totally committed to what I've been saying. And here's a good opportunity to have him understand that face to face.

So, we want to make the case to him directly for complying with the United Nations resolutions, make the case to him from a Secretary of State who's incessantly worked to get this resolution through—the strength of the commitment of the international community—and then try to persuade him to reconsider his position and to take the steps necessary for a peaceful resolution of the crisis. But it isn't a trip of concession. When you've done what he's done, I don't see that there's room for concession, there's room for giving something to save face. That's not the way you treat with aggression. And we're not going to treat with it any differently than I've outlined here.

*   *   *

Q. Mr. President, if you ultimately feel that you have to ask Americans to support the use of force, what that, of course, means is that you have to ask some parents to give up the lives of their children.

A. I know it.

Q. What I was wondering was: We all know how important your children are to you. Do you feel that this issue is important enough to you that you could conceive of giving up one of their lives for it?

A. You know, Maureen [Maureen Santini, New York Daily News], you put your finger on a very difficult question. People say to me, How many lives? How many lives can you expend? Each one is precious. I don't want to reminisce, but I've been there. I know what it's like to have fallen comrades and see young kids die in battle. It's only the President that should be asked to make the decision: Is it worth it? How many lives is it worth? Is it worth it to commit one life, put one life in harm's way to achieve these objectives? And that's why I want to get a peaceful resolution to this question.

You ought to read my mail. It is so heart-moving. Supportive, and yet: Please bring my kid home. Please bring my husband home. It's a tough question. But a President has to make the right decision. These are worldwide principles of moral importance. I will

do my level best to bring those kids home without one single shot fired in anger. And if a shot is fired in anger, I want to guarantee each person that their kid, whose life is in harm's way, will have the maximum support, will have the best chance to come home alive, and will be backed up to the hilt.

Because of that question that weighs on my mind, I added that language this morning about how this will not be a Vietnam. They can criticize me for moving forces. And if we've got one kid that's apt to be in harm's way, I want him backed up to the hilt by American firepower, and others as well. That's why I'm working as hard as I am not only to hold this coalition together but to strengthen it. The best way to safeguard the lives of Americans is for Saddam Hussein to do that what he should have done long ago. And if force has to be used, the best way to safeguard lives is to see that you've got the best and you're willing to use it. That's my posture.

Q. Sir, why do you seem to be avoiding the people's representatives having an opportunity to talk on this and to express their opinion? You know Congress, and yet you're avoiding it. You know that the Constitution gives the power not only to declare war, but to provide the money and to say other things about what shall be done with troops. That's the Constitution. Yet you seem to be avoiding that. The experts on Capitol Hill say that what you have done by prenotification, calling two or three Members and saying we're on the way— you've already made the decision. You're notifying them; that's prenotification. That's not consulting with Congress. They say you should sit down and have a back-and-forth with them.

A. Yes.

Q. And I want to remind you that when Foley speaks as Speaker of the House, he may be Speaker of the House, but he sure as hell doesn't represent Florida and Texas.

A. Sarah, therein, you've properly brought up the dilemma I face. There are 435 Members of the United States Congress, there are 100—

Q. But—

A. May I finish, please? There are 100 Members of the United States Senate. Each one has a view as to what I ought not to do, and that's fine. They have the power under the resolution of adjournment to come back twenty seconds from now and to take a voice, to stand, to take a common position. If they want to come back here and endorse what the President of the United States has done and what the United Nations Security Council has done, come on, we're ready. I'd like to see it happen. But what I don't want to do is have it come back and end up where you have 435 voices in one House and 100 on the other saying what not to do and saying— kind of a hand-wringing operation that would send bad signals. I welcome these hearings. We're having hearings. We're consulting. I've told you I'm consulting. I'll be honest with you: I cannot consult with 535 strong-willed individuals. I can't do it, nor does my responsibility under the Constitution compel me to do that. And I think everyone would agree that we have had more consultations than previous administrations.

Q. Sir, we have a majority rule in this country, and you seem to be afraid of it.

A. No, I'm not afraid of it at all. We have a tripartite form of government. And I know my strengths, and I know the limitations on the Presidency. This is an interesting debate, Sarah. And I know my limitations. And I know what I can do, and I know what previous Presidents have done. And I am still determined to consult the extra mile. You want to continue to debate?

Q. You and Jim Baker give the other countries a chance to talk, and you give the United Nations a chance to talk, but you won't give the United States people a chance to debate with you.

A. Well now, that's an absurd comment, Sarah, from a bright person like you. That is absolutely absurd. They're holding hearings. They're talking. They have the power under the adjournment resolution to reconvene this minute. Some in the House want to come back now, some want to talk about it later on. Some in the Senate want to come right back now and immediately endorse what the President has done and what the Security Council resolution is—and I'm for that—but some don't. And so, consultation is going on. Please do not assign to me improper motives. They're talking right now. They're having endless hearings by endless experts up there, each one with a slightly different view. And that's the American way. And that's fine. And I know what the responsibilities of the

President are, and I am fulfilling those responsibilities.

Secretary Baker's Statement Before the Senate Foreign Relations Committee, December 5, 1990 [10]

Today, I come before you for the third time since August 2 to discuss Iraq's continuing occupation of Kuwait.

I have come here to consult with you because a very dangerous dictator—armed to the teeth—is threatening a critical region at a defining moment in history. He must be stopped—peacefully if possible, but by force if necessary.

We have to face the fact that, four months into this conflict. none of our efforts have yet produced any sign of change in Saddam Hussein.

I would like to focus my prepared remarks on three aspects of the situation:

One, on explaining the President's strategy;

Two, on detailing the reasons that preparations for the possible use of force—and indeed a willingness to use force, if necessary—remain essential to achieving a peaceful resolution; and

Three, on presenting the compelling interests we have in seeing Saddam Hussein's brutal aggression undone.

Strategy

From the outset, the international community has rallied behind four objectives:

First, the immediate, complete, and unconditional Iraqi withdrawal from Kuwait;

Second, the restoration of Kuwait's legitimate government;

Third, the release of all hostages; and

Fourth, a commitment to the security and stability of the Persian Gulf.

The President has stated repeatedly that we want to achieve these objectives peacefully. He has also made

clear that we seek to achieve them at least cost to ourselves and the other members of the international coalition.

From the outset, our strategy to achieve these objectives has been to make Saddam Hussein pay such a high price for his aggression that he would quit Kuwait. We have aimed to impose costs on Saddam for his aggression by taking increasingly harsh steps on a continuum of pressure and pain— politically, economically, and militarily. On this continuum, economic sanctions and military preparations are not *alternatives,* but reinforcing and escalating steps of the same strategy.

Notwithstanding our desire for peace, from the outset we have proceeded with the full realization that if these objectives cannot be achieved peacefully, we must be prepared to use force, given the vital interests at stake.

Thus, starting on August 2, an international coalition led by the United States began to impose costs on Iraq for its aggression.

The day of the invasion the Security Council passed Resolution 660, calling for an immediate Iraqi withdrawal from Kuwait. When this effort and the diplomatic efforts of the Arab League were summarily rejected by Saddam Hussein, on August 6 the Security Council imposed mandatory economic sanctions to increase the pressure on Iraq and make it pay greater costs for its aggression. The hope was that by isolating Iraq politically and economically, Saddam Hussein would withdraw.

While these diplomatic and economic steps were being taken, military forces were deployed in the region to deter further aggression and to support the Security Council Resolutions. As of now, twenty-seven nations have joined in this truly unprecedented multinational force

To date, the international coalition has had considerable success in isolating Iraq and making it pay high costs for its occupation of Kuwait. We regret the pain this causes innocent citizens of Iraq, a people with whom we have no quarrel.

But the question before us now is whether the costs we impose on Saddam Hussein through sanctions alone will be high enough to cause him to withdraw peacefully from Kuwait.

We have to face the fact that, four months into this conflict, none of our efforts have yet produced any sign of change in Saddam Hussein. He shows no signs of complying with any of the Security Council resolutions.

Instead, he seems to be doubling his bets. He has tried to make Kuwait part of Iraq, systematically looting and dismembering a sovereign Arab state. He has been terrorizing the population, his soldiers committing unspeakable crimes against innocent Kuwaitis. He has called for the overthrow of King Fahd of Saudi Arabia and President Mubarak of Egypt. He has threatened to rain terror and mass destruction on his Arab neighbors and on Israel. He has been playing the cruelest of games with hostages and their families and with our diplomats in Kuwait.

Preparing for War to Achieve Peace

After serious and sobering consultations, the United Nations Security Council last Thursday passed by an overwhelming majority a twelfth resolution—one that authorizes all necessary means, including the use of force, to eject Saddam from Kuwait after January 15, 1991. In passing this resolution, the international community is giving Saddam yet another chance—indeed, one last chance—to come to his senses.

In passing Thursday's resolution, the international community sends Saddam the following clear message: "We continue to seek a diplomatic solution. Peace is your only sensible option. You can choose peace by respecting the will of the international community. But if you fail to do so, you will risk all. The choice is yours."

To ensure that Saddam understands this choice, the President has invited the Foreign Minister of Iraq to Washington and has directed me to go to Baghdad.

Put bluntly, this is the last best chance for a peaceful solution. If we are to have any chance of success, I must go to Baghdad with the fullest support of the Congress and the American people behind the message of the international community.

Let me be clear: This meeting will not be the beginning of a negotiation over the terms of the United Nations resolutions. Those terms are clear: a complete, immediate, and unconditional Iraqi withdrawal; the restoration of the legitimate Kuwaiti government; and the release of all foreign nationals.

Nor is this the beginning of a negotiation on subjects unrelated to Iraq's brutal occupation of Kuwait. I will not be negotiating the Palestinian question or the civil war in Lebanon. Saddam did not invade Kuwait to help the Palestinians. He did it for his own self-aggrandizement. As Eduard Shevardnadze has said, you do not enslave one people to free another.

Put simply, my mission to Baghdad will be an attempt to explain to Saddam the choice he faces: comply with the objectives of the Security Council or risk disaster for Iraq.

To give substance to these words, the President has directed the Secretary of Defense, the Chairman of the Joint Chiefs, and me to work with the other members of the international coalition to reinforce the multinational force in the Gulf and coordinate its efforts. Our aim is to ensure that if force must be used, it will be used suddenly, massively, and decisively.

Do the troop reinforcements and the Security Council resolution mean that war is inevitable? Surely not. There is a peaceful outcome possible—one that does not reward aggression—and everyone, including Saddam, knows what it is. He can choose peace by withdrawing unconditionally from Kuwait and releasing all hostages.

He will not make that peaceful choice, however, unless he understands that the alternative to peaceful compliance is to be forced to comply. That is the message we are trying to send him. That is the meaning of the steps the international community has taken over the past month. It is not a new strategy but rather a continuation and reinforcement of the strategy we have pursued since August.

I know that some here and throughout the country are uneasy about the prospects of war. None of us wants war. Not you. Not the President. Not me. None of us have sought this conflict, and we are making every attempt to resolve it peacefully, without appeasing the aggressor.

I know the arguments of those who believe that time and the economic embargo alone will work to resolve this conflict peacefully. But we have to face some hard facts.

If sanctions are to succeed, they must do more than hurt Iraq economically. They must hurt Saddam so much that he changes his behavior and withdraws from Kuwait. That is the criteria of success by which sanctions must be judged.

In considering the role of sanctions in our strategy, we need to ask ourselves:

Can economic sanctions alone compel a dictator like Saddam to make the politically difficult choice of withdrawing from Kuwait?

Absent a credible military threat, will Saddam take the Security Council's actions seriously?

Is there anything in Saddam Hussein's history that could lead us to believe that sanctions alone will get him out of Kuwait?

Let me try to answer these questions, based on the results so far. After four months of a stringent embargo, no one doubts that sanctions are having some effect on the Iraqi economy. But we have to face the difficult fact that no one can tell you that sanctions alone will ever be able to impose a high enough cost on Saddam to get him to withdraw. So far, all available evidence suggests that they have had little if any effect on his inclination to withdraw.

That's in part because Saddam, to a considerable extent, can decide who in Iraq gets hurt by them. And you can bet the Iraqi people will feel the pain first and most deeply—not the Iraqi military or Saddam himself. Saddam has a long history of imposing great pain and suffering on the Iraqi people. It is not new for him to impose economic sacrifices on the Iraqi people in pursuit of his ambitions.

We need to remember who we are trying to get out of Kuwait. Saddam is a ruthless dictator. He has an inflated sense of Iraq's leverage and a high pain threshold. Saddam undoubtedly believes he can endure economic sanctions. However, surely he understands more acutely the consequences of military force.

Waiting not only gives Saddam time to break the sanctions, but it imposes costs on us.

As we wait, Saddam will continue torturing Kuwait, killing it as a nation.

As we wait, he will continue manipulating hostages, attempting to break the coalition.

As we wait he will continue to fortify Kuwait, to build chemical and biological weapons, and to acquire a nuclear weapons capability.

As we wait, he expects other issues to deflect our attention, weaken our resolve, and dissolve the international coalition.

And as we wait, the burden of Saddam's crime weighs heavier on the world.

That is why we must make credible our preparations to use force.

The international community has clearly agreed that force will not be used before January 15 of next year, provided Saddam does not provoke a response. Thus, Mr. Chairman, we need to remind ourselves that for now, no one is making a decision about going to war. Indeed, in asking me to go to Baghdad, the President has made it clear that he will use the next six weeks to exhaust all diplomatic opportunities.

Yet to support these diplomatic efforts, Mr. Chairman, the President has also made it clear that we need continued support for our military preparations to make credible an offensive option to liberate Kuwait. While not prejudging any decision whether force should be used sometime after January 15, I can state unequivocally that failure to continue preparations now has at least three dangerous consequences.

First, it would undercut our diplomatic leverage by removing the other alternative to a peaceful withdrawal: use of force. It would send Iraq exactly the wrong message—that is, "Continue to play for time. You will have lots of it because the Security Council resolution is just a bluff. The international coalition is not even preparing the option to use force, let alone take that option." That is a message we must not send.

We must show Saddam that time is not on his side. He needs to know that even if he believes he can withstand the sanctions, and he may be right in this belief, we can and will impose even greater costs on him through the use of force if necessary.

Second, failure to prepare a credible offensive military option would only tend to reaffirm the status quo and legitimize to some the brutal occupation that Saddam is now carrying out against Kuwait and its people.

Third, failure to prepare adequately now would mean that should conflict come, we would be irresponsibly risking greater casualties—putting the lives of those young Americans already on the front lines in the Persian Gulf at greater risk than they need be. The President will not stand for that. And neither will the American people.

What's at Stake

Mr. Chairman, we do not proceed along this path unaware of the dangers and risks involved. But let there be no doubt that succeeding in this endeavor—hopefully in peace, if necessary by force—is in the vital interest of the American people.

It is often said that there has been no clear answer given to the question of why we are in the Gulf. Much of this results from the search for a single cause for our involvement, a single reason the President could use to explain why the lives of American men and women should be put in harm's way in the sands of Arabia or the seas around it and in the air above it.

Mr. Chairman, let us stop this search. Let us be honest with ourselves and with each other. There are multiple causes, multiple dangers, multiple threats. Standing alone, each is compelling. Put together, the case is overwhelming.

Put bluntly: *A very dangerous dictator—armed to the teeth —is threatening a critical region at a defining moment in history.*

It is the combination of these reasons—who is threatening our interests, what capabilities he has and is developing, where he is carrying out aggression, and when he has chosen to act— that make the stakes so high for all of us.

Let me explain.

Strategically, Saddam is a capricious dictator whose lust for power is as unlimited as his brutality in pursuit of it. He has invaded two neighbors, is harboring terrorists, and now is systematically exterminating Kuwait. Saddam uses poisonous gas —even against his own people; develops deadly toxins; and seeks relentlessly to acquire nuclear bombs. He has built the world's sixth largest army, has the world's fifth largest tank army, and has deployed ballistic missiles.

Geographically, Saddam's aggression has occurred in a political tinderbox that is crossroads to three continents. His success would only guarantee more strife, more conflict, and eventually a wider war. There would be little hope for any effort at peacemaking in the Middle East.

Economically, Saddam's aggression imperils the world's oil lifelines, threatening recession and depression, here and abroad, hitting hardest those fledgling democracies least able to cope with it. His aggression is an attempt to mortgage the economic promise of the post-Cold War world to the whims of a single man.

Morally, we must act so that international laws, not international outlaws, govern the post-Cold War world. We must act so that right, not might, dictates success in the post-Cold War world. We must act so that innocent men and women and diplomats are protected, not held hostage, in the post-Cold War world.

Historically, we must stand with the people of Kuwait so that the annexation of Kuwait does not become the first reality that mars our vision of a new world order. We must stand with the world community so that the United Nations does not go the way of the League of Nations.

Politically, we must stand for American leadership, not because we seek it but because no one else can do the job. And we did not stand united for forty years to bring the Cold War to a peaceful end in order to make the world safe for the likes of Saddam Hussein.

These then are the stakes.

If Saddam is not stopped now, if his aggressive designs are not frustrated, peacefully if possible, or if necessary by force, we will all pay a higher price later.

As the Security Council did last Thursday, this Congress and the American people must tell Saddam Hussein in unmistakable actions and words:

"Get out of Kuwait now or risk all."

Mr. Chairman, now—more than at any time during this conflict —we must stand united with the world community in full support of the Security Council resolutions.

Simply put, it is a choice between right and wrong.

I believe we have the courage and fortitude to choose what's right.

Remarks by Senator Richard J. Lugar Following Secretary Baker's Senate Foreign Relations Committee Statement, December 5, 1990 [10]

Mr. Secretary, I have a comment before I ask a question. On November 14 I made a public suggestion that a special session of the Congress should be called promptly to authorize President Bush to use military force, if necessary, to fulfill the United Nations resolutions regarding Iraqi aggression.

On that same day, Democratic Senate leadership indicated that a special session would not be called, but hearings by the Armed Services Committee and the Foreign Relations Committee would provide useful forums to examine the Persian Gulf situation.

My basic reasoning in calling for focused congressional debate and recorded votes was to make certain that the leaders of Iraq had full confidence of the credibility of the United States position; namely, withdrawal from Kuwait, release all hostages, and prepare to negotiate on the future peace and security of the region by January 15 or face any necessary means to bring about that withdrawal.

After the United Nations Security Council voted 12 to 2 with 1 abstention last Thursday, November 29, to set a deadline to authorize all necessary means to effect Iraqi withdrawal, President Bush met with congressional leaders on Friday. By my count, the President asked those of us assembled on seven occasions during that meeting for action which would indicate clearly to the world that the Congress and the President affirm that the United States is prepared to play the role authorized by the United Nations resolution.

In the sine die adjournment resolution the Congress specifically included the opportunity to return to debate necessary action precipitated by the Persian Gulf developments.

Congress Avoiding a Vote

Many Members of Congress speak out daily, affirming that Congress must act before the United States can employ military force in the Gulf area. Yet both the Speaker of the House and the Republican Leader of the House told the Friday meeting they would strongly oppose calling a special session, and strongly advised the President not to do so.

The Senate Majority Leader took a similar stance. Senator Dole, Senator Simpson, Senator Warner, Senator Kasten, and I spoke in favor of an immediate special session on the focused issue of authorizing the President to use military force if Saddam Hussein

does meet the clear mandates published by the United Nations.

It is now apparent that congressional leadership will not call a special session of the 101st Congress, preferring to wait at least until the swearing in of the 102d Congress on January 3 of next year.

I make this point, Mr. Secretary, because you and many Americans may be confused as you hear so many congressional voices demanding participation in national decision-making, while refusing adamantly to meet in formal session, and undertake the grave responsibilities of official votes.

Instead of formal sessions, Congress says, substitute hearings, which have thus far allowed many witnesses and Senators to propose that Saddam Hussein should suffer a lingering death of his military might and his citizenry through extension of economic sanctions for months, and perhaps, even years, if a single American would thereby be saved from military action.

Arguments Against Waiting

If in fact the alliance of nations arrayed against Iraq lasted that long and the military accidents or terrorism directed the United States or our allies occurred for months or years, and if economic sanctions really remained airtight, the world would witness the starvation first of the remaining Kuwait survivors and other foreign nationals still in harm's way, and then innocent Iraqi citizens victimized by the reckless Iraqi dictator.

Saddam and his army would still be eating and the American people would rightly question: Whoever suggested the virtue of endless sanctions and the hideous starvation of hundreds of thousands of helpless people?

As month by month brings increasing worldwide recession or depression, Americans will rightly wonder whoever suggested holding in place the blockages of world trade and commerce that Saddam's aggression has instituted and which already have affected grievous harm on so many developing nations, and added to the risk of severe recession in our country.

The Washington Post-ABC poll published December 4 asked and I quote the question: "If Iraq does not withdraw from Kuwait, should the United States go to war with Iraq to force it out of Kuwait at some point after January 15 or not?"

Americans answered that poll yes, 63 percent; no, 32 percent; do not know, only 5 percent. With much the same issue stated another way, Americans voted 67 to 29 percent that they agree that the United States should take all necessary action, including the use of military force, to quote the question, to make sure that Iraq withdraws from Kuwait.

Americans approved the Security Council resolution, 69 to 26 percent, and the Washington Post article accompanying the poll adds that two out of three persons questioned now say the embargo will not work.

Need for United Stand

I mention all of this to you, Mr. Secretary, in the event that you and other observers of these Senate hearings are baffled after hearing so many voices suggesting alternative foreign policies, and purporting to represent a majority of American opinion.

After you have explained to Saddam Hussein the comprehensive extent of the United Nations resolutions and the specific capabilities of the array of worldwide military forces readied against him, he may question you and the world as to how solid is that alliance of the United Nations in pressing for unconditional withdrawal, and how solid is the political will of the American people behind you and our President.

Withdrawal, peace and negotiations are most likely to come if Saddam understands that we are rock solid, our credibility is the path to peace.

Eventually the Congress will catch up with the American people, and I believe that the President, you, Secretary Cheney and General Powell have spelled out a strong and successful course of action. A majority of the American people share that view.

Because the reasons for our policies are complex, you and the President must spend important hours in the next few days and weeks communicating with the American people and consulting with the peoples' representatives in the Congress.

I thank you for doing so today, and I thank you for your strong and clear voice.

Saddam Hussein Announces Hostage Release, December 6, 1990 [11]

President Saddam Hussein has called on Speaker and Members of the National Assembly of Iraq to lift the restrictions on the travel of all the foreigners that have not been allowed to entertain the freedom of travel and to adopt a resolution in this respect.

That came in a message sent by the President today to Speaker and Members of the Iraqi National Assembly.

President Saddam Hussein has said in his letter to the National Assembly that one of the most annoying things for the faithful Mujahid, honorable struggler and the courageous fighter, who displays the morals of faithful knights is the overlapping of trenches in the battlefield and thus those who do not intend the duel are wedged in the field between two trenches, and this annoyance changes into a deep cause when harm befalls this category of people as a result of the level and sort of struggle.

The foreigners, President Hussein has further said, who were banned from travel are of this said type in this duel between the right, which the Iraqi people and its armed forces are occupying the vanguard position, and the wrong whose gathering is led by the enemy of God, Bush.

President has further said that he acknowledges and the members of the leadership that withholding freedom of travel for these people despite what has befallen them, has performed new service for the issue of peace.

Since God has taught us, we should not use the embargoed but in the very necessary circumstance and without exaggeration, it has been our duty not to prolong keeping these emergency measures among which is this very measure, the President has added.

President Saddam Hussein has further said that many good people from different nationalities, men and women and from different political tendencies has visited Iraq and some dear brothers from Jordan, Yemen, Palestine, Sudan and the Arab Maghreb have also consulted with us on this issue as well as other issues.

And in the light of our humanitarian feeling, we have found out that time has come to spell out a decisive opinion on this subject, the President added.

President Saddam Hussein has maintained in his letter by saying we have had thought of a timing other than this one, namely, the occasions of Christmas and New Year that have special impression in souls of Christians in the world, including Christians in the West, but appeals made by some brothers, decision of the Democratic majority in the U.S. Senate and invitation extended to our Foreign Minister by the European Parliament for dialogue, all of them encourage us to respond to these positive good changes that would have their big role amidst the Western public opinion in general and the American in particular to curb excessiveness of evildoers rushing to war and those pushing to it as an alternative they chose out of their evil tendency and premeditated intentions for harming others. Thus we have found that the necessities which permitted the embargoed and led to prevent travel of the foreigners has become weak in basis and were replaced by what is stronger than them, namely, this good change in public opinion which would constitute to a certain amount a restriction on intentions and resolutions of the evildoers at the head of whom is the enemy of God, Bush.

Addressing the National Assembly in his letter, President Saddam Hussein has maintained that on this basis I call on you to adopt your just resolution by permitting all the foreigners who are restrained from entertaining the freedom of travel, by lifting this restraint from them, along with our apology for whatever harm caused to any one of them.

President Saddam Hussein has also called for continual watchfulness and caution because armies of aggression are still present on the land of our sanctities in the Arab Peninsula and the evildoers are still blowing the trumpet of war and Bush's call for talks is still up till now carrying preponderance of probabilities of aggression and war and concentrations are still growing. Therefore the steadfast believer, whether among the people or the armed forces should not fall in the trap in which some have fallen before.

President's Remarks to Reporters, December 14, 1990 (Excerpts) [12]

...And now I'd like to take up another subject, a second one. On November 30th, in offering direct meetings between the United States and Iraq, I offered to go the extra mile for a peaceful solution to the Gulf question. And I wanted to make clear to Saddam Hussein the absolute determination of the coalition that he comply fully with the Security Council resolutions. Iraqi aggression cannot be rewarded.

And so, I have asked the Secretary of State to be available to go to Baghdad anytime, up to and including January 3d, which is over five months after the invasion of Kuwait and only twelve days before the United Nations deadline for withdrawal. That deadline is real.

To show flexibility, I have offered any one of fifteen dates for Secretary Baker to go to Baghdad, and the Iraqis have offered only one date. In offering to go the extra mile for peace, however, I did not offer to be a party to Saddam Hussein's manipulation.

Saddam Hussein is not too busy to see on short notice Kurt Waldheim, Willy Brandt, Muhammad Ali, Ted Heath, John Connally, Ramsey Clark, and many, many others on very short notice. It simply is not credible that he cannot, over a two-week period, make a couple of hours available for the Secretary of State on an issue of this importance, unless of course, he is seeking to circumvent the United Nations deadline.

Look, I want a peaceful solution to this crisis. But I will not be a party to circumventing or diluting the United Nations deadline which I think offers the very best chance for a peaceful solution. So, I wanted to get out my feeling about these proposed meetings.

Q. What's wrong with the January 12th date that he set? Why would that dilute it unless you're afraid that he might come up with some offer or something?

A. In the first place, the United Nations resolutions that pertain say that he has to be out of Kuwait. I wish now that I had been a little more explicit in my first announcement of what I mean by mutually convenient dates. But I was not then, and am not now prepared to have this man manipulate the purpose of the Secretary of State's visit. So, we've made an offer of many, many dates. But remember, the United Nations resolution calls for total withdrawal by this date.

Q. **Does your statement today indicate that you would not accept January 5th or 7th or 9th?**

A. Yes, we've offered fifteen days, and he ought to get moving and do something reasonable, if he really wants to move for peace.

Q. **Mr. President, is there a date at which you would withdraw the offer to meet? The Senators this morning say you're willing to forgo talks now.**

A. We're not going to do them on terms that would appear to the world to be an effort to circumvent the United Nations resolution. I mean, he's got a massive force there, and that force has to be out on the 15th day of January under the United Nations resolutions. So, we'll see, we'll see how it goes.

I would say that we've given so many alternatives here that he ought to accept one of these if he's serious. Now, if it's simply that he's trying to manipulate, that is what I will have no part of.

* * *

Q. **You said the deadline is real. Does that mean you think you have carte blanche to start a war after January 15th, or on January 15th?**

A. I'm saying that the United Nations resolution is very clear as it regards January 15th. And I will continue now to work for a peaceful solution.

Q. **You do think you can go to war after that. Is that right?**

A. What do you mean, "can go to war"?

Q. **You can start a war.**

A. I think that the United Nations resolutions should be fully implemented.

Q. **Mr. President, when Congress comes back in January, will you ask Congress for specific authority to take offensive action?**

A. We're talking about that, and I'm very pleased with the support we've had in Congress. And I'm very pleased with the level of support from the American people. You see, as these hostages have come home, I think the people have understood—the American people—much more clearly

what's at stake. As they've seen the testimony about the brutality to the Kuwaiti people that was so compelling at the United Nations, I think people have said, Wait a minute this policy deserves support. So, I'm pleased with the support. I think that's being manifested in more support by the Congress.

But I will be talking to the leaders, continuing to consult. What I told the leaders in the Cabinet Room a few weeks ago: If you want to come in here and strongly endorse what I'm doing or endorse the United Nations resolution, I welcome that because I think it would send a very strong, clear signal to the world.

Q. **Sir, why are you afraid to go before Congress and consult with them and get their advice and get their approval?**

A. Hey, listen, Sarah [Sarah McClendon, McClendon News], I was consulting with them as recently as this morning, five Members of Congress. And we will continue to consult with them.

Q. **That's not 535.**

A. We re doing it all the time. I'm on the phone almost every day to them. We've had leadership meeting after leadership meeting. Oh, listen, I explained this to you in the press room a while back. This same question. Come on.

Q. **Yes, sir. You should see my mail.**

A. You ought to see mine.

Q. **My mail is against war.**

Final Remarks From European Community Summit Meeting, Rome, December 16, 1990 [13]

1. The European Community and its Member States remain firmly committed to full implementation of the U.N. Security Council resolutions. Complete Iraqi withdrawal from Kuwait and the restoration of Kuwaiti sovereignty and of its legitimate government remain the absolute conditions for a peaceful solution of the crisis.

2. Security Council Resolution 678 sends the clearest possible signal to Iraq that the international community is determined to ensure full restoration of international legality. The responsibility lies on the Iraqi Government to ensure peace for its people by comply-

ing fully with the demands of the U.N. Security Council, in particular by a complete withdrawal from Kuwait by 15 January.

3. The European Community and its Member States earnestly hope that implementation of the U.N. Security Council resolutions can be peacefully secured. To this end, they support a dialogue of the sort President Bush has offered. They also favor action by the U.N. Secretary-General and hope that the U.N. Security Council's Permanent Members will remain actively involved as well. They wish Arab countries to continue to play an important role in the efforts for a peaceful solution. The European Community and its Member States underline the value of a contact between the Presidency and the Foreign Minister of Iraq, aimed at securing, in coordination with other members of the international community, full compliance with U.N. Security Council resolutions.

4. The European Council expresses relief at Iraq's decision to release all foreign hostages, but underlines its deep concern at Iraq's failure to withdraw, at its oppressive and inhuman occupation of Kuwait and its attempt to destroy the fabric of the country.

Declaration on the Middle East

1. The European Council expresses its dismay at the continuing lack of clear prospects for a solution to the Arab-Israeli conflict and to the Palestinian problems, and at the renewed acts of terrorism and violence. It expresses its deep concern at the rising incomprehension and tension in the Occupied Territories. It renews its call to the parties concerned to refrain from violence that can only engender new violence. It expresses its concern about the Israeli practices of collective reprisals, such as the destruction of houses or restrictions on freedom of movement, and deplores the recent decision to place moderate Palestinians under Administrative arrest.

The European Council calls once again on Israel to comply with Resolutions 672 and 673 of the U.N. Security Council, to act in conformity with its obligations under the Fourth Geneva Convention on the Protection of the Civilian Population, and to cooperate with the United Nations. It welcomes the recommendations by the U.N.

Secretary-General in this regard and fully supports every effort of the U.N. Security Council to achieve a better protection of the Palestinian population and to promote peace in the area. It reaffirms the determination of the European Community and its Member States to further assist the Palestinian population in its serious plight.

2. The European Council reiterates its longstanding commitment to a just and lasting solution to these problems, in conformity with the relevant resolutions of the U.N. Security Council and with the principles expressed by the European Community in its previous Declarations. To this end, the European Council reaffirms its support for the principle of convening, at an appropriate time, an international peace conference under the auspices of the U.N.

3. The serious deterioration in the economic situation in the Occupied Territories is a source of great concern to the Community. In this connection, the European Council reaffirms its commitment to the economic and social development of the Palestinian people and considers that, in the new circumstances, the doubling of Community aid to the Occupied Territories decided on by the Strasbourg European Council appears particularly appropriate and timely.

The European Council also considers it vital for all efforts to be made to create the conditions for facilitating and increasing trade between the Occupied Territories and the Community.

4. As expressed in its Declaration of 28 October 1990, the European Council remains convinced that relations of mutual confidence and cooperation must be encouraged among the countries of the region, with a view to establishing a situation of stability, security, economic and social well-being, and respect for civil and political rights, to forestalling the recurrence of crises, and to preventing the spread of weapons of mass destruction. The European Community and its Member States remain ready actively to cooperate with the concerned countries to achieve these goals and to contribute to the success of the task entrusted by relevant resolutions to the U.N. Secretary-General to examine measures to enhance security and stability in the region. In this connection, the European Council reaffirms

the importance of meaningful and constructive Euro-Arab Dialogue.

Declaration on Lebanon

The European Council expresses its satisfaction at the implementation of the security plan in greater Beirut following the withdrawal of all militias from the Lebanese capital. It expresses the hope that the recent developments can foster the process of national reconciliation and lead to the full implementation of the Taif Agreements, thus bringing about the restoration of the sovereignty, independence, unity and territorial integrity of a Lebanon free of all foreign troops and enabling the Lebanese people to express their will through free elections.

It appeals to the parties concerned to release all remaining hostages.

The European Community and its Member States reaffirm their commitment to help provide Lebanon with the assistance needed to build its future and view favourably the participation of the Community in the pledging conference for the creation of a Lebanon Assistance Fund.

North Atlantic Council Statement on the Gulf, Brussels, December 17, 1990 [13]

1. Iraq's invasion and brutal occupation of Kuwait represent a flagrant violation of international law and the Charter of the United Nations and pose a fundamental challenge to international order. We condemn Iraq's persistent contempt for the resolutions of the United Nations Security Council, which reflect the overwhelming solidarity and commitment of the international community. Iraq's behaviour threatens peace. It jeopardizes the unprecedented opportunity for the United Nations to realize the original vision of its role in promoting global peace and stability.

2. The responsibility now lies with the Government of Iraq to ensure peace by complying fully with the mandatory United Nations decisions. Iraq has at last released the foreign citizens whom it had, illegally, detained as hostages.

However, complete Iraqi withdrawal from Kuwait and the res-

toration of the sovereignty and legitimate government of Kuwait are unequivocal conditions for a peaceful solution. There can be no partial solutions.

3. We firmly support Resolution 678 and all other relevant resolutions adopted by the Security Council and reiterate our hope that their implementation can be achieved by peaceful means. We are confident that a contact between the Presidency of the European Community and the Foreign Minister of Iraq, among other initiatives can make a contribution to this purpose. We also encourage action by the U.N. Secretary General to this end. In particular, we support efforts for a dialogue, such as those made by President Bush, to provide Iraq through direct high-level contacts, with the clearest possible understanding of the consequences of further postponing the fulfillment of its obligations. We agree that Iraq must not use these initiatives to delay meeting the January 15th date established by the United Nations.

The countries of the Gulf region, and in particular the Arab countries, also continue to bear a special responsibility in the efforts towards a solution.

4. Security Council Resolution 678 has authorized the use of all necessary means if Iraq does not comply before that date, and has expressly called on all governments to provide appropriate support in implementing the resolutions adopted by the Security Council. Our countries will continue to respond positively to this United Nations request. Each of us, to the best of our ability, undertakes to provide further support for this continuing effort, in line with evolving requirements. Furthermore, each of us will continue to maintain and enforce the economic sanctions and to provide financial assistance to those countries most directly affected.

5. We note that the crisis in the Gulf poses a potential threat to one of our allies having common borders with Iraq, and we reaffirm our determination to fulfill the commitments stipulated in Article 5 of the Washington Treaty whereby an armed attack against one of our states shall be considered an attack against them all. We reiterate our firm commitment to the security of the entire Southern Region, the strategic importance of which is highlighted by this crisis.

President's Remarks to Reporters with Prime Minister John Major of the United Kingdom, December 22, 1990 (Excerpt) [14]

Q. Mr. President, do you have any doubt, given the changes that are now occurring in the Soviet Union and the turmoil there, that if you need to make a decision to use force in the Gulf that they will be fully behind you?

A. No, I think they—every indication we've gotten is that there will be no change in their Gulf policy.

Do you want to comment on that one?

The Prime Minister. Well, we've seen no indication of a change in Gulf policy. There was no indication of that in the immediate comments after Mr. Shevardnadze's resignation. We hope there won't be.

Q. If I could ask you both, Saddam Hussein says he's not about to leave Kuwait. If he doesn't change his mind, is the world doomed for war?

President Bush. Do you want to go first?

The Prime Minister. Well, if there's going to be a conflict in Kuwait, that's really a matter for Saddam Hussein. He knows what the Security Council resolutions say. They couldn't be clearer. They've had an almost unprecedented amount of support internationally. I think one has to bear in mind what he's done is unforgivable. What he and his colleagues are doing in Kuwait at this very moment is unforgivable, as you will have seen from the Amnesty [International] report.

I hope he takes seriously the fact that the Security Council resolutions will be enforced. If he moves out, there won't be a conflict. If he doesn't, well, he knows what the consequences may be.

The President. That says it all. And that's exactly the way we feel. We are totally together on this point. And I think we're both still hoping that there will be a peaceful resolution. But I am convinced that Saddam Hussein hasn't got the message yet, for some odd reason, the message as to what he's up against and the message that all of us are determined to fulfill to the letter the United Nations resolutions. But let's hope he does get the message.

White House Statement on the Deployment of North Atlantic Treaty Organization Forces to Turkey, January 2, 1991 [15]

NATO decided today, at a meeting of its Defense Planning Committee, to deploy the air component of the Allied Command Europe Mobile Force to Turkey. Turkey asked the alliance for this help in order to deter the threat posed by Iraq and demonstrate NATO's solidarity with Turkey in this crisis. The NATO unit that will go to Turkey includes squadrons of aircraft from Germany, Italy, and Belgium. This alliance move is significant in three respects: First, the Allied Command Europe mobile Force has never before been deployed in a crisis to defend an ally. Second, the decision demonstrates the alliance's support for the coalition effort and Turkey's part in it against Saddam Hussein. Third, the deployment confirms the importance and effectiveness of the alliance in the post-Cold War era.

President's Statement on Proposed Meeting Between Iraqi Foreign Minister Tariq Aziz and Secretary Baker, January 3, 1991 [15]

More than one month ago, on November 30, I proposed that Iraqi Foreign Minister Aziz travel to Washington to meet with me late in the week of December 10, to be followed shortly thereafter by a trip to Baghdad by Secretary of State James Baker. I did so "to go the extra mile for peace" and to demonstrate our commitment to all aspects of U.N. Security Council Resolution 678, including its pause for goodwill, designed to give Iraq one final opportunity to withdraw unconditionally from Kuwait on or before January 15.

While I offered fifteen days during which Secretary Baker was prepared to travel to Baghdad, including Christmas, Saddam Hussein showed himself to be more interested in manipulating my offer to his advantage than in a serious response. He was not too busy to see on short notice a wide range of individuals, including Kurt Waldheim,

Willy Brandt, Muhammad Ali, Ted Heath, John Connally, and Ramsey Clark, but he was too busy to find even a few hours to meet with the Secretary of State of the United States. Today marks the last of the fifteen dates we suggested, and that effort is therefore at an end.

Secretary Baker is departing on January 6 for several days of close consultations with coalition partners as the UNSC [United Nations Security Council] date of January 15 approaches. While I am not prepared to repeat my previous offer, rejected by Saddam Hussein, I am ready to make one last attempt to go the extra mile for peace. I have therefore offered through CDA [Charge d'Affaires] Joe Wilson in Baghdad to have Secretary Baker meet with Iraqi Foreign Minister Aziz in Switzerland during the period January 7-9, while he is traveling on his consultations.

This offer is being made subject to the same conditions as my previous attempt: no negotiations, no compromises, no attempts at face-saving, and no rewards for aggression. What there will be if Iraq accepts this offer is simply and importantly an opportunity to resolve this crisis peacefully.

President's Meeting with Reporters on Geneva Discussions with Iraq, January 4, 1991 (Excerpts) [15]

As you all know, Iraq has accepted my initiative for a meeting between Secretary Baker and Foreign Minister Aziz. The meeting will take place on Wednesday, January 9th, in Geneva. And this is a useful step.

I hope that Iraq's acceptance of the meeting indicates a growing awareness of the seriousness of the situation and a willingness to heed the international community's will as expressed in twelve United Nations Security Council resolutions. There can be no compromise or negotiating on the objectives contained in those U.N. resolutions. And so, it is now for Saddam Hussein to respond to the international community's plea for reason.

I took this initiative yesterday with the view of going the extra mile to achieve a peaceful solution to the current crisis in the Gulf. Secretary Baker's mission to Geneva is to convey to Iraq the gravity of the situation and the determination of the international community to overcome Iraq's aggression against Kuwait.

Iraq knows what is necessary: The complete and unconditional and immediate withdrawal of all Iraqi forces from all of Kuwait, and the restoration of the legitimate government of Kuwait. And now let me just take a couple of questions and I'll be on my way.

Helen [Helen Thomas, United Press International]?

Q. Mr. President, do you back up Baker's statement that there would be no retaliation against Iraq if it complies with the resolutions?

A. I think it's been made clear to Iraq not only by Secretary Baker but by others that if they totally comply they will not be attacked. And as I have said, when they totally withdraw there still remains some problems to be solved, but they will not be under attack.

Q. Mr. President, what is in the letter you are sending to Saddam Hussein? And are you willing to have Secretary Baker go on to Baghdad if that proves an option?

A. Well, the answer to your question is that letter has not been finalized yet. I'm working on it. I have a copy I'm carrying with me now. I want to talk to the Secretary of State some more about it. And the second part of the question is no.

Q. Why not, sir?

Q. Mr. President, you said you wanted Secretary of State Baker to speak eye-to-eye with Saddam Hussein. And he was willing to meet you on the 12th. You're willing to talk on the 9th. Why not wait 3 days and have that direct meeting?

A. Because we have exhausted that option. We put forward fifteen different dates. And I believe that the message that both Secretary Baker and I want to convey can be done in this matter.

Q. You said you wanted him speaking directly and not to his intermediaries so he would know you were serious.

A. That was rejected by the Iraqi President, and so we're going to try it this way. And I hope that it will have the same result.

Q. Does three days mean that much, Mr. President?

A. I hope this will have the same result. Yes?

Q. Mr. President, in diplomacy, as you so well know, it is often the art of give and take. The Iraqis are already saying that they will talk about getting out of Kuwait, but they want to also talk in Geneva about the Palestinian problem, about Israel's occupation of the West Bank. How are you instructing Secretary Baker to handle that portion?

A. I don't need to instruct him because he and I are in total sync on this, and so are the rest of the alliance. There will be no linkage on these two questions.

Q. If I may follow up, Mr. President: Quite apart from linkage—whether it's called linkage or not—the Iraqis want to pursue these discussions. Is there room for some discussion on these other issues?

A. There will be no linkage on these other issues. We can't tell anybody what he can bring up at a discussion, but there will be no linkage.

Q. Mr. President, what do you make of today's French proposal in which, outside of linkage, the French are saying that they think a deal is possible if you tell the Iraqis that sometime down the road you'll discuss the Middle East? How do you react to that?

A. I haven't seen the French proposal, so I wouldn't care to comment on it.

Q. Do you think that undercuts what you're trying to say here?

A. No, I think François Mitterrand [President of France], if it has anything to do with him, has been a steadfast coalition partner. And I would want to know exactly what his feelings are on this before I commented.

Q. Mr. President, there have been several suggestions, including one by Mr. Mitterrand, that perhaps there's room for one more Security Council meeting before there is any military force used. Will you tell Perez de Cuellar [Secretary-General of the United Nations] that you would approve of anything like that, or do you think at this point the United Nations sanctions ought to stand with no clarification?

A. I don't think any further U.N. action is required. I would be interested if the Secretary-General feels to the contrary. I, again, wouldn't comment on what President Mitterrand has suggested. Somebody told me he responded to some questions—some-

body putting the question to him—and he said, well, maybe it would have some utility. There has been no formal proposal by the French Government to its coalition partners.

*   *   *

Q. Mr. President, would you look without favor on a trip to Baghdad by some other members of the coalition right now, say a European representative?

A. Look, these coalition members are free to do whatever they want. Several have gone to Baghdad, I believe. I'd have to think back to the actual members of the coalition—representatives of governments there. I know there's a French representative there right now, I believe. So, they have to make that determination. But I am pleased with the way the EC has approached this matter, giving priority to the Baker-Aziz meeting in Geneva. I am very pleased with the comments coming out of the EC by Mr. Poos [Foreign Minister of Luxembourg and current President of the European Community], just as I was by the comments coming out from Andreotti [Prime Minister of Italy] and De Michelis [Foreign Minister of Italy] who had the Presidency—the Italians having the Presidency beforehand. So, I have no hangups on that.

Many people have tried to talk sense to the Iraqis and make them understand what they're facing. So, that's for others to determine. We're not trying to dictate to anybody what they do.

*   *   *

Q. Mr. President, does your meeting tomorrow with Perez de Cuellar offer some new hope?

A. I can't say that. I don't want to mislead the American people or the people around the world that are concerned and growing increasing concerned about this situation. But I go back with Perez de Cuellar for a long time. We were Ambassadors at the United Nations together in 1971 or '2. And I've known him, and I know him very favorably, and I have great respect for what he has tried to do, including a trip to that area of the Middle East to make the Iraqis understand that the United Nations was serious.

I talked to him in Paris, and I am very anxious to see him and to compare notes with him. But I don't want to mislead you in answering the question. I don't have in mind any new initiative. But I do think that he stays in close touch with it. I heard what he had to say yesterday about things he is doing privately, keeping up with the key players on this Gulf situation. And so, I think it's more of a getting together and comparing notes. And he knows of my determination and our coalition position. So, I don't need to reiterate that there. But I think it's more getting together, and if some new initiative, he has it in mind, why, I'm most anxious to hear what it might be.

President's Letter to Congressional Leaders Requesting Resolution on the Persian Gulf, January 8, 1991 [16]

Identical letters were sent to Thomas S. Foley, Speaker of the House of Representatives; Senate majority leader George J. Mitchell; Senate minority leader Robert Dole; and House minority leader Robert H. Michel.

The current situation in the Persian Gulf, brought about by Iraq's unprovoked invasion and subsequent brutal occupation of Kuwait, threatens vital U.S. interests. The situation also threatens the peace. It would, however, greatly enhance the chances for peace if Congress were now to go on record supporting the position adopted by the U.N. Security Council on twelve separate occasions. Such an action would underline that the United States stands with the international community and on the side of law and decency; it also would help dispel any belief that may exist in the minds of Iraq's leaders that the United States lacks the necessary unity to act decisively in response to Iraq's continued aggression against Kuwait.

Secretary of State Baker is meeting with Iraq's Foreign Minister on January 9. It would have been most constructive if he could have presented the Iraqi government a resolution passed by both houses of Congress supporting the U.N. position and in particular Security Council Resolution 678. As you know, I have frequently stated my

desire for such a resolution. Nevertheless, there is still opportunity for Congress to act to strengthen the prospects for peace and safeguard this country's vital interests.

I therefore request that the House of Representatives and the Senate adopt a resolution stating that Congress supports the use of all necessary means to implement U.N. Security Council Resolution 678. Such action would send the clearest possible message to Saddam Hussein that he must withdraw without condition or delay from Kuwait. Anything less would only encourage Iraqi intransigence; anything else would risk detracting from the international coalition arrayed against Iraq's aggression.

I therefore request that the House of Representatives and the Senate adopt a resolution stating that Congress supports the use of all necessary means to implement U.N. Security Council Resolution 678.

Mr. Speaker, I am determined to do whatever is necessary to protect America's security. I ask Congress to join with me in this task. I can think of no better way than for Congress to express its support for the President at this critical time. This truly is the last best chance for peace.

Secretary Baker's Press Conference Following Meeting with Iraqi Foreign Minister Aziz, Geneva, January 9, 1991 [17]

Ladies and gentlemen: I have just given President Bush a full report of our meeting today. I told him that Minister Aziz and I had completed a serious and extended diplomatic conversation in an effort to find a political solution to the crisis in the Gulf.

I met with Minister Aziz today not to negotiate, as we have made clear we would not do—that is, negotiate backwards from United Nations Security resolutions—but I met with him today

to communicate. And communicate means listening as well as talking, and we did that—both of us.

The message that I conveyed from President Bush and our coalition partners was that Iraq must either comply with the will of the international community and withdraw peacefully from Kuwait or be expelled by force. Regrettably, ladies and gentlemen, I heard nothing today that—in over six hours I heard nothing that suggested to me any Iraqi flexibility whatsoever on complying with the United Nations Security Council resolutions.

There have been too many Iraqi miscalculations. The Iraqi government miscalculated the international response to the invasion of Kuwait, expecting the world community to stand idly by while Iraqi forces systematically pillaged a peaceful neighbor.

It miscalculated the response I think, to the barbaric policy. of holding thousands of foreign hostages, thinking that so cynically doling them out a few at a time would somehow win political advantage. And it miscalculated that it could divide the international community and gain something thereby from its aggression. So let us hope that Iraq does not miscalculate again.

The Iraqi leadership must have no doubt that the twenty-eight nations which have deployed forces to the Gulf in support of the United Nations have both the power and the will to evict Iraq from Kuwait. If it should choose—and the choice is Iraq's—if it should choose to continue its brutal occupation of Kuwait, Iraq will be choosing a military confrontation which it cannot win and which will have devastating consequences for Iraq.

I made these points with Minister Aziz not to threaten but to inform, and I did so with no sense of satisfaction, for we genuinely desire a peaceful outcome, and, as both President Bush and I have said on many occasions, the people of the United States have no quarrel with the people of Iraq.

I simply wanted to leave as little room as possible for yet another tragic miscalculation by the Iraqi leadership. And I would suggest to you, ladies and gentlemen, that this is still a confrontation that Iraq can avoid.

The path of peace remains open, and that path is laid out very clearly in twelve United Nations Security Council resolutions adopted over a period of over five months.

But now the choice lies with the Iraqi leadership. The choice really is theirs to make, and let us all hope that that leadership will have the wisdom to choose the path of peace.

Q. What do your allies plan to do next to bring this message home?

A. Well, you say, "What do the allies plan to do next," and I think it's important for everyone to note that this is a coalition. This is not Iraq versus the United States. This is Iraq versus the international community. This happens to have been the first time that we've had an opportunity to find agreement on meeting—U.S. and Iraq.

So I don't know what the next steps are, Jim [Anderson, UPI]. I do know this: that time is running on, as I said a day or so ago. After five months and twelve United Nations Security Council resolutions, it seems to me that it is almost evident that the time for talk is running out. It's time for Iraq to act and to act quickly by getting out of Kuwait.

But this is a coalition, and we are seeking to implement solemn resolutions of the United Nations. And so perhaps there may be a way that the Secretary-General of the United Nations could use his good offices here in the remaining six or so days that we have left.

I will say that—I've already mentioned that I didn't hear anything that to me demonstrated flexibility, nor did I hear any new proposals. But I would like to take note of the fact that the Minister did restate their proposal that the United States pick a day for him to come to the United States and Iraq pick a day for me to go to Baghdad.

Those of you who have been traveling with us know what our answer is to that. We've given it over the past four or five days, and I gave it to the Minister tonight. We offered fifteen separate days for a visit to Baghdad. The President of the United States made the proposal for face-to-face discussions. We're glad that Iraq accepted this one, because we did have six hours during which we could make our position known to them; they could make their position known to us.

But as far as next steps are concerned, it seems to me that because we are talking about a coalition and we are talking about implementing resolutions of the United Nations, that perhaps there could be—I don't know what the position of the Government

of Iraq would be on this—but perhaps there would be some room for us to seek the use of the good offices of the Secretary-General of the United Nations.

Regrettably,...in over six hours I heard nothing that suggested to me any Iraqi flexibility whatsoever...

Q. Mr. Secretary, did the Iraqi Foreign Minister reiterate his demands for what he calls "justice and fairness" for the Palestinians? I mean, was there any wavering in the U.S. position, as you may have expressed it to him, that the two issues are not related, are not linked?

A. No. There was—he expressed his position. There was no change in our position, which is that the two issues are not linked. I did make the point that I don't think many people believe that Iraq invaded Kuwait in order to help the Palestinians, and if they did, it was another miscalculation, because it hasn't helped the Palestinians.

I think most people believe that Iraq invaded Kuwait for Iraq's own aggrandizement, and I think most people realize that Iraq is trying to use the Palestinian issue to shield its aggression against Kuwait, which in my view at least remains an obstacle to broader peace in the region rather than a catalyst for achieving that broader peace.

And I made the point as well that rewarding Iraq's aggression with a link to the Arab-Israeli peace process would really send a terrible signal not only to genuine peacemakers in the region but also to other would-be aggressors at what we think is a defining moment in history.

Q. Mr. Secretary, are you willing—is the United States willing to talk again to Iraq before the January 15 deadline, and did you discuss with the President the possibility that you may still go to Baghdad?

A. I had already discussed that with President Bush, and I had already told you what our view was. And the President himself, I think, said, "There will be no trip to Baghdad." The proposal

which he originally made was in effect rejected by Iraq. We offered fifteen separate days. They continued to insist upon only one—the 12th of January—which we think was and still is an obvious effort to avoid the deadline of January the 15th, and we're not interested in that.

We think this deadline is real, and our coalition partners think the deadline is real.

Q. Did you discuss this with the President today?

A. I reported fully to the President, of course.

Q. Could you run through for us—you spoke for six hours—could you give us a sense of how the discussions evolved over those six hours? What did you begin with? What did he counter with? Why did you feel it necessary after two hours to call the President?

A. Well, we broke for lunch. (Laughter) And I think this meeting is sufficiently important that I should call the President, and so I did, just as I did as soon as we were finished.

Q. Did you begin by reading your letter —

A. But I began by saying that I was here to—not to negotiate but to communicate, as I've just told you—that I was here for a serious dialogue in an effort to find a political and peaceful solution, but that they should not expect that we would be prepared to walk backwards from U.N. Security Council resolutions; that the terms of those resolutions had already been set.

And I told the Minister I wanted to handle the meeting in whatever way he wanted. And I gave him the choice, and he chose for me to go first, just as he—I gave him the choice as well as to how to report to you, and he suggested that I come down here first.

So that's how we got where we are here tonight. But let me say that I talked to him about how we saw the situation, about the history of the Security Council resolutions, about what I thought could happen in the event of observance of those resolutions, and what I feared would happen in the event Iraq's nonobservance of those resolutions.

He then presented the position of the Government of Iraq, and he will be down here in a few moments, and he can— Now, we can't run through six hours of dialogue here. Nobody else would get to ask any questions.

Q. One quick follow-up: How detailed were you about the extent of force that would be used against Iraq if it does not comply with the U.N. resolutions by January 15?

A. Well, I didn't get into things that would properly be in the realm of operational security matters. I hope I effectively made the case with respect to what at least our opinion was of the 28-nation multinational force that is there in the Gulf.

Q. Mr. Secretary, is the United States interested in any sort of phased withdrawal, be it one supervised by the United Nations? And if this withdrawal began by January 15, will the United States guarantee there will be no military attack on Iraq?

A. Let me say—I should have said this in answer to Tom's question—I assured the Minister that if they implement the United Nations resolutions, and if they withdraw from Iraq and permit the restoration—from Kuwait and permit the restoration of the legitimate Government of Kuwait, that I could assure him that there would be no military action by the United States. And that I felt that there would, under those circumstances, be no military action by any other elements of the international coalition.

*   *   *

Q. Mr. Secretary, in the remaining six days before the U.N. deadline, would you welcome an initiative by some other European allies or even Arab countries such as Algeria that would perhaps include sending a European Foreign Minister to Baghdad to seek a peaceful resolution?

A. Well, this is an international coalition—let me say it one more time—and therefore, as I've just indicated to you, it's an international coalition seeking to implement solemn resolutions of the world's peacekeeping and security body. And, therefore, there might, it seems to me, be some useful purpose served by perhaps the Secretary General—Secretary General's good offices.

But I said last night, and I have said for months, we welcome any and all diplomatic efforts to solve this crisis peacefully and politically. We want it solved peacefully and politically. I'm disappointed, of course, that we did not receive any indications today whatsoever of any flexibility in the position of Iraq.

So we would welcome any and all diplomatic efforts. We do think if there are efforts by members of the international coalition, that the message should be uniform, as it has been for five months, and it should not be a mixed message. But we want a peaceful and political solution.

Q. Mr. Secretary, can you tell us—you keep saying you saw no indication of flexibility. Did the Foreign Minister actually tell you that Iraq intends to keep Kuwait and will not withdraw from Kuwait?

A. He did not make that statement, but he did not indicate that there was any chance that they would withdraw, Mary. But I did not see, frankly, any flexibility in their position. You can ask him questions when he gets down here.

Q. Mr. Secretary, did you discuss—in answer to any of the discussion about the problems raised elsewhere in the Middle East by the Iraqi Foreign Minister, did you discuss efforts the United States has made in the past to seek Arab/Israeli peace —

A. Yes.

Q. —to persuade Iraq that the United States was serious, genuinely interested, in resolving those problems?

A. Yes. We went through a good bit of the history of the personal efforts that I made for fourteen months to bring about a dialogue between Arab—between Palestinians and Israelis. We went through the experience of the United States in bringing about the Camp David Accords and in bringing about peace between Israel and Egypt, and we had a full discussion of that issue—a complete discussion of it.

I want to make it clear that I made it very clear throughout that there would be no linkage here of that issue to Iraq's withdrawal from Kuwait. And we would not agree as a condition of their withdrawing to any subsequent specific steps to be taken with respect to that. But we did have—they brought it up, and we had a very full discussion.

Q. Well, what was their answer?

A. We disagree. We frankly disagree with respect to that, as I think you know. And I've already told you why I think linkage is a bad idea. I think that it would tend to be read as a reward for aggressors, and it would jeopardize future peace in the region.

Q. Mr. Secretary, what did you tell the Foreign Minister about the willingness of the American people to go to war and the impact of political pressure on the President's decision-making?

A. I said, "Don't miscalculate the resolve of the American people who are very slow to anger but who believe strongly in principle and who believe that we should not reward aggression, and that big countries with powerful military machines should not be permitted to invade, occupy, and brutalize their peaceful neighbors."

Q. Mr. Secretary, you've told us what you didn't hear. You didn't hear any flexibility, and you told us that there was quite a bit of discussion of history. Could you tell us what you did hear? Did you hear justifications from the Foreign Minister? Did you hear a repeat of what they've been saying in public for some time?

Q. I heard some things that I quite frankly found very hard to believe, but I'll let him go into the detail here. I heard, for instance, that their action in invading Kuwait was defensive in nature; that they were being threatened by Kuwait. And I will tell you the same thing I told the Minister which is I found it very hard to believe that any nation in the world will believe that.

Q. Mr. Secretary, even though you did spend six hours here today talking to Foreign Minister Aziz, in the past five-and-a-half months you haven't had much contact with Iraq. What's to prevent the historians of this conflict from concluding that there was a failure of diplomacy here and we slid toward war without trying?

A. There's been a lot of conversations with the leadership of Iraq, all to no avail. The Secretary-General has already had one failed mission. There have been any number of Arab efforts to solve this crisis, all to no avail. There have been efforts by other Western governments. The Soviet Union has tried very hard. They've had meetings. We have now had a meeting. So people can write whatever they decide they might want to write.

But the truth of the matter is, we have been very, I think—the international coalition—very responsible and measured in our approach to this. We have not, as some might suggest, gone off half-cocked. We have gone through the United Nations patiently, working for consensus within the Security

Council. And it is only after five-and-a-half months and the passage of twelve Security Council resolutions that we find ourselves at the point of use of force, David.

So I think that there's been more diplomacy exercised in this crisis than in almost any that I can think of. The one thing I would ask you all not to do is to equate diplomacy and appeasement. We made that mistake in the Thirties, at least, for our part. We don't intend to make it again.

Q. Mr. Secretary, in a sense, two questions. Did the Foreign Minister suggest Iraq might withdraw from Kuwait if there were linkage as, let us say, the French have suggested or others have suggested? And, if he did, is linkage—the principle of linkage—a reason for the loss of—and the insistence on that principle—a reason for the loss of lots of lives?

A. Well, I don't think he said that explicitly, Saul. I think perhaps it was implicit in his comments. But he'll be here and you can ask him. It's more than just the principle of linkage, as I understand their position. There would have to be agreement to conferences, and that sort of thing, that gets you beyond just the simple fact of linkage.

Q. Mr. Secretary, did Minister Aziz make a specific proposal under which Iraq would get out of Kuwait, however unacceptable it was to you? Was there a specific proposal?

A. No. There was no specific proposal. He restated the positions that Iraq has stated publicly in the past. He defended their action in invading and occupying Kuwait. He explained how he feels that was justified. Again, he'll be down here and you can ask him yourselves.

Q. Mr. Secretary, you made it clear that you were not going to Baghdad. But did you and the Foreign Minister talk about future diplomatic contacts at your level between the United States and Iraq? Or did this one six-and-one-half-hour meeting represent the conclusion of diplomatic initiatives by the United States?

A. We will maintain our diplomatic contacts through our Charge in Baghdad until the 12th of January. I asked for and received the personal assurance of the Minister that Joe Wilson and the four other Americans in our Embassy there will be permitted to leave Baghdad on the 12th of January and will not be restrained from so doing.

Q. Mr. Secretary, your mood, if I may say, seems pretty somber at this point. Can you kind of describe your state of mind and your mood after what has occurred today?

A. Somber.

Q. Somber?

A. You got it.

Q. Are you advising an evacuation?

A. I'm not saying that. I'm telling you that we have asked for and received assurances for our remaining five diplomatic personnel to leave on the 12th of January, which is a date that you well know is very close to the January 15 deadline and happens to be the date that Iraq has been insisting on for three weeks for the meeting.

Q. What about other Americans?

A. I think most all Americans are out of Iraq. All that want to leave are gone, as far as I know.

*   *   *

Q. Mr. Secretary, do you have any reason to believe that there is a way to avoid a war as of right now?

A. Yes, I hope there is. There has been no decision taken for that eventuality. I would simply refer you to my opening statement where I made the point that I hope we do not have yet one more miscalculation by the Government of Iraq.

I would also refer you to the statements which President Bush and I and other members of the coalition have made over the course of the last several days or weeks and which I repeated today to the Minister, not in a threatening way but simply so that he would know where our head is and how we feel and what we think and that is that this January 15 deadline, in our minds, is real.

Iraq can choose to believe that or not, but it is real in our minds and in the minds of our coalition partners. We hope that they will believe that we think it's real and that they will act to implement the solemn resolutions of the United Nations.

Q. Mr. Secretary, do you regret that you would have still liked to go, even on the 12th, and meet—instead of Mr. Tariq—Saddam himself? It's still a difference of three days.

A. We've said for the last three weeks, the 12th of January was unacceptable to us because it is just an ef-
fort to avoid the deadline. It's obvious. That's why the 12th was originally suggested. We've said for a long time that date is unacceptable to us. It remains unacceptable to us.

Q. Mr. Secretary, did you spell out your vision of what the Gulf would look like if they withdrew peacefully? In other words, some of the restrictions that you have talked about that must be imposed upon Iraq even if they did withdraw? Did you lay that plan out for him in some way?

A. Yes, I did in my original presentation this morning, John. I don't have time to go through all of that with you now. But that falls right in the category of the assurance that there would not be military force used against Iraq by the United States if they withdrew from Kuwait and permitted the restoration of the legitimate Government of Kuwait.

Q. Did you talk about the nuclear weapons, the chemical weapons, the size of the Iraqi military—things that are of concern to many in the Western coalition beyond the occupation of Kuwait?

A. We had a full discussion of the questions about weapons of mass destruction. I pointed out the interest of the United States, as we have expressed before in addressing that issue and addressing that subject. We talked about the multinational presence there and the fact that President Bush has said we do not desire nor want a permanent military ground presence in the Middle East—I mean in the Gulf. We want to see our troops come home just as fast as the security situation will allow. Those are the kinds of things that we discussed, as you might expect.

Q. Mr. Secretary, could you just please describe to us the point at which the meeting broke off? Why and how did it happen? Was it that you finished off? Did Mr. Aziz finish off? Or was there just nothing to talk about anymore? Please describe that.

A. It was simply a case, I think, that over six hours of discussion, we had both had pretty well made the points that we had come to make, and that was it. I don't believe that there was anything left unsaid. He said everything, I think, he came to say and I had said everything that I had come to say.

I think, frankly, it lasted longer than many of you might have anticipated at the beginning.

Q. Mr. Secretary, you mentioned that you are going to call back the American diplomats. Are you also asking the Iraqi diplomats to leave the United States on January 12th?

A. No. We will ask the Iraqi government to draw down their diplomatic presence in the United States on the 12th. As I indicated to the Minister, we would be willing to permit the presence of a small diplomatic contingent in Washington.

Q. Mr. Secretary, do you feel that if you would have accepted the fact of the linkage, there could have been a proposition of Iraq retiring from Kuwait?

A. I don't know. Why don't you ask the Minister that. Because when you say "accepted linkage," I'm not entirely sure exactly what you mean. Do you mean if we had accepted—if we had indicated a willingness to go to an international conference to handle the question of the Middle East, ask him the question. It would be very interesting.

You know what our position has been for a long time. It would set an extraordinarily unfortunate precedent, we think, and would not, in the long run, contribute to peace in the region but would contribute to instability because aggressors would be seen to be rewarded for their aggression. It's something we simply cannot consider.

Q. Mr. Secretary, was there any single issue on which the difference between the United States and Iraq was narrowed during this six-and-one-half hours?

A. Well, let me say that I think that the discussions—I've already indicated it was a serious one. I think that the tone of it was good, Norm; as good as you could expect under the circumstances. We weren't pounding the table and shouting at each other. It was a very reasoned and, I think, responsible discussion by two diplomats who really would like to find a peaceful and political solution to this problem. I've already said tô you, I did not detect flexibility in the position of Iraq, as they have stated it over the past several days.

Again, I invite you to my opening statement. We still have six days. I just hope that they will think about this meeting; that they will focus on it; that when Foreign Minister Aziz gets back and reports to his President, that per-

haps there could be some change in their position.

There cannot be a negotiation here because the terms of the United Nations Security Council resolutions were worked out in the debate in the United Nations, and the international coalition is bound to those resolutions.

Q. Mr. Secretary, would you be willing to meet Saddam somewhere else, apart from Baghdad? And was that suggested?

A. That was not discussed. It has never been proposed by Iraq. The Iraqi proposal, as you know, for some weeks has been, we pick a date for Baker to come to Baghdad; you pick a date for Aziz to come to Washington, and we'll work it that way. That's been out there for a long, long time. There's never been any suggestion of the other.

Excerpts from Press Conference of Iraqi Foreign Minister Aziz Following Meeting with Secretary Baker, Geneva, January 9, 1991 [18]

When I arrived last night in Geneva, I said that I have come with open-mindedness, and that was my intention. And I also came in good faith. The most important fact about these talks I would like to draw your attention to is that they are taking place after five months of the occurrence of the latest events in the Gulf. If we had an earlier opportunity, several months ago, I told the Secretary that we might have been able to remove a lot of misunderstandings between us. There was a chance, or there is a chance, for that. Because he spoke at length about his government's assumptions of miscalculations by Iraq, and when I came to that point, I made it clear to him that we have not made miscalculations. We are very well aware of the situation. We have been well aware of the situation from the very beginning. We know what the deployment of your forces in the region means. We know what the resolutions you imposed on the Security Council mean...

What's at stake is the fate of the whole region, that region which has been suffering from wars, instabilities, hardships for several decades. If you are ready to bring peace to the region—

comprehensive, lasting, just peace to the whole region of the Middle East—we are ready to cooperate.

*   *   *

Q. Do you believe that war with the United States is inevitable?

A. Well, that is up to the American administration to decide. I told Mr. Baker that we are prepared for all expectations. We have been prepared from the very beginning...if the American administration decides to attack Iraq militarily, Iraq will defend itself in a very bold manner.

Q. Mr. Foreign Minister, in your opening statement, and in fact up to this very moment you have not mentioned Iraq's annexation of Kuwait. I'm curious to know whether you actually ever discussed the question of withdrawal from Kuwait during the course of six or so hours of talks with Secretary Baker?

A. Yes. Mr. Baker spoke a lot about the situation in the Gulf, and I made our position very clear. I told him this situation is part and parcel of a general situation in the region. If you are ready to address it on the same principles, on the same criteria, I am ready to do the same.

Q. Mr. Foreign Minister, if the war starts in the Middle East, in the Gulf, will you attack Israel?

A. Yes, absolutely, yes.

Letter from President Bush to Saddam Hussein (Not Accepted by Iraq), January 9, 1991 [19]

Mr. President:

We stand today at the brink of war between Iraq and the world. This is a war that began with your invasion of Kuwait; this is a war that can be ended only by Iraq's full and unconditional compliance with U.N. Security Council Resolution 678.

I am writing you now, directly, because what is at stake demands that no opportunity be lost to avoid what would be a certain calamity for the people of Iraq. I am writing, as well, because it is said by some that you do not understand just how isolated Iraq is and what Iraq faces as a result. I am not in a position to judge whether this impression is correct; what I can do, though, is try in this letter to reinforce what Secretary of State Baker told your Foreign Minister and eliminate any uncertainty or ambiguity that might exist in your mind about where we stand and what we are prepared to do.

The international community is united in its call for Iraq to leave all of Kuwait without condition and without further delay. This is not simply the policy of the United States; it is the position of the world community as expressed in no less than twelve Security Council resolutions.

We prefer a peaceful outcome. However, anything less than full compliance with U.N. Security Council Resolution 678 and its predecessors is unacceptable. There can be no reward for aggression. Nor will there be any negotiation. Principle cannot be compromised. However, by its full compliance, Iraq will gain the opportunity to rejoin the international community. More immediately, the Iraqi military establishment will escape destruction. But unless you withdraw from Kuwait completely and without condition, you will lose more than Kuwait. What is at issue here is not the future of Kuwait—it will be free, its government will be restored—but rather the future of Iraq. This choice is yours to make.

The United States will not be separated from its coalition partners. Twelve Security Council resolutions, twenty-eight countries providing military units to enforce them, more than one hundred governments complying with sanctions—all highlight the fact that it is not Iraq against the United States, but Iraq against the world. That most Arab and Muslim countries are arrayed against you as well should reinforce what I am saying. Iraq cannot and will not be able to hold on to Kuwait or exact a price for leaving.

You may be tempted to find solace in the diversity of opinion that is American democracy. You should resist any such temptation. Diversity ought not to be confused with division. Nor should you underestimate, as others have before you, America's will.

Iraq is already feeling the effects of the sanctions mandated by the United Nations. Should war come, it will be a far greater tragedy for you and your country. Let me state, too, that the United States will not tolerate the use of chemical or biological weapons or the destruction of Kuwait's oil fields and installations. Further, you will be

held directly responsible for terrorist actions against any member of the coalition. The American people would demand the strongest possible response. You and your country will pay a terrible price if you order unconscionable acts of this sort.

I write this letter not to threaten, but to inform. I do so with no sense of satisfaction, for the people of the United States have no quarrel with the people of Iraq. Mr. President, U.N. Security Council Resolution 678 establishes the period before January 15 of this year as a "pause of good will" so that this crisis may end without further violence. Whether this pause is used as intended, or merely becomes a prelude to further violence, is in your hands, and yours alone. I hope you weigh your choice carefully and choose wisely, for much will depend upon it.

President's Press Conference Following Baker-Aziz Meeting, January 9, 1991 (Excerpt) [20]

I have spoken with Secretary of State Jim Baker, who reported to me on his nearly seven hours of conversation with Iraqi Foreign Minister Tariq Aziz. Secretary Baker made it clear that he discerned no evidence whatsoever that Iraq was willing to comply with the international community's demand to withdraw from Kuwait and comply with the United Nations resolutions.

Secretary Baker also reported to me that the Iraqi Foreign Minister rejected my letter to Saddam Hussein—refused to carry this letter and give it to the President of Iraq. The Iraqi Ambassador here in Washington did the same thing. This is but one more example that the Iraqi Government is not interested in direct communications designed to settle the Persian Gulf situation.

The record shows that whether the diplomacy is initiated by the United States, the United Nations, the Arab League, or the European Community, the results are the same, unfortunately. The conclusion is clear: Saddam Hussein continues to reject a diplomatic solution.

I sent Secretary Jim Baker to Geneva not to negotiate but to communicate. And I wanted Iraqi leaders to know just how determined we are

that the Iraqi forces leave Kuwait without condition or further delay. Secretary Baker made clear that by its full compliance with the twelve relevant United Nations Security Council resolutions, Iraq would gain the opportunity to rejoin the international community. And he also made clear how much Iraq stands to lose if it does not comply.

Let me emphasize that I have not given up on a peaceful outcome—it's not too late. I've just been on the phone, subsequent to the Baker press conference, with King Fahd, with President Mitterrand—to whom I've talked twice today—Prime Minister Mulroney. And others are contacting other coalition partners to keep the matter under lively discussion. It isn't too late. But now, as it's been before, the choice of peace or war is really Saddam Hussein's to make.

Q. Mr. President, you said in an interview last month that you believed in your gut that Saddam Hussein would withdraw from Kuwait by January 15th. After the failure of this meeting today, what does your gut tell you about that? And in your gut, do you believe that there's going to be war or peace?

A. I can't misrepresent this to the American people. I am discouraged. I watched much of the Aziz press conference, and there was no discussion of withdrawal from Kuwait. The United Nations resolutions are about the aggression against Kuwait. They are about the invasion of Kuwait, about the liquidation of a lot of the people in Kuwait, about the restoration of the legitimate government to Kuwait. And here we were listening to a 45-minute press conference after the Secretary of State of the United States had six hours worth of meetings over there, and there was not one single sentence that has to relate to their willingness to get out of Kuwait.

And so, Terry [Terrence Hunt, Associated Press], I'd have to say I certainly am not encouraged by that, but I'm not going to give up. And I told this to our coalition partners—and I'll be talking to more of them when I finish here—we've got to keep trying. But this was a total stiff-arm. This was a total rebuff.

Q. Let me follow up on that. Let me follow up. Have you decided in your mind to go to war if he's not out of there by the 15th?

A. I have not made up my decision on what and when to do. I am more determined than ever that the United Nations resolutions including 678 is implemented fully.

Q. Mr. President, Aziz made a pledge that he would not make the first attack. Would you match that? And also, what's wrong with a Middle East conference if it could avoid a bloody war?

A. No, I wouldn't make it. And we oppose linkage. The coalition opposes linkage. And the argument with Saddam Hussein is about Kuwait. It is about the invasion of Kuwait, the liquidation of a member of the United Nations, a member of the Arab League. And it has long been determined by not just the Security Council but by the entire United Nations that this is about Kuwait. And that is the point that was missing from his explanations here today. And so, there will be no linkage on these items. And that's been the firm position of all of the allies, those with forces there, and, indeed, of the United Nations—the General Assembly.

White House Statement on President's Conversation with U.N. Secretary-General, January 10, 1991 [20]

The President spoke with U.N. Secretary-General Perez de Cuellar late this afternoon to discuss the Secretary-General's upcoming visit to Baghdad. The President wished him well and stated that he was pleased that the Secretary-General is undertaking this mission for peace. The President noted that the United Nations has played a key role in building and maintaining the international coalition against the Iraqi aggression. The discussion centered on the U.N. resolutions dealing with the Iraqi aggression against Kuwait and on securing Iraq's compliance with them.

President's Exchange with Reporters on Telephone Conversation with Soviet President Mikhail Gorbachev, January 11, 1991 (Excerpt) [20]

Q. Mr. President, what can you tell us about the Gorbachev phone call?

A. We've had a very interesting morning here and a very interesting phone call with President Gorbachev, Prime Minister Toshiki Kaifu of Japan, and then a meeting with a lot of the Members of the House of Representatives on the Gulf situation. Now we're shifting our gears to this luncheon with two of our new Cabinet-level officers and, obviously, with one existing Cabinet member, Carla Hills, where our conversation will be both domestic and international. So, it's been a full day.

On the Gorbachev phone call—I won't give you the details of it—but it is very important as we move down the path here that we stay in close touch. And I was very pleased—this was his call to me—and it was a discussion of the Gulf situation mainly. We also talked about the internal problems that he's facing. But I think the very fact he called in the true spirit of consultation says a lot not just about the U.S.-Soviet relationship but about the fact that it is not simply Iraq versus the United States; it is Iraq, indeed, versus the whole world. I think that's the symbolism of Mr. Gorbachev's call. And he had some ideas he wanted to discuss with me. And I respect his confidentiality, but it's the best sense of consultation. We are leaving no stone unturned to try to find a peaceful resolution of this question.

Q. Tass said, Mr. President, that the conversation would be continued.

A. Well, as you may know, I left out one meeting, and that is that I did meet with the Soviet Ambassador here following the Gorbachev call. But whether President Gorbachev and I talk again I'm not—we didn't set a time. Perhaps we will. We've been in touch, and I will continue to stay in touch with him and with other world leaders to see if we cannot resolve this matter peacefully.

I might, as long—take advantage of you all, but to say that I still feel that it would be very helpful to the last step for peace if the Congress would move and would support the so-called U.N.

resolutions that are before the House now and will be before the Senate.

---

1 Text from Weekly Compilation of Presidential Documents of November 12, 1990.

2 Released by the Office of the Majority Leader, November 13, 1990.

3 Released by Senator Lugar's office, November 13, 1990.

4 Text from Weekly Compilation of Presidential Documents of November 19, 1990.

5 Text from Weekly Compilation of Presidential Documents of December 3, 1990.

6 Department of State Press Release 198. November 24, 1990.

7 Text provided by United Nations Information Center, Washington.

8 Department of State Press Release 204, November 29, 1990.

9 Department of State Press Release 205, November 29, 1990.

10 Department of State Press Release 209, December 5, 1990.

11 Text as released by Iraqi [official] News Agency.

12 Text from Weekly Compilation of Presidential Documents of December 17, 1990.

13 Text from Weekly Compilation of Presidential Documents of December 24, 1990.

14 Text from Weekly Compilation of Presidential Documents of December 31, 1990.

15 Text from Weekly Compilation of Presidential Documents of January 7, 1991.

16 Text from Weekly Compilation of Presidential Documents of January 14, 1991.

17 Department of State Document Number 4, January 9, 1991.

18 Transcribed by Foreign Policy Bulletin staff from television coverage, January 9, 1991.

19 Text from Weekly Compilation of Presidential Documents of January 21, 1991. Foreign Minister Aziz refused to deliver the letter, which was dated January 5.

20 Text from Weekly Compilation of Presidential Documents of January 14, 1991.

Some Highlights of Congressional Hearings and Debates on Persian Gulf Policy

Statement by Admiral William J. Crowe, Jr. (Retired), Former Chairman of the Joint Chiefs of Staff, Before the Senate Armed Services Committee, November 28, 1990 [1]

Given U.S. interest in the Persian Gulf and Saddam Hussein's brutal takeover of Kuwait, I strongly believe that the subject of U.S. policy in the region is of utmost importance to all Americans, and I applaud these hearings, Mr. Chairman...

You would think that we would have a decent interval to celebrate the end of the Cold War and the vindication of our policies and values, but the recent events in the Middle East have demonstrated at least to my mind that the globe is still a very dangerous place and that new threats may very well replace the U.S.-Soviet contest which we lived with for so long.

Our difficulties with Iraq certainly suggest the type of challenge that the post-Cold War era may confront. The most distinguishing feature of the agreement or disagreement, I believe, is that the Soviets are not backing Saddam Hussein. For the first time in forty years, we are confronting a major international crisis and not working at cross-purposes with the Kremlin. We should not overlook the importance of that fact. This development has given the President an unprecedented latitude for maneuver and, in turn, has severely constrained Baghdad's options. This is the first time that a postwar President has had such a luxury.

In turn, President Bush has taken full advantage of the newfound maneuvering room. He acted quickly and, in my opinion, correctly to constrain Hussein militarily, to defend Saudi Arabia, and to clamp a tight economic quarantine on Iraq.

Some of the most important early achievements were ones that the President had a large hand in himself, I understand even on the telephone: for example, gaining access to Saudi Arabia for our forces was a previously unheard-of concession and one that we never received throughout the Persian Gulf convoying operations; forging a rough political consensus among the leaders of NATO, the U.S.S.R. and Japan; and encouraging a pan-Arab military effort in support of Saudi Arabia.

If deposing Saddam Hussein would sort out the Middle East and permit the United States to turn its attention elsewhere...the case for initiating offensive action immediately would be considerably strengthened. The Middle East, however, is not that simple.

We are for the time being witnessing a rather remarkable display of collective political and financial support which is unprecedented in the postwar era. President Bush deserves full credit for this achievement, and I believe that the country has extended it to him.

Militarily, the United States has mounted an impressive deployment with air, sea, and ground forces. I would submit that no other nation in the world could have in sixty days moved this size force 8,000 miles and put it in the field, not to mention the rather trying climate and topography in which it must operate. On balance, the original deployment went extremely well.

As for the economic embargo, it is the first time we have been able to mount truly unified sanctions; consequently, I do not believe the previous analogies are too applicable today. No embargoed material is moving into Iraq by sea, and the air blockade is proving relatively effective. Undoubtedly there is some leakage, modest I would hope, probably on the ground from Jordan and Iran, but I know of no significant breaks in the encirclement.

Embargo's Effectiveness

I strongly believe it is important to recognize what has been achieved thus far. Some pundits contend that Saddam Hussein's primary goal is to control the bulk of the Middle East oil and to dictate the price of crude to the West. If that is correct, any such design has been frustrated. He has been served clear notice that he will not be allowed to capture the Saudi oil fields either now or in the future. A definite line has been drawn constraining him and his inflated ambitions.

The increased oil income Saddam had in mind has not materialized. In fact, Baghdad has forfeited $20 billion of foreign exchange earnings per year. As Secretary [James R.] Schlesinger [former Secretary of Defense, Secretary of Energy, and Director of Central Intelligence] pointed out, this figure would be $30 billion at the current oil price. In a country the size of Iraq, that is not chopped liver.

Moreover, it has been graphically demonstrated that the West can live rather well without Iraqi and Kuwaiti oil after we had survived the initial shock. Granted, some special areas of refined products are strapped, but these deficiencies are not having a heavy impact on the industrial nations. The price swings we see have been generated as much by psychological factors as by supply and demand.

The embargo is biting heavily, in my judgment. Given the standard of living Iraq is used to and the increasing sophistication of Iraqi society, it is dead wrong to say that Iraq is not being hurt. It is being damaged severely. That also, I believe, goes for the Iraqi military, which depends on outside support.

I will not elaborate. Secretary Schlesinger discussed this with you in some detail yesterday. I would say, though, it is the most effective peacetime blockade that I have personally witnessed. Granted, the embargo is not working as rapidly as many would prefer, but if we wanted economic results in two or three months then a quarantine was the wrong way to go about it. Most experts I note, however, do believe that it will work with time. Estimates range in the neighborhood of twelve to eighteen months. In other words, the issue is not whether an embargo will work but whether we have the patience to let it take effect.

Ultimately, these trends will translate into political pressure. I generally believe we have already seen the first subtle hints that Saddam Hussein is seeking a way out; in other words, a face-saving way to withdraw. While he did not intend it originally, I believe he has laid the groundwork for a long term alliance structure to contain Iraq. When I say long term, I mean beyond the term of this crisis. He has legitimated in some form for the long term a U.S. military presence in the region. I do not know the shape or the disposition of it, but I really believe that.

Moreover, the logistic support that Iraq used to enjoy will never return to the past levels of generosity, if at all. Hussein has excited the resentment, contempt, and suspicion of the nations he historically depended upon. In essence, under no circumstances can he return to the world he left on August 2. When the dust clears, I hope that we will make vigorous efforts to reinforce that outcome.

In sum, the President's initial moves have already achieved a great deal. The argument that Saddam is winning and being rewarded I believe is both weird and wrong. Obviously this fact is often overlooked by those calling for more direct action.

Going to War

It is true that the trauma is by no means over. I believe the burning question now confronting the President as well as our public is what next. This is no mean question, nor is it an easy one. In its most extreme form, we are talking about deliberately initiating offensive military operations; in other words, war.

War is always a grave decision and one which deserves both deep thought and wide public discussion, and I suspect that is the primary purpose of these hearings, Mr. Chairman.

If Saddam Hussein initiates an attack on Saudi Arabia or U.S. forces, we have no choice but to react vigorously and to use force to bring Iraq to heel. It is imperative once we engage that we bring it to a successful conclusion no matter what it requires. It would be disastrous to do otherwise. I believe such a response would be defensible and ac-

ceptable to all constituencies, domestic and international.

For that reason alone, it is unlikely that Saddam Hussein will initiate further military action. Certainly everything we see to date suggests he is hunkering down for the long haul. If that prediction proves correct, President Bush will be confronted with some very painful choices.

If deposing Saddam Hussein would sort out the Middle East and permit the United States to turn its attention elsewhere and to concentrate on our very pressing domestic problems, the case for initiating offensive action immediately would be considerably strengthened. The Middle East, however, is not that simple. I witnessed it firsthand. I lived in the Middle East for a year.

Middle East's Chronic Instability

Put bluntly, Saddam's departure or any other single act I am afraid will not make everything wonderful. In fact, a close look at the Middle East is rather depressing. While we may wish it otherwise, the fact is that the region has been, is, and will be for the foreseeable future plagued with a host of problems, tensions, enmities, and disagreements.

For instance, the Arab-Israeli dispute is alive and well. To say the least, the Palestinians have been irrevocably alienated by the Israeli Government's policies. There will never be true stability in the area until this dispute is sorted out ultimately. As Henry Schuler phrased it, "Neither the feudal monarchies nor the oppressive dictatorships enjoy the stability of an institutionalized popular mandate of political participation." This suggests that political maturity and, in turn, stability is still a long way off.

Income differences on both national and individual levels are a constant source of tensions and envy throughout the region, and I witnessed this friction at close hand when I lived in Bahrain.

Moslem fundamentalism is spreading, and the process highlights the cultural, religious, and ethnic differences that abound in the area as well as the widespread distrust of the West.

Boundary disputes are legion and have been a part of the region for many years: Qatar versus Bahrain; Abu Dhabi versus Oman and Saudi Arabia; Yemen versus Saudi Arabia; Kuwait

versus Iraq; and many of the Emirates versus Iran.

United States links to Israel and the dominant position of American oil companies have turned large segments of the Arab world against the U.S. in particular. The American public is well aware of this, of course.

The current crisis has divided the "moderate" Arab states for the first time. For example, Saudi Arabia has now split with its traditional friends, Jordan and Yemen. Incidentally, Yemen is now the most populous state on the peninsula—some 10 million plus. This does not bode well for the causes of stability or pluralism, both of which are also U.S. interests.

These frictions, singly or collectively, have resulted in a succession of explosions, assassinations, global terrorism, coups, revolutions, embargoes, and full-scale war on occasion. Secretary Schlesinger summed it up when he said, "The noncombat costs of recourse to war will be substantial."

Like it or not, the process of bringing stability to the Middle East will be painful and protracted with or without Saddam Hussein. Moreover, the United States, both as a leader of the free world and as the world's number one consumer of crude oil, will be integrally involved in the region politically and economically for the foreseeable future, just as we have been for the past 40 years.

That conclusion may not make us comfortable, but frankly I see no way we can avoid this burden. It comes with our affluence and global reach. This reality suggests that anything we do in that part of the world should be consistent with our past policies and our future role as an international leader.

Put another way, today's problem is a great deal more complex than merely defeating Saddam Hussein. In my view, the critical foreign policy questions we must ask are not whether Saddam Hussein is a brutal, deceitful, or as Barbara Bush would put it, a dreadful man—he is all of those things. Whether initiating conflict against Iraq will moderate the larger difficulties in the Gulf region and will put Washington in a better position to work with the Arab world in the future is, in my estimation, the more important question.

I would submit that posturing ourselves to promote stability for the long term is our primary national interest in the Middle East. May I repeat it: that posturing ourselves to promote stability for the long term is our primary national interest in the Middle East. It is not obvious to me that we are currently looking at the crisis in this light. Our dislike for Hussein seems to have crowded out many other considerations.

The Arab Perspective

In working through the problems myself, I am persuaded that the U.S. initiating hostilities could well exacerbate many of the tensions I have cited and perhaps further polarize the Arab world. Certainly, many Arabs would deeply resent a campaign which would necessarily kill large numbers of their Muslim brothers and force them to choose sides between Arab nations and the West.

From the Arab perspective, this fight is not simply a matter between bad and good. It is a great deal more complex than that and includes political and social perspectives deeply rooted in their history. The aftermath of such a contest will very likely multiply manyfold the anti-American resentment which we already see in the Middle East. In essence, we may be in a certain sense on the horns of a no-win dilemma. Even if we win, we lose ground in the Arab world and generally injure our ability to deal in the future with the labyrinth of the Middle East.

I firmly believe that Saddam Hussein must be pushed out of Kuwait. He must leave Kuwait. At the same time, given the larger context, I judge it highly desirable to achieve this goal in a peaceful fashion, if that is possible. In other words, I would argue that we should give sanctions a fair chance before we discard them. I personally believe they will bring him to his knees ultimately, but I would be the first to admit that is a speculative judgment.

If, in fact, the sanctions will work in twelve to eighteen months instead of six months, a tradeoff of avoiding war, with its attendant sacrifices and uncertainties, would in my estimation be more than worth it. A part of this effort, however, must be a strong military posture, both to underwrite our determination and to give effect to the embargo. Secretary Shultz used to say our military provides the umbrella underneath which all our diplomatic cards are played.

Incidentally, it may be necessary in this case to return to a rotation policy to sustain our presence. If the sanctions do not live up to their promise, or if they collapse, then a military solution would be the only recourse and we will be well placed if we continue our policy to mount such a campaign.

In any event, I am convinced that such an action will be much better received if we have visibly exhausted our peaceful alternatives. If we elect a military option—and I know that many are advocating that—I have utter confidence that our forces can prevail. It will not be cost-free, of course. Casualties and the time schedule will depend on our innovativeness, our military objectives, as well as Iraqi determination. I do not believe that we can assume that Iraq will roll over, although many hope that it will.

Defining Objectives

Let me say a word about objectives. It was my experience as Chairman that in such crises to get decision-makers to settle on specific military objectives was difficult, at best. There is a strong tendency, in these circumstances, to talk in generalities when contemplating combat, but frankly, that is not satisfactory when you make a decision of that moment.

In this case, what will we expect our commanders to do? Drive to Baghdad, occupy Iraq, free Kuwait, destroy Iraqi forces, eliminate their nuclear capability, or all of the above, et cetera? The character of your objectives influences the whole operation and your tactical plans, so they must be specific. The more ambitious the goals are, the less likely a peaceful solution can be found, the greater the casualties, the lengthier the campaign, and the more difficult postwar reconstruction.

If we come to that point, I would strongly advise that our combat objectives call for an intense air campaign aimed at disrupting his war-making industry, including nuclear installations, his chemical warfare and biological weapons facilities, a subsequent ground campaign designed to take advantage of the air operations, a subsequent ground campaign to cut off Kuwait and subsequently free it, and to destroy the effectiveness of the Iraqi forces both in Kuwait and on the southern border of Iraq.

At that point, I would strongly recommend reassessing the situation before continuing further operations. Also, instituting a vigorous postwar crisis effort to maintain allied unity and to control war material to Baghdad for the future.

I recognize that some would consider these objectives too limited. I disagree. These goals, if achieved, would deal Saddam Hussein a crushing political and military blow, and dispel any further ambitions he might have to dominate either the Middle East or the global oil market. The point is to succeed with minimum effort, casualties and political cost that we can engineer.

Need for Patience

I understand that many believe our troops, our people, and our allies do not have the necessary patience to wait out the quarantine, or for that matter the necessary patience to do anything for a long period of time. Militarily, we have already lost the element of surprise. Saddam Hussein knows we are there. He knows what strength we are in.

I believe our relative military position improves every day. It is curious that some expect our military to train soldiers to stand up to hostile fire, but doubt its ability to train them to occupy ground and to wait patiently.

I am aware, of course, that there is sincere concern about the task of holding the domestic and international consensus together. While there will be grumbling, I am sure, I believe—and I get this sense from my speaking, and I speak widely around this country—I believe the bulk of the American people are willing to put up with a great deal to avoid war and to avoid casualties a long ways from home. In fact, in my judgment, we are selling our country short by jumping to the conclusion that we cannot stare down our opponent.

Similarly, I cannot understand why some consider our international alliances strong enough to conduct intense hostilities but too fragile to hold together while we attempt a peaceful solution. As General [David C.] Jones [another former Chairman of the Joint Chiefs of Staff who testified] mentioned, I see no indications that there are cracks, significant cracks, coming in our alliance structure. Actually, I sense more nervousness among our allies

PERSIAN GULF

about our impetuousness than about our patience.

In closing, I would make a few observations that perhaps we should keep in mind as we approach this process. Using economic pressure may prove protracted, but if it could avoid hostilities or casualties, those also are highly desirable ends. As a matter of fact, I consider them also national interests. I seldom hear them referred to in that fashion.

It is curious that just as our patience in Western Europe has paid off and furnished us the most graphic example in our history of how staunchness is sometimes the better course in dealing with thorny international problems, a few armchair strategists are counseling a near-term attack on Iraq. It is worth remembering that in the 1950s and 1960s, individuals were similarly advising an attack on the U.S.S.R. Would not that have been great?

Time often has a way of achieving unexpected results. Already there are reports that the Palestinians in Kuwait, having witnessed Saddam's cruelty and having been abused themselves, are turning away from him, and that others in Jordan are also having second thoughts. We should not forget that autocrats often have a talent for alienating even their friends and supporters. I am reminded of how time changed the Panamanian population's view of Noriega.

Mr. Chairman, it may be that Saddam Hussein's ego is so engaged that he will not bend to an embargo or other peaceful deterrents such as containment and we will have to take further action, which I would support strongly. But I believe we should thoroughly satisfy ourselves that that is in fact the case and that hostilities would best serve our interests before resorting to unilateral offensive action against Iraq.

It would be a sad commentary if Saddam Hussein, a two-bit tyrant who sits on 17 million people and possesses a gross national product of $40 billion, proved to be more patient than the United States, the world's most affluent and powerful nation.

Statement by Secretary of Defense Richard B. Cheney Before the Senate Armed Services Committee, December 3, 1990 (Excerpt) [1]

The heart of our effort, if there is a theme underlying U.S. policy over the last four months, has been the fact that we have not "gone it alone," if you will. We have not operated unilaterally. But we have, indeed, functioned as part of a worldwide international coalition.

This coalition did not exist on August 2. It has been assembled through the leadership of the President and the diplomatic skills of my colleague, Jim Baker. I think it is formidable, indeed.

If we look at the map, of course, the heart of the problem that we faced on August 2 was when Saddam Hussein had a couple of hundred thousand troops in Kuwait, he was within 200 to 300 miles of the bulk of the Saudi oil facilities and oil supplies. Nearly all of the oil production of Saudi Arabia is over there on the Persian Gulf. Again, remember Saudi Arabia has some 28 percent of the world's proven reserves. He was within a few hundred miles more of the United Arab Emirates, Qatar, and the other Gulf oil producing states.

As of August 2, when he took Kuwait, the only thing between Saddam Hussein and those oil fields was a battalion of the Saudi Arabian National Guard. There was no significant military obstacle to his further move south.

I personally am convinced that if we had not responded as rapidly as we did, he would, indeed, have continued his aggression, and it was only the speed of the U.S. response that gave him pause and gave us the opportunity to deploy the forces that are now in the field.

Putting the Coalition Together

Saudi Arabia was crucial. Until the Saudis agreed to invite U.S. forces onto their territory, there was absolutely no way the United States could respond with sufficient military force in order to safeguard our interest in that part of the world.

You cannot operate, even if you do, from an aircraft carrier against heavy, massed land divisions, armored divisions, as the committee well knows. The key to the military strategy was to have access to Saudi Arabia and, subsequently, to the other nations of the Gulf—Oman, the United Arab Emirates, Qatar and Bahrain. We were able to achieve that.

Also key to the strategy was Egypt, because, of course, if you look at Egypt, it is important to remember that President Mubarak has been, along with King Fahd, one of the outstanding leaders of this venture. But Egypt is the home of half of all the Arabs in the world. It also, of course, is the location of the Suez Canal.

The only logistical task that I can think of that would have been more difficult than what we have already done, Mr. Chairman, in deploying forces to Saudi Arabia would have been to try to deploy forces in Saudi Arabia if we could not use the Suez Canal. This is because, of course, we would have had to come clear around the Horn of Africa.

In addition to that, Egypt was key because President Mubarak provided the leadership that led to the support of the Arab League with the majority of the members of the Arab League joining and supporting King Fahd and supporting the President in our deployment of forces to the region. Egypt also has been vital in the military sense, in terms of sending significant forces of their own to be deployed in Saudi Arabia.

If we look at the situation from the standpoint of the nations around Iraq, one begins to see that it is a fairly disparate group. Certainly, if you had told me six months ago that by December 1990, the United States would be on the same side of an issue in the Middle East with Iran, and Syria, and Saudi Arabia, and the Soviet Union, and Egypt, I would not have believed it. But the fact is, the effort that is now underway, from an economic standpoint, turns very much as well upon the capacity and willingness of those nations around Saudi Arabia to participate in the venture.

To the east of Iraq, of course, is Iran, a major oil exporter. Currently, there is no way to move oil from Iraq to Iran. But if Iran were not part of the coalition today, it would be a relatively simple matter to build a pipeline from southern Iraq over to southern Iran, comingle Iraqi production with Iranian production, and sell it on the world market, thereby breaking the embargo. It is important that Iran stay as a part of the coalition.

If we go to the north, to Turkey, President Ozal has been one of the leaders in the effort. Turkey shares a border with Iraq. Turkey has suffered significantly as a result of this venture because only about half of their lost revenues from closing the Iraqi oil pipeline to the Mediterranean has been replaced.

Syria, of course, has now been a significant player. There is a pipeline across Syria which is also closed, and Syria is deploying troops to Saudi Arabia to support the effort.

Jordan is a key player in the operation simply because of their geographic location. I will come back to the Jordanian situation in a moment.

The point is today, Mr. Chairman, in the Gulf states, with the single exception of Yemen, to the north of Iraq and virtually the entire region, where we have nations bordering Iraq, we have been able to assemble a coalition to put together both the military support, the public opinion support through the Arab League and Egypt, and the economic support to bring maximum pressure to bear on Saddam Hussein.

The debate we have had focuses to some extent—and I want to spend just a moment on that, if I might—on the question of if we have been this successful to date, if we have been able to assemble this kind of coalition to enforce an embargo against Iraq, why not wait indefinitely, then, for the sanctions to work?

Sanctions Evaluated

I will say just a word about sanctions. General [Colin L.] Powell [Chairman of the Joint Chiefs of Staff] may want to say a word or two more in his presentation.

But we think, at this point, that we have been able to shut off Iraqi ability to export oil. The only oil that we know of that is leaving the country is a small amount that moves by truck to Jordan. It's basically in payment for past debts owed. But it does not appear at present that Saddam Hussein can earn any foreign exchange by exporting oil.

We think we have shut down much of the flow of goods into Iraq from outside. We don't think it is totally successful. But, clearly, he cannot get anything through the Persian Gulf or through

the Red Sea. There's a little bit of air traffic going in and there's some smuggling, no doubt. There's probably always smuggling in that part of the world. And, given the price and the value of commodities now, it is probably even more profitable.

But, basically, in terms of major international commerce, we think we have been able to pretty well dry that up.

The question that comes up with respect to sanctions, though, is I think it is important for us to focus upon what our objective is. Of course, that is the goal of getting Saddam Hussein out of Kuwait.

"Sanctions working" does not mean just destruction of the Iraqi economy. It means getting Saddam Hussein out of Kuwait. That is our goal; that is our objective. That is why the sanctions have been employed.

So, when you talk about sanctions and about sanctions working, I think it has to be with that caveat—that "sanctions working" does not mean just destruction of the Iraqi economy. It means getting Saddam Hussein out of Kuwait. That is our goal; that is our objective. That is why the sanctions have been employed.

In terms of trying to assess whether or not that will happen, we have to look at several things. We have to look at circumstances inside Iraq. There are different pieces of evidence. But I think the overwhelming conclusion I reach in assessing the situation is that we do not have an indefinite period of time to wait for sanctions to produce the desired result.

He does have a command economy. We have watched over the years during the Iran-Iraq War, when he was able clearly to divert resources from the civilian side of the economy to the military side. There is no question about his ability to do it. He continues to do it today.

Iraq has been through an eight-year war with Iran. They clearly have the capacity to hunker down, if you will, and operate on a subsistence basis. It has been suggested that, if you com-

pare the pain, the economic pain, that he feels now, with the pain that the population felt during the Iraq-Iran War, today the pain is not as significant as it was then. Of course then, not only were they faced with the burden of the war, but they were also faced with the propositions of casualties and attacks on Iraqi territory.

We think we clearly have been successful in closing off the flow of spare parts, military supplies from the Soviet Union and France which, previously, were his major suppliers.

But with respect to food and agriculture, the picture is somewhat murkier. Many have argued that the sanctions will work because Iraq previously has imported a very significant portion of their agricultural commodities. But if you analyze the situation carefully, it would appear that he has the capacity to significantly increase his agricultural expansion. Iraq is not a desolate country by any means. In the valley of the Tigris and the Euphrates, there is a lot of good farmland, and there were three occasions in the last twenty-five years when they have been able to double from one year to the next the total amount of cereal production, for example, in country.

The key to bad agricultural performance in the past and significant imports has been bad management of the economy. It has a Stalinist economy, and the Iraqi agricultural sector did not work any better than the Soviet agricultural sector has worked. But he is now offering prices 40 percent higher than previously to Iraqi farmers to produce, and the expectation has to be that they will be able significantly to expand their food production, and that the prospect of the embargo on agricultural commodities going into Iraq, while it is not going to be that appealing a diet, does not appear to be an insurmountable obstacle for them.

Side Effects of Sanctions Elsewhere

Another key element from the standpoint of the sanctions that we have to keep in mind is that sanctions do not impose pain just on Iraq. They impose pain on everybody who used to do business with Iraq.

So, to say that we are going to shut off the flow of commerce, it is important for us to remind ourselves that commerce is a two-way street, and that when you close the pipeline from Iraq across Turkey, Turkey loses the value and the benefits and the earnings of having operated that pipeline, a significant loss to a nation that obviously is very important to us and a key partner in the coalition.

When we close down trade between Iraq and Kuwait on the one hand and Jordan on the other, we are affecting approximately 50 percent of the Gross National Product of Jordan. That is, about 50 percent of Jordanian GNP in the past has been tied up in trade with Iraq and Kuwait. That trade, for all intents and purposes, has been shut down today. While there is still some smuggling going on, Jordan does give indications that they are doing their best to comply with the international sanctions.

We can look at issues that the President has talked about in terms of the situation in Eastern Europe. President Havel told the President when he was in Czechoslovakia recently that the cost to Czechoslovakia of the continued crisis in the Gulf is about $1.5 billion a year, significant for the Czech economy.

In Poland, where I go tomorrow for a visit, information I have is that the Polish economy was scheduled to receive about 20 percent of its oil from imports from Iraq. That was payment by Iraq of past debts owed to the Polish Government. That is no longer available.

So at the same time, the Poles have to make up that difference by purchasing oil on the world market. They are also faced with two other important considerations.

One is the fact that the Soviets are going to a hard currency system for the oil they sell to Poland as of the first of January because of their own internal economic problems. And, of course, the third key point is that the Poles are right smack in the middle of one of the most difficult economic transitions any nation has ever attempted.

So there are consequences, costs, if you will, to the rest of the world and to our coalition partners in the venture. The evidence is not all on the side of the notion that we can wait indefinitely for sanctions to work.

Consequences of Waiting

There are other problems that have to be kept in mind as we contemplate

what the right course of action might be. While we wait for sanctions to work, Saddam Hussein continues to obliterate any trace of Kuwait and her people. While we wait, he continues to dig in, in Kuwait, to send more forces south, to deploy and mobilize additional manpower, to dig more formidable fortifications. So it is possible that at some point the military effort that might be required to get him out will be more difficult in the future than it is today.

While we continue to wait, he also continues, obviously, his efforts to improve his weapons arsenal. He continues to work to see if he can acquire more weapons of mass destruction.

And, while we wait, he continues to hold hundreds of Americans hostage.

So, the questions, it seems to me, Mr. Chairman, that have been asked by this Committee and that have been addressed over the last few days are vital ones. But the notion that we can, in fact, wait a year or two, as some have suggested, that we can wait indefinitely for him to withdraw, comes back again to a couple of very basic, fundamental propositions. Can we make the judgment that sanctions will achieve the desired result of forcing him out of Kuwait?

I don't know. I don't think we can make that judgment. They might. But then again, there is a lot of evidence that they won't.

Will the coalition hold? Will this relatively fragile, complex enterprise that we have organized internationally produce the kind of ongoing support, international effort for the next year or two that it has for the last four months? Will the economic pain be greater for Saddam Hussein than it will be for members of the coalition or for some of our other friends around the world?

Will we be in a better position ourselves, as a coalition and as a nation, to use military force in the future than we are now?

I think it is important, Mr. Chairman, as I close and before I ask General Powell for his presentation, for us to keep in mind the consequences if we fail. If Saddam wins, if he keeps Kuwait, if the coalition falls apart, if economic sanctions do not work, if we do not use military force, if that is the only way to achieve our objective to force him out, then we have a hell of a problem. This is because, of course, he will, given his current loca-

tion and his ability to dominate the Gulf, constitute a significant threat to the world economy. He clearly will constitute, and does today, a significant threat to our friends in the region, especially to those Arab governments who have had the courage to stand by us to try to stop Saddam Hussein.

He clearly represents a threat to Saudi Arabia, to the Gulf State governments and, I would argue as well, to President Mubarak's government in Egypt. We have already had, of course, one assassination in Egypt since the onset of this crisis. We don't know who is responsible. But we do know that the President of the Egyptian Parliament was assassinated.

He clearly constitutes a significant threat to Israel. The United States has a long-standing, deep commitment and an important strategic relationship with the State of Israel. If I were to look at that part of the world today, I would have to conclude, and I think most people would, that the most significant threat to Israel is Saddam Hussein.

My own personal view is that it is far better for us to deal with him now, while the coalition is intact, while we have the United Nations behind us, while we have some twenty-six other nations assembled with military forces in the Gulf, than it will be for us to deal with him five or ten years from now, when the members of the coalition have gone their disparate ways and when Saddam has become an even better armed and more threatening regional super power than he is at present.

Statement by William Webster, Director of Central Intelligence, Before the House Armed Services Committee, December 5, 1990 [1]

I appreciate the opportunity to address this committee on what the intelligence community believes the sanctions have already accomplished and what we believe the sanctions are likely to accomplish over time. Of course, sanctions are only one type of pressure being applied on Iraq, and their impact cannot be completely distinguished from the combined impact of military, diplomatic and economic initiatives in Iraq. At the technical level, economic sanctions and the embargo against Iraq have put Saddam Hussein on notice that he is isolated from the world community and have dealt a serious blow to the Iraq economy.

More than 100 countries are supporting the U.N. resolutions that impose economic sanctions on Iraq. Coupled with the U.S. Government's increased ability to detect and follow up attempts to circumvent the blockade, the sanctions have all but shut off Iraq's exports and reduced imports to less than 10 percent of the pre-invasion level. All sectors of the Iraq economy are feeling the pinch of sanctions and many industries have largely shut down. Most importantly, the blockade has eliminated any hope Baghdad had of cashing in on higher oil prices or its seizure of Kuwaiti oil fields.

Despite mounting disruptions and hardships resulting from sanctions, Saddam apparently believes that he can outlast international resolve to maintain those sanctions. We see no indication that Saddam is concerned at this point that domestic discontent is growing to levels that may threaten his regime or that problems resulting from the sanctions are causing him to rethink his policy on Kuwait. The Iraqi people have experienced considerable deprivation in the past. Given the brutal nature of the Iraqi security services, the population is not likely to oppose Saddam openly. Our judgment has been and continues to be that there is no assurance or guarantee that economic hardships will compel Saddam to change his policies or lead to internal unrest that would threaten his regime. Now, let me take a few minutes to review briefly with you some of the information that led us to these conclusions as well as to present our assessment of the likely impact of sanctions over the coming months.

Effects of Embargo to Date

The blockade and embargo have worked more effectively than Saddam probably expected. More than 90 percent of imports and 90 percent of exports have been shut off. Although there is smuggling across Iraq's borders, it is extremely small relative to Iraq's pre-crisis trade. Iraqi efforts to break sanctions have thus far been largely unsuccessful. What little leakage has occurred is due largely to a relative-

ly small number of private firms acting independently. And we believe that most countries are actively enforcing the sanctions and plan to continue doing so.

Industry appears to be the hardest hit so far. Many firms are finding it difficult to cope with the departure of foreign workers and with the cutoff of imported industrial inputs, which comprised nearly 60 percent of Iraq's total imports prior to the invasion. These shortages have either shut down or severely curtailed production by a variety of industries, including many light industrial and assembly plants as well as the country's only tire manufacturing plant.

Our judgment has been and continues to be that there is no assurance or guarantee that economic hardships will compel Saddam to change his policies or lead to internal unrest that would threaten his regime.

Despite these shutdowns, the most vital industries, including electric power generation and refining, do not yet appear to be threatened. We believe they will be able to function for some time because domestic consumption has been reduced, because Iraqi and Kuwaiti facilities have been cannibalized, and because some stockpiles and surpluses already existed. The cutoff of Iraq's oil exports and success of sanctions have also choked off Baghdad's financial resources. This too has been more effective and more complete than Saddam probably expected.

In fact, we believe that a lack of foreign exchange will in time be Iraq's greatest economic difficulty. The embargo has deprived Baghdad of roughly $1.5 billion of foreign exchange earnings monthly. We have no evidence that Iraq has significantly augmented the limited foreign exchange reserves to which it still has access. And as a result, Baghdad is working to conserve foreign exchange, and to devise alternative methods to finance imports.

We believe Baghdad's actions to forestall shortages of food stocks, including rationing, encouraging smuggling and promoting agricultural production are adequate for the next

several months. The fall harvest of fruits and vegetables is injecting new supplies into the market, and will provide a psychological as well as tangible respite for mounting pressures. The Iraqi population in general has access to sufficient staple foods. Other food stocks, still not rationed, also remain available. However, the variety is diminishing and prices are sharply inflated. For example, sugar purchased on the open market at the official exchange rate went from $32 per 50 kilogram bag in August, to $580 per bag last month. Baghdad remains concerned about its foodstuffs and continues to try to extend stocks and increasingly to divert supplies to the military.

In late November, Baghdad cut civilian rations for the second time since the rationing program began while announcing increases in rations for military personnel and their families. So on balance, the embargo has increased the economic hardships facing the average Iraqi. In order to supplement their rations, Iraqis must turn to the black market where most goods can be purchased but at highly inflated prices. They are forced to spend considerable amounts of time searching for reasonably priced food, or waiting in lines for bread and other rationed items.

In addition, services ranging from medical care to sanitation have been curtailed. But these hardships are easier for Iraqis to endure than the combination of economic distress, high casualty rates and repeated missile and air attacks that Iraqis lived with during the eight year Iran-Iraq War.

During this war, incidentally, there was not a single significant public disturbance, even though casualties hit 2.3 percent of the total Iraqi population—about the same as the percentage of U.S. casualties during the Civil War.

Looking Ahead

Looking ahead, the economic picture changes somewhat. We expect Baghdad's foreign exchange reserves to become extremely tight, leaving it little cash left with which to entice potential sanctions busters. At current rates of depletion, we estimate Iraq will have nearly depleted its available foreign exchange reserves by next spring.

Able to obtain even a few key imports, Iraq's economic problems will begin to multiply as Baghdad is forced to gradually shut down growing numbers of facilities in order to keep critical activities functioning as long as possible. Economic conditions will be noticeably worse and Baghad will find allocating scarce resources a significantly more difficult task. Probably only energy related and some military industries will still be functioning by next spring. This will almost certainly be the case by next summer. Baghdad will try to keep basic services such as electric power from deteriorating.

The regime will also try to insulate critical military industries to prevent an erosion of military preparedness. Nonetheless, reduced rations coupled with rapid inflation and little additional support from the government will compound the economic pressures facing most Iraqis.

By next spring Iraqis will have made major changes in their diets. Poultry, which is a staple of the Iraqi diet, will not be available. Unless Iraq receives humanitarian food aid or unless smuggling increases, some critical commodities such as sugar and edible oils will be in short supply. Distribution problems are likely to create localized shortages. But, we expect that Baghdad will be able to maintain grain consumption, mainly wheat, barley, and rice, at about two-thirds of last years's level until the next harvest in May.

The spring grain and vegetable harvest will again augment food stocks, although only temporarily. To boost next year's food production, Baghdad has raised prices, paid the farmers for their produce, and decreed that farmers must cultivate all available land. Nonetheless, Iraq does not have the capability to become self-sufficient in food production by next year.

Weather is the critical variable in grain production, and even if it is good, Iraqis will be able to produce less than half the grain they need. In addition, Iraq's vegetable production next year may be less than normal because of its inability to obtain seed stock from abroad. Iraq had obtained seed from the United States, the Netherlands, and France.

Although sanctions are hurting Iraq's civilian economy, they are affecting the Iraqi military only at the margins. Iraq's fairly static posture will reduce wear and tear on the military equipment and, as a result, extend the life of its inventory of spare parts and maintenance items.

Under noncombat conditions, Iraq ground and air forces can probably maintain near-current levels of readiness for as long as nine months. We expect the Iraqi air force to feel the effects of sanctions more quickly and to a greater degree than the Iraqi ground forces because of its greater reliance on high technology and foreign equipment and technicians. Major repairs to sophisticated aircraft like the F-1 will be achieved with significant difficulty, if at all, because of the exodus of foreign technicians. Iraqi technicians, however, should be able to maintain current levels of aircraft sorties for three to six months.

The Iraqi ground forces are more immune to sanctions. Before the invasion, Baghdad maintained large inventories of basic military supplies, such as ammunition, and supplies probably remain adequate. The embargo will eventually hurt Iraqi armor by preventing the replacement of old fire control systems and creating shortages of additives for various critical lubricants. Shortages will also affect Iraqi cargo trucks over time.

Mr. Chairman, while we can look ahead several months and predict the gradual deterioration of the Iraqi economy, it is more difficult to assess how or when these conditions will cause Saddam to modify his behavior. At present, Saddam almost certainly assumes that he is coping effectively with the sanctions. He appears confident in the ability of his security services to contain potential discontent, and we do not believe he is troubled by the hardships Iraqis will be forced to endure. Saddam's willingness to sit tight and try to outlast the sanctions, or in the alternative, to avoid war by withdrawing from Kuwait, will be determined by his total assessment of the political, economic and military pressures arrayed against him.

Statement by Dr. Zbigniew Brzezinski, Former National Security Adviser to President Carter, Before the Senate Foreign Relations Committee, December 5, 1990 [1]

If I may, I would like to begin with a brief personal comment. As many of

you know, I supported President Bush in the 1988 elections and I have supported his foreign policy all along. Moreover, I do not subscribe to the notion that the use of force is altogether precluded in international affairs. I mention this at the outset because I would not want my views to be interpreted as motivated either by political or ideological biases.

Let me also say right off that I have supported and still support the initial decisions of the President regarding both troop deployments to deter any further Iraqi aggression and the imposition of sanctions on Iraq for the flagrant aggression that it did commit. The President and his team are to be commended for the skill with which the international coalition has been put together and for the impressively prompt deployment of American power. The policy of punitive containment of Iraq rightly gained almost universal international and domestic support.

What Dialogue Might Achieve

Most Americans, I am sure, share the hope that the President's recent and laudable decision to initiate a direct dialogue with the Iraqi Government will lead to a serious and comprehensive exploration of a nonviolent solution to the ongoing crisis. Wisely, the President indicated that the purpose of such a dialogue is not to merely convey an ultimatum but to convince Iraq that its compliance with the U.N. resolution is the necessary precondition for a peaceful settlement. It is thus not an accident that those who so fervently have been advocating war have promptly denounced the President's initiative.

To be meaningful, such a dialogue has to go beyond demands for unconditional surrender but involve also some discussion of the consequences of Iraqi compliance with the U.N. resolutions. That means that Iraq, in the course of the ensuing discussions, will have to be given some preliminary indications of the likely political, territorial, and financial aftermath of its withdrawal from Kuwait.

I stress these points because those who favor only a military solution will now exercise pressure on the President to reduce the incipient dialogue essentially to a mere transmittal of an ultimatum. That, I trust, everyone recognizes would be pointless and counterproductive. It would simply accelerate the drift to war.

While it is premature to detail here the substance of a nonviolent solution to the crisis that could emerge from the proposed dialogue, it is possible to envisage a series of sequential but linked phases, all premised on Iraq having satisfied the necessary preconditions regarding Kuwait. First, coercive sanctions would be maintained until Iraq implements its willingness to comply with the U.N. resolutions regarding a withdrawal from Kuwait.

Two, binding arbitration by a U.N.-sanctioned body within a specified timeframe would be accepted by the Governments of Iraq and Kuwait regarding territorial delimitation, conflicting financial claims, and other pertinent matters.

Three, an international conference would be convened to establish regional limitations on weapons of mass destruction, pending which a U.N.-sponsored security force would remain deployed in Kuwait and perhaps in Saudi Arabia to secure needed security.

It is important to note, Mr. Chairman, that any dialogue to the above effect would be conducted while Iraq is being subjected to severe sanctions. The United States would be therefore conceding nothing while conducting the talks. It is Iraq that is under duress, not us. It is Iraqi power that is being attritted, while ours is growing. It is Iraq that is isolated and threatened with destruction, not us.

Nor would any such outcome as the one outlined above be tantamount to rewarding aggression. Those who argue that do so because they desire only one outcome, no matter what the price to America—the destruction of Iraq. Withdrawal from Kuwait would represent a massive setback for Saddam Hussein and a victory for the international order. It would be a dramatic reversal of aggression, humiliating and painful to the aggressor.

However, it is quite possible, perhaps even probable, that the talks will initially prove unproductive. In my view, that should not be viewed as a casus belli. Instead, we should stay on course, applying the policy of punitive containment. This policy is working. Iraq has been deterred, ostracized, and punished. Sanctions, unprecedented in their international solidarity and more massive in scope than any ever adopted

in peacetime against any nation—I repeat, ever adopted against any nation—are inflicting painful costs on the Iraqi economy.

Sanctions Inevitably Take Time

"Economic sanctions," by their definition, require time to make their impact felt, but they have already established the internationally significant lesson that Iraq's aggression did not pay. By some calculations, about 97 percent of Iraq's income and 90 percent of its imports have been cut off, and the shutdown of the equivalent of 43 percent of Iraq's and Kuwait's GNP has already taken place.

President Bush's initial commitment to punish Iraq and to deter it remains the wisest course and one which this nation can resolutely and in unity sustain over the long haul.

This is prompting the progressive attrition of the country's economy and warmaking capabilities. Extensive rationing is a grim social reality. Over time, all this is bound to have an unsettling effect on Saddam Hussein's power.

The administration's argument that the sanctions are not working suggests to me that in the first instance the administration had entertained extremely naive notions regarding how sanctions actually do work. They not only take time, they are by their nature an instrument for softening up the opponent, inducing in the adversary a more compliant attitude toward an eventual nonviolent resolution. Sanctions are not a blunt instrument for promptly achieving total surrender.

Worse still, the administration's actions and its rhetoric have conveyed a sense of impatience that in fact has tended to undermine the credibility of long term sanctions. Perhaps the administration felt that this was necessary to convince Saddam Hussein that it meant business. But the consequence has been to make the administration the prisoner of its own rhetoric, with American options and timetable thereby severely constricted.

The cumulative result has been to move the United States significantly

beyond the initial policy of punitive containment, with the result that the conflict of the international community with Iraq has become over-Americanized, over-personalized, and over-emotionalized. The enormous deployment of American forces, coupled with talk of no compromise, means that the United States is now pointed toward a war with Iraq that will be largely an American war, fought predominantly by Americans, in which, on our side, mostly Americans will die—and for interests that are neither equally vital nor urgent to America and which, in any case, can be and should be effectively pursued by other less dramatic and less bloody means.

Deterring Nuclear Danger

Yet to justify military action the administration, echoing the advocates of war, has lately been relying on the emotionally charged argument that we confront a present danger because of the possibility that Iraq may at some point acquire a nuclear capability. In other words, not oil, not Kuwait, but Iraq's nuclear program has become the latest excuse for moving toward war.

This argument deserves careful scrutiny. But, once subjected to it, this latest case for war also does not meet the tests of vitality or urgency to the American national interest. First of all, it is relevant to note that when the United States was threatened directly by the far more powerful and dangerous Stalinist Russia or Maoist China, it refrained from engaging in preventive war. Moreover, Israel already has nuclear weapons and can thus deter Iraq, while the United States has certainly both the power to deter or to destroy Iraq.

Deterrence has worked in the past, and I fail to see why thousands of Americans should now die in order to make sure that at some point in the future—according to experts, some years from now—Iraq does not acquire a militarily significant nuclear capability.

Second, it is within our power to sustain a comprehensive embargo on Iraq to impede such an acquisition. Unlike India or Israel, Iraq does permit international inspection of its nuclear facilities. This gives us some insight into its program. Moreover, much can happen during the next several years, including Saddam's fall from power. Hence, the precipitation of war now on these grounds meets neither the criterion of urgency nor vitality.

Uncertainties of War

More than that, war would be highly counterproductive to the American national interest. A war is likely to split the international consensus that currently exists. The United States is likely to become estranged from many of its European allies. And it is almost certain to become the object of widespread Arab hostility. Indeed, once started, the war may prove not all that easy to terminate, given the inflammable character of Middle Eastern politics. It could be costly in blood and financially devastating.

This prospect is all the more tragic because the United States would thereby be deprived of the fruits of its hard-earned victory in the Cold War. We stand today on the threshold of a historic opportunity to shape a truly cooperative world order based on genuine cooperation and respect for human rights. Yet our overreaction to the crisis in the Persian Gulf is now adversely affecting both our priorities and our principles.

In any case, Mr. Chairman, it is war that soon we may have to face because of the combined pressures resulting from Iraqi intransigence, the imposition of a deadline, the lack of patience in the application of sanctions, and the consequences of massive troop deployments. Given the possibility, therefore, that the United States might be plunged by Presidential decision into a war with Iraq, I would urge this committee to examine carefully in its deliberations and to press the administration for answers regarding the following three clusters of critically important issues.

One, what are the political limits and the likely geopolitical dynamics of war once the President decides to initiate it? For example, we have to be concerned over the use of air power, that in order to mitigate casualties for U.S. ground forces, killing not only the hostages but also thousands, perhaps tens of thousands and even more, of Iraqi civilians, who are not to be held responsible for Saddam Hussein's flagrant misconduct, might be required. Is this politically viable? Is this morally admissible?

Also, how does the administration envisage the termination of the war?

Do we expect a total surrender? Are we counting on a negotiated outcome after a spasm of violence? Are we prepared to occupy all of Iraq, including the huge city of Baghdad? Are we logistically prepared for a war that is not promptly resolved by air power? And are we psychologically prepared for heavy American casualties?

And once war begins, Iran and Syria may not remain passive and the war could thus spread. One has to anticipate the possibility that Iraq will seek to draw Israel into the war. Does the administration have a contingency plan in the event Jordan becomes a battlefield? What might be the United States reaction if some Israeli leaders seek to take advantage of an expanded war to effect the expulsion of all Palestinians from their homes on the West Bank? The Gulf crisis and the Arab-Israeli conflict would thus become linked, our efforts to the contrary notwithstanding.

I believe, Mr. Chairman, that the administration is paying insufficient attention to these inherent uncertainties of war. The war could prove more destructive, more bloody, and more difficult to terminate than the administration spokesmen, not to speak of sundry private advocates of war, seem to think.

I also believe the administration has not given sufficient thought to the geopolitical disruptive consequences of a war in a region that is extraordinarily incendiary. An American military invasion of Iraq would be likely to set off a chain reaction that could bog America down in a variety of prolonged security operations, in a setting of intensified political instability

Aftereffects of War

Second, what are the likely broader aftereffects of the war? The administration has yet to move beyond vague generalities regarding its concept of the postwar Middle East. Yet considerable anxiety is justified that subsequent to the war the United States might not be able to extricate itself from the Middle Eastern cauldron, especially if in the meantime the Arab masses have become radicalized and hostile to the Arab regimes that endorsed the U.S. military action.

How will that affect America's global position? I would think it likely that with the United States embroiled in a Middle Eastern mess for years to come both Europe and Japan, free to promote their own agendas, will pursue the enhancement of their economic power. And in the region itself it is probable that fundamentalist Iran will become the dominant power in the Persian Gulf and that terrorist Syria will inherit the mantle of leadership among the Arabs.

It is also possible that the destruction of Iraq by America and the resulting radicalization of the Arabs might leave Israel, armed as it already is with nuclear weapons, more tempted to use its military force to impose its will in this volatile region. How will all this affect the area's sensitive balance of power?

I believe that none of the above possible developments would be in American interest. Yet I do not sense that sufficient strategic planning has been devoted by the administration in an analysis of the wider shock effects of a war that is bound to be exploited by other parties for their own selfish ends.

Allies Should Assume More of the Burden

Third and finally, what is being done to ensure that the war's burdens and sacrifices are more fairly distributed among its potential beneficiaries or participants if war must come? One cannot help but be struck by the relatively limited contributions of our allies. Moreover, as I understand it, some states with forces in Saudi Arabia have indicated that they will not participate in offensive operations.

The American public certainly is not satisfied with the financial support extended by Germany and Japan. Is the administration satisfied? What additional financial contribution can be expected from the Saudis and the Kuwaitis? It is noteworthy that Saudi Arabia has already benefitted very substantially from the oil crisis, and that the Amir of Kuwait and his family are in the forefront of those arguing for Americans to initiate military action.

Are we thus, despite all of our rhetoric about the new international order, not running the risk of becoming the mercenaries in this war, applauded and financed by others, to do the fighting and the dying for them? I believe that it is already evident that the principal sacrifices of war, both financial and in blood, will in fact have to be borne by America, and to a massively disproportionate degree

Such evident unfairness will inevitably have a very adverse impact on American attitude toward its allies, with deleterious consequences for American public support for the so-called international order.

These are tough issues, and unless the administration responds to them satisfactorily the war will lack domestic support while generating polarizing political passions. Even worse, unless the administration thinks hard about such questions, it could embark on a course deeply damaging to our national interest.

Mr. Chairman, let me conclude with a brief word about the lessons of history. It is important to apply them with a sense of proportion. To speak of Saddam Hussein as a Hitler is to trivialize Hitler and to elevate Saddam. Iraq is not Germany, but a middle-sized country on the scale of, say, Romania, dependent on the export of one commodity for most of its income, unable on its own either to fully feed itself or to construct its own weapons. It is a threat to regional peace, a threat with wider global economic implications, but it is a threat we can contain, deter, or repel as the situation dictates.

Therefore, in my view neither an American war to liberate Kuwait nor a preventive war to destroy Iraq's power is urgently required, be it in terms of the American national interest or of the imperatives of world order. President Bush's initial commitment to punish Iraq and to deter it remains the wisest course and one which this Nation can resolutely and in unity sustain over the long haul. By any rational calculus, the tradeoffs between the discomforts of patience and the costs of war favor patience.

Both time and power are in our favor, and we do not need to be driven by artificial deadlines, deceptive arguments, or irrational emotion into an unnecessary war.

[Also See: Secretary Baker's Statement Before Senate Foreign Relations Committee, December 5, 1990]

Senate Majority Leader George J. Mitchell, January 10, 1991 [2]

Today the Senate undertakes a solemn constitutional responsibility: To decide whether to commit the nation to war. In this debate, we should focus on the fundamental question before us: What is the wisest course of action for our nation in the Persian Gulf crisis?

The question is should war be truly a last resort when all other means fail?

In its simplest form, the question is whether Congress will give the President an unlimited blank check to initiate war against Iraq, at some unspecified time in the future, under circumstances which are not now known and cannot be foreseen, or whether, while not ruling out the use of force if all other means fail, we will now urge continuation of the policy of concerted international economic and diplomatic pressure.

This is not a debate about whether force should ever be used. No one proposes to rule out the use of force. We cannot and should not rule it out. The question is should war be truly a last resort when all other means fail? Or should we start with war, before other means have been fully and fairly exhausted?

This is not a debate about American objectives in the current crisis. There is broad agreement in the Senate that Iraq must, fully and unconditionally, withdraw its forces from Kuwait. The issue is how best to achieve that goal.

Most Americans and most Members of Congress, myself included, supported the President's initial decision to deploy American forces to Saudi Arabia to deter further Iraqi aggression. We supported the President's effort in marshaling international diplomatic pressure and the most comprehensive economic embargo in history against Iraq.

I support that policy. I believe it remains the correct policy, even though the President abandoned his own policy before it had time to work.

The change began on November 8, when President Bush announced that he was doubling the number of American troops in the Persian Gulf to 430,000 in order to attain a "credible offensive option."

The President did not consult with Congress about that decision. He did not try to build support for it among the American people. He just did it. In so doing, President Bush transformed the U.S. role and its risk in the Persian Gulf crisis.

In effect, the President—overnight, with no consultation and no public debate—changed American policy from being part of a collective effort to enforce economic and diplomatic sanctions into a predominantly American effort relying upon the use of American military force. By definition, sanctions require many nations to participate and share the burden. Despite the fact that his own policy of international economic sanctions was having a significant effect upon the Iraqi economy, the President, without explanation, abandoned that approach and instead adopted a policy based first and foremost upon the use of American military force.

As a result, this country has been placed on a course toward war.

This has upset the balance of the President's initial policy, the balance between resources and responsibilities, between interests and risks, and between patience and strength.

Opposition to aggression is not solely an American value. It is universal. If there is to be war in the Persian Gulf, it should not be a war in which Americans do the fighting and dying while those who benefit from our effort provide token help and urge us on. Yet, as things now stand, that is what it would be.

The armed forces in the region should reflect the worldwide concern about the problem, but they do not. Americans now make up more than three-fourths of the fighting forces in the region. That is wrong and unfair. If this is to be an international effort, it should be an international effort in more than name only. Yet, as things now stand, that is what it could be: an international effort in name only.

Iraq must leave Kuwait. There is no disagreement about that. Iraq must leave Kuwait. If necessary, it must be expelled; if need be, by force of arms. There is no disagreement on that.

But in the event of war, why should it be an American war, made up largely of American troops, American casualties, and American deaths? We hope there is no war, but if there is, we hope and pray it will not be prolonged with many casualties.

Certainly, the United States has a high responsibility to lead the international community in opposing aggression, but this should not require the United States to assume a greater burden and a greater responsibility than other nations with an equal or even greater stake in the resolution of the crisis. That is what is happening, and it is wrong.

It may become necessary to use force to expel Iraq from Kuwait, but because war is such a grave undertaking with such serious consequences, we must make certain that war is employed only as a last resort.

House Minority Leader Robert H. Michel, January 10, 1991 [2]

I am happy and proud that the resolution which I support, the bipartisan resolution, is one that is in the form of a joint resolution that would obviously go to the other body, require the signature of the President, and then we would all be speaking with one voice.

Mr. Speaker, as this debate opens, the United States of America has over 370,000 troops in the Gulf area. They are face to face with troops of a ruthless dictator. Our troops will be aware of every word we say in this debate. So will the dictator.

The question we have to ask ourselves is this: When this debate is finished, will the House be seen as a tower of strength or as a tower of Babel? I speak from the prejudice of being a combat veteran of World War II and those of our generation know from bloody experience that unchecked aggression against a small nation is a prelude to international disaster. Saddam Hussein today has more planes and tanks, and frankly, men under arms, than Hitler did at the time when Prime Minister Chamberlain came back from Munich with that miserable piece of paper. I will never forget that replay of that movie in my life. I have an obligation, I guess, coming from that generation, to transmit those thoughts

I had at the time to the younger generation who did not experience what we did.

Saddam Hussein not only invaded Kuwait, he occupied, terrorized and murdered civilians, systematically looted, and turned a peaceful nation into a wasteland of horror. He seeks control over one of the world's most vital resources, and he ultimately seeks to make himself the unchallenged anti-Western dictator of the Mideast. Either we stop him now and stop him permanently, or we will not stop him at all.

Stay what course? A course that allows Saddam to know that he is free from surprise attack, free from sudden offensive movements for six months, a year, or more?

Now, the President has clearly presented the reasons why we cannot stand by idly in his words: "We're in the Gulf because the world must not and cannot reward aggression. And we're there because our vital interests are at stake."

Now, we are told by some that we must show patience. We must wait for sanctions to work. We must wait six months or a year before forces are used. We must stay the course. My question is this: Stay what course? A course that allows Saddam to know that he is free from surprise attack, free from sudden offensive movements for six months, a year, or more? I guess to Members who advocate that course, I would say to those Members, what would they do about the attitude of the American people in that interval period of time? How long will the American people put up with that? How long would that delicate coalition last that we have pulled together, currently? How long will they stay that kind of course? Not to mention our troops abroad an extended period of time, in that kind of an environment, when, frankly, over an extended period of time we would have to be thinking seriously of rotation and all that that implies.

Therefore, I think during the course of this debate, those who advocate that course are going to have to answer some of those questions.

Patience and delay can be virtues when they help bring military or diplomatic goals, but when patience and delay become foreign policy goals in themselves, as I fear they have with some of our colleagues, they are no longer virtues.

I understand principled pacifism which holds that nothing justifies the taking of a human life. I grew up in that tradition, and I respect it, because World War II caused me to come to grips with the very same question in my mind and in my conscience. However, what I cannot understand is a policy that asks Members to believe that after six months or one year, that the alliance will still hold, our sophisticated equipment will be in better shape after frying in the desert, our troops will have higher morale and better readiness. Such a policy is not just an uncertain trumpet to the men and women in our armed services, it is a veritable brass choir of indecision, doubt, and confusion. Patience at any price is not a policy. It is a cop-out.

We will be told by those who want delay that they do not want to risk American lives in combat. Let no one in this Chamber or anyone else lecture me on the horrors of war. I see my friend, the gentleman from Florida and several others, including the gentleman from Ohio similarly, who know all the horrors of war. We have seen it at its worst. The memory will remain within our heart and minds for the rest of their lives.

It is Saddam Hussein who will be responsible for those who make the supreme sacrifice, and Saddam Hussein himself. If Saddam Hussein convinces his neighbors he can survive this crisis, he will become something more than a former hit man with delusions of grandeur. He will become someone who has triumphed over a worldwide coalition. If Members seriously think that that wouldn't be a sinister event in the history of the 20th century, I think those Members are fooling themselves.

In our democracy, we elect our President to speak and act for Members, primarily in foreign affairs, that our message might be clear and unmistakable. We in Congress have our role to play, and we cannot shirk our responsibility. This is the time, it seems to me, for Members to rally around the Chief and give him the support he deserves for our well-crafted bipartisan resolution.

Senator Paul Simon, January 10, 1991 [2]

...When Senator Mitchell and our small group came back from the Middle East after visiting Saudi Arabia, Egypt, and Israel, we met later that day with the President for more than an hour and had a good discussion. I applaud the President for meeting with us. The President said, "Finally, let me just give you this message," and he particularly looked at Senator Mitchell and me as he said this. He said, "Let me give you this final message. If we use the military, we can make the United Nations a really meaningful, effective voice for peace and stability in the future."

I said, "Mr. President, can I give you a 30-second response? If Libya invades Chad, you are not going to send 400,000 troops. What you would be willing to do, and what other nations would be willing to do, is to vote sanctions. If we stick with sanctions, and the sanctions work, then we have a mechanism that the community of nations can use again and again and again, and it is a shared burden."

Senator Orrin G. Hatch, January 10, 1991 [2]

I have been watching this debate with a great deal of interest today. Frankly, I am very concerned about some of the comments that have been made. I think President Bush has gone the extra mile in trying to avoid the use of force. I do not think there is any question about that. I think it is time for Congress to help rather than hinder the President. I think it is time for the Congress to join with the President and get behind him and our young men and women over there sitting in the sand, and show that we are willing to back the use of force.

I never thought I would see the day when a timid organization like the United Nations would come out and authorize the use of force by January 15, and our own Members of Congress are unwilling to back that resolution—some of them. Unless Saddam Hussein believes that the threat of war is real, he will not budge. The only way to avoid war, in my opinion, in this particular situation, is to be prepared to go

to war and to show that our resolve is for real.

If Hussein will not even accept a letter from President Bush, he certainly is not going to accept congressional pleas that Iraq pull out from Kuwait. Our actions should be decisive. If we back the President overwhelmingly, we will maximize the pressure on Iraq. We will enhance the chances that we can avoid war. If the vote is close, Saddam Hussein can conclude that he can divide our country if he will only hold out. If we fail to back the President, war will become inevitable...

If Congress stalls, we will be responsible for the loss of thousands of lives, not only American casualties, but the others as well.

The argument that the United States should simply give the sanctions more time to work is fatally flawed. None of its advocates explain how much time would be needed. Six months? One year? Two years? No one offers a straight answer. If we wait, we will find that time means even more casualties.

Even if we wait a few more months, the cost in terms of U.S. lives will escalate dramatically. That will give Iraq's forces more time to build up the greatest fortified work since the Maginot Line. He has already put in place vast mine fields, fire ditches, dug in armor, infantry positions with overlapping fields of fire, all designed to channel attacking forces into preplanned killing zones. If we wait, he gains time to thicken and strengthen those defenses. If Congress stalls, we will be responsible for the loss of thousands of lives, not only American casualties, but the others as well. There are approximately 250,000 troops from other countries, and we seem to forget that, too.

Those who urge us to wait a year or more portray this conflict as a kind of waiting game. They foolishly believe that things can only get worse for Saddam Hussein and better for us, but that is not the case. There are any number of scenarios that would undercut the position of the United States without a shot being fired. We could see sanc-

tion-evading foreign firms, which already number several hundred, devise better ways to smuggle the goods that Baghdad wants. We could see them. We know that we are seeing it now, through Iran, through Syria, through Jordan. I suspect some others as well.

We could see Iran agree to hook up the oil pipeline network with Iraq and sell Iraqi oil on behalf of Baghdad, giving Saddam Hussein much-needed hard currency, and much more than that if Hussein becomes the darling of the Arab world.

And we could see political turbulence in the Soviet Union, which has already led to the resignation of Shevardnadze, lead to a change in Soviet support in the international effort against Iraq. Right now, one of the most amazing things of this whole century is their support. I do not believe it is going to last if we keep playing these games in the Congress. We could see Saddam Hussein succeed in subverting some of the moderate members of the coalition, such as Egypt and perhaps even Saudi Arabia.

Giving more time for the sanctions to work also carries risks. What looks like the safe course of action could quickly become the more perilous.

House Majority Leader Richard A. Gephardt, January 11, 1991 [2]

Mr. Speaker, let us be clear about the lines being drawn in this debate. This is not a choice between those who want to force Saddam Hussein out of Iraq and those who want to talk him out. All Americans agree: Saddam Hussein must be driven out of Kuwait. And driving him out will take more than words. It will take force. I realize that. The President realizes that. All the world recognizes that.

And so the choice is not between action and inaction: it is a choice between two different courses of action—two different methods of applying force. It is a choice between the headlong rush to combat, and the policy of patient strength.

Make no mistake about it: the use of sanctions is the use of force. Indeed, the stranglehold we have placed upon Iraq is more like a medieval siege than the word "sanction." Iraq is under siege, cut off from all the world and all supplies. Saddam Hussein leads a small country against which all the world is arrayed. The question is not whether he will give up, but when.

Sanctions will force him to give up. They are backed up by an armada as fearful and formidable as any ever assembled. America alone has more than 50 warships, 3 aircraft carriers, and thousands of the finest sailors in the world in the region to enforce the U.N. sanctions.

With our allies, American forces have already made 6,662 interceptions, 796 times they have stopped and boarded ships, and 35 times they have forced ships to divert from their planned destination: Iraq. And, when circumstances called for it, they have fired shots across the bow of offending ships. We've already used force—when force was necessary.

And on the land we have more troops facing off against Iraq across the line in the Saudi sand than we had facing off against the Soviet Union across the Iron Curtain in Central Europe.

The force of these sanctions is indeed severe. We have cut off food from a nation that imports 70 percent of its food. We have stopped the shipment of material that supports Saddam's war machine. And we have cut off Iraq's only real export: oil, the source of 90 percent of its trade revenue.

The force with which we have responded to Iraq's aggression is truly awesome. The grain embargo and Olympic boycott with which America responded to the Soviet's unprovoked aggression against Afghanistan seem puny in comparison.

The strength of these sanctions is truly historic. The Institute for International Economics recently released an exhaustive analysis of each one of the 115 times in which sanctions have been used since World War I. Their conclusion is: "The current U.N. sanctions are by far the strongest and most complete ever imposed against any country by other nations."

Sanctions are choking off half the Gross National Product of Iraq—an amount twenty times greater than the average impact of history's most successful sanctions.

Sanctions can squeeze even the most intransigent regimes into making changes—or the people of those countries will make the changes for them. Again, according to the Institute

for International Economics, the U.N. embargo against Rhodesia helped bring about the demise of the regime of Ian Smith. Sanctions helped bring down dictators like Rafael Trujillo in the Dominican Republic in the 1960s, and Idi Amin in the 1970s, and accelerated the economic chaos that brought down the Sandinista government. Sanctions are force. Sanctions are effective.

Will we have the courage to keep slowly applying force? Or will we allow ourselves to be swept up in the frenzy to win this thing quickly—even if the price of victory is American blood?

It is said that sanctions alone will never force Saddam Hussein to leave; that the political climate created by this crisis will not allow him to leave. But sanctions far weaker than those faced by Saddam Hussein helped to destabilize Idi Amin and Daniel Ortega. How can you be certain they won't destabilize Saddam—or at least force him to retreat in order to feed his people?

If your concern is over how sanctions will politically allow Saddam Hussein to withdraw, then the answer is that sanctions change the political and economic terrain on which Saddam must operate. That's because sanctions hurt—they cause real pain. And, as we've seen in other cases, even in a dictatorship, the pain of the people eventually gets transferred to the leader.

It is also said that the Moslem world will not tolerate American troops on its soil. If we are worried about Arab resentment against a peacekeeping force in a defensive posture, why are we not more worried about the recriminations that will follow a bloody war on Arab soil?

Let no one misunderstand me—least of all Saddam Hussein. I do not rule out the use of force. And if we must fight, we must ensure that we win as quickly and as decisively as possible. But testimony from a variety of military experts suggests that with each day of sanctions and embargo, the Iraqi war machine grows weaker.

Saddam's war machine has been cut off from spare parts: each bullet fired in training or maneuvers or practice is one less bullet he has if and when

war comes. By contrast, we have the option of rotating troops to maintain a fresh force; our supply lines, although long, are unimpeded; our troops are adapting to the desert, and each training exercise makes them better prepared to engage on that hostile and unforgiving terrain. I've been to the front lines in the desert, and I've talked to our troops. Their morale is high—and I have enough faith in them to know it will remain high. They will not be discouraged as long as they know they have the strong support of the folks back home...

Yes, sanctions do take time—there's no doubt about it. Can it be that we are not willing to ask the American people to wait for success, but we are willing to sacrifice their sons and daughters to achieve success? Is our patience really that thin? Is our resolve really that frail?

It is a cruel irony that those who originally designed the policy of sanctions are now the only ones who doubt their effectiveness, and question our resolve. No one else does.

No. It is not the American people who lack resolve.

For forty-five years the American people stood eyeball to eyeball with the communist threat, until finally the bear blinked. For three decades the American people have sent their sons and daughters to keep the peace in Korea—and still their resolve has not waned. It is only the patience and the resolve of our policymakers and our politicians—not our people—that is in doubt. Will we have the strength to stay the course? Will we have the courage to keep slowly applying force? Or will we allow ourselves to be swept up in the frenzy to win this thing quickly—even if the price of victory is American blood?

Senator John McCain, January 11, 1991 [2]

Mr. President, during this debate we hear references time and time again to the Vietnam War and how people want no more Vietnams. We hear that from the President. No one wants another Vietnam. The President does not, and neither does anybody in this body who has addressed the issue. Clearly, neither we nor the American people seek a replay of that tragic chapter in our nation's history.

Yet, this resolution [to give sanctions more time] could force a "Vietnam" upon us. If we drag out this crisis and do not act decisively and bring it to a successful resolution, we face the prospect of a much longer and bitter war.

If we must use force, we must use it quickly and decisively. We must never again drift into a major conflict in slow stages, denying its seriousness, and setting political rules and constraints that make victory impossible.

Representative Stephan J. Solarz, January 12, 1991 [2]

Mr. Speaker, as we come to the close of this historic debate, I find myself in a somewhat anomalous position. It was almost twenty-five years ago that I got my start in politics as the campaign manager for one of the first antiwar candidates for Congress in the country. It never occurred to me then that I would be speaking on the floor of the House of Representatives a quarter of a century later in support of a bipartisan resolution that many whom I respect fear could lead to another Vietnam.

Yet, I believe there are some fundamental differences between the situation in which we found ourselves in Vietnam then and the situation we confront in the Persian Gulf today.

In Vietnam, vital American interests were never at stake. In the Gulf, they are. In Vietnam, the cost in blood and treasure was out of all proportion to the expected benefits of a successful defense of South Vietnam. In the Gulf, the enormous benefits of a successful effort to get Iraq out of Kuwait far exceed the admitted price we will have to pay if force must be used.

We have heard a lot of talk in this debate about the need for patience. We were patient when Japan invaded Manchuria in 1931. We were patient when Italy attacked Ethiopia in 1936. We were patient when Germany overran France in 1940. We were patient, Mr. Speaker, right up to December 7, 1941, when Japan attacked us at Pearl Harbor, by which time Germany had conquered almost all of Europe and Japan controlled much of Asia.

The great lesson of our time is that evil still exists, and when evil is on the march, it must be confronted.

In the Persian Gulf, almost half a year after the brutal and unprovoked annexation of Kuwait, the time for patience has ended and the time for firmness has arrived. Saddam Hussein represents a clear and present danger, not only to the region, but to the world. He has gone to war twice in the last ten years. He has used chemical weapons not only against his enemies, but against his own people, and he is well on the way toward acquiring nuclear weapons as well.

Saddam Hussein does not have to run for reelection in 1992. He does not have to worry about a contentious Congress or a critical press. He will hunker down. He will wait.

Driven by a megalomaniacal lust for power, he is determined to dominate the entire Middle East, and if he is not stopped now, we will have to stop him later under circumstances where he will be much more difficult and dangerous to contain.

None of us wants war. Yet the truth is that not until Saddam Hussein is stripped of any lingering illusions he may have about our willingness to use force will there be any real chance of a peaceful resolution of this crisis.

That is why, with only three days left before the expiration of the U.N. deadline, this bipartisan resolution, by confronting Saddam Hussein with a choice between leaving and living and staying and dying, represents the last best chance for peace.

The vote for the Gephardt-Hamilton resolution a short while ago demonstrates that a majority of the House believes that the protracted application of sanctions is a formula for failure rather than a strategy for success.

Judge [William H.] Webster, the head of the CIA, does not believe the sanctions will be sufficient to get Iraq out of Kuwait. Nor do the British, nor the French, nor the Egyptians, nor the Saudis. Not one of our coalition partners believes that sanctions will be sufficient to get Iraq out of Kuwait.

The reason they do not believe sanctions will be sufficient is because they know that Saddam Hussein does not give a whit for the welfare of his own people. All he cares about is the maximization of his own power. However great the economic impact of the sanctions may be, they know, as we know, that Saddam Hussein does not have to run for reelection in 1992. He does not have to worry about a contentious Congress or a critical press. He will hunker down. He will wait. And while he waits, there is a very real possibility that this inherently fractious and fragile coalition will begin to unravel, and the sanctions will erode, and he will prevail.

With the adoption of the bipartisan resolution, however, we should be in a position to achieve our objectives by peaceful means if possible, but, yes, by the use of force if necessary.

If we prevail, as surely we will, we will have prevented a brutal dictator from getting his hands on the economic jugular of the world. We will have protected and stabilized the Arab governments courageous enough to have opposed him. We will have eliminated his weapons of mass destruction and greatly reduced his conventional military power. We will have enhanced the prospects for progress in the peace process between Israel and its Arab neighbors. And perhaps most importantly of all, by demonstrating that aggression does not pay, and that the international community will uphold the sanctity of existing borders, we will have established a precedent that could lead to the creation of a new world order governed by the rule of law rather than by the law of the jungle, and in which nations shall not make war against other nations anymore.

Senator Sam Nunn, Chairman of the Senate Armed Services Committee, January 11, 1991 [2]

...[W]hen the President made the decision to build up the forces, double the forces in November, and couple that with an announcement there would be no rotation, at that time the die was cast. I am not certain that the President intended that the die be cast then, and that was the reason I raised the question immediately about the lack of rotation and about the size of the force not being sustainable and about the sanctions policy being discarded.

As the Senator will recall, at that time the administration vigorously denied the die had been cast, and that the sanctions policy had been discarded. But in practical terms, when you cannot rotate forces and you do not have enough troops left back home and around the world to rotate, and your forces certainly cannot stay out there in the desert for a year to eighteen months at a time without degrading their military capability, then the die in effect was cast...

The first question I try to ask when it comes to matters of war and peace is the question of whether a particular situation is vital to our nation's security? In this case, is the liberation of Kuwait vital to our nation's security?

We all agree with the goal of restoring Kuwaiti sovereignty; no doubt about that. But have we concluded here that the liberation of Kuwait in the next few weeks is so vital to our nation's security that we must take military action now instead of waiting a few months, waiting a period of time to allow the economic embargo and the blockage to take its toll?

Back in August and September when the embargo was successfully and, I would say, skillfully brought about by President Bush, through what I think was his superb leadership, no one thought or predicted that the embargo was really going to have much effect before April or May of 1991 and almost all of them said it would take at least a year.

There was no surprise about that. I am absolutely amazed when people say, well, we have waited four months and five months and the embargo is not working. They must not have been there at the beginning or they must not have talked to anybody at the beginning about how long it was going to take. It is very puzzling to me how someone could give up on the embargo after five months when nobody that I know predicted that it was going to last less than nine months to a year, and most people said a year to eighteen months from the time of inception, which was August of last year.

When we talk about the question of "vital"—a lot of times we in Washington throw that word around as if it is just another word. Sometimes we use so many words in the course of debate that we do not think carefully about what we mean. I recall very clearly President Reagan's 1982 declaration that Lebanon was vital to the security of the United States—Lebanon.

I am absolutely amazed when people say, well, we have waited four months and five months and the embargo is not working. They must not have been there at the beginning or they must not have talked to anybody at the beginning...

Shortly thereafter, following the tragic death of more than 200 Marines, we pulled out of Lebanon, we pulled out of a country that only a few weeks before had been declared "vital." Today, we debate this eight years later while pursuing our newly proclaimed vital interest in Kuwait. It was not vital before August 2. Nobody said it was vital then. There was no treaty. In fact, when we were protecting Kuwaiti vessels coming out of the Gulf for several years in the Iran-Iraq war, the Kuwaitis did not even let us refuel, as I recall. I would have to be checked on that one but that is my recollection.

All of a sudden it is vital—vital. And, while this embargo has been undertaken since August 2, and while we have seemed to take for granted now that the liberation of Kuwait is vital, not just in general but in the next two or three or four weeks—while that has been going on our government has watched passively and said very little, if anything, while our former enemy, a nation on the terrorist list for years and years and I believe it still is, Syria, used its military power to consolidate its control over Lebanon, the same country that was our vital interest in 1982. So one of our so-called vital interests, Lebanon, eight years ago, is now under the control of Syria, while we have pursued another vital interest.

The point is. not all these things are simple. The point is we ought to be careful about defining "vital." A lot of things are important, very important, that are not vital, vital in the sense of young men and young women being called to put their lives on the line...

Mr. President, weighing the cost of the military option, one must also consider our long term interests in the region. Has there been any in-depth analysis in the administration about what happens in the Middle East after we win? And we will win. The President's declared goals include establishing stability in the Persian Gulf and protecting United States citizens abroad.

Considering the wave of Islamic reaction, anti-Americanism, and terrorism that is likely to be unleashed by a highly disruptive war with many Arab casualties, it is difficult to conceive of a Middle East as a more stable region where Americans will be safe.

Finally, the administration has argued there is no guarantee that economic hardships will in the end compel Saddam Hussein to withdraw from Kuwait. Mr. President, I have attended intelligence community as well as Defense and State Department briefings for eighteen years. I have been thinking back. I cannot recall one instance where I ever came out of those briefings with any guarantee of anything. For the intelligence community to say they cannot guarantee that Iraq is going to get out of Kuwait because of the sanctions, which is going to reduce its gross national product by 70 percent and cut off all the hard currency, for them to say that is true—nobody can guarantee it.

But what else are they guaranteeing? I have not seen any guarantees on any subject from the intelligence community. It is not their fault. They are not in the business of guaranteeing. The CIA is not the FDIC. They give you the facts, and then you use common sense to come to the conclusions.

In summary, Mr. President, I believe that on balance there is a reasonable expectation that continued economic sanctions, backed up by the threat of force and international isolation, can bring about Iraq's withdrawal from Kuwait. I believe that the risks associated with the continued emphasis on sanctions are considerably less than the very real risk associated with war and, most importantly, the aftermath of war in a very volatile region of the world.

Senate Minority Leader Robert J. Dole, January 12, 1991 [2]

Mr. President, we are not going to change any minds. I think everybody's mind has been made up. But I think in addition to a lot of hopes, there is a real world out there. I am not certain any of us can predict with certainty, if there should be a conflict, how many lives would be lost, how much of a cost, how long it would last.

I do believe that our best chance for peace and best hope for peace is to strengthen the President's hand in every way we can.

The Senator from Illinois just indicated it is going to be closely divided. That is unfortunate. I wish it were not. I wish we could get consent, after the vote, to do it on a voice vote that everybody would support. I said I would not ask for that consent.

I am not so concerned about the message we send to the White House. I am more concerned about the message we send to Saddam Hussein. Somehow he has been forgotten in this debate. He started it. He can end it right now.

I agree with the Majority Leader that there is not one Senator in this body who wants war, not one on either side of the aisle who wants war. I assume, by the same token, there is not one who does not want peace and a peaceful settlement.

Some have strong convictions following one path and some have strong convictions on another path, but I think the bottom line is that this is not a blank check, as far as this Senator is concerned. I intend to use my influence, if any, in every way that I can to find some peaceful way to resolve the current crisis.

It just seems to me that when we authorize, we do not mandate. We do not say that it has to be today, tomorrow, or next week. We authorize. I believe that President Bush understands that it is an authorization. It is only an authorization.

After we vote, there will be a vote in the House on this same resolution. It is going to be a massive vote of support for President Bush, true bipartisanship in the House of Representatives, and I commend them for it.

I commend my colleagues on the other side who will support this resolution. It is not contradictory. It

demonstrates again that the primary message coming from the Congress today is to Saddam Hussein. The last time I checked, he was the real villain of this piece.

Mr. President, for many reasons, this is an important vote. It is a very important time in history. The Senator from Connecticut pointed out that things in the Mideast are always difficult. But if we postpone it for six weeks or six months or one year, is it going to be any less difficult? If we have a conflict at that time, will there be fewer casualties, or more? Will the stakes be higher or lower?

I am more concerned about the message we send to Saddam Hussein. Somehow he has been forgotten in this debate. He started it. He can end it right now.

It seems to me that if we could encourage more of our colleagues—and I know that everyone has the same goal, and that is for Saddam Hussein to get out of Kuwait. But if he draws the same conclusion as the Senator from Illinois has drawn, that America is divided, that Congress is divided, he may think he is going to get a free ride; he is going to be rescued, maybe, by the Congress; we are going to throw him an anchor. But if we throw him one, I want it to go down.

Mr. President, I would hope my colleagues would support this resolution, the resolution offered by the distinguished Senator from Virginia, the distinguished Senator from Connecticut, and others of us on both sides of the aisle. This is the time. Oh, there will be other times, but this is the time to send the message. There is not much time left.

There is not much time left, and to President Bush I say, as I said earlier, this is to strengthen your hand; this is to give you every resource we can in the final 48 or 72 hours to send the message that we want a peaceful settlement.

And to Saddam Hussein, again, to underscore that same message, plus to send him an additional message that Congress has acted. We have had bipartisan debate, and we have had some partisan debate. But we are going to have

a bipartisan result in the House of Representatives and the U.S. Senate.

So for all of us who want peace; for all of us who want to strengthen the President of the United States, along with 82 percent of the American people, the vote on this resolution should be yes.

Speaker of the House Thomas S. Foley, January 12, 1991 [2]

I take the well in what will be an unusual and only occasional circumstance, to speak to my colleagues as a Member rather than as Speaker. But as I leave the chair and come to the well, I hope I may for just a moment speak to you as the Speaker, and tell you that I think this general debate—the longest in the modern history of the House of Representatives, extending over twenty hours—has done great credit to each Member who has spoken to the House, to all those who have taken opposing and difficult views, and in the highest tradition of this body fulfills our constitutional responsibilities and our obligations to those Americans for whom we stand and speak.

But I would not feel it right to stand behind the usual custom of the Speaker not to vote and not to speak on a question of this importance. I do not ask anyone to follow me, but I do feel the need to explain to my constituents, to those who have sent me here, why I will cast a vote for the Hamilton-Gephardt resolution and against the Michel-Solarz resolution.

I will vote this way not because I do not have the greatest respect for those who take an opposing view. I do. And I know what a difficult choice this is for each of us. I will not go over the arguments again. They have been articulated so well and so ably on both sides.

But let me suggest what this debate is not about. It is not about a lack of determination to see Saddam Hussein, a brutal dictator who has taken a country by force and violence and holds it today, removed from Kuwait. We will not permit him to stay. We are committed to his removal.

This debate is not about who supports the President of the United States and who does not. I honor and respect the President. I know his determination and I also know the awful loneliness and terrible consequence of the decisions that he must make.

In a letter to Thomas Jefferson, James Madison wrote that, "The Constitution supposes what the history of all governments demonstrate, that the Executive is the branch...most interested in war, and most prone to it. It has accordingly...vested the question of war in the legislature."

I do not believe the President wants war. I believe that he devoutly wishes peace and will continue to hope and work for it. But it is wrong to suggest that we who have taken our own oath can burden him further by giving to him alone the responsibility that also must be ours today. We have been elected to do it. The Constitution mandates it, and we would shirk our duty if we easily acquiesce in what the President decides. That is unfair to him, as it is to our constituents and to our responsibilities.

The President deserves, more than any single person in this country, not our agreement given casually or automatically, but our informed and conscientious judgment. And each Member should strive to give that to the President and the country today.

This debate is not about who supports our troops. We hear constant references that they are eager, almost anxious to fight and to sacrifice and perhaps to die. And I must say a respectful thank God. Thank God we have young men and women who are so committed to this country, to its values, and to its service that they are ready to lay down their very lives for it, and for their fellow citizens. That is a tremendous gift to this country. And each of us who has seen our troops in the field, our young men and women, and noted their morale and enthusiasm, and, as I say, even eagerness, ought not just respect and thank them for it; we have a duty not to rush into an early and precipitous war as a way of recognizing their willingness to make that sacrifice.

This debate is not about supporting the coalition that the President has so successfully organized. It is not about supporting the United Nations that has a new and revived role in promoting international order.

It is not about standing with our allies. All of these things can be done in support of the Hamilton-Gephardt resolution.

The debate is not about the use of force. Force is being used every day. Ships are being stopped. Iraq is being surrounded, its military potential has been hedged. We only reserve the right to give final approval to the President to initiate the maximum offensive force in our command, the terrible, terrible force that this country has the power to inflict.

Let us come together after the vote with the notion that we are Americans here, not Democrats and Republicans, all anxious to do the best for our country, without recrimination as to motive, without anything but the solemn pride that on this great decision day we voted as our conscience and judgment told us we should.

Eight years ago, in the 98th Congress, this House was asked to adopt a resolution providing for the continued peacekeeping presence of U.S. Marines and other servicemen in Lebanon. The Speaker of the House, Thomas P. O'Neill, took the well and asked all Members to support the President's request that we should continue the American peacekeeping presence in Lebanon. I voted for that resolution. I regret that vote today, not because one could not honorably support such a resolution; not because I wanted to back the President or I wanted to stand firm with the leadership on both sides of the aisle. Those were all decent reasons. I regret that vote today not just because, as we all regret, 300 Marines lost their lives. I regret it also because I cast that vote feeling doubtful, uncertain, unwilling to commit myself fully to its consequence. And those who believe that the President must now be armed with what unquestionably—as [Congressman] Dante Fascell so honorably and candidly has told this House—is the virtual declaration of war, should not hesitate to vote that way, should not hesitate to give him that power.

But if you feel that more can be done; if you feel that the sanctions have not yet wasted their opportunity; if you believe that Saddam Hussein is growing weaker every day under their impression; if you believe the international coalition will hold; if you believe this nation's leadership is best expressed in this body and in the other body, and in the coalition of constitutional consent, then vote for Hamilton-Gephardt.

But however you vote, as the Majority Leader has said, let us come together after the vote with the notion that we are Americans here, not Democrats and Republicans, all anxious to do the best for our country, without recrimination as to motive, without anything but the solemn pride that on this great decision day we voted as our conscience and judgment told us we should. And though our opinion may change over years, we will then not bear the burden of a harsh judgment on our honor and our actions at this moment.

And though I too was raised in a tradition that honored silent and private prayer, I offer a public prayer for this House, for all of us, for the Congress, for our President—and he is our President—and for the American people, particularly those young Americans who stand willing to make the supreme sacrifice. May God bless us and guide us and help us in the fateful days that lie ahead.

---

1 The complete transcripts of the hearings from which these excerpts were taken are published by the committees involved and may be obtained from the Superintendent of Documents, U.S. Government Printing Office, Washington, D.C. 20420.

2 Complete transcripts of these Congressional debates can be found in the *Congressional Records* for January 10, 11, and 12, 1991. The record for January 11 is in two sections; while the second section is labelled "Part II," there is no comparable label, at least on our copies, for Part I. Copies may be obtained from the Government Printing Office, using the address in the previous footnote.

War and Peace in the Gulf
Part II: January 12, 1991 - February 27, 1991

Text of Joint Congressional Resolution, January 12, 1991 [1]

Whereas the Government of Iraq without provocation invaded and occupied the territory of Kuwait on August 2, 1990;

Whereas both the House of Representatives (in H.J. Res. 658 of the 101st Congress) and the Senate (in 5. Con. Res. 147 of the 101st Congress) have condemned Iraq's invasion of Kuwait and declared their support for international action to reverse Iraq's aggression;

Whereas Iraq's conventional chemical, biological, and nuclear weapons and ballistic missile programs and its demonstrated willingness to use weapons of mass destruction pose a grave threat to world peace;

Whereas the international community has demanded that Iraq withdraw unconditionally and immediately from Kuwait and that Kuwait's independence and legitimate government be restored;

Whereas the United Nations Security Council repeatedly affirmed the inherent right of individual or collective self-defense in response to the armed attack by Iraq against Kuwait in accordance with Article 51 of the United Nations Charter;

Whereas in the absence of full compliance by Iraq with its resolutions the United Nations Security Council in Resolution 678 has authorized member states of the United Nations to use all necessary means, after January 15, 1991, to uphold and implement all relevant Security Council resolutions and to restore international peace and security in the area; and

Whereas Iraq has persisted in its illegal occupation of, and brutal aggression against Kuwait:

Now, therefore, be it

Resolved by the Senate and House of Representatives of the United States of America in Congress Assembled,

SECTION 1. SHORT TITLE.

This joint resolution may be cited as the "Authorization for Use of Military Force Against Iraq Resolution."

SEC. 2. AUTHORIZATION FOR USE OF UNITED STATES ARMED FORCES

(a) AUTHORIZATION—The President is authorized, subject to subsection (b) to use United States Armed Forces pursuant to United Nations Security Council Resolution 678 (1990) in order to achieve implementation of Security Council Resolutions 660, 661, 662, 664, 665, 666, 667, 669, 670, 674, and 677.

(b) REQUIREMENT FOR DETERMINATION THAT USE OF MILITARY FORCE IS NECESSARY.—Before exercising the authority granted in subsection (a), the President shall make available to the Speaker of the House of Representatives and the President pro tempore of the Senate his determination that—

(1) the United States has used all appropriate diplomatic and other peaceful means to obtain compliance by Iraq with the United Nations Security Council resolutions cited in subsection (a); and

(2) that those efforts have not been and would not be successful in obtaining such compliance.

(c) WAR POWER RESOLUTION REQUIREMENTS.—

(1) Specific Statutory Authorization.—Consistent with section 8(aX1) of the War Powers Resolutions, the Congress declares that this section is intended to constitute specific statutory authorization within the meaning of section 5(b) of the War Powers Resolution.

(2) APPLICABILITY OF OTHER REQUIREMENTS.—Nothing in this resolution supersedes any requirement of the War Powers Resolution.

SEC. 3. REPORTS TO CONGRESS.

At least once every 60 days, the President shall submit to the Congress a summary on the status of efforts to obtain compliance by Iraq with the resolutions adopted by the United Nations Security Council in response to Iraq's aggression.

President's Press Conference Following Vote in Congress, January 12, 1991 (Excerpts) [2]

First, let me just say that I am gratified by the vote in the Congress supporting the United Nations Security Council resolutions. This action by the Congress unmistakably demonstrates the United States commitment to the international demand for a complete and unconditional withdrawal of Iraq from Kuwait. This clear expression of the Congress represents the last, best chance for peace.

As a democracy we've debated this issue openly and in good faith. And as President I have held extensive consultation with the Congress. We've now closed ranks behind a clear signal of our determination and our resolve to implement the United Nations resolutions. Those who may have mistaken our democratic process as a sign of weakness now see the strength of democracy. And this sends the clearest message to Iraq that it cannot scorn the January 15th deadline.

Throughout our history we've been resolute in our support of justice, freedom, and human dignity. The current situation in the Persian Gulf demands no less of us and of the international community. We did not plan for war, nor do we seek war. But if conflict is thrust upon us we are ready and we are determined. We've worked long and hard, as have others including the Arab League, the United Nations, the European Community, to achieve a peaceful solution. Unfortunately, Iraq has thus far turned a deaf ear to the voices of peace and reason.

Let there be no mistake: Peace is everyone's goal. Peace is in everyone's prayers. But it is for Iraq to decide.

Q. Mr. President, does this mean now that war is inevitable—

A. No—

Q. ——and have you made the decision in your own mind?

A. No, it does not mean that war is inevitable. And I have felt that a statement of this nature from both Houses of the United States Congress was, at this late date, the best shot for peace. And so, let us hope that that message will get through to Saddam Hussein.

Q. Have you made the decision in your mind?

A. I have not because I still hope that there will be a peaceful solution.

Q. Mr. President, there's only three days left until the deadline, which isn't enough time for Saddam Hussein to pull out his troops. In fact, you, yourself, wouldn't let Jim Baker go to Baghdad on this date because there wouldn't be enough time. Do you see the possibility of anything happening in these last few days that could avert war or any chance that he will pull his troops out?

A. Well, in terms of the chance, I'd have to say I don't know. And in terms of what could avert war, you might say an instant commencement of a large-scale removal of troops with no condition, no concession, and just heading out could well be the best and only way to avert war, even though it would be, at this date, I would say almost impossible to comply fully with the United Nations resolutions.

Q. Sort of a followup: Have you heard from the U.N. Secretary-General Perez de Cuellar today, and is there any hope on that front?

A. No—well, I don't know whether there is hope on it because I haven't heard from him today.

Q. Mr. President, are you satisfied that countries in the international coalition like France, Syria, and Egypt will take part in offensive operations in the event of hostilities in the Gulf?

A. Yes.

Q. The second part of that question, sir, you've said that if hostilities come it will not be another Vietnam. What kind of assumptions are you making about the duration of a conflict, and can you assure the American

people that hostilities would not expand beyond the current theater of operations?

A. Well, I am not making any assumptions in terms of numbers of days, but I have said over and over again that the differences between what is happening in the Gulf and what happened in Vietnam are enormous in terms of the coalition aligned against the Iraqis, in terms of the demographics, in terms of the United Nations action, and I am convinced in terms of the force that is arrayed against Iraq. So, I just don't think there is a parallel.

But I would like to say that I have gone over all of this with our Secretary of Defense and with the Chairman of the Joint Chiefs; and all three of us, and everybody else involved in this, are determined to keep casualties to an absolute minimum. And that's one of the reasons that I authorized Secretary Cheney to move the additional force several weeks ago.

*   *   *

Q. Sir, can you explain why sooner is better than later?

A. Yes, because I think that's been a major part of the debate on the Hill. And I think it is very important that he knows that the United States and the United Nations are credible. I don't want to see further economic damage done to the Third World economies or to this economy. I don't want to see further devastation done to Kuwait. This question of when was debated in the United Nations, and these countries came down saying this is the deadline. And I don't want to veer off from that for one single iota. And I certainly don't want to indicate that the United States will not do its part in the coalition to fulfill these resolutions.

Q. Mr. President, you spoke of the debate. It was a very somber day up there.

A. Yes.

Q. People talked about the cost of war. I wondered if you watched it and what effect it had on you.

A. That's a good question. On the parts of it I saw I couldn't agree more. It was somber, properly somber. It was, I thought, with very little rancor. I thought it was conducted for the most part—not entirely—in a very objective manner in terms of the subject, and yet subjective in terms of the individual speaking. The compassion and the con-

cern, the angst of these Members, whether they agreed with me or not, came through loud and clear.

And so, I guess I shared the emotion. I want peace. I want to see a peaceful resolution. And I could identify with those— whether they were on the side that was supporting of the administration or the other—with those who were really making fervent appeals for peace. But I think it was historic. I think it was conducted showing the best of the United States Congress at work. And I keep feeling that it was historic because what it did and how it endorsed the President's action to fulfill this resolution—when you go back and look at war and peace I think historians will say this is a very significant step. I am pleased that the Congress responded. I'm pleased that they have acted and therefore are a part of all of this.

But I didn't sense—you know, when you win a vote on something you work hard for, sometimes there's a sense of exhilaration and joy, pleasure. I didn't sense that at all here. I was grateful to the Members that took the lead in supporting the positions that I'm identified with. I could empathize with those who didn't vote for us. So, I guess my emotion was somber itself. I didn't watch the whole thing—I didn't watch the whole debate. But what I saw I appreciated because there was very little personal rancor, assigning motives to the other person, or something of that nature. So, it was quite different than some of the debates that properly characterize the give-and-take of competitive politics.

President's Statement on Signing Resolution Authorizing Use of Military Force Against Iraq, January 14, 1991 [2]

Today I am signing H.J. Res. 77, the "Authorization for Use of Military Force Against Iraq Resolution." By passing H.J. Res. 77, the Congress of the United States has expressed its approval of the use of U.S. armed forces consistent with U.N. Security Council Resolution 678. I asked the Congress to support implementation of U.N. Security Council Resolution 678 because such action would send the clearest possible message to Saddam

Hussein that he must withdraw from Kuwait without condition or delay. I am grateful to those of both political parties who joined in the expression of resolve embodied in this resolution. To all, I emphasize again my conviction that this resolution provides the best hope for peace.

The debate on H.J. Res. 77 reflects the profound strength of our constitutional democracy. In coming to grips with the issues at stake in the Gulf, both Houses of Congress acted in the finest traditions of our country. This resolution provides unmistakable support for the international community's determination that Iraq's ongoing aggression against, and occupation of, Kuwait shall not stand. As I made clear to congressional leaders at the outset, my request for congressional support did not, and my signing this resolution does not, constitute any change in the long-standing positions of the executive branch on either the President's constitutional authority to use the armed forces to defend vital U.S. interests or the constitutionality of the War Powers Resolution. I am pleased, however, that differences on these issues between the President and many in the Congress have not prevented us from uniting in a common objective. I have had the benefit of extensive and meaningful consultations with the Congress throughout this crisis, and I shall continue to consult closely with the Congress in the days ahead.

Statement by White House Press Secretary Marlin Fitzwater on Allied Military Action in the Persian Gulf, January 16, 1991 [2]

I have a statement by the President of the United States:

The liberation of Kuwait has begun. In conjunction with the forces of our coalition partners, the United States has moved under the code name Operation Desert Storm to enforce the mandates of the United Nations Security Council. As of 7 p.m. Eastern Standard Time, Operation Desert Storm forces were engaging targets in Kuwait and Iraq.

President Bush will address the Nation at 9 p.m. tonight from the Oval Office. I'll try to get you more as soon as we can. Thank you very much.

President's Address to Nation Announcing Allied Military Action, January 16, 1991 [2]

Just two hours ago, allied air forces began an attack on military targets in Iraq and Kuwait. These attacks continue as I speak. Ground forces are not engaged.

Tonight, the battle has been joined.

This conflict started August 2d when the dictator of Iraq invaded a small and helpless neighbor. Kuwait—a member of the Arab League and a member of the United Nations—was crushed; its people, brutalized. Five months ago, Saddam Hussein started this cruel war against Kuwait. Tonight, the battle has been joined.

This military action, taken in accord with United Nations resolutions and with the consent of the United States Congress, follows months of constant and virtually endless diplomatic activity on the part of the United Nations, the United States, and many, many other countries. Arab leaders sought what became known as an Arab solution, only to conclude that Saddam Hussein was unwilling to leave Kuwait. Others traveled to Baghdad in a variety of efforts to restore peace and justice. Our Secretary of State, James Baker, held an historic meeting in Geneva, only to be totally rebuffed. This past weekend, in a last-ditch effort, the Secretary-General of the United Nations went to the Middle East with peace in his heart—his second such mission. And he came back from Baghdad with no progress at all in getting Saddam Hussein to withdraw from Kuwait.

Now the twenty-eight countries with forces in the Gulf area have exhausted all reasonable efforts to reach a peaceful resolution—have no choice but to drive Saddam from Kuwait by force. We will not fail.

As I report to you, air attacks are underway against military targets in Iraq. We are determined to knock out Saddam Hussein's nuclear bomb poten-

tial. We will also destroy his chemical weapons facilities. Much of Saddam's artillery and tanks will be destroyed. Our operations are designed to best protect the lives of all the coalition forces by targeting Saddam's vast military arsenal. Initial reports from General Schwarzkopf are that our operations are proceeding according to plan.

Our objectives are clear: Saddam Hussein's forces will leave Kuwait. The legitimate government of Kuwait will be restored to its rightful place, and Kuwait will once again be free. Iraq will eventually comply with all relevant United Nations resolutions, and then, when peace is restored, it is our hope that Iraq will live as a peaceful and cooperative member of the family of nations, thus enhancing the security and stability of the Gulf.

Some may ask: Why act now? Why not wait? The answer is clear: The world could wait no longer. Sanctions, though having some effect, showed no signs of accomplishing their objective. Sanctions were tried for well over five months, and we and our allies concluded that sanctions alone would not force Saddam from Kuwait.

While the world waited, Saddam Hussein systematically raped, pillaged, and plundered a tiny nation, no threat to his own. He subjected the people of Kuwait to unspeakable atrocities—and among those maimed and murdered, innocent children.

While the world waited, Saddam sought to add to the chemical weapons arsenal he now possesses, an infinitely more dangerous weapon of mass destruction—a nuclear weapon. And while the world waited, while the world talked peace and withdrawal Saddam Hussein dug in and moved massive forces into Kuwait.

While the world waited, while Saddam stalled, more damage was being done to the fragile economies of the Third World, emerging democracies of Eastern Europe, to the entire world, including to our own economy.

The United States, together with the United Nations, exhausted every means at our disposal to bring this crisis to a peaceful end. However, Saddam clearly felt that by stalling and threatening and defying the United Nations, he could weaken the forces arrayed against him.

While the world waited, Saddam Hussein met every overture of peace with open contempt. While the world prayed for peace, Saddam prepared for war.

I had hoped that when the United States Congress, in historic debate, took its resolute action, Saddam would realize he could not prevail and would move out of Kuwait in accord with the United Nation resolutions. He did not do that. Instead, he remained intransigent, certain that time was on his side.

Saddam was warned over and over again to comply with the will of the United Nations: Leave Kuwait, or be driven out. Saddam has arrogantly rejected all warnings. Instead, he tried to make this a dispute between Iraq and the United States of America.

Well, he failed. Tonight, twenty-eight nations—countries from five continents, Europe and Asia, Africa, and the Arab League—have forces in the Gulf area standing shoulder to shoulder against Saddam Hussein. These countries had hoped the use of force could be avoided. Regrettably, we now believe that only force will make him leave.

Prior to ordering our forces into battle, I instructed our military commanders to take every necessary step to prevail as quickly as possible, and with the greatest degree of protection possible for American and allied service men and women. I've told the American people before that this will not be another Vietnam, and I repeat this here tonight. Our troops will have the best possible support in the entire world, and they will not be asked to fight with one hand tied behind their back. I'm hopeful that this fighting will not go on for long and that casualties will be held to an absolute minimum.

This is an historic moment. We have in this past year made great progress in ending the long era of conflict and Cold War. We have before us the opportunity to forge for ourselves and for future generations a new world order—a world where the rule of law, not the law of the jungle, governs the conduct of nations. When we are successful—and we will be—we have a real chance at this new world order, an order in which a credible United Nations can use its peacekeeping role to fulfill the promise and vision of the U.N.'s founders.

We have no argument with the people of Iraq. Indeed, for the in-

nocents caught in this conflict, I pray for their safety. Our goal is not the conquest of Iraq. It is the liberation of Kuwait. It is my hope that somehow the Iraqi people can, even now, convince their dictator that he must lay down his arms, leave Kuwait and let Iraq itself rejoin the family of peace-loving nations.

Thomas Paine wrote many years ago: "These are the times that try men's souls." Those well-known words are so very true today. But even as planes of the multinational forces attack Iraq, I prefer to think of peace, not war. I am convinced not only that we will prevail but that out of the horror of combat will come the recognition that no nation can stand against a world united. No nation will be permitted to brutally assault its neighbor.

No president can easily commit our sons and daughters to war. They are the Nation's finest. Ours is an all-volunteer force, magnificently trained, highly motivated. The troops know why they're there. And listen to what they say, for they've said it better than any President or Prime Minister ever could.

Listen to Hollywood Huddleston, Marine lance corporal. He says, "Let's free these people, so we can go home and be free again." And he's right. The terrible crimes and tortures committed by Saddam's henchmen against the innocent people of Kuwait are an affront to mankind and a challenge to the freedom of all.

Listen to one of our great officers out there, Marine Lieutenant General Walter Boomer. He said: "There are things worth fighting for. A world in which brutality and lawlessness are allowed to go unchecked isn't the kind of world we're going to want to live in."

Listen to Master Sergeant J.P. Kendall of the 82d Airborne: "We're here for more than just the price of a gallon of gas. What we're doing is going to chart the future of the world for the next 100 years. It's better to deal with this guy now than five years from now."

And finally, we should all sit up and listen to Jackie Jones, an Army lieutenant, when she says, "If we let him get away with this, who knows what's going to be next?"

I have called upon Hollywood and Walter and J.P. and Jackie and all their courageous comrades-in-arms to do what must be done. Tonight, America and the world are deeply grateful to them and to their families. And let me

say to everyone listening or watching tonight: When the troops we've sent in finish their work, I am determined to bring them home as soon as possible.

Tonight, as our forces fight, they and their families are in our prayers. May God bless each and every one of them, and the coalition forces at our side in the Gulf, and may He continue to bless our nation, the United States of America.

White House Statement Confirming Iraqi Missile Attacks on Israel and Saudi Arabia, January 17, 1991 [2]

The Department of Defense has confirmed the firing of missiles from Iraq into Israel and Saudi Arabia. Damage assessments are being made.

President Bush was informed of this action by NSC [National Security Council] adviser Brent Scowcroft earlier this evening. The President has also discussed this matter with Secretary of State Baker and Secretary of Defense Cheney. The President is outraged at, and condemns, this further aggression by Iraq.

Coalition forces in the Gulf are attacking missile sites and other targets in Iraq.

White House Statement on United States Response to Iraqi Missile Attacks on Israel, January 17, 1991 [2]

The United States has been in touch with the Government of Israel to express its outrage over the missile attacks by Iraq. Secretary Baker discussed the matter with Prime Minister Shamir by telephone from the White House tonight. The Secretary assured the Prime Minister that the United States is continuing its efforts to eliminate this threat.

The United States expects to remain in close consultation with Israel on this issue. The U.S. has also been in contact with its coalition partners.

The President has been kept informed of these developments and remains in the Residence.

President's Press Conference, January 18, 1991 [2]

We're now some 37 hours into Operation Desert Storm and the liberation of Kuwait and so far, so good. U.S. and coalition military forces have performed bravely, professionally, and effectively. It is important, however, to keep in mind two things: First, this effort will take some time. Saddam Hussein has devoted nearly all of Iraq's resources for a decade to building up this powerful military machine. We can't expect to overcome it overnight—especially as we want to minimize casualties to the U.S. and coalition forces and to minimize any harm done to innocent civilians.

Second, we must be realistic. There will be losses. There will be obstacles along the way. War is never cheap or easy. And I said this only because I am somewhat concerned about the initial euphoria in some of the reports and reactions to the first day's developments. No one should doubt or question the ultimate success, because we will prevail. But I don't want to see us get overly euphoric about all of this.

Our goals have not changed. What we seek is the same as what the international community seeks—namely, Iraq's complete and unconditional withdrawal from Kuwait and then full compliance with the Security Council resolutions.

I also want to say how outraged I am by Iraq's latest act of aggression—in this case, against Israel. Once again, we see that no neighbor of Iraq is safe. I want to state here publicly how much I appreciated Israel's restraint from the outset, really from the very beginning of this crisis. Prime Minister Shamir and his government have shown great understanding for the interests of the United States and the interests of others involved in this coalition.

Close consultations with Israel are continuing. So, too, are close consultations with our coalition partners. Just a few minutes ago I spoke to Prime Minister Brian Mulroney of Canada. And in that vein, I also had a long and good conversation this morning with Soviet President Gorbachev in which we thoroughly reviewed the situation in the Gulf. And, of course, I took the opportunity from that call to express again my concern, my deep concern,

over the Baltics and the need to ensure that there is a peaceful resolution to the situation there.

Let me close here by saying how much we appreciate what our fighting men and women are doing. This country is united. Yes, there's some protest, but this country is fundamentally united. And I want that message to go out to every kid that is over there serving this country.

I saw in the paper a comment by one who worried—from seeing demonstrations here and there in this country on television—that that expressed the will of the country. So, to those troops over there, let me just take this opportunity to say your country is supporting you—the Congress overwhelmingly endorsed that. Let there be no doubt in the minds of any of you: You have the full and unified support of the United States of America. So, I salute them. They deserve our full support, and they are our finest.

And now I'd be glad to take a few questions.

Q. Mr. President, has the United States asked Israel not to retaliate against Iraq for its attack, what commitments has the United States received in these consultations that we've had with Israel, and how long do you think Israel can stay on the sidelines if these attacks continue?

A. These questions, questions of what we're talking to Israel about right now, I'm going to keep confidential. No question that Israel's Scud—the attack on Israel was purely an act of terror. It had absolutely no military significance at all. And it was an attack that is symptomatic of the kind of leader that the world is now confronting in Saddam Hussein and that, again, I repeat, the man that will be defeated here.

But Israel has shown great restraint, and I've said that. I think we can all understand that they have their own problems that come from this. But I don't want to go further into it because we are right in the midst of consultations with Israel. I think they, like us, do not want to see this war widened out, and yet they are determined to protect their own population centers. And I can tell you that our defense people are in touch with our commanders to be sure that we are doing the utmost we can to suppress any of these missile sites that might wreak

havoc not just on Israel but on other countries that are not involved in this fighting. So, I'm going to leave it there, and I am confident that this matter can be resolved.

Q. Are you worried that it could change the course of the war?

A. I think that we ought to guard against anything that can change the course of the war. So, I think everybody realizes what Saddam Hussein was trying to do—to change the course of the war, to weaken the coalition. And he's going to fail. I want to say when the Soviet Union made such a strong statement, that was very reassuring. We are in close touch with our coalition partners, and this coalition is not going to fall apart. I'm convinced of that.

Q. Mr. President, two days ago you launched a war, and war is inherently a two-way street. Why should you be surprised or outraged when there is an act of retaliation?

A. Against a country that's innocent and is not involved in it—that's what I'm saying. Israel is not a participant. Israel is not a combatant. And this man has elected to launch a terroristic attack against the population centers in Israel with no military design whatsoever. And that's why. And it is an outrage, and the whole world knows it, and most of the countries in the world are speaking out against it. There can be no—no—consideration of this in anything other than condemnation.

Q. Why is it that any move for peace is considered an end run at the White House these days?

A. Well, you obviously—what was the question?

Q. That—--

A. End run?

Q. Yes, that is considered an end run—that people who still want to find a peaceful solution seem to be running into a brick wall.

A. Oh, excuse me. The world is united, I think, in seeing that these United Nations resolutions are fulfilled. Everybody would like to find a way to end the fighting. But it's not going to end until there is total cooperation with and fulfillment of these U.N. resolutions. This man is not going to pull a victory off by trying to wage terrorist attacks against a country that is not a participant in all of this, and I'm talking about Israel.

And so, I think everyone would like to see it end, but it isn't going to end short of the total fulfillment of our objectives.

Q. Mr. President, you gave assurances on this platform a few weeks ago—reiterated here today—that the coalition would withstand an attempt to engage Israel, or perhaps even Israel's retaliation against an attack. Can you give us some better idea today, sir, of what the basis for your assurance is on that point?

A. Well, a lot of diplomacy has gone on behind the scenes in this regard, and I feel very confident about what I've said.

Q. If I could follow up, sir, a particularly touchy situation obviously exists with regard to Jordan, whose position in the neighborhood is particularly sensitive, sir. Can you update us on any understandings that may exist, any diplomatic initiatives that may be ongoing to assure the Jordanians or to convince them to take no action, or about what would happen if they did?

A. Brit [Brit Hume, ABC News], I don't think there are any understandings on that with Jordan at this point, and so I can't elaborate on that.

Q. Mr. President, there was some indication last night—I appreciate you not wanting to tell us what is going on right now— but last night it appeared that Israeli planes got off the ground and headed toward Iraq. Did this government stop an Israeli retaliation that was underway?

A. No.

Q. Secondly, are we trying to kill Saddam Hussein? We have blown out several buildings where he could have been last night— yesterday.

A. We're not targeting any individual.

Q. Mr. President, do you have any message of reassurance to the people of Israel that the restraint being shown by their government doesn't place them in risk?

A. I think that they know of our determination to safeguard them following this attack—or prior to this attack. And we are going to be redoubling our efforts in the darnedest search-and-destroy effort that has ever been undertaken out in that area. And I hope that that is very reassuring to the citizens of Israel.

Q. Mr. President, are you trying to caution against overconfidence with your statement in—by concern that Saddam Hussein may have a lot more

staying power than was originally thought, or is it based on a upcoming land warfare that is apt to be protracted?

A. No, I don't think there is any conclusion that he has a lot more staying power than anybody thought. But what I am cautioning against is a mood of euphoria that existed around here yesterday because things went very, very well—from a military standpoint, exceptionally well. This was received all around the world with joy, but I just would caution again that it isn't going to be that easy all the time. But we have not changed our assessment as to how difficult the task ahead is.

Q. Sir, you said the Israelis have shown restraint. Are you confident that they will show restraint?

A. Well, we are working on that, and I am very hopeful that they will. They've been most cooperative. Secretary Baker talked to Prime Minister Shamir last night. I'll probably be on the phone with him in not so many minutes from now, and I could answer the question better after that. But I think they realize the complexity of this situation; we certainly do. But whatever happens, I'm convinced that this coalition will hold together.

Q. Sir, will you be able to tell Prime Minister Shamir with any confidence that you have knocked out these missile sites?

A. Well, the problem, John [John Cochran, NBC News], on that is we can tell him with confidence what we've done in terms of some of the missile sites but not all, because you're dealing with mobile missiles that can be hidden.

I'm getting a little off of my turf here because I've vowed to permit the Defense Department to respond to these military questions. But I think that one is rather clear—that when you can hide a mobile missile the way they've done, it's awfully hard to certify that all of them have been taken care of.

Q. Mr. President, granted you say that there are some rough days ahead. But there's also been a considerable amount of discussion as to the relatively unexpectedly low rate of response on the part of the Iraqis—you've had some briefings on this. What are your thoughts? What do you think explains this?

A. Well, I don't know. But my thoughts are that as each hour goes by, they're going to be relatively less able to respond. And I say that with no

bravado. I just simply say that because that's what's happening over there.

So, he may well have been holding his mobile missiles back, for example—wheeling them out there when he thinks they will be undetected and then firing a few of these missiles into the heart of downtown Haifa to try to make some political statement. But there may be some more of that ahead for—maybe aimed at other countries. Who knows? But in terms of his ability to respond militarily, I can guarantee the world that, as every hour goes by, he is going to be less able to respond, less able to stand up against the entire world—the world opinion as expressed in these United Nations resolutions.

Q. Mr. President, if I may follow: Do you have any hard intelligence information that would indicate to you that there is indeed still a live chemical weapons threat from Saddam Hussein?

A. I'd have to refer that to the—well, I would expect there is a threat because chemical weapons have been dispersed. He's used them on his own people. And that's something that our troops have been warned against, the people of Israel have been warned against, obviously, and others in the area have been warned against. So I can't say that every chemical weapon has been destroyed. But I think I said the other night in the speech from—comments from the Oval Office there that his ability to make chemical weapons will not exist. I can't tell you exactly where that stands, but I would refer you to the Pentagon.

Q. This is the first time there's been sustained combat between American soldiers and Arab forces. There's been an enormous amount of concern about what the reaction of the Arab world would be. Now that the war is underway, how concerned are you about that problem? Is there anything that could be done by you to minimize the damage to the links between Arab countries and the United States?

A. You're not talking about in—this in relationship to the attack on Israel.

Q. More in terms of the Arab matter—

A. Gerry [Gerald Seib, Wall Street Journal], you see, I've never believed that the Arabs would oppose what's going on right now. I believe when you see the Arab League and Egypt itself—which I guess is the largest in population of Arab countries—strongly supporting what we're doing, that this idea that all Arabs—the idea that he tried to sell, Saddam did, that Arabs versus America is phony, it's a phony argument.

There are Arab forces in the air probably right now—Kuwaiti or Saudi forces. There is a strong Arab element in this coalition. There are many countries in the Arab League that are opposed to Saddam Hussein and have long felt that he was the bully of the neighborhood. And it is about time that his aggression come to heel. And so I don't worry about it, long run. I do think when this is over we will have some very sophisticated diplomacy to do. But I believe at this point that most people in the Arab world understand and approve of what the United Nations tried to do and is trying to do now. So it doesn't concern me.

Now, there are some elements that, clearly, you might say, are on the other side. And that would worry me in a sense, but it worries me for the future, not so much for the present. I think when all this is over, we want to be the healers. We want to do what we can to facilitate what I might optimistically call a new world order.

But that new world order should have a conciliatory component to it. It should say to those countries that are on the other side at this juncture—and there aren't many of them—look, you're part of this new world order. You're part of this. You can play an important part in seeing that the world can live at peace in the Middle East and elsewhere. So, there are some that oppose us. There are some of the more radical elements that will always oppose the West and the United States.

But there are countries involved there that may have leaned—tilted, to use an old diplomatic expression, towards Saddam Hussein and towards Iraq that will clearly be in the forefront of this new world order. I am not going to write off Jordan. We've had a long-standing relationship with King Hussein, but he's in a very difficult position there. I have had some differences with him, but they've been respectful, but I would like to see him be more publicly understanding of what it is the United Nations is trying to do here and the United States role. We're not going to suggest that Jordan, because they've taken this position, can't continue to be a tremendously important country in this new world order.

So, I don't accept the premise that Saddam Hussein tried to sell the world that it was the Arabs against the United States. There is overwhelming evidence to show that he is wrong. What he was trying to do, obviously, is divert world attention away from the brutal aggression against Kuwait. You heard it in the Aziz press conference. I mean, if there ever was evidence as to what I'm saying, it was the way he conducted himself in that press conference.

So, so far, Gerry, I think there has been understanding as to why we're doing what we are doing. And I'd like to think respect for the coalition because I think they see, as I do—the Arab world—that out of this there's a chance for a lasting peace.

President's Letter to Congressional Leaders, January 18, 1991 [2]

Dear Mr. Speaker: (Dear Mr. President:)

On January 16, 1991, I made available to you, consistent with section 2(b) of the Authorization for Use of Military Force Against Iraq Resolution (H.J. Res. 77, Public Law 102-1), my determination that appropriate diplomatic and other peaceful means had not and would not compel Iraq to withdraw unconditionally from Kuwait and meet the other requirements of the U.N. Security Council and the world community. With great reluctance, I concluded, as did the other coalition leaders, that only the use of armed force would achieve an Iraqi withdrawal together with the other U.N. goals of restoring Kuwait's legitimate government, protecting the lives of our citizens and reestablishing security and stability in the Persian Gulf region. Consistent with the War Powers Resolution, I now inform you that pursuant to my authority as Commander in Chief, I directed U.S. Armed Forces to commence combat operations on January 16, 1991, against Iraqi forces and military targets in Iraq and Kuwait. The Armed Forces of Saudi Arabia, Kuwait, the United Kingdom, France, Italy, and Canada are participating as well.

Military actions are being conducted with great intensity. They have been carefully planned to accomplish

our goals with the minimum loss of life among coalition military forces and the civilian inhabitants of the area. Initial reports indicate that our forces have performed magnificently. Nevertheless, it is impossible to know at this time either the duration of active combat operations or the scope or duration of the deployment of U.S. armed forces necessary fully to accomplish our goals.

The operations of U.S. and other coalition forces are contemplated by the resolutions of the U.N. Security Council, as well as H.J. Res. 77, adopted by Congress on January 12, 1991. They are designed to ensure that the mandates of the United Nations and the common goals of our coalition partners are achieved and the safety of our citizens and forces is ensured.

As our united efforts in pursuit of peace, stability, and security in the Gulf region continue, I look forward to our continued consultation and cooperation.

State Department Statement on Iraq's Legal Obligations Regarding Prisoners of War, January 20, 1991 [3]

The Department of State tonight called in the Iraqi Charge to protest the apparent treatment of members of the United States Armed Forces and other coalition forces held by the Government of Iraq.

In a diplomatic note presented to the Charge, the United States strongly protested Iraq's apparent treatment of U.S. prisoners of war as contrary to the Third Geneva Convention of 1949 relative to the treatment of prisoners of war.

The Department of State reminded Iraq that the mistreatment of POWs is a war crime. The United States demanded full Iraqi compliance with the Convention and requested immediate access for the International Committee of the Red Cross to any prisoners of war held by Iraq.

Interview of Prime Minister Yitzhak Shamir of Israel, January 20, 1991 [4]

Q. You said this morning that in Israel, life must return to normal to the extent possible. Does this mean that the danger from Iraqi missiles has passed, or that we must learn to live with it?

A. No, I did not mean to say that the danger has passed. In my last interview with you I said that the danger is still before us. Since then, we have gone through two days of war, of an ugly war, if there is such thing as a war that is not ugly. I say ugly because this is a war which is not directed at fighting armies; its goals are not to alter borders or impose a certain regime. It has one single goal: to kill and murder as much as possible. We have come through these days, and despite the damage caused, I can say that we have reason to be proud of the way in which the public accepted this trial, overcame and contended with it. Men, women, and children—they all acted with dignity, in an orderly fashion, despite the cruelty of this war. This war is very similar to the war being waged against us by terrorists. Arafat and his ilk, for example. The aim is to murder, especially civilians. It does not matter which civilians, what their age or status. We must face this, and we will. We will contend and overcome. But at the same time, we must lead normal lives, so that the enemy does not think that he is weakening us and ruining our economic infrastructure through attacks on us. We remember cases from history, including recent ones, when entire nations — England during the blitz — faced a barrage of bombs day and night. People went to work and produced and carried on. To a large extent, thanks to that, they overcame. There is no other way for us, either.

Q. Is there still a danger of a chemical attack?

A. I don't know if there is a danger of a chemical attack or not. No one can give convincing answers. There are no assurances. It is true that there is no threat to our existence, a threat of destruction, but someone can get hurt. The more we behave in a more normal way and continue our normal lives, the more strictly we heed civil defense regulations, the fewer casualties we will sustain, and the less damage.

Q. Why has Israel decided not to respond for the time being?

A. There is a certain misunderstanding here . We have not changed our policy. Since the establishment of the state, perhaps even before, Israel has had no other way but to defend itself from attacks forcefully, with intelligence, with courage. This we will do. But to defend ourselves, to fight, does not mean to do so without wisdom and discretion, without evaluating the conditions under which we are operating. We have never been in this type of situation. The enemy is not standing near our borders. We have here a long distance missile war. A large army, that of the U.S. and its allies, stands between us and him. We must take all this into account and act — and we will act — in the most efficient manner and the one most damaging to the enemy, one capable of removing the danger. This is how we will act. It is not a question of ping-pong—you hit me, I'll hit you. The principle of our action has been preserved.

Q. You had three conversations with President Bush. What did you discuss?

A. It's hard to keep track, but they were good conversations . They were very friendly, I would even say heart-to-heart discussions. The President tried to explain to me, and did explain in a fairly convincing way, the situation of the U.S., of the fighting in Iraq; his concern for us, and everything he is doing in order to reinforce that part of the front which relates especially to us; what he expects of Israel; and what we can expect from him. He talked about the consultations he is holding, whom he is consulting with. He suggested sending [Deputy Secretary of State Lawrence] Eagleburger's delegation to Israel again, and described what, in his opinion, the delegation should do, and what we can do with this delegation. He told me about the Patriot missiles that he instructed be sent to us in order to increase our defensive capabilities. We have been talking about the Patriot for a long time. But this latest delivery, which was carried out with such speed, and for which we thank the U.S., came at the initiative of the U.S. He said that he is at my disposal at any time; that we should be in constant touch in order to clarify all the problems. He asked that I relate to Eagleburger as his personal envoy, that I relate to him with full confidence, as he himself

does, and that he is the most reliable channel of communication between us.

Q. Is there any change in the U.S.'s approach to cooperation with Israel in this campaign?

A. These were definitely talks of coordination. This was the third meeting with Eagleburger, and I think that I will be meeting with him tomorrow. These are talks that do reflect the strategic cooperation between us and the U.S., especially with regard to the present conflict, but also with regard to the future.

Statement by Deputy Secretary of State Lawrence S. Eagleburger, Tel Aviv, January 21, 1991 [5]

Last week Iraq launched an unprovoked attack on Israel, using Scud missiles. President Bush expressed the outrage of the United States over this reckless act of terror and aggression, as did leaders of all civilized nations. The President has taken a number of concrete steps to help Israel deal with this threat. These include amongst others:

- the continued devotion by the United States and coalition partners of enormous, persistent military and intelligence assets to the objective of destroying Iraqi Scud missile launchers;
- and, in an unprecedented action, the immediate transfer to Israel of Patriot antimissile units, with their U.S. crews and with PAC II missiles.

This period has been marked by constant and intensive consultations between our two governments. President Bush and Prime Minister Shamir have talked with each other often and intimately during these crucial days.

The United States stands with Israel in defending against Iraqi aggression. The United States is—as it has been for many years—committed to the security of Israel. We recognize and respect the right of every sovereign nation to defend itself, and thus have never questioned Israel's right to respond to attack. We also recognize and respect Israel's desire not to be drawn into this conflict, and greatly admire Israel's restraint in the face of Iraq's deliberate and murderous effort to widen the conflict caused by its aggression against Kuwait.

The President has, at this time of trial for both our nations, sent us to consult with Israeli leaders. My colleagues and I are proud to be here.

Excerpt from President's Press Conference, January 25, 1991 [6]

Q. Mr. President, what can you do about the Iraqi dumping of oil in the Gulf? Is there any way you can offset it?

A. Well, there's a lot of activity going on right now trying to figure out what the best course of action is to clean this mess up, to stop this spill.

Saddam Hussein continues to amaze the world. First, he uses these Scud missiles that have no military value whatsoever. Then, he uses the lives of prisoners of war, parading them and threatening to use them as shields; obviously, they have been brutalized. And now he resorts to enormous environmental damage in terms of turning loose a lot of oil—no military advantage to him whatever in this. It's not going to help him at all.

Q. It won't stop an invasion?

A. Absolutely not. It has nothing to do with that. And so I don't know. I mean, he clearly is outraging the world.

President's Address Before Joint Session of Congress on the State of the Union, January 29, 1991 [7]

Mr. President and Mr. Speaker and Members of the United States Congress:

I come to this House of the people to speak to you and all Americans, certain that we stand at a defining hour. Halfway around the world, we are engaged in a great struggle in the skies and on the seas and sands. We know why we're there: We are Americans, part of something larger than ourselves. For two centuries, we've done the hard work of freedom. And tonight, we lead the world in facing down a threat to decency and humanity.

What is at stake is more than one small country; it is a big idea: a new world order, where diverse nations are drawn together in common cause to achieve the universal aspirations of mankind—peace and security, freedom, and the rule of law. Such is a world worthy of our struggle and worthy of our children's future.

The community of nations has resolutely gathered to condemn and repel lawless aggression. Saddam Hussein's unprovoked invasion—his ruthless, systematic rape of a peaceful neighbor—violated everything the community of nations holds dear. The world has said this aggression would not stand, and it will not stand. Together, we have resisted the trap of appeasement, cynicism, and isolation that gives temptation to tyrants. The world has answered Saddam's invasion with twelve United Nations resolutions, starting with a demand for Iraq's immediate and unconditional withdrawal, and backed up by forces from 28 countries of six continents. With few exceptions, the world now stands as one.

The end of the Cold War has been a victory for all humanity. A year and a half ago, in Germany, I said that our goal was a Europe whole and free. Tonight, Germany is united. Europe has become whole and free, and America's leadership was instrumental in making it possible.

Our relationship to the Soviet Union is important, not only to us but to the world. That relationship has helped to shape these and other historic changes. But like many other nations, we have been deeply concerned by the violence in the Baltics, and we have communicated that concern to the Soviet leadership. The principle that has guided us is simple: Our objective is to help the Baltic peoples achieve their aspirations, not to punish the Soviet Union. In our recent discussions with the Soviet leadership we have been given representations which, if fulfilled, would result in the withdrawal of some Soviet forces, a reopening of dialogue with the Republics, and a move away from violence.

We will watch carefully as the situation develops. And we will maintain our contact with the Soviet leadership to encourage continued commitment to democratization and reform. If it is possible, I want to continue to build a lasting basis for U.S.-Soviet cooperation—for a more peaceful future for all mankind.

The triumph of democratic ideas in Eastern Europe and Latin America and the continuing struggle for freedom elsewhere all around the world all confirm the wisdom of our nation's founders. Tonight, we work to achieve another victory, a victory over tyranny and savage aggression.

We in this union enter the last decade of the 20th century thankful for our blessings, steadfast in our purpose, aware of our difficulties, and responsive to our duties at home and around the world. For two centuries, America has served the world as an inspiring example of freedom and democracy. For generations, America has led the struggle to preserve and extend the blessings of liberty. And today, in a rapidly changing world, American leadership is indispensable. Americans know that leadership brings burdens and sacrifices. But we also know why the hopes of humanity turn to us. We are Americans; we have a unique responsibility to do the hard work of freedom. And when we do, freedom works.

The conviction and courage we see in the Persian Gulf today is simply the American character in action. The indomitable spirit that is contributing to this victory for world peace and justice is the same spirit that gives us the power and the potential to meet our toughest challenges at home. We are resolute and resourceful. If we can selflessly confront the evil for the sake of good in a land so far away, then surely we can make this land all that it should be. If anyone tells you that America's best days are behind her, they're looking the wrong way.

*　　　*　　　*

As Americans, we know that there are times when we must step forward and accept our responsibility to lead the world away from the dark chaos of dictators, toward the brighter promise of a better day. Almost 50 years ago we began a long struggle against aggressive totalitarianism. Now we face another defining hour for America and the world.

There is no one more devoted, more committed to the hard work of freedom than every soldier and sailor, every marine, airman, and coastguardsman, every man and woman now serving in the Persian Gulf. Oh, how they deserve [applause] and what a fitting tribute to them.

You see—what a wonderful, fitting tribute to them. Each of them has volunteered, volunteered to provide for this nation's defense, and now they bravely struggle to earn for America, for the world, and for future generations a just and lasting peace. Our commitment to them must be equal to their commitment to their country. They are truly America's finest.

The war in the Gulf is not a war we wanted. We worked hard to avoid war. For more than five months we—along with the Arab League, the European Community the United Nations—tried every diplomatic avenue. U.N. Secretary-General Perez de Cuellar; Presidents Gorbachev, Mitterrand, Ozal, Mubarak, and Bendjedid; Kings Fahd and Hassan, Prime Ministers Major and Andreotti—just to name a few—all worked for a solution. But time and again, Saddam Hussein flatly rejected the path of diplomacy and peace.

The world well knows how this conflict began and when: It began on August 2d, when Saddam invaded and sacked a small defenseless neighbor. And I am certain of how it will end. So that peace can prevail we will prevail. [Applause] Thank you.

Tonight I am pleased to report that we are on course. Iraq's capacity to sustain war is being destroyed. Our investment, our training, our planning—all are paying off. Time will not be Saddam's salvation.

Our purpose in the Persian Gulf remains constant: to drive Iraq out of Kuwait, to restore Kuwait's legitimate government, and to ensure the stability and security of this critical region.

Let me make clear what I mean by the region's stability and security. We do not seek the destruction of Iraq, its culture, or its people. Rather, we seek an Iraq that uses its great resources not to destroy, not to serve the ambitions of a tyrant, but to build a better life for itself and its neighbors. We seek a Persian Gulf where conflict is no longer the rule, where the strong are neither tempted nor able to intimidate the weak.

Most Americans know instinctively why we are in the Gulf. They know we had to stop Saddam now, not later. They know that this brutal dictator will do anything, will use any weapon, will commit any outrage, no matter how many innocents suffer.

They know we must make sure that control of the world's oil resources does not fall into his hands, only to finance further aggression. They know that we need to build a new, enduring peace, based not on arms races and confrontation but on shared principles and the rule of law.

And we all realize that our responsibility to be the catalyst for peace in the region does not end with the successful conclusion of this war.

Democracy brings the undeniable value of thoughtful dissent, and we've heard some dissenting voices here at home—some, a handful, reckless; most responsible. But the fact that all voices have the right to speak out is one of the reasons we've been united in purpose and principle for 200 years.

Our progress in this great struggle is the result of years of vigilance and a steadfast commitment to a strong defense. Now, with remarkable technological advances like the Patriot missile, we can defend against ballistic missile attacks aimed at innocent civilians.

Looking forward, I have directed that the SDI program be refocused on providing protection from limited ballistic missile strikes, whatever their source. Let us pursue an SDI program that can deal with any future threat to the United States, to our forces overseas, and to our friends and allies.

The quality of American technology, thanks to the American worker, has enabled us to successfully deal with difficult military conditions and help minimize precious loss of life. We have given our men and women the very best. And they deserve it.

We all have a special place in our hearts for the families of our men and women serving in the Gulf. They are represented here tonight by Mrs. Norman Schwarzkopf. We are all very grateful to General Schwarzkopf and to all those serving with him. And I might also recognize one who came with Mrs. Schwarzkopf, Alma Powell, the wife of the distinguished Chairman of the Joint Chiefs. And to the families, let me say our forces in the Gulf will not stay there one day longer than is necessary to complete their mission.

The courage and success of the RAF pilots, of the Kuwaiti, Saudi, French, the Canadians, the Italians, the pilots of Qatar and Bahrain all are proof that for the first time since World War II, the international community is united. The leadership of the United Nations, once only a hoped-for ideal is now confirming its founders' vision.

I am heartened that we are not being asked to bear alone the financial burdens of this struggle. Last year, our friends and allies provided the bulk of the economic costs of Desert Shield. And now, having received commitments of over $40 billion for the first three months of 1991, I am confident they will do no less as we move through Desert Storm.

But the world has to wonder what the dictator of Iraq is thinking. If he thinks that by targeting innocent civilians in Israel and Saudi Arabia, that he will gain advantage he is dead wrong. If he thinks that he will advance his cause through tragic and despicable environmental terrorism, he is dead wrong. And if he thinks that by abusing the coalition prisoners of war he will benefit, he is dead wrong.

We will succeed in the Gulf. And when we do, the world community will have sent an enduring warning to any dictator or despot, present or future, who contemplates outlaw aggression.

The world can, therefore, seize this opportunity to fulfill the long-held promise of a new world order, where brutality will go unrewarded and aggression will meet collective resistance.

Yes, the United States bears a major share of leadership in this effort. Among the nations of the world, only the United States of America has both the moral standing and the means to back it up. We're the only nation on this earth that could assemble the forces of peace. This is the burden of leadership and the strength that has made America the beacon of freedom in a searching world.

This nation has never found glory in war. Our people have never wanted to abandon the blessings of home and work for distant lands and deadly conflict. If we fight in anger, it is only because we have to fight at all. And all of us yearn for a world where we will never have to fight again.

Each of us will measure within ourselves the value of this great struggle. Any cost in lives—any cost—is beyond our power to measure. But the cost of closing our eyes to aggression is beyond mankind's power to imagine. This we do know: Our cause is just; our cause is moral; our cause is right.

Let future generations understand the burden and the blessings of freedom. Let them say we stood where duty required us to stand. Let them know that, together, we affirmed America and the world as a community of conscience.

The winds of change are with us now. The forces of freedom are together, united. We move toward the next century more confident than ever that we have the will at home and abroad to do what must be done—the hard work of freedom.

May God bless the United States of America. Thank you very, very much.

Joint Statement by Secretary of State Baker and Soviet Foreign Minister Alexander Bessmertnykh, January 29, 1991 [8]

In the course of the discussions held in Washington on January 26-29, 1991, U.S.S.R. Minister of Foreign Affairs Alexander Bessmertnykh and U.S. Secretary of State James Baker devoted considerable attention to the situation in the Persian Gulf.

The Ministers reiterated the commitment of their countries to the U.N. Security Council resolutions adopted in connection with Iraq's aggression against Kuwait. They expressed regret that numerous efforts of the United Nations, other international organizations, individual countries, and envoys were all rebuffed by Iraq. The military actions authorized by the United Nations have been provoked by the refusal of the Iraqi leadership to comply with the clear and lawful demands of the international community for withdrawal from Kuwait.

Secretary of State Baker emphasized that the United States and its coalition partners are seeking the liberation of Kuwait, not the destruction of Iraq. He stressed that the United States has no quarrel with the people of Iraq, and poses no threat to Iraq's territorial integrity. Secretary Baker reiterated that the United States is doing its utmost to avoid casualties among the civilian population, and is not interested in expanding the conflict. Minister of Foreign Affairs Bessmertnykh took note of the American position and agreed that Iraq's withdrawal from Kuwait must remain the goal of the international com-

munity. Both sides believe that everything possible should be done to avoid further escalation of the war and expansion of its scale.

The Ministers continue to believe that a cessation of hostilities would be possible if Iraq would make an unequivocal commitment to withdraw from Kuwait. They also believe that such a commitment must be backed by immediate, concrete steps leading to full compliance with the Security Council resolutions.

The Iraqi leadership has to respect the will of the international community. By doing so, it has it within its power to stop the violence and bloodshed.

The Ministers agreed that establishing enduring stability and peace in the region after the conflict, on the basis of effective security arrangements, will be a high priority of our two governments. Working to reduce the risk of war and miscalculation will be essential, particularly because a spiraling arms race in this volatile region can only generate greater violence and extremism. In addition, dealing with the causes of instability and the sources of conflict, including the Arab-Israeli conflict, will be especially important. Indeed, both Ministers agreed that without a meaningful peace process — one which promotes a just peace, security, and real reconciliation for Israel, Arab states, and Palestinians — it will not be possible to deal with the sources of conflict and instability in the region. Both Ministers, therefore, agreed that in the aftermath of the crisis in the Persian Gulf, mutual U.S.-Soviet efforts to promote Arab-Israeli peace and regional stability, in consultation with other parties in the region, will be greatly facilitated and enhanced.

The two Ministers are confident that the United States and the Soviet Union, as demonstrated in various other regional conflicts, can make a substantial contribution to the achievement of a comprehensive settlement in the Middle East.

King Hussein of Jordan Addresses His Nation, February 6, 1991 (Excerpt) [9]

Brother Citizens, Brother Arabs, Brother Muslims, you who uphold your faith and refuse to see your nation

humiliated; you who are truly sincere within yourselves and in your hearts and minds, and in your objectives, ideas and attitudes; you who are concerned for the present as well as the future generations of our nation, I greet every one of you with all affection.

I choose to address you at this very difficult moment, motivated by Arab honor and religious duty. I address you on the eve of the fourth week of this savage and large scale war which was imposed on brotherly Iraq, and which is aimed at Iraq's existence, its role, its progress and its vitality. It is also aimed at Iraq's right to a life of freedom and dignity, and its determination to fulfill its historic, cultural and human role which started in Babylon, Baghdad and Basra, and which contributed to human civilization, scientific progress and culture.

Iraq, fellow Arabs and Muslims, now pays the price in pure and noble blood of belonging to its nation. Iraq had always hastened, without hesitation, to make sacrifices in all the battles which the Arabs fought, or which were forced upon them in defense of Arab land in Palestine, Syria, Egypt and Jordan. Arab blood was always dear to Iraq and shouldn't the blood of Iraqi men, women and children be dear to us?! How shamed will be the Arabs who let Arab blood be split in this unjust war?!

The world has known cruel wars, but never one like this that is waged against Iraq and the lives of which may never happen again. The armies of the biggest and most powerful nations have gathered and unleashed their modern and dangerous weapons on the land, in the sea, and in the sky. These weapons had originally been arrayed by the present international military alliance against an opposing alliance led by another super power. They are all now arrayed against the Baghdad of Haroun al Rashid, the Basra of Islamic studies and poetry, the Kufa of Ali, may God's peace be upon him, the holy Hajaf, Karbala, al Diwaniyeh, Mosul, Kerkouk, and every Iraqi city and village. Fire rains down upon Iraq from airplanes, from battleships, from submarines and rockets, destroying mosques, churches, schools, museums, hospitals, powdered milk factories, residential areas, bedouin tents, electricity generating stations, and water networks. This bombing started from the first hours and took the form of a war that aims to destroy all the achievements of Iraq and return it to primitive life, by using the latest technology of destruction. The first victims of this war were justice, righteousness and peace. Its first casualties were the aspirations of all humanity since the end of the Second World War, hoping that that war would be the last human tragedy, and that man would no longer be killer or victim. All the hopes of our nation and the world community were thwarted the day the land of Iraq was turned into the arena of the third world war.

Brother Citizens, Brother Arabs, Brother Muslims,

The irony of this war is that it is waged under the cloak of international legitimacy, and in the name of the United Nations, which was created to preserve peace, security and justice, and to resolve disputes through dialogue, negotiations and diplomacy. If this is an example of the future role of the United Nations in the new world order, what an ominous future lies before all nations! What international legitimacy will there be to protect the less powerful against the more powerful who seek to subjugate them, humiliate them, kill them, and usurp all their rights that were granted by God and protected by Charter of the United Nations? We now realize fully the real reason why we, the Arabs, were deprived of our right to solve our problems, and why the United Nations was prevented from fulfilling its role, and why the doors were shut against any sincere political attempt to resolve the Gulf crisis. It is claimed that every effort possible was made to solve the crisis during the five months before the war. This is not true. If the effort that was spent in preparing for the war had been devoted to the quest for a peaceful settlement, this disaster would not have taken place. Moreover, the ongoing war, with its destructive outcome, is incompatible with the humanitarian objectives of the United Nations resolutions which were adopted to restore peace and security to the Gulf region.

By contrast the Arab-Israeli conflict remained far from any honest and real attempt to resolve it justly. The Arab Palestinian people and the Arab nation still await the implementation of a single United Nations resolution, which rejects Israeli occupation and calls for an end to it. Twenty-four years have passed since the occupation of the West Bank, Gaza and the Golan Heights, and nine years have passed

since the occupation of south Lebanon, but none of our hopes were fulfilled. Nevertheless, we did not despair of the United Nations. The major powers persisted in assuring us that a peaceful solution was possible. As regards the Gulf crisis, the Arab parties concerned chose from the beginning to reject any political Arab dialogue with Iraq, and to block any attempt that could prevent the internationalization of the crisis and its resolution by directly dealing with all its causes and results. All the good offices of Jordan and others who were concerned for the future of our nation were aborted. Why? Because the real purpose behind this destructive war, as proven by its scope, and as attested to by the declarations of the parties, is to destroy Iraq, and rearrange the area in a manner far more dangerous to our nation's present and future than the Sykes-Picot agreement. This arrangement would put the nation, its aspirations and its resources under direct foreign hegemony and would shred all ties between its parts, thus further weakening and fragmenting it.

The talk about a new world order, whose early feature is the destruction of Iraq, and the persistence of this talk as the war continues, lead us to wonder about the identity of this order and instill in us doubts regarding its nature.

The new world order to which we aspire holds all people equal in their right to freedom, progress and prosperity. It deals with their causes with the same standards and under the same principles, regardless of any consideration or influence. The required new order would not mete out injustice to any one nation. It would not discriminate between nations but draw them together within the framework of mutual respect and fruitful cooperation for the benefit of our planet and all people in it. It must be an order that believes in public freedom and protects private freedoms, respects human rights and strengthens the principles of democracy. It should not deny the Arab people their right to all this.

The nature of the military alliance against Iraq betrays its near and long-term objectives. For when Israel supports this alliance; when two countries, one Arab and other Islamic, both of which have normal political relations with Israel, whose leaders compete for prominence in this alliance and reiterate their desire and enthusiasm for the destruction of Iraq, it becomes

easy to realize that this war is a war against all Arabs and Muslims, not only against Iraq. When Arab and Islamic lands are offered as bases for the allied armies from which to launch attacks to destroy Arab Muslim Iraq, when Arab money is financing this war with unprecedented generosity unknown to us and our Palestinian brothers, while we shoulder our national responsibilities; when this takes place, I say that any Arab or Muslim can realize the magnitude of this crime committed against his religion and his nation. . .

Baker Statement to House Foreign Affairs Committee, February 6, 1991, and Senate Foreign Relations Committee, February 7, 1991 (Excerpt) [10]

The Gulf War

The international coalition has been waging war against Iraq for three weeks now with very clear objectives: to expel Iraq from Kuwait; to restore the legitimate government of Kuwait; and to ensure the stability and security of this critical region. I want to make several observations about the course of the conflict so far.

First, the international coalition has held steadily to its purpose and its course. An outstanding achievement of the current crisis has been the ability of the United Nations to act as its founders intended. Before January 15, a dozen Security Council resolutions guided the United States and other nations as together we waged a concerted diplomatic, political, and economic struggle against Iraqi aggression. We did so because we all share a conviction that this brutal and dangerous dictator must be stopped and stopped now. Since January 16, in actions authorized by Security Council Resolution 678, we have been able to wage war because we are equally convinced that all peaceful opportunities to end Saddam's aggression had been explored and exhausted.

Let me give you some idea of those exhaustive efforts, both by the United States and other nations. In the 166 days between the invasion of Kuwait on August 2, 1990 and the expiration of the U.N. deadline for Iraqi withdrawal on January 15, 1991, I personally held over 200 meetings with foreign dignitaries, conducted 10 diplomatic missions, and travelled over 100,000 miles. For over six and one half hours, I met with the Iraqi Foreign Minister — six and one-half hours in which the Iraqi leadership rejected the very concept of withdrawal from Kuwait, even the mention of withdrawal. As you know, many others also tried — the Arab League, the European Community, the U.N. Secretary-General, Kings, Presidents, and Prime Ministers.

None succeeded because Saddam Hussein rejected each and every one.

Second, the coalition is sharing responsibility for the economic burdens of conflict. Support for U.S. military outlays covers both 1990 commitments for Desert Shield and 1991 commitments for the period of January through March for Desert Shield/Storm. In addition, funds have also been forthcoming to offset the economic costs confronting the front line states in the region.

To date, we have pledges of over $50 billion to support our military efforts and over $14 billion to assist the front line states and others with their economic needs.

Third. our unfolding military strategy fully reflects our political purposes. This is the place to restate, as the President has done so often, that we have no quarrel with the Iraqi people. Our goal is the liberation of Kuwait, not the destruction of Iraq or changes in its borders.

A thoroughly professional and effective military campaign is underway. Our young men and women and the forces of our coalition partners are writing new annals of bravery and skill. But the task is formidable, and no one should underestimate Saddam's military capabilities. Iraq is not a third rate military power. Billions have been diverted from peaceful uses to give this small country the fourth largest army in the world. Iraq has more main battle tanks than the United Kingdom and France combined. It has more combat aircraft than either Germany, France, or the United Kingdom. Ejecting Iraq from Kuwait will not be easy, but, as the President said, "So that peace can prevail, we will prevail."

We are also trying our best to wage a just war in a just way. Our targets are military, and we are doing all we can to minimize civilian casualties and avoid damage to religious and cultural sites. And as General Schwarzkopf has pointed out, the coalition forces are even putting themselves in danger to minimize the risk to innocent lives.

In shocking contrast, Saddam Hussein's conduct of the war has been not unlike his conduct before the war: a relentless assault on the values of civilization. He has launched missiles against Israeli cities and Saudi cities, missiles aimed not at targets of military value but fully intended to massacre civilians. He has abused and paraded prisoners of war and he says he is using them as "human shields" — actions totally in violation of the Geneva Convention. And he has even attacked nature itself, attempting to poison the waters of the Persian Gulf with the petroleum that is the patrimony of the region's economic future.

We have heard, and we take at face value, Saddam's threats to use chemical and biological weapons. We have warned him — and he would be well advised to heed our warning — that we will not tolerate the use of such weapons. Any use of chemical or biological weapons will have the most severe consequences. And we will continue to insist that Iraq fulfill its obligations under the Geneva Convention with respect to coalition POWs.

I think that our conduct of the war is in itself a great strength, the strength that comes from doing the right thing in the right way. And Saddam's continuing brutality redoubles our resolve and the entire coalition's conviction about the rightness of our course. Ending Saddam's aggression will also be a blow to state-sponsored terrorism.

Israel's Restraint

This is also the place to note our deep appreciation and great admiration for the extraordinary restraint of the Government of Israel. Israeli cities have been attacked by Saddam Hussein because part of his strategy has been to consolidate his aggression by turning the Gulf crisis into an Arab-Israeli conflict. Despite its clear right to respond, the Israeli government has acted with restraint and responsibility. The United States has been and will continue to be in close contact at the highest levels with Israel. We have offered and Israel has accepted batteries of Patriot missiles — some with American crews — to defend against Scud attacks. We continue to devote special military efforts to destroying the Scuds and their launchers.

Everyone should know: when we speak about our unshakable commitment to Israeli security, we mean it.

The fourth observation I would make is this: the great international coalition that is now winning the war must also be strong enough to secure the peace. Winston Churchill once observed that "We shall see how absolute is the need of a broad path of international action pursued by many states in common across the years, irrespective of the ebb and flow of national politics." If we are going to redeem the sacrifices now being made by the brave men and women who defend our freedom with their lives, then we must fashion a peace worthy of their struggle. And that can be done if we can hold together in peace the coalition tempered by war.

I believe that when Congress voted the President authority to use force in support of the United Nations resolutions, it voted also for peace—a peace that might prevent such wars in the future. I believe that the American people support our role in the coalition not only to defeat an aggressor but to secure a measure of justice and security for the future.

Post-War Challenges

Mr. Chairman, we and every nation involved in this conflict are thinking about the post-war situation and planning for the future. It would be irresponsible not to do so. At the same time, it would be both premature and unwise for us to lay out a detailed blueprint for the postwar Gulf or, for that matter, the region as a whole.

The war itself and the way it ends will greatly influence both the security of the Gulf and the rest of the area. The deepest passions have been stirred. The military actions now underway necessarily involve many casualties, great hardships, and growing fears for the future. Tough times lie ahead.

We should therefore approach the postwar problems with a due sense of modesty. Respect for the sovereignty of the peoples of the Gulf and Middle East must be uppermost. In any event, modern history has shown that no single nation can long impose its will or remake the Middle East in its own image. After all, that is partly why we are fighting Saddam Hussein.

Yet among all the difficulties we face, one fact stands out: The peoples of the Gulf and indeed the entire

Middle East desperately need peace. I truly believe that there must be a way, working in consultation with all of the affected nations, to set a course that brings greater security for all and enduring peace. We should therefore make every effort not just to heal the Persian Gulf after this war but also to try to heal the rest of the region which needs it so badly.

So I would like to discuss several challenges that I believe we must address in the post war period.

One challenge will be greater security for the Persian Gulf. After two wars in ten years, this vital region needs new and different security arrangements. In our view, there are three basic issues to be resolved: the purposes or principles of the security arrangements; the role of the local states, regional organizations, and the international community; and in the aftermath of the war, the military requirements until local stability is achieved, and thereafter.

I think we would find already a wide measure of agreement on the principles. They would include:

- Deterrence of aggression from any quarter.
- Territorial integrity. There must be respect for existing sovereignty of all states and for the inviolability of borders.
- Peaceful resolution of disputes. Border problems and other disputes that have long histories — and there are many beyond the Iraq-Kuwait example — should be resolved by peaceful means, as prescribed by the U.N. Charter.

These principles must be put into action first and foremost by the local states so that conflicts can be prevented and aggression deterred. We would expect the states of the Gulf and regional organizations such as the Gulf Cooperation Council (GCC) to take the lead in building a reinforcing network of new and strengthened security ties. No regional state should be excluded from these arrangements. Post war Iraq could have an important contribution to play. And so could Iran as a major power in the Gulf.

There is a role, too, for outside nations and the international community, including the United Nations, to encourage such arrangements and to stand behind them.

As for the United States, we have deployed small naval forces in the Persian Gulf ever since the Truman Administration in 1949. We had and continue to have very strong bilateral ties with Saudi Arabia and other local states. And through the years, we have conducted joint exercises with and provided military equipment for our friends in the region. The President has said that we have no intention of maintaining a permanent ground presence on the Arabian Peninsula once Iraq is ejected from Kuwait and the threat recedes.

Before security is assured, however, important questions must be answered. We will be going through an important transitional phase in the immediate aftermath of the war as we try to establish stability. Let me list just a few of the questions that need to be answered.

- Should there be a permanent, locally stationed ground force made up of local troops under U.N. auspices or under regional auspices, such as the GCC?
- How can the international community reinforce deterrence in the Gulf, whether by contributing forces or through other political arrangements, such as resolutions or security commitments?

No one has the answers yet to these and other questions. Some may never be answered. But however we eventually proceed, we will conduct extensive consultations among all of the concerned parties to such arrangements.

A second challenge will surely be regional arms proliferation and control. This includes both conventional weapons and weapons of mass destruction. The terrible fact is that even the conventional arsenals of several Middle Eastern states dwarf those of most European powers. Five Middle Eastern countries have more main battle tanks than the United Kingdom or France. The time has come to try to change the destructive pattern of military competition and proliferation in this region and to reduce arms flows into an area that is already overmilitarized. That suggests that we and others inside and outside the region must consult on how best to address several dimensions of the problem:

- How can we cooperate to constrain Iraq's postwar ability to retain or rebuild its weapons of mass destruction and most destabilizing conventional weapons?
- How can we work with others to encourage steps toward broader regional restraint in the acquisition and use of both conventional armaments and weapons of mass destruction? What role might the kinds of confidence building measures that have lessened conflict in Europe play in the Gulf and the Middle East?
- Finally, what global actions would reinforce steps toward arms control in the Gulf and Middle East? These could include rapid completion of pending international agreements like the Chemical Weapons Convention, as well as much tighter supply restraints on the flow of weapons and dual-use technology into the region. And what implications does that have for arms transfer and sales policies?

A third challenge will be economic reconstruction and recovery. An economic catastrophe has befallen the Gulf and the nations trading with it. Kuwait has been looted and wrecked. Hundreds of thousands of workers have lost jobs and fled. Trade flows and markets have been disrupted.

I am confident that the people of Kuwait will rebuild their country. As we have worked with the Kuwaitis in their moment of trial so we shall look forward to cooperating with them in their hour of recovery.

And no one should forget that for the second time in a decade, the people of Iraq will be recovering from a disastrous conflict. The time of reconstruction and recovery should not be the occasion for vengeful actions against a nation forced to war by a dictator's ambition. The secure and prosperous future everyone hopes to see in the Gulf must include Iraq.

Of necessity, most of the resources for reconstruction will be drawn from the Gulf. Yet, should we not be thinking also of more than reconstruction? It might be possible for a coalition of countries using both local and external resources to transform the outlook for the region — in expanding free trade and investment, in assisting development, and in promoting growth-oriented economic policies which have taken root across the globe.

Any economic effort must have a special place for water development. Well over half the people living in the Middle East draw water from rivers that cross international boundaries or depend on desalination plants. We have all been incensed by Saddam Hussein's deliberate poisoning of the Gulf waters, which could affect a large portion of Saudi Arabia's desalinized drinking water.

Finally, we will want to consult with governments both from the Middle East and from other regions about specific arrangements that might best serve the purposes of region-wide economic cooperation. Such cooperation would surely be helpful in reinforcing our overall objective: reducing one by one the sources of conflict and removing one by one the barriers to security and prosperity throughout the area.

A fourth challenge is to resume the search for a just peace and real reconciliation for Israel, the Arab states, and the Palestinians. By reconciliation, I mean not simply peace as the absence of war, but a peace based on enduring respect, tolerance, and mutual trust. As you know, I personally had devoted considerable effort before the war to facilitating a dialogue between Israel and the Palestinians — an essential part of an overall peace process. Let's not fool ourselves. The course of this crisis has stirred emotions among Israelis and Palestinians that will not yield easily to conciliation. Yet in the aftermath of this war, as in earlier wars, there may be opportunities for peace — if the parties are willing. And if they really are willing, we are committed to working closely with them to fashion a more effective peace process.

The issues to be addressed are of course familiar and more challenging than ever.

- How do you go about reconciling Israelis and Palestinians? What concrete actions can be taken by each side?
- What will be the role of the Arab states in facilitating this process and their own negotiations for peace with Israel?
- How will regional arms control arrangements affect this process?

- What is the best diplomatic vehicle for getting the process underway?

Again, we will be consulting and working very closely with our friends and all parties who have a constructive role to play in settling this conflict.

A fifth and final challenge concerns the United States: we simply must do more to reduce our energy dependence. As the President has stressed, only a comprehensive strategy can achieve our goals. That strategy should involve energy conservation and efficiency, increased development, strengthened stockpiles and reserves, and greater use of alternative fuels. We must bring to this task the same determination we are now bringing to the war itself.

As you can see, Mr. Chairman, some of these elements are political, some are economic, and some of necessity are related to security. That suggests that we should view security not just in military terms but as part and parcel of the broader outlook for the region. We're not going to have lasting peace and well-being without sound economic growth. We're not going to have sound economic growth if nations are threatened or invaded — or if they are squandering precious resources on more and more arms. And surely finding a way for the peoples of the Middle East to work with each other will be crucial if we are to lift our eyes to a better future.

Statement by Soviet President Mikhail Gorbachev, February 9, 1991 (Excerpt) [11]

The developments in the Gulf are taking an ever more alarming and dramatic turn. The war, the largest during the past several decades, is gaining in scope. The number of casualties, including among the civilian population, is growing. Combat operations have already inflicted enormous material damage. Whole countries—first Kuwait, now Iraq, then, perhaps, other countries—are facing the threat of catastrophic destruction. The discharge of an enormous amount of oil into the Gulf can develop into an extremely grave ecological disaster,

The Soviet leadership reiterates its commitment, in principle, to the U.N. Security Council resolutions, which

reflect the will of the majority of countries and the hopes of nations for a new world order that would rule out aggression and infringement on other countries' territory and natural resources.

However, the logic of the military operations and the character of the military actions are creating a threat of going beyond the mandate defined by those resolutions. Provocative attempts to expand the scope of the war, to draw Israel and other countries into it, thus giving the conflict another destructive dimension, the Arab-Israeli one, are also extremely dangerous.

Judging by some statements on a political level and those made by influential mass media organs, attempts are being made to condition people by both sides of the conflict to the idea of a possibility and permissibility of the use of mass destruction weapons. If this happened, the whole of world politics, the world community in general would be shaken to the foundation.

The development of events connected with this war evokes great concern in Soviet society and among the country's leadership, the more so that it is taking place close to the Soviet Union's borders.

White House Statement on Civilian Casualties in Baghdad, February 13, 1991 [12]

Last night, the coalition forces bombed a military command-and-control center in Baghdad that, according to press reports, resulted in a number of civilian casualties.

The loss of civilian lives in time of war is a truly tragic consequence. It saddens everyone to know that innocent people may have died in the course of military conflict. America treats human life as our most precious value. That is why even during this military conflict in which the lives of our service men and women are at risk, we will not target civilian facilities. We will continue to hit only military targets.

The bunker that was attacked last night was a military target, a command-and-control center that fed instructions directly to the Iraqi war machine, painted and camouflaged to avoid detection, and well documented as a military target. We have been systematically attacking these targets since the war began.

We don't know why civilians were at this location. But we do know that Saddam Hussein does not share our value in the sanctity of life. Indeed, he, time and time again, has shown a willingness to sacrifice civilian lives and property that further his war aims.

Civilian hostages were moved in November and December to military sites for use as human shields. POWs reportedly have been placed at military sites. Roving bands of execution squads search out deserters among his own ranks of servicemen. Command-and-control centers in Iraq have been placed op top of schools and public buildings.

Tanks and other artillery have been placed beside private homes and in small villages. And only this morning, we have documentation that two MIG-21s have been parked near the front door of a treasured archeological site which dates back to the 27th century B.C.

His environmental terrorism spreads throughout the Persian Gulf, killing wildlife and threatening human water supplies.

And finally, Saddam Hussein aims his Scud missiles at innocent civilians in Israel and Saudi Arabia. He kills civilians intentionally and with purpose.

Saddam Hussein created this war. He created the military bunkers. And he can bring the war to an end. We urge him once again to save his people and to comply with the U.N. resolutions.

Iraqi Statement Concerning Withdrawal of Troops from Kuwait, February 15, 1991 (Excerpt) [13]

The Revolutionary Command Council has decided to declare the following:

First, Iraq's readiness to deal with Security Council Resolution Number 660 of 1990 with the aim of reaching an honorable and acceptable political solution, including withdrawal. The first step that is required to be implemented as a pledge by Iraq regarding withdrawal will be linked to the following:

A. A total and comprehensive cease-fire on land, air and sea.

B. For the Security Council to decide to abolish from the outset resolutions 661, 662, 664, 665, 666, 667, 669, 670, 674, 677 and 678 and all the effects resulting from all of them, and to abolish all resolutions and measures that were adopted by certain countries against Iraq unilaterally or collectively before 2 August 1990, which were the real reasons for the Gulf crisis, so that things may return to normal as if nothing had happened. Iraq should not receive any negative effects for any reasons.

C. For the United States and the other countries participating in the aggression, and all the countries that sent their forces to the region to withdraw all forces, weapons and equipment which they have brought to the Middle East region before and after 2 August 1990, whether on land, sea, ocean, or the Gulf, including the weapons and equipment that certain countries provided to Israel under the pretext of the crisis in the Gulf, provided that these forces, weapons, and equipment are withdrawn during a period not exceeding one month from the date of cease-fire.

D. Israel must withdraw from Palestine and the Arab territories it is occupying in the Golan [Heights] and southern Lebanon in implementation of the U.N. Security Council and the U.N. General Assembly resolutions. In case Israel fails to do this, the U.N. Security Council should then enforce against Israel the same resolutions it passed against Iraq.

E. Iraq's historical rights on land and at sea should be guaranteed in full in any peaceful solution.

F. The political arrangement to be agreed upon should proceed from the people's will and in accordance with a genuine democratic practice and not on the basis of the rights acquired by the Al-Sabah family [which governs Kuwait]. Accordingly, the nationalist and Islamic forces should primarily participate in the political arrangement to be agreed upon.

Second, the countries that have participated in the aggression and in financing the aggression undertake to reconstruct what the aggression has destroyed in Iraq in accordance with the best specifications regarding all the enterprises and installations that were targeted by the aggression and at their expense. Iraq should not incur any financial expenses in this regard.

Third, all the debts of Iraq and countries of the region—which were harmed by the aggression and which did not take part in the aggression, either directly or indirectly—to the Gulf countries and to the foreign countries that took part in the aggression should be written off.

Besides, relations between the rich nations and poor nations in the region and the world should be based on justice and fairness in such a way that puts the rich nations before clear commitments regarding the realization of development in poor nations, and thus removes their economic sufferings. This should be based on the saying that the poor have a share to claim in the wealth of the rich. Moreover, the duplicitous approach pursued in handling the issues of peoples and nations should be halted, whether this approach is being pursued by the United Nations Security Council or by this or that country.

Fourth, the Gulf states, including Iran, should be given the task of freely drawing up security arrangements in the region and of organizing relations among them without any foreign interference.

Fifth, to declare the Arabian Gulf [Persian Gulf] region a zone free of foreign military bases and from any form of foreign military presence.

Everybody must undertake to observe this.

This is our argument, which we declare before the world, clear and shining against the traitors and their imperialist masters.

Our basic source of confidence, in addition to our reliance on the one and only God, will remain to be our great Iraqi people, our valiant and struggling armed forces, and those who believe in the path that we have chosen in fighting oppression and the oppressors.

Victory will certainly be realized against the oppressors in the coming days, as it had been certain in past times. God is with us. May the despicable be damned.

President's Comments on Iraqi Statement, February 15, 1991 [12]

When I first heard that statement, I must say I was happy that Saddam Hussein had seemed to realize that he must now withdraw unconditionally from Kuwait, in keeping with the relevant U.N. resolutions. Regrettably, the Iraq statement now appears to be a cruel hoax, dashing the hopes of the people in Iraq and, indeed, around the world.

It seems that there was an immediate celebratory atmosphere in Baghdad after this statement, and this reflects, I think, the Iraqi people's desire to see the war end, a war the people of Iraq never sought.

Not only was the Iraq statement full of unacceptable old conditions, but Saddam Hussein has added several new conditions. We've been in touch with members of the coalition, and they recognize there is nothing new here, with the possible exception of recognizing for the first time that Iraq must leave Kuwait.

Let me state once again: They must withdraw without condition. There must be full implementation of all the Security Council resolutions, and there will be no linkage to other problems in the area, and the legitimate rulers of Kuwait must be returned to Kuwait.

Until a massive withdrawal begins, with those Iraqi troops visibly leaving Kuwait, the coalition forces, acting under United Nations Resolution 678, will continue their efforts to force compliance with all the resolutions of the United Nations.

But there's another way for the bloodshed to stop and that is for the Iraqi military and the Iraqi people to take matters into their own hands—to force Saddam Hussein, the dictator, to step aside and to comply with the United Nations resolutions and then rejoin the family of peace-loving nations.

We have no argument with the people of Iraq. Our differences are with Iraq's brutal dictator. And the war, let me just assure you all, is going on schedule. Of course, all of us want to see the war ended soon and with a limited loss of life. And it can, if Saddam Hussein would comply unconditionally with these U.N. resolutions

and do now what he should have done long, long ago.

White House Statement, February 21, 1990 [15]

President Gorbachev called President Bush at 6:47 p.m. this evening to discuss his conversation with Iraqi Foreign Minister Tariq Aziz. President Gorbachev outlined all the major points of a Soviet initiative developed by himself and the Foreign Minister. President Bush thanked President Gorbachev for his intensive and useful efforts, but raised serious concerns about several points in the plan.

President Bush said the United States will consult with its coalition partners on the proposal. We are in the process of examining the Soviet initiative tonight. The United States and its coalition partners continue to prosecute the war. That is the sum and substance of the situation that we have at this point.

Six-Point Soviet Plan for Iraq's Withdrawal, February 22, 1991 [16]

- Iraq agrees to implement, without delay and without conditions, U.N. Security Council Resolution 660, calling for an immediate and unconditional withdrawal of its troops from Kuwait to positions they occupied on August 1, 1991.
- The troop withdrawal would begin the day after a cease-fire in all military operations in the area on land, sea, and in the air.
- The withdrawal would be completed within 21 days, including the withdrawal from Kuwait City within the first four days.
- Immediately after the withdrawal from Kuwait has been completed, the reason for all other U.N. Security Council resolutions would lose their meaning and would be lifted.
- All POWs would be released and repatriated within three days after the cease-fire.
- Control and supervision over the cease-fire and troop withdrawal would be conducted by observers or peacekeeping forces, deter-

mined by the U.N. Security Council.

Statement by the President Setting Deadline to Avoid Ground Action, February 22, 1991 [17]

The United States and its coalition allies are committed to enforcing the United Nations resolutions that call for Saddam Hussein to immediately and unconditionally leave Kuwait. In view of the Soviet initiative, which, very frankly, we appreciate, we want to set forth this morning the specific criteria that will ensure Saddam Hussein complies what the United Nations mandate.

Within the last twenty four hours alone we have heard a defiant, uncompromising address by Saddam Hussein, followed less than ten hours later by a statement in Moscow that on the face of it appears more reasonable. I say on the face of it because the statement promised unconditional Iraqi withdrawal from Kuwait only to set forth a number of conditions. And needless to say, any conditions would be unacceptable to the international coalition and would not be in compliance with the United Nations Security Council Resolution 660's demand for immediate and unconditional withdrawal.

More importantly and more urgently, we learned this morning that Saddam has now launched a scorched-earth policy against Kuwait, anticipating perhaps that he will now be forced to leave. He is wantonly setting fires to and destroying oil wells, the oil tanks, the export terminals and other installations of that small country. Indeed, they're destroying the entire oil production system of Kuwait. At the same time that the Moscow press conference was going on and Iraq's Foreign Minister was talking peace, Saddam Hussein was launching Scud missiles.

After examining the Moscow statement and discussing it with my senior advisors here late last evening and this morning, and after extensive consultation with our coalition partners, I have decided that the time has come to make public with specificity just exactly what is required of Iraq if a ground war is to be avoided.

Most important, the coalition will give Saddam Hussein until noon

Saturday to do what he must do—begin his immediate and unconditional withdrawal from Kuwait. We must hear publicly and authoritatively his acceptance of these terms. The statement to be released, as you will see, does just this and informs Saddam Hussein that he risks subjecting the Iraqi people to further hardship unless the Iraqi Government complies fully with the terms of the statement.

We will put that statement out soon. It will be in considerable detail. And that's all I'll have to say about it right now.

Statement by White House Press Secretary Marlin Fitzwater, February 22, 1991 [18]

The Soviet announcement yesterday represents a serious and useful effort which is appreciated. But major obstacles remain.

The coalition for many months has sought a peaceful resolution of this crisis in keeping with the U.N. resolutions. As President Bush pointed out to President Gorbachev, the steps the Iraqis are considering would constitute a conditional withdrawal, and would also prevent full implementation of relevant U.N. Security Council resolutions.

Also, there is no indication that Iraq is prepared to withdraw immediately.

Full compliance with the Security Council resolutions has been a consistent and necessary demand of the international community. The world must make sure that Iraq has, in fact, renounced its claim to Kuwait and accepted all relevant U.N. Security Council resolutions,

Indeed, only the Security Council can agree to lift sanctions against Iraq, and the world needs to be assured in concrete terms of Iraq's peaceful intentions before such action can be taken.

In a situation where sanctions have been lifted, Saddam Hussein could simply revert to using his oil resources again—not to provide for the well-being of his people, but instead to rearm.

So in a final effort to obtain Iraqi compliance with the will of the international community, the United States, after consulting with the Government of Kuwait and her other coalition partners, declares that a ground campaign will not be initiated against Iraqi forces if prior to noon Saturday, February 23, New York time, Iraq publicly accepts the following terms, and authoritatively communicates that acceptance to the United Nations.

First, Iraq must begin large-scale withdrawal from Kuwait by noon New York time, Saturday February 23. Iraq must complete military withdrawal from Kuwait in one week. Given the fact that Iraq invaded and occupied Kuwait in a matter of hours, anything longer than this, from the initiation of withdrawal, would not meet Resolution 660's requirement of immediacy.

Within the first 48 hours, Iraq must remove all of its forces from Kuwait City and allow for the prompt return of the legitimate Government of Kuwait.

It must withdraw from all prepared defenses along the Saudi-Kuwait and Saudi-Iraq borders, from Bubiyan and Warba Islands, and from Kuwait's Rumalia oil field. Iraq must return all its forces to their positions of August 1 in accordance with Resolution 660.

In cooperation with the International Red Cross, Iraq must release all prisoners of war and third-country civilians being held against their will and return the remains of killed and deceased servicemen.

This action must commence immediately with the initiation of the withdrawal and must be completed within 48 hours.

Iraq must remove all explosives or booby traps, including those on Kuwaiti oil installations, and designate Iraqi military liaison officers to work with Kuwaiti and other coalition forces on the operational details related to Iraq's withdrawal, to include the provision of all data on the location and nature on any land or sea mines.

Iraq must cease combat air fire, aircraft flights over Iraq and Kuwait, except for transport aircraft carrying troops out of Kuwait, and allow coalition aircraft exclusive control over and use of all Kuwaiti airspace.

It must cease all destructive actions against Kuwaiti citizens and property and release all Kuwaiti detainees.

The United States and its coalition partners reiterate that their forces will not attack retreating Iraqi forces, and further will exercise restraint so long as withdrawal proceeds in accordance with the above guidelines and there are no attacks on other countries.

Any breach of these terms will bring an instant and sharp response from coalition forces in accordance with United Nations Security Council Resolution 678.

That's the conclusion of our prepared statement.

Let me add just a couple of points.

First of all, that a copy of this document was provided to Iraqi diplomats here in Washington about noon today. President Bush and Secretary Baker spoke with President Gorbachev for over an hour and fifteen minutes this morning to discuss the situation.

Secretary Baker spoke with Soviet Foreign Ministry officials both yesterday and today, and we have consulted with all of our allies and coalition partners last night or this morning. The coalition remains strong and united.

White House Statement, February 23, 1991 [18]

CENTCOM reports that they have detected no military activity which would indicate any withdrawal of Saddam Hussein from Kuwait. Similarly, there has been no communication between Iraq and the United Nations that would suggest a willingness to withdraw under the conditions of the coalition plan. Iraq continues its scorched-earth policy in Kuwait, setting fire to oil facilities. It's a continuing outrage that Saddam Hussein is still intent upon destroying Kuwait and its people, still intent upon destroying the environment of the Gulf, and still intent upon inflicting the most brutal kind of rule on his own population; yet appears to have no intention of complying with the U.N. resolutions. Indeed, his only response at noon was to launch another Scud missile attack on Israel.

The coalition forces have no alternative but to continue to prosecute the war.

As we indicated last night, the withdrawal proposal the Soviets discussed with Tariq Aziz in Moscow was unacceptable because it did not constitute an unequivocal commitment to an immediate and unconditional withdrawal. Thus, the Iraqi approval of the Soviet proposal is without effect.

President Bush today spoke with Prime Minister Kaifu of Japan, President Ozal of Turkey, and President Gorbachev of the Soviet Union. The phone call from President Gorbachev occurred at 11:15 a.m. and lasted for approximately 28 minutes. President Gorbachev informed the President that he had asked for a U.N. review of his proposal and said that he had talked to Prime Minister Major and President Mitterand about his plan. Both of the allied leaders indicated full support for the coalition withdrawal plan. President Bush thanked President Gorbachev for his extensive efforts and reflected our general disappointment that Saddam Hussein has chosen not to respond positively.

President's Statement to the Nation After Deadline, February 23, 1991 [19]

Yesterday, after conferring with my senior National Security Advisers and following extensive consultations with our coalition partners, Saddam Hussein was given one last chance, set forth in very explicit terms, to do what he should have done six months ago—withdraw from Kuwait without condition or further delay and comply fully with the resolutions passed by the United Nations Security Council.

Regrettably, the noon deadline passed without the agreement of the Government of Iraq to meet demands of United Nations Security Council Resolution 660 as set forth in the specific terms spelled out by the coalition to withdraw unconditionally from Kuwait.

To the contrary, what we have seen is a redoubling of Saddam Hussein's efforts to destroy completely Kuwait and its people. I have therefore directed General Norman Schwartzkopf, in conjunction with coalition forces, to use all forces available, including ground forces, to eject the Iraqi army from Kuwait.

Once again, this was a decision made only after extensive consultations within our coalition partnership. The liberation of Kuwait has now entered a final phase. I have complete confidence in the ability of the coalition

forces swiftly and decisively to accomplish their mission.

Tonight, as this coalition seeks to do what is right and just, I ask only that all of you stop what you were doing and say a prayer for the coalition forces and especially for our men and women in uniform, who at this very moment are risking their lives for their country and all of us. May God bless and protect each and every one of them, and may God bless the United States of America.

Iraqi Announcement of "Withdrawal Order," February 25, 1991 [20]

An official spokesman announces the following:

In the name of God, the almighty, the compassionate, our armed forces have completed their duty of jihad, of rejecting compliance with the logic of evil, force and aggression. They have been engaged in an epic, valiant battle which will be recorded by history in letters of light.

The leadership has stressed its acceptance to withdraw in accordance with U.N. Security Council Resolution 660 when it agreed to the Soviet proposal. On this basis, and in compliance with this decision, orders were issued to the armed forces for an organized withdrawal to the positions in which they were before the 1st of August 1990. This is regarded as practical compliance with Resolution 660.

The spokesman emphasized that our forces, which have proved their fighting and steadfastness ability, will confront any attempt to attack them while implementing the withdrawal order. They will fight with force and courage to make their withdrawal organized and honorable.

The Iraqi News Agency has learned that the Foreign Minister informed the Soviet Ambassador of this decision, which constitutes a compliance with the U.N. Security Council's Resolution 660. The Foreign Minister asked that a message be conveyed from leader President Saddam Hussein and the Revolutionary Command Council to President Gorbachev requesting him to exert efforts at the U.N. Security Council to achieve a cease-fire and put an end to the criminal behavior of the United States and its allies and collaborators.

White House Statement Commenting on Announcement, February 25, 1991 [19]

We continue to prosecute the war. We have heard no reason to change that. And because there is a war on, our first concern must be the safety and security of United States and coalition forces.

We don't know whether this most recent claim about Iraqi withdrawal is genuine. We have no evidence to suggest the Iraqi army is withdrawing. In fact, Iraqi units are continuing to fight. Moreover, we remember when Saddam Hussein's tanks pretended to surrender at Khafji, only to turn and fire. We remember the Scud attacks today, and Saddam's many broken promises of the past. There are at least an additional 22 dead Americans [killed in the Scud missile attack] who offer silent testimony to the intentions of Saddam Hussein.

The statement out of Baghdad today says that Saddam Hussein's forces will fight their way out while retreating. We will not attack unarmed soldiers in retreat, but we will consider retreating combat units as a movement of war.

The only way Saddam Hussein can persuade the coalition of the seriousness of his intentions would be for him personally and publicly to agree to the terms of the proposal we issued on February 22. And because the announcement from Baghdad referred to the Soviet initiative, he must personally and publicly accept explicitly all relevant U.N. Security Council resolutions, including especially U.N. Security Council [Resolution] 662, which calls for Iraqi recision of its purported annexation of Kuwait, and U.N. Security Council Resolution 674, which calls for Iraqi compensation to Kuwait and others.

Excerpt from Speech by Saddam Hussein, February 26, 1991 [21]

As of today our noble armed forces will complete their withdrawal from Kuwait. Today, our fight against aggression and atheism in a thirty-country coalition that has officially waged a U.S.-led war against us, will have lasted from the night of January 16-17 until this moment—two months of legendary showdown.

This showdown is a clear evidence of what God meant it to be: a lesson that would lead the believers to faith, immunity and capability, and to the unfaithful, criminals, traitors, evil and depraved, to abyss, weakness and humiliation.

This is the time of military and nonmilitary showdown, including a military and economic embargo imposed on Iraq from 1990 until God knows when. This showdown has been staged for years with other means. It was a struggle of epic proportions between right and wrong, and we have elaborated on this on another occasion...

The Iraqis will remember and will never forget that on 8/8/90 A.D. [Kuwait] became a meaningful part of Iraq. Legally, constitutionally, and actually it continued to be so until last night, when the withdrawal began, and today we will complete the withdrawal of our forces, God willing.

President's Statement Reacting to Saddam's Withdrawal Announcement, February 26, 1991 [19]

Saddam's most recent speech is an outrage. He is not withdrawing. His defeated forces are retreating. He is trying to claim victory in the midst of a rout. And he is not voluntarily giving up Kuwait.

He is trying to save the remnants of power and control in the Middle East by every means possible. And here too, Saddam will fail.

Saddam is not interested in peace but only to regroup and fight another day. And he does not renounce Iraq's claim to Kuwait. To the contrary, he makes it clear that Iraq continues to claim Kuwait. Nor is there any evidence of remorse for Iraq's aggression or any indication that Saddam is prepared to accept the responsibility for the awful consequences of that aggression.

He still does not accept U.N. Security Council resolutions or the coalition terms of February 22, including the release of our POWs, all POWs, third-country detainees, and an

end to the pathological destruction of Kuwait.

The coalition will therefore continue to prosecute the war with undiminished intensity. As we announced last night, we will not attack unarmed soldiers in retreat. We have no choice but to consider retreating combat units as a threat and respond accordingly. Anything else would risk additional United States and coalition casualties.

The best way to avoid further casualties on both sides is for the Iraqi soldiers to lay down their arms as nearly 30,000 Iraqis already have. It is time for all Iraqi forces in the theater of operations—those occupying Kuwait, those supporting the occupation of Kuwait—to lay down their arms. And that will stop the bloodshed.

Kuwait is liberated. Iraq's army is defeated. Our military objectives are met.

From the beginning of the air operation nearly six weeks ago, I have said that our efforts are on course and on schedule. This morning, I am very pleased to say that coalition efforts are ahead of schedule. The liberation of Kuwait is close at hand.

And let me just add that I share the pride of all the American people in the magnificent, heroic performance of our armed forces. May God bless them and keep them.

Letter from Iraq's Permanent Representative to the United Nations Abdul-Amir Al-Anbari to the President of the Security Council [22]

Upon instruction from my Government I have the honor to inform you that all Iraqi forces have withdrawn from Kuwait at dawn today 27 February 1991 local time. The American and other pro-aggressor forces continued to attack our forces during their withdrawal.

I will appreciate it if your Excellency would have this letter circulated as a document of the Security Council.

Letter from Iraqi Foreign Minister Tariq Aziz to President of Security Council, Transmitted February 27, 1991 (Dated February 28) [22]

I have honor to inform you officially that the Government of Iraq agrees to comply fully with Security Council Resolution 660 (1990) and all the other Security Council resolutions.

You are kindly requested to transmit this letter to the Members of the Security Council and to have it circulated as an official document of the Security Council.

President's Address to Nation Announcing Cease-Fire, February 27, 1991 [19]

Kuwait is liberated. Iraq's army is defeated. Our military objectives are met. Kuwait is once more in the hands of Kuwaitis, in control of their own destiny.

We share in their joy, a joy tempered only by our compassion for their ordeal. Tonight, the Kuwaiti flag once again flies above the capital of a free and sovereign nation, and the American flag flies above our embassy.

Seven months ago, America and the world drew a line in the sand. We declared that the aggression against Kuwait would not stand. And tonight, America and the world have kept their word.

This is not a time of euphoria, certainly not a time to gloat. But it is a time of pride—pride in our troops, pride in our friends who stood with us during the crisis, pride in our nation and the people whose strength and resolve made victory quick, decisive and just.

And soon we will open wide our arms to welcome back home to America our magnificent fighting forces.

No one country can claim this victory as its own, for it's not only a victory for Kuwait but a victory for all the coalition partners.

This is a victory for the United Nations, for all mankind, for the rule of law and what for what is right.

After consulting with Secretary of Defense Cheney, the Chairman of the Joint Chiefs of Staff, General Powell, and our coalition partners, I am pleased to announce that at midnight tonight, Eastern Standard Time, exactly 100 hours since ground operations commenced and six weeks since the start of Operation Desert Storm, all United States and coalition forces will suspend offensive combat operations.

It is up to Iraq whether this suspension on the part of the coalition becomes a permanent cease-fire.

Coalition political and military terms for a formal cease-fire include the following requirements:

- Iraq must release immediately all coalition prisoners of war, third country nationals and the remains of all who have fallen.
- Iraq must release all Kuwaiti detainees.
- Iraq must also inform Kuwaiti authorities of the location and nature of all land and sea mines.
- Iraq must comply fully with all relevant United Nations Security Council resolutions. This includes a rescinding of Iraq's August decision to annex Kuwait and acceptance in principle of Iraq's responsibility to pay compensation for the loss, damage and injury its aggression has caused.

The coalition calls upon the Iraqi Government to designate military commanders to meet within 48 hours with their coalition counterparts at a place in the theater of operations to be specified to arrange for military aspects of the cease-fire.

Further, I have asked Secretary of State Baker to request that the United Nations Security Council meet to formulate the necessary arrangements for the war to be ended.

This suspension of offensive combat operations is contingent upon Iraq's not firing upon any coalition forces and not launching Scud missiles against any other country.

If Iraq violates these terms, coalition forces will be free to resume military operations.

At every opportunity, I have said to the people of Iraq that our quarrel was not with them but instead with their leadership, and above all with Saddam Hussein. This remains the case.

You, the people of Iraq, are not our enemy. We do not seek your destruction. We have treated your POWs with kindness.

Coalition forces fought this war only as a last resort and look forward to the day when Iraq is led by people prepared to live in peace with their neighbors.

We must now begin to look beyond victory in war. We must meet the challenge of securing the peace. In the future, as before, we will consult with our coalition partners. We have already done a good deal of thinking and planning for the postwar period, and Secretary Baker has already begun to consult with our coalition partners on the region's challenges.

There can be, and will be, no solely American answer to all these challenges. But we can assist and support the countries of the region and be a catalyst for peace.

In this spirit, Secretary Baker will go to the region next week to begin a new round of consultations.

This war is now behind us. Ahead of us is the difficult task of securing a potentially historic peace.

Tonight, though, let us be proud of what we have accomplished. Let us give thanks to those who have risked their lives. Let us never forget those who gave their lives. May God bless our valiant military forces and their families, and let us all remember them in our prayers.

Good night, and may God bless the United States of America.

_____

1 Congressional Record, January 12, 1991.
2 Text from Weekly Compilation of Presidential Documents of January 21, 1991.
3 Provided to news media by Department of State spokesman Margaret Tutwiler.
4 Text provided by Embassy of Israel, Washington. The interview was broadcast on Israel TV's "Mabat" evening news program.
5 Released by the United States Information Service, Tel Aviv, January 21, 1991.
6 Text from Weekly Compilation of Presidential Documents of January 28, 1991.
7 Text from Weekly Compilation of Presidential Documents, February 4, 1991.
8 Department of State Document 21, January 29, 1991.
9 Text provided by Embassy of Jordan, Washington.
10 Department of State Document 22, February 6 and 7, 1991.
11 Text provided by Novosti Information Agency, U.S.S.R.
12 Text from Weekly Compilation of Presidential Documents of February 18, 1991.
13 Foreign Broadcast Information Service.
14 Text from Weekly Compilation of Presidential Documents of February 18, 1991. The President was speaking to the American Association for the Advancement of Science in Washington.
15 Released by the Office of the Press Secretary, The White House, February 21, 1991.
16 Official translation from Tass, February 22, 1991.
17 Weekly Compilation of Presidential Documents of February 25, 1991.
18 Released by the Office of the Press Secretary, The White House, February 22, 1991.
19 Weekly Compilation of Presidential Documents of March 4, 1991.
20 Baghdad Radio Announcement, February 25, 1991.
21 Text as carried by the Iraqi [official] News Agency.
22 Text provided by United Nations Information Center, Washington.

Paris Summit:
"A Grand Turn in the Course of History"

Remarks by President Bush to CSCE Summit, November 19, 1990 [1]

Mr. Chairman, this is a glorious day for Europe. This morning I signed for my country an arms control agreement which ends the military confrontation that has cursed this continent for decades. This afternoon we welcome a summit document, a Charter of Paris, which expresses the common aspirations of our society. It is right that we gather here in this magnificent city, a city of civilization, to declare our hopes for the future and to mark a grand turn in the course of history.

Today we do justice to the original framers of the Helsinki Final Act. The goals they set have proven their worth, thanks to the courage of so many who dared not merely to hope but to act. We salute men of courage — Havel and Mazowiecki and Antall,[2] here with us today, and all the other activists—who took Helsinki's goals as solemn commitments and who suffered so that these commitments would be honored. And we salute all those individuals and private groups in the West who showed that the protection of human rights is not just the business of governments; it's everyone's business—nongovernmental organizations, the press, religious leaders, and ordinary citizens.

Their dreams are being realized before our eyes. The new democracies of Central and Eastern Europe have ended decades of repression to rediscover their birthright of freedom. In the Soviet Union, the seeds of democracy and human rights have found new soil. And at long last, the cruel division of Germany has come to an end. A continent frozen in hostility for so long has become a continent of revolutionary change. To assure that this change occurs in a secure framework, we've completed a conventional arms control treaty that transforms the military map of this continent. We are adopting confidence and security building measures that will contribute to lasting peace through

openness. This morning, twenty-two of us signed a solemn undertaking on the nonuse of force.

Agenda for the Future

But today, as old political divisions disappear, other sources of tension—some ancient, some new—are emerging. National disputes persist. Abuses of minority and human rights continue. Where millions had once been denied the freedom to move, now millions feel compelled to move to escape economic or political hardship.

We are witnessing in several countries the ugly resurgence of anti-Semitism and other ethnic, racial, and religious intolerance. Bigotry and hatred have no place in civilized nations. Minorities enrich our societies. Protection of their rights is a prerequisite for stability.

We've established a framework for regular political consultations and institutions to reinforce that framework.

Europe is entering unknown waters the CSCE [Conference on Security and Cooperation in Europe] is ideally suited to help its member states navigate. We have articulated fine standards for national behavior; and now it is our task to bring CSCE down to earth, making it part of everyday politics, building and drawing on its strength to address the new challenges. My government put forward some ideas for the future development of the CSCE earlier this year, and I hope that they contributed to the initiatives that the members of the North Atlantic Alliance announced at our London Summit in July. And I am pleased to see that so many of the ideas discussed there have emerged in a Summit declaration that we will sign this week.

Let me highlight how we think some of these initiatives and others will

help the CSCE put its principles into practice. The declaration we will sign establishes an agenda to guide our work until we meet again in Helsinki. This is important work on issues vital to all of us. The peaceful settlement of disputes, the role of minorities in our societies, the construction of democratic institutions and, most fundamental of all, enhancement of human rights.

We've also agreed that we must deepen the security of our community by extending our talks on conventional forces, expanding the benefits of confidence building measures, and successfully concluding an agreement on "open skies."

New CSCE Institutions

Finally, we recognize that, as Europe mends its wounds, so CSCE can mature. We've established a framework for regular political consultations and institutions to reinforce that framework. The Secretariat, the Office of Free Elections, and the Center for the Prevention of Conflict—let's face it, they are modest, but significant steps towards the new order we all seek. We welcome, too, the call for a new parliamentary dimension in CSCE which can give another voice to the democratic values that we all share.

Two days ago in Prague, I called on Europe and America to work in common cause toward a new commonwealth for freedom based on these shared principles: a belief in the fundamental dignity and rights of the individual, a belief that governments can be empowered only by the people and must answer to them, a belief that individuals should be able to enjoy the fruits of their labor, and a belief that governments and nations must live by a rule of law as a prerequisite for human progress. These are the principles that guide our nations and the CSCE. And yet to secure them in our two continents, they must be secure in the world as a whole.

As we consecrate those principles here today, those same principles are grossly violated in the Persian Gulf. I'd like to quote a sentence from the joint statement issued by President Gorbachev and myself in September at Helsinki. And here's the quote: "Nothing short of complete implementation of the United Nations Security Council resolutions is acceptable."

Well, can there be room for any other view here, in a continent that has suffered so much from aggression and its companion, appeasement? The principles that have given life to CSCE, that have guided our success in Europe have no geographic limits. Our success here can be neither profound nor enduring if the rule of law is shamelessly disregarded elsewhere.

As we entered the Cold War in the spring of 1947, the American Secretary of State, George Marshall—he made an important point which I'd like to quote: "Problems which bear directly on the future of our civilization cannot be disposed of by general talk or vague formulae. They require concrete solutions for definite and extremely complicated questions—questions that have to do with boundaries, with power to prevent military aggression, with people who have bitter memories, with the production and control of things which are essential to the lives of millions of people."

We in the CSCE have come far in the last few months in finding those concrete solutions, and now we should build on this success here, and we should stand on it squarely everywhere.

Remarks by Soviet President Mikhail Gorbachev to CSCE Summit, November 19, 1990 ³

Our meeting is taking place at a turning point between epochs and is in itself a major part of it.

Hardly anyone can today visualize all the consequences of this turning point, extending perhaps for centuries to come. One thing, however, can be said with certainty: this year has been crucial in the outgoing epoch which was marked by two world wars and by nearly half a century of nuclear antagonism between two social systems.

We are entering a world of different dimensions, where common human values mean one and the same to all, where human freedom and welfare, the intrinsic value of human life, must become both the basis for general security and the highest criterion of progress.

Two or three years ago some of the ideas which began to be incorporated in policy seemed illusory to many. Even when a program for this meeting was prepared, there were doubts if we were setting the bar too high and whether the tasks were realistic enough. Now it is clear that such a meeting itself is a sign of profound changes, which for the first time offer a chance of establishing a world order not yet seen before.

Effects of Historic Changes in the Soviet Union

Among the major changes in the world—and it is now generally recognized—is the historic turn in the Soviet Union: from totalitarianism to freedom and democracy, from the command and bureaucratic system to a law-based state and political pluralism, from a state monopoly in the economy to an equality and diversity of ownership forms and market relations, from unitarism to a union of sovereign states based on federation principles.

A breakthrough in relations between the U.S.S.R. and the U.S. was decisive here.

Our country, while remaining great, has become different and will never be the same. We have opened ourselves to the world and the world opened itself to us. This predetermined the radical turn along the main direction of international relations—towards an entirely new perception by states of each other.

A breakthrough in relations between the U.S.S.R. and the U.S. was decisive here. Exactly five years, day for day, separate us from the first Soviet-American summit meeting—with President Reagan in Geneva. This is how far the world has moved since then. The question then was one of stopping the slide towards a nuclear catastrophe. Today the Soviet Union and the U.S. are not adversaries, but partners. The level of their mutual understanding is such that they share a common responsibility for world peace and security.

Rapprochement, openness, and ever closer interconnection and contacts between two such countries, governments and peoples in the interest of themselves and positive changes all over the world are all a contribution to modern civilization. By constantly cooperating in all affairs connected with the formation of a new type of world politics, with the advance towards a new and peaceful period of history, we are discharging our duty to other nations.

Linked with this choice, a general improvement of the international situation saved Europe from serious upheavals, because precisely at this time a number of countries approached the time of revolutionary social and political transformations. But in the Cold War conditions, these transformations could not have been kept within a relatively peaceful framework. This was, moreover, fraught with military confrontation. Tested on that touchstone, the principles of new thinking—freedom of choice, freedom of interstate relations from ideology, the unquestioned equality of all countries without exception, and noninterference in internal affairs—all this passed the examination and provided the world community with such a phenomenon as confidence.

In this context unification of Germany came as a major event of European and world significance. It marked the end of 40 years of separation of a great nation and Europe into two camps. Reconciliation between the peoples of the Soviet Union and united Germany, sealed in a treaty, has become a long term factor for cooperation and confidence in building Europe.

We regard joint declarations and treaties concluded recently by the U.S.S.R. with France, Italy, Spain and Finland as a substantial and inalienable contribution to creating a new international political system in Europe. These documents are of a fundamentally new type and they ultimately deprive confrontation between Eastern and Western Europe of any sense whatever.

Achieving the Helsinki Act's Goals

Gentlemen, the goals proclaimed in the Helsinki Final Act remain invariable guidelines for us. The act arrived ahead of its time. Then it was an attempt to achieve detente within the framework of a system based on Yalta and Potsdam. But the ideological incompatibility of the regimes, which determined interstate relations, made itself felt. The detente of the seventies fell victim to psychological warfare.

Now the ideas proclaimed in Helsinki are assuming tangible form and we can speak of a legally defined European space in the areas of security, human rights, economy, ecology and information as something quite attainable. Similar ideas for a European home, a European confederation and a European peace order are becoming ingredients of a kind of political project upon which we are all expected to work in the nineties.

A united democratic and prosperous Europe, a community and commonwealth not only of nations and states but also of millions of its citizens, has been a dream of great Europeans. Our generation is destined to start turning this dream into irreversible realities of the coming century.

The world around Europe, constantly remembering that Europe is only a part of the world and that its destiny is decided not only within its borders, has likewise begun moving in many respects— with the vector of movement being directed towards a world order that is safer, more civilised and one based not on the strength of arms, but on an equal dialogue and a balance of interests, on a combination of sovereignty and integrity of modern mankind. Concern for survival of the human race is no longer focused solely and almost exclusively on removal of the threat of nuclear war, as has been the case recently. We are getting increasingly concerned with "peaceful" global issues - ecology, power, nutrition, water supplies, social disease, crime, mass poverty, foreign debts, and so on and, what is particularly significant, efforts to achieve international solidarity on all these problems.

Dangers of "Militant Nationalism and Reckless Separatism"

We would, however, yield to unforgivable euphoria if, basing ourselves on that truly great achievement that the threat of a major war in Europe is practically eliminated, we would come to the conclusion that sharp conflict situations are now ruled out here entirely.

There is an active search under way now among countries for a place in the future system. But the search may be fruitful only provided one understands two major realities of the modern world: the inevitable and even fruitful diversity of social-political development, without which the principle of freedom of choice is rendered valueless, and at the same time the need for and importance of partnership, of each other's adaptation, incompatible with nationalist selfishness and provincial isolationism.

Ignoring this diversity, attempting to impose some or other way of life as a condition for cooperation will cause suspicion and mistrust. Militant nationalism and reckless separatism are fraught with conflicts and enmity, with the Balkanization, and worse still, Lebanization of whole regions. Either will hamper the building of a common Europe, and is counterindicated to the European process.

For these reasons it is desirable that immediately after the Paris meeting we should start creating structures and institutions really able to ensure the formation of economic, ecological, and technological groundwork for a new Europe.

This also creates the sole democratic possibility of exercising a beneficial influence on the domestic development of some countries, safeguarding them from dangerous outbursts on the soil of nationalism and separatism. Claims to redivide territory arising from the same source are particularly unacceptable. Here one need only to start acting for a reverse destructive process to flare up, which would throw Europe back to the days already known in its history.

Europe, becoming a voluntary system of states, remains a Europe of motherlands and nations—given mutual openness and multiplicity of their cooperation. Here are two processes balancing each other and giving stability even in the new conditions.

The European space transcends the geographical boundaries from the Atlantic to the Urals. It comprises the Soviet Union, which stretches to the Pacific Coast, the transatlantic U.S. and Canada, inseparably linked with the old world by a common historical destiny. And if the European process gains the required pace, then in the foreseeable future each people and each country—provided they make an appropriate contribution —will dispose of the potential of an unprecedentedly vast community encircling in effect the entire upper part of the globe.

How do we visualize the process of creating European structures, the framework of a European home?

Next Steps to be Taken

It is our desire that the Vienna talks with all 34 countries involved continue without delay and in an active fashion. In addition to making further cuts in the armed forces and changing their structure to fit the level of reasonable sufficiency, the negotiators would engage in charting new and comprehensive confidence building measures. It is advisable that the two negotiating processes of the first round be fused together. It is time to broaden the range of their subjects by covering new types of armaments, primarily naval armaments.

The political and psychological changes which we all note and welcome bring to the fore, quite naturally, the issue of tactical nuclear weapons in Europe. We would be ready for talks on that problem in one-two months. Our suggestion that the parties jointly determine what "minimum deterrence" means and where the limit is beyond which the nuclear deterrence capability turns into an attack capability bears witness to the readiness to embark on a gradual elimination of weapons of that category without overemphasising the existing differences over the role of nuclear weapons in general.

We are ready to continue without delay a meaningful discussion of the "open skies."

European affairs are in the phase of transition. In all probability, it will be necessary to analyse the substance of this period. But our common awareness that it should be peaceful is important. This is why one of the most important results of our meeting is the beginning of the institutionalization of the CSCE process. Among the innovative decisions on creating a three-element mechanism I would like to mention specially the Conflict Prevention Center as a sort of regulator of the military and political situation. We predict that it will have a great future and gradually turn into a kind of "European Security Council" having at its disposal efficient means for extinguishing the flames of any conflict.

The remaining two years before Helsinki-2 will be a test period for the mechanism of European interaction put into operation here, in Paris, and having no precedent in history.

In conditions of the transitional period a common understanding of and accord with regard to the role of the U.S. and the U.S.S.R. is vitally important. No matter what difficulties the Soviet Union is facing today, it will remain a great world and European power, will take the initiative and play a stabilizing role consistent with its enormous potentialities.

Regarding the military alliances — the Warsaw Treaty Organization (WTO) and NATO, the Warsaw Pact countries will evidently make important decisions even before the year is out on transforming the WTO and changing its character.

The question concerning NATO is to be resolved by those who make up the organization. One would like to see, however, the deep-running and evidently irreversible changes in Europe being taken into account in a bolder fashion in its future transformation which has already been announced.

The future of the decisions which we will make here largely depends on the position of and the activities of the existing international structures which have proved their efficiency and accumulated valuable experience which is useful for all. I am referring to the European Communities and the Council of Europe, the European parliamentary institutions, West European and international economic agencies, public, scientific and information centers and, of course, associations of parties and trade unions.

The adaptation to the new conditions on the one hand and the readiness and ability to cooperate with those beyond the boundaries of such organizations on the other is, to be sure, a very difficult problem which requires time. Especially so in view of the enormous difference in the social and economic heritage of the European countries and the crisis-stricken state of many of them. The desire to meet one another halfway—an objective and imperative demand of solidarity—is what we vitally need. It is the message which this forum, convened for the benefit of the whole of Europe, is sending to those who will be involved in European construction along these directions.

The reforms in the U.S.S.R. will create more and more conditions for its closer relations with the EC. I am

also duty bound to say that a sphere of cooperation which we have begun to create in the northern hemisphere is inconceivable without new relations between the U.S.S.R. and Japan.

Strengthening the United Nations

And, finally, the last point, although the matter is not on our agenda. The Iraqi aggression has become a second serious test at the beginning of the road to a new and peaceful period in history. Our unity in condemning it and our shared concern at the outcome of the crisis are also a sign of radical change in the mode of thinking and in the understanding of the goals and means of world politics. Any military attack, wherever it takes place, is now uniting us rather than placing us on the opposite sides of the barricade.

Demanding the aggressor's withdrawal from Kuwait, we are simultaneously upholding the hope of millions for the ability of the international community to settle the worst of conflicts. Otherwise a great deal of what has been achieved in recent years will be imperiled. We are ready to be patient in the quest for a political solution, but we shall be firm and resolute in fulfilling the will of the United Nations.

Ladies and gentlemen, the people of Europe, the U.S.A. and Canada opted for the establishment of a historical entity on the basis of the same principles and goals—those of democracy and humanism. Let me congratulate all of you on this great undertaking and wish everyone every success.

The revival of the spirit of international solidarity which was born in the years of the Second World War and inspired the founders of the United Nations Organization shows promise that the ideas conceived back then will triumph.

It is exceptionally important that the U.N. and its Security Council are at long last acquiring the form which was devised for them from the very outset. Let me greet here our distinguished guest, Mr. Perez de Cuellar, who has done so much for invigorating the role of the U.N.

I would like to express gratitude to the leadership of France and personally to President Francois Mitterrand for the warm welcome, hospitality and the conditions created for our meeting.

Treaty on Conventional Armed Forces in Europe: White House Fact Sheet, November 19, 1990 [4]

Today the twenty-two members of NATO and the Warsaw Pact signed a landmark agreement limiting conventional armed forces in Europe (CFE). The CFE treaty will establish parity in major conventional armaments between East and West in Europe from the Atlantic to the Urals. The treaty will limit the size of Soviet forces to about one third of the total armaments permitted to all the countries in Europe. The treaty includes an unprecedented monitoring regime, including detailed information exchange, on-site inspection, challenge inspection, and monitoring of destruction.

The treaty sets equal ceilings from the Atlantic to the Urals on key armaments essential for conducting surprise attack and initiating large-scale offensive operations. Neither side may have more than:

20,000 tanks
20,000 artillery pieces
30,000 armored combat vehicles (ACV's)
6,800 combat aircraft
2,000 attack helicopters.

To further limit the readiness of armed forces, the treaty sets equal ceilings on equipment that may be with active units. Other ground equipment must be in designated permanent storage sites. The limits for equipment each side may have in active units are:

16,500 tanks
17,000 artillery pieces
27,300 armored combat vehicles (ACV's).

In connection with the CFE treaty, the six members of the Warsaw Pact signed a treaty in Budapest on November 3, 1990, which divides the Warsaw Pact allocation by country. The members of NATO have consulted through NATO mechanisms and have agreed on national entitlements. These national entitlements may be adjusted.

Country Ceilings

The treaty limits the proportion of armaments that can be held by any one country in Europe to about one third of the total for all countries in Europe—the "sufficiency" rule. This provision constrains the size of Soviet forces more than any other in the treaty. These limits are:

  13,300 tanks
  13,700 artillery pieces
  20,000 armored combat vehicles
    (ACV's)
  5,150 combat aircraft
  1,500 attack helicopters.

Regional Arrangements

In addition to limits on the number of armaments in each category on each side, the treaty also includes regional limits to prevent destabilizing force concentrations of ground equipment.

Destruction

Equipment reduced to meet the ceilings must be destroyed or, in a limited number of cases, have its military capability destroyed, allowing the chassis to be used for nonmilitary purposes. After the treaty enters into force, there will be a four-month baseline inspection period. After the four-month baseline period, 25 percent of the destruction must be complete by the end of one year, 60 percent by the end of two years, and all destruction required by the treaty must be complete by the end of three years. Parties have five years to convert limited amounts of equipment.

Large amounts of equipment will be destroyed to meet the obligations of the CFE treaty. The Soviet Union alone will be obliged to destroy thousands of weapons, much more equipment than will be reduced by all the NATO countries combined. NATO will meet its destruction obligations by destroying its oldest equipment. In a process called "cascading," NATO members with newer equipment, including the U.S., have agreed to transfer some of this equipment to allies with older equipment. Cascading will not reduce NATO's destruction obligation. Under the cascading system, no U.S. equipment must be destroyed to meet CFE ceilings. Some 2,000 pieces of U.S. equipment will be transferred to our NATO allies.

Verification

The treaty includes unprecedented provisions for detailed information exchanges, on-site inspections, challenge inspections, and on-site monitoring of destruction. At the initiative of the U.S., NATO has established a system to cooperate in monitoring the treaty. Parties have an unlimited right to monitor the process of destruction.

The CFE treaty is of unlimited duration and will enter into force ten days after all parties have ratified the agreement.

Declaration of the States Parties to the Treaty with Respect to Personnel Strength [4]

In connection with the signature of the Treaty on Conventional Armed Forces in Europe of November 19, 1990, and with a view to the follow-on negotiations referred to in Article XVIII of that Treaty, the States Parties to that Treaty declare that, for the period of these negotiations, they will not increase the total peacetime authorized personnel strength of their conventional armed forces pursuant to the Mandate in the area of application.

Declaration of the States Parties to the Treaty with Respect to Land-Based Naval Aircraft [4]

To promote the implementation of the Treaty on Conventional Armed Forces in Europe, the States Parties to the Treaty undertake the following political commitments outside the framework of the Treaty.

1. No one State will have in the area of application of the treaty more than 400 permanently land-based combat naval aircraft. It is understood that this commitment applies to combat aircraft armed and equipped to engage surface or air targets and excludes types designed as maritime patrol aircraft.

2. The aggregate number of such permanently land-based combat naval aircraft held by either of the two groups of States defined under the terms of the Treaty will not exceed 430.

3. No one State will hold in its naval forces within the area of application any permanently land-based attack helicopters.

4. The limitations provided for in this Declaration will apply beginning 40 months after entry into force of the Treaty on Conventional Armed Forces in Europe.

5. This Declaration will become effective as of entry into force of the Treaty on Conventional Armed Forces in Europe.

Joint Declaration of Twenty-Two States, November 19, 1990 [4]

The Heads of State or Government of Belgium, Bulgaria, Canada, the Czech and Slovak Federal Republic, Denmark, France, Germany, Greece, Hungary, Iceland, Italy, Luxembourg, the Netherlands, Norway, Poland, Portugal, Romania, Spain, Turkey, the Union of Soviet Socialist Republics, the United Kingdom and the United States of America

—greatly welcoming the historic changes in Europe,

—gratified by the growing implementation throughout Europe of a common commitment to pluralist democracy, the rule of law and human rights, which are essential to lasting security on the continent,

—affirming the end of the era of division and confrontation which has lasted for more than four decades, the improvement in relations among their countries and the contribution this makes to the security of all,

—confident that the signature of the Treaty on Conventional Armed Forces in Europe represents a major contribution to the common objective of increased security and stability in Europe, and

—convinced that these developments must form part of a continuing process of cooperation in building the structures of a more united continent,

Issue the following Declaration:

1. The signatories solemnly declare that, in the new era of European relations which is beginning, they are no longer adversaries, will build new partnerships and extend to each other the hand of friendship.

2. They recall their obligations under the Charter of the United

Nations and reaffirm all of their commitments under the Helsinki Final Act. They stress that all of the ten Helsinki Principles are of primary significance and that, accordingly, they will be equally and unreservedly applied, each of them being interpreted taking into account the others. In that context, they affirm their obligation and commitment to refrain from the threat or use of force against the territorial integrity or the political independence of any State, from seeking to change existing borders by threat or use of force, and from acting in any other manner inconsistent with the principles and purposes of those documents. None of their weapons will ever be used except in self-defense or otherwise in accordance with the Charter of the United Nations.

3. They recognize that security is indivisible and that the security of each of their countries is inextricably linked to the security of all the States participating in the Conference on Security and Cooperation in Europe.

4. They undertake to maintain only such military capabilities as are necessary to prevent war and provide for effective defense. They will bear in mind the relationship between military capabilities and doctrines.

5. They reaffirm that every State has the right to be or not to be a party to a treaty of alliance.

6. They note with approval the intensification of political and military contacts among them to promote mutual understanding and confidence. They welcome in this context the positive responses made to recent proposals for new regular diplomatic liaison.

7. They declare their determination to contribute actively to conventional, nuclear and chemical arms control and disarmament agreements which enhance security and stability for all. In particular, they call for the early entry into force of the Treaty on Conventional Armed Forces in Europe and commit themselves to continue the process of strengthening peace in Europe through conventional arms control within the framework of the CSCE. They welcome the prospect of new negotiations between the United States and the Soviet Union on the reduction of their short range nuclear forces.

8. They welcome the contribution that confidence and security building measures [CSBMs] have made to lessening tensions and fully support the further development of such measures. They reaffirm the importance of the "Open Skies" initiative and their determination to bring the negotiations to a successful conclusion as soon as possible.

9. They pledge to work together with the other CSCE participating States to strengthen the CSCE process so that it can make an even greater contribution to security and stability in Europe. They recognize in particular the need to enhance political consultations among CSCE participants and to develop other CSCE mechanisms. They are convinced that the Treaty on Conventional Armed Forces in Europe and agreement on a substantial new set of CSBMs, together with new patterns of cooperation in the framework of the CSCE, will lead to increased security and thus to enduring peace and stability in Europe.

10. They believe that the preceding points reflect the deep longing of their peoples for close cooperation and mutual understanding and declare that they will work steadily for the further development of their relations in accordance with the present Declaration as well as with the principles set forth in the Helsinki Final Act.

The original of this Declaration of which the English, French, German, Italian, Russian and Spanish texts are equally authentic will be transmitted to the Government of France which will retain it in its archives.

The Government of France is requested to transmit the text of the Declaration to the Secretary-General of the United Nations with a view to its circulation to all the members of the organization as an official document of the United Nations, indicating that it is not eligible for registration under Article 102 of the Charter of the United Nations. Each of the signatory States will receive from the Government of France a true copy of this Declaration.

In witness whereof the undersigned High Representatives have subscribed their signatures below.

Charter of Paris for a New Europe, November 21, 1990 [4]

A NEW ERA OF DEMOCRACY, PEACE AND UNITY

We, the Heads of State or Government of the States participating in the Conference on Security and Cooperation in Europe have assembled in Paris at a time of profound change and historic expectations. The era of confrontation and division of Europe has ended. We declare that henceforth our relations will be founded on respect and cooperation.

Europe is liberating itself from the legacy of the past. The courage of men and women, the strength of the will of the peoples and the power of the ideas of the Helsinki Final Act have opened a new era of democracy, peace and unity in Europe.

Ours is a time for fulfilling the hopes and expectations our peoples have cherished for decades: steadfast commitment to democracy based on human rights and fundamental freedoms; prosperity through economic liberty and social justice; and equal security for all our countries.

The Ten Principles of the Final Act will guide us towards this ambitious future, just as they have lighted our way towards better relations for the past fifteen years. Full implementation of all CSCE commitments must form the basis for the initiatives we are now taking to enable our nations to live in accordance with their aspirations.

Human Rights, Democracy and Rule of Law

We undertake to build, consolidate and strengthen democracy as the only system of government of our nations. In this endeavour, we will abide by the following:

Human rights and fundamental freedoms are the birthright of all human beings, are inalienable and are guaranteed by law. Their protection and promotion is the first responsibility of government. Respect for them is an essential safeguard against an over-mighty State. Their observance and full exercise are the foundation of freedom, justice and peace.

Democratic government is based on the will of the people, expressed regularly through free and fair elections. Democracy has as its foundation respect for the human person and the rule of law. Democracy is the best safeguard of freedom of expression, tolerance of all groups of society, and equality of opportunity for each person.

Democracy, with its representative and pluralist character, entails accountability to the electorate, the obligation of public authorities to comply with the law and justice administered impartially. No one will be above the law.

We affirm that, without discrimination, every individual has the right to:

freedom of thought, conscience and religion or belief,
freedom of expression,
freedom of association and peaceful assembly,
freedom of movement;

no one will be:

subject to arbitrary arrest or detention,
subject to torture or other cruel, inhuman or degrading treatment or punishment;

everyone also has the right:

to know and act upon his rights,
to participate in free and fair elections,
to fair and public trial if charged with an offense,
to own property alone or in association and to exercise individual enterprise,
to enjoy his economic, social and cultural rights.

We affirm that the ethnic, cultural, linguistic and religious identity of national minorities will be protected and that persons belonging to national minorities have the right freely to express, preserve and develop that identity without any discrimination and in full equality before the law.

We will ensure that everyone will enjoy recourse to effective remedies, national or international, against any violation of his rights.

Full respect for these precepts is the bedrock on which we will seek to construct the new Europe.

Our States will cooperate and support each other with the aim of making democratic gains irreversible.

Economic Liberty and Responsibility

Economic liberty, social justice and environmental responsibility are indispensable for prosperity.

The free will of the individual, exercised in democracy and protected by the rule of law, forms the necessary basis for successful economic and social development. We will promote economic activity which respects and upholds human dignity.

Freedom and political pluralism are necessary elements in our common objective of developing market economies towards sustainable economic growth, prosperity, social justice, expanding employment and efficient use of economic resources. The success of the transition to market economy by countries making efforts to this effect is important and in the interest of us all. It will enable us to share a higher level of prosperity which is our common objective. We will cooperate to this end.

Preservation of the environment is a shared responsibility of all our nations. While supporting national and regional efforts in this field, we must also look to the pressing need for joint action on a wider scale.

Friendly Relations Among Participating States

Now that a new era is dawning in Europe, we are determined to expand and strengthen friendly relations and cooperation among the States of Europe, the United States of America and Canada, and to promote friendship among our peoples.

To uphold and promote democracy, peace and unity in Europe, we solemnly pledge our full commitment to the Ten Principles of the Helsinki Final Act. We affirm the continuing validity of the Ten Principles and our determination to put them into practice. All the Principles apply equally and unreservedly, each of

them being interpreted taking into account the others. They form the basis for our relations.

In accordance with our obligations under the Charter of the United Nations and commitments under the Helsinki Final Act, we renew our pledge to refrain from the threat or use of force against the territorial integrity or political independence of any State, or from acting in any other manner inconsistent with the principles or purposes of those documents. We recall that noncompliance with obligations under the Charter of the United Nations constitutes a violation of international law.

We reaffirm our commitment to settle disputes by peaceful means. We decide to develop mechanisms for the prevention and resolution of conflicts among the participating States.

With the ending of the division of Europe, we will strive for a new quality in our security relations while fully respecting each other's freedom of choice in that respect. Security is indivisible and the security of every participating State is inseparably linked to that of all the others. We therefore pledge to cooperate in strengthening confidence and security among us and in promoting arms control and disarmament.

We welcome the Joint Declaration of Twenty-Two States on the improvement of their relations.

Our relations will rest on our common adherence to democratic values and to human rights and fundamental freedoms. We are convinced that in order to strengthen peace and security among our States, the advancement of democracy, and respect for and effective exercise of human rights, are indispensable. We reaffirm the equal rights of peoples and their right to self-determination in conformity with the Charter of the United Nations and with the relevant norms of international law, including those relating to territorial integrity of States.

We are determined to enhance political consultation and to widen cooperation to solve economic, social, environmental, cultural and humanitarian problems. This common resolve and our growing interdependence will help to overcome the mistrust of decades, to increase stability and to build a united Europe.

We want Europe to be a source of peace, open to dialogue and to cooperation with other countries, welcoming exchanges and involved in the search for common responses to the challenges of the future.

Security

Friendly relations among us will benefit from the consolidation of democracy and improved security.

We welcome the signature of the Treaty on Conventional Armed Forces in Europe by twenty-two participating States, which will lead to lower levels of armed forces. We endorse the adoption of a substantial new set of Confidence and Security Building Measures which will lead to increased transparency and confidence among all participating States. These are important steps towards enhanced stability and security in Europe.

The unprecedented reduction in armed forces resulting from the Treaty on Conventional Armed Forces in Europe, together with new approaches to security and cooperation within the CSCE process, will lead to a new perception of security in Europe and a new dimension in our relations. In this context we fully recognize the freedom of States to choose their own security arrangements.

Unity

Europe whole and free is calling for a new beginning. We invite our peoples to join in this great endeavour.

We note with great satisfaction the Treaty on the Final Settlement with respect to Germany signed in Moscow on 12 September 1990 and sincerely welcome the fact that the German people have united to become one State in accordance with the principles of the Final Act of the Conference on Security and Cooperation in Europe and in full accord with their neighbors. The establishment of the national unity of Germany is an important contribution to a just and lasting order of peace for a united, democratic Europe aware of its responsibility for stability, peace and cooperation.

The participation of both North American and European States is a fundamental characteristic of the CSCE; it underlies its past achievements and is essential to the future of the CSCE process. An abiding adherence to shared values and our common heritage are the ties which bind us together. With all the rich diversity of

our nations, we are united in our commitment to expand our cooperation in all fields. The challenges confronting us can only be met by common action, cooperation and solidarity.

The CSCE and the World

The destiny of our nations is linked to that of all other nations. We support fully the United Nations and the enhancement of its role in promoting international peace, security and justice. We reaffirm our commitment to the principles and purposes of the United Nations as enshrined in the Charter and condemn all violations of these principles. We recognize with satisfaction the growing role of the United Nations in world affairs and its increasing effectiveness, fostered by the improvement in relations among our States.

Aware of the dire needs of a great part of the world, we commit ourselves to solidarity with all other countries. Therefore, we issue a call from Paris today to all the nations of the world. We stand ready to join with any and all States in common efforts to protect and advance the community of fundamental human values.

GUIDELINES FOR THE FUTURE

Proceeding from our firm commitment to the full implementation of all CSCE principles and provisions, we now resolve to give a new impetus to a balanced and comprehensive development of our cooperation in order to address the needs and aspirations of our peoples.

Human Dimension

We declare our respect for human rights and fundamental freedoms to be irrevocable. We will fully implement and build upon the provisions relating to the human dimension of the CSCE.

Proceeding from the Document of the Copenhagen Meeting of the Conference on the Human Dimension, we will cooperate to strengthen democratic institutions and to promote the application of the rule of law. To that end, we decide to convene a seminar of experts in Oslo from 4 to 15 November 1991.

Determined to foster the rich contribution of national minorities to the life of our societies, we undertake further to improve their situation. We

reaffirm our deep conviction that friendly relations among our peoples, as well as peace, justice, stability and democracy, require that the ethnic, cultural, linguistic and religious identity of national minorities be protected and conditions for the promotion of that identity be created. We declare that questions related to national minorities can only be satisfactorily resolved in a democratic political framework. We further acknowledge that the rights of persons belonging to national minorities must be fully respected as part of universal human rights. Being aware of the urgent need for increased cooperation on, as well as better protection of, national minorities, we decide to convene a meeting of experts on national minorities to be held in Geneva from 1 to 19 July 1991.

We express our determination to combat all forms of racial and ethnic hatred, anti-Semitism, xenophobia and discrimination against anyone as well as persecution on religious and ideological grounds.

In accordance with our CSCE commitments, we stress that free movement and contacts among our citizens as well as the free flow of information and ideas are crucial for the maintenance and development of free societies and flourishing cultures. We welcome increased tourism and visits among our countries.

The human dimension mechanism has proved its usefulness, and we are consequently determined to expand it to include new procedures involving, inter alia, the services of experts or a roster of eminent persons experienced in human rights issues which could be raised under the mechanism. We shall provide, in the context of the mechanism, for individuals to be involved in the protection of their rights. Therefore, we undertake to develop further our commitments in this respect, in particular at the Moscow Meeting of the Conference on the Human Dimension, without prejudice to obligations under existing international instruments to which our States may be parties.

We recognize the important contribution of the Council of Europe to the promotion of human rights and the principles of democracy and the rule of law as well as to the development of cultural cooperation. We welcome moves by several participating States to join the Council of Europe and adhere to its European Convention on Human Rights. We welcome as well the readiness of the Council of Europe to make its experience available to the CSCE.

Security

The changing political and military environment in Europe opens new possibilities for common efforts in the field of military security. We will build on the important achievements attained in the Treaty on Conventional Armed Forces in Europe and in the Negotiations on Confidence and Security Building Measures. We undertake to continue the CSBM negotiations under the same mandate, and to seek to conclude them no later than the Follow-up Meeting of the CSCE to be held in Helsinki in 1992. We also welcome the decision of the participating States concerned to continue the CFE negotiation under the same mandate and to seek to conclude it no later than the Helsinki Follow-up Meeting. Following a period for national preparations, we look forward to a more structured cooperation among all participating States on security matters, and to discussions and consultations among the thirty-four participating States aimed at establishing by 1992, from the conclusion of the Helsinki Follow-up Meeting, new negotiations on disarmament and confidence and security building open to all participating States.

We call for the earliest possible conclusion of the convention on an effectively verifiable, global and comprehensive ban on chemical weapons, and we intend to be original signatories to it.

We reaffirm the importance of the Open Skies initiative and call for the successful conclusion of the negotiations as soon as possible.

Although the threat of conflict in Europe has diminished, other dangers threaten the stability of our societies. We are determined to cooperate in defending democratic institutions against activities which violate the independence, sovereign equality or territorial integrity of the participating States. These include illegal activities involving outside pressure, coercion and subversion.

We unreservedly condemn, as criminal, all acts, methods and practices of terrorism and express our deter-

mination to work for its eradication both bilaterally and through multilateral cooperation. We will also join together in combating illicit trafficking in drugs.

Being aware that an essential complement to the duty of States to refrain from the threat or use of force is the peaceful settlement of disputes, both being essential factors for the maintenance and consolidation of international peace and security, we will not only seek effective ways of preventing, through political means, conflicts which may yet emerge, but also define, in conformity with international law, appropriate mechanisms for the peaceful resolution of any disputes which may arise. Accordingly we undertake to seek new forms of cooperation in this area, in particular a range of methods for the peaceful settlement of disputes, including mandatory third-party involvement. We stress that full use should be made in this context of the opportunity of the Meeting on the Peaceful Settlement of Disputes which will be convened in Valletta at the beginning of 1991. The Council of Ministers for Foreign Affairs will take into account the Report of the Valletta Meeting.

Economic Cooperation

We stress that economic cooperation based on market economy constitutes an essential element of our relations and will be instrumental in the construction of a prosperous and united Europe. Democratic institutions and economic liberty foster economic and social progress, as recognized in the Document of the Bonn Conference on Economic Cooperation, the results of which we strongly support.

We underline that cooperation in the economic field, science and technology is now an important pillar of the CSCE. The participating States should periodically review progress and give new impulses in these fields.

We are convinced that our overall economic cooperation should be expanded, free enterprise encouraged and trade increased and diversified according to GATT rules. We will promote social justice and progress and further the welfare of our peoples. We recognize in this context the importance of effective policies to address the problem of unemployment.

We reaffirm the need to continue to support democratic countries in transition towards the establishment of

market economy and the creation of the basis for self-sustained economic and social growth, as already undertaken by the Group of twenty-four countries. We further underline the necessity of their increased integration, involving the acceptance of disciplines as well as benefits, into the international economic and financial system.

We consider that increased emphasis on economic cooperation within the CSCE process should take into account the interests of developing participating States.

We recall the link between respect for and promotion of human rights and fundamental freedoms and scientific progress. Cooperation in the field of science and technology will play an essential role in economic and social development. Therefore, it must evolve towards a greater sharing of appropriate scientific and technological information and knowledge with a view to overcoming the technological gap which exists among the participating States. We further encourage the participating States to work together in order to develop human potential and the spirit of free enterprise.

We are determined to give the necessary impetus to cooperation among our States in the fields of energy, transport and tourism for economic and social development. We welcome, in particular, practical steps to create optimal conditions for the economic and rational development of energy resources, with due regard for environmental considerations.

We recognize the important role of the European Community in the political and economic development of Europe. International economic organizations such as the United Nations Economic Commission for Europe (ECE), the Bretton Woods Institutions, the Organization for Economic Cooperation and Development (OECD), the European Free Trade Association (EFTA) and the International Chamber of Commerce (ICC) also have a significant task in promoting economic cooperation, which will be further enhanced by the establishment of the European Bank for Reconstruction and Development (EBRD). In order to pursue our objectives, we stress the necessity for effective coordination of the activities of these organizations and emphasize the need to find methods for all our States to take part in these activities.

Environment

We recognize the urgent need to tackle the problems of the environment and the importance of individual and cooperative efforts in this area. We pledge to intensify our endeavours to protect and improve our environment in order to restore and maintain a sound ecological balance in air, water and soil. Therefore, we are determined to make full use of the CSCE as a framework for the formulation of common environmental commitments and objectives, and thus to pursue the work reflected in the Report of the Sofia Meeting on the Protection of the Environment.

We emphasize the significant role of a well-informed society in enabling the public and individuals to take initiatives to improve the environment. To this end, we commit ourselves to promoting public awareness and education on the environment as well as the public reporting of the environmental impact of policies, projects and programs.

We attach priority to the introduction of clean and low-waste technology, being aware of the need to support countries which do not yet have their own means for appropriate measures.

We underline that environmental policies should be supported by appropriate legislative measures and administrative structures to ensure their effective implementation.

We stress the need for new measures providing for the systematic evaluation of compliance with the existing commitments and, moreover, for the development of more ambitious commitments with regard to notification and exchange of information about the state of the environment and potential environmental hazards. We also welcome the creation of the European Environment Agency (EEA).

We welcome the operational activities, problem-oriented studies and policy reviews in various existing international organizations engaged in the protection of the environment, such as the United Nations Environment Program (UNEP), the United Nations Economic Commission for Europe (ECE) and the Organization for Economic Cooperation and Development (OECD). We emphasize the need for strengthening their cooperation and for their efficient coordination.

Culture

We recognize the essential contribution of our common European culture and our shared values in overcoming the division of the continent. Therefore, we underline our attachment to creative freedom and to the protection and promotion of our cultural and spiritual heritage, in all its richness and diversity.

In view of the recent changes in Europe, we stress the increased importance of the Cracow Symposium and we look forward to its consideration of guidelines for intensified cooperation in the field of culture. We invite the Council of Europe to contribute to this Symposium.

In order to promote greater familiarity amongst our peoples, we favor the establishment of cultural centers in cities of other participating States as well as increased cooperation in the audiovisual field and wider exchange in music, theatre, literature and the arts.

We resolve to make special efforts in our national policies to promote better understanding, in particular among young people, through cultural exchanges, cooperation in all fields of education and, more specifically, through teaching and training in the languages of other participating States. We intend to consider first results of this action at the Helsinki Follow-up Meeting in 1992.

Migrant Workers

We recognize that the issues of migrant workers and their families legally residing in host countries have economic, cultural and social aspects as well as their human dimension. We reaffirm that the protection and promotion of their rights, as well as the implementation of relevant international obligations, is our common concern.

Mediterranean

We consider that the fundamental political changes that have occurred in Europe have a positive relevance to the Mediterranean region. Thus, we will continue efforts to strengthen security and cooperation in the Mediterranean as an important factor for stability in Europe. We welcome the Report of the Palma de Mallorca Meeting on the Mediterranean, the results of which we all support.

We are concerned with the continuing tensions in the region, and renew our determination to intensify efforts towards finding just, viable and lasting solutions, through peaceful means, to outstanding crucial problems, based on respect for the principles of the Final Act.

We wish to promote favorable conditions for a harmonious development and diversification of relations with the nonparticipating Mediterranean States. Enhanced cooperation with these States will be pursued with the aim of promoting economic and social development and thereby enhancing stability in the region. To this end, we will strive together with these countries towards a substantial narrowing of the prosperity gap between Europe and its Mediterranean neighbours.

Nongovernmental Organizations

We recall the major role that nongovernmental organizations, religious and other groups and individuals have played in the achievement of the objectives of the CSCE and will further facilitate their activities for the implementation of the CSCE commitments by the participating States. These organizations, groups and individuals must be involved in an appropriate way in the activities and new structures of the CSCE in order to fulfill their important tasks.

NEW STRUCTURES AND INSTITUTIONS OF THE CSCE PROCESS

Our common efforts to consolidate respect for human rights, democracy and the rule of law, to strengthen peace and to promote unity in Europe require a new quality of political dialogue and cooperation and thus development of the structures of the CSCE.

The intensification of our consultations at all levels is of prime importance in shaping our future relations. To this end, we decide on the following:

We, the Heads of State or Government, shall meet next time in Helsinki on the occasion of the CSCE Follow-up Meeting 1992. Thereafter, we will meet on the occasion of subsequent follow-up meetings.

Our Ministers for Foreign Affairs will meet, as a Council, regularly and at least once a year. These meetings will provide the central forum for political consultations within the CSCE process. The Council will consider issues relevant to the Conference on Security and Cooperation in Europe and take appropriate decisions.

The first meeting of the Council will take place in Berlin.

A Committee of Senior Officials will prepare the meetings of the Council and carry out its decisions. The Committee will review current issues and may take appropriate decisions, including in the form of recommendations to the Council.

Additional meetings of the representatives of the participating States may be agreed upon to discuss questions of urgent concern.

The Council will examine the development of provisions for convening meetings of the Committee of Senior Officials in emergency situations.

Meetings of other Ministers may also be agreed by the participating States.

In order to provide administrative support for these consultations we establish a Secretariat in Prague.

Follow-up meetings of the participating States will be held, as a rule, every two years to allow the participating States to take stock of developments, review the implementation of their commitments and consider further steps in the CSCE process.

We decide to create a Conflict Prevention Center in Vienna to assist the Council in reducing the risk of conflict.

We decide to establish an Office for Free Elections in Warsaw to facilitate contacts and the exchange of information on elections within participating States.

Recognizing the important role parliamentarians can play in the CSCE process, we call for greater parliamentary involvement in the CSCE, in particular through the creation of a CSCE parliamentary assembly, involving members of parliaments from all participating States. To this end, we urge that contacts be pursued at parliamentary level to discuss the field of activities, working methods and rules of procedure of such a CSCE parliamentary structure, drawing on existing experience and work already undertaken in this field.

We ask our Ministers for Foreign Affairs to review this matter on the occasion of their first meeting as a Council.

Procedural and organizational modalities relating to certain provisions contained in the Charter of Paris for a New Europe are set out in the Supplementary Document which is adopted together with the Charter of Paris.

We entrust to the Council the further steps which may be required to ensure the implementation of decisions contained in the present document, as well as in the Supplementary Document, and to consider further efforts for the strengthening of security and cooperation in Europe. The Council may adopt any amendment to the supplementary document which it may deem appropriate.

The original of the Charter of Paris for a New Europe, drawn up in English, French, German, Italian, Russian and Spanish, will be transmitted to the Government of the French Republic, which will retain it in its archives. Each of the participating States will receive from the Government of the French Republic a true copy of the Charter of Paris.

The text of the Charter of Paris will be published in each participating State, which will disseminate it and make it known as widely as possible.

The Government of the French Republic is requested to transmit to the Secretary-General of the United Nations the text of the Charter of Paris for a New Europe, which is not eligible for registration under Article 102 of the Charter of the United Nations, with a view to its circulation to all the members of the Organization as an official document of the United Nations.

The Government of the French Republic is also requested to transmit the text of the Charter of Paris to all the other international organizations mentioned in the text.

Wherefore, we, the undersigned High Representatives of the participating States, mindful of the high political significance we attach to the results of the Summit Meeting, and declaring our determination to act in accordance with the provisions we have adopted, have subscribed our signatures below.

---

1 Text from Weekly Compilation of Presidential Documents of November 26, 1990. The quotation in the section heading is from the President's remarks.

2 President Vaclav Havel of Czechoslovakia, Prime Minister Taduesz Mazowiecki of Poland, and Prime Minister Jozsef Antall of Hungary.

3 Text provided by Novosti Information Agency, U.S.S.R.

4 Text from Weekly Compilation of Presidential Documents of November 26, 1990.

French President Mitterand Evaluates Paris Summit Results

Press Conference of French President Francois Mitterand following CSCE Summit, November 21, 1990 (Excerpts). [1]

The CSCE, the Conference on Security and Cooperation in Europe, brought together thirty-four countries of which thirty-two are European. The only one missing was Albania, and even so she had a sort of observer status. As had been planned, the United States of America and Canada were also both present and joined in the discussion. So thirty-four countries took part in the sessions and discussed on the basis of an extremely thorough preparation that had gone on for months and had enabled practically all the obstacles to be removed, not without difficulty as you can imagine.

Let me give you an idea of what this conference represents and above all its success: the approval the thirty-four gave to a series of agreements, treaties that I am going to take the liberty of listing. We began by signing the Treaty on Conventional Forces in Europe, on their reduction, the reduction of the conventional forces agreed by the sixteen member states of the Atlantic Alliance and six Warsaw Pact States. We shall go into the details in a moment.

So there was the signature of this treaty on the reduction of conventional weapons and that of a joint declaration of the twenty-two States directly involved solemnly proclaiming that they no longer considered themselves adversaries. Just think: the Atlantic Pact and Warsaw Pact—just think about everything that went through our minds, everything we have experienced, those who are old enough to have lived through that whole era, everything you have written on that latent conflict known as the Cold War that could at any moment have erupted into a hot one. This had followed wars that had been so hot that they had developed into two world conflicts that had led to Europe's separation into several zones of influence. Yalta has been brought to a close today in Paris.

That's the distance that's been covered. If a more subtle analysis is wanted one might say that a state of in-

security had been created in Europe, to simplify things, starting with the advent of Hitler in Germany, or to be clearer still starting with the Anschluss and Munich, then the war. Since that time Europe has never known any rest—not that we intend to rest from now onwards—but the threat was there, after the atrocious conflict that wounded all our countries and so many of our families. All this has been resolved in Paris over the last few days and this morning with the Treaty on the Reduction of Conventional Forces and the Joint Declaration of the twenty-two member States of the two alliances. Let's not talk any more about one bloc being against the other. All peace-lovers, who know what this represents, will know, even if they have not often been told, that we are genuinely entering a new era, when peace in Europe appears certain, the risks seem to be disappearing and dialogue is taking precedence over confrontation.

For the first time, an agreement of this type has been achieved without victor or vanquished and without a share-out of spoils. We have not wound up a war, we have founded a genuine understanding.

At the end of the Summit, the thirty-four, adopted, signed this morning what we have called the Paris Charter for a New Europe, which has three parts: the announcement of a New Era of Democracy, Peace and Unity, a series of considerations on the Guidelines for the Future and New Structures and Institutions. We shall very probably talk about this during this meeting.

We also expressed the wish, as I myself had in my opening speech since I was chairing this conference on France's behalf, that what is known as the CSCE method or process may serve as an example—I'm not saying "be extended to", that's not the same thing—to other world regions which would do

well to start discussing the reduction of their own arms and begin organizing regular meetings so that countries which are still antagonistic towards each other may build the foundations necessary for their peace, which is conducive to that of the world.

Q. The Western countries wanted all the nations in Europe to be independent, they are now concerned about the rise in nationalism. The Western countries wanted the borders to open, they are now concerned about the possibility of influxes of new immigrants. Are we not in the process of changing, exchanging an unfair order for potentially dangerous disorders?

A. Life is dangerous, international life is not a bed of roses, interests still clash, ambitions too, human nature is not always conducive to harmony and conciliation even in personal relations, so don't go and imagine that today has finally seen the birth of a world which has at last become that dreamt of by philosophers, a sort of new-found paradise. But as far as Europe is concerned we have just brought to an end the tragic situation we have experienced in war or in fear and dread of it, with all that implies in the way of grief, despair, anguish, deaths, all those families torn apart. Although the period of peace that is opening entails risks, I myself have said we must not let yesterday's bloody rivalries give way to a sort of two-speed Europe made up of rich countries enjoying their prosperity and countries lagging behind and suffering from indifference.

It is imperative that we now complete the measures we have taken by working in a spirit of active solidarity to harmonize living standards. We are going to work on this. There is obviously the problem which must not be ignored. It is sometimes good to be pessimistic, it stops us being dozy and complacent. This diplomatic meeting is unprecedented. For the first time an agreement of this type has been achieved without victor or vanquished and without a share-out of spoils. We have not wound up a war, we have founded a genuine understanding. Everyone has played a part, the members of the pacts, military blocs, neutrals, nonaligned, everyone...

Moreover, by playing her part like the others, the Soviet Union, who representing one of the two great powers heading one of the two blocs has just, in my view, anchored herself very firmly and on a long term basis to the European continent.

Q. A question on the Baltic countries. Can't one say, at the end of the CSCE, that the Baltic countries have been, if not the Paris Conference's great losers, at least its forgotten ones—and how do you personally see their destiny in this new Europe whose foundations have been laid today?

A. How can you say that? The Baltic countries were absent because they are still not member states of the United Nations and not recognized as such by international society. I can speak all the more freely as France is one of the countries which is continuing to recognize the sovereignty of the rights of the Baltic countries whose abolition by conquest, by either the Germans or the Russians, we have never recognized. You know that Lithuania entrusted her gold to us, she did so to other countries as well, but especially to us. The other countries either returned the part they held to the Soviet Union or did I know not what with it. France held on to everything in order to be able to return it to Lithuania. That shows you that our attitude is beyond reproach, but our position with respect to the Baltic countries, that they are sovereign states, is not currently that recognized either in Europe or the United Nations.

That's the reality. We pressed our point because at the Paris Summit Preparatory Committee in Vienna it had been agreed that the Baltic States would be invited by the Executive Secretary as "distinguished guests." That seemed to me a reasonable solution, but there was opposition. In particular, the Soviet Union considered that in the current state of her negotiations and talks with, among others, the Baltic countries, it had not been decided that they had become sovereign states and there had been no severance of their ties with the Soviet Union. This conference could but note international law as it stands today. Invitations could be issued only to all the sovereign states. We could not invite the others. So we did our best to deal in a friendly and very correct way with the three Baltic countries' envoys without being able to let them into the conference room.

There are today a great many regions, I say regions because I don't know what to call them. As regards the Baltic countries, they are countries and, in our eyes, states seeking to obtain their right to sovereignty. They still need to be supported and to convince the states in which they are inserted in order to achieve this progress in international law. That is not yet their situation today, even though I regret it, I note it. The fact that France was in the chair does not mean she could decide for all the others.

Q. What's your feeling today?

A. I am very happy for Europe. I feel I have experienced with all the other European countries a very great moment in our joint history. It's an unprecedented event giving cause for great hopes while knowing of course that there will always be obstacles. So we shall have to have courage, a spirit of initiative, a will for peace and then what has been undertaken today will succeed. We have taken a great step forward. The next summit of Heads of State and Government will be in Helsinki... There will be an annual meeting of the Ministers of Foreign Affairs, with the next one in Berlin. There will be a Committee of Senior Civil Servants. There will be a Permanent Secretariat in Prague, and a Conflict Prevention Center in Vienna. There will be an Office for Free Elections in Warsaw which will verify the exercise of democracy. There will be, there is agreement on the principle, a Parliamentary Assembly. So all this has been agreed in order to give structures to what just three days ago was only a hope. So I am very happy for Europe. I am very confident that peace will prevail and am very pleased about this effort that so many countries have made to take the same road and share the same values.

---

1 Text provided by the Embassy of France, Washington.

Update on the Sudan and Liberia Crises

by Herman J. Cohen

Statement before the Subcommittee on African Affairs of the Senate Foreign Relations Committee, November 27, 1990. Mr. Cohen is Assistant Secretary of State for African Affairs. [1]

It is a pleasure to be here this morning to discuss Sudan and Liberia with you. The situations in both these countries are tragic because of the needless and massive loss of human life involved. Many of those who have survived have fled their homelands—refugees from hunger and atrocity. I will address events in Sudan first, then turn to Liberia.

The Food Crisis in Sudan

Events in the Middle East and stories of an impending food shortage have focused attention on Sudan recently. I would like to discuss first the food crisis, since it will have an immense human impact. This is a matter of extreme concern for us. As you know, we brought our Ambassador to Sudan, James Cheek, back to Washington in September to discuss this very issue.

Sudan's rainy season has now ended and the main harvest is underway. It became apparent in mid-August that this year's rains were failing badly over many areas of the country. As a result, the harvest will be substantially below normal. The precise extent of the deficit cannot be stated until the harvest is finished. Rough estimates are that the harvest will be at least 500,000 tons—and perhaps as much as 1 million tons—below normal. At that upper limit, 8-9 million people across Sudan would be at risk. This would include the 3 million people displaced by the civil war and currently fed by the U.N.-sponsored Operation Lifeline Sudan (OLS) relief effort, as well as some 400,000 refugees receiving international assistance.

The United States, the other donors, and the U.N., have raised this issue with the Government of Sudan. We have told the Government of Sudan, in the most forceful terms, that a major emergency is pending in Sudan, that it can be handled only by a coordinated international relief effort, and that Sudan must request such an effort. Our Ambassador to Sudan has raised this directly with General [Omar] Al-Bashir, and we have raised it with numerous other Sudanese Government officials.

The needed relief program will not be possible unless the Government of Sudan agrees to such a program and takes the practical steps to facilitate it.

The Sudanese Government apparently is aware that there is a problem, but has downplayed its magnitude. The Government of Sudan has requested a food assistance program from the United States for next year at the level of $150 million ($100 million Title I/loan and $50 million Title II/grant). This would be channeled through the Government for distribution or sale. What the Government has not done is to request a food relief program, which would involve the donors, the U.N., and various nongovernmental organizations that would get the food to elements of the population most in need. Our estimate is that if 1 million tons of food are needed, 300,000 tons could be moved through the relief network to reach those most in need, and the remaining 700,000 tons could be moved through the normal Sudanese commercial distribution network. A relief program will be necessary to prevent widespread starvation in Sudan next year.

The United States is not waiting, however, but has begun planning to deal with the emergency. As I said, we have told the Government of Sudan what it must do to energize an international response; we have been in contact with other donors and the U.N.; and we are prepared to supply up to 100,000 tons of relief food, plus additional food for commercial distribution, subject to budgetary limitations. What I must emphasize, however, is that the needed relief program will not be possible unless the Government of Sudan agrees to such a program and takes the practical steps to facilitate it. I know that you are familiar with the history of Operation Lifeline Sudan, which has managed, with great difficulty and at great expense, to move relief food into southern Sudan. Khartoum's attitude toward OLS has ranged from ambiguity to outright hostility. The Government of Sudan has harassed nongovernmental organizations, interfered with relief flights, and—in September and again this month—bombed a number of relief sites in southern Sudan. The Government of Sudan must do better in 1991. If it does not, we will not be able to move the amounts of food needed. We will, of course, also need SPLA [Sudanese Peoples' Liberation Army] cooperation.

As you know, OLS moves a substantial amount of food into southern Sudan from Kenya and Uganda. We intend to continue to move food in this fashion, and to increase the amount, but it cannot be a substitute for a nationwide program. At the most, cross-border food could reach perhaps a quarter of those in need. In addition, logistical difficulties will put a cap on the amount of food that could be moved in this way.

Sudan and the Persian Gulf Crisis

Let me turn next to the impact on Sudan of the Middle East crisis. The Omar Al-Bashir government has had friendly relations with Iraq since it came into power in June 1989. Iraq became one of Sudan's principal military suppliers shortly after the coup. As Sudan's traditional sources of military assistance dried up, the Iraqi connection became even more important. We believe it was this military assistance relationship which led Sudan to its current ambiguous stance on the Iraq/Kuwait issue.

To be specific, Sudan has refused to condemn Iraq for its occupation of Kuwait. Sudan insists on characterizing the issue as solely an intra-Arab dispute, which should be settled by the Arab states without outside interference, and has stated that outside forces have no legitimate role in the Gulf. Sudan refused to go along with the Cairo Arab League resolution condemning Iraq. Sudan has stated, however, that Iraqi troops should leave Kuwait and the legitimate Kuwaiti government should be restored. Sudan endorsed, after a period of time, the Security Council resolutions and promised to obey them. Sudan has stated that it believes its policy of not condemning Iraq will place it in a position of mediating between the two sides. In pursuit of this goal, Sudanese President Al-Bashir has engaged in some shuttle diplomacy, flying between Baghdad, Amman, and other Middle Eastern capitals without any discernible results.

Press reports that Sudan has engaged in sanction-busting, and that Iraq has stationed troops, fighters, and missiles in Sudan are—to the best of our knowledge—unsubstantiated.

The United States has impressed upon the government of Sudan, both in Khartoum and in Washington, that we consider its stance on Iraq unhelpful. We have told Sudan that it should line up firmly with the world community in opposition to Iraqi aggression. Unfortunately, it has not done so.

Sudan's stance has gravely affected its relations with other Middle Eastern countries—particularly its traditional friends, Egypt and Saudi Arabia. These countries have made it clear that they, just as we, consider Sudan's position and its explanations for that position unsatisfactory. Egyptian President Mubarak recently stated publicly that if Iraqi missiles were stationed in Sudan, Egypt would take action against them.

I would like to emphasize that Sudan's position on the Iraq/Kuwait crisis does not affect in any way our decisions on the provision of relief food to Sudan. This food goes to feed hungry people in Sudan—not to the Government. We are not using food as a weapon.

Sudanese Domestic Politics

There has been little improvement in the domestic political situation in Sudan. The Bashir government is narrowly based, drawing support only from a segment of the military and the Islamic fundamentalist National Islamic Front (NIF). The NIF has over time assumed a greater role in the government, and NIF appointees now fill numerous key positions in the bureaucracy. This has led to greater opposition from other political forces within Sudan.

A government-sponsored conference on Sudan's future political system has just ended in Khartoum. The conference rejected both one party dictatorship and multiparty democracy in favor of a system similar to the current set-up of local "popular committees." It is not clear how or when this system will be implemented. It does seem clear that without a settlement of the civil war and the participation of the SPLA, there can be no final decision of Sudan's future political system. General Al-Bashir, for his part, has stated that he does not intend to return Sudan to a multiparty democracy. All political parties remain banned in Sudan.

The human rights situation has not improved in any significant way. Sudanese citizens are still subject to detention without charge by the security forces, and we estimate there are currently 200-300 political prisoners. Some prisoners are occasionally released, but new ones replace them. Perhaps the only hopeful sign is that physical and psychological abuse of detainees has decreased. Reports of torture—common earlier in the year— are now rare. But many detainees are still held in sub-standard conditions in isolated areas and do not receive proper medical care.

We have told the Government of Sudan numerous times that the human rights situation there is unacceptable and must be improved. In particular, we have said that all detainees should be either charged or released, that they should be treated humanely, and that if charged, they should receive prompt and fair judicial process.

Potential opponents of the Government have been intimidated by the regime's harsh measures against dissent, including the execution in April of a number of military officers who took part in a coup attempt. In September, however, five former Sudanese army generals, including the chief of staff under the Sadiq Al-Mahdi government, announced that they were forming an opposition alliance with the SPLA. It is not yet clear whether they have any significant following, however.

The U.S. Government has been engaged in a dialogue with both the Government of Sudan and the rebel SPLA on restarting the peace process. Unfortunately, there has been little progress. We have suggested to both sides that a military disengagement and partial withdrawal followed by political

talks could be a fruitful procedure. Unfortunately, the two sides were unable to agree on the parameters of a disengagement/withdrawal. On the political side, they disagree on who should participate in political talks. The Government insists that it and the SPLA only should take part. The SPLA, on the other hand, insists that other Sudanese political forces—the banned political parties, the trade unions, etc.—should also participate.

In truth, we have seen little evidence that either side is willing to make the difficult concessions that will be necessary to make peace possible.

It is obvious from what I have said that we and the Government of Sudan have differences on many issues. Our influence in Khartoum has obviously diminished, particularly as our once substantial assistance program has wound down. But we do discuss issues with Khartoum and look for ways to move forward where we can. Our immediate interests in Sudan are peace and relief, and we will continue to work in these areas, as well as in human rights. In the longer term, we want to see economic reform and a return to representative government. Progress in these areas does not appear likely soon, but we remain ready to work with the Government of Sudan in the future.

Civil War in Liberia

The civil war in Liberia is now beginning its 12th month. Suffering throughout the country has been massive, with 80% of Liberia's 2.2 million people either displaced, experiencing severe food shortages, or now refugees in neighboring countries.

The war is stalemated between the three opposing Liberian forces and the armed forces of the ECOMOG [the military forces of ECOWAS—the Economic Community of West African States]. Charles Taylor's National Patriotic Front of Liberia (NPFL) has been pushed out of the city of Monrovia by the ECOMOG with assistance from Prince Johnson's Independent National Patriotic Front of Liberia (INPFL). Remnants of former President Doe's Armed Forces of Liberia (AFL) continue to play a negative role within the city and have been linked to continued looting and civilian harassment there. Both the INPFL and AFL have now handed over civil power to the interim government of Liberia headed by Amos Sawyer. Mr. Sawyer arrived in Monrovia on Wednesday, November 21, and was warmly received by Prince Johnson and, to a lesser extent, by AFL commander Bowen. To the extent that there is room for optimism, we hope that the interim government's presence in Monrovia, coupled with the proposed ECOWAS talks in Bamako [Mali] with President Traore [of Mali] and Charles Taylor, will begin some movement toward lasting peace. This will, however, be a difficult process as many destabilizing forces have been unleashed throughout Liberia. The U.S. Government stands ready to facilitate the process in realistic ways.

U.S. Steps Toward Liberian Peace

My testimony today is focused on the diplomatic efforts we have undertaken to facilitate a Liberian peace process. Between the beginning of the conflict in December 1989 and the early summer of 1990, the U.S. Government conducted a vigorous initiative to bring about reconciliation between the opposing forces in Liberia. All of the groups involved sent delegations to the State Department at different times. Our message was always the same: Liberia's problems must be settled by Liberians on the basis of democratic values.

While Samuel Doe was still in power, we urged him to move up the date of the next presidential election so that the insurgents could feel that their grievances could be addressed. You will recall that Samuel Doe had agreed to an election within one year—or mid-1991—and had also agreed not to run for reelection. Unfortunately, these concessions were insufficient for the National Patriotic Front which demanded Doe's immediate resignation and exile. Throughout the process, the U.S. Government offered to evacuate Samuel Doe and his family from Liberia to another African country whenever he wished to leave, but he failed to take up the offer.

During the first five months of 1990, the administration also made a major effort to evacuate American citizens living in Liberia who were in danger of being caught up in the fighting. The United States military forces stationed offshore played an important role in our successful effort to evacuate every American who wished to leave as well as nationals of 58 other countries.

During the spring of 1990, the ECOWAS—concerned about the danger to thousands of their nationals living in Liberia; the hundreds of thousands of Liberian refugees who had taken refuge in Cote d'Ivoire, Guinea, and Sierra Leone; and the overall threat to regional stability caused by the conflict—decided to offer its mediation services to the parties to the conflict. The ECOWAS mediation commission proposed that Liberia be governed, after a cease-fire, by an interim government whose leaders would not be eligible to run for office. The role of the interim government would be to restore peace and social services and prepare for a free and fair democratic election. The U.S. Government issued a public endorsement of the objectives of the ECOWAS mediators.

The U.S. military forces stationed offshore played an important role in our successful effort to evacuate every American who wished to leave as well as nationals of 58 other countries.

Under ECOWAS auspices, certain Liberian political parties held a conference in Banjul [The Gambia] which elected the leaders of an interim government, headed by Amos Sawyer as the President. That process was flawed by the absence of the NPFL from the conference. Despite its absence, the interim government offered Charles Taylor the post of Speaker of the National Assembly, and offered the NPFL six seats in the national assembly—more than any other political organization. They also assured Mr. Taylor that he could run for office in a democratic election, even though he held the post of Speaker in the interim government. Charles Taylor refused to accept the offer.

In the absence of a Liberian political consensus, the war continued, mainly in prolonged siege of central Monrovia by the NPFL and the breakaway INPFL. Despite many weeks of combat, it was clear that Samuel Doe's dwindling band of troops could not be defeated in central Monrovia. The continued stalemate guaranteed that the city of Monrovia would slowly starve to

death. Worried about their nationals and the growing tragedy, the members of the ECOWAS mediation commission decided to send troops to Monrovia. The military group dispatched to Monrovia was called ECOMOG, which stands for monitoring group of ECOWAS. The military force hoped to be received peacefully but was vigorously opposed by Charles Taylor's NPFL. A number of ECOWAS governments that did not participate in the decision to send troops to Liberia objected to the action as being contrary to the rules of the organization, which is an economic grouping. In view of the split within ECOWAS on the issue of military intervention, the United States maintained its neutrality while continuing to support the stated goals of ECOWAS—cease-fire, interim government, and democratic elections.

Throughout the period December 1989 to August 1990, the United States has been actively engaged in humanitarian relief. Wherever and whenever possible, we have assisted those inside Liberia and the Liberian refugees in other countries. Whatever one may feel about the armed intervention of ECOMOG forces, we can state that their ability to open up the port of Monrovia and their pacification of much of the city allowed us to arrest the starvation of that city.

By September 1990, it was clear that the ECOWAS effort was not making progress in building a political consensus for Liberian national reconciliation. For that reason, I made a tour of the region, where I discussed the problem with a number of chiefs of state. I found general agreement that Liberians should solve their own problem through negotiations without any preconditions.

My trip was followed by a tour undertaken by Liberian task force director Don Petterson, former Ambassador to Somalia and Tanzania He urged all of Liberia's neighbors to foster national reconciliation among Liberians. We both informed the President of Burkina Faso that we disapproved of his sending arms to the NPFL in transit from Libya, and that any continuation of that activity could only result in a deterioration of our bilateral relations. We also informed all of the governments that Charles Taylor must play a leading role in any solution, and that no political process can succeed unless Charles Taylor cooperates. My feeling is that since our two visits there has been a greater determination to seek a regional consensus about Liberia. The upcoming regional summit scheduled to be held in Bamako will demonstrate whether that cautious optimism is correct.

A Regional Framework for Peace

Creating a regional framework for peace is one of the primary necessities for a successful end to the mediation committee's mandate. To that end, Charles Taylor has been invited by Malian President Moussa Traore to meet with him in Bamako; Mr. Taylor has also indicated his intention to meet with the ECOWAS mediation committee during the course of his visit to Bamako. Just a few days ago, Mr. Taylor told us he may also agree to stay in Bamako during the ECOWAS summit. In addition to such a meeting, Mr. Taylor's stay in Bamako could provide an opportunity for discussions with interim government president Amos Sawyer.

These developments are hopeful portents of peace, but, for the moment, they represent only intentions. The United States will continue to support the ECOWAS stated goals and does so in the belief that ECOWAS mediation in the peace process supports our goals of regional solutions to regional problems.

During our conversations, Charles Taylor indicated to me great concern with the problems of interim governance and with ECOMOG neutrality. I discussed with him ways that these issues could be dealt with within a negotiating structure. While I am encouraged by Mr. Taylor's stated willingness to show flexibility, this remains declaratory policy unaccompanied, for the moment, by diplomatic action or demonstrable desire to achieve an enforceable, lasting cease-fire.

With respect to the role of ECOMOG, the stated primary purpose of the military force has been to stop the fighting and achieve a cease-fire. I hope that all sides show flexibility and negotiate a solution to the war. Failing that, it is difficult to see how Liberian lives can be saved.

The costs of the war are measured in lost lives, refugees, and displaced persons. We believe that more than 600,000 Liberians are living outside their country today, many of them in makeshift camps in Guinea, Sierra Leone, Cote d'Ivoire, Ghana, and Nigeria. Their fate is part of what drives American policy in the Liberian conflict. For the time being, these people's needs are being met by massive assistance programs but they need more than that. They need peace in Liberia.

---

1 The complete transcript of the hearings will be published by the committee and will be available from the Superintendent of Documents, U.S. Government Printing Office, Washington, D.C. 20420.

Economic Challenges in the U.S.-Japan Relationship

By Richard McCormack

Remarks before the North Carolina-Japan Forum, Raleigh, November 1, 1990. Mr. McCormack is Under Secretary for Economic Affairs. [1]

I am pleased to have the opportunity to open this conference, which addresses a number of key topics affecting the U.S.-Japan economic relationship. Both countries face economic challenges. The way we respond to them will have a significant impact on the world economy and our two countries. I hope that in these next few days, you will be able to thoroughly explore the problems—and the opportunities—our two countries face and begin to identify productive solutions as well.

On the U.S. side, we have had to deal with two major difficulties since the summer—the conflict in the Gulf and the budget crisis. Our diplomatic and military responses have moved smoothly and rapidly to meet the Iraqi challenge. However, on the domestic side, our ability to deal with the budget has been anything but smooth and rapid. Our success in solving both challenges will define the country we will be—and the world we will live in—as we move into the 21st century.

Today, I would like to discuss the challenges Japan is now facing in its economic and political affairs. On the economic side, Japan is facing a new kind of economic adjustment. It is struggling to find ways to allow consumers to share the benefits of the phenomenal postwar growth and wealth increases. Japanese citizens have supported the industrial successes by hard work, high savings, and postponed increases in living standards. Many Japanese feel it is now their turn for a greater share in the results. Economic challenges are nothing new to the Japanese, and though there may be some rough spots in the short term, experience shows that the Japanese economy often emerges from difficulties, like the 1970s oil shocks, in an even stronger position. This is partly because when the Japanese government and business establishment believe change is necessary, a plan is developed, and it is implemented.

Japan's International Challenge

What is new today is the international political challenge Japan is now facing. The Persian Gulf crisis is challenging the Japanese to go quickly beyond their economic role in the world to a political one. Their response to the crisis has, therefore, forced the Japanese to confront some very basic issues—about themselves and the kind of country they would like to be.

When the Japanese government and business establishment believe change is necessary, a plan is developed, and it is implemented.

In the early days of the crisis, Japan acted quickly—before the U.N. resolution—to impose economic sanctions on Iraq and freeze Kuwaiti assets in Japan. Our government then sought to work with Japan and other countries to develop a true multinational effort in the Persian Gulf. Japan is in a position to make important economic contributions to the Gulf effort, and it also is considering how it can provide some forms of noncombat personnel support.

They have decided to provide a total financial contribution of $4 billion, including $2 billion to the multinational defense force for transport, housing, and purchases—largely from U.S. sources—of other nonmilitary goods for use by U.S. and other multinational troops in Saudi Arabia. Also they have pledged $2 billion in economic assistance to "frontline states"—Egypt, Turkey, and Jordan—and approximately $22 million in aid to refugees stranded in Jordan. This Japanese contribution is substantial and second only to Saudi Arabia and Kuwait in size. Yet Japan has been repeatedly criticized by the Congress, the public, and even by Doonesbury for not contributing enough to the defense of its economic interests. A large part of the problem is, I think, that Japan's announcement of its contribution came too slowly for many Americans who value swift and decisive action. It took six weeks from the time of the Iraqi invasion for Japan to announce its full package. During that time, congressional impatience grew, and Congress passed a harsh resolution against Japan. Unfortunately, the timing of the congressional action and the timing of the Japanese announcement only reinforced the perception in this country that harsh action and pressure are the only ways to move the Japanese.

How Japan responds to the crisis in the Persian Gulf has broad implications for Japan's international role and the world's view of Japan. The Japanese are now in the process of defining their role in an interdependent world. They must decide on Japan's future and the kind of country Japan wants to become. Japan is a country which rightfully should be a player in world affairs, not a spectator or merely a financial underwriter. We support its active participation in world affairs and look forward to developments over the next few months.

Economic Problems

Turning to the economic side, I note that Japan's economy is facing some strains and problems. Given Japan's heavy dependence on imported energy, the crisis in the Gulf may add to existing inflationary pressures. Since the first oil shock of 1973, Japan has taken steps to decrease its dependence on oil from 77% to less than 60% of total energy needs. But of this oil, 68% comes from the Middle East, and 53% is shipped through the Strait of Hormuz. With appropriate economic policies, the consensus view is that Japan's economy can take prices at $30-$40 per barrel in stride.

Latest projections following Iraq's invasion of Kuwait show that [Japan's] GNP growth will remain at 5.1% this year, falling to 3.9% in 1991; projections show that inflation will increase slightly due to higher energy prices but will remain relatively low at 2.8% for 1990 and 1991.

In addition to solid projections of continued growth, Japan has two economic cushions: a trade surplus and budget surplus, each equal to 2% of

GNP. Japan's strong economic performance, combined with its dependence on imported oil, leads naturally to high expectations with respect to Japan's contributions to multinational efforts in the Persian Gulf.

In spite of the solid growth of the Japanese economy, the financial structure in Japan has been a source of concern, particularly the prices of corporate stocks and land. Land prices in Japan have exploded to the point that the total market value of all the small mountainous islands of Japan is, I am told, ten times the total value of all the land in the entire United States. The small estate of a few acres in Tokyo where the Emperor has his palace is worth, in pure square yardage, more than the entire state of Florida. A single yard of land can cost a quarter of a million dollars. The price of land continues to rise. The latest figures show that land costs in September were up more than 13% [over] the previous year. To young families, the stratospheric price of land means that affordable housing is almost impossible to find. Japanese birth rates are collapsing as young couples are increasingly unwilling to raise children in present cramped conditions. Many Japanese spend hours commuting each day, and yet, in the face of an excruciating shortage of land, there are still thousands of acres of land being used to grow rice within the Tokyo metropolitan area. These stratospheric Japanese land prices are almost entirely the result of artificial shortages created by archaic tax and zoning regulations coupled with a speculative fever unlike anything that has been seen in my lifetime.

During the 1920s, however, the United States had an overheated stock market. There were booms and busts in land—for example in Florida— which wiped out thousands of investors. Last year, it became clear that Japan was running the risk of repeating the U.S. experience of 1929. The Bank of Japan and the Ministry of Finance have begun to take steps to limit the speculative excesses and let the air out of the stock market and land bubbles before they burst in an uncontrollable fashion with economic damage extending far beyond Japan. The easy flow of financing has been somewhat tightened. The stock market, which had risen to levels that bore no relationship whatsoever to price/earning ratios, has now fallen about 35% since its high at the beginning of the year, erasing nearly $2 trillion from the market's collective value.

The difficulty, as I have mentioned, is to let air out of the bubble without it bursting, with potentially great damage to the economy. Since banks own stocks, their assets decline with the stock market. Because of the recent fall in stock prices, there are indications that many banks will not now meet new capital adequacy requirements by 1993. Banks will have to face up to a liquidity crunch by selling assets, raising new capital, and cutting back on lending.

Japan and the U. S. must make changes in our domestic economies—the U.S. to make our economy more competitive and the Japanese to make their markets more open to the world.

Capital Outflow Slows

On the heels of these developments came the Gulf crisis, bringing with it uncertainty over higher oil prices and increased inflationary expectations. These developments exacerbated banking sector problems and are further affecting Japanese patterns of financial investment. Although the market has not yet digested all these changes, the Japanese enthusiasm for investments in foreign financial instruments has been dampened. Some funds invested abroad have been pulled back to Japan to cover stock loans and to seek higher interest rates. One possible implication for the United States is upward pressure on interest rates; the same holds for many Japanese borrowers, including the manufacturing sector. Some companies, for example some major automobile manufacturers, have built up large cash reserves which will provide a competitive edge as capital costs rise.

The outflow of Japanese capital is definitely slowing down. There are obvious reasons: Japan's global current account surplus declined from a peak of $87 billion in 1987 to $49 billion in 1989 and moved to $22.6 billion in the first 7 months of this year. Japan's interest rates are rising, and previous exchange rate risks further decreased the attractiveness of some U.S. holdings.

The Japanese did not actively participate in recent Treasury bill auctions. There are reports that Japanese institutions were net sellers of American securities this year. They are now moving more to direct investment, which is aimed at industries here and in Europe that can strengthen their competitive position.

This brings me to the second part of my speech. Japan has become a domestic issue in the United States. We see polls which label Japan as a greater threat to this country than the Soviet Union is. Part of the reason for this is the correct perception that the Soviet military threat has decreased. But it also reflects a twofold concern about our economic position: apprehension that the United States is in decline and that the Japanese have gained economic strength against us.

We see fears of Japanese investment despite the fact that European purchases of U.S. companies are still considerably higher than those of Japan. Japan now owns $55 billion in U.S. assets—a small sum compared to the close to the $8 trillion total. What catches attention and generates fear is the idea that this investment is concentrated in leading-edge technology companies, or in famous American companies, the so-called trophy investments. If we go beyond the surface exchanges, a hard question is why such assets are for sale, and why American companies are not willing or able to make these purchases themselves. It may be that the Japanese are taking the longer term view more into account than Americans who are tied to short term profit accountability.

Both countries are undergoing structural change, and much of the tension in our relationship can be attributed to the new realities of the relationship and the difficulties in adjusting to it. Japan and the United States must make changes in our domestic economies—the United States to make our economy more competitive and the Japanese to make their markets more open to the world.

Japan has benefitted greatly from the open world trading system and is also now a financial superpower. But we believe Japan still has not provided a reciprocal degree of openness in its trade and financial systems. While some are fixated on the amount of our trade deficit with Japan—about $40 billion last year alone—the real problem is not merely the number but the degree of access foreigners have to Japanese domestic markets. The Japanese system still is not nearly as open as ours. The former West Germany also has a large global trade surplus, greater in 1989 than Japan's, though Japan's GNP is twice as large. Yet West Germany has not been subject to the same kinds of criticism as Japan receives. People have different perceptions about the openness and fairness of the two countries, and facts indicate that this view may be valid.

For example, foreign direct investment in West Germany accounted for 17% of its assets. The same figure in Japan is 1% and acquisitions are not getting any easier. German cars are highly competitive, yet 30% of the autos sold in Germany are imports. In Japan, the figure is 4%, and, incidentally, a large majority of the 4% are German cars. The question is access and fairness. Americans believe that they are getting access to the German market and that they are getting a fair deal there.

A Many-Sided Relationship

The United States has a many-sided relationship with the Japanese—cooperation in aid, in multilateral forums, on political issues, and in terms of their contributions to U.S. forces in Japan. But the weakness in our relationship has, for years, been in trade and economic matters. Unless our economic relationship is on a sound footing, our two countries cannot have a true partnership, especially in an era when economics and the importance of markets are crowding out the Cold War as mass-based issues of concern. Our deficit with Japan is coming down, but a $40 billion trade deficit with Japan is still politically unsustainable.

Our trade policy toward Japan has several parts. A **main emphasis** is coordination in multilateral fora, with successful conclusion of the Uruguay Round next month our major concern.

A **second part** of our economic strategy is coordination of macroeconomic policies to foster improved economic balance, bilaterally and multilaterally. This coordination is likely to gain importance given the uncertainties we all face due to oil price increases and supply disturbances, threat

of inflation, and possible recessionary pressures.

A **third part** of our strategy is negotiations on specific market access problems. In the last few months, we have had successful resolution of several Super 301 cases on satellites, wood products, and supercomputers, and other agreements on amorphous metals and telecommunications. Our trade negotiators have a solid record of progress on market access problems, and we will continue to press for resolution of problem areas.

Finally, the U.S. government is working with the Japanese on questions of structural changes that will identify and remove barriers to market-determined trade and investment flows. We need to reduce Japan's export orientation and free up access for imports. A major part of this policy is the Structural Impediments Initiative (SII). In June, the United States and Japan concluded a year of intensive talks with a joint report which commits both countries to comprehensive measures to reduce structural impediments to the flow of trade and investment and which will help foster balance of payments adjustment. The report is not an end in itself but the beginning of an ongoing process. It contains a blueprint for action that must be fully implemented by both countries before we can claim success for this diplomatic exercise.

SII is a two-way street. On the U.S. side, we are committed to addressing our budget deficit, low savings rate, and educational and worker training questions. The Japanese have committed to change in six areas of structural impediments: savings and investment imbalance, the distribution system, land use policies, *keiretsu* [hierarchy], exclusionary business practices, and pricing.

As someone who has spent his life in the political side of U.S. foreign policy, at the White House, Treasury, State Department, and Congress, I have observed that every decade or so political parties must look at themselves and the world around them and ask if their program is still suitable for a changing external environment. The Reagan administration, and now the Bush administration, have made a conscious effort to broaden the constituency of the Republican Party, include new groups, and address new issues and concerns.

Many observers believe that the Liberal Democratic Party of Japan faces a similar challenge, to address the needs and interests of the new generation of Japanese urban voters. In any political system, changes can come from the bottom up or from the top down. However, statesmanship at the top is easier and less socially wrenching than the alternative.

Many Japanese believe that it is not a sustainable situation politically for a country like Japan—one of the richest nations on earth—to have its wealth so unevenly deployed that less than half of Japanese homes are hooked to a sewer system. Japanese pay 40% more than Americans for the same goods traded between the two countries. The Japanese people have worked long and hard to build up their country and wealth. This massive wealth should, in the view of many Japanese, produce more benefits and a better life for the Japanese people. More internal consumption will also encourage Japanese imports and reduce trade imbalances in the international economy. That is what we are trying to achieve in the Structural Impediments Initiative talks.

Today, I have surveyed some of the important facets of our relationship with Japan—the constructive Japanese response to the crisis in the Persian Gulf, our close economic ties, and the need for better balance in our economic relations. Through the Structural Impediments Initiative and other bilateral and multilateral contacts, we have been working toward this better balance. For us to achieve the economic and foreign policy goals that our countries share, both of our countries—the United States and Japan—will have to make a major sustained effort throughout the decade of the 1990s.

---

1 Text provided to news correspondents by Department of State spokesman Margaret Tutwiler.

January U.S.-Japan Ministerial Meeting

U.S.-JAPAN JOINT PRESS STATE-MENT FOLLOWING MINISTERIAL, JANUARY 14, 1991 [1]

Japanese Foreign Minister [Taro] Nakayama met in Washington with Secretary Baker on January 14, 1991. They agreed that the United States and Japan share a responsibility to promote peace and prosperity among nations and to respond to violations of international law. They pledged to continue their efforts in support of the United Nations resolutions to block back Iraq's aggression against Kuwait. They reaffirmed that they desire a peaceful resolution to the Gulf crisis, but that the only way to achieve such an outcome is for Iraq to comply promptly and completely with the U.N. resolutions.

Secretary Baker expressed appreciation for Japan's political support and financial and other commitments to the multinational effort in the Gulf, which to date exceed $4 billion. This includes financial assistance and in-kind provision of equipment and transportation services for countries in the multinational defense force; special economic assistance to the front line countries; and significant financial support for the refugee effort. Foreign Minister Nakayama told Secretary Baker that Japan would continue to consider additional steps it could take as the situation in the Gulf evolves. Secretary Baker welcomed Japan's announcement that it would fully fund UNDRC's [U.N. Disaster Relief Organization] call for $38 million to finance immediate start-up needs for new eventualities in the refugee area.

The ministers agreed that the Treaty of Mutual Cooperation and Security remains the foundation of the U.S.-Japan relationship and that it has long served, and has long been welcomed throughout the region, as a guarantor of peace and stability and will continue to fulfill that role in the post-Cold War period.

Secretary Baker expressed appreciation for Japan's strong commitment to maintain and enhance the U.S.-Japan security relationship through the new special agreement, signed today, that increased support for American forces in Japan. The ministers also agree to seek an early meeting of the Security Consultative Committee to review a broad range of security and related issues.

The ministers discussed recent Soviet actions in the Baltic States, including the violence against innocent people, which both ministers found deeply disturbing.

Both ministers underscored the importance of continuing the good cooperation on economic issues demonstrated in the past year. They agreed that smooth and effective followup in the Structural Impediments Initiative is central to our bilateral economic relationship and also beneficial to the rest of the world. They expressed strong agreement that the failure of the Uruguay Round would have severe and adverse effects on the stable development of the world economy. They emphasized the critical need for all participants to redouble their efforts to lead the Round to a successful conclusion, and expressed their determination to work together, actively and positively, in all areas toward this goal.

The Secretary welcomed Japan's decision to create a fund, with an endowment of 50 billion yen, to further U.S.-Japan global partnership and promote increased dialogue and interchange between the peoples of our two countries.

STATE DEPARTMENT STATEMENT FOLLOWING MINISTERIAL, JANUARY 14, 1991 (EXCERPT) [1]

On January 14, 1991, Foreign Minister Taro Nakayama and Secretary Baker signed a new multi-year agreement on special measures related to the expenses of maintaining U.S. forces in Japan.

Japan currently pays over $3 billion per year in host nation support. This currently includes housing for U.S. military personnel, the improvement of facilities used by U.S. forces, and more than 50% of the cost of Japanese workers at U.S. facilities. At the present time, this represents about 40% of the total cost of maintaining U.S. forces in Japan.

This new "host nation support" agreement provides for Japan to assume, over 5 years beginning in Japanese fiscal year 1991 (starting April 1, 1991), payments for 100% of the Japanese labor and utilities costs currently borne by U.S. forces in Japan.

As Japan increases its contribution for the expenses of maintaining U.S. forces in Japan, the Government of Japan will be paying, when Japanese labor and utilities costs are fully borne by that government at the end of Japanese FY 1995, about 50% of the total cost of stationing U.S. forces in Japan (based on current cost projections and exchange rates). Such willingness to assume an even greater share of the cost of maintaining U.S. forces in Japan is an important contribution to strengthening our security partnership and is appreciated.

---

1 Department of State Dispatch, January 21, 1991.

President Meets with Chinese Foreign Minister

Exchange With Reporters Prior to Receiving Foreign Minister Qian Qichen of China, November 30, 1990 [1]

Q. Mr. President, has China atoned for Tiananmen Square?

A. Have they what?

Q. Have they atoned for Tiananmen Square?

A. Well, I think the Chinese Government knows that we have some differences on this whole broad question of human rights, but we have many things in common. And one good thing is, we have a very frank relationship with this Foreign Minister and an ability to discuss things openly. He's got some problems with some things, perhaps, we've done, and in this area there are some differences. But that's one of the purposes of this kind of meeting—is to reduce these differences and to go forward.

We've worked closely on the broad concept of stopping aggression. And of course, that is something that we have in common with this very important country, China. So, I'm looking forward to full discussions with this Foreign Minister.

Q. Are you thinking of eliminating sanctions?

A. We're going to discuss a wide array of questions, and I think it will go very well. And, as I say, both sides are trying to strengthen and build on this relationship that both recognize as important. And I will have every opportunity to express to the Foreign Minister, and I expect he will report that back very accurately to the leaders in Beijing, how strongly I feel on some of these questions. And he'll have every opportunity today to present China's views on these important questions.

I'm always inclined to emphasize the positive. And there are many positive and very important aspects to this relationship—very important. And not the least of which is that China and the United States have made common ground in terms of standing up against aggression. And that is important to every American; it is important, I think, to the Chinese side as well.

---

1 Text from Weekly Compilation of Presidential Documents of December 3, 1990.

Department of State Statements on Dissident Trials in China

JANUARY 9, 1991 [1]

We are deeply concerned over the news of the conviction and sentencing in the People's Republic of China of seven persons who, as far as we know, were guilty of nothing other than the peaceful advocacy of democracy. We are concerned that these persons were apparently charged, tried, and convicted for actions which, under the Universal Declaration of Human Rights, any person should be allowed to take without fear of punishment. We are concerned about the secretive process under which the trials were conducted, which raises serious questions about whether they were afforded the opportunity of even-handed justice as provided for in the Universal Declaration. Finally, we are concerned over the length of the prison sentences. No sentences of any length on purely political charges can be characterized as lenient.

The American people feel nothing other than friendship toward the Chinese people. That is why the American public is greatly concerned about the fate of those who exercised internationally recognized rights. That is why we sincerely hope that the facts behind the sentences which were handed down last week will be fully explained, and anyone convicted solely for the exercise of their right to express peacefully their views will be released. We hope that the other political prisoners now held for nonviolent activities protected by the Universal Declaration will be released without having to stand trial.

JANUARY 28, 1991 [2]

We are disappointed by the convictions of Wang Dan and four others. We have seen no evidence that their offenses consisted of more than the nonviolent expression of political views. If so, these convictions would appear to violate the U.N.'s Universal Declaration of Human Rights, which guarantees the right of political expression. Naturally, we welcome the release of some 66 others.

We are disappointed as well that these trials are being conducted without any independent observers present, which invariably raises concerns as to whether the trials meet internationally recognized standards of due process and fairness.

We have advised Chinese authorities of our position on the trials on numerous occasions, most exhaustively during the December visit to China of Assistant Secretary [of State for Human Rights and Humanitarian Affairs Richard] Schifter. We have urged them not to punish further those who did not engage in violent actions and to open the trials to foreign observers.

Officers of our embassy in Beijing have attempted, so far without success, to attend the trials, as have journalists and other interested persons.

We are particularly concerned by reports that in some cases even relatives of the accused were prevented from attending the trials and that some defendents, reportedly including Mr. Wang, were not allowed to choose their own defense attorneys.

---

1 Statement by Department of State deputy spokesman Richard Boucher, January 9, 1991.

2 Statement by Department of State spokesman Margaret Tutwiler, January 28, 1991.

Mongolian President Visits Washington

Remarks by President Bush and President Punsalmaagiyn Ochirbat of Mongolia, January 23, 1991 [1]

President Bush

Mr. President, it's been my great honor to welcome you to the White House for this historic visit to our country, the first ever by the Head of State of Mongolia. Mr. President, Mongolia and the United States are countries separated by thousands of miles and a world of differences—in culture, history, and outlook. And yet, in this past year, our two nations have moved closer together, drawn toward one another by universal principles and ideals.

In the past year, Mongolia has opened its controlled economy to free market reform, opened its closed political system, and opened its doors to the world. Opposition parties are now legal. Mongolia held its first multiparty elections in July—a free and fair vote that produced the first popularly elected legislature in Mongolia's history. This transition toward broader political freedom has a parallel in increased freedom of belief as well, with the reopening of several monasteries. Mr. President, your party's positive approach toward reform has meant peaceful change.

In our discussions today, I made clear the strong support the United States is ready to offer as Mongolia moves forward toward greater freedom. President Ochirbat said he appreciated our support for Mongolia's efforts at democracy and restructuring, and he hopes to lay a firm foundation for positive development of bilateral relations, based on mutual benefit, noninterference in each other's internal affairs.

Already, the United States has begun a program of technical assistance to Mongolia. Just this month, a team from AID [U.S. Agency for International Development] traveled to Ulan Bator to brief 20 midlevel managers on free market reform and found 200 officials ready to exchange ideas, including many members of the Mongolian legislature. And this summer, for the first time ever, Peace Corps volunteers will begin working in Mongolia.

Later this afternoon, our two countries will sign agreements opening the way to expanded trade and closer contact in the areas of science and technology. And today, I have issued the waiver to open the door granting Mongolia most-favored-nation status, a step that I hope will spur increased trade between our two countries.

In addition to these matters of mutual interest, I reviewed with President Ochirbat world affairs of surpassing concern, including Operation Desert Storm. Mongolia was among the very first to condemn Iraq's brutal invasion of Kuwait and to call for Iraq's complete and unconditional withdrawal. Mr. President, after our talks, I know that you believe as I do that no nation must be permitted to assault and brutalize its neighbor. The action of Iraq's dictator—the actions of one misguided man—cannot obscure mankind's bright destiny of democracy and freedom. The future lies with the process of revolution and renewal now taking place in your nation—a democratic revolution that is destined to bring peace, freedom and prosperity to the people of Mongolia, as it has to

this country and so many others around the world.

So, once again, sir, it has been my distinct pleasure to welcome you to Washington and to this White House. And God bless you, and may God bless the people of Mongolia.

President Ochirbat

Mr. President, ladies and gentlemen, at the outset, let me express our sincere thanks to Your Excellency Mr. President, for the invitation to pay an official working visit to the United States of America and the warm welcome accorded to us. Availing myself of this opportunity to address you, the representatives of mass media, in this room of the White House—a house which has witnessed many outstanding historical events—I bring the friendly greeting of the Mongolian people to the American people.

This is the first visit ever paid by the Head of State of Mongolia to the United States of America. It is an evidence of a dynamic development of Mongol-American bilateral relations— particularly if you will recall that formal relations were established between the two countries only four years ago.

President Bush and I had a frank exchange of views on bilateral relations and international issues of mutual interest. And I am extremely pleased to say that this meeting opened up broad vistas for furthering ties between the two countries. We highly appreciate the full support voiced during our meeting by President Bush on behalf of the U.S. administration for democratic processes that are gaining momentum in Mongolia.

President Bush and I agreed to see to it that the Mongol-American relations be developed vigorously on the basis of the universally recognized principles of state sovereignty, independence, noninterference in each other's internal affairs, equality, and mutual benefit.

We have also agreed that there is a broad possibility for cooperation in encouraging U.S. investment and carrying out technological renovation in Mongolia, expanding bilateral trade, facilitating Mongolia's switch to a market economy, and training qualified personnel. I believe that the trade agreement and the agreement on scientific and technological cooperation between the two countries, which are to

be signed today, will be of much importance in making the best of these potentialities.

And, of course, of the exchange of views on international issues, both sides unanimously emphasize the importance of pulling together the efforts of all states in order to strengthen the positive changes that are taking place in the world.

As for the Persian Gulf crisis, we deeply regret the outbreak of an armed conflict there which is jeopardizing international stability. Should the Iraqi leadership meet the demands of the international community and withdraw its troops from Kuwait, this situation would not have occurred. The Mongolian People's Republic strongly hopes that the military operations by allied forces aimed at restoring Kuwait's independence and sovereignty would not escalate, and peace and tranquillity will prevail soon in the Persian Gulf region. Just as democracy, freedom, and human rights are the lofty ideals that should be upheld by all, this is what the Mongolian Government is strongly committed to in its domestic and foreign policies.

Thank you very much, Mr. President, for the warm welcome accorded to us, the delegates of the Mongolian people. I wish you and the American people happiness and well-being.

---

1 Text from Weekly Compilation of Presidential Documents of January 28, 1991.

U.S.-Economic Community Consulations: Institutional Harmony, Uruguay Round Discord

Joint Press Conference Following U.S.-EC Ministerial

Excerpt from Joint Press Conference of Secretary of State Baker, Secretary of Agriculture Clayton Yeutter, Secretary of Commerce Robert Mosbacher, U.S. Trade Representative Carla Hills, EC President Jacques Delors, EC Vice President Andriessen, and EC Commissioners Pandolfi and MacSharry following meeting, Brussels, November 16, 1990. [1]

President Delors. Good afternoon ladies and gentlemen. We had a working session this morning. We have such a working session every six months, bringing together the Secretary of State Jim Baker and his colleagues, together with a number of members of the Commission, and we are very pleased this meeting could take place now, two days after the visit of the President of the Commission and the President of the Council, Mr. Andreotti, to President Bush.

There was a certain link between the two because there's the question of the solidarity of the free world to ensure that international law is respected. That was one link. And then there was the other problem that we had, that might be an obstacle to the freeing of world trade, so that the two links were there. This meeting was a very workmanlike one. We dealt with very specific subjects, and I'll give the floor straight away to Jim Baker.

Secretary Baker. Let me simply say, ladies and gentlemen, that I have a short statement that I'd like to make, and then my colleagues and I would be delighted to respond to your questions, as I'm sure the President and his colleagues will.

First of all, let me say that we value very much our increasingly close ties with the European Community, and we appreciate the key role that the EC plays in bolstering democracy, stability, and prosperity in Europe. Today's meeting is one of a series of biannual consultations that were agreed to last February in order to ensure that the EC-U.S. consultations and cooperation are commensurate with our international role and our international obliga-

tions. As you know, Prime Minister Andreotti of Italy, acting in his EC presidency capacity, accompanied by President Delors, met with us on Tuesday in Washington. We had some very good discussions then, and we have had some very good discussions today on a wide range of issues. The Persian Gulf, the Uruguay Round, the U.S.-EC bilateral relations — all of these issues figured very prominently on our agenda.

On the Uruguay Round, we discussed our goals for the Round, and we discussed our strong conviction that we have got to succeed in substantial trade liberalization and in strengthening the multilateral trading system. Many problems do remain and not much time remains. But I think that it is fair to say that all of us are committed to intense discussions at the highest level to resolve our differences. On the Gulf, I think that there is an unwavering consensus on the critical importance of maintaining international unity against the aggression of Saddam Hussein. All of us, I think, would resist short of full, anything short of full, implementation of the U.N. Security Council resolutions.

The United States and the Community share a deep concern, of course, for the transition of the nations of Central and Eastern Europe to full democracy and to market economies. That course is an arduous course. It's full of challenge; but the United States and the EC are determined to help these nations succeed. And I think we have been cooperating very effectively within the G-24 process and in other ways to help the nations of Central and Eastern Europe succeed. Similarly, I think we both want to do what we can to encourage the ongoing political and economic reform in the Soviet Union, recognizing that the key choices and efforts are going to have to be made by the Soviet people themselves.

I'd like to emphasize that U.S.-EC cooperation can prove valuable outside of the Continent and the immediate environs of this Continent, and that's why we welcome very much the Community's interest in exploring with us and with Japan and with Canada and

some of our Latin neighbors a new way to help Central America, through a Partnership for Democracy and Development that builds on the G-24 model.

I'm also pleased to note agreements that were made today to advance specific U.S.-EC cooperation projects in science and technology, and in education, culture and training. As European integration proceeds, it's important that Europe, the United States and Canada pay very close attention to strengthened transatlantic ties.

As I noted in a speech in Berlin last December, I think we need to enrich, to expand and to evolve the institutional basis for our cooperation so that we can meet changing needs. So I particularly welcome the concrete steps that we are now taking on that Berlin agenda through our development of a U.S.-EC declaration that will outline an institutional framework for U.S.-EC relations. When this is completed, this can represent an important step in giving more structure to our relations and in encouraging consultations on an expanding agenda of U.S.-EC contacts.

I also spoke in Berlin in December about CSCE and about NATO. In a few days our Presidents and Prime Ministers will meet in Paris to advance CSCE's role, and I am pleased that our actions at this year's London NATO Summit have underscored that the NATO alliance is and will continue to be the transatlantic forum in which we address security issues together. Indeed the United States, the EC members who are in NATO, will call attention in this declaration to their commitment to the North Atlantic Alliance. So, as we face new uncertainties and potential challenges, I think it's fair to note that the alliance will remain the vital foundation of stability in Europe and the means through which the fact of our mutual security interests takes practical form.

Jacques, thank you very much for your hospitality and the opportunity to consult closely here today.

The European Community (EC)

The treaty creating the European Economic Community was signed in Rome in March 1957.

▶ **Original Members:**
- Belgium
- France
- Germany
- Italy
- Luxembourg
- The Netherlands

▶ **Later Members:**
- Denmark (1973)
- Greece (1981)
- Ireland (1973)
- Portugal (1986)
- Spain (1986)
- United Kingdom (1973)

Boundary representations are not necessarily authoritative.

Q. I'd like to put a question to both the Secretary of State and Mr. Andriessen. Could they be a bit more specific about what was discussed this morning in connection with the Uruguay Round and of course more specifically what was said about the agricultural aspect of the Uruguay Round? And a second point, I'd like to know whether you discussed the corn conflict, the maize conflict? And even if you didn't discuss that point, would both gentlemen like to spell out their position on the subject, and a more specific question to Mr. Andriessen, does he believe that it will be possible to find a solution to that particular conflict before the end of the year, in order to avoid American sanctions or reprisals.

Secretary Baker. Let me say that I'm going to ask Ambassador Hills to respond to your questions since she has the primary jurisdiction over this issue within the U.S. Government. We did have, as I indicated in my opening remarks, extensive discussions about the Uruguay Round and we had indeed extensive discussions about the question of agriculture. Ambassador Hills.

Ambassador Hills. I thought the time we spent on agriculture was useful. The United States is concerned that there be adequate address of the problem of export subsidies whereby markets are bought by governments for their farmers, and adequate opening of markets around the world. We listened to the European representatives describe how their proposal in dealing

with internal supports might have an effect on both the reduction of export subsidies and the increase of market access. We're going to continue to try to understand better those consequential effects and to see whether or not there could be more express effects; so that we have not concluded our negotiations.

You asked about the corn agreement. In our country we call that the enlargement agreement. The United States had certain tariff concessions as a result of the accession of Spain and Portugal to the European Community. And under the GATT rules, as we understand them, those tariff concessions are permanent. And when they are taken away, then concessions that have been given on the other side are removed. We have been trying to resolve our differences of view this year and, of course, we hope very much that we can obtain a resolution by the end of the year so that we will not have to withdraw concessions earlier made. That would be our first preference. So we, on our side, will move very rapidly and work very hard to achieve a successful resolution. I think it could be done.

Vice President Andriessen. I suppose I'll have to now. On your point about the Uruguay Round, I think we had fruitful discussions. There are major difficulties between the United States and the European Community, not only, by the way, between the United States and the European Community, but also with other countries. But from today, from this morning's discussion, I come away with the conviction that there is a constructive mentality or atmosphere afoot to deal with this matter multilaterally, not bilaterally, but to find a multilateral solution to the problems. But there are problems. I wouldn't deny that.

On your second question, this is really a question of the interpretation of an article of the GATT. It's our view that we have in fact honored our commitments and we hope, as you put it, that that problem won't raise its ugly head. If that were to happen, then we would have to look into the question of how we should respond to the matter. But obviously we shall do our level best to prevent it cropping up.

Q. I should like to direct my question directly to Mrs. Carla Hills, and I apologize, I leave out Secretary of State Baker. You have spoken of useful discussions and everyone has reiterated the fact that these discussions were useful. Now to go straight to the concrete point, at this stage are the EC and United States ready to send a message to the Secretary General of the GATT to the effect that negotiations can finally begin on agricultural matters, in particular? Because it seems to me that up to now it was first the EC that slowed things down in coming forward with its proposal, but then there were further delays. Are you ready to negotiate now?

Ambassador Hills. We are always ready to negotiate, and most assuredly so in agriculture. The suspension of negotiations in Geneva was not instigated by the United States. I think, as Vice President Andriessen has said correctly, this is a multilateral problem,

not a bilateral problem, and the debate over agriculture is not solely between the United States and the European Community, but perhaps more so between the European Community and those nations that export agricultural products, which includes the United States.

Vice President Andriessen. There is just one comment I wanted to make. The European Community was surprised that a meeting held to discuss agriculture was canceled. And I have pressed for the talks on agriculture in Geneva to be resumed as soon as possible in the framework and in the greenroom where these things are normally discussed.

Q. A question for Mr. Yeutter and Mr. MacSharry. Mr. Yeutter, you met the French farm minister yesterday, and after you did, you were very pessimistic about the prospects for an outcome. Now today, Mr. MacSharry had a chance to explain the EC proposal to you, face to face. How do you feel, now that you've had that conversation? And I wonder, Mr. MacSharry, if you could add what your perception was of your discussion with Mr. Yeutter.

Secretary Yeutter. I am still very pessimistic. I am no more optimistic today than I was yesterday, and I am usually an optimist. I have been doing speeches over the last couple of months indicating that Ambassador Hills suggests the probability for success in the Uruguay Round has been about 51-49, 51 probability of success. I have been saying I am more of an optimist than Ambassador Hills is, and I call it 52-48. But that was before the European Community proposal, and I would assess the probabilities at much, much less than 50-50 at the moment. But I don't believe we should give up on the process. It is too important to do so, and so we should all do our very best to achieve an agreement, and it is certainly the intent of the United States to do that.

But the reason I am still pessimistic is that there are some very crucial elements to a successful agricultural negotiation, not only crucial for the United States, but for a lot of other countries in the world, too. And I would just identify two of them very quickly. One is effective, meaningful, definitive discipline of export subsidies in quantitative terms—and by that I mean tonnages or the amount of product that is moved onto the world

market through export subsidies. And I have yet to see any indications of willingness on the part of the European Community to make the kind of specific commitments on export subsidy discipline that will be required by a number of countries. The second one is market access, that is the exposure of European agriculture to global competition. The developing countries in particular have a very strong interest in opening up markets around the world, and so do we, not just in the European Community, but in a lot of other countries around the world.

One of the principal objectives of this whole exercise is to open up additional market opportunities for everybody, and let farmers compete with each other around the world. And in our judgment, the European Community proposal on market access does not meet the criteria for success in that area. In other words, there is little if any additional opportunity for farmers around the world to compete with European farmers in the European Community market place.

Commissioner MacSharry. Ladies and gentlemen, insofar as the discussions have been described already, I think we can too agree that they have been useful; but what we are involved in and wanted to be involved in since we finally got our proposal on the table, was a clarification process demonstrating to all concerned, and the opportunity to state to the U.S. delegation, exactly what is contained in our proposal and how it does impact on internal support, market access, and export subsidies. And that is a process that will continue. There is, I think everybody will accept in this room and I think on the platform, that there is still quite an amount of detailed technical and expert examination required, of both proposals, for the United States and the European Community, as well as many other contracting parties. That process will continue. This afternoon, I intend to have further bilaterals with Secretary Yeutter, and whatever others are necessary. We will ensure that they continue. As Vice President Andriessen has said, we do hope that we can get into meaningful dialogue in the context of the overall discussion in Geneva.

Joint Declaration on U.S.-EC Relations, November 23, 1990 [2]

The United States of America on one side and, on the other, the European Community and its member States,

Mindful of their common heritage and of their close historical, political, economic and cultural ties,

Guided by their faith in the values of human dignity, intellectual freedom and civil liberties, and in the democratic institutions which have evolved on both sides of the Atlantic over the centuries,

Recognizing that the transatlantic solidarity has been essential for the preservation of peace and freedom and for the development of free and prosperous economies as well as for the recent developments which have restored unity in Europe,

Determined to help consolidate the new Europe, undivided and democratic,

Resolved to strengthen security, economic cooperation and human rights in Europe in the framework of the CSCE, and in other fora,

Noting the firm commitment of the United States and the EC member states concerned to the North Atlantic Alliance and to its principles and purposes,

Acting on the basis of a pattern of cooperation proven over many decades, and convinced that by strengthening and expanding this partnership on an equal footing they will greatly contribute to continued stability, as well as to political and economic progress in Europe and in the world,

Aware of their shared responsibility, not only to further common interests but also to face transnational challenges affecting the well-being of all mankind,

Bearing in mind the accelerating process by which the European Community is acquiring its own identity in economic and monetary matters, in foreign policy and in the domain of security,

Determined to further strengthen transatlantic solidarity through the variety of their international relations,

Have decided to endow their relationship with long-term perspectives.

Common Goals

The United States of America and the European Community and its member States solemnly reaffirm their determination further to strengthen their partnership in order to:

- support democracy, the rule of law and respect for human rights and individual liberty, and promote prosperity and social progress worldwide;
- safeguard peace and promote international security, by cooperating with other nations against aggression and coercion, by contributing to the settlement of conflicts in the world and by reinforcing the role of the United Nations and other international organizations;
- pursue policies aimed at achieving a sound world economy marked by sustained economic growth with low inflation, a high level of employment, equitable social conditions, in a framework of international stability;
- promote market principles, reject protectionism and expand, strengthen and further open the multilateral trading system;
- carry out their resolve to help developing countries by all appropriate means in their efforts towards political and economic reforms;
- provide adequate support, in cooperation with other states and organisations, to the nations of Eastern and Central Europe undertaking economic and political reforms and encourage their participation in the multilateral institutions of international trade and finance.

Principles of U.S.-EC Partnership

To achieve their common goals, the European Community and its member States and the United States of America will inform and consult each other on important matters of common interest, both political and economic, with a view to bringing their positions as close as possible, without prejudice to their respective independence. In appropriate international bodies, in particular, they will seek close cooperation.

The U.S.-EC partnership will, moreover, greatly benefit from the mutual knowledge and understanding acquired through regular consultations as described in this declaration.

Economic Cooperation

Both sides recognized the importance of strengthening the multilateral trading system. They will support further steps towards liberalization, transparency, and the implementation of GATT [General Agreement on Tariffs and Trade] and OECD [Organization for Economic Cooperation and Development] principles concerning both trade in goods and services and investment.

They will further develop their dialogue, which is already underway, on other matters such as technical and non-tariff barriers to industrial and agricultural trade, services, competition policy, transportation policy, standards, telecommunications, high technology and other relevant areas.

Education, Scientific and Cultural Cooperation

The partnership between the European Community and its member States on the one hand, and the United States on the other, will be based on continuous efforts to strengthen mutual cooperation in various other fields which directly affect the present and future well-being of their citizens, such as exchanges and joint projects in science and technology, including, inter alia, research in medicine, environment protection, pollution prevention, energy, space, high energy physics, and the safety of nuclear and other installations, as well as in education and culture, including academic and youth exchanges.

Transnational Challenges

The United States of America and the European Community and its member States will fulfill their responsibility to address transnational challenges, in the interest of their own peoples and of the rest of the world. In particular, they will join their efforts in the following fields:

- combatting and preventing terrorism;
- putting an end to the illegal production, trafficking and consumption of narcotics and related criminal activities, such as the laundering of money;

- cooperating in the fight against international crime;
- protecting the environment, both internationally and domestically, by integrating environmental and economic goals;
- preventing the proliferation of nuclear armaments, chemical and biological weapons, and missile technology.

Institutional Framework for Consultation

Both sides agree that a framework is required for regular and intensive consultation. They will make full use of and further strengthen existing procedures, including those established by the President of the European Council and the President of the United States on 27th February 1990, namely:

biannual consultations to be arranged in the United States and in Europe between, on the one side, the President of the European Council and the President of the Commission, and on the other side, the President of the United States;

biannual consultations between the European Community Foreign Ministers, with the Commission, and the U.S. Secretary of State, alternately on either side of the Atlantic;

ad hoc consultations between the Presidency Foreign Minister or the Troika and the U.S. Secretary of State;

biannual consultations between the Commission and the U.S. Government at cabinet level;

briefings, as currently exist, by the Presidency to U.S. Representatives on European Political Cooperation (EPC) meetings at the Ministerial level.

Both sides are resolved to develop and deepen these procedures for consultation so as to reflect the evolution of the European Community and of its relationship with the United States.

They welcome the actions taken by the European Parliament and the Congress of the United States in order to improve their dialogue and thereby bring closer together the peoples on both sides of the Atlantic.

GATT Negotiations in Brussels End Without Agreement

White House Statement on Uruguay Round Negotiations, December 7, 1990 [3]

The United States went to Brussels prepared to conclude ambitious market-opening agreements in all areas of the Uruguay Round.

Unfortunately, the Brussels meeting has ended without result due to the inability of nations with substantial economic strength—the European Community (EC), Japan, and Korea—to negotiate fundamental agricultural reform. This is all the more disappointing given the very constructive attitude taken by many developing countries, particularly many of our friends in Latin America.

The United States remains committed to maintaining and strengthening the multilateral trading system and to a timely and successful conclusion of the round. We will do all we can to bring this about while continuing to insist upon agreements that genuinely liberalize trade. Accordingly it is our hope that participants, especially the EC, will take this opportunity to reflect upon their position on agriculture and develop the political will to negotiate real market-opening agreements while there is still time to do so.

---

1 Department of State Press Release 190, November 16, 1990.

2 Department of State Dispatch, November 26, 1990.

3 Text from Weekly Compilation of Presidential Documents of December 17, 1990.

President Visits Prague on First Anniversary of Revolution

Meetings with National Leaders

Statement by Press Secretary Fitzwater, November 17, 1990 [1]

President Bush and President [Vaclav] Havel met at 10 o'clock this morning at Hradcany Castle in the first meeting of the visit. President Havel welcomed President Bush on this historic occasion, the first-year anniversary of the revolution. The two leaders discussed the economic development of Czechoslovakia, including the need to get U.S. investment. President Bush said the United States is concerned about the international oil situation. President Bush said there is a disruption in supply, but it is the speculation about the Persian Gulf that has driven up prices. President Havel said their economy depends on an uninterrupted flow of oil from the Soviet Union, and that has been a problem in the current situation.

The two leaders discussed the CSCE [Conference on Security and Cooperation in Europe] and the prospects for locating a new Secretariat in Prague. Both leaders stressed the interest in seeing a successful CSCE meeting, particularly on issues of arms control and human rights.

Federal Leaders

President Bush met at approximately 10:40 with Federal leaders to discuss economic conditions. The President said the talks with the IMF [International Monetary Fund] and World Bank are progressing well. They also discussed oil supplies and their impact on this country. They emphasized the important role of private investment in improving the economy of Czechoslovakia.

Czech Leaders

President Bush met with Czech leaders at approximately 11 a.m. They emphasized that they wanted to help themselves economically as much as they can. One of the leaders quoted Mark Twain by saying "a helping hand is usually found at the end of your arm."

President Bush spoke of the strength of the U.S. system in which fifty States have strong views, but cooperate comfortably with the Federal Government. President Bush also spoke of the need for stability in Czechoslovakia as they deal with private investors from the United States. President Bush also raised the matter of the environment, saying that pollution is a high cost that we must be concerned about.

Slovak Leaders

President Bush met at approximately 11:30 with Slovak leaders. He wished them success and emphasized the need for stability. The Slovak leaders commented on the United States as a melting pot that has accepted nationalities from all over the world. They pointed out they are working hard to get private investment and asked if more of their people could come to the United States for training in various production skills.

President Bush said "our vision is a Europe whole and free." President Bush remarked on the warm welcome of the crowds that lined the streets on the way into Prague from the airport.

Alexander Dubcek

At approximately 12:15 President Bush called on Alexander Dubcek, President of the Federal Assembly, and greeted him warmly, acknowledging his historic role in the move towards freedom in Czechoslovakia. President Dubcek recalled his visit to the United States and said that President Bush's visit constitutes a most prominent day for U.S.-Czechoslovak relations. President Bush and President Dubcek discussed the role of the Federal Assembly and its important role in the building of democracy. President Bush concluded the meeting by signing a large, brown leather guest book, giving the signing pen to President Dubcek. President Bush signed: "With great happiness and warm best wishes, George Bush, November 17, 1990."

President's Remarks to Federal Assembly, November 17, 1990 [1]

President Havel, thank you, sir, for greeting us with such warmth today. And to Chairman Dubcek, thank you, sir, for that really warm and generous introduction. May I salute the Prime Ministers of the Czech and Slovak Republics; the Members of the Assembly; and most of all, the people of Czechoslovakia. It is an honor for me, the first American President ever to visit your country, to bring you the greetings of the American people on this, the first anniversary of Czechoslovakia's return to freedom.

Events One Year Ago

One year ago today, in the streets and squares of this city, the people of Prague gathered, first by twos and threes, and then by thousands—in the night air, an autumn chill; in their minds, memories of a spring twenty years past. The Velvet Revolution had begun.

That revolution succeeded without a single shot. Your weapons proved far superior to any in the state's arsenal. In the face of force, you deployed the power of principle. Against a wall of lies, you advanced the truth. Out of a thousand acts of courage, Czech and Slovak, emerged a single voice. Its message: The time had come to bring freedom home to Czechoslovakia.

Your revolution was also a renewal: a renewal of the deeply held principles that bind my country, the United States of America, to yours; principles enshrined in your Declaration of Independence, issued in the United States in 1918 by Tomas Masaryk, your first President, and Milan Stafanik, proud Slovak patriot; principles inspired by the ringing words of our own Thomas Jefferson more than two centuries ago.

In my homeland, those principles were put into practice when we adopted our Constitution and its Bill of Rights. And last night, I carried copies of those documents as we flew from Washington to Prague, copies that I guess were passed out to you as you came in today. And during this historic time, as you consider the adoption of your own federal system and bill of rights, I offer them to you in friendship, for the common principles and common bonds our peoples have long shared.

Generations of Americans, Czechs, and Slovaks sustained these common bonds. In the battle to defeat Nazi tyranny, America stood with the courageous Czech and Slovak partisans fighting for freedom. Through the long dark decades after 1948, we, like you, refused to accept Europe's division. Through Radio Free Europe and the Voice of America, we held aloft the ideal of truth, and we spoke a common language of hope.

At long last, the grip of the dictators weakened; Czechoslovakia seized its chance to rise up, to reclaim your rights as a free people and as a sovereign nation.

Today, as fellow citizens of free governments, we share the fruits of our common resolve. Europe, East and West, stands at the threshold of a new era: an era of peace, prosperity, and security unparalleled in the long history of this continent. Today Europe's long division is ending. Today, once more, Czechoslovakia is free.

Czechoslovakia's revolution is over, but its renaissance has just begun. Your work and ours is far from complete. Your nation, like your neighbors to the north and south, faces the unprecedented task of building a stable, democratic rule and a prosperous market economy on the ruins of totalitarianism. I am here today to say that we will not fail you in this decisive moment. America will stand with you to that end.

Agreements for Economic Help

America stands ready to help Czechoslovakia realize the progress and prosperity now within reach. Today our two countries will conclude agreements giving Czechoslovakia the fullest access to American markets, American investment, and American technology. To help unleash the creativity and drive of the Czechs and Slovak people, I will urge our Congress to authorize a $60-million Czechoslovak-American Enterprise Fund. In addition, to help build your private sector, the United States will extend prompt economic assistance from the $370 million now committed to Central and Eastern Europe for the coming year.

We also welcome the active involvement of the American private sector. I am pleased to see that yesterday your government entered into a promising, multimillion-dollar joint venture with Bell Atlantic and U.S. West to modernize your country's communications network. I am sure this will be the first of many large-scale investments in the future of a free Czechoslovakia.

In response to this region's severe energy problems, we expect the IMF [International Monetary Fund]—at our initiative—to lend up to $5 billion in 1991 to Central and Eastern Europe, and the World Bank will commit an additional $9 billion over the next three years.

In addition to these economic initiatives, we seek to renew the free and open exchange denied our peoples for so many years. I am pleased to announce the reopening of the American consulate in Bratislava in the Republic of Slovakia and, just yesterday, the selection of a site for our new cultural center in Prague. Our newly established International Media Fund promises to contribute expertise and encouragement to your nation's free and independent media. And I am gratified that your government and my country's Institute for East-West Security Studies will soon open a European Studies Center in Stirin, an important partnership of the intellect between European and American scholars.

And let me say once again: Prague should be the home to the permanent Secretariat of the Conference on Security and Cooperation in Europe. In Paris, I am confident that I will find unanimous support for this initiative. It is right that this city, once on the fault line of cold war and conflict, now at the heart of the new and united Europe, play a central role as the CSCE seeks to expand the frontiers of freedom in Europe.

A New Commonwealth of Freedom

At the Paris summit of the CSCE, the nations of North America and Europe will sign historic documents: a treaty to provide deep reductions in conventional armed forces in Europe, a CSCE summit declaration charting the future role of CSCE in ending Europe's division. The Atlantic alliance, the foundation of European stability, has pledged itself to the same goal.

Working together, we can fulfill the promise of a Europe that reaches its democratic destiny, a Europe that is truly whole and free. But this continent's reconciliation is only part of the larger vision for our world, a vision which I ask you to share.

Let me draw on the life and writings of the gentleman that is sitting over my right shoulder, President Havel—let me draw on those just to make my point. Several years ago, Mr. Havel wrote about the Western visitors who came to see your so-called dissidents, asking how they could help your cause. He wondered about that question, wondered why visitors from the West couldn't see that your cause was their cause, too. Mr. Havel wrote, and I quote: "Are not my dim prospects or my hopes his dim prospects and hopes as well? Is not the destruction of humans in Prague a destruction of all humans? Is not indifference to what is happening here a preparation for the same kind of misery elsewhere?"

Dissident Havel—now President Havel— spoke then of a shared destiny, spoke out of a sure sense that the fate of all mankind is linked. Czechs and Slovaks understand this vision and the challenge. For half a century, your struggle for freedom was cut short not by one but by two of the cruelest tyrannies history has ever known. You know what it means to live under regimes whose vision of world order holds no place for freedom. As heirs of Jan Hus, whose statue stands just a few blocks from us, as countrymen of Comenius, the son of Moravia, whose name graces your great University of Bratislava, you have always looked to the far horizon to take your bearings from principles that are universal. As small nations, whose very existence demands constant vigilance, you have always understood that your future depends not only on your own heroic actions here but on the broader principles that govern the greater world in which you live. We must recognize that no people, no continent, can stand alone, secure unto itself. Our fates, our futures are intertwined.

That, you see, is why Europe's celebration of freedom brings with it a new responsibility. Now that democracy has proven its power, Europe has both the opportunity and the challenge to join us in leadership, to work with us in common cause towards this new commonwealth of freedom.

This commonwealth rests on shared principles, upon four cornerstones that constitute our common values: an unshakable belief in the dignity and rights of man, and the conviction that just government derives its power from the people; the belief that, men and women everywhere must be free to enjoy the fruits of their labor and that the rule of law must govern the conduct of nations.

The United States welcomes the new democracies of Central and Eastern Europe fully into the commonwealth of freedom, a moral community united in its dedication to free ideals. We wish to encourage the Soviet Union to go forward with their reforms, as difficult as the course may seem. They will find our community ready to welcome them and to help them as they, too, commit themselves to this commonwealth of freedom.

Every new nation that embraces these common values, every new nation that joins the ranks of this commonwealth of freedom, advances us one step closer to a new world order, a world in which the use of force gives way to a shared respect for the rule of law. This new world will be incomplete without a vision that extends beyond the boundaries of Europe alone. Now that unity is within reach in Europe is no time for our vision of change to stop at the edge of this continent.

The principles guiding our two nations, the principles at work in our two revolutions, are not Czech or Slovak or American alone. These principles are universal, rooted in the love of liberty and the rights of man.

[Concluding remarks on Persian Gulf omitted.]

Presidents Bush and Havel Meet with Reporters, November 17, 1990 [1]

President Havel. Dear friends, let me welcome you to this brief meeting with our honored guest, President Bush, and myself. We are ready to answer your questions. But before doing so, perhaps I should briefly explain what President Bush and I have been discussing.

We have touched upon a number of different matters, but we focused primarily on the following subjects. We have presented our information on the present situation in Czechoslovakia, and possibilities of possible assistance or cooperation on the part of the United States have been discussed. Secondly, we have dwelled upon the future of Europe in the light of the forthcoming CSCE Summit in Paris and upon the future of the Helsinki process. And on that score, we have found that our views there are very close to each other, if not even identical. And sadly, we have talked at some length about the situation in the Persian Gulf.

You can ask us questions that shall be answered alternately by President Bush and myself, with me being the one to answer the first question.

U.S. Assistance for Czechoslovakia

Q. President Havel, are you satisfied with the assistance you're getting? You seem to not be saying that your views are identical on that subject with the President.

A. President Bush shows a lot of understanding for our problems, and he has already pledged certain forms of assistance in the statement he delivered in the Federal Assembly, which you have [certainly] had.

Q. President Bush, even though you did outline some assistance today in your speech, proportionally it's fairly miniscule compared to what Czechoslovakia needs. Are you prepared to consider further direct U.S. assistance?

President Bush. Well, I think we've spelled out what we can do in terms of direct assistance right now. The thing that is of most import to Czechoslovakia is increased support from the IMF and the World Bank. And I made clear to President Havel that we will be very supportive in that connection.

In addition, the thing that would be of most benefit to Czechoslovakia and to the United States would be increased investment and increased private-sector help. And that we've discussed; and then that, I think we both agree, would be the best answer—certainly long range answer—for the vitality and growth of Czechoslovakia.

President Havel. I think we should give an opportunity, also, to the Czechoslovak media.

Q. Mr. President Bush, have you spoken to Mr. Havel about American assistance in the science and technology fields and especially in education of the people? Would you be more concrete?

President Bush. We didn't discuss S&T as much. We did talk about educational exchanges, but we did not dwell on the science and technology. Certainly, I would say we would be ready to cooperate in every way in that field, however.

Soviet Union and Eastern Europe

Q. President Havel, can I ask you about the situation in the Soviet Union, as you watch it—the tensions that we see that Mr. Gorbachev is facing? What concerns do you have about the breakup of the Soviet Union and how that would affect Central European countries?

President Havel. The fact that the Soviet Union is currently undergoing the most sweeping, the most far-reaching changes in its entire history is more than evident, but it is not yet clear what the future arrangement of the Soviet Union will be. But it is our firm belief that the changes may be accomplished in a rapid and peaceful way without any bloodshed and that they may give the individual Republics and the peoples of the Soviet Union the measure of autonomy which they desire.

Q. President Bush, what's your opinion on the plan of economic help to U.S.S.R. through Eastern Europe which was proposed by Minister Dienstbier [Foreign Minister of Czechoslovakia] in his speech at Harvard University earlier this year? And was this topic on the program of your talks in Czechoslovakia?

President Bush. I'm sorry, I didn't hear the first part.

We didn't discuss that in great detail, but I am convinced that the United States—and I tried to say this in our speech to the joint session—has an enormous stake. We do not want to see Czechoslovakia, Poland, and Hungary off in some kind of no man's land. Thus, we did discuss future security arrangements. It is my view—and I would let the Czechoslovakian Government speak for itself—that some more active role in the CSCE process will contribute to the stability of Europe and fully include Czechoslovakia in the decisions that lie ahead for Europe.

Persian Gulf Crisis

Q. President Bush, in your speech in Parliament, you said we Czechoslovaks understand better than any other nation the Kuwaiti situation. Suppose that something similar happens in our part of the world. What attitude U.S. would adopt since we have no oil here?

President Bush. I'm glad you raised that, because one thing that is very clear to me is that what Saddam Hussein has done in taking over Kuwait is devastating to the economies of Eastern Europe, [to] say nothing of the economies of the West and every other part of the world. This naked aggression against Kuwait has clearly had an adverse effect on the economies of every single country because of the disproportionate amount of the GNP that is assigned to energy. So, I am very clear that it is not simply the United States and other countries in the West that are getting hurt by Saddam Hussein's aggression and what that means in terms of higher oil prices but every country as well. Clearly, this is true in Eastern Europe.

Your question, other than that, is too hypothetical for me to say what we might do under some hypothetical situation. But I can guarantee you, we are going to continue to stand against this aggression and do our level best to see that the United Nations resolutions are fully implemented—hopefully, in a peaceful manner. But Saddam Hussein has got to withdraw from Kuwait without condition, and the legitimate leaders have to be restored, and the hostages—and Czechoslovakia has some, and so does the United States—must be freed. This inhumane treatment of hostages is unacceptable. And then there must be a stable order in the Gulf.

So, these objectives will be fulfilled. And my little few hours I've had here on this visit convinced me that it's everybody that's being hurt by this aggression.

Q. President Havel, do you agree with President Bush's views on the Gulf, and do you believe the United States is acting responsibly in the Gulf?

President Havel. Czechoslovakia has made it very clear on a number of occasions that it is necessary to resist evil, that it is necessary to resist aggression, because our own history has taught us ample lessons about the consequences of appeasement.

Dear friends, unless you want the winds to carry us away, you have to accept the situation that there is room for one more question only. [Laughter]

Q. President Havel, do you fear that the Gulf situation is taking too much money away from the kind of problems that it could solve in Eastern Europe?

President Bush. —talking about oil prices?

President Havel. It is my opinion that all the resources that are expended on resisting aggression anywhere in the world finally turned to the good of all humankind.

President Bush. Thank you very much. You heard our host.

President Havel. Thank you all for your attention.

Q. President Bush, there is some feeling that you are too much in a hurry. What do you think of a moratorium that's being called for, in terms of hostilities in the Gulf, by Mubarak [President of Egypt] and other leaders?

President Bush. Mr. Mubarak and I see eye to eye on this situation in the Gulf.

President's Remarks at Ceremony Commemorating End of Communist Rule, November 17, 1990 [1]

Thank you, Mr. President, and thank you, my Czech and Slovak friends. It is a tremendous honor to me to be the first sitting American President to visit this proud and beautiful country and to be able to join you on the first anniversary of the extraordinary Velvet Revolution. What a powerfully moving sight it is.

There are no leaves on the trees, and yet it is Prague Spring. There are no flowers in bloom, and yet it is Prague Spring. The calendar says November 17th, and yet it is Prague Spring.

Your Declaration of Independence proclaims: "The forces of darkness have served the victory of light. The longed-for age of humanity is dawning." Today the freedom-loving people of the world can bear witness that this age of humanity has now finally and truly dawned on this splendid nation.

Seven decades ago, an unprecedented partnership began between two Presidents: the philosopher, Tomas Masaryk, and the idealistic scholar, Woodrow Wilson. It was a partnership as well among Czechs and Slovaks to

join together in federation. And, yes, it was a long, hard road from their work on your Declaration of Independence to this magnificent celebration today. I am proud to walk these last steps with you as one shared journey ends and another begins.

Our countries share a history. We share a vision. And we share a friendship, a friendship Masaryk described to Czech-American soldiers seventy years ago. He said: 'Do not forget that the same ideals, the same principles ever unite us. Do not forget us as we shall never forget you." That is why I'm here today. We have not forgotten.

The world will never forget what happened here in this square where the history of freedom was written—the days of anguish, the days of hope. So many times, you came here bearing candles against the dark night, answering the call of Comenius to follow "the way of light." These brave flames came to symbolize your fiercely burning national pride.

A year ago, the world saw you face down totalitarianism. We saw the peaceful crowds swell day by day in numbers and in resolve. We saw the few candles grow into a blaze. We saw this square become a beacon of hope for an entire nation as it gave birth to your new era of freedom.

This victory owes its heart to two great heroes. Alexander Dubcek—twenty-two years ago, he led this nation in its first sweet taste of liberty. His are the will and compassion that are the living Czechoslovakia. And then President Havel, a man of wisdom, a man of tremendous moral courage. In the dark years, on one side stood the state; on the other side, Havel. On one side, tyranny; on the other, this man of vision and truth. Among the first was Havel, and now there are millions.

Today a Europe whole and free is within our reach. We've seen a new world of freedom born amid shouts of joy; born full of hope, barreling with confidence toward a new century; a new world born of a revolution that linked this square with others—Gdansk, Budapest, Berlin—a revolution that joined together people fueled by courage and by humanity's essential quest for freedom.

For four decades, our two nations waited across the divide between East and West, two peoples united in spirit, in vision, and yet separated by conflict. Today the United States and

Czechoslovakia stand together, united once more in our devotion to the democratic ideal.

Now, with the division of Europe ending and democracy ascending in the East, the challenge is to move forward. In Czechoslovakia: from revolution to renaissance, across this continent toward a new Europe in which each nation and every culture can flourish and breathe free. On both sides of the Atlantic: toward a commonwealth based on our shared principles and our hopes for the whole world, a commonwealth inspired by the words of your great Comenius written three centuries ago: "Let us have but one end in view: the welfare of humanity."

A thousand miles to the south, this new commonwealth of freedom now faces a terrible test. Czechoslovakia was one of the first nations to condemn the outrage in the Persian Gulf, one of the first to measure the magnitude of the wrong committed in the name of territorial ambition. It is no coincidence that appeasement's lonely victim half a century ago should be among the first to understand that there is right and there is wrong, there is good and there is evil, and there are sacrifices worth making.

There is no question about what binds our nations, and so many others, in common cause. There is no question that ours is a just cause and that good will prevail. The darkness in the desert sky cannot stand against the way of light. I salute your courageous President when he joins us in saying that Saddam Hussein's aggression must not be rewarded.

Earlier today I told your Parliament, we know this is a difficult time for you, but also a time of extraordinary optimism. As you undertake political and economic reform know one thing: America will not fail you in this decisive moment. America will stand with you. We will continue along the road mapped out by our Presidents more than seventy years ago, a road whose goal was described by Woodrow Wilson: "to bring peace and safety to all nations and make the world itself at last free."

For the past seventy years, your Declaration of Independence has been preserved and cherished in our Library of Congress. I say, it is time for Masaryk's words to come home. And as humanity and liberty return to Czechoslovakia, so, too, will this treasured document.

On behalf of the people of the United States, I am proud to be able to tell the people of Czechoslovakia: 1989 was the year that freedom came home to Czechoslovakia; 1990 will be the year your Declaration of Independence came home to the golden city of Prague. May it be for future generations a reminder of the ties that bind our nations and the principles that bind all humanity.

In 1776, when our Declaration of Independence was first read in public, a bell tolled to proclaim the defiant thrill of that moment. That bell—we call it, at home, the Liberty Bell—has for 200 years symbolized our nation's deepest dedication to freedom—dedication like your own. Inscribed on this bell are the words: "Proclaim liberty throughout all the land." We want to help you proclaim your new liberty throughout all this proud and beautiful land, and so today we give to you our last replica of the Liberty Bell. You know, one of our patriotic songs proclaims, "Sweet land of liberty—from every mountainside, let freedom ring."

And so, when bells ring in Wenceslas Square or in Bratislava or anywhere in this glorious country, think of this bell and know that all bells are tolling for your precious liberty, now and forever. And so, now I am proud to ring this bell three times. Once for your courage, once for your freedom, and once for your children.

[At this point, the President rang the bell.]

May God bless Czechoslovakia. Thank you all very much.

U.S.-Czechoslovakia Trade Agreement

Statement by Press Secretary Fitzwater, November 17, 1990 [1]

The United States and Czechoslovakia today exchanged diplomatic notes bringing into force the trade agreement signed by the two Governments last April. The agreement extends most-favored-nation (MFN) tariff treatment to Czechoslovak exports to the United States and U.S. exports to Czechoslovakia. President Bush expressed his hope that the mutual extension of MFN tariff treatment will "provide the impetus for greatly expanded trade be-

tween our two countries and the first step toward a normalization of our bilateral trade relations. The exchange follows approval of the agreement on November 16, 1990, by the Czechoslovak Federal Assembly. The U.S. Congress approved the extension of MFN on October 23.

The agreement, along with its side letters on trade and financial matters, intellectual property, and tourism, contains important guarantees for American businesses, including the right to nondiscrimination in renting office space, paying for local goods, and establishing bank accounts. Through this agreement, the Czechoslovak Government has also committed to upgrade substantially its protection of intellectual property rights, bringing its intellectual property regime to a level on a par with that of other industrialized nations.

The implementation of this agreement coincides with the next phase of Czechoslovakia's concerted efforts at market reform and trade liberalization. The Government of Czechoslovakia has announced plans to activate a number of important reform measures in January 1991, including price liberalization through the delinking of retail and wholesale prices, internal currency convertibility, and the privatization of large state enterprises through the establishment of joint ventures with foreign entities.

President Bush praised Czechoslovakia's reform efforts as "impressive initiatives, heralding a new age in Czechoslovakia's relations with the international trading system." The President also expressed his hope that Czechoslovakia's reforms would continue to move the country towards full trade liberalization.

Combined with the current and planned reforms in Czechoslovakia, the extension of MFN should result in the threefold increase in bilateral trade over the next few years, setting the stage for a strong trade relationship between our two countries.

---

1 Text from Weekly Compilation of Presidential Documents, November 26, 1990.

Waiver of Jackson-Vanik Amendment and U.S. Economic Assistance to the Soviet Union

President's Remarks After Meeting with Soviet Foreign Minister Eduard Shevardnadze, December 12, 1990 (opening remarks deleted) [1]

I have just had an opportunity to discuss with Foreign Minister Shevardnadze a number of issues of U.S.-Soviet relations, including our cooperation in the Gulf. And I'm pleased with the great progress that we made on START [Strategic Arms Reduction Talks] and hopeful that we will be ready to sign a treaty at a summit in Moscow on February 11 through 13th.

We also talked at length about the situation in the Soviet Union and the response of the United States to the economic problems there. I asked Minister Shevardnadze to convey to President Gorbachev my desire to respond both to the short term needs of the Soviet Union and to contribute to fundamental economic reform—[I have] long supported *perestroika*, and continue to.

We discussed frankly the relationship of economic change in the Soviet Union to the critical task of democratization. And I reiterated our strong desire to see both political and economic reform continue because they are inextricably linked. I outlined specific and important steps that we're willing to take in support of reform. And after consulting closely with Secretary [of Agriculture] Yeutter as well as Secretaries Brady and Baker, I told Minister Shevardnadze that I am prepared to respond to a Soviet request for credit guarantees for purchase of agricultural commodities through a waiver of the Jackson-Vanik amendment.

While I've taken this step I still look forward to a passage of the Soviet emigration law codifying the generally excellent practices of the past year. And this then will permit us to make further progress toward the normalization of the U.S.-Soviet economic relationship.

In addition, we have proposed to the Soviets a special technical assistance project to help in assessing their food distribution problem and to support market reforms. I will also authorize a joint public-private medical assistance effort to help the Soviet Union cope with immediate shortages of pharmaceuticals and basic medical supplies.

In the longer term, only steps that the Soviet Union itself takes can assure the economic health there. Thus, to promote fundamental economic reform I will propose that the World Bank and the IMF work out with the Soviet Union a special association to give the U.S.S.R. access to the considerable financial and economic expertise of those institutions. I have asked Secretary of the Treasury Nick Brady, as U.S. Governor of both institutions, to pursue this proposal with them and also with our other allies, who I'm sure will be in accord.

As I have said before, I want *perestroika* to succeed. The Soviet Union is facing tough times, difficult times. But I believe that this is a good reason to act now in order to help the Soviet Union stay the course of democratization and to undertake market reforms. The United States has an interest in the Soviet Union—able to play a role as a full and prosperous member of the international community of states. And I am hopeful that these initiatives will further that goal.

White House Fact Sheet on Waiver of the Jackson-Vanik Amendment, December 12, 1990 [1]

The President has decided to waive for the Soviet Union application of the freedom of emigration provisions contained in the Jackson-Vanik amendment (section 402) to the 1974 Trade Act. The Jackson-Vanik amendment effectively bars access to official credit and credit guarantee programs to countries which restrict emigration. The President made this decision:

- based on the liberalization of Soviet emigration policy in recent years by which an estimated 360,000 people will emigrate in 1990;
- after receiving assurances that this policy will continue, and
- to make food available to the Soviet Union in the form of up to $1 billion in Commodity Credit Corporation (CCC) credit guarantees for the purchase of U.S. agricultural products.
- The President's waiver will be valid until at least July 1991, at which time he will need to determine whether to extend the waiver.

While the President has taken this action on Jackson-Vanik, he does not plan at this time to send the U.S.-Soviet trade agreement, signed during the Washington Summit in June 1990, to the Congress. Only when the trade agreement is approved by Congress and takes effect could the Soviet Union receive most-favored-nation trading status.

The immediate effect of the President's action is to make the Soviet Union eligible for export credit guarantees under the CCC General Sales Manager program for the purchase of American agricultural products. This form of food assistance responds to Soviet requests for credit guarantees and will help the Soviet authorities address current food shortages. The waiver will also restore Soviet eligibility for Export-Import Bank credits and credit guarantees. However, the Stevenson amendment to the Ex-Im Bank Act and the Byrd Amendment to the 1974 Trade Act limit credits and guarantees to $300 million, with a subceiling of $40 million and other restrictions on Ex-Im Bank credits or guarantees in support of the fossil fuel industry.

In accordance with the requirements of Jackson-Vanik, before formally executing a waiver the President will report to Congress his determination that a waiver will substantially promote its freedom of emigration objectives in the Soviet Union. This report will also state that he has received the required assurances on Soviet emigration practices.

White House Fact Sheet on the Medical Assistance Program for the Soviet Union, December 12, 1990 [1]

The President has decided to establish a mixed public-private medical assistance effort to help the Soviet Union deal with acute, immediate shortages of pharmaceutical and basic medical supplies. The effort would rely on private voluntary organizations with U.S. Government support, to provide and distribute medicines and medical supplies within the Soviet Union. At least initially, these medicines and supplies would be donated by U.S. firms.

A U.S. task force, with representatives from the U.S. Government and private voluntary organizations, will be set up to coordinate and facilitate the overall relief effort.

• The Agency for International Development (AID) will contact private voluntary organizations and pharmaceutical firms to solicit donations. AID will provide financial assistance to participating private voluntary organizations.

• U.S. private voluntary organizations will organize, deliver, and distribute privately donated medical and pharmaceutical supplies in the Soviet Union.

• The U.S. Embassy in Moscow, working with Soviet authorities in the central government and at the republic and city level, and with U.S. private voluntary organizations already in the Soviet Union, will work to identify specific needs and medical assistance priorities.

The magnitude of the program and the specific materials to be provided will depend on both this detailed assessment of needs and the extent of private interest in this effort.

Ideally, U.S. assistance will be targeted at specific groups in the population needing medical supplies (e.g., disposable syringes for infants, insulin for diabetics, drugs for those with leukemia, etc.).

White House Fact Sheet on Technical Assistance in Food Distribution and Marketing for the Soviet Union, December 12, 1990 [1]

The United States is prepared to send to the Soviet Union this month a team of private and public sector experts in the field of food distribution and marketing. The team's mission will be to assess the problems of food distribution, and provide technical assistance to central, republic, and local authorities in the Soviet Union.

The team will identify ways to strengthen and support market forces in the Soviet Union's food marketing system, consider alternatives to assist vulnerable populations, and recommend measures to improve the availability of food to the Soviet people.

The team will include experts from the U.S. private sector, universities, private voluntary organizations, and the U.S. Government. Team members will work closely with Soviet Government officials, as well as officials of the republic governments.

White House Fact Sheet on the Soviet Union and International Financial Institutions, December 12, 1990 (Excerpt) [1]

The President has proposed a special association of the Soviet Union with the International Monetary Fund (IMF) and the World Bank that will give Moscow access to the economic and financial expertise in those institutions. He has asked Secretary of the Treasury Brady, as U.S. Governor of the IMF and World Bank, to pursue this proposal with the institutions and other countries and to develop with them the necessary new arrangements.

We believe it is best for the Soviet Union to establish such a relationship with these institutions before addressing the issue of full membership.

---

1 Text from Weekly Compilation of Presidential Documents of December 17, 1990.

Challenges Facing the Atlantic Alliance

Excerpts from Secretary Baker's North Atlantic Council Intervention, Brussels, December 17, 1990 [1]

[Secretary Baker began by reiterating Persian Gulf policy and concluded those remarks as follows.]

Before discussing the Soviet Union I would like to make a critical point about responsibility-sharing in the Gulf, a region that is vital to all of us. When I last spoke with you on this subject, we had not yet augmented our forces in the Gulf to provide a credible offensive capability. That was a very big decision for us—not in abstract but human terms. It meant calling up reserves and dividing tens of thousands of families. It means significant new economic burdens for us. And it means real risks and real sacrifices by the American people. It is in this context that we will be coming to you again to discuss how we might responsibly share these additional costs and risks.

Politically, we need to share responsibilities in helping our publics understand this crisis as a test of a new world order and our hopes for a new era of peace.

Economically, we need to share equitably the responsibility to absorb the massive costs of this crisis for us, for the coalition facing Iraq, and for nations which have suffered the most for supporting the United Nations. I have spoken to you before about the impact on one of our member states, Turkey. It's essential that the commitments made to Turkey are fulfilled, and even enhanced.

Militarily, we share responsibility to show Saddam Hussein the choice he really faces and to carry through with the United Nations' commitments.

Soviet Union and Eastern Europe

I would like to turn now to another great challenge facing the West—our relations with a rapidly changing Soviet Union.

Let me make several observations:

First, as my Houston meeting with Foreign Minister Shevardnadze [prior to Mr. Shevardnadze's meeting with President Bush on December 12] demonstrates, Moscow continues to act as a solid partner on many important issues. The new thinking has, in fact, become increasingly the new Soviet policy. We have a partnership in the Gulf. On the Middle East, our discussions suggest that the Soviets will support a practical, not simply a rhetorical or symbolic approach to the peace process. On Angola, Afghanistan, and El Salvador, we are moving closer to ending bloodshed and achieving peace.

On START, we made good progress toward closing out our remaining differences on some highly technical issues. We remain confident that we will have a START Treaty ready for signing when President Bush travels to Moscow in February to meet with President Gorbachev.

Second, our response to the deteriorating Soviet internal situation has been to provide short term assistance to help the Soviets get over this critical transition period. As the President announced last Wednesday, our assistance will take the form of medical supplies, guarantees for food credits, including a Jackson-Vanik waiver, and technical economic help. We have also proposed granting the Soviets special associate status in the IMF and World Bank. Our assistance complements that undertaken by many other members of the Alliance and the European Community.

In providing this assistance, we have sought to make it clear to the Soviets that this must be transitional aid. We continue to press them to ensure that any assistance the West provides is consistent with their long term objectives of democracy and a market economy. This is especially important given the new, critical stage we now see the Soviets entering domestically.

Third, the short term question the Soviet leadership faces now is not so much whether reform can succeed, but whether anarchy and chaos can be prevented. There is the danger that any effort to respond to chaos by strengthening those sectors of Soviet society that are more committed to centralized, command-style solutions,

especially the military and KGB, could have unintended consequences.

Fourth, and finally, instability and chaos in the Soviet Union are in no one's interest. But we are convinced that the only way to ensure long term stability is to continue, indeed accelerate, both political and economic reform. It would be disastrous, for example, for Moscow to crack down on the cooperatives and informal markets that are springing up. That could have a chilling effect on economic and political reform, exacerbating the problems Moscow faces.

Reform in Central and Eastern Europe has also reached a critical stage. The easy steps have been taken. Only hard choices remain. We must work together to ensure that the democratic breakthroughs of 1989 do not become the breakdowns of 1991. As we find billions for transitional assistance for the Soviet Union, we cannot ignore those countries that have made the difficult decisions for reform and have become laboratories for the success of this democratic experiment.

The Alliance must ensure that our liaison missions to the East actually fulfill their purpose of drawing our former adversaries into the democratic community of nations. The members of the Alliance, bilaterally and within CSCE, must continue their efforts to support democracy and market reforms in Central and Eastern Europe. The Gulf crisis has hit those governments particularly hard.

Guiding NATO's Continuing Adaptation

The third challenge is to guide NATO's continuing adaptation. Our work over the past 18 months, especially at the London Summit, has accomplished a great deal and charted a course for further change.

Yet our most fundamental tasks still lie ahead: We need to manage our success; we need to adapt ourselves to handle new threats to our common security that we and our publics are still only beginning to recognize.

My comments about Iraq, the Soviet Union, and Central and Eastern Europe should leave no doubt that the world—indeed, the world of Europe and its immediate environs—remains a place of turmoil and danger.

Whereas our security focus has been riveted for 40 years on the

preponderant Soviet military threat to the east, I would contend that today, and in the future, our collective focus must swing through a wider arc.

I believe our task is fivefold:

First, we need to continue to offer insurance for our members against dangers posed by the Soviet Union and its still considerable conventional and nuclear capabilities. The nature of this danger has undoubtedly changed, and our immediate task is to deal with Soviet power, present and potential, by finding ways to bring the U.S.S.R. into a European order that supports democracy and stability.

Second, we have a strong common interest in promoting a stable security environment throughout Europe—and especially in Central and Eastern Europe—based on the growth of democratic institutions and commitment to peaceful resolution of disputes. Indeed, European security has been threatened many times before by the spillover of political instability and conflict from lands just outside your borders. The challenges —political, economic, and security—of the struggling nations of Central and Eastern Europe are our challenges, too. It's in our interest that those nations not relive the bleak chapters of their history.

Third, we need to recognize that our member states face real and potential direct threats to their territory from other directions—in particular, from the south and the southeast. This is evident in Turkey. It should be evident in the Mediterranean.

Fourth, Iraq's aggression in the tinderbox of the Middle East certainly poses a danger to Western Europe that could be as important as any direct threat to NATO territory. If we let formalistic logic paralyze our efforts to adapt this Alliance to meet these kinds of dangers, we will simply repeat the deadly errors of earlier generations. And this is not likely to be the last challenge we face from that neighboring region.

Fifth, this Alliance can serve—as provided for in Article IV of the North Atlantic Treaty—as a transatlantic forum for Allied consultations on any issue that affects our vital interests and for coordinating our efforts at arms procurement and arms control. This should include work against the proliferation of weapons of mass destruction, a danger that may be one of the most significant and difficult security threats we face in the 1990's.

I am pleased that the London and Paris Summits, through a blend of political and security measures, have already marked much progress for us in reorienting our Alliance to meet this five point agenda. In particular, our evolving ties of peaceful cooperation with the Soviet Union and the nations of Central and Eastern Europe are healthy beginnings on which we must build.

But I think our strategy review is also revealing that to reorient the Alliance to meet this wider arc of security questions, we also need to evaluate how Europe and North America will organize their common security effort in years ahead. Our new realism about a broader security agenda needs to be complemented by a realistic appreciation of the interest in a European security identity.

The United States has long supported a strengthened European role within the Alliance. So we welcome the prospect of sustaining the transatlantic partnership on security affairs with a more confident and united Europe—a partnership consonant with the North Atlantic Treaty. We know that the common values that bind us offer greater cohesion than any external threat.

Indeed, I believe a stronger European identity within the Alliance is all the more important given the changing security agenda. We would be especially interested in how a European defense identity might help meet those challenges I noted above upon which NATO traditionally has not acted. In this respect, we have noted with particular interest suggestions that the WEU —an organization that has twice responded to threats in the Gulf region—might form the basis of such an identity. A European pillar for the Alliance building on the experience of the WEU could help us rise above the old and sterile debate about "out-of-area" roles.

Developments on this issue are, of course, of fundamental importance to the WEU and the EC. These developments also affect every individual ally seated at this table.

The path we take to arrive at a more mature security relationship will have serious and enduring consequences for our mutual relations and common security interests. We have to get it right.

I recognize that the history of European integration has often successfully relied on the launching of a visionary idea, pursued thereafter through multiple, incremental, and difficult negotiations. In this case, I believe the European process needs to proceed in a fashion that ensures detailed consideration of its effects on related institutions and allies.

A world order creating peace, ensuring stability, and fostering prosperity and liberty cannot rest on a Europe divided from North America. The new world order cannot afford an "insular" Europe or an "isolationist" North America.

I am confident that if Europe intends to develop a security identity, we can produce a more clearly defined, visible European pillar that contributes to NATO's ability to handle its new security challenges. To do so, I look forward to continuing close consultations here as NATO's strategy review and parallel EC processes proceed in coming months. It is imperative, as we proceed along these new pathways, that our deliberations are open and that our conclusions are arrived at through close, reinforcing consultations among all of the nations and institutions involved. The consensus of the past must be carried forward to the future.

We need to work together to make sure we get the transatlantic relationship as right in the next forty years, as it has been for the past forty. If we coordinate now—at a time when many embryonic ideas are on the table—we can ensure that a durable and mature transatlantic partnership can emerge.

_____

1 Department of State Press Release 221, December 17, 1990

Soviet Foreign Minister Shevardnadze's Resignation

The Trials Which Await Our People

by Eduard A. Shevardnadze

Delivered before the Fourth Congress of the People's Deputies, Moscow, U.S.S.R., December 20, 1990. [1]

Comrade deputies! I have perhaps the shortest and the most difficult speech of my life. I did not ask for the floor, but since certain deputies have insisted—the reasons, what it is about, are known to me, why this particular group has insisted on my speaking.

I have drawn up the text of such a speech, and I gave it to the secretariat, and the deputies can acquaint themselves with it— what has been done in the sphere of current policy by the country's leadership, by the President and by the Ministry of Foreign Affairs, and how the current conditions are shaping up for the development of the country, for the implementation of the plans for our democratization and renewal of the country, for economic development and so on.

A certain amount has been done, and this is spoken of in the speech. I would like to make a short statement, consisting of two parts.

Yesterday there were speeches by some comrades—they are our veterans—who raised the question of the need for a declaration to be adopted forbidding the President and the country's leadership from sending troops to the Persian Gulf. That was the approximate content, and this was not the first or the second occasion— there are many such notes and items in the press and on television and so on. And these speeches yesterday, comrades, filled the cup of patience, to overflowing.

I'll put it bluntly. What, after all, is happening with the Persian Gulf? On about ten occasions, both in the country and abroad, I have had to speak and explain the attitude and the policy of the Soviet Union toward this conflict. This policy is serious, well considered, sensible and in accordance with all present standards of civilized relations between states.

We have friendly relations with the state of Iraq. They have been built up over years. These relations are being preserved, but we have no moral right to reconcile ourselves to aggression and the annexation of a small, defenseless country. In that case we would have had to strike through everything that has been done in recent years by all of us, by the whole country and by all of our people in the field of asserting the principles of the new political thinking. That is the first thing.

Second, I have explained repeatedly, and Mikhail Sergeyevich spoke of this in his speech at the Supreme Soviet, that the Soviet leadership does not have any plans—I do not know, maybe someone else has some plans, some group—but official bodies, the Ministry of Defense—charges are made that the Foreign Minister plans to land troops in the Persian Gulf, in the region.

I explained that there are no such plans. They do not exist. Nobody is going to send a single military man, or even a single representative of the Soviet armed forces there. This has been said. But someone needed to raise this issue, this problem again. And I know what is happening in the corridors of the Congress.

The third issue. I said there, and I confirm it and state it publicly, that if the interests of Soviet people are encroached upon, if just one person suffers—wherever it may happen, in any country, not just in Iraq but in any other country—yes, the Soviet Government, the Soviet side will stand up for the interests of its citizens.

I think that deputies should back up the Soviet leadership in this. But I would like to raise another question.

Excuse me, is it all accidental? Is it an accident that two members of the Parliament make a statement saying that the Minister of Internal Affairs was removed successfully and that the time has come to settle accounts with the Foreign Minister? This statement has been circulated literally throughout the world press and our newspaper.

Are they such daredevils, these lads—I will call them that, age permits me to because they are really boys in colonel's epaulets—to address such statements to a Minister, to a Member of the Government?

Look in the newspaper. I will not name a single surname today. And what is surprising, and I think we should think seriously: who is behind these comrades, and why is no one rebuffing them and saying that this is not so and that there are no such plans? But perhaps there are such plans?

In this connection permit me to say a few words about the personal

worth of the man, about his personal sufferings.

Because many people think that the Ministers who sit there or the Members of the Government or the President, or someone else, are hired, and that they can do what they like with them. I think that this is impermissible.

In this connection, I remember the Party Congress. Was this really a chance phenomenon? Because at the Congress a real struggle developed, a most acute struggle, between the reformers and—I will not say conservatives, I respect the conservatives because they have their own views which are acceptable to society— but the reactionaries, precisely the reactionaries.

And this battle, it must be stated bluntly, was won with merit by the progressive section, the progressive members, delegates, the progressively minded delegates to the Congress.

I would like to recall that it was against my will, without my being consulted, that my name, my candidacy was included for secret voting. And I had 800 against, 800 delegates voted against. What then—is this random or on purpose? Is the policy the Ministry of Foreign Affairs conducts not good enough? Or am I personally undesirable? This is a serious matter, more than serious.

I say that, all the same, this is not a random event. Excuse me, I am now going to recall the session of the Supreme Soviet. on Comrade Lukyanov's initiative, literally just before the start of a meeting, a serious matter was included on the agenda about the treaties with the German Democratic Republic.

As it happened, I was traveling, and they called in deputies, and people found themselves in a totally stupid position, and the issue was a flop. I had to speak myself the following week.

And how did it turn out? The same people who are now speaking as the authors came out with serious accusations against the Minister of Foreign Affairs, of unilateral concessions, of incompetence, lack of skills and so on and so forth.

Not one person could be found, including the person in the chair, to reply and say simply that this was dishonorable, that this is not the way, not how things are done in civilized states. I find this deeply worrying. Things went as far as personal insults. I endured that, too. Comrades, a hounding is taking place.

I will not name the publications, all manner of publications, the Pamyat Society—I add the Pamyat Society to

these publications —but what statements: Down with the Gorbachev clique! And they also add Shevardnadze and several other names.

Who are they, the so-called reformers? I'll put it bluntly, comrades, I was shaken, I was shaken by the events of the first day, of the start of the work of our Congress: by the pressing of a button, the fate not only of the President but of *perestroika* and democratization was decided. Is that normal?

Democrats, I'll put it bluntly: Comrade democrats! In the widest meaning of this word: you have scattered. The reformers have gone into hiding. A dictatorship is approaching—I tell you that with full responsibility. No one knows what this dictatorship will be like, what kind of dictator will come to power and what order will be established.

I want to make the following statement. I am resigning. Let this be—and do not react and do not curse me—let this be my contribution, if you like, my protest against the onset of dictatorship.

I would like to express sincere gratitude to Mikhail Sergeyevich Gorbachev. I am his friend. I am a fellow thinker of his. I have always supported, and will support to the end of my days, the ideas of *perestroika*, the ideas of renewal, the ideas of democracy, of democratization.

We did great work in international affairs. But I think that it is my duty. As a man, as a citizen, as a communist I cannot reconcile myself with what is happening in my country and to the trials which await our people.

I nevertheless believe that the dictatorship will not succeed, that the future belongs to democracy and freedom.

Thank you very much.

Secretary Baker's Press Briefing After Mr. Shevardnadze's Resignation, December 20, 1990 [2]

Ladies and gentlemen, I have a brief statement on the resignation of Foreign Minister Shevardnadze, and then I'll be glad to respond to your questions.

Minister Shevardnadze's resignation and warning, I think, has to be taken seriously. In my experience, Minister Shevardnadze has always worked as a professional who served his country's interests. He was in the forefront of the new thinking in foreign policy and democratization at home, and I think that he has earned the respect of leaders all around the world.

We are pleased that President Gorbachev has said that there will be no change in Soviet foreign policy. Since the United States-Soviet partnership serves the interests of peace internationally and the process of reform domestically, we, of course, expect that to be the case, and we will be watching events closely in the weeks ahead.

As the President has often stated, our new relationship with the Soviet Union depends on its continuing commitment to democratization and to reform. On a personal note, let me say that I have known Eduard Shevardnadze to be a man of his word, a man of courage, conviction and principle. I'm convinced that he is committed to peaceful reform, political and economic, in the Soviet Union, and I'm also convinced that the dramatic moves toward democratization and freedom in Central and Eastern Europe and the new thinking in Soviet foreign policy would never have happened without his and President Gorbachev's courageous leadership.

Q. Mr. Secretary, you and he appeared to have quite a close personal rapport. With the disappearance of that personal relationship, do you think there will be any impact on the progress of arms control negotiations?

A. Well, we hope not, and we frankly do not think so. President Gorbachev has said there will be no change, as a consequence of this resignation, in Soviet foreign policy. And if there is no change, then we would expect that the agreement with respect to START would move forward to the end that President Gorbachev and President Bush could sign it at their February summit.

Q. Could I just follow that up? Do you think the difficulties that he mentioned this morning in his resignation speech may explain some of the hiccups and false starts in the recent negotiations?

A. I just don't know, Jim. That's not something I really can speculate on.

Q. Mr. Secretary, various Sovietologists have already speculated that this is not good news for U.S. policy in the Persian Gulf, particularly if someone more inclined toward the Gulf view comes in to take that job over. Do you foresee any problem, any change there?

A. No, I don't. And the reason I don't is, again, that President Gorbachev has said that Soviet foreign

policy will not change. President Gorbachev himself has assured President Bush on several occasions that the Soviets do not intend to diverge from the United Nations position on this issue.

*   *   *

Q. Mr. Secretary, is there a possibility that this will open a window of opportunity to those forces within the Soviet Union that are not precisely enthusiastic about what has been happening in Eastern Europe and the rapprochement with the West?

A. Well, we don't know, and we certainly hope not. As I said Monday in Brussels, we have seen some worrying signs for a period of time now, and, as I said in my statement, we would obviously be foolish, I think, not to take the warning in Minister Shevardnadze's resignation statement seriously.

But following up on that, we have made it very clear over the 23 months that we have been dealing with the Soviet Union in its efforts at reform, that legitimacy depends on further democratization and not on a return to authoritarian rule. And I said as recently as two or three days ago that we certainly hope that there's nothing done to snuff out these rudimentary markets that are beginning to develop in the Soviet Union on the economic side.

Q. A follow-up on that, sir?
A. Yes.

Q. Is there a possibility that we will review the waiver in Jackson-Vanik because of this?

A. I don't think so. Not as we stand here today, certainly. Just as a pure consequence of this resignation, the answer would be no.

Q. Does this indicate that the ball of string is now beginning to unravel in the Soviet Union? Is this seen by the Bush administration, when you look at the level of the turmoil now within Gorbachev's administration, that really profound difficulties now lie ahead beyond the scope that you would —

A. I don't think we would put it that way, John. We have said for some time that there are significant difficulties that they are facing in their efforts to reform politically and economically.

Certainly, this, I think, points up that there are differences of view and differences of opinion. It's not something that we haven't seen before in public debate coming out of the Supreme Soviet. It's not something we

haven't seen before, and something we haven't spoken to before.

Q. Mr. Secretary, have you this morning or has President Bush this morning spoken with either Minister Shevardnadze or President Gorbachev, or have either of you tried to?

A. No. I have called Minister Shevardnadze, and I have not reached him as yet. I don't think that's surprising, given the circumstances of his announcement.

Q. And if I could just follow up. You have had many, many meetings with him and most recently about a week ago. Was there any indication that you had in your hours of conversation with him that he was contemplating such a move?

A. No.

Q. Mr. Secretary, you said that Secretary Gorbachev said that the foreign policy wouldn't change. But if you look back at the last few months, after Minister Shevardnadze made his speech at the U.N., he was widely criticized in the Supreme Soviet. Recently, President Gorbachev was criticized by military deputies, quite forcefully. It seems that Minister Shevardnadze was one of the leading advocates of standing up to the military and getting concessions from the Soviet military. Isn't it obvious that Soviet foreign policy has changed and is changing here beyond this resignation, and that the military is sort of resurgent in Soviet foreign policy?

A. No. I think it's obvious that there has been for some time an internal debate within the Soviet Union, but this is not surprising, and it is something that we have spoken to, as I said before, on a number of occasions. I think that debate continues. We have no reason whatsoever to doubt President Gorbachev's statement that Soviet foreign policy will not change.

Q. Mr. Secretary, I wonder if you'd talk a little bit about the personal relationship you had with Minister Shevardnadze, and what, if any, impact that did have on the last two years of diplomacy. Obviously, the Soviets did what they did out of their own interests.

A. Sure.

Q. But, nevertheless, I wondered if you'd talk about what difference do you feel that that personal relationship made.

A. Well, I spoke in my opening remarks to the fact that he was a professional who I think was totally focused on representing his country and its interests as he saw them. I certainly think that's what's motivated me in my relationship with the Soviet Union. Having said that, however, I am proud to call this man a friend. I think that we achieved some significant things during the 23 months that we were able to work together, and on a purely personal note, I would have to tell you that I'm going to miss him.

Q. Can I just have a quick follow-up on that?

A. Sure.

Q. Of all the issues you dealt with, from arms control to the Gulf, are there one or two where you'd point to where Shevardnadze's input into the Soviet decision-making was really decisive?

A. The Gulf is one. I think that, as I've said in my statement, I mean I don't think that you can separate him from President Gorbachev. They both exhibited, in my view, courageous leadership in taking some positions that were not always and still are not totally popular within the Soviet Union.

But look what's happened in Central and Eastern Europe. And when they told us that they would not use force to hold Central and Eastern Europe, many people did not believe that, but they did not use force. And we have seen—we have really seen—externally we've seen the reunification of Germany, the ending of the division of Europe, a partnership in terms of our policy on the Gulf, and I think that—again, without trying in any way to suggest that there was any difference between President Gorbachev and Minister Shevardnadze, because I don't think there was—I'm not sure that that would have happened, had he not been the Foreign Minister of the Soviet Union.

Q. Mr. Secretary, what, if anything, more should the United States do to keep this policy that Minister Shevardnadze exemplified going?

A. I think we should continue to make the case to our interlocutors in the Soviet Union that our policy approach of searching for mutual advantage is a good approach. It is one that has paid off in the manner that I've just outlined to you externally for both the Soviet Union and the United States. I think it has the potential for paying off in terms of internal reform, democratization and economic reform within the Soviet Union, and it's a policy approach that we should both continue. And that's why we are heartened when we hear President Gorbachev say there will be no change in foreign policy.

*　　*　　*

Q. You spoke to the Foreign Minister in Houston about the possibility of a step back toward a possible repression. We are told you, again, stated it very strongly—the U.S. position on this. Did he give you any indication that there might be a move in this direction toward some kind of crackdown? And what is your own assessment of the prospects for moving away from democratization in the Soviet Union?

A. Well, I've just said a minute ago that we certainly hope that that will not be the case. We really are not in a position today, I don't think, to stand up here and absolutely guarantee that it won't be the case, just as we haven't been in a position to do that over the course of the past 23 months and just as we were not in a position to guarantee that force would not be used to hold Central and Eastern Europe.

Again, I think it's important we all understand what we mean when we start using terms like "crackdown," and we must, I think, appreciate the desire to employ measured force to protect citizens against inter-ethnic violence, armed militias, and things like that, versus using that force to suppress or stifle peaceful dissent or peaceful expression of opinion.

Q. Can you tell us what his assessment was when you raised it with him recently?

A. I simply said that we were concerned about reports that there would be some resort to force that might be legitimate in the first instance but would get out of hand. We were concerned that it might spill over and get out of hand.

I think it's fair to say that they are committed to reform—"they" being the President and the Foreign Minister—and they would not want to see that happen either. That's what he indicated.

*　　*　　*

Q. Mr. Secretary, some European officials have said that Shevardnadze's resignation and his warning show the need for increased economic assistance for the Soviet Union to help the reformers and help the reforms. Do you agree?

A. The President has just announced a package of economic assistance. One important thing to realize, when you talk about that, is that what's done now should be transitional in na-ture—transitional aid—and that it should be linked to continued reform efforts. I think that what the United States and what some European countries have done here recently, in order to assist in terms of humanitarian assistance and aid to get through a very difficult winter, is substantial. But that kind of assistance must be linked to taking the steps that are necessary to reform that economy so it can support itself.

Q. But should there be more?

A. No. I think for the time being, at least, the Europeans, the United States, and others have been very forthcoming in that regard.

*　　*　　*

Q. Mr. Secretary, do you think perhaps you staked too much on your relationship with Minister Shevardnadze? And will the United States now attempt to forge closer relationships with the leaders of the republics?

A. The answer to your first question is no. In my view, clearly no. We have not risked anything because we have developed a good, personal relationship with the Foreign Minister of the Soviet Union. In fact, I would argue to you that we were able to make some rather significant gains and achievements during that 23 months. But our policy toward the Soviet Union does not rest on personalities. Never has. Still doesn't. It rests on the overriding principle of mutual advantage, as I said before. We think that what has been accomplished during this period of time is in the best interest of the Soviet people and it's in the best interest of the American people. That principle will continue to guide our policy toward the Soviet Union.

We have been willing to, and we said sometime ago that we were going to, see representatives from the republics. We hope very much that the Soviet Union will work out the differences between the center and the republics and an all-union treaty of some sort that will define the relationship. That's going to be essential to economic reform.

But our approach to the Soviet Union is not one that's based on personalities.

---

1 Text provided by Novosti Information Agency, U.S.S.R.

2 Department of State Press Release 223, December 20, 1990.

Presidents Bush and Gorbachev Exchange Videotaped New Year's Day Greetings [1]

President Bush

It's a great pleasure to wish President and Mrs. Gorbachev and all the peoples of the Soviet Union a happy and healthy New Year. In your country and in mine, the start of the New Year is a good time to reflect on the many achievements of the past and to look ahead with hope.

This year, our two countries as well as those around the world, have much to be grateful for. First and foremost, the improved and strengthened relations between the United States and the Soviet Union. Our countries have made great progress, particularly in important political and arms control areas. And we've taken a common approach to a new challenge in the name of stability and peace. I applaud, the world applauds, the decisive action of the Soviet Union in strongly opposing Saddam Hussein's brutal aggression in the Gulf.

But just as important as these new areas of cooperation between our two nations are the increased contacts between the American and Soviet peoples. Tens of thousands of Soviets have had contact with Americans now, and the numbers are growing. Barbara and I are thrilled to see our two peoples meeting and getting to know one another as friendly neighbors.

On this New Year's Day, as you celebrate with your friends and family, I also want to applaud the Soviet Union for the important steps you've taken in building a new society, for the determination with which you are pressing forward with difficult political and economic reforms. It's an arduous journey, but one well worth making, for it is a path that leads to a brighter future for your nation.

The American people look with hope to the year ahead. Our two nations have set out on a new course making a better life for both our peoples and a better world of peace and understanding.

On behalf of the American people, I wish President Gorbachev and all the wonderful people of the Soviet Union a happy, prosperous New Year.

President Gorbachev

Esteemed citizens of the United States of America: on behalf of the Soviet people, I send you New Year's greetings.

The year 1990 is over, and with it the 1980s. They have been full of events of enormous importance. The Cold War has gone. Gone, too, is the direct threat of nuclear disaster. Horizons of peace have begun to open. And Europe, together with the United States and Canada, has been first to take advantage of this by collectively agreeing on how it will enter the 21st century.

Much has yet to be completed. Many questions still worry both Europeans and Asians, everyone in this world—in a world awakened to the quest for its future. The nations and states have moved toward new shores. That path will not be without danger or pain.

At its very beginning, this world community is facing a serious test—aggression in the Persian Gulf. And it must find in itself the strength to overcome it in such a way as not to wreck the movement, which has begun, toward a peaceful period of civilization.

The main thing now, at this turning point in history, is to achieve a firmer realization that only by joint efforts, only through cooperation and by taking account of the mutual dependence of interests, can we expect progress and security for all and, therefore, also for ourselves.

The many encouraging things which have occurred in the world during these years and in the outgoing year are connected with the improvement in Soviet-American relations. The trust and mutual understanding between the leaderships of our two states have led to an improvement in the international situation. I will soon meet again with President George Bush, and I am confident that it will strengthen the constructive beginning of our relations even more.

Not all the old obstacles have been eliminated. Economic and scientific-technical ties still do not meet with the spirit of the times. Nevertheless, Soviet-American interaction is gaining an ever more reliable basis in contacts between the peoples. In the past, it was only our politicians, and sometimes sportsmen, who went to each other's countries. Now, the mood is changing in the business world.

Contacts between business people have become regular. Those in the military are conducting a dialogue in a frank manner. Trips by scientists, performers, artists, and writers, and just travel itself are becoming the norm. We have begun to get to know each other better. That is why a beneficial feeling of solidarity is emerging.

The past year has been a hard one for the Soviet Union. But this has been a year of fundamental changes in society, and a year of the most difficult, but most necessary, decisions. They will enable our great country—and it will remain great—to overcome the crisis situation and march confidently along the path of steady democratic progress.

Life for us all now is no carefree stroll.

In greeting the citizens of America, I wish you a happy New Year, and I wish you success in everything you do, prosperity to your families, and peace to your great country.

---

1 Department of State Dispatch, January 7, 1991.

Soviet Military Actions in the Baltic States

WHITE HOUSE STATEMENT, JANUARY 8, 1990 [1]

The United States is monitoring carefully the Soviet Government's decision to send additional military forces to Moldavia, the Ukraine, Georgia, Armenia, and the three Baltic States—Latvia, Lithuania, and Estonia. This action represents a serious step toward an escalation of tension within the U.S.S.R. and makes the peaceful evolution of relations among the people of the Soviet Union more difficult.

The United States is especially concerned that the Soviet decision to send military units into the Baltic States, which we view as provocative and counterproductive, could damage the prospects for peaceful and constructive negotiations on the future of those States. The United States urges the U.S.S.R. to cease attempts at intimidation and turn back to negotiations that are conducted free of pressure and the use of force.

The United States, which has never recognized the forcible incorporation of the Baltic States into the Soviet Union, supports the aspirations of the Baltic people to control and determine their own future.

PRESIDENT'S REMARKS TO PRESS ON SOVIET MILITARY ACTION IN LITHUANIA, JANUARY 13, 1991 [2]

Well, I've been following the situation in Lithuania and the other Baltic States closely. The turn of events there is deeply disturbing. There is no justification for the use of force against peaceful and democratically elected governments. And the brave people and the leaders of the Baltic States have, indeed, acted with dignity and restraint. The thoughts and prayers of the people of the United States are with them, and particularly with the Lithuanian people who have experienced a great tragedy.

For several years now, the Soviet Union has been on a course of democratic and peaceful change. And we've supported that effort and stated repeatedly how much we admire the

Soviet leaders who chose that path. Indeed, change in the Soviet Union has helped to create a basis for unprecedented cooperation and partnership between the United States and the Soviet Union.

The events that we're witnessing now are completely inconsistent with that course. The progress of reform in the U.S.S.R. has been an essential element in the improvement of U.S.-Soviet relations. Events like those now taking place in the Baltic States threaten to set back or perhaps even reverse the process of reform which is so important in the world and the development of the new international order.

We condemn these acts, which could not help but affect our relationship. At this hour, the United States and the West will redouble our efforts to strengthen and encourage peaceful change in the Soviet Union. Legitimacy is not built by force; it's earned by the consensus of the people, by openness, and by the protection of basic human and political rights. So, I ask the Soviet leaders to refrain from further acts that might lead to more violence and loss of life. I urge the Soviet Government to return to a peaceful course of negotiations and dialogue with the legitimate governments of the Baltic States.

And I did have an opportunity when I talked to President Gorbachev not so many hours ago to encourage the peaceful change there and not the use of force.

Q. Mr. President, was Gorbachev directly behind this military crackdown? Is there any reason to believe the military acted without complete Presidential decree on this?

A. I cannot answer that question. I just don't know the facts of—

Q. Is there any official explanation for what happened in Lithuania?

A. Not an official explanation, but we have a good deal of information on it.

Q. And what about the fallout here? Is the summit off at this point?

A. Well, I've just expressed this statement here, and I just expressed my sentiments in this statement I made, so I can't go beyond that.

Q. Any consideration of export credit guarantees or any other—

A. I'm just not going to go further than what I've said here. I've just laid it out, and people can interpret it any way they want.

Q. Mr. President, if the crackdown continues in the Baltics, will you go to Moscow on February 11th?

A. Well, I would simply— that's too hypothetical. What I'm saying is I hope the crackdown will not continue.

Q. Mr. President, did you get any reassurances from leader Gorbachev about whether he will continue or halt the act, consider reassurances about what he will do next?

A. Well, I heard a statement I was just asking our Soviet experts about in here, where he was talking about curtailing the use of force. I hope that's true, but I did not get direct affirmation from them.

*　　*　　*

Q. Mr. President, do you think that the Soviet Union is striking out on Lithuania at this moment because they think our attention and the attention of the world has been diverted by the Persian Gulf crisis?

A. No.

Q. Are you concerned that by speaking out now that you may jeopardize your support from Mr. Gorbachev in the Persian Gulf crisis?

A. No, I believe the Soviet support for the United Nations approach is solid and firm. And President Gorbachev told me that not so long ago— just when I had the last conversation.

Q. Are you talking about the Friday phone call? Just to clarify—

A. Yes, yes.

*　　*　　*

Q. Mr. President, you remonstrated with Gorbachev last week not to use force in the Baltics, and just yesterday Gorbachev said he was sending emissaries from his Federation Council to mediate. A few hours later the tanks were rolling. Are you afraid that he has lost control in the Soviet Union?

A. Well, I am concerned about the internal affairs there—and he, himself, is very much concerned about that. But let's hope that there will be a peaceful—a return to peace, no more use of force, and that they can peacefully negotiate their differences. That's what I hope for.

I think that's what President Gorbachev—I know that's what he told me he wanted before, and I hope that still holds, and I hope that will obtain. But I am very much concerned about the loss of life there.

SECRETARY BAKER'S STATEMENT, JANUARY 13, 1991 [3]

President Bush has spoken to President Gorbachev about his concerns on the Baltics. As you know, when I was in Milan I expressed my concerns about Soviet actions as well. Moreover, I conveyed those concerns directly to Minister Shevardnadze.

The events of the last twenty-four hours are deeply disturbing and make us even more concerned.

Let me make several points:

- *First*, the United States has never recognized the forcible incorporation of the Baltic States into the Soviet Union.
- *Second*, we have supported *perestroika* and *glasnost* and democratization in the Soviet Union because they have offered the best prospects for lasting improvement in U.S.-Soviet relations and for a better, freer future for the Soviet peoples.
- *Third,* the use of force by the Soviet Government in the Baltics fundamentally and tragically contradicts the basic principles of *perestroika*, *glasnost*, and democratization. *Perestroika* is based on the rule of law, not rule by force.
- *Fourth*, we will continue to monitor the situation closely. Soviet interests, above all else, require the reform process to go forward. Only with continued reform will progress and hope in the Soviet Union be possible. And, in the end, enduring U.S.-Soviet cooperation, indeed, partnership, depends upon continued reform—for partnership is impossible in the absence of shared values.
- *Fifth*, it's hard for me—and many of the colleagues that I've been speaking to on this trip—to understand how force can be used, especially now, to suppress newly emerging democratic institutions.

- *Finally,* let me just simply say I am deeply disturbed and saddened by these developments. Peaceful dialogue, not force, is the only path to long term legitimacy and stability.

NORTH ATLANTIC COUNCIL STATEMENT ON BALTICS, JANUARY 14, 1991 [4]

The Member Nations of the Atlantic Alliance are deeply concerned by developments in the Baltic Republics, in particular the use of military force against Lithuanian institutions and citizens with resulting loss of life. Allies strongly condemn the use of violence by the Soviet armed forces and actions to undermine the democratically elected authorities of Lithuania, as well as actions of intimidation against the other Baltic Republics.

Allies appeal to the Soviet authorities to implement fully the Soviet Union's CSCE commitments, most recently reflected in the Charter of Paris for a New Europe, and to pursue the process of peaceful reform and democratic change. Allies reiterate their support for this process.

Allies strongly reiterate the views expressed in the communique issued on December 18, 1990 by the North Atlantic Council meeting in ministerial session in which they supported the expectations and legitimate aspirations of the Baltic peoples through open dialogue by the Soviet authorities with democratically elected leaders which would lead to a negotiated solution based on the principles of the Helsinki Final Act, and for all concerned to exercise restraint.

Allies agree that the continuation of these alarming developments, in particular the use of force, would have negative consequences for the political situation in Europe as a whole and on their relations with the Soviet Union.

The North Atlantic Council will continue to monitor the situation in Lithuania and the other Baltic Republics very closely.

STATE DEPARTMENT STATEMENT ON SITUATION IN THE BALTICS, JANUARY 22, 1991 [5]

The United States condemns all intimidation and use of force in the Baltic States and regrets deeply the loss of

innocent lives. As the President said yesterday, we urge the Soviet Government to act to end its use of force and turn back to seeking a peaceful, political solution of the conflict.

We have instructed [U.S.] Ambassador [Jack] Matlock to follow up in Moscow on the contacts made here in Washington concerning Sunday's events in Riga. Embassy Moscow also is in contact with various Soviet Government and republic leaders.

In recent days, we have engaged in intensive consultations with our European allies and friends concerning the situation in the Baltic States.

Among member states of CSCE, for example, there is nearly universal condemnation of the recent violence in the Baltics. In concert with a number of other states, we plan in the next few days to invoke the human dimension mechanism, in response to what we view as serious violations of the Soviet Government's human dimension commitments under various CSCE documents, including the Copenhagen Document and the Charter of Paris adopted last November.

The mechanism usually begins with one or more member states formally requesting another member state to explain how its actions conform to its commitments on human and political rights under CSCE. The latter state must respond to the inquiry.

The state or states invoking the mechanism may request a bilateral meeting with the other party. They also may bring their inquiry to the attention of other CSCE states and raise their concerns at CSCE meetings related to the human dimension.

We also note the decision by the EC to postpone this week's scheduled meeting of the EC-U.S.S.R. Joint Commission. We understand that the EC is reviewing its assistance to the U.S.S.R., including the package of measures announced last December. We are undertaking a similar review.

As for direct contacts with the Baltic States, our Consul General in Leningrad, Richard Mills, visited all three capitals over the weekend and consulted with each of the Baltic presidents. We are seeking to maintain U.S. Government official presence in all three Baltic capitals on a continuous basis.

This afternoon Secretary Baker will be meeting with three Baltic leaders: Vice President Kuzmickas of

Lithuania, Deputy Prime Minister Ivans of Latvia, and Minister Lippmaa of Estonia. The Secretary will convey this administration's strong support for the freely and democratically elected governments in the three states and for a peaceful settlement through dialogue.

REMARKS TO PRESS BY SECRETARY BAKER DURING MEETING WITH BALTIC OFFICIALS, JANUARY 22, 1991 [4]

Q. You've had a number of meetings on this subject in the last few days. Has the administration come to a conclusion about how it ought to respond to the way the Soviets have been behaving in the Baltics?

A.The United States and Soviet Union have made tremendous progress over the course of the last two years in improving the relationship between our two countries, and the events of the last ten days to two weeks or so, I'm afraid to say, could have the effect of putting that progress in jeopardy.

We've made known our position to the Soviet Union at a number of levels, including from President Bush to President Gorbachev. I have expressed our concern over the fact that we are deeply disturbed to the new [Soviet] Foreign Minister [Alexander] Bessmertynkh.

So, we'll continue to make our views known to the Soviet Union in the hopes that there can be a peaceful resolution to this situation and that the hopes and aspirations of the Baltic peoples to determine their own future can be given effect. We've always said for a long time that the only way to resolve this problem is through some sort of negotiation or some sort of dialogue.

Q. What about steps? What about a cutoff, for example, of the very recent and fresh economic benefits that the United States planned for the Soviet Union?

A. All of these matters are being reviewed by the United States, as, indeed, I think they are by other countries around the world, including those in Western Europe.

Q. But the summit date is only a couple of weeks away. When are you going to make a decision about this, and would you be planning some sort

of ministerial with the Foreign Minister?

A. As you know, we are engaged right now, have been during the course of the day, in discussions on the strategic arms treaty. [Soviet Deputy Foreign Minister Aleksey] Obukhov is in Washington. He has been meeting with [Under Secretary for International Security Affairs Reginald] Bartholomew. I might just say here that with respect to arms control particularly, we think it is important to move that process forward. But with respect to the summit, we will be discussing this internally and as well with the Soviet Union.

Q. Some people feel maybe you've been a little preoccupied with the situation in the Gulf and haven't been able to fully focus on the situation in the Baltics. Have you been able to do that, and—

A. We've been focusing on it. You know, because you've been travelling with me. I think you know what I had to say during the course of our last trip to the Gulf and to Europe. I think that constitutes focusing on the situation.

STATEMENT BY SOVIET PRESIDENT MIKHAIL GORBACHEV, MOSCOW, JANUARY 22, 1991 [6]

Ladies and Gentlemen,
Comrades,

The crisis, moral and political tension in society, and developments that led to the loss of life require a straightforward and frank talk. A lack of understanding and even unwillingness to understand the policy of the President are manifesting themselves.

I deeply feel the tragic turn the confrontation in Lithuania and in recent days in Riga has taken. I convey most heartfelt condolences to all families affected by misfortune. The circumstances connected with the use of weapons must be thoroughly investigated and judged according to law.

The first and most important thing that I want to say is the following: The developments in Vilnius and in Riga are by no means the manifestation of the policy line of the presidential authority, for the sake of which it was instituted. I therefore resolutely put aside all speculation, all suspicions, and calumnies on that score.

Neither domestic nor foreign policy has undergone changes. Everything remains intact as it was formulated in the documents and official statements of the Soviet leadership.

The developments in the Baltic republics evolved in an atmosphere of the severest crisis. Unlawful acts, trampling on the constitution itself, disregard for presidential decrees, the flagrant violation of civil rights, discrimination against people of a different nationality, irresponsible behavior with regard to the army, to servicemen, and to their families have created an environment and an atmosphere in which this kind of clash can flare up very easily over [the] most unexpected things.

This is precisely the source of the tragedy, not some mythical orders from higher authorities. This is how it happened in both the first and second instances.

As the President, I perceive that the main tasks are preventing an escalation of the antagonism, normalizing the situation, and securing civil accord and cooperation.

In this connection the following are necessary:

- The anticonstitutional laws formulated by the Supreme Soviets of the republics and the resolutions promulgated by the republican governments—above all, those that violate human rights—should be abrogated.
- Any public organization, committee, or front, whatever its program, may seek to take office only constitutionally, without the use of violence. Any attempts to appeal to the armed forces are inadmissible in the political struggle.
- An absolute end should be put to discriminatory measures with regard to military units stationed on the territories of the republics and to the utterly disgraceful attitude toward the families and children of servicemen. In accordance with the current union laws, troops are stationed wherever their presence is prompted by the requirements of defense and of national security.
- Relations between civilian authorities and the military should be based on the laws of the U.S.S.R. At the same time, unwarranted actions by troops are

impermissible. It is the duty and the honor of commanders at all levels to act by order alone, to show restraint, not to bow to provocations, and to strengthen discipline among their subordinates.

- Confirming the constitutional right of a republic to secede from the union, we cannot allow spontaneity or arbitrariness even on the part of elected bodies. Secession is only possible on the basis of the will of the entire population—a referendum—and as a result of a process envisaged by law.

In connection with what has been said, the Federation Council must again take up the discussion of the situation in the Baltics.

Certain circles have capitalized on the events of the past few days to stir up tensions under the pretext that there is a danger of a right-wing turnaround and a dictatorship.

I resolutely reject these conjectures. The gains of *perestroika,* democratization, and glasnost were and will remain lasting values, safeguarded by presidential power.

This certainly does not mean that we can close our eyes when propaganda—yes, precisely propaganda; lets's call things by their names—is intentionally used to provoke chaos, panic, ethnic strife, to pit the army against the people, and for calls to disregard laws.

Events in the Baltics are being used speculatively as a pretext to dismember our armed forces and to propose establishing republican armies.

Such irresponsible statements are fraught with serious dangers, especially when they come from the Russian leadership.

I believe every sensible person understands what this would bring to our country and to the entire world.

Bows to foreign countries and to the United Nations with invitations to decide for us matters that we can and should decide ourselves are strange and ridiculous, to say the least.

We have opened our society to cooperation and interaction with the world, and we will continue to adhere to our foreign policy. The country's internal problems, however, should be decided exclusively by the Soviet people.

I must say that the events are receiving a lopsided interpretation abroad—and in some cases in a manner reminiscent of the ideological war of the past. Many people there and here perceive them inadequately, seeing in them a shift in the policy of the Soviet leadership.

It would be regrettable and dangerous if such an incorrect interpretation threatened recent achievements in international relations.

In the course of acute polemics in the country over the past few days, somber voices have reminded us to give priority to political stability, firm legal order and discipline, economic normalization, resolute movement toward a market, and democratic reforms in our multinational state. I side with this position.

Society is increasingly aware that conscientious work and civil accord, rather than demonstrations, rallies, strikes, the instigation of political passions, and confrontation will lead the country out of the crisis.

I call on all citizens of my country to heed this.

---

1 Text from Weekly Compilation of Presidential Documents of January 14, 1991.
2 Text from Weekly Compilation of Presidential Documents of January 21, 1991.
3 Department of State Document 17, January 13, 1991.
4 Department of State Dispatch, January 28, 1991.
5 Provided to news correspondents by State Department spokesman Margaret Tutwiler.
6 Soviet Embassy Press Release, Washington, January 23, 1991. Text from Tass, U.S.S.R.

U.S.-Soviet February Summit Rescheduled

Statement by Secretary of State Baker, January 28, 1991. [1]

By mutual agreement, Presidents Bush and Gorbachev will be rescheduling their summit in Moscow, originally planned for February, to a later date in the first half of this year.

The Gulf war makes it inappropriate for President Bush to be away from Washington. In addition, work on the START Treaty will require some additional time.

Both Presidents look forward to seeing an exact summit date as soon as it becomes feasible to do so.

---

1 Department of State Document 20, January 28, 1991.

Interview of Alexander Bessmertnykh, New Soviet Foreign Minister, on U.S.-Soviet Relations

Interviewed by Pravda correspondent Vitaly Gan and Tass correspondent Vladimir Matyash after talks in Washington with President Bush and Secretary of State Baker, January 31, 1991. [1]

Q. Alexander Alexandrovich, you have come to this post in an extremely critical period. Could you share your opinion of events in the world?

A. I believe that much in our foreign policy after World War II was determined by what I call a nuclear paradox. I mean that traditional political trends were somewhat distorted by the need to ensure security, taking into account the nuclear factor. That is why great attention was paid to relations with countries having nuclear potential.

It was absolutely necessary, but I believe that at the same time, traditional relations with neighbors were somewhat de-emphasized. I believe that now that we have entered a new stage of arms reductions, strategic balance of forces and parity, we should pay particular attention to neighboring countries, at the same time not depreciating our relations with the United States and other great countries.

In other words, it is necessary to broaden good-neighborly relations focusing on economic, social and cultural tasks. This is our line that should be part of state and national interests. Our country should not be isolated.

There is also another line, concerning relations not only with neighboring countries but with other leading countries of the world. Many people say that because of domestic problems, it has become more difficult to pursue an active policy in such regions as Latin America, Africa and the Pacific, and it should be curtailed. I believe we should retain the current active and dynamic attitude in our foreign policy.

I have always believed that the connection between domestic and foreign policy is not merely philosophical. People justly say that politics is the concentrated expression of economy. This is right, and this is the philosophical side of the matter. But there is also a purely specific, everyday connection between domestic and foreign policy.

There are two aspects here. The first aspect is well known to everybody. Foreign policy helps domestic policy, creating favorable conditions for *perestroika* and all the reforms we are carrying out.

With the United States, we have reached a level of trust and openness that permits us to discuss things that we do not like or that we oppose. The very tone of our dialogue is conducive to the open discussion of mutual problems and even the most delicate issues.

But we should not forget that domestic policy can also promote foreign policy, actively supporting it and being a firm and reliable foundation, or seriously deteriorate it.

Unfortunately, the latter situation exists. I mean that all our difficulties surely provoke an international response. Take, for example, the Baltics. It is easy to fall prey to emotions, which is happening in the West. But the West does not fully understand what is going on there or the Soviet leadership's real stand.

I will say sincerely that during my visit, the Baltics were discussed very keenly, along with other issues. And they were mainly discussed because the West does not fully understand events there. They are prone to look at events there superficially, without going into detail and sources, i.e. theirs is mostly an emotional response. I believe that such a response has the right to exist.

We also regret what is happening there, but it is necessary to gain an understanding of the reasons for such events. Why has President Mikhail Gorbachev's inclination for dialogue failed in Lithuania, while it works in Latvia and Estonia? Why are republics that strive for independence not moving in constitutional ways?

Alexander Alexandrovich Bessmertnykh [1]

Mr. Bessmertnykh, the son of a civil servant, was born November 10, 1933, in Biysk, in south-central Siberia. He graduated in 1957 from the Moscow State Institute of International Relations and has a degree in international law and political science.

Mr. Bessmertnykh (his name is pronounced byeh-SMERHRT-nikh) worked at the United Nations in the Secretariat during the 1960s, served at the Soviet Embassy to the United States from 1970 to 1983, and was later head of the Foreign Ministry department responsible for the United States and Canada.

As one of three First Deputy Foreign Ministers from 1988 to early 1990, Mr. Bessmertnykh was responsible for North America and the Middle East. In those years, he visited Iran, Iraq, Syria and Turkey, among other countries.

From May 1990 to January 1991, when he was appointed Foreign Minister, Mr. Bessmertnykh was Ambassador Extraordinary and Plenipotentiary of the U.S.S.R. to the United States.

---

1 Edited version of biographic data provided by the Soviet Embassy, Washington.

Nobody is saying that independence is impossible. The West should be more attentive and cautious in its assessments. It is extremely easy in politics to mess things up. It is necessary to correlate everything with changes in Europe and with qualitative changes in the world. It is dangerous and inadmissible to expend effort expressing emotions about events, especially since everything in these republics could take place in line with the Constitution.

Thus, in our foreign policy we should first and foremost focus on security issues, i.e. on our relations with nuclear countries having powerful military structures, and on the economic factor, as we are interested in our country being surrounded with partners rather than opponents.

The world is interdependent. No single country can fully provide for itself, including the United States. Political contacts and friendliness should develop. By removing ideology from our relations, we do not mean that there should be no political ties. We simply should not perceive relations between countries through a stereotyped ideological prism, as we did previously.

We considered some countries in Africa, Asia and Latin America close to us because their leaders said things that sounded ideologically pleasant to us. The ideological factor was most important here. But later we discovered that we had a distorted impression of the real state of affairs.

Major large states wishing to develop relations with us remained on the sidelines. Other countries, no less respected, suddenly received special status simply because their leaders made ideologically more pleasant statements. We have already removed all this from our diplomacy. Our relations with states are versatile.

Some people say that our activities in disarmament weakened us. This is certainly a nonprofessional point of view, although it sometimes comes from extremely professional spheres. Eliminating military-political opposition is the most important factor in ensuring security.

What is the sense in stockpiling more and more weapons and engendering new enemies? I believe that this variant is absolutely unacceptable and extremely dangerous. To remove Pershing missiles from the country's temple, to see inveterate enemies become opponents, then neutral entities and finally even partners — such an evolution is very useful.

Q. Let us return to the second part of the question. How would you assess the current state of Soviet-U.S. relations?

A. I have always believed that we should consider them as vitally important for several reasons. First, the United States is a superpower, on which the nature of the world situation depends. It is leading in the Western world and, naturally, our relations with it — to a great extent, but not 100 percent — determine Soviet diplomatic approaches with respect to other states.

It should certainly be a focus of our foreign policy, but it should not overshadow all other things. I believe the United States thinks about us in the same way and understands that we are also a focus of world politics.

My concept is that, admitting the key role of the United States in our relations, we should not consider it as a force prevailing over all the rest. All other regions should play their role and have their own significance. Relations with other countries should not develop in the shadow of Soviet-U.S. relations.

With the United States we have reached a level of trust and openness that permits us to discuss things that we do not like or that we oppose. The very tone of our dialogue is conducive to the open discussion of mutual problems and even the most delicate issues.

Q. Alexander Alexandrovich, some people in the United States speak about a recession in Soviet-U.S. relations and about the possibility of their return to positions like the second half of the 1970s, when the two countries deviated from detente. What can you say about such opinions?

A. Nothing can be excluded. We cannot guarantee the course of events. But I believe that we have reached a level of relations with the United States and the West as a whole that will guarantee qualitative changes and will be able to make the 21st century a century of a completely new world community.

The period between the end of the Cold War and the current new stage has been very short. We are surrounded by people having strong Cold War thinking. I believe we have wrongly spoken about the end of the Cold War and the transition to a period of a broad, active and even absolute partnership.

I believe there should be a transition period between the Cold War and the developed period of partnership. It is natural because it is necessary to do away with Cold War stereotypes that still determine the positions of politicians, parliamentarians and the public. There is an absolute chance of moving relations in the world and our relations with the United States to a qualitatively new level.

There are dangers, especially if the other side is locked into a purely emotional response and into immediate political calculations, at the same time, overlooking the possibility of destroying the historic trend toward the positive development of the world. Unfortunately, all this exists.

That is why our diplomacy and our foreign policy should inspire vigilance and should be a dynamic force. Nothing can be guaranteed in this world. Our policy has a good chance and a sound basis and has created normal living conditions. But it is necessary to protect all this, and we are now busy doing it.

Q. During talks in the U.S. capital, you discussed finishing work on the treaty on strategic offensive weapons. There are reports saying that both sides are experiencing something like despair because there has not been a breakthrough. What were the results of the discussion?

A. There is no despair. On the contrary, I am deeply satisfied with what happened. It is better to postpone the summit than to make a hash of such an important meeting. Circumstances such as the Gulf war and problems with the START treaty impose certain obligations upon us.

I should note that when we, both sides, said it is necessary to continue work on the treaty, this by no means can be interpreted as some crisis in our efforts to finish work on it. We have few unresolved issues.

But when we counted the number of days before the summit and when we had taken into consideration the great amount of work to be done on the treaty, which textually has not been elaborated, not brushed up, we understood that although we can resolve all issues, we will not be ready by the summit.

Practically speaking, we can finish work on the treaty in two to three weeks. In other words there is some progress, and the delay was caused by purely technical reasons. There is not any crisis here. We will try to move things ahead.

Q. **Have you discussed the possibility of economic sanctions by the West in response to events in the Baltics?**

A. I had read about this and heard it before I arrived here. However the issue of sanctions has not been raised. The word itself was not pronounced. The West wanted to signal its dissatisfaction with events in the Baltics. It should be noted that emotions overshadowed the need to understand the course pursued by the Soviet Government.

Of course, events are occurring beyond the control of the President and local authorities themselves. The situation is heated, and some leaders who wish to profit personally by dramatizing the situation are consciously aggravating it. Anything can happen in such conditions.

In short, we did discuss the issue. I believe the established level of relations permits discussing any issue.

Q. **What do you think about regional conflicts? The Gulf war is one of the planet's hot spots. Can Soviet-U.S. interaction put out the flame of such conflicts?**

A. I think it is impossible to pin all hopes on the Soviet Union and the United States, and it is impossible to present things as if everything depends upon them. The conflicting states should resolve conflicts themselves, but our two countries are ready to help where it is possible. It is very important to strengthen the United Nations and give it priority in settling regional conflicts, rather than be drawn into conflicts ourselves.

Q. **The world is at the turn of the 21st century. What can you say about our near future?**

A. It is hard to predict, but I believe that the bipolar world is coming to an end. It is becoming multipolar. It is a positive phenomenon. Stability has been reached in Soviet-U.S. relations. We have reached a considerable level of understanding. Unfortunately, our interaction lacks a concrete foundation, so to speak. But there is a basis, and it is rather firm.

I would like to note that we are still moving away from the idea of having extreme arms potentials. The world is beginning to pay more attention to resolving social, economic and ecological problems. Political directions are changing. Thank God our diplomacy understands this and is beginning to pay more attention to these issues.

Will there be conflicts in the future? Probably, yes. But we are now involved in a very important issue, creating precedents for dealing with them. The situation in the Gulf is contradictory. It was hard for us to choose such conduct, but it is necessary to behave this way, as we are creating a precedent for dealing with aggression.

The fact that the international community has united against the aggression shows that such conduct has prospects. Security should include not only factors such as the number of weapons, missiles or artillery, but the whole complex of state power, including the economy and social stability of society.

I would like to note that the Soviet foreign political course aims fully toward peaceful development, along peaceful channels. This will help us concentrate on resolving our own complicated domestic tasks.

---

1 Pravda, January 31, 1991.

Security Council Passes Another Resolution on Israel, Occupied Territories

U.N. SECURITY COUNCIL RESOLUTION 681, DECEMBER 20, 1990 [1]

The Security Council,

Reaffirming the obligations of Member States under the United Nations Charter,

Reaffirming also the principle of the inadmissibility of the acquisition of territory by war set forth in Security Council Resolution 242 (1967) of 22 November 1967,

Having received the report of the Secretary-General submitted in accordance with Security Council Resolution 672 (1990) of 12 October 1990 on ways and means of ensuring the safety and protection of the Palestinian civilians under Israeli occupation (S/21919), and taking note in particular of paragraphs 20 to 26 thereof,

Taking note of the interest of the Secretary-General to visit and send his envoy to pursue his initiative with the Israeli authorities, as indicated in paragraph 22 of his report, and of their recent invitation extended to him,

Gravely concerned at the dangerous deterioration of the situation in all the Palestinian territories occupied by Israel since 1967, including Jerusalem, and at the violence and rising tension in Israel,

Taking into consideration the statement made by the President of the Security Council on 20 December 1990 (S/22027) concerning the method and approach for a comprehensive, just, and lasting peace in the Arab-Israeli conflict,

Recalling its resolutions 607 (1988) of 5 January 1988, 608 (1988) of 14 January 1988, 636 (1989) of July 1989 and 641(1989) of 30 August 1989, and alarmed by the decision of the Government of Israel to deport four Palestinians from the occupied territories in contravention of its obligations under the Fourth Geneva Convention,

1. Expresses its appreciation to the Secretary-General for his report;

2. Expresses its grave concern over the rejection by Israel of Security Council resolutions 672 (1990) of 12 October 1990 and 673 (1990) of 24 October 1990;

3. Deplores the decision by the Government of Israel, the occupying power, to resume deportations of Palestinian civilians in the occupied territories;

4. Urges the Government of Israel to accept de jure applicability of the Fourth Geneva Convention, of 1949, to all the territories occupied by Israel since 1967, and to abide scrupulously by the provisions of the said Convention;

5. Calls upon the high contracting parties to the Fourth Geneva Convention of 1949 to ensure respect by Israel, the occupying power, for its obligations under the Convention in accordance with Article l thereof;

6. Requests the Secretary-General, in cooperation with the International Committee of the Red Cross, to develop further the idea expressed in his report of convening a meeting of the high contracting parties to the Fourth Geneva Convention and to discuss possible measures that might be taken by them under the Convention and for this purpose to invite these parties to submit their views on how the idea could contribute to the goals of the Convention as well as on other relevant matters, and to report thereon to the Council;

7. Also requests the Secretary-General to monitor and observe the situation regarding Palestinian civilians under Israeli occupation, making new efforts in this regard on an urgent basis, and to utilize and designate or draw upon the United Nations and other personnel and resources present there, in the area and elsewhere, needed to accomplish this task and to keep the Security Council regularly informed;

8. Further requests the Secretary-General to submit a first progress report to the Security Council by the first week of March 1991 and every four months thereafter, and decides to remain seized of the matter as necessary.

STATEMENT BY THE PRESIDENT OF THE SECURITY COUNCIL, DECEMBER 20, 1990 [1]

The members of the Security Council reaffirm their determination to support an active negotiating process in which all relevant parties should participate, leading to a comprehensive, just and lasting peace to the Arab-Israeli conflict through negotiations which should be based on resolutions 242 (1967) and 338 (1973) of the Security Council and which should take into account the right to security of all states in the region, including Israel, and the legitimate political rights of the Palestinian people.

In this context they agree that an international conference, at an appropriate time, properly structured, should facilitate efforts to achieve a negotiated settlement and lasting peace in the Arab-Israeli conflict.

However, the members of the Council are of the view that there is not unanimity as to when would be the appropriate time for such a conference.

In the view of the members of the Council, the Arab-Israeli conflict is important and unique and must be addressed independently, on its own merits.

STATEMENT BY THE PERMANENT MISSION OF ISRAEL TO THE UNITED NATIONS CONCERNING SECURITY COUNCIL RESOLUTION 681, DECEMBER 20, 1990 [2]

Israel expresses its dismay at the one-sided U.N. Security Council Resolution [681] which does not advance the peace process, tranquility or an atmosphere for negotiations. Moreover, this resolution may be interpreted as a license to encourage violence and extremism.

Israel persists in its efforts to promote the peace process and within this framework extended an invitation to the U.N. Secretary-General and his envoy to visit Israel and discuss the situation in the region.

STATEMENT TO THE SECURITY
COUNCIL BY AMBASSADOR
THOMAS R. PICKERING, U.S. PER-
MANENT REPRESENTATIVE TO
THE U.N., DECEMBER 20, 1991 [3]

Mr. President [Al-Ashtal, Permanent
Representative for Yemen], the United
States has supported this text
[Resolution 681]. However, I want to
make it perfectly clear that there are a
number of elements in the text which
cause us concern. There are also elements that are not in the text which
ought to have been. The Council ought
to be willing to say to the Palestinians
that any use of violence to achieve their
ends is plain wrong. We lament the continued violence, particularly in Israel,
where innocent people have been the
victims of numerous stabbings.

The Security Council began this
debate several months ago with the intention of achieving a resolution concerning the protection of Palestinians
in the occupied territories, and that is
what we have achieved today. This has
only been accomplished after long, excruciating, intensive consultations
among members of this Council. It has
taken us far too long to reach this
point. Far too much of our energy was
spent to the detriment of the other
pressing issues facing this Council, including having to deal with proposals
that would have done nothing to improve the situation in the occupied territories.

Nonetheless, I express my appreciation to those of my colleagues who
engaged in these intensive consultations in good faith to achieve a text we
all could support, especially Ambassadors Tornudd [Permanent Representative for Finland] and Razali
[Deputy Permanent Representative for
Finland].

Let there be no mistake, however,
our vote for this resolution is designed
to demonstrate—as we have done all
along—our deep concern about the
situation in the occupied territories.
Our vote today in no way indicates a
change in U.S. policy on any issue related to the Arab-Israeli conflict.

First, we have made clear that the
United States has not changed its position on an international conference on
the Arab-Israeli dispute. Secretary
Baker has said, and I quote: "We have
not in any way or to any extent or to
any degree shifted our policy regarding

the question of an international conference.

First of all we have taken the position for a long time that an international conference, properly structured,
at an appropriate time, might be useful...."

We are not now recommending
that an international conference on the
Arab-Israeli conflict be held, nor are
we supporting a resolution in the
Security Council that would seek to
convene such a conference.

Precisely because of our consistent
position that we will not link the Gulf
crisis and the Arab-Israeli dispute, this
is certainly not an appropriate time for
an international conference.

Indeed, in consultations on the
resolution before us today, we have
turned aside efforts that would have
linked this resolution to the crisis in
the Gulf. Saddam Hussein has tried to
link the idea of an international conference to his invasion of Kuwait, and
the Council has deprived him of any
satisfaction in this regard. Saddam Hussein did not invade Kuwait to benefit
Palestinians; he did so for his own self-
aggrandizement. Nor should Saddam
be rewarded for this aggression by
being made to appear as a savior of the
Palestinian people. Nothing could be
further from the truth. If anything,
Saddam's actions have set back the pursuit of peace and taken Palestinians farther than ever from their goal. Linkage
of the solution to the Gulf crisis with
the Arab-Israeli conflict would not
only be wrong; it undercuts the efforts
of the international community to
reverse Iraq's aggression as evidenced
by the twelve resolutions this body had
passed against the Iraqi invasion of
Kuwait.

Second, the United States has consistently maintained that the Fourth
Geneva Convention applies to all of
the territories occupied by Israel since
1967. The United States has supported
the position here at the United Nations, and we urge the government of
Israel—in fulfillment of its obligation
as a high contracting party, and in accordance with its responsibilities under
Article 1 of the convention—to ensure
respect for the convention and to accept its de jure application and its
provisions. As stated in the past, the
United States regards the phrase
"Palestinian territories occupied by Israel since 1967," which appears in this

resolution, as being merely
demographically and geographically
descriptive and not indicative of
sovereignty.

Finally, Mr. President, the U.S.
position on deportations has not
changed. Indeed, during the course of
the Council's consideration of this
issue, the Government of Israel announced its intention to resume deportations. The United States deplores
this decision. We believe that such
deportations are a violation of the
Fourth Geneva Convention as it pertains to the treatment of inhabitants of
occupied territories. We condemn the
increasing attacks on Israelis and the
deaths which have resulted, just as we
condemn attacks on Palestinians.
Violence is not the way forward;
neither, however, are deportations an
effective or acceptable answer to
violence. We strongly urge the Government of Israel to immediately and permanently cease deportations, and to
comply fully with the Fourth Geneva
Convention in all of the territories it
has occupied since June 5, 1967.

The tragic events that have
prompted this latest round of Security
Council resolutions on the dangerous
deterioration of the situation in the occupied territories occurred against a
background of increasing violence. We
call on all sides to exercise maximum
restraint so as to avoid further violence
and bloodshed.

I also want to take this opportunity
to clarify for the record U.S. views on
several elements of this resolution. The
resolution requests the Secretary-
General to invite the high contracting
parties to the Geneva conventions to
submit their views on the idea of convening a meeting of the high contracting parties and looks forward to
receiving those views. As a high contracting party, my government has
serious questions whether such a meeting realistically can help to improve the
conditions of the Palestinians in the occupied territories. A premature
decision to convene such a conference
invites uncertainty and confusion that,
in the end, could undermine rather
than contribute to the safety and
protection of the Palestinians under Israeli occupation and, more generally,
could have adverse impacts on the future implementation of the conventions.

The United States strongly supports the ongoing efforts of the Secretary-General to monitor and report on the situation in the occupied territories. Nonetheless, my government wants to explain its view regarding the scope of the Council's request that the Secretary-General utilize available personnel of various U.N. organizations in the region and elsewhere for this purpose. U.N. personnel in the area are mostly employees of UNTSO [United Nations Truce Supervision Organization] and UNRWA [United Nations Relief and Works Agency (for Palestine Refugees in the Near East)], organizations with separate and well-defined mandates. No activity should be undertaken that would alter those mandates, which remain in force, and we would oppose any attempt to alter them.

We are pleased to note that the Government of Israel has invited the Secretary General to send his envoy again to Israel and the occupied territories. We strongly hope this visit will take place soon and that his efforts can lead to a genuine amelioration of the situation for Palestinians in the territories and an end to the bloodshed between Israelis and Palestinians.

For our part, the U.S. reaffirms its commitment and determination to support an active negotiating process leading to a comprehensive, just and lasting peace to the Arab-Israeli conflict based on U.N. Security Council Resolutions 242 (1967) and 338 (1973) of the Security Council, and which should take into account the right to security of all states in the region, including Israel, and the legitimate political rights of the Palestinian people. This process of negotiations between the parties concerned is the only way that will advance the cause of peace in the Arab-Israeli conflict, and all of our efforts should be actively focused on renewing this process.

---

1 Text provided by United Nation Information Center, Washington.

2 Text provided by Embassy of Israel, Washington.

3 Department of State Dispatch, December 24, 1990.

Key Challenges Facing South Asia

by John H. Kelly

Statement before the Subcommittee on Asian and Pacific Affairs, House Foreign Affairs Committee, November 2, 1990. Mr. Kelly is Assistant Secretary of State for Near Eastern and South Asian Affairs. [1]

Thank you for this opportunity to discuss developments in South Asia at a time of change and turmoil.

Before discussing each of the South Asian countries in turn, I would like to reflect on the key challenges facing us in South Asia.

First and most important is the search for regional peace and stability. You are familiar with our efforts to reduce the risk of conflict over Kashmir last spring. I am pleased to note that tensions between Pakistan and India have eased since that time. Both countries continue to maintain diplomatic and military contacts. We continue to urge both countries to adopt confidence building measures, and we remain ready to work with them if they should find that helpful.

Bitterness and violence continue to plague the Kashmir Valley, however. A cycle of violence and repression has set in, retarding the ability of Indians, Kashmiris, and Pakistanis to address the underlying issues. The human rights picture is a disturbing one. The Kashmiri militants have exacerbated this situation through tactics we find repugnant. But the Indian authorities have a special responsibility not to depart from due process of law and to maintain law and order in a humane manner.

Closely related is our interest in reducing the proliferation of weapons of mass destruction. The crisis in the Gulf and the high tensions last spring over Kashmir have made us and our friends in South Asia acutely aware that these weapons present a real danger, not just an abstract one. U.S.-Soviet progress in nuclear arms control and the groundbreaking U.S.-Soviet agreement to destroy the vast majority of chemical weapons stockpiles is another positive step toward ridding the world of potentially devastating weapons. It would be ironic if our success in reducing the arms race were ac-companied by an acceleration of this wasteful competition elsewhere. We will continue to work on these issues with the countries of the region and others whose interests are strongly engaged.

As you are aware, our continuing review of the issues relating to the Pressler amendment certification for Pakistan is part of this effort. In keeping with our longstanding friendship, we expect to engage the new Pakistani government early on in discussions of these issues. Meanwhile, we have complied with the law and suspended all military assistance and new economic aid to Pakistan because of the absence of certification at the beginning of the new fiscal year.

Maintaining and advancing democracy in the region is a challenge for the countries of the region themselves but we have a strong interest in their efforts. Pakistan's recent elections arose in circumstances that strained the fragile democratic system in that country. In its preliminary assessment, the 40-member international observer team announced that it found the elections to have been generally open, orderly, and well administered. A new government should be formed shortly. Peaceful transfer between the roles of government and opposition is part of the democratic process, and we hope that the roots of democracy will continue to deepen in Pakistan.

India's government is dealing with stubborn social and political controversies that have led to tragic loss of life and to the breakup of the government coalition. India's strong democratic traditions augur well for constitutional resolution of this crisis, but uncertain times lie ahead. Sri Lanka continues to try to maintain its democratic tradition in the face of a challenge to its national integrity by the Liberation Tigers of Tamil Eelam (LTTE). The stress has taken its toll in the form of human rights violations by both sides. Debate continues in Nepal over aspects of the new democratic constitution, which we believe will be promulgated soon.

Opposition political activity appears to be picking up in Bangladesh. Bangladesh and Nepal continue to move toward more representative institutions, with our encouragement.

All the countries in the region face the challenge of economic development. For most, their economic difficulties are magnified by the impact of the Gulf crisis and their decisions to maintain sanctions. Development assistance is an important element in our relationship with most of the countries of the region. But they will have to rely on their own efforts to evolve sound economic policies and unleash the productive power of the private sector.

Finally, and most generally, the United States faces the challenge of maintaining friendly relations throughout the region. We have sought over the years to free our ties in South Asia, and especially with India and Pakistan, from the "zero sum" mentality which suggests that strong relations with one must come at another's expense. This will continue to be our goal as we move into the post-Cold War period.

Pakistan

In recent months, Pakistan has been preoccupied with elections for the National Assembly. These were held as scheduled on October 24 with the IJI [Islami Jamhuri Ittihad] winning 105 seats and the PPP [Pakistan People's Party] winning 45 seats.

The National Democratic Institute-sponsored 40-member international observer delegation said the elections were generally open, orderly, and well administered. They observed some flaws in the voting, which in their judgment were not of sufficient magnitude to alter the overall results. Other observer groups, including the Canadians, provided similar assessments.

Based on the information available now, the national election seems to us to have given the Pakistani people a generally fair opportunity to choose their government. It was not without flaws or controversy, but the process of dealing with irregularities and controversies is critical to a functioning democracy. We will review all available information to implement the recently enacted requirement to certify the election as condition for certain U.S. aid.

As you are aware, charges were filed against former Prime Minister [Benazir] Bhutto and members of her government. Court proceedings have begun. We hope that the process will be marked by fairness and judicial independence.

History's final judgment of the process will take into account how complaints are dealt with and the process of accountability. We hope the government formation process will move forward peacefully and that the Pakistanis can put this difficult political period behind them and begin addressing the very serious challenges facing the country. We expect the National Assembly to be convened shortly, elect a Speaker and Deputy Speaker, and then select a Prime Minister.

The United States places great value on its longstanding relationship with Pakistan. Pakistan and the United States continue to share important interests in regional peace and stability and in an honorable political settlement in Afghanistan. We also are partners in a common enterprise in trying to reverse the effects of Iraq's aggression in the Gulf. Pakistan has contributed to that effort, sending over 2,000 troops and upholding the U.N. sanctions. We have faced challenges in our relationship before and will do so again; our aim is to build on this solid base of shared interests.

India

A year ago, India held elections which peacefully replaced the long dominant Congress (I) Party with a minority government led by Prime Minister V. P. Singh. The new government weathered a series of domestic and foreign challenges. Since early August, violent demonstrations have swept through northern and eastern India over the government's decision to pursue a broad "affirmative action" plan, reserving about half of all government jobs for the lower castes. The drastic reduction in job opportunities for other groups has led to bitter political protest, with 63 deaths and more than 150 attempted suicides.

More recently, the Bharatiya Janata Party [BJP] withdrew its support from the governing National Front coalition. This decision resulted from a longstanding religious conflict centered on the BJP campaign to build a Hindu temple dedicated to the Hindu god Ram on a site which houses a 16th century mosque. The government has insisted that temple construction await a decision by the Uttar Pradesh high court. The BJP insisted on beginning work on October 30. BJP leader L.K. Advani has led a month-long, 6,000 mile chariot procession through north-

ern India to gain support for this endeavor. Singh attempted to reach a compromise but failed. Advani's arrest on October 23, intended to prevent potentially violent communal confrontation, led to the BJP withdrawal of support from Singh's coalition.

At this point, the government has neither resigned nor been asked to resign by President Venkataraman. The President has, however, called parliament into session on November 7 to test the government's strength. The next step could be formation of a new government, if one can command a parliamentary majority, or new elections.

In addition to the government crisis, unrest and violence persist in Punjab and Kashmir. We have expressed our concern about human rights abuses in both states.

In Punjab, continuing violence has taken nearly 3,500 lives so far this year and has dashed hopes for new state assembly elections. In early October, parliament extended the President's rule, which has been in effect since 1987, for an additional six months. No date has been set for new elections.

India's support for U.N. Security Council sanctions against Iraq is one example of an opportunity for convergence between Indian and U.S. policies. We seek to continue in this direction as the world adjusts to the end of the Cold War. We place particular importance on the evolution of India's economic and trade policies, and we hope that economic liberalization policies will continue in spite of the present uncertain political environment.

Indo-Pakistani Relations

One of our key goals in South Asia is to reduce tensions and promote regional stability. The 40-year Indo-Pakistani rivalry has been a primary threat to peace in the area. Tensions over Kashmir have led to two wars, and since last December that troubled area has again been the focus of concerns.

Within Kashmir, the Indian government has had little success in establishing a political dialogue with Kashmiris. Attacks by militants against security forces often provoke retaliatory action that harms civilians.

In early October, fires destroyed hundreds of dwellings in Srinagar and surrounding areas. Jammu and Kashmir Governor Saxena has acknowledged the possibility of the security

forces' responsibility for some of these blazes and promised to investigate. We expressed to the government our concern over security force excesses and the use of "collective punishment" against unarmed civilians.

Last spring, the conflict in Kashmir escalated Indo-Pakistani tensions to an alarming level. American diplomacy was actively engaged on this issue. Following the May mission to both countries by Deputy National Security Adviser Robert Gates, the two sides initiated a series of talks at the foreign secretary level designed to improve government-to-government communications and explore ways of reducing tensions.

The immediate risk of conflict between India and Pakistan has subsided, but tensions remain high. We hope that the two governments will continue their contacts through diplomatic and military channels and will institute other confidence-building measures to reduce the risk of conflict. We will continue to urge implementation of the 1988 India-Pakistan agreement prohibiting attacks on each other's nuclear facilities. Finally, we encourage both sides to discuss other ways to limit the risk of proliferation and the possibility of conflict on the subcontinent.

We intend to work with other interested parties, such as the Soviet Union and China, on this issue.

Bangladesh

Bangladesh faces presidential and parliamentary elections in the next two years. The opposition has not yet agreed to contest the elections, but we hope that they and the government will be able to agree on a set of arrangements which will encourage full participation. Meanwhile, at least eight people have been killed in scattered violence related to an antigovernment protest movement that began October 10. We hope Bangladesh will follow the lead of the new democracies in Eastern Europe, Nicaragua, and elsewhere by leaving the past and searching in good faith for a peaceful way to make its elections free, fair, and representative.

In August, Bangladesh agreed to an IMF enhanced structural adjustment agreement designed to address its deteriorating macroeconomic situation. The country has made progress in privatization and liberalization of trade, but additional steps must be taken to make it competitive in the world market.

Bangladesh has been fully supportive of international efforts in the Gulf. The Government has sent 2,300 troops to Saudi Arabia, adhered to sanctions, and condemned Iraq despite the presence of over 100,000 of its citizens in Iraq and Kuwait. Their remittances totaled more than 40% of the country's import capital. The Gulf crisis has further aggravated Bangladesh's poverty. The administration estimates the cost of the crisis to Bangladesh for the rest of 1990 at about $350-375 million.

Nepal

Nepal continues its transition to democratic government. The constitutional reforms commission presented a draft constitution to King Birendra September 10. An extensive cabinet review, which resulted in some changes, was completed on October 11. Since then, the interim government has been considering additional changes proposed by the King. Tensions in Kathmandu deepened during this third phase in the constitutional reforms process. On October 25, however, the palace announced that the constitution would be promulgated on November 9. This step will pave the way for elections, which are tentatively scheduled for spring 1991.

From the drafts we have seen, the new constitution appears to represent fundamental political change. It charters a multiparty parliamentary democracy and constitutional monarchy in place of the previous "partyless" [panchayat] system, which recognized the King as the sole source of political power. The constitution also guarantees many fundamental rights. We believe it is a major step forward in the process to develop democratic institutions, which are essential to a workable, thriving democratic system.

The United States has encouraged and supported Nepal's democratic transition from its beginnings last spring in Kathmandu. Through the Democratic Pluralism Initiatives program, we provided more than $800,000 in FY 1990 to support constitutional reform and the development of pluralistic democratic institutions. We will continue to offer our experience of democratic systems in whatever way the Nepalese find useful as the political transition continues.

Sri Lanka

Sri Lanka embodies one of South Asia's starkest paradoxes. On the one hand, Sri Lanka takes pride in a strong, democratic tradition and dynamic economic policies that brought a 6% annual growth rate for the first half of 1990.

But Sri Lanka's continuing separatist strife has placed strains on the political system and the economy. It also has raised troubling human rights issues. Since the revival of fighting with the LTTE last June, we estimate that over 4,700 people have been killed. The military picture is still ambiguous.

We are deeply concerned by alleged abuses by all parties to Sri Lanka's conflict—Tamil separatists, the JVP (a Maoist revolutionary group apparently subdued in 1989), and government security forces. The United States continues to insist, clearly and unequivocally, that human rights and humanitarian law must be respected by all. We have underscored this point on many occasions, including at the donor consultative group meeting in Paris on October 25. Other delegations, including the European Community, expressed similar concerns in their statements. Sri Lankans themselves—Sinhalese, Muslims, and Tamils—hold the key to peace and thus to a brighter future.

Afghanistan

Our efforts to lay the groundwork for a political settlement have made some progress. We are continuing our discussions with the Soviets on a transition process, which would allow the Afghan people to determine their own future. The United States and the Soviet Union believe that there should be a transition period, culminating in self-determination, to select a government for a nonaligned Afghanistan. Our principal difference with the Soviets concerns the Najibullah regime's transition role and the powers of a transition mechanism. The fundamental decisions and responsibilities for restoring peace ultimately rest with the Afghans themselves.

Within the Afghan resistance, *mujahidin* commanders have recently demonstrated increasing willingness to cooperate across party, ethnic, and religious lines. The most notable example of this trend was the October 9-13 meeting of several major

commanders near the Pakistan-Afghanistan border.

Over the past month, resistance groups have increased military pressure on the government, taking the provincial capital of Tarin Kot (Oruzgan Province) in early October through a combination of military attack and induced defections. Another provincial capital, Qalat (Zabul Province), is under siege, with a small garrison holding only the town's central fort.

We welcome increased resistance unity and military effectiveness. So do the Pakistanis, as evidenced by the high-level reception given to Masood by Pakistani leaders when he visited Islamabad October 16. However, we have no favorites in the resistance, and we continue to consult closely with resistance and Pakistani leaders.

---

1 The complete transcript of the hearings will be published by the committee and will be available from the Superintendent of Documents, U.S. Government Printing Office, Washington, D.C. 20402.

State Department Statement on Aid to Pakistan [1]

Since total foreign assistance funding has declined in fiscal year (FY) 1991, most non-earmarked programs have had to be reduced. Since Pakistan's assistance program is not earmarked in FY 1991 (it was in previous years), its cuts are part of that general deline in non-earmarked programs.

Under the Pressler amendment, Pakistan is not eligible to receive assistance unless the President certifies to the Congress that Pakistan "does not possess a nuclear explosive device and that the proposed U.S. assistance program will reduce significantly the risk that Pakistan will possess a nuclear explosive device."

Since the President has not yet made such a certification for FY 1991, no assistance can be provided to Pakistan at this time. The issue remains under discussion between the United States and Pakistan.

---

1 Statement by Department of State spokesman Margaret Tutwiler, January 28, 1991.

Survey of U.S. Relations with South American Nations

President Bush's written responses to questions submitted by South American press, November 30, 1990. [1]

Chile-U.S. Relations

Q. In the relations between the United States and Chile, what are the main items that you would like to see resolved and in what manner?

A. More than anything else, I would like to convey to the Chilean people my most heartfelt congratulations and support for their transition to civilian democracy. It is a transition which was fraught with difficulties and challenges, but the people of Chile have carried it off with great courage, intelligence, and dignity. Those of us who hoped and worked for this objective feel that the democratic ideal throughout the world has been enhanced by Chile's example. Equally important, Chile has managed to bring about its democratic transition without undermining the economic progress that it has made in recent years.

It is important to keep this larger context in mind as we look at specific items on our bilateral agenda. It is no secret that our agenda during the first months of President Aylwin's term has been dominated by issues left over from the past, principally by the questions of restoration of GSP [Generalized System of Preferences] to Chile and a framework for settlement of the issues generated by the Letelier case.

Many Chileans have felt frustration or even irritation about the slowness with which these questions have been resolved. All I can say is that in democracies, things don't move as fast as they do under other systems; that is the price we pay for consultation and deliberation. The reassuring thing is that decisions do get made, however. I am happy that we have been able to begin the process of restoring GSP to Chile and that the Chilean Congress has passed the "Cumplido" Law transferring jurisdiction over the Letelier case from military to civilian courts. This will make it possible to eliminate restrictions on defense cooperation, something we want to do.

Enterprise for the Americas and Agricultural Trade Negotiations

Q. How do you plan to implement the Enterprise for the Americas Initiative, especially concerning trade, since you have a mainly Democratic Congress with protectionist attitudes and no trade agreement has been reached in Uruguay Round GATT talks? How will you address both issues? How do you expect Latin America to believe in a free market economy if measures are taken in the U.S. Congress to protect your economy?

A. The short answer to your question is that we have to work hard to get the results we want and believe are right, which will provide economic growth for both the United States and our hemispheric partners. We need our Congress to approve legislation for certain parts of the Enterprise for the Americas. This includes legislation for the restructuring of official debt and for the investment fund we would like to see in the Inter-American Development Bank. Fortunately, the reaction in the Congress to the Enterprise initiative has been very positive, which pleases me enormously. We have already succeeded in getting one piece of the Enterprise legislation passed through our Congress, regarding P.L. 480 debt, despite our budget problems and the crunch of legislation that we always face at the end of a legislative term. We are taking steps to implement this legislation, and we are prepared to enter into negotiations with countries eligible under the legislation to reduce their P.L. 480 debt.

You have my commitment that I will be back to the Congress when it reconvenes in January 1991, seeking passage of the other portions of the Enterprise legislation. I feel confident that a bipartisan spirit will prevail, because I am convinced that the vast majority of the Members of Congress recognize the mutual benefits such an agreement could bring and support good relations between the United States and our partners in this hemisphere. This is not to say that protectionist pressures do not exist. They do in our Congress, as they do in all legislatures of democratic countries. I have used my veto power (for example, with the textile bill earlier this year) to

prevent protectionist pressures at home from hurting our economy or damaging important foreign policy interests.

The other point you touched on is the Uruguay Round. I want you to know that I am making every effort to ensure that these talks produce an outcome that results in expanding world trade substantially. Our position is clear: We all need a successful conclusion to the Uruguay Round, one that opens markets worldwide. I am glad that other countries in this hemisphere share this view and have worked hard to bring it about. We look forward to working closely with Chile and other trading nations to achieve good market-opening agreements and substantial agricultural reforms.

Brazil-U.S. Relations

Q. Mr. President, many Brazilians think that the prospect of better relations between Brazil and the United States that emerged from your personal contacts with President Collor earlier this year are fading under the difficulties of new trade frictions and the old debt problem. I would like to ask you two questions in this regard: Your government has recently joined the other G-7 members in demanding that Brazil "resolve its debt arrears problem with the commercial banks" before any further long term financial agreements can be negotiated. The Brazilian Government argues that this approach is not acceptable because it would compromise the market-oriented economic stabilization program that you have endorsed. The issue is likely to be central to your talks in Brasilia. How will you deal with it?

A. You've posed a very complex question, and I will try to do it justice. In the first place, I would like to tell you that I have the highest respect for President Collor and what he is trying to do to reform and modernize the economy of Brazil. To bring about such dramatic change in a huge country like Brazil, which has more than 150 million people, deserves respect and admiration. Our relations with Brazil are based on the solid appreciation that we share a common commitment to democratic civilian rule and economic prosperity for our citizens. With such large, competitive, and varied economies as those of the United States and Brazil, there will always be some trade frictions. What most of you may not realize is the progress we have made in addressing these trade issues. As other problems crop up, they will need to be worked on. As long as I am President, the United States will seek to address these problems in a spirit of creative problem-solving.

With regard to your question about Brazil's debt, the United States is eager to see a long term solution that is consistent with the international debt strategy and will give Brazil the opportunity to grow and trade its way to economic health. This is a process of negotiation and has to be seen as such. While I will want to discuss this issue with President Collor, I do not see it as central to my discussions in Brazil. This is one of many issues we will want to discuss, with the goal of understanding each other's position well and looking for ways to advance common objectives.

U.S. Trade With South America

Q. The United States has proposed a framework trade agreement to Brazil and three other South American nations but has rejected a Brazilian proposal to discuss such an important issue as the access to advanced U.S. technology in the context of the agreement. Why? Is it a commercial problem or a security related problem?

A. First of all, I must point out that the inspiration for doing a five-country framework agreement came from Brazil, Argentina, Uruguay, and Paraguay. Much as I might like to claim credit for this innovative suggestion, I cannot; it came from South America. We were pleased to move forward on this suggestion because it clearly advances the goals of regional and hemispheric economic integration that are at the heart of the Enterprise for the Americas proposal.

Second, I think you may be reading more into our position than there really is. The framework agreements we have negotiated with other countries are directed at trade and investment. There is plenty that we can do and need to do in these areas. While we are indeed willing to talk about trade-related technology questions, we were concerned that if we tried to do too much, we would end up with a struc-

ture that was too difficult to manage. There's a saying in English which says, "Don't bite off more than you can chew." I understand there is a similar phrase in Spanish which says, *"El que mucho abarca, poco aprieta."* We want the framework agreements to work on difficult issues, but not to have them solve all the issues.

Latin America-U.S. Relations

Q. Mr. President, in Latin America there are numerous questions about the motives and objectives that led you to launch the Enterprise for the Americas Initiative. Would you explain your view of Latin America today, the motives that brought you to propose the initiative and, if you could be more specific, in what fields and during what time period do you expect the most important aspects of the initiative to be achieved?

A. With regard to this hemisphere, the first year of my administration was devoted largely to two subjects: restoration of democracy in Central America and the war on drugs. With the triumph of democracy in Nicaragua, the end of dictatorship in Panama, and with the drug strategy launched, I became convinced that the United States needed to take a longer range look at relations in this hemisphere. In part, I was also reacting to concerns expressed to me by the region's leaders, who told me they worried that the amazing events in Central and Eastern Europe would cause us to forget this hemisphere and devote all our resources to Europe.

I gave these Latin American and Caribbean leaders my commitment that the United States would remain engaged in this hemisphere. As I told several leaders, the Americas are our common homeland, and we cannot forget this. For this reason, I asked my top economic and policy advisers to examine our policy in the region and give me ideas on innovative approaches the United States could take to complement economic reforms being implemented by Latin American and Caribbean governments.

The result of this review was the June 27 Enterprise for the Americas Initiative. My goal was to propose a mix of long term and short term objectives, covering the areas of trade, investment, debt, and the environment. In trade, I set out a challenge: that we act

together to create a free trade area for the entire hemisphere. To get there, we are already working on a free trade agreement with Mexico, and we have signed bilateral framework agreements with Bolivia, Colombia, Ecuador, Chile, Honduras, and Costa Rica. In response to a suggestion from Brazil, Uruguay, Paraguay, and Argentina, we have agreed to negotiate a multi-country framework agreement.

In the investment area, we suggested creation of new Inter-American Development Bank programs and an additional multilateral investment fund to improve the hemisphere's investment potential. We are seeking congressional approval of funding to contribute to multilateral [investment]. On debt, we have secured passage through the U.S. Congress of the first element of our package for reducing official debt. As you know, one of the features of this proposal is to use interest paid on the remaining debt stock to fund environmental projects. As soon as the U.S. Congress reconvenes in January, we will be working for passage of the rest of the legislative package.

As we look to the future, however, we should not be doing so in terms of unrealistic deadlines saying that "on such-and-such a date, all of the region's problems will be solved." What we are offering is a commitment to work actively and creatively with this hemisphere, to consult frequently, and to seek solutions which lead to greater prosperity and well-being for all, in what we hope will be the world's first "hemisphere of democracy."

Uruguay-U.S. Relations

Q. Uruguay is a tiny country that, despite its important democratic tradition, [seems] many times to have been ignored by the United States. This Presidential visit, for example, is the first one in 30 years. What brought Latin America to your attention, created an interest in visiting Uruguay, and what benefits might Uruguay gain from this new relationship with the U.S.?

A. It has been too long since a President of the United States visited Uruguay. President Eisenhower visited Montevideo in 1960, and President Lyndon Johnson made a brief trip to Punta del Este in 1967, I believe.

Uruguay may be a small country, but it is one which has throughout its history played a creative and innovative role in world affairs. It is also a nation of immigrants, a fact that serves as a point of linkage with the United States. For example, I recently accepted the credentials of your Ambassador to the United States, Eduardo Mac-Gillycuddy. Ambassador Mac-Gillycuddy is a distant cousin of a United States Senator from Florida, Connie Mack. Ambassador MacGillycuddy's grandfather was a brother of the Philadelphia Phillies baseball legend by the same name.

Let me offer another example. As I mentioned above, we are in the midst of trying to complete the most ambitious trade expansion program in decades. If this effort succeeds, it could expand world trade by $500 billion. It is no accident that this round of world trade talks is called the Uruguay Round, after the country which served as sponsor for its launching.

I can point to other things as well. President Lacalle was the first President of this region to telephone me after I announced the Enterprise for the Americas Initiative on June 27. His support has been a strong stimulus to me to make this proposal work. To make it work, we will need the help of institutions such as the Inter-American Development Bank, which is headed by another Uruguayan, Enrique Iglesias.

For all these reasons, I am eager to visit Uruguay, to consult with President Lacalle, and speak to the Uruguayan Congress. I would not speak only in terms of benefits to Uruguay from the visit. We are looking for answers that will benefit the whole hemisphere, such as the ones we can derive from a successful Uruguay Round and a free trade area stretching from Alaska to Tierra del Fuego.

Argentine Economy

Q. Argentina is working on the economic integration with Brazil and other countries in the Southern Cone and, at the same time, has started a process of deep restructuring of its economy and its institutional frame. What is your impression of the fact that privatization of two big state corporations (an airline and a telephone company) has been achieved with the participation of American capital, but not of American management or technology?

A. I think the most important part of your question relates to what is going on in Argentina today. Difficult, sometimes painful, economic choices are being made by President Menem. These choices involve the transformation of very large sectors of the Argentine economy. Like many other leaders of this hemisphere, President Menem is making the difficult choices and implementing economic reform policies to make Argentina more competitive and guarantee the country's long term economic health.

Privatization has played a part in this economic restructuring. As your question noted, instead of continuing to have the economy dominated by an inefficient state apparatus, which has stifled initiative and blocked economic growth, the Government of Argentina has adopted policies aimed at privatizing businesses such as the airline and the telephone company. This has reduced Argentina's debt burden and brought back to these companies the incentive to compete for investment and for clients. Quite frankly, I believe that good airlines can and should depend on their passengers for their revenues and not depend on the taxpayers.

As for the participation of United States investors—whether this be in the form of capital, of technology, or of management— as long as there is a level playing field, and by that I mean that the rules are the same for all investors, I think that rational economic choices will be made. That's what freedom to compete is all about, whether it is in Argentina or Alaska.

U.S. Trade Policies

Q. At the final stage of the Uruguay Round of GATT, the U.S. is standing again against subsidies and all kinds of protectionist trade barriers for agricultural products. Nevertheless, the Government is subsidizing some grain exports, with potential harm for Argentina and other countries in the hemisphere, and is keeping some tariffs that make difficult the entrance of products like, for example, Argentine leathers. Is it possible that the administration could modify these policies in favor of a more consistent attitude with respect to all forms of protectionism?

A. I know that the Commerce Department's decision to impose countervailing duties on Argentine

leather was unpopular with the leather industry in Argentina. But here are some economic facts: By forbidding the export of hides from Argentina, prices for these hides in Argentina are driven down because they can only be sold in the domestic market. This means that leather exported from Argentine commerce to other markets, such as the United States, is priced artificially low.

Argentina's competitors in the U.S. thought this was unfair and complained to our authorities. Following a very detailed and open process in accordance with our law, in which the Argentine industry was represented by experienced counsel, the Commerce Department agreed that a subsidy was being provided by virtue of the Argentine Government's policy prohibiting the export of hides. This is not an issue where the President of the United States can intervene to tip the scales one way or another. The solution is for Argentina to allow exports of hides, so that its leather will be priced according to the forces of the international market.

I should note that this has been a longstanding sore point in our bilateral relationship. Several years ago, we had negotiated a solution under the section 301 provision, but because the agreement was not fulfilled by Argentina, U.S. industry felt it had no recourse but to seek relief under U.S. trade laws.

With regard to wheat, I assume you are referring to the Export Enhancement Program. This program was designed to keep U.S. wheat competitively priced with the wheat being sold by other producers, primarily the European Community. We hope that a successful outcome of the agricultural talks in the Uruguay Round will make this and other export subsidy programs superfluous.

Petroleum

Q. Venezuela has increased its oil production by half a million barrels daily to help in the Gulf crisis and is opening its doors again to U.S. private investment in the oil sector. Recently, President Carlos Andres Perez stated that his country deplored the speculation which was driving oil prices up and hurting the American consumer. He said it was not in Venezuela's interest, either, to be subject to ups and downs in prices and appealed for a meeting between the major oil producing nations and the leading consumer countries to work out some kind of stabilization program for international oil prices. The U.S. has not reacted to this proposal, made first two months ago.

Although your country supports a market economy, it has joined in stabilization agreements in the past for various products. Would you consider this for oil especially now that the market has been disrupted by the Gulf crisis and the future well-being of the Gulf nations, as well as other producers such as Venezuela, not to mention various of your own States which produce oil, and are dependent upon a steady and reasonable oil income?

A. You have posed a detailed question which requires a detailed reply. In the first place, I must pay tribute to the extremely positive role that Venezuela, and particularly President Carlos Andres Perez, has played in the months since Iraq invaded Kuwait. He worked hard with Saudi Arabia to ensure that members of the Organization of Petroleum Exporting Countries (OPEC) increased supplies to cover the shortfall caused by the loss of Kuwaiti oil and the embargo on Iraqi exports. Venezuela and CAP have been a force for stability in oil supplies.

We have also welcomed President Perez' efforts to prevent wild swings in world oil prices. As he has correctly pointed out, these are bad for producers, and they are bad for consumers. A recession in the industrialized world will not help OPEC members such as Venezuela, and far-sighted leaders such as President Perez have been among the first to realize this.

I know that Venezuela has suggested convening a meeting between oil producing countries and oil consumers. Our reaction has been rather guarded. If there were an absence of communication between producing countries and consuming countries, bringing the two sides together might be worth studying. In the case of the oil market, however, producers and consumers are talking to each other all the time, sharing statistics and projections regarding both supply and demand, and doing so in a number of different contexts. These bilateral and other channels are in my opinion working sufficiently well that we do not have to create another formal medium of communication.

As for your suggestion for joint action by producers and consumers to stabilize the price, I do not believe this is an idea which is workable. Even if

producers and consumers could agree on what a stable price should be, and I think this in itself would prove impossible, I have a more fundamental objection. I believe that in general market mechanisms are more efficient and effective, and this includes the market for oil.

One final point. I agree with President Perez that we need to increase the production of oil from areas of the world such as Latin America and the Caribbean in order to diversify world supplies. I believe that private investment funds are available for this effort and will go to countries which have hospitable investment climates. There is more that we can do in this area, and I look forward to discussing this issue with President Perez and his advisers when I am in Caracas.

[Last question and answer, concerning U.S. Persian Gulf policy, omitted.]

---

1 The questions were submitted by El Mercurio of Chile, Estado de Sao Paulo of Brazil, El Pais of Uruguay, La Nacion of Argentina, and El Nacional of Venezuela. The Office of the Press Secretary issued the text as a press release on December 3. Text from Weekly Compilation of Presidential Documents of December 10, 1980.

President's Visits to Brazil, Uruguay, Argentina, Chile, and Venezuela

REMARKS TO JOINT SESSION OF BRAZILIAN CONGRESS, BRASILIA, DECEMBER 3, 1990 [1]

It is a privilege, it is an honor to join you in this great hall of democracy.

My thoughts today could have no better forum than this National Congress; my words, no better audience than the people of Brazil. We meet at an extraordinary moment in our shared history, a time of serious challenges and important choices that calls for mutual respect, candor, and collective will. I've met with many Latin and Caribbean leaders. And beyond any single issue that we've discussed, all of us have been galvanized by a new era of hope and opportunity throughout the Americas, especially here in Brazil.

By pioneering bold new economic reforms and consolidating its democracy, Brazil today is poised to enter the 21st century as a leader among nations. That is a tribute to a leader whose friendship and vision I value and respect, a man who represents a new generation of democratic leadership now sweeping across Latin America, your dynamic new President, Fernando Collor de Mello. President Collor has spoken eloquently of Brazil's rightful place at the table of the First World, and I agree. I believe it is time, in fact, to end the false distinctions between the First World and Third World that have too long limited political and economic relations in the Americas. Let us instead speak of the New World.

This hemisphere has always found strength in diversity. After all, here I stand, addressing Portuguese speakers in English, because of an Italian sailing on behalf of Spain five centuries ago. What we hold in common transcends borders and translates into any language. The nations of the Americas all struggled and gained independence from the old ways of the Old World, ended the injustice of slavery and colonialism, and built republics of promise and renewal around the dignity and the power of the individual and the rule of law.

Now, as we approach the 500th anniversary of Columbus' discovery of Americas and the arrival of Cabral's Portuguese fleet in Brazil, this is our moment to chart the course for the New World, a course of freedom, a course of democracy, a course of prosperity. We've all witnessed in wonder the dawn of democracy in Eastern Europe. But in the Americas, we, too, have seen extraordinary political and economic change that is transforming the face of this hemisphere—nowhere more so than right here, no more so than in the great nation of Brazil. The changes you are carrying out in your economy—reducing the size of the state, privatizing enterprises, combating inflation, and liberalizing trade—are the keys to growth and prosperity in a global economy of the 21st century, whose outlines we already see today. I am here to tell you that you are not only on the right path but the United States wants you to succeed and supports your efforts every step of the way. I believe that we've just begun to press forward toward the real promise of the Americas.

Territories may end at borders, but mankind's capacity for progress knows no bounds. Continents may end at the water's edge, but human potential knows only those limits set by human imagination. The Americas' role in the world is not defined by geography; it is defined by its people and its ideals. I truly believe that we are approaching a new dawn in the New World.

Our thinking must be bold; our will, resolute. Our challenge now is to hew out of a wilderness of competing interests a new kind of opportunity in the Americas. To fulfill the New World's destiny, all of the Americas and the Caribbean must embark on a venture for the coming century: to create the first fully democratic hemisphere in the history of mankind, the first hemisphere devoted to the democratic ideal—to unleash the power of free people, free elections, and free markets.

Two weeks ago in Czechoslovakia, I spoke to a people that had paid dearly for its freedom. I talked about a new commonwealth of freedom based on four key principles. This hemisphere already shares these convictions: an unshakable belief in the dignity and rights of man, the conviction that just government derives its power from the people, the belief that men and women everywhere must be free to enjoy the fruits of their labor, and four, that the rule of law must govern the conduct of nations. Every nation that joins this commonwealth of freedom advances us

one step closer to a new world order. We must persist until this victory for freedom and democracy is won completely.

Free Trade in the Americas

It is also within our power to make this hemisphere the largest free trading partnership of sovereign nations in the world. From the northernmost reaches of Canada to the tip of Cape Horn, we see a future where growing opportunity, the power of technology, and the benefits of prosperity are developed and shared by all. Change will not come easily. Economies now dependent on protection and state regulation must open to competition. The transition, for the time being, will be painful. Many in the Americas will have to make serious adjustments to compete with Southeast Asia and to take advantage of the European market after 1992. But we are confident that solutions will be found—by Brazilians, by Chileans, by Venezuelans—by all of the Americas.

And the results—growing economies and sound currencies—will bring unprecedented prosperity and growth for all our citizens to share. That was the vision of the Enterprise for the Americas Initiative that we announced last June. And Deputy [Ricardo] Fiuza, I listened very carefully to your strong speech in this regard, and I thank you for those frank and forceful comments. The initiative calls for a major hemispheric effort to unify the New World in the three key areas of trade, investment, and debt.

In trade, our first priority should be to promote long term growth. And the most effective first step is the successful conclusion of the Uruguay Round, now in its final stages in Brussels. An end to export subsidies on agricultural goods and new openings for developing country exports mean new market opportunities and a higher standard of living for the farmer in Para, the textile worker in Santa Catarina, and the engineer in Sao Paulo.

But the Uruguay Round and bilateral trade agreements are only first steps. The Southern Cone Common Market, now developing under the leadership of your President and his colleagues in neighboring countries, is another major step toward the world's first hemispheric free trade zone.

Investment and Debt Restructuring

To promote new investment in the Americas, the dead hand of state control must be lifted. We must allow entrepreneurs the flexibility to adapt, create, and produce. So, as we chart a course for the future of the New World, let us hold firmly in our minds an unshakable conviction in the importance and benefit of free enterprise. Let us work together so that any man or woman who wants to launch a new enterprise views the state as an ally, not as an obstacle, and all who pursue the fruits of the free market see other nations not as threats to sovereignty but as partners in trade and mutual prosperity.

Individuals cannot succeed if government is burdened by debt. So, the third leg of our Enterprise for the Americas Initiative is a comprehensive commitment to work with Brazil and others in Latin America to restructure U.S. official debt. Our new approach to official debt will complement commercial debt restructuring through the Brady plan. I understand the importance to Brazil and, indeed, to the international financial community of reaching a new and effective agreement on commercial debt. I believe, through your program of economic reform, you have taken the first crucial step toward that goal. Global capital flows will be vital to your development, and we are ready to assist wherever possible.

Environmental Protection

We've submitted a request to our Congress for the authority to implement our proposals. But we know that real solutions must involve all of us in the Americas. That's why we envision a permanent partnership between all the nations of the Americas to confront challenges that know no borders. We envision a hemisphere where a collaborative commitment is shared to protect our environmental legacy. There can be no sustained economic growth without respect for the environment. That's why the Enterprise for the Americas Initiative joins environmental protection with bilateral debt relief not as a challenge to national sovereignty—not as a challenge to the sovereignty, in this case, of Brazil—but as an affirmation of shared international interests. Senator [Ronan] Tito—and I do appreciate, sir, your using this podium for a frank exchange here—talked about partners in growth, I believe you said sir, partners in growth rather than shareholders of misery. That is what you want, and that is what we want.

I encourage Brazil and other creditor nations to convert debt into funds for the environment. The entire world stands in awe of Brazil's unique endowment of wildlife, trees, and plants in the Amazon and the Atlantic rain forests. No nation on Earth—none—is as rich in flora and fauna, with all of their potential to provide future medicines and foods and crops and fibers. Your hosting of the United Nations Conference on Environment and Development in 1992 places Brazil in a position of true global leadership. We hope that conference will mark the culmination of a number of initiatives to protect and wisely utilize the world's resources.

Threat of Narcotics Trade

We also are challenged to make ours a hemisphere where sovereign nations are joined in collective determination to eradicate the disease of drugs. On this one, the time for blame is long over. We in the United States recognize that we must do more to reduce what seems to you as insatiable demand. And you understand that the spreading tentacles of the drug trade threaten any democratic society. President Collor has taken a strong position against drugs for the sake of youth in Brazil. I know full well it is a demand problem as well as a supply problem for my country, and I pledge the full efforts of my government to continue to dampen demand. There is only one answer to the drug problem in this hemisphere, and that is to defeat these narco traffickers who prey on our children, once and for all.

Nuclear Nonproliferation

And finally, in this era of great challenges around the world, we want the Western Hemisphere to be a model to the world for security, stability, and peace. Together, let us ensure that this hemisphere stands united to prevent the spread of nuclear weapons or new, more dangerous ballistic missiles anywhere in the world. We hope that all countries in this hemisphere will follow Brazil's and Argentina's recent

decision to bring the nonproliferation treaty, Tlatelolco, into force. I want to applaud, as many other nations have done, the recent announcement by Brazil and Argentina that together they will ensure that no nuclear program in their countries is used for anything but peaceful purposes. We applaud your decision to move forward on full-scope nuclear safeguards.

But your leadership today goes beyond this hemisphere. Just as Brazil made valiant contributions to the cause of freedom in World War II, you were among the very first to implement the sanctions against Iraq. I realize the sacrifices that Saddam [Hussein]'s brutality has caused this nation and its people, has caused many nations around the world. In this country, I was told this morning, the impact—$5 billion in higher oil prices alone for 1 year—$5 billion to your economy, struggling to move forward, because of the brutality and the aggression of Saddam Hussein. In Czechoslovakia, a country that knows about aggression, [President] Vaclav Havel told me, $1.5 billion just because of the aggression of Saddam Hussein. I salute your leadership in the world's community and united stand against Iraq's aggression and in defense of the rule of law.

[Concluding remarks omitted.]

REMARKS TO JOINT SESSION OF URUGUAY'S CONGRESS, MONTEVIDEO, DECEMBER 4, 1990 (EXCERPTS) [1]

Here in Uruguay, President Lacalle has set forth a bold program to restructure the economy, changes which will improve Uruguay's overall strength and prosperity. In time, the economy will produce more goods and services, provide more jobs for all and, in short, improve Uruguay's very quality of life.

*   *   *

Trade and Investment

In order to promote trade, we are working toward a framework agreement with Uruguay, Brazil, Argentina, and Paraguay that commits us to explore practical ways to reduce trade and investment barriers. A strong multilateral trading system is the cornerstone of a healthy, expanding

world economy, benefiting both developing and developed nations alike. That's why I have made the successful conclusion of the Uruguay Round of the GATT a top trade priority, and that's why it has such a prominent place in my Enterprise for the Americas Initiative. It presents us an extraordinary opportunity for unparalleled economic growth for all nations, well into the 21st century.

In the final talks at the GATT this week, we stand firmly with you and other Latin nations in insisting that countries sharply reduce the agricultural subsidies that distort world trade. The land has historically been at the heart of both our economies; and from Montevideo to Montana, our farmers and our ranchers enjoyed shared traditions, shared interests, and shared concerns.

As our trade ministers meet in Brussels this week, I want to speak to them from the place where the round began. It began with a commitment to expansion of world trade, so let us finish the round in the same spirit, translating good intentions into firm commitments that will benefit us all by substantially expanding world trade. As the traveler in "The Purple Land" says: "We lose half our opportunities in life through too much caution." The new dawn is breaking. The stakes are high. Let's successfully conclude the GATT round, and that means opening up Europe's market to this hemisphere's agricultural products.

The Enterprise for the Americas Initiative also acknowledges that improved trade must be bolstered by assistance with investment and with debt. To promote investment, we've been working with the Inter-American Development Bank to create a sectoral loan program. The IDB's response has been outstanding. That's no surprise; it's led by an Uruguayan, Enrique Iglesias. We will also help countries committed to economic and investment reform to shake loose the burden of debt.

Uruguay's Debt Agreement

First, I want to congratulate President Lacalle on his successful negotiation of a debt agreement with the commercial banks under the Brady plan. That is a vote of confidence in Uruguay's economic policies by the international financial community. And we've also asked our Congress to approve a new package to reduce Uruguay's official debt. This will allow us to convert other payments to investment in industry and to swap debt for nature to protect your natural beauty. Environmental destruction knows no borders. And it is our responsibility to leave future generations not only a more prosperous world but a cleaner and a safer world.

A safer world also means a world free from the scourge of this hemisphere, the scourge called cocaine. And for the sake of our kids, every country must do its part to stop the explosive cycle of drugs, dependency, and dollars. And let me assure you, we are doing our level best to reduce demand in the United States for these outrageous illegal narcotics.

And finally, a safer world also means a world safe for freedom, a world governed by the rule of law. And just a few minutes ago, I was privileged to meet with your Supreme Court. A free, honest, and impartial judicial system is fundamental to the freedom of a democracy, just as the rule of law is fundamental to the freedom of the world.

* * *

I want to just say a special word in tribute to your President and to your proud democracy. Uruguay has shown great courage and commitment in support for United Nations sanctions against Iraqi aggression. Some may not realize this, but Uruguay paid a double price, a double price for upholding these sanctions: first, in higher oil prices, but also in substantial markets lost for now for your products. And yet you never flinched; your country never flinched. You never wavered in support of these U.N. sanctions.

REMARKS TO JOINT SESSION OF ARGENTINA'S CONGRESS, BUENOS AIRES, DECEMBER 5, 1990 [2]

I am honored to be with you in this very beautiful Hall of Democracy, with so many Members of your Congress. And I am privileged to be with you at this special time in history—both your own history and the history we share as members of the same hemisphere—for we live in an era of dramatic change.

Some may have thought that the events of Monday [an uprising by some army officers that was suppressed]

would make me change my plans. To the contrary, they strengthened my resolve to come to Argentina, to stand shoulder to shoulder with President Menem and the Argentine people, who love democracy and refuse to see it subverted.

The message today from Argentina is clear: Democracy is here to stay. Too many brave people sacrificed and died to bring democracy back to Latin America. Let those who would attack constitutional democracy understand: In Latin America the day of the dictator is over. Violent assaults upon the rule of law represent the old way of thinking, the old way of acting that history has left behind. It is time to think anew.

No longer should we think in terms of the Old World, where our roots lie, or of the First World or the Third World. No, we must move beyond the labels that once separated us to grasp the common future that unites us. Argentina, the United States, and the other nations in this continent share the promise of a new dawn in a new world.

So, I have come to Argentina to speak about change—you heard it first from the Vice President—the kind of positive, hopeful change symbolized by the Sun of the Spirit of May in your dramatic seal.

There's an old saying that when North Americans meet Argentines, they look into a mirror. I've felt that. Much here seems familiar: the cattle, the seas of grass, the love of liberty, the shared belief in the dignity of the individual, our common European roots and shared colonial past, the warm energy and the spirit of the people, even our interest in sport—we look forward to welcoming your team to the United States in 1994 for our first hosting of the World Cup, for example. But above all, above all, we share a devotion and a commitment to our respective nations that would have pleased General San Martín, who wrote: "Love for one's native land fuels noble souls."

All of this is part of the unique bond between our countries, but it's also recent history that unites us. Your return of democracy has brought our peoples closer than ever before. Your sacrifice during past decades caused us deep anguish and concern. But your people did not lose faith in the democratic ideal, and the United States did not lose faith in you.

Enhancing International Security

As we prepare, with optimism and anticipation, for the challenges facing this hemisphere and the rest of the world, some things are clear. We all know that we want to live in a new world that is a model of security and stability. This means regional arms control—as well as nuclear, missile, and chemical nonproliferation—and the collective determination to face down aggression.

As I said the day before yesterday in Brasília, the United States applauds the decision announced November 28th by the leaders of Argentina and Brazil to move forward on nuclear safeguards and to bring the Treaty of Tlatelolco into force. We hope you will move quickly to realize both of these commitments, as they have a direct, measurable impact on regional and world security. Such action will also allow the United States and other countries to expand significantly the range of our nuclear and other technical cooperation. We are eager and we are ready to do so.

In the current crisis halfway around the world in the Gulf, you have also shown strength and vision by helping to lead international efforts to stop Saddam [Hussein]'s brutal aggression. Your contribution to the multinational force in the Gulf is a statement of your commitment to peace and a commitment to the rule of law and a clear sign that you are assuming your rightful place as a leader among freedom-loving nations.

Restoring Argentina's Economy

Argentina and President Menem have not limited their efforts to promoting international security. Here in this great country, you have embarked on another courageous action: the restoration of your economic dynamism. Your President, Carlos Menem, has defined the challenge that we face to day. He said: "To take advantage of democratic experiences, to propel economic growth and progress, is the principal crossroads and challenge for our peoples and governments."

It is a difficult challenge, as I believe few Presidents have ever taken office under more testing circumstances than did President Menem. And yet he and his colleagues in this Congress did not shrink from the task at hand. Instead, you've set into motion a forward-looking structural, economic, and social transformation of this great country.

We know of the painful, short term sacrifices that you are being called upon to make, in what your own President has called surgery without anesthesia. For this tremendous undertaking to succeed, it will not take miracles; it will take work. But know that the United States is prepared to work with you every step of the way.

Just yesterday we signed two new agreements, a mutual legal assistance treaty and a mutual customs cooperation agreement. And last June, to help this movement in your nation and the others of this continent, we proposed the Enterprise for the Americas Initiative, which calls for a major hemispheric effort to expand trade and investment and to reduce debt; to unleash energy; to encourage initiative; and to let the incentive of reward inspire people to better themselves, their families, and their futures. We are absolutely committed to this initiative as a major priority. It will give impetus to the essential economic restructuring which you already have underway, and it will sustain and deepen this process in tangible ways.

The initiative is our hemisphere's new declaration of interdependence. For economic revolution is the equal of political revolution, and economic cooperation must be embraced not as a threat to privilege for a few but as the key to prosperity for all. We know that prosperity in our hemisphere depends on trade, not aid. And it is within our power to make our region the largest trading center of sovereign nations in the world. Already, the Southern Cone common market is moving us closer to our ultimate objective: a free trade system that links all of the Americas. We support you in this and look forward to completing a framework agreement on trade and investment between the United States and the Southern Cone.

But to promote long term growth, we need the successful conclusion of the Uruguay Round. The negotiators must succeed in their efforts to reduce or eliminate tariffs, subsidies, and other barriers to agricultural products. This will mean new market opportunities for the farmer in Buenos Aires Province, the agricultural workers in Jujuy, and the engineer in Rosario.

No act could be more significant for your nation than the move toward a market-oriented economy, a move cru-

cial to attracting foreign investment. You see, it lays the groundwork for your future, building a road that leads to a modern, growing Argentina. A free enterprise economy will encourage capital investment, greater individual initiative, and real prosperity for this and future generations. With the help of the Inter-American Development Bank, we want to encourage the reform and the opening of investment regimes. The spirit of enterprise will unleash your great potential and assure this nation of its position as one of the most vigorous nations in the world.

The reforms that you are carrying out in your economy, including your bold program of privatization, are not only the key to economic growth and expanded opportunity; they are also the first crucial steps under the Brady plan to achieve debt reduction with your commercial creditors. I understand the burden of debt that weighs on Argentina, but I believe that today— like Mexico, Venezuela, Uruguay, and Costa Rica—Argentina is on the right road to reduce that burden under the Brady plan.

The way we deal with our common economic realities can be a stepping-stone to a permanent partnership among all the nations of the Americas. I believe we are on the brink of something unprecedented in world history— the first wholly democratic hemisphere. Think of it: the first hemisphere devoted to freedom—to free speech, to free elections, free enterprise, free trade, free markets.

And that's why I've come to your country: to celebrate what we share, to recommit the United States of America to the movement toward democracy and prosperity all throughout the Americas, to stress the vital importance of mutual cooperation and understanding among traditional friends. For we read in Martin Fierro: "brothers should stand by each other, because this is the first law." And he goes on: "keep a true bond between you at each and every time."

You know, Argentina is a great nation with enormous resources, but none more impressive than the Argentinean people themselves. When this century began, Argentina was among the most prosperous and productive nations in the entire world. And I am totally confident that Argentina will be such an economic leader again and continue to lead this hemisphere.

Together, yet from our own beloved lands, we will watch freedom, democracy, and prosperity grow. We will watch it from the vantage point of two countries strong in liberty and expanding in economy. And we can look forward together with shared optimism to the 21st century, to the brilliant new dawn of a splendid new world.

Thank you all very much for this warm welcome. I am delighted to have been your guest here today.

REMARKS TO JOINT SESSION OF CHILEAN CONGRESS, VALPRAISO, DECEMBER 6, 1990 (EXCERPT) [2]

Chileans can take great pride in the role they have played in Latin America's democratic renaissance. Since the plebiscite of October 1988, Chile has undergone a political transformation every bit as far-reaching as the revolutions that changed the face of Eastern Europe. When others, frustrated by the long years under autocratic rule, might have engaged in recrimination, you, Chile, chose reconciliation. When others might have consumed themselves with settling scores, Chile chose to draw a positive lesson from the agony and the pain of the past.

Every year under autocratic rule served only to deepen your devotion to freedom and tolerance and respect for human rights, to strengthen Chile's collective resolve to make this return to democracy permanent and to make it irreversible. Chile's peaceful return to the way of democracy owes much to the leadership of a man of vision, a man of great moral courage, President Patricio Aylwin. But as President Aylwin understands, as everyone in this chamber knows, democracy's ultimate success rests not on the shoulders of one man alone but on the collective commitment of every Chilean— every citizen in every region, from every station in society—to put allegiance to democracy above any differences that divide you.

Chile has also been a part of a greater collective commitment through your steadfast participation in the international coalition now facing down aggression in the Persian Gulf. Chile, at considerable expense to your own economy, is upholding the sanctions against Iraq, despite the costs, because of the far greater cost to world stability should brutal aggression go unchecked. You understand, through hard experience, the fundamental importance of the rule of law.

As a friend of Chile, as a representative of a fellow democracy, I have deep respect for all that this nation has done to move forward, in peace, to this new day of freedom.

What is happening here in Chile is part, you see, of a larger movement that is sweeping this continent. Centuries ago, the Americas represented to the explorers of Europe the New World, an uncharted territory of promise and possibility. In the dawn of Chile's own independence, Bernardo O'Higgins, the Chilean patriot and patron of liberty for all of Latin America, spoke of the Americas' shared destiny when he wrote: "The day of liberty has arrived for the Americas. From the Mississippi to Cape Horn, an area comprising almost half the world, we now proclaim the independence of the New World."

At long last, the new world O'Higgins wrote about is dawning across the Americas, a new dawn of democracy in which all men and women are free to live, work, and to worship as they please. My travels these past few days have made me more certain than ever that the Americas share a common democratic destiny and that Latin America's future lies with free government and free markets.

Chile, now returned to the democratic path, has long recognized the merits of a free-market economy. From the day Diego de Almagro first set foot on what is now Chilean soil, your lifeblood and link to the world has been trade. What has been true for Chile throughout its long history is today increasingly true for all nations.

Chile has moved farther, faster than any other nation in South America toward real free-market reform. The payoff is evident to all: seven straight years of economic growth; in exports alone, a 15 to 20 percent increase in value in each of the past five years.

This explosive growth has secured for Chile a growing impact on the world economy. Today the farmer in San Fernando labors not just to feed his family, or even his village, but to deliver products to the dinner tables of Japan, Europe, and the United States. From the miner in Calama, the world obtains the raw materials it puts to use in everything from new homes to skyscrapers to space shuttles.

Chile's success—your success—is the product of wise policy, a comprehensive plan to transform this nation's economy into an engine for growth. Chile has worked to create an open and inviting investment climate for foreign capital. Since 1985 about $2.5 billion in new investment has flowed into Chile. Capital flight, which has sapped the economic strength of so many Latin nations, has now reversed itself, turned around, with returning funds spurring new investment here at home. And Chile has pioneered some of the world's most creative debt-reduction programs—these debt-for-equity swaps, exchanges that have transformed debt from a deadweight on development into new opportunities for growth.

WHITE HOUSE FACT SHEET ON U.S.-VENEZUELA SCIENCE AND TECHNICAL COOPERATION AGREEMENT, DECEMBER 8, 1990 [2]

On Thursday, December 6, 1990, the Government of the United States of America and the Government of Venezuela agreed to enter into a five-year agreement on cooperation in science and technology. This agreement renews the United States-Venezuela agreement for scientific and technical cooperation which expired in July 1988. It will serve as an important instrument to revitalize scientific and technical cooperation between the two countries.

The agreement was signed at the Ministry of Foreign Affairs by Dr. D. Allan Bromley, Assistant to the President for Science and Technology and Director of the White House Office of Science and Technology Policy, for the United States and by Minister Dulce Arnao de Uzcategui for the Government of Venezuela.

The principal objective of the agreement is to provide additional opportunities to exchange ideas, information, skills, and techniques and to collaborate on problems of mutual interest. Cooperation may include exchanges of scientific and technical information, exchanges of scientists and technical experts, the convening of joint seminars and meetings, and the conduct of joint research projects in the basic and applied sciences.

The agreement will serve as an important catalyst to improve and enhance scientific technical cooperation between the two countries, particularly in areas such as environment and global change—including biodiversity, forestry management, and mining pollution in the Venezuelan Amazon—geosciences, and materials and standards research.

The agreement contains two annexes covering intellectual property and security obligations. The intellectual property annex ensures adequate and effective protection of intellectual property and equitable allocation of intellectual property rights arising from cooperative S&T activities. Certain areas of cooperation (drinks and food products for humans or animals, medicines of all kinds, pharmaceutical and chemical preparations, reactions, and compounds) are excluded from cooperation because the Venezuelan patent law does not provide adequate protection in these areas.

The security obligations annexes provide protection for any classified material that might inadvertently result from S&T cooperation and protection for any national security export-controlled equipment or technology involved in the cooperation.

Considering our common interest in promoting scientific research and technological development and recognizing the benefits which will be derived as a result of enhanced close cooperation, the United States and Venezuela look forward to implementation of the agreement.

REMARKS AT LUNCHEON OF VENEZUELAN-AMERICAN CHAMBERS OF COMMERCE, CARACAS, DECEMBER 8, 1990 [2]

This marks my last stop on the South American continent on this trip, and so, I thought it only appropriate to speak today not just of the relations of our two countries but of our shared concern for the future of our hemisphere. After all, Venezuela has always been a South American leader, and so, I might add, has this President of yours.

President Carlos Andres Perez is justly proud of his past successes. But again, Cap wants to do more than strengthen the democratic traditions of one country. He's a tireless promoter of universal liberty, and that's why he is respected and admired throughout the world.

Our working relationship as heads of state is strong; our friendship a bridge between our nations. But something even more profound is at work here. The United States and Latin America are developing a new understanding of each other. We are, at long last, working together in a spirit of mutual respect, for the greater good of the Americas.

This is only natural. Like your country, the United States won its liberty from European princes and powers. From the vision of Bolivar to that of George Washington, our nations were born for the sake of freedom.

As we near the 500th anniversary of Christopher Columbus' epic voyage, we are making a discovery of our own, of a new relationship between North and South. As I've said during this journey, we should not speak of a First World or a Third World but of our New World.

No nation has been a stronger voice for freedom than Venezuela. It was, after all, here in Caracas that many of today's democratic leaders from across the continent found safe harbor. When Caracas looks south, you behold a continent in which all leaders have, for the first time, been chosen by their people and have faith in their people.

Latin America: A Profile in Courage

This trip has reinforced what I have long believed: Latin America today is a profile in courage because the people of this continent—shopkeepers and students, political leaders and trade unionists—have struggled, sacrificed, and died to restore the rule of law and to defend democracy. Cities once under martial law, peoples once living in fear are now reborn in hope.

Look at the recent flareup in Argentina. A handful of army officers tried to settle a dispute with superior officers by force. And President Menem moved quickly, and the people never wavered in support of their elected government. The vast majority of the Armed Forces defended their Constitution and obeyed their civilian Commander in Chief.

Latin America today is also a profile in courage because the leaders and people of this hemisphere have thrown off the shackles of an outmoded set of ideas about how to promote economic growth. They've embarked instead on a bold new course.

Two decades ago, Latin America followed an economic model based on the flawed idea that the people of this continent could not compete in a modern marketplace and that the state had to shelter local industries and protect them behind high tariff walls and protectionist barriers, and that an increasingly intrusive state, rather than a liberated people, was the formula for economic growth.

Those policies were promoted as the path to development, particularly for the poor. You and I know, regrettably, that the opposite was true. For the closed economic systems that were created smothered growth and thwarted upward mobility for ordinary people. They instead created a rigged system based on privilege in which only a handful could prosper through their connections with the state.

Today, throughout this hemisphere, a new generation of bold democratic leaders has confronted that sterile status quo, and they have breathed new life into Latin America. I've met with five of these leaders: Carlos Menem, Fernando Collor, Luis Alberto Lacalle, and Patricio Aylwin and, of course, here in your country, Carlos Andres Perez. You're the bold pioneers of a new path to development in this continent: stripping away state controls, selling off inefficient state-owned enterprises, realigning overvalued exchange rates, and bringing down tariff walls. These leaders understand that the road to growth, jobs, and rising income is through new investment, expanded trade, and unleashing the energy of entrepreneurs.

Enterprise from the Americas Initiative

I want to work in partnership with this new breed of leadership. And that is why I have proposed our Enterprise for the Americas Initiative: to open doors to the free movement of goods and ideas between our countries; to work for a sound financial footing, reduce debt burdens, and increase trade, investment, and opportunity for all Americans. And so, the Enterprise for the Americas seeks to promote open investment policies through new lending in the Inter-American Development Bank, as well as the creation of a multilateral fund to support investment reform.

Venezuela has already embarked on the difficult path of economic reform. Your President recognizes these steps have created hardship for many Venezuelans. President Perez correctly believes that in the long run all Venezuelans will benefit and prosper from reform.

Trade ties between our nations also continue to broaden and to strengthen. And that doesn't mean only oil but an impressive array of new products that are helping to create jobs. And more, much more, lies ahead. Under the Enterprise for the Americas Initiative, we are negotiating a framework agreement on trade and investment to resolve specific problems and to identify new areas of cooperation. This is a first step toward free and open trade throughout the Americas.

Trade and investment are only two pillars of our Enterprise for the Americas Initiative. We recognize that the burden of external debt weighs heavily on efforts to breathe new life into Latin America and Caribbean economies. And for that reason— as the third pillar in this comprehensive approach—the United States will help countries committed to free market reform shake loose this burden of debt.

You can be proud that, under President Carlos Andres Perez's leadership, Venezuela—in the lead—has reached a debt-reduction agreement with the commercial banks under the Brady plan. This agreement is a vote of confidence by the international financial community in Venezuela's economic policies.

Our Enterprise for the Americas Initiative is more than a slogan; it is more than just another program. It is a challenge to commit ourselves to free markets and to the free flow of capital, central to achieving economic growth and lasting prosperity. And that's why I've come to Latin America this week, to extend my hand in an offer of a new partnership, based on mutual respect and mutual responsibility. Ours is more than an economic partnership; it is a moral partnership.

War on Drugs

Your President and I stand together on serious challenges facing all civilized nations, challenges that ask us to choose, literally, between right and wrong, between good and evil. Our country is the world's largest buyer of cocaine, and so, we're fighting hard at home to reduce demand. We're doing it through increased education and treatment efforts that are already showing positive results. Your neighbors are the world's largest suppliers. Little surprise, then, that as much as 80 tons of cocaine a year move through Venezuela. Carlos Andres Perez and I agree, there can be no compromise with this obscene traffic in human addiction and human lives. We are committed to nothing less than decisive victory over the drug lords. Just a few weeks ago, we signed a bilateral money laundering agreement to help sever the flow of cash from the back streets to the banks. President Perez and I are standing firm, and we will win this war on drugs.

On another important moral question, Venezuela has already shown magnificent leadership by working with the world community to counter the aggression of Saddam Hussein. You acted resolutely and responsibly in denouncing Iraq's conquest of Kuwait in the United Nations, and as a reliable supplier of oil, you have demonstrated determination at a time when the dictator of Iraq threatens the world's economy through economic blackmail. And I applaud your leadership.

A New Partnership with Latin America

Among the many shared challenges I've addressed today, there is one vision: In the Americas, we are many nations with a single destiny. We see a new dawn, where ordinary men and women decide who shall govern and where economic freedoms are not threats to privilege but keys to prosperity.

And that's what our Enterprise for the Americas is all about, and that is what the new partnership we seek is all about. It's a partnership with Latin America to strengthen democratic institutions and defend the rule of law; a partnership to move forward together to safeguard our environmental heritage, to protect the children of the Americas from the scourge of drugs, to prevent the spread of deadly chemical or nuclear weapons of war; a partnership to bring down debt, promote investment, and expand free trade so that all the citizens of the Americas can enjoy rising incomes and expanding opportunities. If we seize this opportunity, the partnership between the

United States and Latin America can become a model for all nations into the 21st century.

Some may dismiss this vision as a dream. I am confident that it is already becoming a reality. You see, I believe the day will soon come when every man and woman in the Americas is a citizen of the world's first completely democratic hemisphere, a hemisphere in which human rights are respected: The strong are just; the weak, secure; and the rule of law prevails. And I believe the day will soon come when

Latin America and the United States unite together in the world's first hemisphere in which trade is free, technology shared, and the benefits of prosperity are open to all. This week in South America—ending with this inspiring visit to Venezuela—leaves me more dedicated than ever to work with you to make that dream come true.

---

1 Text from Weekly Compilation of Presidential Documents of December 10, 1990.
2 Text from Weekly Compilation of Presidential Documents of December 17, 1990.

U.S.-Mexican Relations: Joint Statement by Presidents Bush and Salinas de Gortari

Issued at the conclusion of President Bush's state visit to Mexico, Monterrey, November 27, 1990. [1]

At the invitation of President Carlos Salinas de Gortari, President George Bush of the United States of America paid a state visit to Mexico, November 26-27, 1990. During this visit the two Presidents exchanged views on an extensive agenda of common interest.

Both Presidents, reflecting the climate of friendship and cordiality of relations between the two countries and the intention reaffirmed by both heads of state in previous meetings for this climate to materialize in concrete results to enhance the symbols of good neighborliness, held a friendly and cordial dialogue on the most important issues on the bilateral agenda as well as on regional and global matters.

Presidents Bush and Salinas de Gortari underscored that the best means to strengthen bilateral relations in the future is through dialogue with mutual respect for each other's sovereignty. They stressed their conviction that bilateral relations should be evaluated as a whole, without allowing any single issue, regardless of its complexity, to detract from the need for maintaining such a dialogue, in order to ensure that relations remain at their present optimum level.

The diversity and complexity of Mexico-United States affairs should be viewed as a challenge and as an opportunity that encourage nations to pay unceasing attention to this relationship

and to take effective measures to solve problems still pending.

In reviewing recent achievements, the Presidents noted the progress achieved in areas such as trade, financial cooperation, border issues, the fight against international drug traffic and abuse, cooperation for environmental protection, and strengthening of cultural and educational exchange, and tourism. The Presidents also stated that such achievements are largely due to the excellent cooperation between the Governments within the framework of the binational commission, through which a substantial number of Cabinet members of both countries and leaders of U.S. agencies and Mexican decentralized organizations can meet to hold a dialogue at least once a year.

Free Trade Agreement

In the area of the rapidly expanding trade and investment, the Presidents reaffirmed their commitment in regard to the need to promote trade liberalization and to continue consultations towards a free trade agreement between Mexico and the United States, contemplating the way in which Canada might consider joining such negotiations.

Enterprise for the Americas and Uruguay Round

The Presidents also focused on the current status of consultations with Latin

American countries about the Enterprise for the Americas, and reaffirmed their commitment to a successful conclusion of the Uruguay Round.

Border Issues

The Presidents' discussion included a general examination of issues concerning their common border, noting that it is one of the most heavily utilized in the world.

Both governments. having agreed to facilitate the rapid passage through ports of entry, and conscious of the vital importance for border communities of both nationalities of prompt attention in the ports of entry of the two countries, and affirming their interest in achieving improved facilitation of services, including operating hours, expressed their satisfaction with the establishment of new border ports, and with the progress in the construction of the Zaragoza-Ysleta, Colombia-Dolores and Lucio Blanco-Los Indios bridges, as well as the authorization for nine new ports of entry.

The Presidents shared their concern about the cases of violence on both sides of the border. They strongly condemned such acts of violence and instructed their respective authorities to propose, through the subgroup on consular affairs and protection of the binational commission and other timely high-level meetings, joint recommendations calling for new specific mechanisms with the objectives of arriving at a satisfactory solution of pending cases and creating awareness in order to prevent the repetition of such incidents in the future.

Tuna Exports

President Salinas informed President Bush of his concern about the impact of the tuna embargo on Mexico. President Bush noted the recent judicial action in support of the administration's position that the embargo be stayed, and pledged to work cooperatively with Mexico bilaterally and other nations to seek alternative solutions to this problem, including a multilateral convention.

On the same subject, President Salinas ratified his Government's intention of taking part in multilateral agreements—based on equity and appropriate scientific evidence—for the conservation of marine species, including tuna and marine mammals.

The War Against Drug Trafficking and Drug Abuse

In reference to the fight against international drug trafficking, Presidents Salinas and Bush reaffirmed their conviction that only through efficient international cooperation, based on strict respect for each country's sovereignty, can drug trafficking be fought, and at the same time the demand for drugs reduced.

The Presidents underscored that in this war it is the exclusive responsibility of each country to reinforce in its respective jurisdiction applicable national laws.

The Presidents also reaffirmed once more their recognition of the courage shown by officials waging the war on drug trafficking in each country.

The Governments of Mexico and the United States further reaffirmed their intention of continuing the expeditious consultations concerning the exchange of the instruments of ratification of the mutual legal assistance agreement. President Salinas de Gortari pointed out that the Mexican Senate would have to be informed of the results of such consultations in accordance with the Mexican Constitution.

Environmental Cooperation

The Presidents emphasized the need for ongoing cooperation in the area of environmental protection.

Both Presidents instructed the authorities responsible for environmental affairs of their countries to prepare a comprehensive plan designed to periodically examine ways and means to reinforce border cooperation in this regard, based on the 1983 bilateral agreement. Such a mechanism should seek ways to improve coordination and cooperation, with a view to solving the problems of air, soil, and water quality and of hazardous wastes. State and municipal authorities of both governments and private organizations in both countries should participate in such tasks as appropriate.

Educational Cooperation

The Presidents expressed their satisfaction with the signing of an agreement to create the United States-Mexico Commission for Educational and Cultural Exchange for Scholarships, stressing the significant participation of the private sector in the Executive Board of said Commission.

Financial Cooperation

The Presidents examined the measures adopted against money laundering, as well as those designed to avoid double taxation, and agreed to pursue negotiations on issues in this area.

Tourism

The Presidents agreed on the need to facilitate tourist exchange and transportation even further. To that end they agreed to support mechanisms such as the signing of a memorandum of understanding for charter buses to bring tourists into Mexico and to encourage and promote investments in this area.

World Affairs

In the area of regional and global matters, the two Presidents held an extensive exchange of views and information. President Salinas de Gortari informed President Bush of Mexico's intention to cooperate in the search for a negotiated solution to the conflict in El Salvador, in support of the measures taken by the Secretary-General of the U.N. based on resolutions of the Security Council.

In turn, President Bush provided a detailed explanation and assessment of the Persian Gulf situation from the U.S. perspective after his recent visit to that area. The two Presidents once again expressed the desire for a peaceful resolution to the situation in accord with U.N. resolutions, and exhorted the Government of Iraq to effect an immediate unconditional withdrawal from Kuwait and to release at once all hostages that still remain in that country. Both Presidents expressed their satisfaction with the prevailing spirit of a frank and positive dialogue, both between themselves and their administrations, reflecting the unswerving will to sustain and strengthen the friendly relations between Mexico and the United States.

1 Text from Weekly Compilation of Presidential Documents of December 3, 1990.

U.S., Canada, and Mexico Begin Negotiations for North American Free Trade Agreement [1]

The President of the United States, George Bush; the President of the United Mexican States, Carlos Salinas de Gortari; and the Prime Minister of Canada, Brian Mulroney, announced today [February 5, 1991] their intention to pursue a North American free trade agreement creating one of the world's largest liberalized markets.

Following consultations among their ministers responsible for international trade, the three leaders concluded that a North American free trade agreement would foster sustained economic growth through expanded trade and investment in a market comprising over 360 million people and $6 trillion in output. In so doing, the agreement would help all three countries meet the economic challenges they will face over the next decade.

Accordingly, the three leaders have agreed that their trade ministers should proceed as soon as possible, in accordance with each country's domestic procedures, with trilateral negotiations aimed at a comprehensive North American free trade agreement. The goal would be to progressively eliminate obstacles to the flow of goods and services and to investment, provide for the protection of intellectual property rights, and establish a fair and expeditious dispute settlement mechanism.

---

1 Joint statement issued by the three countries, February 5, 1991.

Organization of American States Repudiates Suriname Military Coup

STATEMENT TO OAS PERMANENT COUNCIL BY LUIGI R. EINAUDI, U.S. PERMANENT REPRESENTATIVE, DECEMBER 28, 1990 [1]

On the night of December 24, the leaders of the armed forces of Suriname forced the Surinamese executive and cabinet to "turn in their portfolios." At the same time, they ordered the Surinamese people to stay in their homes. In doublespeak worthy of Orwell's worst nightmare, a military spokesman accused the constitutionally elected government of failing to hold free elections and, in a clumsy attempt to break the inevitable wave of repudiation from within Suriname and from abroad, promised free elections to the Surinamese people in "100 days." Soldiers armed under constitutional authority and sworn to uphold the constitution have arrogated to themselves the right to interpret the constitution unilaterally and abrogate it in the process.

We have seen this all before. I do not believe there is a person in this chamber who wants to see it again. The history of our hemisphere has long been written as a history of civil-military conflicts. Yet despite recurring rumors and even outright coup attempts, the last successful coup d'etat took place in Guatemala in 1982, eight years ago; last use of military force to seize power from civilians took place in 1980 in Bolivia and in Suriname. Ten years without a coup against civilian rule had led many of us to hope that a new era was dawning. As President Bush said in Buenos Aires on December 5:

"Too many brave people sacrificed and died to bring democracy back to Latin America. Let those who would attack constitutional democracy understand: In Latin America the day of the dictator is over."

There is, of course, the possibility that with the end of the Cold War, the day of the dictator is ending throughout the world. As we meet here today, 28 nations, including some from this hemisphere, have military units on duty in the Persian Gulf supporting the United Nations against a military dictator who has sought to impose the law of the bully (la ley del maton) on his people and his neighbors.

Recent Pattern of Civil-Military Cooperation in the Hemisphere

In the Americas, the situation is both clearer and better. Anachronisms aside, the day of the dictator is indeed over. Moreover, substantial progress is taking place to build the foundation of civil-military cooperation in fundamental areas of human rights, security, and national development in a new democratic era.

Argentina and Brazil have moved forward to give effect to the Treaty of Tlatelolco by agreeing to negotiate an agreement on nuclear safeguards. Lauding the decisions of these states to bring the Tlatelolco Treaty on nuclear nonproliferation into force, President Bush said on December 3 in Brasilia:

"We hope that all countries in this hemisphere will follow Brazil's and Argentina's recent decision to bring the nonproliferation treaty . . . into force."

In Central America, the Esquipulas process has contributed decisively to a reduction of military tensions. The Central American Security Commission, created by the June 1990 Antigua accords, is bringing senior political and military leaders together to discuss shifting resources from military to humanitarian needs and is looking ahead to negotiating real reductions in conventional arms.

In Nicaragua and in Haiti, the Organization of American States has over the past year—and yes, it is only a year since representatives of the Secretary General were fully engaged in monitoring the election campaign in Nicaragua—helped to shape an environment of peaceful conflict resolution. The successful elections in Haiti earlier this month were marked by the impartiality and confidence generated by international observers. The OAS International Commission for Support and Verification (CIAV) is still bringing essential impartiality and confidence to the processes of repatriation and national reconciliation in Nicaragua

In short, real progress—generating tangible results—has been made in our hemisphere toward new levels of international cooperation to achieve regional peace and security. This progress is uneven. Narcotics trafficking, terrorism, and clandestine arms smuggling are still major obstacles to regional peace and security. The December 4-5, 1990, rebellion in Panama demonstrates that much remains to be done to advance professionalism even in a case where major advances have taken place. Economic achievements and opportunities are still too often obscured by poverty and lack of competitiveness. Perhaps most importantly, human rights concerns remain a top priority for us in far too many countries.

This said, my government believes we have a major opportunity to build a new era of civil-military cooperation in changing, newly democratic societies. On balance, we are seeing unprecedented respect on the part of military leaders and institutions for the democratic process. On balance, we are seeing an appreciation on the part of civilian political leaders for the institutional interests of the military and a recognition of the important place reserved for the armed forces in a democratic society.

Suriname Military Must Accept Civilian Authority

And now, like an ominous and spiteful rejection of this future to which we are all committed, we have the events that have occasioned this meeting. For five years following independence from the Netherlands in 1975, Suriname was a functioning democracy with an excellent human rights record. Then, in 1980, the legitimate government was overthrown.

By late 1982, the Bouterse junta institutionalized repression of civilian opposition, culminating in the murders of 15 civic leaders. Some were beaten to death, others tortured and shot in cold blood. Because of the appalling Bouterse human rights record, in 1982 both the United States and the Netherlands suspended economic and military aid to Suriname.

Suriname's 1988 return to civilian rule was not respected by military leaders. Continuing human rights

abuses, military harassment of civilians, interference with government activities and with shipments of food and medicine outside the capital, together with other "emergency powers" with no apparent legal basis, are powerful reminders of the Surinamese military's callous disregard for civilian authority and human rights. On June 4,1990, President Ramsewak Shankar of Suriname addressed the OAS General Assembly in Asuncion, Paraguay. He said, among other things:

"The process of peace which is taking place in Suriname, which I have been called upon to lead, aims, in the first place, at putting an end to the armed approach of settling disputes and is, furthermore, geared toward guaranteeing the participation of every subgroup at the national level, as well as realizing the integral development of the nation."

We cannot be silent about the events in Suriname that deprive the Surinamese people of their rights. We cannot allow these illegal acts to threaten the post-Cold War democratic equilibrium now developing. The United States condemns the violation of constitutional order in Suriname and calls on the Surinamese military to restore power immediately to the democratically elected authorities of that country. The United States is proud to cosponsor the resolution drafted by Venezuela and the other members of the Group of Rio.

RESOLUTION 554 OF THE PERMANENT COUNCIL OF THE OAS, DECEMBER 28, 1990 [1]

The Permanent Council of the Organization of American States,
Considering:
That the Charter of the Organization establishes that "the true significance of American solidarity and good neighborliness can only mean the consolidation on this continent, within the framework of democratic institutions, of a system of individual liberty and social justice based on respect for the essential rights of man;"
That democratically elected President Mr. Ramsewak Shankar was deposed by a military coup on December 24, 1990; and
That this act of force violently disturbs the democratic institutional order of a member state, violates the right of its people to elect its governors

freely, and deals a severe setback to the democratization process in the Hemisphere,
Resolves:
1. To categorically repudiate the military coup in Suriname, which thwarts the fundamental right of the people of that country to live in a system of freedom and democracy.
2. To issue an appeal for reestablishment of the democratic institutional order and the avoidance of any act that could aggravate the situation and impair the full enjoyment of human rights.
3. To keep the situation in Suriname under review, without violation of the principle of nonintervention, and to request the Secretary General to inform the Permanent Council on the course of events in that member state.

VOTE: 26 of the 27 members present. Suriname did not join the consensus.

---

1 Department of State Dispatch, January 7, 1991.

U.S. Hails Inauguration of Haitian President Jean-Bertrand Aristide [1]

The people of Haiti, after decades of oppression and deprivation, celebrate the inauguration on February 7 of President Jean-Bertrand Aristide, who they themselves chose in free elections. This inauguration marks the end of the difficult transition period from dictatorship that began with the departure of Jean-Claude Duvalier exactly five years ago.

We offer our congratulations to President Aristide and to the Haitian people for their well-deserved victory, which they accomplished in spite of the actions of determined enemies of democracy.

The Government of the United States of America looks forward to building a close and cooperative relationship, based on mutual respect and common interests, with the newly elected democratic Government of Haiti.

---

1 Statement by Department of State spokesman Margaret Tutwiler, February 7, 1991.

President's Conditional Release of Military Aid to El Salvador

White House Statement, January 15, 1991 [1]

The President is sending a report to Congress on Salvadoran Government and FMLN guerrilla compliance with the terms set forth in the Fiscal Year 1991 Foreign Operations Appropriation Act. [2] Today, the President determined that $42.5 million, the 50 percent of FY 1991 military aid for El Salvador that has been withheld under the law, may be released. The President's decision was based on the FMLN's violation of the conditions against "engaging in acts of violence directed at civilian targets" and acquiring or receiving "significant shipments of lethal military assistance from outside El Salvador," contained in Sections 531 (D) and (E) of the Act.

The President has decided to suspend delivery of this aid for 60 days in the interest of promoting a peaceful settlement to El Salvador's tragic conflict. Despite the FMLN's intransigence in negotiating with the Government and its clear violation of standards which Congress has established, we must give the peace negotiations under U.N. mediation every possible chance to succeed. The end of the 60-day period will coincide with the elections in March for the Salvadoran National Assembly. If the FMLN takes a serious and constructive approach to the peace talks so that they result in a political settlement and a U.N. supervised cease-fire within 60 days, these funds will not need to be released for the defense of El Salvador's security.

The United States is prepared to go the last mile for peace in El Salvador. We are not prepared to sacrifice the security of the elected government or of American citizens. The United States will monitor carefully security conditions in El Salvador, and the President may release military assistance sooner than 60 days in case of a compelling security need.

The President would strongly prefer not to have to use these funds for military purposes, but rather, as the legislation permits, to help monitor a cease-fire and assist in demobilizing combatants and returning them to civilian life. An internationally verified cease-fire would assist greatly in assuring the fullest possible participation in the election and allow us to use our assistance to support a peace settlement and national reconstruction. The time for war in El Salvador is over; the time for a peace settlement is now.

---

1 Text from Weekly Compilation of Presidential Documents of January 21, 1991.

2 See *Foreign Policy Bulletin*, November/December 1990, p. 71.

Department of State Statement on Killing of U.S. Servicemen in El Salvador [1]

We are appalled to learn that Tutela Legal, a human rights organization in El Salvador, has apparently termed the January 2 killing of two American servicemen whose helicopter was downed by FMLN gunfire a "mercy killing."

According to press reports from San Salvador, the director of this organization interviewed the two guerrillas held by the FMLN in connection with the crime. The director of Tutela Legal reportedly said the guerrillas' crime would be "mercy killing," because they allegedly killed the Americans to put them out of their misery. This is at odds with the U.S. medical examiners' report, which found that two of the three crewmen survived the landing of the helicopter, after which one died from multiple gunshot wounds, and another from a single gunshot to the back of the head.

We find it unacceptable that a human rights group would accept without question the account of those implicated in the crime, present it to the press, and then attempt to issue a verdict on the crime the guerrillas committed.

Anyone accused of a crime in El Salvador should have to answer to the legitimate judicial system. Once again we call on the FMLN, if it is serious about justice, to turn the accused over to the Salvadoran judicial system.

The Department of Justice is continuing to investigate and collect information in this case to determine if the killings of U.S. servicemen in El Salvador violated U.S. law. If the Justice Department determines that there are grounds for prosecution of the suspects in the U.S., the possible location for prosecution would be a matter for discussion and agreement between the U.S. and Salvadoran Governments.

---

1 Statement by Department of State spokesman Margaret Tutwiler, February 7, 1991.

Current Actions:

November, December, 1990; January 1991

These listings were released by the Department of State as "Treaty Actions" on, respectively, December 17, 1990; January 14, 1991; and February 11, 1991.

I. November 1990

MULTILATERAL

Antarctica
The Antarctic treaty. Signed at Washington Dec. 1, 1959. Entered into force June 23, 1961. TIAS 4780.
Accession deposited: Switzerland, Nov. 15, 1990.

Germany
Agreement concerning the convention of Oct. 23, 1954 (TIAS 3426), on the presence of foreign forces in the Federal Republic of Germany. Effected by exchanges of notes at Bonn Sept. 25, 1990. Entered into force Sept. 25, 1990.

Declaration suspending the occupation of quadripartite rights and responsibilities. Signed at New York Oct. 1, 1990. Entered into force Oct. 3, 1990.
Signatures: US, France, Federal Republic of Germany, German Democratic Republic, USSR, UK.

Maritime Matters
International convention on tonnage measurement of ships, 1969, with annexes. Done at London June 23, 1969. Entered into force July 18, 1982; for the US Feb. 10, 1983. TIAS 10490.
Accession deposited: Oman, Sept. 24, 1990.

Pollution
Annex V to the international convention for the prevention of pollution from ships, 1973. Done at London Nov. 2, 1973. Entered into force Dec. 31, 1988. [Senate] Treaty Doc. 100-3.
Acceptance deposited: Bahamas, Oct. 12, 1990; Turkey, Oct. 10, 1990.

Protocol of 1978 relating to the international convention for the prevention of pollution from ships, 1973. Done at London Feb. 17, 1978. Entered into force Oct. 2, 1983.
Accession deposited: Singapore, Nov. 1, 1990.[1] Turkey, Oct. 10, 1990.

Protocol to the 1979 convention on long-range transboundary air pollution (TIAS 10541) concerning the control of emissions of nitrogen oxides or their transboundary flukes, with annex. Done at Sofia Oct. 31, 1988.
Ratification deposited: Germany, Nov. 16, 1990.
Enters into force: Feb. 14, 1991.

Taxation — Assistance
Convention on mutual administrative assistance in tax matters. Done at Strasbourg Jan. 25, 1988.[2]
Senate advice and consent: Sept. 18, 1990.[3]

Treaties
Vienna convention on the law of treaties, with annex. Done at Vienna May 23, 1969. Entered into force Jan. 27, 1980.[4]
Accession deposited: Poland, July 2, 1990.

BILATERAL

Cote d'Ivoire
Agreement regarding the consolidation and rescheduling of certain debts owed to, guaranteed by, or insured by the US government and its agencies, with annexes. Signed at Abidjan Sept. 29, 1990. Entered into force Nov. 16, 1990.

Czechoslovakia
Investment incentive agreement. Signed at Prague Oct. 18, 1990. Entered into force Oct. 18, 1990.

Finland
Convention for the avoidance of double taxation and the prevention of fiscal evasion with respect to taxes on income and on capital. Signed at Helsinki Sept. 21, 1989.[2]
Senate advice and consent: Sept. 18, 1990.[5]

Germany
Convention for the avoidance of double taxation and the prevention of fiscal evasion with respect to taxes on income and capitol and to certain other taxes, with a related protocol, exchanges of notes, and memorandum of understanding. Signed at Bonn Aug. 29, 1989.[2]
Senate advice and consent: Sept. 18, 1990.[5]

Agreement concerning air services to and from Berlin. Effected by exchange of notes at Bonn Oct. 9, 1990. Entered into force Oct. 9, 1990.

Memorandum of understanding concerning air navigation services in Berlin, with related exchange of letters. Signed at Bonn Oct. 23, 1990. Entered into force Oct. 23, 1990.

Greece
Agreement extending the interim agreement on air services, with memorandum of understanding, of Apr. 9, 1985, as amended and extended. Effected by exchange of note at Athens Oct. 17 and Nov. 9, 1990. Entered into force Nov. 9, 1990; effective Oct. 25, 1990.

Honduras
International express mail agreement with detailed regulations. Signed at Buenos Aires Sept. 11, 1990. Entered into force Nov. 15, 1990.

Agreement for the exchange of information with respect to taxes. Signed at Washington Sept. 27, 1990. Enters into force upon an exchange of notes confirming that both sides have met all constitutional and statutory requirements.

India
Convention for the avoidance of double taxation and the prevention of fiscal evasion with respect to taxes on income. Signed at New Delhi Sept. 12, 1989.[2]
Senate advice and consent: Sept. 18, 1990.

Indonesia
Convention for the avoidance of double taxation and the prevention of fiscal evasion with respect to taxes on income, with protocol and exchange of notes. Signed at Jakarta July 11, 1988.[2]
Senate advice and consent: Sept. 18, 1990.

Japan
Agreement extending the agreement of Sept. 26, 1985, concerning Japanese participation in the commission for the study of alternatives to the Panama Canal, with attachment. Effected by exchange of notes at Panama Sept. 25, 1990. Entered into force Sept. 25, 1990; effective Sept. 26, 1990.

Korea
Agreement relating to trade in textiles and textile products, with attachment. Effected by exchange of notes at Washington Sept. 14, 1990. Entered into force Sept. 14, 1990; effective Jan. 1, 1990.

New Zealand
Agreement extending the agreement of Feb. 27, 1974 (TIAS 7806), as extended, for scientific and technological cooperation. Effected by exchange of notes at Wellington Sept. 13 and 17, 1990. Entered into force Sept. 17, 1990; effective Aug. 27, 1990.

Panama
Agreement extending the agreement of Sept. 26, 1985, concerning the establishment of the commission for the study of alternatives to the Panama Canal, with attachment. Effected by exchange of notes at Panama Sept. 25, 1990. Entered into force Sept. 25, 1990; effective Sept. 26, 1990.

Philippines
Grant agreement for local development assistance program. Signed at Manila Sept. 28, 1990. Entered into force Sept. 28, 1990.

Project grant agreement for Philippine capital infrastructure support project. Signed at Manila Sept. 28, 1990. Entered into force Sept. 28, 1990.

Saudi Arabia
Agreement amending and extending the technical cooperation agreement of Feb. 13, 1975 (TIAS 8072), as amended and extended. Signed at Washington Sept. 26, 1990. Entered into force Sept. 26, 1990; effective Feb. 13, 1990.

Spain
Convention for the avoidance of double taxation and the prevention of fiscal evasion with respect to taxes on income, with protocol. Signed at Madrid Feb. 22, 1990.
Entered into force: Nov. 21, 1990.

Memorandum of understanding concerning lease of equipment and exchange of technical information for the XXV Olympiad. Signed at Madrid Oct. 19, 1990. Entered into force Oct. 19, 1990.

Treaty on mutual legal assistance in criminal matters, with attachments. Signed at Washington Nov. 20, 1990. Enters into force on the last day of the month following the exchange of instruments of ratification.

Sweden
Agreement amending and extending the agreement of Sept. 9, 1980, as extended, concerning a cooperative program in the field of management of radioactive wastes. Signed at Stockholm Sept. 13, 1990. Entered into force Sept. 13, 1990; effective Sept. 9, 1990.

Switzerland
Extradition treaty. Signed at Washington Nov. 14, 1990. Enters into force 180 days after the exchange of instruments of ratification.

Tunisia
Convention for the avoidance of double taxation and the prevention of fiscal evasion with respect to taxes on income, with exchange of notes. Signed at Washington, June 17, 1985.[2]

Supplementary protocol to the convention for the avoidance of double taxation and the prevention of fiscal evasion with respect to taxes on income of June 17, 1985. Signed at Tunis Oct. 4, 1989.[2]
Senate advice and consent: Sept. 18, 1990.

USSR
Memorandum of cooperation in the fields of environmental restoration and waste management. Signed at Vienna Sept. 18, 1990. Entered into force Sept. 18, 1990.

United Kingdom
Agreement extending the application of the treaty of July 3, 1986, concerning the Cayman Islands relating to mutual legal assistance in criminal matters to Anguilla, the British Virgin Islands, and the Turks and Caicos Islands. Effected by exchange of notes at Washington Nov. 9, 1990. Entered into force Nov. 9, 1990.

Venezuela
Agreement regarding cooperation in the prevention and control of money laundering arising from illicit trafficking in narcotic drugs and psychotropic substances, with attachment. Signed at Washington Nov. 5, 1990. Enters into force Jan. 1, 1991.

Zambia
Agreement regarding the consolidation and rescheduling of certain debts owed to, guaranteed by, or insured by the US government and its agencies, with annexes. Signed at Lusaka Sept. 14, 1990. Entered into force Nov. 5, 1990.

---

1 Does not accept optional annexes III, IV and V.
2 Not in force.
3 With reservations.
4 Not in force for US.
5 With understanding.

II. December 1990

MULTILATERAL

Agriculture
Convention on the inter-American institute for cooperation on agriculture. Done at Washington Mar. 6, 1979. Entered into force Dec. 8, 1980. TIAS 9919.
Ratification deposited: St. Kitts and Nevis, July 27, 1990.

Aviation
Convention on international civil aviation. Done at Chicago Dec. 7, 1944. Entered into force Apr. 4, 1947. TIAS 1591.

Protocol on the authentic trilingual text of the convention on international civil aviation (TIAS 1591), with annex. Done at Buenos Aires Sept. 24, 1968. TIAS 6605.
Adherence deposited: Belize, Dec. 7, 1990.

Conservation
Convention on wetlands of international importance especially as waterfowl habitat. Done at Ramsar Feb. 2, 1971. Entered into force Dec. 21, 1975; for the US Dec. 18, 1986. (Senate) Treaty Doc. 99-28.
Accessions deposited: Chad, June 13, 1990; Ecuador, Sept. 7, 1990; Guatemala, June 26, 1990; Guinea

Bissau, May 14, 1990; Kenya, June 5, 1990; Sri Lanka, June 15, 1990.

Customs
Convention establishing a customs cooperation council, with annex. Done at Brussels Dec. 15, 1950. Entered into force Nov. 4, 1952; for the US Nov. 5, 1970. TIAS 7063.
Accession deposited: Angola, Sept. 26, 1990.

Fisheries
Convention for the establishment of an inter-American tropical tuna commission. Signed at Washington May 31, 1949. Entered into force Mar. 3, 1950. TIAS 2044.
Notification of adherence: Vanuatu, Sept. 10, 1990.

Judicial Procedure
Convention on the civil aspects of international child abduction. Done at The Hague Oct. 25, 1980. Entered into force Dec. 1, 1983; for the US July 1, 1988. (Senate) Treaty Doc. 99-11 . Signature: Ireland, May 23, 1990.
Acceptance deposited: Netherlands, June 12, 1990.[1,2]

Pollution
Convention for the protection of the ozone layer, with annexes. Done at Vienna Mar. 22, 1985. Entered into force Sept. 22, 1988. (Senate) Treaty Doc. 99-9.

Montreal protocol on substances that deplete the ozone layer, with annex. Done at Montreal Sept. 16, 1987. Entered into force Jan. 1, 1989. (Senate) Treaty Doc. 100-10.
Accession deposited: Bulgaria, Nov. 20, 1990.

Protocol to the 1979 convention on long-range transboundary air pollution (TIAS 10541) concerning the control of emissions of nitrogen oxides or their transboundary flukes, with annex. Done at Sofia Oct. 31, 1988. Enters into force Feb. 14, 1991.
Ratification deposited: Spain, Dec. 4, 1990.

Red Cross
Protocol additional to the Geneva conventions of Aug. 12, 1949 (TIAS 3362,3363,3364, 3365), and relating to the protection of victims of international armed conflicts (protocol I), with annexes. Adopted at Geneva June 8, 1977. Entered into force Dec. 7, 1978.[3]

Protocol additional to the Geneva conventions of Aug. 12, 1949 (TIAS 3362,3363,3364, 3365), and relating to the protection of victims of non-international armed conflicts (protocol II). Adopted at Geneva June 8, 1977. Entered into force Dec. 7, 1978.[3]
Ratifications deposited: Ukrainian Soviet SSR, Jan. 25, 1990;[4] Czechoslovakia, Feb. 14, 1990; Yemen Arab Republic, Apr. 17, 1990.
Accession deposited: Barbados, Feb. 19, 1990.

Refugees
Protocol relating to the status of refugees. Done at New York Jan. 31, 1967. Entered into force Oct. 4, 1967; for the US Nov. 1, 1968. TIAS 6577.
Accession deposited: Belize, June 27, 1990.

Satellite Communications Systems
Convention on the international maritime satellite organization (INMARSAT), with annex. Done at London Sept. 3, 1976. Entered into force July 16, 1979. TIAS 9605.
Accession deposited: Monaco, Oct. 1, 1990; Romania, Yugoslavia, Sept. 27, 1990.
Ratification deposited: Cameroon, Oct. 23, 1990.

Operating agreement on the international maritime satellite organization (INMARSAT), with annex. Done at London Sept. 3, 1976. Entered into force July 16, 1979. TIAS 9605.
Signatures: Monaco, Oct. 1, 1990; Romania, Yugoslavia, Sept. 27, 1990.

Sugar
International sugar agreement, 1987, with annexes. Done at London Sept. 11, 1987. Entered into force provisionally Mar. 24, 1988.
Accession deposited: Switzerland, Nov. 20, 1990.

Terrorism
International convention against the taking of hostages. Adopted at New York Dec. 17, 1979. Entered into force June 3, 1983; for the US Jan. 6, 1985.
Accession deposited: Grenada, Dec. 10, 1990.

Timber
International tropical timber agreement, 1983, with annexes. Done at Geneva Nov. 18, 1983.

Entered into force provisionally Apr. 1, 1985; for the US Apr. 26, 1985.
Accession deposited: Nepal, July 3, 1990; Zaire, Nov. 20, 1990.

Trade
United Nations convention on contracts for the international sale of goods. Done at Vienna Apr. 11, 1980. Entered into force Jan. 1, 1988. [52 Fed. Reg. 6262]
Acceptance deposited: Netherlands, Dec. 13, 1990.

Bilateral

Argentina
Treaty on mutual legal assistance in criminal matters, with attachments. Signed at Buenos Aires Dec. 4, 1990. Enters into force upon exchange of instruments of ratification .

Brazil
Memorandum of understanding concerning environmental cooperation. Signed at Washington Nov. 16, 1990. Entered into force Nov. 16, 1990.

Canada
Memorandum of understanding on cooperation in the field of forestry-related programs. Signed at Washington May 17, 1990. Entered into force May 17, 1990.

Agreement extending the agreement of Oct. 28 and Dec. 5, 1980, relating to coordination between the United States and Canadian Coast Guards of icebreaking operations in the Great Lakes and St. Lawrence Seaway system (TIAS 9950; 32 UST 4334). Effected by exchange of notes at Washington Dec. 4, 1990. Entered into force Dec. 5, 1990.

Hong Kong
Agreement concerning the confiscation and forfeiture of the proceeds and instrumentalities of drug trafficking. Signed at Hong Kong Nov. 23, 1990. Enters into force on the date on which the parties have notified each other in writing that their respective requirements have been complied with.

Spain
Agreement concerning the free pursuit of gainful employment by dependents of employees of diplomatic missions, consular posts, or missions to international organizations, with exchange of notes.

TREATIES

Signed at Madrid July 25, 1990. Entered into force provisionally July 25, 1990; definitively, when each party has notified the other of the fulfillment of its internal requirements.

Turkey
Air transport agreement, with annexes. Signed at Washington on Nov. 7, 1990. Enters into force after fulfillment of the constitutional requirements by each party, on the date of an exchange of notes.

United Kingdom
Agreement extending the agreement of May 14, 1987, as extended concerning Montserrat and narcotics activities. Effected by exchange of notes at Washington Nov. 29, 1990. Entered into force Nov. 29, 1990; effective Dec. 1, 1990.

Agreement amending the memorandum of understanding of Oct. 5 and 11, 1984, concerning the provision of mutual logistic support, supplies, and services. Signed at London and Stuttgart-Vaihingen June 29 and Aug. 9, 1990. Entered into force Aug. 9, 1990.

---

1 With reservations.
2 Applicable to the Kingdom in Europe.
3 Not in force for US.
4 With declaration to protocol I.

III. January 1991

MULTILATERAL

Aviation
Convention for the suppression of unlawful acts against the safety of civil aviation. Done at Montreal Sept. 23, 1971. Entered into force Jan. 26, 1973. TIAS 7570.
Accession deposited: Equatorial Guinea, Jan. 2, 1991.

Convention for the suppression of unlawful seizure of aircraft. Done at The Hague Dec. 16, 1970. Entered into force Oct. 14, 1981. TIAS 7192.
Accession deposited: Equatorial Guinea, Jan. 2, 1991.

Conservation
Convention on wetlands of international importance especially as waterfowl habitat, as amended by the Protocol of Paris (Dec. 3, 1982). Done at Ramsar

Feb. 2, 1971. Entered into force Dec. 21, 1971; for the U.S. Dec. 18, 1986. (Senate) Treaty Doc. 99-28.
Accessions deposited: Burkina Faso, June 27, 1990; Chad, June 13, 1990; Czechoslovakia, July 2, 1990; Ecuador, Sept. 7, 1990; Guatemala, June 26, 1990; Guinea-Bisseau, May 14, 1990; Kenya, June 5, 1990; Sri Lanka, June 15, 1990.

Defense
Memorandum of understanding concerning a cooperative program for full integration of a radar in the AV-8B weapon system and the production of life cycle support of a radar-equipped AV-8B (AV-8B Harrier II Plus), with annexes. Signed at Rome, Washington, and Madrid Aug. 8 and 31 and Sept. 28, 1990. Entered into force Sept. 28, 1990.
Signatures: Italy, Aug. 8, 1990; Spain, Sept. 28, 1990; United States, Aug. 31, 1990.

Finance
UNIDROIT convention on international factoring. Done at Ottawa May 28, 1988. Enters into force on the first day of the month following the expiration of 6 months after the date of deposit of the third instrument of ratification, acceptance, approval, or accession.
Signature: United States, Dec. 28, 1990.

UNIDROIT convention on international financial leasing. Done at Ottawa May 28, 1988. Enters into force on the first day of the month following the expiration of 6 months after the date of deposit of the third instrument of ratification, acceptance, approval, or accession.
Signature: United States, Dec. 28, 1990.

Maritime Matters
International convention on standards of training, certification, and watchkeeping for seafarers, 1978. Done at London July 7, 1978. Entered into force Apr. 28, 1984. [1]
Accession deposited: Saudi Arabia, Nov. 29, 1990.

Pollution
Protocol of 1978 relating to the international convention for the prevention of pollution from ships, 1973. Done at London Feb. 17, 1978. Entered into force Oct. 2, 1983.
Accession deposited: Seychelles, Nov. 28, 1990.

Convention for the protection and development of the marine environment of the wider Caribbean region, with annex, with protocol concerning cooperation in combating oil spills in the wider Caribbean region, with annex. Done at Cartagena Mar. 24, 1983. Entered into force Oct. 11, 1986. (Senate) Treaty Doc. 98-13.
Accessions deposited: Dominica, Oct. 5, 1990; St. Vincent and the Grenadines, July 11, 1990.

Convention for the protection of the ozone layer, with annexes. Done at Vienna Mar. 22, 1985. Entered into force Sept. 22, 1988. (Senate) Treaty Doc. 99-9.
Accession deposited: Czechoslovakia, October 1, 1990; Malawi, Jan. 9, 1991.

Montreal protocol on substances that deplete the ozone layer, with annex. Done at Montreal Sept. 16, 1987. Entered into force Jan. 1, 1989. (Senate) Treaty Doc. 100-10.
Ratification deposited: Argentina, Sept. 18, 1990.
Accessions deposited: Czechoslovakia, Oct. 1, 1990; Yugoslavia, Jan. 3, 1991; Malawi, Jan. 9, 1991.

Rubber
International natural rubber agreement, 1987, with annexes. Done at Geneva Mar. 20, 1987. Entered into force provisionally Dec. 29, 1988; definitively Apr. 3, 1989. (Senate) Treaty Doc. 100-9.
Ratification deposited: Thailand, Sept. 24, 1990.

Safety at Sea
International convention for the safety of life at sea, 1974, with annex. Done at London Nov. 1, 1974. Entered into force May 25, 1980. TIAS 9700.
Accessions deposited: Iraq, Dec. 14, 1990.

Women
Convention on the elimination of all forms of discrimination against women. Adopted at New York Dec. 18, 1979. Entered into force Sept. 3, 1981. [1]
Ratification deposited: Grenada, Aug. 30, 1990.

BILATERAL

Argentina
Agreement on the development and facilitation of tourism. Signed at Buenos Aires Sept. 25, 1990. Entered into force Sept. 25, 1990.

Memorandum of understanding for the exchange of technical information directly applicable to the safety of operating civil power and research reactors, with appendix. Signed at Buenos Aires Nov. 30, 1990. Entered into force Nov. 30, 1990.

Agreement regarding mutual assistance between customs services. Signed at Buenos Aires Dec. 4, 1990. Entered into force provisionally Dec. 4, 1990; definitively, upon notification by the parties that national legal requirements have been fulfilled.

Bolivia
Agreement regarding the consolidation and rescheduling of certain debts owed to, guaranteed by, or insured by the US government and its agencies, with annexes. Signed at La Paz Nov. 27, 1990. Enters into force upon receipt by Bolivia of written notice from the US that all necessary domestic legal requirements have been fulfilled.

Brazil
Agreement extending the memorandum of understanding of May 8, 1984, as extended, concerning the Landsat system. Effected by exchange of notes at Brasilia Sept. 3 and Oct. 18, 1990. Entered into force Oct. 18, 1990; effective May 8, 1990.

Brunei
International express mail agreement, with detailed regulations. Signed at Bandar Seri Begawan and Washington Dec. 15, 1990 and Jan. 8, 1991. Enters into force Feb. 18, 1991.

Bulgaria
Agreement concerning the establishment of a Peace Corps program in Bulgaria. Signed at Washington Sept. 27, 1990. Entered in force Sept. 27, 1990.

Chile
Agreement concerning the reciprocal exemption from income tax of income derived from the international operation of aircraft. Effected by exchange of notes at Washington and Santiago Aug.

6 and December 4, 1990. Entered into force Dec. 4, 1990; effective with respect to taxable years beginning on or after Jan. 1, 1987.

Czechoslovakia
Agreement on trade relations, with related exchanges of letters. Signed at Washington April 12, 1990. <u>Entered into force:</u> Nov. 17, 1990.

Agreement on the program of the United States Peace Corps in Czechoslovakia. Signed at Prague June 25, 1990. Entered into force June 25, 1990.

Dominican Republic
International express mail agreement, with detailed regulations. Signed at Santo Domingo and Washington Dec. 3, 1990 and Jan. 8, 1991. Enters into force Feb. 18, 1991.

Finland
Memorandum of understanding for cooperation in energy research and development. Signed at Washington Oct. 23, 1990. Entered into force Oct. 23, 1990.

France
Agreement for the exchange of technical information and cooperation in the regulation of nuclear safety, with patent addendum. Signed at Paris Sept. 4, 1990. Entered into force Sept. 4, 1990.

Agreement extending the agreement of Dec. 12 and 19, 1988, for cooperation in high energy laser-matter interaction physics research and development. Effected by exchange of letters at Washington and Paris Nov. 6 and Dec. 6, 1990. Entered into force Dec. 6, 1990.

Germany
Agreement extending the technical exchange and cooperative arrangement of Dec. 20, 1974, as amended and extended (TIAS 9067, 10040), in the field of management of radioactive wastes. Effected by exchange of letters at Bonn and Washington Sept. 3 and Oct. 10, 1990. Entered into force Oct. 10, 1990; effective Dec. 3, 1989.

Haiti
Agreement amending and extending the agreement of Sept. 26 and 30, 1986, as amended, relating to trade in cotton, wool and man-made fiber textiles and textile products. Effected by exchange of notes at Port-au-Prince July 18, Nov.

19 and 28, 1990. Entered into force Nov. 28, 1990; effective Jan. 1, 1990.

Honduras
Agreement regarding the consolidation and rescheduling or refinancing of certain debts owed to, guaranteed by, or insured by the US government and its agencies, with annexes. Signed at Tegucigalpa Dec. 20, 1990. Enters into force upon receipt by Honduras of written notice from the US that all necessary domestic legal requirements have been fulfilled.

Hungary
Arrangement for the exchange of technical information and cooperation in nuclear safety matters, with patent addendum. Signed at Budapest Sept. 24, 1990. Entered into force Sept. 24, 1990.

Jamaica
Agreement amending the agreement of Aug. 27, 1986, as amended and extended, relating to trade in textiles and textile products. Effected by exchange of notes at Kingston Oct. 29 and 31, 1990. Entered into force Oct. 31, 1990.

Agreement regarding the consolidation and rescheduling or refinancing of certain debts owed to, guaranteed by, or insured by the US government and its agencies, with annexes. Signed at Kingston Dec. 20, 1990. Enters into force upon receipt by Jamaica of written notice from the US that all necessary domestic legal requirements have been fulfilled.

Korea
Agreement amending the agreement of Nov. 21 and Dec. 4, 1986, as amended and extended, concerning trade in certain textiles and textile products. Effected by exchange of letters at Washington Nov. 30 and Dec. 3, 1990. Entered into force Dec. 3, 1990.

Mexico
Agreement amending the agreement of Feb. 13, 1988, as amended, concerning trade in cotton, wool, and man-made fiber textiles and textile products. Effected by exchange of notes at Mexico April 20, July 25, and Aug. 1, 1990. Entered into force Aug. 1, 1990.

Agreement amending the agreement of Aug. 28, 1972, as amended (TIAS 7438), to eradicate screw-worms. Effected by exchange of notes at Mexico

Oct. 19 and Dec. 7, 1990. Entered into force Dec. 7, 1990.

Mongolia
Agreement relating to scientific and technical cooperation, with annex. Signed at Washington January 23, 1991. Entered into force January 23, 1991.

Nepal
Agreement, with memorandum of understanding, amending the agreement of May 30 and June 1, 1986, relating to trade in cotton textiles and the administrative arrangement of July 28 and Aug. 18, 1986, relating to a visa system for exports of Nepalese textile products. Effected by exchange of notes at Kathmandu Nov. 19 and 28, 1990. Entered into force Nov. 28, 1990; effective Jan. 1, 1991.

Pakistan
Agreement amending the agreement of May 20 and June 11, 1987, as amended, concerning trade in textiles and textile products. Effected by exchange of notes at Washington Nov. 30 and Dec. 20, 1990. Entered into force Dec. 20, 1990.

Peru
Agreement amending the agreement of Jan. 3, 1985, relating to trade in cotton, wool, and man-made fiber textiles and textile products. Effected by exchange of notes at Washington July 11 and Oct. 4, 1990. Entered into force Oct. 4, 1990.

International express mail agreement, with detailed regulations. Signed at Lima and Washington Oct. 29 and Nov. 30, 1990. Entered into force Jan. 14, 1991.

Thailand
Agreement extending the memorandum of understanding of Oct. 3, 1985, on logistic support. Effected by exchange of notes at Bangkok Sept. 26 and Oct. 3, 1990. Entered into force Oct. 3, 1990.

Agreement relating to the reciprocal granting of authorizations to permit licensed amateur radio operators of either country to operate their station in the other country. Effected by exchange of notes at Bangkok Oct. 11 and 30, 1990. Entered into force Dec. 14, 1990.

Memorandum of understanding concerning interoperability management of tactical command and control procedural standards, with annex. Signed at Bangkok Dec. 3, 1990. Entered into force Dec. 3, 1990.

Trinidad & Tobago
Agreement amending and extending the agreement of Oct. 15 and 23, 1986, relating to trade in cotton, wool, and man-made fiber textiles and textile products. Effected by exchange of notes at Port-au-Spain Dec. 5, 1989 and Nov. 8 and Dec. 14, 1990. Entered into force Dec. 14, 1990.

Venezuela
Agreement for scientific and technological cooperation, with annex. Signed at Caracas Dec. 8, 1990. Enters into force on the date on which the parties notify each other that they have complied with the necessary constitutional and statutory requirements.

---

1 Not in force for the US.

Department of State

PLEASE NOTE: Beginning January 1991 the State Department's Office of Press Relations started a new category of releases, "Documents," which will in most instances be used instead of Press Releases for significant texts. Therefore, starting January 1991 we are listing what we will call Press Documents under this heading.

Press Releases

No.	Date	Subject
*174	11/4	Baker: remarks to U.S. troops, Saudi Arabia, November 4.
175	11/6	Release of *Foreign Relations of the United States,* 1955-57, volume XXI, East Asian Security; Cambodia, Laos.
*176	11/6	Leonard H. Robinson, Jr., Deputy Assistant Secretary for African Affairs (biographic data).
177	11/8	Release of *Foreign Relations of the United States,* 1961-63, volume II, Vietnam, 1962.
*178	11/9	Program for the official working visit of Giulio Andreotti, President of the Council of Ministers of the Italian Republic and President of the Council of the European Community, November 13.
*179	11/4	Baker: remarks with Foreign Minister Bin Mubarak Al Khalifa of Bahrain, Manama, November 4.
*180	11/7	Baker: departure remarks after meetings in Turkey, Ankarra, November 7.
*181	11/8	Baker: remarks with Soviet Foreign Minister Eduard Shevardnadze, Moscow, November 8.
*182	11/9	Baker: interview on "Good Morning America," ABC-TV, Moscow, November 9.
*183	11/9	Baker: interview on "Today," NBC-TV, Moscow, November 9.
*184	11/9	Baker: interview by Ralph Begleiter, CNN, Moscow, November 9.
*185	11/9	Baker: remarks with British Prime Minister Margaret Thatcher, London, November 9.
*186	11/10	Baker: remarks with French Foreign Minister Roland Dumas, Paris, November 10.
*187	11/10	Baker: press briefing, Paris, November 10.
*188	11/13	Baker: remarks with Canadian Foreign Minister Joe Clark, November 13.
*189	11/14	Baker: press briefing prior to Paris Summit, November 14.
190	11/16	Baker: press conference with Secretary of Agriculture Clayton Yeutter, Secretary of Commerce Robert Mosbacher, U.S. Trade Representative Carla Hills, President of the European Community Jacques Delors, Vice-President of the European Community Andriessen, and European Community Commissioners Pandolfi and MacSharry, November 16.
*191	11/18	Baker: interview on "This Week with David Brinkley," ABC-TV, Paris, November 18.
*192	11/18	Baker: remarks with French Foreign Minister Roland Dumas, Paris, November 18.
*193	11/18	Baker: remarks with Soviet Foreign Minister Eduard Shevardnadze, Paris, November 18.
*194	11/20	Baker: remarks with Soviet Foreign Minister Eduard Shevardnadze, U.S.S.R., Paris, November 20.
*195	11/22	Baker: remarks following meetings in Saudi Arabia, Jeddah, November 22.
*196	11/22	Baker: press conference with President of Yemen Ali Abdallah Saleh, Sanaa, November 22.
*197	11/24	Baker: remarks with Foreign Minister Jaramillo of Colombia following meeting with President Gaviria, Bogota, November 24.
198	11/24	Baker: statement calling for meeting of U.N. Security Council, Houston, November 24.
*199	11/28	Baker: remarks with Soviet Foreign Minister Eduard Shevardnadze, U.S.S.R., New York, November 28.
*200	11/29	Baker: remarks with Foreign Minister Joe Clark of Canada, New York, November 29.
*201	11/29	Baker: remarks with Foreign Minister Dinka Tesfaye of Ethiopia, New York, November 29.
*202	11/29	Baker: remarks with British Foreign Minister Douglas Hurd, New York, November 29.
*203	11/29	Baker: remarks with French Foreign Minister Roland Dumas, New York, November 29.
204	11/29	Baker: statement opening U.N. Security Council debate, New York, November 29.
205	11/29	Baker: statement following U.N. Security Council vote, New York, November 29.
*206	11/29	Baker: press conference following U.N. Security Council meeting, November 29.
*207	11/30	Baker: interview on "Good Morning America," ABC-TV, November 30.
*208	12/2	Baker: interview on "Meet the Press," NBC-TV, December 2.
209	12/5	Baker: statement before Senate Foreign Relations Committee, December 5.
210	12/6	Baker: statement before House Foreign Affairs Committee, December 6 (same text as P.R. 209).

No.	Date	Subject
*211	12/7	Release of *American Foreign Policy: Current Documents*, 1989.
*212	12/9	Baker: interview on "This Week with David Brinkley," ABC-TV, December 9.
*213	12/9	Baker: remarks to press at Ellington Air National Guard Base, Houston, December 9.
*214	12/9	Baker: remarks upon arrival of Soviet Foreign Minister Eduard Shevardnadze, Houston, December 9.
*215	12/10	Baker: remarks with Foreign Minister Shevardnadze before meeting, Houston, December 10.
*216	12/10	Baker: remarks with Foreign Minister Shevardnadze at Space Station Mock-up, Johnson Space Center, Houston, December 10.
*217	12/10	Baker: remarks with Foreign Minister Shevardnadze at Mission Control, Johnson Space Center, Houston, December 10.
*218	12/11	Baker: press briefing with Foreign Minister Shevardnadze, Houston, December 11.
*219	12/14	Baker: remarks with Ambassador Nathaniel Howell upon greeting the Ambassador and the U.S. Embassy Kuwait staff, December 14.
*220	12/17	Remarks by Acting Secretary of State Larry S. Eagleburger, Ambassador Edward J. Perkins, and Ambassador Nathaniel Howell upon return of U.S. Embassy Kuwait staff, December 17.
221	12/17	Baker: excerpts from intervention at North Atlantic Council ministerial, December 17.
*222	12/18	Baker: press conference following North Atlantic Council ministerial, December 18.
223	12/20	Baker: press briefing following resignation of Soviet Foreign Minister Shevardnadze, December 20.

Press Documents

No.	Date	Subject
*1	1/3	Baker: remarks at swearing-in of U.S. Ambassador to Kuwait Edward W. Gnehm, Jr.
*2	1/3	Baker: interview on "Prime Time Live," ABC-TV.
*3	1/6	Baker: interview on "This Week with David Brinkley," ABC-TV.
4	1/9	Baker: press conference following meeting with Iraqi Foreign Minister Tariq Aziz.
*5	1/7	Baker: remarks with U.K. Foreign Secretary Douglas Hurd, London.
*6	1/7	Baker: remarks with Luxembourg Foreign Minister Jacques Poos, London.
*7	1/8	Baker: remarks with German Foreign Minister Hans-Dietrich Genscher, Bonn.
*8	1/8	Baker: remarks with French Foreign Minister Roland Dumas, Paris.
*9	1/8	Baker: remarks with Italian Foreign Minister Gianni de Michelis, Milan.
*10	1/10	Baker: departure remarks, Geneva.
*11	1/11	Baker: remarks with Amir Sheikh Jabir of Kuwait, Saudi Arabia.
*12	1/11	Baker: remarks to U.S. troops, Saudi Arabia.
*13	1/11	Baker: departure remarks, Saudi Arabia.
14	1/12	Baker: remarks with Syrian Foreign Minister Farouk Al-Shara, Damascus.
*15	1/12	Baker: remarks with Egyptian Foreign Minister Abdel-Meguid, Cairo.
*16	1/13	Baker: remarks with Prime Minister John Major, Alconbury RAF, United Kingdom.
17	1/13	Baker: statement concerning events in the Baltic States.
*18	1/14	Baker: remarks with Canadian Prime Minister Brian Mulroney, Ottawa.
*19	1/26	Baker: announcement of pledge from Saudi Arabia to help defray Gulf operations.
20	1/28	Baker: statement announcing rescheduling of U.S.-Soviet summit.
21	1/29	Baker: Joint statement with Soviet Foreign Minister Bessmertnykh.
22	2/6 2/7	Baker: statement to House Foreign Affairs Committee February 6 and Senate Foreign Relations Committee February 7 (as prepared.)
*22A	2/6	Baker: statement to House Foreign Affairs Committee (as delivered.)
*23	2/10	Baker: interview on "Face the Nation," CBS-TV.
*24	2/11	Baker: interview by Connie Chung, CBS-TV.
*25	2/17	Baker: interview on "Newsmaker Sunday," CNN.
*26	2/20	Baker: toast remarks at luncheon in honor of Queen Margrethe II and Prince Henrik of Denmark.
*27	2/24	Baker: interview on "This Week with David Brinkley," ABC-TV.

Copies may be obtained from the Office of Press Relations, Department of State, Washington, D.C. 20520-6810.

*Not printed in the Bulletin. Researchers should be aware that many of the "remarks" are no more than one page and of limited research value.

New Publications from the Institute for the Study of Diplomacy

The Diplomatic Record 1989-1990

Edited by David D. Newsom

This is Volume I of an annual work of review and reference covering principal developments in the field of diplomacy. Regular features will include article-length case histories by scholars and practitioners on major international negotiations, summaries of negotiations in progress, information on changes in diplomatic practice, a chronology of important diplomatic events, and a bibliography of recent books and articles relating to diplomacy.

The contents of this volume consist of: ESSAYS. What Works in Diplomacy?—Allan E. Goodman and David D. Newsom. Peacemaking in Southern Africa: The Namibian-Angola Settlement of 1988—Chester A. Crocker. The Afghanistan Negotiations—Riaz Mohammad Khan. INF Treaty in Perspective—Leo Reddy. U.S.-Soviet Bilateral Relations Since Reykjavik—John M. Evans. Ending the Iran-Iraq War—Sohrab C. Sobhani. The Negotiations on a Chemical Weapons Ban in 1989—Barend ter Haar. International Negotiations on Environmental Issues: The Year Ahead—Andrew Sens. Ozone Diplomacy—Richard Elliot Benedick. Antartic Treaty Diplomacy: Problems, Prospects, and Policy Implications—Christopher C. Joyner. DEPARTMENTS. Looking Ahead: Diplomatic Challenges of 1991. Developments in Diplomatic Practice—Harold E. Horan. Diplomatic Chronology (arranged topically). Bibliography. Acronyms and Abbreviations. Index. The volume was released in December 1990.

The Institute for the Study of Diplomacy is affiliated with the Edmund A. Walsh School of Foreign Service at Georgetown University in Washington. The editor, David D. Newsom, is Director of the Institute and a former U.S. Ambassador to Libya, Indonesia, and the Philippines. He was Under Secretary of State for Political Affairs from 1978 to 1981 and is the author of numerous books and articles.

The Diplomatic Record was published in cooperation with Westview Press. The paperback edition may be purchased for $24.95 from the Institute for the Study of Diplomacy, Georgetown University School of Foreign Service, Washington, D.C. 20057. The hardcover edition may be purchased for $49.95 from Westview Press, 5500 Central Avenue, Boulder, Colorado 80301.

Ozone Diplomacy: New Directions in Safeguarding the Planet

by Richard Elliot Benedick

In September 1987, diplomats from over 60 countries completed negotiations on the landmark Montreal Protocol on Substances That Deplete the Ozone Layer, hailed as the most significant international environmental agreement in history. It sounded the death knell for an important part of the international chemical industry by mandating significant cutbacks—with billion dollar implications—in the use of fluorocarbons (CFCs) and halons, substances with wide applications in thousands of products synonomous with modern lifestyles.

The drive to protect the planet against the effects of ozone layer depletion began not long ago with the derided theories of a handful of iconoclastic scientists. Most observers believed that an international accord to limit the use of chemicals essential to modern life would be impossible in the face of scientific uncertainties and the opposition of powerful commercial interests. In Ozone Diplomacy, Ambassador Benedick, chief U.S. negotiator for the treaty, offers an insider's view of the politics, the economics, the science and the diplomacy surrounding the negotiations. He explores the elements that contributed to the treaty's success and offers glimpses behind the scenes before and during the negotiating conferences—including those in Vienna, Montreal, Helsinki, and the climactic June 1990 meeting in London. In this process he finds useful models for international approaches to other emerging scientific-technological-environmental issues, such as the threat of global warming, that call for action in advance of scientific certainty.

As Deputy Assistant Secretary of State for environment, health, and natural resource issues, Ambassador Benedick was assigned by Secretary of State George Shultz to coordinate U.S. preparations for the negotiations and to be chief U.S. negotiator. In 1988 he received the Presidential Distinguished Service Award for his innovative negotiating strategy.

Ozone Diplomacy was published by Harvard University Press in cooperation with the Institute for the Study of Diplomacy and the World Wildlife Fund & The Conservation Foundation. The paperback edition ($10.95) and the hardcover edition ($27.95) may be purchased from the Institute for the Study of Diplomacy, Georgetown University School of Foreign Service, Washington, D.C. 20057.

Department of State Releases Three Foreign Relations Volumes and Current Documents, 1989

The Department of State, on November 6, 1990, released Foreign Relations of the United States, 1955-1957, volume XXI, East Asian Security; Cambodia; Laos. [1]

The documents on East Asian security demonstrate U.S. efforts to solidify its extensive alliance relationships and bilateral arrangements in the area, while simultaneously seeking to reassure neutral nations such as India and Burma of its good will and willingness to supply some economic aid. Policy conflicts arose within the alliance systems as well as within the U.S. Government over such issues as security guarantees, joint military planning, and U.S. military assistance. Despite these tensions, throughout the period the United States held fast to its fundamental conviction that the independence of mainland Southeast Asia was essential to U.S. national security.

U.S. policy toward Cambodia revolved around King Norodom Sihanouk who abdicated his throne to concentrate on the political administration of his country. The principal U.S. concern during the period was Sihanouk's experimentation with neutralism. His visit to Peking in February 1956 and Cambodian recognition of the People's Republic of China and acceptance of Chinese aid prompted calls for an end to U.S. assistance to Cambodia. Ambassador to Cambodia Robert McClintock, however, convinced the Department of State that support of Sihanouk was the key to maintaining Cambodia's independence. During this three-year period, the tempestuous U.S. relationship with Sihanouk maintained a relative calm.

The overriding U.S. goal in Laos was to keep the Pathet Lao, the local Communists, out of the Lao Government and confined to two northern provinces where they had regrouped under the terms of the Geneva Agreement of 1954. Neutralist Prince Souvanna Phouma formed a government in March 1956 with the intention of inviting the Pathet Lao into a coalition. The United States reluctantly agreed to continue support of Souvanna's Government even after the Pathet Lao joined the cabinet. The United States also kept open its links with anticommunist Lao, and looked to the 1958 elections to limit neutralist and Pathet Lao strength.

Documentation in this 1,096-page volume was selected from previously classified records of the White House, Department of State, and other government agencies. In selecting documents, primary emphasis was placed on high level discussions within the U.S. Government, significant policy papers, consultations and meetings between the United States and other members of SEATO and ANZUS, and materials illustrating major developments in the relationship between the United States and the Governments of Cambodia and Laos.

An expanded preface to volume XXI provides information on the methodology followed in preparation of the volume and includes guides to the files and lists of materials consulted in its preparation. The preface also provides information on the method of indicating in the volume the absence of material withheld in the declassification review process and other editorial methodology. The preface also outlines particular problems encountered in the course of the compilation.

Copies of volume XXI (Department of State Publication No. 9760; GPO Stock No. 044-000-02289-3) may be purchased for $45.00 (domestic postpaid) or $56.25 (foreign postpaid) from the Superintendent of Documents, U.S. Government Printing Office, Washington, D.C. 20402. Checks or money orders should be made out to the Superintendent of Documents.

The Department of State, on November 8, 1990, released Foreign Relations of the United States, 1961-1963, volume II, Vietnam, 1962. [2]

This volume presents the official documentary record of U.S. policy toward Vietnam for the year 1962. In 1962, the U.S. commitment to Vietnam took on more of the form it was to have for the next 13 years. The programs initiated by the Kennedy administration in 1961 were beginning to have an effect on the conduct of the war. Disenchantment with the entrenched government of President Ngo Dinh Diem, which would lead to its overthrow in 1963, had yet to set in. The most important and lasting step was the establishment of the Military Assistance Command, Vietnam (MACV), through which hundreds of thousands of U.S. combat troops would eventually be funneled into Vietnam. Creation of MACV occasioned extensive and heated discussion within the U.S. Government, since its place in both the military and civilian chains of command was unclear. It was not until the end of February that the status of MACV was finally determined.

During the year, continuing evaluations by civilian, military, and intelligence officials reached contradictory conclusions on the ability of the Diem regime to defeat the Viet Cong. All the reports stressed, however, that the government was making some progress and none offered alternatives. Support for Diem was based on the belief that the strategic hamlet program and governmental reform which he had initiated would strengthen South Vietnam. But the attack on the Presidential Palace at the end of February cooled Diem's ardor for reform, and Viet Cong control of the countryside called into question the success of the strategic hamlet program. As the year passed, reports from Vietnam became more critical of Diem, and by the end of the year, U.S. policymakers were beginning to question U.S. support for him.

This is the second of four volumes covering U.S. relations with Vietnam during the 1960-1963 triennium. Documents included in this volume were selected from the Departments of State and Defense, the John F. Kennedy Library, and the National Defense University. Nearly all of the documents selected were declassified for this publication.

An expanded preface to Volume II provides information on the methodology followed in preparation of the volume and includes guides to the files and lists of materials consulted in its preparation, and outlines particular problems encountered in the course of compilation. The preface also provides information on the method of indicating in the volume the absence of material withheld in the declassification review process.

Copies of volume II (Department of State Publication No. 9790: GPO Stock No. 044-000-02264-8) may be purchased for $36.00 (domestic postpaid) or $45.00 (foreign postpaid) from the Superintendent of Documents, U.S. Government Printing Office, Washington, D.C. 20402. Checks or money orders should be made out to the Superintendent of Documents.

The Department of State, on February 15, 1991, released Foreign Relations of the United States, 1958-1960, volume II, United Nations and General International Matters. [3]

This volume presents 936 pages on U.S. participation in the United Nations, negotiations leading to a treaty on Antarctica, two conferences on the Law of the Sea, and exploration of outer space.

At the United Nations, the paramount issue for the U.S. at this time was to prevent the seating of the People's Republic of China at the expense of the Republic of China. The volume also documents the debate and subsquent major decision taken by the U.S. not to push for rejection of the credentials of the Hungarian Delegation, outlines the U.S. position favoring enlargement of the world body as former territories became independent, and details the stormy visit of Soviet Premier Nikita Khrushchev to the United Nations in October 1960.

Other topics are the successful efforts of the United States to obtain a treaty on Antarctica, in which the twelve signatories abandoned their territorial claims and agreed that the continent should be reserved for peaceful and scientific purposes alone; the 1958 and 1960 Law of the Sea Conferences, which ended without agreement on the breadth of the territorial sea and fishery rights in a continguous zone; and the intense debate in the U.S. Government and at the United Nations about policy on outer space.

The volume also contains an expanded preface that provides information on the methodoloy followed in preparing it as well as guides to the

files and other materials consulted in its preparation. The preface explains the method of indicating material withheld in the declassification review process and other editorial methodology. Documents for the volume were gathered from the Department of State, the Dwight D. Eisenhower Library, and the U.S. Mission to the United Nations.

Copies of Volume II (Department of State Publication No. 9833; GPO Stock No. 044-000-02280-0) may be purchased for $35.00 (domestic postpaid) or $43.75 (foreign postpaid) from the Superintendent of Documents, U.S. Government Printing Office, Washington, D.C. 20420.

Checks or money orders should be made out to the Superintendent of Documents.

The Department of State, on December 7, 1990, released American Foreign Policy: Current Documents, 1989. [4]

Major themes covered in the volume are U.S. support for democratic revolution and self-determination, peaceful changes in the communist world, the spread of free enterprise, economic assistance to Poland and Hungary, and the unification of Europe and of Germany. It documents the Baker-Shevardnadze meetings in Moscow and Jackson Hole, and the Bush-Gorbachev summit in Malta. Other topics covered in the volume include multilateral discussions on arms control, regional security, and economic and trade policy: the unfolding crisis in Panama; human rights and refugees issues; and efforts to combat terrorism and atmospheric pollution.

Significant diplomatic initiatives highlighted in the volume include the Bipartisan Accord on Central America and the Brady plan on Third World Debt. Also printed are documents detailing the Paris International Conference on Cambodia, the calls for restraint and nonviolence during the student demonstrations in China, NATO's efforts to develop a new security structure, and the reaffirmation of the U.S. commitment to the Conference on Security and Cooperation in Europe process as a forum for East-West cooperation.

Nearly all of the documents included here were previously published or released. The texts of foreign affairs "background" briefings have been

released for publication in the volume. This 800-page volume, arranged chronologically within 15 geographic and topical chapters, includes a list of documents, editorial annotations, lists of names and abbreviations, and an index.

A microfiche supplement to this volume, consisting of the complete series of Department of State Daily Press Briefings held in 1989, posted statements, special "on-the-record" and "background" press briefings held by senior Department or White House officials, and bilateral and multilateral treaties to which the United States was a signatory in 1989, will be released in early 1991. The editors have included the most important of these briefings and statements in this volume.

Copies of this volume (Department of State Publication No. 9815; GPO Stock No. 044-000-02290-7) may be purchased for $35.00 (domestic postpaid) from the Superintendent of Documents, U.S. Government Printing Office, Washington, DC 20402. Checks or money orders should be made out to the Superintendent of Documents.

---

1 Department of State Press Release 175, November 6, 1990.

2 Department of State Press Release 177, November 8, 1990.

3 Edited version of Office of the Historian announcement, February 15, 1991.

4 Department of State Press Release 211, December 7, 1990, with minor deletions.

INDEX

INDEX

Name Index

Subscribe to
THE FOREIGN POLICY BULLETIN

for only $35 a year

Use the order form below
and/or submit your own purchase order
— or you may enter your subscription
through a subscription agency

For further information, call: (202) 686-5230

FOREIGN POLICY BULLETIN ORDER FORM
(Photocopy to send)

TO: **FOREIGN POLICY BULLETIN**
4812 Butterworth Place, N.W.
Washington, D.C. 20016

Please enter _____ subscription(s) for _____ year(s) to the FOREIGN POLICY BULLETIN at $35.00 per year or $53.00 outside the U.S. and Canada.

_____ Payment is enclosed.

_____ Please send an invoice.

Please Type or Print
Organization or Personal Name _____

Additional Address/Attention Line _____

Street Address _____

City, State, Zip Code _____

Daytime Phone, Including Area Code _____

FOREIGN POLICY BULLETIN
4812 Butterworth Place, N.W.
Washington, D.C. 20016

Foreign Policy

bulletin

The Documentary Record of United States Foreign Policy / Volume 1 / Number 6

With this issue:
ANNUAL INDEX

May/June 1991
Volume 1 Index

MIDDLE EAST POLICY AFTER THE GULF WAR

Also in this issue:

U.S.-Soviet Relations: Three Perspectives

Lech Walesa's Washington Visit

"Fast Track" Trade Legislation

BULLETIN SPECIALS: Congressman Gray at African/African-American Summit, Violeta Chamorro at Joint Session of Congress, Gorbachev Addresses Japanese Parliament, President Bush on New World Order

A Mediacom, Inc. publication with editorial autonomy • No government affiliation

Foreign Policy
bulletin

Volume 1/Number 6
May/June 1991
Annual Index

PHOTO AND
GRAPHIC CREDITS:

1) Cover photo of Marine Expedition-ary Unit Service Support Group 24 providing medical services to Kurdish refugees at clinic set up in Zakhu, Iraq, Department of Defense.

2) Page 3 photo of General Norman Schwartzkopf and General Khalid of Saudi Arabia at cease-fire meeting with Iraqi officers, March 3, 1991, Depart-ment of Defense.

The **FOREIGN POLICY BULLETIN** is published bimonthly (plus annual index) as a private publication of Mediacom, Inc. It uses the same for-mat as the discontinued "Department of State Bulletin" and maintains con-tinuity with that publication while of-fering additional materials as well. Its purpose is to provide a timely and sys-tematic record of United States foreign policy and of complementary docu-ments from international sources. The **BULLETIN's** coverage of official U.S. documents includes major addresses, diplomatic statements, and press con-ferences of the President and the Secretary of State; statements and con-gressional testimony by the Secretary and other administration officials; treaties and other agreements to which the United States is or may become a party; special reports; and selected press releases issued by the White House, the Department of State, and other agencies. Special features in-clude speeches and other statements by foreign officials concerning U.S. policy; reports and other materials from inter-national organizations relating to major issues confronting U.S. policy-makers; and background information about countries of particular interest to U.S. foreign relations.

PAUL E. AUERSWALD
Editor and Publisher

PHILIP AUERSWALD
Assistant Editor/Business
Manager

HUGUETTE NIZARD
Subscriptions Manager

HOPE FUNG
Layout and Typesetting

J. LEONARD MAZUR
Research and Marketing
Consultant

Printed by
PRINTING SERVICE INTERNA-TIONAL

ISSN 1052-7036

SUBSCRIPTIONS: Annual subscrip-tions to the **BULLETIN** are $39.00; outside the U.S. and Canada $53.00. Subscription orders should be sent to: Subscriptions, Foreign Policy Bulletin, 4812 Butterworth Place N.W., Washington, D.C. 20016.
To subscribe by phone, call (202) 686-5230.

SINGLE COPIES: Single copies, if still in print, can be obtained for $10.00 a copy plus postage by writing to the ad-dress below.

CORRESPONDENCE should be ad-dressed to: Foreign Policy Bulletin, 4812 Butterworth Place N.W., Washington, D.C. 20016.
Telephone: (202) 686-5230

INDEXING: Included in the PAIS (Public Affairs Information Service) in-dexes: the PAIS Bulletin, PAIS on CD-ROM, and online through Dialog, BRS, and Data-Star. Information about other indexing services will be provided in subsequent issues.

CONTENTS

FEATURE: MIDDLE EAST POLICY AFTER THE GULF WAR

Middle East Policy After The Gulf War

"...(W)e've kicked the Vietnam syndrome once and for all."

Conclusion of President's Remarks to American Legislative Exchange Council, March 1, 1991. [1]

I know you share this wonderful feeling of joy in my heart. But it is over-welmed by the gratitude I feel—not just the troops overseas but to those who have assisted the United States of America, like our Secretary of Defense, like our Chairman of Joint Chiefs, and so many other unsung heroes who've made all this possible. It's a proud day for America. And, by God, we've kicked the Vietnam syndrome once and for all.

President's Press Conference, March 1, 1991 [1]

Good afternoon. In the hours since we suspended military operations in the Kuwaiti theater of war, considerable progress has been made in moving towards a cease-fire and postwar planning. As our forces moved into Kuwait City, and as the faces of these jubilant Kuwaiti citizens have warmed our hearts, the coalition leaders started the arduous task of addressing the next stages of the Persian Gulf situation.

As a first order of business this afternoon, I want to thank the American people for the affection and support that they have shown for our troops in the Middle East. In towns and cities across this nation, our citizens have felt a sense of purpose and unity in the accomplishment of our military that is a welcome addition to the American spirit. And as our service men and women begin coming home, as they will soon, I look forward to the many celebrations of their achievement.

In the meantime, we are focused on the many diplomatic tasks associated with ending this conflict. General Khalid, General Schwarzkopf and other coalition military leaders of our forces in the Gulf will meet with

representatives of Iraq tomorrow afternoon, March 2nd, in the theater of operations to discuss the return of POWs and other military matters related to the cease-fire. We will not discuss the location of the meeting for obvious security reasons. But this is an important step in securing the victory that our forces have achieved.

Work is proceeding in New York at the United Nations on the political aspects of ending the war. We've welcomed here in Washington this week the envoys of several of our close friends and allies. And shortly, Secretary Baker will be leaving for a new round of consultations that I am confident will advance planning for the war's aftermath. Again, and as I said Wednesday evening, the true challenge before us will be securing the peace.

So, thank you very much. And now who has the first question? Helen [Helen Thomas, United Press International]?

Q. Mr. President, you've always said that you were not targeting Saddam [Hussein] under the U.N. mandate and that the coalition has no claim on Iraqi territory. Is that still the case?

A. We are not targeting Saddam, and we have no claim on Iraqi territory.

Q. Well, will you try to hunt him down for any kind of war crimes trial?

A. No, I'm not going to say that. Not hunt him down, but nobody can be absolved from the responsibilities under international law on the war crimes aspect of that.

Q. Mr. President, along that line, the reports of atrocities in Kuwait apparently go far beyond the horror stories that you've already described in recent weeks. Who will be held accountable for those, perhaps, other than Saddam? And do you think that the allied forces will hold any part of southern Iraq as a security zone for any time?

A. I think on the first question, the first part, I agree that the reports are just sickening that are coming out of Kuwait. We have been concerned about it. Early on in all of this I expressed the concerns that I felt. But I think we'll just have to wait and see because I think the persons that actually

perpetrated the tortures and the insidious crimes will be the ones that are held responsible. Now, how you go about finding them—but I think back to the end of World War II; that process took a long time to evolve, but justice was done...

And what was the second part, Terry [Terence Hunt, Associated Press]?

Q. The second part was about a security zone. You've had all this destruction. Is there any thought of establishing a security zone to protect—

A. On the question of security zone and arrangements out there, these matters will be discussed when Jim Baker is out there with the coalition partners. I don't believe they will be discussed at the military meeting tomorrow.

*   *   *

Q. Mr. President, today you declared an end to the Vietnam syndrome and, of course, we've heard you talk a lot about the new world order. Can you tell us, do you envision a new era now of using U.S. military forces around the world for different conflicts that arise?

A. No, I think because of what has happened, we won't have to use U.S. forces around the world. I think when we say something that is objectively correct, like don't take over a neighbor or you're going to bear some responsibility, people are going to listen because I think out of all this will be a newfound—put it this way, a reestablished credibility for the United States of America.

So, I look at the opposite. I say that what our troops have done over there will not only enhance the peace but reduce the risk that their successors have to go into battle someplace.

Q. But surely, you don't mean that you would be reluctant to do this again.

A. Do what again?

Q. Send troops if you thought you needed to.

A. I think the United States is always going to live up to its security requirements.

*   *   *

"General Schwartzkopf and other coalition military leaders of our forces in the Gulf will meet with representatives of Iraq tomorrow afternoon, March 2nd ..."

President Bush
March 1, 1991

Q. Going into the security talks with the countries of the Middle East, are you willing to consider a long term presence of American troops as a peacekeeping force, or do you think that would be better handled by Arab nations?

A. I think it would be better handled by Arab nations. There will be a United States presence. There was before this. But there will be—one of the things that Secretary Baker is talking about is all these different security arrangements. Perhaps there will be a role for a U.N. force; perhaps there will be a role for an all-Arab force. Certainly there will be some security role for the United States. But I would repeat here I do not want to send out the impression that U.S. troops will be permanently stationed in the Gulf. I want them back.

So, we're still working—we're just beginning to work out these security arrangements, but a part of it will not be a continued presence of substantial quantities of U.S. troops. I'd like to see them all out of there as soon as possible. But there's some shorter-run security problems that I don't want to underestimate.

*   *   *

Q. Mr. President, you've said that the true challenge now is securing the peace. Do you detect any chinks of light either on the Arab side or on the Israeli side which really would lead to a lasting settlement in the Middle East?

A. It's a little early because these consultations are just beginning. But what I really believe is that the conditions are now better than ever. And it's

not simply the restored credibility of the United States, for example. There are a lot of players out there. There's a lot of people that know a lot about the Middle East. And the British and the French and other coalition partners are very interested in moving forward. So I can't tell you that anything specific in what went on in the last 100 days will contribute to this. But I can tell you that each of the people I have talked to have said, now let's get on with this. And so we want to do it. It is in the interest of every country. It's in the interest of the Arab countries. It's in the interest of Israel. It's in the interest of the Palestinian people. So I sense a feeling—look, the time is right; let's get something done. But I can't tie it to— maybe I missed the thrust of your question—I can't tie it to any specific happening.

Q. Do you feel it's a more workable scenario now than it has been for some years?

A. I think so. And I've been wrestling with this—some role or another since U.N. days back in '71 and '72. And part of this is the newfound viability of the United Nations. Part of it is that even though we had some nuances of difference here with the Soviets, that that veto-holding power is together with us in feeling that there must be an answer. China is different than it was in those early days when it first came to the U.N., and they've been supportive of the resolutions against Iraq. And so you've got a whole different perspective in the United Nations and, I'd say, in countries out there. There's still some historic prejudices; historic differences exist. But I think your question is on to something. I think there is a better climate now. And we're going to test it. We're going to probe. We're going to try to lead to see whether we can do something.

*   *   *

Q. What do you see is the role of the Soviet Union in this, postwar?

A. Well, the Soviet Union is a major, significant country that should be treated, as we would other countries, with the proper respect. They have a longstanding knowledge of and interest in the Middle East. And so we will deal with the Soviets with mutual respect—for that reason as well as for the fact that to have the new United Nations be viable and meaningful in its so-called peacekeeping function, the Soviet Union is necessary to be working with them.

I don't want to see the U.N. in 1991 go back to the way it was in 1971, where every vote we found ourselves—put it this way— the U.N. found itself hamstrung because of the veto from the Soviet Union or sometimes from the United States. So as we work with them on common goals in foreign policy, although we have great differences with them on some things—we've spelled it out here on the Baltics and use of force in the Baltics and all of that—I want to continue to work with them, and we'll try very hard to work with them. Because, one, they have some good ideas.

I never resented the idea that Mr. Gorbachev was trying to bring a peaceful resolution to this question. I told him that. I've seen some cartoons that suggested I was being something less than straightforward, but I really didn't. The trouble was it stopped way short of what we and the rest of the coalition could accept. So they will be important players. And I'm very glad— I'll say this—that we wrestle with this whole problem of the Gulf today—yesterday—with Soviet cooperation, as opposed to what it would have been like a few years ago in the Cold War days when every American was absolutely convinced that the only thing the Soviets wanted was access to the warm water ports of the Gulf.

And so the problem, which is highly complex in diplomacy, has been much easier to work because of the cooperation between the five veto-holding powers of the United Nations. And I want to continue that because the U.N. will have a role. It's not going to have the only role. We've got a coalition role; we've got a bilateral diplomacy role; we've got a certain military role in encouraging the stability of the Gulf. But the United Nations can be very helpful.

And the Soviet Union is important. And when I have differences with Mr. Gorbachev, or when we have differences with the Soviets, we'll state them. We'll state them openly. But we will treat them—we will deal with them with respect. And we will iron out our bilateral differences, and then I will reassure them that they are necessary to continue this multilateral diplomacy that has made a significant contribution to the solution to the Middle East problem.

U.N. Security Council Resolution 686, March 2, 1991 [2]

<u>The Security Council,</u>

<u>Recalling</u> and <u>reaffirming</u> its resolutions 660 (1990), 661(1990), 662 (1990), 664 (1990), 665 (1990), 666 (1990), 667 (1990), 669 (1990), 670 (1990), 674 (1990), 677 (1990), and 678 (1990),

<u>Recalling</u> the obligations of Member States under Article 25 of the Charter,

<u>Recalling</u> paragraph 9 of Resolution 661(1990) regarding assistance to the Government of Kuwait and paragraph 3(c) of that resolution regarding supplies strictly for medical purposes and, in humanitarian circumstances, foodstuffs,

<u>Taking</u> note of the letters of the Foreign Minister of Iraq confirming Iraq's agreement to comply fully with all of the resolutions noted above (S/22275), and stating its intention to release prisoners of war immediately (S/22273),

<u>Taking</u> note of the suspension of offensive combat operations by the forces of Kuwait and the Member States cooperating with Kuwait pursuant to resolution 678 (1990),

<u>Bearing</u> in mind the need to be assured of Iraq's peaceful intentions, and the objective in Resolution 678 (1990) of restoring international peace and security in the region,

<u>Underlining</u> the importance of Iraq taking the necessary measures which would permit a definitive end to the hostilities,

<u>Affirming</u> the commitment of all Member States to the independence, sovereignty and territorial integrity of Iraq and Kuwait, and noting the intention expressed by the Member States cooperating under paragraph 2 of Security Council Resolution 678 (1990) to bring their military presence in Iraq to an end as soon as possible consistent with achieving the objectives of the resolution,

<u>Acting</u> under Chapter VII of the Charter,

1. <u>Affirms</u> that all twelve resolutions noted above continue to have full force and effect;

2. <u>Demands</u> that Iraq implement its acceptance of all twelve resolutions noted above and in particular that Iraq:

(a) Rescind immediately its actions purporting to annex Kuwait;

(b) Accept in principle its liability under international law for any loss, damage, or injury arising in regard to Kuwait and third States, and their nationals and corporations, as a result of the invasion and illegal occupation of Kuwait by Iraq;

(c) Immediately release under the auspices of the International Committee of the Red Cross, Red Cross Societies, or Red Crescent Societies, all Kuwaiti and third country nationals detained by Iraq and return the remains of any deceased Kuwaiti and third country nationals so detained; and

(d) Immediately begin to return all Kuwaiti property seized by Iraq, to be completed in the shortest possible period;

3. <u>Further demands</u> that Iraq:

(a) Cease hostile or provocative actions by its forces against all Member States, including missile attacks and flights of combat aircraft;

(b) Designate military commanders to meet with counterparts from the forces of Kuwait and the Member States cooperating with Kuwait pursuant to Resolution 678 (1990) to arrange for the military aspects of a cessation of hostilities at the earliest possible time;

(c) Arrange for immediate access to and release of all prisoners of war under the auspices of the International Committee of the Red Cross, Red Cross Societies, or Red Crescent Societies, and return the remains of any deceased personnel of the forces of Kuwait and the Member States cooperating with Kuwait pursuant to Resolution 678 (1990); and

(d) Provide all information and assistance in identifying Iraqi mines, booby traps and other explosives as well as any chemical and biological weapons and material in Kuwait, in areas of Iraq where forces of Member States cooperating with Kuwait pursuant to Resolution 678 (1990) are present temporarily, and in the adjacent waters;

4. <u>Recognizes</u> that during the period required for Iraq to comply with paragraphs 2 and 3 above, the provisions of paragraph 2 of Resolution 678 (1990) remain valid.

5. <u>Welcomes</u> the decision of Kuwait and the Member States cooperating with Kuwait pursuant to resolution 678 (1990) to provide access and to commence immediately the release of Iraqi prisoners of war as required by the terms of the Third Geneva Convention of 1949, under the auspices of the International Committee of the Red Cross;

6. <u>Requests</u> all Member States, as well as the United Nations, the specialized agencies and other international organizations in the United Nations system, to take all appropriate action to cooperate with the Government and people of Kuwait in the reconstruction of their country;

7. <u>Decides</u> that Iraq shall notify the Secretary-General and the Security Council when it has taken the actions set out above;

8. <u>Decides</u> that in order to secure the rapid establishment of a definitive

end to the hostilities, the Security Council remains actively seized of the matter.

Statement by U.N. Security Council President, March 3, 1991 [2]

The Council welcomes the decisions taken to date relating to food and medical needs by the committee established under Resolution 661 including those just taken to facilitate the provision of humanitarian assistance including infant formula and water purification material.

It urges the committee to pay particular attention to the findings and recommendations on critical medical/public health and nutritional conditions in Iraq which have been and will continue to be submitted to it by the World Health Organization, UNICEF, the International Committee of the Red Cross, and other relevant organizations consistent with the relevant resolutions, and urges these humanitarian agencies to play an active role in this process and cooperate closely with the committee in its work.

It calls upon the committee to continue to act promptly on requests submitted to it for humanitarian assistance.

The Council welcomes the Secretary-General's announcement that he plans to send urgently a mission led by Under Secretary-General Martti Ahtisaari, comprising representatives of the appropriate U.N. agencies, to Iraq and Kuwait to assess the humanitarian needs arising in the immediate post crisis environment. The Council invites the Secretary-General to keep it informed in the shortest possible time on the progress of his mission on which it pledges to take immediate action.

General H. Norman Schwartzkopf's Press Briefing Following Meeting with Iraqi Military, March 3, 1991 (Opening Statement) [3]

Let me just say that we have just completed what I think were very frank, very candid, and very constructive discussions with the Iraqi military. The

purpose of this meeting, as stated previously by the President of the United States, was so that we could agree on certain conditions that were necessary to continue with the cessation of hostilities and the cessation of coalition offensive operations. I am very happy to tell you that we agreed on all matters.

Some of the subjects that were discussed were control measures to ensure that units, armed units of the coalition do not come in contact with armed units of the Iraqi military that result in any more deaths. We received information on the location of minefields in Kuwait and minefields in international waters so that we can begin operations immediately to make those areas safe. We have also made it very clear that upon the signing of a ceasefire, but not before, all coalition forces will be drawn back from Iraqi territory that we currently occupy.

The most important point that we discussed was the immediate release of all prisoners of war. We have agreed that this release should be immediate. We have agreed that the details of this release must be worked out by the International Red Cross. But both sides have agreed that we'll do everything we can to work with the Red Cross to as rapidly as possible determine locations and times. We have also asked that as a token of good faith on both sides that we have a symbolic release immediately, and I feel sure, based upon our discussions, that such a symbolic release should take place.

We have provided the Iraqis with the names of all of the missing in action, and we have asked for as much information as we can get concerning those missing in action. We've also asked them to provide us with the names of anyone who may have died while in their custody, and we have also asked for the return of the remains.

I would just say that I think we have made a major step forward in the cause of peace, and I have every expectation that if we continue the open and frank and cooperative dialogue that we had today—and I would say very candidly that the Iraqis came to discuss and to cooperate, with a positive attitude—that we are well on our way to a lasting peace.

President's Address to a Joint Session of Congress, March 6, 1991 [4]

Speaker of the House Thomas S. Foley. Mr. President, it is customary at joint sessions for the Chair to present the President to the Members of Congress directly and without further comment. But I wish to depart from tradition tonight and express to you on behalf of the Congress and the country, and through you to the members of our Armed Forces, our warmest congratulations on the brilliant victory of the Desert Storm operation.

Members of the Congress, I now have the high privilege and distinct honor of presenting to you the President of the United States.

President Bush. Mr. President. And Mr. Speaker, thank you, sir, for those very generous words spoken from the heart about the wonderful performance of our military.

Members of Congress, five short weeks ago I came to this House to speak to you about the state of the Union. We met then in time of war. Tonight, we meet in a world blessed by the promise of peace.

From the moment Operation Desert Storm commenced on January 16th until the time the guns fell silent at midnight one week ago, this nation has watched its sons and daughters with pride—watched over them with prayer. As Commander in Chief, I can report to you our armed forces fought with honor and valor. And as President, I can report to the nation aggression is defeated. The war is over.

This is a victory for every country in the coalition, for the United Nations. A victory for unprecedented international cooperation and diplomacy, so well led by our Secretary of State, James Baker. It is a victory for the rule of law and for what is right.

Desert Storm's success belongs to the team that so ably leads our Armed Forces: our Secretary of Defense and our Chairman of the Joint Chiefs, Dick Cheney and Colin Powell. And while you're standing, this military victory also belongs to the one the British call the "Man of the Match"—the tower of calm at the eye of Desert Storm— General Norman Schwarzkopf.

And recognizing this was a coalition effort, let us not forget Saudi General Khalid, Britain's General de la Billiere, or General Roquejoffre of France—and all the others whose leadership played such a vital role. And most importantly, most importantly of all, all those who served in the field.

I thank the Members of this Congress— support here for our troops in battle was overwhelming. And above all, I thank those whose unfailing love and support sustained our courageous men and women—I thank the American people.

Our commitment to peace in the Middle East does not end with the liberation of Kuwait.

Tonight, I come to this House to speak about the world—the world after war. The recent challenge could not have been clearer. Saddam Hussein was the villain; Kuwait, the victim. To the aid of this small country came nations from North America and Europe, from Asia and South America, from Africa and the Arab world—all united against aggression. Our uncommon coalition must now work in common purpose: to forge a future that should never again be held hostage to the darker side of human nature.

Tonight in Iraq, Saddam walks amidst ruin. His war machine is crushed. His ability to threaten mass destruction is itself destroyed. His people have been lied to— denied the truth. And when his defeated legions come home, all Iraqis will see and feel the havoc he has wrought. And this I promise you: For all that Saddam has done to his own people, to the Kuwaitis, and to the entire world, Saddam and those around him are accountable.

All of us grieve for the victims of war, for the people of Kuwait and the suffering that scars the soul of that proud nation. We grieve for all our fallen soldiers and their families, for all the innocents caught up in this conflict. And, yes, we grieve for the people of Iraq—a people who have never been our enemy. My hope is that one day we will once again welcome them as friends into the community of nations. Our commitment to peace in the Middle East does not end with the liberation of Kuwait. So tonight, let me outline four key challenges to be met.

Postwar Challenges

First, we must work together to create shared security arrangements in the region. Our friends and allies in the Middle East recognize that they will bear the bulk of the responsibility for regional security. But we want them to know that just as we stood with them to repel aggression, so now America stands ready to work with them to secure the peace. This does not mean stationing U.S. ground forces in the Arabian Peninsula, but it does mean American participation in joint exercises involving both air and ground forces. It means maintaining a capable U.S. naval presence in the region—just as we have for over 40 years. Let it be clear: Our vital national interests depend on a stable and secure Gulf.

Second, we must act to control the proliferation of weapons of mass destruction and the missiles used to deliver them. It would be tragic if the nations of the Middle East and Persian Gulf were now, in the wake of war, to embark on a new arms race. Iraq requires special vigilance. Until Iraq convinces the world of its peaceful intentions— that its leaders will not use new revenues to rearm and rebuild its menacing war machine—Iraq must not have access to the instruments of war.

And **third,** we must work to create new opportunities for peace and stability in the Middle East. On the night I announced Operation Desert Storm, I expressed my hope that out of the horrors of war might come new momentum for peace. We've learned in the modern age geography cannot guarantee security and security does not come from military power alone.

All of us know the depth of bitterness that has made the dispute between Israel and its neighbors so painful and intractable. Yet, in the conflict just concluded, Israel and many of the Arab States have for the first time found themselves confronting the same aggressor. By now, it should be plain to all parties that peacemaking in the Middle East requires compromise. At the same time, peace brings real benefits to everyone. We must do all that we can to close the gap between Israel and the Arab states—and between Israelis and Palestinians. The tactics of terror lead absolutely nowhere. There can be no substitute for diplomacy.

A comprehensive peace must be grounded in United Nations Security Council Resolutions 242 and 338 and the principle of territory for peace. This principle must be elaborated to provide for Israel's security and recognition and at the same time for legitimate Palestinian political rights. Anything else would fail the twin test of fairness and security. The time has come to put an end to Arab-Israeli conflict.

The war with Iraq is over. The quest for solutions to the problems in Lebanon, in the Arab-Israeli dispute, and in the Gulf must go forward with new vigor and determination. And I guarantee you: No one will work harder for a stable peace in the region than we will.

Fourth, we must foster economic development for the sake of peace and progress. The Persian Gulf and Middle East form a region rich in natural resources—with a wealth of untapped human potential. Resources once squandered on military might must be redirected to more peaceful ends. We are already addressing the immediate economic consequences of Iraq's aggression. Now, the challenge is to reach higher—to foster economic freedom and prosperity for all the people of the region.

By meeting these four challenges we can build a framework for peace. I've asked Secretary of State Baker to go to the Middle East to begin the process. He will go to listen, to probe, to offer suggestions—to advance the search for peace and stability. I've also asked him to raise the plight of the hostages held in Lebanon. We have not forgotten them, and we will not forget them.

To all the challenges that confront this region of the world there is no single solution—no solely American answer. But we can make a difference. America will work tirelessly as a catalyst for positive change.

But we cannot lead a new world abroad if, at home, it's politics as usual on American defense and diplomacy. It's time to turn away from the temptation to protect unneeded weapons systems and obsolete bases. It's time to put an end to micromanagement of foreign and security assistance programs—micromanagement that humiliates our friends and allies and hamstrings our diplomacy. It's time to rise above the parochial and the pork barrel, to do what is necessary, what's right, and what will enable this nation to play the leadership role required of us.

The Emerging World Order

The consequences of the conflict in the Gulf reach far beyond the confines of the Middle East. Twice before in this century, an entire world was convulsed by war. Twice this century, out of the horrors of war hope emerged for enduring peace. Twice before, those hopes proved to be a distant dream, beyond the grasp of man. Until now, the world we've known has been a world divided—a world of barbed wire and concrete block, conflict, and Cold War.

Now, we can see a new world coming into view. A world in which there is the very real prospect of a new world order. In the words of Winston Churchill, a world order in which "the principles of justice and fair play protect the weak against the strong...." A world where the United Nations—freed from Cold War stalemate—is poised to fulfill the historic vision of its founders. A world in which freedom and respect for human rights find a home among all nations. The Gulf war put this new world to its first test. And my fellow Americans, we passed that test.

For the sake of our principles—for the sake of the Kuwaiti people—we stood our ground. Because the world would not look the other way, Ambassador al-Sabah, tonight, Kuwait is free. And we're very happy about that.

Tonight, as our troops begin to come home, let us recognize that the hard work of freedom still calls us forward. We've learned the hard lessons of history. The victory over Iraq was not waged as "a war to end all wars." Even the new world order cannot guarantee an era of perpetual peace. But enduring peace must be our mission. Our success in the Gulf will shape not only the world order we seek, but our mission here at home.

[Section on domestic programs omitted.]

I'm sure that many of you saw on the television the unforgettable scene of four terrified Iraqi soldiers surrendering. They emerged from their bunker—broken, tears streaming from their eyes, fearing the worst. And then there was an American soldier. Remember what he said? He said: "It's okay. You're all right now. You're all right now." That scene says a lot about America, a lot about who we are. Americans are a caring people. We are a good people, a generous people. Let us always be caring and good and generous in all we do.

Soon, very soon, our troops will begin the march we've all been waiting for—their march home. And I have directed Secretary Cheney to begin the immediate return of American combat units from the Gulf. Less than two hours from now, the first planeload of American soldiers will lift off from Saudi Arabia, headed for the U.S.A. It will carry men and women of the 24th Mechanized Infantry Division bound for Fort Stewart, Georgia. This is just the beginning of a steady flow of American troops coming home. Let their return remind us that all those who have gone before are linked with us in the long line of freedom's march.

Americans have always tried to serve, to sacrifice nobly for what we believe to be right. Tonight, I ask every community in this country to make this coming Fourth of July a day of special celebration for our returning troops. They may have missed Thanksgiving and Christmas, but I can tell you this: For them and for their families we can make this a holiday they'll never forget.

In a very real sense, this victory belongs to them—to the privates and the pilots, to the sergeants and the supply officers, to the men and women in the machines, and the men and women who made them work. It belongs to the regulars, to the reserves, to the National Guard. This victory belongs to the finest fighting force this nation has ever known in its history.

We went halfway around the world to do what is moral and just and right. We fought hard and, with others, we won the war. We lifted the yoke of aggression and tyranny from a small country that many Americans had never even heard of, and we shall ask nothing in return.

We're coming home now—proud, confident, heads high. There is much that we must do, at home and abroad. And we will do it. We are Americans.

May God bless this great nation, the United States of America. Thank you all very, very much.

White House Statement on Weapons of Mass Destruction, March 7, 1991 [4]

The United States has taken a major step in its continuing efforts to halt the spread of weapons of mass destruction with the issuance of regulations extending export controls over chemicals, equipment, and other assistance that can contribute to the spread of missiles and chemical and biological weapons.

Saddam Hussein's use of chemical weapons against his own citizens, his use of Scud missiles to terrorize civilian populations, and the chilling specter of germ warfare and nuclear weapons have brought home the dangers proliferation poses to American interests and global peace and stability.

Our continuing efforts to stem the spread of weapons of mass destruction will contribute to the construction of a new world order. The new regulations will enhance our ability to head off these dangers so that in the future we will not be forced to confront them militarily as we have in Iraq. At the same time, the new regulations are sensitive to the importance of U.S. exports to our economic vitality and will not unfairly restrict legitimate commerce.

The expanded U.S. export controls apply to equipment, chemicals, and whole plants that can be used to manufacture chemical or biological weapons, as well as to activities of U.S. exporters or citizens when they know or are informed that their efforts will assist in a foreign missile or chemical or biological weapon program.

But the United States cannot do the job alone. Our experience in the Gulf has reinforced the lesson that the most effective export controls are those imposed multilaterally. The administration has therefore initiated vigorous efforts to obtain allied support for chemical and biological weapon export controls in the Australia Group, missile export controls in the Missile Technology Control Regime, and nuclear export controls through consultations with all major nuclear suppliers. These efforts will take advantage of the growing international consensus to redouble our efforts to stem the spread of weapons of mass destruction.

The proliferation of weapons of mass destruction may profoundly challenge our national security in the 1990s. The new regulations issued today and our multilateral initiatives will enhance our ability to meet that challenge squarely.

Excerpts from Secretary Baker's Press Conferences in the Middle East, March 10-14, 1991

EN ROUTE FROM RIYADH TO CAIRO, MARCH 10, 1991 [5]

Let me say that I think we've had a good series of meetings today, particularly the meeting with the Gulf Cooperation Council (GCC) foreign ministers, the Foreign Minister of Egypt, and myself. After that, I had separate bilaterals with the ministers from Syria and from Egypt, and before the plenary meeting, I had separate bilaterals with each of the GCC foreign ministers.

Two-Track Approach

I know you are interested in the peace process, so let me say a word or two about that, and then I'll try and respond to your questions. First of all, as you know, we have been trying to work a two-track approach. I've been exploring with our Arab coalition partners what steps they might be able to take to signal their commitment to peace and reconciliation with Israel. Before this trip began, we had communicated to Israel the general outlines of our two-track approach, and I am now going to have the opportunity, when we get to Israel, to talk in detail and specifically with their leadership about what steps they might be willing to consider. Let me say, I am not going to go into the specific steps now because we are still exploring that. We still have a long way to go. It is very, very early. We are trying to get a process going, and I would simply say that I have a sense that even though it is early, there is a greater willingness to be active on this issue in the aftermath of the Gulf crisis than there was before.

Q. Reading the statement tonight, both the Arab portion of it and the latter part, there doesn't appear to be anything here on the track of direct contacts with Israel, state to state. It all refers to the Palestinian issue, and I ask you—also, I should tell you that in the public statement of the ministers today, there was no indication of a willingness to go on that track. We have been told over and over again, this is a two-track process. Did you hear anything in private that would dissuade us from the view that the Arab foreign ministers and Gulf ministers were only talking about one track?

A. Well, we talked at length about two tracks, and I made it very clear, at a very early stage in what we hope will be a process, we have not as yet even arrived in Israel. We have not had detailed discussions with the Israeli Government about what steps they might be willing to consider and so, therefore, I don't think it is surprising that you don't have Arab governments coming out and unilaterally making statements about steps that they would be willing to take in the absence of knowing a little bit more about what might develop as the process moves forward.

Q. You still are not really saying though whether the two-track approach is still alive and the second half of the question is in your statement: You say that the United States plans to signal peace and reconciliation to Israel. Is there any signal here beyond their traditional approach?

A. Well, you read the language. The wording you just read sounds to me like it's like a signal. In terms of whether it's still alive, let me simply say that it was only born very, very recently, so please don't declare it dead until it's actually dead. I happen to think that it's at least alive until we explore the concept and the possibilities with the leadership of Israel. Let me say that I think that the Arab governments with whom we talked generally about this today exhibited, as I have just indicated to you, a greater willingness to be active than they had in the past or than they did before the Gulf crisis was resolved, and I would interpret that to be a willingness to be active along both tracks, assuming it is a process that is embraced by others, including, most importantly, Israel...

Gulf Security Structure

Q. Can you talk in a little more detail about the Gulf security structure? What kind of role are we going to have, what kind of role would they like us to have, what are your concerns about

Iran, and how are we going to get 637,000 troops home?

A. On the last question, I'm not going to get into that because that's basically an operational matter that the Defense Department could better answer for you, except to say that the President continues to make it clear that he wants to bring all of our forces home at the earliest possible opportunity. He continues to make the point that we do not desire a permanent ground presence in the Gulf, a fact that has been communicated in the meetings that I've had with all of these representatives—all of the governments that I've met with here—and one that I feel comfortable telling you that they not only accept but agree with.

With respect to the security structure, let me say that we're talking about various levels. We're talking about an enhanced GCC. We're talking about an Arab force much as was indicated by the Damascus communique of these very countries that I've just met with that would be, in addition to GCC forces, would contain Egyptian and Syrian elements. We are talking about a role for the United Nations in terms of observers, particularly with respect to the Iraq-Kuwait border. We are talking about as well the possibility that the United States—not the possibility but the probability—that the United States will continue its naval presence in the Gulf which it has maintained for over 40 years, perhaps enhanced. We will be discussing with some countries in the Gulf the prepositioning of equipment. We will be discussing as well, joint participation in training exercises and things like that.

WITH ISRAELI FOREIGN MINISTER DAVID LEVY, JERUSALEM, MARCH 11, 1991 [6]

Q. Mr. Secretary, either in your talks tonight or in your meeting tomorrow with Prime Minister Shamir, have you or will you ask Israel to commit itself in principle to trading land for peace?

A. I have not asked that during the course of the discussions tonight with David Levy. I don't think it comes as any surprise to all to know that the U.S. policy position calls for a comprehensive settlement based on direct negotiations on the basis of [U.N. Resolutions] 242 and 338. And of course, President Bush made specific reference to this policy position in his address to the Congress several nights

ago. Let me say that I do not come to Israel, to the region, with any specific, particular blueprint with regard to peace. But I do come with ideas. I come with a desire and a willingness to explore ideas that might be generated by others. I have corresponded with the minister about the importance of our developing ideas that might lead to peace. I told the minister and his colleagues this evening that I think that there are great opportunities in the aftermath of the recently concluded war, that I think the time is now for us to try and seize the moment to try and take advantage of these opportunities; that I sensed during my two days in Riyadh the beginnings of perhaps a bit of a different attitude on the part of some countries; that we would like to pursue the possibilities of peace on a dual track—moving in parallel on the track of Arab state-Israeli relations and on the path of Israeli-Palestinian relations, dialogue, and so forth.

We think the PLO made a substantial error in supporting Saddam Hussein in his brutal invasion and suppression of an Arab nation.

Political Rights for Palestinians

Q. Mr. Secretary, when your Administration speaks of political rights for the Palestinians, do you mean self-determination or do you consider self-rule, autonomy in the territories, as political rights?

A. Well, I think that discussions of self-government fall within the definition of political rights. I think that the term is one that needs further definition and is subject to further definition, and perhaps further definition through direct negotiation between the parties...

Q. Mr. Baker, you are interested in the Palestinian-Israeli dialogue. There are Palestinians who are facing major problems in the occupied territories, both in the sense that political discourse is not allowed—it is illegal to have any kind of political meetings—and economic problems are very difficult with more than 120,000 people out of work. Will you nudge or cajole or plead with the Israelis to legitimize

political discourse, including legitimizing support or sympathy with the Palestine Liberation Organization (PLO)?

A. Including what?

Q. Would you encourage them to legitimize political discourse, including sympathy or support or membership of the PLO, which is illegal now? And secondly, would you encourage them to ease the economic strain on the Palestinians in the occupied territories?

A. Certainly we would like to see the economic strain and burden eased. Certainly we could like to see—being people who believe as strongly as we believe in democracy and knowing that Israel is the only real democracy now in the region—we would like to see freedom of expression; we would like to see democratic principles permitted to flourish. We have our problems with the PLO, as you know. We used to have a dialogue with the PLO. That dialogue is terminated. We think the PLO made a substantial error in supporting Saddam Hussein in his brutal invasion and suppression of an Arab nation.

Foreign Minister Levy. With your permission I would like to add to the question which was put to you here. Israel aspires to see to it that the Arab population in Judea, Samaria, and Gaza may have the benefit of the freedom, of true freedom, which Israel only has in this part of the world. In other words, we would like to enable this population to improve its economic situation, just as Israel makes it possible for the Arab population to do. All of these aspirations can be realized. This can be done and the affairs of the population can be managed by the population itself. Israel has proposed this, and continues to do so, provided of course, the population we are referring to behaves in keeping with what such an approach would require.

When this population is incited to lash out against Israel, to wreak destruction, to kill people, to commit murders, as you saw with your own eyes just yesterday in that heinous and barbarous act, the slaughter of women, innocent women without protection, in a manner which is unspeakable, and in fact cannot even be compared with what an animal would do because no animal would commit such a murder. When such a population then is incited to such deeds, and to murder of fellow Arabs as well—in fact 500 men and women were killed in this manner, barbarously—when anyone thinks that on the one hand such tactics can be adopted, terrorist tactics coupled with destruction, while on the other hand benefiting from full rights—this does not even exist in the world to come. It simply cannot be. So that Israel cannot but adopt measures designed to protect its own security and the security of its population.

Our desire is to see a different era open—an era in which this population no longer follows the incitement of these terrorists, of these wreakers of destruction who have led them into an impasse—who have led the population into a road which spells no hope. If, indeed, they decide to follow the course of peace, and we do, indeed, offer the course of peace to them—we strive for peace—and we have reiterated this point—we have repeatedly reiterated the peace initiative of the Government of Israel in 1989. If they are responsive to this, they will discover that Israel is at the forefront of those who have offered this population the possibility of taking part in determining their own fate.

No one proposed this before Israel did—no one, not the British, certainly not the Jordanians, and we are in fact interested in resolving the problem. We will not give in. We will not be brought to our knees by terrorism. We will stand firm. We will stand up to any attempt to lash out against our citizens, and against that population itself, while at the same time holding out our hand to them, offering them freedoms and liberties and the possibility of managing their own affairs—the affairs of the population—sitting around the same table and discussing this peacefully, not in a manner which is marked by murder and destruction.

Therefore, the option is open to this population—the option to choose to respond to this population—the option to choose to respond to this initiative at long last. It is time that this came to pass, just as my friend, the Secretary of State Mr. Baker said, we find ourselves following two parallel courses—two lines of action—both of which offer a definite hope of making progress toward peace. As far as Israel is concerned, peace is the greatest victory of all. To date, there was a refusal among the Arab states to talk face to face with Israel about peace.

I am pleased that they are beginning to show signs of change, and we will have to work together, patiently and courageously, with a sense of faith and hope in order to move towards the goal which is best for all of us—peace in this region.

As far as Israel is concerned, peace is the greatest victory of all. To date, there was a refusal among the Arab states to talk face to face with Israel about peace.

PRIOR TO MEETING WITH PALESTINIAN REPRESENTATIVES, MARCH 12, 1991 [7]

Q. And your meeting today with Palestinian representatives, what does that represent?

A. Well, it represents certainly an effort on our part to show that we intend to do what we can, the United States. We intend to use whatever enhanced credibility we might have coming out of this crisis to work diligently for peace. And, I am just saying here to the group that I am very pleased that they have seen fit to ask for this meeting and that we can have this meeting and hope it can be productive and that we can find a way, again, to take advantage of this window — this window of opportunity.

WITH SYRIAN FOREIGN MINISTER FAROUK AL SHARA, DAMASCUS, MARCH 14, 1991 [8]

I will start by telling you that in the meeting last night with President Assad and Minister Shara, we covered a number of different topics and subjects. Of course, we discussed in detail the four broad issue areas that I have been discussing during the course of my trip in the region, and I will continue to discuss as we move on now to Moscow. Those four issue areas being regional security in the Gulf; arms control and proliferation; economic cooperation; and the Arab-Israeli conflict. We also talked about hostages; we talked about Lebanon and the importance of implementing in both letter and spirit the Taif agreement. We talked, as well, about terrorism.

With respect to the question of the Arab-Israeli conflict, I think that the minister would agree with me that we find ourselves in agreement with respect to sharing a commitment to seek a comprehensive settlement based on U.N. Security Council Resolutions 242 and 338. We find ourselves in agreement with respect to the fact that there is, we think, a window of opportunity now in the aftermath of the Gulf crisis that should be seized, if at all possible—a window of opportunity which could make it possible for us to make significant progress in resolving the Arab-Israeli conflict. I sense a very serious intent on the part of the Syrian Government to pursue an active peace process and to continue to work toward that end with the coalition countries that worked together to reverse Saddam Hussein's aggression.

Q. Mr. Secretary, after the Gulf crisis has ended, now there is determination by the international community to implement U.N. resolutions regarding the Arab-Israeli conflict, as the Italian foreign minister said here a few days ago, that there should be no double standard in dealing with this issue. What are you going to do as the United States on this respect?

A. I agree that there should be no double standard, and I would submit to you that, indeed, there is not. The United States, as evidenced by the activity in which I have been engaged over the past four or five days, is going to be very vigorous in attempting to use whatever influence and good offices it might have to pursue a comprehensive settlement based on those U.N. Resolutions, 242 and 338...

Q. Mr. Secretary, can you please tell me why the United States has not dealt with or talked with the Iraqi opposition which has just been meeting in Beirut, even though the Turks have and the British have? Are we, are your people authorized to talk with the Iraqi opposition that is [inaudible] together?

A. The question of what government Iraq ends up with in the aftermath of this crisis is a matter for, and we have said, for the Iraqi people to determine. Now, I don't want to comment any further beyond saying that.

White House Statement on Saddam Hussein's Use of Force Against the Iraqi People, March 13, 1991 [9]

Saddam Hussein has a track record of using his military against his own population. We have received information over the past week that he has been using helicopters in an effort to quell civil disturbances against his regime. We are obviously very concerned about this. President Bush expressed his concern at the news conference. This behavior is clearly inconsistent with the type of behavior the international community would like to see Iraq exhibiting. Iraq has to convince the world that its designs, both against the international community and its own population, are not military and aggressive.

President's Press Conference with French President Mitterrand, Martinique, March 14, 1991 (Excerpt) [9]

Q. A question for both Presidents about Iraq. With no cease-fire in place and concern about civil unrest in Iraq, what will the coalition forces do if Saddam continues to try to put down unrest with his military machine?

President Mitterrand. That's just what is happening right now. That's what he's doing, so it would appear. It seems to be what is happening with varying degrees of success. I, personally, am not sufficiently informed to be able to tell you who is winning the battle in various parts of the country of Iraq. I think with this sort of situational logic which is such that Mr. Saddam Hussein will end up by understanding that his errors of judgment and that his very serious military defeat will make his situation very difficult as a head of state in the future to discuss with other countries how to rebuild his country.

But right at the outset, we said that it was not our intention to conquer Iraq but to liberate Kuwait. That at the outset, we said that we aren't heading for Baghdad, we are not aiming for Baghdad. So, it's perfectly clear that it is not our intention, even if very often what we're seeing is a very sorry spec-

tacle very often, but at the same time, we cannot arbitrate by military means all the conflicts in that part of the world or in other parts of the world. But the fact remains that there are certain rules—not to the cease-fire yet, but to the temporary armistice. And if that was to be violated—but I think that will not be the case—the matter is over.

But the rules indicate clearly that Iraq is not free just to do anything. As far as France is concerned, that particular period of our intervention in the Middle East is now terminated.

President Bush. I listened very carefully to that answer, and I agree with it. I mean, we are not in there trying to impose a solution inside Iraq. So, I would agree with the way President Mitterrand phrased that. I would only add that I am concerned, and I expect he is, too, about the reports coming out of there. But what President Mitterrand said in the beginning is true: Nobody has all the information about what's going on there, who's trying to emerge. But he cited the coalition goals, and I agree with him.

Testimony by John H. Kelly, Assistant Secretary of State for Near Eastern and South Asian Affairs, March 20, 1991 [10]

Secretary Baker's Trip

In his conversations in the Middle East, Secretary Baker discussed various mechanisms which could help to guarantee against a repetition of Iraq's aggression against other Gulf states. The Damascus declaration, issued on March 6 [1991] by the Foreign Ministers of Syria, Egypt, and the six Gulf Cooperation Council [GCC] states, noted agreement on creation of an Arab peace force—including troops from Egypt and Syria—which would be stationed in Saudi Arabia and other Gulf states.

Secretary Baker consulted with a number of our coalition partners concerning how to win the peace now that we have won the war. We currently are developing those key elements of a U.N. resolution which would establish a cease-fire, among other issues. We shortly will be consulting with the

other members of the Security Council concerning this resolution.

GCC Self-Defense

We expect that the six member states of the Gulf Cooperation Council will also be taking steps among themselves to improve their capability for cooperative self-defense. In addition, we discussed potential future arrangements for a U.S. role in the Gulf. We included a continued—and perhaps enhanced—American naval presence, maintaining the U.S. naval presence which has existed in the Gulf since 1949. We are also exploring what might be done to increase our air defense presence in the region. President Bush has stated publicly that we seek no permanent ground force presence in the Gulf region. We discussed the potential prepositioning of military materials and equipment in the region which would be available for U.S. forces in a future emergency. We also discussed combined training exercises which would improve our ability to work together with the states in the region, building on the successful experiences of Operation Desert Storm.

All of those governments we consulted agreed on the need to eliminate weapons of mass destruction in Iraqi hands—whether or not Saddam Hussein remains in power. We will be working with our coalition partners on ways to address Iraqi weapons of mass destruction. All the officials with whom we met also agreed on the need to address the issue of weapons of mass destruction on a region-wide basis.

Arab-Israeli Dispute

Secretary Baker discussed, in each meeting, the Arab-Israeli dispute. We talked of the potential benefit of an approach on two tracks: one at the state to state level between Israel and its Arab neighbors and the second between Israel and Palestinians. The Secretary's discussions led to no instant decisions by the parties to the conflict. We did hear, from all those with whom we met, a new openness to consider fresh steps to address the Arab-Israeli dispute. We will be in contact with all parties in the days and weeks ahead to see if we can advance the process.

Our principles remain the same: the goal of a comprehensive settlement achieved through direct negotiations based on U.N. Security Council Resolutions 242 and 338, including the principles of territory for peace, security for Israel, and the legitimate political rights of Palestinians.

We do not underestimate the difficulty of the task which confronts all of us who seek to advance the cause of peace. We do believe that there are new opportunities in the aftermath of the unprecedented international cooperation which led to the liberation of Kuwait.

Economic Cooperation

Secretary Baker discussed, in each meeting, the question of economic cooperation in the Middle East region. On a preliminary basis there was general agreement that this issue needs to be addressed. Again, there were no decisions reached by the parties consulted, but there was agreement that there is a need to enhance the basis of economic cooperation among the states. We noted that the GCC summit in December [1990] adopted a special program for the creation of a new development fund. It may be that this GCC fund can provide the base for expanded international cooperation for countries inside and outside the region.

U.S. Policy Toward Iraq

As the President has made clear, we believe that Iraq requires special vigilance. Iraq must not have access to the instruments of war. Moreover, Iraq has acknowledged its liabilities for damage resulting from its invasion of Kuwait. The international community will have to decide on appropriate reparations and the conditions for the lifting of economic sanctions.

We believe the Iraqi people should decide Saddam Hussein's fate. The current strife derives from his disastrous policies. Clearly, the international community's relations with Iraq will be significantly affected by the resolution of this issue. As Secretary Baker has noted, we are not providing arms to Iraqi opposition groups, and we believe other states should refrain from interfering in Iraq's internal affairs. We support Iraq's territorial integrity as do other members of the coalition.

President's Exchange with Reporters, April 3, 1991 (Excerpt) [11]

Q. Do you feel frustrated at not being able to help the Iraqis?

A. Well, I feel frustrated any time innocent civilians are being slaughtered. And I feel very frustrated about that. But the United States and these other countries with us in this coalition did not go there to settle all the internal affairs of Iraq.

I have said that there will not be normalized relations with Iraq as long as Saddam Hussein is in power. And of course I feel a frustration and a sense of grief for the innocents that are being killed brutally. But we are not there to intervene. That is not our purpose; it never was our purpose. I can understand the frustration of some who think it should have been our purpose, some who never supported this in the first place on military action. I share their frustration, but I am not going to commit our forces to something of this nature. I'm not going to do that.

We will proceed along the diplomatic channels, working at the United Nations, getting security forces.

Q. Why let their helicopters continue?

A. Because I do not want to see us get sucked into the internal civil war inside Iraq, that's why.

Q. Isn't that a violation of the informal cease-fire?

A. I don't know whether technically, Lori [Lori Santos, United Press International], it's in violation or not. It is in [violation for] the fixed wing planes to fly, but if it is a violation, that doesn't necessarily mean that we are going to commit our young men and our young women into further combat. I will do my level best to use all diplomatic channels to bring this fighting to a halt. But I do not want to push American forces beyond our mandate. We've done the heavy lifting. Our kids performed with superior courage, and they don't need to be thrust into a war that's been going on for years in there. That's my view.

Q. Given the recent success of his forces, are you still confident that Saddam Hussein will not be there in less than a year?

A. Yes. I'm still confident he won't be. I don't think he can survive, and I don't think he should survive. He's not going to have the kind of relations that Iraq should have with other countries as long as he's there. And I haven't changed my view on that at all.

Most of the people I talk to and hear from around the world, in that part of the world, feel the same way I do about that, incidentally.

U.N. Security Council Resolution 687, April 3, 1991 [2]

The Security Council,

Recalling its resolutions 660 (1990), 661(1990), 662 (1990), 664 (1990), 665 (1990), 666 (1990), 667 (1990), 669 (1990), 670 (1990), 674 (1990), 677 (1990), 678 (1990) and 686 (1991),

Welcoming the restoration to Kuwait of its sovereignty, independence and territorial integrity and the return of its legitimate Government,

Affirming the commitment of all Member States to the sovereignty, territorial integrity and political independence of Kuwait and Iraq, and noting the intention expressed by the Member States cooperating with Kuwait under paragraph 2 of resolution 678 (1990) to bring their military presence in Iraq to an end as soon as possible consistent with paragraph 8 of resolution 686 (1991),

Reaffirming the need to be assured of Iraq's peaceful intentions in the light of its unlawful invasion and occupation of Kuwait,

Taking note of the letter sent by the Minister for Foreign Affairs of Iraq on 27 February 1991 (S/22275, annex) and those sent pursuant to resolution 686 (1991) (S/22273, S/122276, S/22320, S/22321 and S/22330),

Noting that Iraq and Kuwait, as independent sovereign States, signed at Baghdad on 4 October 1963 "Agreed Minutes Between the State of Kuwait and the Republic of Iraq Regarding the Restoration of Friendly Relations, Recognition and Related Matters," thereby recognizing formally the boundary between Iraq and Kuwait and the allocation of islands, which were registered with the United Nations in accordance with Article 102 of the

Charter of the United Nations and in which Iraq recognized the independence and complete sovereignty of the State of Kuwait within its borders as specified and accepted in the letter of the Prime Minister of Iraq dated 21 July 1932, and as accepted by the Ruler of Kuwait in his letter dated 10 August 1932,

Conscious of the need for demarcation of the said boundary,

Conscious also of the statements by Iraq threatening to use weapons in violation of its obligations under the Geneva Protocol for the Prohibition of the Use in War of Asphyxiating, Poisonous or Other Gases, and of Bacteriological Methods of Warfare, signed at Geneva on 17 June 1925, [League of Nations, Treaty Series, vol. XCIV (1929), No. 2138] and of its prior use of chemical weapons and affirming that grave consequences would follow any further use by Iraq of such weapons,

Recalling that Iraq has subscribed to the Declaration adopted by all States participating in the Conference of States Parties to the 1925 Geneva Protocol and Other Interested States, held in Paris from 7 to 11 January 1989, establishing the objective of universal elimination of chemical and biological weapons,

Recalling further that Iraq has signed the Convention on the Prohibition of the Development, Production and stockpiling of Bacteriological (Biological) and Toxin Weapons and on their Destruction, of 10 April 1972, [General Assembly Resolution 2826 (XXVI), annex],

Noting the importance of Iraq ratifying this Convention,

Noting moreover the importance of all States adhering to this Convention and encouraging its forthcoming Review Conference to reinforce the authority, efficiency and universal scope of the Convention,

Stressing the importance of an early conclusion by the Conference on Disarmament of its work on a Convention on the Universal Prohibition of Chemical Weapons and of universal adherence thereto,

Aware of the use by Iraq of ballistic missiles in unprovoked attacks and therefore of the need to take specific measures in regard to such missiles located in Iraq,

Concerned by the reports in the hands of Member States that Iraq has attempted to acquire materials for a nuclear weapons program contrary to its obligations under the Treaty on the Nonproliferation of Nuclear Weapons of 1 July 1968, [General Assembly Resolution 2373 (XXII)]

Recalling the objective of the establishment of a nuclear-weapon-free zone in the region of the Middle East,

Conscious of the threat which all weapons of mass destruction pose to peace and security in the area and of the need to work towards the establishment in the Middle East of a zone free of such weapons,

Conscious also of the objective of achieving balanced and comprehensive control of armaments in the region,

Conscious further of the importance of achieving the objectives noted above using all available means, including a dialogue among the States of the region,

Noting that resolution 686 (1991) marked the lifting of the measures imposed by resolution 661(1990) in so far as they applied to Kuwait,

Noting that despite the progress being made in fulfilling the obligations of resolution 686 (1991), many Kuwaiti and third country nationals are still not accounted for and property remains unreturned,

Recalling the International Convention against the Taking of Hostages, [General Assembly Resolution 34/146] opened for signature at New York on 18 December 1979, which categorizes all acts of taking hostages as manifestations of international terrorism,

Deploring threats made by Iraq during the recent conflict to make use of terrorism against targets outside Iraq and the taking of hostages by Iraq,

Taking note with grave concern of the reports of the Secretary-General of 20 March 1991 (S/22366) and 28 March 1991, (S/22409) and conscious of the necessity to meet urgently the humanitarian needs in Kuwait and Iraq,

Bearing in mind its objective of restoring international peace and security in the area as set out in recent Council resolutions,

Conscious of the need to take the following measures acting under Chapter VII of the Charter,

1. Affirms all thirteen resolutions noted above, except as expressly

changed below to achieve the goals of this resolution, including a formal cease-fire;

A

2. Demands that Iraq and Kuwait respect the inviolability of the international boundary and the allocation of islands set out in the "Agreed Minutes Between the State of Kuwait and the Republic of Iraq Regarding the Restoration of Friendly Relations, Recognition and Related Matters," signed by them in the exercise of their sovereignty at Baghdad on 4 October 1963 and registered with the United Nations and published by the United Nations in document 7063, United Nations, Treaty Series, 1964;

3. Calls on the Secretary-General to lend his assistance to make arrangements with Iraq and Kuwait to demarcate the boundary between Iraq and Kuwait, drawing on appropriate material, including the map transmitted by Security Council document S/22412 and to report back to the Security Council within one month;

4. Decides to guarantee the inviolability of the above-mentioned international boundary and to take as appropriate all necessary measures to that end in accordance with the Charter;

B

5. Requests the Secretary-General, after consulting with Iraq and Kuwait, to submit within three days to the Security Council for its approval a plan for the immediate deployment of a United Nations observer unit to monitor the Khor Abdullah and a demilitarized zone, which is hereby established, extending ten kilometres into Iraq and five kilometres into Kuwait from the boundary referred to in the "Agreed Minutes Between the State of Kuwait and the Republic of Iraq Regarding the Restoration of Friendly Relations, Recognition and Related Matters" of 4 October 1963; to deter violations of the boundary through its presence in and surveillance of the demilitarized zone; to observe any hostile or potentially hostile action mounted from the territory of one State to the other; and for the Secretary-General to report regularly to the Council on the operations of the

unit, and immediately if there are serious violations of the zone or potential threats to peace;

6. Notes that as soon as the Secretary-General notifies the Council of the completion of the deployment of the United Nations observer unit, the conditions will be established for the Member States cooperating with Kuwait in accordance with resolution 678 (1990) to bring their military presence in Iraq to an end consistent with resolution 686 (1991);

C

7. Invites Iraq to reaffirm unconditionally its obligations under the Geneva Protocol for the Prohibition of the Use in War of Asphyxiating, Poisonous or Other Gases, and of Bacteriological Methods of Warfare, signed at Geneva on 17 June 1925, and to ratify the Convention on the Prohibition of the Development, Production and Stockpiling of Bacteriological (Biological) and Toxin Weapons and on Their Destruction, of 10 April 1972;

8. Decides that Iraq shall unconditionally accept the destruction, removal, or rendering harmless, under international supervision, of:

(a) all chemical and biological weapons and all stocks of agents and all related subsystems and components and all research, development, support and manufacturing facilities;

(b) all ballistic missiles with a range greater than 150 kilometres and related major parts, and repair and production facilities;

9. Decides, for the implementation of paragraph 8 above, the following:

(a) Iraq shall submit to the Secretary-General, within fifteen days of the adoption of this resolution, a declaration of the locations, amounts and types of all items specified in paragraph 8 and agree to urgent, on-site inspection as specified below;

(b) the Secretary-General, in consultation with the appropriate Governments and, where appropriate, with the Director-General of the World Health Organization (WHO), within forty-five days of the passage of this resolution, shall develop, and submit to the Council for approval, a plan calling for the completion of the following acts within forty-five days of such approval:

(i) The forming of a Special Commission, which shall carry out immedi-

ate on-site inspection of Iraq's biological, chemical and missile capabilities, based on Iraq's declarations and the designation of any additional locations by the Special Commission itself;

(ii) The yielding by Iraq of possession to the Special Commission for destruction, removal or rendering harmless, taking into account the requirements of public safety, of all items specified under paragraph 8 (a) above including items at the additional locations designated by the Special Commission under paragraph 9 (b) (i) above and the destruction by Iraq, under supervision of the Special Commission, of all its missile capabilities, including launchers, as specified under paragraph 8 (b) above;

(iii) The provision by the Special Commission of the assistance and cooperation to the Director-General of the International Atomic Energy Agency (IAEA) required in paragraphs 12 and 13 below;

10. Decides that Iraq shall unconditionally undertake not to use, develop, construct or acquire any of the items specified in paragraphs 8 and 9 above and requests the Secretary-General, in consultation with the Special Commission, to develop a plan for the future ongoing monitoring and verification of Iraq's compliance with this paragraph, to be submitted to the Security Council for approval within 120 days of the passage of this resolution;

11. Invites Iraq to reaffirm unconditionally its obligations under the Treaty on the Nonproliferation of Nuclear Weapons of 1 July 1968;

12. Decides that Iraq shall unconditionally agree not to acquire or develop nuclear weapons or nuclear-weapons-usable material or any subsystems or components or any research, development, support or manufacturing facilities related to the above; to submit to the Secretary-General and the Director-General of the International Atomic Energy Agency (IAEA) within fifteen days of the adoption of this resolution a declaration of the locations, amounts, and types of all items specified above; to place all of its nuclear-weapons-usable materials under the exclusive control, for custody and removal, of the IAEA, with the assistance and cooperation of the Special Commission as provided for in the plan of the Secretary-General discussed in paragraph 9 (b) above; to accept, in ac-

cordance with the arrangements provided for in paragraph 13 below, urgent on-site inspection and the destruction, removal or rendering harmless as appropriate of all items specified above; and to accept the plan discussed in paragraph 13 below for the future ongoing monitoring and verification of its compliance with these undertakings;

13. Requests the Director-General of the International Atomic Energy Agency, through the Secretary-General, with the assistance and cooperation of the Special Commission as provided for in the plan of the Secretary-General in paragraph 9(b) above, to carry out immediate on-site inspection of Iraq's nuclear capabilities based on Iraq's declarations and the designation of any additional locations by the Special Commission; to develop a plan for submission to the Security Council within forty-five days calling for the destruction, removal, or rendering harmless as appropriate of all items listed in paragraph 12 above; to carry out the plan within forty-five days following approval by the Security Council; and to develop a plan, taking into account the rights and obligations of Iraq under the Treaty on the Non-Proliferation of Nuclear Weapons of 1 July 1968, for the future ongoing monitoring and verification of Iraq's compliance with paragraph 12 above, including an inventory of all nuclear material in Iraq subject to the Agency's verification and inspections of the IAEA to confirm that the Agency's safeguards cover all relevant nuclear activities in Iraq, to be submitted to the Security Council for approval within one hundred and twenty days of the passage of the present resolution;

14. Takes note that the actions to be taken by Iraq in paragraphs 8, 9, 10, 11,12 and 13 of the present resolution represent steps towards the goal of establishing in the Middle East a zone free from weapons of mass destruction and all missiles for their delivery and the objective of a global ban on chemical weapons;

D

15. Requests the Secretary-General to report to the Security Council on the steps taken to facilitate the return of all Kuwaiti property seized by Iraq, including a list of any property which Kuwait claims has not been

returned or which has not been returned intact;

E

16. Reaffirms that Iraq, without prejudice to the debts and obligations of Iraq arising prior to 2 August 1990, which will be addressed through the normal mechanisms, is liable under international law for any direct loss, damage, including environmental damage and the depletion of natural resources, or injury to foreign Governments, nationals and corporations, as a result of Iraq's unlawful invasion and occupation of Kuwait;

17. Decides that all Iraqi statements made since 2 August 1990 repudiating its foreign debt are null and void, and demands that Iraq adhere scrupulously to all of its obligations concerning servicing and repayment of its foreign debt;

18. Decides also to create a Fund to pay compensation for claims that fall within paragraph 16 above and to establish a Commission that will administer the Fund;

19. Directs the Secretary-General to develop and present to the Security Council for decision, no later than thirty days following the adoption of the present resolution, recommendations for the Fund to meet the requirement for the payment of claims established in accordance with paragraph 18 above and for a program to implement the decisions in paragraphs 16, 17 and 18 above, including administration of the Fund; mechanisms for determining the appropriate level of Iraq's contribution to the Fund based on a percentage of the value of the exports of petroleum and petroleum products from Iraq not to exceed a figure to be suggested to the Council by the Secretary-General, taking into account the requirements of the people of Iraq, Iraq's payment capacity as assessed in conjunction with the international financial institutions taking into consideration external debt service, and the needs of the Iraqi economy; arrangements for ensuring that payments are made to the Fund; the process by which funds will be allocated and claims paid; appropriate procedures for evaluating losses, listing claims and verifying their validity and resolving disputed claims in respect of Iraq's liability as specified in paragraph 16 above; and the composition of the Commission designated above;

F

20. Decides, effective immediately, that the prohibitions against the sale or supply to Iraq of commodities or products, other than medicine and health supplies, and prohibitions against financial transactions related thereto contained in resolution 661 (1990) shall not apply to foodstuffs notified to the Committee established by resolution 661(1990) concerning the situation between Iraq and Kuwait or, with the approval of that Committee, under the simplified and accelerated "no-objection" procedure, to materials and supplies for essential civilian needs as identified in the report of the Secretary General dated 20 March 1991, (S/22366) and in any further findings of humanitarian need by the Committee;

21. Decides that the Council shall review the provisions of paragraph 20 above every sixty days in the light of the policies and practices of the Government of Iraq, including the implementation of all relevant resolutions of the Security Council, for the purpose of determining whether to reduce or lift the prohibitions referred to therein;

22. Decides that upon the approval by the Council of the program called for in paragraph 19 above and upon Council agreement that Iraq has completed all actions contemplated in paragraphs 8, 9, 10, 11, 12 and 13 above, the prohibitions against the import of commodities and products originating in Iraq and the prohibitions against financial transactions related thereto contained in resolution 661(1990) shall have no further force or effect;

23. Decides that, pending action by the Council under paragraph 22 above, the Committee established by resolution 661(1990) shall be empowered to approve, when required to assure adequate financial resources on the part of Iraq to carry out the activities under paragraph 20 above, exceptions to the prohibition against the import of commodities and products originating in Iraq;

24. Decides that, in accordance with resolution 661(1990) and subsequent related resolutions and until a further decision is taken by the Council, all States shall continue to prevent the sale or supply, or the promotion or facilitation of such sale or supply, to Iraq by their nationals, or from their

territories or using their flag vessels or aircraft, of:

(a) arms and related materiel of all types, specifically including the sale or transfer through other means of all forms of conventional military equipment, including for paramilitary forces, and spare parts and components and their means of production, of such equipment;

(b) items specified and defined in paragraphs 8 and 12 above not otherwise covered above;

(c) technology under licensing or other transfer arrangements used in the production, utilization or stockpiling of items specified in subparagraphs (a) and (b) above;

(d) personnel or materials for training or technical support services relating to the design, development, manufacture, use, maintenance or support of items specified in subparagraphs (a) and (b) above;

25. Calls upon all States and international organizations to act strictly in accordance with paragraph 24 above, notwithstanding the existence of any contracts, agreements, licences or any other arrangements;

26. Requests the Secretary-General, in consultation with appropriate governments, to develop within sixty days, for approval of the Council, guidelines to facilitate full international implementation of paragraphs 24 and 25 above and paragraph 27 below, and to make them available to all States and to establish a procedure for updating these guidelines periodically;

27. Calls upon all States to maintain such national controls and procedures and to take such other actions consistent with the guidelines to be established by the Security Council under paragraph 26 above as may be necessary to ensure compliance with the terms of paragraph 24 above, and calls upon international organizations to take all appropriate steps to assist in ensuring such full compliance;

28. Agrees to review its decisions in paragraphs 22, 23, 24 and 25 above, except for the items specified and defined in paragraphs 8 and 12 above, on a regular basis and in any case 120 days following passage of this resolution, taking into account Iraq's compliance with the resolution and general progress towards the control of armaments in the region;

29. Decides that all States, including Iraq, shall take the necessary measures to ensure that no claim shall lie at the instance of the Government of Iraq, or of any person or body in Iraq, or of any person claiming through or for the benefit of any such person or body, in connection with any contract or other transaction where its performance was affected by reason of the measures taken by the Security Council in resolution 661(1990) and related resolutions;

G

30. Decides that, in furtherance of its commitment to facilitate the repatriation of all Kuwaiti and third country nationals, Iraq shall extend all necessary cooperation to the International Committee of the Red Cross, providing lists of such persons, facilitating the access of the International Committee of the Red Cross to all such persons wherever located or detained and facilitating the search by the International Committee of the Red Cross for those Kuwaiti and third country nationals still unaccounted for;

31. Invites the International Committee of the Red Cross to keep the Secretary-General apprised as appropriate of all activities undertaken in connection with facilitating the repatriation or return of all Kuwaiti and third country nationals or their remains present in Iraq on or after 2 August 1990;

32. Requires Iraq to inform the Council that it will not commit or support any act of international terrorism or allow any organization directed towards commission of such acts to operate within its territory and to condemn unequivocally and renounce all acts, methods and practices of terrorism;

H

33. Declares that, upon official notification by Iraq to the Secretary-General and to the Security Council of its acceptance of the provisions above, a formal cease-fire is effective between Iraq and Kuwait and the Member States cooperating with Kuwait in accordance with resolution 678 (1990);

34. Decides to remain seized of the matter and to take such further steps as may be required for the implementation of the present resolution and to secure peace and security in the area.

President's Statement Following Passage of Resolution 687, April 3, 1991 [11]

I am extremely pleased that the Security Council has voted in favor of Resolution 687. Fourteen times now the United Nations has demonstrated its determination to contribute significantly to the prospects for lasting peace and security in the Gulf region.

This latest resolution creates the basis for a formal cease-fire in the Gulf. It comes eight months since Iraq invaded Kuwait. During these eight months, the world community has stood up for what is right and just. It is now up to Iraq's government to demonstrate that it is prepared to respect the will of the world community and communicate its formal acceptance of this resolution to the Security Council and the Secretary-General.

The resolution is unprecedented. It creates a force to monitor the legal border between Iraq and Kuwait; it also provides a U.N. guarantee of that border. Once this observer force arrives, all remaining U.S. ground forces will be withdrawn from Iraqi territory.

Certain sanctions will remain in force until such time as Iraq is led by a government that convinces the world of its intent both to live in peace with its neighbors and to devote its resources to the welfare of the Iraqi people.

The resolution establishes a fund to compensate Kuwait and other claimants for the damage caused by Iraq's aggression. The resolution also includes provisions designed to ensure that Iraq cannot rebuild its military strength to threaten anew the peace of the region. Weapons of mass destruction and the means to deliver them are to be destroyed; this is to be confirmed by on-site inspection.

Certain sanctions will remain in force until such time as Iraq is led by a government that convinces the world of its intent both to live in peace with its neighbors and to devote its resources to the welfare of the Iraqi people. The resolution thus provides the necessary latitude for the international community to adjust its relations with Iraq depending upon Iraq's leadership and behavior.

I also want to condemn in the strongest terms continued attacks by Iraqi government forces against defenseless Kurdish and other Iraqi civilians. This sort of behavior will continue to set Iraq apart from the community of civilized nations. I call upon Iraq's leaders to halt these attacks immediately and to allow international organizations to go to work inside Iraq to alleviate the suffering and to ensure that humanitarian aid reaches needy civilians. As a result of these cruel attacks, Turkey is now faced with a mounting refugee problem. The United States is prepared to extend economic help to Turkey through multilateral channels, and we call upon others to do likewise.

Statement by Turkey's Foreign Minister H.E. Ahmet Kurtcebe Alptemocin, April 4, 1991 [12]

It appears that the conflict which has been raging in northern Iraq for some time has, during the last couple of days, deteriorated into a punitive operation against the civilian population of the region aimed at compelling them to leave the country. This attitude of the Baghdad authorities is both intolerable and unacceptable be it in terms of legality or in those of human and citizenship rights.

The tragic plight of the civilian population in the region which has unfolded as a result of the operations being conducted by the Iraqi Government forces causes profound indignation in Turkey as it does among other members of the international community who are genuinely concerned about respect for human rights.

Moreover, these military operations carried out in the immediate vicinity of our borders and directed towards our frontiers threaten not only the physical, but also the economic and social security of our country due to the potentiary of a massive exodus they have thus provoked.

In our opinion, the internal peace and stability of Iraq to the maintenance of whose sovereignty and territorial integrity we attach importance cannot be ensured by chastising and forcing to emigrate a portion of the Iraqi citizenry. To put an immediate end to this situation which further aggravates the difficulties confronting Iraq as a result of the damage inflicted upon it by the Gulf war for which it is responsible, and disrupts the efforts aimed at restoring the environment of stability, reconciliation and confidence badly needed in the region, is within the duties and powers of the administration in Baghdad.

This understanding and approach of our Government has been made known to the competent authorities in Iraq with the necessary clarity.

Turkey remains convinced that in order to ensure a speedy elimination of the inadmissible consequences, humanitarian as well as social, of these operations, the military campaign directed against the civilian population of the country from the viewpoint of preserving peace and security in the region, the entire international community should consider it an inescapable duty, individually and collectively, effectively to urge the Government of Iraq, by addressing the necessary warnings to the authorities in Baghdad.

With these considersations in mind, we have brought the issue to the attention of the U.N. Security Council. We expect the U.N. Security Council, as well as all countries who respect the U.N. Charter and human rights, to tackle this critical situation which calls for urgent solution in an earnest and speedy manner commensurate with their responsibilities.

Turkey is aware of the facts that the Gulf crisis and the subsequent war has subjected the Iraqi people to immense suffering and that the entire population of Iraq is in need of humanitarian assistance. We are prepared to continue in a progressive manner our ongoing assistance to alleviate that suffering within the limits allowed by this country's capabilities.

However, the plight and requirements of the hundreds of thousands of people who have today converged immediately across our borders as a consequence of the treatment meted out to its citizens in northern Iraq by the Iraqi leadership, features a particularity which deserves priority beyond the bounds of this general framework. Our Government, having adopted the necessary measures aimed at ensuring the delivery of the humanitarian assistance urgently needed by these people to maintain their livelihood in their own country, has forthwith proceeded to implement them within the constraints imposed by the physical circumstances prevalent in the region. Other countries and organizations who might wish to render those Iraqi nationals ex-clusively humanitarian assistance on the basis of the same understanding will enjoy our full support and cooperation in the facilitation of their efforts.

Apart from such assistance, in case third countries desire to receive as emigrants Iraqi citizens from among those who have presently converged on our borders, as a country which has magnanimously provided temporary shelter to tens of thousands of Iraqi citizens since 1988 by stretching to the utmost her limited means, Turkey will afford them the necessary cooperation.

We expect the U.N. Security Council, as well as all countries who respect the U.N. Charter and human rights, to tackle this critical situation...

U.N. Security Council Resolution 688, April 5, 1991 [2]

The Security Council,

Mindful of its duties and its responsibilities under the Charter of the United Nations for the maintenance of international peace and security,

Recalling Article 2, paragraph 7, of the Charter of the United Nations,

Gravely concerned by the repression of the Iraqi civilian population in many parts of Iraq, including most recently in Kurdish populated areas which led to a massive flow of refugees towards and across international frontiers and to cross border incursions, which threaten international peace and security in the region,

Deeply disturbed by the magnitude of the human suffering involved,

Taking note of the letters sent by the representatives of Turkey and France to the United Nations dated 2 April 1991 and 4 April 1991, respectively (S/22435 and S/22442),

Taking note also of the letters sent by the Permanent Representative of the Islamic Republic of Iran to the United Nations dated 3 and 4 April 1991, respectively (S/22436 and S/22447),

Reaffirming the commitment of all Member States to the sovereignty, ter-ritorial integrity and political independence of Iraq and of all States in the area,

Bearing in mind the Secretary-General's report of 20 March 1991 (S/22366),

1. Condemns the repression of the Iraqi civilian population in many parts of Iraq, including most recently in Kurdish populated areas, the consequences of which threaten international peace and security in the region;

2. Demands that Iraq, as a contribution to removing the threat to international peace and security in the region, immediately end this repression and expresses the hope in the same context that an open dialogue will take place to ensure that the human and political rights of all Iraqi citizens are respected;

3. Insists that Iraq allow immediate access by international humanitarian organizations to all those in need of assistance in all parts of Iraq and to make available all necessary facilities for their operations;

4. Requests the Secretary-General to pursue his humanitarian efforts in Iraq and to report forthwith, if appropriate on the basis of a further mission to the region, on the plight of the Iraqi civilian population, and in particular the Kurdish population, suffering from the repression in all its forms inflicted by the Iraqi authorities;

5. Requests further the Secretary-General to use all the resources at his disposal, including those of the relevant United Nations agencies, to address urgently the critical needs of the refugees and displaced Iraqi population;

6. Appeals to all Member States and to all humanitarian organizations to contribute to these humanitarian relief efforts;

7. Demands that Iraq cooperate with the Secretary-General to these ends;

8. Decides to remain seized of the matter.

President's Statement on Aid to Iraqi Refugees, April 5, 1991 [11]

The human tragedy unfolding in and around Iraq demands immediate action on a massive scale. At stake are not only the lives of hundreds of thousands of innocent men, women, and children but the peace and security of the Gulf.

Since the beginning of the Gulf war on August 2, the United States has contributed more than $35 million for refugees and displaced persons in the region. Many other countries have also contributed. It is clear, however, that the current tragedy requires a far greater effort. As a result, I have directed a major new effort be undertaken to assist Iraqi refugees.

Emergency Airdrops

Beginning this Sunday, U.S. Air Force transport planes will fly over northern Iraq and drop supplies of food, blankets, clothing, tents, and other relief-related items for refugees and other Iraqi civilians suffering as a result of the situation there.

I want to emphasize that this effort is prompted only by humanitarian concerns. We expect the Government of Iraq to permit this effort to be carried out without any interference.

I want to add that what we are planning to do is intended as a step-up in immediate aid, such as is also being provided by the British, the French, and other coalition partners. We will be consulting with the United Nations on how it can best provide for the many refugees in and around Iraq on a long term basis as necessary. We will continue consulting with our coalition partners in this and in other efforts designed to alleviate the plight of the many innocent Iraqis whose lives have been endangered by the brutal and inhumane actions of the Iraqi Government.

I also want to add that this urgent air drop is but one of several steps the United States is taking to deal with this terrible situation. I will shortly be signing an order that will authorize up to $10 million from the Emergency Refugee and Migration Assistance Fund. These funds will help meet the needs of the burgeoning refugee population in the region. Our military forces in southern Iraq will continue to assist refugees and displaced persons. We are also providing considerable economic and food assistance to the Government of Turkey, to help it sustain the many refugees who have taken refuge there. We are prepared as well to deploy a U.S. military medical unit to the border area in southern Turkey to meet emergency needs.

Refugees in Iran

The United States is also concerned about the welfare of those Iraqi refugees now fleeing to Iran. We will be communicating, through our established channel, to the Government of Iran our willingness to encourage and contribute to international organizations carrying out relief efforts aiding these individuals.

I have asked Secretary Baker to travel to Turkey, en route to the Middle East,...to assess the refugee situation and report back to me.

In an effort to help innocent people and especially the children of Iraq, we will be donating $869,000 to UNICEF for child immunizations in Iraq. We will also be providing a further $131,000 and 1,000 tons of food to the International Committee of the Red Cross (ICRC). In all cases, funds and goods provided to international organizations will be distributed by the organizations themselves to civilian in Iraq.

Finally, I have asked Secretary Baker to travel to Turkey, en route to the Middle East, to meet with President Ozal and visit the border area to assess the refugee situation and report back to me.

Remarks by Secretary Baker and Turkish Foreign Minister Alptemocin, Diyarbakir, Turkey, April 8, 1991 [13]

Foreign Minister Alptemocin. We've just come back from the border area where we observed with Secretary Baker the tragedy inflicted by Iraq on its own people. What we are seeing is inhuman and totally unacceptable. It is a challenge that defies the international community to stand together and act effectively. That is what Turkey and the United States are doing.

We have decided to issue a joint statement with Secretary Baker. It reflects our impressions of the situation which continues to worsen. It reflects our position and our resolve to do everything in our power to contribute first, to the alleviation and, then, to the solution of this massive human tragedy. It also confirms our appeal to the world to join in efforts to ensure the safe return of the Iraqi people amassed on our borders to their hometowns without fearing further repression by Saddam Hussein. The civilized world is duty bound not to permit the Iraqi regime to get away with what it is doing to its own civilian people and the threat that it constitutes for peace, security, and stability in the region. Thank you.

Secretary Baker. As the Minister has just indicated, we have a written statement that will be distributed. But before that's done, let me simply say that today we have witnessed the suffering and despair of the Iraqi people. We have seen examples of cruelty and human anguish that really do defy description. Women and children up there are battling hunger, thirst, and the elements to escape repression in Iraq. And as you heard up there—those of you who were in the briefing—may have heard, many of those innocents [are] losing this battle. People are suffering, and, tragically, some of them are dying. Only the generosity and the humanity of the American and Turkish people, as well as the international community, stands between these souls and complete despair and complete tragedy.

President Bush, of course, has asked that I come here and see this human drama and report back first hand on the situation. I will be doing that as soon as I can reach him by telephone.

Our relief efforts, including air drops of supplies, have begun, but they alone are not going to be enough. We cannot do this alone. We cannot do this alone with the Turkish Government. Together, we simply cannot cope with this mounting human tragedy.

So the international community, as the Minister has indicated, has to respond. And it must respond quickly and effectively. Basic supplies are going to have to arrive soon to sustain these people. And the organization and distribution that are required are going to have to be provided both in Turkey as well as in northern Iraq. Most importantly, as the Minister indicated, hope of returning home has got to be given to these people. And that means freedom from threat by the Iraqi Government and safety from further repression.

Statement by Secretary Baker and Turkish Foreign Minister Alptemocin, Diyarbakir, Turkey, April 8, 1991 [14]

We have just returned from a tour of areas where we witnessed the great tragedy suffered by the Iraqi people, most of whom are women and children who have been forcibly uprooted from their homes and villages. The dimensions of this tragedy require the urgent and generous compassion and contribution of the international community. It is with the aim of bringing this situation to the attention of the world that we decided to issue the present statement.

Once again, the brutality and folly of the Iraqi regime has created yet another gruesome tragedy: hundreds of thousands of refugees and many deaths among Iraqi citizens who sought only their democratic rights. The Saddam regime has not contented itself with more repression but has acted with excessive force, driving its own citizens out of their own land.

And, once again, the world is reacting swiftly and with determination to counter Saddam's indecent use of force. On Friday [April 5], the Security Council, acting at Turkish and French request, condemned Iraq in Resolution 688 and called for a large program of international relief. The international community has once again closed ranks in insisting that Iraq end its repression and allow immediate and unimpeded access by international organizations to all in need of aid throughout the country.

Turkey and the United States will cooperate closely to give effect to this resolution. We do not propose armed intervention in a civil war, but we will not tolerate any interference of our humanitarian relief efforts.

Support for Relief Efforts

From the initial stages of the arrival in areas on both sides of the Turkish-Iraqi border of the cold and hungry men, women, and children, Turkey has offered generous humanitarian aid in the form of food, shelter, and medical care within the limits of her capabilities. These capabilities obviously cannot match the vast dimensions and requirements of the situation. To raise the large sums that are needed, the United States is working closely with the EC [European Community] and others and with the U.N. Secretary General. So far—in the last few days—$67 million has been pledged to support relief efforts in Turkey and elsewhere.

We do not propose armed intervention in a civil war, but we will not tolerate any interference of our humanitarian relief efforts.

In addition, working with Turkey, the United States is now moving quickly to provide tents, food, medicine, and other supplies by a dramatic airdrop to groups inside Iraq. Turkey will also cooperate with a relief effort by international organizations to supply food along and across its borders into Iraq—where the greatest and most vulnerable population of displaced persons is located.

Turkey and the United States agree that the goal of relief efforts should be to enable these people to return to their homes. The plight of these refugees creates—as the Security Council Resolution says—a threat to international peace and security and has thus become another important issue in the full implementation of the cease-fire resolution.

British Prime Minister John Major's Press Conference After Meeting of European Council, Luxembourg, April 8, 1991 (Opening Statement) [15]

This meeting of the European Council was planned some time ago at the request of [French] President Mitterand. What has become apparent in the last week or so has been that the need—it has become urgent as the events have unfolded in Iraq in front of all of us on television and elsewhere. I wrote last week to Prime Minister Santer asking him to put the plight of the refugees in Iraq at the top of our agenda for today's meeting. He did so and I would like to record my gratitude to him for his action in that respect.

This afternoon we have seen a meeting that has been characterized amongst all those who spoke at it by real anger at what has been happening in Iraq in recent days, not only real anger but an agreement on practical action to relieve the suffering of the refugees and a determination to stop the blood-letting that has been going on.

Four Point Action Plan

At Prime Minister Santer's invitation I spoke at the beginning of the meeting at which point I put forward an action plan of four main points that are intended to build on Security Council Resolutions 687 and 688.

The **first** of those was that we should agree today to a generous Community contribution to the international appeal which has also been launched today by the Secretary-General of the United Nations. Britain has taken the lead last week in pledging 20 million pounds sterling (approximately $35.4M) to the relief fund. The Community today as a whole will now contribute on a level which matches that sum, a total of 150 million ECU (approximately $202.5M). I urged in discussion this afternoon that the money should be disbursed as quickly as possible. It is needed now and we should not get bogged down in budgetary procedures. I am confident in the light of discussion that the money will be made available speedily and will get where it is most needed within a matter of days.

One of the most frightening things about Iraq under [Saddam Hussein's] leadership has been the ability of a tin pot dictator to acquire high technology weapons as well as conventional weapons on a truly massive scale.

The Royal Air Force have been dropping supplies into Iraq today. That air drop will continue for as long as is necessary. But although it is valuable and worthwhile it is not in itself a substitute for organized relief on the ground.

The **second** suggestion was to propose the establishment of a safe haven in northern Iraq under United Nations control where refugees, particularly Kurds, although there would be some of course who would not necessarily be Kurds, would be safe from attack and able to receive relief supplies in a regular and in an orderly way.

Thirdly, I said that sanctions must remain in force until Saddam Hussein's offer of an amnesty is made permanent and the persecution of the Iraqi Kurds ceases.

Fourthly, I proposed to colleagues a total arms embargo must be maintained on Saddam Hussein's Iraq for as long as he remains in power. One of the most frightening things about Iraq under his leadership has been the ability of a tin pot dictator to acquire high technology weapons as well as conventional weapons on a truly massive scale. As a result of this I proposed a register of arms sales at the United Nations to monitor and control the scale of arms buildup in any one country. This is a vexed and difficult issue and it is one in the past where honest feeling has not always applied, but with all the means open to us I believe it would be possible to get an early warning of a country that was building up an offensive rather than a defensive capacity in military weapons and then put ourselves in a position where the international community could do something about it.

I wanted to put those ideas to our Community partners this afternoon and we put them in parallel to our American partners as well also this afternoon. At the same time I instructed our Ambassadors in the capitals of the five Permanent Members of the Security Council to discuss them with those Governments. I also instructed our Ambassador at the United Nations to put my proposals to the Secretary-General and to discuss them with the Permanent Five in New York. This action is underway as we speak.

I am glad to say that in this afternoon's meeting all of those four points were agreed. We then went on to discuss other issues including longer term support for stability in the Middle East and the lessons for European policy that we need to learn from the Gulf war. We have shown that we have learned one lesson very clearly. When faced with a human tragedy of appalling dimensions we need a response that is swift, generous, and determined. I believe the Community have agreed precisely that this afternoon.

U.N. Security Council Resolution 689, April 9, 1991 [2]

The Security Council,

Recalling its resolution 687 (1991),
Acting under Chapter VII of the Charter of the United Nations,
1. Approves the report of the Secretary-General on the implementation of paragraph 5 of Security Council resolution 687 (1991) contained in document S/22454 and Add. 1-3 of 5 and 9 April 1991, respectively;
2. Notes that the decision to set up the observer unit was taken in paragraph 5 of resolution 687 (1991) and can only be terminated by a decision of the Council; the Council shall therefore review the question of termination or continuation every six months;
3. Decides that the modalities for the initial six month period of the United Nations Iraq-Kuwait Observation Mission shall be in accordance with the above-mentioned report and shall also be reviewed every six months.

...[W]e are dealing here with an extraordinarily intractable problem of very, very long standing.

Secretary Baker Comments on His Second Trip to the Middle East Since the Gulf War, Damascus, April 12, 1991 [16]

Q. Mr. Baker, how different is your trip, this one, from the last one?...
A. ...I have said at earlier stops on this trip that I believe there has been some progress made, but that we are dealing here with an extraordinarily intractable problem of very, very long standing. And we're not going to solve it with one trip, or even two trips, overnight. We're just not going to. We're only going to solve it provided there is genuine desire on the part of all the parties to the conflict for true reconciliation and provided we really keep laboring and working at it and pushing

the envelope. And that's what we intend to try and do.

I've said I think there's an opportunity here. I have said, and I think all will agree, nobody can impose peace in the Middle East. But perhaps we can serve, to some extent, as a catalyst. And that's what we want to do. And I appreciate the statement that the Minister [Syrian Foreign Minister Al Shara] just made just then. Because I felt that there was a genuine desire to move forward. There are still some questions that have to be resolved. There are questions that have been posed to me. And there are questions which I have posed at each and every one of these stops on this trip. And, therefore, the name of the game now is to keep working on these issues, and pushing them, and seeing if we can contribute to bringing the parties together. That's what we intend to do.

Remarks by Prince Sadruddin Aga Khan, U.N. High Commissioner for Refugees, After Meeting with Secretary Baker, Geneva, April 12, 1991 (Excerpt) [17]

Well, Mr. Secretary, I'd like to thank you, on behalf of all my colleagues here in Geneva, for giving us so much of your time, and for listening to the point of view of the U.N. agencies as we face this monumental human tragedy. I think you have identified the problems, the suffering. You were there. Many of us are going to the area in the coming days and weeks, and I think we will share your assessment.

We now need the support of the international community as a whole. We cannot achieve lasting solutions without the help of many donor countries. And I think the High Commissioner for Refugees, which will play a leading role in this operation, is looking for the opportunity of creating incentives for people to go home.

There is no better solution than voluntary repatriation. It's easier to open camps that to close them. And what we have to do is to look down the road, make sure that people are being helped now, that they don't die of hunger and exposure, that women and children can survive on both sides of the border—all the vulnerable groups—

but then look for lasting solutions. I think the talks today will help us to chart the way. And with your support and the support of so many major donor countries, the United Nations will certainly, in the coming days, do everything it can to go toward a solution of this disastrous, monumental human tragedy.

President's Press Conference, April 16, 1991 (Excerpts) [18]

Eleven days ago, on April 5th, I announced that the United States would initiate what soon became the largest U.S. relief effort mounted in modern military history. Such an undertaking was made necessary by the terrible human tragedy unfolding in and around Iraq as a result of Saddam Hussein's brutal treatment of Iraqi citizens.

Within 48 hours, our operation was providing scores of tons of food, water, coats, tents, blankets, and medicines to the Iraqi Kurds in northern Iraq and southern Turkey. The scale of this effort is truly unprecedented. Yet the fact remains that the scale of the problem is even greater. Hundreds of thousands of Iraqi Kurds are in difficult to reach mountain areas in southern Turkey and along the Turkish-Iraq border.

The Government of Turkey, along with U.S., British, and French military units, and numerous international organizations, have launched a massive relief operation. But despite these efforts, hunger, malnutrition, disease, and exposure are taking their grim toll. No one can see the pictures or hear the accounts of this human suffering— men, women, and most painfully of all, innocent children—and not be deeply moved.

It is for this reason that this afternoon following consultations with [British] Prime Minister Major, [French] President Mitterrand, President Ozal of Turkey, [German] Chancellor Kohl this morning, U.N. Secretary-General Perez de Cuellar, I'm announcing a greatly expanded and more ambitious relief effort. The approach is quite simple: If we cannot get adequate food, medicine, clothing, and shelter to the Kurds living in the mountains along the Turkish-Iraq border, we must encourage the Kurds to move to

areas in northern Iraq where the geography facilitates rather than frustrates such a large scale relief effort.

Consistent with United Nations Security Council Resolution 688 and working closely with the United Nations and other international relief organizations and our European partners, I have directed the U.S. military to begin immediately to establish several encampments in northern Iraq where relief supplies for these refugees will be made available in large quantities and distributed in an orderly way.

I have directed the U.S. military to begin immediately to establish several encampments in northern Iraq...

I can well appreciate that many Kurds have good reason to fear for their safety if they return to Iraq. And let me reassure them that adequate security will be provided at these temporary sites by U.S., British, and French air and ground forces, again consistent with United Nations Security Council Resolution 688. We are hopeful that others in the coalition will join this effort.

I want to underscore that all that we are doing is motivated by humanitarian concerns. We continue to expect the Government of Iraq not to interfere in any way with this latest relief effort. The prohibition against Iraqi fixed or rotary wing aircraft flying north of the 36th parallel thus remains in effect.

And I want to stress that this new effort, despite its scale and scope, is not intended as a permanent solution to the plight of the Iraqi Kurds. To the contrary, it is an interim measure designed to meet an immediate, penetrating humanitarian need. Our long term objective remains the same: for Iraqi Kurds and, indeed, for all Iraqi refugees, wherever they are, to return home and to live in peace, free from repression, free to live their lives.

I also want to point out that we're acutely concerned about the problem of the Iraqi refugees now along the Iran-Iraq border and in Iran. I commend the members of the European Community for their efforts to alleviate

hardship in this area. We, ourselves, have offered to contribute to international efforts designed to meet this humanitarian challenge.

As I stated earlier, the relief effort being announced here today constitutes an undertaking different in scale and approach. What is not different is basic policy. All along, I have said that the United States is not going to intervene militarily in Iraq's internal affairs and risk being drawn into a Vietnam-style quagmire. This remains the case. Nor will we become an occupying power with U.S. troops patrolling the streets of Baghdad.

We intend to turn over the administration of and security for these sites as soon as possible to the United Nations, just as we are fulfilling our commitment to withdraw our troops and hand over responsibility to U.N. forces along Iraq's southern border, the border with Kuwait.

But we must do everything in our power to save innocent life. This is the American tradition, and we will continue to live up to that tradition.

Q. Mr. President, your administration estimates that up to 1,000 Kurds are dying each day. How do you respond to critics who say that you've acted too little, too late, and that you've turned your backs on the very people that you inspired to rise up against Saddam Hussein?

A. I don't think we have responded too little, too late. It is an extraordinarily difficult logistical problem. And we have been, as I said in my statement, sending lots of humanitarian relief in there—not just the United States, incidentally, other countries as well, a lot of private relief organizations helping out. So, this has been our policy. But I think we have a better chance to facilitate the relief and to get the Kurds in more sanitary conditions by this new program I've announced here today. There's been an awful lot of consultation with the Turks and others going into this. And in terms of the other, I simply don't accept that.

Q. How long do you think that it will be before the United Nations forces can take over from the U.S. and other allies?

A. You mean in this new operation? We don't know that. We don't know that, but clearly the sooner the better. The United Nations forces will be coming down into the south—the Blue Helmets. And we hope and expect that to be accomplished in a very few days. But this one we're just starting, but we'll have to see what we do. And it may require for a U.N. peacekeeping force in there or U.N. Blue Helmets—a new resolution from the Security Council. And that's a complicated problem, given the fact that some of the members who were steadfastly with us in the coalition might have problems with something of this nature.

Were Kurds and Shiites Misled?

Q. Mr. President, you keep absolving yourself of any responsibility, and yet time after time you are on the record of calling on the Iraqis to take the matter in their own hands, and you never said, not you the Kurds, not you the Shiites. So, how can you really continue to justify that in your own mind when the world's conscience—go ahead.

The President. No, go ahead, finish your question.

Q. Well, the world's conscience has been aroused by this, and we are seeing pictures of this terrible suffering.

The President. Well, I think all Americans—yes—

Q. Obviously, you were taken by surprise, and you have no long term policy for what is going to happen eventually. Will they be refugees for the rest of their lives?

A. I hope not. We've got enough— what looks like permanent refugees, and we're trying to do something about that in various areas. The objectives were set out very early on. And the objectives never included going into Baghdad, never included the demise and destruction of Saddam personally. You had many people that were telling me early on, let sanctions work. Let sanctions work. Don't do anything about the aggression at all. We led an international coalition of unprecedented, historic proportions and achieved objectives.

And you're asking me if I foresaw the size of the Kurdish refugee problem? The answer is: No, I did not. But do I think that the United States should bear guilt because of suggesting that the Iraqi people take matters into their own hands, with the implication being given by some that the United States would be there to support them militarily? That was not true. We never implied that. Do I think the answer is now for Saddam Hussein to be kicked out? Absolutely. Because there will not be—

Q. Is he —-

A. May I finish, please? There will not be normalized relations with the United States—and I think this is true for most coalition partners—until Saddam Hussein is out of there. And we will continue the economic sanctions.

Q. Do you concede you encouraged the revolt and the exodus?

A. I don't concede encouraging an exodus. I did suggest—and it's well documented—what I thought would be good is if the Iraqi people would take matters into their own hands and kick Saddam Hussein out. I still feel that way, and I still hope they do.

*   *   *

Duration of Commitment

Q. You said before that you didn't like the idea of a protected enclave within Iraq itself. But doesn't this, in effect, establish for months and the foreseeable future the United States military protecting Kurdish refugees in that area? And do you want to continue to leave it ambiguous what the U.S. would do in case there is any effort by the Iraqis against the Kurdish refugees?

A. I hope we're not talking about a long term effort. We're working with the French, who've taken a leadership role in a policy to encourage the Kurds to return to the cities. There's some talk about trying to get a U.N. presence along these various way stations as they go back. That would be a very useful idea, and I told Mr. Mitterrand I supported him strongly on that.

But in this one, I don't think it has to be long term. The main thing, long term or short term, from the very beginning we've been trying to save the lives of these women and children and men, and now this is a logical next step to get it done much more sanitarily—get it done in a safe and sensible way.

And some might argue that this is an intervention into the internal affairs of Iraq. But I think the humanitarian concern, the refugee concern is so overwhelming that there will be a lot of understanding about this.

*   *   *

Q. Mr. President, you haven't mentioned anything about the situation in the south where there are thousands of Shiites who are equally concerned about what happens when Americans withdraw.

The President. Exactly.

Q. Can we offer the same kind of assurances that they won't be attacked?

A. The United Nations will be in there soon, and we think that will be very good assurance that they will not be attacked. People forget that the United States has been doing a wonderful job for those refugees for a long time. I've seen no credit given to our troops that are handling that with great concern and compassion. They have done a superb job. So, what we want to do is see—in that neutral zone—see the Blue Helmets come in there, and then I will continue to keep moving our people out as rapidly as possible. I want to bring them home.

Q. But if the U.N. forces aren't enough to deter Iraqi problems down there, is there some kind of an allied coalition commitment to those people as well?

A. I think there will be enough. I think that we're operating on the assumption that they will not be attacked with the United Nations in there. I think that would be a serious problem for Saddam Hussein if he took on the entire United Nations, having agreed to these cease-fire conditions. So, I would just stand with that.

Crisis of Refugees and Displaced Persons of Iraq

Statement by Princeton N. Lyman before the Subcommittee on Immigration and Refugee Affairs of the Senate Judiciary Committee, April 15, 1991. Mr. Lyman is Director, Bureau for Refugee Programs, Department of State. [19]

I appreciate this opportunity to address the crisis of the refugees and displaced people of Iraq. As you know, I have just returned from a trip to the region and to Geneva regarding this important and urgent issue.

Everyone here has likely seen the TV footage of the people affected and the horrors of it. From cities and villages; from all across the north and parts of the south of Iraq; Kurds, Assyrians, Chaldeans, Shias, and Sunnis; 1 million people have had to flee their homes. Many, too many by even one, have died in mountain passes shorn of support or before even making it there.

Background to the Crisis

I would note that movements of refugees and displaced persons during the Persian Gulf crisis can be divided into three stages:

- From August 2, the date of the invasion, through mid-January 1991;

- The armed conflict, January 17-February 28; and

- Post-war.

From August to mid-October, more than 1 million people of numerous nationalities fled Iraq and Kuwait into the neighboring states of Jordan, Syria, Turkey, Iran, and Saudi Arabia. Except for the Kuwaitis, who fled to Saudi Arabia and other Gulf states, these people were overwhelmingly third-country nationals. With the aid of the international community or their own governments, it was possible to repatriate these expatriate workers in Iraq and Kuwait out of the region and to their home countries.

The international community organized rapidly to provide humanitarian relief to this sudden and large flow of people. There were no confirmed reports of death due to starvation or disease. Food and water supplies as well as sanitation and health care in the camps were adequate. Finally, the international effort to repatriate the displaced persons, directed by the International Organization for Migration, went very, very well. By mid-October, the flow of displaced persons from Iraq and Kuwait slowed to a trickle, and the burden on the neighboring states and the international community subsided. The international community provided nearly $300 million for the operation.

From October to January, as the potential for hostilities increased, the international community began to plan for a second large migration of refugees and displaced persons. Under the coordination of the United Nations Disaster Relief Organization (UNDRO), the U.N. developed a Regional Action Plan to move adequate supplies into the area, upgrade and expand camp sites, and provide a management system in Jordan, Syria, Turkey, and Iran. The International Committee of the Red Cross (ICRC), which had played an important role in the previous assistance activities, also

drafted an operational plan. Both UNDRO and ICRC issued funding appeals—for $175 million and $112 million, respectively—predicated on 400,000 refugees. Donors pledged about $136 million to both appeals. The United States provided $7.6 million in cash and food aid.

Migration from Iraq and Kuwait following January 16 was extremely low, which is why the appeals were not fully funded. By the end of March, only about 65,000 people had fled to the neighboring states, most of them (about 45,000) to Iran. Iraq's closure of its border with Turkey, coalition air activity against Scud and other military sites in western Iraq, and the concentration of ground combat to the south all served to limit the migration.

Although some relief infrastructure was, thus, already in place in Turkey and Iran, and more was planned, no one foresaw the magnitude of the civil conflict which caused the latest massive migration of Kurds and other Iraqi civilians.

In addressing the current crisis, I would like to focus on three particular facets of this situation that bear upon how we respond: the magnitude of the problem, the rapidity of the buildup, and the difficulties in reaching these people.

Magnitude. Today, there are more than 1.4 million people who have crossed into Iran and the Turkey border region, and many more displaced from their homes who are fleeing to the border areas. About 1 million of the above have fled to Iran and 500,000-700,000 are just across the border. There are some 400,000 people on the Turkey-Iraq border and perhaps 300,000 more approaching it. The U.N. places the number of displaced who may need urgent assistance at 1.5 million, but that is only what has been clearly identified so far. Witnesses report empty cities in northern Iraq, suggesting perhaps half or more of northern Iraq's population of 3-5 million may be in flight.

In the south, there are some 27,000 people getting assistance from U.S. forces. Although the numbers here are smaller, there are special problems of protection that I will discuss below.

Rapidity of the buildup. It is not just the numbers but the rapidity of the build-up with which this crisis has unfolded that has made it so enormous. A month after the hostilities ended, February 28, there were no more than

50,000 refugees in surrounding countries. Just two weeks before April 8, the day Secretary Baker looked out on 40,000 refugees at Cukurca, Turkey, a U.N. team had surveyed the same spot and found no one there. Since Secretary Baker's visit, one week ago, the number at Cukurca may have doubled. The numbers are mounting so fast that estimates change daily if not by the hour. Perhaps 20,000 persons enter the Turkey-Iraq border area every day. In Iran, the number of refugees went from 300,000 to 700,000 in five days and to 900,000 three days later. Preparations by the U.N. as far back as January, to receive even as many as 400,000 refugees in the entire region, were swamped by this explosion of human need. A U.N. appeal issued on April 6 had to be revised dramatically upward April 9, and already it is out of date.

Difficulties. It is not uncommon for refugees to flee into areas bereft of support, areas without good land, water, roads. Refugees cannot choose. In many cases, they are fleeing for their lives. But in this instance, the problems posed are especially difficult. The border areas of Turkey and Iraq are mountainous; the weather is cold; snow and rain are still falling. Few of the areas of concentration are reachable by roads. People are not in camps but stretched out along a line 165 miles long. This is, in short, a logistics nightmare. In Iran, the conditions are only somewhat better, but the numbers are even greater.

Mounting a sufficient relief effort in these conditions takes tremendous resources and—unfortunately—time. There can be shortcuts, such as air drops, and others I will mention below. But to establish a sustained and steady pipeline of the most basic human services for the number of people in this region—food, shelter, water, minimum health care—demands a logistics effort of enormous scope. This is what the world is rushing to provide.

A major turning point in addressing this crisis was the passage of U.N. Security Council Resolution 688 on April 5. This resolution condemns Saddam's oppression of the civilian population as a threat to international peace and security in the region. It insists that Iraq allow immediate access by international humanitarian organizations to "all those in need of assistance in all parts of Iraq."

It requests the Secretary-General to pursue humanitarian efforts in Iraq, to use all relevant U.N. agencies to address the critical needs of the refugees and displaced, and to report on the plight of all those, especially the Kurds, suffering from the repression. The resolution appeals to all member states and humanitarian organizations to contribute to the relief efforts. Finally, UNSC [Resolution] 688 demands that Iraq cooperate with the Secretary-General to these ends.

This resolution gives exceptional scope as well as urgency to the U.N. humanitarian effort both within Iraq's borders and for the refugees. The Secretary-General has appointed Prince Sadruddin Aga Khan as his Executive Delegate [for Humanitarian Assistance for Iraqi Refugees] to oversee the humanitarian programs for Iraq, Kuwait, and border areas. Prince Sadruddin has designated UNHCR [Office of the U.N. High Commissioner for Refugees] as the lead agency. The Secretary-General also has designated Ambassador [Eric] Suy to assess the plight of the repressed and displaced. Donor nations are already providing assistance at increasingly significant levels, in direct response to UNSC [Resolution] 688, requests of the United Nations for assistance, our own approaches to donor governments. It is in this context that I would like to turn to the efforts underway in each theater.

Turkey-Iraq border. I will start with Turkey from which I have just returned following Secretary Baker's visit. As I mentioned, there are more than 400,000 people now in this region and more arriving every day. They are stretched along a border 165 miles long, in perhaps 10-16 concentrations. They are on both sides of the border: in some cases, the border is irrelevant as concentrations spread over both sides.

The Government of Turkey has not distinguished between those on either side of the border in this region. Assistance and protection are being provided to all. The Turkish Red Crescent Society, a highly proficient organization, is devoting much of its personnel and resources to this effort and is serving as a principal channel for assistance from many parts of the world. The regional governor is diverting resources from the Turkish population in his area of responsibility to the needs of refugees. Roadbuilding crews are working through the dark of night to open up relief routes. Turkish villagers and citizens from all over the

country are donating food, clothing, and other items for the refugees.

But there is no way the Government and people of Turkey could manage this crisis alone. A massive international effort is underway. Because of the urgency and magnitude of the crisis, a two-pronged strategy is being employed.

●A massive effort by the U.S. military is underway at this very moment to save the lives of up to 700,000 people in this region for the next 30 days. This operation involves more than 40 C-130s, close to 60 helicopters, 75-100 small tactical vehicles, a civil affairs battalion, two medical holding companies, a Seabees construction battalion, and massive amounts of food, tents, blankets, and medical supplies. Air drops began over one week ago. But the present effort will deliver supplies much more efficiently, directly to sites, first by helicopter and as soon as possible by ground transport.

●Other donors are joining in this effort. Australia, Austria, Denmark, Germany, Italy, Japan, New Zealand, Spain, and the EC [European Community] are all participating with planes and helicopters as well as supplies. An international task force coordinates this effort, just as it did during Desert Storm. This past weekend, supplies from this operation began arriving at Uludere, one of the worst sites in the region. Visited last Wednesday by our Ambassador, Mort Abramowitz, together with Governor Kozakcioglu, Uludere contains 80,000 people mired in rain and mud with virtually no shelter or sources of support.

●Private agencies such as *Medecins Sans Frontieres*, Save the Children, the International Rescue Committee, CARE, and others are flying in supplies and personnel as well.

The second prong is an international effort under U.N. leadership. The U.S. military and allied operation is a massive but short term effort. It is designed to save people's lives until the international relief effort, led by the U.N., is fully operational. The military effort will greatly facilitate the U.N. program, by building storage facilities, opening up roads, and stabilizing the condition of the refugees. The U.N. must take over with a fully organized pipeline of support, reaching down to the refugees, with logistics, health and sanitation personnel, and with the

funds to fully support and sustain the program.

The U.N. effort, supported by donors from all over the world, is already under way. As part of earlier preparations under the U.N. Regional Plan of Action, the U.N. had food for 20,000 persons and other supplies for 100,000 when the crisis began. Those, of course, are all now depleted. Millions of dollars of additional supplies are coming in; the international staff is expanding; an information system with donors [is] being established; coordination mechanisms [are] being put in place. A USAID [U.S. Agency for International Development] Disaster Assistance Reconnaissance Team is on the ground in Turkey assisting the U.S. military and providing a technical bridge from the U.S.-led to the U.N.-led program. Finally, our embassy in Ankara has deployed teams to the field, to provide essential liaison between USAID and DOD [U.S. Department of Defense] officials and Turkish authorities.

Iran. Iran was in some ways better prepared to meet the crisis than Turkey. Its Red Crescent organization had large scale relief experience from the eight year Iran-Iraq war and from devastating earthquakes. As many as 10,000 Iranians have had disaster relief training. The buildup also began earlier there, and the U.N. and the ICRC had begun expanding supplies and personnel as the numbers grew. As noted earlier, the terrain has not been as formidable as that on the Turkish side.

Iran has now called for massive international help. It has announced readiness to receive international relief flights. The ICRC, by the end of this week, will be caring for 200,000 people in this theater, the UNHCR 100,000. More, of course, must be done urgently. Our contributions to date have been through international agencies, primarily the U.N. and the ICRC. We have asked Iran to define their needs.

Southern Iraq. The area occupied by U.S. forces poses a special problem. Some 27,000 persons have been receiving food, medical care, and other help in this area, and more have received supplies to take to other areas.

The UNHCR has accepted the responsibility for taking over assistance and protection of people in this area once U.S. forces withdraw. The ICRC also will have a presence here. The U.N. also will have an observer force patrolling a 15-kilometer wide demilitarized zone along the border. We are concerned that Iraq not violate the rights of the people in this area when U.S. forces withdraw. UNSC [Resolution] 688 demands that Iraq cooperate with the U.N. in carrying out relief and assistance programs. The U.N. presence will hopefully act as more than a witness to Iraqi behavior but as deterrence to any persecution.

The Scope of the Effort

I noted at the beginning of my testimony that there have been three stages of refugee or displaced persons movement since Iraq's invasion of Kuwait August 2 of last year. The first involved 1 million foreign workers who were repatriated to their home countries. The international community mobilized nearly $300 million for this effort. The second stage, during the hostilities January-February of this year, addressed the needs of 65,000 persons and stockpiled materiel for many more. This stage cost $136 million. Thus, even before the third, current crisis occurred, over $400 million had been spent on refugees and displaced persons in this region.

Now facing this overwhelming new wave of humanity, we are only beginning to grasp its requirements. New U.N. and Red Cross/Red Crescent appeals have been issued for $700 million, and these cover in most cases no more than three months. The costs will surely rise dramatically by year's end.

So far, in a space of two weeks, over $270 million has been pledged for this latest period, and more pledges are coming in constantly. The U.S. contribution to the above is over $53 million and growing. Over $28 million of this total has been contributed in food aid, OFDA [Office of U.S. Foreign Disaster Assistance] assistance, and drawdowns from the Emergency Refugee and Migration Assistance fund. U.S. military assistance to the effort for the refugees from northern and southern Iraq, including operational costs of the massive relief effort, is estimated to be in excess of $26 million and, further, is expected to increase substantially over the next 30 days.

Perhaps one of the most acute shortages is relief management and logistics expertise. The international community was providing protection and assistance to 15 million refugees worldwide when this crisis erupted. The U.N., NGOs [non-governmental organizations], and other repositories of such skills were already heavily engaged. Now we need many more such people.

Problems. Even as this major effort gets underway, three special problems will complicate further our task. In the current circumstances, the Turkish Government has readily acknowledged the need for international assistance and has asked the U.N. to organize the relief effort that will succeed current U.S. activities. Problems remain on both the Turkish and U.N. sides, however, especially in deploying international relief workers into the region and to refugee concentration points. But we are hopeful they will soon be overcome.

Obstacles to repatriation. Everyone agrees that the desired outcome of this situation is for these people to be able to return home voluntarily. Maintaining them on the border for any long period of time conjures up visions of another Gaza Strip. Yet, what is required for people who fled a killer regime to be able to return home safely? One step is to establish a U.N. and ICRC presence not only to where people have moved but also in the areas from which people fled, under the authority of UNSC [Resolution] 688. Coupled with humanitarian assistance from these organizations, it is hoped that this will enable people to return home safely. We are at the very beginning of this process, and it is too early to know exactly how it will unfold. It goes beyond the concept of an "enclave." It aims at providing an international humanitarian presence and relief wherever needed in the country, so that people can stay as close to, and eventually return, home. We have added to our earlier warning to Iraq that it is not to take any actions which interfere with relief activities in any part of the country.

This crisis has attracted world attention and rightfully world sympathy. Unfortunately, it comes at the same time as other less publicized crises also demanding our attention. Civil unrest in Somalia has uprooted 350,000 people into Ethiopia whose condition is perilous. The number of Liberian refugees has grown beyond the expectations and budget of UNHCR. A drought in Sudan threatens famine of massive proportions. These crises also demand our attention and our resources. Both in money and personnel, international humanitarian responses and capability—and, indeed, attention—will be stretched thin. Yet, as much as possible, we must endeavor to respond to this emergency in Iraq without doing it at the cost of others.

Press Conference After European Economic Community Consultation with Secretary Baker, Luxembourg, April 17, 1991 (Excerpt) [20]

Luxembourg Foreign Minister Jacques Poos. We are facing a tragedy in north Iraq, which we agree is one of the greatest human tragedies of this century. This exceptional situation requires exceptional measures on the part of the international community.

Humanitarian Assistance

This is the reason why EC Commission President Jacques Delors has reported the implementation of the decisions of the informal Council of Luxembourg regarding the humanitarian assistance of the Twelve, and we have also heard a brief report of the Acting President of the WEU [Western European Union], Roland Dumas, whose organization was entrusted with the logistics of the distribution of the Community's assistance.

We have noted that the international assistance and the EC assistance is being organized presently [on site] with certain difficulties and we have asked ourselves about the advisability of the creation of a single coordinating organ. It has to do with organizing first the survival, then the protection and finally the return to their homes of the Kurdish refugees.

The Twelve and the U.S. also agree on interpreting in an extensive manner U.N. Resolution 688 regarding the protection of the security camps inside Iraq itself. Finally, the Twelve and the U.S. are in agreement on maintaining the complete isolation of Saddam Hussein's regime, maintaining sanctions as long as all the problems relating to the protection of the population and the return of democracy in Iraq are not yet resolved.

The Peace Process

Second subject: the peace process in the Middle East. As far as the new mission, the third one undertaken by Mr. Baker in Israel and the Arab countries, he can be sure of the clear and unanimous support of the Twelve for his peace efforts. One of the participants in our discussion pointed out the immense credit of the U.S. in the region. We hope that Mr. Baker will succeed in initiating the peace conference. It is important that this conference begin, because time is pressing. Each party — on the one hand the U.S., the EC and the member states on the other — maintain their fundamental position as far as the Israeli/Palestinian issue is concerned.

The Community believes that it could be useful, that it can contribute to the success of the peace process. This is why it believes it should be associated with it. Peace once restored, the Community can contribute to the development of the entire region by providing its enormous resources and opening its huge market.

* * *

Q. Mr. Secretary, John Palmer, the Guardian. I wonder whether or not I could ask you whether you were able to give any assurances to your European colleagues that you'll be able to pursuade Israel to accept the Community as a full participant and not merely an observer in the proposed regional peace conference? Secondly, whether you have any further observations to make about the practicality of the Community's call for President Saddam Hussein [to] be brought to international trial?

Secretary Baker. I'll be glad to comment on both of those. Let me take the first one and say that it has been our view from the beginning of this process that it would be better if it were inclusive, rather than if it were exclusive. We are not particularly interested in participating in a process that seeks to exclude. At the same time, we are interested in seeking to create and establish—and contribute to the creation and establishment—of a process that has some reasonable chance of success, and that has some reasonable chance of being begun in the first place.

So, I think my colleagues know of the view of the United States on this question. We would like to see the process be one of inclusion rather than exclusion. I agree with my colleague Jacques Poos here when he says that the Community should be associated. I think they should be as well. And I would expect to continue to explore that subject in my discussions in Jerusalem in the forthcoming days.

Proposal for War Crimes Trial

Now, with respect to the question of war crimes, let me comment on that. Iraq is a signatory to the Third and Fourth Geneva Conventions, as well as to the Genocide Convention, and it is certainly liable for any violations of those conventions. Therefore, on moral grounds and substantively and legally, we completely agree with the suggestion that has been made and the recommendation that the Twelve have embraced with respect to this issue.

The Community believes that it could be useful, that it can contribute to the success of the peace process. This is why it believes it should be associated with it.

Having said that, I do think it is important that we at least think through the issue of a trial in absentia with some degree of caution, because this could result in an international tribunal with no one to prosecute. The United States has indicated that it is not prepared to take military steps to obtain custody of Saddam Hussein or any of the other members of the Iraqi leadership. Some individuals who, according to the evidence, might be charged with war crimes, I understand are presently in the custody of Kuwait and/or Saudi Arabia. It may be that these countries—countries of the region—might be best equipped to take the lead in any endeavor such as this.

There's one other consideration that I think ought to be kept in mind. President Bush, I think, alluded to this last night in his press conference. That is, to the extent there is any possibility at all Saddam Hussein might desire to step aside in order to rejoin his family in some other country or to seek to avoid the consequences of his actions in that way, I think at the very least we should weigh the number of lives that might be saved if he were to leave Iraq and to leave the leadership of that Government.

Every day that he hangs on as leader of the Iraqi Government more Iraqis will die. So we support the call of the Community for this type of action on a moral basis 100 percent. We support it substantively. But we do think it is worthwhile at least considering the possible consequences of a trial in absentia, and the possibility that there might be a way to rid the Iraqi people—and indeed the world—of this brutal tyrant through other means.

Not Intervention in Civil War

Q. In the north of Iraq today, a number of Kurdish fighters have told our reporters there that they feel the United States has sided with their cause by creating guarded enclaves where their women and children can be safe. They feel that this is a call for them to rearm and attack Iraq. Could you speak to that?

A. Well, it's just as I said it was, which is an effort to save lives. It is strictly a humanitarian effort. It is not a conscious intervention in a civil war in Iraq. It is intended as a temporary relief measure until such time as the international agencies—the United Nations and others—can achieve a presence there on the ground and take over these relief centers and administer them and provide adequate security for the innocent civilians that will be using these relief centers.

Excerpts from Secretary Baker's Press Conferences in the Middle East, April 20-24, 1991

WITH KING HUSSEIN OF JORDAN, AQABA, APRIL 20, 1991 [21]

King Hussein. Ladies and gentlemen, I would like to say how pleased I have been, together with my colleagues, to welcome in Jordan Secretary Baker on this visit and I believe, although the time has been short, we have covered much ground. And I believe that this is a milestone in terms of relations between our two countries that have grown and developed over many, many years, suffered greatly in recent times, but this is a relationship based on mutual respect, a friendship and a commitment towards a better future for people in this region in the world and to safeguard our mutual interests.

I am very happy with the Secretary's visit and with our talks, and we hope that this offers us the opportunity to begin again intensive, frank, constructive dialogue that is so needed in the times ahead.

We particularly view the fact that the United States President Bush, my old friend, and the Secretary are so involved in the problems of the area, particularly the Arab/Israeli problem, Palestinian/Israeli problem, as extremely encouraging.

Needless to say, we will always be committed to the cause of peace, a just and lasting peace, in this region and we hope that it won't be long before we see some real progress towards achieving this goal which is so dear to all of us. Thank you very, very much.

Secretary Baker. Thank you very much, your Majesty. First of all, let me thank you for your superb hospitality in receiving me and my delegation here at your home in Jordan on my first ever visit to Jordan. I, too, your Majesty, am very pleased with the talks that we conducted. I think that they were very productive and very useful and I, too, would like to see a strengthening of the relationship between the United States and Jordan which has, indeed, suffered in the recent past.

We had occasion, ladies and gentlemen, to have a very full discussion of the talks which I have had with Palestinians in the territories respecting the peace process, respecting the Israeli/Palestinian problem, and respecting the Arab/Israeli conflict in general. We also had an opportunity to discuss the bilateral relationship, the pluses as well as the minuses, and discussed ways in which we can, in the future, strengthen that relationship in an effort to try and bring it back to the status which it enjoyed in the past.

Again, your Majesty, thank you very much for your gracious hospitality. It's a pleasure to be here with you.

Q. King Hussein, your Majesty, if I may, a few years ago, you said —you virtually backed out of the U.S. peacemaking effort. You were quoted as saying the United States is hopelessly one-sided in Israel's favor and you virtually washed your hands of the process. And, here you are, back again. What has changed, or have you changed your view of the U.S. as a mediator, or have your needs changed?

A. The needs have not changed. The needs have always been for genuine efforts to achieve peace in this region so that future generations can live with. But the (inaudible) has never changed nor has my position over the fact that the United States can contribute, if it chose to—and I believe it does sincerely more so than any in this world—towards a resolution for the problems of this region, particularly the Palestinian/Israeli and Arab/Israeli problems that have been with us.

I believe that we should move away from old cliches. We should set our sights to ensure that this window of opportunity is not lost.

It has been my dream and my hope that somehow we can see an end to this sad and tragic chapter and the beginning of hope and the beginning of peace and all the opportunities that this offers to all concerned. This will be our contribution for those who follow and nothing has changed in that regard.

*　　*　　*

Meeting with Palestinians

Q. Mr. Secretary, can you describe for us whether or not you have heard some new views from the Palestinians today when you were discussing what they are willing to do? Is there something different that you heard this morning than in past meetings?

Secretary Baker. We got into quite a bit more detail this morning than we have in the past meetings and I would refer you to their characterization of the meeting, because I don't want to put words in their mouths, but they indicated to me during the course of it that they thought it was a more extended, extensive and fruitful meeting than past meetings.

We discussed some of the problems. We talked about, just as I have talked about here today with His Majesty, the importance of breaking the taboos that have existed for so long prohibiting contact and discussion between Arabs and Israelis on the one hand and between Israelis and Palestinians on the other.

Q. Your Majesty, are you prepared at this point to declare that Jordan is ready to join a regional peace conference, sit at the table and negotiate, first in a group setting and then directly with Israel?

King Hussein. I believe that the Secretary was kind enough to refer to our talks and to refer to the question of taboos but, personally, I have never believed that in all the years that have passed that these taboos should be an impediment to making real progress towards attainment of peace. I don't know what its name will be. Will it be a peace conference? Will it be a — this is still something that the Secretary and our friends in the world are concerned with.

I believe that we should move away from old cliches. We should set our sights to ensure that this window of opportunity is not lost and when you have a situation where people, our people, have been under occupation for so many years and they have on a regular basis have had to deal with them—Israelis—and meet with Israelis, I mean, what makes one a better Arab to sort of stay out of it and say that I am Arab because I am not involved? No.

There is a lot of question of meetings, contacts and old taboos, but the question is the question of responsibility in the times ahead and I believe that if these are some of the impediments, then they should be removed. People should talk. There have been many stories and suggestions about contracts and meetings, but nobody has ever been able to say that we gave in on Palestinian rights. The Palestinian dimension has to be addressed by the Palestinian people. We will support them.

We are now talking about a possibility of a conference. If they want to go their own way, we are perfectly happy to support them. If they want to approach us to be a part of a joint delegation, then if it begins with a conference and ends with a conference, fine. We will look at that. We will have to be flexible enough, imaginative enough. There has to be a process of education regarding peace, both on the level of the Palestinians and the Israelis. Arabs and Israelis—what does peace really mean, what does it offer this region in terms of the present and in terms of the future.

So believe me, we are looking very open-mindedly at everything and we will not let, if we can, and we suggest to others not to stick to old cliches. Let us join together in terms of trying to look at the future and look at what our responsibilities are towards future generations and try to find the solutions that, as responsible people, we are here to try to find with the support of our people everywhere and the world as well.

* * *

Q. Mr. Secretary, why was the idea of an international conference dropped for a regional peace conference which (inaudible) of the U.N.?

Secretary Baker. The primary reason is because we want to develop and create a process that will work. No one can impose peace in this situation. Peace will only come if the parties are determined to make it happen. It can't be imposed by the United Nations. It can't be imposed by the Soviet Union. It can't be imposed by a collection of all of those entities, organizations, and countries and a whole lot more.

It is only going to happen if there is a true desire for reconciliation on the part of the parties involved. And the term has become a buzzword, frankly, that I would characterize falls within the definition of—His Majesty's definition—of a cliche. I am not suggesting that he would agree with that but that's the way I look at the term. It had developed into a cliche—international conference. It was anathema to Israel. It still is —the term. The term "autonomy" is a like term. That is a term that has developed a buzzword characteristic, and is anathema to Palestinians. So we don't use that term anymore, just like we don't use the term "international conference."

Q. In your discussions with the Israelis, sir, what were their answers concerning the new settlements that are now uprising in the Occupied Territories of the West Bank?

A. The answer is that the policy of the Government of Israel is well known in this regard. The answer back from the United States is, we disagree with that policy.

Q. So?

A. We see settlements as an obstacle to peace. The answer to your question—So?—is let's get a peace process going so that we can begin to take, to take some action on problems such as these. We have in force, today, a boycott against Israel. Let's get a peace process going and maybe we can do something about that. Maybe we can do something—I don't know whether we can or not—about settlements. Again, it's not something that is going to be stopped by fiat—by the United States or the United Nations or any other group of countries. So, we badly need a peace process.

King Hussein. Thank you very much.

We see settlements [in the Occupied Territories] as an obstacle to peace.

WITH EGYPTIAN FOREIGN MINISTER ABDEL MEGUID, CAIRO, APRIL 21, 1991 [22]

Foreign Minister Meguid. The peace process that the United States is actively involved in I can say, from our perspective, that it is very important. Yes, there are still issues that are to be addressed, and at the same time, there is a very strong will to find solutions to these issues. And from our part, in Egypt, we are keen in finding solutions to this issue and start the whole process.

The principle of a conference is certainly accepted by Egypt, encouraged by Egypt, and we have no problem in attending this conference to move forward achieving a just peace in the area...And I can assure you that President Mubarak is very keen on reaching a successful negotiation establishing peace between Israel and her neighbors, just as there is peace between Egypt and Israel. The peace that we are attached to, we are maintaining, and that is there to stay. Our hope is to reach the same peace concerning the solution of the Palestinian problem, putting an end to the occupation of the Arab territories and moving toward the conference. This is my introduction in which I am trying to bring to you the position of the Egyptian Government. Thank you.

Secretary Baker. Ladies and gentlemen, I would simply echo what my colleague and friend has said and I want to thank the Government of Egypt, President Mubarak, Minister Meguid for their very constructive and helpful approach to the peace process. I agree with the Minister that we have had a very fruitful and productive visit this morning with President Mubarak. Both President Mubarak and Minister Meguid, as well as other officials in the Egyptian Government, are actively helping move this process forward through diplomatic channels, through political contacts, and we are very appreciative of that.

The United States and Egypt were partners in the recent events in the Gulf and we are partners in this effort to move this peace process forward, in this effort to produce a conference which will serve as a catalyst for direct bilateral negotiations between Israel and her Arab neighbors and between Israel and Palestinians, and thereby break taboos that have existed for many years.

* * *

Q. It has been suggested that neighbors of Israel are among those who feel that the Gulf states, including Saudi Arabia, need not be at the table when this peace conference begins. What is the Government of Egypt's position on whether Saudi Arabia and the Gulf states should be at the table when the peace conference now under discussion convenes?

Minister Meguid. Well, if I can share with you our point of view [which] is that all the countries of the region are interested in the peace process—all of them. Some of them have a special status or relation with the peace process more than others, so I really cannot exclude any country from the objective of achieving peace. I am sure the Gulf states, exactly as the Arab countries neighboring Israel, as Israel itself are interested in having peace in the region. I think—I want to make that very clear and also I cannot speak in the name of any other country than myself. They are all, all of them, keen to have this peace process succeed.

SAUDI PRESS AGENCY RELEASE AFTER MEETING WITH KING FAHD, APRIL 22, 1991 (EXCERPT) [23]

Talks between the custodian of the Two Holy Mosques King Fahd Ibn Abdulaziz and U.S. Secretary of State James Baker focused on efforts undertaken to reach a just solution to the Palestinian cause, Foreign Minister Prince Saud Al-Faisal said.

In a statement following his meeting with Baker here yesterday [April 22] Prince Saud said, "It is time to put an end to the Arab-Israeli conflict, and to achieve a just and comprehensive solution to the Palestinian question." Prince Saud ... expressed the Kingdom['s] support to American efforts to achieve peace. Asked about the Kingdom['s] participation in the proposed peace conference, Prince Saud named Egypt, Syria, Jordan, Lebanon and Israel as the countries concerned with participation in the said conference.

Prince Saud said the Kingdom wants a solution to the Palestinian question, a solution that would guarantee the rights of the Palestinian people. In this context, Prince Saud said the Kingdom welcomes international efforts undertaken to solve the Palestinian question and supports peace in the region. Prince Saud welcomed [the] Baker visit to the Kingdom and praised his talks with King Fahd.

WITH SAUDI FOREIGN MINISTER SAUD, APRIL 22, 1991 (EXCERPT) [24]

Q. Foreign Minister, given what you have just said, would Saudi Arabia be prepared to sit down for direct peace talks with Israel, either in the context of a peace conference or working groups, either before the Israelis stop settlements or afterwards? Under any conditions, would Saudi Arabia be ready to enter into direct talks with Israel?

A. Minister Saud. The important thing to concentrate on — and this is the focus of the initiative by the United States, as it were, in the interest and support of this country and the other Arab countries — is to focus on ending the Palestinian problem and ending this conflict because once that issue is tackled in the conference and it is underway, that in itself would open the region for peace and stability in the region. We cannot go ahead of ourselves. We are just now beginning to talk about the peace conference and we wish that there would be (inaudible).

Q. Mr. Baker, what happened to your two-track approach?

Secretary Baker. There is still a two-track approach. We will still have, if the conference takes place, Arab na-

tions sitting down and dealing directly with Israel — face to face negotiations with respect to the problems that exist between them. In addition to that you will have — again if the conference takes place — Israelis and Palestinians at the same table. I am pleased to hear what his Royal Highness said about once the issue of the Israelis and Palestinians have been tackled, I think he said, that would open up the possibility for peace and for dealing with some of the other issues that exist.

FOLLOWING MEETING WITH THE AMIR AND CROWN PRINCE OF KUWAIT, APRIL 22, 1991 [25]

Human Rights in Kuwait

The following three paragraphs were responses to three questions recorded as "inaudible."

...(W)e talked about the importance of democraticization and the Amir made the point to me that he, in a speech, has called for elections. I asked him if there were any dates scheduled for those. He said no, but he has said that the elections would be held in 1992. He said that they had been giving consideration to granting the vote to women. He said on human rights that there were some abuses early on following liberation, that the Government was firmly committed to acting affirmatively to protect minorities in Kuwait, whether they were Palestinians or anybody else. He expressed a willingness—the Crown Prince did—a willingness to permit the international human rights agencies to come into Kuwait and interview representatives of the minority groups.

What I said was that the ability of the United States to continue to support Kuwait politically and from a security standpoint, in a manner in which we supported them against the brutal aggression of Saddam Hussein, would be enhanced if they evidenced full respect and commitment to the preservation of human rights.

I think when you consider that they would be radically transforming their political system, certainly we would not have any objection to the fact that the elections will take place in 1992. That would not be a problem, at least as I see.

Q. On the question of security, apparently some key Sabah leaders are

involved in these guerrilla groups that are going around and rounding up Palestinians. Did you get into that kind of detail?

A. I was told that those practices occurred in the aftermath of the liberation, but are no longer occurring, and haven't been occurring recently, that they have stopped, that there continues to be—I told you we talked about the national security questions involving Kuwait, but we also discussed the internal security questions. They are still making efforts to gain full control of the internal security situation in Kuwait, because when the Iraqis left, they left a lot of weapons in the hands of a lot of different people and groups, and the Kuwaiti government has not felt that it was feasible to try and forcefully relieve those people of those weapons through actions of the military or security forces, that it would be better to approach that problem from another standpoint, because the people continue to be fearful having lived through the aftermath of the Iraqi invasion.

Q. Mr. Secretary, did you discuss the secondary boycott of Israel, and whether they are going to waive that for particular American firms?

A. I'm not going to comment on that.

WITH SYRIAN FOREIGN MINISTER FAROUK AL SHARA, DAMASCUS, APRIL 24, 1991 [26]

Q. Mr. Secretary, what are the differences on the modalities between the Syrians and Israelis? Several issues, in particular: One, will the conference simply be a ceremonial opening or will it have some kind of permanent structure? Two, what will be the role of the United Nations? The Israelis want them out, the Syrians want them in. Three, whether outsiders will be involved—the Europeans and others? Can you say right now that you have either narrowed or closed those gaps in these ten hours of discussion?

A. I think I just said that we are working on these issues, I think, in a constructive way.

[Question recorded as "inaudible"]

A. Is that the way you interpret that—that working through these issues in a constructive way is a "no"?

Q. Yes.

A. Okay, you put your interpretation on it, but we are working — you know, I am not going to conduct these negotiations through the press because we want the negotiations to succeed. They are serious negotiations and it is better if we do not conduct them— as much as it might disappoint you, Bill— if we don't conduct them through you. I know it is disappointing, but of necessity, it has to be the way it is. I am sorry to say that.

But in answer to Tom's question, we are working through these issues in a constructive way. That, I would think, might connote progress. Exactly how much and whether or not you put a "yes" or a "no" on your question, that's really up to you.

Israel's Settlement Policy

Q. President Bush and yourself are working together very seriously and sincerely to bring about a Middle East peace settlement. But isn't Israel's refusing to withdraw from occupied Arab territories, refusing the United Nations, refusing the European Community participation in the conference, continuing the settlements in occupied Arab lands—what is the next step you are going to take to push forward the peace process?

A. Well, I will be going from here today to the Soviet Union to meet with the Soviet Foreign Minister on this subject, primarily on this subject, and not on the other broad range of issues that normally characterize the meetings between the Soviet Union and the United States Foreign Ministers.

Let me say—you made reference to settlements. I have to say to you that we were very disappointed to learn this morning that there is yet another—a new settlement—that has been established in the Occupied Territories, and I think that probably points up rather vividly the fact that it is easier to obstruct peace than it is to promote it, and that the establishment of these settlements certainly does not help the efforts of those of us who are interested in peace.

Q. Mr. Secretary, you said that the United States or anyone else can't impose peace—that it is only when the parties directly involved really and truly want peace themselves will these issues be solved. Can you say now, having met with each of the key players at least three times, that each of the key players in this dispute really want

to make peace and is prepared to make the kinds of concessions necessary to achieve it?

A. I can't say that yet. I can say I certainly hope so. I can say that I, having spent this time, do see evidence of a new approach and of a new willingness in the aftermath of the Gulf conflict to address these extraordinarily intractable issues in a serious and determined fashion. I certainly do see that. And let me say that if I didn't, I don't think I would still be out here.

*   *   *

Q. Mr. Foreign Minister, can you tell us if Syria is now ready to go to a peace conference, number one? And number two, if they are not, why not? What are the objections that you see to going to a peace conference?

I wouldn't call a conference where the United States of America and the Soviet Union and the Europeans and the United Nations [are present] a regional conference.

Foreign Minister Shara. Well, we in Syria have been calling for a peace conference for so many years. Of course we will attend a peace conference where the United States, the Soviet Union, the Europeans and the U.N. will be there.

Q. Do you have any other objections in terms of how the Palestinian delegation could come to a conference—to the sort of thing that Secretary Baker has been talking about? Is it only the U.N. and the Europeans; and after that is resolved, you could come?

Minister Shara. When I said that all these would be present in the peace conference, of course, all the parties directly involved in the conflict would participate as well, including the Palestinians...[W]e would have no objection to an independent Palestinian presentation. I want to clarify this point by saying that it is up to the Palestinian people to traditionally say who their representatives are in this peace conference.

Q. Is the peace conference still going to be called a regional conference?...

Minister Shara. Well, it is no longer going to be a regional conference. I wouldn't call a conference where the United States of America and the Soviet Union and the Europeans and the United Nations presence in such a conference would be called a regional conference.

Secondly, it is obvious that such a conference where its nature, its characteristics, are obviously of an international dimension. It should be obvious to everybody from now on that we will call this a peace conference.

President's Exchange with Press on Middle East, April 26, 1991 [27]

Q. Sir, has Secretary Baker made my progress in the Middle East as far as moving forward the—

A. Yes, he's made progress. I just talked to him. There's sadness in his family—his mother just passed away, so he will be coming home, stopping short of the two meetings that he had hoped to have in Israel...But he did have a meeting with Prime Minister Shamir. And I think it's fair to say that, though problems remain, I think the bottom line is there's some reason for optimism. I don't want to state why; I'm not going to go into details of it. I will get debriefed by him when he gets here. And there are still some sticky problems, but we're not going to give up. We're going to continue to try to bring peace to that troubled corner of the world.

Q. Mr. President, are you confident that the Iraqis, in fact, will keep their military out of the refugee zones?

A. Yes, they're not going to—that they don't want to tangle with the U.S. again. They—

Q. Do you think their promise is good?

A. —learned that the hard way, and the forces are there to be sure that it's good; put it that way. We're not looking for any fight. We want to help these Kurds, and we are. What the United States has done in terms of bringing relief to these pitiful people is just—we all ought to take great pride in the way our country is responding— and I might say at considerable cost. We're doing it because it's right.

But I do not want to intervene and get our troops hauled into some conflict that's going on for years. But when it comes to helping people, the United States is today doing what it's always done—being out in front of the relief effort. But I don't expect, Rita [Rita Beamish, Associated Press], any complication. I don't think Saddam Hussein is dumb enough to want to run into the U.S. troops again.

Q. What about the long term prospects?

A. This isn't a press conference.

Q. What about the long term prospects, Mr. President? What happens when the U.S. leaves, even if there's a small U.N. force there?

A. I don't know that there's going to be lasting peace in Iraq. Peace has escaped those people for years. So, I would hope, though, that the lesson having been taught to Saddam Hussein about aggression, that some of that lesson might spill over in terms of his own internal problems. I would hope that maybe out of the talks he's having with the Kurdish leaders you'll see some long sought-after peace. But I can't certify that. And I would hope that—I would hope—

Q. How long will the troops stay there?

A. They're going to stay there as long as it takes to be sure these refugees are taken care of, and not a minute longer. We're continuing to pull troops back. I want these kids home, and so do the American people want them more. P.S. We will do what's necessary to see that this refugee aid gets there so that they can have it in safety. And then beyond that, we talked yesterday to the Secretary-General and the U.N. has a major role to play here. Some of the United Nations critics ought to open their eyes, because the United Nations not only had a significant role in the repelling of aggression, which was our objective, but it is also playing a significant role in this refugee relief. So, we're going to continue on that track. I've got to—this is the last one.

"We Want Him Out of There"

Q. Do you still think that Saddam Hussein will be deposed? And what do you think—

A. I'm confident he will because there will not be normal relationships with the United States or many other countries as long as he is in power. Those sanctions are going to stay there as far as we're concerned, and undoing some evil that is not going to—by that, I mean working out something possibly with the Kurds—that's only part of the problem. And so, there will not be normal relations with this man as long as I'm President of the United States. I'll guarantee you that.

They're going to stay there as long as it takes to be sure these refugees are taken care of, and not a minute longer.

Q. Sir, he's lasted this long. What's going to put him out of power? What's it going to—

A. The fact that he's been whipped bad in the military. His aggression—he's been forced to that which he said he would never do. His people don't like him, and it's only terror that's keeping him in power. And someday history will show you these things manage to take care of themselves. And I hope it happens soon because we want him out of there.

We don't have any fight with the Iraqi people. I've said that from day one. Go back and look at the text back in August, September, October. Our fight is not with the Iraqi people. Our objective was to repel aggression, and we did it. And the American troops deserve enormous credit, and they're getting it every single day they come home. But beyond that, this internal matter has been going on for years—years and years. And I'd like to see it ended. And one good way to end it is to have somebody with a little more compassion as President of Iraq. But let them worry about that problem. I worry about it because there won't be normal relations until he's gone. But history has a way of taking care of tyrants.

---

1 Text from Weekly Compilation of Presidential Documents of March 4, 1991.

2 Text provided by United Nations Information Center, Washington.

3 Transcript of CENTCOM News Briefing, Safwan, Saudi Arabia, March 3, 1991 made available to the press by the Department of Defense.

4 Text from Weekly Compilation of Presidential Documents of March 11, 1991.

5 Department of State Document 35, March 10, 1991.

6 Department of State Document 36, March 11, 1991.

7 Department of State Document 37, March 12, 1991.

8 Department of State Document 40, March 14, 1991.

9 Text from Weekly Compilation of Presidential Documents of March 18, 1991.

10 Excerpt from opening statement before the Subcommittee on Europe and the Middle East of the House Foreign Affairs Committee, March 20, 1991. The complete transcript of the hearings will be published by the committee and will be available from the Superintendent of Documents, U.S. Government Printing Office, Washington, D.C. 20402.

11 Text from Weekly Compilation of Presidential Documents of April 8, 1991.

12 Text provided by the Turkish Embassy, Washington.

13 Department of State Document 48, April 8, 1991.

14 Department of State Dispatch, April 15, 1991.

15 British Information Services (New York) Policy Statement 16/91, April 9, 1991.

16 Excerpt from press conference with Syrian Foreign Minister Al Shara. Department of State Document 53, April 12, 1991.

17 Department of State Document 54, April 12, 1991.

18 Text from Weekly Compilation of Presidential Documents of April 22, 1991.

19 The complete transcript of the hearings will be published by the committee and will be available from the Superintendent of Documents, U.S. Government Printing Office, Washington, D.C. 20402.

20 Department of State Document 57, April 17, 1991.

21 Department of State Document 58, April 20, 1991.

22 Department of State Document 59, April 21, 1991.

23 Text (dated April 23, 1991) provided by Embassy of Saudi Arabia, Washington.

24 Department of State Document 60, April 22, 1991.

25 Department of State Document 61, April 22, 1991.

26 Department of State Document 63, April 24, 1991.

27 Text from Weekly Compilation of Presidential Documents, April 29, 1991.

The New World Order: Relations with Europe and the Soviet Union

Address by President Bush at Maxwell Air Force Base War College, Montgomery, Alabama, April 13, 1990 (opening remarks omitted). [1]

Here at Air University it's your business to read the lessons of the past with an eye on the far horizon. And that's why I wanted to speak to you today about the new world taking shape around us, about the prospects for a new world order now within our reach. For more than four decades we've lived in a world divided, East from West; a world locked in a conflict of arms and ideas called the Cold War. Two systems, two superpowers separated by mistrust and unremitting hostility.

For more than four decades, America's energies were focused on containing the threat to the free world from the forces of communism. That war is over. East Germany has vanished from the map as a separate entity. Today in Berlin, the wall that once divided a continent, divided a world in two, has been pulverized, turned into souvenirs. And the sections that remain standing are but museum pieces. The Warsaw Pact passed into the pages of history last week, not with a bang but with a whimper—its demise reported in a story reported on page A16 of the Washington Post.

In the coming weeks I'll be talking in some detail about the possibility of a new world order emerging after the Cold War. And in recent weeks I've been focusing not only on the Gulf but on free trade—on the North American Free Trade Agreement, the Uruguay Round trade negotiations, and the essentiality of obtaining from the United States Congress a renewal of Fast Track authority to achieve our goals. But today I want to discuss another aspect of that order—our relations with Europe and the Soviet Union.

The "New Order" Defined

Twice this century, a dream born on the battlefields of Europe died after the shooting stopped. The dream of a world in which major powers worked together to ensure peace; to settle their disputes through cooperation, not con-frontation. Today a transformed Europe stands closer than ever before to its free and democratic destiny. At long last, Europe is moving forward, moving toward a new world of hope.

At the same time, we and our European allies have moved beyond containment to a policy of active engagement in a world no longer driven by Cold War tensions and animosities. You see, as the Cold War drew to an end we saw the possibilities of a new order in which nations worked together to promote peace and prosperity. I'm not talking here of a blueprint that will govern the conduct of nations or some supernational structure or institution. The new world order does not mean surrendering our national sovereignty or forfeiting our interests. It really describes a responsibility imposed by our successes. It refers to new ways of working with other nations to deter aggression and to achieve stability, to achieve prosperity and, above all, to achieve peace.

The new world order really is a tool for addressing a new world of possibilities.

It springs from hopes for a world based on a shared commitment among nations large and small to a set of principles that undergird our relations: peaceful settlements of disputes, solidarity against aggression, reduced and controlled arsenals, and just treatment of all peoples.

Iraq: The First Test

This order, this ability to work together, got its first real test in the Gulf war. For the first time, a regional conflict—the aggression against Kuwait—did not serve as a proxy for superpower confrontation. For the first time, the United Nations Security Council, free from the clash of Cold War ideologies, functioned as its designers intended—a force for conflict resolution in collective security.

In the Gulf, nations from Europe and North America, Asia and Africa and the Arab world joined together to stop aggression, and sent a signal to would-be tyrants everywhere in the world. By joining forces to defend one small nation, we showed that we can work together against aggressors in defense of principle.

We also recognized that the Cold War's end didn't deliver us into an era of perpetual peace. As old threats recede, new threats emerge. The quest for the new world order is, in part, a challenge to keep the dangers of disorder at bay.

Today, thank God, Kuwait is free. But turmoil in that tormented region of the world continues. Saddam's continued savagery has placed his regime outside the international order. We will not interfere in Iraq's civil war. Iraqi people must decide their own political future.

Looking out here at you and thinking of your families, let me comment a little further. We set our objectives. These objectives, sanctioned by international law, have been achieved. I made very clear that when our objectives were obtained that our troops would be coming home. And yes, we want the suffering of those refugees to stop, and in keeping with our nation's compassion and concern, we are massively helping. But yes, I want our troops out of Iraq and back home as soon as possible.

Internal conflicts have been raging in Iraq for many years. And we're helping out, and we're going to continue to help these refugees. But I do not want one single soldier or airman shoved into a civil war in Iraq that's been going on for ages. And I'm not going to have that.

I know the coalition's historic effort destroyed Saddam's ability to undertake aggression against any neighbor. You did that job. But now the international community will further guarantee that Saddam's ability to threaten his neighbors is completely eliminated by destroying Iraq's weapons of mass destruction.

And as I just mentioned, we will continue to help the Iraqi refugees, the hundreds and thousands of victims of this man's— Saddam Hussein's— brutality. See food and shelter and safety and the opportunity to return unharmed to their homes. We will not tolerate any interference in this massive international relief effort. Iraq can return to the community of nations only when its leaders abandon the brutality and repression that is destroying their country. With Saddam in power, Iraq will remain a pariah nation, its people denied moral contacts with most of the outside world.

We must build on the successes of Desert Storm to give new shape and momentum to this new world order, to use force wisely and extend the hand of compassion wherever we can. Today we welcome Europe's willingness to shoulder a large share of this responsibility. This new sense of responsibility on the part of our European allies is most evident and most critical in Europe's eastern half.

The Challenge in Eastern Europe

The nations of Eastern Europe, for so long the other Europe, must take their place now alongside their neighbors to the west. Just as we've overcome Europe's political division, we must help to ease crossover from poverty into prosperity.

The United States will do its part— we always have—as we have already in reducing Poland's official debt burden to the United States by 70 percent, increasing our assistance this year to Eastern Europe by 50 percent. But the key to helping these new democracies develop is trade and investment.

The new entrepreneurs of Czechoslovakia and Poland and Hungary aren't looking to government, their own or others, to shower them with riches. They're looking for new opportunities, a new freedom for the productive genius strangled by forty years of state control.

Yesterday, my esteemed friend, a man we all honor and salute, President Vaclav Havel of Czechoslovakia called me up. He wanted to request advice and help from the West. He faces enormous problems. You see, Czechoslovakia wants to be democratic. This man is leading them towards perfecting their fledgling democracy. Its economy is moving from a failed socialist model

to a market economy. We all must help. It's not easy to convert state owned and operated weapons plants into market-driven plants to produce consumer goods. But these new democracies can do just exactly that with the proper advice and help from the West. It is in our interest, it is in the interest of the United States of America, that Czechoslovakia, Poland, and Hungary strengthen those fledgling democracies and strengthen their fledgling market economies.

NATO's Continued Importance

We recognize that new roles and even new institutions are natural outgrowths of the new Europe. Whether it's the European Community or a broadened mandate for the CSCE [Conference on Security and Cooperation in Europe], the U.S. supports all efforts to forge a European approach to common challenges on the Continent and in the world beyond, with the understanding that Europe's long term security is intertwined with America's and that NATO—NATO remains the best means to assure it.

America's policy toward the Soviet Union in these troubled times is, first and foremost, to continue our efforts to build the cooperative relationship...

And we look to Europe to act as a force for stability outside its own borders. In a world as interdependent as ours, no industrialized nation can maintain membership in good standing in the global community without assuming its fair share of responsibility for peace and security.

But even in the face of such welcome change, Americans will remain in Europe in support of history's most successful alliance, NATO. America's commitment is the best guarantee of a secure Europe, and a secure Europe is vital to American interests and vital to world peace. This is the essential logic of the Atlantic alliance which anchors America in Europe.

This century's history shows that America's destiny and interests cannot be separate from Europe's. Through

the long years of Cold War and conflict, the United States stood fast for freedom in Europe. And now, as Eastern Europe is opening up to democratic ideals, true progress becomes possible.

The Soviet Union

The Soviet Union is engaged in its own dramatic transformation. The policies of confrontation abroad, like the discredited dogma of communism from which those policies sprang, lies dormant, if not mortally wounded. Much has changed. The path of international cooperation fostered by President Gorbachev and manifested most clearly in the Persian Gulf marks a radical change in Soviet behavior. And yet, the course of change within the Soviet Union is far less clear.

Economic and political reform there is under severe challenge. Soviet citizens, facing the collapse of the old order while the new still struggles to be born, confront desperate economic conditions—their hard-won freedoms in peril. Ancient ethnic enmities, conflict between republics and between republics and the central government add to these monumental challenges that they face.

America's policy toward the Soviet Union in these troubled times is, first and foremost, to continue our efforts to build the cooperative relationship that has allowed our nations and so many others to strengthen international peace and stability. At the same time, we will continue to support a reform process within the Soviet Union aimed at political and economic freedom—a process we believe must be built on peaceful dialogue and negotiation. This is a policy that we will advocate steadfastly, both in our discussions with the central Soviet Government and with all elements active in Soviet political life.

Let there be no misunderstanding, the path ahead for the Soviet Union will be difficult and, at times, extraordinarily painful. History weighs heavily on all the peoples of the U.S.S.R.— liberation from 70 years of communism, from 1,000 years of autocracy. It's going to be slow. There will be setbacks. But this process of reform, this transformation from within, must proceed. If external cooperation and our progress toward true international peace is to endure, it must succeed.

Only when this transformation is complete will we be able to take full measure of the opportunities presented by this new and evolving world order.

The New World Facing Us

The new world order really is a tool for addressing a new world of possibilities. This order gains its mission and shape not just from shared interests but from shared ideals. And the ideals that have spawned new freedoms throughout the world have received their boldest and clearest expression in our great country, the United States. Never before has the world looked more to the American example. Never before have so many millions drawn hope from the American idea. And the reason is simple: Unlike any other nation in the world, as Americans we enjoy profound and mysterious bonds of affection and idealism. We feel our deep connections to community, to families, to our faiths.

But what defines this nation? What makes us America is not our ties to a piece of territory or bonds of blood; what makes us American is our allegiance to an idea that all people everywhere must be free. This idea is as old and enduring as this nation itself—as deeply rooted, and what we are as a promise implicit to all the world in the words of our own Declaration of Independence.

The new world facing us—and I wish I were your age—it's a wonderful world of discovery, a world devoted to unlocking the promise of freedom. It's no more structured than a dream, no more regimented than an innovator's burst of inspiration. If we trust ourselves and our values, if we retain the pioneer's enthusiasm for exploring the world beyond our shores, if we strive to engage in the world that beckons us, then and only then will America be true to all that is best in us.

May God bless our great nation, the United States of America. And thank you all for what you have done for freedom and for our fundamental values. Thank you very much.

---

1 Text from Weekly Compilation of Presidential Documents of April 22, 1991.

The New World Order in the Gulf

Excerpt from President's interview with Middle Eastern journalists, March 8, 1991 [1]

Q. Mr. President, the Gulf war is the first of its kind to take place in the context of the new world order. How did the new world order influence the way the world dealt with this crisis? And what is the main lesson learned from the Gulf war?

A. The new world order said that a lot of countries—disparate backgrounds, with differences—can come together, standing for a common principle, and that principle is: You don't take over another country by force. So, the new world order, to the degree it's emerged, so far, has been enhanced by this single concept that we're going to unite, no matter what other differences we may have had, what the bilateral problems may have been, and we're going to stand up against aggression.

It was enhanced by a more viable United Nations, a United Nations where the big powers didn't automatically go against each other. In the Cold War days, we'd say this is black and the Soviets would say, hey, that's white. And you'd have a veto, and nothing would happen. And the peacekeeping dreams of the founders of the U.N. were dashed.

So, part of this new world order has been moved forward by a United Nations that functioned. We might have still been able to stand up and come to the assistance of Kuwait—the United States. I might have said to hell with them, it's right and wrong, it's good and evil, he's evil, our cause is right; and without the United Nations, sent a considerable force to help. But it was an enhanced—it is far better to have this collective action where the world—not just the Security Council but the whole General Assembly stood up and condemned it.

So, part of it is these more viable international organizations. And that is where we are now. Then how we build on it as the questions that will be coming up, trying to give our share of the answers when Jim Baker comes back from these consultations [in the Middle East].

Q. And what is the lesson which we learned from this crisis?

A. Well, the one key lesson is: Aggression will not stand. You don't bully your neighbor. You don't swagger around the neighborhood with an arrogance and back it up by overwhelming force without paying a price. Same thing you learned in the school yard when you were over there in Egypt. One guy came out and tried to beat the hell out of you when you're in the third grade, and you'd wait for a while, and then somebody would hit him and he'd go back into his shell and he wouldn't do it again. And that is what happened in this case. Same thing.

---

1 Full text in Weekly Compilation of Presidential Documents of March 18, 1991. Participants in the interview were Nadir Yata of Al-Bayan, Morocco; Said Sonbol of Al-Akhbar, Egypt; Mohammed Rumaihi of Sawt Al-Kuwait, Kuwait; and Othman Al-Omeir of Al-Sharq Al-Awsat, Saudi Arabia.

Perestroika in Europe and Asia, and the Situation in the Soviet Union

by Mikhail Gorbachev

Text of Soviet President Gorbachev's speech to the Japanese Parliament, April 17, 1991 (opening remarks omitted).

Without Japan it is inconceivable to imagine contemporary progress and a new international order, the first steps toward which have already been taken. Hence the objective need for new Soviet-Japanese relations.

Great Changes in the World

It is precisely from this point of view, that is, from the viewpoint of the importance of and potential for Soviet-Japanese cooperation that I will begin with world issues. I shall not hide the fact that I would like to take the opportunity of addressing such an authoritative forum to try to sum up some of the results of the great changes that have taken place in the world before our very eyes.

Having launched *perestroika,* which required the revision of our entire domestic and foreign policy, we came up with the idea of a comprehensive system of international security whereby the arms race and confrontation would be replaced by competition and cooperation. Thus the foundations of the new ways of thinking in the sphere of foreign policy were laid.

The main elements of the new thinking are probably known to you. They are these: the elimination of nuclear weapons, the limitation of conventional arms to the level of defense sufficiency, respect for the freedom of socio-political choice by every people and state, the primacy of universal human values, the exclusion of a messianic approach in world politics, the de-ideologization of relations between states, and national security based on understanding of the interdependence of everyone in the world community.

This is not a comprehensive list, but the essence of it is that precisely such ideas have been adopted as a basis for the Soviet Union's constructive, predictable and clear-cut policy. This has aroused response throughout the world and predetermined the restructuring of international relations and paved the way for the elimination of the Cold War.

We do not intend to depart from this policy of ours. Any doubts and speculations that have appeared of late are unfounded. They are either the outcome of lack of understanding, lack of information or are prompted by ill will with regard to us.

I do not know of any serious political forces in our country that would favor return to the old approaches in foreign policy.

Striking changes have occurred in the world. Their scope and rapidity would have seemed simply fantastic a few years ago. The foundation has been laid for progress toward a new epoch in the life of the world community. This progress will of course be long and difficult.

Soviet-American relations are pivotal in this process. They have evolved from confrontation to cooperation and even partnership. Real disarmament, including nuclear disarmament, has been started. The face of Europe has changed. The 1990 Paris Charter, signed at summit level, has set new parameters for the continent's development. Germany has become united. Reconciliation between the Soviet and German peoples is a historic event. The foundation has been laid for developing friendly relations between them.

Hence, fundamental changes in East-West relations are quite obvious. They give us hope that progress toward a new world order will not grind to a halt, and that it will become irreversible. However, there are still quite a few difficulties, dangers and trials ahead.

Two Trials for the World Community

The world community has already withstood two serious trials.

The first one, figuratively speaking, was the collapse of the Berlin Wall, which put an end to the "Iron Curtain" in Europe. Freedom of choice and non-interference in domestic processes, a balance of interests, the priority of political approaches, readiness to take into account new realities, and reliance on everything that is viable and leads to more stable and mutually advantageous relations—all these are the criteria of the new relations which are now taking shape among countries also in the eastern part of Europe. The new political thinking patently showed during this first major trial that it is a factor acting in the interests of the world community as a whole.

The other trial was linked with Iraq's aggression against Kuwait and with the Gulf crisis. This was the first major international crisis after the ending of the Cold War. It appears that the world community is emerging from it without having lost anything it had accumulated over the years of its progress toward a new world order. It is deplorable that force had to be used. But the aggressor left no other choice for the United Nations.

The Gulf crisis affected the vital interests of many states, including the Soviet Union and Japan. One of the most urgent tasks now is to cope fairly with its gravest consequences in the spirit that had prevailed during the drawing up of measures to cut short the aggression. This effort leads us straight to the sources of instability in the region and calls for the settlement of the Middle East conflict as a whole. This is a world problem. A strategic knot of international relations lies in this region. It is the point of juncture of world religions. The vital interests of many countries intertwine in this region—one of the energy mainstays of the world economy.

The experience we have accumulated during this crisis proves the effectiveness of bilateral and multilateral cooperation for the sake of common security, for the sake of U.N. principles and the interests of each of its members. It also proves the need for closer cooperation between the Soviet Union and Japan in international affairs.

Soviet-Japanese Relations

Now I would like to move on directly to the problems of Soviet-Japanese relations. They are not inert, of course. Our relations exist and are active. Interest in each other is growing. However, it is obvious that the dimensions and growth rates of these relations lag behind our mutual potential and, I hope, beyond their desired levels.

Why? Let me invite members of the Japanese Parliament to give some thought to this.

There is hardly a field of international activity today where any of us, at state level, would like to harm another country, or where mutual interests could not be found. Even in the Cold War years neither we in Moscow nor, as far as we know, Tokyo aimed at solving any problems in bilateral relations using military force.

Of course, the Cold War legacy is tenacious. Mistrust is still felt despite Soviet statements that it will never attack Japan. Japan seems to be beginning to overcome fears of the "Soviet military threat." Our new military doctrine, which naturally is also spreading in an "easterly direction," proceeds from the principle of exclusive defensive sufficiency.

Under the INF [intermediate-range nuclear forces] Treaty, the Soviet Union completed the destruction of 424 shorter-range missiles in the Asian part of our country, and 166 intermediate-range missiles deployed here will be destroyed by mid-1991.

There has been no increase in the number of nuclear delivery vehicles in the Asian part of the Soviet Union since July 1987.

By 1991, as we promised, the armed forces in the east of the country had been cut by 200,000 people. In the far east, land forces are being reduced by 12 divisions. Eleven air regiments are being disbanded. Sixteen naval vessels, including nine large surface vessels and seven submarines, are being removed from the Pacific Fleet. Furthermore, we plan to invite military observers to the maneuvers of the Soviet Pacific Fleet, due to be held this summer.

The withdrawal of Soviet troops from Mongolia will be completed in 1991. Utilization by the Soviet Armed Forces of facilities at Camranh Bay in Vietnam is being reduced.

We will cut the Soviet military presence in the Asia-Pacific region. That process would have been faster if other naval powers had displayed reciprocity.

I think that all this is being closely analyzed here in Tokyo.

I think it is necessary to stress that the Soviet Union is prepared to begin a concrete dialogue with Japan on military issues. This could remove mutual suspicions. Proposals have been conveyed to your government.

I think it might be advisable to begin trilateral Soviet-Japanese-American consultations. We see their goal as being to remove suspicions and building confidence through concrete agreements.

...we say that it is expedient to begin a five-sided conference involving the U.S.S.R., the United States, the People's Republic of China, India and Japan...[and propose holding] a meeting of foreign ministers of all countries of the Asia-Pacific region in 1993.

The Soviet Union is approaching all these difficult and delicate problems in a realistic way. We have no subversive intentions with regard to the current military-political structures in the region. But we proceed from the ultimate inevitability of evolution, in the course of which military aspects in international relations will lessen in importance.

The Asia-Pacific Region

Now about Soviet-Japanese relations in the context of processes in the Asia-Pacific region. History has created the situation whereby the Soviet Union has become a huge Eurasian state with unique features and possibilities. Japan, with its scientific, technical, industrial and financial potential, plays a leading role in the Asia-Pacific region. Thus, it is impossible to imagine the dynamics of the world process over nearly half of the globe without these two states.

Our new concept of the U.S.S.R.'s place in the Asia-Pacific region was set out in 1986 in Vladivostok and later in

Krasnoyarsk. We have invited all countries of the region to take part in dialogue.

Since that time relations existing with some of the region's countries have been continued and brought to a new level and relations with many other countries of the region have been begun and developed.

- Soviet-Chinese relations have been fully normalized and are improving. The Soviet Union and China were the first countries in Asia to take practical steps toward the mutual reduction of armed forces, as well as confidence-building measures on the border.
- Relations with India have been developed further on a durable foundation of solidarity and friendship.
- There are many promising developments in contacts with Indonesia and other ASEAN countries.
- Diplomatic relations have been established with the Republic of Korea and economic relations with it are rapidly developing.
- Considerable progress was reached in a Soviet-Canadian dialogue. There are obvious changes in relations with Australia and New Zealand.
- The new character of Soviet-American relations, whose global importance I have already mentioned, made it possible to begin direct ties between the Soviet Far East, the Chukchi peninsula, Kamchatka and Sakhalin, and Alaska and the west coast of the United States.

So what is the point of giving up the policy of new thinking if it has resulted in such favorable changes, not only in relations with America and Europe, but also in Asia and in the Pacific? Our security in its present definition would not have really been strengthened had it not been for this policy. What is more, it has enabled us to begin to reduce the heavy burden of military expenditure.

Such are the objective reasons behind our new international course. I do not know of any serious political forces in our country that would favor return to the old approaches in foreign policy.

We view with satisfaction the development of Japan's relations with

China, Vietnam, with the Republic of Korea and with ASEAN countries. We would regard it as natural and appropriate to the demands of the time if Japan established diplomatic relations with the Democratic People's Republic of Korea. We understand Japan's striving to play an active role in the Cambodian settlement.

I take this opportunity to express our support for the activity of the United Nations Economic and Social Commission for Asia and the Pacific (ESCAP). At a recent session in Seoul delegations from 48 countries and 70 international organizations declared that, considering the fact that the Cold War is over, the Asia-Pacific region should be turned into a zone of openness, cooperation and prosperity. Surely that is a sign of changes!

A multitude of complicated economic, ethnic, social, religious and ecological problems are awaiting solution in the countries of the region, which is inhabited by half of the world's population. No single country can resolve such problems on its own, and so it is necessary to pool our efforts and make available material and other resources that are still being squandered on armaments.

The realization of this is also growing in Asia-Pacific countries. This is also shown by the intensification of bilateral ties in recent years. This is an inevitable and positive stage in the process which, I believe, will lead to examination of not only economic problems but also those of security in all its aspects. These things are connected everywhere and this connection is increasingly felt.

We are not talking about some mechanism of multilateral cooperation or institutionalization of the process. What we mean are consultations, joint identification and discussion of common problems and the timely prevention of common dangers.

In this sense we say that it is expedient to begin a five-sided conference involving the U.S.S.R., the United States, the People's Republic of China, India and Japan. We attach precisely this sense to our proposal to hold a meeting of foreign ministers of all countries of the Asia-Pacific region in 1993.

The time has come for a practical approach to the idea of creating a zone of cooperation in the Sea of Japan. It could become a good proving ground for economic integration in the Asia-Pacific region.

We are interested in linking the economy of the Far East and Siberia to the economic complex forming in the Asia-Pacific region. Being aware of the difficulties, we also see enormous opportunities. We have specific proposals to this effect, and I set them out at today's meeting with Japanese business people.

Let us do everything we can to prevent the memory of the past from dividing peoples, and rather encourage them to build relations on sound, contemporary, and reasonable foundations.

The Burden of the Past

On the whole, this is the context of Soviet-Japanese relations, their international and regional background. But I must repeat that they remain inadequate even to the existing possibilities.

The reasons are rooted in the past, the burden of which continues to aggravate our relations.

We spoke about all of this with Prime Minister Kaifu, openly and in detail. Moreover, we are going to have talks in private with Mr. Kaifu. I shall not go into detail now, but I shall share the ideas by which I am guided.

There were many things between our countries that left bitter memories in the hearts and minds of both peoples. What can be done? One can continue to dwell on the past and nurse grudges.

But this is futile. It is necessary to choose a different road—to reconsider the common past for the sake of the present and the future.

The Second World War began and was waged in a different world which has receded into the past, along with its notions, laws, "rules of the game." Such is history. The decisions taken then were decisions made by people of other generations and different views. We cannot be held responsible for them. But what was done by them should not be altered without sufficient consideration, or oblivious to the obvious fact that a new reality has

emerged in the decades that have followed and that these realities should be taken into consideration.

Let us do everything we can to prevent the memory of the past from dividing peoples, and rather encourage them to build relations on sound, contemporary, and reasonable foundations.

I believe that now, fifty years after the most horrible war, the memory of its victims, and of all the tragedies caused by the war both in the East and the West should remind us that this should never be repeated. We cannot do much for those who are no longer with us. We can only preserve their memory, and we are obliged to do so. Soviet people are grateful to the Japanese for their care of the graves of Russian soldiers on Japanese soil. I assure you that our people will care in the same way for the graves of Japanese on our soil.

It is the job of historians to examine in detail the causes of the war and its consequences and weigh the share of guilt among those who unleashed it.

The job of politicians is to work to ensure that countries that once warred in various coalitions do not view one another as "enemies," "victors" or "vanquished" ever again.

It is utterly abnormal that the Soviet Union and Japan do not yet have a peace treaty, one which would finally formalize the results of the Second World War. It is essential to begin to move in that direction without excluding anything positive that has been achieved in bilateral negotiations over the years.

The main thing is to replenish the potential of trust and launch all-embracing cooperation—economic, political and humanitarian—at state and regional levels, with republics of the U.S.S.R., primarily with the Russian Federation, the largest republic which has longstanding direct contacts with Japan and which borders it, between enterprises and firms, in tourism and other free contacts between people.

Taking all of this into consideration, I am having talks with the Prime Minister of Japan. I think that the results of the talks and of more than ten joint documents that are to be signed will show that Moscow and Tokyo are taking a resolute step toward reaching full mutual understanding between the two countries and finally settling problems that are the legacy of the war, including the most difficult problem — that of territorial delimitation.

The Situation in the Soviet Union

Now a few words about our own country. You are awaiting, of course, my judgements on this subject as well.

Exactly six years have passed since *perestroika* began. What have we achieved during this period and what have we not achieved?

It took the first two to three years to realize in what position the country found itself and what kind of a world surrounded it, and to work out a policy of *perestroika*. Then at an increasing pace began the dismantling of the administrative command system, which was basically a totalitarian system.

A new, democratic system and way of life are taking shape with great difficulty, sometimes in an atmosphere of fierce struggle. Unprecedented freedom, openness, and the pluralism of parties, movements and opinions are the characteristic signs of our life.

We have set about changing relations of ownership and have begun to make the transition to a mixed market economy. We are on the threshold of fundamental changes in the very nature of the Union as a federation of sovereign states.

In short, we are proceeding toward a new society. But this is a very painful process. Such fundamental changes, revolutionary in their essence, could not, naturally, be drought about smoothly in such a vast and multifaceted country overburdened with problems, with an abnormal economy and a dogmatized social psychology.

We did not manage to avoid a period of crisis, a period of the most difficult transition from one state of society to another.

Transformations have greatly affected the basic interests of various sections of the population and the people as a whole. Arguments as to what is happening with us and where we have found ourselves—in families, in work collectives, at rallies, on public transport, in lines, at scientific conferences and in parliaments, not to mention the media.

An acute political struggle has begun, in which—with our level of democratic culture—"any means will do" is a motto for many. And all this is happening against the background of

an economic slump and discord in our economy. Hence the growing instability in society.

In a word, the situation in the country is complex, even dramatic. Many people are worried, including people in Japan, as to whether *perestroika* has come to a standstill and whether a reverse movement has begun. I think the changes that have taken place in the country are irreversible. Society has already become different and no one is in a position to take it back to its former state. We can solve our problems only on our way forward.

The overcoming of the crisis should be achieved only by means of specific deeds and with consensus on the main issues on the agenda. *Perestroika* can now be saved by the immediate and effective accomplishment of urgent socioeconomic tasks of an anti-crisis nature.

...perestroika is no longer only our national problem. It is a world problem. Events in a country such as the Soviet Union are bound to affect world processes.

This is the essence and objective of a specific anti-crisis program that was worked out on the eve of my visit here. It is intended for one year, with every move scheduled literally by the month. I have no doubt that a strict and coordinated implementation of the program will make it possible to stabilize the situation as early as this year and open up new opportunities for forward movement.

We are not changing and do not intend to change our general line toward radical economic reform, toward the reforming of the Union and the political system and toward the establishment of a law-governed state.

I am confident that this course will make it possible to find an optimum correlation between the stabilization of the situation and the creation of conditions for movement to a market economy, for the functioning of structures of a law-governed state and the solution of the problems of the vast multiethnic state.

We shall promote entrepreneurship in every way, support business initiative and advance medium-sized and small businesses and the service sector. But we cannot allow ourselves to throw everything into the arms of the market in one go.

We intend to act circumspectly. We are now bringing prices into line with economic realities. This is a most difficult and painful operation. Achieving the convertibility of the ruble is the most complex element of the transition to a market economy. We now see that it is essential to proceed to the convertibility of the ruble more quickly. This is essential for the domestic market and is particularly important for cooperation with other countries.

All this is providing us with an objective basis for an in-depth democratic remaking of our entire society. But a market economy and democracy will not come together by themselves. Efforts by political forces are needed, as well as mutual understanding between them and the necessary minimum of consensus. People should come to realize: When sitting in the same boat, they must row in the same direction.

Extremes and adventurism are the danger now. The centrist political line which I uphold is the orientation toward responsibility with an eye to new methods. If this line is not maintained and if democratic trends around it are not consolidated, a serious civil conflict is possible.

Our country may, indeed, descend into chaos, possibly with a dictatorship, if we fail to stop its disintegration, including the collapse of our economy, the undermining of the legal system and the disruption of inter-republican ties, and if we fail to keep our new social processes within peaceful bounds.

This is why it is necessary to take unpopular steps, including administrative measures, within the framework of our Constitution. Many people, including foreigners, assess this as a revision of our course. This is a mistake. Everything we are now doing is intended to continue the *perestroika* policy and simultaneously create prerequisites for its even more resolute promotion.

We must be resolute in order to promote a new political culture, recognizing pluralism, competitiveness of political programs, and discussions within the bounds of the laws in force and the existing legal order. Of course, this requires self-restraint, patience and insusceptibility to pressures both from the right and from the left. A strong government, relying on the law, is needed for the normal functioning of any democracy.

Ladies and gentlemen, you will probably agree that *perestroika* is no longer only our national problem. It is a world problem. Events in a country such as the Soviet Union are bound to affect world processes. After the March 17 referendum on whether the Soviet Union should be preserved or not, we can confidently declare that our state will remain great, and will continue to play its role and bear responsibility for world affairs. The referendum also reflected the attitude of the majority of our population to the country's place in the world structure. Those republics that decide to secede on the basis of legitimate referendums in each republic will have to recognize the need for a proper constitutional process which guarantees the interests of all those who will inevitably be affected by such a dramatic rupture.

The creation of a new, peaceful world order largely depends on the outcome of *perestroika*. This is why it is very important to correctly understand our problems in the world community. I refer primarily to those people who are able to exert a major influence on the main vector of world politics. We expect our efforts to be supported, especially now, at this critical stage of the transition period.

Perestroika and the policy of new thinking will allow us to return our country to world civilization, to world economic relations and to the international division of labor. The country has already turned around to face the outside world. It has acquired many friends and partners and an atmosphere of solidarity with us has now appeared.

We shall draw on the experience of other countries which have overcome the critical stage of modernization before us and have achieved success. But this does not mean that we are ready to forfeit our identity. It is clear to us that we will be able to preserve the integrity of our multinational society only if we take account of the concrete historical and socio-psychological features of our country and the peoples inhabiting it, and if we learn to rely on them in conditions of equality and interaction. Blind imita-

tion or attempts to heal our ailments by means of prescriptions adapted to other conditions would, most probably, produce destructive or even catastrophic results.

"Life on Our Planet is in Danger"

Your country has managed to steer safely around the dangerous reefs of modernization and to reach the pinnacle of technological progress because, though drawing on the experience of others, it was able to retain its national traditions, to meet the outside world's challenges without succumbing to them. It was able to uphold its cultural and spiritual inimitability.

Esteemed Members of Parliament, in conclusion I would like to take a glance into the future. Winston Churchill once said that the difference between statesmen and politicians is that the former think of the future and the latter of the next election.

Unfortunately we often resemble such politicians. In the meantime, we are living in an epoch when those who bear responsibility for the destiny of their countries and peoples must constantly pay attention to problems affecting mankind's future.

Life on our planet is in danger. We first realized this when the danger of nuclear war appeared on the horizon. Today we have been able to put it off. But mankind is now confronted with other grave threats, primarily the ecological menace. Scientists warn us that irreversible changes in the planet's climate, in its entire ecological system are bound to occur if we do nothing about it within the next few decades. This would be tantamount to a delayed nuclear catastrophe. We shall take this into consideration. Nature is warning us in no uncertain terms: It is high time to put an end to the arms race, senseless conflicts and the squandering of resources, and to focus our energy, will and talent on the preservation of mankind's environment, thereby saving life on our planet.

Countries and peoples have for centuries regarded each other as "friends" or "foes", and have obeyed the rules of the game when one was bound to win and the other to lose. No matter how this "philosophy" was explained, our ancestors and we ourselves have paid dearly for it. Today we real-

ize that mankind has a common destiny. And this obliges responsible politicians to think more broadly—in universal dimensions.

The world was built in such a way that rich and poor people are bound to exist in it for a long time to come yet. But let us not forget one thing: Nations find it hard to grasp universal values when they are driven into an impasse and deprived of historical perspective. Desperation and a sense of futility are a grave threat to civilization's progress. Hence, by aiding other states, the advanced countries are actually helping themselves.

Naturally, the great powers and their leaders bear special responsibility. In this light we regard the prospect of Soviet-Japanese cooperation on global problems, of course in interaction with the United States and other northern and southern powers. This envisages, among other things, the enhancement of the role of the United Nations and the streamlining of the entire system of international institutions to meet the challenges of the 21st century.

Nobody can guarantee us success in advance. It can be guaranteed only by sensible policies, by being aware of the dangers, having the ability to overcome them and a readiness to conduct a dialogue and to make compromises.

Let us jointly seek answers to our epoch's challenges and jointly exert efforts to make our common hopes for the future come true.

Leo Tolstoy once said, addressing his Japanese colleague, writer Tokutomi Roka: "You ask me about ways to establish lasting friendship between Russia and Japan. It is necessary. We will be able to achieve this goal only if we're urged on to it by a mutual desire."

May these words be the guiding star indicating the way which will lead our peoples to a real meeting with each other.

---

1 This translation is an amalgamation of two texts, the one provided in English by TASS on April 17, 1991, the other included in the Novosti English-language publication "Visit of Mikhail Gorbachev to Japan," Moscow, 1991. Their content is identical, but in some cases one translation is clearer in English than the other.

Congressman William H. Gray III Addresses
First African/African-American Summit

Representative Gray spoke to the closing session of the conference, Abidjan, Cote d'Ivoire, April 19, 1991. [1]

Dr. Sullivan has given me a job to do, and there's one thing you must understand: Dr. Sullivan is a constituent of mine, and whenever he tells me do something, I'm going to do it.

He has asked me to give a few brief remarks in response to this conference and also to the Declaration. It's a great honor to do so. It's a pleasure to come before you to reaffirm the commitment of the United States Congress to help improve the life of all Africans.

I want to take a moment and compliment Dr. Sullivan personally for convening and organizing this historic conference. Those who know Dr. Sullivan know of his longtime leadership on issues involving Africa, from the Sullivan Principles, right up to OIC International where he first helped bring attention to that terrible scourge called apartheid, and began to bring self-help principles here to the continent of Africa. He is to be commended for his leadership.

My hope is that as a result of this conference Africa and America will create new bonds of friendship and commerce together. I also hope that much of the ligaments binding us together come from the African-American community.

"What is Africa to me?"

So wrote the African-American poet Countee Cullen, born at the beginning of this century:

> What is Africa to me:
> Copper sun or scarlet sea
> Jungle star or jungle track
> Strong bronzed men, or regal black
> Women from whose loins I sprang
> When the birds of Eden sang

In America we have not forgotten from whence our ancestors came. We know that some came from Europe and we also know that some came from this great continent—in the words of poet and historian Lerone Bennett, Jr.,—

"chained, two by two, left leg to right leg from a thousand villages and towns."

We African-Americans are descendants of the Hausas, the Mandingos, the Yorubas and the Ibos, the Ashantis and many others, and we have not forgotten that.

African-Americans find the spirit of this continent embedded in our language, our churches and our family customs back home in America. Indeed we have made a powerful contribution to the music and the arts and every other aspect of American life, and we relish the opportunity to come back across the sea to strengthen the bonds that even three centuries could not erase. This is an historic event, a conference on mutual concerns with African and African-American leadership.

It comes at a time of change, challenge and opportunity.

It is a time of *change* from Eastern Europe to Southern Africa. From Poland to Namibia, the winds of freedom and democracy are freeing tidal waves of change.

It's a time of *challenge*, for the question is: how do we harness the power of that change to create higher standards of opportunity and life for all people? How do we deal with the massive problems of hunger—right now, in the Sudan 300,000 people have died of malnutrition.

It is also a time of *opportunity*, a time when the American people and African people can unite to shape those winds of change and at the same time meet the challenge.

U.S. Aid Program

The United States Government has had for a long time a relationship with the continent of Africa, particularly through its aid programs.

In the past these programs have often been small. They've often been relegated to second class status in our foreign aid budget. However, I'm here to tell you that change is taking place; that in the mid-1980s when Africa was hit by a drought and there was suffering, the United States responded with foreign aid worth $700 million dollars.

And yes, during the 1980s we fully funded our commitment to the African Development Bank so we could build Africa's infrastructure and provide new opportunity. And then we started to create new agencies of self-help, the African Development Foundation to help those in the villages of Africa.

And yes, under the leadership of the Congressional Black Caucus — people like those of my colleagues who are seated here—we did what some people said was not possible. Last year we got the United States Congress to push development assistance to sub-Saharan Africa from $565 million to $800 million in this fiscal year, the largest single increase in any area of the foreign aid budget.

But we're not going to stop there. Those of us who serve on the Foreign Operations and the Foreign Affairs Committee led by the Chairman of the Congressional Black Caucus will be seeking one billion dollars of development assistance for subSaharan Africa.

Not only are we talking about increasing amounts of aid so important for infrastructure; we are also looking at new programs like the IFESH program that Dr. Sullivan has developed where you can exchange debt for development.

Last year in our appropriations bill, we provided about $10 million for a demonstration project. It's our expectation that this year there may be as much as a $100 million which can be leveraged in a multi-billion dollar debt retirement program.

That money will help a lot of countries and a lot of people on the continent.

Human Rights and Democratic Institutions

But our allegiance in the United States Government is to the people of Africa, not to any one government. And for that reason our concern doesn't stop with aid and money. We want to do more. We know we must do more. We have a responsibility to do more. But at the same time we are interested in human rights and democratic institutions.

If African countries are to have positive relations with the United States Congress, then human rights must be in the foreground of our relationship. And, my friends, this principle must apply to all Africa from South Africa to central Africa. When nations adhere to principles of democracy and human rights they will see an overwhelming response from the Government of the United States.

Enlisting the Private Sector

But if we are willing to help Africa, we cannot rely on government alone. We have to enlist America's private sector. We have to convince them in America that Africa is the place for investment. That means getting them to know all of Africa. I mean really knowing Africa.

They should know that black Africa is a continent of 600 million people, more than twice that of the United States; that by 2020 the population of Nigeria may equal that of the United States of America; that there are places in Africa of incredible sophistication; that in Africa there are dozens of examples of substantative economic reform, the kind that should make investors be willing to come and invest money here.

There's Cameroon where they have a new investment code, and Nigeria's structural adjustment program designed to utilize a system of foreign exchange. There's Zimbawe and its reforms and import quotas, and the Congo's willingness to sign a treaty with the United States last year guaranteeing U.S. firms fair treatment.

The winds of change are blowing. These reforms won't bring prosperity overnight. There are already some brilliant success stories that need to be told: Botswana, for example, that model of democracy and stability, or Namibia, whose new constitution reflects the highest ideals in democratic principles, or our host country, today, where last year multiparty elections have sent a signal heard not only throughout Africa but indeed throughout the world.

My friends, there's a lot to give us hope, but there's one thing for sure. The steps may seem small but each step moves us closer toward the goal of liberation, freedom and opportunity for all people.

My friends, this conference has made a major step toward that goal.

I commend Dr. Sullivan. I commend the heads of states, the ministers of states, the delegates from Africa and the United States. The result of your coming together will be big dividends of unity, of understanding and the chance to better the lives of people — not on just one continent either, for indeed, if we can bring America and Africa together there will be mutual benefit to both.

And so this conference may be a precursor of a new set of relations between the continent and America. It can improve the lives not only of those in Africa but those in America. And when we reach that day, as the Lion of Zion will tell you, the lions and the lambs will lie down together and they will dwell at the table of fellowship and study war no more. God bless you. Congratulations.

---

1 Text provided by Congressman Gray's office, Washington.

Civil War and Famine in Ethiopia: U.S. Actions

Excerpt from testimony by Acting Assistant Secretary of State Jeffrey Davidow before the Subcommittee on Africa, Senate Foreign Relations Committee, May 14, 1991. [1]

Recently, the Ethiopian Government called for a roundtable to consider transitional arrangements. The main rebel groups did not accept this offer as such, but they have instituted at least a temporary stand-down of hostilities while the U.S. explores how peace might be given a chance.

We have made it clear to all that we are ready to do anything we can to help lift the burden of conflict. We have been working to facilitate negotiations between the Government and the Eritrean People's Liberation Front. Now we are inviting Addis and the three principal insurgent groups to a meeting in Europe to discuss how a peaceful transition could be achieved.

In the meantime, the U.S. has a full agenda of other issues in Ethiopia. We press the Ethiopian Government to improve its human rights record. Hundreds of political prisoners are being held without trial, and forced

conscription of underaged children is a common occurrence. In the most highly visible of Ethiopia's human rights problems, we are attempting to win for Ethiopian Jews the chance to emigrate to Israel. Last month President Bush asked former Senator [Rudy] Boschwitz to travel to Ethiopia as his personal emissary to express our conviction that all Falashas who wish to do so should be allowed to leave for Israel without further delay. We will continue to work for the resolution of this urgent human rights question...

The famine has extended into 1991. Our relief program has been massive, and has been operational across the constantly-shifting battle lines of a raging civil war. It's good to note that finally, in January of this year, the port of Masawa was opened as the result largely of U.S. pressure and helpful advocacy from this Committee among others. For the first time in a long time large amounts of food are moving in Ethiopia across battle lines. With intense effort we hope to keep abreast of famine again this year. We will continue to keep all options open for moving food. As in Sudan [and Somalia], the best thing that could happen would be an end to the conflicts which create the problems and impede the free movement of food.

---

1 The complete transcript of the hearings will be published by the committee and will be available from the Superintendent of Documents, U.S. Government Printing Office, Washington, D.C. 20402.

Japanese Prime Minister Toshiki Kaifu Meets with President Bush in California

PRESS CONFERENCE, NEWPORT BEACH, APRIL 4, 1991 [1]

The President. Let me just say what a pleasure it's been to have Prime Minister Kaifu here in the United States. In the past year, we've resolved significant trade disputes, and we've moved to ease trade tensions. I think we've made solid progress in opening new markets to satellites and telecommunications, wood products.

We need to move ahead now in other areas—construction services, autos, auto parts, semiconductors, other areas. We need to prove that our efforts under the SII, the Structural Impediments Initiative, produce real results. I think progress has been made. It remains our best hope of fending off those who advocate managed trade between our nations.

In 1990, the U.S. trade deficit with Japan fell for the third straight year. And American exports to Japan continued to rise, up more than 75 percent since 1987. In fact, I think many Americans would be surprised to learn that Japan buys more goods from the U.S. per capita than we buy from Japan.

The Prime Minister and I both agree that we want to see a successful conclusion to the Uruguay Round. And I might take this opportunity to urge the Congress of the United States to take decisive action and send a clear signal that America stands for free trade by extending the Fast Track procedures.

We had full discussions on the Gulf, and I took this occasion to thank, profoundly thank, Prime Minister Kaifu for the assistance that Japan made as a member of this coalition. Japan has provided a substantial level of financial support for Operation Desert Storm.

Just to save time, we will be putting out a more full statement here. [2] But Mr. Prime Minister, I welcome your visit. And it's been a great pleasure having you here—all too brief a visit, but a very important one. Thank you for coming all this way.

The Prime Minister. Thank you, George, for [your] kind remarks. You've shown yourself to be the great leader not just of this great nation, the United States, but of the entire world. Not only that, may I say, you are the private self of a countless number of people across the world who are fighting for the peace and justice, for freedom and democracy.

I am most pleased to see you, here in this beautiful State of California again, since we met over a year ago in a similar setting, and to be able to continue our close dialogue.

I wish to take this opportunity on behalf of the entire Japanese people to pay our deepest respect to the great leadership you exerted as President throughout the Gulf crisis and to the dedication and sacrifice of the American soldiers, men and women, in Operations Desert Shield and Desert Storm.

I'm certainly aware that there are divergent views [about Japan] in the United States. We would like to continue with our efforts so that we will be establishing a relationship of mutual confidence that is unshakable.

The world has just overcome a great challenge in the Gulf region, and now it is time to tackle a truly historic mission, which is to build a new international order in the aftermath of the Cold War. The Gulf crisis has demonstrated beyond anybody's doubt that the United States is the only superpower with the capability to play the most important role in the post-Cold War world and to do so in a responsible way.

At the same time, it has become clear that it is just as important that the like-minded countries work together and support American efforts. We deeply recognize this in Japan. Together with Americans, Europeans, Asians, and other peoples of the world, we seek to participate actively in this endeavor and cooperate for creating a new international order.

Throughout the Gulf crisis, Japan firmly supported the United States and international coalition efforts and cooperated as much as possible. And we are grateful for the appreciation expressed by the President. Nevertheless, sometimes Japan's efforts have not been properly understood and appreciated, and frankly speaking, this reception has caused disappointment among Japanese people. Thinking about the future of Japan-U.S. relationship, which is so important to the peace and prosperity of the world, I firmly believe that we have to rectify this situation.

Japan and the United States are staunch allies, bound together with strong security ties and a close economic interdependence. I believe the world strongly desires to see friendly and cooperative bilateral relations between our two countries, in which both sides will bring their respective strengths in order to meet global challenges, and will tackle problems between our two countries.

We are with you always, standing together as firm allies and friends across the Pacific. I'm convinced that the friendship and the spirit of cooperation between our two peoples will always prevail. Thank you.

Q. I'd like to ask a question of Prime Minister Kaifu. Because of constitutional constraints Japan was not able to send military forces during the Gulf war. However, Japan financed the $9 billion additional contribution through tax increase, and in that respect I believe it is fair to say that Japan has shed its blood in its own way. However, that contribution is not properly valued in the United States. On top of that, more recently, there seems to be a stepping up of Japan-bashing in the United States over trade issues, whereas in Japan there is dissatisfaction amongst the Japanese people. People are grumbling that Japan is not an automatic teller machine of a bank...

The Prime Minister. ... Japan, from the very beginning, showed its basic position that Iraq is wrong. And from Japan's position, we cooperated and made contribution as much as possible. With regard to financial cooperation, we put a bill to the Diet of the Japanese Parliament. We passed a budget bill for that purpose. And for the purpose of funding that budget, we asked the Japanese people to accept an increased tax. And we were aware of the need to make this contribution, and the President has kindly appreciated that contribution that Japan made.

On the other hand, I'm certainly aware that there are divergent views in the United States. We would like to continue with our efforts so that we will be establishing a relationship of mutual confidence that is unshakable.

*　　*　　*

Q. I should like to ask a question of Mr. President with regard to Japanese contribution related to the Gulf war. You said that you profoundly appreciated Japanese important financial contribution. Japan did not send even a medical team, not to speak of self-defense personnel. And I wonder if you feel that it is possible to maintain a relationship of alliance with a country, Japan, which did not make a human contribution at a time of an international crisis. I would appreciate your candid remarks. And also, I wonder what you would expect of Japan to do for the purpose of preserving and further promoting this alliance.

The President. My answer is, yes, not only do I think we will preserve but I think we will strengthen this relationship. I hope most Americans understand the constitutional constraints on Japan in terms of what—I think you called them human forces, or human—human personnel.

But what I would like to emphasize to the American people and the people of Japan is, from day one—from day one, Toshiki Kaifu and the Japanese Government was in strong support of the U.N. resolutions. Japan stepped up early on to a fundamental and substantial monetary contribution. Through those months of diplomacy before force was used, Japan played a key role. And so if we have a difference now over some detail, I would simply say that this relationship is too fundamental, too important to have it on the shoals because of difficulty that I'm confident we can work out.

And to the degree that there's bashing on one side of the Pacific or another, Toshiki Kaifu and I are committed to see that that bashing doesn't go forward because it's in our interest in the United States to have this

relationship strong. And I happen to think it's in Japan's interest.

EXCERPT FROM PRESIDENT'S STATEMENT ON U.S.-JAPAN RELATIONS, APRIL 4, 1991 [1]

Trade is just one dimension of our relationship. Last year, our two nations marked the 30th anniversary of our Mutual Security Treaty. Our commitment to common defense has never been stronger, and yet here, too, our longstanding alliance continues to adjust to new challenges and new realities. Just this January, in keeping with its growing economic might, Japan agreed to increase its share of the costs as host nation to American forces.

Let me be clear: The United States welcomes the broadest possible participation by Japan in world affairs. In the past year, we've seen a significant easing of tensions in Europe. I call on Japan to join with us in seeking solutions to regional conflicts that threaten stability in the Pacific. And I thank Japan as a key member of the coalition that triumphed over the forces of aggression in the Persian Gulf. For the first time, Japan contributed to a multinational peacekeeping effort, and it is providing a substantial level of financial support for Operation Desert Storm.

I welcome the visit of Prime Minister Kaifu. We must do all we can to build public support for our relationship and to promote contacts of every kind between the American and Japanese people. Just this last year, Japan's distinguished former Foreign Minister Abe announced the creation of a new foundation to promote exchanges that bring together academics and artists, that encourage tourism and travel.

For more than 40 years, Japan and the United States have been partners— partners in democracy, partners in prosperity, partners in peace. I am convinced that our meeting today proves that this partnership remains strong, that together we will constitute a source of stability, now and into the next century.

---

1 Text from Weekly Compilation of Presidential Documents of April 8, 1991.

2. President Bush covered most of the statement in his remarks. The rest is excerpted here.

High Seas Driftnet Fishing Agreement: U.S., Japan, and Canada [1]

The United States, Japan, and Canada have reached agreement on scientific monitoring and enforcement programs for Japan's high seas driftnet fisheries for the upcoming fishing season, which begins in June 1991. An exchange of letters to conclude the agreement was signed today [April 23]; representatives of the Department of State's Bureau of Oceans and International Environmental and Scientific Affairs and the National Marine Fisheries Service signed on behalf of the United States. The trilateral accord extends and improves upon monitoring and enforcement programs originally agreed to in 1989 for Japan's driftnet fishery in the North Pacific Ocean.

The agreement is consistent with the provisions of the 1989 U.N. General Assembly resolution on large scale pelagic driftnet fishing. The resolution recommends that, in contemplation of a moratorium on all large scale high seas pelagic driftnet fisheries after June 30, 1992, nations involved in driftnet fishing cooperate with coastal states in the collection and sharing of statistically sound scientific data on driftnet fishing's effects.

The understandings reached are aimed at producing statistically reliable estimates of numbers of fish, marine mammals, turtles, and sea birds killed by driftnet fishing activities. They also include other significant provisions

designed, among other things, to minimize the bycatch of U.S. origin salmon and steelhead trout.

1991-92 Scientific Monitoring Program

Under the terms of the agreement, 30 U.S., 21 Japanese, and 10 Canadian scientific observers will be deployed on 61 Japanese small mesh squid driftnet vessels to monitor over 2,500 driftnet retrievals during the 1991 fishing season. The observers will be deployed to reflect the typical monthly pattern of 1990 fishing effort and will be assigned to vessel types (large and small) in proportion to the 1990 fishing effort by each vessel type: 45 on large type vessels (those over 100 tons) and 16 on small type vessels (those under 100 tons).

It has been possible to reduce the number of observers by 13 from last year through an observer program designed to provide bycatch estimates within plus or minus 10% tolerable error at a confidence interval of 90% based on 1990 fishing effort. The progress of the squid driftnet fishery scientific monoitoring program will be evaluated during the course of the season and adjusted as necessary. The parties will exchange on a weekly basis the number of observations by each deployed observer in order to check the cumulative total numbers of obser-

vations and adjust the coverage as needed.

The number of observers placed on the Japanese large mesh driftnet fleet will be determined by September 30, 1991, after data collected from the 1990-91 program are available. The required number of observations in 1991-92 will be calculated based on those data.

Japan will provide total fishing catch and effort data on the small mesh driftnet fishery by April 1, 1992, two months earlier than specified in the 1990 program. Agreement was also reached to move the date for the final report of the results of the 1991 observer program up by one month to May 1, 1992, as compared to last year's agreement.

1991-92 Enforcement Program

The enforcement program is scheduled to run through June 30, 1992.

Japan agreed to review its regulatory measures regarding the illegal reflagging of Japanese driftnet vessels and, if necessary, to reinforce penalties to deter any reflagging schemes.

Japan also agreed to place satellite transmitters on all Japanese driftnet fishing vessels operating beyond its 200 nautrical mile zone in 1991.

---

1 Statement by Department of State Spokesman Margaret Tutwiler, April 23, 1991.

Sea Turtle Conservation in Commercial Shrimp Fisheries [1]

The Department of State certified yesterday that 13 countries in the wider Caribbean region have taken initial steps to protect sea turtles from capture and drowning in their shrimp fishing operations. The Department's certification is required under a 1989 law (Section 609 of P.L. 101-162) that would ban the import of shrimp from any country not taking adequate measures to conserve sea turtles in commercial shrimp fisheries. The certification by the Department is valid for one year, which will allow countries

to further develop and implement their respective programs. Because a certification could not be made for Suriname, shrimp imports from that country are prohibited as of May 1, 1991.

U.S. Law and Policy

Sea turtles and shrimp share similar habitats in tropical and subtropical waters and, as a result, the air breathing turtles are often caught in shrimp nets and drown. This incidental drown-

ing has been identified as the principal threat to the survival of sea turtles in U.S. waters. To protect turtles, U.S. shrimpers are required to use a piece of equipment in their nets called the turtle excluder device (or TED). These devices have been shown to be effective in allowing more than 97 percent of all turtles that enter shrimp nets to escape unharmed.

The 1989 law is intended to extend the protection given to sea turtles under the U.S. regulations to other areas these turtles inhabit throughout the Gulf of Mexico, Caribbean, and western central Atlantic (the wider Caribbean). The countries affected by the law are Belize, Brazil, Colombia, Costa Rica, French Guiana, Guatemala, Guyana, Honduras, Mexico, Nicaragua, Panama, Suriname, Trinidad and Tobago, and Venezuela. The law provides that, to continue exporting shrimp to the United States beyond May 1, 1991, a country must receive a certification that it has met specific conservation requirements.

In order to receive a certification, a country must either provide evidence of the adoption of a regulatory program comparable to the U.S. program or provide evidence that the fishing environment does not pose a threat to sea turtles. Because the use of TED is the centerpiece of the U.S. regulatory program, its use will eventually be the principal feature of any foreign program determined to be comparable to the U.S. program. By the time the phased-in implementation of the foreign programs is completed in May 1994, the nations affected by this law must require the use of TEDs on all shrimp vessels operating in areas where there is a chance of taking sea turtles or their exports of shrimp to the United States will be embargoed.

International Discussions

Beginning in January 1990, officials of the Departments of State and Commerce began discussions with the affected countries to make each of them aware of the importance of taking the necessary measures to protect sea turtles.

...[T]he State Department emphasized its interest and its commitment to seeing equivalent measures to protect sea turtles implemented on the Pacific coast of North, Central, and South America, and in other areas where sea turtles are taken incidental to commercial shrimp fishing operations. In this regard, the Department specifically recognized the efforts of Mexico, Colombia, and Nicaragua, each of which has indicated that its sea turtle protection program in the commercial shrimp fishery will apply equally to the Atlantic (Gulf of Mexico and Caribbean) and Pacific coasts...

---

1 Statement by Department of State Spokesman Margaret Tutwiler, May 1, 1991.

Climate Change Negotiations Begin

Excerpt from Statement by E.U. Curtis Bohlen before the Intergovernmental Negotiating Committee of the Framework Convention on Climate Change, Washington, D.C., February 5, 1991. Mr. Bohlen is Assistant Secretary of State for Oceans, International Environmental and Scientific Affairs. [1]

It is with great hope and enthusiasm that the United States joins in the start of negotiations on a framework convention on climate change. We are embarking on an ambitious international undertaking, a truly global effort to address what is perhaps the most complex and critical environmental issue we are likely to face for many decades to come. These negotiations are but the first step in what must be a sustained and long term effort.

Climate change presents us with a dilemma of daunting proportions. Since the Industrial Revolution, mankind has been engaged in an enormous unplanned experiment that is slowly changing the composition of the earth's atmosphere. We cannot be certain what the result of this experiment will be, but we are fully aware that its consequences could be far reaching. At the same time, the human activities that are affecting the atmosphere are fundamentally linked to all countries' economic well-being. We do not know what the economic costs would be of efforts to limit greenhouse gas emissions, but we recognize they could be high and could have a significant impact on the global economy.

So we must determine what constitutes a responsible and sound international response to a global environmental concern in the face of a range of uncertainties. While this is not the first time we have been asked to make major policy decisions in the context of uncertainties, it may very well be the first time an issue of such complexity and with such broad-ranging implications has been addressed by the full international community. We are clearly faced with unprecedented challenges to our wisdom, foresight, and scientific capacity.

The U.S. View of the Negotiations

The United States is entering these negotiations with the utmost serious-ness of purpose. We have considered all aspects of this issue and brought to bear all of our experience and knowledge in environmental protection, scientific research, and economic decisionmaking. Based on our deliberations, we will undertake these negotiations with several key principles in mind—principles which we feel are the key to an effective convention and an effective global response to climate change:

First, we believe we must take a comprehensive approach to climate change, one which considers all aspects of this complex issue and which addresses all greenhouse gases and their sources and sinks [e.g., trees, oceans, or other areas where greenhouse gases are trapped or absorbed];

Second, we must continue to pursue aggressively our scientific and economic research efforts and our technology development programs in order to resolve uncertainties and build a solid foundation for innovative responses;

Third, we must not wait for all uncertainties to be resolved, but must pursue cost-effective actions, already justified on other grounds, which will limit net greenhouse gas emissions;

Fourth, we must adopt a long term perspective which takes account of the costs and benefits of our actions for present and future generations; and

Fifth, we must recognize the special needs of the developing countries and design mechanisms for assisting them in securing the scientific and technical tools necessary for their fullest participation in a truly global effort.

We have the opportunity now to translate these principles into innovative and effective solutions by crafting a framework convention that will engage all nations in a concerted international response.

---

1 Department of State Dispatch, February 25, 1991.

2 America's Climate Change Strategy: An Action Agenda, released by the White House on February 4, 1991.

Polish President Lech Walesa Visits Washington

Remarks at White House Welcoming Ceremony, March 20, 1991 [1]

President Bush. Mr. President, to all our Polish and American friends here today: A poet once wrote, "Let me address you in the name of millions." Today, I address you in the name of millions who convey their admiration and love—the people of the United States.

Two years ago, Lech Walesa became only the second private citizen from abroad to address a joint session of the Congress. And he impressed us then with his commitment to goodness, his passion for the hard-fought necessity we call democracy. Today he returns as his nation's first democratically elected President.

Mr. President, you have led by principle and example. You created a solidarity of spirit that inspired millions of Poles to risk their lives in steel mills, shipyards, and tenements and towns. And after winning the fight for independence, you instilled the sense of tolerance essential for letting democracy set down roots in an unsettled world. No wonder your countrymen sing to you, *"Sto lat, sto lat"*—may he live 100 years.

But you also understand that the cause of freedom cannot end at your own borders, and you proved it during the war in the Persian Gulf. You joined us in demonstrating to the entire world that we cannot permit aggression to stand. And you taught your countrymen that the answer to tyranny is international solidarity. And in the process, you helped shape a new world order.

That order, of course, began in Europe with the end of the Cold War and the emergence of a continent whole and free. You played a key role in helping Central and Eastern Europe join the commonwealth of freedom. And you have worked hard to build a prosperous land upon tyranny's ruins.

This is not an easy task. In your New Year's Eve message, you talked of reform: political reform—you've called for fully free parliamentary elections; intellectual reform that can help man begin the hard work of freedom;

spiritual reform, honoring the One through whom all things are possible; and finally, you've spoken of economic reform, upon which so much depends. In your address to Congress, you said, "We are not expecting philanthropy. But we would like to see our country treated as a partner and friend."

Today we rededicate ourselves to the success of free democracy in Poland and throughout Central and Eastern Europe.

Mr. President, we want your economic transformation to succeed, your new democracy to flourish.

Last week, the Paris Club agreed to cut Poland's official debt burden by at least 50 percent. The United States worked long and hard to achieve that unprecedented agreement, and we encourage other creditors to join us in going beyond that 50 percent level. We certainly shall. We will reduce your indebtedness to us by a full 70 percent, a portion of which will help Poland fund a new foundation for the environment.

I am pleased to tell you, Mr. President, that I've asked the Congress to increase next year's grant assistance to these new democracies to $470 million, half again last year's request. And since the real engine of progress is not aid but trade, I am pleased to announce two new economic initiatives designed to help the nations of Central and Eastern Europe proceed along the path to growth and prosperity.

The American Business Initiative and the Trade Enhancement Initiative will encourage businesses to invest in your future. In addition, Commerce Secretary Robert Mosbacher will lead an investment mission to Poland this summer, letting U.S. businesses see the great opportunity the new Poland offers.

So, as you can see, Mr. President, we want your economic transformation to succeed, your new democracy to

flourish. And we call on other nations to follow our example.

For two centuries, the love of liberty has linked our lands. General Kosciusko was a friend to our Founding Fathers, just as you and His Holiness Pope John Paul II are our steadfast friends today. Mr. President, our nations and heroes have long fought together to defend the rights of man. This historic commitment forms the core of the Joint Declaration of Principles that we will sign later today.

Two hundred years ago, gallant Polish freedom fighters praised these principles when they sang, "Poland is not lost while Poles still live." Today we rejoice. Poland is not lost but has once again been found because men like you still live.

God bless you, your beloved land, and our United States of America.

President Walesa. Honored Mr. President, thank you for such a nice welcome. Thank you for your friendly words. I am happy that I stepped again on the hospitable American land.

I come as the President of a sovereign and democratic Republic of Poland, the country which was the first to challenge communism and today is building a system of freedom, democracy, and free enterprise.

It is not a coincidence that it is America which is the target of one of my first trips in my Presidential term of office. The United States has, for over 200 years, been exemplifying to the world how to build a system of freedom. The United States led the free world defending values of democracy and humanism. Your determination and your civilizational bloom were the hope of Poles opposing alien domination. It was America, in the name of the international community, that restored recently peace and justice in the Persian Gulf.

Poland is not a world superpower; her actions do not have a global dimension. But it was Poland first in Central Europe to step upon the path of freedom. Poland is the country which paves the way for other nations liberating themselves from communism.

Poland also took upon itself the burden of leading in the structuring of a market economy. We used in the past the assistance of the United States of America—political, economic, and first of all, moral.

Today, a major part of our debt burden was reduced. Your personal involvement in this cause has, for Poland, a historical dimension. It gives us new, great possibilities. For this help, I most cordially thank the great American nation.

The changes in Poland are not completed yet. The political victory of Solidarity should be reflected in economic success. Our success is important not only to us; it is needed for Europe because it is a condition of order and stability. It is needed by the whole free world, for it extends its boundaries by the central region of the continent, it extends the zone of democracy and security.

The relations between the Republic of Poland and the United States have today reached their peak after the war. One could even say that they reached their peak in the whole of history. Our countries are linked by common values and the same ideals. We are linked by friendly collaboration on the international arena. I would like this to be followed by a development of mutually advantageous economic cooperation.

Free Poland is becoming a country of new economic opportunities. It is worth to broaden the cooperation with it, to trade and to invest. I invite you to this cooperation, for it is going to be advantageous to both sides.

I know, Mr. President, that you're a sincere friend of Poland. I'm grateful to you for your extremely goodwill interest in our problems. Our talks shall contribute to the strengthening of cooperation and the friendship of our nations.

God bless you, Mr. President. God bless America.

Declaration on Relations Between the United States of America and the Republic of Poland, March 20, 1991 [1]

For over 200 years the United States and Poland have been bound by shared values and a commitment to the principles of democracy, human liberty and the rule of law. The American Constitution of 1789 and the Polish Constitution of 1791 are enduring symbols of

this special bond, which survived even during the long periods when Poland's independence and liberty were denied. Our relations have been further sustained and enriched by the millions of Americans of Polish descent who over the generations have helped create a free and prosperous society in the United States.

Poland and the United States share an interest in maintaining stability and security in the new Europe, and in working for the further strengthening of peace on the continent.

Just as Poles supported America's quest for freedom and liberty more than two centuries ago, so has America stood by Poland during her long years of darkness. When the Polish people began to reassert control over their national destinies, the United States committed itself to supporting their pioneering efforts to secure their freedom and to build a market economy and stable democratic rule.

Poland and the United States share an interest in maintaining stability and security in the new Europe, and in working for the further strengthening of peace on the continent. Our relations are based on the United Nations Charter and principles of the Helsinki Final Act and Paris Charter, [2] including sovereign equality, territorial integrity, inviolability of frontiers, nonintervention in internal affairs, and the rule of law. The United States attaches great importance to the consolidation and safeguarding of Poland's democracy and independence, which it considers integral to the new Europe, whole and free.

Relations between Poland and the United States have entered a new era of cooperation and partnership. The United States and Poland are committed to developing their new partnership through an enhanced political dialogue and regular contacts in areas of common interest.

Poland and the United States share the conviction that the development of a market economy in Poland is essential to its stability and security. The United States reaffirms its con-

tinued strong support for Poland's courageous program of economic reform. The Polish Stabilization Fund, the Polish-American Enterprise Fund, and U.S. support in international financial institutions are among the tangible signs of that commitment.

Poland's firm commitment to an economic reform program that enjoys the endorsement and support of the International Monetary Fund has made possible the mobilization of substantial new financial and other economic assistance from the international community. The United States and Poland have concluded a Treaty Concerning Business and Economic Relations and other key agreements that should facilitate trade and investment needed for economic growth and prosperity.

Poland is engaged in an economic transformation of historic proportions in which its economic partners also have a key role in assuring success. We therefore welcome the agreement of the Paris Club on the substantial reduction of Poland's foreign debt obligations, which represents an historic and exceptional step by the international community to reinforce Poland's progress toward democracy and the free market.

The United States and Poland are also committed to developing their new partnership through closer cultural, educational, and scientific contacts.

The United States and Poland are convinced that these principles will further strengthen the bonds of lasting friendship and cooperation between both states, as an integral element of the broader partnership that binds the United States and Europe and of a new world order based on democratic values and the rule of law.

White House Fact Sheet on United States Assistance to Poland, March 20, 1991 [1]

Recent Economic Developments

In 1990, Poland adopted and implemented a comprehensive program of economic reforms more extensive than that of any other country in Central and Eastern Europe. The new government of President Walesa is taking important steps to further the development of a market economy by placing special emphasis on speeding up the pace of reform in general and the process of privatization in particular.

Responding to requests for assistance from the Polish Government, the U.S. Government provided over $300 million in grant assistance in 1990 and offered substantial credits from the Export-Import Bank and the Overseas Private Investment Corporation. The United States has begun projects in agriculture, privatization, technical training, and labor training, and concentrated ventures in clean fossil fuels, and air and water quality in the Krakow region.

All of these activities will continue in 1991, but U.S. technical assistance will expand considerably as we begin new efforts to help restructure the Polish economy. The United States will also substantially increase the amount of funds available for equity investment through the Polish-American Enterprise Fund and will initiate new programs to encourage U.S. private sector investment in Poland.

Assistance Activities

1. *Democratic Initiatives.* U.S. programs in this area will provide:

- Equipment and training for the national legislature, focusing primarily on the establishment of parliamentary procedures and the development of effective research and information systems.
- Training for local and regional legislatures, city and regional managers, and other local public administrators in the basic skills of governance and administration.
- Support for independent media, including the establishment of a Media Resource Center in Poland.

2. *Food Aid.* In 1990, the United States provided over $90 million in food aid to Poland. This assistance was intended to help stem Poland's declining standard of living and ease the budget crunch by improving the efficiency of private agriculture. Thanks in part to the effect of the market on supplies, major food aid will not be needed in 1991.

3. *Stabilization Fund.* The United States granted $200 million to the Polish Stabilization Fund in 1990 as part of a U.S.-led multidonor hard cur-

rency reserve in support of the transformation of the economy. The fund made possible limited convertibility of the Polish zloty by creating a reserve to be used by the Polish Government if additional foreign exchange is needed. Poland has not had to draw on the fund to date, and has earned substantial interest that the Polish Government may use in support of its economic programs.

4. *The Polish-American Enterprise Fund,* to be capitalized at $240 million, received $35 million in FY 1990, and will be given an additional $69 million in FY 1991. This privately managed investment fund can take equity or debt positions in new businesses or recently privatized firms, leveraging private capital and often facilitating joint ventures. For instance, the fund is already financing private banking, new housing construction, and agribusinesses.

5. *Environment and Energy.* U.S. programs carried out by AID [U.S. Agency for International Development], the EPA [U.S. Environmental Protection Agency], and the Department of Energy will provide equipment and technical assistance for clean fossil fuels, technical assistance for air and water quality, and technical assistance to redress decades of environmental degradation. The United States is also providing assistance in improving energy efficiency.

6. *Labor Market Transition.* The Department of Labor is providing help in the development of unemployment insurance, job retraining, the creation of regional unemployment centers, and other "safety-net" mechanisms to assist those most disadvantaged during the transition to a market economy. The AFL/CIO is helping with the strengthening of trade unions and the retraining of the labor force.

7. *Peace Corps.* Approximately 100 volunteers are in Poland teaching English, working on environmental projects, and assisting with small businesses.

8. *Trade and Development Program (TDP).* TDP is financing over $4 million in feasibility studies, consultancies, and training programs for major development projects with large export potential for the U.S. private sector.

9. *International Financial Institutions.* The United States, as lead shareholder, has encouraged the World Bank (IBRD) to provide strong support to Eastern Europe's redevelop-

ment. The Bank already has plans to lend $9 billion to countries of the region. We have also led the way in obtaining an additional $7.5 billion in funding to Eastern Europe by the International Monetary Fund (IMF).

10. The U.S. Agency for International Development is launching a number of new activities which will focus on the development of the private sector in Poland. Some of these projects are:

Privatization and Enterprise Restructuring will provide technical assistance to prepare state-owned enterprises for privatization, to assist private firms to operate more efficiently, and to help Government agencies put in place the policies, laws, and regulations necessary to privatization.

The American Business and Private Sector Development Initiative will stimulate the transfer of U.S. technology and the flow of U.S. capital to Eastern Europe by promoting business opportunities in the region for American firms.

The Competition Policies, Laws, and Regulations project provides technical assistance in rewriting laws and regulations regarding taxation, antitrust, and the ownership and transfer of private property.

In the *Financial Services* sector we will assist in the critical development of a competitive banking industry and help create new financial institutions.

Management Training and Economics Education will help develop the technical, management, and economics skills necessary to operate a market-oriented economy.

In the *Housing* sector we will provide technical assistance for development of housing markets and a competitive housing construction industry.

In *Agriculture and Agribusiness* we are helping to develop a true cooperative system and create the framework for further privatization.

In the *Humanitarian* sector, we are assisting with the improvement of health care and the creation of an improved social safety net.

11. In addition, the *Citizens Democracy Corps [CDC],* a private voluntary organization created with the assistance of a U.S. Government grant, is helping to mobilize the resources of the private sector to assist in the Polish transition. CDC Chairman Drew Lewis is directing a major effort to modernize

the Polish transportation and distribution system. Hundreds of private U.S. organizations are mounting their own programs in Poland as well.

White House Fact Sheet on the Reduction of Poland's Debt, March 20, 1991 [1]

Today President Bush warmly endorsed the historic agreement between the Government of Poland and its government creditors in the Paris Club to reduce Poland's debt obligations to official creditors. This package represents a strong signal of creditor support for Polish economic and democratic reforms. Together with a new three year program with the International Monetary Fund (IMF) and continued reforms, it should help encourage new private investment and capital flows to Poland and provide a sound basis for sustained economic growth. The agreement is the successful culmination of vigorous U.S. efforts to achieve a multilateral agreement offering substantial benefits to Poland.

Specifically, the agreement provides for the reduction of Polish debt by a minimum of 50 percent in real terms. The debt reduction will be formally adopted by the Paris Club once Poland's IMF program has been approved (expected in April). The restructuring will occur in two stages:

- The first stage involves 30 percent relief on a net present value basis and includes cash flow relief of 80 percent for the crucial first three years of the agreement.
- The second stage consists of 20 percent relief on a net present value basis after three years, upon successful completion by Poland of the IMF program.

In each stage, creditor governments will have the option of pursuing equivalent relief through debt reduction, interest reduction, or capitalization of interest on concessional terms.

Governments will also have the option of further reducing Polish obligations beyond the consensus level of 50 percent reduction through (a) additional bilateral relief and (b) the voluntary conversion of up to 10 percent of outstanding claims via debt/equity, debt-for-nature, or other debt swaps.

To lead this effort, the President announced that the United States was prepared to increase U.S. debt relief for Poland beyond the 50 percent level agreed in the Paris Club. We propose to do this in the following two ways:

- Additional bilateral debt reduction within the two stage operation.
- A write-off of 10 percent of Poland's stock of debt to the United States. This action will enable the Government of Poland to provide local currency resources to fund a foundation for the environment.

As a result of these additional steps, Polish debt to the United States would be reduced by a total of 70 percent in real terms.

The unilateral actions by the United States would raise the total debt reduction under the multilateral Paris Club agreement from the agreed minimum consensus level of 50 percent to 52 percent. The President strongly encourages other creditor governments to take similar additional actions and provide bilateral relief beyond the 50 percent level.

White House Fact Sheet on American Business and Private Sector Development Initiative for Central and Eastern Europe, March 20, 1991 [1]

U.S. trade and investment can play a major role in supporting political and economic reforms in Central and Eastern Europe. The American Business and Private Sector Development Initiative is designed to promote the growth of U.S. investment, participation by U.S. firms in infrastructure development, and increased involvement of small and medium sized U.S. companies in bilateral trade.

This initiative is a $45 million two year project carried out by AID, the Department of Commerce, the Overseas Private Investment Corporation [OPIC], and the U.S. Trade and Development Program in partnership with the private sector.

Primary emphasis will be on five key sectors identified by the Central and Eastern European countries and

ourselves as of key importance: agriculture and agribusiness, energy, environment, telecommunications, and housing.

The six elements of the program are:

- An American Business Center in Warsaw, Poland, which will make available office space and technical business services on a user-fee basis in cooperation with the private sector.
- Consortia of American businesses in Eastern Europe which will support groups of mainly small and medium-sized U.S. companies wishing to enter the East European market. Grants will assist U.S. trade and business associations in selected sectors in establishing a presence in the region.
- Expansion of Commerce's Eastern Europe Business Information Center, to develop information and provide assistance to U.S. and East European companies interested in trade and investment.
- An AID Capital Development Initiative, designed to provide assistance to Eastern European Governments and private sector firms in designing infrastructure projects in ways that will encourage the involvement of U.S. companies.
- Additional funding for feasibility studies by the Trade and Development Program related to the five sectors described above.
- We are also seeking legislative authority to expand OPIC's pilot equity investment program to include Eastern Europe, so that OPIC can make direct investments in promising joint ventures.

White House Fact Sheet on Trade Enhancement Initiative for Central and Eastern Europe, March 20, 1991 [1]

From the beginning, U.S. support for political and economic reform in Eastern Europe has emphasized not only aid but trade. The United States has led the way in extending increased access to its own market and in encouraging the European Community and others to do the same. Listed below are additional initiatives in the trade area that the United States is undertaking at this time.

(1) *GSP Duty-free Benefits.*

The President is expected to approve shortly a significant expansion of duty-free benefits covering $182 million in Central and Eastern European country exports under the Generalized System of Preferences (GSP). Czechoslovakia will be added to the list of beneficiaries which already includes Poland, Hungary, and Yugoslavia. These increases are in addition to $500 million in duty-free imports from Central and Eastern Europe at this time. In addition, the President has decided to speed up implementation of $176 million in benefits to May 1 from the traditional July 1 date.

Over half of the expanded Eastern European GSP benefit will go to Poland—$93.3 million of the $182.4 million. This action will more than double the amount of Poland's duty-free exports under GSP.

(2) *Overcoming Informational Barriers to Trade.*

The administration will sponsor a series of seminars designed to ensure Central and Eastern European countries' understanding of U.S. trade laws including antidumping and countervailing duty provisions (AD/CVD); familiarity with the GSP program and procedures; access to data on trade flows and on U.S. quota fill rates; familiarity with open procurement laws and procedures.

AD/CVD. The Department of Commerce will conduct seminars for Eastern European officials on U.S. anti-dumping and countervailing duty laws. These seminars, to which interested enterprise representatives will be welcome, will focus on the methodology used to analyze dumping in non-market economic cases. The Commerce Department will also discuss the implications under AD/CVD laws of the move toward greater market orientation.

GSP. Commerce, State, and USTR [Office of U.S. Trade Representative] representatives will conduct a series of GSP seminars in eligible Central and Eastern European countries to ensure that enterprises are familiar with GSP benefits and procedures for taking full advantage of the program. The next seminar series is scheduled for late March in Prague, Budapest, and Warsaw.

Quotas. Embassies in Central and Eastern European countries will be kept informed on quota fill rates and ensure, in cooperation with responsible host government officials, chambers of commerce, etc., that this information is available to local producers.

Procurement. Commerce and OMB are prepared to organize a series of seminars for Central and Eastern European countries on recommended government procurement laws and transparent procedures which, if adopted, would result in savings, purchase of improved products, and fair competition and would also enable these countries to seek accession to the (GATT) Agreement on Government Procurement.

(3) *Regional Economic Development Initiative (REDI).*

The administration is developing a program to promote new commercial ties between companies and business organizations in comparable economic regions of the United States and Central and Eastern Europe, with a particular focus on promoting trade with the region's burgeoning private sector.

The Commerce Department program will match companies in complementary economic regions in the United States and Central and Eastern Europe. The program, using existing Commerce Department resources and facilities (e.g., the Eastern European Business Information Center and U.S. Foreign Commercial Service offices), will focus on building a data base of regional and local business leaders and groups in the United States and Eastern Europe. This information will be particularly useful in matching small and medium-sized U.S. companies with counterparts in Eastern Europe's burgeoning private sector and in promoting new trade and investment ties among these entities.

(4) *Removal of Impediments to Trade Expansion.*

The President is prepared to send to Poland and other reforming Central and Eastern European countries a team of experts, led by the Office of the U.S. Trade Representative, to conduct a prompt and intensive review of internal and external barriers to expanded trade with the region and to propose specific solutions to problems identified.

(5) *Access to the European Community.*

The President is challenging the European Community, Central and Eastern Europe's largest market, with the largest potential for trade expansion, to redouble its efforts to open its markets to Central and Eastern European countries and to open all sectors (including agriculture) for liberalization under the free-trade area agreements now under negotiation with Poland, Hungary, and Czechoslovakia.

---

1 Text from Weekly Compilation of Presidential Documents of March 25, 1991.

2 Charter of Paris for a New Europe, November 21, 1990. See *Foreign Policy Bulletin*, January-April 1991, p. 75.

The United States and Albania Reestablish Relations

JOINT COMMUNIQUE, MARCH 15, 1991 [1]

The Government of the United States of America and the Government of the People's Socialist Republic of Albania, following consultations between their duly authorized representatives, and having confirmed their commitment to the principles of equality, mutual respect, and mutual benefit, have decided to reestablish diplomatic relations with effect from March 15, 1991, and subsequently to exchange diplomatic missions at the level of Ambassador.

MEMORANDUM OF UNDERSTANDING BETWEEN THE UNITED STATES AND ALBANIA, MARCH 15, 1991 [1]

The Government of the United States of America and the Government of the People's Socialist Republic of Albania, as a result of discussions of their representatives and considering that the Governments have reestablished diplomatic relations effective this date, have agreed as follows:

Article I

1. The Governments shall conduct their diplomatic relations in accordance with the Charter of the United Nations, signed at San Francisco on June 26, 1946, and the Vienna Convention on Diplomatic Relations, signed at Vienna on April 18, 1961, to which both Governments are parties. The Governments shall exchange diplomatic representatives with the rank of Ambassador Extraordinary and Plenipotentiary, as soon as the necessary administrative and legal arrangements in the sending State so permit.

2. The two Governments shall provide all necessary assistance for the early establishment, and performance of the functions, including consular functions, of diplomatic missions in their respective capitals, in accordance with international law and practice. Such assistance shall include, inter alia, consent to the use of wireless transmitters including the use of satellite links, by the respective Embassies for pur-

poses of official communication, subject to compliance with the laws and regulations of the receiving State. Such laws and regulations shall, however, be applied so as to give full effect to the consent hereby recorded.

3. The Governments affirm their intent to respect the fundamental principles on which diplomatic intercourse is based, including, inter alia, the principle of inviolability of the premises of the diplomatic mission.

We intend to send a delegation to Albania in the near future to expand contact with the Albanian government and people and to begin preparations for establishing a diplomatic mission.

---

4. The two Governments shall extend the privileges and immunities of diplomatic agents, as defined in the Vienna Convention on Diplomatic Relations, to those members of their respective administrative and technical staffs of the diplomatic missions accredited to Washington and Tirana, as well as their families. The stated privileges and immunities will not be accorded to persons who are nationals or permanent residents of the receiving State.

5. The two Governments intend to hold discussions on the conduct of consular relations at the earliest practicable time. Until such time, the two Governments agree to the following interim practical arrangement:

> If a citizen of the sending country is arrested or detained in any manner, the authorities of the receiving country shall, within 72 hours, notify the designated representative of the sending country of the arrest or detention of the person and permit within 24 hours of such notification access by a representative of the sending country to the citizen who is under arrest or detained in custody.

Article II

The two Governments intend to promote relations in economic, cultural and other fields.

Article III

The Treaty of Naturalization signed at Tirana on April 6, 1932, shall terminate upon the entry into force of this Memorandum of Understanding. In this connection, the Government of the United States of America notes that the statement made in paragraph 2 of the diplomatic note delivered on June 23, 1922, by the American Commissioner in Tirana to the President of the Council and Minister of Foreign Affairs of Albania concerning the "interpretation and application of laws affecting naturalization in the United States" has for a number of years ceased to be an accurate representation of United States law.

Article IV

Following the reestablishment of relations, the two Governments, upon the request of either side, shall enter into negotiations for the prompt settlement of claims and other financial and property matters that remain unresolved between them, each Government being entitled to raise during such negotiations the matters it wishes to be addressed.

Article V

This Memorandum of Understanding shall enter into force upon signature. Done at Washington, in duplicate, in the English and Albanian languages, this 16th day of March, 1991.

REMARKS AT SIGNING CEREMONY, MARCH 16, 1991 [2]

Raymond G. H. Seitz, Assistant Secretary of State for European and Canadian Affairs and Albanian Foreign Minister Muhamet Kapllani

Assistant Secretary Seitz. I welcome you, Foreign Minister [Kapllani], to Washington and to the Department of State for this historic occasion. Today, after a lapse of 52 years, the United States and Albania are reestablishing diplomatic relations with the hope of building friendly and fruitful ties between our two peoples.

The relationship between our countries goes back to the early years of this century, when President [Woodrow] Wilson extended American support for the young Albanian state. That relationship was never forgotten by the many thousands of Americans of Albanian origin, some of whom are in this room, who kept contact with their homeland over all these years.

Despite differences in political systems, the common interests of our two countries have not altered since President Wilson's time. Both of our countries share an interest in a world in which all states, large and small, can live together without fear. We recognize Albania's independence and territorial integrity within its present borders. We welcome the aspirations of the Albanian people to join the Helsinki process and look forward to the day when Albania will be a full participant in the Conference on Security and Cooperation in Europe (CSCE).

Today, Albania stands on the threshold of a new future. The Albanian people have made clear their hopes for a more democratic and prosperous country. The United States supports and encourages the process of political and economic reform which has begun in Albania. This process will mark an important step forward when multiparty elections are held at the end of this month. We are pleased that Americans will be among foreign groups who will observe them. It will be important to the CSCE community of nations and to the world that these elections are both free and fair. We understand the great social and economic hardships now confronting Albania. We believe that these difficulties can be overcome if all Albanian political parties and citizens pursue their goals through peaceful, democratic dialogue.

The United States hopes to enter into a constructive and productive relationship with Albania on the basis of mutual interests. We intend to send a delegation to Albania in the near future to expand contact with the Albanian government and people and to begin preparations for establishing a diplomatic mission. Along with other countries and international organizations, the United States is prepared to support the efforts of the Albanian government and people to pursue economic and political reforms. Our ability to help will be linked to Albania's own commitment to reform

and to its government's respect for fundamental human rights. We will also encourage private American organizations and individuals to make their own contributions to this process.

I would like to thank all of the many people who made this day possible. Among them are a number of distinguished Americans of Albanian origin in this room today who contributed immensely of their time and efforts to forge a new relationship between our two countries.

Mr. Foreign Minister, welcome again to the United States. We now begin to build a better future for both of our peoples.

Foreign Minister Kapllani. It is a great privilege and honor to have been charged by my government to sign the document on the reestablishment of diplomatic relations between Albania and the United States. We are at a very important ceremony. I call it a historic moment, a big day. It is a big day, for today we are filling a gap which has been felt for too long between us. We are creating the favorable conditions to make up for lost time. This is not simply a symbolic moment of putting a signature in a document. It is a milestone on the road of our relations—a turning point in these relations which we do hope, or I'd rather say, are convinced, will witness successful developments.

Albania is living one of the most exciting periods in its history of post-World War II. It is going through a radical democratic process which covers the political field, the superstructure, the economic field, the infrastructure, and all fields of life. are committed to this process, because it responds to the present and long term interests of the Albanian people to make Albania a truly—and a productive member of the family of the European nations. Albania believes in the CSCE process. The CSCE process has shown that security in the world of today is not simply a security of arms—military security, political security—it is at the same time, if not more than military, economic security—and economic security means economic development.

We in Albania have many difficulties: We are facing economic difficulties, facing difficulties which have to do with political reforms, but these are difficulties which are leading us to a better future. That is why it is worth exerting all our efforts to meet this

challenge of the time. We are fully confident that the Albanian people, along with the other European nations, along with this great country and nation with whom we are today reestablishing diplomatic relations, Albania will march ahead on the road of democracy in the interests of its own people, in the interests of peace and security in the Balkans and beyond.

---

1 Department of State Dispatch, March 18, 1991.

2 Department of State Dispatch, March 25, 1991.

Soviet Disunion: The American Response

by *Robert B. Zoellick*

Statement before the Subcommittee on European Affairs of the Senate Foreign Relations Committee, February 28, 1991. Mr. Zoellick is Counselor of the Department of State. [1]

I am pleased to have this opportunity to report on recent events in the Soviet Union and the American response. I have organized my statement to cover four topics:

- Key tenets of U.S. policy toward the Soviet Union, 1989-90;
- Analysis of recent events;
- Outlook; and
- Implications for US policy.

Key Tenets of U.S. Policy Toward the Soviet Union, 1989-90

In analyzing our future course, it is useful to review the key elements of our present policy. It establishes a baseline and explains the reasoning behind our current path.

The President stated in May 1989 that it was time for us to move "beyond containment." Given the break in traditional patterns of Soviet behavior, we felt it was important to seize the possibility to achieve long term Western goals while also opening the way for the U.S.S.R. to play a constructive part in the international community.

Secretary Baker explained our approach toward the Soviet Union in speeches he gave in April and October 1989; he then reviewed our progress and explained our ongoing strategy in a third speech in October of 1990.

In brief, our strategy has been to explore and develop possible points of mutual advantage for both the United States and the Soviet Union. Our logic has been to probe the "new thinking" in Soviet foreign policy, seeking to shape and, where possible, to alter Soviet policy calculations so that the Soviets might face up to the contradictions between the new thinking and old habits. We sought to formulate proposals in ways that emphasized benefits to both parties. In doing so, we strove to escape from the old East-West, zero-sum logic that a gain for one was a loss for the other.

Our strategy required us to broaden and deepen our agenda with the Soviets. We added new items. We proposed new approaches.

Our first objective was to work with the Soviets to overcome the division of Europe, the original cause of the Cold War. After many decades, Western resolve and NATO's protection had led to free and prosperous countries next door to dictatorship. When the people behind the Iron Curtain—confronted with such disparity—chose freedom, we sought to persuade the Soviets that the peaceful emergence of democratic governments and market economies throughout Central and Eastern Europe would benefit all of us—East and West. The old illegitimate regimes were decaying because they did not reflect the consent of the governed and could not tap the free will of free men; their perpetuation would be costly both in economic terms and in preventing the Soviet Union from achieving the opening to the West that it sought. Our approach was cooperative and reassuring, not threatening. This approach—an effort not to singularize or isolate any party in Europe that respected the moves toward freedom—was important in bringing about German unification peacefully and democratically.

Second, we stressed our common interest in resolving regional conflicts peacefully, often seeking to rely on elections as a means of establishing legitimacy and the local popular will. To create an appropriate context for elections, we sought to use our respective influence to persuade conflicting parties that the use of arms would not produce an enduring solution. This has been the approximate formula for our cooperative efforts in Nicaragua, Cambodia, Angola, and Afghanistan. The experience provided the basis for the immediate joint U.S.-Soviet denunciation of Iraq's attack on Kuwait—the joint statement of Secretary Baker and Minister Shevardnadze on August 3 which in turn provided the basis for unprecedented U.N. and multinational action.

Third, we sought to demonstrate our support for *perestroika* in practical ways. We expanded our human rights agenda with the Soviets through an effort to institutionalize these rights by building the rule of law. We started a program of technical economic cooperation to encourage the development of market reforms. We explored our common interest in addressing transnational challenges, such as narcotics, terrorism, and the environment.

Fourth, we expanded the arms control agenda with two efforts: we pressed to address the imbalance in conventional weapons in Europe, and we explored our mutual interest in halting and reversing the build-up of new weapons of mass destruction. These efforts produced the CFE [conventional armed forces in Europe] and chemical weapons destruction agreements.

A Successful Record

I think this strategy has built a successful record, although there is no doubt that our work is far from finished. The Red Army is departing Central and Eastern Europe. The nations behind the old Iron Curtain now have an opportunity to chart a new course of democracy and market economics. We have taken significant steps toward constraining and channeling the Soviet military threat through arms control. We have seen the Soviet impulse toward adventurism diminish, and we have also helped to foster Soviet cooperation in regional conflicts around the globe. And we demonstrated our good faith commitment to support political and economic reform in the Soviet Union if that is a course to which the Soviet leadership remains committed.

The increased uncertainty about the future course of the Soviet Union has three major implications for this strategy.

One, we should seek to secure those benefits that we have achieved over recent years.

Two, we should continue to explore the possibility of finding new points of mutual advantage between the Soviet Union and the United

States, but do so in a way that recognizes the changed context.

Three, we should try to manage uncertainty by multiplying our channels of information and increasing our points of access with a rapidly changing Soviet society.

Analysis of Recent Events

The Soviet Union is a vast country. The motivations, fears, and interests of its diverse peoples are enormously complex. The Kremlin is certainly not the sole locus of influence, but the political scene has been dominated by the interplay of many forces in Soviet society with the actions of a particular leader. Therefore, I wanted to offer you one possible analysis of how recent changes may have affected President Gorbachev's perspective and the path of Soviet policy.

In October 1989, Secretary Baker made an observation on the Soviet reform effort that is a useful point of departure for reviewing the course of recent events there. He said:

President Gorbachev wants to remake the Soviet Union. That's what *perestroika* and *glasnost* are all about. That may not have been his aim in 1985, but the failures of the early reform efforts convinced him and his colleagues that change must dig deeper into Soviet society. These are utilitarian purposeful, and determined men—we should recognize that they are not pursuing freedom for freedom's sake. Their aim is to modernize the Soviet Union, but their frame of reference is not the Age of Reason or the spirit of the Enlightenment. They are the descendants of other great Russian modernizers—like Peter the Great and Alexander II—fundamentally rooted in the unique Russian experience.

As a modernizer and as a balancer of political forces, President Gorbachev faced success, deterioration, and dilemmas in the late summer of 1990.

By unleashing the truth, he had begun to expose the terrible record of communism. The old system was discredited. Indeed, in July, Gorbachev rallied popular resentment to inflict a stunning defeat of the old guard at the Communist Party congress.

Yet he had nothing to substitute for the party's control of state and society, and problems pressed in from all sides. The new openness seemed to be dismantling institutional

capabilities and societal norms at a rapid pace. State institutions—executive and legislative—appeared unable to step into the breach. There was an erosion of executive power at all levels. Legislatures could debate, but seemed unable to act coherently; their passage of laws did not translate into action.

The economic situation continued to worsen. Movements calling for increased autonomy, or even secession, complicated the difficult tasks of creating a new civil society and new economic relationships. All this disorder, however explicable and perhaps unavoidable, tapped deep-seated Russian fears. The society and economy seemed to be disintegrating, and yet no one seemed to be able to do anything about it.

Still, it is important not to lose sight of some fundamental changes that have taken place in the Soviet Union over the course of the past six years.

Despite the hopes and excitement the reformers generated, they seemed unable to serve as an effective counterweight; they could not yet help balance those forces in society that were frightened and threatened by the changes. That is why [Foreign Minister] Shevardnadze sought to give them a "wake-up call," warning of the need for reformers to pull themselves together.

Solutions From the Right

In contrast, the institutions on the right may have seemed to Gorbachev to offer straightforward, understandable solutions to these problems—even though they are not real answers. Moreover, the army, the KGB, the defense industrial complex, and the Communist Party all remain powerful constituencies. All felt threatened by recent events. Just as important, these are all national institutions, tools that the Soviet leadership might use to counter the forces that it probably perceived as undermining its modernization of the Soviet Union.

In sum, President Gorbachev may have perceived internal economic and political problems that gave him less freedom to maneuver; lack of support

(or even a threat) from radical reformers wanting to move quickly toward real democracy, capitalism, and republic independence; and forces on the right that offered apparent solutions and familiar tools to deal with their own anxieties and those of the society at large.

So Gorbachev turned to the right, in his view, to preserve his credibility as a leader and to preserve the union. In September [1990], Gorbachev rejected Shatalin's "500 Day Plan" and spurned the reformers. He retained Ryzhkov as his prime minister, affirming his intention not to abandon the existing governmental structure. In October, Gorbachev secured adoption of a more vaguely worded compromise economic reform program. In December, he got vast new presidential powers to implement this program. Also in December, Gorbachev made key personnel changes at the interior and justice ministries and secured stronger enforcement powers for the KGB and military to act internally. Foreign Minister Shevardnadze resigned, warning of dictatorship. By the end of the year, almost all of Gorbachev's perestroika team had departed. Finally, in January, the Soviet leadership opted for intimidation in the Baltics, which became a show of force and then violence.

Gorbachev may well believe that, given the pressures he faces, he must act forcefully to restore order so as to "save" reform. But it is important to underscore that this is his conception of reform—of modernization of Soviet society—not the conception of the radical reformers whom he freed to think for themselves. Indeed, President Gorbachev has probably been honestly surprised by the negative reaction in the Soviet Union and in the West to these moves; he may have expected that people would trust him, would give him leeway.

In the face of a strong negative reaction from the West, President Gorbachev appears to have taken steps to limit his responsibility for some of the particularly objectionable characteristics of the rightward turn, most notably in the Baltics. He probably recognizes that his long range hopes for modernization of the Soviet Union require maintaining an opening to the West. But modernization, and the West, are not more important than survival.

Still, it is important not to lose sight of some fundamental changes that have taken place in the Soviet Union over the course of the past six years. Some reforms have planted roots, although it is hard to tell how deep they run. People no longer fear challenging the government and the old ways. Demonstrations of over 200,000 people in the streets of Moscow cannot be dismissed lightly. The cooperative movement, facing incredible adversity, continues to grow. (Over 6% of the Soviet labor force now works in cooperatives or is self-employed.) There are reports that the Soviet military is troubled by the prospect of being employed against its own people in the event of civil unrest. And the new leaders of the republics, although not operating from a common agenda, do seem to share a mutual interest in establishing a more pluralistic system and a more equitable distribution of power between the center and the republics. These are changes we need to encourage; they offer some chance of a different future for the Soviet Union.

Outlook

Perestroika has been a program of political and economic liberalization that was supposed to modernize the Soviet Union. President Gorbachev wanted to end stagnation. He wanted to open the way for new people and fresh thinking. He wanted to lift restraints on information to encourage the development of science and technology. He thought that if he gave the Soviet people an increased role in setting policy, increased freedom to speak and act, that he would generate more energy and commitment to strengthen the Soviet state.

It appears that the Soviet leadership never recognized that increased freedom would enable people to choose how they would focus their energies. Those freed forces moved Soviet society in unforeseen directions. The leadership did not appreciate the long-smoldering embers of nationalism that were ready to flare once the empire loosened its grip of fear. They did not know that, once allowed to express their disdain for the Communist Party, the people would not devote their energies to invigorating state institutions created by the communists. Soviet leaders could not know that they were

creating a crisis of legitimacy that threatened the whole system through which they had risen and which they had mastered.

The Soviet leadership is trying to cope with this crisis of legitimacy by restoring "order." For them, order depends on authority.

So I suspect that the Soviet Union is now in a period of what I would label "authoritarian reform." The state will be willing to use heavy-handed measures to restore what it considers to be the necessary prerequisites for a continued program of economic and social modernization. That program is likely to be marked by a series of incremental changes and a pattern of fits and starts. The greatest danger is that the "authoritarian" elements could overwhelm the reform impulse.

The major issues that President Gorbachev now faces are, first, to work out effective center-republic relations, and second, to improve economic performance.

As the Soviet leadership focuses its attention on these two key problems, it will certainly be willing to tamper with and limit the new political and social freedom. For now, political groups continue to operate within and outside the legislative process. There is still an exchange of ideas that would have been inconceivable six years ago. President Gorbachev may seek to avoid significant limits on this exchange of ideas, because he still believes it is essential for the modernization of the economy and technological growth. But openness is a means to an end in the Soviet Union; it could be curtailed significantly if it impedes the center's ability to cope with those two overriding problems.

The problem of center-republic relations is fundamentally one of negotiating arrangements that achieve satisfactory political legitimacy between different levels of government and the people. It is clear that the old authority of empire operates no longer, so the center is beginning a halting process of determining the degree of autonomy necessary to achieve legitimacy.

Nationalism in the U.S.S.R.

As outsiders viewing this process, we need to be careful not to examine it solely through the lens of our Western conceptions of the nation-state.

Nationalism, one of the momentous movements of the 19th and 20th centuries in much of the rest of the world, has followed a somewhat different course in the Soviet Union. Russian nationalism has existed for some time, but it has been harnessed to serve the ends of Soviet communism. Russian chauvinism has antagonized many other peoples in the U.S.S.R. But the national movements in the borderland republics have only recently been freed to define their own national characters and their origins in culture, literature, language, territory, and history; they are still evolving and still exploring how they relate to one another. The relation between nationalism and the state is frequently not yet well defined.

Moreover, the national movements do not fit neatly within republic boundaries. One in five Soviet citizens lives outside his ethnic republic or area. So there is substantial potential for friction and conflict among the central government, republic governments, and national movements.

The search for political legitimacy, the balance between central authority and autonomy, and the accommodation of nationalism are all questions for the Soviet people to determine. They are not, of course, something that we are in a position to decide.

It may be the case that the new pattern of relations worked out within the Soviet Union may not be easily described in terms of traditional nation-state sovereignty. President Gorbachev has said that the center may need to develop a different treaty relationship with each republic, and that the transitions to these new relationships might differ. It is clear, however, that the Soviet Union has not progressed far in defining appropriate concepts of power-sharing, federalism, or individual rights.

On the economic front, as in the case of center-republic relations, I expect the primary objective will be to reestablish order. Some may believe that order is a prerequisite for moving the system toward market relations. The currency confiscation and the attacks on the shadow economy are designed to foster order. The price increases and compensation proposals are designed to reorder price and wage relationships. Commands to fill state orders are designed to ensure that basic supplier relationships remain in place.

These moves will be complemented with other incremental actions, such as destatization, designed to restructure the industrial organization of the economy to operate more effectively in some type of competitive market format.

Worsening Economic Outlook

This economic program will almost certainly fail. The decline in production will likely accelerate. So will inflation. Large industrial enterprises are likely to move increasingly to barter relationships, unless halted by an extensive discipline campaign. Firms that can produce goods or raw materials for export in exchange for real currencies will seize that opportunity. Firms that produce products that can be bartered for food or other supplies will do so, passing the benefits through to their workforce. Enterprises that produce large, nontradeable goods will be in trouble. Labor that controls sensitive sectors, such as energy and transport, may use its power to secure special benefits. If the agricultural sector cannot get the necessary inputs and machinery, this year's harvest could slip. The Soviet Union has a large amount of debt coming due this year, which it cannot pay, adding to the burden. The men and women at the end of the chain—the consumers—are likely to suffer even more.

One of the greatest dangers of the emphasis on economic order is that it will be particularly damaging to the nascent market sector. Despite incredible obstacles, cooperatives have continued to grow and employ more workers. But they are vulnerable because they operate outside the understood rules of the command economy. Similarly, black markets have arisen to supply goods and services to people at market prices. But the association of some of these activities with the criminal sector—either as victims of it or supplied by it—leave them vulnerable to a discipline campaign. The drive for order may also inhibit some of the barter arrangements that are developing among enterprises. This proto-market system is inefficient, handicapped by lack of competition and established rules, but it is seeking to pick up where the broken-down command economy left off.

In the economic area, too, the Soviet Union needs to establish a basic set of rules governing property rights, contracts, and competition. This is a matter of creating legitimacy and confidence in economic relations, roughly analogous to the task ahead in the political realm. Of course the ability to establish such economic rules of the game is fundamentally tied up with establishing the respective authorities of political units. At present, there is a "war of laws" that leaves producers, investors, workers, and consumers befuddled. Furthermore, there could be a clash between the need to establish efficient market ties over large areas and the devolution of political authority. So these two questions—of political and economic rules—will have to be resolved together.

The present course appears to be one of seeking to reestablish the power of the center. This is the power system that the Soviet leadership knows, and with which the national institutions like the army, the KGB, and the Communist Party are comfortable. But President Gorbachev may sincerely believe he is using this reassertion of central authority to return to the course of *perestroika*.

In part, the conflict is that President Gorbachev, who rose to the top of the old Soviet system, cannot fully understand an irony: that by initiating a new system he did not automatically ensure his legitimate leadership within the new system. The Soviet leadership's concept of legitimacy is limited by their own experience. They may want to reach an end result for the Soviet Union that both they and we can see would be in our mutual interest, but they believe they cannot reach that result unless they are permitted to operate with the power derived from the old system. The forces they must unleash to modernize the Soviet Union challenge their authority. Since they perceive these challenges as threats to modernization, the leadership moves to restore the old order. This could explain the increasing references by some Soviets to models of development like the Republic of Korea or Chile.

We should try to persuade Soviet leaders that a reliance on the methods of the old power system will create unintended consequences that move them away from the very objectives they seek. Both efficient market economics and stable democratic politics depend on public confidence that government and the public will operate according to a set of generally understood rules. Arbitrary assertions of government power threaten such a rule-based system. It is in our interest to urge all parties in the Soviet Union to create and abide by such rules. Their own processes, operating within those rules, will have to establish the legitimacy of relations between the center and the republics, and between governments and the people.

Implications for U.S. Policy

Perhaps for some time, we will need to maintain a flexible approach that can adjust to important problems raised by a major nation in great flux. The Soviet Union remains a military superpower with the capability to destroy the United States and, for that matter, the world as we know it. It still has approximately 30,000 nuclear warheads. Within the past two centuries, its armies have marched from the shores of the Pacific to Paris and Berlin. It has 46 nuclear power reactors of questionable construction that could erupt into an environmental and human catastrophe. Its oil and gas reserves are huge. Its borders mark an arc of other lands in transition: from the struggling democracies of Central and Eastern Europe, through the Islamic lands of the Mideast, on to South Asian countries struggling with their own religious and national conflicts, and extending to the communists of Eastern and Northern Asia who are trying to bolster bankrupt regimes.

As I noted above, conditions in the Soviet Union are likely to worsen, but the specific course of the future is highly uncertain. Therefore, we need to secure the benefits we have achieved, continue to probe for other points of mutual advantage while recognizing the changed context, and seek to manage the uncertainty by multiplying our points of access with a society that is transforming itself.

We need to continue to stress, through both our diplomacy and our foreign economic policy, the importance for East-West stability of the success of the fragile democratic market economies of Central and Eastern Europe. Economic decline and upheaval in the Soviet Union add one more pressure on these countries. Our policies should both help these nations achieve stable democracies and sound market economies and also facilitate their connections with the stabilizing network of Western political and economic institutions. We must do so in a way that encourages the Soviet Union to recognize that it is to its benefit to have successful examples of democratic and market transformations on its borders.

In regional conflicts, it remains in our interest to work constructively with the Soviet Union to resist a reversal of "new thinking' that was designed to define and shape Soviet security differently. That thinking makes it possible to develop cooperative approaches to resolve conflicts peacefully and democratically. Some of the fundamental internal circumstances that produced a Soviet willingness to engage with us on regional issues remain. Soviet involvement in these conflicts was expensive in terms of economic and military resources and in terms of President Gorbachev's desire to improve relations with the West.

We need to recognize, however, that the leadership's preoccupation with internal troubles might lead to a lack of high-level focus on some of these problems around the globe. Moreover, given the strategic readjustment that the Soviet Union has made, powerful groups are likely to be increasingly sensitive about conflicts in regions in bordering areas. It is a geopolitical reality that some in the Soviet Union will perceive that regional problems closer to home involve greater political and security interests than those at issue in Africa, Central America, or Southeast Asia.

The Arms Control Agenda

In arms control, it continues to make sense to reduce and constrain the Soviet military threat by negotiating effectively verifiable agreements. Of course the specific terms of any negotiations must serve our own national interest. We need to send a strong signal that we will not accept the rewriting of agreements already entered into and that faithful implementation will be required.

We also should test whether the Soviet Union is interested in cooperating with us and others on the proliferation agenda—an arms control subject that is likely to be even more important in the future than traditional East-West discussions. The Soviet Union should have a strong interest in stop-

ping and reversing the spread of weapons of mass destruction and missile technology, because a number of those seeking to develop these destabilizing weapons are on its own borders. In any case, as the Gulf crisis highlights, we have a strong interest in vigorously pursuing the proliferation challenge.

Policy Toward the Baltics

Our policy toward the Baltics should focus on two tracks. First, we need to continue to demonstrate our unequivocal support for their aspirations of independence. Of course, we never have accepted their illegal incorporation into the Soviet Union. We have demonstrated this support through words and deeds. We've met at the highest political levels with officials and representatives of the democratically elected governments of the Baltics. The President has met with all of the four top Baltic officials who have visited Washington since last May. We are maintaining a virtually continuous diplomatic presence in all three Baltic capitals. Our consul general in Leningrad supplements this presence with periodic trips to meet top Baltic leaders. We welcome the visits of these leaders to the United States. We are sending humanitarian medical supplies directly to the Baltics. And we work with the other nations of the West, through CSCE [Conference on Security and Cooperation in Europe] and other multilateral bodies, to demonstrate cohesive international support.

But these steps alone will not be sufficient unless we are able to persuade the Soviet leadership to engage in peaceful negotiations to resolve those issues that stand in the way of the Baltics' goal. So our second track is to persuade Soviet leaders that such a course is in their interest. At a minimum, this course involves sending a strong, united Western signal that the use of intimidation and force is unacceptable. It also needs to involve frequent contact with Soviet leaders so we can urge them to establish mechanisms that could achieve, step by step, a result that satisfies the Baltic peoples. We have pointed out that the Baltics involve special circumstances because of their illegal annexation following the Nazi-Soviet pact that a commission of the Supreme Soviet itself denounced.

In addition to our contacts with the center, we have sought out officials of the Soviet republics to explore their perspective on events in the Baltics. A peaceful, democratic result in the Baltics might establish a method that could help the center develop legitimate, consensual ties with the republics.

Finally, it remains in our interest, as well as that of the Soviet leaders, to create a pluralistic society within the Soviet Union. This is a vital step toward the democracy and market economy that we hope will eventually result. We need to honestly recognize that our influence in this historical process will be marginal. But given the importance of the Soviet Union to the world, we should look for ways that might help the process of transformation.

Given the devolution that has already taken place in Soviet society, it is in our interest to have an expanded range of contacts. Of course, these should be with republic and local leaders as well as the center. We have looked for ways to support democrats, free trade unions, and market reformers. These are courageous and admirable pioneers, people who reflect the universal human spirit of freedom and dignity. We hope they can play a greater role in their country's future.

Perhaps less obvious to some, we should also expand our range of contacts with other important groups in the Soviet Union, including the military and the defense industrial sector. These are powerful groups, and we know they have been associated with the rightward swing in Soviet policymaking. But these groups or institutions also reflect the anxiety that has troubled much of Soviet society. No Soviet leader will be able to ignore the military's concern about housing and jobs for the troops withdrawn from Central and Eastern Europe. No economic reform program will be politically successful if it does not address the fears of the skilled and influential workers in the defense industrial sector. Perhaps contacts with us and others in the West can help lead some of those not traditionally associated with the reform movement to recognize the potential benefits of reform and the dim prospects for a program based on old thinking.

We need to face the fact, however, that while it is useful to maintain and

expand these contacts, at times it will
be exceedingly difficult to do so. Given
the turmoil in the Soviet Union, we
should expect actions, some accidental,
some intentional, that offend and outrage us. When those events occur, as
they already have and probably will
again, we will need to send a strong
message to the people involved. We
need to point out that internal conditions will affect the willingness and
capability of Western democracies to
ease the Soviet Union's self-imposed
political and economic isolation. In
doing so, we need to make hard-nosed
calculations about maintaining relations that are in our own national interest and could be in the long term
interest of a reformed Soviet Union.

We need to have the types of
dialogue with the highest levels of
Soviet and republic governments that
enable us to point out the unintended
negative consequences that may flow
from certain actions. These unintended
consequences could block Soviet
leaders' abilities to achieve their own
positive objectives. President Gorbachev has achieved a significant
legacy, but we need to explain that he
risks that legacy by his own actions.

The Soviet Union is in the midst of
a political, economic, and social crisis.
But the Soviet Union cannot solve its
problems through rigid adherence to
an old constitutional and political system that never achieved political
legitimacy. The old system of central
controls will not establish a basis of
legitimacy for the future; nor will the
use of intimidation and force. The
Soviet Union needs to establish new
relations between the government and
the people. It will have to devise the institutions and degrees of autonomy
that appropriately reflect the consent
of the governed.

1 The complete transcript of the hearings
will be published by the committee and will be
available from the Superintendent of Documents,
U.S. Government Printing Office, Washington,
D.C. 20420.

International Trade Agreements: Fast Track Procedures

Foreword to a report to Congress submitted by President Bush, March 1, 1991.

The Fast Track and Why It Is Essential

For the better part of this century, Congress and the executive have recognized that the negotiation and implementation of trade agreements require special cooperation between the two branches. In the aftermath of the record high rates of the Smoot-Hawley Tariff Act of 1930 and the Depression that they helped fuel, both Congress and the executive came to realize that only by working closely together in the exercise of their constitutional responsibilities could the two branches effectively bring down foreign barriers to our trade and open opportunities for U.S. products and services in the international marketplace.

This new partnership was reflected in the Reciprocal Trade Agreements Act of 1934, which gave the President authority not only to conclude tariff-cutting agreements but also to implement them by proclamation without the need for subsequent legislation.

During the following years, when the principal barriers to trade were tariffs, this arrangement proved highly successful and was responsible for the tariff reductions that promoted post-World War II economic growth, particularly in successive rounds of multilateral tariff-cutting negotiations.

As countries began to rely less on tariff protection and more on non-tariff trade barriers, the scope of trade negotiations broadened, and the "fast track" procedures were created by Congress as the necessary complement to this broader trade agenda.

Fast track procedures for approval of trade agreements were included by Congress in trade legislation in 1974, 1979, and again in the Omnibus Trade and Competitiveness Act of 1988 (1988 Act). While giving Congress the assurance of meaningful participation throughout the negotiating process, fast track also provides two guarantees essential to the successful negotiation of trade agreements:

- A vote on implementing legislation within a fixed period of time; and
- No amendments to that legislation.

These procedures reflect an understanding that trade agreements, in which results in one area are often linked to results in others, are particularly vulnerable to multiple amendments that, while possibly small in themselves, could unravel entire agreements. Whether the balance of benefits contained in any trade agreement is in the overall interest of the United States can only be determined by looking at the whole package.

These procedures reflect an understanding that trade agreements, in which results in one area are often linked to results in others, are particularly vulnerable to multiple amendments that, while possibly small in themselves, could unravel entire agreements.

Through the fast track, Congress has given the President the same bargaining power possessed by his counterparts: the ability to assure his negotiating partners that the agreement reached internationally would be the agreement voted on at home. Without fast track, the President cannot give his negotiating partners that assurance. Without that assurance, foreign governments are reluctant to negotiate with the United States and will not make the tough concessions necessary to reach agreements the United States would be willing to sign. No negotiating partner will give its bottom line knowing that the bargain could be reopened.

On the basis of fast track procedures, the United States has negotiated and implemented three remarkable trade agreements, each of which was approved by an overwhelming majority in both Houses of Congress. These agreements—the results of the Tokyo Round of GATT [General Agreement on Tariffs and Trade] negotiations in 1979, the free-trade agreement (FTA) with Israel in 1985, and the FTA with Canada in 1988—have reduced barriers to trade and provided a powerful engine for economic growth in the United States and worldwide.

The United States has much to gain through trade agreements that open markets and provide rules for free and fair trade. Maintaining the fast track will preserve our ability to continue efforts to liberalize trade and open markets through the GATT, through other multilateral agreements, and through bilateral agreements.

Extension of Fast Track Continues a Cooperative Relationship

Fast track procedures preserve Congress' role during the negotiation, approval, and implementation of trade agreements. To ensure congressional and private sector input, the fast track statute contains extensive notification and consultation requirements. At each step along the way, from initiation through implementation, Congress is an active partner.

To use the fast track for any agreement, bilateral or multilateral, the President must notify Congress 90 calendar days before signature. By the time the President gives his 90-day notification, our many private sector advisory committees must report their views on the agreement both to Congress and the President. For bilateral agreements, Congress must be given advance notice of the negotiations; during the following 60 legislative working days, either the Senate Finance or House Ways and Means Committee can vote to deny fast track treatment.

Once an agreement is reached, Congress and the Administration work in close consultation to formulate implementing legislation. The process has involved the full participation of all committees of jurisdiction, and not only those committees traditionally consulted in setting trade negotiating objectives. If the agreement and its implementing legislation are still not acceptable, they can be rejected by majority vote of either house. In fact, as a result of the extensive consultations with Congress and the private sector, the agreements that have been implemented under fast track procedures enjoyed widespread support when they were presented to Congress.

We find ourselves today engaged in bilateral and multilateral trade initiatives that hold unprecedented promise for the advancement of U.S. economic objectives. With such initiatives in the balance, now is not the time to dissolve a partnership that has endured for almost sixty years.

Continuing Fast Track Is Essential to Securing Economic Gains

In incorporating the fast track in the 1988 Act, Congress expressly contemplated that an extension of the provision beyond June 1991 might be necessary and appropriate in order for the President to pursue effectively the trade policy objectives set out in the law.

The continued availability of fast track procedures over the next two years—during which we expect to complete the Uruguay Round of multilateral negotiations, negotiate a North American Free Trade Agreement with Mexico and Canada, and pursue the trade objectives of the Enterprise for the Americas Initiative—will enable our negotiators to bring to Congress for its consideration trade agreements that will enhance the ability of the United States to compete internationally. Supporting fast track now will allow these important negotiations to go forward without in any way detracting from Congress' ability to assess each agreement on its merits when presented for approval.

The Uruguay Round. These complex negotiations with 107 other nations (many of which are not fully integrated into the multilateral trading system) offer rich opportunities to break down trade barriers and expand the scope of international trade rules.

• Since their inception in 1986, the Uruguay Round negotiations have been conducted in 15 areas. Our objectives include more open markets, internationally agreed rules in areas not previously covered by multilateral agreements (services, investment, intellectual property rights), and institutional improvements in the GATT. The negotiations have been difficult, and important issues remain, but

there has been significant progress overall toward our objectives. That progress should not be abandoned.

• The United States had hoped to conclude the Uruguay Round last December at a ministerial level meeting in Brussels. However, the status of the negotiations on several subjects at that time did not warrant conclusion—particularly on agriculture. The unwillingness of the European Community (EC), as well as Japan and Korea, to accept a framework for agricultural reform impeded progress in the negotiations in all areas.

We are encouraged by a recent statement of GATT Director-General Arthur Dunkel that all participants have now agreed to negotiate specific binding commitments in each of the key areas of agricultural reform, thus clearing the way for the resumption of negotiations. However, important differences in agriculture and other areas remain. Much hard bargaining lies ahead.

The United States refused to accept a deficient Uruguay Round package in Brussels. Our high standards have not changed. Although ultimate success in the Uruguay Round cannot be guaranteed, we believe the United States should continue negotiations because a successful Round is overwhelmingly in our long-term economic interests.

North American FTA. We have a historic opportunity to achieve a North American Free Trade Agreement (NAFTA) with Canada and Mexico. The Mexican government has been pursuing a dramatic opening of its trading regime and has introduced market oriented domestic reforms that benefit both Mexico and the United States. Building on those reforms and on the existing FTA we have with Canada, we can create a NAFTA that encompasses some 360 million people with almost $6 trillion in output. A comprehensive NAFTA will create growth and better jobs in all three countries, and will make us more competitive in the global marketplace.

Extension of fast track will be essential for these negotiations, which are expected to begin in late Spring.

Enterprise for the Americas Initiative. An extension of fast track will also enable the United States to take steps

in the next two years toward fulfillment of the trade objectives of the Enterprise for the Americas Initiative (EAI), announced in June 1990. Although it is likely that few Latin American nations will be in a position to enter into FTA negotiations with the United States before June 1993, the United States must continue to be able to respond to the increasing pace of economic liberalization in the region.

The United States has an enormous stake in the future of the global trading system. Exports have become a vital source of strength to the U.S. economy. In 1990, the nearly 8.5 percent growth in U.S. exports accounted for 88% of U.S. GNP [gross national product] growth. Since 1986, expanded exports have accounted for more than 40 percent of the growth in U.S. GNP.

In order to sustain the expansion of exports and consequent growth, we must continue our efforts to open world markets. We must maintain our active leadership role. Without an extension of fast track, those efforts and that role are placed in jeopardy.

Preserving fast track procedures—and the partnership between Congress and the executive branch which fast track represents—will keep on course our joint efforts to liberalize trade and open markets through the initiatives described above and through other multilateral and bilateral agreements. No country stands to gain more from those efforts than the United States.

As we approach the beginning of a new century, we should not hesitate to pursue the opportunities for economic growth and prosperity presented by successful trade negotiations. In order to turn those opportunities into realities, Congress and the executive must continue to work together in the manner envisioned by the fast track.

President's letter to Congressional Leaders on Fast Track Authority Extension and the North American Free Trade Agreement, May 1, 1991 [2]

Through the better part of this century, successive Congresses and Administrations—Republican and Democratic—have worked to open markets and expand American exports. This partnership has resulted in unparalleled growth in world trade and huge economic benefits for the United States. Opening foreign markets means economic growth and jobs for all Americans.

Historically, the fast track procedures established by the Congress have served us well. On March 1, I requested an extension of fast track so that we could continue to realize increased economic growth and the other benefits of expanded trade. The fast track in no way limits the ability of Congress to review any agreement negotiated, including the Uruguay Round or a North American Free Trade Agreement (NAFTA). If Congress is not satisfied, it retains the unqualified right to reject whatever is negotiated. But refusing to extend the fast track would end negotiations before they have even begun and relinquish a critical opportunity for future economic growth.

Initiatives to open markets will enhance the global competitiveness of the United States and create new opportunities for American workers, American exports, and American economic growth. The Uruguay Round offers a vital opportunity to eliminate barriers to our goods, investment, services, and ideas. A NAFTA offers an historic opportunity to bring together the energies and talents of three great nations, already bound by strong ties of family, business, and culture. Prime Minister Mulroney and President Salinas are both leaders of great vision. They believe, as do I, that a NAFTA would enhance the well-being of our peoples. They are ready to move forward with us in this unprecedented enterprise.

Responding to Congressional Concerns

In seeking to expand our economic growth, I am committed to achieving a balance that recognizes the need to preserve the environment, protect worker safety, and facilitate adjustment. In your letter of March 7, you conveyed a number of important Congressional concerns about free trade with Mexico. At my direction, Ambassador [Carla] Hills and my Economic Policy Council have undertaken an intensive review of our NAFTA objectives and strategy to ensure thorough consideration of the economic, labor,

and environmental issues raised by you and your colleagues. The Administration's response is presented in the attached report. Let me emphasize the following:

First, you have my personal commitment to close bipartisan cooperation in the negotiations and beyond. And you have my personal assurance that we will take the time necessary to conclude agreements in which both the Congress and the Administration can take pride.

Second, while economic studies show that a free trade agreement would create jobs and promote growth in the United States, I know there is concern about adjustment in some sectors. These concerns will be addressed through provisions in the NAFTA designed to ease the transition for import-sensitive industries. In addition, my Administration is committed to working with the Congress to ensure that there is adequate assistance and effective retraining for dislocated workers.

Third, based on my discussions with President Salinas, I am convinced that he is firmly committed to strengthened environmental protection, and that there is strong support for this objective among the Mexican people. Because economic growth can and should be supported by enhanced environmental protection, we will develop and implement an expanded program of environmental cooperation in parallel with the free trade talks.

Fourth, President Salinas has also made it clear to me that his objective in pursuing free trade is to better the lives of Mexican working people. Mexico has strong laws regulating labor standards and worker rights. Beyond what Mexico is already doing, we will work through new initiatives to expand U.S.-Mexico labor cooperation.

Thus, our efforts toward economic integration will be complemented by expanded programs of cooperation on labor and the environment. The catalyst for these efforts is the promise of economic growth that a NAFTA can provide, and the key to these efforts is the extension of unencumbered fast track procedures.

There are great challenges ahead. The world is changing dramatically, as nations move toward democracy and free markets. The United States must continue to open new markets and lead in technological innovation, confident

that America can and will prevail in this new and emerging world. By working together, we can negotiate good trade agreements that assure a strong and healthy America as we prepare to meet the challenges of the next century.

Summary of Report Responding to Concerns Raised by Congressional Leaders About a North American Free Trade Agreement, May 1, 1991 [3]

On September 25, 1990, the President notified the Congress of his decision to proceed with free trade negotiations with Mexico. After consultations with Prime Minister Mulroney and President Salinas, the President notified Congress on February 5, 1991, of his decision to include Canada, and so to work towards a North American Free Trade Agreement (NAFTA).

Today, the President responded to a variety of concerns raised last month in letters from Chairmen Bentsen and Rostenkowski and from Majority Leader Gephardt about the effect a NAFTA would have on the economy, on labor. and on the environment. The response, which sets forth detailed action plans for addressing these concerns, as well as views on the economic impact of a NAFTA, is summarized below.

1. A NAFTA Would Benefit the U.S. Economy.

From 1986 to 1990, as Mexico reduced import barriers, our exports more than doubled—from $12.4 billion to $28.4 billion—generating 264,000 additional U.S. jobs. Under a NAFTA, we can do even better. Mexico still has higher trade barriers than the United States. Mexico's average duty is 10 percent compared to 4 percent in the United States. Significant nontariff barriers remain. We, therefore, have much to gain from the elimination of these barriers.

All three major economic analyses done to date corroborate that the United States will benefit from a NAFTA in exports, output, and employment.

We will benefit from Mexican growth: for each dollar Mexico spends on imports, 70 cents is spent on U.S. goods; for each dollar of GNP growth, 15 cents is spent on U.S. goods.

Further, the resulting economic integration will strengthen the ability of the United States to compete with Japan and the EC.

2. A NAFTA Would Include Transition and Safeguard Provisions.

Transition Measures: In order to avoid dislocations to industries and workers producing goods that are import-sensitive, tariffs and nontariff barriers on such products should be eliminated in small increments over a time period sufficient to ensure orderly adjustment.

In determining import sensitivity, we will rely heavily on advice of the International Trade Commission, the Congress, and the private sector.

We will be prepared to consider transition periods beyond those in the U.S.-Canada FTA.

Effective Safeguard Provisions: Even where reductions in tariffs and other trade barriers are staged over a lengthy period, there may be isolated cases in which injurious increases in imports could occur. To prevent injury from such increases, we will seek to include in the agreement a procedure allowing temporary reimposition of duties and other restrictions.

This mechanism should be designed to respond quickly, especially in cases of sudden import increases.

Special "snap-back" provisions should be included to address the unique problems faced by producers of perishable products.

Strict Rules of Origin: We will negotiate rules of origin to ensure that the benefits of a NAFTA do not flow to mere passthrough operations exporting third country products to the U.S. with only minimal assembly in Mexico.

Rules of origin will impose clear, tough, and predictable standards to the benefit of North American products.

We will seek to strengthen the required North American content for assembled automotive products.

We will consult closely with the private sector and the Congress in designing these rules.

3. The Administration Is Committed to Effective Retraining and Worker Adjustment Programs.

Since trade barriers on sensitive products should be decreased over a long timeframe, we do not expect immediate or substantial job dislocations.

Nevertheless, beyond including adjustment provisions in the NAFTA itself, there is a need to assist dislocated workers who may have adjustment difficulties.

The administration is committed to working with Congress to ensure a worker adjustment program that is adequately funded and that provides effective services to workers who may lose their jobs as a result of an agreement with Mexico.

Whether provided through the improvement or expansion of an existing program or through the creation of a new program, worker adjustment measures should be targeted to provide dislocated workers with comprehensive services in a timely fashion.

4. Labor Mobility and Immigration Laws Are Not on the Table.

We have agreed with Mexico that labor mobility and our immigration laws are not on the table in NAFTA talks, with the possible exception of a narrow provision facilitating temporary entry of certain professionals and managers.

5. Mexico's Laws Provide Comprehensive Rights and Standards for Workers.

Protections afforded by Mexican labor law and practice are stronger than generally known.

Mexico's laws provide comprehensive rights and standards for workers in all sectors, including the maquiladoras.

Mexico has ratified 73 International Labor Organization conventions on workers rights, including those on occupational safety and health.

Mexico has a minimum working age of 14 and mandates special protections and shorter working hours for those between the ages of 14 and 16.

A substantially higher proportion of the Mexican workforce is unionized than is the U.S. workforce.

While enforcement problems have resulted largely from a lack of resources, a NAFTA would both raise living standards and create resources for enforcing existing laws.

6. There Will Be Increased U.S.-Mexico Cooperation on Labor Matters.

Memorandum of Understanding: The Secretary of Labor and her counterpart from Mexico are prepared to sign a Memorandum of Understanding providing for cooperation and joint action on a number of labor issues which could be implemented in parallel with our FTA negotiations. These include health and safety measures; work conditions, including labor standards and enforcement; labor conflicts; labor statistics; and other areas of concern to the United States and Mexico.

Specific Projects: U.S. and Mexican officials have agreed on joint projects to address specific concerns in the labor sector. Initial projects include: occupational health and safety, child labor, and labor statistics.

7. Mexico is Committed to Strengthened Environmental Protection.

As President Salinas has made clear, Mexico has no interest in becoming a pollution haven for U.S. companies. Mexico's comprehensive environmental law of 1988, which is based on U.S. law and experience, is a solid foundation for tackling its environmental problems. All new investments are being held to these higher legal standards, and an environmental impact assessment is required to show how they will comply.

Enforcement has in the past been a key problem, but Mexico's record has been improving dramatically. Since 1989, Mexico has ordered more than 980 temporary and 82 permanent shutdowns of industrial facilities for environmental violations, and the budget of SEDUE (Mexico's EPA) has increased almost eightfold.

8. A Number of Environmental Issues Would Be Addressed in the NAFTA.

Protection of Health and Safety: We will ensure that our right to safeguard the environment is preserved in the NAFTA.

We will maintain the right to exclude any products that do not meet our health or safety requirements, and we will continue to enforce those requirements.

We will maintain our right to impose stringent pesticide, energy conservation, toxic waste, and health and safety standards.

We will maintain our rights, consistent with other international obligations, to limit trade in products controlled by international treaties (such as treaties on endangered species or protection of the ozone layer).

Enhancement and Enforcement of Standards: We will seek a commitment to work together with Mexico to enhance environmental, health, and safety standards regarding products, and to promote their enforcement.

We will provide for full public and scientific scrutiny of any changes to standards before they are implemented.

We will provide for consultations on enhancing enforcement capability, inspection training, monitoring, and verification.

9. Expanded U.S.-Mexico Environmental Cooperation Will Be Pursued in Parallel With NAFTA Negotiations.

In parallel to the FTA negotiations, we intend to pursue an ambitious program of cooperation on a wide range of environmental matters.

We will design and implement an integrated border environmental plan to address air and water pollution, hazardous wastes, chemical spills, pesticides, and enforcement.

During the design phase of the border plan, there will be an opportunity for public comment and hearings; during implementation, there will be periodic comprehensive reviews.

We will consult on national environmental standards and regulations, and will provide an opportunity for the public to submit data on alleged noncompliance.

We will discuss expanded cooperative enforcement activities, such as coordinated targeting of environmental violators.

We will establish a program of technical cooperation and training, which will include facilitating sharing of technology for pollution abatement.

10. Environmental Experts Will Be Invited To Participate in the Policy-Making Process.

We will broaden public participation in the formulation and implementation of trade policy to ensure that efforts to liberalize trade are consistent with sound environmental practices.

We will appoint individuals to selected trade policy advisory committees who can contribute both an environmental perspective and substantive expertise.

In consultation with interested members of the public, we will complete a review of U.S.-Mexico environmental issues, with particular emphasis on possible environmental effects of the NAFTA, to enable U.S. officials to consider the results during ETA negotiations and other bilateral efforts.

---

1 Department of State Dispatch, March 4, 1991.

2 Text from Weekly Compilation of Presidential Documents of May 3, 1991. Identical letters were sent to Lloyd Bentsen, Chairman of the Senate Finance Committee; Richard A. Gephardt, House Majority Leader; and Dan Rostenkowski, Chairman of the House Ways and Means Committee.

3 White House Fact Sheet. Text from Weekly Compilation of Presidential Documents of May 3, 1991.

President Violeta Chamorro of Nicaragua Visits U.S.

REMARKS AT WELCOMING CEREMONY, APRIL 17, 1991[1]

President Bush. It gives me great pleasure to welcome to the United States a woman of courage, a leader of conviction, a person of morality and vision: Mrs. Violeta Chamorro, President of Nicaragua.

We stand here at the White House almost a year to the day after the extraordinary moment when you stood at Managua's National Stadium to be sworn in as your nation's first freely elected president.

What a moment that was. In you we saw the exhilarating victory of democracy, of that glorious new breeze that, in one amazing year, swept out oppression and dictatorship from Prague to Managua. In you we saw your nation's peacemaker, the person who would close the books on 11 years of cruel civil war.

In you we saw the symbol of national reconciliation with the inner strength and resolve to turn the face of your country toward the path of healing.

In you we saw what your countrymen saw when they cast their ballots in their first fair, open election. We all saw the person who inspired her people to believe in the triumphant return of peace and freedom.

On that Inauguration Day we saw Dona Violeta, candidate of compassion, become President Chamorro, leader of reconciliation. On that day you closed a painful chapter in your nation's history, and you began to forge a new one. The beautiful land of Ruben Dario had been exhausted by strife, embittered by repression, polarized by government attempts to dominate every single aspect of society, impoverished by a cynical and mismanaged regime.

But you are the leader who once said: "As a mother, I feel with great intensity the obligation to teach while governing and to govern while forming peaceful hearts." And you've begun to bring life and dreams back to your people in your "mission to help them"—as you call it, "mission to help them." Your courageous countrymen are showing that they are ready to dig

in and work hard to reap the benefits of free government and free enterprise.

Following the course of your slogan, "Yes, we can change things," your reforms are realistic—restoration of democratic liberties, religious freedom, economic reconstruction, free market opportunities, reallocation of military funds to vital economic and social programs, and reincorporation of former combatants and refugees.

...as your national anthem says, "the voice of the cannon no longer roars."

But your reforms are also visionary—the restoration of moral values and human dignity. The importance of an inheritance for your children of reconciliation and respect. And the belief in the goodness of a people that still turns for guidance to its patron saint, La Purisima.

And your reforms, your "new sun of justice and freedom," bring hope to the watching world. For with the democratization of Nicaragua, we are one crucial step closer to the incredible goal of becoming this world's first fully democratic hemisphere.

We know that the tasks facing the Nicaraguan people are difficult. Your economic stabilization plan requires hard choices. Economic reform after years of mismanagement is never easy and presents challenges to leadership. But sacrifice in the short run is vital to achieve long term growth and development. And we hope that all elements of Nicaraguan society will work with you for the good of your country.

The Nicaraguan people do not stand friendless and alone to face these challenges. We are confident that as you confront them, all Nicaraguans will enjoy renewed and widely shared prosperity.

Dona Violeta, I am proud to stand with you, and our nation is proud to stand by you. We're offering over $500 million in aid over your first two years as President. And we've joined with

other developed countries to work with the international financial institutions to help Nicaragua. And beyond aid, we're offering opportunities for trade and investment that will benefit both our countries through the Enterprise for the Americas Initiative.

And most of all, we're offering something from our hearts to your proud country, your blue and white Nicaragua, where, as your national anthem says, "the voice of the cannon no longer roars." We are offering you our respect, our admiration, and our friendship.

As your nation renews itself under your leadership, the world shares the view of Nicaraguan poet Pablo Antonio Cuadra, who wrote about your late husband, Pedro Joaquin—who was tragically assassinated for the pure passion of his political idealism. Cuadra said of you: "Pedro's flag could not be in better hands."

Madam President, your nation is fortunate to have you as a leader. I am proud to have you as a friend. We salute you. And may God bless you and your proud and courageous land. And welcome to the United States.

President Chamorro. President Bush, my good friend; Mrs. Barbara Bush, my good friend also; ladies and gentlemen. Many years have elapsed since the President of Nicaragua has made a state visit to the White House.

It is a great honor for me to be here with you this morning, for it represents the establishment of a new and precious relationship between our two nations. The genuine friendship extended by a noble country such as the United States deserves in turn the friendship of democratic governments that respect the rights of their people. For only in this manner can there exist a sincere relationship between both nations.

As we meet today, Mr. President, it is our responsibility as leaders of two democratic nations to begin fertilizing the seed of a new friendship, a friendship based on our shared belief in democracy and mutual respect.

I would also like to take this opportunity to express our gratitude to the people and Government of the United States of America for the assistance they have provided to Nicaragua. That assistance was a decisive factor during my first year in office. And now Nicaragua has begun to recover from the years of political instability and continuous conflict.

I must conclude by reiterating my government's firm commitment to the sacred principles of democracy shared by our peoples. This commitment is, and will continue to be, to work towards consolidating peace, strengthening our democratic institutions, respecting human rights, and putting our economy in order.

I shall work toward achieving this goal without wavering, because I have adopted as my own those universal truths which Abraham Lincoln bequeathed to mankind: "a government of the people, by the people, and for the people."

God bless and protect the peoples and governments of the United States and Nicaragua. Thank you.

ADDRESS BY VIOLETA B. DE CHAMORRO, PRESIDENT OF NICARAGUA, TO A JOINT SESSION OF CONGRESS, APRIL 16, 1991 [2]

Mr. Speaker, Mr. President, Members of Congress, in 1979 I chose to follow the difficult path of politics. I felt that I owed something to the memory of my husband, Pedro Joaquin Chamorro.

I became terribly disillusioned during that year. The Sandinistas deviated from the course of the 1979 Revolution and turned against democracy, against free economic initiatives, and against human rights. That's why I resigned from the Provisional Government Board in April 1980. That's also why I accepted the presidential nomination in 1989.

And we won. And now we're transforming our country and giving it dignity by setting up the framework for a republican democracy. In the past few years, Nicaraguans have shed many tears and much blood. Many thousands of patriots, the equivalent of millions of American lives, died for political causes, for ideological differences, and because basic human rights were restricted and people were prevented from living in peace. Now, in Nicaragua, the war has ended, the majority of Nicaraguans voted so that they could have peace.

More than 20,000 Nicaraguans who fought for liberty surrendered their arms and returned to being civilians, for there was no longer any reason to carry arms. I reduced, by two thirds, the huge army amassed by the previous regime, and I will continue to reduce the army's size as a step forward in my demilitarization scheme.

We did away with the policy of public institutions having to conform to the interests of one political party, one group or one person. We also did away with the delerium of a totalitarian ideology; Nicaraguans no longer have to kneel before the State.

From the moment that I took over the government, the Executive Branch has religiously respected the freedom and the independence of all the Government's powers, the democratic liberties and human rights. We did away with the policy of public institutions having to conform to the interests of one political party, one group or one person. We also did away with the delerium of a totalitarian ideology; Nicaraguans no longer have to kneel before the State. Now the principle of freedom prevails so that people can speak openly, move within their country freely, work and run their own businesses profitably.

The Challenge of Democracy

The last time that I addressed Nicaragua's Congress, I stated that it isn't an easy feat to bring a democracy to a country. But if a democratic system is being built from the ruins of a dictatorship, and a civil war — from the ruins of an economic disaster — the feat is not only difficult, it is almost impossible. However, Nicaraguans have accepted this as their challenge.

Justice is the one element that cannot be missing from this system. Crimes cannot remain unsolved, as we have witnessed in the past.

My government is committed to radically reduce government intervention in the economy and the enormous bureaucratic apparatus that we have in-

herited. Our Congress approved a law that authorizes private banks to operate and encourages foreign investments and is studying the privatization law in order to convert government businesses. We are rapidly advancing toward the establishment of a social-market economy. Restrictions on prices and salaries must be lifted. We have initiated a serious economic stabilization program, accompanied by corresponding tax reforms, to discipline the public to share the burden of real costs, to encourage domestic production, and to stimulate private domestic and foreign investment.

Senators and Representatives, we are raising a Republic from the ashes of a previous period in our history that has left our country saddened, but has taught us a great deal. No path leads to happiness if liberty is oppressed and human rights disrespected. In Nicaragua, an authentic revolution is beginning. It is a revolution for democracy and liberty, a revolution for which Nicaraguans have longed, a revolution that will serve as a model to other countries.

An End to Militarism

The consequences of militarism, which only succeeded in making our country suffer, have forced us to assume the leading role in Central America, to transform our region into a "zone of Peace and Cooperation"; an area of international security, of democracy and of economic prosperity.

In this sense, it is important to reiterate that Nicaragua does not now tolerate, and will not tolerate sending arms to neighboring countries. Our policy is to punish these types of actions. Following this policy, we were able to successfully take action and recuperate the missiles which only last December were in the hands of Salvadorean guerrillas.

Senators and Representatives, when we first heard the news about the fall of the Berlin Wall, I found myself in Washington, D.C. in a working meeting with Speaker Foley and other Members of the House of Representatives. At that time, I was a presidential candidate. I realized then that, in the same way, all of the walls that infringe upon democratic rights and liberties would fall. It pleases us that we have contributed to this current in contemporary history, which no human force is able to distort and prevent.

As I expressed in September 1990, before the United Nations General Assembly, democracy now belongs to all the people. There is no doubt that the United States is playing one of the lead roles in this democratization process that is shaking up the whole planet.

Relations with U.S.

Friends, we have arrived at a time when we can put an end to the conflicting relations between our governments, and we need to concentrate our efforts on constructing a new institutional relationship which reflects the friendship between the peoples of our two countries. Within Nicaragua, we are instituting a policy of national reconciliation—with perseverance and firmness—and of deep respect for human rights. At the same time, we are promoting a policy of reconciliation in our international relations.

The National Assembly of Nicaragua is discussing an initiative that I presented last April 4th, to change previous government legislation that obliged Nicaragua to maintain a confrontational relationship with the United States. The majority of the Nicaraguan people do not believe in this law. All of the people who voted did so not only to achieve internal peace, but also to end international confrontation. We are restoring the friendship between the United States and Nicaragua, and we need to establish a strong common commitment for the future of our countries and our peoples.

Nicaragua is part of a new democratic Central America which is both working for, and hoping to achieve, unification in the near future in order to compete worthily with the rest of the world — one Central America which is becoming a zone of peace, liberty, and free trade, integrated in the near future to Venezuela and Mexico. For a unified Central America, the new decade will be one of transition as we move toward the 21st Century. It is also the decade of exemplary relations between our countries and the United States.

Economic Prosperity the Key

Finally, it is important to note, ladies and gentlemen, that our efforts to strengthen freedom, establish democracy and set up a "State of Law" have to be accompanied by economic prosperity. The people of Latin America applaud the efforts of the Enterprise for the Americas Initiative that President George Bush created as well as the Partnership for Democracy and Development presented during the recent meeting that took place in San Jose, Costa Rica. By the same token, we support the free trade zone between Mexico and the U.S.

I would especially like to thank you, the representatives of the American public, for the generous assistance that you and the Government of the United States have given to the Nicaraguan people for our reconstruction.

Nicaragua needs extraordinary international cooperation. Our economy has been destroyed. Our productive capacity has remained dismantled. Our country was totally de-capitalized. In addition, we have to protect our natural resources and promote policies that will protect the environment. We need steadfast financial assistance from the United States throughout this entire decade to reconstruct our economy, following the terrible damage incurred during the past decade.

We urgently need foreign investment, credit, and international cooperation in order to permit our people to develop their creative talents and to let us rise from the ashes left for us by past dictatorships. Only in this way will we be able to realize the dreams of our people — a people that have heroically suffered in order to strengthen democracy and liberty in their own country.

Senators and Representatives, let me be so bold as to make my own a thought from Abraham Lincoln: "The security that we have is the love of liberty that God has planted in our breast." God Bless America! Thank you very much!

---

1 Text provided by the Embassy of Nicaragua, Washington.

Current Actions:

February, March, April, 1991

These listings were released by the Department of State as "Treaty Actions" on March 11 and April 8, 1991.

I. February 1991

MULTILATERAL

Arbitration
Convention on the recognition and enforcement of foreign arbitral awards. Done at New York June 10, 1958. Entered into force June 7, 1959; for the US Dec. 29, 1970. TIAS 6997.
Accessions deposited: Guinea, Jan. 23, 1991; Cote d'Ivoire, Feb. 1, 1991.

Human Rights
International covenant on civil and political rights. Done at New York, Dec. 16, 1966. Entered into force Mar. 23, 1976.[1]
Accession deposited: Haiti, Feb. 6, 1991.

Judicial Procedure
Convention on the civil aspects of international child abduction. Done at The Hague Oct. 25, 1980. Entered into force Dec. 1, 1983; for the US July 1, 1988. (Senate) Treaty Doc. 99-11.
Signature: Argentina, Jan. 28, 1991.

Maritime Matters
Convention on the International Maritime Organization, as amended. Signed at Geneva Mar. 6, 1948. Entered into force Mar. 17, 1958. TIAS 4044, 6285, 6490, 8606, 10374.
Acceptance deposited: Luxembourg, Feb. 14, 1991.

Nuclear Accidents
Convention on early notification of a nuclear accident. Done at Vienna Sept. 26, 1986. Entered into force Oct. 27, 1986; for the US Oct. 20, 1988. (Senate) Treaty Doc. 100-4.
Accession deposited: Food and Agriculture Organization, Oct. 19, 1990.

Convention on assistance in the case of a nuclear accident or radiological emergency. Done at Vienna Sept. 26, 1986. Entered into force Feb. 26, 1987; for the US Oct. 20, 1988. (Senate) Treaty Doc. 100-4.

Accession deposited: Food and Agriculture Organization, Oct. 19, 1990.
Ratification deposited: Italy, Oct. 25, 1990.[2,3] Approval deposited: Finland, Nov. 27, 1990.[3]

Pollution
Protocol to the 1979 convention on long-range transboundary air pollution (TIAS 10541) concerning the control of emissions of nitrogen oxides or their transboundary flukes, with annex. Done at Sofia Oct. 31, 1988. Entered into force Feb. 14, 1991.
Ratification deposited: Canada, Jan. 25, 1991.

Satellite Communications Systems
Agreement relating to the International Telecommunications Satellite Organization (INTELSAT), with annexes. Done at Washington Aug. 20, 1971. Entered into force Feb. 12, 1973. TIAS 7532.
Accession deposited: Cape Verde, Feb. 19, 1991.

Operating agreement relating to the International Telecommunications Satellite Organization (INTELSAT), with annex. Done at Washington Aug. 20, 1971. Entered into force Feb. 12, 1973. TIAS 7532.
Signature: CTT — Empressa Publica dos Correios e Telecomunicacoes (Cape Verde), Feb. 19, 1991.

Seabed Disarmament
Treaty on the prohibition of the emplacement of nuclear weapons and other weapons of mass destruction on the seabed and the ocean floor and in the subsoil thereof. Done at Washington, London, and Moscow Feb. 11, 1971. Entered into force May 18, 1972. TIAS 7337.
Accession deposited: China, Feb. 28, 1991.[4]

Sugar
International sugar agreement, 1987, with annexes. Done at London Sept. 11, 1987. Entered into force provisionally Mar. 24, 1988.
Ratification deposited: Argentina, Jan. 10, 1991.

Taxation — Assistance
Convention on mutual administrative assistance in tax matters. Done at Strasbourg Jan. 25, 1988.[5] Signature: Netherlands, Sept. 25, 1990.
Ratification deposited: US, Feb. 13, 1991.

Trade
United Nations convention on contracts for the international sale of goods. Done at Vienna Apr. 11, 1980. Entered into force Jan. 1, 1988. (52 Fed. Reg. 6262.)
Accession deposited: Guinea, Jan. 23, 1991.

Treaties
Vienna convention on the law of treaties, with annex. Done at Vienna May 23, 1969. Entered into force Jan. 27, 1980.[1]
Accession deposited: Suriname, Jan. 31, 1991.

Women
Convention on the elimination of all forms of discrimination against women. Done at New York Dec. 18, 1979. Entered into force Sept. 3, 1981.[1]
Signature: Nepal, Feb. 5, 1991.

BILATERAL

Australia
Agreement concerning the Navstar Global Positioning System. Signed at Washington Feb. 7, 1991. Entered into force Feb. 7, 1991.

Colombia
Agreement on measures to prevent the diversion of essential chemicals. Signed at Washington Feb. 25, 1991. Enters into force on the date on which the parties inform each other that they have completed their constitutional and legal requirements.

European Atomic Energy Community (EURATOM)
Agreement extending the agreement of Jan. 28, 1982, as extended (TIAS 10338), in the field of nuclear material safeguards research and development. Signed at Brussels and Washington Dec. 18, 1990, and Feb. 13, 1991. Entered into force Feb. 13, 1991; effective Dec. 31, 1990.

Germany

Agreement extending the agreement of June 8, 1976, as amended and extended (TIAS 8657), in the field of liquid metal-cooled fast breeder reactors. Effected by exchange of letters at Washington and Bonn Jan. 14 and Feb. 7, 1991. Entered into force Feb. 7, 1991; effective Dec. 31, 1990.

Israel

Agreement on the status of Israeli personnel. Signed at Jerusalem Jan. 22, 1991. Enters into force upon an exchange of notes confirming that their respective constitutional requirements have been met.

Agreement on the status of United States personnel, with annexes and related letter. Signed at Jerusalem Jan. 22, 1991. Enters into force upon an exchange of notes confirming that their respective constitutional requirements have been met.

Korea

Agreement amending the agreement of Sept. 14, 1990, relating to trade in textiles and textile products. Effected by exchange of letters at Washington Jan. 24 and Feb. 1, 1991 . Entered into force Feb. 1 , 1991 .

Agreement amending the mutual logistics support agreement of June 8, 1988. Signed at Seoul Feb. 5, 1991. Entered into force Feb. 5, 1991.

Mongolia

Agreement on trade relations, with exchange of letters. Signed at Washington Jan. 23, 1991. Enters into force on the date of exchange of notices of acceptance by the two governments.

USSR

Treaty on the limitation of underground nuclear weapons tests. Signed at Moscow July 3, 1974.

Protocol to the treaty of July 3, 1974, on the limitation of underground nuclear weapon tests. Signed at Washington June 1, 1990.

Treaty on underground nuclear explosions for peaceful purposes, with agreed minute. Signed at Washington and Moscow May 28, 1976.

Protocol to the treaty of May 28, 1976, on underground nuclear explosions for peaceful purposes. Signed at Washington June 1, 1990.
Senate advice and consent to ratification: Sept. 25, 1990.
Instrument of ratification signed by the President: Dec. 8, 1990.
Instruments of ratification exchanged: Dec. 11, 1990.
Entered into force: Dec. 11, 1990.

---

1 Not in force for the US.
2 With declaration(S)
3 With reservation(s).
4 With statements.
5 Not in force.

II. March-April 1991

MULILATERAL

Aviation

Convention on international civil aviation. Done at Chicago Dec. 7, 1944. Entered into force Apr. 4, 1947. TIAS 1 591.

Protocol on the authentic trilingual text of the convention on international civil aviation (TIAS 1591), with annex. Done at Buenos Aires Sept. 24, 1968. TIAS 6605.
Adherence deposited: Albania, Mar. 28, 1991.

Biological Weapons

Convention on the prohibition of the development, production, and stockpiling of bacteriological (biological) and toxin weapons and on their destruction. Done at Washington, London, and Moscow Apr. 10, 1972. Entered into force Mar. 26, 1975. TIAS 8062.
Accession deposited: Zimbabwe, Nov. 5, 1990.

Gas

Protocol for the prohibition of the use in war of asphyxiating, poisonous, or other gases, and of bacteriological methods of warfare. Done at Geneva June 17, 1925. Entered into force Feb. 8, 1928; for the US Apr. 10, 1975. TIAS 8061.
Accession deposited: Angola, Oct. 30, 1990.1

International Court of Justice

Declaration recognizing as compulsory jurisdiction of the International Court of Justice under Art. 36, para. 2 of the statute of the Court. 59 Stat. 1055; TS 993.2
Declaration deposited: Poland, Sept. 25, 1990.

Narcotic Drugs

United Nations convention against illicit traffic in narcotic drugs and psychotropic substances, with annex and final act. Done at Vienna Dec. 20, 1988. Entered into force Nov. 11, 1990. [Senate] Treaty Doc. 101-4.
Ratifications deposited: USSR, Dec. 17, 1990; Egypt, Mar. 15, 1991. Accession deposited: Oman, Mar. 15, 1991.

Pollution

Convention on long-range transboundary air pollution. Done at Geneva Nov. 13, 1979. Entered into force Mar. 1 6, 1983. TIAS 10541.
Ratification deposited: Romania, Feb. 27, 1991.

Convention for the protection of the ozone layer, with annexes. Done at Vienna Mar. 22, 1985. Entered into force Sept. 22, 1988. (Senate) Treaty Doc. 99-9.
Accession deposited: India, Mar. 18, 1991.

Seabed Operations

Memorandum of understanding on the avoidance of overlaps and conflicts relating to deep seabed areas, with annexes. Signed at New York Feb. 22, 1991. Entered into force Feb. 22, 1991.

Terrorism

Convention on the prevention and punishment of the crimes against internationally protected persons, including diplomatic agents. Done at New York Dec. 14, 1973. Entered into force Feb. 20, 1977. TIAS 8532.
Accession deposited: Sri Lanka, Feb. 27, 1991.

Torture

Convention against torture and other cruel, inhuman, or degrading treatment or punishment. Done at New York Dec. 10, 1984. Entered into force June 26, 1987.3
Accession deposited: Romania, Dec. 18, 1990.

Treaties

Vienna convention on the law of treaties, with annex. Done at Vienna May 23, 1969. Entered into force Jan. 27, 1980.3

Accession deposited: Oman, Oct. 18, 1990.[4]

Treaties International Organizations
Vienna convention on the law of treaties between states and international organizations or between international organizations, with annex. Done at Vienna Mar. 21, 1986.[5]
Accession deposited: Czechoslovakia, Oct. 19, 1990.

United Nations
Charter of the United Nations and Statute of the International Court of Justice. Signed at San Francisco June 26, 1945. Entered into force Oct. 24, 1945. 59 Stat. 1031, TS 993.
Admitted to membership: Liechtenstein, Sept. 18, 1990.

BILATERAL

Albania
Memorandum of understanding concerning the re-establishment of diplomatic relations. Signed at Washington Mar. 15, 1991. Entered into force Mar. 15, 1991.

Treaty of naturalization. Signed at Tirana Apr. 5, 1932. Entered into force Jul. 22, 1935. TS 892; 49 Stat, (2) 3241.
Terminated: Mar. 15, 1991.

Bahrain
Agreement concerning the deployment of US forces, with exchange of letters. Signed at Manama Jan. 13, 1991. Entered into force Jan. 1 3, 1991.

Canada
Agreement on air quality, with annexes. Signed at Ottawa Mar. 13, 1991. Entered into force Mar. 13, 1991.

China
Agreement concerning the mutual provision of properties for use of the two countries, with appendices. Signed at Beijing Mar. 23, 1991. Entered into force Apr. 22, 1991.

Costa Rica
Agreement for the exchange of information with respect to taxes, with exchange of notes. Signed at San Jose Mar. 15, 1989. Entered into force Feb. 12, 1991.

Denmark
Memorandum of understanding concerning use of Sondrestrom Aviation Facility, Kulusuk Airfield, and other matters related to US military activities in Greenland. Signed at Copenhagen Mar. 13, 1991. Entered into force Mar. 13, 1991.

Israel
Memorandum of understanding concerning cooperation in the field of environmental protection, with annexes. Signed at Jerusalem Feb. 20, 1991. Entered into force Feb. 20, 1991.

Italy
Protocol amending the air transport agreement of June 22, 1970 (TIAS 6957). Signed at Washington Oct. 25, 1988. Entered into force Mar. 28, 1991.

Korea
Memorandum of understanding for a cooperative technology project concerning coastal/harbor defense, with annex. Signed at Washington and Taejon Nov. 13 and 26, 1990.
Entered into force: Nov. 26, 1990.

Agreement for the establishment of the Joint US Military Affairs Group to the Republic of Korea. Signed at Seoul Jan. 25, 1991. Entered into force Feb. 27, 1991.

Marshall Islands
Agreement for the exchange of information with respect to taxes, with attachment and exchange of notes. Signed at Majuro March 14, 1991. Entered into force Mar. 14, 1991.

United Arab Emirates
Agreement relating to trade in textiles and textile products, with annexes. Effected by exchange of notes at Abu Dhabi Jan. 26 and Feb. 5, 1991. Entered into force Feb. 5, 1991; effective Jan. 1, 1989.

United Kingdom
Memorandum of understanding concerning the measures to be taken for the transfer to, and security and safeguarding of, MK IV radar instrumentation system technical information, software, and equipment in the United Kingdom. Signed at Washington Feb. 6, 1991. Entered into force Feb. 6, 1991.

---

1 With reservation.
2 With conditions.
3 Not in force for the US.
4 With declaration.
5 Not in force.

Department of State

No.	Date	Subject
28	3/1	Baker: remarks with German Foreign Minister Hans-Dietrich Genscher following meeting.
29	3/3	Baker: interview on "Meet the Press," NBC-TV.
30	3/4	Baker: remarks with Italian Foreign Minister Gianna de Michelis following meeting.
31	3/4	Baker: remarks with Canadian Foreign Minister Joseph Clark following meeting.
32	3/5	Baker: remarks with Spanish Foreign Minister Francisco Fernandez following meeting.
33	3/9	Baker: remarks with Kuwaiti Foreign Minister al-Sabah following meeting, Ta'if, Saudi Arabia.
34	3/10	Baker: remarks with Saudi Foreign Minister Prince Saud following GCC + Egypt, Syria, and U.S. ministerial meeting.
*35	3/10	Baker: press briefing en route from Riyadh to Cairo.
*36	3/11	Baker: press conference with Israeli Foreign Minister David Levy.
*37	3/12	Baker: remarks prior to meeting with Palestinian representatives, Jerusalem.
38	3/12	Baker: remarks while visiting Karmiel, Israel.
39	3/12	Baker: remarks with Israeli President Chaim Herzog, Jerusalem.
*40	3/14	Baker: press conference with Syrian Foreign Minister Farouk Shara, Damascus.
41	3/15	Baker: press briefing with Soviet Foreign Minister Alexander Bessmertnyk.
42	3/17	Baker: interview on "This Week with David Brinkley," ABC-TV.
43	3/20	Baker: remarks with Polish President Lech Walesa following working luncheon.
44	3/16	Baker: remarks following meeting with President Ozal of Turkey.
45	4/5	Baker: statement on the death of Senator John Tower.
46	4/7	Baker: arrival remarks, Ankara, Turkey.
47	4/8	Baker: remarks upon departure from Esenboga International Airport, Ankara.
*48	4/8	Baker: remarks with Turkish Foreign Minister Ahmet Kurtcebe Alptemocin, Diyarbakir Airport, Turkey.
49	4/9	Baker: remarks with Israeli Foreign Minister David Levy, Jerusalem.
50	4/10	Baker: remarks after meeting with Israeli President Chaim Herzog.
51	4/10	Baker: remarks with Egyptian Foreign Minister Abel Meguid, Cairo.
52	4/11	Baker: remarks prior to meeting with Foreign Minister Habibben Yahya of Tunisia, Damascus.
*53	4/12	Baker: press conference with Syrian Foreign Minister Farouk Al Shara, Damascus.
*54	4/12	Baker: remarks with Prince Sadruddin Aga Khan, U.N. High Commissioner for Refugees, Geneva.
55	4/12	Baker: remarks prior to meeting with Jordanian Foreign Minister Al Mashi, Geneva.
56	4/16	Baker: remarks with Rumanian Prime Minister Petre Roman, Washington.
*57	4/17	Baker: press conference with Luxembourg Foreign Minister Jacques Poos and EC President Jacques Delors.
*58	4/20	Baker: remarks with King Hussein of Jordan, Aqaba.
*59	4/21	Baker: remarks with Egyptian Foreign Minister Abdel Meguid.
*60	4/22	Baker: remarks with Saudi Foreign Minister Saud Al Faisal, Jeddah.
*61	4/22	Baker: briefing following meeting with the Amir and Crown Prince of Kuwait, Kuwait City.
62	4/22	Baker: remarks at Babtain Palace, Kuwait City.
*63	4/24	Baker: press conference with Syrian Foreign Minister Farouk Al Shara, Damascus.
64	4/25	Baker: press conference with Soviet Foreign Minister Alexander Bessmertnykh, Kislovodsk, U.S.S.R.
64	4/26	Baker: remarks to press, Jerusalem.

Copies may be obtained from the Office of Press Relations, Department of State, Washington, D.C. 20520-6810.

*Printed in full or excerpted in the Bulletin.

New Publications from the Council on Foreign Relations

American Foreign Policy: Foreign Affairs Press Briefings and Treaties, 1987, Supplement

Intervention or Neglect: The United States and Central America Beyond the 1980s

by Linda Robinson
Publication Date: August 22, 1991

Central America stands at a critical juncture: will its fragile democracies flourish or will the region backslide into the violent conflict that characterized the 1980s? How Central America arrived at this point and what part the United States played in its getting there is the subject of this new examination by Linda Robinson, Latin America Correspondent for *U.S. News & World Report* and former Associate Editor (1986-89) of *Foreign Affairs*. Robinson draws on the political and economic record of the region to construct comprehensive studies of Panama, El Salvador, and Nicaragua, and brief profiles of Honduras, Guatemala, and Costa Rica. Reinforcing her research with personal interviews with leading figures in the region and from the U.S. policymaking arena, she traces the key developments of the 1980s—the growth of political opposition, the evolution of regional peace efforts, the rise of drug trafficking, and the influence of external, international actors, including the United Nations, the Soviet Union, and Cuba—and reviews American foreign policy failures and successes during this period. Robinson identifies the most serious obstacles to the consolidation of democracy and maps out the options now available to the United States that would secure American interests at minimal risk and expense.

The volume contains chapters on: Charting a New Course in Central America. Nicaragua—the Sandinistas & Their Opponents. Nicaragua—Diplomacy Takes Over. El Salvador—The Duarte Era & the Advent of ARENA. El Salvador—The War and the FMLN. Panama & the United States—From Symbiosis to Festering Crisis. Central America's Future—New Dangers to Democracy. 176 pp./Paper/$14.95. Send order to: Council on Foreign Relations Press, 58 East 68th Street, New York, NY 10021. (Telephone: 1-212-734-0400.)

Yen for Development: Japanese Foreign Aid & the Politics of Burden-Sharing

Shafiqul Islam, Editor

Japan has just replaced the U.S. as the world's top donor of foreign aid. For a country that was repaying its own World Bank debts until July 1990, this is an astounding feat. Yet, many feel that while Japan is doing more, it is not doing enough. To study the issue, the Council on Foreign Relations convened a group of distinguished Japanese and American aid experts to explore the new, and sometimes surprising, impact of Japan on economic development and on the bilateral politics of foreign aid.

The contents of their volume consists of: Foreword—James D. Robinson III. Introduction—Shafiqul Islam. PART I: GLOBAL CONTEXT. Japan's Global Ride—Takashi Inoguchi; Comment by William H. Gleysteen, Jr. PART II: OFFICIAL DEVELOPMENT ASSISTANCE. Overview—Toru Yanagihara & Anne Emig; U.S.-Japan Aid Alliance?—Julia Chang Bloch; Japanese Perspective on Aid & Development—Masamichi Hanabusa; Comments by Shinji Asanuma, Ernest H. Preeg; Japanese & U.S. Aid to Philippines—Filologo Pante, Jr. & Romero A. Reyes. PART III: PRIVATE SECTOR PARTICIPATION. Japanese Direct Investment & Development Finance—Hiroya Ichikawa; Japanese Banks & Third World Debt—Shoji Ochi; Comment by Barbara Stallings. PART IV: HUMAN DIMENSION. Japan's Leadership Role in Multilateral Development Institutions—Ryokichi Hirono; Comment by Ernest Stern. PART V: YEN DIPLOMACY & U.S. FOREIGN POLICY. Beyond Burden-Sharing—Shafiqul Islam. Bibliography. Index. March 1991. 256 pp./Paper/$18.95. Send order to: Council on Foreign Relations Press, 58 East 68th Street, New York, NY 10021. (Telephone: 1-212-734-0400.)

The Department of State released this microfiche publication on April 9, 1991. Part I contains the transcripts of Department of State daily press briefings and the Department of State and White House Special Briefings and Press Conferences held in 1987. Following many of the daily briefings are "Posted Statements," which are the written responses to reporters' specific inquiries prepared after the daily briefings. Part II contains the treaties, protocols, and agreements signed by the United States in 1987, specifically those international agreements requiring formal Senate consent in the ratification process. An accompanying 111-page printed guide contains lists of all briefings and treaties included in the microfiche, the names and positions of all on-the-record briefers, and a comprehensive index for both parts.

This publication supplements the official record of principal messages, addresses, statements, and briefings in the printed volume *American Foreign Policy: Current Documents, 1987* published in December 1988. The briefings cover major developments in U.S.-Soviet relations including the signing of the Intermediate Range Nuclear Forces Treaty at the Reagan-Gorbachev Summit in Washington, D.C., the establishment of Nuclear Risk Reduction Centers, and reexamination of the Embassy construction project in Moscow. This publication documents U.S. objectives in the Persian Gulf and reactions to events in the region, with special focus on the Iraqi attack on the U.S.S. *Stark*, the reflagging of Kuwaiti ships, and the U.S. attack on the Iranian Rashdat Platform. The Iran arms and Contra aid investigations, the Central American Peace Agreement and American peace efforts in that region, the U.S.-Canadian trade agreement, the Venice Economic Summit, and U.S. policy toward southern Africa also are covered.

Copies of this microfiche publication (Department of State Publication No. 9805, GPO Stock No. 044-000-02297-4) may be purchased for $25.00 from the Superintendent of Documents, U.S. Government Printing Office, Washington, D.C., 20402. Checks or money orders should be made out to the Superintendent of Documents.

Name Index

INDEX: VOLUME 1

Page numbers in this index are identified by the following designations:

July (July/August issue)
Sept (September/October issue)
Nov (November/December issue)
Jan (January-April double issue)
May (May/June issue)

Items under each heading are listed in the order in which they appeared in the *Bulletin*.

C

F

G

FOREIGN POLICY BULLETIN
4812 Butterworth Place, N.W.
Washington, D.C. 20016

BULK RATE
U.S. POSTAGE
PAID
WASHINGTON, D.C.
PERMIT NO. 4393